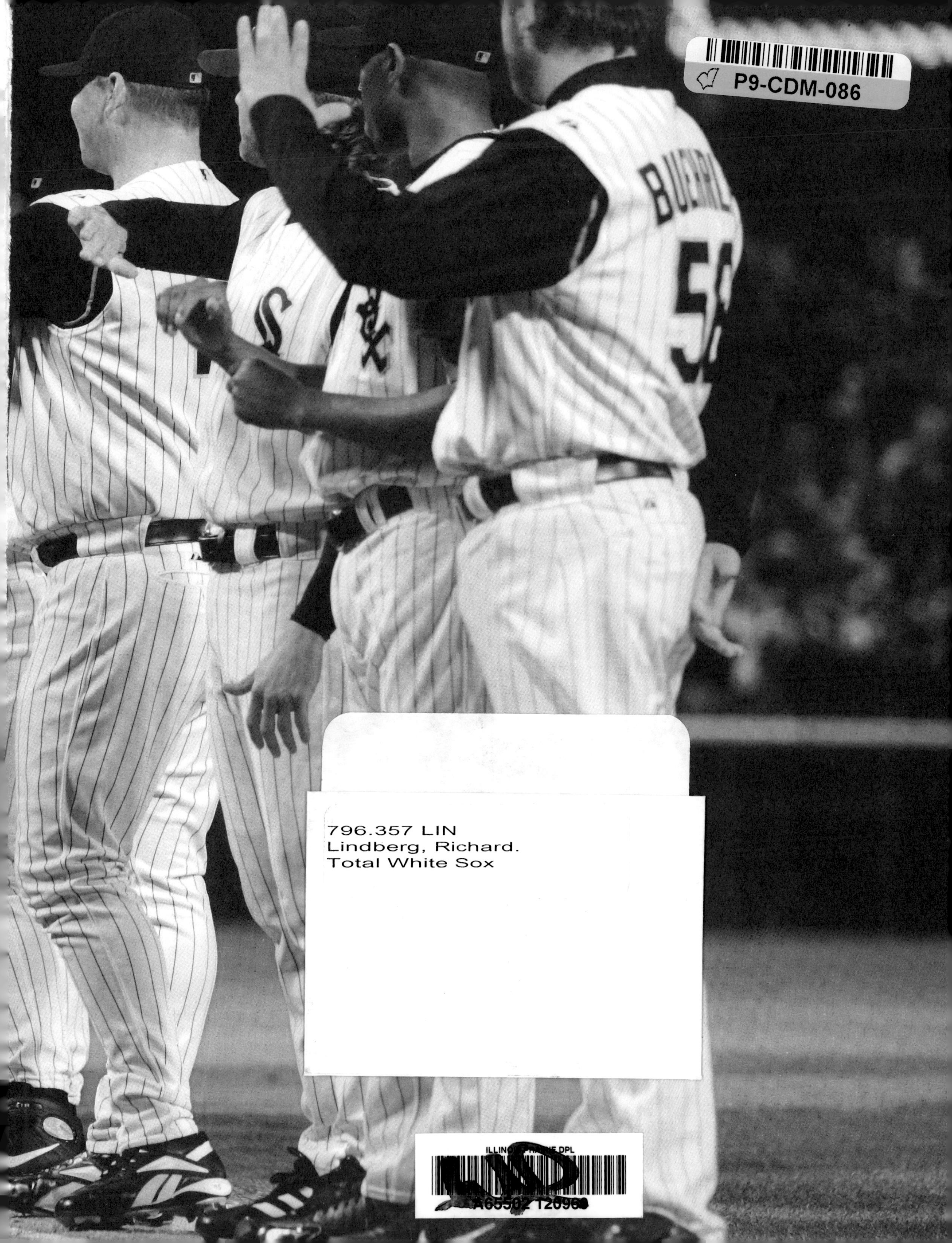

TOTAL WHITE SOX

Richard C. Lindberg

TOTAL WHITE SOX

The Definitive Encyclopedia of the Chicago White Sox

Revised and Expanded

Foreword by Ken "Hawk" Harrelson

TRIUMPH
BOOKS

Originally published by Temple University Press, Philadelphia,
© 1997, as *The White Sox Encyclopedia.*

This book is available in quantity at special discounts for your group or organization. For further information, contact:

Triumph Books
542 South Dearborn Street
Suite 750
Chicago, Illinois 60605
(312) 939-3330
Fax (312) 663-3557
www.triumphbooks.com

Printed in U.S.A.
ISBN: 978-1-60078-404-0
Editorial production by Prologue Publishing Services, LLC

Contents

Foreword

One of the great joys of broadcasting White Sox baseball for as long as I have is an appreciation for the richly defined and colorful history and traditions of the South Side ballclub that I have covered over the years—the many personalities, the gloroious moments, and the forgotten and famous incidents of years gone by. The rhythms of the national pastime are timeless. That is the beauty of baseball. It is essentially the same game our grandfathers and their fathers watched. A generation of fans from the dead-ball era—the first two decades of the 20th century when home runs were scarce and Ed Walsh, Doc White, and Red Faber were White Sox mound aces without peer—would instantly recognize and value the modern game for what it is today.

What is baseball without its history and nostalgia? More than any other sport, this great game endures only because of the living memories we carry with us of the players we remember from childhood, the pride they instilled in all of us, and the glory they achieved. Baseball is a game of comparisons—the records that are set by one generation only to be broken by the next. Baseball is continuity, teamwork, emotion, and in many respects a perfect metaphor of the American spirit. The White Sox are a part of that fabric of continuity. Founded by the "Old Roman," Charles Comiskey, who with his friend and baseball mentor Ban Johnson, envisioned way back in 1899 that a second professional league—the American League—could in fact successfully challenge the National League for supremacy, the White Sox remain a charter franchise of the AL to this day. This ballclub has come a long way since the 1970s—Disco Demolition, short pants, and "Friday night fights"—to become a perennial pennant contender. I cannot emphasize enough the pivotal role that Jerry Reinsdorf has played in restoring the luster of the franchise. By investing his time, resources, and energy to revamp the club, by making commitments to the fans and the city of Chicago, and by providing families with a wonderful entertainment venue year in and year out, the Sox stand on higher ground today than ever before. But what a history it was! Their story is one of adversity overcome; comedy and tragedy; embattled ownerships bucking tough odds and thriving in a fiercely competitive two-team town where family loyalties are often divided and the Sox-Cubs rivalry shows no sign of ever letting up.

In this encompassing third edition of *Total White Sox*, Rich Lindberg presents in precise detail a "living museum," if you will, of Sox history from the team's inception through 110 years of history, spanning the eras of the Hitless Wonders, the Black Sox, the Go-Go Boys, South Side Hit Men, the 1983 Winning Uglies, and all the way through the climactic 2005 World Series and beyond. It's all here: a narrative history of every season through 2010, more than 200 player biographies, the greatest (and zaniest) moments in team history, a collection of "Sox Yarns," the complete postseason, front-office personalities, the history of the minor leagues, the stadiums, stats and more stats, the Sox-Cubs showdowns written up by Biart Williams, and a wonderful collection of photos carefully gathered by Mark Fletcher. This is a true team encyclopedia in every respect that was praised for its originality when it was first conceived back in 1997.

Rich is a familiar figure around U.S. Cellular Field. He's been recognized by many as the official team historian for nearly three decades, and over the years he has contributed greatly to the rebuilding of the historic archive and the preservation of this club's storied past since he began his research work in the days of the second Bill Veeck ownership. Most of all, he's a Sox fan—from the northwest side of Chicago, of all places. He's always been very passionate about his team and has been since his earliest remembrances of Nellie Fox, "Little Louie" Aparicio, and Gary Peters. Rich's volume is written from a dual perspective—as a fan with his own opinions and biases, and as a recognized Chicago historian who has authored 15 earlier books—four of them about his beloved White Sox. So join with me in a celebration of *Total White Sox* baseball—end to end, past, present, and future—our Sox from A to Z.

—Ken "Hawk" Harrelson

Preface and Introduction

Total White Sox began as *The White Sox Encyclopedia,* a research project launched in 1994 for Temple University Press in Philadelphia with the objective of compiling a definitive team history condensed into a single volume—with equal attention paid to all eras and decades—and not just the players and events of recent memory. The first copies of the *Encyclopedia* were delivered to bookstores in July 1997, but the Temple series of major league team histories, conceived in 1992, was abandoned not long after. Eight different volumes made their way into print before the series was canceled.

In 2005 the White Sox and their fans realized an impossible dream. The team that was historically accorded "second-class status in the second city" by the Chicago media stunned the baseball world and copped the World Series in amazing fashion. Not long after, the *White Sox Encyclopedia* was reborn as *Total White Sox* with Triumph Books of Chicago. The 2006 edition reached a far wider audience than it had ever tapped into during the lamentable 1997 season, and the response from Sox fans was gratifying. "Is there any plan to update the 2006 edition?" That was the question I kept hearing during my presentations to city and suburban library patrons, various fan groups, and membership associations about Sox team history. My answer was an unequivocal yes.

So here it is, Sox fans—our third edition of the *Encyclopedia* now called *Total White Sox.* It moves the story of the franchise forward through the 2010 season, building upon the trials, tribulations, and moments of glory of a ballclub interwoven into the fabric of the South Side. The community supported it through years of triumph, the disgrace of the devastating Black Sox Scandal, and the long losing seasons that were to follow. With this new edition we have traced the progress of our favorite team from the last out of the Series through Mark Buehrle's no-hitter and perfect game; the 2008 "Blackout Game," and the amazing June comeback in "2K-10." The volume is packed with a collection of new and rarely seen photographs supplied by Mark Fletcher, Jeff Szynal from the team, and the many great White Sox fans like Mike McKay, Gerry Bilek, Mike McCormick, and Len Maybaum, who were enthusiastic about this project; plus plenty of narrative and statistics to solve the most vexing trivia questions; and, of course, a rich and defining team history to look back on, from Charles Comiskey to Jerry Reinsdorf.

I am a research historian and the author of 15 books about various subject matters all related in some way to Chicago and its remarkable history. But I have written *Total White Sox* from the perspective of being a dedicated, lifelong fan of the White Sox since the early 1960s while I was growing up in a neighborhood inhabited by Cubs fans up on the far Northwest Side of the city. In those days, Gary Peters, Pete Ward, Joe Horlen, Ron Hansen, and Hoyt Wilhelm were the team's biggest stars, and diminutive Nellie Fox was playing his final games in the White Sox pinstripes.

The team—just four years removed from a memorable pennant-winning season—was still challenging the Yankees for supremacy, and as a youth, the American League, with its galaxy of great stars, represented big-time baseball to me, the real deal. And my White Sox were outfitted in their crisp-looking pinstriped uniforms with the old English logo on the jersey, playing in Comiskey Park—a magical place. It was distant. It was majestic. It had an exploding scoreboard, night baseball, and it was just *magnificent.* But it was also far-removed from my insulated world up on the Northwest Side and hard to get to by public transportation.

On the other hand, neighbors in our remote corner of Chicago near O'Hare most often took the CTA bus and elevated line to Clark & Addison to watch the sad-sack, chronic eighth-place finishers managed by a weird "college of coaches" in a ballpark that was almost always empty with no unique attractions to recommend except for the old man who read the starting lineups while standing in front of a microphone in back of home plate. For all of its lore, Wrigley Field held no special appeal for me. The neighborhood was on the downslope, and it is hard to imagine, but a typical weekday crowd at the so-called "Friendly Confines" in those years barely numbered 7,500, and the Sox outdrew them nearly every season. Those were my strongest memories of Chicago baseball during my impressionable years, 1962 to 1966.

The years passed, and my affection for the South Side team only deepened—through some very lackluster seasons in 1968 and 1969 and continuing into the late 1970s. Then I began digging into the nearly forgotten history of the franchise, and that's when my *professional* relationship with the Chicago White Sox organization evolved. It dates back 32 years and is unique in baseball.

These days the White Sox have few advocates or champions left within the Chicago media. The great sportswriters of my youth who professed their admiration and support for the Comiskeys and the South Side team—John Carmichael, Arch Ward, John Justin Smith, and Bill Gleason—have gone on to their reward. I believe that the trend toward a pro-Cubs media first began in the late 1960s and early 1970s, while Leo Durocher was managing the North Side ballclub and Wrigley Field was just beginning to come into its own as a tourist destination and epicenter of Chicago's saloon culture.

The legendary scribes from that earlier generation were succeeded by a younger cadre of reporters, most of them imported from other regions of the country or downstate. Sports journalists matriculating into Chicago from the Sunbelt or points east may have had no pre-conceived notions about the two teams before they arrived. But their attitudes likely changed when they contrasted the empty grandstands at cavernous old Comiskey Park circa 1968–1975, a woebegone, colorless ballclub struggling to draw fans inside its brick and concrete walls against the backdrop of the jazzy North Side and the rather romanticized notion of the "lovable losers" saddled with a fictitious Billy Goat curse—a colorful, but far-fetched yarn dreamed up inside the Billy Goat Tavern one night by newspaper columnists Mike Royko and Dave Condon.

Of course, a heavy schedule of Cubs games aired over WGN-TV every afternoon following *Bozo's Circus* in the 1960s through the 1970s didn't help the White Sox's efforts to bolster their attendance, either. The quirks of TV scheduling minted a whole new generation of baby boomer fans in the 1960s. New York had two local stations, WOR and WPIX, that balanced the scales for the New York teams. In Chicago there was only WGN. The Sox, with their heavy schedule of night games and limited television exposure on Channel 9 in those pivotal years, lost an entire generation of ticket-buying customers, and their attendance suffered.

Like many White Sox fans, I have become sharply critical and frankly fed up with the perceived biases of the Chicago media, the amount of column inches and front-page coverage in the sports section devoted to the North Side team, and the penchant of the television and radio announcers to *always* announce the results of the Cubs game ahead of the Sox. Despite fervent denials of the sports editors and radio program directors that there is no bias, the evidence seems to suggest otherwise. The issue is not new and has been hotly debated for many years. Bill Veeck was attuned to it back in the late 1970s and believed that, as a consequence of second-class treatment of his team by the media, the Sox were no longer viable in the Windy City, thus hastening his decision to sell the team in 1980. In 2010, as the White Sox staged a remarkable, almost unprecedented surge that elevated them from nine games under .500 in late May to 16 games over .500 and in first place by August 1, one of the "Sox Fans on Deck" fan club loyalists astutely observed that if it were the Cubs who had made this fabulous pennant run after being pronounced dead and buried in the standings by Memorial Day, they would be the headlining story. Editorialists would push them ahead of coverage of the Bears' training camp, the Blackhawks' salary cap issues, the Bulls—foreign wars, stock market crashes, the awarding of the Nobel Peace Prize, natural disasters, and what the president of the United States is up to at any given moment. Maybe I'm exaggerating the point, but you get the idea.

My role as historian extends back a number of years. Before instant, computer-generated statistics became commonplace in baseball, I supplied historical tidbits, lost and forgotten team records (beginning in 1978), and helped the team to rebuild a historic archive that had simply vanished by 1981, the year that I first glimpsed the extent of their fragmented holdings at old Comiskey Park. Where did these files go? I chalk it up to the departing ownerships—the Comiskeys, Allyns, and Veecks, who took chunks of the team history with them out the front door. Over the next 20 years, I poured over newspaper microfilm at the downtown Chicago library—examining every game result dating back to 1900. Through four of my White Sox book projects, I interviewed players, fans, and front-office people from the various ownerships, and as the years passed, I managed to compile an archive of forgotten history, trivia, and anecdotes that is presented to you in this all-encompassing volume.

By 1985 my role as team historian was more or less formalized and defined by Paul Jensen, who then headed up media relations and was responsible for the dissemination of statistical and historical information through the yearly press guide, daily media news releases, and assorted team publications. At a Red Cloud banquet one year, Paul introduced me to the audience as the "White Sox team historian," and the moniker has stuck.

The White Sox are the only Chicago team that I write about, and frankly, the only professional sports team in town that matters to me. I am indifferent to hockey. I am only mildly interested in the NBA. I could care less about college football and college hoops, and the only thing the Chicago Bears represent to me is a depressing hiatus from the end of the baseball season to the opening of spring training. I guess you could say that I am *not* a sports fan—just a White Sox fan.

But that's just me. Concerning our South Side team, where are they positioned in the second decade of the new millennium? Are they a big-market team, or a small-market team playing in a large-market city? It can be argued that they have their feet planted in both worlds—and rank somewhere in the middle. In 2010 *Forbes Magazine* elevated the White Sox to 10th place in franchise value—$466 million with estimated revenues of $194 million. That places them ahead of Houston but trailing San Francisco and represents an upward spike from 14th place, where they stood in 2008. They are not the Yankees, the Red Sox, or the Mets—teams with unlimited financial resources and a national following or a "Nation," as the fans of Boston boast. Through conservative fiscal management, the White Sox have survived and prospered against long and tough odds and can likely be classified as a "middle-market" team—keeping company with the Tigers, Braves, Rockies, Mariners, and Rangers. That is not bad company.

More important, Jerry Reinsdorf has restored financial stability to a team teetering on bankruptcy and threatening to leave Chicago on three separate occasions before he purchased the club from Bill Veeck for the sum of $20 million in 1981.

Jerry's tenure of ownership is the second-longest in the major leagues (after the Steinbrenner family in New York), and he is a respected member of baseball's governing inner circle—the Major League Baseball Executive Council. Under his guidance and wisdom and through the commitment, imagination, and dedication of his investors, a talented executive team, the front-office staff, marketing, and baseball operations, the White Sox have been on the winning side of the ledger since 1981, and in most years they manage to field a highly competitive team. The strategy is not to tear the club down and rebuild on five-year cycles, but to *retool* in order to remain in contention and give the fans an exciting on-field product to watch. Jerry and his advisors know they must, because it is understood that U.S. Cellular Field attendance will shrink if the team were to fall into a predictable holding pattern of 90-plus losses every year or engage in perpetual rebuilding programs, as say, the Pittsburgh Pirates, Kansas City Royals, and Baltimore Orioles. The attendance issue is not a new one—it has been problematic in just about every era of White Sox history dating back to the 1920s, and regrettably in our modern age, attendance still dictates the annual payroll budget.

Thus, nervous Sox fans have always kept one eye on the box score and the other focused on the size of the paid crowd; it has been that way since the Great Depression. That has been the unfortunate reality of the situation, but it is a consequence of decades of socioeconomic and demographic factors that came into play. The dynamic of limited television exposure in the early years, negative media perceptions about the contrasting image of the respective neighborhoods in which the two Chicago teams play—the absence of bars and clubs in Bridgeport to congregate in after the game—coupled with some bad marketing decisions and stadium controversies, have all fueled larger problems dating back 60 or more years.

But here's a little-known fact that should cheer White Sox fandom, assuage the old attendance concerns, and chase away the lingering memory of Arthur and John Allyn and Bill Veeck tacking up FOR SALE signs on the front door (thus stirring the darker possibility of franchise relocation to another city). The Sox are identifying new and additional revenue streams through a related sports enterprise they have launched, known as Silver Chalice Ventures. Its purpose is to increase equity positions in different companies to generate profits outside of the normal baseball-related channels.

Because the Cubs draw in the range of 36,000 to 39,000 per game, comparisons are inevitably drawn to the smaller-sized crowds that show up at the Cell, but it is an issue Sox fans need to distance themselves from because it is a specious argument. Here's why.

First, you have to subtract the 10,000 to 15,000 tourists, bus junketeers from Iowa, Wisconsin, Indiana, Missouri, and elsewhere; the twentysomethings and summer break kids from Arlington Heights, Mt. Prospect, and other Northwest suburbs wearing their backward baseball hats and $200 jerseys as they swarm past the bouncers in the Wrigleyville bier stubes; and tourists and fans of the opposing teams who buy tickets months in advance, and what are you left with? An estimated 24,000 to 26,000 hardcore, serious-minded baseball fans—roughly the equivalent number of people who attend games at the Cell on any given night.

The White Sox, because of their abundance of sky suites and party rooms to accommodate large groups and company outings, are less dependent on the walk-up traffic and single-game ticket buyers than the Cubs—but that is not to dismiss the importance of attendance. Sox fans need to get behind this ballclub—support them in the down years. Unless you are the Yankees or Red Sox, losing seasons are inevitable for most teams in this game. Nevertheless, in 2010 it was estimated that 3,000 people per game were simply not showing up at Wrigley because the team was so bad. Minus the number of suites and picnic areas at the Cell, the North Siders were losing on average $27 spent on food and concessions *per person.* If 3,000 of the Wrigley Field faithful are not showing up to buy their $27 worth of beer and hot dogs, the Cubs will likely have problems. So my advice to loyal Sox supporters is to just ignore the Cubs fans that harangue and goad our fans (because there is no other argument they can advance in their team's favor) and just forget about it.

The important thing to remember is we have held on to our White Sox through the rough times—through all the slips and falls—and the moments of grandeur. This is a fabled franchise, and it will continue to endure and thrive in its traditional South Side setting carved out by the "Old Roman," Charles Comiskey, who battled the National League magnates in order to gain an entrée in 1900, the year the former St. Paul Saints came down from Minnesota to be rechristened the Chicago White Sox. During the contentious negotiations that followed, Comiskey held firm against strong NL opposition. He said he would either have his ballclub playing in Chicago on the South Side, or failing in that, he would forsake baseball and solicit an appointment to the Chicago Police Department as a desk sergeant. That is a true story.

There are many more colorful anecdotes and fables of White Sox baseball presented in the current volume. Our ballclub mirrors the "I Will" spirit of the city of Chicago—a city and a team that have defied long odds and thrived. So, to echo the words of Ken "the Hawk" Harrelson, "Settle in, strap it down, and welcome to White Sox baseball!"

—Richard Lindberg

Beginnings of White Sox Baseball

An air of expectation and intrigue hung over the room. The fate of this fledgling confederation of baseball teams hung in the balance as the entrenched National League power brokers pondered their options. Should they placate this upstart Ban Johnson and allow him access to the Chicago market under the auspices of Charles Comiskey—one of the instigators of the great player revolt of 1890? Or was it better to take their chances with Adrian "Cap" Anson, the front man for a St. Louis group intent upon reviving the corpse of the dormant American Association, which had fought a long and costly trade war with the NL through the 1880s?

These weighty matters were very much on their minds as Johnson gathered together his Western League owners for a closed-door conference at Chicago's majestic Great Northern Hotel, the gray afternoon of October 11, 1899.

For seven seasons the overbearing and dictatorial Western League president played the waiting game. He sensed that the National League, riding the crest of baseball monopoly in the 1890s, would soon crumble under the weight of a cumbersome 12-team arrangement, interlocking ownerships controlled by men with dubious political connections, and the public's growing dissatisfaction with "syndicate ball" where the cash-poor losers at the bottom of the standings were utilized as farm clubs for the wealthier teams. Fans in Cleveland were helpless to prevent Frank Robison from shearing the top talent from the hometown Spiders because he believed his other team, the Cardinals, was positioned in a better market. The Spiders had lost 134 games in 1899, then vanished.

Ban Johnson's Western League, formed in the autumn of 1893, prospered through frugal, centralized management in such out-of-the-way locales as Grand Rapids, Michigan; Sioux City, Iowa; and St. Paul, Minnesota, where Comiskey, a star first baseman of former years, had operated his ballclub for five Spartan seasons.

Comiskey and Johnson shared a vision and common purpose. Both men believed that there was ample room for a second major league to break the NL's monopoly of power. The lessons of the past had taught them that such ventures were filled with peril and that the chances of success were less than 50–50. There had been many interlopers since 1876 when the National League was organized.

However, they had all been ground into dust by the Nationals. Some, like the Union Association, went quickly. The American Association, a colorful aggregation of teams that defied baseball's blue laws by selling beer in the grandstand and playing games on the Sabbath, lasted a full decade before the ultimate collapse occurred. Charles Comiskey, known as the Old Roman after his playing days ended, was a major star of the American Association and its shrewdest manager. The St. Louis Browns team that he guided was a league powerhouse in the 1880s and one reason why the league prospered in the second half of the decade.

Now that this fresh opportunity had finally surfaced, Johnson moved with dispatch, employing Trojan-horse tactics to gain entrance into the realm. Johnson never believed for a moment that Cap Anson and his St. Louis backers posed much of a threat to National League hegemony. They were poorly financed and possessed only the Anson name—which struck false terror into the hearts of Robison and National League president Nicholas Young.

The threat of another 10-year trade war with a revived American Association was just too dark a possibility to contemplate. So John T. Brush, the cantankerous New York Giants owner and Comiskey's former employer in Cincinnati, where the Old

Pitcher Jack Katoll, shown here in 1902 at the 39th Street Grounds, was a member of the St. Paul Saints team brought down to Chicago by Charles Comiskey in 1900 to begin play as the White Sox. (Courtesy of Chicago History Museum, SDN–000577, photographer: *Chicago Daily News*)

Roman had managed before rushing off to join the Western League, made peace overtures to Johnson. The National League, Brush explained, was prepared to grant concessions to Johnson's group—provided they agreed to remain within the governance of the sacrosanct National Agreement. In other words, the Western League must continue to operate as a minor league "farm" subject to the normal draft rules and whims of the NL owners.

Using the specter of a rejuvenated American Association as his trump card, Johnson demanded three things from Brush: the right to relocate Comiskey's St. Paul team to Chicago over the stern objections of James Hart, owner of the National League Colts; an increase in payment to the Western League from $500 to $1,000 per player drafted; and an additional year tacked on to the length of service of Western League players before they could be eligible for the NL draft. Brush and his cohorts readily agreed.

The gathering of Western League men at the Great Northern Hotel that October afternoon endorsed Johnson's proposal to move forth with the realignment. W.F.C. Golt, representing the Indianapolis entry, arose from his chair and made a motion to change the name of the association to the American League of Professional Ball Clubs. It was an emotionally charged moment. The tiny Midwestern baseball league was on course with a larger destiny, and the struggling St. Paul team would soon become the league's cornerstone franchise for the next two decades—the Chicago White Stockings.

The formal agreement that landed the St. Paul Saints in Chicago was signed by Comiskey and the adversarial Mr. Hart on March 21, 1900. Hart never doubted Comiskey's ulterior motives, and to allow the wolf in through the back door would only invite ruin, or so he reasoned. There was no doubt in his mind that Comiskey was after a much bigger prize than playing second banana in a minor league—that is, if he could succeed where others had failed.

"Two Chicago clubs? No never!" Hart roared. "You'll see what will become of these divided interests before the season is over!" The owner of the Colts underestimated the resolve of Comiskey, whose heritage was woven into the core of Chicago ward politics. The Old Roman's father served as alderman of the Irish 10th Ward for many years. And if history and experience were any teacher, Comiskey understood that he had to vigorously promote his product to the people he knew best, the Irish-American community on the city's South Side. That is why he had to chuckle to himself when confronted with Hart's "conditions." Before he affixed his signature to the slip of paper, Comiskey understood that he would first have to agree to play his home games south of 35th Street.

Located in Bridgeport just three miles south of downtown, the 35th Street neighborhood was home to thousands of second- and third-generation Irish potato-famine families. Comiskey did not have the slightest reservations. These were his people—salt-of-the-earth simple folk who would welcome a baseball team into their midst. The Old Roman had grown up among them, and he understood their customs and ways.

One other thing, Hart interjected, "You cannot use the good name of the City of Chicago in your business dealings!" Again, Comiskey complied. Since Hart mentioned nothing about nicknames, the Old Roman borrowed the venerable and historic moniker of the White Stockings—Chicago's first professional team that began play in 1870, a year before the great fire. Comiskey had watched them play as an adolescent growing up on the West Side of the city, and since the National League ballclub had abandoned the nickname years earlier, the owner decided to adopt it for his own purposes.

Within a year, the upstart White Stockings were outdrawing their National League counterparts playing in a tiny makeshift wooden stadium that had once served as a cricket field for an amateur team. The success of the infant American League in 1900 convinced Comiskey and Johnson to proceed toward their ultimate objective. After the season had ended and the White Stockings had emerged as champions of the league, the duo decided not to renew the National Agreement for 1901. Henceforth, the American League would no longer allow its players to be farmed to National League teams, and for all intents and purposes the AL would consider itself the second major league.

The Nationals did not view matters in the same light, so another trade war ensued. It was a conflict easily won by the Americans in 1903 after Johnson's league was officially "recognized" and the contracts of disputed players were resolved. Comiskey and Johnson, who had forged a strong friendship in Cincinnati 10 years earlier when the Old Roman was managing the Redlegs and Johnson was a sportswriter for the *Commercial-Gazette* newspaper, were divided in their opinions concerning what to do about the National League. The White Sox owner believed it was within their power to drive the older league out of existence and should do so—with relish. Johnson, a dour-looking man who parted his thinning hair down the middle, was rigid in the belief that competition with the National League was healthy for baseball and beneficial to their common interests. Comiskey disagreed, and therein lay the origin of a historic feud between these two charismatic but strong-willed leaders.

There was no special affection or warm regard between Comiskey and Cubs owner Hart. The Cubs and White Sox nervously coexisted in a market that proved it could sustain two teams. However, the Old Roman recognized that it would be a continuing struggle to thrive in a two-team town if his ballclub suffered through a succession of losing seasons. History has proved him correct.

Indeed, much of White Sox history is underscored by this sometimes grim tug-of-war between the Cubs and White Sox for the loyalties of the Chicago fan. Even though the Sox earned bragging rights by soundly thrashing their crosstown rivals in a celebrated World Series, the annual postseason City Series, and any number of charity games that followed, the White Sox emerged as the classic underdog after the epochal Black Sox Scandal of 1920. The conspiracy to throw the 1919 World Series was a defining moment in baseball—and for the fortunes of a beloved Chicago institution in the coming decades.

OZUNA
88

1

Down through the Seasons

1900

Record: 82–53
Finish: First
Games Ahead: 4
Manager: Charles Comiskey

By any other name the infant American League was still a minor league association subject to the will of the senior circuit. The American League was governed by a "National Agreement" and subject to the drafting of its players by the National League. Therefore, the spirited 1900 pennant race highlighted by a White Sox championship is often overlooked by baseball historians in their discussions of the AL founding.

In Charles Comiskey's final campaign as a field manager, the White Sox energized Chicago baseball with an ensemble cast of players who performed on a converted cricket field at 39th Street and Wentworth Avenue on the South Side.

Up to the final moment on April 21, when fans streamed into the revamped cricket field to preview the inaugural American League baseball game against Connie Mack's Milwaukee Brewers, construction crews were applying the final touches to the tiny wooden grandstand.

The Brewers edged the Sox 5–4 in 10 innings before an estimated crowd of 2,000 to 3,000 fans. William "Dummy" Hoy set the tempo for the game and the future directions of White Sox baseball by leading off the game with a walk and an attempted stolen base. Whatever offense they lacked in 1900, Chicago more than compensated with speed, defense, and abundant pitching—hallmarks of White Sox baseball down through the years.

Hoy's 32 stolen bases provided numerous RBI opportunities for Dick Padden, Frank Shugarts, and Fred Hartman—three middle infielders who generated much of the offensive attack.

After a weak beginning, the White Sox rolled into high gear in mid-June. They grabbed first place on the 19th, just three days after being held hitless by Winford Kellum of Indianapolis. It was the AL's first no-hitter.

The Sox clinched their "unofficial" pennant on September 12, when they rolled over the Cleveland Blues 12–1 behind Roy "Boy Wonder" Patterson, a 17-game winner in 1900.

Charles Comiskey was honored by his players with the gift of a five-foot commemorative bat to mark the occasion of his retirement from active field duty. It was appropriate irony in a year when the Sox won the pennant but finished dead last in hitting.

"Here is the man who will own and manage the Chicago American League ball club!" Thus the *Chicago Inter-Ocean* introduced Charles Comiskey in February 1900.

	G	AB	H	R	2B	3B	HR	RBI	SB	AVG
Frank Isbell	109	399	99	49	14	7	1	NA	22	.248
Dick Padden	130	482	137	84	24	5	1	NA	36	.284
Frank Shugarts	98	377	107	54	21	1	5	NA	16	.284
Fred Hartman	116	450	124	71	21	6	1	NA	15	.276
Herm McFarland	121	460	111	81	23	7	3	NA	31	.241
Dan Lally	138	576	151	71	24	6	1	NA	21	.262
Dummy Hoy	137	547	139	115	16	6	1	NA	32	.254
Joe Sugden	121	459	133	47	23	4	0	NA	15	.290
Dave Brain	8	25	6	3	1	1	0	NA	0	.240
Walt Brodie	64	229	60	41	6	3	0	NA	8	.262
Dick Buckley	40	139	28	10	6	0	0	NA	0	.201
Ed Burke	14	53	11	8	2	0	0	NA	4	.208
G. E. Clayton	2	9	3	1	0	0	0	NA	0	.333
Bob Dillard	28	98	19	13	1	2	0	NA	5	.194
Ed Doheny	6	14	3	3	1	0	0	NA	0	.214
Tom Dowd	98	381	100	47	20	3	0	NA	17	.262
Frank McManus	39	128	30	21	3	1	0	NA	7	.234
Charlie O'Leary	27	92	15	4	3	0	0	NA	0	.163
John Shearon	126	529	140	67	26	11	1	NA	10	.265
Bob Wood	36	127	39	15	11	0	1	NA	3	.307
		4,690	1,455	667	246	63	13	NA	242	.257

Pregame relaxation for the team that history records as the "Black Sox"

	W	L	GS	CG	IP	H	BB	K	ShO	ERA
Jack Katoll	16	14	29	25	282	247	60	81	6	NA
Roger Denzer	20	10	29	24	272	258	55	76	4	NA
Roy Patterson	17	8	27	22	232	211	53	87	5	NA
Chauncey Fisher	19	9	30	27	285	282	51	63	5	NA
Ed Doheny	0	4	4	3	33	31	20	14	0	NA
Frank Isbell	5	2	7	4	53	56	23	5	0	NA
Frank Killen	0	1	1	1	8	12	3	1	0	NA
Willie McGill	3	2	5	3	33	40	14	6	0	NA
Cy Seymour	1	1	2	1	10	8	9	5	0	NA
Tommy Thomas	1	4	5	2	38	45	8	12	0	NA
	82	53	137	112	1,246	1,190	296	350	20	NA

1901

Record: 83–53
Finish: First
Games Ahead: 4
Manager: Clark Griffith

The one-year agreement to honor the harsh terms of the National Agreement expired at the end of the 1900 season, and with Comiskey in accord, AL President Ban Johnson decided not to sign an extension. The gambling duo pushed ahead with their plan to declare major league status in 1901 by offering pay raises and slight modifications to the ancient and unfair reserve clause to National League players desiring to "jump" the NL. Comiskey commenced immediate negotiations with several top stars on the Chicago Orphans (Cubs) roster.

Orphans pitchers Clark Griffith and James Callahan and infielder Sandow Mertes came to terms with Comiskey in March 1901. Comiskey recognized certain leadership abilities in Griffith, an early and strident advocate for player rights. As an added inducement to manage the White Stockings in 1901, Griffith was awarded stock in the ballclub.

Orphans president James Hart downplayed the seriousness of the situation, predicting Griffith and the others would likely return…hat in hand. "They may talk all they want," Hart snorted, "about the city supporting two teams, but they are mistaken. Chicago can only support *one* Chicago club!"

The White Sox proved the imperious Hart dead wrong by drawing 354,350 fans to the 39th Street Grounds, nearly 150,000 more than the Orphans. American League baseball, as it was played on the South Side in 1901, provided fast-paced, high-scoring action with more than the usual amount of surprises.

The season was barely three weeks old when Griffith's team registered the AL's first no-hitter by defeating Cleveland 4–2 on May 9, despite being held hitless by Earl Moore. They pounded 24 singles against these same Clevelanders on April 28, and poled two grand-slam home runs in a 19–9 deluge of the Tigers on May 1. The following day, another American League first was registered when the Sox forfeited a game to Detroit after stalling for an early adjournment in a seesaw contest threatened by encroaching darkness. When umpire Tom Connolly signaled forfeit, the fans stormed the field. Comiskey pushed his way through the crowd trying to mollify his patrons while the police hustled the umpire from the grounds. Such were the rough-and-tumble conditions in 1901.

Comiskey's 1901 champions

President Johnson tried to instill a healthy respect for the umpires, and often had to be firm and uncompromising to enforce this edict. Shortstop Frank Shugarts and pitcher Jack Katoll were blacklisted after engaging in fisticuffs with umpire Jack Haskell in Washington one afternoon. Comiskey supported Johnson, but in the next few years the AL president seemed to go out of his way to scapegoat White Sox players.

Despite a rash of injuries, as well as the angry altercations with umpires, the White Sox fended off a persistent challenge from the Boston Puritans and secured first place for good on July 18. They never relinquished that lead and wrapped up their second consecutive flag on September 24.

Because the National League still refused to sanction a World Series, the White Sox had to content themselves with a split of a four-game postseason "barnstorming" series played against a team of "All American Stars" captained by Nap Lajoie of the Philadelphia Athletics.

The White Sox won Chicago fandom over in 1901 with a daring mix of crowd-pleasing baseball. The local press had ceased calling Hart's team Orphans, preferring instead the more appropriate moniker "Remnants." Charles Comiskey had made good on his promise to reduce the National Leaguers to that very thing—tattered remnants.

	G	AB	H	R	2B	3B	HR	RBI	SB	AVG
Frank Isbell	137	556	143	93	15	8	3	70	52	.257
Sandow Mertes	137	545	151	94	16	17	5	98	46	.277
Frank Shugarts	107	415	104	62	9	12	2	47	12	.251
Fred Hartman	120	473	146	77	23	13	3	89	31	.309
Fielder Jones	133	521	177	120	16	3	2	65	38	.340
Dummy Hoy	132	527	155	112	28	11	2	60	27	.294
Herm McFarland	132	473	130	83	21	9	4	59	33	.275
Billy Sullivan	98	367	90	54	15	6	4	56	12	.245
Jimmy Burke	42	148	39	20	5	0	0	21	11	.264
Jimmy Callahan	45	118	39	15	7	3	1	19	10	.331
Dave Brain	5	20	7	2	1	0	0	5	0	.350
Clarence Foster	12	35	10	4	2	2	1	6	0	.286
Joe Sugden	48	153	42	21	7	1	0	19	4	.275
		4,725	1,318	819	173	89	32	656	280	.279

	W	L	GS	CG	IP	H	BB	K	ShO	ERA
Roy Patterson	20	16	35	30	312⅓	345	62	127	4	3.37
Clark Griffith	24	7	30	26	266⅔	275	50	67	5	2.67
Jimmy Callahan	15	8	22	20	215⅓	195	50	70	1	2.42
Jack Katoll	11	11	25	19	208	231	53	59	0	2.81
Erwin Harvey	3	6	9	5	92	91	34	27	0	3.62
John Skopec	6	3	9	6	68⅓	62	45	24	0	3.16
Wiley Piatt	4	2	6	4	51⅔	42	14	19	1	2.79
John McAleese	0	0	0	0	3	7	1	1	0	9.00
Frank Isbell	0	0	0	0	1	2	0	0	0	9.00
Frank Dupee	0	0	1	0	0	0	3	0	0	0.00
	83	53	136	110	1,218⅓	1,250	309	394	11	2.95

1902

Record: 74–60
Finish: Fourth
Games Behind: 8
Manager: Clark Griffith

The tattered Remnants were made to suffer again in 1902. Outfielder Danny Green abandoned the West Side ballclub to join the Sox for their third title run. The plucky Irish outfielder complemented a lineup already stacked with speed

Clark Griffith

merchants. The 1902 White Sox pilfered a league-leading 265 bases; Green swiped 35. The defense however, was suspect. In a generally weak field the White Sox committed 257 errors, which was the fewest in the league but an indication that the quality of play in the AL was still very sloppy.

Encouraged by his 1901 success, Comiskey spent lavishly in order to bolster his team at the expense of the older league. Sammy Strang, Tom Daly, and Ed McFarland were signed to White Sox contracts. On paper at least, the White Sox appeared even stronger than before.

Chicago built an early, impressive 4½ game lead by July 4, only to have it vanish by month's end. In July the National League conspired with Baltimore manager John McGraw to cripple the American League and force Ban Johnson to sue for peace. McGraw privately negotiated the sale of his team to New York Giants owner John T. Brush. After Baltimore forfeited a game on July 17, Johnson revoked the franchise charter and assumed management of the team. Johnson ordered the other seven American League teams to contribute two players off their roster in order for the Orioles to keep going through the year. The White Sox surrendered Jack Katoll and Herm McFarland, then awaited Johnson's next move.

The immediate repercussions of the foiled McGraw coup damaged the White Sox pennant hopes, but the seeds were already sown for something more spectacular. Secret plans were already afoot to transfer the ailing Baltimore team to New York, where it would begin play as the Highlanders in 1903. In August, when the rumors first surfaced, Johnson conferred with Comiskey. It was decided that for the good of the league, Clark Griffith should take over the managerial duties of the New York team. The Sox manager was unhappy with his situation in Chicago and was pleased to leave Comiskey's employ.

	G	AB	H	R	2B	3B	HR	RBI	SB	AVG
Frank Isbell	137	520	133	65	14	4	4	59	38	.256
Tom Daly	137	489	110	57	22	3	1	54	19	.225
George Davis	132	485	145	76	27	7	3	93	31	.299
Sammy Strang	137	536	158	108	18	5	3	46	38	.295
Danny Green	129	481	150	77	16	11	0	62	35	.312
Fielder Jones	135	532	171	98	16	5	0	54	33	.321
Sandow Mertes	129	497	140	60	23	7	1	79	46	.282
Billy Sullivan	76	263	64	36	12	3	1	26	11	.243
Jimmy Callahan	70	218	51	27	7	2	0	13	4	.234
Herm McFarland	9	29	5	5	0	0	0	4	1	.172
Jimmy Durham	5	15	1	3	0	0	0	0	0	.067
Ed McFarland	73	244	56	29	9	2	1	25	8	.230
Ed Hughes	1	4	1	0	0	0	0	0	0	.250
		4,659	1,251	678	170	50	14	537	265	.268

	W	L	GS	CG	IP	H	BB	K	ShO	ERA
Jimmy Callahan	16	14	31	29	282⅓	287	89	75	2	3.60
Roy Patterson	20	12	30	26	268	262	67	61	2	3.06
Wiley Piatt	12	13	30	22	246	263	66	96	2	3.51
Clark Griffith	15	9	24	20	212⅔	247	47	51	3	4.19
Ned Garvin	9	10	19	16	175⅓	169	43	55	2	2.21
Jimmy Durham	1	1	3	3	20	21	16	3	0	5.85
Sandow Mertes	1	0	0	0	7⅔	6	0	0	0	1.17
Dummy Leitner	0	0	0	0	4	9	2	0	0	13.50
Sam McMackin	0	0	0	0	3	1	0	2	0	0.00
Frank Isbell	0	1	1	0	1	3	1	1	0	9.00
Jack Katoll	0	0	0	0	1	1	0	2	0	0.00
	74	60	138	116	1,221	1,269	331	346	11	3.41

1903

Record: 60–77
Finish: Seventh
Games Behind: 30½
Manager: Jimmy Callahan

Peace between the warring leagues was finally reached on January 10, and everyone seemed happy with the arrangements except Comiskey, who scolded Johnson for failing to drive the ailing National League out of business once and for all.

As a part of the settlement agreement, the contracts of nine disputed players were awarded to the American League, including that of George Stacey Davis, a veteran shortstop who voluntarily left Comiskey's employ in 1902 in order to jump back to the New York Giants.

Upon hearing the news, Davis vowed to sit out the 1903 season. The sulky Davis decided to sit out his early retirement at the Brighton Beach Racetrack not far from New York.

The revamped lineup introduced to Chicago fans a quartet of promising young players destined to play starring roles in the gradually unfolding "Hitless Wonder" era.

Davis' replacement, the light-hitting Louisville recruit Lee Tannehill, committed six errors in a game with the New York Highlanders on September 18. The White Sox were simply awful in the field, and no one suffered the consequences more than Patsy Flaherty, the Louisville pitcher whose 11–25 record remains a benchmark of futility unmatched by any White Sox hurler before or since.

The dead-ball style of play was in full flower, and for the third consecutive year the team batting average dropped. Not until June 17 did a Sox player hit a home run at the 39th Street Grounds. Player/manager Jimmy Callahan's blast off of Bill Wolfe of the New York Highlanders that afternoon was only one of 14 home runs hit by the team all year.

Pat Flaherty lost 25 games in 1903—still a club record.

The Sox ended their business with a dismal 60–77 record despite a first-place showing as late as June 1. The second-half swoon, however, afforded Callahan the luxury of experimenting with a trio of young pitchers destined for mound greatness: Guy "Doc" White, an off-season dentist; Nick Altrock, claimed from Boston after he was given his release; and Frank Owen, an obscure pitcher with Omaha of the Western League until he came to the attention of Comiskey.

Whatever else may be said of Comiskey and his occasional mistreatment of players in his employ, the "Old Roman" was a master at player development. His 1903 acquisitions set the stage for the first golden era of White Sox baseball.

	G	AB	H	R	2B	3B	HR	RBI	SB	AVG
Frank Isbell	138	546	139	52	25	9	2	59	26	.255
George Magoon	94	334	76	32	11	3	0	25	4	.228
Lee Tannehill	138	503	113	48	14	3	2	50	10	.225
Jimmy Callahan	118	439	128	47	26	5	2	56	24	.292
Danny Green	135	499	154	75	26	7	6	62	29	.309
Fielder Jones	136	530	152	71	18	5	0	45	21	.287
Ducky Holmes	86	344	96	53	7	5	0	18	25	.279
Ed McFarland	61	201	42	15	7	2	1	19	3	.209
Tom Daly	43	150	31	20	22	0	0	19	6	.207
Pat "Cozy" Dolan	27	104	27	16	5	1	0	7	5	.260
Harry "Pep" Clark	15	65	20	7	4	2	0	9	5	.308
Bill Hallman	63	207	43	29	7	4	0	18	11	.208
Jack Slattery	63	211	46	8	3	2	0	20	2	.218
Billy Sullivan	32	111	21	10	4	0	1	7	3	.189
		4,670	1,159	516	176	49	14	436	180	.248

	W	L	GS	CG	IP	H	BB	K	ShO	ERA
Doc White	17	16	36	29	300	258	69	135	3	2.13
Patsy Flaherty	11	25	34	29	293⅔	338	50	65	2	3.74
Roy Patterson	14	15	30	26	293	275	69	89	2	2.70
Frank Owen	8	12	20	15	167⅓	167	44	66	1	3.50
Davey Dunkle	5	4	7	6	82	96	31	26	0	4.06
Nick Altrock	4	3	8	6	71	59	19	19	1	2.15
Jimmy Callahan	1	2	3	3	28	40	5	12	0	4.50
	60	77	138	114	1,235	1,233	287	412	9	3.02

1904

Record: 89–65
Finish: Third
Games Behind: 6
Managers: Jimmy Callahan, Fielder Jones

The White Sox owner was personally fond of Jimmy Callahan, but the Sox skipper was an undisciplined hard drinker unable to stay in proper physical condition. As a manager, his inexperience had cost the White Sox many games in 1903. The anticipated changing of the guard occurred on June 7, 1904, when Callahan stepped down in favor of his teammate, Fielder Allison Jones, whose leadership skills were apparent to Comiskey. "I believe I have the best interests of the team at heart," Cal said. "And this is the reason for my act. I will play harder for him than I ever have for myself."

Guy Harris White: five straight shutouts in September 1904

Jones stepped into the fray at a moment in time when White Sox fortunes were on an upswing. The fiery Jones had provided Chicago with steady outfield play since jumping to the Sox in 1901. Like Griffith, he was an agitator for player rights, and he was often quarrelsome in the presence of Comiskey, with whom he was not on speaking terms when the offer to manage came.

As a playing manager, Jones was a brilliant tactician and a motivator of men who was never afraid to experiment with his lineup or some unusual piece of strategy. In 1904 he moved a struggling fourth-place team into the heat of a pennant race within days. The White Sox claimed first place on August 10 and held the top spot for six short-lived days.

In September Doc White twirled five consecutive shutouts to keep his team in the thick of the race. The 45 consecutive scoreless innings established a major league record until Don Drysdale eclipsed the shutout string with six straight whitewashings in 1968.

The remarkable streak was finally snapped on October 2 by Griffith's Highlanders before an overflow crowd of 30,084 patrons who swarmed the field to congratulate Dr. White for his good work.

The Sox pulled to within two games of Boston on September 30, but could draw no closer to the eventual champs.

The 1904 season was also notable for the debut of a tall, rangy pitcher out of the Pennsylvania coalfields possessing an eccentric, exaggerated windup. Edward Augustine Walsh debuted in Philadelphia in relief on May 12, before nailing down his first career victory seven days later in Washington. Walsh was nearly perfect against a Three-I rookie named Beany Jacobsen. Walsh's two-hit shutout that long-ago rain-soaked afternoon in D.C. justified Callahan's preseason prognosis that his pitching staff was a formidable one. "I've got a ball team alright!" he glowed, and indeed he had.

	G	AB	H	R	2B	3B	HR	RBI	SB	AVG
Jiggs Donahue	102	367	91	46	9	7	1	48	18	.248
Gus Dundon	108	373	85	40	9	3	0	36	19	.228
George Davis	152	563	142	75	27	15	1	69	32	.252
Lee Tannehill	153	547	125	50	31	5	0	61	14	.229
Danny Green	147	536	142	83	16	10	2	62	28	.265
Charles Jones	5	17	4	2	0	1	0	1	0	.235
Fielder Jones	154	564	137	74	14	6	3	43	25	.243
Jimmy Callahan	132	482	136	66	23	2	0	54	29	.261
Billy Sullivan	108	371	85	29	18	4	1	44	11	.229
Frank Isbell	96	314	66	27	10	3	1	34	19	.210
Ducky Holmes	68	251	78	42	11	9	1	19	13	.311
Frank Huelsman	4	7	1	0	1	0	0	0	0	.143
Ed McFarland	50	160	44	22	11	3	0	20	2	.275
Mike Heydon	4	10	1	0	1	0	0	1	0	.100
Claude Berry	3	1	0	1	0	0	0	0	0	.000
		5,027	1,217	600	193	68	14	519	216	.242

	W	L	GS	CG	IP	H	BB	K	ShO	ERA
Frank Owen	21	15	36	34	315	243	61	103	4	1.94
Nick Altrock	21	13	36	31	307	274	48	87	6	2.96
Doc White	16	10	30	23	237	201	68	115	7	1.71
Frank Smith	16	10	23	22	202⅓	157	58	107	4	2.09
Roy Patterson	9	9	17	14	165	148	24	64	4	2.29
Ed Walsh	5	5	8	6	110⅔	90	32	57	1	2.60
Patsy Flaherty	1	2	5	4	43	36	10	14	0	2.09
Elmer Stricklett	0	1	1	0	7	12	2	3	0	10.29
Tom Dougherty	0	0	0	0	2	0	0	0	0	0.00
	89	65	156	134	1,389	1,161	303	550	26	2.29

1905

Record: 92–60
Finish: Second
Games Behind: 2
Manager: Fielder Jones

A blazing, down-to-the-wire pennant race and a preview of the great days to come spelled excitement between the white lines for the South Side faithful in 1905.

Year two of the first golden age of White Sox baseball featured great individual accomplishments by a pitching staff without peer in the American League.

Right-hander Frank Smith, who joined the team in 1904 after a stint in the Southern Association, fired the first of two 1905 one-hitters against the Senators on May 21. Smith, who was often at odds with his manager, followed up this bit of pitching mastery with a no-hitter on September 6 against Detroit.

The "Iron Man" quartet of Smith, White, Owen, and Altrock logged more than 1,200 innings between them in 1905, including a brutal stretch of *five doubleheaders* played in five consecutive days against the Philadelphia A's and Boston Pilgrims the final week of August. Chicago won seven of 10 games to close to within a half-game of Connie Mack's A's when the grueling stretch finally ended on August 27.

The White Sox sported the strongest pitching staff in the league. Their glittering 1.99 team earned run average was remarkable, even for those dead-ball years. The A's, on the other hand, were an offensive-oriented team who made their final assault on first place in July, after the Cleveland Naps, who had led the pack in the early going, faded.

Ed Walsh, who was completing his apprenticeship as a spot starter and long-relief man, won both ends of a doubleheader on September 26, after taking over for Doc White in the first inning of game one. Walsh duplicated the efforts of teammate Frank Owen, who also turned the unusual feat in 1905, against the St. Louis Browns on July 1. There seemed to be no limit to the skills and endurance of these pitchers.

The league championship was on the line when the Sox entered Philadelphia's tiny Columbia Park for a decisive showdown on September 28. The three games drew a combined 68,000 fans into a park that comfortably seated only 6,000. Mack's team delighted the hometown fans by winning two of three, thereby claiming a narrow one-game lead over Chicago in the standings.

Even though the Comiskeys were far from finished, Ban Johnson and the ruling National Commission declared Philadelphia the pennant winner and assigned them the World Series home-game dates. "Is that fair to the players, to the public, to myself?" Comiskey protested. "The actions of the Commission are an outrage!"

At the heart of the matter was the growing coolness between Johnson and Comiskey. The two founders were barely civil to each other. Their differences were years in the making, but finally bubbled to the surface on June 5, when Johnson abruptly suspended White Sox outfielder James "Ducky" Holmes for arguing with umpire James "Silk" O'Loughlin at a time when the roster was thinned by injuries.

Ducky Holmes roamed the Comiskey outfield for less than three seasons. He was a constant disciplinary problem to Callahan and Jones. Yet his Chicago legacy was powerfully enduring because it drove a permanent wedge between the two American League founding fathers. How different the course of baseball history might have been if only Comiskey and Johnson had practiced civility and reached some accommodation in order to work for the betterment of the game.

	G	AB	H	R	2B	3B	HR	RBI	SB	AVG
Jiggs Donahue	149	553	153	71	22	4	1	76	32	.287
Gus Dundon	106	364	70	30	7	3	0	22	14	.192
George Davis	157	550	153	74	29	1	1	55	31	.278
Lee Tannehill	142	480	96	38	17	2	0	39	8	.200
Danny Green	112	379	92	56	13	6	0	44	11	.243
Fielder Jones	153	568	139	91	17	12	2	38	20	.245
Ducky Holmes	92	328	66	42	15	2	0	22	11	.201
Billy Sullivan	99	323	65	25	10	3	2	26	14	.201
Frank Isbell	94	341	101	55	21	11	2	45	15	.296
George Rohe	34	113	24	14	1	0	1	12	2	.212
Jimmy Callahan	96	345	94	50	18	6	1	43	26	.272
Ed McFarland	80	250	70	24	13	4	0	31	5	.280
James "Hub" Hart	10	17	2	2	0	0	0	4	0	.118
		5,109	1,212	613	200	55	11	487	194	.237

The 1905 White Sox

	W	L	GS	CG	IP	H	BB	K	ShO	ERA
Frank Owen	21	13	38	32	334	276	56	125	3	2.10
Nick Altrock	22	12	34	31	315⅔	274	63	97	3	1.88
Frank Smith	19	13	31	27	291⅔	215	107	171	4	2.13
Doc White	18	14	33	25	260⅓	204	58	120	4	1.76
Ed Walsh	8	3	13	9	136⅔	121	29	71	1	2.17
Roy Patterson	4	5	9	7	88⅔	73	16	29	1	1.83
	92	60	158	131	1,427	1,163	329	613	16	1.99

1906

Record: 93–58
Finish: First
Games Ahead: 3
Manager: Fielder Jones

On May 1, 1906, Comiskey vacated his offices in the Fisher Building on Dearborn Street, where he had shared space with Ban Johnson for nearly six years. The AL president immediately refurbished the empty office and explained to the newspapermen that Comiskey's quarters were needed for expansion, nothing more.

The differences between the two men reflected another widening gulf—the gap between Cubs and White Sox fans. By nature, the West Side Cubs fan was less likely to charge the field and attack any offending umpire, as was the custom on the South Side in the early years. Boisterous White Sox fans viewed their team as a logical extension of the Bridgeport neighborhood they called home.

"The pikers who crowd into the first-base bleachers and bet nickels on the innings then roast player or umpire, or hurl bottles at them when they lose are responsible for the reputation Chicago has of being the toughest town in either Major League circuit" wrote the *Chicago Tribune* on May 1, 1906.

This 1906 ballclub was not a great team. In fact, until very late in the season, it wasn't even a very *good* team.

Indeed, this was a very unsettled baseball team in spring training. Two-thirds of the starting outfield in 1905 were out of baseball. Ducky Holmes was released over the winter; Jimmy Callahan became part owner of a famous local semi-pro team known as the Logan Squares; and Danny Green had retired.

Comiskey and Jones regrouped and added to the list of spring hopefuls one Ernest "Rube" Vinson, a part-time outfielder who had been suspended by Cleveland in 1905. The cloudy outfield picture, however, would not be resolved until mid-July, when Patsy Dougherty was added to the roster following a fistfight with his manager, Clark Griffith.

Manager Jones was blessed with a marvelous pitching staff—and very little else. Bad weather, outfield inconsistencies, and a rash of early season injuries buried the Sox in sixth place by the time June rolled around. Fielder Jones was forced to improvise with a weak-hitting lineup hobbled by George Davis' sore shoulder, second baseman Gus Dundon's illness, and a case of food poisoning that sidelined catcher Billy Sullivan.

After the clubhouse began resembling a hospital ward, Comiskey hired a specialist in physical conditioning: University of Chicago athletic trainer Hiram "Doc" Connibear. His

"There, Mr. Bear! You Stay Down There!" The Hitless Wonders bag a "West Side Bear" in this front-page cartoon from the *Chicago Daily News*, October 1906.

rigorous exercise regimens restored vitality and gave the team its second wind. Connibear lasted only a half season. He departed the team in early September to accept a coaching job at the University of Washington, but the "Bear" left his imprimatur on this team. Without him, the Sox could not have won in '06.

Fielder Jones was never afforded the luxury of a settled lineup. He had to make due with "situation players" like outfielder Eddie Hahn, who joined the team on May 6 and sparked the offense in the middle of the season. His single off Browns pitcher Barney Pelty on July 6 saved the Sox from being no-hit.

Across town, the Cubs offered a positive contrast to the injury-riddled Sox. The West Siders were turning the National League race into a shambles and were on their way to racking up 116 wins. By July 31, Frank Chance's ballclub stood at 66–28, their pennant on the threshold. The slowly

Comiskey's 1906 misfits were magic.

improving Sox stood at 50–42 by comparison, and they trailed Cleveland and New York by nine games.

It was around this time that the Jones boys acquired the nickname "Hitless Wonders" for the amazing way they won ballgames without benefit of an offense. Consider: their everyday shortstop Lee Tannehill hit .183 for the entire season. It was the lowest figure ever recorded for a starting player who appeared in 100 or more games. On June 10 Chicago nearly won a game without a hit. They scored the only run off of Highlander pitcher Al Orth on a hit batsman, a muffed double play, and an error.

The Sox batted only .230 as a team with six credited home runs until closer research turned up a seventh. The lost roundtripper was hit by catcher Billy Sullivan on August 16.

Sox Homers in 1906

Date	Player	Opposing Pitcher	Team	Inning
1. 5/05/06	Bill O'Neill	Jack Townsend	Cleveland	1st
2. 5/18/06	Fielder Jones	Casey Patten	Washington	1st
3. 5/31/06	Billy Sullivan	Ed Siever	Detroit	9th
4. 8/16/06	Billy Sullivan	Joe Harris	Boston	3rd
5. 8/20/06	Pat Dougherty	Al Orth	New York	7th
6. 9/22/06	Fielder Jones	Jack Doyle	New York	5th
7. 10/04/06	Jiggs Donahue	Addie Joss	Cleveland	7th

A *Tribune* headline from July 14 marveled at the "Hitless Wonders, Who Rally and Turn an Apparent New York Victory Into Defeat."

Maybe it was sportswriter Charles Dryden from that same newspaper who first coined the memorable phrase. No one knows for sure, but Hughie Fullerton, Dryden's sidekick on the baseball beat, added a few choice words of his own in the midst of the team's record-setting 19-game winning streak that erased the nine-game deficit between the two other contenders and the Sox.

"To those who have not seen the Sox in their wonderful winning streak, it is a wonder how they score so many runs on so few hits. Let them see the Sox take every advantage of misplays and let them see them dash daringly around the bases and invite wild throws. Let them follow the quick accurate work of the fielders and their keen teammates. These wonderful fans will then solve for themselves the methods which are winning game after game," the *Chicago Tribune* reported on August 21, 1906.

The logic-defying victory streak ended in Washington on August 25, in the presence of Ban Johnson, who was rooting loudly for the seventh-place Senators.

And still, it was not quite enough to thrust Chicago over the top because Griffith's Highlanders reeled off a 15-game streak of their own that temporarily dropped the White Sox into second place on September 3.

It was a home-and-away series with Detroit from September 5 to 10 that turned the tide of victory in Chicago's favor. The White Sox won four of five amid disturbing allegations that the Detroit players were "laying down" for Chicago and the bookmakers.

The pennant was won on October 3 while the Sox sat out a rain delay in St. Louis. Jones modestly proclaimed that he would not trade his pitching staff for any other in baseball. Who could argue with such irrefutable logic?

The 32 shutouts turned in by this team paced the major leagues. Doc White and Ed Walsh recorded four one-hitters between them. However, the final credit for this triumph against impossible odds rested with Fielder Jones, who maximized the contributions of a moderately talented ballclub laden with dissension.

When comparing the merits of White Sox managers yet to come, few stand as tall as the Napoleon-like field boss from Shinglehouse, Pennsylvania.

The fearsome Chicago Cubs were to provide the opposition in a remarkable World Series showdown that was shaping up to be a war to the finish between the South Side "Davids" and the West Side "Goliaths."

	G	AB	H	R	2B	3B	HR	RBI	SB	AVG
Jiggs Donahue	154	556	143	70	17	7	1	57	36	.257
Gus Dundon	143	549	153	71	21	11	0	57	37	.279
George Davis	133	484	134	63	26	6	0	80	27	.277
Lee Tannehill	116	378	69	26	8	3	0	33	7	.183
Bill O'Neill	94	330	82	37	4	1	1	21	19	.248
Fielder Jones	144	496	114	77	22	4	2	34	26	.230
Ed Hahn	130	484	110	80	7	5	0	27	19	.227
Billy Sullivan	118	387	83	37	18	4	2	33	10	.214
George Rohe	75	225	58	14	5	1	0	25	8	.258
Gus Dundon	33	96	13	7	1	0	0	4	4	.135
Lee Quillan	4	9	3	1	0	0	0	0	1	.333
Patsy Dougherty	75	253	59	30	9	4	1	27	11	.233
Frank Hemphill	13	40	3	0	0	0	0	2	1	.075
Ernest "Rube" Vinson	7	24	6	2	0	0	0	3	1	.250
Frank Roth	16	51	10	4	1	1	0	7	1	.196
James "Hub" Hart	17	37	6	1	0	0	0	0	0	.162
Jay "Babe" Towne	13	36	10	3	0	0	0	6	0	.278
Ed McFarland	7	22	3	0	1	0	0	3	0	.136
		4,924	1,133	567	155	52	7	444	214	.230

	W	L	GS	CG	IP	H	BB	K	ShO	ERA
Frank Owen	22	13	36	27	293	289	54	66	7	2.33
Nick Altrock	20	13	30	25	287⅔	269	42	99	4	2.06
Ed Walsh	17	13	31	24	278⅓	215	58	171	10	1.88
Doc White	18	6	24	20	219⅓	160	38	102	7	1.52
Roy Patterson	10	7	18	12	142	119	17	45	3	2.09
Frank Smith	5	5	13	8	132	124	37	53	1	3.39
Lou Fiene	1	1	2	1	31	35	9	12	0	2.90
Frank Isbell	0	0	0	0	2	1	0	2	0	0.00
	93	58	154	117	1,375⅓	1,212	255	550	32	2.13

1907

Record: 87–64
Finish: Third
Games Behind: 5½
Manager: Fielder Jones

Fielder Jones led a restless and discontented band of White Sox players deep into the Mexican interior, where Comiskey elected to conduct his 1907 spring training. For years it had been the Old Roman's burning ambition to internationalize baseball. His celebrated "World Tour" was seven years away, but for now Comiskey basked in the favorable publicity of this modest excursion organized by Ted Sullivan, Commy's friend and baseball mentor.

There was widespread discontent among the champions when the *Sunset Limited* steamed out of Chicago on March 5, on its way to Parque de la Reforma in Mexico City. The players and the manager were united in the belief that they deserved something more in their contracts than the $15,000 bonus money given out at World Series time. For each player, the bonus worked out to $1,874.01—which Comiskey factored into the 1907 contracts.

Fielder Jones was sullen and contemplative. The skipper pondered retirement until the Old Roman came through

From May until August, Fielder Jones's 1907 edition held down first place.

with a one-year contract extension calling for an adjusted annual salary of $10,000, which Jones accepted. The players however, had to "take it or leave it."

A crew of workmen hoisted the pennant pole into the air on Opening Day, April 18, only to have it come crashing down in the presence of Comiskey, the mayor of Chicago, and a score of local dignitaries. It was that kind of year on the South Side.

Injuries exacted a frightful toll in 1907. The starting lineup was intact for only seven days of the year. Jones was forced to experiment with his lineups, and the team showed surprising success.

George Rohe, the hero of the 1906 World Series, filled in for Lee Tannehill at third base when Tannehill was sidelined with a spike wound and nearly lost his leg. Rohe's disappointing hitting caused Comiskey to release him at the end of the season, despite a guarantee of lifetime employment based on his World Series contributions.

The White Sox took over first place on May 2 and held on to a paper-thin lead until August 6. It was another virtuoso performance by Jones, who was twice ejected from a game and suspended by Johnson. When Johnson sent Comiskey a fresh catch of fish from a recent outdoor expedition as a sign that there were no hard feelings between the two, Comiskey demanded to know, "Am I to play these in the outfield?"

For the fourth straight year, the White Sox battled the league leaders down to the final week of the season. But again, as in 1905, a pivotal road series in Philadelphia in late

September sealed the fate of the ballclub. The Sox dropped two of three to Mack's team September 24–26, and with these losses their fading pennant hopes evaporated.

The Detroit Tigers would square off against Frank Chance's Cubs in the 1907 tilt. It was a bitter finish to an emotionally draining season in which many Sox fans had to be asking themselves whether these Hitless Wonders were actually one-year wonders?

For the embattled Sox manager, 1907 became a season of marked frustration. As the bell tolled on the season, Jones chided a visiting delegation of local reporters in the lobby of the Copley Square Hotel who asked him if the Sox would be satisfied to finish second.

"Take the second husband for instance," Jones snapped. "He's a dead bird before the wedding bells ring out. All the second husband is good for is to wear the old clothes of the first. The Sox are too proud to take anybody's leavings. If we cannot be first, we care not for second, which is but the anteroom to oblivion."

The White Sox obliged and finished third.

	G	AB	H	R	2B	3B	HR	RBI	SB	AVG
Jiggs Donahue	157	609	158	75	16	4	0	68	27	.259
Frank Isbell	125	486	118	60	22	8	0	55	22	.243
George Davis	132	466	111	59	16	2	1	52	15	.238
George Rohe	144	494	105	46	11	2	2	51	16	.213
Ed Hahn	156	592	151	87	9	7	0	45	17	.255
Fielder Jones	154	559	146	72	18	1	0	47	17	.261
Patsy Dougherty	148	533	144	69	17	2	2	59	33	.270
Billy Sullivan	112	339	59	30	8	4	0	36	6	.174
Lee Quillan	49	151	29	17	5	0	0	14	8	.192
Lee Tannehill	33	108	26	9	2	0	0	11	3	.241
Jake Atz	3	7	1	0	0	0	0	0	0	.143
Mike Welday	24	35	8	2	1	1	0	1	0	.229
Charles Hickman	21	23	6	1	2	0	0	8	0	.261
Ed McFarland	52	138	39	11	9	1	0	7	3	.283
James "Hub" Hart	29	70	19	6	1	0	0	0	1	.271
Charlie Armbruster	1	3	0	0	0	0	0	0	0	.000
		5,079	1,205	584	150	35	6	488	175	.237

	W	L	GS	CG	IP	H	BB	K	ShO	ERA
Ed Walsh	24	18	46	37	422⅓	341	87	206	5	1.60
Frank Smith	22	11	37	29	310	280	111	139	3	2.47
Doc White	27	13	35	24	291	270	38	141	7	2.26
Nick Altrock	8	12	21	15	213⅔	210	31	61	1	2.57
Roy Patterson	4	6	13	4	96	105	18	27	1	2.63
Frank Owen	2	3	4	2	47	43	13	15	0	2.49
Lou Fiene	0	1	1	1	26	30	7	15	0	4.15
Frank Isbell	0	0	0	0	⅓	0	0	0	0	0.00
	87	64	157	112	1,406⅓	1,279	305	604	17	2.22

1908

Record: 88–64
Finish: Third
Games Behind: 1½
Manager: Fielder Jones

The "season of second guessing" began when Jimmy Callahan applied for reinstatement after a two-year absence playing in the local semipro circuit. Callahan was turned down by the autocratic National Commission, but if Comiskey's affection for his former manager was any condition, Jimmy would eventually be back in some capacity.

Ed Walsh firing his deadly spitter

The White Sox never lost sight of first place at any point in the 1908 season. During the first half of the season they battled the Cleveland Naps and the improved St. Louis Browns for top honors. After the Fourth of July the focus shifted to the Detroit Tigers, who staged an impressive rally that elevated them from worst to first.

With essentially the same hitless cast of characters who won it all in '06, Comiskey's team threatened to make this an encore performance by winning 13 straight beginning on June 4. They captured first place and held on for 16 tension-filled days before dropping back.

Visions of an all-Chicago World Series were uppermost in the fans' minds as the season progressed. Unfortunately the Sox were still very weak offensively. Fielder Jones, Frank Isbell, and Ed Walsh accounted for all three home runs hit by the White Sox in 1908.

In a year characterized by controversy and finger-pointing, Ed Walsh's 40 victories rank as the greatest pitching performance in team annals. Walsh pitched every two days on the average. He started 49 games and appeared in relief 15 other times. Walsh accounted for seven of his team's last 13 victories of the season. In six of his losses, his mates failed to dent the plate.

Walsh is credited with 40 wins, though with modern scoring rules applied, four of the victories would have to be considered "saves." In their postseason summary of October 7, the *Chicago Tribune* credited the Sox ace with 36 victories—a figure closer to the truth, with all due respect to the achievements of Walsh.

His pride injured beyond repair, Frank Smith jumped the ballclub on July 12 as a result of deep personal resentments toward Fielder Jones, who had criticized his sensitive pitcher for boozing and missing practice. Upon his return to Chicago, Smith brushed aside media criticisms and posted 11 victories during the stretch drive, including a September 20 no-hitter against Philadelphia.

The Smith and Jones acrimony ultimately cost the Sox the pennant and indirectly brought down the curtain on the five-year Hitless Wonder saga.

The stunning climax unfolded in Cleveland on October 2, when Walsh and Addie Joss hooked up in a pitching duel few have ever matched. The handsome young ace of the Cleveland staff struck out four batters in a 1–0 perfect-game performance. Reserve catcher Ossee Schreckengost ruptured tendons in his forefinger trying to hold on to Walsh's sharply breaking spitter. His inability to hang on to Walsh's delivery led to Cleveland's only run when Joe Birmingham scored on a passed ball.

Walsh fanned 15 that afternoon and was nearly as good as Joss, pitch for pitch.

Frank Smith and Doc White won the next two games to pull the White Sox to within a game and a half of the Tigers and Naps with two left to play in Chicago. Ed Walsh returned to the hill on October 5 to shut down the Tigers. Cleveland was eliminated that same day, leaving Detroit and Chicago to settle accounts in a winner-take-all showdown on the final day of the season.

Fielder Jones considered bringing back Walsh on just 24 hours' rest, but Ed did not look good in his pregame warm-ups, forcing Jones to choose between Frank Smith and Doc White. Smith enjoyed greater success against Detroit than Dr. White, who had split eight decisions against them in 1908. Smith also had an extra day's rest, but Jones had not forgiven him for past differences.

Doc White was ordered to the mound on an overcast, gray afternoon in Chicago, where confidence ran high among Sox fans. Comiskey had arrived at the park at 7:00 AM in breathless anticipation of the day. "Our only anxiety was the weather," the Old Roman reported. "I'll venture to say that 90 percent of the crowd this afternoon were as confident as we were."

Too much confidence? It ended quickly. The outcome was decided in the first inning, when Ty Cobb tripled home two runs. White was removed after retiring only one batter in favor of the overworked and arm-weary Ed Walsh. The big "Moose" was unable to contain the Detroit hitters, who cruised to an easy 7–0 victory, and with it they carried the flag back to Tiger town.

Euphoria gave way to gloom. In the postgame interviews, Comiskey described the unexpected outcome to this most exciting of all seasons as a crushing disappointment—the worst of his career.

"That game meant more to me than any game I ever saw," he told the writers. On that last bitter note, the Hitless Wonder era ended, and the slow process of rebuilding began.

	G	AB	H	R	2B	3B	HR	RBI	SB	AVG
Jiggs Donahue	93	304	62	22	8	2	0	22	14	.204
George Davis	128	419	91	41	14	1	0	26	22	.217
Freddy Parent	119	391	81	28	7	5	0	35	9	.207
Lee Tannehill	141	482	104	44	15	3	0	35	6	.216
Ed Hahn	122	447	112	58	12	8	0	21	11	.251
Fielder Jones	149	529	134	92	11	7	1	50	26	.253
Patsy Dougherty	138	482	134	68	11	6	0	45	47	.278
Billy Sullivan	137	430	82	40	8	4	0	29	15	.191
Frank Isbell	84	320	79	31	15	3	1	49	18	.247
Jake Atz	83	206	40	24	3	0	0	27	9	.194
Billy Purtell	26	69	9	3	2	0	0	3	2	.130
John Anderson	123	355	93	36	17	1	0	47	21	.262
Al Shaw	32	49	4	0	1	0	0	2	0	.082
Art Weaver	15	35	7	1	1	0	0	1	0	.200
Ossee Schreckengost	6	16	3	1	0	0	0	0	0	.188
		5,027	1,127	535	145	41	3	430	209	.224

	W	L	GS	CG	IP	H	BB	K	ShO	ERA
Ed Walsh	40	15	49	42	464	343	56	269	12	1.42
Frank Smith	17	16	35	24	297⅔	213	73	129	3	2.03
Doc White	19	13	37	24	296	267	69	126	5	2.55
Frank Owen	6	9	14	5	140	142	37	48	1	3.41
Nick Altrock	3	7	13	8	136	127	18	21	1	2.71
Mark "Moxie" Manuel	3	3	6	3	60⅓	52	25	25	0	3.28
Lou Fiene	0	1	1	1	9	9	1	3	0	4.00
Andy Nelson	0	0	1	0	9	11	4	1	0	2.00
Fred Olmstead	0	0	0	0	2	6	1	1	0	13.50
	88	64	156	107	1,414	1,170	284	623	22	2.22

1909

Record: 78–74
Finish: Fourth
Games Behind: 20
Manager: Billy Sullivan

After nearly a decade of loyal and faithful service to the White Sox as their day-in-and-day-out catcher, Billy Sullivan was appointed manager on April 12. Comiskey waited until the last possible moment for Jones to return, but the colorful and enigmatic manager sent a message to the press that left little room for doubt as to where he stood.

"My desire is to quit the game," he said. "Of course, I should feel obliged to play if Commy meets my figures. He won't, and I'll be glad for it."

Jones was speaking of partial ownership of the ballclub as his price for returning in 1909. Comiskey never gave it a passing thought. He remained confident that the White Sox could weather Jones' departure, but the White Sox failed to respond to Sullivan's laid-back management style and sagged in the standings.

Chicago got off to a rough start and was never a factor in the final outcome of the flag chase. The early season absence of Ed Walsh, who held out for $7,500, set the tone for the season. Big Ed won only 15 games in 1909—his powerful right arm was hampered by strained ligaments.

The 1909 season marked the end of the road for two South Side mainstays—Nick Altrock and Frank Isbell, the last player from the original 1900 cast. Beset by injuries and

Rebuilding with infielder Freddie Parent

	G	AB	H	R	2B	3B	HR	RBI	SB	AVG
Frank Isbell	120	423	97	33	17	6	0	39	23	.224
Jake Atz	119	381	90	39	18	3	0	22	14	.236
Freddy Parent	136	472	123	61	10	5	0	30	32	.261
Lee Tannehill	155	531	118	39	21	5	0	47	12	.222
Ed Hahn	76	287	52	30	6	0	1	16	9	.181
Dave Altizer	116	382	89	47	6	7	1	20	27	.233
Patsy Dougherty	139	491	140	71	23	13	1	55	36	.285
Billy Sullivan	97	265	43	11	3	0	0	16	9	.162
Billy Purtell	103	361	93	34	9	3	0	40	14	.258
George Davis	28	68	9	5	1	0	0	2	4	.132
Barney Reilly	12	25	5	3	0	0	0	3	2	.200
Jiggs Donahue	2	4	0	0	0	0	0	2	0	.000
Hamilton Patterson	1	3	0	2	0	0	0	0	0	.000
Willis Cole	46	165	39	17	7	3	0	16	3	.236
Bobby Messenger	31	112	19	18	1	1	0	0	7	.170
Mike Welday	29	74	14	3	0	0	0	5	2	.189
Gavvy Cravath	19	50	9	7	0	0	1	8	3	.180
Roland "Cutie" Barrows	5	20	3	1	0	0	0	2	9	.150
Frank Owens	64	174	35	12	4	1	0	17	3	.201
Fred Payne	32	82	20	8	2	0	0	12	0	.244
		5,017	1,110	494	145	56	4	399	211	.221

	W	L	GS	CG	IP	H	BB	K	ShO	ERA
Frank Smith	25	17	41	37	365	278	70	177	7	1.80
Jim Scott	12	12	29	19	250⅓	194	93	135	4	2.30
Ed Walsh	15	11	28	20	230⅓	166	50	127	8	1.41
Doc White	10	9	21	14	177⅔	149	31	77	3	1.72
Bill Burns	8	13	19	8	174⅓	169	35	52	3	1.96
Harry "Rube" Suter	2	3	6	3	87⅓	72	28	53	1	2.47
Lou Fiene	2	5	6	4	72	75	18	24	0	4.13
Fred Olmstead	3	2	6	5	54⅔	52	12	21	0	1.81
Frank Owen	1	1	2	1	16	19	3	3	0	4.50
Nick Altrock	0	1	1	1	9	16	1	2	0	5.00
	78	74	159	112	1,436⅔	1,190	341	671	26	2.04

advancing age, Isbell was granted his release in order to fulfill wide-ranging ambitions to manage. He would take over the affairs of the Wichita club of the American Association, and as a minor league magnate of some importance, would conclude numerous player transactions with Comiskey in the years to come.

Nick Altrock, a pixieish southpaw, was traded to Washington for "Sleepy" Bill Burns, a journeyman pitcher deeply involved in the conspiracy to throw the 1919 World Series to the Reds.

An August rally saved the White Sox from falling below the .500 mark in Sullivan's first season. The late-season rush maintained a string of first-division finishes, but Sully was unhappy in the unfamiliar role of field boss. In midseason he notified Comiskey of his intention to step down in the fall.

Losing to the Cubs in the 1909 City Series was a terrible blow to the owner—the postseason games were played for pride and bragging rights. "We lost the pennant in the American League this year and the championship of the City Series because the team didn't fight as hard as it should have fought," Comiskey stated.

Unable to lure Fielder Jones out of his early retirement, Comiskey inveigled 41-year-old Hugh Duffy, a former National League batting champion who had been only marginally successful as manager of the Philadelphia Phillies, to pilot the Sox in 1910.

"Duffy is the right man to turn the trick next year," Comiskey gloated. "I am going to give him a good team and one that can win."

1910

Record: 68–85
Finish: Sixth
Games Behind: 35½
Manager: Hugh Duffy

Weird omens and ancient Irish superstitions preyed upon the Old Roman as construction crews steamed ahead to complete the new Comiskey Park in time for the scheduled July 1 opening. In the company of league president Ban Johnson, the Sox owner narrowly avoided serious injury in a freakish train collision outside Frankfort, Kentucky, two months before the season was scheduled to open. When the American League schedule was drafted over the winter, Comiskey was horrified to discover that July 1 fell on a Friday—traditionally an unlucky day for the Irish. Ban Johnson spitefully refused to revise the schedule to placate his former friend.

The team that inaugurated Chicago's first concrete and steel sports stadium was deeply in transition. An influx of rookies reduced the median age to 27, a drop of five years since 1908. The youth movement sacrificed George Davis, who was released in the preseason, and Frank "Yip" Owen, who was assigned to Minneapolis, the graveyard for washed-up White Sox pitchers.

The disintegration of the Hitless Wonders provided Sox fans with an early preview of a future Black Sox star vying for a spot on the roster: first baseman Arnold "Chick" Gandil, whose erratic play resulted in a demotion to the Eastern League on September 2.

The season began on a high note. Frank Smith tossed the only Opening Day one-hitter in team history when he blanked the Browns on April 14. "Smithie," the unconscious clubhouse comedian, was traded to the Boston Red Sox on August 8 with Billy Purtell for Harry Lord and Ambrose McConnell, a pair of infielders acquired for their defensive skills.

The trade was weeks in the making, but it was nearly canceled when Boston Red Sox owner John I. Taylor demanded Ed Walsh even-up for Lord. Comiskey flatly refused. Taylor relented and agreed to the Old Roman's terms. Smith lasted less than a year in the Hub. All in all, it was a good trade for Chicago and is counted among Comiskey's finest pre–Black Sox deals.

Comiskey Park, the third concrete and steel stadium built in America, opened to rave reviews and great fanfare on July 1. Four military bands and a score of local dignitaries joined in the festive celebrations, which were soured by a 2–0 loss to St. Louis and a costly injury to White Sox captain Rollie Zeider. In the next few days, Chick Gandil and backup catcher Freddie Payne sustained freakish injuries, leading to speculation that this new park had a curse attached to it.

Harry Lord, captain of the White Sox

Nineteen ten was a pretty bleak year all around on the South Side, despite the usual workmanlike efforts put forth by sore-armed Ed Walsh, who tossed 40⅔ consecutive scoreless innings in early August—good for second place on the team's all-time list.

The 1910 edition was the height of futility, never rising above fifth place. The weak-hitting ballclub was shut out 24 times. Their collective .211 team batting average still stands as the worst of any team in the 20th century. The team finished dead last in hitting slugging average, home runs, and doubles, and sixth in fielding. An 11-game losing streak between July 8 and 21 established a new record of failure on the South Side up to this time.

	G	AB	H	R	2B	3B	HR	RBI	SB	AVG
Arnold "Chick" Gandil	77	275	53	21	7	3	2	21	12	.193
Rollie Zeider	136	498	108	57	9	2	0	31	49	.217
Lena Blackburne	75	242	42	16	3	1	0	10	4	.174
Billy Purtell	102	368	86	21	5	3	1	36	5	.234
John "Shano" Collins	97	315	62	29	10	8	1	24	10	.197
Paul Meloan	65	222	54	23	6	6	0	23	4	.243
Patsy Dougherty	127	443	110	45	8	6	1	43	22	.248
Fred Payne	91	257	56	17	5	4	0	19	6	.218
Lee Tannehill	67	230	51	17	10	0	1	21	3	.222
Charles French	45	170	28	17	1	1	0	4	5	.165
Harry Lord	44	165	49	26	6	3	0	10	17	.297
Charlie Mullen	41	123	24	15	2	1	0	13	4	.195
Ambrose McConnell	32	119	33	13	2	3	0	5	4	.277
Freddy Parent	81	258	46	23	6	1	1	16	14	.178
George Browne	30	112	27	17	4	1	0	4	5	.241
Edward "Dutch" Zwilling	27	87	16	7	5	0	0	5	1	.184
Felix Chouinard	24	82	16	6	3	2	0	9	4	.195
Willis Cole	22	80	14	6	2	1	0	2	0	.175
Ed Hahn	15	53	6	2	2	0	0	1	0	.113
Albert "Red" Kelly	14	45	7	6	0	1	0	1	0	.156
Bobby Messinger	9	26	6	7	0	1	0	4	3	.231
Roland "Cutie" Barrows	6	20	4	0	0	0	0	1	0	.200
James "Red" Bowser	1	2	0	0	0	0	0	0	0	.000
Bruno Block	55	152	32	12	1	1	0	9	3	.211
Billy Sullivan	45	142	26	10	4	1	0	6	0	.183
		5,028	1,062	456	115	58	7	351	183	.211

	W	L	GS	CG	IP	H	BB	K	ShO	ERA
Ed Walsh	18	20	36	33	369⅔	242	61	258	7	1.27
Doc White	15	13	29	20	245⅔	219	50	111	2	2.56
Jim Scott	8	18	23	14	229⅔	182	86	135	2	2.43
Fred Olmstead	10	12	20	14	184⅓	174	50	68	4	1.95
Irv Young	4	8	17	7	135⅔	122	39	64	4	2.72
Frank Lange	9	4	15	6	130⅔	93	54	98	1	1.65
Frank Smith	4	9	15	9	128⅔	91	40	50	3	2.03
William "Chief" Chouneau	0	1	1	0	5⅓	7	0	1	0	3.38
Bill Burns	0	0	0	0	⅓	0	1	0	0	0.00
	68	85	156	103	1,430	1,130	381	785	23	2.01

1911

Record: 77–74
Finish: Fourth
Games Behind: 24
Manager: Hugh Duffy

Solid improvement with a reconfigured pitching staff and the most potent team offense since 1902 offered encouragement as the second decade of Sox baseball dawned.

Duffy's team played break-even baseball for much of the season, wavering between fourth and sixth but never losing complete sight of the first division.

Ed Walsh returned to brilliance with 27 victories, including the only nine-inning no-hitter of his career on August 27 against the Red Sox. A walk to Clyde Engle in the fourth inning was all that stood between Big Ed and absolute mound perfection.

It was a most satisfying year for the Sox ace, whose arm was strong and healthy. Walsh put an end to Ty Cobb's 40-game hitting streak on July 4. On September 30 he pocketed an additional $100 after smacking a 419-foot fungo fly that set new records on Charley Comiskey's annual "Field Day" event in Comiskey Park.

At the conclusion of the season Walsh was awarded a $4,000 touring car from his teammates, the fans, and Frank "Wildfire" Schulte of the Cubs, who felt bad that the Sox ace had been overlooked by the committee voting on the Chalmers Award (forerunner of the Most Valuable Player award). The car was presented to Walsh before a special exhibition game against the Cubs on October 26.

As a judge of rookie talent, Comiskey was usually without peer among American League owners. Joe Benz, the Batesville, Indiana, "butcher boy," was a late-season sensation in 1911. Indeed, there were really only three players of future consequence who slipped through the White Sox organization in the first two decades—outfielder Edd Roush and pitchers Horace "Hod" Eller and George Mogridge were given "cup of coffee" tryouts and then released. Mogridge failed to impress during his 1911 appearance and was returned to Frank Isbell's Wichita club for further tuning. George Mogridge would go on to post 134 wins in a 15-year career.

The modest success of the 1911 Sox failed to save Duffy's job. On October 22, Comiskey brought back an old fan favorite in Jimmy Callahan as his choice to manage the ballclub in 1912. Comiskey preferred that his field bosses maintain a year-long residence in Chicago so they could attend to the baseball business in the off-season. Duffy was a resident of Dorchester, Massachusetts, who refused to change his address in order to suit Comiskey.

Hugh Duffy was offered the job of managing the Western League club in Des Moines, Iowa, which Comiskey had recently purchased from John F. Higgins, a Chicago-based printer who had lost money in his baseball operation. The historic purchase marked the first attempt on the part of White Sox management to build their own "farm system" years before Branch Rickey got around to "inventing" the idea of teams on the major league level owning minor league independents.

Manager James J. Callahan

	G	AB	H	R	2B	3B	HR	RBI	SB	AVG
John "Shano" Collins	106	370	97	48	16	12	3	48	14	.262
Ambrose McConnell	104	396	111	45	11	5	1	34	7	.280
Lee Tannehill	141	516	131	60	17	6	0	49	0	.254
Harry Lord	141	561	180	103	18	18	3	61	43	.321
Marty McIntyre	146	569	184	102	19	11	1	52	17	.323
Francesco "Ping" Bodie	145	551	159	75	27	13	4	97	14	.289
Jimmy Callahan	120	466	131	64	13	5	3	60	45	.281
Billy Sullivan	89	256	55	26	9	3	0	31	1	.215
Rollie Zeider	73	217	55	39	3	0	2	21	28	.253
Roy Corhan	43	131	28	14	6	2	0	8	2	.214
Charlie Mullen	20	59	12	7	2	1	0	5	1	.203
William "Tex" Jones	9	31	6	4	1	0	0	4	1	.194
Freddy Parent	3	9	4	2	1	0	0	3	0	.444
Marty Berghammer	2	5	0	0	0	0	0	0	0	.000
Patsy Dougherty	76	211	61	39	10	9	0	32	19	.289
Roland "Cutie" Barrows	13	46	9	5	2	0	0	4	2	.196
Felix Chouinard	14	17	3	3	0	0	0	0	0	.176
Bobby Messenger	13	17	2	4	0	1	0	0	0	.118
Paul Meloan	1	3	1	0	0	0	0	1	0	.333
Jimmy Johnston	1	2	0	0	0	0	0	2	0	.000
Fred Payne	66	133	27	14	2	1	1	19	6	.203
Bruno Block	39	115	35	11	6	1	1	18	0	.304
Ralph Kreitz	7	17	4	0	1	0	0	0	0	.235
Wally Mayer	1	3	0	0	0	0	0	0	0	.000
		5,210	1,399	717	179	92	19	593	201	.269

	W	L	GS	CG	IP	H	BB	K	ShO	ERA
Ed Walsh	27	18	37	33	368⅔	327	72	255	5	2.22
Doc White	10	14	29	16	214⅓	219	35	72	4	2.98
Jim Scott	14	11	26	14	202	195	81	128	3	2.63
Frank Lange	8	8	22	8	161⅔	151	77	104	1	3.23
Fred Olmstead	6	6	11	7	117⅔	146	30	45	1	4.21
Jesse Baker	2	7	8	3	94	101	30	51	0	3.93
Irv Young	5	6	11	2	92⅔	99	25	40	0	4.37
Joe Benz	3	2	6	2	55⅔	52	13	28	0	2.26
Joe Hovlik	2	0	3	1	47	47	20	24	1	3.06
George Mogridge	0	2	1	0	12⅔	12	1	5	0	4.97
	77	74	154	86	1,366⅓	1,349	384	752	15	3.01

1912

Record: 78–76
Finish: Fourth
Games Behind: 28
Manager: Jimmy Callahan

The 1912 White Sox bolted out of the gate with 20 wins in their first 25 games, kindling new hopes for the raising of the third AL flag. Comiskey's faith in Callahan's ability to deliver the goods where others had failed seemed justified by the 5½-game first-place bulge the club had built by May 18. "Pennants are won in June," Al Lopez, a future Sox pilot of renown often said. By the same token, if a team cannot sustain and build upon an early flush of success, "Castle to Outhouse" is likely to become the autumn sonata.

April 11–May 18		May 19–October 6	
Won	Lost	Won	Lost
23	6	55	70

Lack of consistency, the inexperience of youth, and an unsettled outfield doomed the Hose to their familiar post–Hitless Wonder pattern of .500 baseball. However, it was a spirited group of athletes who broke camp in April. They provided an early preview of the great years just up the road. George "Buck" Weaver, for one, made a strong impression on Callahan and was brought north after only two years of minor league ball behind him. The 21-year-old rookie shortstop led the American League in errors in 1912, but he was on his way to stardom.

When the ballclub began its descent into the second division in late June, Comiskey and Callahan shored up the immediate need for a new battery by securing knuckleballing Eddie Cicotte from the Boston Red Sox on July 10, after the temperamental pitcher had quarreled with his manager Jake Stahl and Bosox owner John Taylor. A month and a day later, catcher Ray Schalk reported to Chicago from the Milwaukee club of the American Association. Schalk cost the Sox the services of infielder Lena Blackburne and catcher Jimmy "Bruno" Block. Both Cicotte and Schalk were bargain-basement finds. Schalk was headed for the Hall of Fame; Cicotte might have joined him there if not for the infamy of the Black Sox scandal.

In the day-to-day scheme of things, "Ping" Bodie (née Francesco Pezzullo) emerged as the hitting star of this team in 1912. Bodie was instantly recognizable to the fans and media, and he was a mentor to young Buck Weaver in his rocky maiden season. *Chicago Tribune* columnist Ring Lardner adopted Bodie as the prototypical ballplayer of his era and used him as the inspiration for his "You Know Me Al" columns, which amused and delighted readers of the sports page through much of the dead-ball era.

Ping Bodie

Bodie played with a lot of heart, even though his rabble-rousing habits and streak hitting cost his manager many a sleepless night. Commenting on his subpar baserunning skills, columnist Bugs Baer observed: "There was larceny in his heart, but his feet were honest."

	G	AB	H	R	2B	3B	HR	RBI	SB	AVG
Rollie Zeider	129	420	103	57	12	10	1	42	47	.245
Morrie Rath	157	591	161	104	10	2	1	19	30	.272
George "Buck" Weaver	147	523	117	55	21	8	1	43	12	.224
Harry Lord	151	570	152	81	19	12	5	54	28	.267
John "Shano" Collins	153	575	168	75	34	10	2	81	26	.292
Francesco "Ping" Bodie	137	472	139	58	24	7	5	72	12	.294
Jimmy Callahan	111	408	111	45	9	7	0	52	19	.272
Walt Kuhn	75	178	36	16	7	0	0	10	5	.202
William "Babe" Borton	31	105	39	15	3	1	0	17	1	.371
Jack Fournier	35	73	14	5	5	2	0	2	1	.192
Ernie Johnson	18	42	11	7	0	1	0	5	0	.262
Anton "Mutz" Ens	3	6	0	0	0	0	0	0	0	.000
Lee Tannehill	3	3	0	0	0	0	0	0	0	.000
William "Kid" Gleason	1	2	1	0	0	0	0	0	0	.500
Lena Blackburne	3	1	0	0	0	0	0	0	1	.000
Wally Mattick	88	285	74	45	7	9	1	35	15	.260
Marty McIntyre	45	84	14	10	0	0	0	10	3	.167
Roland "Cutie" Barrows	8	13	3	0	0	0	0	2	1	.231
Joe Berrens	2	4	1	1	0	0	0	0	0	.250
Bruno Block	46	136	35	8	5	6	0	26	1	.257
Billy Sullivan	39	91	19	9	2	1	0	15	0	.209
Ray Schalk	23	63	18	7	2	0	0	8	2	.286
Ted Easterly	30	55	20	5	2	0	0	14	1	.364
Wally Mayer	7	9	0	1	0	0	0	0	0	.000
Howard "Polly" McLarry	2	2	0	0	0	0	0	0	0	.000
Delmar Paddock	1	1	0	0	0	0	0	0	0	.000
Roy "Polly" Wolfe	1	1	0	0	0	0	0	0	0	.000
		5,181	1,321	640	174	80	17	537	205	.255

	W	L	GS	CG	IP	H	BB	K	ShO	ERA
Ed Walsh	27	17	41	32	393	332	94	254	6	2.15
Joe Benz	12	18	31	11	237⅔	230	70	96	3	2.92
Doc White	8	9	19	9	172	172	47	57	1	3.24
Frank Lange	10	10	21	11	165⅓	165	68	96	2	3.27
Eddie Cicotte	9	7	18	13	152	159	37	70	1	2.84
Oscar "Rube" Peters	5	6	11	4	108⅔	134	33	39	0	4.14
George Mogridge	3	4	7	2	64⅔	69	15	31	0	4.04
Jim Scott	2	2	4	2	37⅔	36	15	23	1	2.15
Wiley Taylor	1	1	3	0	20	21	14	4	0	4.95
Ellis Johnson	0	0	0	0	13⅔	11	10	8	0	3.29
Phil Douglas	0	1	1	0	12⅓	21	6	7	0	7.30
Ray "Rip" Jordan	0	0	0	0	10⅓	13	0	0	0	6.10
Jim Crabb	0	1	1	0	8⅔	6	4	3	0	1.04
Ralph Bell	0	0	0	0	6	8	8	5	0	9.00
Harry Smith	1	0	1	0	5	6	0	1	0	1.80
Lee "Flame" Delhi	0	0	0	0	3	7	3	2	0	9.00
Fred Lamline	0	0	0	0	2	7	2	1	0	31.50
	78	76	158	84	1,412	1,397	426	697	14	3.06

1913

Record: 78–74
Finish: Fifth
Games Behind: 17½
Manager: Jimmy Callahan

Summing up the prospects for success on the eve of the 1913 season, *Chicago Tribune* sportswriter Hugh Fullerton offered this sobering assessment to hopeful Sox fans:

"What makes the Sox so hard to figure is this. They have grand fielders who can't bat; great hitters who can't field, and two fellows who hit like fiends as long as the pitching is bad and can't hit at all after about July 4. In short, Callahan has a club composed of material good enough to win a pennant if he could use it all at once, which he can't."

The fence-busting marvel who took dead aim on the "bad pitching" common in April and May was Ping Bodie, who if the season ended on July 4, would have carted home two batting titles in his first two White Sox seasons.

Limpy Jim Scott duplicated his 1911 form...but unfortunately lost 21 to offset the 20 games he won. The dubious achievement has one modern parallel in team history. Wilbur Wood won 24 and lost 20 in 1973. Rookie sensation Ewell "Reb" Russell was drafted out of Fort Worth for $1,200. He paced the pitching staff with 22 victories and a sparkling 1.91 ERA after he was taught how to throw a curveball by first-year coach William "Kid" Gleason. Russell offset the loss of Ed Walsh, whose chronic arm miseries were cutting short his career.

To bolster the infield defense, Comiskey announced the acquisition of "Prince" Hal Chase on June 1 for "Babe" Borton and Rollie Zeider, called the "Bunion and the Onion" by grumbling New York sportswriters who believed the Highlanders were shortchanged.

Chase, however, was a moody, disruptive player often accused of throwing games to gamblers. When the New York Highlanders advertised his availability, only one interested party stepped forward: Charles Comiskey. "He is a grand player, although during the last few seasons he has not played his best," Comiskey admitted, "owing to his desire to get away from New York where he played since 1905. A change is what he needs to bring out his best."

It took Chase a full week to report to Chicago, an ominous sign which Comiskey stubbornly refused to acknowledge in his acclaim for his newfound star.

Winners of 20 of their first 32 games, the White Sox faded at the midpoint and hovered just above the .500 mark until the end of the season. The team offense declined in 1913. In one stretch of games between September 5 and 8, the South Siders were held scoreless for 26 consecutive innings.

Cynics often accused the South Siders of reserving all their strength and energy for the annual postseason showdown against the Cubs—which they won for the third year in a row.

Spring training tour, Oakland, California, March 1913

	G	AB	H	R	2B	3B	HR	RBI	SB	AVG
Hal Chase	102	384	110	49	11	10	2	39	9	.286
Morrie Rath	90	295	59	37	2	0	0	12	22	.200
George "Buck" Weaver	151	533	145	51	17	8	4	52	20	.272
Harry Lord	150	547	144	62	18	12	1	42	24	.263
John "Shano" Collins	148	535	128	53	26	9	1	47	22	.239
Francesco "Ping" Bodie	127	406	107	39	14	8	8	48	5	.264
Wally Mattick	68	207	39	15	8	1	0	11	3	.188
Ray Schalk	128	401	98	38	15	5	1	38	14	.244
Joe Berger	77	223	48	27	6	2	2	20	5	.215
Jack Fournier	68	172	40	20	8	5	1	23	9	.233
William "Babe" Borton	28	80	22	9	5	0	0	13	1	.275
Jim Breton	10	30	5	1	1	1	0	2	0	.167
Rollie Zeider	13	20	7	4	0	0	0	2	3	.350
Larry Chappell	60	208	48	20	8	1	0	15	7	.231
Walter "Biff" Schaller	34	96	21	12	3	0	0	4	5	.219
Johnny Beall	17	60	16	10	0	1	0	3	1	.267
Davy Jones	10	21	6	2	0	0	0	0	1	.286
Edd Roush	9	10	1	2	0	0	0	0	0	.100
Jimmy Callahan	6	9	2	0	0	0	0	1	0	.222
Don Rader	2	3	1	1	0	0	0	0	0	.333
Ted Easterly	60	97	23	3	1	0	0	8	2	.237
Walt Kuhn	26	50	8	5	1	0	0	5	1	.160
Tom Daly	1	3	0	0	0	0	0	0	0	.000
Billy Meyer	1	1	1	0	0	0	0	0	0	1.000
		4,822	1,139	486	157	66	23	410	156	.236

	W	L	GS	CG	IP	H	BB	K	ShO	ERA
Ewell "Reb" Russell	22	16	36	25	316	249	79	122	8	1.91
Jim Scott	20	20	38	27	312⅓	252	86	158	4	1.90
Eddie Cicotte	18	12	30	18	268	224	73	121	3	1.58
Joe Benz	7	10	17	7	151	146	59	79	1	2.74
Doc White	2	4	8	2	103	106	39	39	0	3.50
Ed Walsh	8	3	14	7	97⅔	91	39	34	1	2.58
Frank Lange	1	3	3	0	40⅔	46	20	20	0	4.87
Clarence "Pop Boy" Smith	0	2	2	0	32	31	11	13	0	3.38
Thomas "Buck" O'Brien	0	3	3	0	18⅓	21	13	4	0	3.93
Bill Lathrop	0	0	0	0	17	16	12	9	0	4.24
Bob Smith	0	0	0	0	2	3	3	1	0	13.50
Frank Miller	0	1	1	0	1⅔	2	3	2	0	27.04
	78	74	152	86	1,359⅔	1,189	437	602	17	2.33

1914

Record: 70–84
Finish: Sixth
Games Behind: 30
Manager: Jimmy Callahan

For years it had been Charley Comiskey's singular ambition to internationalize baseball by escorting a ballclub of his own creation to foreign lands.

Comiskey's faithful secretary, Harry Grabiner, succeeded in coaxing New York Giants manager John McGraw to bring along his ballclub and a significant amount of his personal fortune to fund the goodwill junket to Japan, Australia, Ceylon, France, Italy, Egypt, and England, where the two teams performed before King George at London's Wembley Stadium.

Chicago won 24 of the 44 exhibition games against New York before returning to American soil and a raucous hero's welcome on March 6, 1914. Whether Comiskey had broken any ground since Albert Spalding's first European tour was highly doubtful. Back at home, Comiskey was lauded as a man ahead of his times. High tide for the Comiskey dynasty in Chicago was approaching.

The rigors of uninterrupted year-long baseball were self-evident after the White Sox broke camp. There was plenty

The world-touring White Sox and Giants gather in front of the Great Sphinx in Egypt in 1914. Red Faber stands on the far right. Buck Weaver sits in the center, wearing a fez. (Courtesy of the Amateur Athletic Association of Los Angeles)

of dissension, grumbling over salaries, and bad feelings all around, undoubtedly inspired by the rebellious Hal Chase, who inspired his roommate Harry Lord to jump the ballclub without explanation on May 13.

Chase followed Lord out the door on June 21 in order to join up with the Buffalo team of the outlawed Federal League, which began play in 1914 in defiance of National Agreement mandates. Chase served the seldom-used "ten-day clause" on Comiskey, whose battery of lawyers were unable to permanently enjoin Chase from playing elsewhere.

With half his infield blown apart, Callahan had to make due with John Jacques Fournier, a lumbering first baseman with a stone glove. The starting corps of Joe Benz, Ed Cicotte, and Jim Scott was bolstered by the addition of Urban "Red" Faber, a spitball pitcher acquired from Des Moines for the sum of $3,500 on August 25, 1913. Red Faber weakened in the second half of the season but demonstrated competence and a tough attitude.

Competition from the local Federal League team convinced an ailing Comiskey the time was ripe to build a champion after six dormant seasons. The personnel shakeup began on December 8, when the contract of star second baseman Eddie Collins was purchased from the Philadelphia A's for $50,000. Collins finished second in the 1914 batting race to Ty Cobb and was in the prime of his career.

With the arrival of the veteran Collins, Callahan suddenly found his job in jeopardy. It was the owner's custom to negotiate year-to-year contracts with his managers, and Callahan's time was up.

The announcement of the next Sox manager was delayed until December 17, pending the resolution of the final details of the Collins contract. But in the end, neither Collins nor veteran coach Kid Gleason was tendered an offer. Comiskey's surprise choice was a 33-year-old "Busher" from Dubuque, Iowa, named Clarence "Pants" Rowland.

For Rowland, it was the dream of a lifetime come true. "To say I am pleased is entirely too mild an expression," he gushed. "I'm tickled to death. Through my career in baseball, Charles Comiskey has been my staunch friend and supporter. He has been my staunch friend and supporter. He has been my ideal! He is now placing me in a position where I can repay him for helping me in the past. I intend to give him all that I have in me."

	G	AB	H	R	2B	3B	HR	RBI	SB	AVG
Jacques Fournier	109	379	118	44	14	9	6	44	10	.311
Lena Blackburne	144	474	105	52	10	5	1	35	25	.222
George "Buck" Weaver	136	541	133	64	20	9	2	28	14	.246
Jim Breton	81	231	49	21	7	2	0	24	9	.212
John "Shano" Collins	154	598	164	61	34	9	3	65	30	.274
Francesco "Ping" Bodie	107	327	75	21	9	5	3	29	12	.229
Ray Demmitt	146	515	133	63	13	12	2	46	12	.258
Ray Schalk	135	392	106	30	13	2	0	36	24	.270
Hal Chase	58	206	55	27	10	5	0	20	9	.267
Scotty Alcock	54	156	27	12	4	2	0	7	4	.173
Joe Berger	47	148	23	11	3	1	0	3	2	.155
Harry Lord	21	69	13	8	1	1	1	3	2	.188
Howard Baker	15	47	13	4	1	1	0	5	2	.277
Carl Manda	9	15	4	2	0	0	0	1	1	.267
Tom Daly	61	133	31	13	2	0	0	8	3	.233
Robert "Braggo" Roth	34	126	37	14	4	6	1	10	3	.294
Larry Chappell	21	39	9	3	0	0	0	1	0	.231
Roy "Polly" Wolfe	9	28	6	0	0	0	0	0	1	.214
Cecil Coombs	7	23	4	1	1	0	0	1	0	.174
Irv Porter	1	4	1	1	0	0	0	0	0	.250
Hank Schreiber	1	2	0	0	0	0	0	0	0	.000
Wally Mayer	39	85	14	7	3	1	0	5	1	.165
Walt Kuhn	17	40	11	4	1	0	0	0	2	.275
Billy Sullivan	1	0	0	0	0	0	0	0	0	.000
Charlie "Silk" Kavanaugh	5	5	1	0	0	0	0	0	0	.200
Delos Brown	1	1	0	0	0	0	0	0	0	.000
		5,040	1,205	487	161	71	19	390	167	.239

	W	L	GS	CG	IP	H	BB	K	ShO	ERA
Joe Benz	14	19	35	16	283⅓	245	66	142	4	2.26
Eddie Cicotte	11	16	29	15	269⅓	220	72	122	4	2.04
Jim Scott	14	18	33	12	253⅓	228	75	138	2	2.84
Urban "Red" Faber	10	9	20	11	181⅓	154	64	88	2	2.68
Ewell "Reb" Russell	8	12	23	8	167⅓	168	33	79	1	2.90
Mellie Wolfgang	9	5	11	9	119⅓	96	32	50	2	1.89
Bill Lathrop	1	2	1	0	47⅔	41	19	7	0	2.64
Ed Walsh	2	3	5	3	44⅔	33	20	15	1	2.82
Harry "Hi" Jasper	1	0	0	0	32⅓	22	20	19	0	3.34
	70	84	157	74	1,398⅔	1,207	401	660	16	2.48

1915

Record: 93–61
Finish: Third
Games Behind: 9½
Manager: Clarence Rowland

Rowland on strategy, 1915: "Win one game at a time, and the old pennant will be close enough for you to hear its flapping when the curtain drops!

"The old hit and run game still gets 'em. Last year at Peoria we needed only an average of 1.7 hits for each run we score. In 1913 at Dubuque we got around for an average of 1.3 blows. That means speed and a style of play that keeps the other fellas wondering what comes next."

"A Carolina millhand the kids called Shoeless Joe"—Nelson Algren

The coming glory and the ultimate tragedy of the White (to Black) Sox in the second decade were interwoven with the events of 1915.

Comiskey introduced five new position players whose contributions vaulted the White Sox into the upper strata of the American League with a victory total that matched their 1906 output. Rowland employed a hit-and-run offense revolving around the fleet-footed Collins boys (Eddie and Shano). The up-tempo White Sox pilfered 233 bases, the highest total since 1902.

The tendency for developing young teams is to win games in bunches, then fall back. Rowland's White Sox launched a nine-game winning streak on May 17, took over first place five days later, and maintained their lead (with one interruption) until July 19.

The White Sox fell out of serious contention in July and August, giving way to the onrushing Tigers and Red Sox. After the strain of the pennant fight wore off, the Sox regrouped and won 11 games in a row to close out the season on a high note.

Three key acquisitions at the midpoint of the season solidified the ballclub for 1916 and beyond. Veteran outfielder Eddie Murphy was purchased outright from the Philadelphia A's on July 15. In Chicago, Murphy provided strong and capable bench help.

Charles Comiskey built his reputation as a "Western" man. In an era defined by regional loyalties, the White Sox harvested the available talent west of the Mississippi River. Comiskey had agents in the Western League and up and down the Pacific Coast League. In 1915 the name that kept surfacing was Claude Preston Williams, star hurler at Salt Lake City. Williams was sold to Chicago on August 14; he would begin his White Sox career in 1916.

"Bunny" Brief and Jacques Fournier divided first-base responsibilities with little success. With few prospects for immediate improvement at this position, Comiskey dispatched Harry Grabiner to Cleveland to negotiate for the services of "Shoeless" Joe Jackson, an outfielder by trade, who was pound for pound nearly as good a hitter as the fearsome Ty Cobb.

Grabiner outbid Boston, Washington, and New York for Jackson. Three lesser-known players, Robert "Braggo" Roth, Ed Klepfer, Larry Chappell, and $15,000 cash were delivered to Cleveland for Jackson, who finished the season in Chicago at first base.

The problems caused by Hal Chase's sudden desertion in 1914 had a direct effect on Jackson's arrival in the Windy City, all of which raises an interesting "what if" possibility. What if Chase had found contentment in Chicago? Might not future visitors to the Hall of Fame be gazing at a plaque bearing the name of one of the greatest natural hitters the game has ever produced—one Joseph Jefferson Jackson?

	G	AB	H	R	2B	3B	HR	RBI	SB	AVG
Jacques Fournier	126	422	136	86	20	18	5	77	21	.322
Eddie Collins	155	521	173	118	22	10	4	77	46	.332
George "Buck" Weaver	148	563	151	83	18	11	3	49	24	.268
Lena Blackburne	96	283	61	33	5	1	0	25	13	.216
Eddie Murphy	70	273	86	51	11	5	0	26	20	.315
Oscar "Happy" Felsch	121	427	106	65	18	11	3	53	16	.248
John "Shano" Collins	153	576	148	73	24	17	2	85	38	.257
Ray Schalk	135	413	110	46	14	4	1	54	15	.266
Robert "Braggo" Roth	70	240	60	44	6	10	3	35	12	.250
Anthony "Bunny" Brief	48	154	33	13	6	2	2	17	8	.214
Pete Johns	28	100	21	7	2	1	0	11	2	.210
Jim Breton	16	36	5	3	1	0	0	1	2	.139
"Shoeless" Joe Jackson	46	162	43	21	4	5	2	36	6	.265
Tom "Finners" Quinlan	42	114	22	11	3	0	0	7	3	.193
Nemo Leibold	36	74	17	10	1	0	0	11	1	.230
Ray Demmitt	9	6	0	0	0	0	0	0	0	.000
Wally Mayer	22	54	12	3	3	1	0	5	0	.222
Tom Daley	29	47	9	5	1	0	0	3	0	.191
Howard Baker	2	2	0	0	0	0	0	0	0	.000
Larry Chappell	1	1	0	0	0	0	0	0	0	.000
Charlie Jackson	1	1	0	0	0	0	0	0	0	.000
		4,918	1,269	717	163	102	25	598	233	.258

	W	L	GS	CG	IP	H	BB	K	ShO	ERA
Urban "Red" Faber	24	14	32	22	299⅔	264	99	182	3	2.55
Jim Scott	24	11	35	23	296⅓	256	78	120	7	2.03
Joe Benz	15	11	28	17	238⅓	209	43	81	2	2.11
Ewell "Reb" Russell	11	10	25	10	229⅓	215	47	90	3	2.59
Eddie Cicotte	13	12	26	15	223⅓	216	48	106	1	3.02
Mellie Wolfgang	2	2	2	0	53⅔	39	12	21	0	1.84
Ed Walsh	3	0	3	3	27	19	7	12	1	1.33
Harry "Hi" Jasper	0	1	2	1	15⅔	8	9	15	0	4.60
Ed Klepfer	1	0	2	1	12⅔	11	5	3	0	2.84
Frank "Dixie" Davis	0	0	0	0	3	2	2	2	0	0.00
Ellis "Swede" Johnson	0	0	0	0	2	3	0	3	0	9.00
	93	61	155	92	1,401	1,242	350	635	17	2.43

1916

Record: 89–65
Finish: Second
Games Behind: 2
Manager: Clarence Rowland

Clarence Rowland was derided as a "busher" by his press critics and Sox fans who were impatient with the ballclub's lack of progress at the midway point in 1916. A curse or a badge of honor? "I am a bush leaguer, it is no disgrace," Rowland told Harvey Woodruff of the *Tribune.* "But if you call me a bush leaguer at the end of 1916, I may regard it as a reflection."

The veteran ballplayers who played listlessly and without a sense of purpose placed Rowland's job in jeopardy by June 21, when the team was mired in sixth place with a 26–28 record. Through it all he maintained his dignity with a cheerful, enthusiastic outlook.

Rowland was supported by his players through these difficult days. The players sensed that he was an ally against their mutual enemy, Charley Comiskey, whose adherence to the bottom line stirred dissension. They held a clubhouse meeting in

Ewell "Reb" Russell

late May and vowed "never to give up" for Rowland, their likable young manager.

There was no turning back. Joe Jackson's torrid June hitting fueled the speedy comeback. Jackson ripped opposing pitchers at a .524 clip between May 31 and July 4. In July the rejuvenated White Sox won 21 games to draw within a game of the league-leading Bosox.

The schedule favored the White Sox, who were to play 20 of their last 24 games in Comiskey Park, primarily against weaker second-division ballclubs. The White Sox trailed the leaders by a half game on September 16 when Boston arrived in town for a climactic showdown. By virtue of winning two out of three games, Boston increased its lead by 1½ games, and there went the 1916 flag.

A shortstop and a first baseman were high priorities during the coming off-season. Otherwise, if the infield weaknesses could not be corrected over the winter, the misfiring White Sox would likely remain neither "fish nor fowl, nor good red herring," as sportswriter Sy Sanborn noted in his 1916 season summary.

	G	AB	H	R	2B	3B	HR	RBI	SB	AVG
Jacques Fournier	105	313	75	36	13	9	3	44	19	.240
Eddie Collins	155	545	168	87	14	17	0	52	40	.308
Zeb Terry	94	269	51	20	8	4	0	17	4	.190
George "Buck" Weaver	151	582	132	78	27	6	3	38	22	.227
John "Shano" Collins	143	527	128	74	28	12	0	42	16	.243
Oscar "Happy" Felsch	146	546	164	73	24	12	7	70	13	.300
"Shoeless" Joe Jackson	155	592	202	91	40	21	3	78	24	.341
Ray Schalk	129	410	95	36	12	9	0	41	30	.232
Jack Ness	75	258	69	32	7	5	1	34	4	.267
Fred McMullin	68	187	48	8	3	0	0	10	9	.257
Fritz Von Kolnitz	24	44	10	1	3	0	0	7	0	.227
Edward "Ceylon" Wright	8	18	0	0	0	0	0	0	0	.000
Robert "Ziggy" Hasbrook	9	8	1	1	0	0	0	0	0	.125
George Moriarty	7	5	1	1	0	0	0	0	0	.200
Eddie Murphy	51	105	22	14	5	1	0	4	3	.210
Nemo Leibold	45	82	20	5	1	2	0	13	7	.244
Jack Lapp	40	101	21	6	0	1	0	7	1	.208
Byrd Lynn	31	40	9	4	1	0	0	3	2	.225
Ted Jourdan	3	2	0	0	0	0	0	0	2	.000
Joe Fautsch	1	1	0	0	0	0	0	0	0	.000
Ray Shook	1	0	0	0	0	0	0	0	0	.000
		5,081	1,277	601	194	100	17	484	197	.251

	W	L	GS	CG	IP	H	BB	K	ShO	ERA
Ewell "Reb" Russell	17	11	26	16	264⅓	207	42	112	5	2.42
Claude "Lefty" Williams	13	7	25	10	224⅓	220	65	138	2	2.89
Urban "Red" Faber	16	9	25	15	205⅓	167	61	87	3	2.02
Eddie Cicotte	16	7	20	11	187	138	70	91	2	1.78
Jim Scott	9	14	20	8	165⅓	155	53	71	1	2.72
Joe Benz	9	5	16	6	142	108	32	57	4	2.03
Mellie Wolfgang	4	6	14	6	127	103	42	36	1	1.98
Dave Danforth	5	5	8	1	93⅔	87	37	49	0	3.27
Ed Walsh	0	1	1	0	3⅓	4	3	3	0	2.70
	89	65	155	73	1,412⅓	1,189	405	644	18	2.36

1917

Record: 100–54
Finish: First
Games Ahead: 9
Manager: Clarence Rowland

Charles Comiskey looked to the West for his third-base "missing link," as he had so often in the past. The Old Roman located his man playing for the Vernon club of the PCL. The final piece of the Black Sox puzzle was in place with the arrival of Charles "Swede" Risberg.

Risberg's arrival allowed Rowland to shift Buck Weaver back to shortstop, his natural position. The other problem spot on the infield was first base. In 1917 Jacques Fournier was replaced by the capable "Chick" Gandil, who returned to Chicago to spark the 1917 pennant drive with his sparkling, league-leading defensive play. The youngster Risberg and the grizzled Chickie were important pennant catalysts who helped turn the 1916 bridesmaids into champions.

Outfitted in khaki military uniforms and proudly toting their Springfield rifles, a full complement of spit-and-polish White Sox players performed close-order drill in Comiskey Park on August 23, 1917. Baseball was doing its part for the

Coach Kid Gleason (left) and Manager Clarence "Pants" Rowland, 1917

war effort, and these special exhibitions of patriotism helped justify the continuance of the national pastime as an "essential, morale-lifting" wartime industry.

Such were the strange and unfamiliar scenes in the nation's baseball stadiums. The Old Roman supported the war effort by donating 10 percent of his gate receipts at Comiskey Park, or $17,113, to the Red Cross.

When the Rowlands were not drilling in full military regalia, they were methodically winning ballgames. Chicago vaulted out of the gate with nine victories in their first 11 games before suffering through a dry spell in early May that dropped them into third place on May 6. An eight-game winning streak ending in Boston on May 20 returned them to the top. After June 8 the White Sox never fell any lower in the standings than a first-place tie with their closest pursuers, the Boston Red Sox.

This ballclub had been assembled with great care and at considerable expense. Comiskey's four-year rebuilding efforts achieved the perfect balance between youth and experience. The presence of coach Kid Gleason on the sidelines aided Rowland. The younger players called Gleason their "Pop," and the suspicion grew that the Kid—and not manager Rowland—was calling the shots from the dugout.

Lefty Williams won his first nine decisions. White Sox pitchers led the league in team earned run average. Sox ace Eddie Cicotte struck terror in the hearts of opposing batters with his dreaded "shine ball." Cicotte won 28 games for the 1917 edition…the strongest team in Sox history if the won-lost record is taken at face value.

The White Sox rolled into September nursing a four-game lead. With the race still very much in doubt in the minds of the players, a pool was allegedly collected to "reward" the Detroit Tigers for "laying down" in two scheduled doubleheaders played in Comiskey Park on September 2 and 3. Chicago triumphed by scores of 7–2, 6–5, 7–5, and 14–8, effectively quashing the hopes of the runner-up Red Sox. The charges of crookedness were not proven one way or the other, but the presence of gamblers in the nation's ballparks and their steady infiltration of the game were self-evident by 1917.

The White Sox nailed down the pennant in thrilling fashion. Playing in Fenway Park on September 21, against their closest pursuers, Eddie Cicotte induced Babe Ruth to hit into a game-ending double play in the bottom of the 10th inning to preserve a hard-fought 2–1 victory. The championship series was coming home after 11 years.

Charles Comiskey received the happy news over a special telephone hookup from his downtown office to the Hub. He simply could not wait for the results to come in over the slower ticker-tape machine. Recalling other disappointments of years past, Comiskey made note of the fact that "twice I had the pennant all ready to nail to the pole. And both times they snatched it from my hands. This one is mine though, and after 11 years!"

	G	AB	H	R	2B	3B	HR	RBI	SB	AVG
Arnold "Chick" Gandil	149	553	151	53	9	7	0	57	16	.273
Eddie Collins	156	564	163	91	18	12	0	67	53	.289
Charles "Swede" Risberg	149	474	96	59	20	8	1	45	16	.203
George "Buck" Weaver	118	447	127	64	16	5	2	32	19	.284
Nemo Leibold	125	428	101	59	12	6	0	29	27	.236
Oscar "Happy" Felsch	152	575	177	75	17	10	6	102	26	.308
"Shoeless" Joe Jackson	146	538	162	91	20	17	5	75	13	.301
Ray Schalk	140	424	96	48	12	4	3	51	19	.226
Fred McMullin	59	194	46	35	2	1	0	12	9	.237
Ted Jourdan	17	34	5	2	0	1	0	2	0	.147
Bobby Byrne	1	1	0	0	0	0	0	0	0	.000
Robert "Ziggy" Hasbrook	2	1	0	1	0	0	0	0	0	.000
Zeb Terry	2	1	0	0	0	0	0	0	0	.000
John "Shano" Collins	82	252	59	38	13	3	1	14	14	.234
Eddie Murphy	53	51	16	9	2	1	0	16	4	.314
Byrd Lynn	35	72	16	7	2	0	0	5	1	.222
Joe Jenkins	10	9	1	0	0	0	0	2	0	.111
Jacques Fournier	1	1	0	0	0	0	0	0	0	.000
		5,057	1,281	657	152	80	19	535	219	.253

	W	L	GS	CG	IP	H	BB	K	ShO	ERA
Eddie Cicotte	28	12	35	29	346⅔	246	70	150	7	1.53
Urban "Red" Faber	16	13	29	17	248	224	85	84	3	1.92
Claude "Lefty" Williams	17	8	29	8	230	221	81	85	1	2.97
Ewell "Reb" Russell	12	5	24	11	189⅓	170	32	54	5	1.95
Dave Danforth	15	6	9	1	173	155	74	79	1	2.65
Jim Scott	6	7	17	6	125	126	42	37	2	1.87
Joe Benz	6	3	13	7	94⅔	76	23	25	2	2.47
Mellie Wolfgang	0	0	0	0	17⅔	18	6	3	0	5.09
	100	54	156	79	1,424⅓	1,236	413	517	21	2.16

1918

Record: 57–67
Finish: Sixth
Games Behind: 17
Manager: Clarence Rowland

The "work or fight" edict issued by Provost Marshal Enoch Crowder to baseball's governing National Commission on May 22, 1918, required all draft-age, eligible players to choose between military service or full-time employment in an "essential" wartime industry.

In this war-shortened season that tested the mettle of the players who never knew from day to day whether they would be fighting in France or painting battleships in East Coast naval yards, the writers were unanimous in the belief that the Sox were likely to repeat if the government would oblige Comiskey by holding back the draft notices.

When Joe Jackson, Lefty Williams, and catcher Byrd Lynn elected to join the "painter's league" upon receiving their draft notices, Comiskey exploded. "I don't consider them fit to play on my ballclub," he complained. "I would gladly lose my whole team if the players wished to do their duty for the country, as hundreds of thousands of other young men are doing."

It was a disturbing time for Rowland, who contended not only with the loss of his key players to the war—Red Faber joined the navy, Eddie Collins enlisted in the marines in August—but also with serious schisms that had already developed between rival cliques.

Following repeated clashes with Comiskey and several of his own teammates, Hap Felsch jumped the club on July 1.

Close order "preparedness" marching drills at Comiskey Park, minus the rifles and bayonets

He could not get along with Eddie Collins and the faction of players who came to be known as the Clean Sox in the postscandal period.

The Sox played .500 baseball up until June 23, then dropped into the second division after the lineup was depleted. One bright spot on an otherwise bleak landscape was snatched away on August 23, when the National Commission ordered pitcher John Picus Quinn to report to the Yankees after deciding that this minor league player did not have the right to negotiate his services with Comiskey after New York had filed its claim through the proper channels. The controversial decision cost the Sox the services of an outstanding pitcher, and it drove a deeper wedge between the antagonistic Ban Johnson and the White Sox owner.

The ill-fated 1918 season was called off on September 2 because of wartime considerations. The Sox were mired in an eight-game losing streak and plummeting toward the cellar when play was halted.

A dazed and saddened Clarence Rowland knew for some time he would not be called back in 1919. He was blamed for the 1918 collapse—the circumstances over which he had no control.

Comiskey kept the fans guessing until New Year's Eve, when William "Kid" Gleason was appointed manager. It was a logical but somewhat surprising choice, because Gleason had chosen to sit out the 1918 season following some differences with Comiskey. But now all was forgiven, and the Kid was coming back. "That's the best New Year's present I could think of," exulted Eddie Collins from his Philadelphia home. "Mark it down: that in view of the fact that Gleason has been made chief skipper of the Sox, I would not change places with any one on any club in the American League. By this, I mean to say that the White Sox look to me to be the best bet for 1919."

	G	AB	H	R	2B	3B	HR	RBI	SB	AVG
Arnold "Chick" Gandil	114	439	119	49	18	4	0	55	9	.271
Eddie Collins	97	330	91	51	8	2	2	30	22	.276
George "Buck" Weaver	112	420	126	37	12	5	0	29	20	.300
Fred McMullin	70	235	65	32	7	0	1	16	7	.277
Oscar "Happy" Felsch	53	206	52	16	2	5	1	20	6	.252
John "Shano" Collins	103	365	100	30	18	11	1	56	7	.274
Nemo Leibold	116	440	110	57	14	6	1	31	13	.250
Ray Schalk	108	333	73	35	6	3	0	22	12	.219
Charles "Swede" Risberg	82	273	70	36	12	3	1	27	5	.256
Ralph "Babe" Pinelli	24	78	18	7	1	1	1	7	3	.231
Johnny Mostil	10	33	9	4	2	2	0	4	1	.273
Ted Jourdan	7	10	1	1	0	0	0	1	0	.100
Eddie Murphy	91	286	85	36	9	3	0	23	6	.297
Wilbur Good	35	148	37	24	9	4	0	11	1	.250
"Shoeless" Joe Jackson	17	65	23	9	2	2	1	20	3	.354
Otto Jacobs	29	73	15	4	3	1	0	3	0	.205
Al DeVormer	8	19	5	2	2	0	0	0	1	.263
Byrd Lynn	5	8	2	0	0	0	0	0	0	.250
Pat Hargrove	2	2	0	0	0	0	0	0	0	.000
Frank "Kid" Willson	4	1	0	2	0	0	0	0	0	.000
		4,132	1,057	457	136	54	9	375	116	.256

	W	L	GS	CG	IP	H	BB	K	ShO	ERA
Eddie Cicotte	12	19	30	24	266	275	40	104	1	2.64
Frank Shellenback	10	12	20	10	182⅔	180	74	47	3	2.66
Joe Benz	7	8	17	10	154	156	28	30	1	2.51
Dave Danforth	6	15	13	5	139	148	40	48	0	3.43
Ewell "Reb" Russell	6	5	14	10	124⅔	117	33	38	2	2.60
Claude "Lefty" Williams	6	4	14	7	105⅔	76	47	30	2	2.73
Urban "Red" Faber	5	1	9	5	80⅔	70	23	26	1	1.23
Jack Quinn	5	1	5	5	51	38	7	22	0	2.29
Roy Mitchell	0	1	2	0	12	18	4	3	0	7.50
Mellie Wolfgang	0	1	0	0	8⅓	12	3	1	0	5.40
Ed Corey	0	0	0	0	2	2	1	0	0	4.50
	57	67	124	76	1,126	1,092	300	349	10	2.69

1919

Record: 88–52
Finish: First
Games Ahead: 3½
Manager: Kid Gleason

Few of the scribes who covered the White Sox during spring training shared Eddie Collins' optimism. Red Faber was home from the war, but his lame arm sidelined him for much of the year. Reb Russell never regained his winning form and was released to Minneapolis in July.

Ed Cicotte and Lefty Williams returned strong and healthy, but a two-man pitching staff just couldn't cut it in the league. Kid Gleason turned the ball over to Dickie Kerr and Grover Loudermilk, vintage minor leaguers who came through in a big way after Comiskey had exhausted all of his trade possibilities.

The question must be asked in any discussion of the "Black Sox." How badly did these contentious players want to win?

They played with an uncommon intensity through the most difficult circumstances. The White Sox were vilified by fans in opposing stadiums as "slackers" and "shipbuilders" whenever they took the field. This was a formidable ballclub…arguably one of the most talented teams to grace a big league diamond despite an unsettled pitching staff.

Gleason's White Sox combined speed and power into an unpredictable offense revolving around Joe Jackson and Eddie Collins, two of the great money players of the game. Collins battled Ty Cobb for the batting championship in the early months of the season. Jackson's final mark of .351 ranked him fourth among AL hitters. Typical of their hustling, aggressive style of play was a July 13 game against the Red Sox in Comiskey Park, when a routine single by Buck Weaver plated *three* Sox runners. The writers could not recall the last time they had seen such a play.

Ed Cicotte, a 15-game winner by July 8, staked the Sox to a four-game lead by June 1. The improving Yankees knocked the Gleasons out of first place and held the lead until July 9.

Showing flashes of his 1917 brilliance, Red Faber defeated the Philadelphia A's in both ends of a doubleheader on July 9. After Faber's standout performance, the Yankees were done for. Chicago won nine of 10 games on their home field and never looked back. The Cleveland Indians tried to make a race of it in August and early September, but drew no closer to the Sox than 3½ games. And the gap became that narrow only after Gleason elected to rest his starters in the final four games of the season.

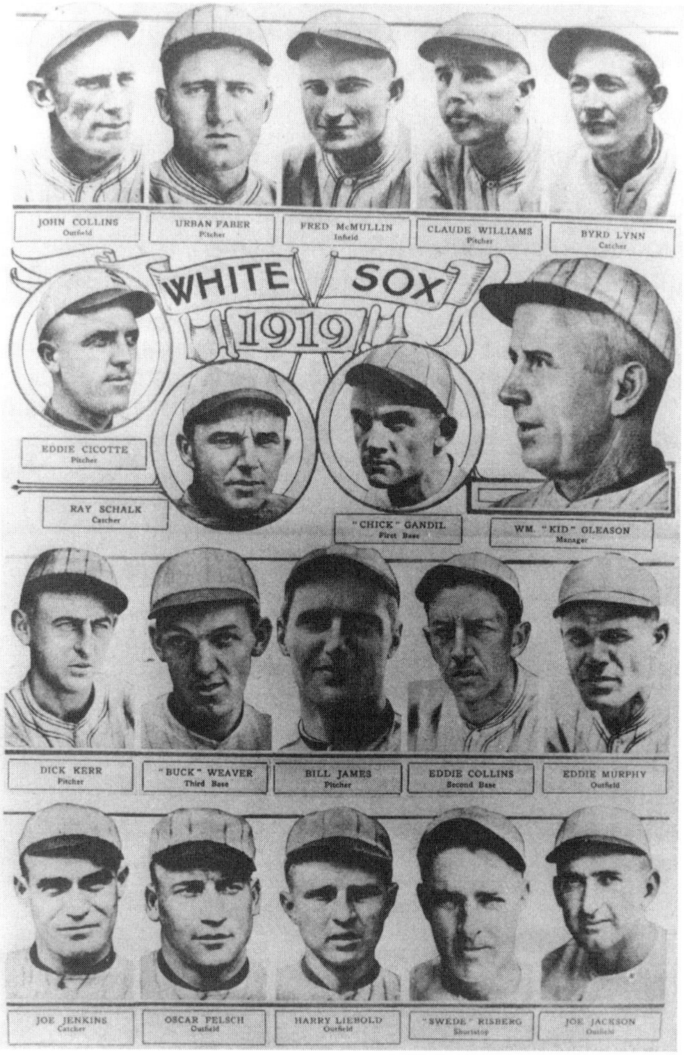

A ballclub that belongs to the ages

Day in and day out the White Sox exhibited their mastery in all phases of the game. The inner defense was superb: an infield without peer in baseball. Gandil, Collins, Risberg, and Weaver traveled at a fast clip, completing dazzling fielding plays that astounded the baseball patrons in every American League port of call.

As the 1919 pennant became that much more of a certainty, off-hours conversation among the players turned to the coming World Series and their likely opponent. The Sox stars looked forward to a rematch with John McGraw's Giants. A New York–Chicago World Series played in the spacious Polo Grounds meant additional gate receipts and a larger bonus for the players.

When the surprising Cincinnati Redlegs pulled away from the Giants in August, clubhouse talk in Chicago seemed to focus on the seating capacity of Redland Field—not the left-handed slants of ace hurler Dutch Ruether or the newfound hitting prowess of former teammate Edd Roush.

If it wasn't already apparent to Comiskey that something rather peculiar was afoot, Kid Gleason should have sensed it. The Collins-Schalk-Faber clique had little to do with the "slacker" element: Williams-Jackson-Felsch-Gandil, to whom Ed Cicotte, Risberg, and Buck Weaver owed their allegiance.

There was a fair amount of regional prejudice existing between the college-bred Collins and the other northern players who tended to view Jackson and company on less than equal terms. Nevertheless, once these players took the field, personal differences were cast aside.

The Ban Johnson–Charles Comiskey feud and the reports of "freak wagers"—even money bet on the vastly superior White Sox—on the eve of the World Series failed to sound an alarm bell that all was not right on the South Side, because the fans loved their ballclub and had every expectation of victory in the Fall Classic.

The gamblers had sensed the deeper significance of the internal divisions on the team, and they exploited it to suit their own purposes. The "outcast" clique of White Sox players initiated contact with gambler Joseph "Sport" Sullivan at Boston's Buckminster Hotel on September 19 to discuss a business proposition—the "fixing" of the 1919 World Series in return for a $100,000 payoff to be divided "among the boys."

Sport Sullivan and "Sleepy" Bill Burns, a White Sox alumnus, were second-level intermediaries. They were the front men for Arnold Rothstein, the "Big Bankroll" in New York who had lost money betting on the White Sox in 1917 and who saw a fast and easy way to even the score.

Abe Attell, a featherweight titleholder during the White Sox Hitless Wonder era, was also friendly with Chick Gandil. Their off-hours collegiality in American League hotel saloons convinced the "Little Champ" that the internal discord could be exploited. Attell and Sullivan would effectively serve as the go-betweens.

The Black Sox. Chicago's shame, baseball's tragedy.

With less than a week to go in this otherwise memorable baseball season, Kid Gleason gloated over the prospects of a White Sox world championship. His exuberance was almost childlike—his confidence unfounded. "There isn't any weak spot on my infield," he beamed. "Take those four fellows with Ray Schalk behind the plate and I don't know how they can be beaten. It won't make any difference to them whether they're playing the Reds for the World's Championship or playing an exhibition game in a hick town."

	G	AB	H	R	2B	3B	HR	RBI	SB	AVG
Arnold "Chick" Gandil	115	441	128	54	24	7	1	60	10	.290
Eddie Collins	140	518	165	87	19	7	4	80	33	.319
Charles "Swede" Risberg	119	414	106	48	19	6	2	38	19	.256
George "Buck" Weaver	140	571	169	89	33	9	3	75	22	.296
Nemo Leibold	122	434	131	81	18	2	0	26	17	.302
Oscar "Happy" Felsch	135	502	138	68	34	11	7	86	19	.275
"Shoeless" Joe Jackson	139	516	181	79	31	14	7	96	9	.351
Ray Schalk	131	394	111	57	9	3	0	34	11	.282
Fred McMullin	60	170	50	31	8	4	0	19	4	.294
Harvey McClellan	7	12	4	2	0	0	0	1	0	.333
John "Shano" Collins	63	179	50	21	6	3	1	16	3	.279
Eddie Murphy	30	35	17	8	4	0	0	5	0	.486
Byrd Lynn	29	66	15	4	4	0	0	4	0	.227
Joe Jenkins	11	19	3	0	1	0	0	1	1	.158
		4,675	1,343	668	218	70	25	571	150	.287

	W	L	GS	CG	IP	H	BB	K	ShO	ERA
Eddie Cicotte	29	7	35	29	306⅔	256	49	110	5	1.82
Claude "Lefty" Williams	23	11	40	27	297	265	58	125	5	2.64
Dickie Kerr	13	7	17	10	212⅓	208	64	79	1	2.88
Urban "Red" Faber	11	9	20	9	162⅓	185	45	45	0	3.83
Grover Lowdermilk	5	5	11	5	96⅔	95	43	43	0	2.79
Dave Danforth	1	2	1	0	41⅔	58	20	17	0	7.78
Bill James	3	2	5	3	39⅓	39	14	11	2	2.52
Frank Shellenback	1	3	4	2	35	40	16	10	0	5.14
Erskine Mayer	1	3	2	0	23⅔	30	11	9	0	8.37
Roy Wilkinson	1	1	1	1	22	21	10	5	1	2.05
John Sullivan	0	1	2	1	15	24	8	9	0	4.20
Wynn Noyes	0	0	1	0	6	10	0	4	0	7.50
Tom McGuire	0	0	0	0	3	5	3	0	0	9.00
Joe Benz	0	0	0	0	2	2	0	0	0	0.00
Charlie Robertson	0	1	1	0	2	5	0	1	0	9.00
Pat Ragan	0	0	0	0	1	1	0	0	0	0.00
	88	52	140	87	1,265⅔	1,244	341	468	14	3.04

1920

Record: 96–58
Finish: Second
Games Behind: 2
Manager: Kid Gleason

In a roadhouse in Bellevue, Kentucky, following the disastrous second game of the 1919 World Series, a sorely disillusioned Ring Lardner, with help from *Tribune* beat writer Jim Crusinberry, penned an ode to failure:

I'm forever blowing ballgames
Pretty ballgames in the air,
I come from Chi,
I hardly try
Just go to bat, and fade and die,
Fortunes coming my way,
That's why I don't care,
I'm forever blowing ballgames,
For the gamblers treat me fair.

Rumors of the "fix" percolated throughout the baseball world and on into the winter despite customary denials from Charles Comiskey, who had his suspicions from the opening pitch of the first game.

Attorney Alfred Austrian (left) and "Shoeless" Joe Jackson confer on the eve of the grand jury hearing.

Commy voiced these concerns to Ban Johnson in a 3:00 AM meeting at Cincinnati's Sinton Hotel after Game 1, but Johnson dismissed his words as the "whelp of a beaten cur." In a more tactful, soothing tone of voice, National League president John A. Heydler told Comiskey not to worry, because "such a thing as crookedness in that game didn't seem possible. I told Comiskey I thought the White Sox were rather taken by surprise, that perhaps they had underestimated the strength of the Cincinnati team."

The day after the series ended, Hugh Fullerton added a few words of his own to the debate: "Yesterday's, in all probability, is the last game that will be played in any World Series. If the club owners and those who have the interest of the game at heart have listened during the Series, they will call off the annual inter-league contest. Yesterday's game also means the disruption of the Chicago White Sox ballclub. There are seven men on the team who will not be there when the gong sounds next spring."

To support these charges, convincing proof was needed. No one was talking, however, and the gamblers had the good sense to lie low. "When the same stories started to make the rounds early this season," the *Tribune* reported in September 1920, "the bookies folded up their bankrolls and turned to other fields."

Only Chick Gandil was absent when the curtain rose on the new season. Acting on the advice of his wife, the ringleader of the fix skipped the 1920 season in order to play for an "outlaw" team in the West.

Minus Gandil, the White Sox charged out of the gate looking like sure winners. A rejuvenated Red Faber joined Lefty Williams, Ed Cicotte, and Dickie Kerr as 20-game winners. Not until 1971, when the Baltimore Orioles' starting four duplicated the feat, did another team match the record of four 20-game winners on the staff.

The hard-hitting trio of Buck Weaver, Eddie Collins, and Joe Jackson recorded 210 or more hits apiece. The 1921 St. Louis Browns were the only other team in the 20th century to showcase three players with 210 safeties.

Chicago occupied third place for much of the season. They began a belated pennant push on August 6, to turn a five-game deficit into a 3½ game first-place advantage. The 1920 White Sox provided every indication that their experience and depth of pitching would be adequate to survive a challenge mounted by Cleveland and New York.

As they neared the end of a 15-game eastern road trip in late August, something went terribly awry for this team. After pounding the Yankees 16–4 on August 26, to bolster their lead to 3½ games, the Sox dropped the next seven in a row. The available evidence suggests that the gamblers pressured the corrupted ballplayers to throw games down the stretch to enable either the Yankees or the Indians to slip past them in the standings.

Contemporary accounts in the *Tribune* from this time paint a clearer picture of a team coming apart at the seams.

- **New York, August 27:** "Cicotte's wildness was responsible for the defeat."
- **New York, August 28:** "Risberg and Weaver were the best players New York had today. They booted in three runs which Faber put on base with passes."
- **Boston, August 30:** "The rest of the bunch were as soft as two-minute eggs most of the time."
- **Boston, August 31:** "The breaks were all against the Gleasons, once in the sloppy third a return throw by Jackson got away from Risberg and cost two runs. Again in the seventh, with runners on first and third and one run down, a sharp bounder to John Collins was a cinch doubleplay but Risberg could not find second after taking the throw so his return was delayed until the batsman beat it and let the runner score."

Eddie Collins voiced his suspicions to Comiskey on September 2, when the team returned to Chicago set to play 22 of the remaining 1920 games on their home field. Comiskey listened patiently, but it was an exasperating, useless rehash of unverifiable information.

Comiskey said he would look into it but was relieved of that heavy burden when a special grand jury was convened by the Cook County state's attorney to look into the allegations of crookedness in baseball. Events moved quickly after that. Subpoenas were issued to Comiskey, his friend George M.

Cohan, and New York Giants pitcher Rube Benton, who named Cicotte, Gandil, Felsch, and Williams as the names that had surfaced in gambling circles.

Trailing the Indians by only a half game with five left to play, Comiskey definitely vowed to play his regulars no matter what Ban Johnson reported to the grand jury. The White Sox played their final home game on September 27, defeating the Tigers 2–0. Hours after the game had ended, a state's attorney's detective appeared at Cicotte's doorstep. The next day he told Comiskey that he got $10,000 for "being a crook."

Without benefit of private counsel, Cicotte and Joe Jackson admitted their complicity in the World Series fix on September 29. Sequestered in his Comiskey Park office and refusing to meet with reporters, the Old Roman dictated a telegram notifying Gandil, Risberg, Freddie McMullin, Cicotte, Williams, Weaver, Jackson, and Felsch of their immediate suspension. "If you are guilty," Comiskey advised, "you will be retired from organized baseball for the rest of your lives if I can accomplish it."

A patchwork-quilt lineup of untested rookies and the remaining Clean Sox quietly dropped two of the final three games of the season in St. Louis, thus allowing the Cleveland Indians to back into the American League championship.

With the scandal out in the open, Eddie Collins spoke on behalf of his uncorrupted teammates. "Hardly any of us have talked with any of those fellows except on the field since the season opened. Even during the batting practice our gang stood in one group waiting our turn to hit and the other gang had their own group. We went along and gritted our teeth and played ball. We had to trail along with those fellows all summer, and all the time felt that they had thrown us down. It was tough. Now the load has been lifted. No wonder you feel like celebrating."

It was all so pointless and tragic. A ballclub of legend belonged to the ages.

Shoeless Joe

Do not be remembering the most natural
man ever to wear spiked shoes—
The canniest fielder and longest hitter,
Who squatted on his heels
In a uniform muddied at the knees,
Till the bleacher shadows grew long behind him.
Who went along with Chick and Buck and Happy
Because they treated him so friendly like—
Hardly like Yankees at all.
With Williams because Lefty was from the South too
And with Risberg because the Swede was such a hard guy—
Who made an X for his name and
couldn't argue with Comiskey's sleepers.
But who could pick a line drive out of
the air ten feet outside the foul line
and rifle anything home from anywhere in the park.
For Shoeless Joe is gone, long gone
A long-yellow grass-blade between his teeth
And the bleacher shadows behind him. . . .

—Nelson Algren, Chicago author, poet, and man of the streets

	G	AB	H	R	2B	3B	HR	RBI	SB	AVG
John "Shano" Collins	133	495	150	70	21	10	1	63	12	.303
Eddie Collins	153	601	222	115	37	13	3	75	19	.369
Charles "Swede" Risberg	126	458	122	53	21	10	2	65	12	.266
George "Buck" Weaver	151	630	210	104	35	8	2	75	19	.333
Nemo Leibold	108	413	91	61	16	3	1	28	7	.220
Oscar "Happy" Felsch	142	556	188	88	40	15	14	115	8	.338
"Shoeless" Joe Jackson	146	570	218	105	42	20	12	121	9	.382
Ray Schalk	151	485	131	64	25	5	1	61	10	.270
Ted Jourdan	48	150	36	16	6	1	0	8	3	.240
Fred McMullin	46	127	25	14	1	4	0	13	1	.197
Harvey McClellan	10	18	6	4	1	1	0	5	2	.333
Amos Strunk	51	183	42	32	7	1	1	14	1	.230
Eddie Murphy	58	118	40	22	2	1	0	19	1	.339
Bibb Falk	7	17	5	1	1	1	0	2	0	.294
Byrd Lynn	16	25	8	0	2	1	0	3	0	.320
Clarence "Bubber" Jonnard	2	5	0	0	0	0	0	0	0	.000
		5,325	1,571	793	263	97	37	692	108	.295

	W	L	GS	CG	IP	H	BB	K	ShO	ERA
Urban "Red" Faber	23	13	39	28	319	332	88	108	2	2.99
Eddie Cicotte	21	10	35	28	303⅓	316	74	87	4	3.26
Claude "Lefty" Williams	22	14	38	26	299	302	90	128	0	3.91
Dickie Kerr	21	9	28	20	253⅔	266	72	72	3	3.37
Roy Wilkinson	7	9	11	9	145	162	48	30	0	4.03
George Payne	1	1	0	0	29⅔	39	9	9	0	5.46
Clarence "Shovel" Hodge	1	1	2	1	19⅔	15	12	5	0	2.29
Spencer Heath	0	0	0	0	7	19	2	0	0	15.43
Grover Lowdermilk	0	0	0	0	5⅓	9	5	0	0	6.75
Joe Kiefer	0	1	1	0	4⅔	7	5	1	0	15.43
	96	58	154	112	1,386⅓	1,467	405	440	9	3.59

1921

Record: 62–92
Finish: Seventh
Games Behind: 36½
Manager: Kid Gleason

Charles Comiskey was done with the Black Sox players long before the conspiracy trial began in July 1921. Barred from major league baseball by decree of Comiskey and Judge Kenesaw Mountain Landis, the eight players cut their own deals with "outlaw" teams. Chicago investment broker George K. Miller capitalized on the box-office value of their names by organizing a barnstorming team revolving around Jackson, Risberg, and Williams.

A bewildering array of college players, career minor leaguers, and sandlot recruits tried out for starting berths in 1921. Harry Grabiner, who spent a busy off-season examining minor league roster sheets, was optimistic about the coming season. Gleason reserved judgment.

Over the winter Comiskey purchased an entire infield from Salt Lake City of the PCL. Earl Sheely, a square-shouldered, lumbering first baseman, was the key acquisition in a deal that also included third baseman Eddie Mulligan and Ernie Johnson, a journeyman shortstop who broke in with the Sox back in 1912.

Among the 50 spring training hopefuls, only Sheely, college slugger Bibb Falk, and Johnny Mostil, a speedy outfielder groomed in the American Association, came through in 1921. Comiskey added a veteran presence to the untested rookie mix by dealing Shano Collins and Nemo Leibold to the Boston Red Sox for outfielder Harry

Hooper, one of the great leadoff hitters of the game, on March 4.

Whatever fears Comiskey had over the winter about the fans returning to his ballpark in the postscandal period were put to rest when 25,000 cheering fans showed up on Opening Day. In the public's mind, it was the eight discredited players—and not Comiskey—who betrayed their interests.

A perfect Opening Day was the singular highlight of an otherwise bleak season for the Pale Hose. After dividing their first six games in April, the team never again reached the .500 mark. They dropped into seventh place on June 23 and remained there for the rest of the season.

Red Faber posted a career year in 1921. The lanky Iowan nailed down his 20th win on July 21, and he had an outside shot at 30. He slumped in the closing weeks, however, and had to "settle" for 25—a remarkable achievement. Rival managers savored the prospect of humbling the neutered White Sox. The team was in Washington on July 27, when Faber, Schalk, Dickie Kerr, the Sox trainer, and two reserves—Roy Wilkinson and Harvey McClellan—were called back to Chicago to testify in the Black Sox trial. Gleason asked Senators owner Clark Griffith to postpone the contest in the interest of sportsmanship. But not even a deluge of rain could force Griffith to cancel this game, "though in the past he has postponed many a contest on a mere sprinkle and put on a doubleheader later," wrote Jim Crusinberry. Despite putting up a good fight, the Sox lost 8–5.

It must have provided Comiskey some small consolation when his team ruined the Cleveland Indians' bid for a second straight pennant by capturing three out of four in a season-ending series, September 29 to October 2.

World Series hero Dickie Kerr was awarded a bouquet of roses, a mahogany chest, and a set of silverware on his special day—Dickie Kerr Day in Chicago, September 29, 1921.

Kerr pitched one of the greatest games of his career, shutting out the Tribe 5–0 on six hits. For one brief, shining moment, the South Side faithful imagined that it was September 1919 and the final thrilling days of the pennant race all over again.

Versatile Shano Collins

	G	AB	H	R	2B	3B	HR	RBI	SB	AVG
Earl Sheely	154	563	171	68	25	6	11	95	4	.304
Eddie Collins	139	526	177	79	20	10	2	58	12	.337
Ernie Johnson	142	613	181	93	28	7	1	51	22	.295
Eddie Mulligan	152	609	153	82	21	12	1	45	13	.251
Harry Hooper	108	419	137	74	26	5	8	58	13	.327
Amos Strunk	121	401	133	68	19	10	3	69	7	.332
Bibb Falk	152	585	167	62	31	11	5	82	4	.285
Ray Schalk	128	416	105	32	24	4	0	47	3	.252
Harvey McClellan	63	196	35	20	4	1	1	14	2	.179
Johnny Mostil	100	326	98	43	21	7	3	42	10	.301
Fred Bratchi	16	28	8	0	1	0	0	3	0	.286
Elmer Leifer	9	10	3	0	0	0	0	1	0	.300
Clarence "Yam" Yaryan	45	102	31	11	8	2	0	15	0	.304
George Lees	20	42	9	3	2	0	0	4	0	.214
Robert "Red" Ostergard	12	11	4	2	0	0	0	0	0	.364
Eddie Murphy	6	5	1	1	0	0	0	0	0	.200
Frank Pratt	1	1	0	0	0	0	0	0	0	.000
		5,319	1,509	677	242	82	35	609	93	.284

	W	L	GS	CG	IP	H	BB	K	ShO	ERA
Urban "Red" Faber	25	15	39	32	330⅔	293	87	124	4	2.48
Dickie Kerr	19	17	37	25	308⅔	357	96	80	3	4.72
Roy Wilkinson	4	20	22	11	198⅓	259	78	50	0	5.13
Clarence "Shovel" Hodge	6	8	11	6	142⅔	191	54	25	0	6.56
Douglas McWeeney	3	6	9	4	97⅔	127	45	46	0	6.08
John Russell	2	5	8	4	66⅓	82	35	15	0	5.29
Dominic Mulrennan	2	8	10	3	56	84	36	10	0	7.23
Joubert "Lum" Davenport	0	3	2	0	35⅓	41	32	9	0	6.88
Edwin "Cy" Twombly	1	2	4	0	27⅔	26	25	7	0	5.86
Jack Wieneke	0	1	3	0	25⅓	39	17	10	0	8.17
George "Sarge" Connally	0	1	2	0	22⅓	29	10	6	0	6.45
Lee Thompson	0	3	4	0	20⅔	32	6	4	0	8.27
Joseph "Bugs" Bennett	0	3	2	1	17⅔	19	16	2	0	6.11
Horace "Hod" Fenner	0	0	1	0	7	14	3	1	0	7.71
Russ Pence	0	0	0	0	5⅓	6	7	2	0	8.44
John Michaelson	0	0	0	0	2⅔	4	1	1	0	10.13
Foster "Babe" Blackburn	0	0	0	0	1	0	1	0	0	0.00
	62	92	154	86	1,365⅓	1,603	549	392	7	4.94

1922

Record: 77–77
Finish: Fifth
Games Behind: 17
Manager: Kid Gleason

The White Sox were back in the news in a positive way despite Comiskey's stubborn refusal to offer Dickie Kerr a three-year guaranteed contract, prompting his huffy exit from the South Side. Kerr's salary demand seemed trifling when measured against the $100,000 Comiskey lavished on the ownership triumvirate of the San Francisco Seals for the services of one William Edward Kamm, a third baseman of great promise.

The Kamm purchase and the deal cut for Earl Sheely a year earlier set a trend for the decade. While nickel-and-diming his rostered veterans, Comiskey spent hundreds of thousands of dollars buying rookie prospects from greedy minor league brokers who advertised their "stable" each year at the annual baseball winter meetings. The college draft and the farm system envisioned by Branch Rickey were years away.

Rookie hurler Charlie Robertson, a spring training dark horse, polished off the Tigers in Detroit on April 30, without giving up a hit, walk, or error. It was baseball's first perfect game since 1908, when Addie Joss blanked the White Sox. Robertson's heart-stopping performance ensured him a spot on the roster longer than one would normally expect of a chronically wild pitcher who struggled to keep his ERA below five.

Charles Robertson: perfect for one day

Until July 31 the White Sox occupied third place, and they were a couple of games over the .500 mark entering the final week of the season. Comiskey's abiding faith in his ability to dip into the minors to solve his long-term problems seemed justified by the team's marked improvement, but the real credit for the modest 1922 success went to Kid Gleason, who maximized the output of a threadbare unit. There was much more to be done before daylight could break through the clouds.

	G	AB	H	R	2B	3B	HR	RBI	SB	AVG
Earl Sheely	149	526	167	72	37	4	6	80	4	.317
Eddie Collins	154	598	194	92	20	12	1	69	20	.324
Ernie Johnson	145	603	153	85	17	3	0	56	21	.254
Eddie Mulligan	103	372	87	39	14	8	0	31	7	.234
Harry Hooper	152	602	183	111	35	8	11	80	16	.304
Johnny Mostil	132	458	139	74	28	14	7	70	14	.303
Bibb Falk	131	483	144	58	27	1	12	79	2	.298
Ray Schalk	142	442	124	57	22	3	4	60	12	.281
Harvey McClellan	91	301	68	28	17	3	2	28	3	.226
Johnny Evers	1	3	0	0	0	0	0	1	0	.000
John Jenkins	5	3	0	0	0	0	0	1	0	.000
Amos Strunk	92	311	90	36	11	4	0	33	9	.289
Elmer Pence	1	0	0	0	0	0	0	0	0	.000
Clarence "Yam" Yaryan	36	71	14	9	2	0	2	9	1	.197
Roy Graham	5	3	0	0	0	0	0	0	0	.000
Jim Long	3	3	0	0	0	0	0	0	0	.000
August Swentor	1	1	0	0	0	0	0	0	0	.000
Harold Bubser	3	3	0	0	0	0	0	0	0	.000
		5,269	1,464	691	245	63	45	635	109	.278

	W	L	GS	CG	IP	H	BB	K	ShO	ERA
Urban "Red" Faber	21	17	38	31	353	334	83	148	4	2.80
Charlie Robertson	14	15	34	21	272	294	89	83	3	3.64
Gorham "Dixie" Leverett	13	10	27	16	224⅔	224	79	50	4	3.32
Clarence "Shovel" Hodge	7	6	8	2	139	154	65	37	0	4.14
Ted Blankenship	8	10	15	7	127⅔	124	47	42	0	3.81
Harry Courtney	5	6	11	5	87⅔	100	37	28	0	4.93
Ferdie Schupp	4	4	12	3	74	79	66	38	1	5.08
Frank Mack	2	2	4	1	34⅓	36	16	11	1	3.67
Joubert "Lum" Davenport	1	1	1	0	16⅔	14	13	9	0	10.80
Jose Acosta	0	2	1	0	15	25	6	6	0	8.40
Roy Wilkinson	0	1	1	0	14⅓	24	6	3	0	8.79
Homer Blankenship	0	0	0	0	13	21	5	3	0	4.85
Larry Duff	1	1	1	0	12⅔	16	3	7	0	4.97
Douglas McWeeney	0	1	1	0	10⅔	13	7	5	0	5.91
John Russell	0	1	1	0	6⅔	7	4	3	0	6.75
Dick McCabe	1	0	0	0	3⅓	4	0	1	0	5.40
Emmett Bowles	0	0	0	0	1	2	1	0	0	27.00
Ernie Cox	0	0	0	0	1	1	2	0	0	18.00
	77	77	155	86	1,406⅔	1,472	529	484	13	3.93

1923

Record: 69–85
Finish: Seventh
Games Behind: 30
Manager: Kid Gleason

Kid Gleason had every expectation that the coming season boded well for his maturing ballclub. The White Sox offense revolved around the two speed merchants, Eddie Collins and Johnny Mostil, who formed the nucleus of a tough, dangerous starting lineup lacking only a long-ball threat sculpted in the image of Babe Ruth.

Even without a Ruth or Jimmy Foxx providing the thrills, the Sox finished only three points below the league average in hitting with .279. Substandard pitching and a horrible rash of injuries, which would plague the Sox through the next two decades, dashed Gleason's soaring preseason expectations.

The White Sox were buried deep in the second division on June 5 when they embarked on a month-long road trip that included stops in every American League city. Playing away from Comiskey Park seemed to have a salutary effect on Gleason's team. They returned to the city tied for third and only a half game out of second after winning 18 of 27 on foreign fields. The trip was a wonderful success, but it exacted a terrible toll for the season. Eddie Collins twisted his knee in St. Louis on July 2 and was out for the next two weeks. "That fellow's misfortunes was what broke us up," Gleason explained. "The team was never right after that."

The July 2 contest in Sportsman's Park offers an interesting historical anecdote. Years later, Theodore Amar Lyons would look upon this unremarkable 7–2 loss to the Browns as his major league debut. Inserted into the game in the eighth inning, Lyons, who was fresh off the Baylor University campus, retired the three batters he faced in one inning of relief.

The Sox tumbled into seventh place on the last day of the season. It was bitter medicine for Kid Gleason, who waited until the conclusion of the City Series on October 17 to announce his resignation. Gleason praised Comiskey as one of the smartest men he had ever known, but offered no explanation for his somewhat surprising decision to step down.

The strain of the scandal on his health forced Gleason to regain his strength in the solitude of his home. For many weeks afterward he could not eat, sleep, or stand to be alone. He had endured more in five White Sox seasons than some baseball men in a lifetime. Gleason would never again manage a big league club.

Eddie Collins, Ray Schalk, and Yankees coach Charley O'Leary were all rumored as possible replacements for Gleason. During the 1922 season Collins was tabbed as the likely successor to Miller Huggins in New York, when the great Yankees manager's job hung by a thread.

But in weighing the merits of Collins versus Schalk, it boiled down to an issue of pride. Could either one of these Hall of Fame–bound veterans accept direction from the other without complaint?

Comiskey demurred and hired Frank Chance, who had just been let out of his job managing the Boston Red Sox. Comiskey and Grabiner were exultant after reeling in Chance, a guaranteed box-office draw. The Sox nabobs gave him a free hand to wheel and deal as he saw fit.

At the winter meetings manager Chance announced Eddie Collins' availability via the trade route. "I did not expect to be placed in the market," he said. "I liked Chicago and would have been delighted to play under Chance, but he is the boss and wants to get rid of me. Oh well, this is all a game. What else can I say?"

	G	AB	H	R	2B	3B	HR	RBI	SB	AVG
Earl Sheely	156	570	169	74	25	3	4	88	5	.296
Eddie Collins	145	505	182	89	22	5	5	67	47	.360
Harvey McClellan	141	550	129	67	29	3	1	41	14	.235
Willie Kamm	149	544	159	57	39	9	6	87	17	.292
Harry Hooper	145	576	166	87	32	4	10	65	18	.188
Johnny Mostil	153	546	159	91	37	15	3	64	41	.291
Bibb Falk	87	274	84	44	18	6	5	38	4	.307
Ray Schalk	123	382	87	42	12	2	1	44	6	.228
John Happenny	32	86	19	7	5	0	0	10	0	.221
Ernie Johnson	12	53	10	5	2	0	0	1	2	.189
Lou Rosenberg	3	4	1	0	0	0	0	0	0	.250
Roy Elsh	81	209	52	28	7	2	0	24	15	.249
Bill Barrett	42	162	44	17	7	2	2	23	12	.272
Maurice Archdeacon	22	87	35	23	5	1	0	4	2	.402
Amos Strunk	54	54	17	7	0	0	0	8	1	.315
Roy Graham	36	82	16	3	2	0	0	6	0	.195
Clyde "Buck" Crouse	23	70	18	6	2	1	1	7	0	.257
Charlie Dorman	1	2	1	0	0	0	0	0	0	.500
John "Shine" Cortazzo	1	1	0	0	0	0	0	0	0	.000
Wyatt "Roxy" Snipes	1	1	0	0	0	0	0	0	0	.000
Leo Taylor	2	0	0	0	0	0	0	0	0	.000
		5,225	1,459	690	255	57	42	604	186	.279

	W	L	GS	CG	IP	H	BB	K	ShO	ERA
Charlie Robertson	13	18	34	18	255	262	104	91	1	3.81
Urban "Red" Faber	14	11	31	15	232⅓	233	62	91	2	3.41
Mike Cvengros	12	13	26	14	215⅓	216	107	86	0	4.39
Ted Blankenship	9	14	23	9	208⅔	219	100	57	1	4.27
Gorham "Dixie" Leverett	10	13	24	9	192⅔	212	64	64	0	4.06
Hollis "Sloppy" Thurston	7	8	12	8	191⅔	223	36	55	0	3.05
Frank Mack	0	1	0	0	23⅓	23	11	6	0	4.24
Ted Lyons	2	1	1	0	22⅔	30	15	6	0	6.35
Claral Gillenwater	1	3	3	1	21⅓	28	6	2	1	5.48
Paul Castner	0	0	0	0	10	14	5	0	0	6.30
George "Sarge" Connally	0	0	0	0	8⅔	7	12	3	0	6.23
Homer Blankenship	1	1	0	0	5	9	1	1	0	3.60
Joubert "Lum" Davenport	0	0	0	0	4⅓	7	4	1	0	6.23
Noah "Red" Proctor	0	0	0	0	4	11	2	0	0	13.50
Charles "Slim" Embry	0	0	0	0	2⅔	7	2	1	0	10.13
Leon Cadore	0	1	1	0	2⅓	6	2	3	0	23.14
Frank Woodward	0	1	1	0	2	5	1	0	0	13.50
	69	85	156	74	1,402	1,512	534	467	5	4.03

1924

Record: 66–87
Finish: Eighth
Games Behind: 25½
Managers: Frank Chance, Johnny Evers, Ed Walsh, Eddie Collins

Frank Chance arrived in Chicago for the 1923–1924 winter meetings weakened to the point of exhaustion. The harsh Chicago climate only aggravated his shaky health and brought on a strain of influenza that developed into bronchial pneumonia.

Hoping to regain his health, Chance traveled to Hot Springs, Arkansas, to formulate plans for the new season. The soothing waters of the resort spa failed to restore his vitality, however, and on February 16 he wired Comiskey of his intention to resign. Unable to comprehend the seriousness of his condition, Comiskey dismissed his retirement plans and promised to keep the chair warm until he could return. "Take as much time as you need to get well, but by all means come back," Comiskey replied.

Frank Chance missed the entire spring training, and his absence created new dilemmas for the younger players who were never sure which of the three supervising coaches—Eddie

Collins, Ed Walsh, and former Cub great Johnny Evers—to take their direction from.

Prior to the opening of the 1924 season, the White Sox played a two-game exhibition series against the New York Giants in Comiskey Park to whip up publicity for the second "Baseball World Tour" that John McGraw and the Old Roman planned for the 1924–1925 off-season. The meaningless games against New York lured Chance out of his sickbed. The "Peerless Leader" contracted a cold in the frigid April climate and as a result underwent emergency surgery at Mercy Hospital the following week. Chance was sent home on the advice of his physicians. Four months later this legendary Chicago sports figure was dead at age 47.

The low-key Johnny Evers was designated to handle the management chores thereafter, but Evers had to undergo an emergency appendectomy on May 14. Evers designated Ed Walsh to guide the club, but the former Sox pitcher's managerial skills left much to be desired. After only two games, Walsh was removed, and Eddie Collins was placed in charge.

Hobbled by injuries for much of the season, the pitching staff received a shot in the arm from young Hollis "Sloppy" Thurston, whose fine work kept the Sox at or near the .500 mark through July 22. The encouraging start was negated by a 13-game losing streak that began on August 9 and continued until the 26th, by which time the ballclub was buried in the cellar. It was the longest losing streak in team history, and for the first time a White Sox team finished last in the standings.

The dreary 1924 campaign had few saving graces. Ray "Cracker" Schalk caught his 1,500th career game on May 25, but a foul tip deflecting off his finger that afternoon reduced his playing time to only 57 games during the year.

Named interim manager on May 22, Eddie Collins performed capably under a difficult set of circumstances. He was awarded the job on a more permanent basis on December 11. "I felt that the public in Chicago wanted Collins to lead the team," Comiskey explained from his suite in New York's Biltmore Hotel. "He's been popular with our patrons ever since he was with the team. I think he's earned the right to become manager." Collins called it a "mighty good Christmas present."

The White Sox and Giants embarked on their European expedition on October 15, with stopovers in London, Dublin, Glasgow, Berlin, Paris, and Rome. The trip was not the same artistic and commercial success as the 1914 junket. Comiskey's fond hope of internationalizing baseball was a goal he never achieved in his lifetime.

Hollis "Sloppy" Thurston: a meticulous dresser

	G	AB	H	R	2B	3B	HR	RBI	SB	AVG
Earl Sheely	146	535	171	84	34	3	3	103	7	.320
Eddie Collins	152	556	194	108	27	7	6	86	42	.349
Bill Barrett	119	406	110	52	18	5	2	56	15	.271
Willie Kamm	147	528	134	58	28	6	6	93	9	.254
Harry Hooper	130	476	156	107	27	8	10	62	16	.328
Johnny Mostil	118	385	125	75	22	5	4	49	7	.325
Bibb Falk	138	526	185	77	37	8	6	99	6	.352
Clyde "Buck" Crouse	94	305	79	30	10	1	1	44	3	.259
Ray French	37	112	20	13	4	0	0	11	3	.179
Ray Morehart	31	100	20	10	4	2	0	8	3	.200
Harvey McClellan	32	85	15	9	3	0	0	9	2	.176
Bud Clancy	13	35	9	5	1	0	0	6	3	.257
Ike Davis	10	33	8	5	1	1	0	4	0	.242
Bill Black	6	5	1	0	0	0	0	0	0	.200
Wally Dashiell	1	2	0	0	0	0	0	0	0	.000
Frank Naleway	1	2	0	0	0	0	0	0	0	.000
Bernie DeViveiros	1	1	0	0	0	0	0	0	0	.000
Maurice Archdeacon	95	288	92	59	9	3	0	25	11	.319
Roy Elsh	60	147	45	21	9	1	0	11	6	.306
Ray Schalk	57	153	30	15	4	2	1	11	1	.196
Johnny "Nig" Grabowski	20	56	14	10	3	0	0	3	0	.250
Joe Burns	8	19	2	1	0	0	0	0	0	.105
Elwood "Kettle" Wirtz	6	12	1	0	0	0	0	0	1	.083
Amos Strunk	1	1	0	0	0	0	0	0	0	.000
		5,240	1,512	794	255	59	41	710	136	.289

	W	L	GS	CG	IP	H	BB	K	ShO	ERA
Hollis "Sloppy" Thurston	20	14	36	28	291	330	60	37	1	3.80
Ted Lyons	12	11	22	12	216⅓	279	72	52	0	4.87
Urban "Red" Faber	9	11	20	9	161⅓	173	58	47	0	3.85
George "Sarge" Connally	7	13	13	6	160	177	68	55	0	4.05
Ted Blankenship	7	6	11	7	125⅓	167	38	36	0	5.17
Mike Cvengros	3	12	15	2	105⅔	119	67	36	0	5.88
Gorham "Dixie" Leverett	2	3	11	4	99	123	41	29	0	5.82
Charlie Robertson	4	10	14	5	97⅓	108	54	29	0	4.99
Leo Mangum	1	4	7	1	47	69	25	12	0	7.09
Douglas McWeeney	1	3	5	2	43⅓	47	17	18	0	4.57
Milton Steengrafe	0	0	1	0	5⅔	15	4	3	0	12.71
Bob Barnes	0	0	2	0	4⅔	14	0	1	0	19.29
August "Happy" Foreman	0	0	0	0	4	7	4	1	0	2.25
Joubert "Lum" Davenport	0	0	0	0	2	1	2	1	0	0.00
John Dobb	0	0	0	0	2	4	1	2	0	9.00
Bob Lawrence	0	0	0	0	1	1	1	1	0	9.00
Webb Schultz	0	0	0	0	1	1	0	0	0	9.00
	66	87	154	76	1,366⅔	1,635	512	360	1	4.75

1925

Record: 79–75
Finish: Fifth
Games Behind: 18½
Manager: Eddie Collins

The White Sox offered positive encouragement to their fans by sweeping the entire card of 19 spring training games played against a ragged collection of Class A and B teams in Shreveport, Louisiana, before heading home with a new sense of purpose. Three talented young hurlers, Ted Lyons, Hollis Thurston, and Ted Blankenship, provided a depth of pitching not seen on the South Side since 1920. Blankenship won 10 straight games after pitching coach Albert "Chief" Bender helped him develop a changeup pitch for his repertoire.

Teddy Lyons was robbed of a no-hitter after Bobby Veach of the Senators dropped a Texas League single over Earl Sheely's head with two outs in the bottom of the ninth inning of a 17–0 White Sox conquest on September 19. Lyons was the workhorse of the staff, twirling 263 innings, including a 14⅓ inning performance against Philadelphia on August 1.

Dickie Kerr was reinstated after a four-year absence from pro ball. Kerr's emotional homecoming on August 15 was marked by a touching pregame ceremony and thunderous applause, but Dickie had lost his effectiveness, and his much publicized 1925 comeback was largely a failure.

Despite a subpar, injury-riddled season, Eddie Collins banged out career hit No. 3,000 on June 6. It was a ringing double hit off ancient Walter Johnson in Washington. Collins became only the sixth major league player in history to reach this historic plateau.

Eddie Collins worked wonders with this team. He molded a doormat into an overnight winner, utilizing a collection of waiver-list players and learning to make due. Harvey McClellan, the regular shortstop, was lost in the closing hours of spring training, forcing Collins to employ Ike Davis, an unskilled Columbus recruit, in his place. Beset with serious stomach ailments dating back more than a year, the popular "Little Mac" was operated on for ulcers. He passed away unexpectedly on November 6 at his Kentucky home, and his death convinced more than a few cynics that this ballclub was tragically cursed.

The White Sox are greeted by King George of England during their 1924 goodwill World Tour. Charlie Robinson (left), Dave Bancroft of the New York Giants (shaking hands with the king), and Bibb Faulk (standing behind Bancroft) are pictured.

	G	AB	H	R	2B	3B	HR	RBI	SB	AVG
Earl Sheely	153	600	189	93	43	3	9	111	3	.315
Eddie Collins	118	425	147	80	26	3	3	80	19	.346
Ike Davis	146	562	135	105	31	9	0	61	19	.240
Willie Kamm	152	509	142	82	32	4	6	83	11	.279
Harry Hooper	127	442	117	62	23	5	6	55	12	.265
Johnny Mostil	153	605	181	135	36	16	2	50	43	.299
Bibb Falk	154	602	181	80	35	9	4	99	4	.301
Ray Schalk	125	343	94	44	18	1	0	52	11	.274
Bill Barrett	81	245	89	44	23	3	3	40	5	.363
John Kane	14	56	10	6	1	0	0	3	0	.179
Spencer Harris	56	92	26	2	2	0	1	13	1	.283
Roy Elsh	32	48	9	6	1	0	0	4	2	.188
Maurice Archdeacon	10	9	1	2	0	0	0	0	0	.111
Julius Mallonee	2	3	0	1	0	0	0	0	0	.000
Clyde "Buck" Crouse	54	131	46	18	7	0	0	25	1	.351
Johnny "Nig" Grabowski	21	46	14	5	4	1	0	10	0	.304
John Bischoff	7	11	1	1	0	0	0	0	0	.091
Leo Tankersley	1	3	0	0	0	0	0	0	0	.000
Bud Clancy	4	3	0	0	0	0	0	0	0	.000
		5,225	1,482	811	299	60	38	738	131	.284

	W	L	GS	CG	IP	H	BB	K	ShO	ERA
Ted Lyons	21	11	32	19	262⅔	274	83	45	5	3.26
Urban "Red" Faber	12	11	32	16	238	266	59	71	1	3.78
Ted Blankenship	17	8	23	16	222	218	69	81	3	3.16
Hollis "Sloppy" Thurston	10	14	25	9	175	250	47	35	0	6.17
Charlie Robertson	8	12	23	6	137	181	47	27	2	5.26
George "Sarge" Connally	6	7	2	0	104⅔	122	58	45	0	4.64
Mike Cvengros	3	9	11	4	104⅔	109	55	32	0	4.30
Jim Joe Edwards	1	2	4	1	45⅓	46	23	20	1	3.97
Dickie Kerr	0	1	2	0	36⅔	45	18	4	0	5.15
Leo Mangum	1	0	0	0	15	25	6	6	0	7.80
Frank Mack	0	0	0	0	13⅓	24	13	6	0	9.45
Arthur "Tink" Riviere	0	0	0	0	4⅔	6	7	1	0	13.50
Ken Ash	0	0	0	0	4	7	0	0	0	9.00
Carl "Jake" Freeze	0	0	0	0	3⅔	5	3	1	0	2.45
Albert "Chief" Bender	0	0	0	0	1	1	1	0	0	18.00
	79	75	154	71	1,367⅔	1,579	489	374	12	4.34

1926

Record: 81–72
Finish: Fifth
Games Behind: 9½
Manager: Eddie Collins

Downtown oddsmakers listed the White Sox as 6–1 long shots to capture the 1926 crown. The odds dipped even further after the usual rash of injuries decimated the lineup. Thus Collins was unable to deliver a pennant winner to the impatient Comiskey, who believed his expensive minor league acquisitions were good enough to rank with the contenders.

Nevertheless, the ballclub remained competitive for much of the 1926 season, though the Sox trailed the Yankees by 10 games when July rolled around.

Hard-hitting outfielder Bill Barrett and third baseman Willie Kamm went down with knee injuries. Ted Blankenship fractured his right thumb on July 29 and missed more than a month. Collins played sparingly, and brittle Everett "Deacon" Scott, who had been coaxed out of retirement to play shortstop for the Comiskeys, made Sox fans long for their beloved "Little Mac."

Johnny Mostil and Bibb Falk feasted on American League pitching for much of the season. Their torrid hitting helped knock off the powerful Yankees 4–3 before a record-setting crowd of 43,000 on June 20. That stood as a single-game attendance mark before Comiskey Park was upper-decked in the off-season.

Eddie Collins was toasted by fans on his special day, June 19, 1926. Cardinal Patrick O'Donnell of Ireland and Mayor William Dever joined with 27,000 in a chorus of praise for the Sox veteran whose loyalty to the owner was never fully repaid. A born competitor whose right to lead was first questioned by the Black Sox faction, and then later by the Old Roman who second-guessed him at every turn, Collins was dismissed on November 11 without so much as the courtesy of a telephone call. Because Collins was no longer an everyday player and his box-office appeal was diminishing, Comiskey desired to make a change.

The battle-scarred backstop Ray Schalk was already in office for 1927 when Collins received formal notice of his release by the ballclub.

Shining lights in a dark time (left to right): Bibb Falk, Earl Sheely, and Willie Kamm

	G	AB	H	R	2B	3B	HR	RBI	SB	AVG
Earl Sheely	145	525	157	77	40	2	6	89	3	.299
Eddie Collins	106	375	129	66	32	4	1	62	13	.344
Bill Hunnefield	131	470	129	81	26	4	3	48	24	.274
Willie Kamm	143	480	141	63	24	10	0	62	14	.294
Bill Barrett	111	368	113	46	31	4	6	61	9	.307
Johnny Mostil	148	600	197	120	41	15	4	42	35	.328
Bibb Falk	155	566	195	86	43	4	8	108	9	.345
Ray Schalk	82	226	60	26	9	1	0	32	5	.265
Ray Morehart	73	192	61	27	10	3	0	21	3	.318
Everett "Deacon" Scott	40	143	36	15	10	1	0	13	1	.252
Moe Berg	41	113	25	4	6	0	0	7	0	.221
Bud Clancy	12	38	13	3	2	2	0	7	0	.342
Art Veltman	5	4	1	1	0	0	0	0	0	.250
Spencer Harris	80	222	56	36	11	3	2	27	8	.252
Tom Gulley	16	35	8	5	3	1	0	8	0	.229
Everett "Pid" Purdy	11	33	6	5	2	1	0	6	0	.182
Clyde "Buck" Crouse	49	135	32	10	4	1	0	17	0	.237
Johnny "Nig" Grabowski	48	122	32	6	1	1	1	11	0	.262
Harry McCurdy	44	86	28	16	7	2	1	11	0	.326
		5,221	1,507	731	314	60	32	666	125	.289

	W	L	GS	CG	IP	H	BB	K	ShO	ERA
Ted Lyons	18	16	31	24	283⅔	268	106	51	3	3.01
Tommy Thomas	15	12	32	13	249	225	110	127	2	3.80
Ted Blankenship	13	10	26	15	209⅓	217	65	66	1	3.61
Urban "Red" Faber	15	9	25	13	184⅔	203	57	65	1	3.56
Jim Joe Edwards	6	9	16	8	142	140	63	41	3	4.18
Hollis "Sloppy" Thurston	6	8	13	6	134⅓	164	36	35	1	5.02
George "Sarge" Connally	6	5	8	5	108⅓	128	35	47	0	3.16
Milton Steengrafe	1	1	1	0	38⅓	43	19	10	0	3.99
Gorham "Dixie" Leverett	1	1	3	1	24	31	7	12	0	6.00
Les Cox	0	1	0	0	5	6	5	3	0	5.40
Pryor McBee	0	0	0	0	1⅓	1	3	1	0	6.75
	81	72	155	85	1,380	1,426	506	458	11	3.74

1927

Record: 70–83
Finish: Fifth
Games Behind: 39½
Manager: Ray Schalk

Charles Comiskey tinkered and fiddled with his ballclub, searching for the right player combinations. He spent vast fortunes on untested rookies only to lose patience with the young men before they were given a fair chance. Comiskey's once formidable skills of developing high-caliber talent abandoned him in the 1920s. Advancing age, the residue of scandal, and the changing complexities of baseball doomed his sincere efforts to rebuild his team.

An off-season trade brought Yankees second baseman Aaron Ward to Chicago for infielder Ray Morehart and catcher John Grabowski, heir apparent to Schalk. Ward teamed with Roger Peckinpaugh, a 1925 MVP winner acquired on January 15 for Sloppy Thurston and Leo Mangum. It was a bad move compounded by a near tragedy.

Johnny Mostil, the speedy center fielder whose superb outfield play was a joy to watch, inflicted 13 razor cuts to his chest and arms in a botched suicide attempt at the team's

Johnny Mostil: a riddle wrapped inside an enigma

spring training hotel on March 9. An agonizing nerve disorder diagnosed as neuritis caused him so many sleepless nights that he was unable to cope with the pain any longer. This was the peculiar explanation handed the press by the Comiskeys.

Mostil hovered at death's doorstep for several days while the fans and media groped for a deeper meaning. Eventually the Sox outfielder regained his strength and returned to Chicago, where he underwent extensive rehabilitation and therapy.

The White Sox began the home season in refurbished Comiskey Park on April 20. The White Sox Rooter's Association staged a massive downtown parade and presented Schalk with a floral horseshoe symbolizing good luck. The "new" Comiskey Park, with its distant outfield upper deck seated 52,000, nearly doubling the size of the original stadium. The architects of the $600,000 renovation vowed that no mere mortal could hit a ball over the roof. "Why, it is not possible by the laws of man!" proclaimed one. They only had to wait until August 16 to witness "Samson" tear apart the temple. On that afternoon Babe Ruth, a cultural icon of the dazzling 1920s, defied the experts by launching a mammoth home run over the right-field roof off Tommy Thomas. The ball landed in an adjacent soccer field after traveling a distance of 474 feet.

The grand unveiling of the modernized stadium was diminished by the Johnny Mostil episode, which cast a pall over everything Schalk hoped to accomplish in his maiden season. Minus Mostil's capable presence, as well as a starting pitcher to back up Ted Lyons and Thomas, Schalk's team was unable to sustain an early flush of success. Only one game separated the second-place White Sox from the league-leading Yankees on June 6. At no other time in this desparing decade (1920 being the lone exception) would a Chicago White Sox team stab at first place so late in a season.

Before another month had passed, the Sox trailed New York by 10 games—the illusory pennant race up in smoke. A 10-game losing streak in September ended the hope for a third consecutive winning season. The real dog days of White Sox baseball were at hand.

	G	AB	H	R	2B	3B	HR	RBI	SB	AVG
Bud Clancy	130	464	139	46	21	2	3	53	4	.300
Aaron Ward	145	463	125	75	25	8	5	56	6	.270
Bill Hunnefield	112	365	104	45	25	1	2	36	13	.285
Willie Kamm	148	540	146	85	32	13	0	59	7	.270
Bill Barrett	147	556	159	62	35	9	4	83	20	.286
Alex Metzler	134	543	173	87	29	11	3	61	15	.319
Bibb Falk	145	535	175	76	35	6	9	83	5	.327
Harry McCurdy	86	262	75	34	19	3	1	27	6	.286
Roger Peckinpaugh	68	217	64	23	6	3	0	23	2	.295
Early Sheely	45	129	27	11	3	0	2	16	1	.209
Ray Flaskamper	26	95	21	12	5	0	0	6	0	.221
Jim Battle	6	8	3	1	0	1	0	0	0	.375
Bob Way	5	3	1	3	0	0	0	1	0	.333
Bernie Neis	45	76	22	9	5	0	0	11	1	.289
Ike Boone	29	53	12	10	4	0	1	11	0	.226
Carl Reynolds	14	42	9	5	3	0	1	7	1	.214
Johnny Mostil	13	16	2	3	0	0	0	1	1	.125
Randy Moore	6	15	0	0	0	0	0	0	0	.000
Frank "Kid" Wilson	7	10	1	1	0	0	0	1	0	.100
Clyde "Buck" Crouse	85	222	53	22	11	0	0	20	4	.239
Moe Berg	35	69	17	4	4	0	0	4	0	.246
Ray Schalk	16	26	6	2	2	0	0	2	0	.231
Lena Blackburne	1	1	1	1	0	0	0	1	0	1.000
		5,157	1,433	662	285	61	36	610	86	.278

	W	L	GS	CG	IP	H	BB	K	ShO	ERA
Ted Lyons	22	14	34	30	307⅔	291	67	71	2	2.84
Tommy Thomas	19	16	36	24	307⅔	271	94	107	3	2.98
Ted Blankenship	12	17	34	11	236⅔	280	74	51	3	5.06
George "Sarge" Connally	10	15	18	11	198⅓	217	83	58	1	4.08
Urban "Red" Faber	4	7	15	6	110⅔	131	41	39	0	4.55
Elmer Jacobs	2	4	8	2	74⅓	105	37	22	1	4.60
Bert Cole	1	4	2	0	66⅔	79	19	12	0	4.73
Charlie Barnabe	0	5	5	1	61	86	20	5	0	5.31
Frank Stewart	0	1	1	0	4	5	4	0	0	9.00
	70	83	153	85	1,367	1,465	439	365	10	3.89

1928

Record: 72–82
Finish: Fifth
Games Behind: 29
Managers: Ray Schalk, Russ Blackburne

If there was one player who symbolized the hope and determination of the White Sox in the first half of the 20th century—a "Mr. White Sox"—it was Ray Schalk, the fireplug catcher who appeared in 100 or more games for 10 straight years. When Schalk donned his mask and chest protector on

July 21, 1925, he shattered Deacon McGuire's record for games caught by appearing in his 1,576th contest.

Comiskey's decision to appoint him manager was born out of loyalty and a sense of obligation. In this instance, however, it would have been more desirable to steer the course with Eddie Collins, whose temperament and disposition were better suited to running a baseball team than "Cracker" Schalk's. His easygoing manner inspired little respect among veteran players like Bill Barrett and Bibb Falk. In an age when the manager very often had to enforce his edicts with a well-timed right hook, Schalk receded into the background, refusing to assess a single fine against these hard-case vets who undermined his authority.

An expensive bumper crop of rookies basked in a harsh glow of media scrutiny in 1928. The big news in camp was the celebrated arrival of Chalmer "Bill" Cissell, a $123,000 shortstop acquired from the Pacific Coast League. The record-setting sum illustrated the exacerbating lengths to which Comiskey would go in order to buy a winner, when the simpler solution might have been to leave well enough alone and allow the manager to manage.

The 1928 youth movement canceled out the failed 1927 strategy of employing aged veterans. Aaron Ward was sold to Cleveland on March 27, and Roger Peckinpaugh retired in order to take over as the new manager of the Indians.

Ed Walsh Jr., right, shown here with his dad, Ed Walsh Sr., made his pitching debut in 1928. (Courtesy of the Amateur Athletic Foundation of Los Angeles)

The White Sox took over the AL cellar in early May and trailed the leader board by a staggering 21½ games when Comiskey finally had enough. On July 4 he coaxed Schalk into relinquishing his duties in favor of Coach Russell "Lena" Blackburne.

"I probably made more mistakes as manager, but I feel sure the team would be far better off right now if we hadn't had the steady run of bad luck since the season started," Schalk said.

Afterward he penned a farewell letter to Comiskey before the White Sox's train departed for Washington to begin an eastern road trip. It marked the first time in 17 years that the venerable Ray Schalk was not among the traveling party.

Lena Blackburne was the antithesis of the likable Schalk. He was a hard-boiled roughneck who subscribed to a fast-paced hit-and-run offense. "Here's your bat! Now use it!" The grumblers who refused to go along with the plan were told to get out or sit down and keep their yaps shut. To enforce his edicts, Lena announced a policy of regimented $50 fines to anyone who dared sass the manager.

On August 20 first baseman Art Shires made his impressive rookie debut in Boston, rapping out a triple and three singles off Red Ruffing. A hard-drinking jazz baby with all the bad habits, Shires epitomized 1920s "Flaming Youth." He was an after-hours reveler who stepped out on the town each night attired in derby hat and spats, with a walking cane. "I'm going to make $250,000 out of baseball before I'm through!" he told the folks back home in Italy, Texas.

Somewhere from afar, Ray Schalk must have been shaking his head in wonderment, saying to himself, "I'm glad it's you and not me, pal," with respect to the care and feeding of young Shires by Lena Blackburne.

	G	AB	H	R	2B	3B	HR	RBI	SB	AVG
Bud Clancy	130	487	132	64	19	11	2	37	6	.271
Bill Hunnefield	94	333	98	42	8	3	2	24	16	.294
Chalmer "Bill" Cissell	125	443	115	66	22	3	1	60	18	.260
Willie Kamm	155	552	170	70	30	12	1	84	17	.308
Alex Metzler	139	464	141	71	18	14	3	55	16	.304
Johnny Mostil	133	503	136	69	19	8	0	51	23	.270
Bibb Falk	98	286	83	42	18	4	1	37	5	.290
Clyde "Buck" Crouse	78	218	55	17	5	2	2	20	3	.252
George "Buck" Redfern	86	261	61	22	6	3	0	35	8	.234
Art Shires	33	123	42	20	6	1	1	11	0	.341
Karl Swanson	22	64	9	2	1	0	0	6	3	.141
Johnny Mann	6	6	2	0	0	0	0	1	0	.333
Carl Reynolds	84	291	94	51	21	11	2	36	15	.323
Bill Barrett	76	235	65	34	11	2	3	26	8	.277
George Blackerby	30	83	21	8	0	0	0	12	2	.253
Randy Moore	24	61	13	6	4	1	0	5	0	.213
Moe Berg	76	224	55	25	16	0	0	29	2	.246
Harry McCurdy	49	103	27	12	10	0	2	13	1	.262
Ray Schalk	2	1	1	0	0	0	0	1	1	1.000
		5,209	1,404	657	231	76	24	592	144	.270

	W	L	GS	CG	IP	H	BB	K	ShO	ERA
Tommy Thomas	17	16	32	24	283	277	76	129	3	3.08
Ted Lyons	15	14	27	21	240	276	68	60	0	3.98
Grady Adkins	10	16	27	14	224⅔	233	89	54	0	3.73
Urban "Red" Faber	13	9	27	16	201⅓	223	68	43	2	3.75
Ted Blankenship	9	11	22	8	158	186	80	36	0	4.61
George Cox	1	2	2	0	89	110	39	22	0	5.26
Ed Walsh, Jr.	4	7	10	3	78	86	42	32	0	4.96
George "Sarge" Connally	2	5	5	1	74⅓	89	29	28	0	4.84
Charlie Barnabe	0	2	2	0	9⅔	17	0	3	0	6.52
Bob Weiland	1	0	1	1	9	7	5	9	1	0.00
Roy Wilson	0	0	0	0	3⅓	2	3	2	0	0.00
John Goodell	0	0	0	0	3	6	2	0	0	18.00
Rudy Leopold	0	0	0	0	2⅓	3	0	0	0	3.86
Al Williamson	0	0	0	0	2	1	0	0	0	0.00
Dan Dugan	0	0	0	0	⅓	0	0	0	0	0.00
	72	82	155	88	1,378	1,516	501	418	6	3.98

1929

Record: 59–93
Finish: Seventh
Games Behind: 46
Manager: Lena Blackburne

Lena Blackburne's first mistake was appointing Shires team captain after he had fomented a spring revolt of the younger players against the manager. The "Great" Shires (he made no secret of his preference for a nickname) convinced Bill Cissell that Blackburne was playing favorites with Falk, Kamm, and Faber. "Why, I just might return to the Texas League," threatened Shires, who went on a bender one night in the team's spring training hotel. Blackburne suspended Shires and sent him back to Chicago for a conference with the Old Roman. "What's the matter with you, Shires?" the Sox owner asked.

"Well, don't forget we got a lot of publicity out of it!"

Shires learned nothing from his suspension. He got into a fistfight in the White Sox clubhouse with Blackburne on May 15 and was knocked cold by the older man. Another 10-day suspension followed. If all this wasn't enough to drive a manager to distraction, Shires was arrested by the Philadelphia police after a drunken row in the Ben Franklin Hotel on September 14. Shires nearly bit off the ring finger of traveling secretary Lou Barbour, who found himself caught in the middle of a wild mêlée between the two Philadelphia cops and Blackburne.

The Shires altercations impeded Lena Blackburne's ability to manage this marginally talented ballclub. In a league dominated by the Yankees and A's, the White Sox found themselves out of the race by Decoration Day. Red Faber was the only White Sox pitcher to win as many games as he lost. Forgotten in the hoopla surrounding Shires was the yeomanlike work of Teddy Lyons, who pitched all 21 innings of a heart-breaking loss to the Detroit Tigers on May 24. Only Jack Coombs of the Philadelphia A's and Joe Harris of the Boston Red Sox, his mound opponent in a 1906 game, matched this record for single-game longevity.

Harry Grabiner, who had been running the White Sox during the period of Comiskey's long illness in 1929, was convinced that either Blackburne or Shires had to go. The rough 1929 season had only four games left on the schedule when former Tiger shortstop Owen "Donie" Bush was summoned to Chicago and, over cocktails at the Edgewater Beach Hotel, was tendered a formal offer to manage the Sox.

"Whattaman!" Art "the Great" Shires

It was Donie's great misfortune to sign a two-year contract hours *before* receiving a counteroffer from Yankees president Ed Barrow, who was looking for a replacement for Miller Huggins, who was not expected to live out the week. The Yanks very badly wanted Bush to manage their club, but American League president Ernest Sargent Barnard gently reminded him of his obligations to the ailing Comiskey, who had just returned from his Wisconsin retreat following a long convalescence.

Even though Lena Blackburne's heart was in the right place, there was nothing he could do to improve a hopeless situation or tame the wild Shires. Could an outsider do any better?

	G	AB	H	R	2B	3B	HR	RBI	SB	AVG
Art Shires	100	353	110	41	20	7	3	41	4	.312
Johnny Kerr	127	419	108	50	20	4	1	39	9	.258
Chalmer "Bill" Cissell	152	618	173	83	27	12	5	62	26	.280
Willie Kamm	147	523	140	72	32	6	3	63	12	.268
Carl Reynolds	131	517	164	81	24	12	11	67	19	.317
Clarence "Dutch" Hoffman	103	337	87	27	16	5	3	37	6	.258
Alex Metzler	146	568	156	80	23	13	2	49	11	.275
Moe Berg	106	351	101	32	7	0	0	47	5	.288
Bud Clancy	92	290	82	36	14	6	3	45	3	.283
Bill Hunnefield	47	127	23	13	5	0	0	9	5	.181
George "Buck" Redfern	21	44	6	0	0	0	0	3	1	.136
Frank Sigafoos	7	3	1	1	0	0	0	1	0	.333
Cliff Watwood	85	278	84	33	12	6	2	18	6	.302
Doug Taitt	47	124	21	11	7	0	0	12	0	.169
Johnny Mostil	12	35	8	4	3	0	0	3	1	.229
Clyde "Buck" Crouse	45	107	29	11	7	0	2	12	2	.271
Martin Autry	43	96	20	7	6	0	1	12	0	.208
Bill Barrett	3	1	0	0	0	0	0	0	0	.000
Karl Swanson	2	1	0	0	0	0	0	0	0	.000
		5,243	1,406	626	240	74	37	558	112	.268

	W	L	GS	CG	IP	H	BB	K	ShO	ERA
Tommy Thomas	14	18	31	24	259⅔	270	60	62	2	3.19
Ted Lyons	14	20	31	21	259⅔	276	76	57	1	4.10
Urban "Red" Faber	13	13	31	15	234	241	61	68	1	3.88
Hal McKain	6	9	10	4	158	158	85	33	1	3.65
Grady Adkins	2	11	15	5	138⅓	168	67	24	0	5.33
Ed Walsh, Jr.	6	11	20	7	129	156	64	31	0	5.65
Dan Dugan	1	4	2	0	65	77	19	15	0	6.65
Bob Weiland	2	4	9	1	62	62	43	25	0	5.81
Ted Blankenship	0	2	1	0	18⅓	28	9	7	0	8.84
Frank "Dutch" Henry	1	0	1	1	15	20	7	2	0	6.00
George "Sarge" Connally	0	0	0	0	11⅓	13	8	3	0	4.76
Jerry Byrne	0	1	1	0	7⅓	11	6	1	0	7.36
Lena Blackburne	0	0	0	0	⅓	1	0	0	0	0.00
	59	93	152	78	1,357⅔	1,481	505	328	5	4.41

Carl Reynolds: long-ball threat

1930

Record: 62–92
Finish: Seventh
Games Behind: 40
Manager: Donie Bush

Donie Bush believed he had the solution to the Shires enigma. "If he comes back, the first time he starts a rumpus will be his finish. That means finished…everywhere!" The Great Shires was a spring training holdout. He demanded $22,500. Comiskey's opening 1930 offer was $6,000.

Shires was not the only salary malcontent. Veteran Willie Kamm boycotted the team until Bush agreed to reappoint him captain, an honor he had surrendered to Shires a year earlier. The team captaincy carried with it an additional $3,600 a year in salary. Kamm could never see eye to eye with Bush, and was benched in June for lackluster play.

Smead Powell Jolley, a strapping PCL outfielder purchased for $50,000, got lost while making his way to the Sox spring training camp in San Antonio. After he reported, Sox officials discovered that Jolley could not field his position. But he supplied offensive punch to the lineup, and that presented a real dilemma.

Teammate Carl Reynolds clouted 22 round trippers in 1930—a Chisox team record that would hold up another four years. Reynolds was one of the few players on the squad who profited from the leadership of Donie Bush. He became the first Sox player to club three home runs in one game on July 2 in New York. In so doing, Reynolds equaled George Kelly's three-year-old record for hitting home runs in successive innings.

Spotty fielding and poor pitching neutralized an improved offense that kept the Sox in the thick of things… until May 2. After winning seven of their first 11 games, fifth, sixth, and finally seventh place beckoned Chicago in their four-month free fall. Bush, as it turned out, was no more successful handling Shires than Blackburne had been. The "Great One" was traded to Washington on June 16 for pitcher Garland Braxton and Bennie Tate, a good-hitting catcher who broke a finger. "It's the ego racket," Shires sniffed. Two years later he was out of baseball for good—his entire career spanned only 291 games.

Better results were obtained later in the year when the Cubs elected to take a pass on shortstop Luke Appling, playing for the Atlanta Crackers of the Southern Association.

A late season call-up, Appling debuted on September 10 in South Chicago. His one-for-four performance against Danny MacFayden of the Boston Red Sox left little impression on *Tribune* sportswriter Edgar Munzel, who noted, "What he did yesterday, however, afforded no line on the possibilities of his living up to expectations."

	G	AB	H	R	2B	3B	HR	RBI	SB	AVG
Bud Clancy	68	234	57	28	8	3	3	27	3	.244
Chalmer "Bill" Cissell	141	561	152	82	28	9	2	48	16	.271
Greg Mulleavy	77	289	76	27	14	5	0	28	5	.263
Willie Kamm	111	331	89	49	21	6	3	47	5	.269
Smead Jolley	152	616	193	76	38	12	16	114	3	.313
Emile "Red" Barnes	85	266	66	48	12	7	1	31	4	.248
Carl Reynolds	138	563	202	103	25	18	22	100	16	.359
Bennie Tate	72	230	73	26	11	2	0	27	2	.317
Cliff Watwood	133	427	129	75	25	4	2	51	5	.302
Johnny Kerr	70	266	77	37	11	6	3	27	4	.289
Art Shires	37	128	33	14	5	1	1	18	2	.258
Irv Jeffries	40	97	23	14	3	0	2	11	1	.237
John "Blondy" Ryan	28	87	18	9	0	4	1	10	2	.207
Bill Hunnefield	31	81	22	11	2	0	1	5	1	.272
Ernie Smith	24	79	19	5	3	0	0	3	2	.241
Luke Appling	6	26	8	2	2	0	0	2	2	.308
Hugh Willingham	3	4	1	2	0	0	0	0	0	.250
Bob "Fats" Fothergill	51	131	40	10	9	0	0	24	0	.305
Dave Harris	33	86	21	16	2	1	5	13	0	.244
Alex Metzler	56	76	14	12	4	0	0	5	0	.184
Jim Moore	16	39	8	4	2	0	0	2	0	.205
Bruce Campbell	5	10	5	4	1	1	0	5	0	.500
Clyde "Buck" Crouse	42	118	30	14	8	1	0	15	1	.254
Martin Autry	34	71	18	1	1	1	0	5	0	.254
Moe Berg	20	61	7	4	3	0	0	7	0	.115
Johnny Riddle	25	58	14	7	3	1	0	4	0	.241
Walter "Butch" Henline	3	8	1	1	0	0	0	2	0	.125
Joe Klinger	4	8	3	0	0	0	0	1	0	.375
		5,408	1,497	729	256	91	63	675	74	.277

	W	L	GS	CG	IP	H	BB	K	ShO	ERA
Ted Lyons	22	15	36	29	297⅔	331	57	69	1	3.78
Pat Caraway	10	10	21	9	193⅓	194	57	83	1	3.86
Urban "Red" Faber	8	13	26	10	169	188	49	62	0	4.21
Tommy Thomas	5	13	27	7	169	229	44	58	0	5.22
Frank "Dutch" Henry	2	17	16	4	155	211	48	35	0	4.88
Ed Walsh, Jr.	1	4	4	4	103⅔	131	30	37	0	5.38
Garland Braxton	4	10	10	2	90⅔	127	33	44	0	6.45
Hal McKain	6	4	5	0	89	108	42	52	0	5.56
Jim Moore	2	1	5	2	40	42	12	11	0	3.60
Bob Weiland	0	4	3	0	32⅔	38	21	15	0	6.61
Ted Blankenship	2	1	1	0	14⅔	23	7	2	0	9.20
Wilbur "Biggs" Wehde	0	0	0	0	6⅓	7	7	3	0	9.95
	62	92	154	67	1,361	1,629	407	471	2	4.71

1931

Record: 56–97
Finish: Eighth
Games Behind: 51½
Manager: Donie Bush

The Donie Bush doghouse looked more like a kennel with each passing day. The irritable, impatient Sox manager made an enemy out of Willie Kamm in 1930. He added Ted Lyons to a growing list of recalcitrants by sending him home in the spring after determining that Teddy's arm was "dead." Lyons was brought back at Comiskey's insistence two weeks later.

Manager Bush turned to the veterans in 1931—sore-armed first baseman Luzurne Blue was purchased from the Browns and drew 127 walks in his first Sox season to set a new team record. Blue was one of the best switch-hitters of his era, with an excellent on-base percentage of .400. The 1931 edition finished last in batting average, slugging average, home runs, and doubles—matching the 1910 White Sox ballclub for offensive futility.

Sox manager Donie Bush greets William Veeck Sr. at Comiskey Park.

The pitching staff wasn't much to speak of—over the hill, out of shape, or wet behind the ears. Cecil Pat Caraway, an elongated right-hander with a bizarre "accordion-style" windup, won six of his first nine decisions in the big leagues, then lost 21 of the next 25. In one brutal three-day stretch beginning July 23 in Boston, Caraway yielded 11 runs to the Red Sox in just 4⅔ innings. He pleaded to be taken out of the game but Bush refused. The manager administered a tongue lashing between innings, telling him to buck up and take it like a man. Three days later in Yankee Stadium, Caraway, his confidence shattered, surrendered *13 runs* in just two innings of work. The Sox lost 22–5. It was the most lopsided loss in team history—a single-game record of futility that still stands.

Neither Harry Grabiner nor his manager addressed the need for a starting pitcher. Instead, they agreed to trade Willie Kamm to the Indians for Lew Fonseca, a former batting champion whose .380 average on May 16 proved irresistible. It was an unnecessary trade and one that Comiskey would probably not have made 20 years earlier when he was still in the prime of his life and sharp in his thinking. Donie Bush experimented with Fonseca at second base with only meager results. In his eagerness to add a marquee star to his sickly lineup, Bush overlooked the possibility that the deal might end up costing him his job.

Lew Fonseca was promoted from the playing ranks on October 12, after Bush had already called it quits. "I don't mind losing ballgames if there is a prospect of better days ahead," he said in his statement to the press. "But I feel that whatever reputation I possess as a manager would be jeopardized by remaining another year."

When asked what Sox fans might expect of him in the coming year, Fonseca shrugged his shoulders and lamented the passing of the "old-fashioned" kind of player: "Ballplayers today aren't the rough and ready type of old. You must handle them to suit their natures. You can call some of them in public and they don't object. Some you must call in private. Others can't take a panning of any kind. Those are the ones you must slap on the back when they're down." Slaphappy days were here again.

	G	AB	H	R	2B	3B	HR	RBI	SB	AVG
Luzurne Blue	155	589	179	119	23	15	1	62	13	.304
Johnny Kerr	128	444	119	51	17	2	2	50	9	.268
Chalmer "Bill" Cissell	109	409	90	42	13	5	1	46	18	.220
Billy Sullivan, Jr.	92	363	100	48	16	5	2	33	4	.275
Carl Reynolds	118	462	134	71	24	14	6	77	17	.290
Cliff Watwood	128	367	104	51	16	6	1	47	9	.283
Lew Fonseca	121	465	139	65	26	5	2	71	4	.299
Bennie Tate	89	273	73	27	12	3	0	22	1	.267
Luke Appling	96	297	69	36	13	4	1	28	9	.232
Irv Jeffries	79	223	50	29	10	0	2	16	3	.224
Willie Kamm	18	59	15	9	4	0	0	9	1	.254
Bob "Fats" Fothergill	109	312	88	25	9	4	3	56	2	.282
Mel Simons	68	189	52	24	9	0	0	12	1	.275
Fred Eichrodt	34	117	25	9	5	1	0	15	0	.214
Smead Jolley	54	110	33	5	11	0	3	28	0	.300
Bill Norman	24	55	10	7	2	0	0	6	0	.182
Bruce Campbell	4	17	7	4	2	0	2	5	0	.412
Frank Grube	88	265	58	29	13	2	1	24	2	.219
Walter "Butch" Henline	11	15	1	2	1	0	0	2	0	.067
Hank Garrity	8	14	3	0	1	0	0	2	0	.214
		5,483	1,423	704	238	68	27	649	94	.260

	W	L	GS	CG	IP	H	BB	K	ShO	ERA
Vic Frazier	13	15	29	13	254	258	127	87	2	4.46
Tommy Thomas	10	14	36	11	242	296	69	71	2	4.80
Pat Caraway	10	24	32	11	220	268	101	55	1	6.22
Urban "Red" Faber	10	14	19	5	184	210	57	49	1	3.82
Hal McKain	6	9	8	3	112	134	57	39	0	5.71
Ted Lyons	4	6	12	7	101	117	33	16	0	4.01
Jim Moore	0	2	4	0	83⅔	93	27	15	0	4.95
Bob Weiland	2	7	8	3	75	75	46	38	0	5.16
Garland Braxton	0	3	3	0	47⅓	71	23	28	0	6.85
Grant Bowler	0	1	3	1	35⅓	40	24	15	0	5.35
Lou Garland	0	2	2	0	16⅔	30	14	4	0	10.26
Wilbur "Biggs" Wehde	0	0	0	0	16	19	10	3	0	6.75
	56	97	156	54	1,387	1,611	588	420	6	5.05

1932

Record: 49–102
Finish: Seventh
Games Behind: 56½
Manager: Lew Fonseca

Beset by the complications of old age and declining health, Charles Comiskey had divorced himself from the daily operation of his team nearly two years earlier. When the news of his passing was sent down from the Eagle River, Wisconsin, resort on October 26, 1931, his loyal followers in the media eulogized him as a wise and benevolent owner shattered both physically and emotionally by the events of 1919–1920. When the verdict of history was handed down years later, it was not nearly as kind.

Diminishing trade returns: Johnny Hodapp

The Old Roman bequeathed control of the team to his only son John Louis, a shy, introverted man afflicted with a malignant case of scarlet fever. What remained to be seen was how interactive Comiskey would be, given the precarious state of his health. At the winter meetings, Comiskey finalized his first trade, sending Carl Reynolds and infielder John Kerr to Washington for pitchers Irving "Bump" Hadley and "Sad" Sam Jones and second baseman Jackie Hayes. It was an outstanding deal from a Chicago viewpoint. J. Louis Comiskey looked confidently to the future by breaking with the past. He phased out the blue traveling uniforms of the dead-ball era and equipped the Sox in a more conservative shade of battleship gray, offset by red trim. New duds for a new day. Would it help?

If Lew Fonseca had left well enough alone, it would have been interesting to see how this team might have turned out. Winners of four of their first five games, the Sox dropped 20 of their next 25 to crash into the cellar by May 20. Fonseca demanded immediate results, and when they were slow in coming, he instigated three costly multiplayer trades within five days in late April. Smead Jolley was dealt to Boston for catcher Charley Berry and outfielder John Rothrock—a terrible trade. Then Fonseca really outsmarted himself by trading Bump Hadley and rookie Bruce Campbell to St. Louis for shortstop Red Kress and pitcher Chad Kimsey—youth for experience. Never a very good idea. Kress, a solid-hitting veteran, was the key to the trade, but he was a Comiskey Park washout. Campbell, on the other hand, became a star in Detroit later in the decade.

And finally, with Grabiner's blessing, Fonseca parted company with the fading Bill Cissell, who joined Willie Kamm in Cleveland. In return, the Sox received Bob Seeds and second baseman Johnny Hodapp, an offensive threat—from the 1920s—who was on the verge of retiring.

Panic moves. Then a last-place finish to top it all off. The White Sox lost their 100th game of the year on September 19—sending a wake-up call to Lou Comiskey, who opened discussions with Connie Mack, who entertained a notion of trading Lefty Grove. A proposed deal that would have sent Teddy Lyons to Philadelphia for Grove or Al Simmons never materialized. Simmons' name, however, kept surfacing in trade talks.

For the future, Lou Comiskey promised Sox fans they would soon be seeing some of the biggest stars in the baseball galaxy playing in Chicago. The owner revealed that the team had spent upward of $1 million in the previous 12 seasons buying unproductive minor league recruits. All that would soon change, he vowed. The money would go toward *proven* players and a revamped scouting system—bold and inspirational words coming in the toughest year of the Depression.

"We've always tried and maybe we've been wrong," sighed the laconic Grabiner. "But we'll keep on trying until we click."

	G	AB	H	R	2B	3B	HR	RBI	SB	AVG
Luzurne Blue	112	373	93	51	21	2	0	43	17	.249
Jackie Hayes	117	475	122	53	20	5	2	54	7	.257
Luke Appling	139	489	134	66	20	10	3	63	9	.274
Carey Selph	116	396	112	50	19	8	0	51	7	.283
Bob Seeds	116	434	126	53	18	6	2	45	5	.290
Elias "Liz" Funk	122	440	114	59	21	5	2	40	17	.259
Bob "Fats" Fothergill	116	346	102	36	24	1	7	50	4	.295
Frank Grube	93	277	78	36	16	2	0	31	6	.282
Billy Sullivan, Jr.	93	307	97	31	16	1	1	45	1	.316
Charlie English	24	63	20	7	3	1	1	8	0	.317
Chalmer "Bill" Cissell	12	43	11	7	1	1	1	5	0	.256
Fabian Kowalik	6	13	5	2	2	0	0	2	0	.385
Greg Mulleavy	1	3	0	0	0	0	0	0	0	.000
Red Kress	135	515	147	83	42	4	9	57	6	.285
Johnny Hodapp	68	176	40	21	8	0	3	20	1	.227
Jack Rothrock	39	64	12	8	2	1	0	6	1	.188
Evar Swanson	14	52	16	9	3	1	0	8	3	.308
Cliff Watwood	13	49	15	5	2	0	0	0	0	.306
Bill Norman	13	48	11	6	3	1	0	2	0	.229
Smead Jolley	12	42	15	3	3	0	0	7	1	.357
Lew Fonseca	18	37	5	0	1	0	0	6	0	.135
Hal Anderson	9	32	8	4	0	0	0	2	0	.250
Bruce Campbell	9	26	4	3	1	0	0	2	0	.154
Mel Simons	7	5	0	0	0	0	0	0	0	.000
Charlie Berry	72	226	69	33	15	6	4	31	3	.305
Bennie Tate	4	10	1	1	0	0	0	0	0	.100
		5,338	1,425	667	273	56	36	608	89	.267

	W	L	GS	CG	IP	H	BB	K	ShO	ERA
Ted Lyons	10	15	26	19	230⅔	243	71	58	1	3.28
Sam Jones	10	15	28	10	200⅓	217	75	64	0	4.22
Milt Gaston	7	17	25	7	166⅔	183	73	44	1	4.00
Vic Frazier	3	13	21	4	146	180	70	33	0	6.23
Paul Gregory	5	3	9	3	117⅔	125	51	39	0	4.51
Urban "Red" Faber	2	11	5	0	106	123	38	26	0	3.74
Pat Caraway	2	5	9	1	64⅔	80	37	13	0	6.82
Pete Daglia	2	4	5	2	50	67	20	16	0	5.76
Tommy Thomas	3	3	3	1	43⅔	55	15	11	0	6.18
Bill Chamberlin	0	5	5	0	41⅓	39	25	11	0	4.57
Phil Gallivan	1	3	3	1	33⅓	49	24	12	0	7.56
Charlie Biggs	1	1	4	0	24⅓	32	12	1	0	6.93
Ed Walsh, Jr.	0	2	4	1	20⅓	26	13	7	0	8.41
Irving "Bump" Hadley	1	1	2	1	18⅔	17	8	13	0	3.86
Art Evans	0	0	0	0	18	19	10	6	0	3.00
Hal McKain	0	0	0	0	11⅓	17	5	7	0	11.12
Chad Kimsey	1	1	0	0	11	8	5	6	0	2.45
Fabian Kowalik	0	1	1	0	10⅓	16	4	2	0	6.97
Archie Wise	0	0	0	0	7⅓	8	5	2	0	4.91
Art Smith	0	1	2	0	7	17	4	1	0	11.57
Grant Bowler	0	0	0	0	6⅓	15	3	2	0	15.63
Les Bartholomew	0	0	0	0	5⅓	5	6	1	0	5.06
Clarence Fieber	1	0	0	0	5⅓	6	3	1	0	1.69
Lew Fonseca	0	0	0	0	1	0	0	0	0	0.00
Jim Moore	0	0	0	0	1	1	1	2	0	0.00
Bob Poser	0	0	0	0	⅔	3	2	1	0	27.00
	49	102	152	50	1,348⅔	1,551	580	379	2	4.82

1933

Record: 67–83
Finish: Sixth
Games Behind: 31
Manager: Lew Fonseca

Happy days were *not quite* here again, but things were starting to look up. "Uncle Lou" made good on his promises by purchasing three of Connie Mack's most venerable stars for the sum of $150,000: slugger Al Simmons, veteran third sacker Jimmie Dykes, and George "Mule" Haas, a capable right fielder. The deal was an eye-opener, and it brought to mind the Old Roman's pre–Black Sox strategy of buying his stars at auction, but this time the results were very different.

J. Louis Comiskey in his office. He spent a fortune trying to build up the 1933 Sox.

Comiskey's financial resources were already stretched thin by the inheritance taxes he had to pay the government after his father's death. In order to satisfy his debt to Connie Mack, Lou secured bank loans to pay the sale price. Was it worth it?

Al Simmons had a wonderful year. However, a great deal of tension existed between Simmons and Fonseca, who ripped his star for failing to hustle. Simmons paced American League hitters in the first half of the '33 campaign and was the top vote-getter in baseball's first All-Star Game, which was awarded to the Comiskeys on May 27.

The White Sox equaled their entire 1932 victory output with win No. 49 on August 10. However, Fonseca was never fully satisfied with the effort put forth by this team. The Sox tumbled into sixth place after climbing to third place in early June. The overall improvement was reflected by the snappy infield play of Jimmie Dykes, who instilled in young Luke Appling the fielding skills he had honed over the course of a 15-year career.

The aging pitching staff, on the other hand, was ready for an overhaul. Ted Lyons dropped 21 games. Red Faber bid hail and farewell to White Sox fans after 20 up-and-down seasons. He ended his career in 1933 No. 1 on the all-time victory list (up to that point) with 254 wins. With a better ballclub playing in back of him in the final 10 years, Faber would have easily surpassed 300. It was another overlooked Black Sox legacy.

"Bucketfoot" Al Simmons

First baseman Zeke Bonura, a .357 hitter for the Dallas Steers in 1932, drew rave reviews and was ready to launch his White Sox career in 1934. His feet were made of clay, and his maneuverability off first base inspired the pundits of the age. His faint, halfhearted stabs at the ball coaxed a smile out of *Tribune* sportswriter Ed Burns, who labeled the deft maneuver the Bonura-Mussolini Salute, with respect to the problems brewing in Europe and the frequency of baseballs whizzing through the right-hand side of the White Sox infield.

	G	AB	H	R	2B	3B	HR	RBI	SB	AVG
Red Kress	129	467	116	47	20	5	10	78	4	.248
Jackie Hayes	138	535	138	65	23	5	2	47	2	.258
Luke Appling	151	612	197	90	36	10	6	85	6	.322
Jimmie Dykes	151	554	144	49	22	6	1	68	3	.260
Evar Swanson	144	539	165	102	25	7	1	63	19	.306
George "Mule" Haas	146	585	168	97	33	4	1	51	0	.287
Al Simmons	146	605	200	85	29	10	14	119	5	.331
Frank Grube	85	256	59	23	13	0	0	23	1	.230
Billy Sullivan, Jr.	54	125	24	9	0	1	0	13	0	.192
Hal Rhyne	39	83	22	9	1	1	0	10	1	.265
Lew Fonseca	23	59	12	8	2	0	2	15	1	.203
Charlie English	3	9	4	2	2	0	0	1	0	.444
Earl Webb	58	107	31	16	5	0	1	8	0	.290
John Stoneham	10	25	3	4	0	0	1	3	0	.120
Milt Bocek	11	22	8	3	1	0	1	3	0	.365
Elias "Liz" Funk	10	9	2	1	0	0	0	0	0	.222
Charlie Berry	86	271	69	25	8	3	2	28	0	.255
Merritt "Mem" Lovett	1	1	0	0	0	0	0	0	0	.000
		5,318	1,449	683	231	53	43	642	43	.272

	W	L	GS	CG	IP	H	BB	K	ShO	ERA
Ted Lyons	10	21	27	14	228	260	74	74	2	4.38
Sam Jones	10	12	25	11	176⅔	181	65	60	2	3.36
Milt Gaston	8	12	25	7	167	177	60	39	1	4.85
Ed "Bull" Durham	10	6	21	6	138⅔	137	46	65	0	4.48
Joe Heving	7	5	6	3	118	113	27	47	1	2.67
Jake Miller	5	6	14	4	105⅔	130	47	30	2	5.62
Paul Gregory	4	11	17	5	103⅔	124	47	18	0	4.95
Chad Kimsey	4	1	2	0	96	124	36	19	0	5.53
Whitlow Wyatt	3	4	7	2	87⅔	91	45	31	0	4.62
Urban "Red" Faber	3	4	2	0	86⅓	92	28	18	0	3.44
Les Tietje	2	0	3	1	22⅓	16	15	9	0	2.42
Vic Frazier	1	1	1	0	20⅓	32	11	4	0	8.85
Hal Haid	0	0	0	0	14⅔	18	13	7	0	7.98
Ira Hutchinson	0	0	1	0	4	7	3	2	0	13.50
George Murray	0	0	0	0	2⅓	3	2	0	0	7.71
	67	83	151	53	1,371⅓	1,505	519	423	8	4.45

1934

Record: 53–99
Finish: Eighth
Games Behind: 47
Managers: Lew Fonseca, Jimmie Dykes

Assessing the strengths of the 1934 Sox, a "gung-ho" Lew Fonseca happily predicted to the media, "We do not expect to finish worse than third!"

The 1934 edition finished last in fielding, last in batting, last in pitching...and last in the American League. The team ERA was a sickening 5.41—an all-time low for the White Sox. The geriatric quartet of Sam Jones, George Earnshaw, Ted Lyons, and Milt Gaston combined for 45 years of major-league diamond experience.

Player/manager Jimmie Dykes reaches for the stars.

Where was the pitching help to come from? The retirement of "Bull" Durham on May 25 opened up a roster spot for 6′5″ Monty Stratton, who made his nervous debut on June 2 against Detroit. After yielding two runs in three innings of work, Stratton was returned to the minors for further seasoning.

The White Sox scouting system consisted solely of Joe Page, a wheezing septuagenarian who once worked for the Old Roman as a batboy in the early 1900s; and Mr. and Mrs. Roy Largent, a husband and wife team from the great state of Texas. Under these tough circumstances, the manager's task was impossible.

For 1934, J. Lou Comiskey moved the Comiskey Park infield 14 feet closer to the walls to aid and abet Al Simmons' assault on Carl Reynolds' team home run record. But it was not Simmons and his menacing 38-inch bat that shattered the mark, but Zeke Bonura, who poled 27 home runs in his rookie season.

Vowing to shake up his roster following a bleak 4–11 record to start the season, J. Lou Comiskey traveled east with his ballclub on May 5—the first time he had made this arduous journey since 1912. The Comiskey son was very candid when he told the press that he was not at all pleased with Lew Fonseca's handling of the pitching staff during spring training.

After his team was outslugged 32–11 by Philadelphia and Washington in the first three games of the trip, Comiskey ordered Fonseca to his hotel suite on May 8 to advise him of his dismissal. "I told him I held no ill feeling toward him and thanked him for his sincerity in trying to make a winner of the White Sox during the two-and-a-half-year period he has been manager. He assured me we were parting good friends," Comiskey said.

Groomed by Connie Mack and seasoned by his experience playing for the champion A's of 1929–1931, Jimmie Dykes was recognized by Comiskey as a natural-born leader and was offered a two-year contract to manage the Sox. The move finally restored stability to the management team after years of casting about for a second Fielder Jones or Kid Gleason.

Dykes held out few hopes for turning around the 1934 season, but he stuck up for his guys and what they had tried to accomplish under Fonseca. "None of the boys actually has been dogging it, but some have lost their confidence and encouragement. Some of the younger ones need a little patient advice, and each man in the outfit needs to understand all the others."

The White Sox already occupied the bottom tier of the ladder when Dykes took over. They remained there until the bitter end, but managed to avoid the humiliation of another 100-loss season by winning two of their last four games.

	G	AB	H	R	2B	3B	HR	RBI	SB	AVG
Zeke Bonura	127	510	154	86	35	4	27	110	0	.302
Jackie Hayes	62	226	58	19	9	1	1	31	3	.257
Luke Appling	118	452	137	75	28	6	2	61	3	.303
Jimmie Dykes	127	456	122	52	17	4	7	82	1	.268
Evar Swanson	117	426	127	71	9	5	0	34	10	.298
George "Mule" Haas	106	351	94	54	16	3	2	22	1	.268
Al Simmons	138	558	192	102	36	7	18	104	3	.344
Ed Madjeski	85	281	62	36	14	2	5	32	2	.221
Bob Boken	81	297	70	30	9	1	3	40	2	.236
Marty Hopkins	67	210	45	22	7	0	2	28	0	.214
Joe Chamberlin	43	141	34	13	5	1	2	17	1	.241
Mark Mauldin	10	38	10	3	2	0	1	3	0	.263
Red Kress	8	14	4	3	0	0	0	1	0	.286
John "Jocko" Conlon	63	225	56	35	11	3	0	16	2	.249
Bernard "Frenchy" Uhalt	57	165	40	28	5	1	0	16	6	.242
Stan "Frenchy" Bordagaray	29	87	28	12	3	1	0	2	1	.322
Ray "Rip" Radcliff	14	56	15	7	2	1	0	5	1	.268
Milt Bocek	19	38	8	3	1	0	0	3	0	.211
Charlie Uhlir	14	27	4	3	0	0	0	3	0	.148
Mervin Shea	62	176	28	8	3	0	0	5	0	.159
Harold "Muddy" Ruel	22	57	12	4	3	0	0	7	0	.211
George Caithamer	5	19	6	1	1	0	0	3	0	.316
Johnny Pasek	4	9	3	1	0	0	0	0	0	.333
Bill Fehring	1	1	0	0	0	0	0	0	0	.000
		5,302	1,395	704	237	40	71	668	36	.263

	W	L	GS	CG	IP	H	BB	K	ShO	ERA
George Earnshaw	14	11	30	16	227	242	104	97	2	4.52
Ted Lyons	11	13	24	21	205⅓	249	66	53	0	4.87
Milt Gaston	6	19	28	10	194	247	84	48	1	5.85
Sam Jones	8	12	26	11	183⅓	217	60	60	1	5.11
Les Tietje	5	14	22	6	176	174	96	81	1	4.81
Phil Gallivan	4	7	7	3	126⅔	155	64	55	0	5.61
Joe Heving	1	7	2	0	88	133	48	40	0	7.26
Whitlow Wyatt	4	11	6	2	67⅔	83	37	36	0	7.18
Harry Kinzy	0	1	2	1	34⅓	38	31	12	0	4.98
Vern Kennedy	0	2	3	1	19⅓	21	9	7	0	3.72
Hugo Klaerner	0	2	3	1	17⅓	24	16	9	0	10.90
Lee Stine	0	0	0	0	11	11	10	8	0	8.18
Monty Stratton	0	0	0	0	3⅓	4	1	0	0	5.40
John Pomorski	0	0	0	0	1⅔	1	2	0	0	5.40
	53	99	153	72	1,355	1,599	628	506	5	5.41

1935

Record: 74–78
Finish: Fifth
Games Behind: 19½
Manager: Jimmie Dykes

An infusion of new players made all the difference in the world in 1935. Veteran backstop Luke Sewell, acquired from the St. Louis Browns (via Washington) proved invaluable as he nurtured a trio of pitching hopefuls slowing coming into their own: Vern Kennedy, Monty Stratton, John Henderson Whitehead, and Lloyd Vernon Kennedy, who fashioned a no-hitter against the Cleveland Indians on August 31.

A spate of injuries failed to halt the rampaging White Sox in the first few months of the season. When doctors diagnosed bone chips in Jackie Hayes' thumb, Grabiner and Dykes filled the hole with Tony Piet, an infielder purchased from the Toronto of the International League on June 5.

Piet established an instant rapport with Sox fans, who turned out in large numbers on his testimonial day, September 1. Piet was always proud of his White Sox association, and years later, when he owned a South Side Pontiac dealership, he could always be counted on to purchase large blocks of tickets to distribute to his customers.

May 28, 1934	May 28, 1935
13–20, 8th Place	21–12, 1st Place

The first-place standing on Decoration Day was a historic occasion in this drab 30-year cycle of failure spanning the Black Sox era and the dawn of the 1950s Go-Go years. It marked the first time since 1920 that the team occupied first place so late in a season.

The White Sox were in third place and only five games out of first on August 2, when Browns manager Rogers Hornsby pronounced the last rites. "Now I predict they will curl up and be an old-fashioned second-division White Sox team at the finish!" The "Curse of the Rajah." But he was right...the team spiraled downward thereafter.

Jimmie Dykes had taken over a ballclub that was the object of unrelenting ridicule in 1934, and he had whipped it into shape by scrapping an over-the-hill pitching staff in favor of livelier, younger arms. "If I stick around here long enough, I'm going to have a ballclub that is in the pennant fight," he predicted. "And for one thing, this club will finish no worse than fifth and may be the surprise of the league."

	G	AB	H	R	2B	3B	HR	RBI	SB	AVG
Zeke Bonura	138	550	162	107	34	4	21	92	4	.295
Jackie Hayes	89	329	88	45	14	0	4	45	3	.267
Luke Appling	153	525	161	94	28	6	1	71	12	.307
Jimmie Dykes	117	403	116	45	24	2	4	61	4	.288
George "Mule" Haas	92	327	95	44	22	1	2	40	4	.291
Al Simmons	128	525	140	68	22	7	16	79	4	.267
Ray "Rip" Radcliff	146	623	178	95	28	8	10	68	4	.286
Luke Sewell	118	421	120	52	19	3	2	67	3	.285
Tony Piet	77	292	87	47	17	5	3	27	2	.298
Marty Hopkins	59	144	32	20	3	0	2	17	1	.222
Glenn Wright	9	25	3	1	1	0	0	1	0	.120
Mike Kreevich	6	23	10	3	2	0	0	2	1	.435
George Washington	108	339	96	40	22	3	8	47	1	.283
John "Jocko" Conlon	65	140	40	20	7	1	0	15	3	.286
Fred Tauby	13	32	4	5	1	0	0	2	0	.125
Mervin Shea	46	122	28	8	2	0	0	13	0	.230
Frank Grube	9	19	7	1	2	0	0	6	0	.368
Daniel "Bud" Hafey	2	0	0	1	0	0	0	0	0	.000
		5,314	1,460	738	262	42	74	690	46	.275

	W	L	GS	CG	IP	H	BB	K	ShO	ERA
John Whitehead	13	13	27	18	222⅓	209	101	72	1	3.72
Vern Kennedy	11	11	25	16	211⅔	211	95	65	2	3.91
Ted Lyons	15	8	22	19	190⅔	194	56	54	3	3.02
Les Tietje	9	15	21	9	169⅔	184	81	64	1	4.30
Sam Jones	8	7	19	7	140	162	51	38	0	4.05
Ray Phelps	4	8	17	4	125	126	55	38	0	4.82
Carl Fischer	5	5	11	3	88⅔	102	39	31	1	6.19
Jack Salveson	1	2	2	2	66⅔	79	23	22	0	4.86
Whitlow Wyatt	4	3	1	0	52	65	25	22	0	6.75
Monty Stratton	1	2	5	2	38	40	9	8	0	4.03
Joe Vance	2	2	0	0	31	36	21	12	0	6.68
George Earnshaw	1	2	3	0	18	26	11	8	0	9.00
Italo Chelini	0	0	2	0	5	7	4	1	0	12.60
Lee Stine	0	0	1	0	2	2	3	1	0	9.00
	74	78	153	80	1,360⅔	1,443	574	436	8	4.38

1936

Record: 81–70
Finish: Third (tie)
Games Behind: 20
Manager: Jimmie Dykes

The unhappy Al Simmons–White Sox union was dissolved on December 10, amid hopeful rumors that Philadelphia strong boy Jimmy Foxx was Chicago bound. Replacing Simmons with old "Double X" would have been a joyous Christmas present for Sox fans. Alas, the rumors were unfounded, and center field was awarded by default to "Iron" Mike Kreevich on a more permanent basis.

Simmons was sold to Detroit for $75,000—far less than the original $400,000 asking price. Another Comiskey austerity movement was afoot.

After a slow beginning, Jimmie Dykes huddled with his coaches and then went to market. The cash purchase of relief specialist Clint Brown from the Cleveland Indians was vintage Dykes. He was at his very best when it came to prying journeymen players from other organizations who could fill a specific role in Chicago. Then, in a straight swap of pitchers with the Browns, the Sox exchanged arthritic Les Tietje for Merritt "Sugar" Cain, who won 14 games for Chicago after joining the Sox on May 5.

Dykes literally pulled Bill "Bullfrog" Dietrich from an Albany-bound train after acquiring his contract from Washington

Senators owner Clark Griffith, who had exiled the right-hander to the minors. With refinements made to his delivery by pitching coach Muddy Ruel, Dietrich became a valuable contributor for the next 10 years. The 1936 trades did not stir the imagination or garner the same publicity as the Simmons purchase four years earlier, but Jimmie Dykes' skillful maneuvering was far more meaningful to the Sox down the road.

The White Sox vacated the second division in late July behind the torrid hitting of Rip Radcliff, who ran neck and neck for the 1936 batting title in the summer months. This was a ballclub that scored runs in bunches. In a four-day period, July 16 to 19, the Sox plated *64 runs* against Washington and Philadelphia. Five .300 hitters in the starting lineup keyed the attack. The high-octane White Sox offense averaged 6.1 runs a game, which remains a single-season franchise record.

Luke Appling salted away the batting championship in the last two months of the season after reeling off a 27-game hitting streak—a record-setting streak that was ended by Red Sox pitcher Wes Ferrell on September 3. Earl Averill of the Indians finished a distant second.

Appling modestly deflected the credit to his manager who helped him overcome his hesitancy in the field. From the left-hand corner of the Sox dugout, Dykes would holler soft words of encouragement: "Hey, fumblefoot! Take your time!"

The Sox faltered at the critical moment of the season when second place was up for grabs. Unable to contain the seventh-place Browns in a critical series played at Sportsman's Park September 17 to 20, the Sox had to settle for a third-place tie, putting a damper on a wonderfully satisfying season.

	G	AB	H	R	2B	3B	HR	RBI	SB	AVG
Zeke Bonura	148	587	194	120	39	7	12	138	4	.330
Jackie Hayes	108	417	130	53	34	3	5	84	4	.312
Luke Appling	138	526	204	111	31	7	6	128	10	.388
Jimmie Dykes	127	435	116	62	16	3	7	60	1	.267
George "Mule" Haas	119	408	116	75	26	2	0	46	1	.284
Mike Kreevich	137	550	169	99	32	11	5	69	10	.307
Ray "Rip" Radcliff	138	618	207	120	31	7	8	82	6	.325
Luke Sewell	128	451	113	59	20	5	5	73	11	.251
Tony Piet	109	352	96	69	15	2	7	42	15	.273
Jo-Jo Morrissey	17	38	7	3	1	0	0	6	0	.184
Les Rock	2	1	0	0	0	0	0	1	0	.000
Larry Rosenthal	85	317	89	71	15	8	3	46	2	.281
Fred "Dixie" Walker	26	70	19	12	2	0	0	11	1	.271
George Washington	20	49	8	6	2	0	1	5	0	.163
George Stumpf	10	22	6	3	1	0	0	5	0	.273
Frank Grube	33	93	15	6	2	1	0	11	1	.161
Mervin Shea	14	24	3	3	0	0	0	2	0	.125
		5,466	1,597	920	282	56	60	862	66	.292

	W	L	GS	CG	IP	H	BB	K	ShO	ERA
Vern Kennedy	21	9	34	20	274⅓	282	147	99	1	4.63
John Whitehead	13	13	32	15	230⅔	254	98	70	1	4.64
Merritt "Sugar" Cain	14	10	26	14	195⅓	228	75	42	1	4.75
Ted Lyons	10	13	24	15	182	227	45	48	1	5.14
Monty Stratton	5	7	14	3	95	117	46	37	0	5.21
Italo Chelini	4	3	6	5	83⅔	100	30	16	0	4.95
Clint Brown	6	2	2	0	83	106	24	19	0	4.99
Bill Dietrich	4	4	11	6	82⅔	93	36	39	1	4.68
Ray Phelps	4	6	4	2	68⅔	91	42	17	0	6.03
Russell "Red" Evans	0	3	0	0	47⅓	70	22	19	0	7.61
Bill Shores	0	0	0	0	17	26	8	5	0	9.53
Whitlow Wyatt	0	0	0	0	3	3	0	0	0	0.00
Les Tietje	0	0	0	0	2⅓	6	5	3	0	27.00
	81	70	153	80	1,365	1,603	578	414	5	5.06

A Yankees runner caught in a pickle in 1936. Jimmie Dykes flips the ball to Jackie Hayes. Luke Appling (middle) appears uncertain about what to do next.

1937

Record: 86–68
Finish: Third
Games Behind: 16
Manager: Jimmie Dykes

A big winter trade involving the Senators, Indians, and White Sox provided Dykes with the quality left-hander he had been seeking for nearly two years. Jack Salveson, a minor league sensation but a major league disappointment, went to Cleveland in return for Thornton Lee, who relied on a sharply breaking sinker pitch. Coach Muddy Ruel specialized in developing down-and-out pitchers like Thornton Lee, Vern Kennedy, and Monty Stratton. All three enjoyed productive seasons in 1937.

Jimmie Dykes listed fourth place as his objective—a somewhat surprising goal coming off a banner 1936 season. His No. 3 starter, John Whitehead, refused to take the game seriously and adhere to physical conditioning. Unsure about the quality of his starting pitching, Dykes received unexpected help from Monty Stratton, who won seven of his first nine decisions, a performance that earned him a berth on the All-Star team. The unlucky Stratton suffered an arm injury on August 7 in Boston that cost him a 20-victory season.

Bill Dietrich's 8–0 no-hit performance against the St. Louis Browns at Comiskey Park on June 1 continued a team winning streak that catapulted the Sox from fifth place to first. Thornton Lee edged the Yankees 5–4 on June 8 to make it a perfect 10 in a row and give the Hose a share of first place—a lead that was relinquished the next day when former teammate Bump Hadley beat Vern Kennedy 10–3.

Lefty Lee was a proverbial Yankees killer who won five of the seven White Sox victories recorded against the Bronx Bombers in 1937. His teammates alternated between second and fourth place through late August before settling into third place on August 15 and remaining there until the end.

Key injuries to Stratton and outfielder Larry Rosenthal, a defensive magician, ruined whatever faint notions Dykes might have entertained about unseating Joe McCarthy, the "Push Button" manager, as the wearer of the AL crown. Given this yearly grind of injuries, the question had to be asked again: Was this White Sox ballclub tragically cursed?

	G	AB	H	R	2B	3B	HR	RBI	SB	AVG
Zeke Bonura	116	447	154	79	41	2	19	100	5	.345
Jackie Hayes	143	473	131	63	27	4	2	79	1	.229
Luke Appling	154	574	182	98	42	8	4	77	18	.317
Tony Piet	100	332	78	34	15	1	4	38	14	.235
Fred "Dixie" Walker	154	593	179	105	28	16	9	95	1	.302
Mike Kreevich	144	583	176	94	29	16	12	73	10	.302
Ray "Rip" Radcliff	144	584	190	105	38	10	4	79	6	.325
Luke Sewell	122	412	111	51	21	6	1	61	4	.269
Louis "Boze" Berger	52	130	31	19	5	0	5	13	1	.238
George "Mule" Haas	54	111	23	8	3	3	0	15	1	.207
Mervyn Connors	28	103	24	12	4	1	2	12	2	.233
Jimmie Dykes	30	85	26	10	5	0	1	23	0	.306
Larry Rosenthal	58	97	28	20	5	3	0	9	1	.289
Hank Steinbacher	26	73	19	13	4	1	1	9	2	.260
Mervin Shea	25	71	15	7	1	0	0	5	1	.211
Tony Rensa	26	57	17	10	5	1	0	5	3	.298
		5,277	1,478	780	280	76	67	726	70	.280

	W	L	GS	CG	IP	H	BB	K	ShO	ERA
Vern Kennedy	14	13	30	15	221	238	124	114	1	5.09
Thornton Lee	12	10	25	13	204⅔	209	60	80	2	3.52
Ted Lyons	12	7	22	11	169	182	45	45	0	4.15
John Whitehead	11	8	24	8	165⅔	191	56	45	4	4.07
Monty Stratton	15	5	21	14	164⅔	142	37	69	5	2.40
Bill Dietrich	8	10	20	7	143⅓	162	72	62	1	4.90
Clint Brown	7	7	0	0	100	92	36	51	0	3.42
Johnny Rigney	2	5	4	1	90⅔	107	46	38	1	4.96
Merritt "Sugar" Cain	4	2	6	1	68⅔	88	51	17	0	6.16
Bill Cox	1	0	2	1	12⅔	9	5	8	0	0.71
Italo Chelini	0	1	0	0	8⅔	15	0	3	0	10.38
George Gick	0	0	0	0	2	0	0	1	0	0.00
	86	68	154	71	1,351⅓	1,435	532	533	14	4.17

Veteran moundsmen Ted Lyons, Bill Dietrich, and Vern Kennedy

1938

Record: 65–83
Finish: Sixth
Games Behind: 32
Manager: Jimmie Dykes

Years ending in eight have been unlucky ones for the White Sox, ever since that fateful afternoon in October 1908 when old Ty Cobb's smoking bat ruined Fielder Jones' quest for a second Hitless Wonder pennant. Nineteen thirty-eight provided a new twist to a painful story.

The run of bad luck began at the winter meetings when Dykes finally outsmarted himself by trading Vern Kennedy,

Monty Stratton in happier days

outfielder "Dixie" Walker, and Tony Piet to Detroit for third baseman Marv Owen, Gee Walker, and catcher Mike Tresh, an ex-Detroit sandlotter. Owen turned out to be a flop compared to the colorful career awaiting Dixie Walker, who moved on to Brooklyn, where he became an instant hero—the "People's Cherce" of Flatbush.

The season was a disaster in the making from the moment spring training began in Pasadena. Heavy flooding made it virtually impossible for Dykes to conduct workouts. Zeke Bonura's arrogant salary holdout was no longer amusing to Dykes or Grabiner, who traded Bonura and his 100 RBIs to Washington for Joe Kuhel, reputed to be the best glove in the American League.

The Curse, Part I: Three-quarters of the starting lineup went down with injuries in 1938. Luke Appling fractured an ankle. Monty Stratton strained his pitching arm. Clint Brown had bone chips removed from his throwing arm and was gone for the year. Gee Walker missed 15 games. Joe Kuhel had to be carried off the field on May 8 after catching his spikes on the bag. Bullfrog Dietrich suffered from an inflamed elbow...and on and on.

The Curse, Part II: Eleven games were lost to the elements by May 24. In June six more games were washed away by monsoon storms. No one could remember another year when the rains played so much havoc on the baseball schedule. The revenue loss was enormous.

In the eighth month the skies over Chicago finally cleared...forcing the Sox to play *13 doubleheaders,* which included 15 games in eight days.

Veteran writer Warren Brown had a pet theory about the South Siders' repeated misfortunes, one he developed after years of careful observation—that is, a "tradition...that things happened to the White Sox that could *only* happen to them."

Then, finally, on November 27 came the shocking news from Greenville, Texas. Monty Stratton was shooting rabbits in a pasture near his home when a bullet from his .32 caliber pistol accidentally discharged in his holster, piercing the femoral artery near his right knee.

The final decision to amputate Stratton's leg was made by Lou Comiskey, who was no stranger to the hardships imposed on the physically handicapped. Downcast and at the point of tears, Comiskey sent word to the surgeons to remove the leg. Monty was too nice of a guy to have such a thing happen to him in the prime of life.

Nineteen thirty-eight. The unkindest year of them all.

	G	AB	H	R	2B	3B	HR	RBI	SB	AVG
Joe Kuhel	117	412	110	67	27	4	8	51	9	.267
Jackie Hayes	62	238	78	40	21	2	1	20	3	.328
Luke Appling	81	294	89	41	14	0	0	44	1	.303
Marv Owen	141	577	162	84	23	6	6	55	6	.281
Hank Steinbacher	106	399	132	59	23	8	4	61	1	.331
Mike Kreevich	129	489	145	73	26	12	6	73	13	.297
Gerald "Gee" Walker	120	442	135	69	23	6	16	87	9	.305
Luke Sewell	65	211	45	23	4	1	0	27	0	.213
Louis "Boze" Berger	118	470	102	60	15	3	3	36	4	.217
Jimmie Dykes	26	89	27	9	4	2	2	13	0	.303
George Meyer	24	81	24	10	2	2	0	9	3	.296
Mervyn Connors	24	62	22	14	4	0	6	13	0	.355
John Gerlach	9	25	7	2	0	0	0	1	0	.280
Tommy Thompson	19	18	2	2	0	0	0	2	0	.111
Jesse Landrum	4	6	0	0	0	0	0	1	0	.000
Ray "Rip" Radcliff	129	503	166	64	23	6	5	81	5	.330
Larry Rosenthal	61	105	30	14	5	1	1	12	0	.286
Tony Rensa	59	165	41	15	5	0	3	19	1	.248
Norm Schlueter	35	118	27	11	5	1	0	7	1	.229
Mike Tresh	10	29	7	3	2	0	0	2	0	.241
Joe Martin	1	0	0	0	0	0	0	0	0	.000
		5,199	1,439	709	239	55	67	657	56	.277

	W	L	GS	CG	IP	H	BB	K	ShO	ERA
Thornton Lee	13	12	30	18	245⅓	252	94	77	1	3.49
Ted Lyons	9	11	23	17	194⅔	238	52	54	1	3.70
Monty Stratton	15	9	22	17	186⅓	186	56	82	0	4.01
John Whitehead	10	11	24	10	183⅓	218	80	38	2	4.76
Johnny Rigney	9	9	12	7	167	164	72	84	1	3.56
Jack Knott	5	10	18	9	131	135	54	35	0	4.05
Frank Gabler	1	7	7	3	69⅓	101	34	17	0	9.09
Bill Dietrich	2	4	7	1	48	49	31	11	0	5.44
Harry Boyles	0	4	2	1	29⅓	31	25	18	0	5.22
Merritt "Sugar" Cain	0	1	3	0	19⅔	26	18	6	0	4.58
Gene Ford	0	0	0	0	14	21	12	2	0	10.29
Clint Brown	1	3	0	0	13⅔	16	9	2	0	4.61
Bill Cox	0	2	1	0	11⅔	11	13	5	0	6.94
Bob Uhle	0	0	0	0	2	1	0	0	0	0.00
George Gick	0	0	0	0	1	0	0	1	0	0.00
	65	83	149	83	1,316⅓	1,449	550	432	5	4.36

1939

Record: 85–69
Finish: Fourth
Games Behind: 22½
Manager: Jimmie Dykes

Monty Stratton returned to the Comiskey Park pitching mound on May 1, 1939, to greet his fans during a touching ceremony honoring the young pitcher struggling to make a valiant comeback on his one good leg. Monty accepted a conciliatory gesture from the Comiskeys to serve as the team's batting practice pitcher, but he also served notice that he viewed his situation as a temporary setback…not the end of the line.

Minus Stratton and John Whitehead, who was shipped to the Browns in June, the Sox began the season certain of only one thing. Ted Lyons, Thornton Lee, and Jack Knott had to come through in a big way if the new kid in camp, John Dungan Rigney, failed to pass muster.

Rigney, a local boy from Chicago's western suburbs, completed an 11-game winning streak in July and August and stole the heart of Dorothy Comiskey, the boss man's only daughter, whom he would wed in October 1941.

Attired in new home uniforms featuring a large red block-letter *S* on the front of the jersey, the White Sox shook off the 1938 doldrums by winning 10 of their first 15 games.

Seeking a new "Yankee killer," Dykes secured Edgar "Gorby" Smith from the A's. Smith's record against the League was a dismal 8–28 entering the season. But as a member of the A's, he notched five of those wins against New York. Smith's final 1939 numbers against the Yanks were 2 and 6. So much for lucky hunches.

Night baseball finally arrived in Chicago on August 14. The 1938 cancellations had undoubtedly convinced Comiskey to do something about improving his profit picture by tapping into a new market. The 144-million-candle-power system was activated by his 14-year-old son, Charles II. Sporting his own Sox uniform, the sprightly lad quipped to reporters, "I think I'll hold out for $10 before I turn 'em."

J. Lou Comiskey never saw the lights go on. A compassionate man who fed an army of hungry tramps during the Depression, he had expired at his Eagle River home on July 18 at age 55. "Uncle Lou's" passing was a terrible blow to the White Sox, who had just begun to right themselves after the long post-scandal malaise the team had fallen into.

Comiskey's legacy was positive and enduring. Beginning in 1939, the White Sox established their own farm system after several false starts. Under the direction of Bob Tarleton, the former business manager of the Dallas Steers, and ex-coach Billy Webb, working agreements were begun with teams in Lubbock and Longview, Texas; Rayne, Louisiana; Kansas City; Milwaukee; Dallas; and Jonesboro, Arkansas.

Lou Comiskey's will designated the First National Bank of Chicago as the executor of his estate until his son Charley attained his 35th birthday. The bank, however, identified a set of "dire circumstances" six months later and announced its intention to sell the team's stock in January 1940. The White Sox had reported a net book loss of $675,029 dating back to 1928.

In a last-ditch effort to keep the team in the family, the widow, Grace Reidy Comiskey, renounced the will and asked for her dower rights. Probate Judge John F. O'Connell ruled in favor of Mrs. Comiskey on February 29, 1940, based on the reasonable assumption that night baseball, a competitive team, and the coming economic prosperity augured well for the Comiskeys in the new decade. Lou's fortuitous decision to install lights in the ballpark helped save the Sox for the next generation of Comiskeys. However, the dangerous ambiguities contained in Lou's will eventually prevented Charley Comiskey from fulfilling his father's most ardent wish—to have his son carry the family name into the next century and beyond.

	G	AB	H	R	2B	3B	HR	RBI	SB	AVG
Joe Kuhel	139	546	164	107	24	9	15	56	18	.300
Ollie Bejma	90	307	77	52	9	3	8	44	1	.251
Luke Appling	148	516	162	82	16	6	0	56	16	.314
Eric "Boob" McNair	129	479	155	62	18	5	7	82	17	.324
Larry Rosenthal	107	324	86	50	21	5	10	51	6	.265
Mike Kreevich	145	541	175	85	30	8	5	77	23	.323
Gerald "Gee" Walker	149	598	174	95	30	11	13	111	17	.291
Mike Tresh	119	352	91	49	5	2	0	38	3	.259
Jackie Hayes	72	269	67	34	12	3	0	23	0	.249
Marv Owen	58	194	46	22	9	0	0	15	4	.237
Bob Kennedy	3	8	2	0	0	0	0	1	0	.250
John Gerlach	3	2	2	0	0	0	0	0	0	1.000
Jimmie Dykes	2	1	0	0	0	0	0	0	0	.000
Ray "Rip" Radcliff	113	397	105	49	25	2	2	53	6	.264
Hank Steinbacher	71	111	19	16	2	1	1	15	0	.171
Ken Silvestri	22	75	13	6	3	0	2	5	0	.173
Norm Schlueter	34	56	13	5	2	1	0	8	2	.232
Tony Rensa	14	25	5	3	0	0	0	2	0	.200
Tommy Thompson	1	0	0	0	0	0	0	1	0	.000
		5,279	1,451	755	220	56	64	679	113	.275

	W	L	GS	CG	IP	H	BB	K	ShO	ERA
Thornton Lee	15	11	29	15	235	260	70	81	2	4.21
Johnny Rigney	15	8	29	11	218⅔	208	84	119	2	3.70
Edgar Smith	9	11	22	7	176⅔	161	90	67	1	3.67
Ted Lyons	14	6	21	16	172⅔	162	26	65	0	2.76
Jack Knott	11	6	23	8	149⅔	157	41	56	0	4.15
Bill Dietrich	7	8	19	2	127⅔	134	56	43	0	5.22
Clint Brown	11	10	0	0	118⅓	127	27	41	0	3.88
Johnny Marcum	3	3	6	2	90	125	19	32	0	6.00
John Whitehead	0	3	4	0	32	60	5	9	0	8.16
Vic Frazier	0	1	1	0	23⅔	45	11	7	0	10.27
Art Herring	0	0	0	0	14⅓	13	5	8	0	5.65
Vallie Eaves	0	1	1	1	11⅔	11	8	5	0	4.63
Harry Boyles	0	0	0	0	3⅓	4	6	1	0	10.80
Jess Dobernic	0	1	0	0	3⅓	3	6	1	0	13.50
	85	69	155	62	1,377	1,470	454	535	5	4.31

1940

Record: 82–72
Finish: Fourth (tie)
Games Behind: 8
Manager: Jimmie Dykes

Deal maker Dykes changed the complexion of this team overnight by peddling Gee Walker to Washington for outfielder Taft Wright and pitcher Pete Appleton, a spot starter acquired as "bait" for a larger trade Jimmie had in mind. Dykes tried to sell the St. Louis Browns on Appleton in return for outfielder Julius "Moose" Solters, but they wanted Rip Radcliff, and the Sox manager obliged. The Walker-for-

Luke Appling (left) holds the winning hand in a game of Hearts against his boss, Jimmie Dykes, in this 1940 scene inside the White Sox locker room.

Wright swap was outstanding. "Taffy" Wright was a good hitter and the everyday right fielder for much of the decade. Solters, unfortunately, was a dismal failure in the outfield and was released to the minors three years later.

The season began inauspiciously for Sox fans on April 16, when Cleveland wunderkind Bob Feller delivered baseball's only Opening Day no-hitter, whitewashing the Hose 1–0 on a bone-chilling afternoon.

Cheer up, Sox fans, urged *Chicago Herald American* columnist Ed Cochrane, because "there is no reason to believe the Sox will stay in any such batting slump, or they will not wind up the schedule in as good a position as expected. In fact the Sox appear very satisfactory."

Winless at Comiskey Park until May 20, the Comiskeys were unable to cash in on various Yankees misfortunes that coincided with the early season Sox swoon. The Yankees occupied last place on May 16...until they graciously sublet the basement to their White Sox cousins two days later.

The Sox were cruelly denied a victory over New York on June 20, when Yankees manager Joe McCarthy protested Julius Solters' shoestring catch of a foul fly in the 11th inning. Umpire George Quinn had taken his eye off the ball—McCarthy contended Quinn's view was partially obscured by Solters' hat, which had flown off his head. Quinn vetoed the protest. The game went into the books as a 1–0 victory until the league upheld McCarthy's protest. A replay was ordered for September 18.

The White Sox improved as summer ran its course. They closed the gap between themselves and the first-place Cleveland Indians to only four games on September 15. Chicago had just swept three consecutive doubleheaders and was roaring down the stretch when the Yankees arrived in town for a series featuring the infamous "replay" game.

Despite the outcome of the June 20 game, the White Sox enjoyed greater success against New York than in any year since 1925. The Sox played with confidence against the Yanks and seemed to have cracked an age-old riddle. But alas the dreaded replay. Again, an umpire's questionable call thwarted the Sox at a crucial hour of the pennant race and set the stage for one of Dykes' most famous tirades.

Chicago nursed an 8–7 lead into the eighth inning before the Yankees pushed across two runs to take a one-run advantage. After the Sox failed to score in their half of the inning, umpire Harry Geisel motioned to the dugouts signaling his intention to call the game because of darkness. Jimmie Dykes was livid. He kicked his hat. He waved his arms wildly and screamed in shrill hysterical tones. Almanacs were produced to demonstrate to Geisel that sunset would occur 47 minutes *after* 6:07 PM, the moment when the game was called off.

The demoralizing loss sent the White Sox into a tailspin that cost them their only legitimate shot at an AL pennant in this 30-year period. They lost seven of 10 to close out the season in a fourth-place tie.

If all this wasn't enough to make a Sox fan's hair stand on end, Luke Appling lost the batting title to Joe DiMaggio on the last day of the season, despite collecting two hits in four at bats. Browns second baseman Johnny Lucadello's one-handed grab of a looping liner denied Appling a 3-for-3 performance and the batting crown.

	G	AB	H	R	2B	3B	HR	RBI	SB	AVG
Joe Kuhel	155	603	169	111	28	8	27	94	12	.280
James "Skeeter" Webb	84	334	79	33	11	2	1	29	3	.237
Luke Appling	150	566	197	96	27	13	0	79	3	.348
Bob Kennedy	154	606	153	74	23	3	3	52	3	.252
Taft Wright	147	581	196	79	31	9	5	88	4	.337
Mike Kreevich	144	582	154	86	27	10	8	55	15	.265
Julius "Moose" Solters	116	428	132	65	28	3	12	80	3	.308
Mike Tresh	135	480	135	62	15	5	1	64	3	.281
Eric "Boob" McNair	66	251	57	26	13	1	7	31	1	.227
Jackie Hayes	18	41	8	2	0	1	0	1	0	.195
Don Kolloway	10	40	9	5	1	0	0	3	1	.225
Larry Rosenthal	107	276	83	46	14	5	6	42	2	.301
Tom Turner	37	96	20	11	1	2	0	6	1	.208
Ken Silvestri	28	24	6	5	2	0	2	10	0	.250
Dave Short	4	3	1	1	0	0	0	0	0	.333
		5,386	1,499	735	238	63	73	671	52	.278

	W	L	GS	CG	IP	H	BB	K	ShO	ERA
Johnny Rigney	14	18	33	19	280⅔	240	90	141	2	3.11
Thornton Lee	12	13	27	24	228	223	56	87	1	3.47
Edgar Smith	14	9	28	12	207⅓	179	95	119	0	3.21
Ted Lyons	12	8	22	17	186⅓	188	37	72	4	3.24
Jack Knott	11	9	23	4	158	166	52	44	2	4.56
Bill Dietrich	10	6	17	6	149⅔	154	65	43	1	4.03
Clint Brown	4	6	0	0	66	75	16	23	0	3.68
Pete Appleton	4	0	0	0	57⅔	54	28	21	0	5.62
Vallie Eaves	0	2	3	0	18⅔	22	24	11	0	6.75
Ed Weiland	0	0	0	0	14⅓	15	7	3	0	8.79
Jack Hallett	1	1	2	1	14	15	6	9	0	6.43
Orval Grove	0	0	0	0	6	4	4	1	0	3.00
	82	72	155	83	1,386⅔	1,335	480	574	10	3.74

1941

Record: 77–77
Finish: Third
Games Behind: 24
Manager: Jimmie Dykes

Grace Reidy Comiskey, the matriarch of American League baseball, was elected team president by unanimous consent on March 3, 1941. The First National Bank of Chicago had resigned as trustee, happy to be out of the baseball business once and for all.

Mrs. Comiskey, an iron-willed dowager who mistrusted the motives of her general manager, Harry Grabiner, accepted the burdensome task of supervising the family business until such time her only son, Charles II, would be ready to assume his rightful duties as policy maker and majority owner.

Charley Comiskey was only 16 years old in 1941. Nearly an entire decade would pass before the "crown prince" would be ready for his big league coronation, and that delay was most unfortunate for Sox fans, whose appetite for winning baseball had been whetted by the exciting, competitive teams of the late 1930s.

It was the decade of making do—do only what it takes to get by and no more. Mrs. Comiskey's conservative fiscal policies doomed the White Sox to a series of second-division finishes in the 1940s. Older players were kept on the roster until their trading value had dwindled to nothing. Very little money was spent on scouting, procuring top talent, or enriching the fledgling farm system, which was dealt a crippling blow by the war. Breaking even became Grace Comiskey's singular obsession. It was a hell of a way to run a railroad—or a baseball team.

It had been a rough spring for Jimmie Dykes. A sense of complacency seemed to permeate the camp. Dykes detected a listless spirit, and an infusion of veteran ballplayers acquired in the opening weeks of the campaign seemed to lack a competitive edge playing for the Comiskeys.

Relief ace Clint Brown was shipped to Cleveland for speed-ball pitcher Johnny Humphries in the early spring. It was another in a long line of Jimmie's patented "spare parts" trades that worked to perfection. The Indians were anxious to dump the right-handed reliever because he had been one of the instigators of the infamous 1940 "Crybaby" revolt against Cleveland manager Oscar Vitt.

In August Humphries tossed three consecutive shutouts after being inserted into the starting rotation. Humphries' string of 35 consecutive scoreless innings was ended by Chet Laabs' booming home run in St. Louis on August 30. However, the streak was good enough to rank him in the top five among Sox pitching immortals in this category.

Some of the other "spare parts" did not perform nearly as well in '41. Dario Lodigiani came over from the A's but was a poor replacement for Jimmie Dykes. Finding a capable third baseman who could combine hitting and fielding skills would continue to vex the Comiskeys for many years to come.

Jimmie Dykes continued to shop the waiver lists after Opening Day. The team played well in April and May and held down second place through June 8 in a generally weak American League field dominated by the Yankees. Manager Dykes, who had not played a game in two years, made his undeclared retirement official in New York the same day when he removed his name from the active-duty roster.

On that same afternoon portly Edgar Smith shut down the Yankees 13–1 on nine hits. Joe DiMaggio produced the only

Sox rookies (left to right) Chet Hajduk, Clyde Lorenz, Don Kolloway, and Bob Kennedy in a mid-winter game of pepper outside the University of Chicago

Yankees run with a first-inning single—and though nobody could possibly suspect it at the time, it was one of the most famous moments in baseball history. It marked the beginning of Joe DiMaggio's 56-game hitting streak.

Smith pitched brilliantly for much of the season, but lack of offensive support cost him a winning record. The roly-poly, hard-luck right-hander was the winning pitcher in the 1941 All-Star Game played in Detroit, and then exhibited his boxing skills in Philadelphia two weeks later by punching Al Simmons in the nose for some unmerciful bench jockeying.

Jimmie Dykes jumped on the back of the Browns' team mascot during a wild, bench-clearing fracas in St. Louis on August 11, resulting in two player suspensions. The brawling 1941 Sox were a perfect reflection of their hot-tempered manager, who was suspended by American League president Will Harridge on July 7 for "obscene and abusive language" directed against umpire Steve Basil. "No manager is bigger than the League. For years Dykes has tried to promote himself at the expense of the League and the president's office," Harridge stated.

Part of the fun of going to Comiskey Park in the 1940s was to observe the fearsome Dykes raging against AL umpires, his players, and the world in general. There would never be another one like him.

	G	AB	H	R	2B	3B	HR	RBI	SB	AVG
Joe Kuhel	153	600	150	99	39	5	12	63	20	.250
Bill Knickerbocker	89	343	84	51	23	2	7	29	6	.245
Luke Appling	154	592	186	93	26	8	1	57	12	.314
Dario Lodigiani	87	322	77	39	19	2	4	40	0	.239
Taft Wright	136	513	165	71	35	5	10	97	5	.322
Mike Kreevich	121	436	101	44	16	8	0	37	17	.232
Myril Hoag	106	380	97	30	13	3	1	44	6	.255
Mike Tresh	115	390	98	38	10	1	0	33	1	.251
Don Kolloway	71	280	76	33	8	3	3	24	11	.271
Bob Kennedy	76	257	53	16	9	3	1	29	5	.206
James "Skeeter" Webb	29	84	16	7	2	0	0	6	1	.190
Jake Jones	3	11	0	0	0	0	0	0	0	.000
Julius "Moose" Solters	76	251	65	24	9	4	4	43	3	.259
Ben Chapman	57	190	43	26	9	1	2	19	2	.226
Larry Rosenthal	20	59	14	9	4	0	0	1	0	.237
Dave Philley	7	9	2	4	1	0	0	0	0	.222
Dave Short	3	8	0	0	0	0	0	0	0	.000
Tom Turner	38	126	30	7	5	0	0	8	2	.238
George Dickey	32	55	11	6	1	0	2	8	0	.200
Stan Goletz	5	5	3	0	0	0	0	0	0	.600
Chester Hajduk	1	1	0	0	0	0	0	0	0	.000
		5,404	1,376	638	245	47	47	567	91	.255

	W	L	GS	CG	IP	H	BB	K	ShO	ERA
Thornton Lee	22	11	34	30	300⅓	258	92	130	3	2.37
Edgar Smith	13	17	33	21	263⅓	243	114	111	1	3.18
Johnny Rigney	13	13	29	18	237	224	92	119	3	3.84
Ted Lyons	12	10	22	19	187⅓	199	37	63	2	3.70
Bill Dietrich	5	8	15	4	109⅓	114	50	26	1	5.35
Lee "Buck" Ross	3	8	11	7	108⅓	99	43	30	0	3.16
Jack Hallett	5	5	6	3	74⅔	96	38	25	0	6.03
John Humphries	4	2	6	4	73⅓	63	22	25	4	1.84
Joe Haynes	0	0	0	0	28	30	11	18	0	3.86
Pete Appleton	0	3	0	0	27⅓	27	17	12	0	5.27
Orval Grove	0	0	0	0	7	9	5	5	0	10.29
	77	77	156	106	1,416	1,362	521	564	14	3.52

1942

Record: 66–82
Finish: Sixth
Games Behind: 34
Manager: Jimmie Dykes

Failing in their efforts to reacquire Bruce Campbell from the Tigers, Dykes parted company with the slumping Mike Kreevich, who was packaged with pitcher Jack Hallet and sent to Philadelphia for Wally Moses, a lifetime .319 hitter up to that point in time. After trading his star pupil to the White Sox, the venerable A's owner Connie Mack said that the White Sox were his choice to win the 1942 pennant.

A horrendous start quickly put to rest *that* illusion. Minus Lefty Lee, who was sidelined with a sore arm until July 25, the Sox plummeted into the cellar before the season was three weeks old. When the team fell into a collective batting slump in April, Dykes threatened to activate his coaching staff. "I'm serious about this," he said. "If our hitters don't show me something…and quick, you are going to see Dykes at third, Muddy Ruel behind the plate, and Mule Haas and Bing Miller in the outfield!"

Well, things did not improve to Jimmie's satisfaction. They got worse. Losers of 18 of their first 22 games, Dykes made good on his promise to bench the entire infield on May 6. "We'll have Murrell Jones at first, Skeeter Webb at second, Leo Wells at short, and Dario Lodigiani at third. They can't be any worse, and maybe they'll be better."

It was a horrible, embarrassing year when the wheels fell off the cart. The team batted out of order in an April 26 game in Cleveland. Edgar Smith dropped 11 of his first 12 decisions, including four shutout losses and two other games lost by a 2–1 margin.

Johnny Rigney was reclassified 1-A by his draft board and was lost to Uncle Sam in May. He was the first White Sox player to join the war effort.

Pitching exclusively on Sundays, 42-year-old Ted Lyons completed every game he started—20 in all. The ageless wonder bagged his 250th victory in Boston on June 21, then joined the service at the end of the season. A four-year hitch in the Marines undoubtedly cost Lyons a shot at 300 wins—hallowed ground that would have established him as one of the game's true immortals.

The Sox capped off a nine-game winning streak in the first week of August that saved the season from complete ruin. After flirting with the first division, the Sox settled into sixth place on August 11 and remained there the rest of the way.

His pitching staff withered by injuries and the war, Dykes' patience with the media and umpires was exhausted. For the second year in a row, President Harridge reprimanded him for conduct unbecoming. This time a written apology was demanded from the Sox manager.

There was no great novelty for an umpire to bounce Jimmie Dykes from a game—it happened all the time in the 1940s. But when 17-year-old Charley Comiskey bolted out of the dugout on July 26 to argue a call after Dykes had

Sox pitchers take aim on the caricature of a Japanese soldier in spring 1942.

been chased by Umpire John Quinn, the 8,556 White Sox partisans stood up and roared their approval. No doubt about it. The kid had pluck. But then, he had a good teacher.

	G	AB	H	R	2B	3B	HR	RBI	SB	AVG
Joe Kuhel	115	413	103	60	14	4	4	52	22	.249
Don Kolloway	147	601	164	72	40	4	3	60	16	.273
Luke Appling	142	543	142	78	26	4	3	53	17	.262
Bob Kennedy	113	412	95	37	18	5	0	38	11	.231
Wally Moses	146	577	156	73	28	4	7	49	16	.270
Myril Hoag	113	412	99	47	18	2	2	37	17	.240
Taft Wright	85	300	100	43	13	5	0	47	1	.333
Mike Tresh	72	233	54	21	8	1	0	15	2	.232
Dario Lodigiani	59	168	47	9	7	0	0	15	3	.280
James "Skeeter" Webb	32	94	16	5	2	1	0	4	1	.170
Leo Wells	35	62	12	8	2	0	1	4	1	194
Jimmy Grant	12	36	6	0	1	1	0	1	0	.167
Jake Jones	7	20	3	2	11	0	0	0	1	.150
Sammy West	49	151	35	14	5	0	0	25	2	.232
Bill Mueller	26	85	14	5	1	0	0	5	2	.165
Val Heim	13	45	9	6	1	1	0	7	1	.200
Harry "Bud" Sketchley	13	36	7	1	1	0	0	3	0	.194
Thurman Tucker	7	24	3	2	0	1	0	1	0	.125
Tom Turner	56	182	44	18	9	1	3	21	0	.242
George Dickey	59	116	27	6	3	0	1	17	0	.233
		4,949	1,215	538	214	36	25	486	114	.246

	W	L	GS	CG	IP	H	BB	K	ShO	ERA
John Humphries	12	12	28	17	228⅓	227	59	71	2	2.68
Edgar Smith	7	20	29	18	215	223	86	78	2	3.98
Ted Lyons	14	6	20	20	180⅓	167	26	50	1	2.10
Bill Dietrich	6	11	26	6	160	173	70	39	0	4.89
Lee "Buck" Ross	5	7	22	4	113⅓	118	39	37	2	5.00
Joe Haynes	8	5	40	1	103	88	47	35	0	2.62
Jake Wade	5	5	15	3	85⅔	84	56	32	0	4.10
Thornton Lee	2	6	11	6	76	82	31	25	1	3.32
Orval Grove	4	6	12	4	66⅓	77	33	21	0	5.16
Johnny Rigney	3	3	7	6	59	40	16	34	0	3.20
Len Perme	0	1	4	1	13	6	4	4	0	1.38
Ed Weiland	0	0	5	0	9⅔	18	3	4	0	7.45
Pete Appleton	0	0	4	0	4⅔	2	3	2	0	3.86
	66	82	148	86	1,314⅓	1,304	473	432	8	3.58

1943

Record: 82–72
Finish: Fourth
Games Behind: 16
Manager: Jimmie Dykes

The onset of World War II imposed numerous hardships on baseball. Finding a suitable place to conduct spring training in the face of wartime travel restrictions was a looming concern. In 1943 the White Sox shared facilities with their hated crosstown rivals, the Cubs, at French Lick, Indiana. When the ballfields at nearby West Baden were flooded, Dykes had no choice but to move the squad indoors—into the ballroom of the French Lick Springs Hotel, where calisthenics were conducted to the jumping rhythms of big band music.

The rapidly depleting rosters of major league teams provided fresh opportunity to players who might not have been given a chance under ordinary circumstances. Outfielder Guy Paxton Curtright bounced around the minor leagues for nine seasons before Dykes summoned him from St. Paul of the American Association. Given a new lease on life, the 30-year-old rookie replaced the injury-prone Moose Solters in left field. Curtright led both leagues in hitting through the first half of the season. His 26-game hitting streak, good for second place on the all-time list behind Appling, was halted by Milo Candini of the Washington Senators on July 2.

Other bargain basement contributors in '43 included second baseman Tony Cuccinello, picked up from the Boston Braves, and Shreveport rookie Gordon Maltzberger, who led the league in saves with 14. "I was always being sold in midseason. I guess I'm a slow starter," he said of his lack of pitching success prior to 1943.

Minus Marine Corps recruit Teddy Lyons and (chronically) sore-armed Lefty Lee, the starting pitchers held up remarkably well. Orval Grove, a former prep star from Chicago's western suburbs, equaled Lefty Williams' 1917 team record by winning his first nine decisions of the 1943 season. On July 8, Grove pitched 8⅔ innings of no-hit ball against the Yankees until Joe Gordon whacked a double down the left-field line to end the kid pitcher's dream.

The White Sox compensated for their offensive shortcomings by reintroducing the walk, the stolen base, and the timely hit to their repertoire. In early July the club took over the league lead in stolen bases, thus surpassing their entire 1942 output in thefts. They were dubbed the Wild West Boys by the media for their base thievery. Wally Moses pilfered 56 bases to establish a new club record. Even old Luke Appling got in on the act, with 27 steals—a career high. Appling won his second American League batting championship in 1943. No White Sox player has duplicated the feat since. In fact, no White Sox player other than Appling has *ever* won a batting title.

A sub-.500 team until late July, the Sox motored their way into the first division with a strong second-half surge, despite losing four of five to the Yankees in a mid-July matchup that all but eliminated them from serious pennant contention.

Lamenting their pop-gun attack against the Bronx Bombers, James S. Kearns of the *Chicago Sun* expressed admiration for the fortitude of Sox fans:

"That is one of the nice things about the South Side fan. He will forget. He will turn the other cheek. He will be firm in his faith that lightning won't strike twice in the same place, or having struck twice, that it won't hit three times...or four...or six. Sometimes you are sorry for him."

	G	AB	H	R	2B	3B	HR	RBI	SB	AVG
Joe Kuhel	153	531	113	55	21	1	5	46	14	.213
Don Kolloway	85	348	75	29	14	4	1	33	11	.216
Luke Appling	155	585	192	63	33	2	3	80	27	.328
Ralph Hodgin	117	407	128	52	22	8	1	50	3	.314
Wally Moses	150	599	147	82	22	12	3	48	56	.245
Thurman Tucker	139	528	124	81	15	6	3	39	29	.235
Guy Curtright	138	488	142	67	20	7	3	48	13	.291
Mike Tresh	86	279	60	20	3	0	0	20	2	.215
James "Skeeter" Webb	58	213	50	15	5	2	0	22	5	.235
Jimmy Grant	58	197	51	23	9	2	4	22	4	.259
Dick Culler	53	148	32	9	5	1	0	11	4	.216
Tony Cuccinello	34	103	28	5	5	0	2	11	3	.272
Don Hanski	9	21	5	1	1	0	0	2	0	.238
Cass Michaels	2	7	0	0	0	0	0	0	0	.000
Julius "Moose" Solters	42	97	15	6	0	0	1	8	0	.155
Tom Turner	51	154	37	16	7	1	2	11	1	.240
Vince Castino	33	101	23	14	1	0	2	16	0	.228
Frank Kalin	4	4	0	0	0	0	0	0	0	.000
		5,254	1,297	573	193	46	33	508	173	.247

	W	L	GS	CG	IP	H	BB	K	ShO	ERA
Orval Grove	15	9	25	18	216⅓	192	72	76	3	2.75
John Humphries	11	11	27	8	188⅓	198	54	51	2	3.30
Edgar Smith	11	11	25	14	187⅔	197	76	66	2	3.69
Bill Dietrich	12	10	26	12	186⅔	180	53	52	2	2.80
Lee "Buck" Ross	11	7	21	7	149⅓	140	56	41	1	3.19
Thornton Lee	5	9	19	7	127	129	50	35	1	4.18
Joe Haynes	7	2	2	1	109⅓	114	32	37	0	2.96
Gordon Maltzberger	7	4	0	0	98⅔	86	24	48	0	2.46
Jake Wade	3	7	9	3	83⅔	66	54	41	1	3.01
Bill Swift	0	2	1	0	51⅓	48	27	28	0	4.21
Don Hanski	0	0	0	0	1	1	1	0	0	0.00
Floyd Speer	0	0	0	0	1	1	2	1	0	9.00
	82	72	155	70	1,400⅓	1,352	501	476	12	3.20

1944

Record: 71–83
Finish: Seventh
Games Behind: 18
Manager: Jimmie Dykes

Luke Appling and his keystone mate Don Kolloway were inducted into the military, creating further hardships for the Comiskeys. The roster of capable wartime replacements was stretched increasingly thin, forcing Dykes to improvise—nothing new for the Sox manager. In November 1943 former Cleveland power hitter Hal Trosky was coaxed out of retirement by Dykes and invited to the Sox camp. Trosky was hailed as one of the great hitters of the game, but migraine headaches forced him out of baseball in 1942. "He'll supply a lot of long-distance power in the cleanup spot that we needed so desperately last year," Dykes promised. In 1944 Trosky contributed—when his rib muscles weren't bothering him. He belted 10 of the 23 home runs hit by the White Sox all year.

Wally Moses, Sox speedster

The White Sox brain trust vested their 1944 hopes in a quartet of minor league recruits: left fielder Eddie Carnett, drafted from the Seattle club of the PCL; Ray Schalk's namesake LeRoy, a second baseman who hoped to finally crack the big time after 12 years of kicking around the minors; Johnny Dickshot, a rangy outfielder who hit .356 with the Hollywood Stars the year before; and Cass Michaels, a shortstop who jumped from American Legion ball to the big leagues in just one year. Michaels had great tools but a poor work ethic. There wasn't much here to work with, but it had to suffice in a year of lean pickings.

Paced by the fine first-half hitting of Thurman Tucker, a sure-handed outfielder who had been ranked fourth in the league in fielding in 1943, the Sox managed to keep their heads above water the first two months of the season. Tucker, a dead ringer for comedian Joe E. Brown, was hitting a torrid .326 on July 16. He was the leadoff hitter for the American League in the All-Star Game but could not sustain his blistering pace. Tucker lost 40 points on his average, ending up at .287.

Given the uncertainty of the times, the 1944 Sox were picked to finish anywhere from second to sixth. They dropped into seventh place on the last day of the season amid accusations that Dykes had lost interest in his ballclub and was asleep at the switch.

Was he? For the second time in three years, the White Sox batted out of order in a regular season game. This latest comic reprisal of Abbott and Costello's famous "Who's On First?" routine occurred in St. Louis on September 15, when coach Mule Haas handed in the wrong lineup card to the umpire. Manager Luke Sewell of the Browns waited until the Sox threatened to bust the game open in the first inning before rushing out of the dugout to lodge a formal protest. Chicago's run was negated—they lost 5–1.

Dykes was labeled the "David Harum of Major League managers" by the Chicagoland media because of his willingness to upset the apple cart on a moment's notice. "The whole White Sox squad is up for trade. We'll trade anybody, everybody...if we can!" There was anger in Dykes' words—which were expressed to the writers in no uncertain terms at the conclusion of the woeful 1944 season.

	G	AB	H	R	2B	3B	HR	RBI	SB	AVG
Hal Trosky	135	497	120	55	32	2	10	70	3	.241
Roy Schalk	146	587	129	47	14	4	1	44	5	.220
James "Skeeter" Webb	139	513	108	44	19	6	0	30	7	.211
Ralph Hodgin	121	465	137	56	25	7	1	51	3	.295
Wally Moses	136	535	150	82	26	9	3	34	21	.280
Thurman Tucker	124	446	128	59	15	6	2	46	13	.287
Eddie Carnett	126	457	126	51	18	8	1	60	5	.276
Mike Tresh	93	312	81	22	8	1	0	25	0	.260
Dick Clarke	63	169	44	14	10	1	0	27	0	.260
Tony Cuccinello	38	130	34	5	3	0	0	17	0	.262
Cass Michaels	27	68	12	4	4	1	0	5	0	.176
Bill Metzig	5	16	2	1	0	0	0	1	0	.125
Guy Curtright	72	198	50	22	8	2	2	23	4	.253
Johnny Dickshot	62	162	41	18	8	5	0	15	2	.253
Myril Hoag	17	48	11	5	1	0	0	4	1	.229
Tom Turner	36	113	26	9	6	0	2	13	0	.230
Vince Castino	29	78	18	8	5	0	0	3	0	.231
Tom Jordan	14	45	12	2	1	1	0	3	0	.267
		5,292	1,307	543	210	55	23	494	66	.247

	W	L	GS	CG	IP	H	BB	K	ShO	ERA
Bill Dietrich	16	17	36	15	246	269	68	70	2	3.62
Orval Grove	14	15	33	11	234⅔	237	71	105	2	3.72
Ed Lopat	11	10	25	13	210	217	59	75	1	3.26
John Humphries	8	10	20	8	169	170	57	42	0	3.67
Joe Haynes	5	6	12	8	154⅓	148	43	44	0	2.57
Thornton Lee	3	9	14	6	113⅓	105	25	39	0	3.02
Gordon Maltzberger	10	5	0	0	91⅓	81	19	49	0	2.96
Lee "Buck" Ross	2	7	9	2	90⅓	97	35	20	0	5.18
Jake Wade	2	4	5	1	74⅔	75	41	35	0	4.82
Don Hanski	0	0	0	0	3	5	2	0	0	12.00
Eddie Carnett	0	0	0	0	2	3	0	1	0	9.00
Floyd Speer	0	0	0	0	2	4	0	1	0	9.00
	71	83	154	64	1,390⅔	1,411	420	481	5	3.58

1945

Record: 71–78
Finish: Sixth
Games Behind: 15
Manager: Jimmie Dykes

The anticipated postseason shake-up never materialized. At the winter meetings in New York, Grabiner and Dykes traded erratic Eddie Carnett to Cleveland for Oris Hockett, another wartime reclamation project flashing an artificially inflated batting average. Hoping to present a few new faces to war-weary Chicagoans, Grabiner invited 38 "independent" players to camp.

"The so-called independents—a term that could mean anything from raw green peas to gents yanked from their grandpappy chairs—are headed by [pitcher] Clay Touchstone who admits he marked his 40th or was it 41st(?) birthday," commented the mirthful Irving Vaughn of the *Tribune.*

Hal Trosky retired over the winter. Gordon Maltzberger was drafted. What new rabbits could Dykes pull out of the hat to save this failing show? Kirby Farrell, an Indianapolis prospect, shared first base duties with Bill Nagel, a good-hit, no-field Milwaukee recruit. Thirty-nine-year-old Earl Caldwell, who hadn't played in a major league game in eight years until Grabiner purchased his contract from the Milwaukee Brewers of the American Association, was assigned to bullpen duties.

Nineteen forty-five: a chaotic year in baseball.

Reliable Bill Dietrich went under the knife in early April and was lost to the Sox until late June. Joe "Hard Luck" Haynes was carried off the field on a stretcher the day Dietrich was finally activated. It was another emergency room nightmare for Dykes, who had become accustomed to losing his regulars in the heat of combat. However, Thornton Lee returned to winning form after four lost years of repeated arm miseries, and posted his best year since his 22-win season in 1941.

Still, the ballclub managed to hold its head above the .500 watermark until August 28, when Cleveland dropped their record to 60–61. The Sox would have to wait six long years before they would again sport a winning record so late in a season.

On September 30, officially the last day of the '45 campaign, rains washed out a scheduled doubleheader in Comiskey Park. The day began with Tony Cuccinello holding down

Tony Cuccinello lost the 1945 batting crown on the last day of the season.

first place in the batting derby by a percentage point over Stuffy Stirnweiss of the New York Yankees. "Cooch" was hitting .308, equaling a career mark in an otherwise lackluster 15-year career. The rainout denied the Sox third baseman a chance to win top batting honors because Stirnweiss collected three scratch hits that day to edge Cooch .309 to .308.

In 1945 four Sox players placed among the top 10 hitters in the league: Cuccinello (.308, second place), Johnny Dickshot (.303, third place), Wally Moses (.295, fifth place), and Oris Hockett (.293, eighth place). Dickshot, Cuccinello, and Hockett were released, never to appear in the big leagues again. Such was the legacy of the wartime baseball player.

"There'll be plenty of changes made before next spring," Dykes avowed. "I was just thinking to myself how many of these guys I won't have to look at again. And you can quote me as saying Mrs. Comiskey is prepared to spend money for ballplayers!"

	G	AB	H	R	2B	3B	HR	RBI	SB	AVG
Kerby Farrell	103	396	102	44	11	3	0	34	4	.258
Roy Schalk	133	513	127	50	23	1	1	65	3	.248
Cass Michaels	129	445	109	47	8	5	2	54	8	.245
Tony Cuccinello	118	402	124	50	25	3	2	49	6	.308
Wally Moses	140	569	168	79	35	15	2	50	11	.295
Oris Hockett	106	417	122	46	23	4	2	55	10	.293
Johnny Dickshot	130	486	147	74	19	10	4	58	18	.302
Mike Tresh	150	458	114	50	11	0	0	47	6	.249
Bill Nagel	67	220	46	21	10	3	3	27	3	.209
Floyd Baker	82	208	52	22	8	0	0	19	3	.250
Danny Reynolds	29	72	12	6	2	1	0	4	1	.167
Luke Appling	18	58	21	12	2	2	1	10	1	.362
Joe Orengo	17	15	1	5	0	0	0	1	0	.067
Guy Curtright	98	324	91	51	15	7	4	32	3	.281
Bill Mueller	13	9	0	3	0	0	0	0	1	.000
Vince Castino	26	37	8	2	1	0	0	4	0	.216
		5,079	1,330	596	203	55	22	544	78	.262

	W	L	GS	CG	IP	H	BB	K	ShO	ERA
Thornton Lee	15	12	28	19	228⅓	208	76	108	1	2.44
Orval Grove	14	12	30	16	217	233	68	54	4	3.44
Ed Lopat	10	13	24	17	199⅓	226	56	74	1	4.11
John Humphries	6	14	21	10	153	172	48	33	1	4.24
Bill Dietrich	7	10	16	6	122⅓	136	36	43	4	4.19
Earl Caldwell	6	7	11	5	105⅓	108	37	45	1	3.59
Joe Haynes	5	5	13	8	104	92	29	34	1	3.55
Frank Papish	4	4	5	3	84⅓	75	40	45	0	3.74
Johnny "Swede" Johnson	3	0	0	0	69⅔	85	35	38	0	4.26
Lee "Buck" Ross	1	1	2	0	37⅓	51	17	8	0	5.79
Clay Touchstone	0	0	0	0	10	14	6	4	0	5.40
	71	78	150	84	1,330⅔	1,400	448	486	13	3.69

1946

Record: 74–80
Finish: Fifth
Games Behind: 30
Managers: Mule Haas, Jimmie Dykes, Ted Lyons

It was the season of change, but not the kind Jimmie Dykes envisioned when he pronounced the last rites on wartime baseball. Harry Grabiner resigned as vice president and general manager on November 15, 1945, after 40 years of loyal and unbroken service to the Comiskey family. Fed up with the nickel-nursing ways of Grace Comiskey and her open hostility toward him, which seemed to grow stronger by the day, Grabiner moved on to Cleveland to help Bill Veeck mold a championship ballclub.

Leslie O'Connor, former longtime legal aide to the late Commissioner Landis, replaced Grabiner, and in the next two years he would concentrate on building up the farm system to produce talent—but with very little success.

Neither O'Connor nor Mrs. Comiskey was inclined to give Jimmie Dykes a renewed vote of confidence. The first reports of Dykes' imminent departure were leaked to the public by *Chicago Times* columnist Gene Kessler five days before Grabiner announced his resignation. Rumors surrounding his dismissal percolated all winter, but no actions were taken.

Shortly after spring training began, Dykes was stricken with a stomach ailment that required surgery. His diet of 15 cigars a day and a nervous, excitable nature finally caught up with the fireplug manager.

Changing of the old guard: Mule Haas and Jimmie Dykes

Mule Haas opened the season as interim manager and guided the Sox until April 30, when Dykes returned to Chicago restored to good health. However, the team managed to win only eight of their first 23 games. Frustrated by another lackluster start, Sox fans vented their displeasure with the status quo in the pages of the local sports sections. One South Side sufferer wrote to Kessler: "Many have given up hope of seeing a winner to represent the Sox so long as Mrs. Comiskey is in charge, unless she changes the present policy of obtaining men only through the draft or waiver route."

Dykes had had enough. On May 24 the worst-kept secret in baseball was revealed by a Los Angeles gossip columnist. Dykes was out as White Sox skipper after nearly 13 years. Only Connie Mack and Joe McCarthy had logged more time with one club among active AL managers. "They have paid me off, and the action speaks for itself." Jimmie Dykes displayed little emotion and left with no regrets. It had been a tough, long road, and now it was Teddy Lyons' turn to see what miracles he could perform.

Grace Comiskey had long coveted the day she could appoint Ted Lyons—a man rich in experience—to pilot the Sox. It was a decision born out of sentiment for the past, as well as a belief that Teddy was what Sox fans wanted all along. "Just tell the fans I'm going to do my best to give them the best White Sox team we ever had out here...and I hope I can fulfill that promise," the new manager beamed.

Ted Lyons recorded his 260th (and final) victory against the Browns in Comiskey Park on April 28. He pitched his last game on May 19 against the Washington Senators, then removed himself from the active roster less than a month later in order to become a full-time manager. The winningest pitcher in White Sox history ended his career with a streak of 28 complete games intact.

The White Sox, who played listless, uninterested baseball under Haas and Dykes the first two months of the season, began to "resemble a major league club again," in the learned opinion of Kessler. The team won 64 and lost 60 the rest of the way despite the usual rash of injuries.

Lyons counted on youth and experience for 1947—rookie outfielder Dave Philley was a top-rated prospect with the American Association Milwaukee Brewers, and the pitching staff was bolstered by the free agent acquisition of former Yankees great Red Ruffing on December 6.

"Give us one distance-hitting outfielder, and we may be up there," Lyons glowed. "Don't forget, we'll have one of the best-looking first basemen in baseball in Murrell Jones!"

	G	AB	H	R	2B	3B	HR	RBI	SB	AVG
Hal Trosky	88	299	76	22	12	3	2	31	4	.254
Don Kolloway	123	482	135	45	23	4	3	53	14	.280
Luke Appling	149	582	180	59	27	5	1	55	6	.309
Dario Lodigiani	44	155	38	12	8	0	0	13	4	.245
Taft Wright	115	422	116	46	19	4	7	52	10	.275
Thurman Tucker	121	438	126	62	20	3	1	36	9	.288
Bob Kennedy	113	411	106	43	13	5	5	34	6	.258
Mike Tresh	80	217	47	28	5	2	0	21	0	.217
Cass Michaels	91	291	75	37	8	0	1	22	9	.258
Joe Kuhel	64	238	65	24	9	3	4	20	4	.273
Leo Wells	45	127	24	11	4	1	1	11	3	.189
Jake Jones	24	79	21	10	5	1	3	13	0	.266
Floyd Baker	9	24	6	2	1	0	0	3	0	.250
Frank Whitman	17	16	1	7	0	0	0	1	0	.063
Ralph Hodgin	87	258	65	32	10	1	0	25	0	.252
Mizell "Whitey" Platt	84	247	62	28	8	5	3	32	1	.251
Wally Moses	56	168	46	20	9	1	4	16	2	.274
Dave Philley	17	68	24	10	2	3	0	17	5	.353
Guy Curtright	23	55	11	7	2	0	0	5	0	.200
Joe Smaza	2	5	1	2	0	0	0	0	0	.200
Frankie "Blimp" Hayes	53	179	38	15	6	0	2	16	1	.212
George Dickey	37	78	15	8	1	0	0	1	0	.192
Ed Fernandes	14	32	8	4	2	0	0	4	0	.250
Tom Jordan	10	15	4	1	2	1	0	0	0	.267
		5,312	1,364	562	206	44	37	515	78	.257

	W	L	GS	CG	IP	H	BB	K	ShO	ERA
Ed Lopat	13	13	29	20	231	216	48	89	2	2.73
Orval Grove	8	13	26	10	205⅓	213	78	60	1	3.02
Joe Haynes	7	9	23	9	177⅓	203	60	60	0	3.76
Edgar Smith	8	11	21	3	145⅓	135	60	59	1	2.85
Frank Papish	7	5	15	6	138	122	63	66	2	2.74
Earl Caldwell	13	4	0	0	90⅔	60	29	42	0	2.08
Johnny Rigney	5	5	11	3	82⅔	76	35	51	2	4.03
Ralph Hamner	2	7	7	1	71⅓	80	39	29	0	4.42
Bill Dietrich	3	3	9	3	62	63	24	20	0	2.61
Al Hollingsworth	3	2	2	0	55	63	22	22	0	4.58
Thornton Lee	2	4	7	2	43⅓	39	23	23	0	3.53
Ted Lyons	1	4	5	5	42⅔	38	9	10	0	2.32
Gordon Maltzberger	2	0	0	0	39⅔	30	6	17	0	1.59
Len Perme	0	0	0	0	4⅓	6	7	2	0	8.31
Emmett O'Neill	0	0	0	0	3⅔	4	5	0	0	0.00
	74	80	155	62	1,392⅓	1,348	508	550	8	3.10

1947

Record: 70–84
Finish: Sixth
Games Behind: 27
Manager: Ted Lyons

Les O'Connor believed his own myth. "The Sox are a real first-division team!"

Based on his team's fine second-half showing in 1946, Lyons was awarded a new two-year contract on Opening Day. He had inherited from Dykes a rickety, injury-prone pitching staff led by 39-year-old relief specialist Earl Caldwell; Thornton Lee, 39; Red Ruffing, 42; and Eddie Smith, 34; a Punch and Judy offense; and a "What me worry?" attitude. This team suspiciously resembled the 1934 edition, and not the exciting Go-Go clubs looming just over the horizon.

Red Ruffing spent two months on the disabled list. Murrell "Jake" Jones, another in a long line of angular, muscle-bound first basemen whose actual abilities belied the favorable scouting reports, was traded to Boston for Rudy York on June 14. Playing against his old teammates in Fenway Park the very next day, Jones banged out four hits in seven at bats, including a grand-slam home run, with seven RBIs. The once-potent bat of York was silenced in cavernous Comiskey Park for the remainder of the season. So much for the year of rising expectations.

Lyons experimented with Don Kolloway at first base and Floyd Baker, a Brownie castoff, at third. Baker was a sure fielder but only an ordinary hitter. His deft moves around the hot corner earned him the nickname "Blotter" and the affection of a generation of '40s Sox fans, but it was his offensive shortcomings that were the greatest concern to Lyons.

It was hard to tell the players without a scorecard, but nobody mistook Luke Appling, who enjoyed another outstanding season in the twilight of his career—at the very moment when Sox management began casting about the minor leagues for a quality replacement shortstop. Appling was honored by the Comiskeys on his own "day," June 8, 1947. Old Luke was awarded a new sedan, paid for by Chicago fans who chipped in a dime apiece. In August Appling took over the league lead in hitting, which put any talk of retirement on hold for the time being.

On July 5 a nervous Cleveland rookie of African American descent pinch-hit for Bryan Stephens in Comiskey Park. The kid outfielder from the Negro Leagues struck out on five pitches delivered by Earl Harrist, a southerner who was surprisingly indifferent to the presence of the first black man to stand in an American League batter's box.

Doby's historic debut before 18,000 applauding Comiskey Park fans shattered the color barrier in the American League. In his own quiet way, Larry Doby was as much a pioneer as Jackie Robinson in the National League, but he was overshadowed for much of his career by the memory of Robinson's earlier, more spectacular debut. He was the second African American player to appear in the big leagues and would later become its second African American manager.

It would be another two years before Charley Comiskey would begin to lay the groundwork for the arrival of the first black player in Chicago.

1947: a mediocre team in a forgettable year

	G	AB	H	R	2B	3B	HR	RBI	SB	AVG
Rudy York	102	400	97	40	18	4	15	64	1	.243
Don Kolloway	124	485	135	49	25	4	2	35	11	.278
Luke Appling	139	503	154	67	29	0	8	49	8	.306
Floyd Baker	105	371	98	61	12	3	0	22	9	.264
Bob Kennedy	115	428	112	47	19	3	6	48	3	.262
Dave Philley	143	551	142	55	25	11	2	45	21	.258
Taft Wright	124	401	130	48	13	0	4	54	8	.324
Mike Tresh	90	274	66	19	6	2	0	20	2	.241
Cass Michaels	110	355	97	31	15	4	3	34	10	.273
Jack Wallaesa	81	205	40	25	9	1	7	32	2	.195
Jake Jones	45	171	41	15	7	1	3	20	1	.240
Thurman Tucker	89	254	60	28	9	4	1	17	10	.236
Ralph Hodgin	59	180	53	26	10	3	1	24	1	.294
Lloyd Christopher	7	23	5	1	0	1	0	0	0	.217
George Dickey	83	211	47	15	6	0	1	27	4	.223
Joe Stephenson	16	35	5	3	0	0	0	3	0	.143
Joe Kuhel	4	4	0	0	0	0	0	0	0	.000
		5,275	1,350	553	211	41	53	519	91	.256

	W	L	GS	CG	IP	H	BB	K	ShO	ERA
Ed Lopat	16	13	31	22	252⅔	241	73	109	3	2.81
Frank Papish	12	12	26	6	199	185	98	79	1	3.26
Joe Haynes	14	6	22	7	182	174	61	50	2	2.42
Orval Grove	6	8	19	6	135⅔	158	70	33	1	4.44
Bob Gillespie	5	8	17	1	118	133	53	36	0	4.73
Earl Harrist	3	8	4	0	93⅔	85	49	55	0	3.56
Thornton Lee	3	7	11	2	86⅔	86	56	57	1	4.47
Pete Gebrian	2	3	4	0	66⅓	61	33	17	0	4.48
Gordon Maltzberger	1	4	0	0	63⅔	61	25	22	0	3.39
Earl Caldwell	1	4	0	0	54⅓	53	30	22	0	3.64
Charles "Red" Ruffing	3	5	9	1	53	63	16	11	0	6.11
Johnny Rigney	2	3	7	2	50⅔	42	15	19	0	1.95
Edgar Smith	1	3	5	0	33⅓	40	24	12	0	7.29
Hi Bithorn	1	0	0	0	2	2	0	0	0	0.00
	70	84	155	47	1,391	1,384	603	522	8	3.64

Eddie Lopat—the one that got away

1948

Record: 51–101
Finish: Eighth
Games Behind: 44½
Manager: Ted Lyons

The Les O'Connor legacy: first he ran the team into the ground, and then out of the league.

Before the 1947 season was complete, the Sox GM signed a Chicago prep star named George Zoeterman to a contract in defiance of a rule barring professional teams from negotiating the services of an athlete playing for a high school team not recognized by the National Federation of High School Associations. Commissioner A. B. "Happy" Chandler levied a $500 fine against O'Connor—which he refused to pay. Chandler immediately suspended the Sox from the American League until the impasse was resolved to his satisfaction. "As long as the suspension stands, the White Sox cannot ask waivers on players, claim players, sign contracts, or participate in baseball's transactions or activities," Chandler warned. The White Sox were out—until Charley Comiskey quietly paid the fine and ended the row.

Maybe the Sox would have been better off sitting this one out after all. With the exception of three days in late April, when they managed to climb into a virtual seventh-place tie, the ballclub languished in the cellar from start to finish. Their .336 winning percentage was second-worst in team history behind the feeble effort put forth by the 1932 edition.

Pitching was the main problem. O'Connor exacerbated the situation by trading junk-baller Eddie Lopat to the Yankees for Bill Wight on February 24. Lopat was a standout pitcher in the American Association in the early 1940s, and he was as good as advertised by the time he finally arrived for his first major league season in 1945. Eddie Lopat won 17 games for the Yankees in 1948. Bill Wight lost 20 for the Sox.

The acquisition of Fat Pat Seerey was another O'Connor gem. Bob Kennedy, in and out of the starting lineup for nearly six seasons, was dealt to the Indians on June 2 for pitcher Allen Gettel and Seerey—a Smead Jolley reincarnation. Kennedy gave the Tribe five good years—Seerey provided one day's worth of thrills, and not even before the hometown fans.

Playing in Philadelphia on July 18, Seerey slugged four mammoth home runs in an 11-inning win over the A's, thus joining Lou Gehrig and Chuck Klein as the only other players to accomplish the feat between 1900 and 1948. Otherwise, Fat Pat was good for 102 strikeouts and a .229 batting average. He was released in early 1949.

The 1948 disaster finally awakened Mrs. Comiskey to the realities. You can't operate a ballclub on a lemonade-stand budget. During the World Series the slumbering front office was given a long-overdue wake-up call.

On the final day of the season, Ted Lyons resigned before he could be fired. The Baylor Bearcat was rumored to be heading to Boston, forever tainted by the two disastrous seasons behind him. Former major league catcher Jack

Onslow was appointed manager hours later, vowing to "tear apart" the entire White Sox roster to achieve results. Onslow had piloted the White Sox farm affiliates in Waterloo and Memphis with some degree of success, and he was brought to Chicago with a vote of confidence from 22-year-old Charley Comiskey, who had been working without a title until his mother allowed him a free hand to "clean house."

As his first order of business, Comiskey decided to accept Les O'Connor's resignation without protest. O'Connor had been a lost soul in the unfamiliar role of charting White Sox policy. He was happy to oblige his employers by vacating his office at 35th and Shields. In his place Charley hired 52-year-old Frank Charles Lane, a human hurricane who was in perfect accord with Comiskey's 1949 theme: "If we're going to lose a hundred games again, let's do it with some new faces!"

	G	AB	H	R	2B	3B	HR	RBI	SB	AVG
Ulysses "Tony" Lupien	154	617	152	69	19	3	6	54	11	.246
Don Kolloway	119	417	114	60	14	4	6	38	2	.273
Cass Michaels	145	484	120	47	12	6	5	56	8	.248
Luke Appling	139	497	156	63	16	2	0	47	10	.314
Taft Wright	134	455	127	50	15	6	4	61	2	.279
Dave Philley	137	488	140	51	28	3	5	42	8	.287
Pat Seerey	95	340	78	44	11	0	18	64	0	.229
Aaron Robinson	98	326	82	47	14	2	8	39	0	.252
Floyd Baker	104	335	72	47	8	3	0	18	4	.215
Jack Wallaesa	33	48	9	2	0	0	1	3	0	.188
Frank Whitman	3	6	0	0	0	0	0	0	0	.000
Ralph Hodgin	114	331	88	28	11	5	1	34	0	.266
Bob Kennedy	30	113	28	4	8	1	0	14	0	.248
Jim Delsing	20	63	12	5	0	0	0	5	0	.190
Herbie Adams	5	11	3	1	1	0	0	0	0	.273
Jerry Scala	3	6	0	1	0	0	0	0	0	.000
Ralph Weigel	66	163	38	8	7	3	0	26	1	.233
Mike Tresh	39	108	27	10	1	0	1	11	0	.250
		5,192	1,303	558	172	39	55	532	46	.251

	W	L	GS	CG	IP	H	BB	K	ShO	ERA
Bill Wight	9	20	32	7	223⅓	238	135	68	1	4.80
Joe Haynes	9	10	22	6	149⅔	167	52	40	0	3.97
Alan Gettel	8	10	19	7	148	154	60	49	0	4.01
Marino Pieretti	8	10	18	4	120	117	52	28	0	4.95
Howie Judson	4	5	5	1	107⅓	102	56	38	0	4.78
Randy Gumpert	2	6	11	6	97⅓	103	13	31	1	3.79
Frank Papish	2	8	14	2	95⅓	97	75	41	0	5.00
Orval Grove	2	10	11	1	87⅔	110	42	18	0	6.16
Glen Moulder	3	6	9	0	85⅔	108	54	26	0	6.41
Bob Gillespie	0	4	6	1	72	81	33	19	0	5.13
Ike Pearson	2	3	2	0	53	62	27	12	0	4.92
Earl Caldwell	1	5	1	0	39	53	22	10	0	5.31
Earl Harrist	1	3	1	0	23⅓	23	13	14	0	5.79
Marv Rotblatt	0	1	2	0	18⅓	19	23	4	0	7.85
Fred Bradley	0	0	0	0	15⅔	11	4	2	0	4.60
Jim Goodwin	0	0	1	0	10⅓	9	12	3	0	8.71
	51	101	154	35	1,346	1,454	673	403	2	4.89

1949

Record: 63–91
Finish: Sixth
Games Behind: 34
Manager: Jack Onslow

"There are no sacred cows on this club!" Frank Lane declared. To reinforce this point, the entire Sox ballclub was placed on waivers over the winter. Only All-Star second baseman Cass Michaels and pitcher Howie Judson (destined to lose 14 straight games in '49) stirred interest.

Lane completed his first trade on November 10, 1948, sending catcher Aaron Robinson to the Detroit Tigers for a kid pitcher named Billy Pierce *and* $10,000. It was a scathing, brilliant stroke of genius. The Tigers believed they owed the Sox a whole lot more than *just* this sandlot pitcher, so they tossed in $10,000 to sweeten the deal.

Gone from the roster were Taffy Wright, Joe Haynes, Orval Grove, and Frank Papish—players who carried the hopes of Sox fans in the past but who no longer fit in with the youth movement. The spotlight this year shifted to Gus Zernial, a power-hitting outfielder who punched 38 Pacific Coast League home runs in 1948. Zernial put up good numbers in his rookie season—but shattered his collarbone in Cleveland on May 29 and missed two-thirds of the campaign.

Unhappy Jack Onslow (left) makes his point to catcher Joe Tipton, Luke Appling, and pitcher Marino Pieretti.

The Sox were on the move, and the fans sensed it. A record-setting crowd 53,325 strong turned out to watch the Sox whitewash the World Champion Indians 10–0 and 2–0 on May 15. Comiskey and Lane celebrated the moment by digging up home plate and mailing it off to Bill Veeck in Cleveland as a souvenir of a memorable Chicago weekend. "They've won over the long-suffering South Side fans by their efforts to bring in young hustling players," commented Leo Fischer of the *Herald-American*.

Gone were the days of complacency and the feeling that it was good enough just to make ends meet. The team sported a conservative white and black uniform featuring an old English "SOX" logo for the first time in 1949, and the resemblance to the Yankees togs was striking. "I stole from the Yankees," Charley Comiskey liked to say. And he was more than happy to do so.

But even as the Sox showed renewed signs of life, there was bad blood between the manager and the general manager. It was Comiskey's job to keep the combative Lane and the quarrelsome Onslow an arm's length apart. One of the two eventually had to go. Who was it going to be?

"Honest" Jack Onslow would have preferred to retire Luke Appling to a desk job next to Lane, but the venerable shortstop refused to step aside until he was good and ready. Appling was benched in favor of Freddie Hancock in June, at a time when Luke was closing in on "Rabbit" Maranville's record of 2,153 games played at shortstop. The sacred mark was tied on August 5 in Washington and surpassed the next day when "Mr. White Sox" banged out two hits and handled four chances in the field flawlessly. The sportswriters had once called the Maranville record unbreakable.

In June the team lost 15 of 20 games to fall out of contention. The absence of Zernial proved devastating. Lane tried to plug the hole with journeyman outfielder George Metkovich, purchased from Oakland in early June, and a succession of minor league prospects, including Jerry Scala, Dick Lane, and Herbie Adams. None were effective.

While the final results might have fallen short of Lane's and Comiskey's expectations, the youthful Sox ballclub made significant strides toward respectability in 1949. More importantly, Charley Comiskey set in motion a long-overdue plan to bring African-American players into the White Sox organization. Veteran Negro League pitcher John Donaldson was hired as a scout on June 28. His task was to locate and sign top-flight youngsters for immediate delivery to the South Side.

	G	AB	H	R	2B	3B	HR	RBI	SB	AVG
Charlie Kress	97	353	98	45	17	6	1	44	6	.278
Cass Michaels	154	561	173	73	27	9	6	83	5	.308
Luke Appling	142	492	148	82	21	5	5	58	7	.301
Floyd Baker	125	388	101	38	15	4	1	40	3	.260
Dave Philley	146	598	171	84	20	8	0	44	13	.286
George "Catfish" Metkovich	93	338	80	50	9	4	5	45	5	.237
Herbie Adams	56	208	61	26	5	3	0	16	1	.293
Don Wheeler	67	192	46	17	9	2	1	22	2	.240
Gordon Goldsberry	39	145	36	25	3	2	1	13	2	.248
Bobby Rhawn	24	73	15	12	4	1	0	5	0	.205
Rocky Krsnich	16	55	12	7	3	1	1	9	0	.218
Fred Hancock	39	52	7	7	2	1	0	9	0	.135
Jim Baumer	8	10	4	2	1	1	0	2	0	.400
Don Kolloway	4	4	0	0	0	0	0	0	0	.000
Steve Souchock	84	252	59	29	13	5	7	37	5	.234
Gus Zernial	73	198	63	29	17	2	5	38	0	.318
John Ostrowski	49	158	42	19	9	4	5	31	4	.266
Jerry Scala	37	120	30	17	7	1	1	13	3	.250
Billy Bowers	26	78	15	5	2	1	0	6	1	.192
Earl Rapp	19	54	14	3	1	1	0	11	1	.259
Dick Lane	12	42	5	4	0	0	0	4	0	.119
Bill Higdon	11	23	7	3	3	0	0	1	1	.304
Pat Seerey	4	4	0	1	0	0	0	0	0	.000
Joe Tipton	67	191	39	20	5	3	3	19	1	.204
Eddie Malone	55	170	46	17	7	2	1	16	2	.271
George Yankowski	12	18	3	0	1	0	0	2	0	.167
		5,204	1,340	648	207	66	43	591	62	.257

	W	L	GS	CG	IP	H	BB	K	ShO	ERA
Bill Wight	15	13	33	14	245	254	96	78	3	3.31
Randy Gumpert	13	16	32	18	234	223	83	78	3	3.81
Billy Pierce	7	15	26	8	171⅔	145	112	95	0	3.88
Bob Kuzava	10	6	18	9	156⅔	139	91	83	1	4.02
Marino Pieretti	4	6	9	0	116	131	54	25	0	5.51
Howie Judson	1	14	12	3	108	114	70	36	0	4.58
Max Surkont	3	5	2	0	96	92	60	38	0	4.78
Mickey Haefner	4	6	12	4	80⅓	84	41	17	1	4.37
Alan Gettel	2	5	7	1	63	69	26	22	1	6.43
Eddie "Specs" Klieman	2	0	0	0	33	33	14	9	0	3.00
Clyde Shoun	1	1	0	0	23⅓	37	13	8	0	5.79
Bob Cain	0	0	0	0	11	7	5	5	0	2.45
Jack Bruner	1	2	2	0	7⅔	10	8	4	0	8.22
Bill Evans	0	1	0	0	6⅓	6	8	1	0	7.11
Ernie Groth	0	1	0	0	5	2	3	1	0	5.40
Alex Carrasquel	0	0	0	0	3⅔	8	4	1	0	14.73
Fred Bradley	0	0	1	0	2	4	3	0	0	13.50
Orval Grove	0	0	0	0	⅔	4	1	1	0	54.00
	63	91	154	57	1,363⅓	1,362	693	502	9	4.30

1950

Record: 60–94
Finish: Sixth
Games Behind: 38
Managers: Jack Onslow, Red Corriden

Jack Onslow was invited back for another year...but with trepidations. "How can you change managers after I lifted the Sox two notches?" Onslow's logic was irrefutable, his disciplinary methods rigid and unyielding. But Lane was unfazed. He complained that Onslow was constantly being outsmarted by rival managers—"too dim" to win. Lane desired to make a change, and by mid-May Charley Comiskey came around to his general manager's way of thinking and admitted that the hiring of Onslow was a mistake. However, Grace Comiskey pulled rank on them both and nixed a plan to replace "Honest Jack" with Paul Richards.

The 1950 White Sox finished in sixth place, but were poised for a great improvement. Young Nellie Fox is shown fourth from the left.

Over the winter, a cabal of 1949 troublemakers, including catcher Joe Tipton, pitcher Max Surkont, and outfielder Steve Souchock, were traded to other teams to placate Onslow. Tipton had exchanged blows with the manager in St. Louis at one point during the 1949 season. The pair had quarreled constantly.

Tipton was traded to Philadelphia on October 19, 1949, for a pint-sized infielder named Nellie Fox, a trade that was made out of spite. No one paid much attention to the deal at the time, and it is doubtful it would have even been made if not for the bad blood existing between Tipton and Onslow. Fate works in strange ways.

Nellie Fox was old Connie Mack's final blessing bestowed upon Chicago, dating back to the Eddie Collins sale of 1914.

The team got off to a horrific start, winning only eight of the first 30 games. When Comiskey told his mother that he was "sick of losing" and threatened to quit unless Onslow was fired, Grace finally caved in. On May 26 Onslow was out—Red Corriden, who had coached the Cubs for nearly a decade back in the 1930s, was in. There were bruised feelings all around, and the press reveled in the public airing of Comiskey dirty laundry.

Four days later Lane completed a blockbuster trade that sent Cass Michaels, Bob Kuzava, and John Ostrowski to Washington for power-hitting first baseman Eddie Robinson, pitcher Ray Scarborough, and Al Kozar. It was dubbed the $600,000 trade, and it was a good one from a Chicago perspective because it opened up second base for Nellie Fox on a full-time basis. By adding one or two quality players to the roster per year, Lane was molding a winner, though it was hardly evident judging by the 1950 results.

For three years the Sox had tried to gently nudge Luke Appling into retirement with little success. In 1950 player/coach Appling celebrated an even 20 years with the Hose, but was resigned to a part-time role. The "Greatest Player" in Sox history (as determined in various fan polls), hung up the spikes for good on the last day of the season, October 1. Appling's career spanned 2,422 games, all of them in a White Sox uniform. In November he accepted an offer to manage a Sox minor league affiliate in Memphis, where he hoped to gain the necessary skills to return to Chicago one day to pilot the Sox.

The Comiskeys had already found their replacement shortstop in the Dodgers farm system, and he was a solid contributor during the 1950 season. His name was Alfonso "Chico" Carrasquel, and Lane pried him loose from Brooklyn after paying Branch Rickey $25,000 and two minor leaguers.

Now they had to come up with someone to lead the young thoroughbreds into the promised land.

	G	AB	H	R	2B	3B	HR	RBI	SB	AVG
Eddie Robinson	119	428	133	62	11	2	20	73	0	.311
Nellie Fox	130	457	113	45	12	7	0	30	4	.247
Alfonso "Chico" Carrasquel	141	524	148	72	21	5	4	46	0	.282
Hank Majeski	122	414	128	47	18	2	6	46	1	.309
Marv Rickert	84	278	66	38	9	2	4	27	0	.237
Dave Philley	156	619	150	69	21	5	14	80	6	.242
Gus Zernial	143	543	152	75	16	4	29	93	0	.280
Phil Masi	122	377	105	38	17	2	7	55	2	.279
Floyd Baker	83	186	59	26	7	0	0	11	1	.317
Cass Michaels	36	138	43	21	6	3	4	19	0	312
Luke Appling	50	128	30	11	3	4	0	13	2	.234
Gordon Goldsberry	82	127	34	19	8	2	2	25	0	.268
Al Kozar	10	10	3	4	0	0	1	2	0	.300
Charlie Kress	3	8	0	0	0	0	0	0	0	.000
Joe Kirrene	1	4	1	0	0	0	0	0	0	.250
Mike McCormick	55	138	32	16	4	3	0	0	3	.232
Herbie Adams	34	118	24	12	2	3	0	10	0	.203
Jerry Scala	40	67	13	8	2	1	0	2	0	.194
John Ostrowski	22	49	12	10	2	1	2	6	0	.245
Jim Busby	18	48	10	5	0	0	0	2	0	.208
Ed McGhee	3	6	1	0	0	1	0	4	0	.167
Bill Wilson	3	6	0	0	0	0	0	0	0	.000
Gus Niarhos	41	105	34	17	4	0	0	0	0	.324
Eddie Malone	31	71	16	2	2	0	0	16	0	.225
Joe Erautt	16	18	4	0	0	0	0	10	0	.222
Bill Salkeld	1	3	0	0	0	0	0	1	0	.000
		5,264	1,368	625	172	47	93	592	19	.260

	W	L	GS	CG	IP	H	BB	K	ShO	ERA
Billy Pierce	12	16	29	15	219⅓	189	137	118	1	3.98
Bill Wight	10	16	28	13	206	213	79	62	3	3.58
Bob Cain	9	12	23	11	171⅔	153	109	77	1	3.93
Randy Gumpert	5	12	17	6	155⅓	165	58	48	1	4.75
Ray Scarborough	10	13	23	8	149⅓	160	62	70	1	5.30
Howie Judson	2	3	3	1	112	105	63	34	0	3.94
Ken Holcombe	3	10	15	5	96	122	45	37	0	4.59
Luis Aloma	7	2	0	0	87⅔	77	53	49	0	3.80
Mickey Haefner	1	6	9	2	70⅔	83	45	17	0	5.73
Bob Kuzava	1	3	7	1	44⅓	43	27	21	0	5.68
Lou Kretlow	0	0	1	0	21⅓	17	14	14	0	3.80
Jack Bruner	0	0	0	0	12⅓	7	5	8	0	3.65
Marv Rotblatt	0	0	0	0	8⅔	11	1	6	0	6.23
John Perkovich	0	0	0	0	5	7	1	3	0	7.20
Bill Connelly	0	0	0	0	2⅓	5	5	0	0	11.57
Gus Keriazakos	0	1	1	0	2⅓	7	3	1	0	19.29
Charlie Cueller	0	0	0	0	1⅓	6	3	1	0	33.75
	60	94	156	62	1,365⅔	1,370	734	566	7	4.41

1951

Record: 81–73
Finish: Fourth
Games Behind: 17
Manager: Paul Richards

For years the empty canyons of Comiskey Park echoed the distant call of "C'mon, Luke!" The game on the field in the listless 1930s and '40s revolved around Luke Appling. And now the "renaissance" of White Sox baseball had dawned. Luke was gone, and a new battle cry was heard across the land. The chant of "Go! Go! Go!" rang loud and clear through the stands.

A younger generation of baseball fans encouraged a supercharged trio of fleet-footed players who dusted off the long-forgotten stolen-base offense. Jim Busby, Chico Carrasquel, and Orestes "Minnie" Minoso paced the American League in stolen bases in 1951. On May 12 the Sox pilfered their 20th base of the year, which was one more than the entire 1950 output. They finished the year with a league-leading 99 thefts. For only the third time in their 50-year history, the 1951 edition led the American League in team batting average. Speed, defense, and timely hitting—it was an exciting, daring brand of baseball, uncommon for the times they played in.

Paul Richards, a former Detroit Tigers catcher who suffered malaria as a youngster, had awaited the White Sox's call for nearly two years. Now his time had come. A tall, taciturn, scholarly figure, Richards was opposite in temperament from the excitable, often profane Frank Lane. For the time being at least, they would work a little magic.

Paul Richards was an excellent motivator and teacher who was skilled in the care and handling of pitchers. In the minors he had been regarded as a "bear-down" manager and a stickler for fundamentals, which is what this club desperately needed. He was hired on October 12, 1950, and awarded a two-year, $25,000 per annum salary plus a nickel a head for every paid admission over 900,000.

Meanwhile, Frank "Trader" Lane continued his behind-the-scenes machinations by peddling Bill Wight and Ray Scarborough to the Boston Red Sox for Al Zarilla, Joe Dobson, and Dick Littlefield at the 1950 winter meetings. The restless Lane kept the pot boiling all winter long, searching for new trading partners. For the first time in years, there was a sense of heightened anticipation as winter gave way to spring.

Paul Richards' club won the Grapefruit League title and began the new season with a flourish by sweeping the first three games of the season, outpointing the Browns and Tigers 35–8. The magic formula was speed and defense, but Lane was not finished.

On April 30 Lane sequestered himself in a New York hotel room as he put the finishing touches on a complex three-cornered trade that packaged Gus Zernial, who had established a new Sox home run record in 1950 with 29, and Dave Philley to the Philadelphia A's via Cleveland for Minnie Minoso, a Cuban-born speedster originally signed by Bill Veeck.

Minoso shattered the White Sox color barrier in spectacular fashion by clouting a home run off Vic Raschi in his first at-bat on May 1. In that same game a Yankees rookie named Mickey Mantle clubbed his first career home run off Randy Gumpert.

Left: After a 14-game winning streak, excited White Sox fans welcome their heroes home from a long road trip at the train station.

Right: The "Go-Go" Sox knock the Yankees off of their first-place perch in the American League standings, May 30, 1951.

The White Sox were off and running, literally and figuratively. They began a 14-game winning streak on May 15. All but three of these victories occurred on foreign soil—Cleveland, Boston, New York, and Washington. When they returned to Chicago on May 28, with the second-longest winning streak in club history still intact, Mayor Martin Kennelly presented Charley Comiskey and his conquering heroes with the keys to the city.

Under Paul Richards' patient tutelage, the pitching jelled. Billy Pierce developed into a star. The youthful ace won 15 that year. Saul Rogovin, a sore-armed washout in Detroit, was acquired for Bob Cain early in the season. Sleepy-eyed Saul paced the junior circuit in earned run average in '51 while backing up "Billy the Kid" as the No. 2 starter.

Nineteen fifty-one was a remarkable, unforgettable year—truly the turning point in the sagging White Sox fortunes. Rescued from near oblivion by the quartet of Comiskey, Lane, Richards, and farm director John Rigney, the resurgent Sox remained in the thick of the pennant fight until July 20, when they dropped into fourth place and remained comfortably secure as a first-division ballclub until season's end.

It would not have turned out this way without the colorful, gregarious Minoso leading the way. He was an instant fan favorite whose presence in the lineup solidified the ballclub, but more importantly, Minnie's arrival in the 50th anniversary year of the White Sox' founding swept away the cobwebs of a troubled past.

A beam of sunlight had finally broken through the clouds. The most exciting, joyous era of White Sox baseball was under way, and the team was no fluke according to Casey Stengel. "I'll let you in on a little secret. The Sox are gonna' be up there a lot longer than most people figured!"

	G	AB	H	R	2B	3B	HR	RBI	SB	AVG
Eddie Robinson	151	564	159	85	23	5	29	117	2	.282
Nellie Fox	147	604	189	93	32	12	4	55	9	.313
Alfonso "Chico" Carrasquel	147	538	142	41	22	4	2	58	14	.264
Bob Dillinger	89	299	90	39	6	4	0	20	5	.301
Al Zarilla	120	382	98	56	21	2	10	60	2	.257
Jim Busby	143	477	135	59	15	2	5	68	26	.283
Orestes "Minnie" Minoso	138	516	167	109	32	14	10	74	31	.324
Phil Masi	84	225	61	24	11	2	4	28	1	.271
Floyd Baker	82	133	35	24	6	1	0	14	0	.263
Joe DeMaestri	56	74	15	8	0	2	1	3	0	.203
Bert Haas	25	43	7	1	0	1	1	2	0	.163
Hank Majeski	12	35	9	4	4	0	0	6	0	.257
Bob Boyd	12	18	3	3	0	1	0	4	0	.167
Gordon Goldsberry	10	11	1	4	0	0	0	1	0	.091
Eddie "Bud" Stewart	95	217	60	40	13	5	6	40	1	.276
Don Lenhardt	64	199	53	23	9	1	10	45	1	.266
Ray Coleman	51	181	50	21	8	7	3	21	2	.276
Paul Lehner	23	72	15	9	3	1	0	3	0	.208
Dave Philley	7	25	6	0	2	0	0	2	0	.240
Gus Zernial	4	19	2	2	0	0	0	4	0	.105
Gus Niahros	66	168	43	27	6	0	1	10	4	.256
Hollis "Bud" Sheely	34	89	16	2	2	0	0	7	0	.180
Joe Erautt	16	25	4	3	1	0	0	0	0	.160
Bob "Red" Wilson	4	11	3	1	1	0	0	0	0	.273
Sam Hairston	4	5	2	1	1	0	0	1	0	.400
Glenn "Rocky" Nelson	6	5	0	0	0	0	0	0	0	.000
		5,378	1,453	714	229	64	86	668	99	.270

	W	L	GS	CG	IP	H	BB	K	ShO	ERA
Billy Pierce	15	14	28	18	240⅓	237	73	113	1	3.03
Saul Rogovin	11	7	22	17	192⅔	166	67	77	3	2.48
Ken Holcombe	11	12	23	12	159⅓	142	68	39	2	3.78
Joe Dobson	7	6	21	6	146⅔	136	51	67	0	3.62
Randy Gumpert	9	8	16	7	141⅔	156	34	45	1	4.32
Lou Kretlow	6	9	18	7	137	129	74	89	1	4.20
Howie Judson	5	6	14	3	121⅔	124	55	43	0	3.77
Harry Dorish	5	6	4	2	96⅔	101	31	29	1	3.54
Luis Aloma	6	0	1	1	69⅓	52	24	25	1	1.82
Marv Rotblatt	4	2	2	0	47⅔	44	23	20	0	3.40
Bob Cain	1	2	4	1	26⅓	25	13	3	0	3.76
Ross Grimsley	0	0	0	0	14	12	10	8	0	3.86
Dick Littlefield	1	1	2	0	9⅔	9	17	7	0	8.38
Hal "Skinny" Brown	0	0	0	0	8⅔	15	4	4	0	9.35
Bob Mahoney	0	0	0	0	6⅔	5	5	3	0	5.40
	81	73	155	74	1,418⅓	1,353	549	572	10	3.50

1952

Record: 81–73
Finish: Third
Games Behind: 14
Manager: Paul Richards

Catching was Paul Richards' Achilles' heel in 1951. Lane corrected the problem in November by trading four players to the Browns for Sherm Lollar, a dependable backstop who drove in as many runs in 1951 as Phil Masi and four other White Sox catchers combined. "Jungle" Jim Rivera, a certifiable zany whom the fans had taken to heart in 1951, was dispatched to St. Louis in the Lollar trade, but was returned to Chicago on July 28 for J.W. Porter, a $40,000 bonus baby, and Ray Coleman.

By virtue of their close dealings with Bill Veeck and Veeck's warm regard for his old hometown, the White Sox enjoyed a consensual relationship with the St. Louis Browns, an American League doormat at this time. The Browns filled the bill as Chicago's unofficial "farm team" from 1951 to 1953. It was a tactic the Yankees would copy to perfection later in the decade in their business dealings with the hapless Kansas City A's.

The White Sox climbed a notch in the standings and closed the gap between themselves and Stengel's Yankees by three full games, but they were unable to improve on their 1951 record, and that failure was most disappointing to Paul Richards and the press, who expected much more out of the maturing Go-Go boys. The ballclub got off to a sluggish start and struggled to remain ahead of the .500 mark through mid-August.

Richards grew impatient with Chico Carrasquel, his chronically overweight shortstop, who fractured a finger and then was benched for poor play in August. Frank Lane dangled Chico before the Cleveland Indians for Larry Doby, but the fish weren't biting.

Having solved the catching dilemma, the Lane-Comiskey brain trust next turned their attention to the third-base muddle, but the best they could come up with was Hector "Hot Rod" Rodriguez, a 31-year-old Cuban who tore up the International League a year earlier. "He could be anywhere from good to the best there ever was!" Richards speculated.

The search for Atlantis...the Ark of the Covenant...and intelligent life in outer space had one modern parallel in the 1950s; and that was finding, someone...anyone...to man the hot corner.

Boys of summers past: Chico Carrasquel, Ferris Fain, Nellie Fox, Minnie Minoso, and Billy Pierce

	G	AB	H	R	2B	3B	HR	RBI	SB	AVG
Eddie Robinson	155	594	176	79	33	1	22	104	2	.296
Nellie Fox	152	648	192	76	25	10	0	39	5	.296
Alfonso "Chico" Carrasquel	100	359	89	36	7	4	1	42	2	.248
Hector Rodriguez	124	407	108	55	14	0	1	40	7	.265
Sam Mele	123	423	105	46	18	2	14	59	1	.248
Ray Coleman	85	195	42	19	7	1	2	14	0	.215
Orestes "Minnie" Minoso	147	569	160	96	24	9	13	61	22	.281
Sherman Lollar	132	375	90	35	15	0	13	50	1	.240
Willie Miranda	70	150	33	14	4	1	0	7	1	.220
Sam Dente	62	145	32	12	0	1	0	11	0	.221
Rocky Krsnich	40	91	21	11	7	2	1	15	0	.231
Leo Thomas	19	24	4	1	0	0	0	6	0	.167
Ken Landenberger	2	5	1	0	0	0	0	0	0	.200
Sammy Esposito	1	4	1	0	0	0	0	0	0	.250
Eddie "Bud" Stewart	92	225	60	23	10	0	5	30	3	.267
Jim Rivera	53	201	50	27	7	3	3	18	13	.249
Tom Wright	60	132	34	15	10	2	1	21	1	.258
Al Zarilla	39	99	23	14	4	1	2	7	1	.232
Jim Busby	16	39	5	5	0	0	0	0	0	.128
Hank Edwards	8	18	6	2	0	0	0	1	0	.333
George "Ted" Wilson	8	9	1	0	0	0	0	1	0	.111
Don Nicholas	3	2	0	0	0	0	0	0	0	.000
Hollis "Bud" Sheely	36	75	18	1	2	0	0	3	0	.240
Phil Masi	30	63	16	9	1	1	0	7	0	.254
Darrell Johnson	22	37	4	3	0	0	0	1	1	.108
Bob "Red" Wilson	2	3	0	0	0	0	0	0	0	.000
		5,316	1,337	610	199	38	80	560	61	.252

	W	L	GS	CG	IP	H	BB	K	ShO	ERA
Billy Pierce	15	12	32	14	255⅓	214	79	144	4	2.57
Saul Rogovin	14	9	30	12	231⅔	224	79	121	3	3.85
Joe Dobson	14	10	25	11	200⅔	164	60	101	3	2.51
Marv Grissom	12	10	24	7	166	156	79	97	1	3.74
Chuck Stobbs	7	12	17	2	135	118	72	73	0	3.13
Harry Dorish	8	4	1	1	91	66	42	47	0	2.47
Lou Kretlow	4	4	11	4	79	52	56	63	2	2.96
Hal "Skinny" Brown	2	3	8	1	72⅓	82	21	31	0	4.23
Bill Kennedy	2	2	1	0	70⅔	54	38	46	0	2.80
Luis Aloma	3	1	0	0	40	42	11	18	0	4.28
Ken Holcombe	0	5	7	1	35	38	18	12	0	6.17
Howie Judson	0	1	0	0	34	30	22	15	0	4.24
Hal Hudson	0	0	0	0	4	7	1	4	0	2.25
Al Widmar	0	0	0	0	2	4	0	2	0	4.50
	81	73	156	53	1,416⅔	1,251	578	774	13	3.25

1953

Record: 89–65
Finish: Third
Games Behind: 11½
Manager: Paul Richards

A February trade with the Red Sox brought Vern Stephens, the supposed missing link, to Chicago. Lane peddled three pitchers, Marv Grissom, Bill Kennedy, and Hal "Skinny" Brown, for Stephens.

Many of Frank Lane's trades looked good on paper and thus encouraged a wild ticket-buying frenzy in the winter months. The arrival of Stephens and Ferris "Burrhead" Fain, the American League batting champion for 1951 and 1952, looked awfully good to Sox fans who religiously followed the sports columns in their afternoon papers. To acquire first baseman Fain, the Sox traded Eddie Robinson, their only real home run threat, to Connie Mack's A's, along with Ed McGhee and Joe DeMaestri.

But it's results that count, and by midseason it was painfully obvious that Lane had been outfoxed by two of the grand old men of the game: Red Sox owner Tom Yawkey and venerable Connie Mack. Fain proved to be a costly flop. Vern Stephens was over the hill at 33 and off the team by July 31.

Ferris Fain was a hard-drinking troublemaker who was accused of shoving a row of lockers on top of Nellie Fox as he changed clothes in the clubhouse in an August series played in Washington. Ferris Fain was slapped with a $600 fine two days after belting a nightclub patron in the snoot in an after-hours altercation that was personally embarrassing to the wholesome family image the Comiskeys expected their athletes to uphold on and off the field.

The team improved despite Fain's repeated disruptions. Billy Pierce tossed a one-hitter in the second game of the season, en route to 18 victories and a glittering 2.72 ERA.

Minnie Minoso paced the junior circuit in thefts for the third season in a row, and the punchless White Sox compensated for a lack of offense by leading the league in fielding.

Paul Richards' team kept pace with the Yankees through the early summer months and trailed the leaders by only 4½ games when August began. Harry Dorish provided the bullpen help. And the St. Louis "express" rolled merrily down the track. Bill Veeck delivered Virgil "Fire" Trucks to Chicago for Lou Kretlow and $95,000 in cash on the eve of the trading deadline. Trucks won 15 of 21 decisions with the Sox in 1953 to become a 20-game winner for the first and only time of his career.

What made the Go-Go Sox so fascinating to watch in the early years of the 1950s was their utter unpredictability. For the second time in three years manager Richards moved a starting pitcher into the field in order to utilize a relief specialist against one or two batters at a decisive moment in the game.

The unusual bit of strategy worked like a charm on June 25, when Billy Pierce was shifted to first base in order to bring in Harry Dorish to face Hank Bauer and Gil McDougald. Pinch-hitter Don Bollweg pushed a bunt toward Pierce, who fielded it flawlessly. Bollweg was safe by an eyelash, but Dorish managed to preserve a hard-earned 4–2 victory over the Yanks.

	G	AB	H	R	2B	3B	HR	RBI	SB	AVG
Ferris Fain	128	446	114	73	18	2	6	52	3	.256
Nellie Fox	154	624	178	92	31	8	3	72	4	.285
Alfonso "Chico" Carrasquel	149	552	154	72	30	4	2	47	5	.279
Bob Elliott	67	208	54	24	11	1	4	32	1	.260
Sam Mele	140	481	132	64	26	8	12	82	3	.274
Jim Rivera	156	567	147	79	26	16	11	78	22	.259
Orestes "Minnie" Minoso	157	556	174	104	24	8	15	104	25	.313
Sherman Lollar	113	334	96	46	19	0	8	54	1	.287
Bobby Boyd	55	165	49	20	6	2	3	23	1	.297
Rocky Krsnich	64	129	26	9	8	0	1	14	0	.202
Vern Stephens	44	129	24	14	6	0	1	14	2	.186
Freddie Marsh	67	95	19	22	1	0	2	2	0	.200
Connie Ryan	17	54	12	6	1	0	0	6	2	.222
Neil Berry	5	8	1	1	0	0	0	0	0	.125
Sam Dente	2	0	0	0	0	0	0	0	0	.000
Tom Wright	77	132	33	14	5	3	2	25	0	.250
Eddie "Bud" Stewart	53	59	16	16	2	0	2	13	1	.271
Bill Wilson	9	17	1	1	0	0	0	1	0	.059
Allie Clark	9	15	1	0	0	0	0	0	0	.067
Bob "Red" Wilson	71	164	41	21	6	1	0	10	2	.250
Hollis "Bud" Sheely	31	46	10	4	1	0	0	2	0	.217
		5,212	1,345	716	226	53	74	669	73	.258

	W	L	GS	CG	IP	H	BB	K	ShO	ERA
Billy Pierce	18	12	33	19	271⅓	216	102	186	7	2.72
Virgil Trucks	15	6	21	13	176⅓	151	67	102	3	2.86
Mike Fornieles	8	7	16	5	153	160	61	72	0	3.59
Harry Dorish	10	6	6	2	145⅔	140	52	69	0	3.40
Saul Rogovin	7	12	19	4	131	151	48	62	1	5.22
Sandy Consuegra	7	5	13	5	124	122	28	30	1	2.54
Joe Dobson	5	5	15	3	100⅔	96	37	50	1	3.67
Bob Keegan	7	5	11	4	98⅔	80	33	32	2	2.74
Connie Johnson	4	4	10	2	60⅔	55	38	44	1	3.56
Gene Bearden	3	3	3	0	58⅓	48	33	24	0	2.93
Luis Aloma	2	0	0	0	38⅓	41	23	23	0	4.70
Lou Kretlow	0	0	3	0	20⅔	12	30	15	0	3.48
Tommy Byrne	2	0	6	0	16	18	26	4	0	10.13
Earl Harrist	1	0	0	0	8⅓	9	5	1	0	7.56
Hal Hudson	0	0	0	0	⅔	0	0	0	0	0.00
	89	65	156	57	1,403⅔	1,299	583	714	16	3.41

1954

Record: 94–60
Finish: Third
Games Behind: 17
Managers: Paul Richards, Marty Marion

"The Yanks are indisputably on the downgrade!" observed Paul Richards just before the new season got going. It was hard to fathom the meaning of Richards' words. The Bronx Bombers were just as formidable as ever, winning 103 ballgames. There was one important difference, however. The Cleveland Indians led by Al Lopez won 111 games in 1954, shattering all existing American League records for winning percentage.

With expectations running high for that elusive pennant, the Sox broke camp no closer to solving the third-base riddle than in the three previous years. Minnie Minoso opened the season at third base—a stopgap measure until Frank Lane could work something out with his fellow GMs.

Finally, a month into the campaign, Lane traded reserve infielder Grady Hatton and $100,000 cash to the Red Sox for George Kell, a solid hitter for many years but well past his prime and suffering from back spasms. It was Lane's 196th transaction as general manager since 1948. The next day he completed No. 197.

Coming to the Sox in a brilliant public relations coup that stunned and annoyed the crosstown Cubbies was free agent first baseman Phil Cavarretta, who had been let go in spring training after 20 years of faithful service to the Wrigleys, first as a player and then winding up as their manager. Cavarretta played well in a part-time role with the Sox and was rewarded by management with his own special night on September 14.

In 1954 Billy Pierce suffered an uncharacteristic off year, but Sandy Consuegra posted a 16–3 record, and Jack Harshman, a converted first baseman who toiled in the Giants farm system for eight years, won 14 games. Harshman struck out 16 Red Sox batters on July 25 to establish a new single-game team record.

Through the early weeks of June, the Sox, the Indians, and the Yankees ran neck and neck. The Hose won 26 of 36 games on the road during one important stretch, but torn knee cartilage hobbled George Kell on July 2. The injury was most costly.

The season was shaping up to be the finest pennant race in many a year, but as the days grew shorter, the White Sox lost their momentum and fell back. When September rolled around, Chicago trailed its two rivals by 9½ games amid rumors of imminent change in the front office.

When Richards demanded a three-year contract calling for $40,000 a year from Mrs. Comiskey, he was politely rebuffed. This rejection was another example of the penny-wise, pound-foolish kind of thinking that had guided Grace Comiskey since she began taking an active role in White Sox policy making in 1940.

On August 27 Frank Lane granted his manager permission to talk to the Baltimore Orioles about the position of general manager in their organization. The "sound and the fury" that had existed for some time between the stormy

Lane and his equally determined manager was hardly a secret to the media. Richards wanted to be his own man with a fresh chance to build a ballclub from scratch. The Orioles afforded him that opportunity.

Paul Richards was lost to Baltimore on September 10 and was immediately replaced by 36-year-old Marty Marion, the ex-Cardinals shortstop who lost his last manager's job in St. Louis when the Browns decamped for Baltimore after the 1953 season. The reticent Marion never warmed up to the city of Chicago or its fans. His heart was in St. Louis, though neither Lane nor Comiskey suspected as much when they hired him. Sometimes, though, you have to take one step back in order to move two steps forward. Such was the case with the unhappy Marty Marion–White Sox union.

	G	AB	H	R	2B	3B	HR	RBI	SB	AVG
Ferris Fain	65	235	71	30	10	1	5	51	5	.302
Nellie Fox	155	631	201	111	24	8	2	47	16	.319
Alfonso "Chico" Carrasquel	155	620	158	106	28	3	12	62	7	.255
Cass Michaels	101	282	74	35	13	2	7	44	10	.262
Jim Rivera	145	490	140	62	16	8	13	61	18	.286
Johnny Groth	125	422	116	41	20	0	7	60	3	.275
Orestes "Minnie" Minoso	153	568	182	119	29	18	19	116	18	.320
Sherman Lollar	107	316	77	31	13	0	7	34	0	.244
George Kell	71	233	66	25	10	0	5	48	1	.283
Phil Cavarretta	71	158	50	21	6	0	3	24	4	.316
Freddie Marsh	62	98	30	21	5	2	0	4	4	.306
Ron Jackson	40	93	26	10	4	0	4	10	2	.280
Grady Hatton	13	30	5	3	1	0	0	3	1	.167
Joe Kirrene	9	23	7	4	1	0	0	4	1	.304
Stan Jok	3	12	2	1	0	0	0	2	0	.167
Ed McGhee	42	75	17	12	1	0	0	5	5	.227
Willard Marshall	47	71	18	7	2	0	1	7	0	.254
Bob Boyd	29	56	10	10	3	0	0	5	2	.179
Bill Wilson	20	35	6	4	1	0	2	5	0	.171
Eddie "Bud" Stewart	18	13	1	0	0	0	0	0	0	.077
Don Nicholas	7	0	0	3	0	0	0	0	0	.000
Matt Batts	55	158	36	16	7	1	3	19	0	.228
Carl Sawatski	43	109	20	6	3	3	1	12	0	.183
Bob "Red" Wilson	8	20	4	2	0	0	1	1	0	.200
		5,168	1,382	711	203	47	94	655	98	.267

Career Cub Phil Cavarretta donned the Sox pinstripes in 1954.

	W	L	GS	CG	IP	H	BB	K	ShO	ERA
Virgil Trucks	19	12	33	16	264⅔	224	95	152	5	2.79
Bob Keegan	16	9	27	14	209⅔	211	82	61	2	3.09
Billy Pierce	9	10	26	12	188⅔	179	86	148	4	3.48
Jack Harshman	14	8	21	9	177	157	96	134	4	2.95
Sandy Consuegra	16	3	17	3	154	142	35	31	2	2.69
Don Johnson	8	7	16	3	144	129	43	68	3	3.13
Harry Dorish	6	4	6	2	109	88	29	48	1	2.72
Morrie Martin	5	4	2	1	70	52	24	31	0	2.06
Mike Fornieles	1	2	6	0	42	41	14	18	0	4.29
Dick Strahs	0	0	0	0	14⅓	16	8	8	0	5.65
Al Sima	0	1	1	0	7	11	2	1	0	5.14
Tom Flanigan	0	0	0	0	1⅔	1	1	0	0	0.00
Vito Valentinetti	0	0	0	0	1	4	2	1	0	54.00
	94	60	155	60	1,383	1,255	517	701	21	3.05

1955

Record: 91–63
Finish: Third
Games Behind: 5
Manager: Marty Marion

Bob Kennedy, the veteran infielder who returned to Chicago on May 30, had this theory about the 1955 season: "We missed the championship by eight inches...the eight-inch incision the surgeon made when he removed Dick Donovan's appendix!"

Richard Edward Donovan was plucked from the obscurity of the Southern Association and thrust into a starting role behind Trucks, Pierce, and Harshman. With a few refinements made to Donovan's deceptive slider pitch, he won 13 of 17 decisions before undergoing an emergency appendectomy in Washington on July 31 at the critical moment when the White Sox protected a one-game, first-place lead.

In a spectacular eruption of power—unparalleled in modern baseball—the White Sox erupted for 29 runs against the hapless Kansas City A's on April 23. Chicago banged out 29 hits and seven home runs that set the tone for the exciting days yet to come.

The White Sox held down first place for 27 hectic days and were in a virtual dead heat with Cleveland and New York on Labor Day. Nellie Fox and Minnie Minoso paced the offense, which had been given an added infusion of home run power with big Walt Dropo installed at first base. The 116 round-trippers set a new team record for a White Sox team that was by far the strongest of the 1950s Go-Go teams to grace the Comiskey diamond.

Marty Marion, who was accused of a defeatist attitude while guiding the Browns at the tail end of their lame-duck season in St. Louis, imposed a series of hefty fines on his athletes for breaking training rules. Marion never shied away from benching unproductive veterans or speaking his mind to the press. Marty did his level best to emulate the Paul Richards style. But he toiled in the shadow.

Frank Lane and Charley Comiskey were disappointed in Marion's performance over the course of the season. They believed they had provided their new manager with the necessary firepower and a balanced pitching staff to finally carry this club over the top after four years of first-division apprenticeship.

Marion saw matters in a different light, even as he was being blamed for the mid-September collapse that cost the Sox the pennant. A managerial change might have occurred sooner if not for Frank Lane's announcement of his resignation on September 21.

His seven-year tenure, which witnessed 241 transactions involving 353 players, ended in a bitter turf dispute with Charley Comiskey, who refused to retract a public reprimand he made against Lane that *Chicago American* columnist Warren Brown played up big in the press.

Frank Lane had been fined $500 by Commissioner Ford Frick for his comments to umpire chief Cal Hubbard and Larry Napp in an explosive tirade during an August 30 game in Comiskey Park. Lane was even more incensed later on: "Here I am sticking up for my club and players, and another official criticizes me for it!" Lane took his verbal punches at Charley Comiskey and moved on to the St. Louis Cardinals, where his career and reputation slowly began to unravel.

	G	AB	H	R	2B	3B	HR	RBI	SB	AVG
Walt Dropo	141	453	127	55	15	2	19	79	0	.280
Nellie Fox	154	636	198	100	28	7	6	59	7	.311
Alfonso "Chico" Carrasquel	145	523	134	83	11	2	11	52	1	.256
George Kell	128	429	134	44	24	1	8	81	2	.312
Jim Rivera	147	454	120	71	24	4	10	52	25	.264
Jim Busby	99	337	82	38	13	4	1	27	7	.243
Orestes "Minnie" Minoso	139	517	149	79	26	7	10	70	19	.288
Sherman Lollar	138	426	111	67	13	1	16	61	2	.261
Bob Kennedy	83	214	65	28	10	2	9	43	0	.304
Ron Jackson	40	74	15	10	1	1	2	7	1	.203
Jim Bridewester	34	58	12	6	3	2	0	4	0	.207
Vern Stephens	22	56	14	10	3	0	3	7	0	.250
Bobby Adams	28	21	2	8	0	1	0	3	0	.095
Carl "Buddy" Peterson	6	21	6	7	1	0	0	2	0	.286
Phil Cavarretta	6	4	0	1	0	0	0	0	0	.000
Sammy Esposito	3	4	0	3	0	0	0	0	0	.000
Stan Jok	6	4	1	3	0	0	1	2	0	.250
Bob Nieman	99	272	77	36	11	2	11	53	1	.283
Johnny Groth	32	77	26	13	7	0	2	11	1	.338
Williard Marshall	22	41	7	6	0	0	0	6	0	.171
Gil Coan	17	17	3	0	0	0	0	1	0	.176
Ron Northey	14	14	5	1	2	0	1	4	0	.357
Ed McGhee	26	13	1	6	0	0	0	0	2	.077
Ed White	3	4	2	0	0	0	0	0	0	.500
Les Moss	32	59	15	5	2	0	2	7	0	.254
Clint Courtney	19	37	14	7	3	0	1	10	0	.378
Earl Battey	5	7	2	1	0	0	0	0	0	.286
Lloyd Merriman	1	1	0	0	0	0	0	0	0	.000
Bob Powell	1	0	0	0	0	0	0	0	0	.000
		5,220	1,401	725	204	36	116	677	69	.268

	W	L	GS	CG	IP	H	BB	K	ShO	ERA
Billy Pierce	15	10	26	16	205⅔	162	64	157	6	1.97
Dick Donovan	15	9	24	11	187	186	48	88	5	3.32
Jack Harshman	11	7	23	9	179⅓	144	97	116	0	3.36
Virgil Trucks	13	8	26	7	175	176	61	91	3	3.96
Sandy Consuegra	6	5	7	3	126⅓	120	18	35	0	2.64
Connie Johnson	7	4	16	5	99	95	52	72	2	3.45
Harry Byrd	4	6	12	1	91	85	30	44	1	4.65
Mike Fornieles	6	3	9	2	86⅓	84	29	23	0	3.86
Millard "Dixie" Howell	8	3	0	0	73⅔	70	25	25	0	2.93
Bob Keegan	2	5	11	1	58⅔	83	28	29	0	5.83
Morrie Martin	2	3	0	0	52	50	22	22	0	3.63
Harry Dorish	2	0	0	0	17	16	9	6	0	1.59
Bob Chakales	0	0	0	0	12⅓	11	6	6	0	1.46
Al Papai	0	0	0	0	11⅔	10	8	5	0	3.86
Ted Gray	0	0	1	0	3	9	2	1	0	18.00
	91	63	155	55	1,378	1,301	499	720	17	3.37

A trio of White Sox—(from left) Minnie Minoso, Jack Harshman, and Jim Rivera—taking life easy in the heat of the 1955 flag chase.

1956

Record: 85–69
Finish: Third
Games Behind: 12
Manager: Marty Marion

Charley Comiskey and John Rigney divided Frank Lane's front-office responsibilities between them, and the business of baseball went on. The White Sox failed to roll over and die on cue as "Frantic Frankie" predicted—or might have even secretly wished.

The 1956 edition continued in a third-place holding pattern, but in so doing they matched the historic accomplishments of the vintage "dead-ball era" Sox who finished in the first division six years in a row (1904–1909).

Hitless Wonder Sox (1904–1909)	Go-Go Sox (1951–1956)
527–385 .578	521–403 .564

The Comiskey-Rigney alliance completed its first trade in October 1955, and it was an eye-opener. Chico Carrasquel was dealt to Cleveland for power-hitting Larry Doby, whom the White Sox had wanted for many years. Doby added left-handed power to the lineup, but more importantly he freed up the shortstop position for Memphis phenom Luis Ernesto Aparicio, a Venezuelan speedster coveted by Clark Griffith and other envious AL magnates who had an occasion to preview Louie's work in the minors. Aparicio was a revelation. He appeared in 152 games, paced the league in stolen bases, and was the hands-down choice for Rookie of the Year.

June 24, 1956. Larry Doby, Billy Pierce, and Sherm Lollar signal three straight over the mighty Yankees after thrashing the Bombers 14–2 in the first game of a twin bill. The Sox went on to complete the sweep.

The 1956 season boiled down to a weekend of thrills in Comiskey Park, June 22–24, when the inspired Go-Go boys swept a four-game series against the Yankees before the largest paying crowds of the year. There were fights galore. Dave Philley scored a TKO in a donnybrook with Yankees pitcher Bob Grim—retaliation for beaning Minnie Minoso in the skull a year earlier. Larry Doby emerged from a season-long slump with three towering home runs and seven RBIs. All in all, it was the most satisfying weekend of baseball in many a year, if only because it afforded Sox fans the rare opportunity to stick the needle into the sides of the Yankees fans who frequented Comiskey Park.

Chicago captured their ninth game in a row on June 26—before losing 11 straight to lesser opponents beginning a week later. When the dust settled, the Sox trailed the Yanks by 12½ games, their pennant hopes up in smoke. Marty Marion had blown his one chance to redeem himself for the 1955 disappointment.

Whenever Marion saw an opportunity to escape to his St. Louis home for an off-day sabbatical, he did so with relish. Toward the end of the season, the Sox manager, whose job hung by the thread to begin with, blew off an important organizational meeting in order to be with his family. And that cinched it for Comiskey, who had been secretly courting Al Lopez for Chicago for weeks. The Indian skipper was on his way out in Cleveland.

Marion submitted his resignation with startling swiftness on October 24. His parting shot: "Chuck, if you're lucky enough to get Lopez, try to get him to bring along his Cleveland pitching staff. That would really give the White Sox a lift." Five days later, "Señor" Lopez inked a one-year contract with the Sox. In six seasons at the Cleveland helm, the easygoing but astute Lopez never finished lower than second. "The Yankees are a good club, but they can be had," Lopez cheerfully predicted. "The White Sox have a chance to go all the way in '57!"

	G	AB	H	R	2B	3B	HR	RBI	SB	AVG
Walt Dropo	125	361	96	42	13	1	8	52	1	.266
Nellie Fox	154	649	192	109	20	10	4	52	8	.296
Luis Aparicio	152	533	142	69	19	6	3	56	21	.266
Fred Hatfield	106	321	84	46	9	1	7	33	1	.262
Jim Rivera	139	491	125	76	23	5	12	66	20	.255
Larry Doby	140	504	135	89	22	3	24	102	0	.268
Orestes "Minnie" Minoso	151	545	172	106	29	11	21	88	12	.316
Sherman Lollar	136	450	132	55	28	2	11	75	2	.293
Dave Philley	86	279	74	44	14	2	4	47	1	.265
Sammy Esposito	81	184	42	30	8	2	3	25	1	.228
George Kell	21	80	25	7	5	0	1	11	0	.313
Ron Jackson	22	56	12	7	3	0	1	4	1	.214
Bob Kennedy	8	13	1	0	0	0	0	0	0	.077
Jim Brideweser	10	11	2	0	1	0	0	1	0	.182
John "Bubba" Phillips	67	99	27	16	6	0	2	11	1	.273
Ron Northey	53	48	17	4	2	0	3	23	0	.354
Jim Delsing	55	41	5	11	3	0	0	2	1	.122
Bob Nieman	14	40	12	3	1	0	2	4	0	.300
Cal Abrams	4	3	1	0	0	0	0	0	0	.333
Les Moss	56	127	31	20	4	0	10	22	0	.244
Earl Battey	4	4	1	1	0	0	0	0	0	.250
		5,286	1,412	776	218	43	128	726	70	.267

	W	L	GS	CG	IP	H	BB	K	ShO	ERA
Billy Pierce	20	9	33	21	276⅓	261	100	192	1	3.32
Dick Donovan	12	10	31	14	234⅔	212	59	120	3	3.64
Jack Harshman	15	11	30	15	226⅔	183	102	143	4	3.10
Jim Wilson	9	12	21	6	159⅔	149	70	82	3	4.06
Bob Keegan	5	7	16	4	105⅓	119	35	32	0	3.93
Gerry Staley	8	3	10	5	101⅔	98	20	25	0	2.92
Millard "Dixie" Howell	5	6	1	0	64⅓	79	36	28	0	4.62
Paul LaPalme	3	1	0	0	45⅔	31	27	23	0	2.36
Sandy Consuegra	1	2	1	0	38⅓	45	11	7	0	5.17
Ellis Kinder	3	1	0	0	29⅔	33	8	19	0	2.73
Howie Pollet	3	1	4	0	26⅓	27	11	14	0	4.10
Jim McDonald	0	2	3	0	18⅔	29	7	10	0	8.68
Morrie Martin	1	0	0	0	18⅓	21	7	9	0	4.91
Mike Fornieles	0	1	0	0	15⅔	22	6	6	0	4.60
Connie Johnson	0	1	2	0	12⅓	11	7	6	0	3.65
Jim Derrington	0	1	1	0	6	9	6	3	0	7.50
Harry Byrd	0	1	1	0	4⅓	9	4	0	0	10.38
Jerry Dahlke	0	0	0	0	2⅓	5	6	1	0	19.29
Bill Fischer	0	0	0	0	1⅔	6	1	2	0	21.60
Dick Marlowe	0	0	0	0	1	2	1	0	0	9.00
	85	69	154	65	1,389	1,351	524	722	11	3.73

1957

Record: 90–64
Finish: Second
Games Behind: 8
Manager: Al Lopez

The Señor spoke freely of a coming pennant, but the golden chalice was still two years away. The unsettled infield situation precluded this team from serious contention.

The White Sox were tight up the middle but very weak at the corners. Nellie Fox and Luis Aparicio were diamond magicians. Bubba Phillips and Jungle Jim Rivera, converted outfielders who were assigned to third and first, respectively, were not. The experiment ended when Charley Comiskey dealt Dave Philley to Detroit for Earl Torgeson, a hard-edged first baseman who solved one-half of the infield problem... for the time being.

The club got off to a spectacular start, winning 22 of the first 30 to claim an early four-game lead. Chicago's first-place margin increased to six games on June 9. It was the South Sider's biggest lead since the ill-fated 1919 pennant year.

The frustration of constantly losing to the Yankees took an early toll on Lopez, who banged his fist on his Comiskey Park desk following a particularly galling 3–2 loss on June 11. "Just one game I'd like to win for these people!" Al Lopez had managed in Casey Stengel's shadow in Cleveland, and so it continued in Chicago.

After Sherm Lollar's right wrist was broken on June 20, the White Sox sputtered. Lollar was lost for 41 days. When he returned, they had fallen behind New York by seven games. They closed the gap to only 4½ games on September 7 but could draw no closer. The Yankees were just too good. They were the only AL ballclub to win a season series against the White Sox in 1957. Six of the 14 losses to New York were by one run.

Finishing second was a refreshing departure for the restructured ownership, who had tired of the monotonous third-place refrain.

Grace Comiskey, beset with a heart ailment and chronic drinking problems that often clouded her judgment, passed away on December 10, 1956. She bequeathed majority control of the ballclub to her daughter Dorothy. This decision was a painful rebuke to her only son; Charley Comiskey had been inching ever closer to the larger role he seemed destined to play in White Sox matters before fate intervened.

The upswing in White Sox fortunes in 1957 had a lot to do with the calming presence of Al Lopez in the dugout, but Charley Comiskey's front-office role in hiring the Señor cannot be overlooked. Charley's failure to reach a suitable accommodation with his whining, bullheaded sister, whose only desire was to exit the public realm, checkmated him at the hour of decision.

	G	AB	H	R	2B	3B	HR	RBI	SB	AVG
Earl Torgeson	86	251	74	53	11	2	7	46	7	.295
Nellie Fox	155	619	196	110	27	8	6	61	5	.317
Luis Aparicio	143	575	148	82	22	6	3	41	28	.257
John "Bubba" Phillips	121	393	106	38	13	3	7	42	5	.270
Jim Landis	96	274	58	38	11	3	2	16	14	.212
Larry Doby	119	416	120	57	27	2	14	79	2	.288
Orestes "Minnie" Minoso	153	568	176	96	36	5	12	103	18	.310
Sherman Lollar	101	351	90	33	11	2	11	70	2	.256
Walt Dropo	93	223	57	24	2	0	13	49	0	.256
Sammy Esposito	94	176	36	26	3	0	2	15	5	.205
Fred Hatfield	69	114	23	14	3	0	0	8	1	.202
Ron Jackson	13	60	19	4	3	0	2	8	0	.317
Jim Rivera	125	402	103	51	21	6	14	52	18	.256
Ted Beard	38	78	16	15	1	0	0	7	3	.205
Dave Philley	22	71	23	9	4	0	0	9	1	.324
Earl Battey	48	115	20	12	2	3	3	6	0	.174
Les Moss	42	115	31	10	3	0	2	12	0	.270
Ron Northey	40	27	5	0	1	0	0	7	0	.185
Bob Kennedy	4	2	0	0	0	0	0	0	0	.000
Bob Powell	1	0	0	1	0	0	0	0	0	.000
		5,265	1,369	707	209	41	106	670	109	.260

Uneasy allies: Bill Veeck and Charley Comiskey ponder a solution to baseball's problems.

	W	L	GS	CG	IP	H	BB	K	ShO	ERA
Billy Pierce	20	12	34	16	257	228	71	171	4	3.26
Dick Donovan	16	6	28	16	220⅔	203	45	88	2	2.77
Jim Wilson	15	8	29	12	201⅔	189	65	100	5	3.48
Jack Harshman	8	8	26	6	151⅓	142	82	83	0	4.10
Bob Keegan	10	8	20	6	142⅔	131	37	36	2	3.53
Bill Fischer	7	8	11	3	124	139	35	48	1	3.48
Gerry Staley	5	1	0	0	105	95	27	44	0	2.06
Millard "Dixie" Howell	6	5	0	0	68⅓	64	30	37	0	3.29
Paul LaPalme	1	4	0	0	40⅓	35	19	19	0	3.35
Jim Derrington	0	1	5	0	37	29	29	14	0	4.86
Jim McDonald	0	1	0	0	22⅓	18	10	12	0	2.01
Barry Latman	1	2	2	0	12⅓	12	13	9	0	8.03
Don Rudolph	1	0	0	0	12	6	2	2	0	2.25
Jim Hughes	0	0	0	0	5	12	3	2	0	10.80
Ellis Kinder	0	0	0	0	1	0	1	0	0	0.00
Stover McIlwain	0	0	0	0	1	2	1	0	0	0.00
	90	64	155	59	1,401⅔	1,305	470	665	14	3.35

1958

Record: 82–72
Finish: Second
Games Behind: 10
Manager: Al Lopez

With Frank Lane back in the American League after a two-year absence (this time with Cleveland), Sox fans did not have to wait long for the kettle to begin to boil. On December 4, 1957, Lane completed his first American League deal with his former employers by shipping Early Wynn and Al Smith—mainstays of the Indian glory years—to Chicago for Minnie Minoso and light-hitting infielder Fred Hatfield. The trade was a shocker, and the howls of fan displeasure in both cities echoed from the shores of Lake Erie all the way to Lake Michigan. "I have just traded the White Sox into the pennant!" Lane grinned. His sarcasm was unmistakable—but his words were prophetic.

Twenty-four hours earlier the Rigney-Comiskey-Lopez alliance had dealt Larry Doby, Jack Harshman, and two minor leaguers to Baltimore for pitcher Ray Moore, outfielder Tito Francona, and third baseman Billy Goodman. The White Sox brain trust was satisfied they had finally solved the third-base puzzle once and for all—at the cost of Doby, who not only disliked Al Lopez, but would later accuse the Señor of racism. It was an accusation that was hard to fathom. Al Lopez was one of the most even-tempered managers the game had ever known, and never before had this charge surfaced.

The controversial trades cleared two roster positions for a pair of highly publicized rookie outfielders Comiskey was anxious to promote from the ballclub's Indianapolis affiliate: Johnny Callison and Jim Landis. Callison, a power-hitting sensation with all the "tools," required further seasoning at Triple-A. After a slow start, however, Jim Landis solved the team's center-field problem nicely. As a glove man, he was without peer. His speed and grace in the spacious outfield pastures of Comiskey Park were reminiscent of Johnny Mostil, who tutored Landis on outfield play.

There wasn't much to say about the 1958 pennant "race." From a White Sox perspective, the issue was settled by May 20, when the gap between New York and Chicago ballooned to 10½ games. The champions won 19 of their first 24, and then awaited the opening of the 1958 World Series.

Beginning on June 13 and continuing through the end of the season, the Sox played at a .588 pace. Unfortunately there was too much ground to overcome in so short a period of time. Chicago claimed second place on August 11, but could draw no closer than to within nine games of the Bombers.

Billy Pierce enjoyed his last truly outstanding White Sox season in 1958. In late June he pitched three consecutive shutouts, including a near-perfect game against the Washington Senators on the 27th. Billy's heroic effort was foiled by pinch-hitter Ed Fitzgerald with two outs in the ninth inning. In all, Pierce recorded eight low-hit games in 1958, but that one ill-fated pitch to Fitzgerald cast a pall over Billy's season and undoubtedly has cost him rightful admission to the Hall of Fame.

The proceedings between the white lines were largely anticlimactic to the larger drama off the field. Unable to reconcile philosophical and personal differences with her brother Charley, Dorothy Comiskey Rigney granted Bill Veeck and his syndicate a 60-day option to purchase her 54 percent controlling interest in the ballclub. A long and bitter stock fight between the Comiskey siblings that dated back to 1957 ended unhappily for Charley when a probate judge paved the way for Veeck and his partners to buy the White Sox on March 6, 1959.

The appeals would drag on into late 1960, but the situation was hopeless for young Comiskey, whose sister knowingly violated a covenant originally set forth by the Old Roman and his son, Lou. Before another three years passed, the Comiskey name would disappear from the corporate masthead altogether.

	G	AB	H	R	2B	3B	HR	RBI	SB	AVG
Earl Torgeson	96	188	50	37	8	0	10	30	7	.266
Nellie Fox	155	623	187	82	21	6	0	49	5	.300
Luis Aparicio	145	557	148	76	20	9	2	40	29	.266
Billy Goodman	116	425	127	41	15	5	0	40	1	.299
Jim Rivera	116	276	62	37	8	4	9	35	21	.225
Jim Landis	142	523	145	72	23	7	15	64	19	.277
Al Smith	139	480	121	61	23	5	12	58	3	.252
Sherman Lollar	127	421	115	53	16	0	20	84	2	.273
John "Bubba" Phillips	84	260	71	26	10	0	5	30	3	.273
Ray Boone	77	246	60	25	12	1	7	41	1	.244
Ron Jackson	61	146	34	19	4	0	7	21	2	.233
Sammy Esposito	98	81	20	16	3	0	0	3	1	.247
Walt Dropo	28	52	10	3	1	0	2	8	0	.192
Don Mueller	70	166	42	7	5	0	0	16	0	.253
Tito Francona	41	128	33	10	3	2	1	10	2	.258
Johnny Callison	18	64	19	10	4	2	1	12	1	.297
Ted Beard	19	22	2	5	0	0	1	2	3	.091
Jim McAnany	5	13	0	0	0	0	0	0	0	.000
Norm Cash	13	8	2	2	0	0	0	0	0	.250
Earl Battey	68	168	38	24	8	0	8	26	1	.226
John Romano	4	7	2	1	0	0	0	1	0	.286
Chuck Lindstrom	1	1	1	1	0	1	0	1	0	1.000
Les Moss	2	1	0	0	0	0	0	0	0	.000
		5,249	1,348	634	191	42	101	594	101	.257

	W	L	GS	CG	IP	H	BB	K	ShO	ERA
Dick Donovan	15	14	34	16	248	240	53	127	4	3.01
Billy Pierce	17	11	32	19	245	204	66	144	3	2.68
Early Wynn	14	16	34	11	239⅔	214	104	179	4	4.13
Jim Wilson	9	9	23	4	155⅔	156	63	70	1	4.10
Ray Moore	9	7	20	4	136⅔	107	70	73	2	3.82
Gerry Staley	4	5	0	0	85⅓	81	24	27	0	3.16
Bob Shaw	4	2	3	0	64	67	28	18	0	4.64
Barry Latman	3	0	3	1	47⅔	27	17	28	1	0.76
Tom Qualters	0	0	0	0	43	45	20	14	0	4.19
Omar "Turk" Lown	3	3	0	0	40⅔	49	28	40	0	3.98
Bill Fischer	2	3	3	0	36⅓	43	13	16	0	6.69
Bob Keegan	0	2	2	0	29⅔	44	18	8	0	6.07
Don Rudolph	1	0	0	0	7	4	5	2	0	2.57
Stover McIlwain	0	0	1	0	4	4	0	4	0	2.25
Hal Trosky, Jr.	1	0	0	0	3	5	2	1	0	6.00
Jim McDonald	0	0	0	0	2⅓	6	4	0	0	19.29
Millard "Dixie" Howell	0	0	0	0	1⅔	0	0	0	0	0.00
	82	72	155	55	1,389⅔	1,296	515	751	15	3.61

1959

Record: 94–60
Finish: First
Games Ahead: 5
Manager: Al Lopez

The season began in a courtroom. It ended in a riotous celebration when 25,000 bleary-eyed celebrants jammed Chicago's Midway Airport to welcome home their conquering heroes who had vanquished the Cleveland Indians 4–2 along the shores of Lake Erie to wrap up the first White Sox pennant since 1919. In many respects, this was a "surprise pennant," given the advancing age of this ballclub, the historic problems at first and third, and of course the Yankees, who had made it all look so easy in 1958.

"The Yankees can be had this year," Lopez drawled. But hadn't he said that once before, in 1957? The Chicago press corps took a more sobering view of the season at hand. Edgar Munzel of the *Sun-Times* declared that second place was the "absolute ceiling" for this team. He added that the Sox could sink as low as fourth.

The *Comiskey* v. *Veeck* and *Comiskey* courtroom contretemps caused the players to take a "watch and wait" attitude concerning the signing of their 1959 contracts. They believed they could finagle more money out of the wild-spending Veeck than the Comiskeys. And these issues, of course, made it hard for Lopez to run his spring training camp. Would tall, rangy Ron Jackson finally be ready to take over first base? What about the kid Norm Cash?

The answer to the first-base question was slow in coming—Sox fans had to wait until August 25, when Ted Kluszewski, a 230-pound home run terror, was claimed on waivers from the Pittsburgh Pirates. But in April Bill Veeck had tried to plug the hole by offering cash-strapped Senators owner Clark Griffith $250,000 for Roy Sievers and pitcher Pedro Ramos. Lopez wisely advised Veeck to relax and enjoy the ride. The deal was put on hold for the time being.

Saddled by injuries and lengthy contract holdouts, the Yankees plummeted into the cellar on May 30. They were never a factor in the 1959 flag chase.

The challenge for AL supremacy revolved around the Cleveland Indians, a ballclub traumatized by the presence of the meddling Frank Lane, who had dealt Early "Gus" Wynn, an ace in the hole, to the White Sox. Gus Wynn compensated for Billy Pierce's off year by winning 22 games en route to a Cy Young Award season. Without Wynn's steadying influence

Victory at hand: Sox clinch.

in Chicago, it is likely that Cleveland, and not the Sox, would have prevailed in 1959.

Nellie Fox, the astounding mighty mite of the 1950s Go-Go Sox, established seven major league records in the pennant year. He ranked among the top five hitters in the circuit for much of the season and was the hands-down choice for the Most Valuable Player award. Luis Aparicio and Gus Wynn finished two and three in the voting. At season's end Fox ranked second behind Ted Williams for career hits among all active players.

In typical "go-going" fashion, the White Sox weaved and bobbed their way into an early lead, then fell back into second place in mid-June. The key to the 1959 season was their ability to take full measure of the Yankees. By winning three of four on their home grounds the weekend of June 26–28, the Sox broke with the past and were in good shape to confront their chief rivals, the Cleveland Indians, a team they had beaten rather handily throughout much of the decade.

In 1959 the Sox captured 15 of 22 games from the Tribe, including a key four-game sweep in Cleveland Stadium, August 28–30. The White Sox entered the series nursing a 1½-game lead. By the time the team charter winged its way back to Chicago at the conclusion of the series, the Cleveland *Plain Dealer* was singing the "Wait Till Next Year" blues: "Go-Go Home White Sox!"

Al Lopez preferred to remain on an even keel. There was a full month of games left to be played. "I don't feel any better about our lead now than when we came here," he said. But for all intents and purposes, the race was over. The White Sox fans sensed it. Ten thousand strong showed up at the airport the night of August 30 to greet the ballclub at the tarmac.

The 1959 pennant was won on the proven White Sox formula of pitching, defense, and scratch hitting. A walk, a stolen base, a wild pitch, and a Texas League single constituted the best offense in this improbable season.

Tuesday, September 22, 1959, 10:30 PM. In the dark of the night, and without warning, the city's air-raid sirens blared for five minutes, marking the momentous occasion of the pennant clinching in Cleveland. The Chicago City Council, with Mayor Richard J. Daley's blessing, had earlier resolved that "bells [should] ring, whistles blow, bands play, and general joy be confined [to Chicago]."

Not everyone in Chicago was a baseball fan, however, and the fear of an atomic blast sent thousands scurrying for their backyard bomb shelters and bungalow basements. An independent poll later determined that a full 33 percent of all Chicagoans believed the world was about to end.

	G	AB	H	R	2B	3B	HR	RBI	SB	AVG
Earl Torgeson	127	277	61	40	5	3	9	45	7	.220
Nellie Fox	156	624	191	84	34	6	2	70	5	.306
Luis Aparicio	152	612	157	98	18	5	6	51	56	.257
John "Bubba" Phillips	117	379	100	43	27	1	5	40	1	.264
Jim McAnany	67	210	58	22	9	3	0	27	2	.276
Jim Landis	149	515	140	78	26	7	5	60	20	.272
Al Smith	129	472	112	65	16	4	17	55	7	.237
Sherman Lollar	140	505	134	63	22	3	22	84	4	.265
Billy Goodman	104	268	67	21	14	1	1	28	3	.250
Norm Cash	58	104	25	16	0	1	4	16	1	.240
Ted Kluszewski	31	101	30	11	2	1	2	10	0	.297
Sammy Esposito	69	66	11	12	1	0	1	5	0	.167
Ray Boone	9	21	5	3	0	0	1	5	1	.238
Ron Jackson	10	14	3	3	1	0	1	2	0	.214
J. C. Martin	3	4	1	0	0	0	0	1	0	.250
Jim Rivera	80	177	39	18	9	4	4	19	5	.220
Johnny Callison	49	104	18	12	3	0	3	12	0	.173
Del Ennis	26	96	21	10	6	0	2	7	0	.219
Harry "Suitcase" Simpson	38	75	14	5	5	1	2	13	0	.187
Larry Doby	21	58	14	1	1	1	0	9	1	.241
Lou Skizas	8	13	1	3	0	0	0	0	0	.077
Joe Hicks	6	7	3	0	0	0	0	0	0	.429
John Romano	53	126	37	20	5	1	5	25	0	.294
Earl Battey	26	64	14	9	1	2	2	7	0	.219
Camilo Carreon	1	1	0	0	0	0	0	0	0	.000
Don Mueller	4	4	2	0	0	0	0	0	0	.500
		5,297	1,325	669	220	46	97	620	113	.250

	W	L	GS	CG	IP	H	BB	K	ShO	ERA
Early Wynn	22	10	37	14	255⅔	202	119	179	5	3.17
Bob Shaw	18	6	26	8	230⅔	217	54	89	3	2.69
Billy Pierce	14	15	33	12	224	217	62	114	2	3.62
Dick Donovan	9	10	29	5	179⅔	171	58	71	1	3.66
Barry Latman	8	5	21	5	156	138	72	97	2	3.75
Gerry Staley	8	5	0	0	116⅓	111	25	54	0	2.24
Omar "Turk" Lown	9	2	0	0	93⅓	73	42	63	0	2.89
Ray Moore	3	6	8	0	89⅔	86	46	49	0	4.12
Rodolfo Arias	2	0	0	0	44	49	20	28	0	4.09
Ken McBride	0	1	2	0	22⅔	20	17	12	0	3.18
Joe Stanka	1	0	0	0	5⅓	2	4	3	0	3.38
Claude Raymond	0	0	0	0	4	5	2	1	0	9.00
Don Rudolph	0	0	0	0	3	4	2	0	0	0.00
Gary Peters	0	0	0	0	1	2	2	1	0	0.00
	94	60	156	44	1,425⅓	1,297	525	761	13	3.29

1960

Record: 87–67
Finish: Third
Games Behind: 8
Manager: Al Lopez

By the mid-to-late 1950s, farm director John Rigney could rightfully boast that after nearly 20 years of experimentation his White Sox minor league system was the envy of the baseball world. Under the patient tutelage of Rigney and Comiskey, a bumper crop of outstanding rookies proliferated within the system, that is, until Bill Veeck and his general manager Hank Greenberg decided to exchange youth for experience in the vain hope of nailing down a repeat pennant in 1960.

Without consulting Comiskey, who had been shunted aside by the new ownership group, Greenberg commenced the destruction of the farm system by trading Bubba Phillips, Norman Cash, and catcher John Romano to Cleveland on December 6, 1959, for the fading Minnie Minoso, Jake Striker, and Dick Brown. Two days later Johnny Callison was

Sox 1960 Winter Promotional Caravan (left to right): Early Wynn, Bob Shaw, Bill Veeck, Al Smith, Ed Short, Al Lopez, and Jim Rivera (seated)

dispatched to the Philadelphia Phillies for the lead-footed Gene Freese—the newest third-base hope.

Most galling of all was the April 5 trade that sent catcher Earl Battey and first baseman Don Mincher to Washington for Roy Sievers. Battey, the heir apparent to the brittle Sherm Lollar, had not developed fast enough to suit Greenberg. Charley Comiskey was angry, and he felt betrayed after hearing the news secondhand at an airport in Puerto Rico.

"Some of us, like me, are not worried about next year," explained Al Lopez in defense of his employers, "because we might not be around then." The scorched-earth strategies of Greenberg devastated the franchise for the next two decades. It would be a tough hole for this team to crawl out of.

Hank Greenberg, beloved in Cleveland for building a perennial pennant contender in the early 1950s, was the inverse of the Frank Lane equation. Lane, successful and popular in Chicago for so many years, was vilified by Cleveland Indian fans for destroying their franchise in a corresponding three-year period. The same accusation could be leveled at Greenberg in Chicago with one exception. He was shielded from criticism by Bill Veeck, the beloved showman who distracted Sox fans with a dazzling array of stunts, promotions, and gimmicks during his two-and-a-half-year tenure on the South Side. For 1960 he installed baseball's first exploding scoreboard in Comiskey Park, and he outfitted his athletes in uniforms with their names stitched on the back—a baseball first.

But even with the added firepower of Sievers, Freese, and Minnie Minoso in the lineup, the 1960 White Sox clubbed only 15 more home runs than the 1959 pennant winners. The team earned run average increased, and the bullpen was not nearly as effective as it had been a year earlier. An early first-place advantage evaporated on May 22. The Sox gamely fought back in late August to claim a share of the top spot, but they were no match for the resurgent Yankees, who quickly re-established hegemony over the rest of the league.

The White Sox ballclub was on the downgrade, but the fans turned out in record-setting numbers just the same. They had high hopes of a repeat pennant, based on the glowing forecasts in the daily newspapers and the pabulum fed to them in the preseason baseball-forecast magazines. But it just wasn't in the cards—for 1960 or beyond. Hank Greenberg and Bill Veeck put to rest that flickering hope, though they could not have possibly anticipated the devastating consequences of their ill-advised player moves.

	G	AB	H	R	2B	3B	HR	RBI	SB	AVG
Roy Sievers	127	444	131	87	22	0	28	93	1	.295
Nellie Fox	150	605	175	85	24	10	2	59	2	.289
Luis Aparicio	153	600	166	86	20	7	2	61	51	.277
Gene Freese	127	455	124	60	32	6	17	79	10	.273
Al Smith	142	536	169	80	31	3	12	72	8	.315
Jim Landis	148	494	125	89	25	6	10	49	23	.253
Orestes "Minnie" Minoso	154	591	184	89	32	4	20	105	17	.311
Sherman Lollar	129	421	106	43	23	0	7	46	2	.252
Ted Kluszewski	81	181	53	20	9	0	5	39	0	.293
Sammy Esposito	57	77	14	14	5	0	1	11	0	.182
Billy Goodman	30	77	18	5	4	0	0	6	0	.234
Earl Torgeson	68	57	15	12	2	0	2	9	1	.263
J. C. Martin	4	20	2	0	1	0	0	2	0	.100
Joe Hicks	36	47	9	3	1	0	0	2	0	.191
Floyd Robinson	22	46	13	7	0	0	0	1	2	.283
Jim Rivera	48	17	5	17	0	0	1	1	4	.294
Stan Johnson	5	6	1	1	0	0	1	1	0	.167
Joe Ginsberg	28	75	19	8	4	0	0	9	1	.253
Dick Brown	16	43	7	4	0	0	3	5	0	.163
Camilo Carreon	8	17	4	2	0	0	0	2	0	.235
Earl Averill, Jr.	10	14	3	2	0	0	0	2	0	.214
Jim McAnany	3	2	0	0	0	0	0	0	0	.000
		5,191	1,402	741	242	38	112	684	122	.270

	W	L	GS	CG	IP	H	BB	K	ShO	ERA
Early Wynn	13	12	35	13	237⅓	220	112	158	4	3.49
Billy Pierce	14	7	30	8	196⅓	201	46	108	1	3.62
Bob Shaw	13	13	32	7	192⅔	221	62	46	1	4.06
Frank Baumann	13	6	20	7	185⅓	169	53	71	2	2.67
Russ Kemmerer	6	3	7	2	120⅔	111	45	76	1	2.98
Gerry Staley	13	8	0	0	115⅓	94	25	52	0	2.42
Herb Score	5	10	22	5	113⅔	91	87	78	1	3.72
Dick Donovan	6	1	8	0	78⅔	87	25	30	0	5.38
Omar "Turk" Lown	2	3	0	0	67⅓	60	34	39	0	3.88
Ray Moore	1	1	0	0	20⅔	19	11	3	0	5.66
Mike Garcia	0	0	0	0	17⅔	23	10	8	0	4.58
Bob Rush	0	0	0	0	14⅓	16	5	12	0	5.65
Al Worthington	1	1	0	0	5⅓	3	4	1	0	3.38
Ken McBride	0	1	0	0	4⅔	6	3	4	0	3.86
Don Ferrarese	0	1	0	0	4	8	9	4	0	18.00
Jake Striker	0	0	0	0	3⅔	5	1	1	0	4.91
Gary Peters	0	0	0	0	3⅓	4	1	4	0	2.70
	87	67	154	42	1,381	1,338	533	695	10	3.60

1961

Record: 86–76
Finish: Fourth
Games Behind: 23
Manager: Al Lopez

Fireworks, fashion shows, cow-milking contests, and weekend S&H Green Stamp giveaways at Comiskey Park, while entertaining and amusing diversions, failed to lessen the disappointment of Sox fans who expected the 1960 "power team" to rebound and win it all in '61.

Illness kept Bill Veeck away from Comiskey Park as his "Slow-Slow" Sox (their league leadership in the stolen base category in 1961 was misleading; Louie Aparicio swiped 53 of them), crash-landed in the cellar on May 24, prompting a City Hall inquiry among certain Chicago aldermen. What's wrong with the Sox? "Give me a combination of good pitching and good hitting, and I'll give you a ballclub!" Lopez shot back.

Bill Veeck had to be disappointed with the results, as he fought to regain his health at the Mayo Clinic in Minnesota early in the season. With his physical condition imperiled and seeing little chance to devote his full-time energies to righting the capsizing ballclub, Veeck decided to put his White Sox stock up for sale. Two groups stepped forward.

Entertainer Danny Thomas fronted an investment group headed by Chicago attorney Bernard Epton, who undoubtedly would have returned Charley Comiskey to the forefront of the baseball operation were it in his power to do so. Sensing an intrigue afoot, Veeck and Greenberg shuffled their deck and dealt an insider's hand to Arthur C. Allyn Jr., the president of a diversified corporation known as Artnell, and his father, who was a longtime Veeck ally in each of his three baseball ownerships.

The sale of Veeck's White Sox stock to this baseball dilettante was completed on June 10 after a week of name-calling and rancor between the parties that was aired out in the press. Charley Comiskey's end-around move to regain control of his dad's ballclub was thwarted, and that defeat was a great loss to Chicago baseball.

The improvement was immediate and dramatic after Veeck left town. The White Sox launched a 12-game winning streak on June 17 behind the pitching of newcomers Ray Herbert and Juan Pizarro, the saving grace of the Hank Greenberg regime. Over the winter, Gene Freese was dealt to Cincinnati for Cal McLish and Pizarro, a sphinxlike lefty who had failed to make the grade in Milwaukee in an earlier try.

In August Hank Greenberg stepped down as general manager, leaving the job to Edwin Short, team publicist and a former radio scriptwriter for broadcaster Bob Elson. Under Greenberg, the Sox farm system had crashed and burned. Now it was up to Short to rebuild the organization with an infusion of younger faces. And that task would require trading away popular career veterans like Billy Pierce, who won his last game in a White Sox uniform on September 24. The "Short answer" to the problem: "We cannot afford to let this team grow too old and fall apart completely."

Floyd Robinson beats Yankees pitcher Bill Stafford to the bag. Sox win 14–9.

	G	AB	H	R	2B	3B	HR	RBI	SB	AVG
Roy Sievers	141	492	145	76	26	6	27	92	1	.295
Nellie Fox	159	606	152	67	11	5	2	51	2	.251
Luis Aparicio	156	625	170	90	24	4	6	45	53	.272
Al Smith	147	532	148	88	29	4	28	93	4	.278
Floyd Robinson	132	432	134	69	20	7	11	59	7	.310
Jim Landis	140	534	151	87	18	8	22	85	19	.283
Orestes "Minnie" Minoso	152	540	151	91	28	3	14	82	9	.280
Sherman Lollar	116	337	95	38	10	1	7	41	0	.282
J. C. Martin	110	274	63	26	8	3	5	32	1	.230
Andy Carey	56	143	38	21	12	3	0	14	0	.266
Sammy Esposito	63	94	16	12	5	0	1	8	0	.170
Billy Goodman	41	51	13	4	4	0	1	10	0	.255
Earl Torgeson	20	15	1	1	0	0	0	1	0	.067
Ted Lepcio	5	2	0	0	0	0	0	0	0	.000
Al Pilarcik	47	62	11	9	1	0	1	6	1	.177
Wes Covington	22	59	17	5	1	0	4	15	0	.288
Mike Hershberger	15	55	17	9	3	0	0	5	1	.309
Dean Look	3	6	0	0	0	0	0	0	0	.000
Camilo Carreon	78	229	62	32	5	1	4	27	0	.271
Bob Roselli	22	38	10	2	3	0	0	4	0	.263
Joe Ginsberg	6	0	0	0	0	0	0	0	0	.000
Jim Rivera	1	0	0	0	0	0	0	0	0	.000
		5,556	1,475	765	216	46	138	704	100	.265

	W	L	GS	CG	IP	H	BB	K	ShO	ERA
Juan Pizarro	14	7	25	12	194⅔	164	89	188	1	3.05
Frank Baumann	10	13	23	5	187⅔	249	59	75	1	5.61
Billy Pierce	10	9	28	5	180	190	54	106	1	3.80
Cal McLish	10	13	27	4	162⅓	178	47	80	0	4.38
Ray Herbert	9	6	20	4	137⅔	142	36	50	0	4.05
Early Wynn	8	2	16	5	110⅓	88	47	64	0	3.51
Omar "Turk" Lown	7	5	0	0	101	87	35	50	0	2.76
Russ Kemmerer	3	3	2	0	96⅔	102	26	35	0	4.38
Don Larsen	7	2	3	0	74⅓	64	29	53	0	4.12
Bob Shaw	3	4	10	3	71⅓	85	20	31	0	3.79
Warren Hacker	3	3	0	0	57⅓	62	8	40	0	3.77
Herb Score	1	2	5	1	24⅓	22	24	14	0	6.66
Gerry Staley	0	3	0	0	18	17	5	8	0	5.00
Joel Horlen	1	3	4	0	17⅔	25	13	11	0	6.62
Gary Peters	0	0	0	0	10⅓	10	2	6	0	1.74
Alan Brice	0	1	0	0	3⅓	4	3	3	0	0.00
Mike Degerick	0	0	0	0	1⅔	2	1	0	0	5.40
	86	76	163	39	1,448⅔	1,491	498	814	3	4.06

1962

Record: 85–77
Finish: Fifth
Games Behind: 11
Manager: Al Lopez

Ed Short took a lot of heat for trading Billy Pierce, Roy Sievers, and Minnie Minoso to the National League for an ensemble cast of players, including Cardinals first baseman Joe Cunningham, pitchers Eddie Fisher and Dom Zanni from the Giants, and righty John Buzhardt, whose combined 11–34 record spanning two seasons in Philadelphia was almost laughable. The housecleaning was necessary for the Sox to preserve their string of 11 straight first-division finishes. And as it turned out, Short came up a winner his first time in the box. The National League castoffs performed well in Chicago.

The 1962 edition was an imperfect blend of youth and experience—a team "under construction." Nellie Fox and Sherm Lollar were holdovers from the Frank Lane era, but these two old warriors who brought honor to the franchise during its Go-Go glory days had slowed considerably. Lollar was relegated to part-time duty behind Camilo Carreon, and in July Fox was benched in favor of Bob Sadowski.

It was a lackluster season from beginning to end. Early Wynn's desperate struggle to nail down his 300th career victory before his arthritic legs gave way was cheapened by Art Allyn and Ed Short's shabby marketing ploy to lure fans into Comiskey Park in the closing days of the season by holding Wynn back from pitching on the road. Working on borrowed time, the 42-year-old competitor dropped his final three decisions to end the year in a holding pattern at 299. Wynn's name was lopped off of the roster on November 20. Short's youth movement showed no mercy.

The vaunted White Sox pitching staff took its lumps during the 1961–1962 rebuilding. Only Ray Herbert, a 20-game winner who nailed down the 1962 All-Star Game for the American League in Wrigley Field, offered encouragement. This was a .500 ballclub at the halfway point, and it remained that way until September, when Lopez's team strung together 15 victories against eight losses—just enough to salt away another winning season and first-division berth in the 10-team league.

	G	AB	H	R	2B	3B	HR	RBI	SB	AVG
Joe Cunningham	149	526	155	91	32	7	8	70	3	.295
Nellie Fox	157	621	166	79	27	7	2	54	1	.267
Luis Aparicio	153	581	140	72	23	5	7	40	31	.241
Al Smith	142	511	149	62	23	8	16	82	3	.292
Mike Hershberger	148	427	112	54	14	2	4	46	10	262
Jim Landis	149	534	122	82	21	6	15	61	19	.228
Floyd Robinson	156	600	187	89	45	10	11	109	4	.312
Camilo Carreon	106	313	80	31	19	1	4	37	1	.256
Charley Smith	65	145	30	11	4	0	2	17	0	.207
Bob Sadowski	79	130	30	22	3	3	6	24	0	.231
Sammy Esposito	75	81	19	14	1	0	0	4	0	.235
Bob Farley	35	53	10	7	1	1	1	4	0	.189
Grover "Deacon" Jones	18	28	9	3	2	0	0	8	0	.321
Ramon Conde	14	16	0	0	0	0	0	1	0	.000
Al Weis	7	12	1	2	0	0	0	0	1	.083
Dick Kenworthy	3	4	0	0	0	0	0	0	0	.000
Charlie Maxwell	69	206	61	30	8	3	9	43	0	.296
Brian McCall	4	8	3	2	0	0	2	3	0	.375
Ken Berry	3	6	2	2	0	0	0	0	0	.333
Sherman Lollar	84	220	59	17	12	0	2	26	1	.268
Bob Roselli	35	64	12	4	3	1	1	5	1	.188
J. C. Martin	18	26	2	0	0	0	0	2	0	.077
		5,514	1,415	707	250	56	92	662	76	.257

	W	L	GS	CG	IP	H	BB	K	ShO	ERA
Ray Herbert	20	9	35	12	236⅔	228	74	115	2	3.27
Juan Pizarro	12	14	32	9	203⅓	182	97	173	1	3.81
Eddie Fisher	9	5	12	2	182⅔	169	45	88	1	3.10
Early Wynn	7	15	26	11	167⅔	171	56	91	3	4.46
John Buzhardt	8	12	25	8	152⅓	156	59	64	2	4.19
Frank Baumann	7	6	10	3	119⅔	117	36	55	1	3.38
Joel Horlen	7	6	19	5	108⅔	108	43	63	1	4.89
Dom Zanni	6	5	2	0	86⅓	67	31	66	0	3.75
Omar "Turk" Lown	4	2	0	0	56⅓	58	25	40	0	3.04
Mike Joyce	2	1	1	0	43⅓	40	14	9	0	3.32
Dean Stone	1	0	0	0	30⅓	28	9	23	0	3.26
Russ Kemmerer	2	1	0	0	28	30	11	17	0	3.86
Dave DeBusschere	0	0	0	0	18	5	23	8	0	2.00
Gary Peters	0	1	0	0	6⅓	8	1	4	0	5.68
Herb Score	0	0	0	0	6	6	4	3	0	4.50
Verle Tiefenthaler	0	0	0	0	3⅔	6	7	1	0	9.82
Frank Kruetzer	0	0	0	0	1⅓	0	1	1	0	0.00
Mike Degerick	0	0	0	0	1	1	1	0	0	0.00
	85	77	162	50	1,451⅔	1,380	537	821	11	3.73

1963

Record: 94–68
Finish: Second
Games Behind: 10½
Manager: Al Lopez

Upon hearing the news that he had been traded to Baltimore with Al Smith for knuckleballing relief ace Hoyt Wilhelm, shortstop Ron Hansen, and two youngsters named Pete Ward and Dave Nicholson, Luis Aparicio planted a curse on the White Sox that grew more ominous with each passing year. "The Sox will need 40 years to win the pennant again!" Louie's unhappiness with the organization was mirrored in his parting shot. He hated leaving Chicago, but the team was headed on a different course, and he no longer fit in.

The new acquisitions afforded Lopez plenty of maneuverability with his infielders. Pete Ward, the son of a former National Hockey League player, provided good power and adequate defense at the hot corner, marking a substantial improvement over the dozens of interim third basemen who held down the position before.

In 1963 Pete Ward finished second in Rookie of the Year balloting behind his teammate Gary Peters, one of the finest hitting pitchers of the 1960s, who finally blossomed into a star in his option year. The emergence of Peters, with his "fluid-motion" pitching delivery, after four failed attempts to make it in Chicago was testament to the patience shown by farm director Glen C. Miller and Ed Short.

However, when Short had to choose between Bruce Howard and Denny McLain, a first-year bonus player from Chicago's Catholic League, for minor league reassignment, the Sox GM selected Howard and released McLain on the last day of spring training. McLain was immediately picked up by the Detroit Tigers.

The White Sox had themselves an outstanding year despite losing first baseman Joe Cunningham, a defensive wizard, for the season on June 3. Cunningham shattered his collarbone in a freakish collision with Charley Dees of the Los Angeles Angels, and this injury occurred at a time when the ballclub was in a virtual first-place tie with the Yankees.

Because Nellie Fox was slowed by advancing age and because Short and Lopez wanted to integrate switch-hitting Al Weis into the everyday lineup, Fox's 1963 playing time was reduced to only 137 games. In 1963 Little Nell became the 40th major leaguer to log 2,500 career hits. He crossed the historic threshold on July 28, with a single off Dave McNally in Baltimore. It was the final milestone of his illustrious White Sox career.

The Fox era ended on December 10, when Short reunited Nellie with his old boss, Paul Richards, who had taken over as general manager of the Houston Colt .45s. In return, the White Sox received pitchers Danny Murphy and Jim Golden, who contributed nothing to the 1964 title drive—or beyond.

Paul Richards valued Nellie's integrity and experience as he tried to mold this expansion team into a contender. Ed Short, on the other hand, seemed eager to unload a salary and create a roster opening. But in the process Short made enemies of White Sox fans whose sentimental regard for Nellie Fox transcended five-year rebuilding programs.

	G	AB	H	R	2B	3B	HR	RBI	SB	AVG
Tommy McCraw	102	280	71	38	11	3	6	33	15	.254
Nellie Fox	137	539	140	54	19	0	2	42	0	.260
Ron Hansen	144	482	109	55	17	2	13	67	1	.226
Pete Ward	157	600	177	80	34	6	22	84	7	.295
Floyd Robinson	146	527	149	71	21	6	13	71	4	.283
Jim Landis	133	396	89	56	6	6	13	45	8	.225
Dave Nicholson	126	449	103	53	11	4	22	70	2	.229
J. C. Martin	105	259	53	25	11	1	5	28	0	.205
Joe Cunningham	67	210	60	32	12	1	1	31	1	.286
Al Weis	99	210	57	41	9	0	0	18	15	.271
Jim Lemon	36	80	16	4	0	1	1	8	0	.200
Don Buford	12	42	12	9	1	2	0	5	1	.186
Grover "Deacon" Jones	17	16	3	4	0	1	1	2	0	.188
Charley Smith	4	7	2	0	0	1	0	1	0	.286
Mike Hershberger	135	476	133	64	26	2	3	45	9	.279
Charlie Maxwell	71	130	30	17	4	2	3	17	0	.231
Gene Stephens	6	18	7	5	0	0	1	2	0	.389
Brian McCall	3	7	0	1	0	0	0	0	0	.000
Ken Berry	4	5	1	2	0	0	0	0	0	.200
Camilo Carreon	101	270	74	28	10	1	2	35	1	.274
Sherman Lollar	35	73	17	4	4	0	0	6	0	.233
Sammy Esposito	1	0	0	0	0	0	0	0	0	.000
		5,508	1,379	683	208	40	114	648	64	.250

AL Rookie of the Year Gary Peters

	W	L	GS	CG	IP	H	BB	K	ShO	ERA
Gary Peters	19	8	30	13	243	192	68	189	4	2.33
Ray Herbert	13	10	33	14	224⅔	230	35	105	7	3.24
Juan Pizarro	16	8	28	10	214⅔	177	63	163	3	2.39
Hoyt Wilhelm	5	8	3	0	136⅓	106	30	111	0	2.64
John Buzhardt	9	4	18	6	126⅓	100	31	59	3	2.42
Joel Horlen	11	7	21	3	124	122	55	61	0	3.27
Eddie Fisher	9	8	15	2	120⅔	114	28	67	1	3.95
Dave DeBusschere	3	4	10	1	84⅓	80	34	53	1	3.09
Jim Brosnan	3	8	0	0	73	71	22	46	0	2.84
Frank Baumann	2	1	1	0	50⅓	52	17	31	0	3.04
Bruce Howard	2	1	0	0	17	12	14	9	0	2.65
Taylor "T-Bone" Phillips	0	0	0	0	14	16	13	13	0	10.29
Fritz Ackley	1	0	2	0	13	7	7	11	0	2.08
Mike Joyce	0	0	0	0	10⅔	13	8	7	0	8.44
Frank Kruetzer	1	0	1	0	5	3	1	0	0	1.80
Joe Shipley	0	1	0	0	4⅔	9	6	3	0	5.79
Dom Zanni	0	0	0	0	4⅓	5	4	2	0	8.31
Fred Talbot	0	0	0	0	3	2	4	2	0	3.00
	94	68	162	49	1,469	1,311	440	932	19	2.97

1964

Record: 98–64
Finish: Second
Games Behind: 1
Manager: Al Lopez

The gentility of Al Lopez, his calm demeanor, and his eternal optimism are what we remember of the character of the man who led the White Sox through some of their most glorious and historic years. And yet, there was another side to Lopez that surfaced again in 1964. From time to time the Señor would banish certain veteran players to a doghouse they were powerless to escape from. Larry Doby, Al Smith, Minnie Minoso, even the mild-mannered Billy Pierce, all vented their displeasure of the field boss. In 1964, Jim Landis, the last of the Go-Go boys, was benched by Lopez after demanding a $50 honorarium from Ed Short for a TV appearance he was asked to make on behalf of the ballclub.

Unlike Pierce and Minoso, members of the Sox "Silent Generation," Landis was vocal in his criticism throughout the "feud." He found a sympathetic ally in *Chicago American* columnist Bill Gleason, who organized a "Jim Landis Night" at Comiskey Park, June 10, 1964. Landis was presented a trophy—Al Lopez was hung in effigy in the players' parking lot. Unmoved by the jeering anger of the fans, Lopez started Minnie Minoso in place of Landis without comment or apology.

The 1964 pennant race was a barn burner. Only the 1904–1908 dead-ball-era seasons—and the 1967 heartbreak yet to come—matched the '64 campaign for heart-pounding intensity. After dropping their first three games of the year, the White Sox won nine of the next 11 and were off and running in hot pursuit of the Yankees and the improved Baltimore Orioles.

Day in and day out the lead changed hands. It was the pitching, however, that kept the Sox in the thick of things against the two power-hitting contenders. The "Big Four" of Gary Peters, Juan Pizarro, Joel Horlen, and John Buzhardt were the reasons why the Sox never dropped any further from the league lead than 4½ games at any given point in this hectic season. Hoyt Wilhelm and Eddie Fisher provided Lopez with amazing depth in the bullpen. To beat the White Sox, it was necessary for an opponent to score runs early and often, and that just didn't happen.

By 1964, Earl Battey and John Callison had already emerged as bona fide major league stars with their respective

Gary Peters (seated), Floyd Robinson, Gene Stephens, and Don Buford cool off in the heat of the pennant race (August 28, 1964).

teams. Their presence in the White Sox lineup that season would undoubtedly have turned the tide of victory in Chicago's favor. As it turned out, the Sox struggled to score runs all season long minus a legitimate 100-RBI man and long-ball threat.

The catching situation was in a shambles. Cam Carreon, J. C. Martin, and Gerry McNertney had their moments defensively but could not put up the offensive numbers when it counted. Earl Battey was sorely missed; one need only recall Lopez's bitter "Let's live for today" message to Sox fans after Earl had been stupidly traded to Washington in 1960.

Bill "Moose" Skowron and "Smoky" Burgess were late-season additions who chipped in, but their contributions failed to slow the Yankees, who had defeated the Sox in their first 11 meetings of the year. Not until August 11 were the Sox able to dent the victory column against their principal rivals. Were the Yankees just that good, or did their manager Yogi Berra have the Sox's number? The hitters were ineffective against southpaw pitching. Berra knew this, so he trotted out White Sox killer Whitey Ford and a trio of lefties to neutralize the Sox "attack"—what little of it there was.

The White Sox won their last nine regular season games against the AL doormats to chip away at a deficit that had ballooned to four games by September 25. Meanwhile, the Yankees captured 13 of 14 games down the stretch to seal their fifth straight AL crown. The 1964 season ended much too quickly for the White Sox and their disappointed followers, who looked no further than to the early season losses to the Yankees to understand the true meaning behind Lopez's sage belief that "pennants are won in June."

	G	AB	H	R	2B	3B	HR	RBI	SB	AVG
Tommy McCraw	125	368	96	47	11	5	6	36	15	.261
Al Weis	133	328	81	36	4	4	2	23	22	.247
Ron Hansen	158	575	150	85	25	3	20	68	1	.261
Pete Ward	144	539	152	61	28	3	23	94	1	.282
Mike Hershberger	141	452	104	55	15	3	2	31	8	.230
Jim Landis	106	298	62	30	8	4	1	18	5	.208
Floyd Robinson	141	525	158	83	17	3	11	59	9	.301
J. C. Martin	122	294	58	23	10	1	4	22	0	.197
Don Buford	135	442	116	62	14	6	4	30	12	.262
Bill "Moose" Skowron	73	273	80	19	11	3	4	38	0	.293
Joe Cunningham	40	108	27	13	7	0	0	10	0	.250
Charley Smith	2	7	1	1	0	1	0	0	0	.143
Dave Nicholson	97	294	60	40	6	1	13	39	0	.204
Gene Stephens	82	141	33	21	4	2	3	17	1	.234
Jeoff Long	23	35	5	0	0	0	0	5	0	.143
Ken Berry	12	32	12	4	1	0	1	4	0	.375
Orestes "Minnie" Minoso	30	31	7	4	0	0	1	5	0	.226
Gerald McNertney	73	186	40	16	5	0	3	23	0	.215
Camilo Carreon	37	95	26	12	5	0	0	4	0	.274
Forrest "Smoky" Burgess	7	5	1	1	0	0	1	1	0	.200
Marv Staehli	6	5	2	0	0	0	0	2	1	.400
Dick Kenworthy	2	2	0	0	0	0	0	0	0	.000
Charlie Maxwell	2	2	0	0	0	0	0	0	0	.000
Jim Hicks	2	0	0	0	0	0	0	0	0	.000
		5,491	1,356	642	184	40	106	586	75	.247

	W	L	GS	CG	IP	H	BB	K	ShO	ERA
Gary Peters	20	8	36	11	273⅔	217	104	205	3	2.50
Juan Pizarro	19	9	33	11	239	193	55	162	4	2.56
Joel Horlen	13	9	28	9	210⅔	142	55	138	2	1.88
John Buzhardt	10	8	25	8	160	150	35	97	3	2.98
Hoyt Wilhelm	12	9	0	0	131⅓	94	30	95	0	1.99
Eddie Fisher	6	3	2	0	125	86	32	74	0	3.02
Ray Herbert	6	7	19	1	111⅔	117	17	40	1	3.47
Fred Talbot	4	5	12	3	75⅓	83	20	34	2	3.70
Frank Kruetzer	3	1	2	0	40⅓	37	18	32	0	3.25
Don Mossi	3	1	0	0	40	37	7	36	0	2.93
Frank Baumann	0	3	0	0	32	40	16	19	0	6.19
Bruce Howard	2	1	3	1	22⅓	10	8	17	1	0.81
Fritz Ackley	0	0	2	0	6⅓	10	4	6	0	8.53
	98	64	162	44	1,467⅔	1,216	401	955	16	2.72

1965

Record: 95–67
Finish: Second
Games Behind: 7
Manager: Al Lopez

Between rounds of golf at his Tampa, Florida, home, Al Lopez pondered early retirement. In Chicago Art Allyn cheerfully predicted a 1965 pennant and never gave a second thought to his manager's desire to escape the daily grind of jet-age baseball. As the season wore on and the pennant became less a certainty, Lopez was all the more determined to escape to the Florida sunshine on a permanent basis.

Ed Short was roundly assailed for a January trade that returned veteran catcher John Romano and two Cleveland rookies to Chicago for Rocky Colavito, who was Sox property for about 10 minutes. The unusual three-team swap involving the Sox, the Indians, and the Kansas City A's cost the Sox the services of Jim Landis, Mike Hershberger, Cam Carreon, and pitcher Fred Talbot. Romano was the main guy from the Sox' point of view, but the two rookie unknowns—pitcher Tommy John and outfielder Tommy Agee—whom nobody counted on at the time, paid much bigger dividends. As a general manager, Ed Short was a mixed blessing. No one, though, faulted him for this bit of genius.

The Sox looked like runaway winners one month into the season. Winners of 23 of their first 31 games, Chicago enjoyed a commanding 4½-game lead on May 18. The Yankees' dominance had finally been broken, and only the Minnesota Twins and the Baltimore Orioles stood in the way of a White Sox pennant. Then, just when the Sox were on the brink of pulling away, injuries set in. Juan Pizarro's torn triceps muscle landed him on the disabled list, and on June 30 Lopez was diagnosed as suffering from enteritis.

The White Sox were never the same after that.

With a year left to go on his contract, Lopez resigned on November 4, but he agreed to remain with the organization as a vice president. The Señor's first task was to guide the appointment of a new field manager. Twins manager Sam Mele, George Strickland of the Indians, and Sox "super scout" Charley Metro were ruled out before Allyn and Lopez settled on 48-year-old firebrand Eddie Stanky, a cross between Billy Martin and Jimmie Dykes, with a wee bit of Leo Durocher thrown in for good measure.

"The way I manage a baseball club is 24 hours a day and 12 months a year," Stanky beamed. "I know how tough that will be for my wife and kids." Not to mention the 25 unhappy athletes about to find out just how *tough* things could be with Sergeant Stanky in charge of the fort.

	G	AB	H	R	2B	3B	HR	RBI	SB	AVG
Bill "Moose" Skowron	146	559	153	63	24	3	18	78	1	.274
Don Buford	155	586	166	93	22	5	10	47	17	.283
Ron Hansen	162	587	138	61	23	4	11	66	1	.235
Pete Ward	138	507	125	62	25	3	10	57	2	.247
Ken Berry	157	472	103	51	17	4	12	42	4	.218
Danny Cater	142	514	139	74	18	4	14	55	3	.270
J. C. Martin	119	230	60	21	12	0	2	21	2	.261
Tommy McCraw	133	273	65	38	12	1	5	21	12	.238
Al Weis	103	135	40	29	4	3	1	12	4	.296
Gene Freese	17	32	9	2	0	1	1	4	0	.281
Floyd Robinson	156	577	153	70	15	6	14	66	4	.265
Dave Nicholson	54	85	13	11	2	1	2	12	0	.153
Bill Voss	11	33	6	4	0	1	1	3	0	.182
Tommie Agee	10	19	3	2	1	0	0	3	0	.158
Jim Hicks	13	19	5	2	1	0	1	2	0	.263
John Romano	122	356	86	39	11	0	18	48	0	.242
Forrest "Smoky" Burgess	80	77	22	2	4	0	2	24	0	.286
Jimmie Schaffer	17	31	6	2	3	1	0	1	0	.194
Duane Josephson	4	9	1	2	0	0	0	0	0	.111
Marv Staehli	7	7	3	0	0	0	0	2	0	.429
Bill Heath	1	1	0	0	0	0	0	0	0	.000
Dick Kenworthy	3	1	0	0	0	0	0	0	0	.000
		5,509	1,354	647	200	38	125	587	50	.246

	W	L	GS	CG	IP	H	BB	K	ShO	ERA
Joel Horlen	13	13	34	7	219	203	39	125	4	2.88
John Buzhardt	13	8	30	4	188⅔	167	56	108	1	3.01
Tommy John	14	7	27	6	183⅔	162	58	126	1	3.09
Gary Peters	10	12	30	1	176⅓	181	63	95	0	3.62
Eddie Fisher	15	7	0	0	165⅓	118	43	90	0	2.40
Bruce Howard	9	8	22	1	148	123	72	120	1	3.47
Hoyt Wilhelm	7	7	0	0	144	88	32	106	0	1.81
Juan Pizarro	6	3	18	2	97	96	37	65	1	3.43
Bob Locker	5	2	0	0	91⅓	71	30	69	0	3.15
Frank Lary	1	0	1	0	26⅔	23	7	14	0	4.05
Greg Bollo	0	0	0	0	22⅔	12	9	16	0	3.57
Ted Wills	2	0	0	0	19	17	14	12	0	2.84
	95	67	162	21	1,481⅔	1,261	460	946	8	2.99

1966

Record: 83–79
Finish: Fourth
Games Behind: 15
Manager: Eddie Stanky

Affectionately known as "the Brat" during his playing days, Eddie Stanky was expected to provide vibrant and colorful, if not controversial, leadership as the 22nd manager of the White Sox. Stanky served up plenty of controversy during his two-plus years at the helm. He made more enemies within the baseball establishment in two years than Al Lopez did in a lifetime.

The season was barely a month old when Stanky berated fellow manager Charley Dressen as "bush." In 1966 he verbally sparred with Sam Mele and Bill Rigney, and ordered his pitchers to throw at opposing batters in order to "send a message." Stanky billed himself the "retaliation manager" and expected his players to carry out his head-hunting mandates. After John Buzhardt drilled Twins pitcher Jim Perry in the head on May 19, a clubhouse spy revealed Stanky's ugly little secret to the press. "We shouldn't get upset if one of our colleagues—our flesh and blood—betrays us!" Stanky countered with sarcasm dripping from his mouth. John Romano was strongly suspected. He was immediately benched.

Dead last in hitting, the White Sox struggled the entire season to score runs in order to escape the wrath of their pugnacious manager, who inspired much fear in the clubhouse. Tommy John, a sinker-ball pitcher who was Stanky's special favorite, paced the staff with 14 wins. Rookie outfielder Tommie Agee won Rookie of the Year honors on the strength of 22 home runs, 44 stolen bases, and a team-leading .273 average.

Indeed, Stanky had restored the Go-Go spirit to the Sox sagging offense. White Sox speedsters swiped 153 bases and played the kind of baseball that won many converts in the early 1950s.

AL President Will Harridge proclaims Eddie Fisher the *Sporting News* Fireman of the Year for 1965.

The fans, however, were unimpressed. Sox home attendance dipped below the million mark for the first time in eight years. Urban rioting on Chicago's South Side scared many fans away from attending night games at Comiskey Park in 1966. But neighborhood safety concerns alone did not entirely account for the set of problems the Allyns were encountering.

The style of baseball personified by the new Go-Go boys—Agee, Tommy McCraw, and Don Buford—began to wear thin with Sox fans bored by the glut of 1–0 and 2–1 games played in cavernous Comiskey Park. Art Allyn and Ed Short groped for answers.

	G	AB	H	R	2B	3B	HR	RBI	SB	AVG
Tommy McCraw	151	389	89	49	16	4	5	48	20	.229
Al Weis	129	187	29	20	4	1	0	9	3	.155
Jerry Adair	105	370	90	27	18	2	4	36	3	.243
Don Buford	163	607	148	85	26	7	8	52	51	.244
Floyd Robinson	127	342	81	44	11	2	5	35	8	.237
Tommie Agee	160	629	172	98	27	8	22	86	44	.273
Ken Berry	147	443	120	50	20	2	8	34	7	.271
John Romano	122	329	76	33	12	0	15	47	0	.231
Bill "Moose" Skowron	120	337	84	27	15	2	6	29	1	.249
Lee Elia	80	195	40	16	5	2	3	22	0	.205
Wayne Causey	78	164	40	23	8	2	0	13	2	.244
Gene Freese	48	106	22	8	2	0	3	10	2	.208
Ron Hansen	23	74	13	3	1	0	0	4	0	.176
Dick Kenworthy	9	25	5	1	0	0	0	0	0	.200
Marv Staehli	8	15	2	2	0	0	0	0	1	.133
Pete Ward	84	251	55	22	7	1	3	28	3	.219
Danny Cater	21	60	11	3	1	1	0	4	3	.183
Ed Stroud	12	36	6	3	2	0	0	1	3	.167
Charles "Buddy" Bradford	14	28	4	3	0	0	0	0	0	.143
Jim Hicks	18	26	5	3	0	1	0	1	0	.192
Bill Voss	2	2	0	0	0	0	0	0	0	.000
J. C. Martin	67	157	40	13	5	3	2	20	0	.255
Forrest "Smoky" Burgess	79	67	21	0	5	0	0	15	0	.313
Gerry McNertney	44	59	13	3	0	0	0	1	1	.220
Duane Josephson	11	38	9	3	1	0	0	3	0	.237
Grover "Deacon" Jones	5	5	2	0	0	0	0	0	0	.400
		5,348	1,235	574	193	40	87	524	153	.231

	W	L	GS	CG	IP	H	BB	K	ShO	ERA
Tommy John	14	11	33	10	223	195	57	138	5	2.62
Joel Horlen	10	13	29	4	211	185	53	124	2	2.43
Gary Peters	12	10	27	11	204⅔	156	45	129	4	1.98
John Buzhardt	6	11	22	5	150⅓	144	30	66	4	3.83
Bruce Howard	9	5	21	4	149	110	44	85	2	2.30
Jack Lamabe	7	9	17	3	121⅓	116	35	67	2	3.93
Bob Locker	9	8	0	0	95	73	23	70	0	2.46
Dennis Higgins	1	0	1	0	93	66	33	86	0	2.52
Juan Pizarro	8	6	9	1	88⅔	91	39	42	0	3.76
Hoyt Wilhelm	5	2	0	0	81⅓	50	17	61	0	1.66
Eddie Fisher	1	3	0	0	35⅓	27	17	18	0	2.29
Fred Klages	1	0	3	0	15⅔	9	7	6	0	1.72
Greg Bollo	0	1	1	0	7	7	3	4	0	2.57
	83	79	163	38	1,475⅓	1,229	403	896	19	2.68

1967

Record: 89–73
Finish: Fourth
Games Behind: 3
Manager: Eddie Stanky

An unforgettable, bittersweet season to those who remember it. In Boston delirious Red Sox fans celebrated an "Impossible Dream." The Minnesota Twins and Detroit Tigers played before packed houses all year. The Chicago White Sox, meanwhile, were greeted by a season-long indifference, even as they stood on the threshold of an American League pennant in the closing days of a historic, four-team flag chase.

What a year for Eddie Stanky. The Brat lashed out at the press for their perceived negativity. He labeled Red Sox star Carl Yastrzemski "moody" and an "All-Star from the neck down." Bill Rigney of the Angels took exception to being called a "television manager." Stanky's enemies accused him

1966 Rookie of the Year Tommie Agee beats Elston Howard to the plate.

of freezing baseballs in a clubhouse refrigerator in order to deaden his opponent's offense.

By Stanky's own admission, the 1967 White Sox were the "dullest ballclub he had ever seen." And yet this much-maligned Sox team played through the constant intrigues and the self-inflicted pressure of trying to please the explosive Stanky. He imposed fines for the slightest infraction of team rules. "Then I know we're doing more things right than wrong," he rhapsodized. "That's the old team spirit!"

The "sockless" Sox (team batting average .225), played the hand they were dealt. Joel Horlen completed a Cy Young year, posting 19 victories, a no-hit performance against the Tigers on September 10, and a league-leading .206 ERA. But he was deprived of his rightful honor by Red Sox hurler Jim Lonborg, whose numbers just didn't compare to those of the soft-spoken Texan.

The pitching staff was the trump card that landed the White Sox in first place on June 10. They held the lead until a heartbreaking loss to the Minnesota Twins knocked them into second place on August 13. Thereafter it was a four-team dogfight.

Sinker-ball specialist Bob Locker teamed with Hoyt Wilhelm and Don McMahon, an early season pickup, to form the nucleus of a tough bullpen. With assembly-line precision, pitching coach Ray Berres "manufactured" live, young arms and rejuvenated the veterans. Berres had supervised the Sox pitchers for nearly 19 years until Stanky replaced him with Marv Grissom in 1967.

Ed Short burned up the telephone lines seeking a capable hitter to beef up the punchless attack. Jim King, Ken Boyer, and Rocky Colavito arrived via the waiver route, but these were desultory moves that upset the delicate chemistry of the ballclub and hurt the morale of the younger players coming down the homestretch.

The fate of the White Sox hung in the balance on September 27—"Black Wednesday"—in Kansas City. Playing in that city for the final time before moving on to Oakland for 1968, Charley Finley's doormat A's knocked off the Sox in a twi-night doubleheader. Stanky's team needed only a split of the two games to place them in an enviable position going into the final three days of the season. The other contenders had all lost that day. "How could they beat us with a lineup like that?" Pete Ward asked. The gloom was pervasive. No one stewed over the misfortune more than Eddie Stanky. "All year long the elephants feared the mouse," he quipped.

Seventeen consecutive first-division finishes—no other major league team except the Yankees and Orioles matched the longevity of the winning White Sox until the crushing finale of the 1967 pennant race signaled "lights out" on the franchise for the next two decades.

Joel Horlen (left), Tommy McCraw, and Gary Peters celebrate another '67 cliffhanger victory.

	G	AB	H	R	2B	3B	HR	RBI	SB	AVG
Tommy McCraw	125	453	107	55	18	3	11	45	24	.236
Wayne Causey	124	292	66	21	10	3	1	28	2	.226
Ron Hansen	157	498	116	35	20	0	8	51	0	.233
Don Buford	156	535	129	61	10	9	4	32	34	.241
Ken Berry	147	485	117	49	14	4	7	41	9	.241
Tommie Agee	158	529	124	73	26	2	14	52	28	.234
Pete Ward	146	467	109	49	16	2	18	62	3	.233
J. C. Martin	101	252	59	22	12	1	4	22	4	.234
Ken Boyer	57	180	47	17	5	1	4	21	0	.261
Jerry Adair	28	98	20	6	4	0	0	9	0	.204
Dick Kenworthy	50	97	22	9	4	1	4	11	0	.227
Marv Staehli	32	54	6	1	1	0	0	1	1	.111
Al Weis	50	53	13	9	2	0	0	4	3	.245
Sandy Alomar	12	15	3	4	0	0	0	0	2	.200
Rich Morales	8	10	0	0	0	0	0	0	0	.000
Charles "Cotton" Nash	3	3	0	1	0	0	0	0	0	.000
Walt "No Neck" Williams	104	275	66	35	16	3	3	15	3	.240
Rocky Colavito	60	190	42	20	4	1	3	29	1	.221
Jim King	23	50	6	2	1	0	0	2	0	.120
Ed Stroud	20	27	8	6	0	1	0	3	7	.296
Bill Voss	13	22	2	4	0	0	0	0	1	.091
Charles "Buddy" Bradford	24	20	2	6	1	0	0	1	1	.100
Jimmy Stewart	24	18	3	5	0	0	0	1	1	.167
Duane Josephson	62	189	45	11	5	1	1	9	0	.238
Gerry McNertney	56	123	28	8	6	0	3	13	0	.228
Ed Herrmann	2	3	2	1	1	0	0	1	0	.667
Forrest "Smoky" Burgess	77	60	8	2	1	0	2	11	0	.133
Bill "Moose" Skowron	8	8	0	0	0	0	0	1	0	.000
		5,383	1,209	531	181	34	89	491	124	.225

	W	L	GS	CG	IP	H	BB	K	ShO	ERA
Gary Peters	16	11	36	11	260	187	91	215	3	2.28
Joel Horlen	19	7	36	13	258	188	58	103	6	2.06
Tommy John	10	13	29	9	178⅓	143	47	110	6	2.47
Bob Locker	7	5	0	0	124⅔	102	23	80	0	2.09
Bruce Howard	3	10	17	1	112⅔	102	52	76	0	3.43
Wilbur Wood	4	2	8	0	5⅓	95	28	47	0	2.45
Don McMahon	5	0	0	0	91⅔	54	27	74	0	1.67
Hoyt Wilhelm	8	3	0	0	89	58	34	76	0	1.31
John Buzhardt	3	9	7	0	88⅔	100	37	33	0	3.96
Jim O'Toole	4	3	10	1	54⅓	53	18	37	1	2.82
Fred Klages	4	4	9	0	44⅔	43	16	17	0	3.83
Francisco Carlos	2	0	7	1	41⅔	23	9	27	1	0.86
Steve Jones	2	2	3	0	25⅔	21	12	17	0	4.21
Dennis Higgins	1	2	0	0	12⅓	13	10	8	0	5.84
Roger Nelson	0	1	0	0	7	4	0	4	0	1.29
Jack Lamabe	1	0	0	0	5	7	1	3	0	1.80
Aurelio Monteagudo	0	1	1	0	1⅓	4	2	0	0	20.25
	89	73	162	36	1,490⅓	1,197	465	927	17	2.45

1968

Record: 67–95
Finish: Eighth (tie)
Games Behind: 36
Managers: Eddie Stanky, Les Moss, Al Lopez

Amid growing rumors that Arthur Allyn was pondering a move to Milwaukee because of the three-year attendance slide, mounting political opposition to Allyn's ambitious plan to build a privately financed domed stadium for the White Sox, and the lingering neighborhood fears, Ed Short addressed the serious need for hitting by completing two trades that looked great on paper but set in motion the White Sox' resounding 1968 collapse.

In November Short traded Don Buford and pitchers Bruce Howard and Roger Nelson to Baltimore for Louie Aparicio and Russ Snyder. Two weeks later Al Weis and Tommie Agee were dispatched to New York for former batting champ Tommy Davis and pitcher Jack Fisher. These ill-advised moves canceled Ed Short's youth movement, which had generally produced results up until this point.

Nineteen sixty-eight began disastrously with 10 straight losses. Roving batting instructor Grover "Deacon" Jones worked with the slumping ballclub, but the anemic Sox regulars were hitting only .176 after the first nine games and had scored only 11 runs. The newcomers—Snyder, Davis, and Aparicio—played tight and rebelled against Stanky's harsh edicts. "To hell with the fines...and him!" grumbled Snyder, who would be gone after only 38 games.

Unaccustomed to losing and sensitive to the criticisms of the Chicago press corps who bristled over a recent Stanky decision to declare his clubhouse off-limits to the media, Arthur Allyn allowed his manager to save face by resigning on July 12. It must have been a bitter pill for the Brat to swallow. Stanky often said that he would never quit—that is, until he was shoved out the door in favor of the man he originally replaced.

Al Lopez was summoned out of retirement to end the locker-room tensions and pick up the pieces. "Stanky nearly took the South Side franchise down the drain with him," wrote Brent Musburger in his *Chicago American* column, rejoicing at Stanky's departure.

Eddie Stanky was not the problem, as it turned out. Confidence emanated from the White Sox camp that Lopez could turn it around in the second half of the season, but the problems only multiplied. Attendance dwindled. The White Sox played 10 "home games" in Milwaukee as a dry run for their expected move to Beer Town. The red ink flowed freely in the ledger book, and suddenly the game of baseball was no longer fun to Art Allyn.

Tommy Davis was a key addition to the 1968 team, but the team still could not generate a good offense.

	G	AB	H	R	2B	3B	HR	RBI	SB	AVG
Tommy McCraw	136	477	112	51	16	12	9	44	20	.235
Sandy Alomar	133	363	92	41	8	2	0	12	21	.253
Luis Aparicio	155	622	164	55	24	4	4	36	17	.264
Pete Ward	125	399	86	43	15	0	15	50	4	.216
Charles "Buddy" Bradford	103	281	61	32	11	0	5	24	8	.217
Ken Berry	153	504	127	49	21	2	7	32	6	.252
Tommy Davis	132	456	122	30	5	3	8	50	4	.268
Duane Josephson	128	434	107	35	16	6	6	45	2	.247
Tim Cullen	72	155	31	16	7	0	2	13	0	.200
Dick Kenworthy	58	122	27	2	2	0	0	2	0	.221
Bill Melton	34	109	29	5	8	0	2	16	1	.266
Wayne Causey	59	100	18	8	2	0	0	7	0	.180
Ron Hansen	40	87	20	7	3	0	1	4	0	.230
Gail Hopkins	29	37	8	4	2	0	0	2	0	.216
Rich Morales	10	29	5	2	0	0	0	0	0	.172
Ken Boyer	10	24	3	0	0	0	0	0	0	.125
Bill Voss	61	167	26	14	2	1	2	15	5	.156
Leon Wagner	69	162	46	14	8	0	1	18	2	.284
Walt "No Neck" Williams	63	133	32	6	6	0	1	8	0	.241
Russ Synder	38	82	11	2	2	0	1	5	0	.134
Carlos May	17	67	12	4	1	0	0	1	0	.179
Woodie Held	40	54	9	5	1	0	0	2	0	.167
Gerry McNertney	74	169	37	18	4	1	3	18	0	.219
Richard "Buddy" Booker	5	5	0	0	0	0	0	0	0	.000
		5,405	1,233	463	169	33	71	431	90	.228

	W	L	GS	CG	IP	H	BB	K	ShO	ERA
Joel Horlen	12	14	35	4	223⅔	197	70	102	1	2.37
Jack Fisher	8	13	28	2	180⅔	176	48	80	0	2.99
Tommy John	10	5	25	5	177⅓	135	49	117	1	1.98
Gary Peters	4	13	25	6	162⅔	146	60	110	1	3.76
Wilbur Wood	13	12	2	0	159	127	33	74	0	1.87
Francisco Carlos	4	14	21	0	122⅓	121	37	57	0	3.90
Bob Priddy	3	11	18	2	114	106	41	66	0	3.63
Hoyt Wilhelm	4	4	0	0	93⅔	69	24	72	0	1.73
Bob Locker	5	4	0	0	90⅓	78	27	62	0	2.29
Don McMahon	2	1	0	0	46	31	20	32	0	1.96
Gerald Nyman	2	1	7	1	40⅓	38	16	27	1	2.01
Dennis Ribant	0	2	0	0	31⅓	42	17	20	0	6.03
Danny Lazar	0	1	1	0	13⅓	14	4	11	0	4.05
Fred Rath	0	0	0	0	11⅓	8	3	3	0	1.59
Billy Wynne	0	0	0	0	2	2	2	1	0	4.50
	67	95	162	20	1,468	1,290	451	834	4	2.75

1969

Record: 68–94
Finish: Fifth (West)
Games Behind: 29
Managers: Al Lopez, Don Gutteridge

The script called for Al Lopez and his coaches to guide the Sox through the first year of divisional realignment and then yield the floor to a new managerial regime carefully screened and evaluated by Ed Short and Art Allyn. Al's nervous stomach canceled out their drawing-board strategies on May 2.

The Lopez resignation was not unexpected. He had suffered in pain since November and had trouble sleeping through the night. "This is it. I'm through as an active manager," he told Short by phone from the White Sox' hotel in Minneapolis.

The selection of first-base coach Don Gutteridge followed. No one was more surprised—or ill-prepared—to manage the White Sox than the likable but inept Gutteridge, who said he had "learned a lot working for Lopez." It was hard to fathom Gutteridge's thinking when he announced the first of his projected personnel changes: "I'm thinking of putting Bill Melton in right field."

Young Melton was a power-hitting third baseman who vied for Rookie of the Year honors with teammate Carlos May. By no stretch of the imagination, however, was he qualified to patrol the outfield pastures with his limited range.

Bill Melton, Carlos May, and the little "fireplug" Walt Williams provided the singular highlights of a forgettable year. After an encouraging start, the Sox dipped below the .500 mark for good on May 25 and hunkered down in the lower tier of the division.

Carlos May's outstanding season was cut short on August 11, when a misfiring mortar blew off a piece of his right thumb at Camp Pendleton, California. The mishap brought to mind the earlier tragedies befalling Monty Stratton and Jackie Hayes, whose White Sox career was cut short by blindness in 1940.

Art Allyn fumed over the League's decision to exile his team into the West Division with the two expansion teams and the West Coast ballclubs. The late-night games from Oakland, Seattle, and California created havoc with the TV ratings and buried the Sox next to the obituaries in the early morning newspapers. Leo Durocher's surprising, winning Cubs enjoyed a monopoly of the Chicago baseball coverage in 1969.

Home attendance fell to a 31-year low. Bud Selig, heading an entrepreneurial group seeking a new baseball team for Milwaukee, pressed Allyn for a firm commitment to move the Sox into empty County Stadium for the 1970 season. Arthur vacillated. He was eager to cut his losses and quit baseball. By the same token, his public image would suffer a blow by abandoning the South Side. At the hour of decision Art did the right thing. He turned down Selig's generous offer and sold his controlling stock to his brother John, who committed his energies and resources toward restoring luster to the franchise. The White Sox were safe at home…for the moment.

	G	AB	H	R	2B	3B	HR	RBI	SB	AVG
Gail Hopkins	124	373	99	52	13	3	8	46	2	.265
Bobby Knoop	104	345	79	34	14	1	6	41	2	.229
Luis Aparicio	156	599	168	77	24	5	5	51	24	.280
Bill Melton	157	556	142	67	26	2	23	87	1	.255
Walt "No Neck" Williams	135	471	143	59	22	1	3	32	6	.304
Ken Berry	130	297	69	25	12	2	4	18	1	.232
Carlos May	100	367	103	62	18	2	18	62	1	.281
Ed Herrmann	102	290	67	31	8	0	8	31	0	.231
Tommy McCraw	93	240	62	21	12	2	2	25	1	.258
Pete Ward	105	199	49	22	7	0	6	32	0	.246
Ron Hansen	85	185	48	15	6	1	2	22	2	.259
Rich Morales	55	121	26	12	0	1	0	6	1	.215
Sandy Alomar	22	58	13	8	2	0	0	4	2	.224
Bob Spence	12	26	4	0	1	0	0	3	0	.154
Charles "Buddy" Bradford	93	273	70	36	8	2	11	27	5	.256
Bob Christian	39	129	28	11	4	0	3	16	3	.217
Angel Bravo	27	90	26	10	4	2	1	3	2	.289
Woodie Held	56	63	9	9	2	0	3	6	0	.143
Jose Ortiz	16	11	3	0	1	0	0	2	0	.273
Don Pavletich	78	188	46	26	12	0	6	33	0	.245
Duane Josephson	52	162	39	19	6	2	1	20	0	.241
Chuck Brinkman	14	15	1	2	0	0	0	0	0	.067
Doug Adams	8	14	3	1	0	0	0	1	0	.214
		5,450	1,346	625	210	27	112	585	54	.247

	W	L	GS	CG	IP	H	BB	K	ShO	ERA
Joel Horlen	13	16	35	7	235⅔	237	77	121	2	3.78
Tommy John	9	11	33	6	232⅓	230	90	128	2	3.25
Gary Peters	10	15	32	7	218⅔	238	78	140	3	4.53
Billy Wynne	7	7	20	6	128⅔	143	50	67	1	4.06
Wilbur Wood	10	11	0	0	119⅔	113	40	73	0	3.01
Paul Edmondson	1	6	13	1	87⅔	72	39	46	0	3.70
Gerry Nyman	4	4	10	2	64⅔	58	39	40	1	5.29
Dan Osinski	5	5	0	0	60⅔	56	23	27	0	3.56
Francisco Carlos	4	3	4	0	49⅓	52	23	28	0	5.66
Don Secrist	0	1	0	0	40	35	14	23	0	6.08
Gary Bell	0	0	2	0	38⅔	48	23	26	0	6.28
Danny Murphy	2	1	0	0	31⅓	28	10	16	0	2.01
Sammy Ellis	0	3	5	0	29⅓	42	16	15	0	5.83
Bart Johnson	1	3	3	0	22⅓	22	6	18	0	3.22
Bob Locker	2	3	0	0	22	26	6	15	0	6.55
Danny Lazar	0	0	3	0	20⅔	21	11	9	0	6.53
Jack Hamilton	0	3	0	0	12⅓	23	7	5	0	11.68
Fred Rath	0	2	2	0	11⅔	11	8	4	0	7.71
Bob Priddy	0	0	0	0	8	10	2	5	0	4.50
Dennis O'Toole	0	0	0	0	4	5	2	4	0	6.75
	68	94	162	29	1,437⅔	1,470	564	810	9	4.21

1970

Record: 56–106
Finish: Sixth (West)
Games Behind: 42
Managers: Don Gutteridge, Billy Adair, Chuck Tanner

Don Gutteridge failed in a number of ways to marshal control of a young ballclub sorely lacking in direction. Among other things, the soft-spoken manager from Pittsburg, Kansas, neither commanded respect nor enforced discipline.

During spring training Gutteridge neglected the fundamentals—teaching run-down plays, the cutoff. Instead, he emphasized batting practice—hours and hours of batting practice.

The White Sox were ill-prepared to begin the 1970 season. Blown out 12–0 by the Minnesota Twins on Opening Day before a tiny gathering of 11,473, they never achieved the .500 mark at any time in 1970. This team could generate offense that in other years would have been enough to carry them over the top. But the pitching staff was horrendous, and the fielding even worse. Gutteridge insisted on playing Bill Melton in right field at the expense of Walt "No Neck" Williams, the team's most popular player and only .300 hitter in 1969. Williams was frequently benched amid outcries from angry Sox fans.

Part of Gutteridge's problems were easily traced to the front office, where Ed Short (who had been elevated to a vice presidency in 1969) virtually ignored the farm system while adhering to a penny-pinching policy that sacrificed good players for little or nothing in return. The off-season trade of Gary Peters to Boston for infielder Sidney Lloyd O'Brien and pitcher Billy Farmer (who failed to report), were characteristic of the panic moves that dragged the team further down.

Amid the wreckage of their worst season ever (loss No. 103 on September 28 established a new record in this department), it was ironic and kind of sad that Luis Aparicio should enjoy a career year under such tough circumstances. Little Louie, rumored as a possible successor to Gutteridge, reached the .300 mark for the only time in his career and was rewarded with his own "day" on July 19. In December a new regime ungraciously traded Louie to Boston.

John Allyn believed he owed his manager the courtesy of one year to try to turn things around after taking over the team from his brother in September 1969. By July, however, Mr. Allyn's patience ended. This team was complacent and unconcerned—very "sportsmanlike" in defeat.

Round one on the road to respectability: Ed Short was fired on September 1 and replaced by Stu Holcomb, a former head football coach at Purdue, and more recently the White Sox public relations maven. The next day Holcomb paid a call on Don Gutteridge in Anaheim and allowed him the choice of quitting now or being fired later. Gutteridge resigned, but said he was "not spiteful."

The task of remaking the White Sox was a formidable one. Holcomb knew it but was up to the challenge. He found the new "Frank Lane–Paul Richards" tandem in 42-year-old Pacific Coast League manager Chuck Tanner and Roland Hemond, an executive hidden away in the California Angels farm system. Holcomb vested complete authority in Hemond as the director of player personnel.

Hemond and Tanner were unknown commodities, as were Lane and Richards 20 years earlier in set of circumstances that was parallel—with one exception: the continuity of the franchise was at stake. There was a greater urgency attached to the mission than ever before. The White Sox had to turn things around fast—or risk going bankrupt and having to leave town.

Staff ace Tommy John in 1970

	G	AB	H	R	2B	3B	HR	RBI	SB	AVG
Gail Hopkins	116	287	82	32	8	1	6	29	0	.286
Bobby Knoop	130	402	92	34	13	2	5	36	0	.229
Luis Aparicio	146	552	173	86	29	3	5	43	8	.313
Bill Melton	141	514	135	74	15	1	33	96	2	.263
Walt "No Neck" Williams	110	315	79	43	18	1	3	15	3	.251
Ken Berry	141	463	128	45	12	2	7	50	6	.276
Carlos May	150	555	158	83	28	4	12	68	12	.285
Ed Herrmann	96	297	84	42	9	0	19	52	0	.283
Sydney O'Brien	121	441	109	48	13	2	8	44	3	.247
Tommy McCraw	129	332	73	39	11	2	6	31	12	.220
Bob Spence	46	130	29	11	4	1	4	15	0	.223
Rich McKinney	43	119	20	12	5	0	4	17	3	.168
Rich Morales	62	112	18	6	2	0	1	2	1	.161
Ossie Blanco	34	66	13	4	0	0	0	8	0	.197
John "Pineapple" Matias	58	117	22	7	2	0	2	6	1	.188
Charles "Buddy" Bradford	32	91	17	8	3	0	2	8	1	.187
Jose Ortiz	15	24	8	4	1	0	0	1	1	.333
Bob Christian	12	15	4	3	0	0	1	3	0	.267
Duane Josephson	96	285	90	28	12	1	4	41	1	.316
Chuck Brinkman	9	20	5	4	1	0	0	0	0	.250
Art Kusyner	4	10	1	0	0	0	0	0	0	.100
Lee Maye	6	6	1	0	0	0	0	1	0	.167
		5,514	1,394	633	192	20	123	587	54	.253

	W	L	GS	CG	IP	H	BB	K	ShO	ERA
Tommy John	12	17	37	10	269	253	101	138	3	3.28
Jerry Janeski	10	17	35	4	206	247	63	79	1	4.76
Joel Horlen	6	16	26	4	172	198	41	77	0	4.87
Wilbur Wood	9	13	0	0	122	118	36	85	0	2.80
Jerry Crider	4	7	8	0	91	101	34	40	0	4.45
Bart Johnson	4	7	15	2	90	92	46	71	1	4.80
Danny Murphy	2	3	0	0	81	82	49	42	0	5.67
Barry Moore	0	4	7	0	70⅔	85	34	34	0	6.37
Bob Miller	4	6	12	0	70	88	33	36	0	5.01
Floyd Weaver	1	2	3	0	62	52	31	51	0	4.35
Jim Magnuson	1	5	6	0	45	45	16	20	0	4.80
Billy Wynne	1	4	9	0	44	54	22	19	0	5.32
Tommie Sisk	1	1	1	0	33	37	13	16	0	5.45
Lee Stange	1	0	0	0	22⅓	28	5	14	0	5.24
Don Secrist	0	0	0	0	15	19	12	9	0	5.40
Gerry Arrigo	0	3	3	0	13	24	9	12	0	13.15
Don Eddy	0	0	0	0	12	10	6	9	0	2.25
Virle "Gene" Rounsaville	0	1	0	0	6	10	2	3	0	10.50
Steve Hamilton	0	0	0	0	3	4	1	3	0	6.00
Dennis O'Toole	0	0	0	0	3	5	2	3	0	3.00
Rich Maloney	0	0	0	0	1	2	0	1	0	0.00
	56	106	162	20	1,430⅓	1,554	556	762	5	4.56

September 14, 1970. Changing of the guard as Stu Holcomb (standing) introduces Roland Hemond as director of player personnel (left) and the team's new manager, Chuck Tanner.

1971

Record: 79–83
Finish: Third (West)
Games Behind: 22½
Manager: Chuck Tanner

Thirteen new players, a change of uniforms, and a new aggressive attitude symbolized by the presence of tell-it-like-it-is Harry Caray in the broadcast booth spelled a rebirth of interest in White Sox baseball.

Roland Hemond, who was the antithesis of the flamboyant Frank Lane but no less effective in identifying "situation" players who could deliver spectacular results for half the going rate, rebuilt from scratch.

More than 43,000 fans jammed Comiskey Park on Opening Day to acquaint themselves with a bevy of Hemond newcomers: Pat Kelly, Jay Johnstone, Rick Reichardt, Mike Andrews, Tom Bradley, Tom Egan, Steve Kealey, Vincente Romo, Tony Muser, and Luis Alvarado.

Chuck Tanner managed with gusto. His sunny, cheerfully optimistic disposition won the media over and appealed to the fans after five years of the Stanky cold war and Don Gutteridge's apathy. Behind closed doors, however, Tanner was nothing like the snoozing Gutteridge. He prodded lazy players and enforced discipline—but he always shielded his players from the prying eyes of the media. In time, the reporters would come to resent Tanner's stonewalling.

The 1971 improvement was gradual. The White Sox were mired in last place on July 8, nine games under .500, before putting it together in an August–September drive spearheaded by the unhittable Wilbur Wood. Pitching coach Johnny Sain shrewdly recognized something in Woody that had been overlooked by three previous managers. After Joe Horlen went down with an injury in the spring, Wood was converted to a starting role. Overnight he became the ace of the staff, relying on a knuckleball pitch taught to him by Hoyt Wilhelm.

September 30, 1971: Going into the last day of the season Bill Melton was deadlocked with Reggie Jackson and Norm Cash for the AL home run championship with 32. Chuck Tanner inserted Melton into the leadoff spot in order to give him one extra shot at a first-ever White Sox home run crown.

In the third inning Melton drilled a line drive into the left-field grandstand off Milwaukee Brewers pitcher Bill Parsons. It was a historic moment for Melton and for the franchise, but like so many of the glories of the "Old Roman" empire, this one occurred on a day when no one was watching. Less than 3,000 fans were present to witness it.

	G	AB	H	R	2B	3B	HR	RBI	SB	AVG
Carlos May	141	500	147	64	21	7	7	70	16	.294
Mike Andrews	109	330	93	45	16	0	12	47	3	.282
Luis Alvarado	99	264	57	22	14	1	0	8	1	.216
Bill Melton	150	543	146	72	18	2	33	86	3	.269
Walt "No Neck" Williams	114	361	106	43	17	3	8	35	5	.294
Jay Johnstone	124	388	101	53	14	1	16	40	10	.260
Rick Reichardt	138	496	138	53	14	2	19	62	5	.278
Ed Herrmann	101	294	63	32	6	0	11	35	2	.214
Rich McKinney	114	369	100	35	11	2	8	46	0	.271
Lee "Bee Bee" Richard	87	260	60	38	7	3	2	17	8	.231
Rich Morales	84	185	45	19	8	0	2	14	2	.243
Steve Huntz	35	86	18	10	3	1	2	6	1	.209
Bob Spence	14	27	4	2	0	0	0	1	0	.148
Tony Muser	11	16	5	2	0	1	0	0	0	.313
Pat Kelly	67	213	62	32	6	3	3	22	14	.291
Mike Hershberger	74	177	46	22	9	0	2	15	6	.260
Ed Stroud	53	141	25	19	4	3	0	2	4	.177
Lee Maye	32	44	9	6	2	0	1	7	0	.205
Ken Hottman	6	16	2	1	0	0	0	0	0	.125
Ron Lolich	2	8	1	0	1	0	0	0	0	.125
Tom Egan	85	251	60	29	11	1	10	34	1	.239
Chuck Brinkman	15	20	4	0	0	0	0	1	0	.200
		5,382	1,346	617	185	30	138	568	83	.250

	W	L	GS	CG	IP	H	BB	K	ShO	ERA
Wilbur Wood	22	13	42	22	334	272	62	210	7	1.91
Tom Bradley	15	15	39	7	285⅔	273	74	206	6	2.96
Tommy John	13	16	35	10	229⅓	244	58	131	3	3.62
Bart Johnson	12	10	16	4	178	148	111	153	0	2.93
Joel Horlen	8	9	18	3	137⅓	150	30	82	0	4.27
Steve Kealey	2	2	1	0	77⅓	69	26	50	0	3.86
Vincente Romo	1	7	2	0	72	52	37	48	0	3.38
Terry Forster	2	3	3	0	49⅔	46	23	48	0	3.96
Jim Magnuson	2	1	4	0	30	30	16	11	0	4.50
Rich Hinton	2	4	2	0	24⅓	27	6	15	0	4.50
Don Eddy	0	2	0	0	22⅔	19	19	14	0	2.35
Stan Perzanowski	0	1	0	0	6	14	3	5	0	12.00
Dennis O'Toole	0	0	0	0	2	0	1	2	0	0.00
Pat Jacquez	0	0	0	0	2	4	2	1	0	4.50
	79	83	162	46	1,450⅓	1,348	468	976	16	3.13

1972

Record: 87–67
Finish: Second (West)
Games Behind: 5½
Manager: Chuck Tanner

Roland Hemond completed the most controversial and talked-about trade in White Sox history at the annual winter meeting: Tommy John and infielder Steve Huntz to the Los Angeles Dodgers for Richie "Dick" Allen, the power-hitting enigma who had worn out his welcome in Philadelphia, St. Louis, and L.A. Allen supplied the Sox with the main ingredient, a deadly No. 3 hitter to sandwich between Pat Kelly, Bill Melton, and Carlos May.

Years later Roland Hemond would often speak of Allen as the "savior of the franchise." Richie gave the White Sox two and a half seasons packed with many thrilling, often unforgettable moments. Allen's 37 home runs in 1972 shattered Bill Melton's team record, and his relentless parade of extra-base hits earned Richie the Most Valuable Player award—a well-deserved honor. However, Tommy John's finest achievements on a baseball diamond would occur long after Allen had retired from the game. As a short-term solution to the White Sox' financial woes, the deal was an outstanding one, if only for the reason that it brought people *back* to Comiskey Park.

The White Sox were the youngest team in the majors when the strike-shortened campaign finally got under way on April 15. Despite losing Bill Melton for the season with a herniated disc, the Sox were a persistent threat to Charley Finley's Oakland A's—an American League juggernaut that surpassed Chicago at nearly every position, except first base where Dick Allen held court.

Chuck Tanner was short a starting pitcher and very weak at both the shortstop and third-base positions. But with Wilbur Wood pitching every three days (sometimes two) the Sox were a real and present danger to the A's. The No. 2 starter was Stan Bahnsen, a fine off-season acquisition who came from the New York Yankees for Rich McKinney, one of the top-rated third-base prospects of the Gutteridge era. McKinney had simply lost his nerve after being asked to convert to shortstop.

Bahnsen won 21 games despite earning the dubious nickname of "Stanley Struggle" because he always seemed to do his best pitching with two men on base and only one out. "How that fellow wins all those ballgames is a mystery to me," pondered Ralph Houk.

The firm of Allyn, Allen, Tanner, & Hemond had restored the mantle of respectability to the franchise following three of the darkest years in team history, 1968 to 1970. Expressing the hopes of Sox fans everywhere, Stu Holcomb looked to 1973 as *the* year: "The way I see it, our goal—an American League pennant—is only 162 games away!"

	G	AB	H	R	2B	3B	HR	RBI	SB	AVG
Dick Allen	148	506	156	90	28	5	37	113	19	.308
Mike Andrews	148	505	111	58	18	0	7	50	2	.220
Rich Morales	110	287	59	24	7	1	2	20	2	.206
Ed Spiezio	74	277	66	20	10	1	2	22	0	.238
Pat Kelly	119	402	105	57	14	7	5	24	32	.261
Rick Reichardt	101	291	73	31	14	4	8	43	2	.251
Carlos May	148	523	161	83	26	3	12	68	23	.308
Ed Herrmann	116	354	88	23	9	0	10	40	0	.249
Luis Alvarado	103	254	54	30	4	1	4	29	2	.213
Bill Melton	57	208	51	22	5	0	7	30	1	.245
Jorge Orta	51	124	25	20	3	1	3	11	3	.202
Tony Muser	44	61	17	6	2	2	1	9	1	.279
Hank Allen	9	21	3	1	0	0	0	0	0	.143
Rudy Hernandez	8	21	4	0	0	0	0	1	0	.190
Hugh Yancy	3	9	1	0	0	0	0	0	0	.111
Jay Johnstone	113	261	49	27	9	0	4	17	2	.188
Walt "No Neck" Williams	77	221	55	22	7	1	2	11	6	.249
Jim Lyttle	44	82	19	8	5	2	0	5	0	.232
Charles "Buddy" Bradford	35	48	13	13	2	0	2	8	3	.271
Lee "Bee Bee" Richard	11	29	7	5	0	0	0	1	1	.241
Jim Qualls	11	10	0	0	0	0	0	0	0	.000
Tom Egan	50	141	27	8	3	0	2	9	0	.191
Chuck Brinkman	35	52	7	1	0	0	0	0	0	.135
		5,083	1,208	566	170	28	108	528	100	.238

	W	L	GS	CG	IP	H	BB	K	ShO	ERA
Wilbur Wood	24	17	49	20	376⅔	325	74	193	8	2.51
Tom Bradley	15	14	40	11	260	225	65	209	2	2.98
Stan Bahnsen	21	16	41	5	252⅓	263	73	157	1	3.60
Terry Forster	6	5	0	0	100	75	44	104	0	2.25
Dave Lemonds	4	7	18	0	94⅔	87	38	69	0	2.95
Rich "Goose" Gossage	7	1	1	0	80	72	44	57	0	4.28
Steve Kealey	3	2	0	0	57⅓	50	12	37	0	3.30
Vincente Romo	3	0	0	0	51⅔	47	18	46	0	3.31
Cecilio "Cy" Acosta	3	0	0	0	34⅔	25	17	28	0	1.56
Eddie Fisher	0	1	4	0	22⅓	31	9	10	0	4.43
Bart Johnson	0	3	0	0	13⅔	18	13	9	0	9.22
Phil Regan	0	1	0	0	13⅓	18	6	4	0	4.05
Jim Geddes	0	0	1	0	10⅓	12	10	3	0	6.97
Moe Drabowsky	0	0	0	0	7⅓	6	2	4	0	2.45
Dennis O'Toole	0	0	0	0	5	10	2	5	0	5.40
Dan Neumeier	0	0	0	0	3⅔	2	3	0	0	7.36
Ken Frailing	1	0	0	0	3	3	1	1	0	3.00
	87	67	154	36	1,386	1,269	431	936	11	3.12

1973

Record: 77–85
Finish: Fifth (West)
Games Behind: 17
Manager: Chuck Tanner

Things are never as they seem. Thirty-eight injuries befell the White Sox in 1973, proving that "the Curse of the Comiskeys" was alive and prospering in the new decade. Dick Allen fractured his kneecap on June 28 in Anaheim and was lost for the season. Ken Henderson, Carlos May, Pat Kelly, Brian Downing, and other members of the supporting cast were shelved at various times, negating a strong 27–15 start that catapulted the Sox into an early lead that looked like it might hold up. Pitching on a steady diet of two days' rest, Wilbur Wood won his 12th game before Memorial Day and was charting a course to a 30-victory season when injuries and dissension befell the ballclub.

The same day Allen went down with his injury, Mike Andrews and Rick Reichardt were released after bickering with Mr. Allyn over their pay. There was a current of dissatisfaction

Stu Holcomb: deposed in a palace coup

and jealousy toward Dick Allen's boxcar-sized salary and exempt status, and it was reflected in the team's play.

A front-office intrigue pitting Stu Holcomb against Chuck Tanner and Roland Hemond led to Holcomb's fast exit on July 27. Fearing the loss of his talented young manager, John Allyn sided against Holcomb, whose authority to chart policy was undermined all season by the manager. Tanner's special set of rules governing his temperamental superstar struck Holcomb as rather unfair, not to mention establishing dangerous precedents for the other players.

"The season starts tomorrow!" glowed Chuck Tanner on August 5. Peace and harmony were restored, even as the losses continued to mount.

	G	AB	H	R	2B	3B	HR	RBI	SB	AVG
Tony Muser	109	309	88	38	14	3	4	30	8	.285
Jorge Orta	128	425	113	46	9	10	6	40	8	.266
Eddie Leon	127	399	91	37	10	3	3	30	1	.228
Bill Melton	152	561	155	85	29	1	20	87	4	.276
Pat Kelly	144	550	154	77	24	5	1	44	22	.280
Johnny Jeter	89	299	72	39	14	4	7	26	5	.241
Bill Sharp	76	196	54	23	8	3	4	22	2	.276
Ed Herrmann	119	379	85	42	17	1	10	39	2	.224
Carlos May	149	553	148	61	20	0	20	96	8	.268
Dick Allen	72	250	79	39	20	3	16	41	7	.316
Luis Alvarado	79	203	47	21	7	2	0	20	6	.232
Mike Andrews	53	159	32	10	9	0	0	10	0	.201
Russell "Bucky" Dent	40	117	29	17	2	0	0	10	2	.248
Hank Allen	28	39	4	2	2	0	0	0	0	.103
Sam Ewing	11	20	3	1	1	0	0	2	0	.150
Rich Morales	7	4	0	1	0	0	0	1	0	.000
Ken Henderson	73	262	68	31	13	0	6	32	3	.260
Jerry Hairston	60	210	57	25	11	1	0	23	0	.271
Charles "Buddy" Bradford	53	168	40	24	3	1	8	15	4	.238
Rick Reichardt	46	153	42	15	8	1	3	16	2	.275
Brian Downing	34	73	13	4	1	0	2	4	0	.178
Chuck Brinkman	63	139	26	13	6	0	1	10	0	.187
Pete Varney	5	4	0	0	0	0	0	0	0	.000
Joe Keough	5	1	0	1	0	0	0	0	0	.000
		5,475	1,400	652	228	38	111	598	84	.256

	W	L	GS	CG	IP	H	BB	K	ShO	ERA
Wilbur Wood	24	20	48	21	359⅓	381	91	199	4	3.46
Stan Bahnsen	18	21	42	14	282⅓	290	117	120	4	3.57
Steve Stone	6	11	22	3	176⅓	163	82	138	0	4.29
Terry Forster	6	11	12	4	172⅔	174	78	120	0	3.23
Eddie Fisher	6	7	16	2	110⅔	135	38	57	0	4.88
Cecillo "Cy" Acosta	10	6	0	0	97	66	39	60	0	2.23
Bart Johnson	3	3	9	0	80⅔	76	40	56	0	4.13
Rich "Goose" Gossage	0	4	4	1	49⅔	57	37	33	0	7.43
Jim Kaat	4	1	7	3	42⅔	44	4	16	1	4.22
Jim McGlothlin	0	1	1	0	18⅓	13	13	14	0	3.93
Ken Frailing	0	0	0	0	18⅓	18	7	15	0	1.96
Dennis O'Toole	0	0	0	0	17	23	3	8	0	5.29
Jim Geddes	0	0	1	0	15⅔	13	14	7	0	2.87
Steve Kealey	0	0	0	0	11⅓	23	7	4	0	15.09
Dave Baldwin	0	0	0	0	5	7	4	1	0	3.60
	77	85	162	48	1,457	1,483	574	848	9	3.87

1974

Record: 80–80
Finish: Fourth (West)
Games Behind: 9
Manager: Chuck Tanner

The useless acquisition of Ron Santo, the great Cubs third baseman of years gone by, was greeted with jubilation by Sox promotions director Millie Johnson: "Ronnie honey, you're going to sell a lot of tickets for us!" (Attendance dropped by more than 150,000 in 1974.)

With Bill Melton and Ron Santo in tow, the Sox were deep at third base but weak in the pitching department. Wilbur Wood, Stan Bahnsen, and lefty Jim Kaat, who arrived via league waivers in late 1973, formed a veteran nucleus of starters the eternally optimistic Chuck Tanner looked to with confidence. "This is the strongest White Sox team in history!" lauded Tanner, whose silly dugout cheerleading chipped away at his sinking credibility.

Rookie pitcher Carl "Bugs" Moran, one of many unsuccessful candidates for the fourth spot in the rotation took the

Sox general manager Roland Hemond (right) celebrates the arrival of Ron Santo, his new second baseman.

mound for the first time on May 13, nervously inquiring of his teammates: "What are they going to play? The National Anthem or taps?"

Top to bottom this was a .500 ballclub, nothing more. Ron Santo alternated between second base and designated hitter with little success. Santo, a gritty campaigner, usurped leadership from Tanner and was vocal in his criticisms of Dick Allen's special privileges. Allen, who led the league in home runs with 32 in 1974, was bothered by a shoulder injury that was slow to heal, and he seemed to resent Santo and the changes he sensed within the organization. With a year to go on his $250,000 contract, the "Sox savior" called the players together on September 14 to tearfully announce his "retirement" from baseball. Allen changed his mind over the winter but did not return to Chicago. If he had to do it all over again, Dick Allen would undoubtedly have chosen to remain in the Windy City where the South Side fans always treated him as a hero—and not as an outcast.

	G	AB	H	R	2B	3B	HR	RBI	SB	AVG
Dick Allen	128	462	139	84	23	1	32	88	7	.301
Jorge Orta	139	525	166	73	31	2	10	67	9	.316
Russell "Bucky" Dent	154	496	136	55	15	3	5	45	3	.274
Bill Melton	136	495	120	63	17	0	21	63	3	.242
Bill Sharp	100	320	81	45	13	2	4	24	0	.253
Ken Henderson	162	602	176	76	35	5	20	95	12	.292
Carlos May	149	551	137	66	19	2	8	58	8	.249
Ed Herrmann	107	367	95	32	13	1	10	39	1	.259
Pat Kelly	122	424	119	60	16	3	4	21	18	.281
Ron Santo	117	375	83	29	12	1	5	41	0	.221
Tony Muser	103	206	60	16	5	1	1	18	1	.291
Lee "Bee Bee" Richard	32	67	11	5	1	0	0	1	0	.164
Eddie Leon	31	46	5	1	1	0	0	3	0	.109
Bill Stein	13	43	12	5	1	0	0	5	0	.279
Lamar Johnson	10	29	10	1	0	0	0	2	0	.345
Luis Alvarado	8	10	1	1	0	0	0	0	0	.100
Hugh Yancy	1	0	0	0	0	0	0	0	0	.000
Jerry Hairston	45	109	25	8	7	0	0	8	0	.229
Charles "Buddy" Bradford	39	96	32	16	2	0	5	10	1	.333
Nyls Nyman	5	14	9	5	2	1	0	4	1	.643
Brian Downing	108	293	66	41	12	1	10	39	0	.225
Pete Varney	9	28	7	1	0	0	0	2	0	.250
Chuck Brinkman	8	14	2	1	0	0	0	0	0	.143
		5,577	1,492	684	225	23	135	633	64	.268

	W	L	GS	CG	IP	H	BB	K	ShO	ERA
Wilbur Wood	20	19	42	22	320⅓	305	80	169	1	3.60
Jim Kaat	21	13	39	15	277⅓	263	63	142	3	2.92
Stan Bahnsen	12	15	35	10	216⅓	230	110	102	1	4.71
Terry Forster	7	8	1	0	134⅓	120	48	105	0	3.63
Bart Johnson	10	4	18	8	121⅔	105	32	76	2	2.73
Lee "Skip" Pitlock	3	3	5	0	105⅔	103	55	68	0	4.42
Rich "Goose" Gossage	4	6	3	0	89⅓	92	47	64	0	4.15
Carl "Bugs" Moran	1	3	5	0	46⅓	57	23	17	0	4.70
Cecilio "Cy" Acosta	0	3	0	0	45⅔	43	18	19	0	3.72
Jack Kucek	1	4	7	0	37⅔	48	21	25	0	5.21
Ken Tatum	0	0	1	0	20⅔	23	9	5	0	4.71
Jim Otten	0	1	1	0	16⅓	22	12	11	0	5.63
Joe Henderson	1	0	3	0	15	21	11	12	0	8.40
Wayne Granger	0	0	0	0	7⅔	16	3	4	0	7.88
Lloyd Allen	0	1	2	0	7	7	12	3	0	10.29
Francisco Barrios	0	0	0	0	2	7	2	2	0	27.00
Stan Perzanowski	0	0	1	0	2⅓	8	2	2	0	22.50
	80	80	163	55	1,465⅔	1,470	548	826	7	3.94

1975

Record: 75–86
Finish: Fifth (West)
Games Behind: 22½
Manager: Chuck Tanner

John Allyn gambled it all on Dick Allen and lost. Without the name of the home run champ to stimulate the turnstiles in 1975, the cupboard was bare both financially and artistically. The farm system, still reeling from the aftershocks of the 1960 Veeck trades, delivered only a handful of noteworthy prospects to the parent ballclub in the mid-1970s. Shortstop Bucky Dent, catcher Brian Downing, and first baseman Lamar Johnson were productive—but they were not "stars" in the usual sense of the word.

As the rumors of an impending sale of the ballclub to the Torco Oil Company and other interested parties bubbled to the surface in mid-June, Allyn demanded a shakeup in personnel. Costly veterans had to go—the owner could no longer afford to pay their salaries. John Allyn's various financial holdings had suffered an aggregate $8 million dollar loss since 1970. Saving the White Sox for Chicago was driving the beleagured owner into bankruptcy.

In the next few days, Roland Hemond once again demonstrated his value to the organization by trading Stan Bahnsen to Oakland for pitcher Dave Hamilton and third baseman Chester Lemon, a top prospect in the Southern Association. The trade augered well for the future and seemed to recharge the team's battery.

Chicago crept to within a game of the .500 mark on August 1. The attendance improved with the team's second-half resurgence. Life was on an upswing for Mr. Allyn, who decided to increase his asking price to $20 million—$6 million for Comiskey Park and $14 million for the ballclub.

In September the Sox tumbled and the crowds dwindled to fewer than 10,000. Home attendance reached a five-year low. Reality hit home when Allyn was faced with the grim prospect of missing his final payroll of the season. The choice boiled down to selling the White Sox to a Seattle-based syndicate that would have moved the team to the Pacific Northwest or to Bill Veeck, whose unconventional methods and sense of whimsy irritated the AL moguls. The owners would rather have moved the Sox out of Chicago than admit Veeck back into the lodge.

The issue went right down to the wire. Veeck's method of financing the purchase was sharply questioned before the owners agreed to a compromise. Bill Veeck was given seven days to raise an additional $1.2 million in capital, or the team would be sent to Seattle. At considerable cost, John Allyn held out for Veeck against the advice of his accountants and certain AL owners anxious to placate the Seattle syndicate.

Somehow or another, Veeck managed to pull a rabbit out of the hat. He hustled up the money and returned to the table a week later, defying the league to turn him down. On December 10, 1975, Allyn's sale to Veeck was approved by a vote of 10–2, with Charley Finley and Gene Autry casting the only negative votes.

After 14 years Veeck and his "Over the Hill Gang" were back in business.

	G	AB	H	R	2B	3B	HR	RBI	SB	AVG
Carlos May	128	454	123	55	19	2	8	53	12	.271
Jorge Orta	140	542	165	64	26	10	11	83	16	.304
Russell "Bucky" Dent	157	602	159	52	29	4	3	58	2	.264
Bill Melton	149	512	123	62	16	0	15	70	5	.240
Pat Kelly	133	471	129	73	21	7	9	45	18	.274
Nyls Nyman	106	327	74	36	6	3	2	28	10	.226
Ken Henderson	140	513	129	65	20	3	9	53	5	.251
Brian Downing	138	420	101	58	12	1	7	41	13	.240
Deron Johnson	148	555	129	66	25	1	18	72	0	.232
Bill Stein	76	226	61	23	7	1	3	21	2	.270
Tony Muser	43	111	27	11	3	0	0	6	2	.243
Mike Squires	20	65	15	5	0	0	0	4	3	.231
Lee "Bee Bee" Richard	43	45	9	11	0	1	0	5	2	.200
Chet Lemon	9	35	9	2	2	0	0	1	1	.257
Lamar Johnson	8	30	6	2	3	0	1	1	0	.200
Gerry Moses	2	2	1	1	0	1	0	0	0	.500
Jerry Hairston	69	219	62	26	8	0	0	23	1	.283
Bobby Coluccio	61	161	33	22	4	2	4	13	4	.205
Charles "Buddy" Bradford	25	58	9	8	3	1	2	15	3	.155
Bill Sharp	18	35	7	1	0	0	0	4	0	.200
Pete Varney	36	107	29	12	5	1	2	8	2	.271
		5,490	1,400	655	209	38	94	604	101	.255

	W	L	GS	CG	IP	H	BB	K	ShO	ERA
Jim Kaat	20	14	41	12	303⅔	321	77	142	1	3.11
Wilbur Wood	16	20	43	14	291⅓	309	92	140	2	4.11
Claude Osteen	7	16	37	5	204⅓	237	92	63	0	4.36
Rich "Goose" Gossage	9	8	0	0	141⅔	99	70	130	0	1.84
Jesse Jefferson	5	9	21	1	107⅔	100	94	67	0	5.10
Dave Hamilton	6	5	1	0	69⅔	63	29	51	0	2.84
Stan Bahnsen	4	6	12	2	67⅓	78	40	31	0	6.01
Dan Osborn	3	0	0	0	58	57	37	38	0	4.50
Bill Gogolewski	0	0	0	0	55	61	28	37	0	5.24
Cecil Upshaw	1	1	0	0	47⅓	49	21	22	0	3.23
Rich Hinton	1	0	0	0	37⅓	41	15	30	0	4.82
Terry Forster	3	3	1	0	37	30	25	32	0	2.19
Pete Vuckovich	0	1	2	0	10⅓	17	7	5	0	13.06
Rick Sawyer	0	0	0	0	6	7	2	3	0	3.00
Lloyd Allen	0	2	2	0	5⅓	8	6	2	0	11.81
Jim Otten	0	0	0	0	5⅓	4	7	3	0	6.75
Ken Kravec	0	1	1	0	4⅓	1	8	1	0	6.23
Jack Kucek	0	0	0	0	3⅔	9	4	2	0	4.91
Chris Knapp	0	0	0	0	2	2	4	3	0	4.50
Tim Stoddard	0	0	0	0	1	2	0	0	0	9.00
	75	86	161	34	1,458⅓	1,495	657	802	3	3.93

1976

Record: 64–97
Finish: Sixth (West)
Games Behind: 25½
Manager: Paul Richards

Given the choice between accepting a diminished role as a roving scout for the White Sox or replacing Alvin Dark as manager of the Oakland A's, Chuck Tanner happily departed for the West Coast, taking along two White Sox coaches.

The selection of 67-year-old Paul Richards as Tanner's replacement was a rare public relations setback for Bill Veeck, who leaned heavily on the Richards name to help lure the fans back to Comiskey Park. As to the length of the contract, Veeck explained, "It will be kind of a Walter Alston…year to year."

Opening Day, 1976. Bill Veeck (right), costumed as the fifer, Rudie Shaffer (middle) as the flag carrier, and Paul Richards (left) as the drummer reprise the *Spirit of '76*, marking the nation's bicentennial celebration.

Recyling the warm and fuzzy memories of 1951 was a poor excuse for hiring Paul Richards, the league's oldest manager. He was out of touch and often distracted.

Of course, there was very little for Richards to work with. Despite a flurry of activity at the winter meetings by Veeck and Hemond, who recognized the necessity of presenting a "new look" to the fans, the 1976 Sox were subpar in every phase of the game. Ralph Garr, Jim Spencer, Jack Brohamer, Alan Bannister, and Clay Carroll replaced Ken Henderson, Jim Kaat, and Bill Melton, with mixed results.

In the case of Melton, Veeck simply could not afford to pay his salary in 1976. It boiled down to Veeck choosing between Melton and Wilbur Wood. One of the two veterans had to go, and Veeck preferred to retain the services of a proven starter. The strategy went up in smoke on May 9, when a line drive off the bat of Ron LeFlore shattered Woody's kneecap and for all intents and purposes ended his career.

A 10-game winning streak in early May instilled false hope and was deceiving. This was a terrible ballclub—almost as lethargic about losing as the 1970 disaster. Chicago dropped into the cellar on August 31, and all the zany sideshows (activating Minnie Minoso at age 54), promotional stunts (Frisbee-catching dogs), and gimmickry (outfitting his players in short pants), which appealed to puerile tastes, proved a poor substitute for a winning, competitive team. Bill Veeck acknowledged the error of his ways and devised a new master plan over the winter.

	G	AB	H	R	2B	3B	HR	RBI	SB	AVG
Jim Spencer	150	518	131	53	13	2	14	70	6	.253
Jack Brohamer	119	354	89	33	12	2	7	40	1	.251
Russell "Bucky" Dent	158	562	138	44	18	4	2	52	3	.246
Kevin Bell	68	230	57	24	7	6	5	20	2	.248
Jorge Orta	158	636	174	74	29	8	14	72	24	.274
Chet Lemon	132	451	111	46	15	5	4	38	13	.246
Ralph Garr	136	527	158	63	22	6	4	36	14	.300
Brian Downing	104	317	81	38	14	0	3	30	7	.256
Pat Kelly	107	311	79	42	20	3	5	34	15	.254
Bill Stein	117	392	105	32	15	2	4	36	4	.268
Lamar Johnson	82	222	71	29	11	1	4	33	2	.320
Sam Ewing	19	41	9	3	2	1	0	2	0	.220
Hugh Yancy	3	10	1	0	1	0	0	0	0	.100
Orestes "Minnie" Minoso	3	8	1	0	0	0	0	0	0	.125
Charles "Buddy" Bradford	55	160	35	20	5	2	4	14	6	.219
Alan Bannister	73	145	36	19	6	2	0	8	12	.248
Jerry Hairston	44	119	27	20	2	2	0	10	1	.227
Rich Coggins	32	96	15	4	2	0	0	5	3	.156
Carlos May	20	63	11	7	2	0	0	3	4	.175
Wayne Nordhagen	22	53	10	6	2	0	0	5	0	.189
Cleon Jones	12	40	8	2	1	0	0	3	0	.200
Nyls Nyman	8	15	2	2	1	0	0	1	1	.133
Jim Essian	78	199	49	20	7	0	0	21	2	.246
Pete Varney	14	41	10	5	2	0	3	5	0	.244
Phil Roof	4	9	1	0	0	0	0	0	0	.111
George Enright	2	1	0	0	0	0	0	0	0	.000
		5,532	1,410	586	209	46	73	538	120	.255

	W	L	GS	CG	IP	H	BB	K	ShO	ERA
Rich "Goose" Gossage	9	17	29	15	224	214	90	135	0	3.94
Bart Johnson	9	16	32	8	211⅓	231	62	91	3	4.73
Francisco Barrios	10	12	26	16	200⅔	171	76	91	1	3.32
Ken Brett	5	9	14	6	141⅔	136	46	81	0	4.31
Terry Forster	2	12	16	1	111⅓	126	41	70	0	4.38
Pete Vuckovich	7	4	7	1	110⅓	122	60	62	0	4.66
Dave Hamilton	6	6	1	0	90⅓	81	45	62	0	3.60
Clay Carroll	4	4	0	0	77⅓	67	24	38	0	2.57
Jesse Jefferson	2	5	9	0	62⅓	86	42	30	0	8.56
Wilbur Wood	4	3	7	5	56⅓	51	11	31	1	2.25
Chris Knapp	3	1	6	1	52⅓	54	32	41	0	4.85
Ken Kravec	1	5	8	1	49⅔	49	32	38	0	4.86
John "Blue Moon" Odom	2	2	4	0	28	31	20	18	0	5.79
Larry Monroe	0	1	2	0	21⅔	23	13	9	0	4.09
Jim Otten	0	0	0	0	6	9	2	3	0	4.50
Jack Kucek	0	0	0	0	4⅔	9	4	2	0	9.00
	64	97	161	54	1,446⅔	1,460	600	802	5	4.26

1977

Record: 90–72
Finish: Third (West)
Games Behind: 12
Manager: Bob Lemon

The answer was deceptively simple. If Bill Veeck could not afford to compete with the Yankees, Angels, and other big spenders for value-driven free agents, the Sox owner would *rent* them, if only for one year.

Exactly a year to the very day after he acquired the White Sox, Veeck traded Terry Forster and fire-balling relief ace Rich Gossage to the Pittsburgh Pirates for Richie Zisk, a power-hitting outfielder entering his option year. Veeck's reasoning: if he couldn't meet Zisk's salary demand in December 1976, at least he had him for one full season, and perhaps during that time he would become so enamored with Chicago and its fans that he would re-up for 1978 and beyond. Was Veeck optimistic or simply naïve?

The final pieces of the puzzle were firmly in place when the White Sox inked "bargain basement" free agent Eric Soderholm to a contract on November 26, 1976, and then waited until the end of spring training before waving goodbye to Bucky Dent, who demanded from Veeck a three-year, guaranteed contract. Dent was traded to the Yankees for outfielder-DH Oscar Gamble and pitchers Dewey LaMarr Hoyt and Bob Polinsky. It was a brilliant masterstroke—Roland Hemond's finest trade, among many, though the writers couldn't see it at the time.

Gamble, Zisk, and Soderholm were the main ingredients of the "South Side Hitmen" summer—a rollicking journey into the first division fueled by a barrage of home runs, amazing comebacks, and heart-pumping nonstop action. The White Sox clubbed 192 home runs, a team record that held up until 1996. Who cared if the team ERA ballooned to a rickety 4.25? The offense was a mother lode—quite uncharacteristic of

Oscar Gamble rattles the Red Sox.

White Sox baseball down through the years. Nineteen seventy-seven was truly a season "apart."

The White Sox battled the Kansas City Royals and the Minnesota Twins through the summer months. They enjoyed a continuous first-place run from July 1 through August 12 amid a chorus of "Na Na Hey Hey Kiss Him Goodbye!" and thunderous standing ovations from the Comiskey Park faithful, who demanded "curtain calls" from their heroes after every home run. It was a gesture of contempt that their arch-enemies—the Kansas City Royals—called "bush" and "unprofessional." The war of words between the two ballclubs erupted into a fistfight, pitting Sox pitcher Bart Johnson against Royals catcher Darrell Porter when they squared off in Kansas City for a first-place showdown on August 5.

After that, the Sox played with hesitation, uncertain of themselves and whether or not they deserved championship consideration. The Royals won the war of words and eventually the division title, but on the final day of the season Eric Soderholm, the Comeback Player of the Year, pronounced the year a success. And it was. "What happened to the club is pretty much what happened to me," he said. "We both went from the depths of despair and came out smelling like a rose. And we did it for the best fans in the world. By far the best. When we start playing next year we'll be contenders, not outcasts."

	G	AB	H	R	2B	3B	HR	RBI	SB	AVG
Jim Spencer	128	470	116	56	16	1	18	69	1	.247
Jorge Orta	144	564	159	71	27	8	11	84	4	.282
Alan Bannister	139	560	154	87	20	3	3	57	4	.275
Eric Soderholm	130	460	129	77	20	3	25	67	2	.280
Ralph Garr	134	543	163	78	29	7	10	54	12	.300
Chet Lemon	150	553	151	99	38	4	19	67	8	.273
Richie Zisk	141	531	154	78	17	6	30	101	0	.290
Jim Essian	114	322	88	50	18	2	10	44	1	.273
Oscar Gamble	137	408	121	75	22	2	31	83	1	.297
Lamar Johnson	118	374	113	52	12	5	18	65	1	.302
Jack Brohamer	59	152	39	26	10	3	2	20	0	.257
Don Kessinger	39	119	28	12	3	2	0	11	2	.235
Kevin Bell	9	28	5	4	1	0	1	6	0	.179
Tim Nordbrook	15	20	5	2	0	0	0	1	1	.250
Mike Squires	3	3	0	0	0	0	0	0	0	.000
John Flannery	7	2	0	1	0	0	0	0	0	.000
Wayne Nordhagen	52	124	39	16	7	3	4	22	1	.315
Royle Stillman	56	119	25	18	7	1	3	13	2	.210
Bobby Coluccio	20	37	10	4	0	0	0	7	0	.270
Jerry Hairston	13	26	8	3	2	0	0	4	0	.308
Henry Cruz	16	21	6	3	0	0	2	5	0	.286
Bobby Molinaro	1	2	1	0	0	0	0	0	1	.500
Cirilio "Tommy" Cruz	4	2	0	1	0	0	0	0	0	.000
Brian Downing	69	169	48	28	4	2	4	25	1	.284
Bill Nahorodny	7	23	6	3	1	0	1	4	0	.261
		5,632	1,568	844	254	52	192	809	42	.278

	W	L	GS	CG	IP	H	BB	K	ShO	ERA
Francisco Barrios	14	7	31	9	231⅓	241	58	119	0	4.13
Steve Stone	15	12	31	8	207⅓	228	80	124	0	4.52
Ken Kravec	11	8	25	6	166⅔	161	57	125	1	4.10
Chris Knapp	12	7	26	4	146⅓	166	61	103	0	4.81
Wilbur Wood	7	8	18	5	122⅔	139	50	42	1	4.98
Lerrin LaGrow	7	3	0	0	98⅔	81	35	63	0	2.45
Bart Johnson	4	5	4	0	92	114	38	46	0	4.01
Ken Brett	6	4	13	0	82⅔	101	15	39	0	4.99
Dave Hamilton	4	5	0	0	67⅓	71	33	45	0	3.63
Steve Renko	5	0	8	0	53⅓	55	17	36	0	3.57
Don Kirkwood	1	1	0	0	40	49	10	24	0	5.18
Jack Kucek	0	1	3	0	34⅔	35	10	25	0	3.60
Bruce Dal Canton	0	2	0	0	24	20	13	9	0	3.75
Dave Frost	1	1	3	0	23⅔	30	3	15	0	3.00
Silvio Martinez	0	1	0	0	21	28	12	10	0	5.57
Clay Carroll	1	3	0	0	11⅓	14	4	4	0	4.91
John Verhoeven	0	0	0	0	10⅓	9	2	6	0	1.74
Larry Anderson	1	3	0	0	8⅔	10	15	7	0	9.00
Randy Wiles	1	1	0	0	2⅔	5	3	0	0	9.00
	90	72	162	34	1,445⅓	1,557	516	842	2	4.25

1978

Record: 71–90
Finish: Fifth (West)
Games Behind: 20½
Managers: Bob Lemon, Larry Doby

Neither Richie Zisk nor Oscar Gamble, who enjoyed their most productive seasons in Chicago, cared to accept Bill Veeck's modest contract extension. Zisk signed with Texas. Gamble fled to San Diego. They were Chicago's first free agent losses, and bellwethers of Veeck's financial miseries in this difficult new era of baseball.

The free agent signing of injury-plagued outfielder Ron Blomberg was suppose to offset the loss of Gamble. Blomberg's game-tying home run on Opening Day was the singular highlight of what amounted to little more than a failed publicity stunt. Blomberg signed for four years at a guaranteed rate, but played in only 61 games. Roland Hemond's annual December blockbuster trade packaged Brian Downing and pitchers Chris Knapp and Dave Frost to the Angels for Bobby Bonds, pitcher Richard Dotson, and outfielder Thad Bosley.

The team just never got off the ground. Bonds was an expensive luxury that Veeck simply could not afford, and after the Sox's record had dipped to 9–20, Bonds was dealt to Texas for gimpy Claudell Washington and Rusty Torres. Washington was damaged goods and did not play until June 16. Veeck filed a protest with the league, but the trade was upheld by Lee McPhail.

Bob Lemon, whose low-key leadership had complemented the Sox' style of play during their 1977 Cinderella season, was on the hot seat the first two months of the '78 season. His imminent dismissal was put on hold when the White Sox suddenly showed signs of life. They won 17 of 19 games between May 28 and June 15. The sustained streak was the best since Al Lopez's 1961 team won 19 of 20, and it was very encouraging to Veeck, whose detractors in the media accused him of sitting on a pile of investor money—money that he refused to spend to acquire star-caliber players to help turn things around.

The team wearing the odd clam-digger pants and softball-style jerseys advertising the name CHICAGO on the front was a mediocre hodgepodge of utility players held together by baling wire, bubble gum, and a wing and a prayer. After flirting with the .500 mark on June 18, the White Sox reverted to their old form, forcing an impatient Bill Veeck to dismiss Lemon on June 30. Rumors were flying that Veeck intended to "trade" managers with the Yankees—Lemon to New York for Billy Martin. It never worked out, and it was just as well…for Martin.

In what amounted to another ill-timed and potentially exploitive publicity stunt, Bill Veeck hired his batting coach,

Veeck's Wrecks gather in Sarasota: Ron Blomberg (far left), Steve Stone, Bill Veeck, Eric Soderholm, unknown

Larry Doby, to lead the Sox the rest of the way. Veeck hoped that baseball's second African American player would stimulate fan interest and help him attain the unrealistic goal of 2 million paid admissions in 1978. Thus Larry Doby followed in the footsteps of another Robinson—Frank Robinson—to become baseball's second African American manager.

In the first month of the Doby regime, the Sox lost 18 of 28. The team demonstrated no improvement thereafter. David Israel, the one sportswriter in town unimpressed by the Veeck mystique, observed, "The only problem is that there is too much suffering, too much vaudevillian comedy, and too little winning."

	G	AB	H	R	2B	3B	HR	RBI	SB	AVG
Lamar Johnson	148	498	136	52	23	2	8	72	6	.273
Jorge Orta	117	420	115	45	19	2	13	53	1	.274
Don Kessinger	131	431	110	35	18	1	1	31	2	.255
Eric Soderholm	143	457	118	57	17	1	20	67	2	.258
Claudell Washington	86	314	83	33	16	5	6	31	5	.264
Chet Lemon	105	357	107	51	24	6	13	55	5	.300
Ralph Garr	118	443	122	67	18	9	3	29	7	.275
Bill Nahorodny	107	347	82	29	11	2	8	35	1	.236
Bobby Molinaro	105	286	75	39	5	5	6	27	22	.262
Greg Pryor	82	222	58	27	11	0	2	15	3	.261
Ron Blomberg	61	156	36	16	7	0	5	22	0	.231
Mike Squires	46	150	42	25	9	2	0	19	4	.280
Alan Bannister	49	107	24	16	3	2	0	8	3	.224
Harry Chappas	20	75	20	11	1	0	0	6	1	.267
Jim Breazeale	25	72	15	8	3	0	3	13	0	.208
Kevin Bell	54	68	13	9	0	0	2	5	1	.191
Alvin "Junior" Moore	24	65	19	8	0	1	0	4	1	.292
Joe Gates	8	24	6	6	0	0	0	1	1	.250
Mike Eden	10	17	2	1	0	0	0	0	0	.118
Thad Bosley	66	219	59	25	5	1	2	13	12	.269
Wayne Nordhagen	68	206	62	28	16	0	5	35	0	.301
Bobby Bonds	26	90	25	8	4	0	2	8	6	.278
Henry Cruz	53	77	17	13	2	1	2	10	0	.221
Tom Spencer	29	65	12	3	1	0	0	4	0	.185
Rusty Torres	16	44	14	7	3	0	3	6	0	.318
Mike Colbern	48	141	38	11	5	1	2	20	0	.270
Marv Foley	11	34	12	3	0	0	0	6	0	.353
Larry Doby Johnson	3	8	1	0	0	0	0	0	0	.125
		5,393	1,423	634	221	41	106	595	83	.264

	W	L	GS	CG	IP	H	BB	K	ShO	ERA
Steve Stone	12	12	30	6	212	196	84	118	1	4.37
Ken Kravec	11	16	30	7	203	188	95	154	2	4.08
Francisco Barrios	9	15	33	9	195⅔	180	85	79	2	4.05
Wilbur Wood	10	10	28	4	168	187	74	69	0	5.20
Jim Willoughby	1	6	59	0	93⅓	95	19	36	0	3.86
Lerrin LaGrow	6	5	52	0	88	85	38	41	0	4.40
Ron Schueler	3	5	30	0	81⅔	76	39	39	0	4.30
Rich Hinton	2	6	29	2	80⅔	78	28	48	0	4.02
Mike Proly	5	2	14	2	65⅔	63	12	19	0	2.74
Richard Wortham	3	2	8	2	59	59	23	25	0	3.05
Pablo Torrealba	2	4	25	1	57⅓	69	39	23	1	4.71
Jack Kucek	2	3	10	3	52	42	27	30	0	3.29
Ross Baumgarten	2	2	7	1	23	29	9	15	1	5.87
Steve Trout	3	0	4	1	22⅓	19	11	11	0	4.03
Britt Burns	0	2	2	0	7⅔	14	3	3	0	12.91
	71	90	161	38	1,409⅓	1,380	586	710	7	4.23

1979

Record: 73–87
Finish: Fifth (West)
Games Behind: 14
Managers: Don Kessinger, Tony LaRussa

After failing to retain seasoned veterans lost to free agency, Bill Veeck looked to the farm system for the long-term salvation of the franchise. However, Veeck failed to sign his first and second picks in the January minor league draft in each of his first four seasons as owner. "You always ask yourself, are you drafting the best player or the player you know you can sign?" wondered Charlie Evranian, who directed the tattered farm system.

Veeck advertised and touted the coming glory of the younger players in the system. Shortstop Harry Chappas, catchers Marvis Foley and Mike Colbern, and pitchers Richard Wortham, Steve Trout, Ken Kravec, Ross Baumgarten, and Randy Scarbery were billed by Veeck as "can't-miss prospects" during the annual season-ticket renewal drive. The youth movement was the final bullet in Veeck's gun. Since he was checkmated by free agency and a peculiar financing arrangement that did not allow him to take advantage of

Are Bill Veeck and his scouts searching the skies for UFOs, a long shot in the fifth at Hialeah, or someone (anyone) to play shortstop?

the available tax breaks, the only thing Veeck could do was baby-sit his kiddie corps and promote the hell out of collective mediocrity labeled the Keystone Sox by *Tribune* columnist David Israel.

Larry Doby was neither surprised nor embittered when he was replaced by shortstop Don Kessinger on October 19, 1978. "I'm in the business of selling tickets to survive," Veeck admitted. "But his popularity was not the overriding factor by any means." In essence, it *was*. Kessinger was a beloved Chicago sports figure playing out the string with the White Sox when he was tendered an offer to manage. Selling tickets was the *only* reason for turning the keys over to Kessinger, who had never been kicked out of a game by an umpire in his 13-year career.

Under his command, the Sox managed a 46–60 record—not good enough in view of all the negative publicity surrounding the "Disco Demolition" riot in Comiskey Park on July 12, 1979. A sarcastic Chicago disc jockey packed the stadium with 50,000 antidisco fanatics who refused to return to their seats after a stack of the offending dance records were blown up in the outfield. When the second game of the scheduled doubleheader could not be played, the American League declared a forfeit. It was a low, embarrassing moment for the ownership, whose credibility waned. Kessinger's abdication followed less than a month later. "If a fellow says he can't run up the sail, then I'll have to respect his wishes," Bill Veeck explained.

Tony LaRussa, the 34-year-old manager of the Sox Triple A affiliate in Des Moines, was summoned to Chicago to replace Kessinger and continue the development of the young prospects he had tutored in the minor leagues. The White Sox played .500 baseball the rest of the way under a new manager few people counted on to be much more than an interim caretaker.

	G	AB	H	R	2B	3B	HR	RBI	SB	AVG
Lamar Johnson	133	479	148	60	29	1	12	74	8	.309
Alan Bannister	136	506	144	71	28	8	2	55	22	.285
Greg Pryor	143	476	131	60	23	3	3	34	3	.275
Kevin Bell	70	200	49	20	8	1	4	22	2	.245
Claudell Washington	131	471	132	79	33	5	13	66	19	.280
Chet Lemon	148	556	177	79	44	2	17	86	7	.318
Rusty Torres	90	170	43	26	5	0	8	24	0	.253
Milt May	65	202	51	23	13	0	7	28	0	.252
Jorge Orta	113	325	85	49	18	3	11	46	1	.262
Mike Squires	122	295	78	44	10	1	2	22	15	.264
Jim Morrison	67	240	66	38	14	0	14	35	11	.275
Eric Soderholm	56	210	53	31	8	2	6	34	0	.252
Wayne Nordhagen	78	193	54	20	15	0	7	25	0	.280
Don Kessinger	56	110	22	14	6	0	1	7	1	.200
Harry Chappas	26	59	17	9	1	0	1	4	1	.288
Joe Gates	16	16	1	5	0	1	0	1	1	.063
Ralph Garr	102	307	86	34	10	2	9	39	2	.280
Alvin "Junior" Moore	88	201	53	24	6	2	1	23	0	.264
Thad Bosley	36	77	24	13	1	1	1	8	4	.312
Rusty Kuntz	5	11	1	0	0	0	0	0	0	.091
Bill Nahorodny	65	179	46	20	10	0	6	29	0	.257
Marv Foley	34	97	24	6	3	0	2	10	0	.247
MIke Colbern	32	83	20	5	5	1	0	8	0	.241
		5,463	1,505	730	290	33	127	680	97	.275

	W	L	GS	CG	IP	H	BB	K	ShO	ERA
Ken Kravec	15	13	35	10	250	208	111	132	3	3.74
Richard "Tex" Wortham	14	14	33	5	204	195	100	119	0	4.90
Ross Baumgarten	13	8	28	4	190⅔	175	83	72	3	3.53
Steven Trout	11	8	18	6	155	165	59	76	2	3.89
Randy Scarbery	2	8	5	0	101⅓	102	34	45	0	4.63
Francisco Barrios	8	3	15	2	94⅔	88	33	28	0	3.60
Mike Proly	3	8	6	0	88⅓	89	40	32	0	3.89
Ed Farmer	3	7	3	0	81⅓	66	34	48	0	2.44
Fred Howard	1	5	6	0	68	73	32	36	0	3.57
Rich Hinton	1	2	2	0	41⅔	57	8	27	0	6.00
Guy Hoffman	0	5	0	0	30⅓	30	23	18	0	5.40
Richard Dotson	2	0	5	1	24⅓	28	6	13	1	3.75
Ron Schueler	0	1	1	0	19⅔	19	13	6	0	7.20
Lerrin LaGrow	0	3	2	0	17⅔	27	16	9	0	9.00
Dewey Robinson	0	1	0	0	14⅓	11	9	5	0	6.43
Gil Rondon	0	0	0	0	9⅔	11	6	3	0	3.60
Pablo Torrealba	0	0	0	0	5⅔	5	2	1	0	1.50
Britt Burns	0	0	0	0	5	10	1	2	0	5.40
LaMarr Hoyt	0	0	0	0	3	2	0	0	0	0.00
Wayne Nordhagen	0	0	0	0	2	2	1	2	0	9.00
Mark Esser	0	0	0	0	1⅔	2	4	1	0	13.50
Jack Kucek	0	0	0	0	⅔	0	3	0	0	0.00
	73	86	159	28	1,409	1,365	618	675	9	4.13

1980

Record: 70–90
Finish: Fifth (West)
Games Behind: 26
Manager: Tony LaRussa

The final year of the Veeck "Second Coming" was weird and unbelievable—business as usual at 35th and Shields. No one suspected that Bill Veeck was about to pull the plug on his ownership when the season began. He was circumspect about his future plans, preferring to dwell on the positive aspects of his youth movement.

Under Tony LaRussa's guidance, outfielder Harold Baines and pitchers Britt Burns, LaMarr Hoyt, and Richard Dotson came through in a major way after the Kevin Bells, Rich Hintons, and Jack Kuceks—the rising hope of the farm system in the 1974–1978 era—wore out their welcome.

The White Sox were still two years and several free agents away from bona fide pennant contention, but the depressing outcome of the 1980 season was livened up by a series of wacky episodes that could only occur during a Veeck ownership.

Much of the controversy this year swirled around announcer Jimmy Piersall, whose play-by-play banter with Harry Caray delighted and amused Sox fans but was a major irritant to Tony LaRussa and the players, who were stung by their on-air barbs. In June Piersall was dismissed from his job as an outfield coach, after offending the manager—and the owner—by calling Veeck's wife a "colossal bore" on a daytime TV talk show. Under fire from all quarters, Piersall exploded in a fit of wild rage in the Sox clubhouse on July 2.

He assaulted Rob Gallas, a suburban sportswriter who made casual reference to Piersall's recent misfortunes. In all likelihood Jimmy Piersall would have been fired on the spot if not for the outpouring of love and support coming from Chicago fans who paraded banners around Comiskey Park in his defense. Veeck gave his announcer one more chance.

The Piersall-Gallas flap predicated an even larger complication as the season wore on.

"Take my team...please!" Borrowing a tired one-liner from Henny Youngman, Bill Veeck secretly shopped the market for the right kind of megamillionaire to take the White Sox off of his hands. Veeck flew to Denver to discuss the sale of the franchise to Marvin Davis, whose interest in the White Sox was guarded. Davis would have surely transferred the Sox to Denver with Veeck's connivance, but thought the better of buying the team (for whatever reason) and said no.

On August 22 Veeck announced the sale of the Sox to Edward DeBartolo of Youngstown, Ohio, for a sum pegged at $20 million dollars. DeBartolo intimated that he would consider moving the Sox to New Orleans, but hedged his bets after he was called into account by the media and the American League owners. DeBartolo's horse-racing interests concerned commissioner Bowie Kuhn, who seemed troubled by other issues—absentee ownership and the specter of organized crime, so often equated with the thoroughbred game. The DeBartolo camp leveled charges of anti-Italian bias against the commissioner.

"You realize, Mr. DeBartolo, that I have veto power," Kuhn asserted. "Yes," DeBartolo replied, "and I have the right to sue you. And I have millions of dollars to do just that."

Bowie Kuhn refused to be threatened or intimidated by DeBartolo's words. The league voted down the sale twice before approving a more palatable offer from Jerry Reinsdorf, the 45-year-old chairman and chief executive officer of Balcor Company, a suburban-Chicago real estate firm. The sale was finalized on January 29, 1981, after six months of hectic and often strained negotiations.

An embittered Bill Veeck took an instant dislike to Reinsdorf and his partner Eddie Einhorn after some unfortunate

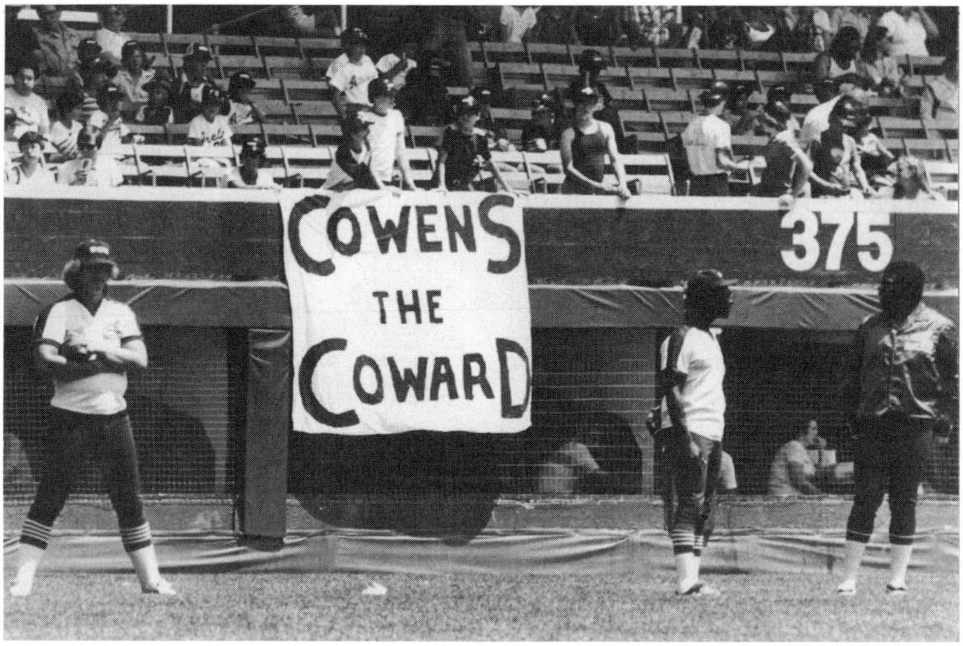

On June 20, 1980, Kansas City outfielder Al Cowens charged Sox pitcher Ed Farmer. The fans react.

comments by Einhorn were taken out of context by the outgoing regime. To say that Veeck was not very happy with the outcome was putting things mildly.

	G	AB	H	R	2B	3B	HR	RBI	SB	AVG
Mike Squires	131	343	97	38	11	3	2	33	8	.283
Jim Morrison	162	604	171	66	40	0	15	57	9	.283
Todd Cruz	90	293	68	23	11	1	2	18	2	.232
Kevin Bell	92	191	34	16	5	2	1	11	0	.178
Harold Baines	141	491	125	55	23	6	13	49	2	.255
Chet Lemon	147	514	150	76	32	6	11	51	6	.292
Wayne Nordhagen	123	415	115	45	22	4	15	59	0	.277
Bruce Kimm	100	251	61	20	10	1	0	19	1	.243
Lamar Johnson	147	541	150	51	26	3	13	81	2	.277
Greg Pryor	122	338	81	32	18	4	1	29	2	.240
Alvin "Junior" Moore	45	121	31	9	4	1	1	10	0	.256
Fran Mullins	21	62	12	9	4	0	0	3	0	.194
Harry Chappas	26	50	8	6	2	0	0	2	0	.160
Randy Johnson	12	20	4	0	0	0	0	3	0	.200
Bobby Molinaro	119	344	100	48	16	4	5	36	18	.291
Thad Bosley	70	147	33	12	2	0	2	14	3	.224
Alan Bannister	45	130	25	16	6	0	0	9	5	.192
Claudell Washington	32	90	26	15	4	2	1	12	4	.289
Leo Sutherland	34	89	23	9	3	0	0	5	4	.258
Ron Pruitt	33	70	21	8	2	0	2	11	0	.300
Rusty Kuntz	36	62	14	5	4	0	0	3	1	.226
Marv Foley	68	137	29	14	5	0	4	15	0	.212
Glenn Borgmann	32	87	19	10	2	0	2	14	0	.218
Rick Seilheimer	21	52	11	4	3	1	1	3	1	.212
		5,442	1,408	587	255	38	91	547	68	.259

	W	L	GS	CG	IP	H	BB	K	ShO	ERA
Britt Burns	15	13	32	11	238	213	63	133	1	2.84
Steve Trout	9	16	30	7	199⅔	229	49	89	2	3.69
Richard Dotson	12	10	32	8	198	185	87	109	0	4.27
Mike Proly	5	10	3	0	146⅔	136	58	56	0	3.06
Ross Baumgarten	2	12	23	3	136	127	52	66	1	3.44
LaMarr Hoyt	9	3	13	3	112⅓	123	41	55	1	4.58
Ed Farmer	7	9	0	0	99⅔	92	56	54	0	3.33
Richard "Tex" Wortham	4	7	10	0	92	102	58	45	0	5.97
Ken Kravec	3	6	15	0	81⅔	100	44	37	0	6.91
Guy Hoffman	1	0	1	0	37⅔	38	17	24	0	2.61
Dewey Robinson	1	1	0	0	35	26	16	28	0	3.09
Randy Scarbery	1	2	0	0	28⅔	24	7	18	0	4.03
Francisco Barrios	1	1	3	0	16⅓	21	8	2	0	5.06
Nardi Contreras	0	0	0	0	13⅔	18	7	8	0	5.79
	70	90	162	32	1,435	1,434	563	724	5	3.92

1981

Record: 54–52
Finish: Third (West, First Half) | Sixth (West, Second Half)
Games Behind: 2½ (First Half) | 6½ (Second Half)
Manager: Tony LaRussa

Reshaping the image of the White Sox required imagination and bold strokes, although not all White Sox fans were in accord. Sales of hard liquor were suspended in Comiskey Park. The embarrassing softball-style uniforms of the late 1970s were mercifully scrapped. And the marketing thrust for 1981 and beyond was aimed at promoting White Sox baseball as wholesome family-oriented entertainment for *all* Chicagoans, not just South Siders.

To bolster the product on the field and lend immediate credibility to the new ownership group, Jerry Reinsdorf entered the free agency market. A marathon West Coast bargaining session with agent Jerry Kapstein reeled in catcher Carlton Fisk on March 10. It was a bold departure from Veeck's "bargain basement" shopping sprees, but Reinsdorf was intent on purging the "Rodney Dangerfield" image that haunted the ballclub in the past. "Eddie [Einhorn] saw the public relations value in getting Carlton immediately," Reinsdorf explained.

In Philadelphia, Greg "the Bull" Luzinski vented his displeasure with management after nearly a decade as a mainstay of their offense. His contract was purchased on March 30.

Fisk, Luzinski, and Tony Bernazard, acquired from Montreal for "Tex" Wortham, complemented a nucleus of youthful players developed in the last year and a half of the Veeck ownership. A better supporting cast behind them—Harold Baines, Britt Burns, and Richard Dotson—provided hope for the future, not idle promise.

In storybook fashion, Carlton Fisk returned to Fenway Park on April 10 to destroy his former teammates in the season opener. Four days later his grand-slam home run in Comiskey Park buried the Milwaukee Brewers before 51,560 exultant fans—a record-setting Opening Day crowd.

Winners of 10 of their first 13 games, the White Sox were on a fast track and keeping exclusive company when baseball's first midseason work stoppage halted play on June 12. Following the resumption of the season on August 10, the club showed no visible signs of a letup, grabbing a temporary first-place lead on August 25.

New for 1981: Carlton Fisk, free agent acquisition. Standing is clubhouse man "Chicken" Willie Thompson.

Title hopes went up in smoke in the last month of the season. Youth and inexperience were the culprits. Promising no more "September swan songs," Einhorn, Reinsdorf, and Roland Hemond traded Chet Lemon to Detroit for Steve Kemp, an option player not likely to remain in Chicago after 1982. Lemon's loss was offset by the acquisition of Tom Paciorek, named Seattle's Most Valuable Player on the strength of a .326 batting performance.

All in all, 1981 was a satisfying debut to a new era.

	G	AB	H	R	2B	3B	HR	RBI	SB	AVG
Mike Squires	92	294	78	35	9	0	0	25	7	.265
Tony Bernazard	106	384	106	53	14	4	6	34	4	.276
Bill Almon	103	349	105	46	10	2	4	41	16	.301
Jim Morrison	90	290	68	27	8	1	10	34	3	.234
Harold Baines	82	280	80	42	11	7	10	41	6	.286
Chet Lemon	94	328	99	50	23	6	9	50	5	.302
Ron LeFlore	82	337	83	46	10	4	0	24	36	.246
Carlton Fisk	96	338	89	44	12	0	7	45	3	.263
Greg Luzinski	104	378	100	55	15	1	21	62	0	.265
Lamar Johnson	41	134	37	10	7	0	1	15	0	.276
Greg Pryor	47	76	17	4	1	0	0	6	0	.224
Bobby Molinaro	47	42	11	7	1	1	1	9	1	.262
Jay Loviglio	14	15	4	5	0	0	0	2	2	.267
Wayne Nordhagen	65	208	64	19	8	1	6	33	0	.308
Rusty Kuntz	67	55	14	15	2	0	0	4	1	.255
Jerry Hairston	9	25	7	5	1	0	1	6	0	.280
Jerry Turner	10	12	2	1	0	0	0	2	0	.167
Leo Sutherland	11	12	2	6	0	0	0	0	2	.167
Jim Essian	27	52	16	6	3	0	0	5	0	.308
Marc Hill	16	6	0	0	0	0	0	0	0	.000
		3,615	982	476	135	27	76	438	86	.272

	W	L	GS	CG	IP	H	BB	K	ShO	ERA
Britt Burns	10	6	24	5	156⅔	139	49	108	1	2.64
Richard Dotson	9	8	24	5	141	145	49	73	4	3.77
Dennis Lamp	7	6	27	3	127	103	43	71	0	2.41
Steve Trout	8	7	20	3	124⅔	122	38	54	0	3.46
Ross Baumgarten	5	9	19	2	101⅔	101	40	52	1	4.06
LaMarr Hoyt	9	3	43	0	90⅔	80	28	60	0	3.56
Ed Farmer	3	3	42	0	52⅔	53	34	42	0	4.58
Kevin Hickey	0	2	41	0	44⅓	38	18	17	0	3.68
Francisco Barrios	1	3	8	1	36⅓	45	14	12	0	4.00
Jerry Koosman	1	4	8	1	27	27	7	21	0	3.33
Lynn McGlothen	0	0	11	0	21⅔	14	7	12	0	4.09
Reggie Patterson	0	1	6	0	7⅓	14	6	2	0	14.14
Juan Agosto	0	0	2	0	5⅔	5	0	3	0	4.50
Dewey Robinson	1	0	4	0	4	5	3	2	0	4.50
	54	52	106	20	940⅔	891	336	529	6	3.50

1982

Record: 87–75
Finish: Third (West)
Games Behind: 6
Manager: Tony LaRussa

Only three players from the 1979 "Keystone Sox" remained on the Opening Day roster in 1982. With Roland Hemond cutting the deals and Jerry Reinsdorf signing the checks, the White Sox were on course for a first-division rendezvous. The farm system was expanded from three to five teams. Charley Lau, recognized as the finest batting coach in baseball, signed a six-year contract at LaRussa's insistence.

Jerry Reinsdorf counted on record-setting attendance in 1982 and no less than a division championship. "I think it's important to the fans that we never lose—on or off the field," he said. If the timetables seemed unrealistic given the woeful state of affairs as recently as 1980, the White Sox provided every indication they would keep faith with the schedule.

Rain and snow forced postponement of the first five games of the season, but when the bell rang on April 11 in New York, the White Sox broke away from the pack like a thundering herd. They opened the campaign with eight straight victories and an early first-place advantage that melted with the spring snows.

The inconsistencies of team play were reflected in the streaky nature of the ballclub, both individually and collectively. Lamarr Hoyt was an early season sensation, equaling Lefty Williams' and Orval Grove's team record of nine straight wins to open a season. Hoyt's poststreak record was a disappointing 10–15.

After the team skidded to the .500 mark on July 29, Jerry Reinsdorf fired pitching coach Ron Schueler. The manager's job hung in the balance in the next few days, but Reinsdorf exercised good judgment by granting LaRussa a vote of confidence at a time when a media second-guesser—Jimmy Piersall—demanded his ouster.

In early August the Sox stormed back into the race, but were swept out of contention just as quickly by the Kansas City Royals in a home-and-away series played in the middle of the month. In 1982 Chicago dropped 10 of 13 games to the Royals, a longtime nemesis of this ballclub dating back to the early 1970s.

	G	AB	H	R	2B	3B	HR	RBI	SB	AVG
Mike Squires	116	195	52	33	9	3	1	21	3	.267
Tony Bernazard	137	540	138	90	25	9	11	56	11	.256
Bill Almon	111	308	79	40	10	4	4	26	10	.256
Aurelio Rodriguez	118	257	62	24	15	1	3	31	0	.241
Harold Baines	161	608	165	89	29	8	25	105	10	.271
Rudy Law	121	336	107	55	15	8	3	32	36	.318
Steve Kemp	160	580	166	91	23	1	19	98	7	.286
Carlton Fisk	135	476	127	66	17	3	14	65	17	.267
Greg Luzinski	159	583	170	87	37	1	18	102	1	.292
Tom Paciorek	104	382	119	49	27	4	11	55	3	.312
Vance Law	114	359	101	40	20	1	5	54	4	.281
Jim Morrison	51	166	37	17	7	3	7	19	0	.223
Chris Nyman	28	65	16	6	1	0	0	2	3	.246
Steve Dillard	16	41	7	1	3	1	0	5	0	.171
Jay Loviglio	15	31	6	5	0	0	0	2	2	.194
Lorenzo Gray	17	28	8	4	1	0	0	0	1	.286
Greg Walker	11	17	7	3	2	1	2	7	0	.412
Ron LeFlore	91	334	96	58	15	4	4	25	28	.287
Jerry Hairston	85	90	21	11	5	0	5	18	0	.233
Ron Kittle	20	29	7	3	2	0	1	7	0	.241
Rusty Kuntz	21	26	5	4	1	0	0	3	0	.192
Marc Hill	53	88	23	9	2	0	3	13	0	.261
Marv Foley	27	36	4	1	0	0	0	1	0	.111
		5,575	1,523	786	266	52	136	747	136	.273

The Sox celebrate the clinching of the AL West Division, September 17, 1983.

	W	L	GS	CG	IP	H	BB	K	ShO	ERA
LaMarr Hoyt	19	15	32	14	239⅔	248	48	124	2	3.53
Richard Dotson	11	15	31	3	196⅔	219	73	109	1	3.84
Dennis Lamp	11	8	27	3	189⅔	206	59	78	2	3.99
Jerry Koosman	11	7	19	3	173⅓	194	38	88	1	3.84
Britt Burns	13	5	28	5	169⅓	168	67	116	1	4.04
Steve Trout	6	9	0	2	120⅓	130	50	62	0	4.26
Salome Barojas	6	6	0	0	106⅔	96	46	56	0	3.54
Kevin Hickey	4	4	2	0	78	73	30	38	0	3.00
Ernesto Escarrega	1	3	1	0	73⅔	73	16	33	0	3.67
Jim Kern	2	1	0	0	28	20	12	23	0	5.14
Warren Brusstar	2	0	2	0	18⅓	19	3	8	0	3.44
Rich Barnes	0	2	0	0	17	21	4	6	0	4.76
Al "Sparky" Lyle	0	0	0	0	12	11	7	6	0	3.00
Eddie Solomon	1	0	1	0	7⅓	7	2	2	0	3.68
Jim Siwy	0	0	0	0	7	10	5	3	0	10.29
Juan Agosto	0	0	0	0	2	7	0	1	0	18.00
	87	75	162	30	1,439	1,502	460	753	7	3.87

1983

Record: 99–63
Finish: First (West)
Games Ahead: 20
Manager: Tony LaRussa

Slowly, the pieces fell into place, and with them came a White Sox divisional championship that wiped clean the "city of losers" stigma that had haunted the residents of Chicago since 1963—the year the Bears won the city's last professional sports title. The free agent signing of Seattle pitcher Floyd Bannister on December 14, 1982, was followed by the ascendance of two Edmonton rookies, outfielder Ron Kittle and first baseman Greg Walker, replacing Steve Kemp and Mike Squires, respectively. Kittle broke the Sox' freshman home run record with 35, and at season's end he was the league's choice for Rookie of the Year.

One month into the season the outlook was not nearly so promising. The White Sox were struggling at 12–13 on May 8, when *Sun-Times* columnist Ron Rapoport complained, "It seems axiomatic that if a month into the season, a team does not have a shortstop, does not have a third baseman, does not have a center fielder, then no matter what its assets may be, it forfeits its right to call itself a contender."

The slow start compromised Tony LaRussa, who heard a neverending cascade of boos from the fans every time he approached the mound to consult with his pitcher. Harry Caray and Jimmy Piersall, gone from the White Sox broadcast booth for over a year, had whipped the LaRussa haters into a booing frenzy that just never let up. Neither Caray nor Piersall could claim credit for the Sox' 1983 success. All of the credit for the turnaround belonged to Roland Hemond and Tony LaRussa, who emerged as one of the finest young managers in the game—despite opinions to the contrary.

It wasn't until after the All-Star break that the Sox ran wild. Their second-half 59–26 stampede easily crushed the meager opposition afforded by the Kansas City Royals and Texas Rangers. LaMarr Hoyt, Richard Dotson, and Floyd Bannister were unbeatable down the stretch. Bannister posted a blistering 13–1 mark after a discouraging 3–9 start. Hoyt (15–2) and Dotson (14–2) were even more spectacular in the second-half surge. Hoyt's quiet toughness and rugged appearance on the mound made him an instant fan favorite. His 1983 Cy Young Award pointed the way to a seemingly limitless future.

Not every opposing manager or out-of-town writer joined in the chorus of praise for the talented young Sox. On the eve of a four-game series in Texas that buried the Rangers' 1983 title hopes, Richard Justice of the *Dallas Times-Herald* wrote, "If the White Sox are the best in the West, they may be no better than fifth place in the East." In that same article Justice quoted Rangers manager Doug Rader, who inadvertently supplied the pennant-hungry Sox with a battle cry…and a motive: "Their bubble has got to burst. They're not playing that well. They're winning ugly. At least that's what our reports say."

"Winning Ugly" became the spiritual theme of the 1983 White Sox, who wrapped up a letter-perfect season by clinching their first AL West Division championship against Seattle in Comiskey Park on September 17. After Harold Baines' sacrifice fly scored Julio Cruz with the winning run in the bottom of the ninth inning, 45,000 fans stormed the field in unrestrained joy. They danced and sang long into the night, dreaming of the exciting days yet to come.

	G	AB	H	R	2B	3B	HR	RBI	SB	AVG
Tom Paciorek	115	420	129	65	32	3	9	63	6	.307
Julio Cruz	99	334	84	47	9	4	1	40	24	.251
Jerry Dybzinski	127	256	59	30	10	1	1	32	11	.230
Vance Law	145	408	99	55	21	5	4	42	3	.243
Harold Baines	156	596	167	76	33	2	20	99	7	.280
Rudy Law	141	501	142	95	20	7	3	34	77	.283
Ron Kittle	145	520	132	75	19	3	35	100	8	.254
Carlton Fisk	138	488	141	85	26	4	26	86	9	.289
Greg Luzinski	144	502	128	73	26	1	32	95	2	.255
Greg Walker	118	307	83	32	16	3	10	55	2	.270
Scott Fletcher	114	262	62	42	16	5	3	31	5	.237
Tony Bernazard	59	233	61	30	16	2	2	26	2	.262
Mike Squires	143	153	34	21	4	1	1	11	3	.222
Lorenzo Gray	41	78	14	18	3	0	1	4	1	.179
Chris Nyman	21	28	8	12	0	0	2	4	2	.286
Aurelio Rodriguez	22	20	4	1	1	0	1	1	0	.200
Tim Hulett	6	5	1	0	0	0	0	0	1	.200
Miguel Dilone	4	3	0	1	0	0	0	0	1	.000
Jerry Hairston	101	126	37	17	9	1	5	22	0	.294
Dave Stegman	29	53	9	5	2	0	0	4	0	.170
Rusty Kuntz	28	42	11	6	1	0	0	1	1	.262
Casey Parsons	8	5	1	1	0	0	0	0	0	.200
Marc Hill	58	133	30	11	6	0	1	11	0	.226
Joel Skinner	6	11	3	2	0	0	0	1	0	.273
		5,484	1,439	800	270	42	157	162	165	.262

	W	L	GS	CG	IP	H	BB	K	ShO	ERA
LaMarr Hoyt	24	10	36	11	260⅔	236	31	148	1	3.66
Richard Dotson	22	7	35	8	240	209	106	137	1	3.23
Floyd Bannister	16	10	34	5	217⅓	191	71	193	2	3.35
Britt Burns	10	11	26	8	173⅔	165	55	115	4	3.58
Jerry Koosman	11	7	24	2	169⅔	176	53	90	1	4.77
Dennis Lamp	7	7	5	1	116⅓	123	29	44	0	3.71
Dick Tidrow	2	4	1	0	91⅔	86	34	66	0	4.22
Salome Barojas	3	3	0	0	87⅓	70	32	38	0	2.47
Juan Agosto	2	2	0	0	41⅔	41	11	29	0	4.10
Kevin Hickey	1	2	0	0	20⅔	23	11	8	0	5.23
Steve Mura	0	0	0	0	12⅓	13	6	4	0	4.38
Guy Hoffman	1	0	0	0	6	14	2	2	0	7.50
Randy Martz	0	0	1	0	5	4	4	1	0	3.60
Al Jones	0	0	0	0	2⅓	3	2	2	0	3.86
Jim Kern	0	0	0	0	⅔	1	0	0	0	0.00
	99	63	162	35	1,445⅓	1,355	447	877	9	3.69

1984

Record: 74–88
Finish: Fifth (West)
Games Behind: 10
Manager: Tony LaRussa

The White Sox's marketing and publicity mill came up with a catchy little jingle to buoy 1984 ticket sales. Reviving a forgotten Chubby Checker rock standard from the early 1960s, the ad agency representing the ballclub heated up the television air waves and the print media with "Let's Do It Again!"

Jerry Reinsdorf chuckled at the painful irony of a fifth-place finish coming in a year when everyone in the organization confidently believed that the regular season was just a World Series tune-up. "I was primarily responsible for creating an attitude in '84 that we couldn't lose. We were making plans in the spring of '84 for how we were going to handle the playoffs in the fall. Everybody in the organization, including the players, thought all we had to do is show up and we'll win the division."

The short-term success of the "Winning Uglies" disguised the inadequacies of a farm system that was still stuck in neutral after 24 years. The best young prospects in the high minors—outfielder Daryl Boston, catcher Joel Skinner, and pitchers Bob Fallon and Edwin Correa—never panned out.

For 1984 Roland Hemond added Hall of Fame–bound Tom Seaver and right-hander Ron Reed to the roster, hoping that these distinguished veterans would provide pitching depth to a staff already overloaded with talent. Seaver paced the team in victories as Richard Dotson and LaMarr Hoyt suffered through losing seasons.

The 1984 White Sox occupied first place at the All-Star break. They were the second most prolific home run–hitting team in club history. They were No. 2 in team fielding, and they established a single-season attendance record for the second time in two years. And still, the Sox were destined to finish in fifth place. "We drew like crazy but didn't play well," LaRussa said. "The way I figure it, we owe the fans one, and we expect to pay that debt off in 1985."

	G	AB	H	R	2B	3B	HR	RBI	SB	AVG
Harold Baines	147	569	173	72	28	10	29	94	1	.304
Daryl Boston	35	83	14	8	3	1	0	3	6	.169
Steve Christmas	12	11	4	1	1	0	1	4	0	.364
Julio Cruz	143	415	92	42	14	4	5	43	14	.222
Jerry Dybzinski	94	132	31	17	5	1	1	10	7	.235
Carlton Fisk	102	359	83	54	20	1	21	43	6	.231
Scott Fletcher	149	456	114	46	13	3	3	35	10	.250
Jerry Hairston	115	227	59	41	13	2	5	19	2	.260
Marc Hill	77	193	45	15	10	1	5	20	0	.233
Tim Hulett	8	7	0	1	0	0	0	0	1	.000
Ron Kittle	139	466	100	67	15	0	32	74	3	.215
Rudy Law	136	487	122	68	14	7	6	37	29	.251
Vance Law	151	481	121	60	18	2	17	59	4	.252
Greg Luzinski	125	412	98	47	13	0	13	58	5	.238
Tom O'Malley	12	16	2	0	0	0	0	3	0	.125
Tom Paciorek	111	363	93	35	21	2	4	29	6	.256
Casey Parsons	1	1	0	0	0	0	0	0	0	.000
Jamie Quirk	3	2	0	0	0	0	0	1	0	.000
Joel Skinner	43	80	17	4	2	0	0	3	1	.213
Roy Smalley	47	135	23	15	4	0	4	13	1	.170
Mike Squires	104	82	15	9	1	0	0	6	2	.183
Dave Stegman	55	92	24	13	1	2	2	11	3	.261
Greg Walker	136	442	130	62	29	2	24	75	8	.294
		5,513	1,360	679	225	38	172	640	109	.247

Tom Seaver's American League debut, April 8, 1984

	W	L	GS	CG	IP	H	BB	K	ShO	ERA
Juan Agosto	2	1	0	0	55⅓	54	34	26	0	3.09
Floyd Bannister	14	11	33	4	218	211	80	152	0	4.83
Salome Barojas	3	2	0	0	39⅓	48	19	18	0	4.58
Tom Brennan	0	1	1	0	6⅔	8	3	3	0	4.05
Britt Burns	4	12	16	2	117	130	45	85	0	5.00
Richard Dotson	14	15	32	14	245⅔	216	103	120	1	3.59
Bob Fallon	0	0	3	0	14⅔	12	11	10	0	3.68
Jerry Don Gleaton	1	2	1	0	18⅓	20	6	4	0	3.44
LaMarr Hoyt	13	18	34	11	235⅔	244	43	126	1	4.47
Al Jones	1	1	0	0	20⅓	23	11	15	0	4.43
Gene Nelson	3	5	9	2	74⅔	72	17	36	0	4.46
Randy Niemann	0	0	0	0	5⅓	5	5	5	0	1.69
Ron Reed	0	6	0	0	73	67	14	57	0	3.08
Bert Roberge	3	3	0	0	40⅔	36	15	25	0	3.76
Tom Seaver	15	11	33	10	236⅔	216	61	131	4	3.95
Jim Siwy	0	0	0	0	4⅓	3	2	1	0	2.08
Dan Spillner	1	0	0	0	48⅓	51	14	26	0	4.10
Mike Squires	0	0	0	0	⅓	0	0	0	0	0.00
	74	88	162	43	1,454⅓	1,416	483	840	6	4.14

1985

Record: 85–77
Finish: Third (West)
Games Behind: 6
Manager: Tony LaRussa

Though far from the storybook comeback Tony LaRussa expected, the modest upswing in White Sox fortunes in 1985 offered a semblance of hope for the future. As in years past, improvement of this nature reflected more favorably upon Roland Hemond and his skills as a general manager than upon the quality of talent in the minors. In truth, the White Sox farm system was barren under the direction of Bobby Winkles, who was always regarded as a shrewd judge of talent by his peers. Thus the time to trade had arrived.

Roland Hemond gambled that LaMarr Hoyt's productive days were for the most part behind him. Seeking a shortstop and pitching help, the Sox GM traded the former Sox ace to San Diego for young Venezuelan shortstop Ozzie Guillen and pitchers Bob Long and Tim Lollar. A day later he sent third baseman Vance Law to Montreal for Bob James, the kind of relief ace the Sox so desperately needed in 1984.

The charismatic Guillen stabilized the infield with his fancy glove work and was the easy choice for Rookie of the Year honors. Bob James' imposing fastball silenced opposing hitters, and Carlton Fisk caught his second wind at age 37, matching Dick Allen's team home run record, which had held up since 1972.

There were moments of crowning glory in 1985. Tom Seaver notched career victory No. 300 on August 4 in New York before a packed house of emotional Yankees fans celebrating Phil Rizzuto Day. The day and the season belonged to Seaver, however. His 16–11 record was exceeded only by Britt Burns, who was on the comeback trail coming off a nightmarish, injury-riddled campaign.

The Sox held first place for nine days in June, and might have claimed the West Division crown if they had had another quality starter to replace Richard Dotson, who underwent season-ending surgery in July.

The toughest loss of the season occurred in Baltimore on July 11, and in hindsight it probably altered the course of White Sox history. With two outs in the bottom of the ninth inning and the Sox leading the Orioles 6–3, Bob James injured his right knee and had to be removed from the game. Tony LaRussa called in Mike Stanton, a journeyman reliever Hemond pulled out of the minors in late June. Stanton failed to retire the four batters he faced. The fatal blow, a three-run

Tony LaRussa: tough days ahead

homer by Fred Lynn, spelled sudden, crushing defeat for the White Sox.

In the TV broadcast booth, announcer Ken "Hawk" Harrelson and his sidekick Don Drysdale questioned Roland Hemond's abilities, if the best pitcher he could make available to LaRussa in an injury crisis situation was Mike Stanton. Stunned by the defeat, Harrelson and Drysdale fell silent. The former Dodgers pitcher shook his head and whispered in frustration: "Um...um...um...."

	G	AB	H	R	2B	3B	HR	RBI	SB	AVG
Harold Baines	160	640	198	86	29	3	22	113	1	.309
Daryl Boston	95	232	53	20	13	1	3	15	8	.228
John Cangelosi	5	2	0	2	0	0	0	0	0	.000
Julio Cruz	91	234	46	28	2	3	0	15	8	.197
Joe De Sa	28	44	8	5	2	0	2	7	0	.182
Carlton Fisk	153	543	129	85	23	1	37	107	17	.238
Scott Fletcher	119	301	77	38	8	1	2	31	5	.256
Oscar Gamble	70	148	30	20	5	0	4	20	0	.203
Mark Gilbert	7	22	6	3	1	0	0	3	0	.273
Ozzie Guillen	150	491	134	71	21	9	1	33	7	.273
Jerry Hairston	95	140	34	9	8	0	2	20	0	.243
Marc Hill	40	75	10	5	2	0	0	4	0	.133
Tim Hulett	141	395	106	52	19	4	5	37	6	.268
Ron Kittle	116	379	87	51	12	0	26	58	1	.230
Rudy Law	125	390	101	62	21	6	4	36	29	.259
Bryan Little	73	188	47	35	9	1	2	27	0	.250
Reid Nichols	51	118	35	20	7	1	1	15	5	.297
Tom Paciorek	46	122	30	14	2	0	0	9	2	.246
Mark Ryal	12	33	5	4	3	0	0	3	0	.152
Luis Salazar	122	327	80	39	18	2	10	45	14	.245
Joel Skinner	22	44	15	9	4	1	1	5	0	.341
Mike Squires	2	0	0	1	0	0	0	0	0	.000
Greg Walker	163	601	155	77	38	4	24	92	5	.258
		5,470	1,386	736	247	37	146	695	108	.253

	W	L	GS	CG	IP	H	BB	K	ShO	ERA
Juan Agosto	4	3	0	0	60⅓	45	23	39	0	3.58
Floyd Bannister	10	14	34	4	210⅔	211	100	198	1	4.87
Britt Burns	18	11	34	8	227	206	79	172	4	3.96
Edwin Correa	1	0	1	0	10⅓	11	11	10	0	6.97
Joel Davis	3	3	11	1	71⅓	71	26	37	0	4.16
Richard Dotson	3	4	9	0	52⅓	53	17	33	0	4.47
Bob Fallon	0	0	0	0	16	25	9	17	0	6.19
Steve Fireovid	0	0	0	0	7	17	2	2	0	5.14
Jerry Don Gleaton	1	0	0	0	29⅔	37	13	22	0	5.76
Bob James	8	7	0	0	110	90	23	88	0	2.13
Al Jones	1	0	0	0	6	3	3	2	0	1.50
Tim Lollar	3	5	13	0	83	83	58	61	0	4.66
Bill Long	0	1	3	0	14	25	5	13	0	10.29
Gene Nelson	10	10	18	1	145⅔	144	67	101	0	4.26
Tom Seaver	16	11	33	6	238⅔	223	69	134	1	3.17
Dan Spillner	4	3	3	0	91⅔	83	33	41	0	3.44
Mike Stanton	0	1	0	0	11⅔	15	8	12	0	9.26
Bruce Tanner	1	2	4	0	27	34	13	9	0	5.33
Dave Wehrmeister	2	2	0	0	39⅓	35	10	32	0	3.43
	85	77	163	20	1,451⅔	1,411	569	1023	6	4.07

1986

Record: 72–90
Finish: Fifth (West)
Games Behind: 20
Managers: Tony LaRussa, Doug Rader, Jim Fregosi

Hawk Harrelson's "blueprint for success" so impressed Jerry Reinsdorf and Eddie Einhorn that they offered him Roland Hemond's job as vice president of baseball operations on October 2, 1985. Dwindling attendance, the crosstown success of the Cubs, and the need for a high-profile figure in the front office convinced the owners to push ahead with this controversial move. Roland Hemond was somber, but he accepted a meaningless assignment in the White Sox front office before joining the commissioner's office in May.

Tony LaRussa was loyal to Hemond, but he remained wary of Harrelson's intentions, even after signing a one-year contract extension. It was an uneasy alliance, one that was doomed to failure from the start. Still, Harrelson believed that he was very close to success with this ballclub, and with LaRussa's cooperation the White Sox could move ahead quickly. "We're not in a rebuilding process at all," he said. "We're just one or two players away."

It boiled down to a power conflict between two strong-willed men. Harrelson was irked by what he perceived as LaRussa's secondhand treatment of *his* players—catcher Ron Hassey and pitchers Neil Allen, Dave Schmidt, and Joe Cowley, whom he had acquired in the off-season. Tony LaRussa, on the other hand, was hurt and angered by press reports of his imminent dismissal following a miserable 7–18 start to the 1986 season. Harrelson had been courting Billy Martin as a possible managerial successor. After the Martin rumors quieted down, the Hawk handed LaRussa a vote of confidence on May 9...before firing him on June 20.

"People can read so many things into this, but the bottom line: it's a baseball decision," explained Harrelson. Hoping to repair the tattered image of the White Sox, and sullied by the LaRussa fiasco and the sudden announcement of Reinsdorf's intention to seek state funding to build a new Comiskey Park in Chicago's western suburbs, Reinsdorf and Har-

Carlton Fisk: pride in performance

relson hired 43-year-old Jim Fregosi to manage the ballclub on June 22.

Under Fregosi, the Sox temporarily ended their dry spell with 11 wins in 15 games to climb back into contention—only to suffer an eight-game losing streak and a rash of player injuries. As the pressures mounted for Harrelson, the colorful ex-player and broadcaster increasingly retreated from the media and his flamboyant persona. Finally, the noble experiment ended on September 25, when the Hawk stepped down as GM. Rebuilding or disorganization? The White Sox front office had lost its focus—and the confidence of the fans—as the season wound down.

Jerry Reinsdorf took his beating from the media and then went out and hired 46-year-old Larry Himes, the director of scouting and player personnel for the California Angels, as his new vice president and general manager. The decision to hire Himes was partly based on Eddie Einhorn's extensive study of the California Angels farm system. "What it revealed was that the Angels, of the contending clubs, had more quality draft choices than anyone else in the past six years," Einhorn explained. "The Angels have a very impressive record of guys who made it to the major leagues, and he [Himes] is the guy who did it."

	G	AB	H	R	2B	3B	HR	RBI	SB	AVG
Harold Baines	145	570	169	72	29	2	21	88	2	.296
Bobby Bonilla	75	234	63	27	10	2	2	26	4	.269
Daryl Boston	56	199	53	29	11	3	5	22	9	.266
Scott Bradley	9	21	6	3	0	0	0	0	0	.286
Ivan Calderon	13	33	10	3	2	1	0	2	0	.303
John Cangelosi	137	438	103	65	16	3	2	32	50	.235
Dave Cochrane	19	62	12	4	2	0	1	2	0	.194
Rodney Craig	10	10	2	3	0	0	0	0	0	.200
Julio Cruz	81	209	45	38	2	0	0	19	7	.215
Carlton Fisk	125	457	101	42	11	0	14	63	2	.221
George Foster	15	51	11	2	0	2	1	4	0	.216
Brian Giles	9	11	3	0	0	0	0	1	0	.273
Ozzie Guillen	159	547	137	58	19	4	2	47	8	.250
Jerry Hairston	101	225	61	32	15	0	5	26	0	.271
Ron Hassey	49	150	53	22	11	1	3	20	0	.353
Donnie Hill	22	19	3	2	0	0	0	0	0	.158
Tim Hulett	150	520	120	53	16	5	17	44	4	.231
Ron Karkovice	37	97	24	13	7	0	4	13	1	.247
Ron Kittle	86	296	63	34	11	0	17	48	2	.213
Bryan Little	20	35	6	3	1	0	0	2	0	.171
Steve "Psycho" Lyons	42	123	25	10	2	1	0	6	2	.203
Russ Morman	49	159	40	18	5	0	4	17	1	.252
Reid Nichols	74	136	31	9	4	0	2	18	5	.228
Jack Perconte	24	73	16	6	1	0	0	4	2	.219
Luis Salazar	4	7	1	1	0	0	0	0	0	.143
Joel Skinner	60	149	30	17	5	1	4	20	1	.201
Wayne Tolleson	81	260	65	39	7	3	3	29	13	.250
Greg Walker	78	282	78	37	10	6	13	51	1	.277
Kenny Williams	15	31	4	2	0	0	1	1	1	.129
		5,406	1,335	644	197	34	121	605	115	.247

	W	L	GS	CG	IP	H	BB	K	ShO	ERA
Juan Agosto	0	2	0	0	4⅔	6	4	3	0	7.71
Neil Allen	7	2	17	2	113	101	38	57	2	3.82
Floyd Bannister	10	14	27	6	165⅓	162	48	92	1	3.54
Steve Carlton	4	3	10	0	63⅓	58	25	40	0	3.69
Bryan Clark	0	0	0	0	8	8	2	5	0	4.50
Joe Cowley	11	11	27	4	162⅓	133	83	132	0	3.88
Joel Davis	4	5	19	1	105⅓	115	51	54	0	4.70
Bill Dawley	0	7	0	0	97⅔	91	28	66	0	3.32
Jose DeLeon	4	5	13	1	79	49	42	68	0	2.96
Richard Dotson	10	17	34	3	197	226	69	110	1	5.48
Pete Filson	0	1	1	0	11⅔	14	5	4	0	6.17
Bob James	5	4	0	0	58⅓	61	23	32	0	5.25
Joel McKeon	3	1	0	0	33	18	17	18	0	2.45
Gene Nelson	6	6	1	0	114⅔	118	41	70	0	3.85
Dave Schmidt	3	6	1	0	92⅓	94	27	67	0	3.31
Ray Searage	1	0	0	0	29	15	19	26	0	0.62
Tom Seaver	2	6	12	1	72	66	27	31	0	4.38
Bobby Thigpen	2	0	0	0	35⅔	26	12	20	0	1.77
	72	90	162	18	1,442⅓	1,361	561	895	4	3.94

1987

Record: 77–85
Finish: Fifth (West)
Games Behind: 8
Manager: Jim Fregosi

An overnight miracle worker he was not. Larry Himes asked for time and a little patience from Sox fans in order for him to fulfill the long-range plan of bringing quality players selected through the amateur draft to Chicago.

In the spring of 1987, Al Goldis, director of scouting and player development, had his eye on Stanford pitcher Jack McDowell. Later that summer, after McDowell led his team to the College World Series, the White Sox selected the young man in the first round of the amateur draft. In September, long after matters were settled in the AL West, the lanky young pitcher brimming with self-confidence reported to Chicago, where he became an immediate sensation. McDowell won three of his four September starts.

The Jack McDowell pick was a harbinger of good things to come and the first of four consecutive outstanding Larry Himes draft picks that returned the White Sox to contention in the 1990s. Robin Ventura, Frank Thomas, and Alex Fernandez waited in the wings.

The remaining "Winning Ugly" holdovers—Floyd Bannister, Richard Dotson, Harold Baines, and Carlton Fisk—sparked a second-half recovery that spared Sox fans the ignominy of another last-place finish. The early going was a disaster. The ballclub was mired in last place on June 30 until Floyd Bannister turned things around after a 3–7 start. In customary fashion, the fire-balling righty who lacked a killer instinct reeled off 13 wins in his next 17 decisions.

Fregosi received unexpected help from veteran pitcher Jose DeLeon, a product of the Harrelson regime acquired at no small cost, in this case outfielder Bobby Bonilla, who had put in a cameo appearance in a Chicago uniform the season before. The blistering September drive, triggered by the arrival of relief specialist Bobby Thigpen from Birmingham, offered little solace and consolation to Sox fans who survived another tense year steamed with controversy. The game on the field took a back seat to the overriding stadium issue, which grew more ominous by the day.

After failing to win voter approval in an advisory referendum to build a new stadium in west suburban Addison, the White Sox ownership stepped up discussions with officials from St. Petersburg, Florida, who were eager to land a tenant for their new Suncoast Dome. Unless swift legislative action was undertaken by the bickering Illinois politicians, the Sox were Florida bound.

	G	AB	H	R	2B	3B	HR	RBI	SB	AVG
Harold Baines	132	505	148	59	26	4	20	93	0	.293
Daryl Boston	103	337	87	51	21	2	10	29	12	.258
Ivan Calderon	144	542	159	93	38	2	28	83	10	.293
Carlton Fisk	135	454	116	68	22	1	23	71	1	.256
Ozzie Guillen	149	560	156	64	22	7	2	51	25	.279
Jerry Hairston	66	126	29	14	8	0	5	20	0	.230
Ron Hassey	49	145	31	15	9	0	3	12	0	.214
Donnie Hill	111	410	98	57	14	6	9	46	1	.239
Tim Hulett	68	240	52	20	10	0	7	28	0	.217
Ron Karkovice	39	85	6	7	0	0	2	7	3	.071
Pat Keedy	17	41	7	6	1	0	2	2	1	.171
Bill Lindsey	9	16	3	2	0	0	0	1	0	.188
Steve "Psycho" Lyons	76	193	54	26	11	1	1	19	3	.280
Fred Manrique	115	298	77	30	13	3	4	29	5	.258
Gary Redus	130	475	112	78	26	6	12	48	52	.236
Jerry Royster	55	154	37	25	11	0	7	23	2	.240
Greg Walker	157	566	145	85	33	2	27	94	2	.256
Kenny Williams	116	391	110	48	18	2	11	50	21	.281
		5,538	1,427	748	283	36	173	706	138	.258

	W	L	GS	CG	IP	H	BB	K	ShO	ERA
Neil Allen	0	7	10	0	49⅔	74	26	26	0	7.07
Floyd Bannister	16	11	34	11	228⅔	216	49	124	2	3.58
Ralph Citarella	0	0	0	0	11	13	4	9	0	7.36
Bryan Clark	0	0	0	0	18⅔	19	8	8	0	2.41
Joel Davis	1	5	9	1	55	56	29	25	0	5.73
Jose DeLeon	11	12	31	2	206	177	97	153	0	4.02
Richard Dotson	11	12	31	7	211⅓	201	86	114	0	4.17
Bob James	4	6	0	0	54	54	17	34	0	4.67
Dave LaPoint	6	3	12	2	82⅔	69	31	43	1	2.94
Bill Long	8	8	23	5	169	179	28	72	2	4.37
Jack McDowell	3	0	4	0	28	16	6	15	0	1.93
Joel McKeon	1	2	0	0	21	27	15	14	0	9.43
Scott Neilsen	3	5	7	1	66⅓	83	25	23	1	6.24
John Pawlowski	0	0	0	0	3⅔	7	3	2	0	4.91
Adam Peterson	0	0	1	0	4	8	3	1	0	13.50
Ray Searage	2	3	0	0	55⅔	56	24	33	0	4.20
Bobby Thigpen	7	5	0	0	89	86	24	52	0	2.73
Jim Winn	4	6	0	0	94	95	62	44	0	4.79
	77	85	162	29	1,447⅔	1,436	537	792	12	4.30

1988

Record: 71–90
Finish: Fifth (West)
Games Behind: 32½
Manager: Jim Fregosi

Loyal Sox fans, torn by their warm nostalgia for old Comiskey Park and their desire to see the stadium funding bill pass effortlessly through the legislature in order to keep the team rooted in Chicago, deserved a Purple Heart for all they were forced to endure in the fractious, stress-filled 1988 season.

The Florida drumbeat grew louder by the day as a coalition of community groups, historical preservationists, Reinsdorf haters, and embittered followers of the late Bill Veeck

Greg Walker: class act

opposed the stadium bill right down to the wire. With the future of the Chicago franchise hanging by a thread, the Illinois General Assembly on June 30 narrowly passed the $150 million funding package seconds ahead of the midnight gavel. Using every ounce of political brinkmanship in his political arsenal, Governor James Thompson steered the shaky legislation through treacherous waters. Without Thompson's guidance and support, the White Sox would be playing in Florida today.

The Sox were here to stay, and the new stadium to be built across the street from old Comiskey Park would be ready by Opening Day 1991.

Over the winter Larry Himes had parted company with Jose DeLeon, Floyd Bannister, and Richard Dotson—three-quarters of the 1987 starting rotation. The DeLeon trade brought Cardinals outfielder Lance Johnson and pitcher Rick Horton to Chicago. The deal had great significance for the future, but it left Himes open for some criticism after Horton failed to provide instant pitching relief.

The unexpected loss of Greg Walker, Carlton Fisk, and outfielder Ivan Calderon placed Fregosi in a tough spot. Fisk's broken right hand sidelined him for 10 weeks. Devoid of the offensive contributions of these veterans at a key point in the season, the White Sox fell apart in July at a time when Jim Fregosi desperately needed a good showing from his squad in order to save his job.

Larry Himes inherited Jim Fregosi, but they never saw eye to eye. Fregosi, considered a good baseball strategist, was more attuned to veteran ballplayers. Himes required his manager to be a wet nurse for the younger players. It hardly came as a surprise when Larry Himes fired Fregosi on October 7. "This is probably best for everybody concerned," Fregosi told reporters from his Florida home. "It's up to somebody else to judge whether I was given a fair chance."

	G	AB	H	R	2B	3B	HR	RBI	SB	AVG
Harold Baines	158	599	166	55	39	1	13	81	0	.277
Daryl Boston	105	281	61	37	12	2	15	31	9	.217
Ivan Calderon	73	264	56	40	14	0	14	35	4	.212
Mike Diaz	40	152	36	12	6	0	3	12	0	.237
Carlton Fisk	76	253	70	37	8	1	19	50	0	.277
Dave Gallagher	101	347	105	59	15	3	5	31	5	.303
Ozzie Guillen	156	566	148	58	16	7	0	39	25	.261
Jerry Hairston	2	2	0	0	0	0	2	0	0	.000
Donnie Hill	83	221	48	17	6	2	0	20	3	.217
Lance Johnson	33	124	23	11	4	1	3	6	6	.185
Ron Karkovice	46	115	20	10	4	0	5	9	4	.174
Steve "Psycho" Lyons	146	472	127	59	28	3	5	45	1	.269
Fred Manrique	140	345	81	43	10	6	0	37	6	.235
Carlos Martinez	17	55	9	5	1	0	0	0	1	.164
Russ Morman	40	75	18	8	2	0	0	3	0	.240
Kelly Paris	14	44	11	6	0	0	3	6	0	.250
Dan Pasqua	129	422	96	48	16	2	20	50	1	.227
James "Sap" Randall	4	12	0	1	0	0	0	1	0	.000
Gary Redus	77	262	69	42	10	4	6	34	26	.263
Mark Salas	75	196	49	17	7	0	3	9	0	.250
Greg Walker	99	377	93	45	22	1	8	42	0	.247
Kenny Williams	73	220	35	18	4	2	8	28	6	.159
Mike Woodard	18	45	6	3	0	1	0	4	1	.133
		5,449	1,327	631	224	35	132	573	98	.244

	W	L	GS	CG	IP	H	BB	K	ShO	ERA
Jeff Bittiger	2	4	7	0	61⅔	59	29	33	0	4.23
Joel Davis	0	1	2	0	16	21	5	10	0	6.75
John Davis	2	5	1	0	63⅔	77	50	37	0	6.64
Shawn Hillegas	3	2	6	0	40	30	18	26	0	3.15
Ricky Horton	6	10	9	1	109⅓	120	36	28	0	4.86
Barry Jones	2	2	0	0	26	15	17	17	0	2.42
Dave LaPoint	10	11	25	1	161⅓	151	47	79	1	3.40
Bill Long	8	11	18	3	174	187	43	77	0	4.03
Ravelo Manzanillo	0	1	2	0	9⅓	7	12	10	0	5.79
Tom McCarthy	2	0	0	0	13	9	2	5	0	1.38
Jack McDowell	5	10	26	1	158⅔	147	68	84	0	3.97
Donn Pall	0	2	0	0	28⅔	39	8	16	0	3.45
Ken Patterson	0	2	2	0	20⅔	25	7	8	0	4.79
John Pawlowski	1	0	0	0	14	20	3	10	0	8.36
Melido Perez	12	10	32	3	197	186	72	138	1	3.79
Adam Peterson	0	1	2	0	6	6	6	5	0	13.50
Jerry Reuss	13	9	32	2	183	183	43	73	0	3.44
Steve Rosenberg	0	1	33	0	46	53	19	28	0	4.30
Jose Segura	0	0	4	0	8⅔	19	8	2	0	13.50
Bobby Thigpen	5	8	68	0	90	96	33	62	0	3.30
Carl Willis	0	0	6	0	12	17	7	6	0	8.25
	71	90	161	11	1,439	1,467	533	754	9	4.12

1989

Record: 69–92
Finish: Seventh (West)
Games Behind: 29½
Manager: Jeff Torborg

Jeff Torborg, Yankees pitching coach for nine seasons, beat out six other applicants for the job of White Sox manager. "Out of all the candidates he was the only one with major league managerial experience," Himes said, adding, "I hope to be here 10 years and I hope to be here with *him* the next 10 years."

Torborg admitted that it would take some time to rebuild this team with youth: "We're going to take some heat. But there are some good young players here."

The youthful White Sox occupied the cellar continuously from April 21 until the last day of the season. The free agent signing of Ron Kittle and a spring training swap with the Detroit Tigers that brought pitcher Eric King to Chicago were not enough to salvage respectability. The pitching-thin, short-circuiting offense registered an 11-game Comiskey Park losing streak in late May, and it wasn't until July 13 that the moribund Sox finally began to exhibit signs of a pulse.

In May White Sox announcer Tom Paciorek promised his TV audience that he would shave his head if the Sox won eight straight. The team came through from July 13 to 22, forcing the affable Paciorek to undergo a buzz cut in front of the Comiskey Park faithful two days later. The second-half improvement was largely a result of the contributions of two newcomers, infielder Scott Fletcher and outfielder Sammy Sosa, acquired from the Texas Rangers along with rookie pitcher Wilson Alvarez for Harold Baines and Fred Manrique on July 29.

The departure of the White Sox all-time home run leader (through 1989) did not set well with many of Baines' loyal fans, who had hoped that Harold would finish his career in Chicago. But it worked out splendidly for the White Sox, and the trade was a telling factor in the team's 1990 resurgence.

Harold Baines bid the fans fond farewell in 1989.

	G	AB	H	R	2B	3B	HR	RBI	SB	AVG
Harold Baines	96	333	107	55	20	1	13	56	0	.321
Daryl Boston	101	219	55	34	3	4	5	23	7	.252
Ivan Calderon	157	622	178	83	34	9	14	87	7	.286
Carlton Fisk	103	375	110	47	25	2	13	68	1	.293
Scott Fletcher	59	232	63	30	11	1	1	21	1	.272
Dave Gallagher	161	601	160	74	22	2	1	46	5	.266
Ozzie Guillen	155	597	151	63	20	8	1	54	36	.253
Jerry Hairston	3	3	1	0	0	0	0	0	0	.333
Lance Johnson	50	180	54	28	8	2	0	16	16	.300
Ron Karkovice	71	182	48	21	9	2	3	24	0	.264
Ron Kittle	51	169	51	26	10	0	11	37	0	.302
Steve "Psycho" Lyons	140	443	117	51	21	3	2	50	9	.264
Fred Manrique	65	187	56	23	13	1	2	30	0	.299
Carlos Martinez	109	350	105	44	22	0	5	32	4	.300
Matt Merullo	31	81	18	5	1	0	1	8	0	.222
Russ Morman	37	58	13	5	2	0	0	8	1	.224
Dan Pasqua	73	246	61	26	9	1	11	47	1	.248
Billy Jo Robidoux	16	39	5	2	2	0	0	1	0	.128
Jeff Schaefer	15	10	1	2	0	0	0	0	1	.100
Sammy Sosa	33	99	27	19	5	0	3	10	7	.273
Robin Ventura	16	45	8	5	3	0	0	7	0	.178
Greg Walker	77	233	49	25	14	0	5	26	0	.210
Eddie Williams	66	201	55	25	8	0	3	10	1	.274
		5,504	1,493	693	262	36	94	661	97	.271

	W	L	GS	CG	IP	H	BB	K	ShO	ERA
Jeff Bittiger	0	1	1	0	9⅔	9	6	7	0	6.52
John Davis	0	1	0	0	6	5	2	5	0	4.50
Richard Dotson	3	7	17	1	99⅔	112	41	55	0	3.88
Wayne Edwards	0	0	0	0	7⅓	7	3	9	0	3.68
Jack Hardy	0	0	0	0	12⅓	14	5	4	0	6.57
Greg Hibbard	6	7	23	2	137⅓	142	41	55	0	3.21
Shawn Hillegas	7	11	13	0	119⅔	132	51	76	0	4.74
Barry Jones	3	2	0	0	30⅓	22	8	17	0	2.37
Eric King	9	10	25	1	159⅓	144	64	72	1	3.39
Bill Long	5	5	8	0	98⅔	101	37	51	0	3.92
Tom McCarthy	1	2	0	0	66⅔	72	20	27	0	3.51
Donn Pall	4	5	0	0	87	90	19	58	0	3.31
Ken Patterson	6	1	1	0	65⅔	64	28	43	0	4.52
Melido Perez	11	14	31	2	183⅓	187	90	141	0	5.01
Adam Peterson	0	1	2	0	5⅓	13	2	3	0	15.19
Jerry Reuss	8	5	19	1	106⅔	135	21	27	1	5.06
Steve Rosenberg	4	13	21	2	142	148	58	77	0	4.94
Jose Segura	0	1	0	0	6	13	3	4	0	15.00
Bobby Thigpen	2	6	0	0	79	62	40	47	0	3.76
	69	92	161	9	1,422	1,472	539	778	5	4.23

Fletcher provided steady infield play—a sorely missed ingredient. Wilson Alvarez was a name for the future.

Given all of the controversy and raw anger surrounding the decision to raze old Comiskey Park, it was shocking that the Sox barely shaded the million mark in home attendance in 1989. Did the fans *really* care that in less than a year's time the old park would be reduced to a dusty pile of rubble? Or was the Comiskey Park issue just a sounding board to vent their displeasure with the ownership?

Looking back on a decade that began with such high hopes but ended so miserably, one is struck by the memory of that galling July 11, 1985, loss to Baltimore triggering the front-office purge that changed the course of Sox history. How different would things have been if Chicago had hung on to its 6–3 advantage instead of losing 7–6? Where would the Sox have been in 1989 if Tony LaRussa and Roland Hemond had kept their jobs?

1990

Record: 94–68
Finish: Second (West)
Games Behind: 9
Manager: Jeff Torborg

The marketing theme for 1990 revolved around the Comiskey Park closing. In their wildest dreams, the front office, the fans, possibly even the manager himself could not conceive of the kind of year awaiting the White Sox. The strong second-half showing in 1989 provided an early preview of the season ahead, though few could possibly suspect it at the time.

Jeff Torborg's club broke camp with four rookies on the 25-man roster. They were the youngest team in baseball and were eager to prove themselves to a skeptical world. At the halfway mark the record stood at 48–30, equaling the Baltimore Orioles' 1988–1989 turnaround as the greatest half-year improvement from one All-Star Game to the next.

The character of this team was measured by the early season struggles of Robin Ventura, a first-round draft pick in the June 1988 draft, who survived an 0–41 drought to raise his average to .249 at season's end. Jack McDowell emerged as the ace of the pitching staff after opponents had roughed him up in 1988 and 1989. The maturing McDowell, a "gamer" in Hawk Harrelson parlance, was supported by an outstanding bullpen led by Bobby Thigpen, whose 57 saves established a major league record.

The White Sox nipped at the heels of the potent Oakland A's all season long. They were the only team to win a season series against the eventual AL champs, silencing some rather pointless bench jockeying directed at McDowell by A's pitcher Dave Stewart.

The season was not without its usual front-office intrigue. Citing personal and philosophical differences, Jerry Reinsdorf inexplicably fired Larry Himes and Al Goldis on September 15. Relations were strained for some time. Himes was criticized for perceived "personality problems." "The fact is, Larry Himes cannot get along with anybody," Reinsdorf told radio talk show host Chet Coppock. "You can hardly find anybody in the Sox organization that wasn't happy when Larry Himes left."

The Himes legacy endured long after his sudden departure. Two of his top draft picks, Frank Thomas and Alex Fernandez, were recalled from the White Sox' Birmingham affiliate on August 2. Fernandez won his first major league start in Milwaukee that same night. The powerfully built Thomas—a future Ted Williams in the making—drove home the winning run in his debut.

The two celebrated rookies offered convincing proof that the 1990 success was no one-year fluke. The festive final weekend at old Comiskey Park, fraught with so much emotion, nostalgia, and tears, offered something more to the fans. And that was continuing hope for the future.

	G	AB	H	R	2B	3B	HR	RBI	SB	AVG
Daryl Boston	5	1	0	0	0	0	0	0	1	.000
Phil Bradley	45	133	30	20	5	1	0	5	7	.226
Ivan Calderon	158	607	166	85	44	2	14	74	32	.273
Carlton Fisk	137	452	129	65	21	0	18	65	7	.285
Scott Fletcher	151	509	123	54	18	3	4	56	1	.242
Dave Gallagher	45	75	21	5	3	1	0	5	0	.280
Craig Grebeck	59	119	20	7	3	1	1	9	0	.168
Ozzie Guillen	160	516	144	61	21	4	1	58	13	.279
Lance Johnson	151	541	154	76	18	9	1	51	36	.285
Ron Karkovice	68	183	45	30	10	0	6	20	2	.246
Ron Kittle	83	277	68	29	14	0	16	43	0	.245
Steve "Psycho" Lyons	94	146	28	22	6	1	1	11	1	.192
Carlos Martinez	92	272	61	18	6	5	4	24	0	.224
Rodney McCray	32	6	0	8	0	0	0	0	6	.000
Dan Pasqua	112	325	89	43	27	3	13	59	1	.274
Sammy Sosa	153	532	124	72	26	10	15	70	32	.233
Matt Stark	8	16	4	0	1	0	0	3	0	.250
Frank Thomas	60	191	63	39	11	3	7	31	0	.330
Robin Ventura	150	493	123	48	17	1	5	54	1	.249
Greg Walker	2	5	1	0	0	0	0	0	0	.200
Jerry Willard	3	3	0	0	0	0	0	0	0	.000
		5402	1,393	682	251	44	106	637	140	.258

	W	L	GS	CG	IP	H	BB	K	ShO	ERA
Wayne Edwards	5	3	5	0	95	81	41	63	0	3.22
Alex Fernandez	5	5	13	3	87⅔	89	34	61	0	3.80
Greg Hibbard	14	9	33	3	211	202	55	92	1	3.16
Shawn Hillegas	0	0	0	0	11⅓	4	5	5	0	0.79
Barry Jones	11	4	0	0	74	62	33	45	0	2.31
Eric King	12	4	25	2	151	135	40	70	2	3.28
Jerry Kutzler	2	1	7	0	31⅓	38	14	21	0	6.03
Bill Long	0	1	0	0	5⅔	6	2	2	0	6.35
Steve "Psycho" Lyons	0	0	0	0	2	2	4	1	0	4.50
Jack McDowell	14	9	33	4	205	189	77	165	0	3.82
Donn Pall	3	5	0	0	76	63	24	39	0	3.32
Ken Patterson	2	1	0	0	66⅓	58	34	40	0	3.39
Melido Perez	13	14	35	3	197	177	86	161	3	4.61
Adam Peterson	2	5	11	2	85	90	26	29	0	4.55
Scott Radinsky	6	1	0	0	52⅓	47	36	46	0	4.82
Steve Rosenberg	1	0	0	0	10	10	5	4	0	5.40
Bobby Thigpen	4	6	0	0	88⅔	60	32	70	0	1.83
	94	68	162	17	1,449⅓	1,313	548	914	10	3.61

Final game at old Comiskey

1991

Record: 87–75
Finish: Second (West)
Games Behind: 8
Manager: Jeff Torborg

Jerry Reinsdorf had his eye on Ron Schueler as a possible successor to Larry Himes long before Himes was advised that it was time to clean out his desk. Schueler, who earned high marks in an executive capacity with the Oakland A's, returned to Chicago as a senior vice president of baseball operations upon completion of the 1990 season. Schueler's task was analogized to a chalkboard strategy cooked up by Reinsdorf to simplify his reasoning to the press. Ron Schueler was called upon to guide the White Sox from "Point B," where Larry Himes had taken them up until he was fired, to the treacherous "Point C," the pennant.

The Sox appeared to be a good bet for 1991 with the addition of outfielders Tim Raines and Cory Snyder and pitcher Charlie Hough. Schueler traded pitcher Barry Jones and outfielder Ivan Calderon to Montreal for Raines. Eric King and Shawn Hillegas were sent to Cleveland for Snyder, who rejected the tutelage of hitting coach Walt Hriniak, whose radical theories did not always meet with the approval of the veteran players.

New Comiskey Park, offering state-of-the-art amenities and a less-than-pleasing upper deck that reached to the heavens, opened for business on time and under budget on April 18. The Detroit Tigers spoiled the fun with a jolting 16–0 whitewash of the Hose before 42,191 deflated fans. The hoopla surrounding a new stadium and the season-long rehabilitation of free agent Bo Jackson boosted home attendance to record levels. Nearly 3 million fans passed through the turnstiles to set a city attendance record at the time.

The April 3 signing of Bo Jackson was a masterful public relations stroke for an ownership that had taken its punches throughout the 1980s. Bo Jackson, an athlete with an unconscious flair for the dramatic, played his first game in Comiskey Park on September 2, following surgery on his left hip. Though he would never attain the level of success he enjoyed early in his career, Bo's heart-rending comeback was a sports fable that will likely be retold down through the years.

A disastrous May and a disappointing August were sandwiched around outstanding performances in June and July. The failure to play consistent ball early and late in the season cost the Sox a chance to make 1991 a truly historic and momentous occasion.

	G	AB	H	R	2B	3B	HR	RBI	SB	AVG
Esteban Beltre	8	6	1	0	0	0	0	0	1	.167
Joey Cora	100	228	55	37	2	3	0	18	11	.241
Carlton Fisk	134	460	111	42	25	0	18	74	1	.241
Scott Fletcher	90	248	51	14	10	1	1	28	0	.206
Craig Grebeck	107	224	63	37	16	2	6	31	1	.281
Ozzie Guillen	154	524	143	52	20	2	3	49	21	.273
Mike Huff	51	97	26	14	4	1	1	15	3	.268
Bo Jackson	23	71	16	8	4	0	3	14	0	.225
Lance Johnson	159	588	161	72	14	13	0	49	26	.274
Ron Karkovice	75	167	41	25	13	0	5	22	0	.246
Ron Kittle	17	47	9	7	0	0	2	7	0	.191
Rodney McCray	17	7	2	2	0	0	0	0	1	.286
Matt Merullo	80	140	32	8	1	0	5	21	0	.229
Warren Newson	71	132	39	20	5	0	4	25	2	.295
Dan Pasqua	134	417	108	71	22	5	18	66	0	.259
Tim "Rock" Raines	155	609	163	102	20	6	5	50	51	.268
Cory Snyder	50	117	22	10	4	0	3	11	0	.188
Sammy Sosa	116	316	64	39	10	1	10	33	13	.203
Frank Thomas	158	559	178	104	31	2	32	109	1	.318
Robin Ventura	157	606	172	92	25	1	23	100	2	.284
Don Wakamatsu	18	31	7	2	0	0	0	0	0	.226
		5,594	1,464	758	226	39	139	722	134	.262

	W	L	GS	CG	IP	H	BB	K	ShO	ERA
Wilson Alvarez	3	2	9	2	56⅓	47	29	32	1	3.51
Jeff Carter	0	1	2	0	12	8	5	2	0	5.25
Brian Drahman	3	2	0	0	30⅔	21	13	18	0	3.23
Tom Drees	0	0	0	0	7⅓	10	6	2	0	12.27
Wayne Edwards	0	2	0	0	23⅓	22	17	12	0	3.86
Alex Fernandez	9	13	32	2	191⅔	186	88	145	0	4.51
Ramon Garcia	4	4	15	0	78⅓	79	31	40	0	5.40
Roberto Hernandez	1	0	3	0	15	18	7	6	0	7.80
Greg Hibbard	11	11	29	5	194	196	57	71	0	4.31
Charlie Hough	9	10	29	4	199⅓	167	94	107	1	4.02
Jack McDowell	17	10	35	15	253⅔	212	82	191	3	3.41
Donn Pall	7	2	0	0	71	59	20	40	0	2.41
Ken Patterson	3	0	0	0	63⅔	48	35	32	0	2.83
Melido Perez	8	7	8	0	135⅔	111	52	128	0	3.12
Scott Radinsky	5	5	0	0	71⅓	53	23	49	0	2.02
Bobby Thigpen	7	5	0	0	69⅔	63	38	47	0	3.49
Steve Wapnick	0	1	0	0	5	2	4	1	0	1.80
	87	75	162	28	1,478	1,302	601	923	8	3.79

1992

Record: 86–76
Finish: Third (West)
Games Behind: 10
Manager: Gene Lamont

It was inevitable that sooner or later Ron Schueler would want to place his own man at the White Sox helm. Private disagreements between Jeff Torborg and Schueler bubbled to the surface after Torborg left the organization to assume command of the New York Mets. With a year to go on Torborg's contract, the White Sox brass *encouraged* him to accept the Mets' offer.

Schueler and Reinsdorf were reluctant to classify this action as a termination, but the handwriting was already on the wall for Torborg, who had showed entirely too much favoritism for Carlton Fisk. The Sox were desperately trying to ease Fisk into retirement. His advancing age, boxcar salary, and declining skills made it imperative for the ballclub to groom his successor—Ron Karkovice—into a starting role. Fisk refused to quit. The all-time record for games played by a catcher loomed on the horizon for the venerable "Pudge."

The Fisk situation was a factor in the decision to part company with Jeff Torborg and bring on Gene Lamont, the Pittsburgh Pirates' third-base coach for the previous six seasons. Lamont was a protégé of Pirates manager Jim Leyland—held in high regard by White Sox executives ever since 1983 when he patrolled the third-base coaching box for Tony LaRussa. Leyland, however, was not available.

Was the reserved, laid-back Lamont a "Point C" manager? Under fire by the fans and second-guessed by Chicago's sports-talkshow hosts all season long for his noncombative management style, Gene Lamont trod water with this ballclub in his maiden season.

With "Point C" uppermost in his mind, Ron Schueler added veterans George Bell and Steve Sax to the roster at the expense of Melido Perez, Bob Wickman, Domingo Jean, Sammy Sosa, and Ken Patterson. Costly, unnecessary trades.

In 1992 Lance "the One Dog" Johnson reeled off a 25-game hitting streak—good for No. 3 on the all-time Sox list. Frank Thomas became just the eighth player in modern baseball history to bat over .300 with 20 home runs, 100 runs scored, 100 RBIs, and 100 walks in consecutive seasons. If there was to be a "Michael Jordan of baseball" in the 1990s, Frank Thomas, "the Big Hurt," qualified.

With all these superlatives, the Sox were just a .500 ballclub when August rolled around. A strong August–September showing ensured a winning season for the third year in a row, but it did not quell the impatience of Sox fans or the stigma of underachievement that haunted this club.

The last time Jack McDowell smiled

	G	AB	H	R	2B	3B	HR	RBI	SB	AVG
Shawn Abner	97	208	58	21	10	1	1	16	1	.279
George Bell	155	627	160	74	27	0	25	112	5	.255
Esteban Beltre	49	110	21	21	2	0	1	10	1	.191
Joey Cora	68	122	30	27	7	1	0	9	10	.246
Chris Cron	6	10	0	0	0	0	0	0	0	.000
Carlton Fisk	62	188	43	12	4	1	3	21	3	.229
Craig Grebeck	88	287	77	24	21	2	3	35	0	.268
Ozzie Guillen	12	40	8	5	4	0	0	7	1	.200
Scott Hemond	8	13	3	1	1	0	0	1	0	.231
Mike Huff	60	115	24	13	5	0	0	8	1	.209
Shawn Jeter	13	18	2	1	0	0	0	0	0	.111
Lance Johnson	157	567	158	67	15	12	3	47	41	.279
Ron Karkovice	123	342	81	39	12	1	13	50	10	.237
Matt Merullo	24	50	9	3	1	1	0	3	0	.180
Warren Newson	63	136	30	19	3	0	1	11	3	.221
Dan Pasqua	93	265	56	26	16	1	6	33	0	.211
Tim "Rock" Raines	144	551	162	102	22	9	7	54	45	.294
Nelson Santovenia	2	3	1	1	0	0	1	2	0	.333
Steve Sax	143	567	134	74	26	4	4	47	30	236
Dale Sveum	40	114	25	15	9	0	2	12	1	.219
Frank Thomas	160	573	185	108	46	2	24	115	6	.323
Robin Ventura	157	592	167	85	38	1	16	93	2	.282
		5,498	1,434	738	269	36	110	686	160	.261

	W	L	GS	CG	IP	H	BB	K	ShO	ERA
Wilson Alvarez	5	3	9	0	100⅓	103	65	66	0	5.20
Brian Drahman	0	0	0	0	7	6	2	1	0	2.57
Mike Dunne	2	0	1	0	12⅔	12	6	6	0	4.26
Alex Fernandez	8	11	29	4	187⅔	199	50	95	2	4.27
Roberto Hernandez	7	3	0	0	71	45	20	68	0	1.65
Greg Hibbard	10	7	28	0	176	187	57	69	0	4.40
Charlie Hough	7	12	27	4	176⅓	160	66	76	0	3.93
Terry Leach	6	5	0	0	73⅔	57	20	22	0	1.95
Kirk McCaskill	12	13	34	0	209	193	95	109	0	4.18
Jack McDowell	20	10	34	13	260⅔	247	75	178	1	3.18
Donn Pall	5	2	0	0	73	79	27	27	0	4.93
Scott Radinsky	3	7	0	0	59⅓	54	34	48	0	2.73
Bobby Thigpen	1	3	0	0	55	58	33	45	0	4.75
	86	76	162	21	1,461⅔	1,400	550	810	5	3.82

1993

Record: 94–68
Finish: First (West)
Games Ahead: 8
Manager: Gene Lamont

The magic number was 1993 after all. The well-armed Sox blended speed, an outstanding four-man pitching rotation, and Frank Thomas to win the American League West Division on the 10-year "Winning Ugly" anniversary.

The White Sox survived the tortuous, humiliating release of Carlton Fisk just six days after celebrating his milestone achievement. Fisk caught his 2,226th career game on June 22, shattering Bob Boone's record for longevity, and then was cut loose during a road trip to Cleveland.

They weathered a barrage of bad publicity after Robin Ventura blew his cool and charged Nolan Ryan—a beloved Texas institution—on August 4. The grizzled Ryan won the fistfight, but the "Good Guys Wear[ing] Black" (the ad firm's marketing campaign for '93), bagged a bigger elephant: sole retention of first place when they left Arlington.

The Sox overcame their self-destructive tendencies and finally shed the underachiever rap. Jack McDowell capped off a 22-win season with a Cy Young Award. Frank Thomas became the first White Sox player to crack the seemingly

A grim-faced Carlton Fisk nearing the end of the road

	G	AB	H	R	2B	3B	HR	RBI	SB	AVG
George Bell	102	410	89	36	17	2	13	64	1	.217
Ellis Burks	146	499	137	75	24	4	17	74	6	.275
Ivan Calderon	9	26	3	1	2	0	0	3	0	.115
Joey Cora	153	579	155	95	15	13	2	51	20	.268
Drew Denson	4	5	1	0	0	0	0	0	0	.200
Carlton Fisk	25	53	10	2	0	0	1	4	0	.189
Craig Grebeck	72	190	43	25	5	0	1	12	1	.226
Ozzie Guillen	134	457	128	44	23	4	4	50	5	.280
Mike Huff	43	44	8	4	2	0	1	6	1	.182
Bo Jackson	85	284	66	32	9	0	16	45	0	.232
Lance Johnson	147	540	168	75	18	14	0	47	35	.311
Ron Karkovice	128	403	92	60	17	1	20	54	2	.228
Mike LaValliere	37	97	25	6	2	0	0	8	0	.258
Doug Lindsey	2	1	0	0	0	0	0	0	0	.000
Norberto "Paco" Martin	8	14	5	3	0	0	0	2	0	.357
Matt Merullo	8	20	1	1	0	0	0	0	0	.050
Warren Newson	26	40	12	9	0	0	2	6	2	.300
Dan Pasqua	78	176	36	22	10	1	5	20	21	.205
Tim "Rock" Raines	115	415	127	75	16	4	16	54	7	.306
Steve Sax	57	119	28	20	5	0	1	8	4	.235
Frank Thomas	153	549	174	106	36	0	41	128	1	.317
Robin Ventura	157	554	145	85	27	1	22	94	0	.262
Rick Wrona	4	8	1	0	0	0	0	1	0	.125
		5,483	1,454	776	228	44	162	731	106	.265

	W	L	GS	CG	IP	H	BB	K	ShO	ERA
Wilson Alvarez	15	8	31	1	207⅔	168	122	155	1	2.95
Tim Belcher	3	5	11	1	71⅓	64	27	34	1	4.40
Jason Bere	12	5	24	1	142⅔	109	81	129	0	3.47
Rod Bolton	2	6	8	0	42⅓	55	16	17	0	7.44
Chuck Cary	1	0	0	0	20⅔	22	11	10	0	5.23
Jose DeLeon	0	0	0	0	10⅓	5	3	6	0	1.74
Brian Drahman	0	0	0	0	5⅓	7	2	3	0	0.00
Alex Fernandez	18	9	34	3	247⅓	221	67	169	1	3.13
Roberto Hernandez	3	4	0	0	78⅔	66	20	71	0	2.29
Chris Howard	1	0	0	0	2⅓	2	3	1	0	0.00
Barry Jones	0	1	0	0	7⅓	14	3	7	0	8.59
Terry Leach	0	0	0	0	16	15	2	3	0	2.81
Kirk McCaskill	4	8	14	0	113⅔	144	36	65	0	5.23
Jack McDowell	22	10	34	10	256⅔	261	69	158	4	3.37
Donn Pall	2	3	0	0	58⅔	62	11	29	0	3.22
Scott Radinsky	8	2	0	0	54⅔	61	19	44	0	4.28
Scott Ruffcorn	0	2	2	0	10	9	10	2	0	8.10
Jeff Schwarz	2	2	0	0	51	35	38	41	0	3.71
David Stieb	1	3	4	0	22⅓	27	14	11	0	6.04
Bobby Thigpen	0	0	0	0	34⅔	51	12	19	0	5.71
	94	68	162	16	1,454	1,398	566	974	11	3.70

insurmountable 40–home run barrier and was the unanimous choice for Most Valuable Player. The "Big Hurt" was in a class all by himself.

The difference between the ho-hum 1992 third-place finish and victory in 1993 was the quality of the starting pitching. Young Wilson Alvarez ended the season with a seven-game winning streak, including the memorable division clincher against Seattle in Comiskey Park on September 27.

Teammate Jason Bere was recalled from Nashville on May 25. The young right-hander, gifted with above-average speed and good self-esteem, duplicated Alvarez's success with seven straight wins to close out a remarkable year. The unswerving commitment to a youth program, initiated under Larry Himes in 1986, was vindicated by the satisfying 1993 finish.

Ozzie Guillen, the senior member of the crew, who cut his eyeteeth under Tony LaRussa in 1985, had come to realize what this game was all about: "It shows you—baseball. It's making a building. You build and build and build until you've made a building."

1994

Record: 67–46
Finish: First (Central)
Games Ahead: 1
Manager: Gene Lamont

"How tragic," wrote *Chicago Sun-Times* columnist Jay Mariotti on July 11, "in a famine capital whose last championship is remembered only by octogenarians, if the most title-equipped team in years isn't allowed the opportunity." A month and a day later the horrible prophecy came true.

Unable to reach an accommodation with the owners over a proposal to implement a salary cap to curb inflated salaries, the Major League Baseball Players Association authorized a strike that wiped out the remainder of an enormously entertaining season, the playoffs, and the World Series.

This was to be *the* White Sox's year. Seasoned by their 1993 playoff experience and strengthened by the addition of free-agent outfielders Julio Franco and Darrin Jackson to replace

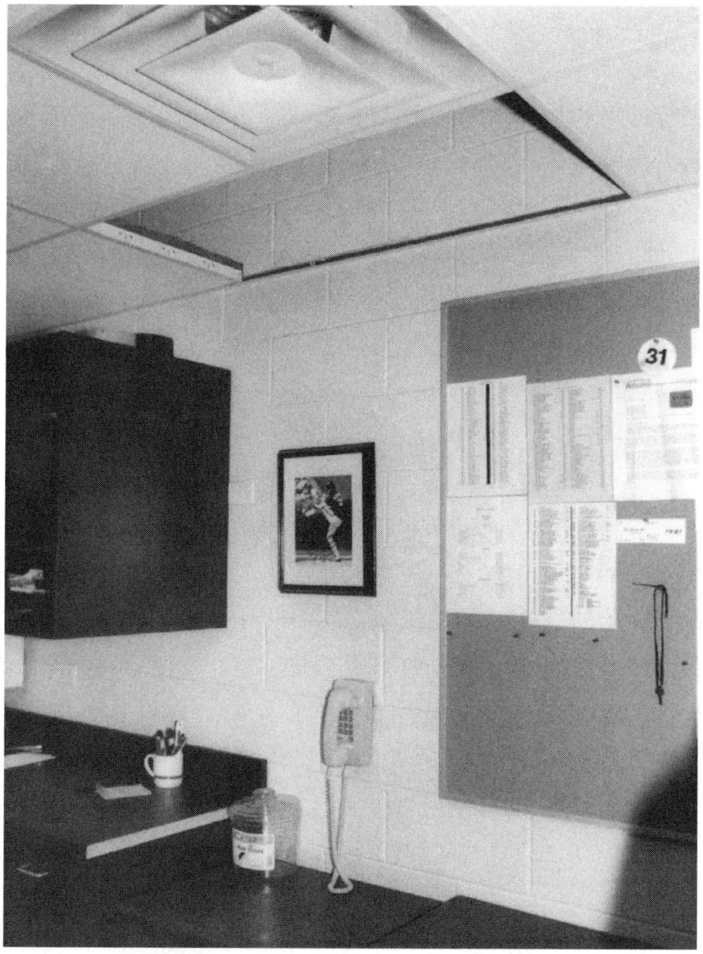

The case of "Batgate." Albert Belle's corked bat was swiped from this room. Note the ceiling panel ajar.

the departed George Bell and Ellis Burks, the White Sox were heavily favored to win the AL Central in the first year of the new divisional alignment.

It promised to be a lively, interesting year, reuniting the Sox with an old rival from the 1950s, the Cleveland Indians, who were much improved and figured to be the only team among the other four in the division to mount a challenge to Chicago.

The Tribe enjoyed an early advantage, but their inexperience caught up with them in mid-July, when the Sox gained their second wind and grabbed first place on July 18. Like two punch-drunk fighters, the White Sox and Indians battled each other to an eight-game draw in a crucial home-and-away showdown July 14–17 and 21–24.

Cleveland's second visit to Comiskey Park in July featured the celebrated "Batgate" incident, when Gene Lamont called for the confiscation of Albert Belle's bat after accusing the Cleveland slugger of corking the barrel. American League president Bobby Brown ordered Belle suspended after a hearing in New York. Several Cleveland players claimed that the White Sox possessed "inside information." Even if that allegation were true, it was a masterstroke of psychological warfare initiated by Lamont, and it earned him the grudging respect of the Chicago media, now squarely in his corner after two years of doubts.

The vaunted Sox pitching staff hit its stride early, despite Jack McDowell's highly publicized two-year salary squabble with Reinsdorf and Schueler. "Black Jack" made his intention known that he would be pitching elsewhere in 1995. After a poor start, McDowell won seven of his last nine decisions. His career winning percentage was third on the all-time list behind Lefty Williams and Juan Pizarro at season's end.

Wilson Alvarez, the "ace heir apparent" in 1995, began the '94 campaign 8–0. Coupled with his seven-game streak to end 1993, his 15 consecutive wins equaled LaMarr Hoyt's team record. Frank Thomas recorded the highest single-season average since Luke Appling nailed down his first batting championship in 1936. Thomas was the MVP of the abbreviated American League season. The team batted .287, a new single-season record.

And yet...

There was great apprehension expressed for the future, even as the fans savored the thrills provided by an exciting ballclub that compared favorably to the legendary Sox teams of yesteryear.

Hitless Wonders (1904–1909)	Go-Go Sox (1951–1956)	Good Guys In Black (1990–1994)
527–385 .578	521–403 .564	428–333 .562

"I might not have an opportunity to have this club again," reflected Ron Schueler as the strike dragged on. "We have a lot of free agents. You don't know what's in store."

Gene Lamont received a one-year contract extension just when it appeared his Chicago days might be numbered. The embattled Sox manager's dream of reaching elusive "Point C" was put on hold pending the outcome of the player strike.

What is overlooked in the heated Lamont debate is a little-known historical footnote. The back-to-back first-place finishes of 1993–94 duplicated the earlier accomplishments of 1900–01, when Charles Comiskey and Clark Griffith were the managers.

It was a good beginning.

	G	AB	H	R	2B	3B	HR	RBI	SB	AVG
Joey Cora	90	312	86	55	13	4	2	30	8	.276
Julio Franco	112	433	138	72	19	2	20	98	0	.319
Craig Grebeck	35	97	30	17	5	0	0	5	8	.309
Ozzie Guillen	100	365	105	46	9	5	1	39	0	.288
Joe Hall	17	28	11	6	3	0	1	5	5	.393
Dann Howitt	10	14	5	4	3	0	0	0	0	.357
Darrin Jackson	104	369	115	43	17	3	10	51	7	.312
Lance Johnson	106	412	114	56	11	14	3	54	26	.277
Ron Karkovice	77	207	44	33	9	1	11	29	0	.213
Mike LaValliere	59	139	39	6	4	0	1	24	0	.281
Norberto "Paco" Martin	45	131	36	19	7	1	1	16	4	.275
Bob Melvin	11	19	3	3	0	0	0	1	0	.158
Warren Newson	63	102	26	16	5	0	2	7	1	.255
Dan Pasqua	11	23	5	2	2	0	2	4	0	.217
Tim "Rock" Raines	101	384	102	80	15	5	10	52	13	.266
Olmedo Saenz	5	14	2	2	0	1	0	0	0	.143
Frank Thomas	113	399	141	106	34	1	38	101	2	.353
Ron Tingley	5	5	0	0	0	0	0	0	0	.000
Robin Ventura	109	401	113	57	15	1	18	78	3	.282
Bob Zupcic	36	92	18	10	4	1	1	8	0	.196
		3,942	1,133	633	175	39	121	602	77	.287

	W	L	GS	CG	IP	H	BB	K	ShO	ERA
Wilson Alvarez	12	8	24	2	161⅔	147	62	108	1	3.45
Paul Assenmacher	1	2	0	0	33	26	13	29	0	3.55
Jason Bere	12	2	24	0	141⅔	119	80	127	0	3.81
Dennis Cook	3	1	0	0	33	29	14	26	0	3.55
Jose DeLeon	3	2	0	0	67	48	31	67	0	3.36
Alex Fernandez	11	7	24	4	170⅓	163	50	122	3	3.86
Atlee Hammaker	0	0	0	0	1⅓	1	0	1	0	0.00
Roberto Hernandez	4	4	0	0	47⅔	44	19	50	0	4.91
Dane Johnson	2	1	0	0	12⅓	16	11	7	0	6.57
Kirk McCaskill	1	4	0	0	52⅔	51	22	37	0	3.42
Jack McDowell	10	9	25	6	181	186	42	127	2	3.73
Scott Ruffcorn	0	2	2	0	6⅓	15	5	3	0	12.79
Scott Sanderson	8	4	14	1	92	110	12	36	0	5.09
Jeff Schwarz	0	0	0	0	11⅓	9	16	14	0	6.35
	67	46	113	13	1,011⅓	964	377	754	9	3.96

1995

Record: 68–76
Finish: Third (Central)
Games Behind: 32
Managers: Gene Lamont, Terry Bevington, Joe Nossek

Ron Schueler's prophetic statements in the middle of baseball's longest and most costly work stoppage foretold the decline and fall of the Chicago White Sox, baseball's *second* most successful pro franchise in the first half of the 1990s.

By the time Dennis "Oil Can" Boyd and the rest of the White Sox "replacement" players were sent packing to make way for Frank Thomas and company, the drive, the thunder, the will to win had vanished. For the fifth time in history, a pennant-caliber White Sox team confounded baseball's sharpest thinkers by tumbling into the second division after almost winning a championship the year before. The 1995 season was a long, grim odyssey into futility, bringing to mind similar misfortunes in 1909, 1921, 1968, and 1984.

The collapse of the 1995 White Sox was a collective failure. Pitching, defense, the bullpen, hitting with men on base—the Sox were dismal in every important phase of the game.

The young and highly talented trio of Wilson Alvarez, Alex Fernandez, and Jason Bere were counted on to overcome the off-season trade of Jack McDowell to the Yankees, but Black Jack had the final chuckle. The fireballing Bere lost both his confidence and control of his fastball and was horrendous from start to finish. Alvarez, out of shape and unprepared in April, finally came around in late August. Young Fernandez fulfilled destiny's call by winning his last seven decisions, but it was too late to rescue the Sox from an oblivion of their own making.

The resurgent Cleveland Indians were on a mission in '95. For all intents and purposes, the fate of the White Sox was sealed by June 2, the day the Sox limped home to Chicago after dropping four straight to the Tribe in Jacobs Field. Gene Lamont was forced to shoulder the blame for the sluggish 11–20 start and was replaced by Terry Bevington, the colorful but occasionally tongue-tied third-base coach who kicked the level of intensity up two notches.

Terry's combativeness with umpires and a notorious fistfight with Brewers manager Phil Garner in midsummer livened up the dreary proceedings of post-strike baseball on the South Side. At times, it actually appeared that the ballclub was on the verge of snapping out of its collective funk, but just when the Sox appeared about to turn a corner, their motor stalled again.

John Kruk

Losing McDowell was only part of the problem. The costly defection of Julio Franco and Darren Jackson to Japan meant that there was no one left to protect the "Big Hurt," who was walked 136 times. Thomas lost 45 points in his batting average but still registered another outstanding season at the plate, becoming the *only* player in major league history to collect 100 walks, 20 homers, and 100 or more RBIs, score 100 runs, and hit .300 in his first five seasons. The consensus of opinion around Chicago is that Big Frank suffered through his first off-year, despite posting numbers that would make most other players envious.

The vastly underrated Joey Cora, a spark plug at second base and one of the genuine clubhouse characters who relieved the collective tensions of the ballclub for nearly five seasons, was not re-signed. He was picked up by Seattle and helped lead the Mariners to a surprise division championship in the AL West. Meanwhile, Joey's replacement, Ray Durham, was inconsistent at the plate and tentative in the field. He was never in the same class as some of the other exceptional rookies making their American League debut this year.

The loss of McDowell, Jackson, Franco, Cora, and long-relief man Paul Assenmacher was a talent drain that proved impossible to overcome.

To soothe angry White Sox fans who believed that the front office had not put forth an honest effort to re-sign the departed players, Ron Schueler signed a bevy of veteran free agents during a frenzied 48-hour period preceding the start of the 1995 season, including Mike Devereaux, Rob Dibble, Chris Sabo, Jim Abbott, and Dave Martinez. But the chemistry was never there, and of the free agents, only the hard-working Martinez made it to the finish line.

Veteran slugger John Kruk ended his early retirement and inked a White Sox contract on May 12, but the injury-prone "designated savior" decided that it was no fun playing DH for a losing ballclub that had no heart. At least that is what he told certain members of the press. After collecting a base hit in Baltimore on July 30, Kruk retreated to the visitors' clubhouse, packed his bags, and left the park while the game was still in progress. It was his last at bat.

When the veterans proved useless and the gap between Cleveland and the Sox swelled to 20 games, Schueler and Reinsdorf abandoned all hope and dipped into the farm system to see what was stirring down in Nashville and Birmingham. In all, 15 rookies made their White Sox debut in 1995. "If anything good comes out of this season," the Sox GM explained, "it's the fact that we've finally been able to see some of our kids."

The White Sox languished in fourth place until the last two weeks of the season, when they staged a rally and finally pushed past their division rivals to the north, the Milwaukee Brewers. Terry Bevington, whose day-to-day status had remained in doubt all year, was rewarded with a contract extension on the last day of the season after managing his ballclub to a respectable 55–54 record.

"It was a nightmare," Bevington said. "But as far as I know having a bad season didn't cause anyone to get sick or die."

	G	AB	H	R	2B	3B	HR	RBI	SB	AVG
Doug Brady	12	21	4	4	1	0	0	3	0	.190
Mike Cameron	28	36	7	4	2	0	1	2	0	.184
Mike Devereaux	92	333	102	48	21	1	10	55	6	.306
Ray Durham	125	471	121	68	27	6	7	51	18	.257
Craig Grebeck	53	154	40	19	12	0	1	18	0	.260
Ozzie Guillen	122	415	103	50	20	3	1	41	6	.248
Lance Johnson	142	607	186	98	18	12	10	57	40	.306
Ron Karkovice	113	323	70	44	14	1	13	51	2	.217
John Kruk	45	159	49	13	7	0	2	23	0	.308
Mike LaValliere	46	98	24	7	6	0	1	19	0	.245
Barry Lyons	27	64	17	8	2	0	5	16	0	.266
Norberto "Paco" Martin	72	160	43	17	7	4	2	17	5	.269
Dave Martinez	119	303	93	49	16	4	5	37	8	.307
Lyle Mouton	58	179	54	23	16	0	5	27	1	.302
Warren Newson	51	85	20	19	0	2	3	9	1	.235
Tim Raines	133	502	143	81	25	4	12	67	13	.285
Chris Sabo	20	71	18	10	5	0	1	8	2	.254
Chris Snopek	22	68	22	12	4	0	1	7	1	.324
Frank Thomas	145	493	152	102	27	0	40	111	3	.308
Chris Tremie	10	24	4	0	0	0	0	0	0	.167
Robin Ventura	135	492	145	79	22	0	26	93	4	.295
		5,060	1,417	755	252	37	146	712	110	.280

	W	L	GS	CG	IP	H	BB	K	ShO	ERA
Jim Abbott	6	4	17	3	112⅓	116	35	45	0	3.36
Wilson Alvarez	8	11	29	3	175	171	93	118	0	4.32
Luis Andujar	2	1	5	0	30⅓	26	14	9	0	3.26
James Baldwin	0	1	4	0	14⅔	32	9	10	0	12.89
Jason Bere	8	15	27	1	137⅔	151	106	110	0	7.19
Mike Bertotti	1	1	4	0	14⅓	23	11	15	0	12.56
Rod Bolton	0	2	3	0	22	33	14	10	0	8.18
Jose DeLeon	5	3	0	0	67⅔	60	28	53	0	5.19
Rob Dibble	0	1	0	0	14⅓	7	27	16	0	6.28
Alex Fernandez	12	8	30	5	203⅔	200	65	159	2	3.80
Tim Fortugno	1	3	0	0	38⅔	30	19	24	0	5.59
Atlee Hammaker	0	0	0	0	6⅓	11	8	3	0	12.79
Roberto Hernandez	3	7	0	0	59⅔	63	28	84	0	3.92
Matt Karchner	4	2	0	0	32	33	12	24	0	1.69
Brian Keyser	5	6	10	0	92⅓	114	27	48	0	4.97
Andrew Lorraine	0	0	0	0	8	3	2	5	0	3.38
Isidro Marquez	0	1	0	0	6⅔	9	2	8	0	6.75
Dave Martinez	0	0	0	0	1	0	2	0	0	0.00
Kirk McCaskill	6	4	1	0	81	97	33	50	0	4.89
Scott Radinsky	2	1	0	0	38	46	17	14	0	5.45
Dave Righetti	3	2	9	0	49⅓	65	18	29	0	4.20
Scott Ruffcorn	0	0	0	0	8	10	13	5	0	7.88
Jeff Shaw	0	0	0	0	9⅔	12	1	6	0	6.52
Billy Simas	1	1	0	0	14	15	10	16	0	2.57
Mike Sirotka	1	2	6	0	34⅓	39	17	19	0	4.19
Larry Thomas	0	0	0	0	13⅔	8	6	12	0	1.32
	68	76	145	12	1,284⅔	1,374	617	892	4	4.85

1996

Record: 85–77
Finish: Second (Central)
Games Behind: 14½
Manager: Terry Bevington

Borrowing a page from the late Bill Veeck, the White Sox marketing department concocted an ingenious series of Wacky Week Night promotions to lure disenchanted White Sox fans back to Comiskey Park. On Romance Night, for instance, prizes were awarded to amorous lovers locked in a torrid grandstand embrace. Ozzie Guillen and his teammates were unamused by the marathon kissing contests going on in the right-field seats with a game in progress.

The carnival-sideshow atmosphere of the Wacky Week Nights may have infuriated the White Sox veterans, but Guillen's criticism in the press of a lighthearted gimmick underscored a tense, season-long cold war pitting the fans against the players and a bewildered ownership that was forced to shoulder the blame for the 1994 strike, which in all likelihood cost the Sox a World Series appearance.

The fans stayed away all season, despite the team's spirited run for a wild-card berth that ended unhappily for Chicago on the next to the last day of the season.

At year's end, owner Jerry Reinsdorf was left to assess the wreckage of a season that began on a high note but ended so miserably. With one of the highest payrolls in all of baseball, the 1996 White Sox were expected to challenge the Cleveland Indians in the Central Division. Up until mid-June at least, the Sox seemed to be every bit as good as advertised.

The free agent signings of Harold Baines, pitcher Kevin Tapani, and veteran outfielder Tony Phillips, who retired and then unretired within a span of 48 hours during spring training, provided manager Terry Bevington with a potent

A tough year for Terry Bevington—and the American League umpires

everyday lineup and a quality third starter backing up Wilson Alvarez and Alex Fernandez. General manager Ron Schueler gambled that the temperamental, injury-prone outfielder Danny Tartabull had some pop left in his bat, and he was willing to trade two farms hands to the Oakland A's for his services. The gamble nearly paid off.

The emergence of rookie pitcher James Baldwin and the overall defensive improvement were mirrored in the team's 40–21 record on June 10, good for a first-place showing. Collectively, the White Sox toppled the seemingly impenetrable all-time team home run mark of 192, set by the 1977 South Side Hitmen. The club finished near the top in team fielding and pitching in an explosive offense-oriented year when the hitters dominated every phase of the game. So what went wrong?

Frank Thomas suffered a stress fracture in mid-July that landed him on the disabled list for the first time in his career. But even with a healthy and productive Thomas relentlessly battering opposing pitchers following his return to active duty, the underachieving Pale Hose struggled to beat even the weakest of their American League rivals. As late as August 14, Chicago enjoyed a comfortable 3½-game lead over Baltimore for the wild-card spot and were poised to mop up the victor's spoils against the AL doormats they were scheduled to play for the next 20 games. Instead, the Sox squandered their opportunity and limped home with a 9–11 record. For all intents and purposes, the season was lost at that point.

The White Sox were vulnerable in two key areas. Bevington's youthful, unproven corps of relief pitchers buckled from overwork and exhaustion. The Sox manager simply refused to allow his starters to go the distance, placing a terrible burden on the inexperienced bullpen tandem of Matt Karchner, Larry Thomas, and Billy Simas.

Karchner, arguably the best set-up man on the staff, ended the season on the disabled list. Even with a healthy and robust Roberto Hernandez enjoying a career year, the bullpen managed to blow 32 saves in 75 opportunities.

The Chicago media vented much criticism at Ron Schueler for coming up empty in his effort to land a capable fifth starter when the season was on the line. Veteran National League castoff Joe Magrane and a collection of ragarm pitchers shuttled to the Windy City direct from the Sox farm system were unable to escape a second- or third-inning shelling in their starting assignments.

Nevertheless, it was a lively, interesting year steamed with the usual controversies and mishaps that seem to beset only the White Sox.

In May Tony Phillips added a new wrinkle to the often bitter White Sox–Brewers rivalry when he punched out a grandstand heckler in County Stadium and ended up in a Milwaukee courtroom explaining his actions to a judge.

Terry Bevington, no amateur scrapper himself, alienated the Chicago press corps all season with his curt, sarcastic answers to the most mundane questions put to him during the postgame interview sessions. The testy Sox manager compounded his image problems and drew more unwanted publicity to the team late one night by exchanging blows with American League umpire Richie Garcia at a Chicago steak house.

There were fisticuffs all around in 1996, including a celebrated dugout altercation between the normally reserved Robin Ventura and Frank Thomas. The biggest battle, however, was the one against fan apathy.

Everyone had their own pet theory for the phenomenon of the empty ballpark, and the issue was hotly debated in the newspapers and sports talkshows all year long. The corporate skyboxes (perceived as elitist by the hard-core Bill Veeck loyalists), criticisms of the steep upper deck in the new Comiskey Park, hostility toward the ownership for the 1994 strike debacle, and the inhospitable location of the stadium for commuting suburbanites were cited as key factors for the alarming drop-off in attendance. The marketing department commissioned a fan survey to get to the root of the problem, but never publicized the results. One thing seemed certain, however, as the players packed it in and headed for home: there would be some wholesale personnel changes made over the winter. The first was a shocker. On November 19 the Sox signed Albert Belle, the villain of "Batgate," to a five-year contract.

When the dust from this weird and wacky season had settled, a beleaguered Jerry Reinsdorf could only shake his head and promise White Sox fans that they would see a kinder, gentler, more fan-friendly team in 1997. But would the South Side faithful *ever* be willing to forgive and forget the sins of the past?

	G	AB	H	R	2B	3B	HR	RBI	SB	AVG
Harold Baines	143	495	154	80	29	0	22	95	3	.311
Pat Borders	31	94	26	6	1	0	3	6	0	.277
Mike Cameron	11	11	1	1	0	0	0	0	0	.091
Domingo Cedeno	12	19	3	2	2	0	0	3	1	.158
Ray Durham	156	557	153	79	33	5	10	65	30	.275
Ozzie Guillen	150	499	131	62	24	8	4	45	6	.263
Ron Karkovice	111	355	78	44	22	0	10	38	0	.220
Chad Krueter	46	114	25	14	8	0	3	18	0	.219
Darren Lewis	141	337	77	55	12	2	4	53	21	.228
Robert Machado	4	6	4	1	1	0	0	2	0	.667
Norberto "Paco" Martin	70	140	49	30	7	0	1	14	10	.350
Dave Martinez	146	440	140	85	20	8	10	53	15	.318
Lyle Mouton	87	214	63	25	8	1	7	39	3	.294
Jose Munoz	17	27	7	7	0	0	0	1	0	.259
Greg Norton	11	23	5	4	0	0	2	3	0	.217
Tony Phillips	153	581	161	119	29	3	12	63	13	.277
Mike Robertson	6	7	1	0	1	0	0	0	0	.143
Don Slaught	14	36	9	2	1	0	0	4	0	.250
Chris Snopek	46	104	27	18	6	1	6	18	0	.260
Danny Tartabull	132	472	120	58	23	3	27	101	1	.254
Frank Thomas	141	527	184	110	26	0	40	134	1	.349
Robin Ventura	158	586	168	96	31	2	34	105	1	.287
		5,644	1,586	898	284	33	195	860	105	.281

	W	L	GS	CG	IP	H	BB	K	ShO	SV	ERA
Wilson Alvarez	15	10	35	0	217⅓	216	97	181	0	0	4.22
Luis Andujar	0	2	5	0	23	32	0	6	0	0	8.22
James Baldwin	11	6	28	0	169	168	57	127	0	0	4.42
Jason Bere	0	1	5	0	16⅔	26	18	19	0	0	10.26
Mike Bertotti	2	0	2	0	28	28	20	19	0	0	5.14
Tony Castillo	3	1	0	0	22⅔	23	4	9	0	1	1.59
Jeff Darwin	0	1	0	0	30⅔	26	9	15	0	0	2.93
Alex Fernandez	16	10	35	6	258	248	72	200	1	0	3.45
Marvin Freeman	0	0	1	0	2	4	1	1	0	0	13.50
Roberto Hernandez	6	5	0	0	84⅔	65	38	85	0	38	1.91
Stacey Jones	0	0	0	0	2	0	1	1	0	0	0.00
Matt Karchner	7	4	0	0	59⅓	61	41	46	0	1	5.76
Brian Keyser	1	2	0	0	59⅔	78	28	19	0	1	4.98
Alan Levine	0	1	0	0	10⅓	22	7	12	0	0	5.40
Joe Magrane	1	5	8	0	53⅔	70	25	21	0	0	6.88
Kirk McCaskill	5	5	4	0	51⅔	72	31	28	0	0	6.97
Scott Ruffcorn	0	1	1	0	6⅓	10	6	3	0	0	11.37
Rich Sauveur	0	0	0	0	3	3	5	1	0	0	15.00
Billy Simas	2	8	0	9	72⅔	75	39	65	0	2	4.58
Mike Sirotka	1	2	4	0	26⅓	34	12	11	0	0	7.18
Kevin Tapani	13	10	34	1	225⅓	236	76	150	0	0	4.59
Larry Thomas	2	3	0	0	30⅔	32	14	20	0	0	3.23
	85	77	162	7	1,461	1,529	616	1,039	4	43	4.52

1997

Record: 80–81
Finish: Second (Central)
Games Behind: 6
Manager: Terry Bevington

The glories of the past and the raging controversies of 1997 collided in unexpected ways; a season primarily remembered for the infamous "White Flag" trade of July 31, sending a trio of talented veterans—Wilson Alvarez, Danny Darwin, and ace closer Roberto Hernandez—to the San Francisco Giants for six minor league unknowns: pitchers Keith Foulke, Ken Vining, Lorenzo Barcelo, Bob Howry, outfielder Brian Manning, and shortstop Mike Caruso. The White Sox were playing .500 baseball and locked in third place at the time, yet trailed the Cleveland Indians by a mere three games.

Still smarting over the injustice of the canceled 1994 season, slow-to-forgive Sox fans were in an uproar over the departure of their top closer and prized Venezuelan lefty Alvarez, who left with nine victories to his credit and a low ERA. The trade was puzzling at the time, but a tacit admission on the part of the front office that the ballclub wasn't nearly good enough to overtake the rampaging Tribe, chasing their second pennant in three seasons. Jerry Reinsdorf admitted as much when he remarked that if Sox fans thought they had a chance to overtake Cleveland, they were crazy. Not exactly words to endear the embattled owner to an increasingly hostile fan base, but a candid assessment of a veteran ballclub that desperately needed to go in another direction in order to seriously challenge for a division crown down the road. Losing two potential free agents at mid-season seemed like a good first step, though the fan base and the media did not exactly see things in the same light.

Attendance rebounded and hit a four-year high with the addition of Albert Belle. The temperamental superstar's season was disappointing and lackluster, although he drove home 116 runs, poled four grand slams to set a new team record, and equaled Luke Appling's franchise record 27-game hitting streak. Minus the injured Robin Ventura who sat out the first 99 games of the season due to a compound fracture in his ankle, the team struggled out of the gate and was a dismal 8–17 and mired in last place on May 1. Thereafter the club went 72–64, with Frank Thomas taking charge. The "Big Hurt" won his second American League batting title with a nifty .347 average—reaching the "high water mark" of his Hall of Fame career.

Interleague play debuted in 1997 and was a resounding success for Sox fans jamming the New Comiskey in mid-June to cheer on the first "official" victories over the hated North Siders. By virtue of winning two of three against the Cubs before record crowds, a frustrating season was partially redeemed, although poor team play would cost Terry Bevington his job. Bypassing an opportunity to sign Roger Clemens as a free agent—the "Rocket" was available for the right price—the Sox chose instead to ink the hapless Jaime Navarro to a four-year contract two days *before* Clemens signed with Toronto. The ex-Cub posted a dismal 9–14 record with a 5.91 earned-run average that rose even higher in 1998. No surprise that the pitching staff was in shambles—the team ERA topped 5.00 for the first time since 1936, and for the second year in a row, the Sox tied for dead last in team fielding.

With such disappointing results, it was a foregone conclusion that the combative manager who was uncommunicative with the media, unpopular with the fans, and losing respect among the players, would not be invited back. Too many times, Bevington let the situation get away from him. In one awful moment, he walked to the mound to summon a new pitcher—but had no one warming up in the bullpen. On September 30 the club chose not to exercise their option on Bevington's contract, beginning the guessing game of who was to lead in '98. "Obviously, Terry was a mistake," Reinsdorf admitted. "He's a terrific third-base coach and instructor, but he Murphy-lawed as a manager. Too bad we couldn't keep him as a third-base coach, but you just can't do that."

From a historical perspective, the '97 campaign was memorable in another way. Carlton Fisk's No. 72 was retired in a special ceremony on September 14. And finally, after so many years of frustration and waiting, Nelson Fox was inducted into the Hall of Fame on August 3. A "Nellie Fox Tribute Day" was held on August 16, a windswept, rain-soaked Saturday afternoon in the Windy City before a packed house. His widow, Mrs. Joanne Fox, and a number of Nellie's former teammates gathered inside the park for a touching ceremony honoring the famous White Sox "Mighty Mite." After so many years of lobbying, campaigning, and letter-writing, the Nellie Fox Society founders were given their just reward and could at last retire or elect to recommit their time and resources to the start-up of the... *Billy Pierce Society.*

	G	AB	H	R	2B	3B	HR	RBI	SB	AVG
Jeff Abbott	19	38	10	8	1	0	1	2	0	.263
Harold Baines	93	318	97	40	18	0	12	52	0	.305
Albert Belle	161	634	174	90	45	1	30	116	4	.274
Mike Cameron	116	379	98	63	18	3	14	55	23	.259
Ray Durham	155	634	172	106	27	5	11	53	33	.271
Jorge Fabregas	100	322	90	31	10	1	7	48	1	.280
Chad Fonville	9	9	1	1	0	0	0	1	2	.111
Ozzie Guillen	142	490	120	59	21	6	4	52	5	.245
Ron Karkovice	51	138	25	10	3	0	6	18	0	.181
Chad Kreuter	19	37	8	6	2	1	1	3	0	.216
Darren Lewis	81	77	18	15	1	0	0	5	11	.234
Robert Machado	10	15	3	1	0	1	0	2	0	.200
Norberto "Paco" Martin	71	213	64	24	7	1	2	27	1	.300
Dave Martinez	145	504	144	78	16	6	12	55	12	.286
Lyle Mouton	88	242	65	26	9	0	5	23	4	.269
Greg Norton	18	34	9	5	2	2	0	1	0	.265
Magglio Ordonez	21	69	22	12	6	0	4	11	1	.319
Tony Pena	31	67	11	4	1	0	0	8	0	.164
Tony Phillips	36	129	40	23	6	0	2	9	4	.310
Chris Snopek	86	298	65	27	15	0	5	35	3	.218
Frank Thomas	146	530	184	110	35	0	35	125	1	.347
Mario Valdez	54	115	28	11	7	0	1	13	1	.243
Robin Ventura	54	183	48	27	10	1	6	26	0	.262
	161	5,491	1,498	779	260	28	158	740	106	.273

	W	L	GS	CG	IP	H	BB	K	ShO	SV	ERA
Wilson Alvarez	9	8	22	2	145⅔	126	55	110	1	0	3.03
James Baldwin	12	15	32	1	200	205	83	140	0	0	5.27
Jason Bere	4	2	6	0	28⅔	20	17	21	0	0	4.71
Mike Bertotti	0	0	0	0	3⅔	9	2	4	0	0	7.36
Carlos Castillo	2	1	2	0	66⅓	68	33	43	0	1	4.48
Tony Castillo	4	4	0	0	62⅓	74	23	42	0	4	4.91
Chris Clemons	0	2	2	0	12⅔	19	11	8	0	0	8.53
Nelson Cruz	0	2	0	0	26⅓	29	9	23	0	0	6.49
Danny Darwin	4	8	17	1	113⅓	130	31	62	0	0	4.13
Jeff Darwin	0	1	0	0	13⅔	17	7	9	0	0	5.27
Doug Drabek	12	11	31	0	169⅓	170	69	85	0	0	5.74
Scott Eyre	4	4	11	0	60⅔	62	31	36	0	0	5.04
Tom Fordham	0	1	1	0	17⅓	17	10	10	0	0	6.23
Keith Foulke	3	0	0	0	28⅔	28	5	21	0	3	3.45
Roberto Hernandez	5	1	0	0	48	38	24	47	0	27	2.44
Matt Karchner	3	1	0	0	52⅔	50	26	30	0	15	2.91
Allan Levine	2	2	0	0	27⅓	35	16	22	0	0	6.91
Chuck McElroy	1	3	0	0	59⅓	56	19	44	0	1	3.94
Jaime Navarro	9	14	33	2	209⅔	267	73	142	0	0	5.79
Billy Simas	3	1	0	0	41⅓	46	24	38	0	1	4.14
Mike Sirotka	3	0	4	0	32	36	5	24	0	0	2.25
Larry Thomas	0	0	0	0	3⅓	3	2	0	0	0	8.10
	80	81	161	6	1,422	1,505	575	961	7	52	4.74

1998

Record: 80–82
Finish: Second (Central)
Games Behind: 9
Manager: Jerry Manuel

Forty-four-year-old Jerry Manuel was anointed the 36th White Sox manager on December 4, 1997. The die was cast for another rebuilding program, this time directed by Jim Leyland's former bench coach after Leyland had led the Florida Marlins to a stunning World Series upset over Cleveland in 1997. The low-key, taciturn Manuel was the polar opposite of Terry Bevington and a calming presence on the field after three tumultuous seasons. Manuel became the third consecutive "freshman" manager provided on-the-job training at the Sox helm, but only the second African American skipper in team history, following in Larry Doby's footsteps by exactly 20 years.

The youth movement was in full bloom with 18 rookies making their debut, but none making much of a lasting impression. The veteran core—Ventura, Thomas, and Belle—formed the nucleus of a power-laden ballclub in a year when all of the attention was focused on the North Side, where Sammy Sosa stroked 66 home runs for the Cubs. The 1992 George Bell–for–Sammy Sosa swap had turned out to be a calamitous miscalculation for the South Side faithful. But a little-known, unheralded trade with the North Siders completed on July 29, 1998, came out all right in the end and would eventually provide a measure of vindication. On that day, Ron Schueler exchanged 30-year-old, right-handed reliever Matt

Mike Caruso, kid shortshop (White Sox photo by Ron Vesely)

Karchner for an unknown minor league prospect still several years away from stardom—pitcher Jon Garland.

The first building block of a coming championship was now firmly in place, but there was still no quick fix for a ballclub in transition. Manuel admitted as much. "I think I fell short," he said. "Once we got into it, I realized there were some things that had to be done. I got real concerned during the All-Star break when we were having lunch in the press room and someone said, 'We are on a pace to lose 100 games.' We already were last. Instead of watching to see how the Cleveland Indians were doing, we were watching to see how the Detroit Tigers were doing." After the break, the Sox improved, ever so slowly. Albert Belle finally delivered the goods—establishing a new team record for home runs, with 49, and 152 RBIs. The mercurial Belle narrowly missed becoming the first player since Stan Musial in 1948 to record 400 total bases, 100 extra-base hits in a season, and fell one homer and two doubles shy of 50-50.

His impressive numbers did little to elevate overall team play, however, and at season's end, Belle elected to exercise a clause allowing him to opt out of the remainder of his contract if he was not the highest paid player on the roster. Needless to say, the Albert Belle experiment did not produce the desired "Point C" results, and Jerry Reinsdorf was not terribly unhappy to part ways with him, either. Belle signed with the Orioles as a $65 million free agent in 1999, but debilitating injuries ended his career two years later.

The 1998 Sox remained a sub-.500 team all season long, but with a strong 18–7 September surge, they narrowly missed achieving the break-even mark. On the last day of the season, as James Baldwin polished off the Kansas City Royals with offensive support from Robin Ventura, who stroked a home run with three driven in, TV announcers Ken Harrelson and Tom Paciorek paid tribute to the all-around best White Sox third baseman since the days of Willie Kamm in the 1920s. Like most Sox fans, Hawk and Wimpy knew in their heart of hearts that Robin was already lost to free agency—and what a shame it was. His replacement, Greg Norton, would provide a few sanguine moments in the year ahead, but the departure of Ventura to the deep pockets of the New York Mets was the most painful loss of them all.

	G	AB	H	R	2B	3B	HR	RBI	SB	AVG
Jeff Abbott	89	244	68	33	14	1	12	41	3	.279
Albert Belle	163	609	200	113	48	2	49	152	6	.328
Mike Cameron	141	396	83	53	16	5	8	43	27	.210
Mike Caruso	133	523	160	80	17	6	5	55	22	.306
Wil Cordero	96	341	91	58	18	2	13	49	2	.267
Ray Durham	158	635	181	125	35	8	19	67	36	.285
Lou Frazier	7	7	0	0	0	0	0	0	4	.000
Mark Johnson	7	23	2	2	0	2	0	1	0	.087
Chad Kreuter	93	245	62	26	9	1	2	33	1	.253
Robert Machado	34	111	23	14	6	0	3	15	0	.207
Greg Norton	105	299	71	38	17	2	9	36	3	.237
Charlie O'Brien	57	164	43	12	9	0	4	18	0	.262
Magglio Ordonez	145	535	151	70	25	2	14	65	9	.282
Ruben Sierra	27	74	16	7	4	1	4	11	2	.216
Brian Simmons	5	19	7	4	0	0	2	6	0	.368
Chris Snopek	53	125	26	17	2	0	1	4	3	.208
Frank Thomas	160	585	155	109	35	2	29	109	7	.265
Robin Ventura	161	590	155	84	31	4	21	91	1	.263
Craig Wilson	13	47	22	14	5	0	3	10	1	.468
	163	5,585	1,516	861	291	38	198	806	127	.271

	W	L	GS	CG	IP	H	BB	K	ShO	SV	ERA
Jim Abbott	2	0	2	0	31⅔	35	12	14	0	0	4.55
James Baldwin	4	4	12	1	159	176	60	108	0	0	5.32
Jason Bere	1	4	7	0	83⅔	98	58	53	0	0	6.45
Chad Bradford	2	1	0	0	30⅔	27	7	11	0	1	3.23
Larry Casian	0	0	0	0	4	8	1	6	0	0	11.25
Carlos Castillo	3	1	2	0	100⅓	94	35	64	0	0	5.11
Tony Castillo	0	0	0	0	27	38	11	14	0	0	8.00
Scott Eyre	2	3	9	0	107	114	64	73	0	0	5.38
Tom Fordham	1	1	3	0	48	51	42	23	0	0	6.75
Keith Foulke	3	1	0	0	65⅓	51	20	57	0	1	4.13
Mike Heathcott	0	0	0	0	3	2	1	3	0	0	3.00
Bob Howry	0	1	0	0	54⅓	37	19	51	0	9	3.15
Matt Karchner	1	3	0	0	36⅔	33	19	30	0	11	5.15
Jaime Navarro	5	7	14	0	172⅔	223	77	71	0	1	6.36
Jim Parque	5	2	11	0	113	135	49	77	0	0	5.10
Todd Rizzo	0	0	0	0	6⅔	12	6	3	0	0	13.50
Billy Simas	4	2	0	0	70⅔	54	22	56	0	18	3.57
Mike Sirotka	7	6	16	3	211⅓	255	47	128	0	0	5.06
John Snyder	3	1	6	0	86⅓	96	23	52	0	0	4.80
Bryan Ward	1	0	0	0	27⅓	30	7	17	0	1	3.33
	80	82	163	8	1,439	1,569	580	911	4	42	5.24

1999

Record: 75–86
Finish: Second (Central)
Games Behind: 21½
Manager: Jerry Manuel

How is it possible for a team to shave nearly a half a run off of an ERA topping 5.00 one year earlier and elevate its accumulated batting average six points but finish with a worse record than the year before? Chalk it up to the inexperience of youth and a leaky defense on the left-hand side of the infield that brought back horrifying memories of the Alan Bannister years of the late 1970s. Second-year shortstop Mike Caruso, the key to the "White Flag" trade, regressed after a promising rookie season. His 24 fielding miscues were exceeded only by Greg Norton, the Robin Ventura stand-in at third base, who muffed 27 plays. The marketing slogan this year was "The Kids Can Play." Well, at least some of them could. The White Sox began the campaign as the second-youngest team in all of baseball behind the Florida Marlins and were flirting with the .500 mark and respectability in the first half of the season until the bottom fell out.

Nineteen more rookies made their debut in 1999, including nine pitchers and Paul Konerko, acquired from the Cincinnati Reds for the disappointing center fielder Mike Cameron on November 10, 1998. It was Ron Schueler's finest trade as general manager. Konerko was a minor league sensation but a big-league washout deemed expendable by the Dodgers and then the Reds, who simply gave up on the power-hitting first-sacker who could also play third. Cameron, who arrogantly boasted that he was "only 10 hits from being one of the best in the game," eventually drifted from Cincinnati to Seattle to the Mets.

Second-year pitching coach Nardi Contreras, who made a cup-of-coffee appearance with "Veeck's Wrecks" back in 1980, sharpened the bullpen by turning the ball over to late-inning closer Bobby Howry and set-up man Keith Foulke, whose brilliant work silenced critics of the infamous "White Flag" trade. But the starting tandem of James Baldwin, Mike Sirotka, Jim

Mike Sirotka lowered his ERA by a full run in 1999, but he fell short of a winning record. (White Sox photo by Ron Vesely)

Parque, John Snyder, and Jaime Navarro were inconsistent and, at times, flat-out terrible. Nineteen ninety-nine was an explosive year offensively, with a record number of home runs hit in each league, and Sox hitters rose to the challenge. Outfielders Magglio Ordonez and Carlos Lee were two home-grown products who made good that summer. Lee was named the organization's top prospect and *Baseball America's* "Best Power Hitter" for 1998. He made an immediate and lasting impression by stroking a home run off of Oakland's Tom Candiotti in his first major league at-bat on May 7—becoming the first White Sox player to ever accomplish the rare feat. Lee played his way into the starting lineup, drilled 16 home runs, and received consideration for Rookie of the Year honors in his freshman season, while Venezuelan-born Ordonez, a second-year man, joined Albert Belle and Frank Thomas as only the third player in team history to stroke 30 home runs, drive in 100 runs, and score 100 runs in a single season.

However, Thomas fell short of attaining his yearly goal of 30 home runs and 100 RBIs as a result of a chronic bone-spur injury to his ankle. When he refused to pinch hit in the second game of a doubleheader in Texas on September 6, Jerry Manuel was incensed and blew up at his ailing slugger in the dugout. "I would have been fine and had no problem with it if he had told me before the game or even had been on the bench and said he couldn't go. But just to say you can't go when you already pinch hit the game before…I let the bench and the team know," Manuel told reporters. The next day Thomas had surgery in Chicago and was lost for the rest of the season. The second half of his great career was comprised by one nagging injury after another, beginning in 1999 when the manager, the media, and White Sox fans called into question his commitment and dedication to team play—a selfish, inner-directed player only interested in statistics, some would argue. At the yearly Cubs-Sox showdown, filled with the tension and high drama of a World Series game, North Side fans derisively chanted "the Big *Skirt*" whenever Thomas came to bat. *The Big Hurt* took the shots in stride and played on as best he could. A disappointing season came to an inglorious end with many unanswered questions on a rain-soaked early October afternoon. In the Sunday drizzle, the Sox and Twins played to a 1–1 rain-shortened tie before a sparse crowd. Season attendance dipped below 1.4 million, the lowest in the history of the New Comiskey.

Following a predictable four-decade pattern, the Pale Hose closed out the 1990s on a downgrade, repeating old and bad habits from 1969, 1979, and 1989. Pondering the ups and downs of the two-year youth movement, Manuel looked ahead to 2000 with trepidation. "I think we have more questions in the sense that we went into this season thinking certain things were in place," he said. "Now we have to look back and view it differently." As he packed up his locker on the final day, Jaime Navarro had a few choice words for management. "This isn't a team," he grumbled. "The kids all go their own ways and do different things. I want to be in a place where I'm comfortable. A place where I know I'll be a starter and not in the bullpen. I've had it with this place…this organization." To the delight of Sox fans everywhere, Navarro was granted this last request.

	G	AB	H	R	2B	3B	HR	RBI	SB	AVG
Jeff Abbott	17	57	9	5	0	0	2	6	1	.158
Mike Caruso	136	529	132	60	11	4	2	35	12	.250
McKay Christensen	28	53	12	10	1	0	1	6	2	.226
Jason Dellaero	11	33	3	1	0	0	0	2	0	.091
Ray Durham	153	612	181	109	30	8	13	60	34	.296
Brook Fordyce	105	333	99	36	25	1	9	49	2	.297
Darren Jackson	73	149	41	22	9	1	4	16	4	.275
Mark Johnson	73	207	47	27	11	0	4	16	3	.227
Paul Konerko	142	513	151	71	31	4	24	81	1	.294
Carlos Lee	127	492	144	66	32	2	16	84	4	.293
Jeff Liefer	45	113	28	8	7	1	0	14	2	.248
Greg Norton	132	436	111	62	26	0	16	50	93	.255
Magglio Ordonez	157	624	188	100	34	3	30	117	13	.301
Josh Paul	6	18	4	2	1	0	0	1	0	.222
Liu Rodriguez	39	93	22	8	2	2	1	12	0	.237
Brian Simmons	54	126	29	14	3	3	4	17	4	.230
Chris Singleton	133	496	149	72	31	6	17	72	20	.300
Frank Thomas	135	486	148	74	36	0	15	77	3	.305
Craig Wilson	98	252	60	28	8	1	4	26	1	.238
	162	5,644	1,563	777	298	37	162	742	110	.277

	W	L	GS	CG	IP	H	BB	K	ShO	SV	ERA
James Baldwin	12	13	16	1	199⅓	219	81	123	0	0	5.10
Chad Bradford	0	0	0	0	3⅔	9	5	0	0	0	19.64
Carlos Castillo	2	2	2	0	41	45	14	23	0	0	5.71
Pat Daneker	0	0	2	0	15	14	6	5	0	0	4.20
Joe Davenport	0	0	2	0	1⅔	1	2	0	0	0	0.00
Scott Eyre	1	1	0	0	25	38	15	17	0	0	7.56
Keith Foulke	3	3	0	0	105⅓	72	21	123	0	9	2.22
Bob Howry	5	3	0	0	67⅔	58	38	80	0	28	3.59
Sean Lowe	4	1	0	0	95⅔	90	46	62	0	0	3.67
David Lundquist	1	1	0	0	22	28	12	18	0	0	8.59
Aaron Myette	0	2	3	0	15⅔	17	14	11	0	0	6.32
Jaime Navarro	8	13	27	0	159⅔	206	71	74	0	0	6.09
Jim Parque	9	15	30	1	173⅔	210	79	111	0	0	5.13
Jesus Pena	0	0	0	0	20⅓	21	23	20	0	0	5.31
Todd Rizzo	0	2	0	0	1⅓	4	3	2	0	0	6.75
Billy Simas	6	3	0	0	72	73	32	41	0	2	3.75
Mike Sirotka	11	13	32	3	209	236	57	125	1	0	4.00
John Snyder	9	12	25	1	129⅓	167	49	67	0	0	6.68
Tanyon Sturtze	0	0	1	0	6	4	2	2	0	0	0.00
Bryan Ward	0	1	0	0	39⅓	63	11	35	0	0	7.55
Kip Wells	4	1	7	0	35⅔	33	15	29	0	0	4.04
	75	86	162	6	1,438⅓	1,608	596	968	3	39	4.92

2000

Record: 95–67
Finish: First (Central)
Games Ahead: 5
Manager: Jerry Manuel

The Cleveland Indians seemed invincible, and the inexperienced White Sox were a desperate long shot as a new millennium of Pale Hose baseball began. But the Indians suffered a big-market payroll in what must be viewed as a small-market town. They could fill up Jacobs Field every night, set impressive attendance records, and allow Tribe fans to feel good about themselves and their ballclub for the short term, but when all was said and done, local revenue alone would not be enough to sustain a dynasty. Nor would it be enough to enable Cleveland to hang on to Manny Ramirez, Albert Belle, and other members of the supporting cast who made this team such an unstoppable juggernaut in the second half of the 1990s. The Indians were fading fast in 2000, and the White Sox, universally praised for the depth of a farm system that had yet to live up to its promise, thundered out of the gate and held down first place in the Central Division from April 19 until the close of the season.

Off to their best start since 1973, the youthful White Sox demonstrated that the kids could not only play, they could fight, as well. It was classic Saturday afternoon base-brawl at Comiskey that caught the attention of the national media on April 22. Two bench-clearing fights erupted after one of Jim Parque's inside pitches grazed Dean Palmer of the Tigers. The brushback followed two earlier beanings by Jeff Weaver, a former Sox draft prospect who never came to terms with the club. It was a real "pier-six donnybrook," to quote the late Jack Brickhouse. When the dust settled, 11 players were ejected, with suspensions later handed down to Magglio Ordonez, Bob Howry, Carlos Lee, Jim Parque, Tanyon Sturtze, and Jerry Manuel, whose normal passivity had earned him the nickname "Manager Gandhi" among White Sox Internet bloggers. And oh, by the way, the Sox won the game 14–6 against a toothless Tigers team that seemed so formidable for so many years.

But in the changing fortunes of baseball, old Sox tormentors like the Kansas City Royals and the Detroit Tigers were

Soft-throwing lefty Jim Parque played for the 1996 U.S. Olympic Team, and he had a .684 winning percentage in 2000—a career best. (White Sox photo by Ron Vesely)

the new doormats of the Central Division as a result of poor management and small-market revenues that did not allow them to effectively compete. It could be argued that the White Sox were also a small-market club playing in a big-market town, based on their low payroll and subpar attendance—with one important difference. They had a multitalented front-office tandem in place with general manager Ron Schueler, his assistant GM, Danny Evans, and Kenny Williams, vice president of player development. The Sox brain trust was never afraid to roll the dice and make the deals. The real key to the Cinderella 2000 season was a bit of off-season larceny they perpetrated against the Milwaukee Brewers, who were finding new and interesting ways to stumble and fall in the National League Central Division, their new home. In January Schueler dealt the sulky, underachieving Jaime Navarro, his $5-million-per-year salary, and pitcher John Snyder to Milwaukee for shortstop Jose Valentin and veteran pitcher Cal Eldred, who was recovering from reconstructive arm surgery. It seemed at the time to be an exchange of damaged spare parts, but Valentin's inspired play drove Mike Caruso out of the organization, and Eldred won 10 of 12 decisions in the first half before he was sidelined with ulnar neuritis on July 17. Jose Valentin, despite a penchant for striking out in tight spots and some occasionally slipshod glove work, shattered Ron Hansen's 36-year-old team record for home runs by a shortstop in a season.

Herbert Perry, the Florida "Milkman," was acquired from Tampa Bay via the waiver route on April 22, the same day the Sox and Tigers were throwing punches at one another. Perry took over for the erratic Greg Norton and bench sub Craig Wilson played through a hamstring injury and gave the Sox a career-best season and steady, reliable play at the hot corner right on through to the playoffs.

The fast start to the season left many unconvinced, but the true believers emerged from the woodwork, and home attendance spiked upward only after the White Sox returned to Chi-town on June 19 after completing a perfect 7–0 march through Cleveland and New York. The three-game shellacking of the Tribe on their home grounds raised eyebrows, given the recent history of poor play in the Jake, but the trip to Yankee Stadium featured an unforgettable 17–4 blowout of Joe Torre's Bombers on the last day of the trip. Sox hitters touched Orlando "El Duque" Hernandez for nine runs in the first inning, the most for a White Sox team in the first inning of play since 1962. When the team returned home the next night to face Cleveland in a rematch, 43,062 pumped-up fans greeted them—the season's first sellout not involving the Cubs.

The 2000 Sox were an explosive, offense-oriented ballclub—the first in team history to cross the magic threshold of 200 home runs in one season. Right down to Ray Durham, who became one of only two second baseman (the other being Nellie Fox) to score 100 runs in four consecutive seasons, the Sox dented the plate early and often. The pitching was another matter. Eldred was lost to the team after July 17. Mike Sirotka, the workhorse of the staff, developed elbow problems in the home stretch. James Baldwin complained of a tired arm and missed nearly the entire month of September with soreness. By late July the heat was already on Schueler to shore up the brittle pitching, but there was natural hesitation on his part to sacrifice the live young arms darting back and forth between the minor leagues and Chicago all season long—Mark Buehrle, Jon Garland, Josh Fogg, and Kip Wells. Finally, on July 29, he pulled the pin and acquired a catcher, Charles Johnson, and 41-year-old Harold Baines, now making his third and final return to Chicago, for Brook Fordyce and three undistinguished pitching prospects going to the Baltimore Orioles. Johnson was a free agent with World Series experience and reportedly an excellent handler of pitchers. That was the logic for the trade, the Sox GM explained, but efforts to pry loose John Wetteland from the Rangers or Shane Reynolds from Houston to bolster the starting staff came up empty. The Sox would have to go the rest of the way with a hospital corps, the kids, and their high-octane offense.

They wrapped up the Central Division in Minnesota on September 24 despite an extra-inning loss to the Twins. Only a handful of fans and media made the trek north to help the Sox uncork the champagne inside the cavernous but mostly empty Hubert H. Humphrey Metrodome. With one or two exceptions, the TV stations and the print guys were off covering college football that weekend. The team simply wasn't getting the respect it deserved for achieving this level of success in only the third year of the rebuilding program. The reasons were complex and far-reaching, but the Sox faithful cherished the moment nevertheless and breathed a collective sigh of relief as they awaited the outcome of a frenzied American League wild-card race. Would it be the Tribe, the Yankees, or Seattle? The fans feared division rival Cleveland the most, much preferring the Seattle Mariners as a first-round opponent the battered pitching staff might be able to silence. But did the opponent really matter, looking back on it? "The good thing is, we know we are in," sighed Jerry Manuel.

	G	AB	H	R	2B	3B	HR	RBI	SB	AVG
Jeff Abbott	80	215	59	31	15	1	3	29	2	.274
Harold Baines	24	61	13	2	5	0	1	9	0	.213
McKay Christensen	32	19	2	4	0	0	0	1	1	.105
Joe Crede	7	14	5	2	1	0	0	3	0	.357
Ray Durham	151	614	172	121	35	9	17	75	25	.280
Tony Graffanino	57	148	40	25	5	1	2	16	4	.270
Charles Johnson	44	135	44	24	8	0	10	36	0	.326
Mark Johnson	75	213	48	29	11	6	3	23	3	.225
Paul Konerko	143	524	156	84	31	1	21	97	1	.298
Carlos Lee	152	572	172	107	29	2	24	92	13	.301
Jeff Liefer	5	11	2	0	0	0	0	0	0	.182
Greg Norton	71	201	49	25	6	1	6	28	1	.244
Magglio Ordonez	153	588	185	102	34	3	32	126	18	.315
Josh Paul	36	71	20	15	3	2	1	8	1	.282
Herbert Perry	109	383	118	69	29	1	12	61	4	.308
Chris Singleton	147	511	130	83	22	5	11	62	22	.254
Frank Thomas	159	582	191	115	44	0	43	143	1	.328
Jose Valentin	144	568	155	107	37	6	25	92	19	.273
Chris Wilson	28	73	19	12	3	0	0	4	1	.260
	162	5,646	1,615	978	325	33	216	926	119	.286

	W	L	GS	CG	IP	H	BB	K	ShO	SV	ERA
James Baldwin	14	7	28	2	178	185	59	116	1	0	4.65
Lorenzo Barcelo	4	2	1	0	39	34	9	26	0	0	3.69
Kevin Beirne	1	3	1	0	49⅔	50	20	41	0	0	6.70
Lee "Rocky" Biddle	1	2	4	0	22⅔	31	8	7	0	0	8.34
Chad Bradford	1	0	0	0	13⅔	13	1	9	0	0	1.98
Mark Buehrle	4	1	3	0	51⅓	55	19	37	0	0	4.21
Cal Eldred	10	2	20	2	112	103	59	97	1	0	4.58
Scott Eyre	1	1	1	0	19	29	12	16	0	0	6.63
Keith Foulke	3	1	0	0	88	66	22	91	0	34	2.97
Jon Garland	4	8	13	0	69⅔	82	40	42	0	0	6.46
Matt Ginter	1	0	0	0	9⅓	18	7	6	0	0	13.5
Ken Hill	0	1	1	0	3	5	6	0	0	0	24.0
Bob Howry	2	4	0	0	71	54	29	60	0	7	3.17
Sean Lowe	4	1	5	0	70⅔	78	39	53	0	0	5.48
Aaron Myette	0	0	0	0	2⅔	0	4	1	0	0	0.00
Jim Parque	13	6	32	0	187	208	71	111	0	0	4.28
Jesus Pena	2	1	0	0	23⅓	25	16	19	0	0	5.40
Bill Simas	2	3	0	0	67⅔	69	22	49	0	0	3.46
Mike Sirotka	15	10	32	1	197	203	69	128	0	0	3.79
Tanyon Sturtze	1	2	1	0	15⅔	25	15	6	0	0	12.06
Kip Wells	6	9	20	0	98⅔	126	58	71	0	0	6.02
Kelly Wunsch	6	3	0	0	61⅓	50	29	51	0	1	2.93
	95	67	162	5	1,450⅓	1,509	614	1,037	7	43	4.66

2001

Record: 83–79
Finish: Third (Central)
Games Behind: 8
Manager: Jerry Manuel

Less than a month after the division championship run, Ron Schueler stepped down as general manager, concluding a stellar 10-year run. It came as no surprise within the organization, because "Schu" had been hinting at leaving for the previous three years. "The future of this club is very bright, and most of the thanks goes to Ron, his abilities, and the impressive baseball organization he has helped us develop," praised Jerry Reinsdorf with no exaggeration. The ballclub was a respectable 817–734 (.527) during his regime and had made the postseason twice. In 2000 *USA Today* and Howe Sports Data honored the Sox for building the minor league organization of the year, a testament to his abilities. Schueler, who simply desired to move on with his life, became the team's latest victim of cheap-shot journalism, practiced by a certain foaming-at-the-mouth *Chicago Sun-Times* sports columnist who had made the owner and the front-office support staff his personal whipping boys in a tiresome decade-long diatribe. The writer accused Schueler of walking away from "unfinished business, hardly a noble decision." Schueler did not deserve the dig. He had a family to think of and now was as good a time as any to exit the front office.

Bypassing the hard-working and energetic Danny Evans, who had waited in the wings for nearly two decades, Reinsdorf turned to former Sox third baseman/outfielder Kenny Williams as Schu's replacement, with Roland Hemond brought back into the organization to provide counsel and mentorship. Affirming the team's commitment to advancing minorities into key management positions, the White Sox thus became the first major league organization to feature an African American manager and general manager.

"If we do not bring a world's championship to Chicago, I will have failed," Williams told reporters during the organizational meeting in Phoenix. "We are about to embark on a four- to five-year window where we are going to be pretty darn competitive." Kenny's words were prophetic, but his early forays into the trade market were less than auspicious. On January 14, 2001, he sent sore-armed Mike Sirotka, outfielder Brian Simmons, and three lesser prospects to Toronto for David "Boomer" Wells, the burly, tattooed lefty, fresh off a 20-win season for the Jays. Wells seemed to be just what the doctor ordered: a quality No. 1 starter capable of winning 15–20, who could mentor the younger guys on the staff along the way. The portly ace, whose mother once dated a member of the Hell's Angels according to published reports, tutored Mark Buehrle on the mechanics of pitching, but he also had a lot to say on a wide range of subjects, including some poorly timed barbs directed at the ailing Frank Thomas over the WMVP-AM airwaves. Thomas went down with a torn right tricep and was lost for the season on April 27. Adding his two cents' worth, Wells said, "You need to be somewhere else and learn to play this game with guts

2001: a David Wells Odyssey

and glory. Frank has put his foot in his mouth a lot of times and doesn't know what he's saying. Playing hurt will get you a lot more respect from your fellow players." The inappropriate comment came just as Thomas received word that his father had passed away in Georgia. But Wells had less to say after he went down with a lower strained back that required surgery in early July.

Admitting that the January trade was a flop, Williams bought out the final year of David Wells' contract, not figuring that he had a few more good seasons left in him. However, the opinionated pitcher returned to his winning form with the Yankees a year later (naturally!). But his lackluster record with the 2001 White Sox set the tone for a difficult and challenging year. Plagued by injuries and losers of 15 of the first 23 games, the Sox dug themselves a deep trench before showing improvement. Beginning in late May, however, the club started to win, and win consistently, becoming the first team since the 1991 Milwaukee Brewers to reach the .500 mark after slipping 15 games under the break-even mark at any point in a season.

Selected in the 38th round of the June 1998 First Year Player Draft, 22-year-old rookie left-hander Mark Buehrle blossomed into a bona fide pitching star for the 2001 White Sox, topping all American League southpaws with a 3.29 ERA. Shortstop Royce Clayton, picked up from Texas for two minor leaguers, steadied the inner defense while shattering Ron Hansen's 38-year-old fielding mark with a .988 percentage. Free agent Jose Canseco was signed in mid-June. The former Bash Brother chipped in 16 home runs and stirred some fan interest, but he did not figure in long-range plans and was given no guarantee past 2001, just a minor league contract for 2002. The small-ball, hustling, speed-oriented style of play that vaulted the Minnesota Twins past the White Sox into second place should have served as an alarm to management that a return to the tried-and-true 1950s "Go-Go" format might better serve the interests of the team than the recent over-reliance on home runs. Small ball was still several years away from becoming a reality.

	G	AB	H	R	2B	3B	HR	RBI	SB	AVG
Sandy Alomar, Jr.	70	220	54	17	8	1	4	21	1	.245
Harold Baines	32	84	11	3	1	0	0	6	0	.131
Jose Canseco	76	256	66	46	8	0	16	49	2	.258
McKay Christensen	2	4	1	0	0	0	0	0	0	.250
Royce Clayton	135	433	114	62	21	4	9	60	10	.263
Joe Crede	17	50	11	1	1	1	0	7	1	.220
Mark Dalesandro	1	0	0	0	0	0	0	0	0	.000
Ray Durham	152	611	163	104	42	10	20	65	23	.267
Tony Graffanino	74	145	44	23	9	0	2	15	4	.303
Mark Johnson	61	173	43	21	6	1	5	18	2	.249
Paul Konerko	156	582	164	92	35	0	32	99	1	.282
Carlos Lee	150	558	150	75	33	3	24	84	17	.269
Jeff Liefer	83	254	65	36	13	0	18	39	0	.256
Magglio Ordonez	160	593	181	97	40	1	31	113	25	.305
Josh Paul	57	139	37	20	11	0	3	18	6	.266
Herbert Perry	92	285	73	38	21	1	7	32	2	.256
Julio Ramirez	13	37	3	2	0	0	0	1	2	.081
Aaron Rowand	63	123	36	21	5	0	4	20	5	.293
Chris Singleton	140	392	117	57	21	5	7	45	12	.298
Frank Thomas	20	68	15	8	3	0	4	10	0	.221
Jose Valentin	124	438	113	74	22	2	28	68	9	.258
	162	5,464	1,463	798	300	29	214	770	123	.268

	W	L	GS	CG	IP	H	BB	K	ShO	SV	ERA
James Baldwin	7	5	16	2	95⅔	109	38	42	1	0	4.61
Lorenzo Barcelo	1	0	0	0	21	24	8	15	0	0	4.71
Lee "Rocky" Biddle	7	8	21	0	128⅔	137	52	85	0	0	5.39
Mark Buehrle	16	8	32	4	221⅓	188	48	126	2	0	3.29
Cal Eldred	0	1	2	0	6	12	3	6	0	0	13.50
Alan Embree	1	2	0	0	34	31	7	34	0	0	5.03
Josh Fogg	0	0	0	0	13⅓	10	3	17	0	0	2.03
Keith Foulke	4	9	0	0	81	57	22	75	0	42	2.33
Jon Garland	6	7	16	0	117	123	55	61	0	0	3.69
Matt Ginter	1	0	0	0	39⅔	34	14	24	0	0	5.22
Gary Glover	5	5	11	0	100⅓	98	32	63	0	0	4.93
Bob Howry	4	5	0	0	78⅔	85	30	64	0	5	4.69
Sean Lowe	9	4	11	0	127	123	32	71	0	3	3.61
Antonio Osuna	0	0	0	0	4⅓	8	2	6	0	0	20.77
Jim Parque	0	3	5	0	28	36	10	15	0	0	8.04
Bill Pulsipher	0	0	0	0	8	11	7	4	0	0	7.88
Ken Vining	0	0	0	0	6⅔	15	7	3	0	0	17.55
David "Boomer" Wells	5	7	16	1	100⅔	120	21	59	0	0	4.47
Kip Wells	10	11	20	0	133⅓	145	61	99	0	0	4.79
Dan Wright	5	3	12	0	66⅓	78	39	36	0	0	5.70
Kelly Wunsch	2	1	0	0	22⅓	21	9	16	0	0	7.66
	83	79	162	8	1,433⅓	1,465	500	921	7	51	4.55

2002

Record: 81–81
Finish: Second (Central)
Games Behind: 13½
Manager: Jerry Manuel

It was the summer of *Ligue*, and another shockingly low moment endured by the embattled South Siders who were expected to contend for the Central Division crown but faltered midway through the season and had to settle for another humdrum .500 finish. *Ligue.* The shirtless fan and his 15-year-old son attacked Kansas City Royals first-base coach Tom Gamboa in a meaningless September night game, thus earning the Sox unwanted national publicity and the attention of David Letterman who listed the "Top 10 Shirtless Father-and-Son Explanations" on a segment of the *Late Show.* William Ligue Jr., the 34-year-old "fan," if that term can be loosely applied to the perpetrator of this vicious, unprovoked assault aided and abetted by his teenaged son, bolted out of his seat and drove the 54-year-old Gamboa to the ground from behind. Speaking of his ordeal later, Gamboa told Sporting News Radio, "I have never at any time ever verbally or physically acknowledged the people in the stands, and I encourage players to just tune them out. To respond to it in any manner lets that idiot know that he is getting to you, and common sense tells you that it will just escalate."

Despite the bad publicity surrounding the ugly event, incidences of this nature were thankfully few and far between. In fact, 42 years had elapsed since the last time a fan in the stands jumped the wall to physically attack a player on the Comiskey playing field. In 1960 it had more to do with fan frustration over the outcome of a close game than a crazy, drunken, "I dare you!" stunt. After Sox infielder Sammy Esposito booted a certain double-play ball against the Yankees in the heat of the pennant race, fan Willie Harris took matters into his own hands and charged little Sammy, but security guards wrestled Harris to the ground before a blow could be struck. The

Ligue affair was an unsettling, but isolated, example of fan behavior more consistent with the late 1970s, when repeated acts of rowdyism earned old Comiskey Park the surly reputation as the "World's Largest Outdoor Saloon." The Reinsdorf group had fought hard to dispel that image since taking over in 1981, but some old habits die slowly.

The 2002 Sox were heavily favored to win the Central Division title in a cakewalk. Preseason expectations ran high. The players believed they were the best in the division, and certain disparaging comments to the effect that the Twins were unworthy pretenders for the title became bulletin-board motivation inside the Minnesota clubhouse. It was a season of underachievement. Youngsters like outfielder Aaron Rowand and third basemen Joe Crede were given a lot of playing time in the second half. Their hustle and determination pointed the way toward a brighter future. The missing link, however, was a veteran mound presence Williams dreamed about since taking over in 2000, although Mark Buehrle had emerged as the "stopper" and narrowly missed out on a 20-win season in 2002. Over the winter, Williams shuffled the deck and pulled out his next "ace in the hole" at the annual winter meetings. Instead he was saddled with another joker, courtesy of the Pittsburgh Pirates, who were very eager to part ways with veteran sinkerball specialist Todd Ritchie for Kip Wells and Josh Fogg, two of the highest-rated prospects in the farm system. Ritchie received a hefty raise and earned $3.5 million in 2002. In return he gave them a Jaime Navarro–like 5–15 record (exacerbated by an enflamed right shoulder) with a 6.23 ERA in 23 starts before Williams had enough and declined to pick up his 2003 option.

The free agent signing of 34-year-old center fielder Kenny Lofton was expected to create RBI opportunities for Frank Thomas (finally healthy, but stewing over the "diminished skills" clause in his contract) and Magglio Ordonez, enjoying his best all-around White Sox season. Williams hedged his bets, though, by signing Lofton to a one-year, incentive-laden contract. The ex-Cleveland speed merchant started strong, faded just as quickly, and was dealt to San Francisco in late July after the Twins' lead in the Central ballooned to double digits. The next Sox free-agent-to-be, Ray Durham, a blue-chip second baseman for seven years, was traded to Oakland for pitcher Jon Adkins and a bundle of cash—more white-flagging in 2002. When the trading frenzy ended, one-third of the Opening Day lineup was gone. As the bags were packed up on the last day, Paul Konerko, who enjoyed a terrific all-around campaign, put matters into their proper perspective: "We should look at playing six months of solid baseball, and maybe we'll be in contention the whole time. If that means we get knocked out in the last week, we get knocked out. But, I mean, this stuff of being knocked out at the half and playing three months of meaningless games is not too fun."

Jerry Manuel took solace in a winning August–September record, but a vote of confidence and a hearty slap on the back was not forthcoming. Williams vented his displeasure by dismissing three members of Jerry's original coaching staff, making it clear to all interested parties that patience was wearing thin as "Point C" goals once again eluded his grasp.

	G	AB	H	R	2B	3B	HR	RBI	SB	AVG
Sandy Alomar, Jr.	51	167	48	21	10	1	7	25	0	.287
Joe Borchard	16	36	8	5	0	0	2	5	0	.222
Royce Clayton	112	342	86	51	14	2	7	25	5	.251
Joe Crede	53	200	57	28	10	0	12	35	0	.285
Ray Durham	96	345	103	71	20	2	9	48	20	.299
Tony Graffanino	70	229	60	35	12	4	6	31	2	.262
Willie Harris	49	163	38	14	4	0	2	12	8	.233
D'Angelo Jimenez	27	108	31	22	4	3	1	11	7	.287
Mark Johnson	86	263	55	31	8	1	4	18	0	.209
Paul Konerko	151	570	173	81	30	0	27	104	0	.304
Carlos Lee	140	492	130	82	26	2	26	80	1	.264
Jeff Liefer	76	204	47	28	8	0	7	26	0	.230
Kenny Lofton	93	352	91	68	20	6	8	42	22	.259
Miguel Olivo	6	19	4	2	1	0	1	5	0	.211
Magglio Ordonez	153	590	189	116	47	1	38	135	7	.320
Josh Paul	33	104	25	11	4	0	0	11	2	240
Aaron Rowand	126	302	78	41	16	2	7	29	0	.258
Frank Thomas	148	523	132	77	29	1	28	92	3	.252
Jose Vanentin	135	474	118	70	26	4	25	75	3	.249
	162	5,502	1,475	856	289	29	217	819	75	.268

	W	L	GS	CG	IP	H	BB	K	ShO	SV	ERA
James Baldwin	0	1	0	0	6	9	1	1	0	0	9.00
Lee "Rocky" Biddle	3	4	7	0	77⅔	72	39	64	0	1	4.06
Mark Buehrle	19	12	34	5	239	236	61	134	2	0	3.58
Keith Foulke	2	4	0	0	77⅔	65	13	58	0	11	2.90
Jon Garland	12	12	33	1	192⅔	188	83	112	1	0	4.58
Matt Ginter	1	0	0	0	54⅓	59	21	37	0	1	4.47
Gary Glover	7	8	22	0	138⅓	136	52	70	0	1	5.20
Bob Howry	2	2	0	0	50⅔	45	17	31	0	0	3.91
Damaso Marte	1	1	0	0	60⅓	44	18	72	0	10	2.83
Antonio Osuna	8	2	0	0	67⅔	64	28	66	0	11	3.86
Jim Parque	1	4	4	0	25⅓	34	16	13	0	0	9.95
Mike Porzio	2	2	0	0	43	40	23	33	0	0	4.81
Jon Rauch	2	1	6	0	28⅔	28	14	19	0	0	6.59
Todd Ritchie	5	15	26	0	133⅔	176	52	77	0	0	6.06
Dan Wright	14	12	33	1	196⅓	200	71	136	1	0	5.18
Kelly Wunsch	2	1	0	0	31⅔	26	19	22	0	0	3.41
	81	81	162	7	1,423	1,422	528	945	7	35	4.53

2003

Record: 86–76
Finish: Second (Central)
Games Behind: 4
Manager: Jerry Manuel

A strong sense of urgency and the expectation of better days to come filtered through the organization as a new season unfolded. On January 31 naming rights to the new Comiskey Park were sold to U.S. Cellular, a Chicago-based wireless company, whose CEO, John Rooney, was a dyed-in-the-wool Sox fan. The 23-year agreement was worth an estimated $68 million, and it provided the necessary working capital to address the original design flaws of the 10-year-old stadium and to improve the overall fan experience. The six-year renovation project (kicking off in 2001) reduced the upper-deck seating capacity, flattened the sloped canopy-style roofline, added a Bullpen Sports Bar, and replaced the blue seating with a more pleasing forest green color scheme, among lesser improvements.

Meanwhile, over the winter of 2002–2003, Williams, Roland Hemond, and the player development team retooled and delivered a new-look White Sox team to the fans—one that seemed capable of unseating the annoyingly arrogant

Gone in a flash: Bartolo Colon, 2003 (White Sox photo by Ron Vesely)

Twins, who had supplanted the Indians as the dominant force in the Central Division. Minnesota relied on a pop-gun offense, lights-out starting pitching, and a "grinder" attitude worth copying. Keith Foulke was dealt to Oakland for Billy Koch, a flame-throwing bullpen closer who was anything but his old self after donning the black and white (although Neal Cotts, the throw-in player, redeemed the clunker trade two years later).

More immediate results were achieved by Williams in a tricky three-cornered trade with Montreal and the Yankees that brought Bartolo Colon to Chicago for Rocky Biddle, Antonio Osuna, and Jeff Liefer, three expendable situational players. Colon, a 240-pound "meat locker," was Williams' latest veteran pick-up auditioning for the No. 1 spot in the rotation. He passed the test—then passed out of the organization as quickly as he had come, opting for the free-agency riches doled out by the Anaheim Angels at season's end.

Esteban Loaiza, the real No. 1 for 2003, arrived in town cheaply and with far less fanfare. In fact, this non-roster invitee was off the radar when spring training convened. Loaiza, a so-so right-handed starter who bounced around Pittsburgh, Toronto, and Texas for more than a decade with limited success, was just happy to be here after agreeing to a minor league contract in January. Ten months later he was named the runner-up for the Cy Young Award after notching 21 wins, a league-leading strikeout total, and the honor of all of Mexico as he joined Fernando Valenzuela as the only other Mexican-born pitcher with 21 victories in a season. Fame is fleeting for so many journeymen players, and Esteban Loaiza was the proverbial one-year wonder, but what a year it was! He became the first White Sox pitcher to start an All-Star Game since Early Wynn in 1959 (and the ninth all time to start in his home park), when the mid-season classic returned to the South Side for the fourth time in its history. Loaiza tossed two flawless innings. "He was starting in front of his home crowd, and he was unflappable," said a beaming Jerry Manuel. "[He] wasn't excited, wasn't overhyping anything. Obviously, he had family there. He had media attention. He had everything you can have to disrupt someone, and he wasn't disrupted."

Before the season began, Jerry Manuel intimated that if his Sox won a World Series title in 2003, he just might take early retirement, knowing the mission was accomplished. The flip side of the coin, of course, was management's intention to let him go if the mission wasn't accomplished. But with a rejuvenated Frank Thomas hitting to the opposite field, battering down fences, and making his peace with Manuel, the Sox jelled in mid-season and grabbed first place on August 20. Smelling victory in the air, Williams acquired a quartet of veterans—Robby Alomar, Scott Schoeneweis, Carl Everett, and Scott Sullivan—for the late-season push via the trade route. The ball was now in Manuel's corner to bring them across the finish line—his job depended on it.

And so, the White Sox came roaring down the stretch and were in an enviable position on September 9. They were all alone in first place, a game up on the Twinkies after taking the first of a crucial three-game set in Chicago, and were ahead 8–2 in the bottom of the ninth in Game 2, when Manuel opened the final frame with Jose Paniagua, plucked off of the waiver wire earlier in the week. Paniagua promptly surrendered four runs, retiring only one batter in one of the shortest stints in team history. Questioning balls and strikes, he directed an obscene gesture toward the home-plate umpire and was tossed. The Sox managed to hang on for a narrow 8–6 victory, but the momentum had already shifted. For embarrassing the club so egregiously, Jose Paniagua was handed his release papers the next day. But Manuel's bad decision to bring this guy in for mop-up work seemed to reawaken the struggling Minnesota ballclub.

Sometimes an entire season can turn on the fortunes of one bad game, and the call to the bullpen for Paniagua seemed to completely unhinge the Sox, who dropped the next three and fell out of the race the following week after the Twins swept them inside the Metrodome. Too often the long-ball hitters would go cold, and when Lee, Maggs, and Thomas ended their home run barrage, the rest of the offense simply shut down. Soft throwers like Seattle's Jamie Moyer and Kansas City's Brian Anderson gave the Sox big guns their comeuppance. They paid a price for all of this hitting inconsistency. In the end, Jerry Manuel's team was lucky to fend off the on-rushing Kansas City Royals and clinch second place the final weekend of the season. Coming on the heels of the mid-September Minnesota debacle, the poorly guarded secret was let out of the bag. The calm and soothing Sox manager would not be invited back to the dance in 2004. "This isn't the end," shrugged Manuel, "just a pause. You push the button in again when the season starts." Looking back on the six unfulfilling years of "Manager Ghandi," a new twist to the old baseball adage coined by Leo Durocher many years ago seems most apropos: "Nice guys *do not* finish last, they finish *second*." Or the really successful ones know how to push the *right* buttons.

	G	AB	H	R	2B	3B	HR	RBI	SB	AVG
Sandy Alomar, Jr.	75	194	52	22	12	0	5	26	0	.268
Roberto Alomar	67	253	64	42	11	1	3	17	6	.253
Joe Borchard	16	49	9	5	1	0	1	11	0	.184
Jaime Burke	6	8	3	0	0	0	0	0	0	.375
Joe Crede	151	536	140	68	31	2	19	75	1	.261
Brian Daubach	95	183	42	26	11	0	6	21	1	.230
Carl Everett	73	256	77	40	14	0	10	41	4	.301
Tony Graffanino	90	250	65	51	15	3	7	23	8	.260
Willie Harris	79	137	28	19	1	1	0	5	12	.204
D'Angelo Jimenez	73	271	69	35	5	5	7	26	4	.255
Paul Konerko	137	444	104	49	19	0	18	65	0	.234
Carlos Lee	158	623	181	100	35	1	31	113	18	.291
Aaron Miles	8	12	4	3	3	0	0	2	0	.333
Miguel Olivo	114	317	75	37	19	1	6	27	6	.237
Magglio Ordonez	160	606	192	95	46	3	29	99	9	.317
Josh Paul	13	17	6	6	0	0	0	4	0	.353
Armando Rios	49	104	22	4	3	0	2	11	0	.212
Aaron Rowand	93	157	45	22	8	1	6	24	0	.287
Frank Thomas	153	546	146	87	35	0	42	105	0	.267
Jose Valentin	144	503	119	79	26	2	28	74	8	.237
	162	5,487	1,445	791	303	19	220	766	77	.263

	W	L	GS	CG	IP	H	BB	K	ShO	SV	ERA
Jon Adkins	0	0	0	0	9⅓	8	7	3	0	0	4.82
Mark Buehrle	14	14	35	2	230⅓	250	61	119	0	0	4.14
Bartolo Colon	15	13	34	9	13⅓	223	67	173	0	0	3.87
Neal Cotts	1	1	4	0	191⅔	15	17	10	0	0	8.10
Jon Garland	12	13	32	0	3⅓	188	74	108	0	0	4.51
Matt Ginter	0	0	0	0	35⅔	2	1	0	0	0	13.5
Gary Glover	1	0	0	0	35⅔	43	14	23	0	0	4.54
Tom "Flash" Gordon	7	6	0	0	74	57	31	91	0	12	3.16
Billy Koch	5	5	0	0	53	59	28	42	0	11	5.77
Esteban Loaiza	21	9	34	1	236⅓	196	56	207	0	0	2.90
Damaso Marte	4	2	0	0	79⅔	50	34	87	0	11	1.58
Jose Paniagua	0	0	0	0	⅓	3	1	0	0	0	108.00
Mike Porzio	1	1	3	0	14	18	1	9	0	0	6.43
David Sanders	0	0	0	0	22	25	11	14	0	0	6.14
Scott Schoeneweis	2	1	0	0	26	26	9	27	0	0	4.50
Josh Stewart	1	2	5	0	25⅔	28	16	13	0	0	5.96
Scott Sullivan	0	0	0	0	14⅓	9	6	13	0	0	3.77
Rick White	1	2	0	0	47⅔	56	13	37	0	1	6.61
Dan Wright	1	7	15	0	86⅓	91	46	47	0	1	6.15
Kelly Wunsch	0	0	0	0	36	17	25	33	0	0	2.75
	86	76	162	12	1,431	1,364	518	1,056	4	36	4.17

2004

Record: 83–79
Finish: Second (Central)
Games Behind: 9
Manager: Ozzie Guillen

And slowly the pieces of the puzzle fell into place, beginning with the announcement of Ozzie Guillen's appointment as the 37th Sox manager on November 3, 2003. The news was greeted with a mixture of surprise and bewilderment. To some it smacked of a publicity stunt worthy of Bill Veeck, given Ozzie's reputation as a fun-loving player who liked to clown around; but nothing in the house of Comiskey is as it seems. The former Sox shortstop, who continued the "Venezuelan Connection" of infield excellence (Chico Carrasquel, Luis Aparicio, then Guillen) through the 1980s and 1990s, impressed Jerry Reinsdorf and Kenny Williams with his outspoken candor during job interviews after Jerry received a strong thumbs-up and personal recommendation from former Sox skipper Jeff Torborg, who had groomed Ozzie as his third-base coach with Montreal in 2001. "He's ready to manage," Torborg said. "But he hasn't managed," retorted Reinsdorf. "I know, but he's been outstanding coaching third base," Torborg assured the chairman. Given a free hand to move the club to "Point C" for however long it might take, Guillen surrounded himself with a coaching staff that was a veritable White Sox alumni association: Harold Baines, Greg Walker, Tim Raines, Joey Cora, Kevin Hickey, and old reliable Art Kusnyer.

The new manager inherited a club that lived and died by the home run and the big inning. This wasn't exactly the kind of "Point C," "grinder" team Guillen had in mind when he accepted the job, but home runs were exciting to fans. In 2004 the Sox led the major leagues and set a new franchise record with 145 round trippers hit in their home park and "launching pad," U.S. Cellular Field. They clouted 242 long-distance shots to tie the Yankees with the most in baseball. New York and Chicago went into the record books as the first teams to record five consecutive seasons of 200 or more home runs—an amazing feat for the Chicago White Sox franchise given their past "Go-Go" history—and one they would extend to six seasons in 2005.

Remarkably, the home run onslaught was accomplished without the services of either Frank Thomas or Magglio Ordonez, both of whom were lost to the team early in the campaign. Ordonez went down with a severely bruised left knee in a freakish collision with teammate Willie Harris, as both players chased a routine pop fly in Cleveland on May 19. Maggs was in his option year, but the hopes of re-signing the perennial All-Star faded by the day. His differences with Guillen were pronounced—an ugly feud erupted between the front office and their star player. On top of that, the dollar amount of agent Scott Boras' contract demand exceeded the limits of Reinsdorf's mid-revenue payroll—and his patience.

In 2002 a handful of Chicago writers pronounced the last rights on Frank Thomas' Sox career, but the Big Hurt

Shingo Takatsu: one-year wonder

enjoyed a big comeback year in 2003 and was gamely working toward meeting his goal of 500 career home runs when he suffered a partial stress fracture of the navicular bone of the left ankle in July and had to go under the knife to clear away bone chips. Without Maggs in the lineup, the Sox held down first place for 53 days in 2004 and were snapping at the heels of the Twins (they trailed the leader by only 1½ games) when Thomas was sent home. No team, no matter how talented, can easily withstand the loss of its two best offensive players.

Another three-game sweep at the hands of the Twins from July 26 to 28 rekindled bad memories of the 2003 collapse, and it turned out to be the 2004 knockout punch for this ballclub, stocked with a plethora of slow, right-handed hitters and not much of a bench to compensate for the injured stars. After Mark Buehrle took his turn on the mound, it was white-knuckles time for Sox fans, as the rest of the starting rotation proved woefully ineffective, and the team ERA soared. Scott Schoeneweis struggled as a starter after a promising start, and what can one possibly say about Danny Wright's 8.15 ERA?

Although it was probably too late to make much of a dent on the outcome of the 2004 season, Kenny Williams shored up the pitching staff by executing two fine mid-season trades that would set the table for the exciting year to come. Catcher Miguel Olivo, who had shown a glimmer of promise but not much more, was packaged with minor league outfielder Jeremy Reed and shipped off to Seattle on June 27 for pitcher Freddy Garcia, a quality starter married to Ozzie Guillen's wife's niece, and throw-in catcher Ben Davis. In a separate deal, Williams gambled that Esteban Loaiza's 2003 Cinderella season was not likely to be duplicated and dealt him to the Yankees for Jose Contreras, one of Cuba's top right-handed pitchers who had defected in October 2002 during the Americas Cup tournament in Santillo, Mexico. As it turned out, Contreras held the keys in his hand to the successful championship run of 2005, but his shaky, often erratic performance in the second half of 2004 was not encouraging.

The club said good-bye to the fading Jose Valentin at season's end after he posted the worst batting and on-base percentages of his career, despite clouting 30 home runs. The brilliant freshman season of Japanese closer Shingo Takatsu earned him second place in American League Rookie of the Year balloting, but once AL hitters figured out a way to lay back on his 80 mph fastball, it was lights out for the personable Takatsu and his "Gong Show." And when the gong finally sounded on the 2004 campaign, Williams and Guillen added up the pluses and minuses and hunkered down for a long winter with only one certainty: next year's team would look a whole lot different than this one come Opening Day 2005. A miracle in the making was at hand.

	G	AB	H	R	2B	3B	HR	RBI	SB	AVG
Sandy Alomar, Jr.	48	146	35	15	4	0	2	14	0	.240
Roberto Alomar	17	61	11	4	1	0	1	8	0	.180
Joe Borchard	63	201	35	26	4	1	9	20	1	.174
Jaime Burke	47	120	40	22	9	0	0	15	0	.333
Joe Crede	143	490	117	67	25	0	21	69	1	.239
Ben Davis	50	160	37	21	9	0	6	16	1	.231
Kelly Dransfeldt	15	30	10	5	0	0	0	4	0	.333
Carl Everett	43	154	41	21	7	1	5	21	1	.266
Ross Gload	95	234	75	28	16	0	7	44	0	.321
Willie Harris	127	409	107	68	15	2	2	27	19	.262
Paul Konerko	154	563	156	84	22	0	41	117	1	.277
Carlos Lee	153	591	180	103	37	0	31	99	11	.305
Miguel Olivo	43	141	38	21	7	2	7	26	5	.270
Magglio Ordonez	52	202	59	32	8	2	9	37	0	.292
Timo Perez	100	293	72	38	12	0	5	40	3	.246
Aaron Rowand	137	487	151	94	38	2	24	69	17	.310
Frank Thomas	74	240	65	53	16	0	18	49	0	.271
Juan Uribe	131	502	142	82	31	6	23	74	9	.283
Wilson Valdez	18	43	10	8	1	0	1	4	1	.233
Jose Valentin	124	450	97	73	20	3	30	70	8	.216
	162	5,534	1,481	865	284	19	242	823	78	.268

	W	L	GS	CG	IP	H	BB	K	ShO	SV	ERA
Jon Adkins	2	3	0	0	62	75	20	44	0	0	4.65
Jeff Bajenaru	0	1	0	0	8⅓	15	6	8	0	0	10.80
Mark Buehrle	16	10	35	4	245⅓	257	51	165	1	0	3.89
Jose Contreras	5	4	13	0	74⅔	73	42	68	0	0	5.30
Neal Cotts	4	4	1	0	65⅓	61	30	58	0	0	5.65
Vic Darensbourg	0	0	0	0	1⅓	1	1	0	0	0	0.00
Felix Diaz	2	5	7	0	49⅓	62	16	33	0	0	6.75
Freddy Garcia	9	4	16	0	103	96	32	102	0	0	4.46
Jon Garland	12	11	33	1	217	223	76	113	0	0	4.89
Jason Grilli	2	3	8	1	45	52	20	26	0	0	7.40
Mike Jackson	2	0	0	0	46⅔	55	15	26	0	0	5.01
Billy Koch	1	1	0	0	23⅓	24	16	25	0	8	5.40
Esteban Loaiza	9	5	21	2	140⅔	156	45	83	1	0	4.86
Damaso Marte	6	5	0	0	73⅔	56	34	68	0	6	3.42
Arnie Munoz	0	1	1	0	14⅓	20	12	11	0	0	10.05
Cliff Politte	0	3	0	0	51⅓	52	22	48	0	1	4.38
Jon Rauch	1	1	2	0	8⅔	16	4	4	0	0	6.23
Scott Schoeneweis	6	9	19	0	112⅔	129	49	69	0	0	5.59
Josh Stewart	0	1	2	0	7⅔	16	3	5	0	0	15.26
Shingo Takatsu	6	4	0	0	62⅓	40	21	50	0	19	2.31
Dan Wright	0	4	4	0	17⅔	24	11	6	0	0	8.15
Kelly Wunsch	0	0	0	0	2	2	1	1	0	0	0.00
	83	79	162	8	1,432⅓	1,505	527	1,013	2	34	4.91

2005

Record: 99–63
Finish: First (Central)
Games Ahead: 6
Manager: Ozzie Guillen

With the miracle season behind them and the autumn leaves falling, the time had come for the White Sox brain trust to reflect back on the wild, magical romp through the 2005 playoffs and World Series. Kenny Williams shared his thoughts on the season just passed with Terry Ryan, general manager of the third-place Minnesota Twins, who called to extend congratulations for overturning the 88-year-old Comiskey Curse the year after the Boston Red Sox put to rest their own real or imagined "Curse of the Bambino."

"I told Terry Ryan, 'Congratulations, my ass! You forced me to do this. I was tired of second place. We had to play your game.'" The challenge posed to Williams and assistant GM Rick Hahn by the Twins during their tenuous three-year lock on the Central Division was to come up with a ballclub mirroring the success of the Minnesota team—and accomplish the objective while operating with a limited mid-market payroll.

Lacking the deep pockets of the Yankees, Red Sox, and Mets, who were bunched one, two, three in the annual rankings, the White Sox payroll topped out at a modest $75.2 million in 2005, placing them in 13th position. But with a scrappy, young, and hungry group of players out to prove their worth to themselves and the fans, the 2005 club adopted "Don't Stop Believin'," a 1980s rock standard by Journey as the appropriate fight song to carry them through the tense days of the playoffs and into the ledger of history's great White Sox teams.

The evolution from the big inning to small ball began in earnest in September 2004 with a series of high-level meetings between Reinsdorf, Williams, Hahn, Roland Hemond, and Dan Fabian, a computer systems maven who programmed the scouts and the prospects in the field into a central intranet. Technology, coupled with the wisdom of veteran talent evaluators at all levels of the organization, yielded a bountiful harvest of new faces in the off-season. At first Williams believed the team could get by with Ben Davis behind the plate, but Guillen disagreed, thus hastening the arrival of free agent and ex-Twin A. J. Pierzynski, a poster-boy for grinder-style baseball. Unwanted by his former team, the San Francisco Giants, Pierzynski led all AL catchers in fielding percentage in 2005. Outfielder Jermaine Dye, the son of a Georgia church deacon and a veteran of postseason play, replaced departing right fielder Magglio Ordonez.

The decision to trade slugger Carlos Lee to Milwaukee for speed merchant Scott Podsednik was the biggest gamble of all. Was this a disaster in the making or the steal of the century? Losing C. Lee's 30-plus home runs for a guy who hit only .244 the year before seemed like a high price to pay, but Guillen was down on the big man after he failed to slide hard into second base in a July 2004 encounter with the Twins in retaliation for Tori Hunter upending Jaime Burke in a brutal home-plate collision. Guillen believed that Lee wasn't working hard enough to achieve success. The deal worked out well for both teams, as it turned out. Podsednik pilfered 59 bases and added strength to the top of the lineup, batting ahead of second baseman Tadahito Iguchi, the latest Japanese import acquired from the Fukoka Daiei Hawks sight unseen. The Chicago White Sox roared out of the gate and occupied first place all by themselves 175 of 182 days of the season. They never trailed in the division race and went wire-to-wire for the first time in team history, while tying an obscure major league record for most consecutive games (37) with a lead at some point in the game. This year's marketing slogan, "Win or Die Trying," affirmed the GM's "World Series or Bust" mandate announced on day one of Williams' regime.

From their heart-pounding 1–0 Opening Day victory over Cleveland, bookended by a 1–0 whitewash of Houston in the final game of the World Series, the Sox played a fluid, nearly

flawless brand of baseball. Not since the days of the "Black Sox" had a White Sox team won so effortlessly and with so much expectation of victory as this club. They rolled through the All-Star break in command of the Central, leaving the Twins and every other division opponent in the dust as they amassed a staggering 15½-game lead in early August after sweeping the Baltimore Orioles four straight in Camden Yards for the first time since 1956. Three eight-game winning streaks highlighted the stampede to the postseason.

The starting five of Mark Buehrle, Jon Garland, Freddy Garcia, Orlando Hernandez, and Jose Contreras were simply outstanding, day-in and day-out, and if "perfect team play" could ever be applied to one ballclub, it was the 2005 White Sox. Contreras, written off as over-the-hill following a disappointing 4–5 record in the first half, went 11–2 the rest of the way after assuring Guillen that he was a steady second-half pitcher. Mark Buehrle ran off a streak of 49 consecutive games going six or more innings. Frank Thomas missed two-thirds of the season with chronic ankle problems, but provided the June spark and considerable moral support by drilling 12 home runs in limited play. Jon Garland, shown greater patience by Guillen than by Manuel, came of age as a starter, making the Cubs rue the day they traded him to the South Siders. Perennial fan favorite Paul Konerko joined Thomas as only the second player in franchise history to hit 40 or more home runs in a season twice. And as much as the emphasis was on small ball, the club poled 200 homers, continuing the record-breaking pace of six consecutive seasons with 200 or more distance shots shared with the Yankees.

But for all of their star-studded accomplishments in 2005, the White Sox were never the lead story in the national media and an afterthought to ESPN, obsessed with the Red Sox, Yankees, and Mets—three East Coast prima donnas in their own Bristol, Connecticut, backyard. Closer to home certain local columnists, refusing to endorse the coming celebration of Chicago's first World Series appearance in 46 years, chose instead to rain on the fans' parade all season long with a chorus of unrelenting negativity and second-guessing. One infamous piece penned by *Sun-Times* man Greg Couch early in the season ruffled the feathers of the front office and struck a raw nerve among a majority of players and fans who embraced Guillen, chuckled over his verbal flaps, and respected his sense of style and personal charisma. "Don't buy what Ozzie is selling!" screeched Couch, but the 2.3 million fans surging through the gates in 2005 saw matters differently. The columnists miscalculated Ozzie's managerial brilliance, as he invalidated the annoying criticisms and the invectives leveled by Jay Mariotti, the back-page *Sun-Times* columnist, against the front office and the television broadcast team.

The snide remarks of armchair quarterbacks, Jerry Reinsdorf bashers, skeptics, and nay-sayers were mostly silenced after the Sox fended off a late-season rush by the rebuilding Cleveland Indians, who managed to shave their 15½-game deficit in early August to a razor-thin one and a half games in the final week of the season. The last 10 days of the season were sheer heart-pounding suspense for Sox fans as the division title hung in the balance with each pitch. The Tribe was playing at a .700 clip, knocking down opponents like trees in a forest by the time the Sox regrouped and dug in. The entire season turned on a dime Sunday afternoon, September 25, when Buehrle stifled the Twins in U.S. Cellular Field by a 4–1 count. Meanwhile, Cleveland dropped a 5–4 heartbreaker to the last-place Kansas City Royals after Grady Sizemore lost Paul Phillips' deep pop fly in the sun, allowing the winning run to score. One play, one game is all it took to reverse the momentum.

Chicago won five of the next seven games, clinching the division on September 29 inside empty Comerica Park after Konerko slammed his 40th homer of the season. How appropriate to wrap it up in Detroit with Magglio Ordonez on hand to witness the raucous party from the other dugout. And Sox fans drew enormous satisfaction from the knowledge that nearly every preseason baseball forecaster had predicted that the Tigers would finish ahead of Chicago in the 2005 standings. In the glorious final weekend of the year, they swept away the Tribe in the Jake to put an exclamation point on a spectacular run, while putting Cleveland's last flickering hope of gaining a wild-card berth to rest.

When the cheering was finally over and fans had the chance to ponder what it all meant, they could take pride knowing what this championship season portended for the future. After so many disheartening seasons of playing in the shadow of the Cubs, it offered Sox fans hope and the unique opportunity to achieve parity in a two-team town, while firmly anchoring them to the South Side of Chicago. The value of the franchise soared to an estimated $327 million in 2005, a 20–30 percent increase, according to the estimates of sports economists. The impact on the bottom line translated into increased sponsorship revenue, enhanced national prestige, and the inherent desire of people to associate with a winner. The White Sox could aspire to top the magical 3 million attendance mark consistently and gain the ability to sign Type A free agents and retain their star players instead of losing quality athletes like Magglio Ordonez, Bartolo Colon, Robin Ventura, and Ray Durham to the open market.

Going beyond wins, losses, and dreary baseball economics, the 2005 White Sox united a city in common purpose; they provided excitement and joy in a time of war and a season of deadly hurricanes and, for many, a temporary escape from the ordinary grind of big-city living. Addressing the Chicago City Council following a ticker-tape parade through the ethnic working class neighborhoods of Bridgeport, Pilsen, Chinatown, Greektown, and Bronzeville, and past the throngs of cheering spectators lining LaSalle Street, Jerry Reinsdorf paused to reflect on the real meaning of this momentous event. "I kept thinking," he said, "these people have problems that we don't even know about. And yet they're forgetting their problems today. They're out and they're happy. That was the best part—knowing that we brought joy to a lot of people." A final footnote to the 2005 lovefest: the White Sox chairman can at last find comfort and personal satisfaction by knowing that he mended his fences with fandom and was mostly forgiven after taking his hits for so many long and contentious years.

	G	AB	H	R	2B	3B	HR	RBI	SB	AVG
Brian Anderson	13	34	6	3	1	0	2	3	1	.176
Geoff Blum	31	95	19	6	2	1	1	3	0	.200
Joe Borchard	7	12	5	0	2	0	0	0	0	.417
Raul Casanova	6	5	1	0	0	0	0	0	0	.200
Joe Crede	132	432	109	54	21	0	22	62	1	.252
Jermaine Dye	145	529	145	74	29	2	31	86	11	.274
Carl Everett	135	490	123	58	17	2	23	87	4	.251
Ross Gload	28	42	7	2	2	0	0	5	0	.167
Willie Harris	56	121	31	17	2	1	1	8	10	.256
Tadahito Iguchi	135	511	142	74	25	6	15	71	15	.278
Paul Konerko	158	575	163	98	24	0	40	100	0	.283
Pedro Lopez	2	7	2	1	0	0	0	2	0	.286
Pablo Ozuna	70	203	56	27	7	2	0	11	14	.276
Timo Perez	76	179	39	13	8	0	2	15	2	.218
A.J. Pierzynski	128	460	118	61	21	0	18	56	0	.257
Scott Podsednik	129	507	147	80	28	1	0	25	59	.290
Aaron Rowand	157	578	156	77	30	5	13	69	16	.270
Frank Thomas	34	105	23	19	3	0	12	26	0	.219
Juan Uribe	146	481	121	58	23	3	16	71	4	.252
Chris Widger	45	141	34	18	8	0	4	11	0	.241
	162	5,529	1,450	741	253	23	200	713	137	.262

	W	L	GS	CG	IP	H	BB	K	ShO	SV	ERA
Jon Adkins	0	1	0	0	8⅓	13	4	1	0	0	8.64
Jeff Bajenaru	0	0	0	0	4⅓	10	0	3	0	0	6.23
Mark Buehrle	16	8	33	3	236⅔	240	40	149	1	0	3.12
Jose Contreras	15	7	32	1	204⅔	177	75	154	0	0	3.61
Neal Cotts	4	0	0	0	60⅓	38	29	56	0	0	1.94
Freddy Garcia	14	8	33	2	228	225	60	146	0	0	3.87
Jon Garland	18	10	32	3	221	212	47	115	3	0	3.50
Dustin Hermanson	2	4	0	0	57⅓	46	29	58	0	34	2.04
Orlando "El Duque" Hernandez"	9	9	22	0	128⅓	137	50	91	0	1	3.61
Bobby Jenks	1	1	0	0	39⅓	34	15	50	0	6	2.75
Brandon McCarthy	3	2	12	0	67	62	17	48	0	0	4.03
Damaso Marte	3	4	0	0	45⅓	45	33	54	0	4	3.77
Cliff Politte	7	1	0	0	67⅓	42	21	57	0	1	2.00
David Sanders	0	0	0	0	2	3	1	1	0	0	13.5
Shingo Takatsu	1	2	0	0	28⅔	30	16	32	0	8	5.97
Luis Vizcaino	6	5	0	0	70	74	29	43	0	0	3.73
Kevin Walker	0	1	0	0	7	10	5	5	0	0	9.00
	99	63	162	9	1,477⅓	1,392	459	1,040	10	54	3.61

2006

Record: 90–72
Finish: Third (Central)
Games Behind: 6
Manager: Ozzie Guillen

How do you measure success? Back-to-back 90-win seasons (the first for a White Sox team since 1964–1965); record-setting attendance; a franchise record for fielding percentage (.9848); or, oh yes, a major league–leading 236 home runs? By chasing the wild-card into September, they even managed to end the season with higher TV ratings than the Cubs—a miracle in its own right—but then the Cubs had finished with the worst record in the National League.

Perhaps in earlier eras, with expectations riding not quite so high, such breathtaking accomplishments as these would stir feelings of jubilation, even ecstasy among the fans in a pennant-starved city such as Chicago. But after a ridiculously easy postseason run in 2005 and a World Series championship that banished forever (or at least seemed to) the "Comiskey Curse," the 2006 season began with such high hopes but ended in crushing disappointment. In some ways it was an eerie repeat of the 1960 post-pennant letdown. Both seasons featured a power-laden offense with an overreliance on the long ball, success in the first half of the season, a collapse in the closing weeks and new attendance records established in the process. The celebrated Roy Sievers arrived in Chicago in 1960 to batter down the fences—Jim Thome, a player cast in the same image, reprised the same familiar role for Ozzie Guillen's ballclub. Sievers and Thome delivered the goods as they were expected to, but somehow the two teams were never quite the same high-octane engines the year after winning pennants in 1959 and 2005, respectively. Of course, winning back-to-back titles is arguably the hardest goal of them all to attain in professional sports, minus the parity one sees in the NFL and the NHL.

Javier Vazquez: inconsistent strikeout ace (© 2006 finalshot.com)

Thome, acquired to boost the chances of a repeat, was a run-scoring machine in the first half—setting a major league record by scoring a run in each of the first 17 games of the season. On June 22 his home run was the only hit the Sox collected against the Cardinals, but it was good enough to salt away a 1–0 victory. There were smiles all around at the All-Star break as Ozzie Guillen led seven White Sox regulars into the All-Star Game in Pittsburgh. Big Jim was one of them. He had already poled 30 homers and driven home 77 runners—but after the July break, his numbers dipped precipitously to 12 and 32, reflecting the up-and-down fortunes of Thome and the entire team. On July 9 the 57–31, second-place Sox trailed the rejuvenated Tigers by only two games. In the second half, it was an entirely different story. The July–October record fell to 33–41 as they surrendered the wild-card and were easily overtaken by the on-rushing Twins. The Sox fell into third place for good on September 4, while Minnesota and Detroit battled down to the final weekend of the season. For all the thrills and excitement that go with 236 White Sox home runs, 127 of them were solo shots. And this was to become a worsening, chronic problem over the next several seasons. It was feast-or-famine time—home run or nothing, although the heart of the 2006 batting order—Thome, Konerko, and Dye combined to hit .317 with 129 homers, 393 RBIs, and 356 runs scored.

The offensive firepower in the middle of the lineup disguised inadequate pitching and a shaky bullpen. Flame-throwing Javier Vazquez, acquired from Arizona in the off-season, was given the lead in 26 of his 32 starts, but was inconsistent and unreliable—very strong in the early innings of the game but coming completely unglued by the fifth or sixth. "He throws the ball too good to get him out of the rotation," Guillen said in defense of his starter. "Sometimes you wonder what it is." Indeed. Pitching wins pennants—that was the storyline of 2005. Bad pitching spells third place, although Ken Williams desperately tried to stave off the inevitable plummet by acquiring Matt Thornton, David Riske, and Mike MacDougal to bolster the bullpen. But a bullpen staff that was so effective in '05 with a combined 3.23 ERA saw its earned run average swell to an unacceptable 4.55 in '06. Thornton was a terrific acquisition—for the future—but

MacDougal was a bust, and Riske was no risk, but no gain either. The rumor mill had outfielder Alfonso Soriano, a 40–40 leadoff hitter for the Washington Nationals coming to Chicago—but Williams hesitated and reportedly nixed a deal that would have sent Brandon McCarthy, an over-hyped pitching prospect to D.C. That left Scott Podsednik, whose 2006 season was a wash, as the igniter—but when the ignition stalled, his White Sox future appeared to be in jeopardy at season's end.

In a year when the Sox unveiled statues of Hall of Fame heroes Nellie Fox and Louie Aparicio in the center-field concourse and the players and front-office staff received their 14-carat gold, black onyx, World Series rings with 95 inlaid diamonds, so much more than a third-place finish was expected. "It's disappointing," Guillen reflected on the last day. "I'd rather be setting up my starting rotation for the playoffs than sitting at home watching [his son] Ozney play. My job is to try to get into the playoffs, and unfortunately I didn't do it. I don't feel disappointed about the players. I feel disappointed about the season"—as we all did.

	G	AB	H	R	2B	3B	HR	RBI	SB	AVG.
Sandy Alomar, Jr.	19	46	10	5	3	0	1	8	0	.217
Brian Anderson	134	365	82	46	23	1	8	33	4	.225
Alex Cintron	91	288	82	35	10	3	5	41	10	.285
Joe Crede	150	544	154	76	31	0	30	94	0	.283
Jermaine Dye	146	539	170	103	27	3	44	120	7	.315
Josh Fields	11	20	3	4	2	0	1	2	0	.150
Ross Gload	77	156	51	22	8	2	3	18	6	.327
Tadahito Iguchi	138	555	156	97	24	0	18	67	11	.281
Paul Konerko	152	566	177	97	30	0	35	113	1	.313
Rob Mackowiak	112	255	74	31	12	1	5	23	5	.290
Jerry Owens	12	9	3	4	1	0	0	0	1	.333
Pablo Ozuna	79	189	62	25	12	2	2	17	6	.328
A.J. Pierzynski	140	509	150	65	24	0	16	64	1	.295
Scott Podsednik	139	524	137	86	27	6	3	45	40	.261
Chris Stewart	6	8	0	0	0	0	0	0	0	.000
Ryan Sweeney	18	35	8	1	0	0	0	5	0	.229
Jim Thome	143	490	141	108	26	0	42	109	0	.288
Juan Uribe	132	463	109	53	28	2	21	71	1	.235
Chris Widger	27	76	14	6	3	0	1	7	0	.184
		5,657	1,586	868	291	20	236	839	93	.280

	W	L	GS	CG	IP	H	BB	K	SHO	SV	ERA
Mark Buehrle	12	13	32	1	204	247	48	98	0	0	4.99
Jose Contreras	13	9	30	1	196	194	55	134	1	0	4.27
Neal Cotts	1	2	0	0	54	64	24	43	0	1	5.17
Freddy Garcia	17	9	33	1	216⅓	228	48	135	0	0	4.53
Jon Garland	18	7	32	1	211⅓	247	41	112	1	0	4.51
Charlie Haeger	1	1	1	0	18⅓	12	13	19	0	1	3.44
Dustin Hermanson	0	0	0	0	6⅔	6	1	5	0	0	4.05
Bobby Jenks	3	4	0	0	69⅔	66	31	80	0	41	4.00
Boone Logan	0	0	0	0	17⅓	21	15	15	0	1	8.31
Mike MacDougal	1	1	0	0	25	19	6	19	0	0	1.80
Brandon McCarthy	4	7	2	0	84⅔	77	33	69	0	0	4.68
Agustin Montero	1	0	0	0	14	15	2	7	0	0	5.14
Jeff Nelson	0	1	0	0	2⅔	3	5	2	0	0	3.38
Cliff Politte	2	2	0	0	30	47	15	15	0	0	8.70
David Riske	1	1	0	0	34⅓	32	14	23	0	0	3.93
Matt Thornton	5	3	0	0	54	46	21	49	0	2	3.33
Sean Tracey	0	0	0	0	8	4	5	3	0	0	3.38
Javier Vazquez	11	12	32	1	202⅔	206	56	184	0	0	4.84
	90	72	162	5	1,449	1,534	433	1,012	11	46	4.61

2007

Record: 72–90
Finish: Fourth (Central)
Games Behind: 24
Manager: Ozzie Guillen

Was the 2007 debacle an aberration, or were the warning signs of a letdown already in place? Should we have sensed that a gradual talent decline was coming? To be fair, no one could have foreseen the spate of injuries vexing the White Sox. Joe Crede was out for the season on June 6 with a bad back. Scott Podsednik was gone for most of July with a strained rib cage, and Jim Thome suffered the same problem in May. For five seasons, Sox trainer Herm Schneider had kept the ballclub in tip-top shape. They were the healthiest team in baseball from 2002 to 2006, but 11 trips to the disabled list in 2007 turned the White Sox clubhouse into a M.A.S.H. unit field hospital.

After a winning April, the team foundered through the next four months and was in last place as late as September 18. The vaunted offense of 2006 went south, although 190 home runs attested to the enduring firepower of this club. But home runs alone, as evidenced in 2006, are largely meaningless if the supporting cast stands around and waits for one of the big boppers to unload the long ball. It was this lack of situational hitting, and the inability to score runners from second and third base with less than two outs that really plagued this team in 2007—and beyond. The Sox finished dead last in the league with a .243 average with runners in scoring position. Their 693 runs scored were the fewest for a Sox team since 1990, and the .246 team batting average the worst since the Jim Fregosi days of 1988.

Outfielder Brian Anderson, the "can't miss" rookie prospect everyone counted on to attain stardom in '06 was optioned to Charlotte on April 29 after hitting an anemic .118. The fans were more than patient with this likeable blond-haired youngster and sincerely believed he would come around with the bat if only he was given the proper chance. But after 90 strikeouts in just 365 at-bats in 2006, patience had worn thin. Brian appeared hopelessly overmatched at the plate and uncertain of himself, although few people questioned his defensive abilities. The kid "threw some leather," as it were, but baseball is not a one-dimensional game. Anderson was gone from the organization in 2009, but he attempted to resurrect his stalled career as a pitcher in the Royals farm system.

The free agent pickup of Darin Erstad, an Angels outfielder long coveted by the White Sox, looked good on paper. Erstad replaced Anderson in center field, but two trips to the DL in '07 and advancing age minimized his contributions. Signaling that for all intents and purposes the season was over before the August "dog days" arrived, Ken Williams traded Tadihito Iguchi, one of the heroes of '05 to Philadelphia on July 27 for a rookie pitcher of no great consequence. Meanwhile, Danny Richar, a young Dominican infielder, was summoned from Charlotte to take his place at second, but he made no lasting impression. Jerry Owens, a speedy outfield prospect from the

Jim Thome launches his 500th career home run, September 15, 2007. (Courtesy of the Chicago White Sox)

Knights, pilfered 32 bases in his debut season—but he was not the hoped-for salvation, either. Josh Fields, tabbed as Joe Crede's heir apparent, garnered mixed reviews during his lengthy 2007 audition at third base following Crede's trip to the DL. Fields was ranked by *Baseball America* as the No. 2 prospect in the Sox system and had showcased some natural power, but as is so often the case with White Sox prospects, expectations and real-time performance are two different yardsticks.

Few teams can sustain winning ways year-in and year-out without a steady infusion of talent coming from the minor league system. (The Minnesota Twins offer the best example of consistently building from within.) And as the first decade of the new millennium wore on, it was becoming painfully evident that as a consequence of trading youth for veterans, bad scouting and other factors mixed in, the system was edging ever closer to the same unenviable position it had been in during the mid-1960s after Bill Veeck had drained the talent well dry through his bad trades. The struggle to build a viable talent incubator in the minor leagues only intensified and continued on through the mid-1980s.

On a brighter note, Javier Vazquez rebounded from a lackluster '06 campaign to lead the team in wins while notching 213 strikeouts—sixth highest in White Sox history behind spitballer Ed Walsh (who holds down the top four spots) and southpaw Gary Peters. Jim Thome gave the fans at U.S. Cellular Field a thrill to remember on September 16 with a walk-off, game-winning home run against the Angels—his 500th career shot—a great milestone for him as he set his sights on the Hall of Fame. Veteran ace Mark Buehrle demonstrated why he was the master of the house by twirling the 16th no-hitter in team history against Texas on April 18—the first for a Sox pitcher at home since Joel Horlen's masterpiece on September 10, 1967. And Bobby Jenks redeemed a horrendous bullpen that ranked 12th in the American

League by posting back-to-back 40-save seasons. The suspense surrounding Buehrle and Jermaine Dye, both in the last year of their contracts, was happily resolved when both players re-signed with the club in mid-season, ending a frenzy of media trade speculation.

It is not so surprising to see that in this Cubs-obsessed city, a White Sox team that stumbles out of the gate in the early weeks of a season quickly becomes fodder for gloomy and dire gossip mostly emanating from the press box that the team is about to be "blown up," and that "it's only a matter of days" before the veteran players are sent packing—bound for the contending teams in exchange for minor league unknowns and future considerations. The fans have been warned, or so these "experts" like to remind us. In fact, the writers seem to revel in this kind of talk. That was essentially the steady drumbeat served up to Sox fans by *Sun-Times* beat writer Joe Cowley on a daily basis from the month of June through September 2007. Perhaps it is just one more example of media bias favoring the Chicago National League team in this town, because rarely do we hear these same negative rumors swirling around the Cubs front office in *their* down years. Does any knowledgeable fan truly believe that the Cubs are *always* buying and the Sox on the other hand must *always* be looking to dump salary at the slightest hint of trouble? Thankfully, the media is usually wrong on this issue, but it makes one wonder who their sources are.

Unless his back is pressed to the wall, Ken Williams does not like to make mid-season fire sales for the sake of gutting the team, driving down the payroll, and starting over. With the Dye and Buehrle signings in 2007, he made that point abundantly clear amid the tatters of a lost season. "We'll look to supplement a lot of things over the next few years to make the product even better," Kenny promised. "But we're not interested in a complete rebuilding plan because we have too much talent." By not hitting the panic button in '07 and keeping the arrow pointing forward, it proved to be a prudent and wise decision, as far as the fortunes of the 2008 White Sox were concerned.

	G	AB	H	R	2B	3B	HR	RBI	SB	AVG.
Brian Anderson	13	17	2	3	1	0	0	0	0	.118
Alex Cintron	68	185	45	23	7	1	2	19	2	.243
Joe Crede	47	167	36	13	5	0	4	22	0	.216
Jermaine Dye	138	508	129	68	34	0	28	78	2	.254
Darrin Erstad	87	310	77	33	13	1	4	32	7	.248
Josh Fields	100	373	91	54	17	1	23	67	1	.244
Andy Gonzalez	67	189	35	17	6	0	2	11	1	.185
Toby Hall	38	116	24	8	4	0	0	3	0	.207
Tadahito Iguchi	90	327	82	45	17	4	6	31	8	.251
Paul Konerko	151	549	142	71	34	0	31	90	0	.259
Donny Lucy	8	15	3	0	0	0	0	0	0	.200
Rob Mackowiak	85	237	66	34	11	2	6	36	3	.278
Gustavo Molina	10	18	1	0	0	0	0	1	0	.056
Jerry Owens	93	356	95	44	9	2	1	17	32	.267
Pablo Ozuna	27	78	19	9	3	0	0	3	3	.244
A.J. Pierzynski	136	472	124	54	24	0	14	50	1	.263
Scott Podsednik	62	214	52	30	13	4	2	11	12	.243
Danny Richar	56	187	43	30	9	3	6	15	1	.230
Ryan Sweeney	15	45	9	5	3	0	1	5	0	.200
Luis Terrero	61	117	44	27	2	0	5	12	4	.231
JimThome	150	513	119	79	19	0	35	96	0	.275
Juan Uribe	150	513	120	55	18	2	20	68	1	.234
		5,441	1,341	693	249	20	190	667	78	.246

	W	L	GS	CG	IP	H	BB	K	SHO	SV	ERA
David Aardsma	2	1	0	0	32⅓	39	17	36	0	0	6.40
Lance Broadway	1	1	1	0	10⅓	5	5	14	0	0	0.87
Mark Buehrle	10	9	30	3	201	208	45	115	1	0	3.63
Ryan Bukvich	1	0	0	0	35⅔	36	24	18	0	0	5.05
Jose Contreras	10	17	30	2	189	232	62	113	2	0	5.57
John Danks	6	13	26	0	139	160	54	109	0	0	5.50
Dewon Day	0	1	0	0	12	19	9	7	0	0	11.25
Gavin Floyd	1	5	10	0	70	85	19	49	0	0	5.27
Jon Garland	10	13	32	2	208⅓	219	57	98	1	0	4.23
Charlie Haeger	0	1	0	0	11⅓	17	8	1	0	0	7.15
Bobby Jenks	3	5	0	0	65	45	13	56	0	40	2.77
Boone Logan	2	1	0	0	50⅔	59	20	35	0	0	4.97
Mike MacDougal	2	5	0	0	42⅓	50	33	39	0	0	6.80
Nick Masset	2	3	1	0	39⅓	52	26	21	0	0	7.09
Mike Myers	1	0	0	0	13⅔	21	7	6	0	0	11.20
Heath Phillips	1	1	0	0	7⅓	10	4	2	0	0	3.68
Brett Prinz	0	0	0	0	3⅓	4	2	1	0	0	8.10
Andrew Sisco	0	1	0	0	14	19	11	13	0	0	8.36
Matt Thornton	4	4	0	0	56⅓	59	26	55	0	2	4.79
Javier Vazquez	15	8	32	2	216⅔	197	50	213	0	0	3.74
Ehren Wasserman	1	1	0	0	23	20	7	14	0	0	2.74
	72	90	162	9	1,440⅔	1,556	499	1,015	9	42	4.77

2008

Record: 89–74
Finish: First (Central)
Games Ahead: 1
Manager: Ozzie Guillen

The product *did* get better, more so than anyone could have reasonably expected it to or possibly hoped for in the off-season after Williams completed two questionable trades with West Coast teams—dispatching Jon Garland to the Angels for 2007 Gold Glove shortstop Orlando Cabrera and three prospects to Oakland for Nick Swisher, the goofy, but spirited A's right fielder. Keeping Buehrle and Dye anchored to their home base was a major factor in the surprising '08 turnaround. Both Sox veterans rebounded after just so-so seasons in 2007. It would be nice to say that the Cabrera trade provided the Sox with a seasoned and capable shortstop for the long haul, but his one season on the South Side was stormy and filled with controversy and distractions. Ozzie Guillen did not appreciate his shortstop calling the press box to question the official scorer's decision concerning an error that was charged against him, or his decision to leave the clubhouse early in order to avoid media interviews. Worse, Cabrera questioned the Sox's desire to win. But, pushing aside these negatives, Cabrera was not nearly as volatile a presence as Albert Belle had been 11 years earlier, and his .978 fielding percentage in '08 ranks fourth highest in team history. There is little doubt that Cabrera steadied the Sox inner defense and saved a few games with his glove.

Nick Swisher, who tattooed the initials of his paternal grandmother to his chest—was another story. He hit just .191 in the second half and was a season-long disappointment to Guillen, who benched him in September, explaining, "I have to put the best lineup out there to win the game.... To me, the best lineup right now is without [Swisher]." The Swisher trade was a disaster. Better results were achieved with the installation of Cuban defector Alexei Ramirez at second base. Dubbed the "Cuban Missile," the string-bean right-handed hitter slugged a club-record four grand slams and was runner-up for Rookie of the Year honors.

Second-year pitchers John Danks and Gavin Floyd blossomed into promising young mound stars, as injuries and ineffectiveness befuddled Jose Contreras and eased the veteran out of the equation. Fire-balling Matt Thornton, acquired from Seattle for rookie bust-out Joe Borchard a year earlier, became the perfect late-inning setup man for Bobby Jenks, and free agent acquisitions Octavio Dotel and D.J. Carrasco were significant long-relief improvements over the 2007 tandem of Mike MacDougal and Boone Logan. On July 31 the Sox traded for Ken Griffey Jr., marking only the second time in history that a player with more than 500 career home runs was involved in a mid-season deal (Willie Mays being the first). Between Griffey and Jim Thome, the two had accumulated more than 1,100 career home runs. Junior was closing in on retirement, and his contributions were negligible, but the move was good for a few headlines in the press. Even in this exciting dash to the playoffs, the Pale Hose still needed as much favorable coverage as they could get, God knows.

The Sox occupied first place for 148 days—but it was a tight, neck-and-neck battle with the Minnesota Twins all the way down to the final day of the season, even though the Twins had lost their two best players, Torii Hunter and Johan Santana, to other teams. Chicago claimed the third-best home winning percentage in the AL—winning 54 games and losing only 28 for a strong .659 percentage, although their road record was dismal for a division-winning ballclub.

U.S. Cellular Field was their homer haven, and for the second time in three years the White Sox led the major leagues in home runs with 234 on the strength of newcomer Carlos Quentin's 36 long-distance blows. Quentin, a fiercely intense, highly focused former college All-American, arrived from the Arizona Diamondbacks in a "sleeper" trade for low-level infield prospect Chris Carter over the winter. At the time of his self-inflicted (stupid!) season-ending injury on September 1—a fractured right wrist resulting from slamming his fist into his bat in a moment of pique after fouling off a Cliff Lee pitch in Cleveland—Quentin led the league in home runs and was the leading candidate to win the Most Valuable Player Award. "It's a freak thing that happened," was all he could say. Quentin missed out on winning the home run crown after Detroit's Miguel Cabrera finally overtook him on September 27, but he earned a nice consolation prize—an AL Silver Slugger Award.

With Joe Crede also lost for the balance of the season, the White Sox were considerably weakened heading into the stretch run. The Twins were odds-on favorites to wrest the division crown away from the Sox, but because Minneapolis was the host city of the Republican National Convention, the schedule maker had sent them packing on a physically draining 14-game road trip. Still, the Sox did all they could do after dropping three straight in the Humphrey Dome September 23–25, dumping them into second place and trailing by a half-game by the time they returned to Chicago the next day. This set the stage for the most dramatic and improbable season climax since the dead-ball days of Ed Walsh and Fielder Jones in 1908.

After dropping the first two games of the homestand to Cleveland on September 26–27—the Tribe scored in double digits against Danks and Vazquez on successive days—the White Sox found themselves a half-game behind Minnesota for the top slot. Mark Buehrle held down the Indians the next night, 5–1, inducing four double plays and looking very much like the Buehrle of old. The Tigers arrived in town on September 29 for a one-game makeup, and they sent an old friend, Freddy Garcia (attempting a comeback with Detroit) to the bump against Gavin Floyd, who was enjoying a breakout year. Alexei Ramirez connected for his record-setting fourth grand slam of the season, powering the Sox to an 8–2 rout. This lifted the South Siders into a tie with the Twins, necessitating a one-game playoff at U.S. Cellular Field.

It was just the 12th time in major league history that two teams ended the regular season in a tie and needed an additional game to crown a champion. Game location was determined by a flip of the coin with Minnesota, which the Sox had won in early September. More than 40,000 fans jammed the Cell—the largest home crowd since August 4, 2003—to see Danks square off against Nick Blackburn in Game No. 163 for all the money. The showdown was billed as the "Blackout Game" because fans were encouraged to wear their black-and-white Sox T-shirts and jerseys. However, it was the Twins who suffered a blackout spell, or shall we say the proverbial black eye, after Jim Thome drilled a 461-foot home run in the seventh inning. It was the only run of the game, but it was enough to claim the Central Division title as Bobby Jenks nailed down the save with a perfect ninth inning. The three-game season finale marked the first time in major league history that a team won each of its last three games against three different opponents.

As the Sox prepared to square off against the Tampa Bay Rays, a young, talent-rich (but cash-poor) team that was built the old-fashioned way—through effective scouting, good draft choices, and a strong minor league system—Ken Williams heaped more useless praise on the annoying Twins and their "formula for success," that this up-and-coming Rays team seemed to emulate. "Early on I thought throwing talent at the wall would bring a championship, and for three or four years, on paper, we had the best team in our division," he said. "There were at least two or three of those years where Minnesota won the division and came out and said, 'That team there [the Sox] had more talent than us.' That really made me rethink some of the things we were doing, the approach we were taking."

Jim Thome and Ken Griffey Jr. The two have amassed 1,100 home runs between them. (Courtesy of the Chicago White Sox)

	G	AB	H	R	2B	3B	HR	RBI	SB	AVG.
Brian Anderson	109	181	42	24	13	0	8	26	5	.232
Jason Bourgeosis	6	3	1	0	1	0	0	0	0	.333
Orlando Cabrera	161	661	186	93	33	1	8	57	19	.281
Joe Crede	97	335	83	41	18	1	17	55	0	.248
Jermaine Dye	154	590	172	96	41	2	34	96	3	.292
Josh Fields	14	32	5	3	1	0	0	2	0	.156
Chris Getz	10	7	2	2	0	0	0	1	1	.286
Ken Griffey Jr.	41	131	34	16	10	0	3	18	0	.260
Toby Hall	41	41	33	7	3	0	2	7	0	.260
Paul Konerko	122	438	105	59	19	1	22	62	2	.240
Jerry Owens	12	16	4	1	0	0	0	1	2	.250
Pablo Ozuna	32	64	18	5	3	0	0	6	0	.281
Paul Phillips	4	2	0	0	0	0	0	0	0	.000
A.J, Pierzynski	134	534	150	66	31	1	13	60	1	.281
Carlos Quentin	130	480	138	96	26	1	36	100	7	.288
Alexei Ramirez	136	480	139	65	22	2	21	77	13	.290
Nick Swisher	153	497	109	86	21	1	24	69	3	.219
Jim Thome	149	503	123	93	28	0	34	90	1	.245
Juan Uribe	119	324	80	38	22	1	7	40	1	.247
Dewayne Wise	57	129	32	20	4	2	6	18	9	.248
		5,553	1,458	811	296	13	235	785	67	.263

	W	L	GS	CG	IP	H	BB	K	SHO	SV	ERA
Lance Broadway	1	0	1	0	14	20	5	7	0	0	7.07
Mark Buehrle	15	12	34	1	218⅔	240	52	140	0	0	3.79
D.J. Carrasco	1	0	0	0	38⅔	30	14	30	0	0	3.96
Jose Contreras	7	6	20	1	121	130	35	70	0	0	4.54
John Danks	12	9	33	0	195	182	57	159	0	0	3.32
Octavio Dotel	4	4	0	0	67	52	29	92	0	1	3.76
Gavin Floyd	17	8	33	1	206⅓	190	70	145	0	0	3.84
Bobby Jenks	3	1	0	0	61⅔	51	17	38	0	30	2.63
Scott Linebrink	2	2	0	0	46⅓	41	9	40	0	1	3.69
Esteban Loaiza	0	0	0	0	3	3	0	1	0	0	3.00
Boone Logan	2	3	0	0	42⅓	57	14	42	0	0	5.95
Mike MacDougal	0	0	0	0	17	16	12	12	0	0	2.12
Nick Masset	1	0	1	0	44⅔	55	21	32	0	0	4.63
Horatio Ramirez	0	3	0	0	13	24	8	2	0	0	7.62
Clayton Richard	2	5	8	0	47⅔	61	13	29	0	0	6.04
Adam Russell	4	0	0	0	26	30	10	22	0	0	5.19
Matt Thornton	5	3	0	0	67⅓	48	19	77	0	1	2.67
Javier Vazques	12	16	33	1	208⅓	214	61	200	0	0	4.67
Ehren Wasserman	1	2	0	0	19⅔	27	14	9	0	0	7.78
	89	74	4.06	4	1,457⅔	1,471	460	1,147	10	34	4.06

2009

Record: 79–83
Finish: Third (Central)
Games Behind: 7½
Manager: Ozzie Guillen

The White Sox attained perfection—for exactly one day in an otherwise drab season of lackluster .500 play to close out a winning, highly successful decade of South Side baseball. A leaky inner defense dropped them into a tie for dead last in team fielding, and they were next to last in hitting. How many runners were left stranded at third base with less than two outs by the middle of the lineup? Although they ranked sixth in home runs with 184, the team averaged just 4.47 runs per game—third lowest in the American League.

Up in the broadcast booth there was little Hawk Harrelson or Steve Stone could do to paint a more optimistic and pleasing picture for the fans. However, the pitching was as good as it could be against tough American League hitting, finishing second to Seattle. Mark Buehrle's perfect game masterpiece against Tampa Bay on July 23 earned him a cover shot on *Sports Illustrated* and front-office accolades on August 4 in what the organization billed as "The Mark Buehrle Appreciation Series." Credit utility outfielder Dewayne Wise with the defensive gem of the year—perhaps even the decade. Wise made a spectacular over-the-wall grab of Gabe Kapler's long drive in the ninth inning to preserve Mark's perfect game.

Wise, a luckless career minor leaguer since 1997 with a handful of unsuccessful tryouts in Cincinnati, Atlanta, and Toronto to his name before inking a deal as a White Sox free agent on March 5, 2008, was penciled in as Guillen's Opening Day leadoff hitter after the speedy but light-hitting Jerry Owens failed to stick. It was revealing and perhaps indicative of the declining fortunes of the Sox that there was no one better on the roster or inside the system to step up to provide a necessary spark at the top of the lineup. Ken Williams addressed this situation by summoning back Scott Podsednik, who was out of work and sitting on the couch at his home in Texas, waiting for someone to call with a job offer. Podsednik promised Williams that he was healthy and ready to go. After working out the kinks in Charlotte, Scotty Pods rejoined the White Sox on May 1 and seemed to be a man on a mission—a mission to jump-start his stalled career. No one expected him to lead the team in hitting, let alone avoid his usual and customary spate of aggravating injuries. But he gave the team and the fans a solid, productive year, hitting .304 and contributing three walkoff, game-winning hits, although it was strictly a one-year, stop-gap arrangement.

Williams had great expectations entering the 2009 campaign and had eased off the gas pedal as far as making aggressive preseason moves. "You can't just throw as much talent against the wall and formulate a club strictly on talent," he said. "Sometimes what appears to be the most obvious move because Player X is the star or has been the star could ultimately be the worst thing you do." Was this a thinly veiled reference to the Javier Vazquez deal or even Jim Thome? The Sox hovered at or dropped a few games below the .500 mark all season long. Then the GM went back to work and made a series of moves he believed was necessary to improve the team.

Veteran utility catcher Ramon Castro arrived from the Mets on May 29 via the trade route after "Corky" Miller, acquired along with Tyler Flowers and Brent Lillibridge for Vazquez in the off-season, showed why he was not the answer. Flowers was tabbed as A.J. Pierzynski's future replacement, but Miller and Lillibridge were washouts in a disappointing trade with Atlanta. In August, in a surprise move, outfielder Alex Rios was claimed off waivers from the financially strapped Toronto Blue Jays. Rios, a two-time All-Star who could hit, field, and run with the best of them, endured a painful period of adjustment in Chicago and struggled to hit .200. Nevertheless, better results were anticipated for him in 2010.

Williams failed to pry loose 2007 Cy Young Award–winner Jake Peavy from San Diego in late May after Peavy exercised his no-trade clause with a firm no. Trader Kenny resumed negotiations with Padres GM Kevin Towers later in the summer and this time succeeded, sending four prospects—including two promising young pitchers, Aaron Poreda, a 2007 first-round draft pick, and Clayton Richard—to the Padres on July

Gordon Beckham strokes his first career home run in the annual Civil Rights Game played at Cincinnati's Great American Ballpark, June 20, 2009. (Courtesy of Mike McKay)

31. Peavy, his trade value diminished by injury, finally agreed to join the White Sox. "In May we didn't think the time was right," the power right-hander explained. "Now things are a little bit different on a lot of fronts. I'm excited about going to an organization that has made winning a priority." There was only one problem, however: Jake had been sent to the disabled list by the Padres with a strained ankle tendon in June and would not be added to the White Sox active duty roster until September 18. He won all three of his starts in the closing weeks, but by then it was meaningless.

The season was shot, and all that could be said of the 2009 Sox is that the April-to-September adventure was draining, underachieving, and disappointing. So much more was expected, but so little was delivered. A road trip to Boston, the new Yankee Stadium, and a farewell visit to the Minnesota Humphrey Dome, commencing on August 24, was the litmus test—and the last chance for the 63–61, second-place White Sox to redeem themselves or pack it in for the year. When the dust settled, the Sox limped home to Chicago with a 2–8 record after being hammered in all three cities.

A disgusted Williams did not hesitate and did what he had to—waving good-bye to Jim Thome and Jose Contreras on August 31. The two aging veterans were deemed expendable and shipped to the National League for prospects. The slow-footed Thome was clogging up the base paths, and Contreras was simply awful as he tried to regain a measure of consistency on the comeback trail. Rookies Daniel Hudson and Jhonny Nunez filled the vacated roster spots, as Sox fans looked to the farm system for future salvation.

That hoped-for salvation arrived early when the contract of rookie infielder Gordon Beckham was purchased on June 4 from Charlotte. A June 2008 first-round pick (eighth overall) in the Major League Baseball First-Year Player Draft, Beckham was a junior shortstop for the University of Georgia Bulldogs, hitting a torrid .397 and ranked among the NCAA Division I leaders in most offensive categories when the phone call from Chicago came. It was the first time since 1990 that the club had picked in the top 10 of the draft—and the signing of Beckham was a much ballyhooed event in Soxland. "We're thrilled to land a player of Gordon's caliber at that spot," Doug Laumann, director of amateur scouting said at the time. "He brings a lot to the table, and he was the guy we had targeted early on in the process." In his short time at Charlotte, the kid was hitting the ball at a .464 clip.

Despite misgivings from Ozzie Guillen, who sourly noted that he was "in trouble if he had to count on Beckham" at this point in the season, Gordon was fast-tracked to the parent ballclub—to relieve the disappointing Josh Fields of his duties at third—and not at his natural position at shortstop, where Alexei Ramirez had been moved prior to 2009. The 22-year-old rookie from Atlanta, Georgia, broke in with a flourish and showed a lot of chutzpah as he adjusted to life in the big leagues and his new position. He was named AL Rookie of the Month for July after hitting .330, and at season's end was awarded the *Sporting News* Rookie of the Year award, and the Player's Choice AL Outstanding Rookie Award, although he narrowly missed out on the baseball writers' award.

With Beckham and Peavy in the fold, there was room for cautious optimism as the chill of autumn set in. The White Sox minor league affiliates enjoyed a combined 425–346 (.551) record in 2009, third-best overall behind the Giants and Yankees, but still you had to wonder whether the prospects were bona fides...or not. "Winning isn't the ultimate goal," explained Buddy Bell, the new White Sox director of minor league instruction, who seemed to be the right man to turn things around and deliver the prospects. "It is an indication that these players are talented, and you can't win without talent. We emphasize development, but it is important in the minor leagues. You don't want guys who don't know how to win."

	G	AB	H	R	2B	3B	HR	RBI	SB	AVG.
Brian Anderson	65	185	44	25	9	0	2	13	3	.238
Gordon Beckham	103	378	102	58	28	1	14	63	7	.270
Wilson Betemit	20	45	9	2	5	0	0	3	0	.200
Ramon Castro	31	76	14	8	3	0	4	12	0	.184
Jermaine Dye	141	503	126	78	19	1	27	81	0	.250
Josh Fields	79	239	53	29	5	2	7	30	2	.222
Tyler Flowers	10	16	3	3	1	0	0	0	0	.188
Chris Getz	107	375	98	49	18	4	2	31	25	.261
Paul Konerko	152	546	151	75	30	1	28	88	1	.277
Mark Kotsay	40	113	33	12	7	0	3	18	1	.282
Brent Lillibridge	46	95	15	9	2	0	0	3	6	.158
Abraham "Corky" Miller	14	39	8	5	3	0	0	5	0	.205
Jayson Nix	94	255	57	36	11	0	12	32	10	.224
Jerry Owens	12	12	1	0	0	0	0	0	1	.083
A.J. Pierzynski	138	504	151	57	22	1	13	49	1	.300
Scott Podsednik	132	537	163	75	25	6	7	48	30	.304
Carlos Quentin	99	351	83	47	14	0	21	56	3	.236
Alexei Ramirez	148	542	150	71	14	1	15	68	14	.277
Alex Rios	41	146	29	11	6	0	3	9	5	.199
Jim Thome	107	345	86	55	15	0	23	74	0	.249
Dewayne Wise	84	142	32	17	8	3	2	11	4	.225
		5,463	1,410	724	246	20	184	695	113	.258

	W	L	GS	CG	IP	H	BB	K	SHO	SV	ERA
Lance Broadway	0	1	0	0	16	19	9	9	0	0	5.06
Mark Buehrle	13	10	33	1	213⅓	222	45	105	1	0	3.84
D.J. Carrasco	5	1	1	0	93⅓	103	29	62	0	0	3.76
Bartolo Colon	3	6	12	0	62⅓	69	21	38	0	0	4.19
Jose Contreras	5	13	21	0	114⅔	121	45	89	0	0	5.42
John Danks	13	11	32	1	200⅓	184	73	149	0	0	3.77
Octavio Dotel	3	3	0	0	62⅓	54	36	75	0	0	3.32
Jack Egbert	0	0	0	0	2⅔	8	2	0	0	0	27.00
Gavin Floyd	11	11	30	1	193	178	59	163	0	0	4.06
Freddy Garcia	3	4	9	0	56	56	12	37	0	0	4.34
Jimmy Gobble	0	0	0	0	12	14	7	10	0	0	7.50
Daniel Hudson	1	1	2	0	18⅔	16	9	14	0	0	3.38
Bobby Jenks	3	4	0	0	53⅓	52	16	49	0	29	3.71
Scott Linebrink	3	7	0	0	56	70	23	55	0	2	4.66
Mike MacDougal	0	0	0	0	4⅓	7	7	3	0	0	12.46
Jhonny Nunez	0	0	0	0	5⅔	10	2	3	0	0	9.53
Jake Peavy	3	0	3	0	20	11	6	18	0	0	1.35
Tony Pena	1	2	0	0	36	40	9	29	0	1	3.75
Aaron Poreda	1	0	0	0	11	9	8	12	0	0	2.45
Clayton Richard	4	3	14	1	89	94	37	66	0	0	4.65
Matt Thornton	6	3	0	0	72⅓	58	20	87	0	4	2.74
Carlos Torres	1	2	5	0	28⅓	30	17	22	0	0	6.04
Wes Whisler	0	0	0	0	1⅓	0	3	2	0	0	13.50
Randy Williams	0	1	0	0	17⅔	13	12	22	0	0	4.58
	79	83	162	4	1,439⅔	1,438	507	1,119	11	36	4.14

2010

Record: 88–74
Finish: Second (Central)
Games Behind: 6
Manager: Ozzie Guillen

Interesting parallels can be drawn between two seasons separated by nearly 50 years. In 1961, the year the Yankees and Roger Maris rewrote the record books, the Al Lopez–led White Sox stumbled out of the gate and were left for dead on June 11 with a 15–33 record. Then they went on a 19–4 tear that included a 12-game winning streak.

On June 6, 2010, Ozzie Guillen's ensemble were in the dumps with a 24–33 record, trailing the Tigers by 9½ games. The starting pitching had foundered. The hitting was tepid and the bullpen shaky. Jake Peavy, counted on to be the messiah of the starting rotation, gave every indication by his mediocre outings that he was better suited pitching to weaker National League hitters than in the talent-rich American League. Peavy was getting rocked nearly every time out while Sox fans lamented, 'Where was Clayton Richard when we needed him?' Answer: the 2009 compensation for Peavy was winning some big games out west for the Padres.

By late May, the Chicago press corps in their daily briefings reported that Kenny Williams was fed up with losing and ready to blow up the entire team. Paul Konerko—"he'll be gone soon, and so will A.J.," was the word on the street. The two Sox veterans meant everything to the franchise—but both were playing through the final year of their contracts, and the beat writers and columnists kept telling us it was just a matter of time and that we had better face up to it—the geniuses! To be sure, Williams was upset with his underperforming cast, and change seemed to be in the air. With a high payroll, Jerry Reinsdorf and his investors had a huge financial stake in this team's success. But would the GM actually gut the team in June or July? It was something that had not happened on the South Side since the white flag days of 1997. The answer, of course, was, not on his watch! "We are always trying to add," Williams said on June 22. "Even in 2007 you guys didn't believe it, but we were actively in the trade market to add. We knew we would have a tough time coming back that year, but sometimes you add for the year after that, thinking you have a good core. Even if the perception is, we are moving this player or that player, it's still with the mindset to win the next year. We have not been in the mode for selling for the sake of selling for a long, long time. We are incapable as long as I'm sitting in this chair of thinking any other way."

Eleven days earlier the Sox had begun their annual interleague junket, and immediately they turned a corner and reversed their fortunes against hapless National League opponents by torching the Cubs four out of six and posting a sparkling 15–3 mark against the senior circuit. On June 15 they commenced an 11-game winning streak during an extended eastern road trip to NL ports of call and would stay hot through mid-July by following up the 11-game run with a nine-game streak, thus notching a stunning 25–5 record leading into the All-Star break. The impressive string of wins equaled a mark originally set by the 1975 Reds and the 1990 Mets for the best record leading into the All-Star Game. Suddenly the White Sox had erased an impossible deficit and climbed past the Twins and Tigers to grab first place on July 11 after barbecuing the Royals 16–5 at the Cell. Detroit was incapable of winning on the road in 2010 and quickly fell away. For the moment, the Twins were sputtering, leaving the White Sox in command of the Central...and their own fate. Guillen and his troops clung to the top spot for exactly 30 days—reaching their high-water mark of the season by establishing a 3½-game bulge on July 20.

That lead quickly evaporated during a disastrous road trip to Baltimore, where they dropped three of four to a terrible Orioles club in early August and were then swept away in Minnesota a week later. Catching their second wind, Minnesota caught fire and went on a 45–17 run between July 16 and September 21 just as the White Sox were cooling off. August was the key month, but the South Siders managed only a 13–15 record after going 18–8 in July. They struggled mightily against three of the worst teams in the AL—the Indians, Orioles, and Royals. On the other hand, they handled the always-tough Angels and the once-ferocious Red Sox with ease. Go figure.

It was another oddball season fraught with the usual high tension, zany front-office tilts, press second-guessing, Ozzie verbal outbursts, and nonstop high-wire drama. Beginning in spring training with the "Twitter-gate" fiasco—pitting Guillen and his sons against Kenny Williams and several front-office executives in an online verbal sparring match that reached nonsensical proportions—through the dog days of summer when the Sox manager and the Sox GM again clashed over Guillen's anger over his son's being drafted low in the free agent draft, there was no end in sight to the controversies. The soap opera aspects overshadowed so many of the superlatives normally associated with a winning team challenging for a title.

Ken Williams had given Guillen the benefit of the doubt and delivered to him the kind of small-ball, speed-oriented offense he had longed for since coming on board in 2004. Against his better judgment, Williams went along with Guillen's scheme to implement a designated-hitter-by-committee approach, meaning that the chance to reacquire Jim Thome as a free agent was forever lost when the Sox manager publicly vetoed the idea at the 2010 Sox Fest. Mark Kotsay, a journeyman utility outfielder who punched many bus tickets shuttling from team to team before joining the Sox in 2009, was penciled in as the left-handed DH with the fading veteran Andruw Jones on the right side—and that turned out to be just a bad, bad idea.

So it was inevitable, of course, that Thome (who would have jumped at the chance to rejoin the Sox) would sign with the opportunistic Twins and deliver the key long-distance blows that would help salt away the Central Division title for Minnesota late in the season. His 25 home runs in part-time play—several of them game-winners against the Sox—rejuvenated Minnesota just as their star first baseman Justin Morneau was lost for the season. Guillen, meanwhile, snorted at his critics who dared to question the wisdom of his decision to turn away the popular and well-liked slugger in favor of Kotsay, who hit a miserable .239, and the committee approach to doing things. "If I have to wear this the rest of my life because Jimmy is a fan favorite, player favorite, manager favorite, owner favorite...I mean everyone loves Jim Thome in this organization," Ozzie snapped. "Meanwhile, even when we were struggling, I continued to keep my head up and say, 'I think we did the right thing.'... I don't regret it at all, no."

Guillen earned a measure of redemption for the Thome misfire in his insistence that Williams trade for Juan Pierre, the 32-year-old former Marlin and Dodger with Maury Wills–like speed. Pierre was impressive. He was the hardest-working player in spring training and earned praise as a "table-setter and mood-setter" by hitting coach Greg Walker. Pierre made Sox fans forget all about their departed favorite, Scott Podsednik, by providing even greater speed at the top of the lineup than "Pods." His 68 stolen bases led the league, and Juan became the first Sox player to achieve that since Luis Aparicio in 1961—that "parallel year" again. Juan was a real grinder, just as Guillen had promised. The 2010 White Sox swiped 160 bases, the most since 1992, when Tim Raines and Steve Sax were running loose on the base paths. "Go-Go" baseball had returned to the South Side after a long absence with a rejuvenated Alex Rios chipping in 34 steals.

On the other hand, Gordon Beckham (shifted over to play second base to make room for the disappointing Mark Teahen), who was counted on to be a "doubles machine" and a budding franchise superstar, regressed. He struggled to keep his average above .200 until a late summer spurt pushed him up to the .250 mark before a hand injury in early September closed him down for the final three weeks. The Sox were plagued by these kinds of nuisance injuries all year—the garden-variety muscle pulls, foot problems, sore arms, and beanball bruises (Carlos Quentin finished second to teammate and league leader Juan Pierre in getting hit by pitches in 2010 and also missed time), capped off by Jake Peavy's weird season-ending latissimus dorsi muscle tear in his right posterior shoulder on July 6. In layman's language the muscle pulled away from the bone, and the fans could only wonder if this was a career-ender despite Peavy's solemn vow to come back strong in 2011.

Bobby Jenks tested the patience of his employers with another season of arm problems and more blown saves. By year's end he had written the unlikely ending chapter to his once promising Chicago career. The bullpen was further devastated by injuries to workhorse Matt Thornton—a 2010 All-Star selection. J.J. Putz, a fine free agent pickup who recorded 27 straight scoreless appearances, and Erick Threets, who looked impressive, however briefly, went on the disabled list in August, forcing the Sox to summon the inexperienced Lucas Harrell, Carlos Torres, and Chris Sale, their prized June 2010 First-Year Player Draft pick out of Florida Gulf Coast University, from Charlotte. The 21-year-old Sale, the first rookie draft choice to make it up to the parent club in his first year of pro ball since Alex Fernandez in 1990, showed a lot of poise on the mound and, by the end of the year, was closing games in place of the wounded Jenks.

Andruw Jones slugged his 400th career home run on July 11 as a member of the 2010 Sox. (Courtesy of the Chicago White Sox)

With Peavy down for the count, Williams went to market on July 30 and traded top-rated prospect Daniel Hudson to Arizona for Edwin Jackson, a hard-throwing right-hander who had tossed a no-hitter for the D'backs against Tampa Bay earlier in the season. Letting go of Hudson was a calculated gamble. But no one expected the kid to step it up during a hot pennant chase like this one, so Williams elected to roll the dice and opted for a pitcher instead of going after the Washington Nationals' lead-footed slugger Adam Dunn, who was made available but at a high cost. With some fine-tuning from Don Cooper, Jackson seemed to have found himself—winning his first three decisions and tying a franchise record shared by Floyd Bannister and Ed Walsh by fanning 10 batters in at least three consecutive games.

Although the Sox had dramatically improved upon their ability to score runs with two outs—a chronic problem in recent years—the offense continued its struggles. Power from the left side was absent. Thome, for all of his strikeouts, base-running problems, and slowness afoot, was sorely missed, forcing Williams to take desperate measures. On August 30, the GM acquired 12-time All-Star Manny Ramirez from the Dodgers on waivers—a clear repudiation of Guillen's DH-by-committee stratagem. Would Manny be Manny, the RBI machine everyone remembered from his productive Cleveland and Boston days, or a manager's headache? "This guy's been there and done that," explained Williams. "It's just a matter of him getting his timing back, and he'll be effective." At his introductory media press conference, he addressed the reporters in Spanish—another amusing, if not puzzling example of Manny being Manny.

As it turned out, Ramirez left behind no negative vibes in the clubhouse or on the field. He went about his business quietly, too quietly as a matter of fact, delivering only one home run and just two measly RBIs—he was a non-factor however you want to look at it. A seven-game winning streak—including a stunning three-game sweep of the Red Sox in Fenway in early September—stirred fans' hopes, but that was followed by an eight-game losing streak, which nailed the coffin lid shut for the 2010 White Sox. Finishing up 5–13 against the Twins didn't help matters, either—the Sox simply gave away some easily winnable games to Minnesota. A better record against the two dregs of the division, and the Twins would have assured the Sox of a postseason appearance, but that is just hindsight.

Nevertheless, it was an exciting, but otherwise emotionally draining season—on paper a success, but in reality a frustrating, worrisome year for no other reason than the impending threat of losing Paul Konerko and A.J. Pierznski to free agency. Konerko, who had put up MVP numbers in his walk year, finished fifth in balloting for the league's highest award after the votes were in. Paulie had been the heart and soul of the franchise for 12 seasons, and A.J. was the face of White Sox toughness. In a year when management retired Frank Thomas' No. 35 and honored him with his special day, and when Chicago said their fond farewells to the beloved team organist Nancy Faust, who retired after 40 stellar seasons, the fate of the two heroes of '05 hung in the balance as the curtain came down on 2K-10. But as every Sox fan knew and understood, it all boiled down to economics. With a bloated payroll of $108 million in 2010, the White Sox ranked seventh in all of Major League Baseball. They were exceeded in this category only by the Yankees, Red Sox, Cubs, Phillies, Mets, and Tigers. But for the fourth straight year, home attendance sagged, so how could anyone reasonably expect the front office to reconcile or even try to match the salaries Paulie and A.J. were likely to command on the open market when cutbacks seemed to be a moral certainty in 2011? That issue was quietly and happily settled in the off-season when the Sox stretched their thinning financial resources and re-signed both players to extended contracts and added Washington Nationals slugger Adam Dunn for the next four years at a hefty $56 million price tag. Where was this money coming from?

Nothing had ever come easy for this team or its fan base, and not even a solid winning season like this one could assuage or put to rest our collective anxieties. For at least some fans, there was one small consolation prize left to enjoy. The Minnesota Twins went stone cold in the AL Division Series and were once again devoured by the Yankees in one easy swallow. Jim Thome made the final out in the first two losses at Target Field and went 1-for-10 in the Yankees' sweep, leaving the many Minnesota-haters to gloat: who's your daddy now, Twins fans? Finally, the tiresome media praise heaped on the Twins' system, the Twins' way of doing things, the "Gee, look how smart the Twins are," ad nauseam was silenced…for the moment. Payback (supplied by the Yankees in this instance) was most satisfying. Could it just be that the Twins' system wasn't that great after all?

	G	AB	H	R	2B	3B	HR	RBI	SB	AVG.
Gordon Beckham	128	444	112	58	25	2	9	49	4	.252
Ramon Castro	36	115	32	18	2	0	8	21	1	.278
Alejandro De Aza	19	30	9	7	3	0	0	2	2	.300
Tyler Flowers	8	11	1	2	0	0	0	0	0	.091
Andruw Jones	95	278	64	41	12	1	19	48	9	.230
Paul Konerko	149	548	171	89	30	1	39	111	0	.312
Mark Kotsay	107	327	78	30	17	2	8	31	1	.239
Brent Lillibridge	64	98	22	19	5	2	2	16	5	.224
Donny Lucy	7	15	5	2	3	0	1	2	1	.333
Brent Morel	21	65	15	9	3	0	3	7	2	.231
Jayson Nix	22	49	8	3	1	0	1	5	0	.163
Juan Pierre	160	651	179	96	18	3	1	47	68	.275
A.J. Pierzynski	128	474	128	43	29	0	9	56	3	.270
Carlos Quentin	131	453	110	73	25	2	26	87	2	.243
Alexei Ramirez	156	585	165	83	29	2	18	70	13	.282
Manny Ramirez	24	69	18	6	1	0	1	2	0	.261
Alex Rios	146	567	161	89	29	3	21	88	34	.284
Mark Teahen	77	233	60	31	13	2	4	25	3	.258
Dayan "the Tank" Viciedo	38	104	32	17	7	0	5	13	1	.308
Omar Vizquel	99	344	95	36	11	1	2	30	11	.276
		5,484	1,467	752	263	21	177	710	160	.267

	W	L	GS	CG	IP	H	BB	K	SHO	SV	ERA
Mark Buehrle	13	13	33	3	210⅓	246	49	99	0	0	4.28
John Danks	15	11	32	1	213	189	70	162	1	0	3.72
Gavin Floyd	10	13	31	1	187⅓	199	58	151	0	0	4.08
Freddy Garcia	12	6	28	0	157	171	45	89	0	0	4.64
Lucas Harrell	1	0	3	0	24	34	17	15	0	0	4.88
Daniel Hudson	1	1	3	0	15⅔	17	11	14	0	0	6.32
Gregory Infante	0	0	0	0	4⅔	2	4	5	0	0	0.00
Edwin Jackson	4	2	11	0	75	73	18	77	0	0	3.24
Bobby Jenks	1	3	0	0	52⅔	54	18	61	0	27	4.44
Scott Linebrink	3	2	0	0	57⅓	59	17	52	0	0	4.40
Jeff Marquez	0	0	0	0	1	2	0	0	0	0	18.00
Jake Peavy	7	6	17	1	107	98	34	93	1	0	4.63
Tony Pena	5	3	3	0	100⅔	108	45	56	0	0	5.10
J.J. Putz	7	5	0	0	54	41	15	65	0	3	2.83
Chris Sale	2	1	0	0	23⅔	15	10	32	0	4	1.93
Sergio Santos	2	2	0	0	51⅔	53	26	56	0	1	2.96
Matt Thornton	5	4	0	0	60⅔	41	20	81	0	8	2.67
Erick Threets	0	0	0	0	12⅓	9	3	6	0	0	0.00
Carlos Torres	0	1	1	0	13⅔	23	9	13	0	0	8.56
Randy Williams	0	1	0	0	25	37	21	22	0	0	5.40
	88	74	162	6	1,446⅓	1,471	490	1,149	10	43	4.10

2

Player Profiles

Baseball is a game of timeless comparisons, uniting fans of all ages in a multigenerational debate as old as the sport itself. In the warm twilight of a July evening in Chicago, fans of the White Sox and Cubs proudly defended their team—and their neighborhood turf—in unwinnable arguments for bragging rights. Who was *really* the better shortstop pound for pound, Louie Aparicio or Ernie Banks?

There is no easy answer to this and other unsolvable baseball riddles. But perhaps we can mediate matters somewhat by presenting an All-Star cast of White Sox players representing 10 decades of South Side baseball.

Not every player selected for inclusion is Hall of Fame material. Many are long forgotten. However, each player left behind his imprimatur on Sox history, in a moment of diamond brilliance or throughout an entire career. We have chosen major award winners, the players who lingered in Chicago for 10 or more seasons, perennial fan favorites, the Black Sox (because the scandal is a defining epoch of team history), and a sprinkling of human interest stories.

We have tried to avoid the natural inclination to attach greater significance to the players and events of recent memory, preferring to draw equally from all eras. We hope we have succeeded in bringing the past alive by introducing to younger fans some of the men who thrilled and delighted previous generations of White Sox fans.

Agee, Tommie

White Sox: 1965–67
Outfielder
Birthplace: Magnolia, Alabama

B: August 9, 1942
D: January 22, 2001
Batted right, threw right
Ht. 5–11; **Wt.** 195

Agee, Tommie

White Sox	G	AB	H	AVG	RBI	R	2B	3B	HR	SA	SB
1965	10	19	3	.158	3	2	1	0	0	.211	0
1966	160	629	172	.273	86	98	27	8	22	.447	44
1967	158	529	124	.234	52	73	26	2	14	.371	28
Career	1,129	3,912	999	.255	433	558	170	27	130	.412	167

Signed by the Cleveland Indians and awarded a $60,000 bonus in 1960, Tommie Agee was a late bloomer. The Tribe simply lost patience after the speedy outfielder failed to make the grade in three separate trials.

The nervous rookie, who had broken both his hands in a minor league brawl in 1963, was added to the list of players changing teams in the big winter trade that brought Tommy John to Chicago on January 20, 1965. Al Lopez had big plans for Agee, but he broke his hand in a preseason exhibition game, further delaying his arrival until 1966. That spring the new Sox manager, Eddie Stanky, said to Agee, "You're my center fielder, no matter what!" Ken Berry, who was Al Lopez's center fielder the year before, was shifted to left for the time being.

Manager Eddie Stanky demonstrates the finer points of bunting to rookie Tommie Agee in 1966.

Agee cracked a home run off of Dean Chance of the California Angels on Opening Day 1966. It was a confidence-building moment for the young speedster out of Grambling University, and it provided the impetus for him to go on and win Rookie of the Year honors. He was only the third White Sox player so honored by the Baseball Writers of America. And in so doing, Tommie became the first Sox

Gus Zernial (catching) and Joe Dobson (enjoying) help Marilyn Monroe perfect her swing, Pasadena, California, 1951.

player to swat 20 home runs and steal 20 bases in the same season.

Tommie lost 40 points off his batting average in 1967, and this decline was a factor in Ed Short's poorly-thought-out decision to trade Agee and Al Weis to the New York Mets for Tommy Davis, Jack Fisher, and Buddy Booker on December 15, 1967. Short hand-delivered a future pennant to the Mets. Eighth place was the Sox's 1968 destiny with this trio of veterans added to the roster.

Allen, Dick

White Sox: 1972–74
First baseman
Birthplace: Wampum, Pennsylvania

B: March 8, 1942
Bats right, throws right
Ht. 5–11; **Wt.** 187

Allen, Dick (Richie)

White Sox	G	AB	H	AVG	RBI	R	2B	3B	HR	SA	SB
1972	148	506	156	.308	113	90	28	5	37	.603	19
1973	72	250	79	.316	41	39	20	3	16	.612	7
1974	128	462	139	.301	88	84	23	1	32	.563	7
Career	1,749	6,322	1,848	.292	1,556	894	320	79	351	.534	133

The passage of time has failed to dim the memory of the diamond thrills provided by one Richard Anthony Allen. There are fans who still maintain that Dick Allen was the greatest White Sox first baseman to grace the Comiskey Park infield, though his batting exploits were compressed into only two and a half seasons.

Controversy followed Dick Allen wherever he played. In Philadelphia, the city where Allen began his career, the boos cascaded out of the stands every time he took the field. He was forever branded a malcontent—a sullen, moody player who marched to his own drummer.

Contrasting his unhappy experiences in the City of Brotherly Love to Chicago, where the fans openly embraced their "antiestablishment" hero, Allen remarked: "I feel more a part of this team than any other place I've been. There's a different feeling around here. In Philadelphia you play your heart out and if you come up a loser they really give it to you. Here the people make excuses for you if you lose. The guys around here are a lot easier to talk to without them getting mad or offended."

Efforts to bring Allen to Chicago were initiated on September 15, 1970, by Roland Hemond, when he placed a phone call to Cardinals general manager Bing Devine from his hotel room in Kansas City. The new Sox manager, Chuck Tanner, knew the Allen family, and he believed that Richie might be agreeable to playing for his old friend in Chicago. Tanner lived in New Castle, Pennsylvania, a stone's throw from Wampum, the small town where Allen had starred in prep basketball.

However, it wasn't until December 2, 1971, that a deal for Allen could be finalized. Richie was playing in Los Angeles and was as unhappy as ever when he received word that he was going to Chicago for pitcher Tommy John and infielder Steve Huntz. At first Allen balked. He demanded a $135,000

Dick Allen always wore a helmet in the field—a habit acquired in Philadelphia when the fans threw objects at him.

contract from his new employers. The Sox said yes. Allen agreed—then he failed to show up for spring training. Finally, when the players decided to call a strike and head for home, Dick Allen showed up in camp, bat in hand and ready to play.

In 1972 Allen won two-thirds of a Triple Crown. He smashed two inside-the-park home runs against the Minnesota Twins on July 31 to tie a major league record. He shattered Bill Melton's one-year-old home run record, drove home 113 runs, and provided levels of excitement not seen in Comiskey Park in many a year. Allen reinvigorated a dying franchise. Hemond conceded as much when he called Allen the "savior of the franchise."

By virtue of an MVP season, Dick Allen was accorded special favors from Tanner, whose dual set of clubhouse rules wore thin with the veteran players who endured pay cuts in order to help owner John Allyn to pay Dick's boxcar salary. Things really unraveled after Tanner's prize pupil sustained a season-ending leg fracture on June 28, 1973.

The following year Allen led the league in home runs, but he crossed swords with Ron Santo, who had just come over from the Cubs. Santo was not the kind of player to put up with a lot of bull. Then, after Tanner decided to stiffen his training rules, Allen, bothered by a nagging shoulder injury, decided he had had enough and walked out on his teammates on September 14. As it turned out, Chuck Tanner was no more capable of "handling" the contentious Dick Allen than any of his previous managers in three different cities.

Roland Hemond was only partially correct when he praised this highly gifted but enigmatic player as a White Sox "savior." By the same token, Dick Allen nearly destroyed that which he had built up.

Aloma, Luis

White Sox: 1950–53
Pitcher
Birthplace: Havana, Cuba

B: June 19, 1923
D: April 7, 1997
Batted right, threw right
Ht. 6–2; **Wt.** 195

Aloma, Luis

White Sox	W	L	Pct	ERA	G	CG	IP	H	BB	K	ShO	Sv
1950	7	2	.778	3.80	42	0	87⅔	77	53	49	0	4
1951	6	0	1.000	1.82	25	1	69⅓	52	24	25	1	3
1952	3	1	.750	4.28	25	0	40	42	11	18	0	6
1953	2	0	1.000	4.70	24	0	38⅓	41	23	23	0	2
Career	18	3	.857	3.44	116	1	235⅓	212	111	115	1	15

The short but sweet pitching career of Luis Aloma was filled with many superlatives. Louie owns the best career winning percentage among Sox hurlers if you include pitchers with fewer than 500 innings.

Aloma was discovered in 1944 by Joe Cambria, the legendary Washington Senators scout who signed more than

Luis Aloma

400 Cuban ballplayers following the close of World War II. Louie drifted through the Senators' minor league system in the 1940s, until the Buffalo club of the International League claimed him in 1949.

Sox general manager Frank Lane purchased his contract on April 19, 1950, primarily because he needed a Spanish-speaking interpreter for star shortstop Chico Carrasquel and pitcher Mike Fornieles. In order to acquire Aloma for the Sox, Lane also shipped pitcher Alex Carrasquel—Chico's uncle—to Buffalo, where Paul Richards was managing at the time.

Used primarily in emergency relief when he wasn't conveying messages from Richards to Carrasquel, Louie was very effective. "His No. 1 stock-in-trade is courage," Richards said of Aloma. "He throws strikes out there. He isn't afraid to get the ball over."

Altrock, Nicholas

White Sox: 1903–09
Pitcher
Nickname: Nick
Birthplace: Cincinnati, Ohio

B: September 15, 1876
D: January 20, 1965
Batted right and left, threw left
Ht. 5–10; **Wt.** 178

Altrock, Nick

White Sox	W	L	Pct	ERA	G	CG	IP	H	BB	K	ShO
1903	4	3	.571	2.15	12	6	71	59	19	19	1
1904	20	15	.571	2.96	38	31	307	274	48	87	6
1905	22	12	.647	1.88	38	31	315⅔	274	63	97	3
1906	21	12	.636	2.06	38	25	287⅔	269	42	99	4
1907	8	12	.400	2.57	30	15	213⅔	210	31	61	1
1908	3	7	.300	2.71	23	8	136	127	18	21	1
1909	0	1	.000	5.00	1	1	9	16	1	2	0
Career	84	74	.532	2.67	218	128	1,515	1,455	272	425	16

Baseball has had its share of zany comedians—Germany Schaefer, Al Schacht, Max Patkin, and myriad others. Nick Altrock, however, was famous for his clowning antics that amused Washington Senators fans long after this once-famous pitcher retired from active duty. It is in his familiar role as the lovable, goofing clown who pranced along the sidelines before and after Senators games that the fans best remember Altrock.

As a mainstay of the White Sox pitching staff during the glorious Hitless Wonder era, the gnomelike lefty recorded 20-win seasons in 1904, 1905, and 1906. In the 1906 World Series he won the opener after Frank Owen and Doc White, the two pitchers ahead of him in the rotation, turned up sick. Nick lost the fourth game 1–0 to "Three-Finger" Brown.

Altrock was apprenticed to a shoemaker and patiently worked at his craft until 1898, when he saw his chance to play baseball with a team in Grand Rapids, Michigan. In 1902 he was sold to the Boston Pilgrims after spending much of the year with the Milwaukee Brewers of the American Association.

In his first and only start against the White Sox on June 5, 1903, in Boston, Altrock surrendered eight runs in the first

Nick Altrock: Baseball's funny man was also a star pitcher.

inning. Nick was released two days later by his manager, Jimmy Collins, who ridiculed him as "excess baggage." With tears welling in his eyes, Altrock hunted up Comiskey after the game and begged for a tryout. Despite the poor showing (Altrock was suffering from an illness at the time), Charles Comiskey recognized a diamond in the rough and signed the 28-year-old southpaw to a White Sox contract.

Superstitious to the point of near paranoia, Nick Altrock would not sit for a picture on Friday or pass a cemetery in full moon at midnight. But he was a tough competitor and the workhorse of the White Sox staff before the arrival of Ed Walsh. "He is one of the pitchers who believes in a return of the old order of pitching," commented his manager Fielder Jones, "...the day when a twirler was worked in every other game, or even successive games." Overwork and age caught up with him in 1909. He was traded to Washington with Jiggs Donahue and outfielder Gavvy Cravath on May 16, 1909, for pitcher "Sleepy" Bill Burns—an intermediary between the gamblers and the Black Sox players prior to the 1919 World Series. It was one of the 10 worst trades in Chicago White Sox history.

The wit and wisdom of Nick Altrock were showcased nationwide in the Hearst newspapers during the early years of the Great Depression. Altrock's ruminations amused and delighted a generation of readers who tried to make sense of his daffiness. "Our Washington club's success this season," he wrote in 1930, "is due to its *esprit de corps*. That's French for hash-browned potatoes."

Alvarez, Wilson

White Sox: 1991–97
Pitcher
Birthplace: Maracaibo, Venezuela

B: March 24, 1970
Bats left, throws left
Ht. 6–1; **Wt.** 235

Alvarez, Wilson

White Sox	W	L	Pct	ERA	G	CG	IP	H	BB	K	ShO
1991	3	2	.600	3.51	10	2	56⅓	47	29	32	1
1992	5	3	.625	5.20	34	0	100⅓	103	65	66	0
1993	15	8	.652	2.85	31	1	207⅔	168	122	155	1
1994	12	8	.600	3.45	24	2	161⅔	147	62	108	1
1995	8	11	.421	4.32	29	3	175	171	93	118	0
1996	15	10	.600	4.22	35	0	217⅓	216	97	181	0
1997	9	8	.529	3.03	22	2	145⅔	126	55	110	1
Career	102	92	.526	3.96	355	12	1747⅔	1,624	805	1,330	5

Wilson Alvarez was the "long-term dividend" paid to the White Sox by the Texas Rangers when they acquired Harold Baines for the stretch drive on July 29, 1989. The hard-throwing southpaw, who was only 19 at the time, had tossed *12 no-hitters* between 1981 and 1986, when he was pitching in Venezuelan youth baseball. Now he is a national celebrity in his homeland, and he enjoys the distinction of being the winningest (single-season) Venezuelan pitcher in the big leagues. His 15 victories in 1993 set the standard, which he equaled in 1996.

Early in his career some doubts were expressed as to whether Wilson's performance would match his enormous potential. These concerns were put to rest in 1993, when he ended the season with seven consecutive wins and then helped the Sox stay alive in the playoffs by whipping the Blue Jays 6–1 in Game 3, played at the Toronto Skydome. Second-guessing Sox fans wondered why manager Gene Lamont had not simply opened the playoffs with Wilson instead of

Wilson Alvarez

waiting until the third game when they found themselves down two games to none. In 1994 Alvarez picked up where he had left off, beginning the strike-shortened season with eight straight wins to run his streak to a franchise-record-tying 15 in a row.

Alvarez broke in spectacularly in 1991. In his second major league start in Baltimore on August 11, Wilson no-hit the Orioles to become the eighth-youngest pitcher in history to accomplish the feat.

Through the 2010 season, Alvarez ranked fourth all-time among Venezuelan-born pitchers with 102 victories. In 2006 he joined the Pittsburgh Pirates organization as a pitching instructor. He was appointed pitching coach for their State College minor league affiliate a year later.

Aparicio, Luis

White Sox: 1956–62; 1968–70
Shortstop
Nickname: Little Louie
Birthplace: Maracaibo, Venezuela

B: April 29, 1934
Bats right, throws right
Ht. 5–9; **Wt.** 160

Aparicio, Luis

White Sox	G	AB	H	AVG	RBI	R	2B	3B	HR	SA	SB
1956	152	533	142	.266	56	69	19	6	3	.341	21
1957	143	575	148	.257	41	82	22	6	3	.332	28
1958	145	557	148	.266	40	76	20	9	2	.345	29
1959	152	612	157	.257	51	98	18	5	6	.332	56
1960	153	600	166	.277	61	86	20	7	2	.343	51
1961	156	625	170	.272	45	91	24	4	6	.352	53
1962	153	581	140	.241	40	72	23	5	7	.334	31
1968	155	622	164	.264	36	55	24	4	4	.334	17
1969	156	599	168	.280	51	77	24	5	5	.362	24
1970	146	552	173	.313	43	86	29	3	5	.404	8
Career	2,599	10,230	2,677	.262	791	1,335	394	92	83	.343	506

The arrival of Louie Aparicio continued a long-standing White Sox tradition of excellence at the shortstop position dating back to 1930.

The eldest of six children, Louie was the son of Luis Aparicio Sr., Venezuela's greatest shortstop, who spurned an offer from the Washington Senators in 1939 in order to remain in his homeland. His son Louie played amateur ball around Maracaibo in the late 1940s while working as an accountant for a local pharmacy. Ticketed for certain stardom, Aparicio replaced his father as the starting shortstop for the Gavilanes club of the Venezuelan Association on November 18, 1953. The ballclub was co-owned by Aparicio Sr. and managed by Red Kress, who played briefly for the White Sox in the early 1930s.

Kress, who was moonlighting from his job as a Cleveland Indians coach, tipped off his employers about the young Venezuelan prospect. After the Tribe failed to act on the tip, Frank Lane purchased Louie's contract from the Caracas club of the Venezuelan Winter League. Aparicio was barely 20 years old when he stepped off the plane in Miami, where he was met by Glen Miller, one of the executives in the Sox farm system.

Luis Aparicio. Above: rookie sensation, 1956; bottom: the second time around

The Venezuelan Connection—Aparicio, Ozzie Guillen, and Chico Carrasquel

He completed a two-year apprenticeship in the minors before replacing Chico Carrasquel as the White Sox' everyday shortstop in 1956. Sox Manager Marty Marion, a former star shortstop, refined Louie's fielding after noticing that he was taking way too much time removing the ball from his glove and firing to first. Marion suggested that Louie switch to a smaller glove, and the change worked. Aparicio was now ready to step in and replace Chico.There was great irony in the situation Louie found himself in. As a kid, Aparicio used to stand outside the ballpark in Maracaibo hoping to catch a glimpse of his baseball hero—Chico Carrasquel—hoping that he might pause to sign an autograph.

Yankees manager Casey Stengel joined Marty Marion in a chorus of praise for the 22-year-old rookie who played more games than any other major league shortstop that year. In 1956 Aparicio led the American League in stolen bases—and for the next eight years after that. Speed and defense were his special gifts.

As a shortstop Louie had no equals. Playing side by side with Nellie Fox for seven years, he formed the nucleus of one of the slickest fielding double-play combos the game has ever seen. In 1959 Louie finished second in Most Valuable Player voting to his pal Nellie Fox, whom he would name a son after. Aparicio led the league in assists from 1956 through 1961. For eight years running (1959–1966), statistics proved that Louie was the circuit's top shortstop. It was Aparicio who converted Vic Power's ground ball into a pennant-clinching double play on September 22, 1959.

Louie believed he was a White Sox player for life, but general manager Ed Short had other ideas. On January 14, 1963, Short traded Louie and Al Smith to Baltimore for four players, including Hoyt Wilhelm and Pete Ward. Bitter and angry over what he considered a betrayal of his loyalty, Aparicio predicted that the Sox would not win another pennant for 40 years. His prophecy held up…it was 42.

Returning to Chicago in 1968, Aparicio enjoyed some of his finest and most productive years. He topped the .300 mark for the only time in his career in 1970. Dispelling the myth that players do little on their testimonial "day," Louie collected four hits in nine at-bats on "Aparicio Day"—July 18, 1970. "When I came to this country as a 19-year-old, I was mighty scared," he told the crowd. "But everyone has always been real good to me." In that otherwise forgettable season, Louie eclipsed Luke Appling's record of longevity by playing in his 2,219th game on September 25.

Rumors circulated that Louie might become the next Sox manager, but this notion was put to rest when Roland Hemond traded him to Boston for Mike Andrews and Luis Alvarado on December 1, 1970. He retired after the 1973 season and returned to his home in Venezuela to start anew as vice president and owner of a Triple-A team.

Considered by many to be the greatest shortstop of his time, Louie is credited by baseball historians with resurrecting the stolen base as an offensive weapon at a time when teams traditionally relied on the home run and the big inning.

On August 14, 1984, Louie returned to Comiskey Park to take part in homecoming festivities honoring him on the occasion of his Hall of Fame induction. His familiar No. 11 was retired by Sox management in a pregame ceremony. In poor health at the time, Louie reacquainted himself with White Sox fans by participating in a spring training "fantasy camp" with several of his 1950s teammates in 1986.

In a surprise move that stunned older White Sox fans, Louie's No. 11 was officially "unretired" on February 8, 2010. The move came as a welcoming gesture to free agent shortstop Omar Vizquel who asked his fellow countryman if he would mind his wearing it for the 2010 season, after Ozzie Guillen refused to give up his No. 13, Vizquel's traditional number. Aparicio was most gracious. "If there is one player who I would like to see wear my uniform number with the White Sox, it is Omar Vizquel," he said. "I have known Omar for a long time. Along with being an outstanding player, he is a good and decent man." After banging out a single up the middle against James Shields of the Tampa Bay Rays on May 30, 2010 (his last season before retiring), Vizquel passed up Aparicio in career hits for a shortstop with 2,675—which placed him second behind Derek Jeter on the all-time list.

Luis Ernesto Aparicio restored the Go to "Go-Go" in the second half of the 1950s—an era that culminated in a 1959 AL pennant.

Appling, Luke

White Sox: 1930–43; 1945–50
Shortstop
Nickname: Old Aches and Pains
Birthplace: High Point, North Carolina

B: April 2, 1907
D: January 3, 1991
Batted right, threw right
Ht. 5–10; **Wt.** 183

Appling, Luke

White Sox	G	AB	H	AVG	RBI	R	2B	3B	HR	SA	SB
1930	6	26	8	.308	2	2	2	0	0	.385	2
1931	96	297	69	.232	28	36	13	4	1	.313	9
1932	139	489	134	.274	63	66	20	10	3	.374	9
1933	151	612	197	.322	85	90	36	10	6	.443	6
1934	118	452	137	.303	61	75	28	6	2	.405	3
1935	153	525	161	.307	71	94	28	6	1	.389	12
1936	138	526	182	.388	128	111	31	7	6	.508	10
1937	154	574	182	.317	77	98	42	8	4	.439	18
1938	81	294	89	.303	44	41	14	0	0	.350	1
1939	148	516	162	.314	56	82	16	6	0	.368	16
1940	150	566	197	.348	79	96	27	13	0	.442	3
1941	154	592	186	.314	57	93	26	8	1	.390	12
1942	142	543	142	.262	53	78	26	4	3	.341	17
1943	155	585	192	.328	80	63	33	2	3	.407	27
1945	18	58	21	.362	10	12	2	2	1	.517	1
1946	149	582	180	.309	55	59	27	5	1	.378	6
1947	139	503	154	.306	49	67	29	0	8	.412	8
1948	139	497	156	.314	47	63	16	2	0	.354	10
1949	142	492	148	.301	58	82	21	5	5	.394	7
1950	50	128	30	.234	13	11	3	4	0	.320	2
Career	2,422	8,857	2,749	.310	1,116	1,319	440	102	45	.398	179

Voted the greatest White Sox player of all time in two separate fan polls commissioned in 1949 and 1969, Luke Appling was a small-town southern boy who arrived in Chicago with little fanfare on September 9, 1930. The Pullman porter aboard the afternoon train from Atlanta advised him to detrain at 47th Street on Chicago's South Side and catch a cab to Comiskey Park. With a battered suitcase in hand, Appling wandered into the park just in time to see his future teammates complete the final out of a 10–1 victory over Boston. Appling was overwhelmed by the size of the park and the thousands of fans who streamed past him toward the exit. "Atlanta was never like that," Appling later remembered. "And I wasn't sure I'd ever like Chicago after such a jostling."

The gangly young shortstop was penciled into the starting lineup the next day by manager Donie Bush after fielding 500 practice grounders and fungo flies during an exhausting pregame workout. When it was over, Appling was advised to take his shower and suit up. "I was so weary I could hardly pull off my uniform." Vintage Appling. Aches, pains, and complaints. It never let up. "I swear that [Comiskey] park must have been built on a junkyard!" (As it turned out, he was right.)

But there were few people in Atlanta who doubted his abilities. Luke Appling was encouraged to play professional ball by his dad, his Uncle Lon, and his high school coach Lucien Hopa. At the end of his sophomore year at Oglethorpe University, Appling signed a bonus contract with the Atlanta Crackers of the Southern Association, where he would play less than a year. One morning his manager, Jimmy Dobbs, awakened him with the news that his contract had been picked up by the Chicago Cubs.

"Old Man" Luke Appling, seated in a rocking chair in his 20th season, 1950

After he finished packing, Appling was advised that the Cubs deal was off. As it turned out, the Chicago White Sox, and not the Cubs, were the interested party. The Comiskeys traded outfielder Douglas Taitt to the Wrigleys, along with $20,000 of their cash, to secure Appling. The deal was engineered by Milt Stock, Eddie Stanky's father-in-law.

Appling was a defensive liability those first few years of his career. He was rushed into the majors much too quickly, and his anxiety often got the best of him. *Chicago Tribune* sportswriter Ed Burns labeled him the Pneumatic Glove. Luke fumbled his way into such notoriety that the fans began calling him Kid Boots. Luckily, the Pneumatic Glove was willing to accept direction from his managers and coaches. By the late 1930s, Appling was a gem of consistency thanks to Jimmie Dykes' counsel and advice. It was his hitting abilities, however, that elevated Appling to stardom. In 1933, his first great year, Appling batted .322. Playing in hot, muggy St. Louis on August 5 of that year, Luke pounded out five hits in six at-bats off Bump Hadley and three other Brownie pitchers. All afternoon, the St. Louis players heaped abuse upon Appling from the bench, but his composure held. The kid had matured in his thinking and wouldn't let anything bother him. The Sox eventually lost 10–9 in 12 innings, but Appling often referred to this particular contest as the greatest game of his career.

There were many other fine individual accomplishments. Appling won the American League batting championship in 1936 and again in 1943. No other Sox player has laid claim to a batting title before or since, and his .388 average in 1936 stands as an all-time club record. Luke's 27-game hitting streak, which began on August 31, 1936, and ended on September 26, was seriously challenged on only two other occasions in team history. Gifted with a great batting eye, Appling could drive a pitcher to exhaustion by fouling off pitch after pitch before selecting the right one to drive into the gap. Ted Lyons swore that he once saw Appling spoil 14 consecutive pitches delivered by Red Ruffing.

The "iron man" rule suited the nature of Old Aches and Pains. On August 5, 1949, he surpassed Rabbit Maranville's record of 2,153 games played at shortstop. It was a record the "experts" claimed would never be broken.

Despite a groundswell from White Sox fans, the Comiskeys refused to bend to pressure and name Appling team manager when his playing days ended after the 1950 season. In 1951 he accepted their consolation offer to manage the Sox' Memphis affiliate, but after a few seasons his contract was not renewed. He later served as a base coach under Don Gutteridge and Chuck Tanner in 1970 and 1971. Luke was a minor league hitting instructor for the Atlanta Braves at the end of his life.

Luke Appling was elected to baseball's Hall of Fame in 1964. Another high point in his career occurred at the Cracker Jack Old Timer's Classic held in Washington on July 19, 1982, when the 75-year-old ex-Sox-great slammed a home run off 61-year-old Warren Spahn. During his entire 20-year career, Appling hit only 45. "It was a good pitch," he explained. "And I just swung away." For Luke Appling, that was quite an admission.

Bahnsen, Stan

White Sox: 1972–75
Pitcher
Birthplace: Council Bluffs, Iowa

B: December 15, 1944
Bats right, throws right
Ht. 6–2; **Wt.** 185

Bahnsen, Stan

White Sox	W	L	Pct	ERA	G	CG	IP	H	BB	K	ShO
1972	21	16	.568	3.60	43	5	252⅓	263	73	157	1
1973	18	21	.462	3.57	42	14	282⅓	290	117	120	4
1974	12	15	.444	4.71	38	10	216	230	110	102	1
1975	4	6	.400	6.01	12	2	67⅓	78	40	31	0
Career	146	149	.495	3.61	574	73	2,528	2,440	924	1,359	16

Stanley (aka "Struggle") Bahnsen did his best pitching with two men on base—no exaggeration. White Sox fans who watched Bahnsen win 20 in his first season with the ballclub, then lose 20 the next, recall his many harrowing moments pitching out of one jam after another.

In one of the most remarkable games in the otherwise forgettable 1970s, Bahnsen fired a *12-hit* shutout against the World Champion Oakland A's on June 21, 1973, at Comiskey Park.

Twice Bahnsen flirted with no-hit glory. Two months after his 12-hit masterpiece, Stan carried a no-hitter into the ninth inning at Cleveland's Municipal Stadium when former teammate Walt Williams chopped a single over Bill Melton's head.

Bahnsen was particularly adept at beating the Yankees—the team that signed him to his first professional contract in 1965. Three years later he won American League Rookie of the Year honors on the strength of a fine 17–12 record.

Desperate for third-base help, the Yankees took Rich McKinney straight up for Bahnsen on December 2, 1971.

Stan Bahnsen

McKinney was the top-rated infield prospect within the Sox organization but a bust at the major league level. It was a good short-term trade for Chicago that paid handsome trade dividends down the road.

After a brilliant 1972 season with the Sox, Bahnsen's career went into a permanent tailspin. Announcer Harry Caray heaped a ton of verbal abuse on him for what he considered indifferent play. Jarred by Harry's comments, Bahnsen only allowed his performance to worsen. He was dealt to the Oakland A's on June 15, 1975, for Chet Lemon and Dave Hamilton. After ending his career in 1982, Bahnsen went to work for a Pompano Beach, Florida, electronics firm.

Baines, Harold

White Sox: 1980–89; 1996–97; 2000–01
B: March 15, 1959
Outfielder, designated hitter
Bats left, throws left
Birthplace: St. Michaels, Maryland
Ht. 6–2; **Wt.** 175

Baines, Harold

White Sox	G	AB	H	AVG	RBI	R	2B	3B	HR	SA	SB
1980	141	491	125	.255	49	55	23	6	13	.405	2
1981	82	280	80	.286	41	42	11	7	10	.482	6
1982	161	608	165	.271	105	89	29	8	25	.469	10
1983	156	596	167	.280	99	76	33	2	20	.443	7
1984	147	569	173	.304	94	72	28	10	29	.541	1
1985	160	640	198	.309	113	86	29	3	22	.467	1
1986	145	570	169	.296	88	72	29	2	21	.465	2
1987	132	505	148	.293	93	59	26	4	20	.479	0
1988	158	599	166	.277	81	55	39	1	13	.411	0
1989	96	333	107	.321	56	55	20	1	13	.505	0
1996	143	495	154	.311	95	80	29	0	22	.503	3
1997	93	318	97	.305	52	40	16	0	12	.475	0
2000	24	61	21	.213	9	2	5	0	1	.344	0
2001	32	84	11	.131	8	3	1	0	0	.143	0
Career	2,830	9,908	2,866	.289	1,628	1,299	488	49	384	.465	34

Quiet, reflective, and guarded in his choice of words—especially around reporters—Harold Baines shunned publicity at all costs. "Harold could have owned this town…if he wanted to!" complained one radio broadcaster who reserved his harshest criticism for White Sox owner Jerry Reinsdorf, who ordered Baines' uniform No. 3 retired on August 20, 1989, thus making him only the third active player (Frank Robinson and Phil Niekro were the others) to be accorded such an honor. Maybe Baines *could* have taken the town by storm. He just didn't want to.

For nine years Harold Baines provided steady, even-handed play while patrolling right field. He was a solid contributor at the plate and was the White Sox' all-time leader in home runs for four seasons until Carlton Fisk finally surpassed his mark in 1990. Possessing a batting style reminiscent of Mel Ott, Baines led the American League in game-winning hits with 22 in 1983.

His center-field bullpen shot off of Milwaukee's Chuck Porter on May 9, 1984, ended the longest American League game in history—a 25-inning, eight-hour-and-six-minute marathon won by Chicago 7–6. Harold was named the American League's Designated Hitter of the Year for two consecutive seasons (1987–88) after a knee injury forced manager Jim Fregosi to retire him to the bench. Indeed, the placid Baines enjoyed many fine career moments with the Sox. He was Chicago's perennial All-Star selection from the forgettable White Sox teams of the late 1980s. As he approached the plate on those warm summer nights of 1983 when the stadium was full and the stands were rocking, the fans would greet him with a rhythmic chorus of "Har-old! Har-old! Har-old!" to the musical accompaniment of organist Nancy Faust.

Stardom came slowly for Harold Baines. It was a slow, painful process of maturation and coping with media pressure. Not until his third season did he begin to live up to the glowing expectations set forth by White Sox owner Bill Veeck, who scouted the 12-year-old Baines when the youngster was playing Little League ball on the eastern shore of Maryland. After the White Sox had selected Baines as their first pick in the June 1977 amateur draft, Paul Richards tossed his own log on the fire by predicting that Harold "was on his way to the Hall of Fame. He just stopped by Comiskey Park for 20 years or so."

By the late 1980s, Harold Baines evolved into the league's top designated hitter.

The prophecy was never fulfilled. Harold Baines was traded to the Texas Rangers with infielder Fred Manrique on July 29, 1989, for Sammy Sosa, Wilson Alvarez, and Scott Fletcher. Harold shuttled through Texas, Oakland, and Baltimore before re-signing with the White Sox as a free agent on December 11, 1995. The Sox dusted off his uniform number, and he posted solid numbers as the everyday designated hitter in 1996.

He enjoyed his last productive year in 1999, dividing the season between Cleveland and Baltimore while earning a berth on the American League All-Star team at age 40. Harold is one of seven players to appear in a White Sox uniform on three separate occasions, but in his final go-around in 2001, Baines was a shadow of his former self; another sad case of a veteran star sticking around one year too many. When longtime coach Joe Nossek resigned from the organization, Ozzie Guillen invited his old pal back to U.S. Cellular Field to serve as his bench coach in 2004. That year, while Guillen served a pair of two-game suspensions, Baines managed the White Sox to a 1–3 record. Harold, the silent White Sox star for so many years, is a hero in his hometown of St. Michaels, Maryland, where every January 9 the residents celebrate "Harold Baines Day."

Floyd Baker was the human blotter around the hot corner.

Baker, Floyd

White Sox: 1945–51
Third baseman
Nickname: The Blotter
Birthplace: Luray, Virginia
B: October 10, 1916
Bats left, throws right
Ht. 5–9; **Wt.** 160

Baker, Floyd

White Sox	G	AB	H	AVG	RBI	R	2B	3B	HR	SA	SB
1945	82	208	52	.250	19	22	8	0	0	.288	3
1946	9	24	6	.250	3	2	1	0	0	.292	0
1947	105	371	98	.264	22	61	12	3	0	.313	9
1948	104	335	72	.215	18	47	8	3	0	.257	4
1949	125	388	101	.260	40	38	15	4	1	.327	3
1950	83	186	59	.317	11	26	7	0	0	.355	1
1951	82	133	35	.263	14	24	6	1	0	.323	0
Career	874	2,280	573	.251	196	285	76	13	1	.297	23

Vastly underrated during the years he played on the South Side and all but forgotten by subsequent generations of Sox fans, Floyd Baker led the league in fielding percentage only one time (that was 1949), but he was steady, dependable, and a tremendous asset during some gray years of White Sox baseball. Looking back on his 40-year career in the White Sox organization, general manager Harry Grabiner pointed to the Baker acquisition as his most satisfying player move.

Floyd Baker spurned a football scholarship at George Washington University in order to sign with the St. Louis Browns as a shortstop in 1938. He made it up to the majors in 1943 but played sparingly for the Brownies over the next two seasons. Baker was the "player to be named later" when Grabiner sold backup catcher Tom Turner to the Browns for $12,500 and the privilege of selecting one of the St. Louis utility men for $2,500. Harry picked Baker on December 30, 1944, and deposited the $10,000 in the Sox's cash reserve.

Economics may have been behind many of Harry's "rummage sale" player transactions in the 1930s and 1940s, but this one stands out. After playing for the Sox's Milwaukee affiliate in 1946, Baker arrived in Comiskey Park to stay a year later. It was a testament to Floyd's abilities that he was able to survive Frank Lane's 1948–49 housecleaning when so many veterans were traded or released. Baker hit .317 for the 1950 Sox in a part-time role and was a member of Paul Richards' Go-Go squad that revived the franchise. He was traded to the Washington Senators on October 24, 1951, for infielder Willie Miranda.

Baker came to the plate 2,280 times spanning 874 major league games. He hit only one home run in all those years, and it came as a member of the White Sox in 1949.

Baldwin, James

White Sox: 1995–2001
Pitcher
Nickname: J.B.
Birthplace: Southern Pines, North Carolina

B: July 15, 1971
Bats right, throws right
Ht. 6–3; **Wt.** 210

Baldwin, James

White Sox	W	L	Pct	ERA	G	CG	IP	H	BB	K	ShO	Sv
1995	0	1	.000	12.89	6	0	14⅔	32	9	10	0	0
1996	11	6	.647	4.42	28	0	169	168	57	127	0	0
1997	12	15	.444	5.26	32	1	200	205	83	140	0	0
1998	13	6	.684	5.32	37	1	159	176	60	108	0	0
1999	12	13	.480	5.10	35	1	199⅓	219	81	123	0	0
2000	14	7	.667	4.65	29	2	178	185	59	116	1	0
2001	7	5	.583	4.61	17	2	95.7	109	38	42	1	0
Career	79	74	.516	5.01	266	7	1,322⅔	1,443	486	844	2	2

James Baldwin the ballplayer—not the author—was a power pitcher playing in the time of the power hitters. Offense was on the rise in the mid- to late 1990s, and pitcher earned-run averages took a beating. In different times J.B. might have been far more effective than what his White Sox statistics otherwise indicate. Inconsistency was his biggest problem. At various intervals in his career, Baldwin looked like a world-beater and the "ace-in-waiting." At other times, he tested the patience of Manager Jerry Manuel by pitching up in the strike zone, resulting in frequent home runs by opponents. But when he was on, he was as good as any right-handed pitcher in the league and the unsung hero of the 2000 American League Division Series.

Photo courtesy of Major League Baseball

James Baldwin: No. 37 shows us the two-seamer.

Baldwin was a three-sport athlete at Pine Crest (N.C.) High School and was recruited by several Division I schools for football. Selected in the fourth round of the June 1990 free agent draft, J.B. broke camp with the 1995 White Sox and was penciled into the starting rotation until he was shelled by the Tigers in late May and sent back down for more seasoning. *Baseball America* described his breaking pitch as the best in the American Association, but he showed very little at Nashville to merit a return engagement in Chicago until a year later, when Baldwin adjusted to big-league life and vaulted out of the gate with a 9–1 record in his first 17 starts. Although he faltered just as quickly in the second half, J.B. was named American League Rookie Pitcher of the Year by the *Sporting News*. He led the league in wild pitches in 1997 and was exiled to the bullpen in 1998 as hopes for this strapping right-hander faded. But the relief stint helped him regain command of his curveball. After he rejoined the rotation in mid-June, J.B. closed the year on an 11–3 run with a 3.45 ERA in 17 starts.

The 2000 season would mark another 90-degree turn in his up-and-down fortunes. His 10–1 start was the best since Joel Horlen in 1967—it earned him his first All-Star selection and a victory in the mid-summer classic in Atlanta. Baldwin was the fifth White Sox hurler to win the All-Star Game, and the first since Jack McDowell in 1993. After the break, he complained of a tired arm and recurring shoulder problems that would plague him throughout the second half, limiting his effectiveness and ultimately sidelining him from late August through late September. On August 17 he tied an AL record by plunking four Orioles batsmen. Previously, he had hit only one in 154 innings of work. Baldwin simply fell apart in the second half as problems of inconsistency caught up with him. The White Sox pitching staff was in shambles by the time the 2000 Division Series rolled around. Devastated by injuries and the ineffectiveness of its starters, the team was ill-prepared for postseason play, but Baldwin delivered a surprising and heroic performance in Game 3 at Seattle when their backs were against the wall. J.B. allowed the Mariners just three hits and one run over six innings, but his teammates mustered no offense as Seattle scratched out a tie-breaking run in the bottom of the ninth.

After the season, Baldwin underwent arthroscopic surgery to remove a bone chip and repair his ailing shoulder. Under the circumstances, the White Sox were unwilling to lock him up with a long-term contract, choosing instead to move him to Los Angeles, where Danny Evans had recently taken over as the new Dodgers general manager and was eager to make an immediate impression by fleecing his former employer. Evans, who recognized Baldwin's potential while he was serving under Ron Schueler, had every confidence that J.B. could resurrect his career in a new setting, but it wasn't to be. The Sox received three minor leaguers in return, but none of them were ever called up. The trade was a wash. His best years behind him, Baldwin drifted from the Dodgers to the Mariners to the Twins, then to the Mets, Rangers, and finally the Orioles, where he came out of the bullpen to work a handful of games in the 2005 campaign. James Baldwin, Mike Sirotka, and Jim Parque were expected to become the "Big Three" of the New Millennium who would ease the pain of Sox fans mourning the loss of Jack McDowell and Alex Fernandez to free agency and Wilson Alvarez in the "White Flag" trade. Replacing the three pitchers who helped mold the White Sox into a perennial contender early in the decade with this trio was too much to expect, and the team's subpar seasons at the end of the 1990s illustrate that top-notch front-line pitching is the most precious commodity of all. The new "Big Three" each had their shining moments, but in the end none had the staying power or physical stamina to consistently produce at the big-league level.

Bannister, Alan

White Sox: 1976–80
Infielder, outfielder
Birthplace: Montebello, California
B: September 3, 1951
Bats right, throws right
Ht. 5–11; **Wt.** 175

Bannister, Alan

White Sox	G	AB	H	AVG	RBI	R	2B	3B	HR	SA	SB
1976	73	145	36	.248	8	19	6	2	0	.317	12
1977	139	560	154	.275	57	87	20	3	3	.338	4
1978	49	107	24	.224	8	16	3	2	0	.290	3
1979	136	506	144	.285	55	71	28	8	2	.383	22
1980	45	130	25	.192	9	16	6	0	0	.238	5
Career	972	3,005	811	.269	288	430	143	28	19	.355	107

Alan Bannister faced the toughest challenge of his short baseball career when he was called upon on the last day of the 1977 spring training sessions to take over the duties of shortstop full-time, following the 11th-hour trade of the popular and effervescent Bucky Dent to the Yankees.

Alan Bannister

Bannister made the best of his opportunities—at the plate. He generated the offense that Dent was unable to provide, but his glove work was another matter. Banny committed an astounding 40 errors in 1977, and the most routine throw across the infield quickened the pulse of the most reserved White Sox fan. But in all fairness to this heralded collegiate athlete, Alan was never exactly sure where he would be playing from day to day.

Bannister was one of the highest rated players to come out of Arizona State University, where he was a two-time All American for manager Bobby Winkles. He established three NCAA records and was drafted No. 1 in the 1973 free agent draft by the Philadelphia Phillies. He had been a shortstop in his collegiate career, but the Phils converted him to third base and then second base, because there was little chance for him to unseat the incumbent shortstop Larry Bowa.

Banny played six different positions with the 1976 White Sox after coming over in a December 10, 1975, trade that sent Jim Kaat, a luxury Bill Veeck could not afford, to the Phillies.

While the Sox were clicking on all six cylinders in the 1977 "South Side Hitmen" summer, it was easy to overlook Alan's faltering play in the infield. Through late July, Bannister maintained a .315 batting average, and he was a great "table setter" for the big RBI men in the lineup—Richie Zisk, Oscar Gamble, and Eric Soderholm.

But sooner or later, things have a way of catching up; the best laid plans of Veeck and company to coast by with a shortstop who commanded half the salary of Bucky Dent quickly went awry. An ailing shoulder limited Bannister's playing time in 1978, a problem corrected by surgery in August. Meanwhile, Don Kessinger, Mike Eden, Greg Pryor, and Harry Chappas did the best they could to stabilize a jittery, Triple-A caliber infield defense.

Banny opened the 1979 season at second base but was shifted to the outfield after the All-Star break. Offensively, 1979 was his best all-around season, but without a steady position, all he could look forward to in his future White Sox career was a utility role.

This is what it boiled down to when Bannister failed to perform at satisfactory levels after being awarded the starting third baseman's job by manager Tony LaRussa in 1980.

On June 14, 1980, Roland Hemond traded him to the Cleveland Indians for Ron Pruitt, another jack-of-all-trades utility man without a well-defined role. Bannister was actually excited about leaving one dispirited ballclub to join another. "I'm not going to rip the trade as some of my teammates think I should," he proclaimed, "because they might cancel it before I get there, if I do."

Alan reprised his six-position role with the Tribe and provided them with better-than-average depth on the bench until the spendthrift Indians could no longer afford the luxury of a $350,000 substitute. They sold him to the Houston Astros in March 1984.

Bannister, Floyd

White Sox: 1983–87
Pitcher
Birthplace: Pierre, South Dakota
B: June 10, 1955
Bats left, throws left
Ht. 6–2; **Wt.** 189

Bannister, Floyd

White Sox	W	L	Pct	ERA	G	CG	IP	H	BB	K	ShO
1983	16	10	.615	3.35	34	5	217⅓	191	71	193	2
1984	14	11	.560	4.83	34	4	218	211	80	152	0
1985	10	14	.417	4.87	34	4	210⅔	211	100	198	1
1986	10	14	.417	3.54	28	6	165⅓	162	48	92	1
1987	16	11	.592	3.58	34	11	228⅔	216	49	124	2
Career	117	131	.471	4.07	345	51	2,098	2,040	766	1,347	14

Floyd Bannister was a standout college pitcher at Arizona State University—one of the top prospects in the United States—who won 38 and lost only six in three seasons with the Sun Devils. In 1976 he was voted the *Sporting News* College Player of the Year before being selected by the Houston Astros as the No. 1 pick in the draft. Big league scouts likened Bannister's fastball to Nolan Ryan's. It was a valid comparison, but speed alone did not translate into major league success.

After playing out his option with the Seattle Mariners, Banny signed a record-setting five-year $4.8 million contract with the White Sox on December 13, 1982. His addition assured the Sox of a formidable starting pitching staff going into the 1983 season. However, Floyd was a first-half disappointment who dropped nine of his first 12 decisions.

Carlton Fisk worked with the former All-American and convinced him that he did not have to throw the perfect pitch every time in order to be effective. After reviewing old game films, Bannister corrected a few flaws and became the catalyst of Chicago's second-half assault on the Western Division title by winning 13 of 14 to establish a new career high. His career waned after that.

Frequently victimized by the long ball and unwilling to use his imposing fastball to brush back opposing hitters, Bannister became just another .500 pitcher following his impressive 1983 showing. Floyd lacked the killer instinct, and he paid for it with subpar performances. After an injury-plagued campaign in 1986, Banny improved his record to 16–11 in '87. Larry Himes capitalized on his increased market value by dealing him to Kansas City on December 10, 1987, for a quartet of promising young players, including Greg Hibbard and Melido Perez.

Floyd Bannister

Barrett, Bill

White Sox: 1923–29
Outfielder
Nicknames: Whispering Bill; Wild Bill
Birthplace: Cambridge, Massachusetts
B: May 28, 1900
D: January 26, 1951
Batted right, threw right
Ht. 6–0; **Wt.** 200

Barrett, Bill

White Sox	G	AB	H	AVG	RBI	R	2B	3B	HR	SA	SB
1923	42	162	44	.272	23	17	7	2	2	.377	12
1924	119	406	110	.271	56	52	18	5	2	.355	15
1925	81	245	89	.363	40	44	23	3	3	.518	5
1926	111	368	113	.307	61	46	31	4	6	.462	9
1927	147	556	159	.286	83	62	35	9	4	.403	20
1928	76	235	65	.277	26	34	11	2	3	.379	8
1929	3	1	0	.000	0	0	0	0	0	.000	0
Career	716	2,395	690	.288	328	318	151	30	23	.405	80

Crippled by injuries, the 1923 White Sox resembled a hospital emergency ward by midsummer. Desperate to bolster a patchwork lineup that was not very good to begin with, secretary Harry Grabiner trolled the waters of the International League in search of fresh faces. Bill Barrett, one of the players high on Grabiner's list of "can't miss" prospects, was hitting .450 for the Reading, Pennsylvania, club, but his fielding skills were considered well below average.

Barrett was exiled to the minors by Philadelphia Athletics manager Connie Mack, who had lost patience with the lad for turning the most routine ground balls into nail-biting

Bill Barrett

adventures. As it turned out, the soft-spoken and gentlemanly Barrett was better suited to play in the outfield than as a shortstop.

With his contract secured for the White Sox a few days later, Whispering Bill reported to Chicago on August 18, 1923. The next day he collected two hits and a stolen base in his sensational Chicago debut before 33,000 Comiskey Park patrons who had come out to see Babe Ruth and the Yankees wrecking crew. Based on his performance that afternoon, the Chicago sportswriters predicted a great future for the new recruit.

Barrett put up good offensive numbers over the next five seasons. Batting sixth in the lineup, he prevented opposing hitters from pitching around Earl Sheely, Eddie Collins, Bibb Falk, and Johnny Mostil—the heart of a potent mid-1920s White Sox lineup. In a matchup with the Cleveland Indians along the shores of Lake Erie on May 1, 1924, Barrett collected four hits and stole home *twice* in a 13–7 rout of the Tribe.

As befits every White Sox team since time immemorial, there were the usual setbacks and controversy. Manager Johnny Evers moved Whispering Bill back to the shortstop position in 1924 after slick-fielding Harvey McClellan suffered an ulcer attack and had to undergo surgery. Bill finished dead last in fielding with a miserable .904 percentage that season, and the experiment was canceled. Barrett was returned to left field, but in 1925 and 1926 he suffered chronic knee problems, which curtailed his playing time.

Despite his fine numbers, Barrett was not altogether happy with his situation in Chicago. He married his sweetheart after the 1928 season and purchased a home in Cambridge, Massachusetts, with the expectation of someday playing for a team closer to home—possibly a contender.

When the time came to report to the White Sox spring training camp, Whispering Bill badgered Grabiner to trade him to one of the Boston teams. A deal with the Red Sox was consummated via a long-distance telephone hookup on May 23, 1929. The White Sox received the otherwise forgettable Douglas Taitt for the unhappy Barrett. Within a year's time, Taitt would be dispatched to the Atlanta Crackers of the Southern Association—for rookie shortstop Luke Appling.

Barrios, Francisco

White Sox: 1974; 1976–81
Pitcher
Birthplace: Hermosillo, Mexico

B: June 10, 1953
D: April 9, 1982
Batted right, threw right
Ht. 6–3; **Wt.** 195

Barrios, Francisco

White Sox	W	L	Pct	ERA	G	CG	IP	H	BB	K	ShO
1974	0	0	.000	27.00	2	0	2	7	2	2	0
1976	5	9	.357	4.31	35	6	142	136	46	81	0
1977	14	7	.667	4.13	33	9	231	241	58	119	0
1978	9	15	.375	4.05	33	9	195⅔	180	85	79	2
1979	8	3	.727	3.60	15	2	95	88	33	28	0
1980	1	1	.500	5.06	3	0	16	21	8	2	0
1981	1	3	.250	4.00	8	1	36	45	14	12	0
Career	38	38	.500	4.15	129	27	717⅔	718	246	323	2

Frankie Barrios' rookie pose, 1975. He died before his 30th birthday.

Life in the major leagues proved too much for Frankie Barrios, an excitable, occasionally hotheaded youngster born and raised in Mexico's interior.

Barrios's 90 mph heater caught the attention of Sox general manager Roland Hemond during one of his frequent scouting expeditions south of the border. Frankie was signed to a contract by Hemond after he won the Mexican League Rookie of the Year Award for the Jalisco club in 1973.

In 1976 he became a regular on the Chicago squad. He saved a no-hitter in Oakland for Blue Moon Odom on July 28. Between the veteran and the kid, they walked 11 A's batters but managed to preserve a hard-fought 2–1 win.

Barrios earned a spot in the 1977 rotation. His 14–7 record ranked fourth among AL pitchers in percentage that year. But his personality and temperament were ill-suited to the rigors of baseball. He constantly goaded home plate umpires over balls and strikes and allowed minor setbacks to rattle his composure on the mound.

He slugged it out with teammate Steve Trout in a Cleveland hotel, and he had to be restrained from punching Ralph Garr in the mouth during an eventful overnight flight to Seattle in 1979.

Barrios's career ended in 1981 after he was arrested on a narcotics charge in a Rush Street nightclub. A year later Frankie died of a heart attack—a life in the fast lane played out to a sad conclusion.

Baumann, Frank

White Sox: 1960–64
Pitcher
Nickname: Beau
Birthplace: St. Louis, Missouri

B: July 1, 1933
Bats left, throws left
Ht. 6–1; **Wt.** 180

Baumann, Frank

White Sox	W	L	Pct	ERA	G	CG	IP	H	BB	K	ShO	Sv
1960	13	6	.684	2.67	47	7	185⅓	169	53	71	2	3
1961	10	13	.435	5.61	53	5	187⅔	249	59	75	1	3
1962	7	6	.538	3.38	40	3	119⅔	117	36	55	1	4
1963	2	1	.667	3.04	24	0	50⅓	52	17	31	0	1
1964	0	3	.000	6.19	22	0	32	40	16	19	0	1
Career	45	38	.542	4.11	244	19	797⅓	856	300	384	4	13

Frankie Baumann was a high school pitching sensation in St. Louis during the early 1950s when Bill Veeck still owned the financially strapped Browns. Recognizing Baumann's enormous marketing value to the hometown team, Veeck entered into a competitive bidding war with the Boston Red Sox for the young man's service. "I made an all-time high bonus offer for him. It was $30,000," Veeck later recalled. "The way things were going for us, that was the same as a $450,000 offer from almost any other major league club. If my bid was accepted, I intended to pitch him the next Sunday and get most of it back."

Things never worked as Veeck planned because the Boston Red Sox tripled the bonus money and signed the young southpaw to an impressive salary. They tagged him with a silly nickname (Beau) in order to inflate preseason publicity and then waited out the next six seasons for Baumann to live up to his press clippings. Unable to maintain his proper weight, the "Beau" flopped in Beantown, but Veeck never forgot about the former St. Louis prodigy.

Frank Baumann and sons

A month after the 1959 World Series, Veeck and Hank Greenberg dealt 6′7″ first baseman Ron Jackson to Boston for Baumann. Neither player had shown very much in repeated tries, despite possessing all the tools for success. But the trade turned out to be a good one for Chicago—at least in that first year.

Baumann shed 10 pounds. Al Lopez and pitching coach Ray Berres corrected his delivery by forcing him to convert from sidearm to three-quarter-arm. Alternating between the bullpen and the starting rotation, Frankie's glittering 2.67 earned run average paced the team and the American League in a pitching-thin year, which seemed to validate Veeck's highest expectations.

Veeck, Lopez, and the White Sox brain trust counted on Baumann to become the next veteran castoff to win 20 games for the aging Pale Hose, but he was already past his peak. Baumann began dipping his shoulder, his fastball flattened out, and at the 1961 All-Star break, his earned run average was a stratospheric 6.10.

His failure mirrored the general collapse of the team that season, despite one historic and unusual moment occurring on July 13. Baumann and Sherm Lollar became only the third pitcher-catcher duo to wallop back-to-back home runs in a game. The blows were struck off of Yankees pitcher Bill Stafford in the fifth inning of a 6–2 Sox loss.

Baumann figured in one other bit of Chicago baseball history. When he was traded to the Cubs for reserve catcher Jimmie Schaffer on December 1, 1964, it marked the first time that the two Chicago baseball teams completed a direct exchange of players. It was always the rule of Cubs owner Phil Wrigley to refuse to deal with the White Sox because he believed that doing so would wipe out the distinct identity of each team. The Schaffer-Baumann swap proved to be of no consequence—for either Chicago team.

Belle, Albert

White Sox: 1997–98
Outfielder
Birthplace: Shreveport, Louisiana

B: August 25, 1966
Bats right, throws right
Ht. 6–2; **Wt.** 210

Belle, Albert

White Sox	G	AB	H	AVG	RBI	R	2B	3B	HR	SA	SB
1997	161	634	174	.274	116	90	45	1	30	.491	4
1998	163	609	200	.328	152	113	48	2	49	.655	6
Career	1,539	5,853	1,726	.295	1,239	974	389	21	381	.564	88

It was never clear whether the departure of Albert Belle from Cleveland on November 20, 1996, was Chicago's gain or the Tribe's loss. One seemed to cancel out the other

Albert Belle passed through Chicago just long enough to establish a new team home run record.

when the final results of the headline-grabbing free agent signing were tallied three years later. Never has one player done so much, yet contributed so little, to effect an overall outcome than Albert (aka Joey) Belle, the 1995 American League home run champion whose raw talent and abilities were tragically overshadowed by a series of unfortunate incidents in Cleveland that alienated the player from the fans, the media, and the organization. While still a Tribesman, Belle was suspended for destroying part of a bathroom, firing a baseball at the chest of a heckling fan, and more infamously, using a corked bat against the White Sox in the 1994 "Batgate" affair. In all, he was suspended five times in six seasons by the American League. In 1996 he struck Brewers infielder Fernando Vina with his forearm. A year earlier he chased down some neighborhood kids with his sports utility vehicle after Halloween trick-or-treaters egged his home. Was he a sadly misunderstood rebel certain to benefit in new surroundings or a hostile, spoiled millionaire and clubhouse malcontent likely to destroy the delicate chemistry of a ballclub?

"I want a fresh start," pleaded Belle at his press conference. "I'd like to put some of the things that happened in Cleveland behind me. It took the fans there a while to embrace me, and it probably will take a while for the fans in Chicago to embrace me." Outbidding the Florida Marlins, the Sox signed Belle for an estimated $55 million, spread over five years. Albert Belle represented Jerry Reinsdorf's biggest financial gamble since his acquisition of the White Sox in 1981. "People in Chicago showed that with the fellow with the pink hair [Dennis Rodman of the Bulls]. They said, 'If you play hard for us, we'll embrace you.' They did with Dennis. They will with Albert," predicted Reinsdorf. While it was true that the White Sox uniform tended to have a calming influence on earlier franchise malcontents—most notably Jimmy Callahan, Al Simmons, and Dick Allen—what could Chicago reasonably expect from Belle? They glimpsed the truth at the annual winter SoxFest, when Belle extended churlish greetings to the fans by delivering a stern warning that he would not, under any circumstances, affix his autograph to any baseball card or photograph showing him in a Cleveland uniform. In his first visit to Jacobs Field that year, the sulky outfielder delivered an obscene gesture to the fans after being showered with dollar bills and enduring a brutal hazing. He delivered a solid performance in 1997, but his batting average was not quite up to earlier standards of play with the Tribe. With the quiet and dignified Jerry Manuel at the helm in 1998, Belle produced better results despite a sluggish first half. After the All-Star break, Belle went on a hitting tear for the ages, batting .387 with 31 home runs and a stupefying .816 slugging average. For the season, he established new team home run and RBI records with 49 roundtrippers and 152 driven in, yet he received no consideration from the media for postseason awards. His "bad boy" antics were never forgotten by the baseball people who mattered the most when the votes were being cast for MVP.

In 1998 Belle exacerbated his situation with his arrest on a domestic battery charge in south suburban Alsip after winning a Player of the Week award. The Cook County State's Attorney's office informed the White Sox flagship radio station AM 1000 that Belle was additionally charged with criminal damage to property and interfering with a report of domestic battery. White Sox general manager Ron Schueler told reporters: "Albert said there is no validity to the charge." Belle also said that he was very happy playing in Chicago and preferred to remain with the White Sox. But he had a clause in his contract to the effect that if he wasn't one of the three highest-paid players in baseball after the second year of his contract, he could demand a salary increase or file for free agency. Jerry Reinsdorf wasn't interested in reupping at any price, not after all the attending controversies and dismal results.

On December 1, 1998, Albert Belle inked a five-year, $65 million contract with the Baltimore Orioles, with a blanket no-trade clause for the first three years after Reinsdorf rebuffed three requests from Belle to match the O's final offer. With the image-conscious O's, Belle was suspended by team officials after a fan sent a letter to owner Peter Angelos complaining that the player allegedly raised his finger and grabbed his crotch while facing in the direction of right-field fans in Camden Yards on June 6. After two years of mixed reviews in Baltimore, Albert Belle suffered a degenerative right hip and retired from baseball with three years left on his contract, leaving behind considerable ill-will and bruised feelings in the three cities where he hung his spikes.

The "Butcher Boy" Benz (right) with teammates Lefty Williams, Ed Cicotte, and Mellie Wolfgang, 1917

Benz, Joe

White Sox: 1911–19
Pitcher
Nicknames: Blitzen; Butcher Boy
Birthplace: New Alsace, Indiana

B: January 21, 1886
D: April 22, 1957
Batted right, threw right
Ht. 6–1½; **Wt.** 196

Benz, Joe

White Sox	W	L	Pct	ERA	G	CG	IP	H	BB	K	ShO
1911	3	2	.600	2.26	12	2	55⅔	52	13	28	0
1912	12	18	.400	2.92	41	11	237⅔	230	70	96	3
1913	6	10	.375	2.74	33	7	151	146	59	79	1
1914	15	19	.441	2.26	48	16	283⅓	245	66	142	4
1915	15	11	.577	2.11	39	17	238⅓	209	43	81	2
1916	9	5	.643	2.03	28	6	142	108	32	57	4
1917	6	3	.667	2.47	19	7	94⅔	76	23	25	2
1918	7	8	.467	2.51	29	10	154	156	28	30	1
1919	0	0	—	0.00	1	0	2	2	0	0	0
Career	73	76	.490	2.42	250	76	1,358⅔	1,224	334	538	17

Joe Benz was working in his father's meat market in Batesville, Indiana, and playing for a local sandlot team known as the Royals when he came to the attention of the White Sox. Joe's dad took him to Chicago to see the Old Roman, not really thinking the boy had much of a chance. "My son here believes that he is a baseball player. I don't. If he isn't one, don't waste any time but send him back to Batesville." Comiskey reserved judgment. He assigned a minor league scout named Hoyer to keep track of Benz. Impressed with the young man's abilities, Hoyer offered him a contract with the Clarksburg, West Virginia, team of the Mountain State League. Benz finished the 1909 season with the White Sox' Des Moines affiliate and remained in Iowa the next two seasons sharpening his skills.

Included in his assortment of pitches was a knuckleball and a spitter, which he employed with varying degrees of success following his arrival in the majors in September 1911. Years later, when Benz reviewed the highlights of his career, he would tell his listeners that he "had it" over Walter Johnson in the days when the "Big Train" was in his prime. "Who can beat Johnson?" inquired White Sox manager Jim Callahan one afternoon. "I can!" Benz replied. Joe loved the game, and he showed grit and nerve at every turn.

However, the record shows that Benz won only two of 10 decisions against Johnson over the years, but one of them was a nearly flawless gem. But let's backtrack to May 1, 1914, when Benz took his regular turn against the Cleveland Naps. That afternoon "Blitzen" Benz fired a no-hitter despite three White Sox errors. Then on June 6 Benz limited the New York Highlanders to a pair of hits in a rain-shortened nine-inning 1–1 draw. Six days later in Chicago he squared off against the mighty Johnson. For eight innings he held Washington hitless while his teammates accumulated two scratch runs. But in the fateful ninth inning, Eddie Ainsmith of the Senators hit a chopper toward Buck Weaver at short. Weaver was positioned to make the play, but third baseman Scotty Alcock cut him off and deflected the ball into left field to ruin a potential no-hitter. It ended right after that—a one-hitter over Johnson to cap off a remarkable month of pitching.

Joe's earned run average rose no higher than 2.92 during any single season of his eight-year White Sox career. Unfortunately he was the No. 3 starter for the lackluster pre–Black Sox teams that struggled to score runs on his behalf. In 1915, with a better supporting cast behind him, Benz finished the year 15–11, his best effort. Plagued by recurring arm troubles, Benz was released after one appearance in the 1919 season. He missed out on a second World Series, but never believed for a moment that his teammates threw games to the Reds that year. After he retired from the game, Benz worked as a mechanical engineer in Chicago and coached Little Leaguers on the side. He maintained his lifelong friendship with George "Buck" Weaver until death claimed the least culpable of the Black Soxers in 1956.

Berg, Moe

White Sox: 1926–30
Shortstop, catcher
Birthplace: New York City

B: March 2, 1902
D: May 29, 1972
Batted right, threw right
Ht. 6–1; **Wt.** 185

Berg, Moe

White Sox	G	AB	H	AVG	RBI	R	2B	3B	HR	SA	SB
1926	41	113	25	.221	7	4	6	0	0	.274	0
1927	35	69	17	.246	4	4	4	0	0	.304	0
1928	76	224	55	.246	29	25	16	0	0	.317	2
1929	106	351	101	.288	47	32	7	0	0	.308	5
1930	20	61	7	.115	7	4	3	0	0	.164	0
Career	662	1,812	441	.243	206	150	71	6	6	.299	11

"He could speak 12 different languages, but could not hit in any of them" adequately sums up the playing skills of Morris "Moe" Berg, a student of ancient Sanskrit, linguist, and America's premier OSS spy who gathered high-level intelligence information on Nazi Germany's top scientists during World War II. The Moe Berg story has been retold in countless articles, books, and documentaries dealing with baseball. Not to be overlooked in any discussion of the brilliant but eccentric Berg are the four years he spent in Chicago as a second-string infielder and catcher.

Moe Berg was a minor league shortstop from the Reading, Pennsylvania, club of the International League trying to catch on as a utility infielder when he reported to Eddie Collins in the spring of 1926 following completion of his law courses at Columbia University. He played sparingly in 1926, but caught a break the next year when the two regular catchers, Harry McCurdy and Clyde Crouse, suffered injuries just before the Yankees came to town. Manager Ray Schalk faced a dilemma. "I told Ray that I had caught during high school and a bit in college," Berg related in 1964. "He just looked at me. He said I didn't know the signals or how to give them. He was wrong about that. I'd been watching him give them and how he gave them long enough to know. If I do say so, I was then and still am a quick student."

Moe Berg: scholar, spy, diplomat, .230 hitter

With Berg crouching behind the plate for the first time on May 9, 1927, Red Faber shut down the Yankees 2–1 in 10 innings. Given a chance to play every day in 1929, he hit a very respectable .288—a career high. Moe was a fair handler of pitchers, but his law studies inevitably delayed his arrival in spring training each year. In the scheme of things, Berg just didn't fit in with the players of that era. He lasted until April 2, 1931, the day when Comiskey sold him to the Cleveland Indians for the league waiver price.

Years later, at a gathering of the old-timers, Ray Schalk recalled that long-ago afternoon when Berg donned the "tools of ignorance" for the first time: "Moe wasn't exactly the best infielder the Sox ever owned. In fact, we were just about ready to let him go when he volunteered to catch in that 1927 emergency. As a catcher he added 13 more years to his career." Until he died, Berg retained among his possessions the weather-beaten mitt that Schalk had presented to him.

Berry, Ken

White Sox: 1962–70
Outfielder
Nickname: The Bandit
Birthplace: Kansas City, Missouri

B: May 10, 1941
Bats right, throws right
Ht. 6–0; **Wt.** 175

Berry, Ken

White Sox	G	AB	H	AVG	RBI	R	2B	3B	HR	SA	SB
1962	3	6	2	.333	0	2	0	0	0	.333	0
1963	4	5	1	.200	0	2	0	0	0	.200	0
1964	12	32	12	.375	4	4	1	0	1	.500	0
1965	157	472	103	.218	42	51	17	4	12	.347	4
1966	147	443	120	.271	34	50	20	2	8	.379	7
1967	147	485	117	.241	41	49	14	4	7	.330	9
1968	153	504	127	.252	32	49	21	2	7	.343	6
1969	130	297	69	.232	18	25	12	2	4	.327	1
1970	141	463	128	.276	50	45	12	2	7	.356	6
Career	1,383	4,136	1,053	.255	343	422	150	23	58	.344	45

Ted Lyons spotted Ken Berry playing for a semipro team in Liberal, Kansas, in 1960. His extraordinary speed and defensive skills evoked memories of Johnny Mostil and compared favorably to Jim Landis—then the incumbent White Sox center fielder.

Berry was one of the top prep athletes coming out of Kansas in the late 1950s. He was enrolled at Wichita University on a football scholarship when Lyons and midwestern scout Jack Sheehan coaxed him into signing with the White Sox in 1960. While patrolling the outfield grounds at Victory Stadium in Indianapolis, Berry picked up his "Bandit" nickname because of his leaping, diving grabs of apparent doubles and triples.

Ken Berry was the centerfield "Bandit."

Groomed as the heir apparent to Jim Landis, Berry made it up to stay in 1965. His hitting was weak—but he kept at it and batted a respectable .271 in 1966. In the spring of 1967 he reeled off a 20-game hitting streak, but finished up at .241—which was the highest average among the regulars in the "Year of the Pitcher."

Berry was not paid to hit. It was his skill in the outfield and his knack for pulling back center-field bullpen home runs that made him valuable to the organization. Ken Berry matched the standards set by Jim Landis in this department, and in many ways exceeded his illustrious predecessor. In 1969, a year when Berry voiced dissatisfaction to the front office and demanded to be traded, he did not commit an error in 222 chances for a perfect 1.000 fielding percentage.

Unhappy with Sox GM Ed Short and his decision to shift from a hit-and-run, speed-oriented offense to a "power" team, Berry pressed his demand for a trade. Short, however, was already gone when Ken was traded to the California Angels with Sid O'Brien and Billy Wynne on November 30, 1970, for catcher Tom Egan and pitcher Tom Bradley. Berry returned to the organization in 1988 as a minor league hitting instructor and outfield coach before being named manager of the Sox's Double A affiliate at Birmingham in 1989. He was a featured extra in the 1988 motion picture *Eight Men Out,* playing a leather-lunged Comiskey Park heckler.

Blankenship, Ted

White Sox: 1922–30
Pitcher
Birthplace: Bonham, Texas

B: May 10, 1901
D: January 14, 1945
Batted right, threw right
Ht. 6–1; **Wt.** 170

Blankenship, Ted

White Sox	W	L	Pct	ERA	G	CG	IP	H	BB	K	ShO
1922	8	10	.444	3.81	24	7	127⅔	124	47	42	0
1923	9	14	.391	4.27	44	9	208⅔	219	100	57	1
1924	7	6	.538	5.17	25	7	125⅓	167	38	36	0
1925	17	8	.680	3.16	40	16	222	218	69	81	3
1926	13	10	.565	3.61	29	15	209⅓	217	65	66	1
1927	12	17	.414	5.06	37	11	236⅔	280	74	51	3
1928	9	11	.450	4.61	27	8	158	186	80	36	0
1929	0	2	.000	8.84	8	0	18⅓	28	9	7	0
1930	2	1	.667	9.20	7	0	14⅔	23	7	2	0
Career	77	79	.494	4.32	241	73	1,320⅔	1,462	489	378	8

Ted Blankenship was one of the White Sox's most dependable starting pitchers throughout the bleak 1920s. This former Oklahoma sandlotter, whose brother Homer also broke in with the Sox at the same time, was purchased from the Sherman club of the Texas League in the fall of 1921. Blankenship broke his finger in an automobile accident and was laid up until June 30, 1922, when Comiskey added him to the roster. Manager Kid Gleason moved Teddy into the starting rotation three days later after he pitched 12 dazzling innings of relief against the Detroit Tigers, only to lose 7–6 in the 14th.

With better support in back of him, Blankenship might have improved on his career 77–79 mark. But as it turned out, he played his entire career in Chicago, posting a 17–8 record in 1925. He broke a finger in 1926 and was never quite the same afterward.

Ted Blankenship

Bonura, Henry

White Sox: 1934–37
First baseman
Nicknames: Zeke; Banana Nose; the Physique
Birthplace: New Orleans, Louisiana
B: September 20, 1908
D: March 9, 1987
Batted right, threw right
Ht. 6–0; **Wt.** 210

Bonura, Henry

White Sox	G	AB	H	AVG	RBI	R	2B	3B	HR	SA	SB
1934	127	510	154	.302	110	86	35	4	27	.545	0
1935	138	550	162	.295	92	107	34	4	21	.485	4
1936	148	587	194	.330	138	120	39	7	12	.482	4
1937	116	447	154	.345	100	79	41	2	19	.573	5
Career	917	3,582	1,099	.307	704	600	232	29	119	.487	19

Sportswriters who observed Henry Bonura in action when he was a top-rated college football player at Notre Dame University picked up on something coach Knute Rockne said one afternoon after observing the husky youth taking his shower: "Gee, get a load of that fellow's physique!" Hence, "Zeke" for short. The nickname remained with him throughout his career.

Bonura broke in with the White Sox in spectacular fashion in 1934. He clubbed 27 home runs, which set a new team record at the time. His career .315 White Sox average ranks fifth on the all-time list. Bonura was a power-hitting first baseman beloved by the fans, but a source of constant irritation to his manager and the front office.

Zeke led the league in fielding three times during his big-league career, but his range was limited, and he didn't always give it the old college try. Bonura would remain transfixed at his station, waving the patented "Mussolini Salute" with his glove hand as ground balls whizzed by him into right field. *Chicago Tribune* writer Ed Burns coined the phrase "Mussolini Salute," which referred to the troubles boiling over in fascist Italy and to Zeke's faculty for missing the ball by a rabbit's whisker. "Zeke would have found out that you can't get killed by a batted ball," sighed Jimmie Dykes. "If he had only learned that early, there's no telling how great he might have become."

Zeke Bonura interviewed by Bob Elson

Colorful and always outspoken, Zeke was rumored to be interested in Dorothy Comiskey, the eldest daughter of the White Sox owner. In addition, his annual salary holdout delayed his arrival in spring training each year. Lou Comiskey finally had enough. Zeke was traded to the Washington Senators on March 18, 1938, for first baseman Joe Kuhel—the best glove man in the league.

Bradley, Tom

White Sox: 1971–72
Pitcher
Birthplace: Asheville, North Carolina
B: May 16, 1947
Bats right, throws right
Ht. 6–2½; **Wt.** 180

Bradley, Tom

White Sox	W	L	Pct	ERA	G	CG	IP	H	BB	K	ShO	Sv
1971	15	15	.500	2.96	45	7	286	273	74	206	6	0
1972	15	14	.517	2.98	40	11	260	225	65	209	2	0
Career	55	61	.474	3.72	183	27	1,017⅔	999	311	691	10	2

The scholarly right-hander earned a degree in Latin from the University of Maryland, then enjoyed a brief flurry of success with the White Sox before fading away, illustrating just how fleeting fame can sometimes be at the major league level.

Tom Bradley and a pretty "Soxette," April 18, 1972

Nearly blind without his thick-lens glasses, Bradley was signed by the California Angels in May 1969 after turning pro. He was a capable performer for Chuck Tanner when the Sox skipper still managed Hawaii of the Pacific Coast League, and it was on Tanner's advice that Roland Hemond insisted that Bradley be included in a November 30, 1970, trade that sent Ken Berry, Sid O'Brien, and pitcher Billy Wynne to the Angels.

Pitching coach Johnny Sain worked with Bradley's mechanics, tutoring him on the controlled breaking pitch, which complemented an above-average fastball. With a better ballclub behind him than the youthful, rebuilding White Sox, Bradley might have easily won 20 games in 1971. As it turned out, he registered six shutouts and fanned 206 batters, joining Ed Walsh, Gary Peters, and Wilbur Wood as the only Sox pitchers to strike out more than 200 hitters in a single season up to that time. Possessing good control of his fastball, the bespectacled righty seemed destined for a bright and limitless future. But it was not to be.

Bradley won 10 of his first 15 decisions in 1972, then suffered through some tough, one-run losses. For the second straight year he topped the 200 strikeout mark by fanning 10 Texas Rangers in his last start of the season. Over the winter he worked for the White Sox as a ticket salesman at a time when many players still found it necessary to supplement their baseball salaries with off-season jobs.

It seemed almost inconceivable that the Sox would trade a player with this much heart—and promise. But the center field position was a serious problem in 1972, a year in which the Sox battled Oakland right down to the final two weeks of the season for the top spot.

At the winter meetings in Hawaii, Roland Hemond opened trade talks with the San Francisco Giants, who were interested in the White Sox pitching. They shopped Ken Henderson, a switch-hitting outfielder considered by many to be the next Willie Mays. Hemond wanted Henderson badly, but he refused to part with Wilbur Wood, who was the Giants' first choice.

Hemond turned down their bid, but offered 21-game winner Stan Bahnsen as a compromise. The Giants wouldn't go for Bahnsen, but they liked Bradley despite his occasional inconsistency on the mound. The deal was struck on November 19, 1972, and pitcher Steve Stone accompanied Henderson to Chicago.

Bradley lost his effectiveness and struggled through three seasons in the National League before being cast adrift by the Giants. Ken Henderson provided a few stellar moments in Chicago, but he was injury prone and frequently criticized for indifferent play by Sox announcer Harry Caray. The much-talked-about trade proved to be a washout for both parties.

Bradley launched his coaching career in 1978 as a pitching coach for St. Mary's College, and later coached at Jacksonville University. He joined the Toronto Blue Jays organization in 2001 as manager of the rookie-level Pioneer League team in Medicine Hat, Alberta, Canada. In 2005 he was appointed pitching coach for the San Diego Padres' Midwest League affiliate at Fort Wayne, Indiana.

Brown, Clint

White Sox: 1936–40
Pitcher
Birthplace: Blackash, Pennsylvania

B: July 8, 1903
D: December 31, 1955
Batted left, threw right
Ht. 6–1½; **Wt.** 180

Brown, Clint

White Sox	W	L	Pct	ERA	G	CG	IP	H	BB	SO	ShO	Sv
1936	6	2	.750	4.99	38	0	83	106	24	19	0	5
1937	7	7	.500	3.42	53	0	100	92	36	51	0	18
1938	1	3	.250	4.61	8	0	13⅔	16	9	2	0	2
1939	11	10	.524	3.88	61	0	118⅓	127	27	41	0	18
1940	4	6	.400	3.68	37	0	66	75	16	23	0	10
Career	89	92	.492	4.26	434	62	1,485⅔	1,740	368	410	7	64

Over the years some of the finest relief specialists in the game have passed through Comiskey Park at one time or another. Clint Brown, who was a very capable starting pitcher for the Cleveland Indians in the early 1930s, was one of them. Brown was acquired by the Sox in a straight cash transaction on April 11, 1936, when a trio of rookie pitchers, Jack Salveson, Ray Phelps, and Les Tietje, failed to make the grade in spring training. He threw a slow, tantalizing curveball and a deceptive sidearm pitch, which he put to good use as an emergency reliever for Jimmie Dykes. "Dr." Brown led the American League with 18 saves and 53 appearances in 1937.

Clint Brown was the relief ace of the 1930s.

Hobbled by bone chips in his pitching arm the following season, Brown made a great comeback in 1939 by shattering the AL record for appearances, originally set by Garland Braxton of the Washington Senators in 1927. Brown eclipsed Braxton's mark of 58 by answering the call 61 times.

Sensing that the 37-year-old veteran was fast approaching the end of the line, the Sox traded Brown back to Cleveland on February 7, 1941, for Johnny Humphries—a former relief ace whom Jimmie Dykes converted to the starting rotation.

Buehrle, Mark

White Sox: 2000–
Pitcher
Birthplace: St. Charles, Missouri

B: March 23, 1979
Bats left, throws left
Ht. 6–2; **Wt.** 220

Buehrle, Mark

White Sox	W	L	Pct	ERA	G	CG	IP	H	BB	SO	ShO	Sv
2000	4	1	.800	4.21	28	0	51⅓	55	19	37	0	0
2001	16	8	.667	3.29	32	4	221⅓	188	48	126	2	0
2002	19	12	.613	3.58	34	5	239	236	61	134	2	0
2003	14	14	.500	4.14	35	2	230⅓	250	61	119	0	0
2004	16	10	.615	3.89	35	4	245⅓	257	51	165	1	0
2005	16	8	.667	3.12	33	3	236⅔	240	40	149	1	0
2006	12	13	.480	4.99	32	1	204	247	48	98	0	0
2007	10	9	.526	3.63	30	3	201	208	45	115	1	0
2008	15	12	.556	3.79	34	1	218⅔	240	52	140	0	0
2009	13	10	.565	3.84	33	1	213⅓	222	45	105	1	0
2010	13	13	.500	4.28	33	3	210⅓	246	49	99	0	0
Career	148	110	.574	3.85	359	27	2,271⅓	2,389	519	1,287	8	0

Workhorse of the staff of the 2000s, ace lefty Mark Buehrle was cut twice by his high school baseball coach. He was a lowly junior college pitcher and a 38th-round pick in the June 1998 First Player Draft—one of those rare "sleepers" who escaped early notice by nearly everyone, except perhaps his family and friends back home. As a boy, Mark attended carnivals in rural Missouri with his parents. At an early age, he showed amazing accuracy firing baseballs at beanbag targets in the carnival games. "We used to go home with all kinds of stuffed animals," Buehrle would recall. This obscure Missouri country boy spent less than a year and a half in the high minors before answering an emergency call from the parent club on July 16, 2000. Cal Eldred had just gone down with a lingering arm ailment, and reliever Jesus Pena was demoted to Double A following a shocking admission that he had fired a pitch at the head of Cardinals first baseman Eduardo Perez in an interleague game. Mark won his first start in Minnesota but saw limited action in the division title chase that year. He became a permanent fixture in the White Sox starting rotation in 2001 and never looked back.

Glib, opinionated, and guilty of committing the occasional verbal faux pas (in 2005 he implied to the radio audience on a sports call-in show that a Cubs pitcher, likely Greg Maddux, was "loading up"—that is, throwing an illegal spitball), Buehrle is a whimsical throwback to the colorful, quotable characters of yesteryear who delighted fans with their irreverence. His belly-flopping slides on the rain-soaked tarp during rain delays at U.S. Cellular Field amused the fans but caused his managers and coaching staff apoplexy. On the mound, however, he was all business. A quick worker whose games were the shortest in length among all AL hurlers in 2004 and 2005, Buehrle became the first Sox pitcher to lead the league in innings (2004) since Wilbur Wood in 1973. Although he never added the knuckleball to his repertoire, there are similarities between Woody and Buehrle. In 2005, one of his best all-around seasons, Buehrle started (and won) the All-Star Game in Detroit. He was the first Pale Hose pitcher since Wood (1971–1975) to record 10 wins, 100 strikeouts, and 200 innings pitched in five consecutive seasons.

A winner of 10 of 12 decisions at home in 2005, Buehrle ran off a streak of 49 consecutive starts between May 11, 2004, and July 26, 2005, in which he threw six or more innings—the most since Steve Carlton's 69 straight in 1979–82. Mark's streak was abruptly halted in Baltimore on August 1 when umpire Brian Gorman ejected him without issuing a prior warning for hitting B.J. Surhoff with a pitch. The ump's call was questionable and infuriating, but if Buehrle was indeed aiming at Surhoff, he was only doing it to protect his teammates. He ended the regular season with the third-highest winning percentage in team history, ahead of fellow southpaws Claude "Lefty" Williams (.648) and Juan Pizarro (.615), and was game-ready when the postseason bell sounded.

Buehrle was crisp in the playoffs, winning two games. Having grown up a fan of the Cardinals, particularly of pitcher Todd Worrell, he was eager for St. Louis to slip past Houston in the NLCS in order to fulfill a boyhood dream. "To be able to play in Busch, go there for the last few games at Busch, would have been special," he said, but it wasn't to be. Mark failed to record a decision against the Astros in the World Series, and he admitted that he wasn't as sharp as he would have liked, but he came out to save the 14-inning marathon victory in Game 3 after Ozzie Guillen had exhausted his bullpen. It was a cold-blooded job of pitching, but what else could you expect from a "gamer" like Buehrle? Although he was shut out on postseason awards, despite sporting the third-lowest ERA in the league, Mark enjoyed the unique distinction of seeing his image adorn a Wheaties cereal box. No one could remember the last time a White Sox player was accorded such an unusual honor.

Maybe when all is said and done, Mark's superstitious habit of purchasing a Rockstar energy drink at a Shell gas station at Kingery Highway and I-55 on his scheduled day to pitch was the magical ju-ju necessary for him to etch his name into the roster of Hall of Fame pitchers and the great names in Sox history who forged an unforgettable legacy. But first a six-game losing streak midway through the 2006 season and a penchant for surrendering an alarming number of long balls (the 36 home runs he yielded that year were second to Floyd Bannister's club record 38 in 1987) resulted in his first losing campaign with the Pale Hose. Mark rebounded during the 2007 collapse and posted a winning record, despite poor offensive support through 11 no-decisions. His no-hitter against the Texas Rangers on April 18 was a first in U.S.

Mark Buehrle, no-hit ace of the first decade of the new millennium. (Courtesy of the Chicago White Sox)

Cellular Field and the 16th in team history. He retired the first 13 batters in the game, and only a one-out walk to Sammy Sosa in the fifth inning stood in the way of perfection. (Mark picked the former Cubs slugger off of first base moments later, meaning he faced the minimum 27 batters.) With his contract expiring, the fans were pensive as the mid-season trading deadline approached. Would Kenny Williams pull the plug and trade away their hero of '05 for prospects rather than risk losing him to free agency? Buehrle's affection for the Cardinals was well known, and the rumor mill had him St. Louis–bound when Mark and his agent, Jeff Berry, ended the suspense and happily agreed to a four-year contract extension on July 8.

It stood to reason that you just can't part ways with the staff workhorse who delivered 200 or more innings nine years in a row to become only the second pitcher in franchise history to win 10 or more games a season in that corresponding nine-year time frame. He joined "Doc" White of the Hitless Wonder Era as the only other pitcher to notch that record. Also in 2007 Buehrle won his 100th career game. Ed Walsh, Red Faber, Ted Lyons, and Joel Horlen are the only White Sox hurlers to win their first 100 games in a Sox uniform. With all these stellar accomplishments, his wonderful pitching for the White Sox failed to elevate him into his rightful place in the national spotlight. Despite four All-Star Game appearances (second only to Billy Pierce in team history), Mark was rarely included in the mention of the game's premier, elite pitchers—until he became a *Sports Illustrated* poster boy after notching the 18th perfect game in major league history on July 23, 2009. Under a clear summer sky, the quick-working Buehrle was masterful against the hard-hitting Tampa Bay Rays—his fastball, curve, and change-up were pinpoint and razor-sharp.

"Buehrle dominates you with tempo," observed White Sox pitching coach Don Cooper. "His rhythm and the rhythm of the game met. It was a perfect storm." Coop's description was apropos, and the magic continued into Buehrle's next start against the Minnesota Twins at the Humphrey Dome on July 28. Mark retired the first 17 Twins hitters he faced, eclipsing teammate Bobby Jenks' major league record (established only a year earlier) by retiring 45 straight batters spanning his last three starts. A two-out walk to Alexi Casilla in the sixth inning ended the streak. But after that remarkable stretch, Buehrle was plagued by inconsistency and limped home with a 2–7 second-half record and a sky-high ERA. A strange season of highs and lows had come to a rather startling but humbling close, although when the awards were passed out, one final accolade awaited him. Mark reeled in a Gold Glove award, joining Jim Kaat as the only other Sox pitcher to be so honored for excellence in fielding. Buehrle is a brilliant fielding pitcher—no one would argue the point.

He opened the 2010 season in dramatic fashion—surpassing Pierce for the most Opening Day starts by a Sox pitcher (eight) and retiring Indians catcher Lou Marson with the fielding gem of the decade—flipping the ball *between his legs* to Paul Konerko while tumbling to the ground near first base. No one could recall seeing such a play. But after the first week, Mark settled in to another .500 season. He led the league in the most hits given up, and worse, he was unable to establish any particular rhythm or dominance over opposing hitters. With one year left to go on his contract, Buehrle was a sure bet to return in 2011, but he strongly intimated that he would retire from the game at the end of the '11 campaign.

Buford, Don

White Sox: 1963–67
Third baseman, second baseman
Birthplace: Linden, Texas

B: February 2, 1937
Bats both, throws right
Ht. 5–7; **Wt.** 160

Buford, Don

White Sox	G	AB	H	AVG	RBI	R	2B	3B	HR	SA	SB
1963	12	42	12	.286	5	9	1	2	0	.405	1
1964	135	442	116	.262	30	62	14	6	4	.348	12
1965	155	586	166	.283	47	93	22	5	10	.389	17
1966	163	607	148	.244	52	85	26	7	8	.349	51
1967	156	535	129	.241	32	61	10	9	4	.316	34
Career	1,286	4,553	1,203	.264	418	718	457	44	93	.379	200

Originally signed as an outfielder in 1960, Don Buford was asked to make the switch to third base—until Pete Ward came over from Baltimore and broke in spectacularly at the hot corner in 1963. Buford, a compactly built speedster who had starred in football at the University of Southern California and won the International League Rookie of the Year Award, was coming into his own when Al Lopez asked him to work out at a new position—second base. "We traded Nellie Fox because we believe Buford can take over the second-base job," Lopez explained in the spring of 1964. "I'm going to play him the same way I did with Pete Ward at third last year. He can't play with somebody breathing down his neck, so I'm going to put him at second and keep him there."

Sox speedster Don Buford

Nevertheless, Eddie Stanky moved Buford back to third base as one of his first official acts as an incoming Sox manager in 1966. Don swiped 51 bases that season and tied an American League record by appearing in 163 games. Buford, Tommy McCraw, and Tommie Agee keyed a motion offense revolving around walks, stolen bases, sacrifice bunts, and perfectly timed base hits—"little ball" if you will. Their unique chemistry is not adequately reflected in the sagging batting averages the trio posted in 1966 and 1967, but once the tandem had been broken up by trades, the White Sox were never the same hustling, winning ballclub.

Don Buford was traded to Baltimore on November 29, 1967, in a package deal that returned Louie Aparicio to Chicago. Don's versatility paid handsome dividends for the Orioles, who moved him to left field, where he starred for the next five seasons.

Buford returned to Comiskey Park on Memorial Day 1971 to do battle with Sox pitcher Bart Johnson and a heckling fan who booed him for charging the mound after a Johnson fastball brushed by his head. Johnson avoided a serious injury, but the railbird in the front-row seats took a licking from Don's Oriole teammates after he jumped the fence and charged Buford. The next night a brigade of fans paraded banners in the left-field stands jeering the ex-Sox infielder. "Buford Is a Bum!" read one sign. "The Orioles Are Psychotic!" proclaimed a second bedsheet banner. It was the most famous White Sox fistfight of the 1970s.

Burgess, Forrest

White Sox: 1964–67
Pinch-hitter, catcher
Nickname: Smoky
Birthplace: Caroleen, North Carolina
B: February 6, 1927
D: September 15, 1991
Batted left, threw right
Ht. 5–8½; **Wt.** 198

Burgess, Forrest

White Sox	G	AB	H	AVG	RBI	R	2B	3B	HR	SA	SB
1964	7	5	1	.200	1	1	0	0	1	.800	0
1965	80	77	22	.286	24	2	4	0	2	.416	0
1966	79	67	21	.313	15	0	5	0	0	.388	0
1967	77	60	8	.133	11	2	1	0	2	.250	0
Career	1,718	4,471	1,318	.295	673	485	230	33	126	.389	13

Old Smoky—that was his father's nickname also—was a National League All-Star with three different teams. His long and meritorious career began in 1944 when he played with Lockport, New York, in the Pony League and ended two decades later with Eddie Stanky's White Sox. Burgess is remembered as one of the best pinch-hitters of his era, but he had been an outstanding catcher with the Cubs, Phillies, Reds, and Pirates.

Ed Short purchased Smoky's contract from the Pittsburgh Pirates for the $30,000 waiver price on September 13, 1964. The Yankees were unable to block the deal because they were ahead of the Sox in the standings, but they were fighting to hang on to a paper-thin lead in a torrid three-team pennant race. Burgess contemplated retirement but decided to join the Sox in Detroit instead, on September 15.

Smoky Burgess: the little round man who was terrific in the pinch

Trailing the Tigers by a score of 2–1 in the eighth inning, manager Al Lopez summoned Burgess from the bench and told him to get in there and hit for Joel Horlen. Smokehouse had never hit American League pitching in a regular season game, but in his first appearance he homered off Dave Wickersham to send the game into extra innings. The Sox prevailed in the 10th to keep their slim pennant hopes alive.

Burgess supplied many thrilling moments over the next two seasons. Cool, calm, and collected, the round little man who wore No. 2 on his back thrived in pressure-packed situations. He led the American League in emergency safeties in 1965 and 1966 and still holds the club single-season mark for most pinch hits in a season. Smoky broke Red Lucas's 27-year-old record for career pinch hits on July 25, 1965, in Detroit with a patented line single up the middle. In his three-plus seasons on the South Side, Smoky appeared in 243 games but donned the mask and chest protector only seven times.

Burgess retired after the 1967 season in order to run his North Carolina car dealership. He returned to the game late in life as a coach for the Atlanta Braves' rookie team in Pulaski, Tennessee.

Burns, Britt

White Sox: 1978–85
Pitcher
Nickname: Hoss
Birthplace: Houston, Texas
B: June 8, 1959
Bats right, throws left
Ht. 6–5; **Wt.** 215

Burns, Britt

White Sox	W	L	Pct	ERA	G	CG	IP	H	BB	K	ShO
1978	0	2	.000	12.91	2	0	7⅔	14	3	3	0
1979	0	0	—	5.40	6	0	5	10	1	2	0
1980	15	13	.536	2.84	34	11	238	213	63	133	1
1981	10	6	.625	2.64	24	5	157	139	49	108	1
1982	13	5	.722	4.04	28	5	169⅓	168	67	116	1
1983	10	11	.476	3.58	29	8	173⅔	165	55	115	4
1984	4	12	.250	5.00	34	2	117	130	45	85	0
1985	18	11	.621	3.96	36	8	227	206	79	172	4
Career	70	60	.538	3.66	193	39	1,094⅔	1,045	362	734	11

Shoeless Joe Jackson collected hairpins for good luck. Britt Burns used them regularly to keep his hat in place. The really interesting thing about this towering, baby-faced left-hander is the manner in which he was discovered. *Chicago Tribune* book critic and talk show host Bob Cromie was passing through Birmingham, Alabama, in April 1978 when he noticed a clipping in the *Post-Herald* about a local whiz kid who fanned 18 batters in one game. Cromie, who was a friend of Bill Veeck, mailed the clipping to the Sox owner with a note attached: "Dear Bill: For your dream file. Best, Bob Cromie."

Britt Burns was signed to a Sox contract that year and was an August call-up. He was unimpressive in his debut and would require two full seasons of minor league work before the Cromie "dream" kid lived up to advance billing. Burns was named *Sporting News* Rookie Pitcher of the Year in 1980

Britt Burns: A damaged hip ended his career.

after winning 15 games. He tossed 30 consecutive scoreless innings in 1981 and was selected to the AL All-Star team. The year was marred by the sudden death of his father—a tragedy that exacted a toll on young Burns, both physically and emotionally. During his dad's two-month fight for life, Britt commuted from his bedside back to Chicago.

A 1982 shoulder injury and streaks of inconsistency hurt Burns at a time when an infusion of new players restored respectability to the franchise. Britt was a member of a pitching staff White Sox co-owner Eddie Einhorn called the "best in the history of baseball." Nineteen eighty-three was a lost year for Britt. But he pitched his heart out in Game 4 of the 1983 American League Championship Series. In a do-or-die situation, Burns blanked the Orioles for nine innings until Tito Landrum's ninth-inning home run ended all hope.

After a sterling "comeback" performance in 1985, Burns was traded with two minor leaguers to the Yankees on December 12, 1985, for Ron Hassey and Joe Cowley. Sox general manager Ken Harrelson seized an opportunity and peddled Burns to New York, knowing that his career was jeopardized by a chronic, degenerative hip condition. Britt underwent surgery in the spring of 1986, but his career was already over. He never again pitched in the big leagues, but he has remained a White Sox fan, even while serving as a minor league pitching coach for the Florida Marlins for nine seasons, the Detroit Tigers affiliates for six years, and currently as the Houston Astros minor league pitching coordinator.

Busby, Jim

White Sox: 1950–52; 1955
Outfielder
Nickname: Buzzer
Birthplace: Kenedy, Texas

B: January 8, 1927
D: July 8, 1996
Batted right, threw right
Ht. 6–1; **Wt.** 175

Busby, Jim

White Sox	G	AB	H	AVG	RBI	R	2B	3B	HR	SA	SB
1950	18	48	10	.208	4	5	0	0	0	.208	0
1951	143	477	135	.283	68	59	15	2	5	.354	26
1952	16	39	5	.128	0	5	0	0	0	.128	0
1955	99	337	82	.243	27	38	13	4	1	.315	7
Career	1,352	4,250	1,113	.262	438	541	162	35	48	.350	97

Jim Busby was the first of the Go-Go boys who helped inaugurate the most exciting era of White Sox baseball since the Black Sox era. The "Buzzer" was a fleet-footed halfback at Texas Christian University who turned down a pro football contract to sign with the White Sox prior to the 1948 season.

He was a minor league sensation at Waterloo, Iowa, and Sacramento, California, where his blinding speed on the

Jim Busby

base paths convinced Paul Richards (then managing Seattle of the PCL), that when his turn to manage at the big-league level came, he would have the hustling Busby on his team one way or another.

"Buzzer" stepped off the 100-yard dash at TCU at 9.8 seconds. It was Busby—and not Minnie Minoso—who inspired the famous "Go-Go" chant that echoed through the stands at Comiskey Park in the 1950s. His 26 stolen bases in 1951 seem rather unimpressive today, but in the early 1950s the speed offense revolving around stolen bases and the hit-and-run play was virtually forgotten. Busby, Minoso, and Jim Rivera reintroduced this vital element to the game.

Jim was a tremendous fan favorite and should have remained with the organization for a few more years at least, but Frank Lane was not the kind of general manager to let well enough alone. He traded Buzzer to Washington on May 3, 1952, for Sam Mele—a trade that misfired for Chicago. Jim led the American League twice in putouts and once in percentage and maintained his batting average for the Senators and the other teams he played for in the decade, including the Sox, who reacquired him on June 7, 1955, in a trade with the Senators. Jim was hitting only .230 at the time, but acknowledging that he had erred in judgment, Lane told the press that "the only way I could get him back was when he was in a slump."

A cousin of Kansas City Royals ace Steve Busby, Jim coached for Paul Richards in Baltimore, Houston, Atlanta, and back home on the South Side in 1976.

Buzhardt, John

White Sox: 1962–67
Pitcher
Birthplace: Prosperity, South Carolina

B: August 15, 1936
D: June 15, 2008
Batted right, threw right
Ht. 6–2½; **Wt.** 195

Buzhardt, John

White Sox	W	L	Pct	ERA	G	CG	IP	H	BB	K	ShO	Sv
1962	8	12	.400	4.19	28	8	152⅓	156	59	64	2	0
1963	9	4	.692	2.42	19	6	126⅓	100	31	59	3	0
1964	10	8	.556	2.98	31	8	160	150	35	97	3	0
1965	13	8	.619	3.01	32	4	188⅔	167	56	108	1	1
1966	6	11	.353	3.83	33	5	150⅓	144	30	66	4	1
1967	3	9	.250	3.96	28	0	88⅔	100	37	33	0	0
Career	71	96	.425	3.66	326	44	1,490⅔	1,425	457	678	15	7

When he moved up to the Cubs late in the 1958 season, this lanky sinkerball specialist from the Carolinas was called BUZZ-HART by the Wrigley Field faithful. Coming to the White Sox on November 28, 1961, in an experience-for-youth trade that sent Roy Sievers to the Philadelphia Phillies, the phonetic pronunciation of his last name was mysteriously changed by the White Sox marketing geniuses. In his five-year run on the South Side, big John was henceforth called BAZAAR-'D.

By any other name, John Buzhardt's baseball career was in a shambles by the time White Sox pitching coach Ray Berres got ahold of him. His one redeeming moment was dubious at best. In 1961 Buzhardt put a stop to the Phillies embarrassing 23-game losing streak. The die-hard Phillies faithful greeted him with a standing ovation when the team plane touched down at the airport. Otherwise there was little to recommend him to manager Al Lopez and the White Sox, whose winning tradition was based on the quality of the starting pitching and the relief corps.

"Buzhardt is a hard thrower with a good sinker, and under Ray Berres' coaching we believe we can turn him into a winner," Lopez predicted after hearing that Sievers, one of his least favorite players who never really blended into the Sox run-and-gun offense, was gone.

Pitching coach Berres was indeed a miracle worker. Buzhardt was no exception. Despite a losing record in 1962, he showed great poise by whipping New York three times that year. During his Sox career, Johnny became the latest "Yankee Killer" by virtue of winning seven decisions without a loss.

A sore shoulder limited his playing time in 1963, but he moved easily into the rotation and was a very capable fourth starter for Lopez in the pitching-rich 1960s.

Over the winter of 1965–66, Sox general manager Ed Short tried to package Buzhardt with Eddie Fisher and Floyd

John Buzhardt

Robinson in a trade with Cincinnati that would have brought Frank Robinson and his potent bat to the South Side. Short nearly pulled it off, but Reds GM Bill DeWitt vetoed it at the last minute to bargain with the Baltimore Orioles, who eventually sent the fading Milt Pappas to Cincinnati. In hindsight, DeWitt probably should have accepted Short's more generous offer, given the disastrous consequences of this trade for Cincinnati.

Under Eddie Stanky's militaristic regimens, which included a ban on watching television in the clubhouse, Buzhardt's performance slipped precipitously in 1966, despite four shutouts. A new pitching coach, Marv Grissom, altered John's stance on the mound so that his body moved toward the third-base line, allowing him to conserve some effort before releasing his overhand sinker—a deadly delivery when it was working.

But after absorbing an Opening Day shellacking at the hands of the Boston Red Sox to inaugurate the bittersweet 1967 season, Buzhardt was of no further use to Stanky. He was sold to Baltimore for the $20,000 waiver price on August 21 to make room for the young pitching phenom Francisco Carlos.

Ivan Calderon

Calderon, Ivan

White Sox: 1986–90; 1993
Outfielder
Birthplace: Fajardo, Puerto Rico

B: March 19, 1962
D: April 8, 1997
Batted right, threw right
Ht. 6–1; **Wt.** 220

Calderon, Ivan

White Sox	G	AB	H	AVG	RBI	R	2B	3B	HR	SA	SB
1986	13	33	10	.303	2	3	2	1	0	.341	0
1987	144	542	159	.293	83	93	38	2	28	.526	10
1988	73	264	56	.212	35	40	14	0	14	.424	4
1989	157	622	178	.286	87	83	34	9	14	.437	7
1990	158	607	166	.273	74	85	44	2	14	.422	32
1993	9	26	3	.115	3	1	2	0	3	.193	0
Career	924	3,312	901	.272	444	470	200	25	104	.442	97

A series of nagging injuries curtailed Ivan Calderon's playing time with the Seattle Mariners and the White Sox throughout his career. The hard-hitting outfielder was a top contender for Rookie of the Year honors in 1985 when his season was cut short by a hand injury. With his value to the Mariners organization diminished as a result, Calderon was traded to the Sox on June 26, 1986, for catcher Scott Bradley. It was probably Ken Harrelson's smartest trade in his short-lived tenure as general manager.

Ivan blasted 28 home runs in 1987—none of them were cheap. A big man, possessing surprising speed, Calderon paced the ballclub in 10 different offensive categories but made the defensive play of the year, and perhaps the decade, when he climbed the left-field wall at old Tiger Stadium on July 27 to pull back an Alan Trammell home run that was already in the stands.

The injury jinx came back to haunt Calderon in 1988 when he pulled a muscle in the rib cage. With his average hovering in the low .200 range, the Sox decided to have his chronically ailing shoulder repaired by the renowned Dr. Frank Jobe.

Ivan came back strong in 1989 and 1990, and was the team's most formidable offensive threat before Frank Thomas arrived from the minors. With the "Big Hurt" on board, Calderon suddenly became expendable. He was traded to Montreal on December 24, 1990, for Tim Raines, which turned out to be one of Ron Schueler's best trades as GM.

Carrasquel, Alfonso

White Sox: 1950–55
Shortstop
Nickname: Chico
Birthplace: Caracas, Venezuela

B: January 23, 1928
D: May 26, 2005
Batted right, threw right
Ht. 6–0; **Wt.** 170

Carrasquel, Alfonso

White Sox	G	AB	H	AVG	RBI	R	2B	3B	HR	SA	SB
1950	141	524	148	.282	46	72	21	5	4	.365	0
1951	147	538	142	.264	58	41	22	4	2	.331	14
1952	100	359	89	.248	42	36	7	4	1	.298	2
1953	149	552	154	.279	47	72	30	4	2	.359	5
1954	155	620	158	.255	62	106	28	3	12	.368	7
1955	145	523	134	.256	52	83	11	2	11	.348	1
Career	1,325	4,644	1,199	.258	474	568	172	25	55	.342	31

The son of a Venezuelan beer salesman, Chico had been playing baseball since he was 15 years old when Branch Rickey's agents approached him about a shortstop opening with the Dodgers affiliate at Fort Worth, Texas, in 1949. The shrewd Rickey signed Carrasquel to his first professional contract, but Chico would remain in the Brooklyn system for only one year. White Sox general manager Frank

Lane managed to convince Rickey that Chico wasn't going to amount to much—knowing all along that just wasn't the case.

The language barrier may have hastened Rickey's decision to unload Chico to the White Sox on September 30, 1949, for $35,000 and two obscure minor leaguers, Fred Hancock and Charles Eisenmann. The communication problem was easily remedied by Lane when he dealt pitcher Alex Carrasquel—Chico's uncle—to Buffalo of the International League for relief pitcher Luis Aloma, whose real value to the organization in the next few years was as Chico's translator.

Beginning in his rookie year of 1950 when he unseated Luke Appling as the starting shortstop, young Carrasquel overcame the hardships of playing in a foreign land with teammates who did not understand a word of what he was saying by becoming a premier player in the American game. Chico reeled off a 24-game hitting streak in 1950. A year later he shattered an American League record by accepting 297 chances without committing an error. Carrasquel was one of the spark plugs of the team's 1951 resurgence.

A solid defensive player who led the league in fielding in 1951, 1953, and 1954, and who was named to three AL All-Star squads, Carrasquel was an "off and on again" kind of hitter prone to hot streaks and prolonged dry spells. His inconsistency was traced to a weight problem that he seemed unable to control. Manager Paul Richards benched him for lethargic play in 1952. Earlier in the year he had shown up in spring training without so much as cab fare. The Chico "problem" continued in 1955 under Marty Marion, the new Sox manager. "I don't know what is the matter," complained Marion one afternoon. "You'd think benching a player would make him angry. Not Chico. He just goes along as if nothing happened."

Tiring of these antics, but very pleased with the steady progress of minor league sensation Luis Aparicio, Chuck Comiskey and John Rigney traded Chico and outfielder Jim Busby to Cleveland for Larry Doby on October 25, 1955. Carrasquel was angry and upset with both Marion and Comiskey upon hearing the news. He told reporters that the youthful White Sox VP had promised him "lifetime employment" in the organization. According to Carrasquel there was nothing he could do to please the hypercritical Marion. "I'm glad to be in Cleveland," he added.

Chico Carrasquel

A national hero in his homeland, Chico broadcast the Venezuelan Winter League for 10 years before joining the White Sox Spanish-language radio network as a commentator in 1990.

Cicotte, Eddie

White Sox: 1912–20
Pitcher
Birthplace: Detroit, Michigan

B: June 19, 1884
D: May 5, 1969
Batted right, threw right
Ht. 5–9; **Wt.** 175

Cicotte, Ed

White Sox	W	L	Pct	ERA	G	CG	IP	H	BB	K	ShO
1912	10	10	.500	3.50	29	15	198	217	52	90	1
1913	18	12	.600	1.58	41	18	268	224	73	121	3
1914	13	16	.448	2.04	45	15	269⅓	220	72	122	4
1915	13	12	.520	3.02	39	15	233⅓	216	48	106	1
1916	15	7	.682	1.78	44	11	187	138	70	91	2
1917	28	12	.700	1.53	49	29	346⅔	246	70	150	7
1918	12	19	.387	2.64	38	24	266	275	40	104	1
1919	29	7	.806	1.82	40	29	306⅔	256	49	110	5
1920	21	10	.677	3.26	37	28	303⅓	316	74	87	4
Career	210	149	.585	2.37	502	248	3,224⅓	2,897	827	1,374	36

Eddie Cicotte paid dearly for his sins against baseball. For 40 years the former White Sox ace lived with the knowledge that he was one of the eight crooked players who conspired to "throw" the 1919 World Series to the Cincinnati Redlegs. Late in life Cicotte was interviewed by baseball writer Joe Falls of the *Detroit Free Press.* When asked about the burden of guilt he shouldered, Cicotte replied, "I admit I did wrong, but I've paid for it."

Cicotte (pronounced SY-cot-tee) played baseball with independent teams in the metropolitan Detroit area before signing a minor league contract with the Tigers in 1904. In 1905 he had an outstanding season with Augusta in the South Atlantic League but was bypassed for promotion because his roommate, Ty Cobb, was setting the league on fire. Eddie drifted through the American Association and the Western League for the next two years until the Red Sox purchased his contract in 1907. His American League debut followed a year later.

In Boston Cicotte acquired a reputation as a surly troublemaker after repeated run-ins with Red Sox manager Jake Stahl and owner John Taylor. After Cicotte was suspended by Stahl, Boston management placed him on waivers. The White Sox were the only team to submit a claim, and the sale was consummated on July 10, 1912.

For the next four years Cicotte delivered his knuckleball to opposing hitters with varying degrees of success. He led the league in winning percentage and was second in earned run average in 1916, but was never properly acknowledged as

Knuckleball and "shineball" ace Ed Cicotte

one of the top three pitchers of the league. Not until a year later did the accolades begin to pour in, and only because of a trick pitch he allegedly developed over the winter called the "shine ball." It was not so much a pitch as a brilliant piece of psychological warfare employed by the veteran moundsman to frustrate opposing hitters.

Cicotte was accused of concealing a sticky substance inside his uniform to doctor a ball illegally. During the pennant-winning 1917 season, the year Eddie twirled a no-hitter against the Browns among his 28 victories, 12 sets of uniforms were seized by suspicious umpires. They could not find any evidence of an illegal substance, however. Cicotte claimed there was no such thing as a "shine ball." "So long as the batters thought they were batting against something they didn't know anything about, I had an advantage," he said at the time. "If you can bluff a fellow into believing that you know more than he knows or have more than he has, you have him licked."

At the age of 35, Cicotte led the Sox to their second pennant in three years. A marvelously conditioned athlete at the top of his game, Eddie was the workhorse of Gleason's 1919 staff. His 29 victories topped the league, and they were the main reason why the Sox were heavily favored to knock off the Cincinnati Redlegs in the World Series. But a consortium of East Coast gamblers tied to New York gangster Arnold Rothstein had other ideas.

Eddie and teammate Joe Jackson were the key to a World Series fix that sullied baseball's image as the last "clean" sport in America. In his appearance before the grand jury on September 29, 1920, Cicotte told of the pressure put upon him by his teammates. "Risberg and Gandil and McMullin were at me for a week before the World Series started. They wanted me to go crooked. I don't know. I needed the money. I had the wife and kids. I don't know what they'll think," he said.

Cicotte's integrity was compromised—with the promise of $10,000 that he planned to use to pay off a mortgage on his new farm. "The eight of us got together in my room three or four days before the games started," he said. "Gandil was the master of ceremonies. We talked about throwing the series—decided we could get away with it."

Eddie signaled the gamblers that the fix was on when he plunked Morrie Rath, the Reds' leadoff batter in Game 1, between the shoulder blades. Though his earned run average for the series was a respectable 2.91, Cicotte lost the first and fourth games. His guilt was clearly established, but the motivation for putting his career in jeopardy is less clear.

There is no hard and fast evidence to support author Eliot Asinof's contention that Cicotte was "held back" by manager Kid Gleason in the final weeks of the 1917 and 1919 seasons in order to save Comiskey from paying his ace pitcher a $10,000 bonus if he won his 30th game. If Comiskey reneged on a promise, it was not due to any deliberate intrigue on his part to shortchange Cicotte in this manner. Cicotte's 1919 base salary was $9,075—well above the league average.

Ed Cicotte was acquitted of criminal charges by a Cook County jury in August 1921, but stood convicted in the mind of Judge Kenesaw Mountain Landis, baseball's first commissioner. Cicotte and his seven Black Sox teammates were banned from baseball for life. An outcast to the bitter end, Eddie returned to Detroit, where he worked in a Ford plant for many years. In his declining years Eddie tended to his strawberry patch and patiently answered letters sent to him by baseball fans all around the country. When the subject of the Black Sox scandal came up, as it usually did, Cicotte never shied away from the truth. He admitted he made a mistake, but hastily added, "I don't know of anyone who ever went through life without making a mistake. Everybody who has ever lived has committed sins of his own."

Cissell, Chalmer

White Sox: 1928–32
Shortstop
Nicknames: Bill; Spider Bill
Birthplace: Perryville, Missouri

B: January 3, 1904
D: March 15, 1949
Batted left, threw right
Ht. 5–11; **Wt.** 170

Cissell, Chalmer

White Sox	G	AB	H	AVG	RBI	R	2B	3B	HR	SA	SB
1928	125	443	115	.260	60	66	22	3	1	.330	18
1929	152	618	173	.280	62	83	27	15	5	.387	26
1930	141	561	152	.271	48	82	28	9	2	.364	16
1931	109	409	90	.220	46	42	13	5	1	.284	18
1932	12	43	11	.256	5	7	1	1	1	.395	0
Career	956	3,706	990	.267	423	516	173	43	29	.360	114

Bill Cissell's tragic life provides an object lesson about the pitfalls of coping with instant fame and fast money in the world of baseball.

"Spider Bill" was serving with the 14th U.S. Cavalry stationed in Des Moines, Iowa, when he decided to switch careers and become a ballplayer. He signed a minor league contract with the Des Moines team in 1925, but attained his stardom with Portland of the Pacific Coast League two years later. Cissell earned rave reviews for his fancy glove work and was purchased by Comiskey for $123,000 in cash—a record-breaking sum that overshadowed the Willie Kamm consideration five years earlier. "The ballyhoo I got after Portland sold me for that sum was the greatest burden any player ever carried into the majors," he once said.

Bill Cissell was one of the many tragic figures who dot the pages of White Sox history.

Cissell collected six hits in his first 11 at bats—a good beginning—but success was fleeting for this rangy shortstop who waged a losing battle against alcohol and the impulse to carouse in nightclubs with fellow fun seeker Art Shires. Bill Cissell's Chicago misfortunes ended on April 24, 1932, when he was traded to Cleveland for Johnny Hodapp and Bob Seeds.

In 1949 Cissell and his young son Gary were located in a dingy South Side rooming house. The ex-Sox bonus player was broke, destitute, and suffering from malnutrition. A serious nerve condition cost him the use of both of his legs. It was rumored that Cissell had been working in Comiskey Park as an electrician prior to his death, but no one could verify these reports.

Bill Cissell suffered a heart attack in March 1949. He remained in an oxygen tent until his passing on the 15th of that month. Travel expenses for Cissell's son and the cost of the funeral were paid by Chuck and Dorothy Comiskey when it was determined that the family had no money to pay for a decent burial. His remains were shipped back to his hometown in Perryville—where this strange baseball odyssey began in 1918 when a kid shortstop named Chalmer Cissell came looking for a job with the local nine.

Collins, Eddie

White Sox: 1915–26
Second baseman
Nickname: Cocky
Birthplace: Tarrytown, New York

B: May 2, 1887
D: March 25, 1951
Batted left, threw right
Ht. 5–9; **Wt.** 175

Collins, Eddie

White Sox	G	AB	H	AVG	RBI	R	2B	3B	HR	SA	SB
1915	155	521	173	.332	77	118	22	10	4	.436	46
1916	155	545	168	.308	52	87	14	17	0	.396	40
1917	156	564	163	.289	67	91	18	12	0	.363	53
1918	97	330	91	.276	30	51	8	2	2	.330	22
1919	140	518	165	.319	80	87	19	7	4	.405	33
1920	153	601	222	.369	75	115	37	13	3	.489	19
1921	139	526	177	.337	58	79	20	10	2	.424	12
1922	154	598	194	.324	69	92	20	12	1	.403	20
1923	145	505	182	.360	67	89	22	5	5	.453	47
1924	152	556	194	.349	86	108	27	7	6	.455	42
1925	118	425	147	.346	80	80	26	3	3	.442	19
1926	106	375	129	.344	62	66	32	4	1	.459	13
Career	2,826	9,949	3,311	.333	1,299	1,818	437	187	47	.428	743

Baseball purists and East Coast historians remember Eddie Collins as the glue of Connie Mack's fabled "Million Dollar Infield," a quartet of enormously gifted Philadelphia A's that also included Stuffy McInnis, Franklin "Home Run" Baker, and Jack Barry. Often overlooked by these same historians, who equate Collins' diamond exploits solely with his Philadelphia years, is that Eddie played for the White Sox for a longer period of time and with greater distinction.

Eddie Collins collected his 3,000th career hit with the Sox.

He was one of the great money players of the game, a natural-born hitter whose leadership on and off the field was greatly valued by a succession of White Sox managers. "That fellow Eddie Collins is the greatest player I ever seen in my long career, and I have seen a lot of them," offered umpire Billy Evans in 1919. "Never saw him do a dumb thing in his life, and incidentally he is forever keeping some of his teammates from making a slip."

Feeling threatened by the marauding tactics of Chicago's Federal League team and declining fan interest in the South Side ballclub, Charles Comiskey loosened the purse strings and bought Eddie Collins from the A's on December 8, 1914, following weeks of intense negotiation.

A graduate of Columbia University who made his major league debut playing against the White Sox under the pseudonym "Sullivan" on September 16, 1906, Collins shrewdly negotiated a record-setting five-year contract for himself, calling for a $15,000 signing bonus and $15,000 per annum. The Old Roman was said to have paid Mack $50,000 to secure Collins' release—a titanic sum of money.

In the next 10 years Eddie Collins pulled down an aggregate sum of $175,000 from Comiskey, which included $6,000 in each of those 10 seasons for serving as White Sox team captain. Considered to be a management-oriented player who made no bones about his desire to pilot a big-league club someday, Collins was never very popular with the eight Black Sox players who were eventually banned from baseball for life. Returning from an eastern road trip on September 2, 1920, Eddie reported his suspicions of wrongdoing to Comiskey but was scolded for rumormongering. Collins was a witness for the prosecution when the Black Sox conspiracy trial convened in July 1921.

Comiskey was keenly aware that the Eddie Collins name meant good box office. For these reasons alone, the Old Roman hired him to manage the Sox on December 11, 1924. Eddie proved up to the task and guided the Sox through two winning seasons in one of the darkest periods of team history. When advancing age and knee problems set in, Comiskey dumped Collins in favor of Ray Schalk. No one came to the park to see Eddie Collins manage, Comiskey reasoned.

So in 1927 Collins returned to Philadelphia and a warm welcome from his old boss Connie Mack, who hired him as a player/coach. He was a steadying clubhouse influence who was neither bored nor hysterical in his dealings with the players. Collins waited patiently for Mack to retire, but when the opportunity failed to materialize, he moved on to Boston, where he became part owner of the Red Sox with his former prep school classmate Tom Yawkey. Elected to the Hall of Fame in 1939 (the year of its founding), Eddie Collins always traveled the high road in life. He was one of the great gentlemen of the game who was badly mistreated by Charles Comiskey in the twilight of his career.

Collins, John

White Sox: 1910–20
Outfielder, first baseman
Nickname: Shano
Birthplace: Charlestown, Massachusetts

B: December 4, 1885
D: September 10, 1955
Batted right, threw right
Ht. 6–0; **Wt.** 175

Collins, John

White Sox	G	AB	H	AVG	RBI	R	2B	3B	HR	SA	SB
1910	97	315	62	.197	24	29	10	8	1	.289	10
1911	106	370	97	.262	48	48	16	12	3	.395	14
1912	153	575	168	.292	81	75	34	10	2	.397	26
1913	148	535	128	.239	47	53	26	9	1	.327	22
1914	154	598	164	.274	65	61	34	9	3	.376	30
1915	153	576	148	.257	85	73	24	17	2	.368	38
1916	143	527	128	.243	42	74	28	12	0	.342	16
1917	82	252	59	.234	14	38	13	3	1	.321	14
1918	103	365	100	.274	56	30	18	11	1	.392	7
1919	63	179	50	.279	16	21	6	3	1	.363	3
1920	133	495	150	.303	63	70	21	10	1	.392	12
Career	1,798	6,386	1,687	.264	705	746	309	133	21	.364	225

Versatile and eager to please, "Shano" (a Gaelic variation of Sean, meaning John) was an unselfish athlete who cheerfully accepted his role as a "situation player" for a decade without complaint.

Collins began his career with the Haverhill, Massachusetts, club of the New England League in the fall of 1907. He was out of baseball the following year, but back with Springfield of the Connecticut League in 1909, hitting a robust .322. Shano was signed by Charles Comiskey at the conclusion of the 1909 season. He showed manager Hugh Duffy some real pluck by remaining in the spring training lineup despite a severe attack of the grippe. Shano Collins had come to play, but his first-base work was spotty. Two weeks into the 1910 season Duffy converted him to the outfield. By 1913 he had established himself as one of the defensive specialists in the league.

John "Shano" Collins played in the shadow of his teammates but was a star in his own right.

Long and rangy, Collins covered vast amounts of ground. His throwing arm was strong and accurate, but a tendency to overswing at the ball cost him a few points on his batting average. Manager Clarence Rowland moved Collins back to first base in 1915 when the situation became critical, but after Jacques Fournier regained his health, Shano was returned to the outfield.

When the Sox clinched the pennant in Boston on September 21, 1917, it was appropriate that Collins (as the senior man on the roster in terms of service) delivered the game-winning hit. Relegated to part-time duty in the outfield by this point, Collins collected Chicago's first hit and first run in the 1917 World Series.

Chick Gandil's stubborn refusal to report to the White Sox spring training camp in 1920 forced Gleason to shift Collins to first base as an everyday player after rookie Ted Jourdan was found wanting. Management expressed its appreciation for the veteran's stellar effort under these difficult circumstances by declaring September 11, 1920, "Shano Collins Day" in Chicago. A purse of $2,000 was collected from long-time White Sox fans and presented to him as a token of their esteem. Two weeks later the full revelations of the Black Sox scandal appeared in the press, and Collins' job status changed overnight.

Shano was one of the few players left on the roster that Comiskey could reasonably expect to receive something for in a trade. On March 4, 1921, Collins was packaged to Boston along with Nemo Leibold for future Hall of Famer Harry Hooper.

Consuegra, Sandy

White Sox: 1953–56
Pitcher
Birthplace: Potrerillos, Las Villas, Cuba

B: September 3, 1920
Bats right, throws right
Ht. 5–11; **Wt.** 165

Consuegra, Sandy

White Sox	W	L	Pct	ERA	G	CG	IP	H	BB	K	ShO
1953	7	5	.583	2.54	29	5	124	122	28	30	1
1954	16	3	.842	2.69	39	5	154	142	35	31	2
1955	6	5	.545	2.64	44	3	126⅓	120	18	35	0
1956	1	2	.333	5.17	28	0	38⅓	45	11	7	0
Career	51	32	.614	3.37	248	24	809⅓	811	246	193	5

Happy-go-lucky Sandy was discovered playing ball in Havana, and he was signed to a Senators contract in 1950 at a time when the Washington ballclub monopolized the Cuban baseball market. The little right-hander, who enjoyed betting on cockfights during the off-season, was purchased from the Senators in a straight cash deal on May 12, 1953. It was one of Frank Lane's best acquisitions as general manager.

Sandy Consuegra

Alternating between the bullpen and the starting rotation during the 1954 season, Sandy scaled the heights with his new ballclub. He posted the highest winning percentage in White Sox history and became only the fourth Chisox pitcher (up to that time) to lead the American League in that category. Sandy was a perfect 8–0 in Comiskey Park, and his earned run average was second in the league to Mike Garcia of the Cleveland Indians.

A marvelous control pitcher, the Cuban righty was named to the 1954 All-Star team, but he was rocked for five hits and five runs in only one-third of an inning. Consuegra was not nearly as effective in 1955 and was relegated to part-time duty in the bullpen. He was sold to the Baltimore Orioles on May 14, 1956.

Contreras, Jose

White Sox: 2004–09
Pitcher
Birthplace: La Martinas, Cuba

B: December 6, 1971
Bats right, throws right
Ht. 6–4; **Wt.** 245

Contreras, Jose

White Sox	W	L	Pct	ERA	G	CG	IP	H	BB	K	ShO	Sv
2004	5	4	.556	5.30	13	0	74⅓	73	42	68	0	0
2005	15	7	.682	3.61	32	1	204⅓	177	75	154	0	0
2006	13	9	.591	4.27	30	1	196	194	55	134	1	0
2007	10	17	.370	5.57	32	2	189	232	62	113	2	0
2008	7	6	.538	4.54	20	1	121	130	35	70	0	0
2009	5	13	.278	5.42	21	0	114⅔	121	45	89	0	0
Career	77	67	.535	4.55	258	5	1,140⅓	1,145	410	856	3	4

Jose Contreras

By their own admission, the New York Yankees blundered badly when they traded Jose Contreras, the star Cuban pitcher, to the White Sox for Esteban Loaiza on July 31, 2004. Ken Williams was the only general manager in baseball interested in acquiring Jose, who suffered control problems and a lack of confidence in the pressure cooker that is New York City. "Sometimes we might be too quick to judge because of the New York mentality; the patience level isn't there," admitted Yankees GM Brian Cashman after assessing the big Cuban righty's newfound success in Chicago and his outstanding 2005 campaign. "We've been guilty of pitchers not handling the situation. Sometimes pitchers get hurt; sometimes guys have come here and thrived."

And sometimes they resurrect their careers elsewhere, as was the case with Contreras, who played seven years for the Cuban National Team before defecting to the United States on October 25, 2002, while in Santillo, Mexico, for the Americas Cup. Jose was a gold medalist at the 1999 Pan-American Games in Canada and an admired international star in Latin America with an amazing 117–50 record before the Yankees upstaged and outbid Boston for his services on February 6, 2003. At the time the signing was announced, Red Sox president and CEO Larry Lucchino excoriated the Yankees as "the Evil Empire" for their ability to overpay and out-hustle every other team for Type A free agents and players with so much potential, as Contreras' numbers in the Cuban League seemed to suggest. Even the most evil of empires screw up from time to time, and what better beneficiary of their shortsightedness than the Pale Hose? Contreras became the 13th Cuban to play for the White Sox and, arguably, the most notable since Minnie Minoso, Luis Aloma, and Sandy Consuegra back in the early 1950s.

But in 2004 he led the league in wild pitches, and he couldn't hold runners on first base very well, either. It was obvious that the erratic Contreras possessed "all the tools," but harnessing his skills at this level would prove to be the real challenge for pitching coach Don Cooper going into the 2005 season. Contreras started poorly: his 4–5 record at the All-Star break for a team playing at a .625 clip tested Ozzie Guillen's patience, but the Wizard of Oz never lost hope. With a little help from Orlando "El Duque" Hernandez, who mentored his teammate and fellow countryman, Contreras settled down and made the necessary adjustments that turned his season around. In the second half Contreras was unstoppable. Although he still couldn't hold runners on to save his soul, Jose moved from the outhouse to the castle on the strength of an 11–2 post–All-Star break record.

He turned it around by making necessary but simple adjustments to his pitching mechanics. Contreras dropped his arm slot to a low, three-quarter angle, delivering his split-finger fastball with deadly accuracy. Credit "El Duque" with suggesting he change his delivery. Credit team massage therapist John Louis with a treatment program that made Contreras feel "loose." "In Cuba I didn't have that," Jose said through his interpreter. "I haven't gotten an injury. Thank God I gave that man a chance to massage me." In September Contreras roared down the stretch with a perfect 6–0 record in six starts and was named American League Pitcher of the Month. He had emerged as the most dominant pitcher on the staff and continued his string of success into the postseason, winning three of four, including Game 1 of the World Series against his former Yankees teammate, mentor, and friend Roger Clemens, who had welcomed him to New York in 2003 as a scared rookie unable to communicate in English. "He taught me a lot of things, a couple of pitches," Jose said. "We pitch mostly the same way, and just facing him is an honor. I wish I had him on my team, but too bad we have to face him." The "Rocket," old and gimpy, suffered engine failure and was removed early in the game. Jose Contreras gutted out a tough win and emerged the victor.

Awarded a three-year, $29 million contract extension on April 1, 2006, Jose picked right up where he left off in 2005. He tied a team record by winning his first nine decisions in 2006—and set a new team mark for Sox hurlers with 17 consecutive wins—a streak that extended from August 21, 2005, to July 4, 2006, when the Yankees put an end to it. Contreras had already tied Johan Santana and Dave McNally for the second-longest winning streak in the past 40 years, but after that moment of glory, the wheels completely fell off. Ozzie Guillen and Don Cooper showed remarkable patience, but the Cuban righty's career, simply put, went from penthouse to outhouse after the 2006 All-Star break. Was his age catching up with him? Demoted to the bullpen late in the 2007 season, Contreras was unable to regain the old magic. An angry Jerry Reinsdorf expressed understandable frustration and publicly chided himself for going against his strong convictions against signing pitchers to long-term contracts. "He certainly isn't living up to his money," the Sox chairman snapped. "I've said how many times over the years, when you go more than one year with a pitcher you are sticking your neck out. If you go more than three years, it's probably suicide."

Jose's struggles were exacerbated by a ruptured Achilles tendon suffered on August 9, 2008, while attempting to field a weakly hit ground ball and cover first against the Boston Red Sox. It looked like a career-ending injury, and the odds weighed heavily against his return in 2009. But if anything, Jose was determined. He was ready when the bell rang in 2009, and his physical recovery from so devastating an injury seemed nothing short of miraculous—that is, until he faced live action. His mended leg could not stave off a string of five losses to start the season and a rapid demotion to Triple A Charlotte on May 12. He was summoned back to Chicago on June 8, but after hopeful signs that he could once again effectively shut down American League hitting, expectations for a full recovery and a return to stardom proved to be premature.

His shabby 2009 performance must surely rank as the worst single-season pitching exhibition by a Sox starter since the days of Jaime Navarro in the late 1990s, or going back even further than that to the luckless right-hander Joel Davis in the 1980s (picked ahead of Roger Clemens in the amateur draft). Of course, no discussion about bad Sox starting pitching over the past 40 years is complete without a tip of the cap to Jesse Jefferson and his incredibly bad mound work in 1976. But in this case, Contreras had sparkled in 2005–06 only to suffer a complete collapse. It was a bitter if not vexing disappointment to the many fans who will never forget his contributions in better days. On August 31, 2009, Jose was dealt to Colorado for pitcher Brandon Hynick, and with that bit of news came an enormous sigh of relief in the White Sox Nation. Jose appeared in the 2009 National League Division Series then signed with the Phillies as a free agent on January 28, 2010. In the role of long reliever, his velocity improved, and he was used extensively out of the pen by manager Charlie Manuel. In the 2010 NLDS, Contreras won Game 2 in relief.

Crede, Joe

White Sox: 2000–08
Infielder
Birthplace: Jefferson City, Missouri

B: April 26, 1978
Bats right, throws right
Ht. 6–2; **Wt.** 195

Crede, Joe

White Sox	G	AB	H	AVG	RBI	R	2B	3B	HR	SA	SB
2000	7	14	5	.357	3	2	1	0	0	.429	0
2001	17	50	11	.220	7	1	1	1	0	.280	1
2002	53	200	57	.285	35	28	10	0	12	.515	0
2003	151	536	140	.261	75	68	31	2	19	.433	1
2004	144	490	117	.239	69	67	25	0	21	.418	1
2005	132	432	109	.252	62	54	21	0	22	.454	1
2006	150	544	154	.283	94	76	31	0	30	.506	0
2007	47	167	36	.216	22	13	5	0	4	.317	0
2008	97	335	83	.248	55	41	18	1	17	.460	0
Career	888	3,101	787	.254	470	392	159	5	140	.444	4

Joe Crede waited a long time for his major league call-up, but so, too, did his cousin and fellow Missourian, the big righty Dennis Higgins, who toiled in the White Sox farm system for eight seasons before making his successful pitching debut as a handy middle reliever for Eddie Stanky in 1966. Joe didn't have to wait quite as long as Cousin Dennis, but year after year it seemed, Sox fans read with great interest the accomplishments of this rookie third baseman and wondered why the bus had not yet left Charlotte bound for Chicago. His press clippings and lengthening list of minor league awards made us all want to believe that the second coming of Brooks Robinson was close at hand.

Selected in the fifth round of the June 1996 free agent draft out of Fatima High School in Westphalia, Missouri, Crede was originally ticketed for shortstop, but team priorities changed. Joe was given a tryout in center field, but the experiment was scrapped after he was diagnosed with a depth-perception problem by team physicians. He settled in at third base thereafter and captured the 1998 Carolina League MVP at Class A Winston-Salem. The accolades poured in. He was named *Baseball America*'s Best Defensive Third Baseman of the Southern League in 1999; the MVP of the Southern League for a second time in 2000; and *Baseball America*'s No. 10 Prospect and Best Defensive Third Baseman of the International League in

2002. So where was Joe? Inquiring columnists wanted to know. "There is nothing else Crede can accomplish in Class AAA. Because Crede was ready for the major leagues, if not last season, then certainly at the beginning of this season. Because Crede currently has a stratospheric slugging percentage of .575 and is turning into an old man while he awaits a call-up to the majors. But what will [Ken] Williams do with Crede?" wondered Carol Slezak, *Sun-Times* columnist, at the mid-point of the 2002 campaign.

The question boiled down to opening a roster spot in the lineup. The Sox were in no particular hurry to rush the kid along with Jose Valentin playing third and hitting his home runs. Tony Graffanino spelled Valentin at the hot corner, and Royce Clayton plugged the defensive hole at shortstop. So, at that point, it seemed pointless to bring Crede up and see him waste away on the bench. Ultimately, however, Slezak's wish became Williams' command. In 2002 Crede was summoned from Charlotte. Not long after, he earned his first award in the big time, American League Player of the Week honors for August 26–September 1, and was in a hitter's groove. Everyone in the organization was excited because the arrival of Joe Crede made the free agent loss of Robin Ventura in 1998 that much easier to swallow. Then Royce Clayton departed. Valentin moved back to short, and Joe became the everyday third baseman, exhibiting excellent range, although his hot hitting in 2002 trailed off the following year with more playing time.

It was plain to see that he was destined to become a better glove man than big-time slugger. But that was okay in a lineup

Joe Crede

dominated by right-handed power hitters like Frank Thomas, Carlos Lee, and Magglio Ordonez. The Sox could live with a third-sacker hitting in the .250–.270 range if he could maintain the defense on the left-hand side of the infield in the same fine tradition as Robin Ventura. And this was the important dimension that Crede brought with him to the team. Joe proved his value in other ways, as well. He is a tremendous clutch hitter with a flair for the dramatic. When a key hit was needed at a crucial stage of a ballgame—preferably a home run—Joe always seemed to find a way to come through. He has five game-ending, "walk-off" home runs to his credit (through 2005), but none more spectacular or important than his 10th-inning shot off of Indians' reliever David Riske on September 20 to hold the rampaging Tribe at bay and extend the Sox' tissue-thin lead to 3½ games. The decisive shot was one of the keys to final victory in the championship season. This followed a short stint on the disabled list for a hairline fracture of the right middle finger.

But it was in the postseason that Crede came of age as a world-class third baseman. Slowed by a pair of herniated disks in his lower back that bothered him for most of the season, Joe gave the White Sox the lead with another clutch home run in Game 1 of the World Series and then saved the day with his glove. Throughout the playoffs and into the Series, Crede made a strong case for awards consideration. He put on a fielding clinic the entire show, exhibiting great range and tremendous instinct. Those idyllic images of "the next Brooks Robinson" seemed close to fulfilling the prophecy, even as the distant rumblings of Crede's eventual free agency echoed in Sox Nation and a prized rookie challenger out of Oklahoma State named Josh Fields waited patiently in the wings. Meanwhile, back in Westphalia, where Crede is just "good ol' Joe" to his neighbors, the townsfolk threw their favorite son a parade when he returned home from his World Series adventures.

Joe reached the pinnacle of his White Sox career in 2006, reeling in a Silver Slugger award while joining Bill Melton as the only third-sacker in team history to slug 20-plus home runs in three straight seasons. His All-Star appearance in '06 was his first—and last. Back surgery ended his 2007 season on June 12—an ominous indicator that Robin Ventura's successor's career on the South Side was likely to be curtailed. It became a self-fulfilling prophecy when he was sidelined with lumbar inflammation from July 25 to August 24, 2008. On September 2 he left a game in Cleveland, complaining of back stiffness. At that point it was painfully clear to an increasingly frustrated Ozzie Guillen that Crede was playing in the twilight—his physical health notwithstanding. Joe committed 20 errors to lead the AL in limited play. It was the most miscues at the hot corner since the hapless Greg Norton muffed 25 in 1999.

At season's end, the gimpy Crede who once said that *Seinfeld* was the one TV show he "never could miss," underwent back surgery and filed for free agency. There was plenty of time now for him to catch up on his *Seinfeld* reruns. He was picked up by the Minnesota Twins on February 21, 2009, and signed for half the salary he made in his last season with the White Sox. The Sox archrivals to the north were desperate for an "interim" third baseman—Minnesota had burned through 19 different starters at third since Corey Koskie left in 2004, and the Crede signing was strictly a Band-Aid move to shore up the hot corner while Danny Valencia, one of the Twinkies' top prospects, completed his minor league apprenticeship. In spring training 2009 Valencia was mentored by Joe. "You can see from the way he catches ground balls and plays defense that he's really good," the rookie said of his mentor. "And he knows what he's really talking about so I really listen." However, Crede was really plagued by various injuries—his right shoulder, a bruised hand, a sore hamstring—and appeared in only 90 games, posting a meager .225 average. Agent Scott Boras talked to the Twins about tendering Joe a 2010 contract, but Crede was preparing to undergo his third back surgery in three years, and the club backed off. Joe was out of work—and out of baseball.

Joe Cunningham: the "India Rubber Man"

Cunningham, Joe

White Sox: 1962–64
First baseman
Birthplace: Paterson, New Jersey

B: August 27, 1931
Bats left, throws left
Ht. 6–0; **Wt.** 180

Cunningham, Joe

White Sox	G	AB	H	AVG	RBI	R	2B	3B	HR	SA	SB
1962	149	526	155	.295	70	91	32	7	8	.428	3
1963	67	210	60	.286	31	32	12	1	1	.367	1
1964	40	108	27	.250	10	13	7	0	0	.315	0
Career	1,141	3,362	980	.291	436	525	177	26	64	.417	16

Minnie Minoso and Joe Cunningham were attending the same sports banquet in Joliet, Illinois, the night of November 27, 1961, when word was sent down that the two players had been traded for one another. Minoso arose from the dais and announced to the dinner guests that he would be playing for the St. Louis Cardinals in 1962. Minnie kept his chin up, but he was shattered by the news. Cunningham, a balding, scrappy first baseman who hit .345 in 1959 for the Cards, was philosophical and seemed to welcome the change.

By acquiring Cunningham, Ed Short plugged a hole at first base and added to the roster a lifetime .304 hitter who fit into the Sox's aggressive hit-and-run mold—a style of play temporarily abandoned by Bill Veeck in 1960.

Joe was a studious hitter who paid attention to detail. After every game he reviewed his little black book containing data on opposing pitchers. He updated the profiles, based upon the pitches he had seen that day. Cunningham was an acrobat around first base who led the league in fielding in 1962. His leaping catches of errant throws from across the infield and his unfailing ability to dig the ball out of the dirt mesmerized the fans and the media. In 1962 he reached base 268 times and led the team in walks, runs, sacrifice flies, and bunt hits. Joe always found a way to get on base.

Nineteen sixty-three was a lost season for "Jumpin' Joe." He shattered his collarbone in a collision with Charley Dees of the Los Angeles Angels on June 3 and was on the disabled list until September. The injury was costly to the Sox in the stretch drive, and it had a debilitating effect on Cunningham's career. Joe was traded to the Washington Senators in a waiver deal for power-hitting Bill "Moose" Skowron and pitcher Frank Kruetzer on July 13, 1964.

In the 1980s Cunningham worked for the St. Louis Cardinals as their director of community relations and group sales.

Curtright, Guy

White Sox: 1943–46
Outfielder
Birthplace: Holliday, Missouri

B: October 18, 1912
D: August 23, 1997
Batted right, threw right
Ht. 5–11; **Wt.** 200

Curtright, Guy

White Sox	G	AB	H	AVG	RBI	R	2B	3B	HR	SA	SB
1943	138	488	142	.291	48	67	20	7	3	.379	13
1944	72	198	50	.253	23	22	8	2	2	.343	4
1945	98	324	91	.281	32	51	15	7	4	.407	3
1946	23	55	11	.200	5	7	2	0	0	.236	0
Career	331	1,065	294	.276	108	147	45	16	9	.374	20

Guy Curtright waited nine years for a chance to don a major league uniform. He paid his dues and bounced from one minor league team to the next following his graduation from Kirksville, Missouri Teacher's College in 1934. If not for World War II and the depletion of the big-league rosters, he might have settled into a comfortable but obscure life as a Missouri mathematics teacher—his occupation during the off-season. Curtright, originally scouted and signed by the talent-laden Detroit Tigers, was plucked off the St. Paul Saints roster following the 1942 season but was accorded only a 50–50 chance of making the grade the following spring.

Wartime baseball created strange folk heroes. One of them was the rookie long shot Curtright, who was a South Side hitting sensation for exactly a half-season. Batting third in the Sox's lineup that year, Guy led both leagues in batting average

Guy Curtright was brilliant for one season.

through June and July of 1943. His .362 average outpaced such luminaries as Vern Stephens of the Browns and Dick Wakefield, another wartime prospect belonging to the Detroit Tigers.

More important, Curtright reeled off a 26-game hitting streak that was abruptly snapped by Milo Candini in a tough July 2 extra-inning loss to the Washington Nationals at Comiskey Park. Curtright's improbable streak has withstood the test of time. Only Luke Appling's record of 27 straight, set in 1936, tops Guy's mark. However, his torrid hitting proved illusory. Curtright's average plummeted in the second half of the 1943 season. He never duplicated his early success and was dropped from the roster after 1946.

Danforth, Dave

White Sox: 1916–19
Pitcher
Nickname: Dauntless Dave
Birthplace: Granger, Texas

B: March 7, 1890
D: September 19, 1970
Batted left, threw left
Ht. 6–0; **Wt.** 167

Danforth, Dave

White Sox	W	L	Pct	ERA	G	CG	IP	H	BB	K	ShO	Sv
1916	5	5	.500	3.27	28	1	93⅔	87	37	49	0	2
1917	15	6	.714	2.65	50	1	173	155	74	79	1	7
1918	6	15	.286	3.43	39	5	139	148	40	48	0	2
1919	1	2	.333	7.78	15	0	41⅔	58	20	17	0	1
Career	74	67	.525	3.89	114	44	1,186	1,235	455	484	3	20

The era of specialization was still decades away when this well-traveled lefty arrived at Mineral Wells, Texas, in the spring of 1916 to showcase his talents for Sox manager Clarence Rowland, who was busy previewing two other newcomers of note—Claude "Lefty" Williams and Hod Eller.

Danforth, a situational pitcher with an exaggerated windup and an interesting new kind of pitch known as the shine ball, was acquired in the off-season by Charles Comiskey from the Louisville club of the American Association.

In front of 25 carloads of friends and family from nearby Granger, Danforth fanned 15 collegians from Southwestern University in a spring pickup game. He pitched well thereafter and was added to the Opening Day roster when the team broke camp in April.

Danforth was penciled in as a starting pitcher, but in the coming weeks he demonstrated an alarming tendency to fall apart in the early innings. In those days players were counted on to go the full limit. Relegated to bullpen by Rowland more out of frustration than necessity, Danforth enhanced his value to the team as someone who could come in and put out fires, particularly in the later innings when the game was on the line. Dave's role as one of baseball's first closers drew comment, and it stirred controversy. Opposing teams registered complaints to the league office about his usage of the deadly shine ball—a doctored pitch that Ed Cicotte added to his repertoire in 1917.

Dauntless Dave—the nickname he acquired years later when he pitched through considerable arm pain as a member of the St. Louis Browns—led the American League in winning percentage, appearances, and saves in 1917. He was a big factor in the Sox's pennant-winning success that year, but the old complaints about his limitations kept surfacing. Kid Gleason, who took over for Clarence Rowland, hoped that Danforth could overcome his mental block and become a valued fourth starter in 1919. But he was routed in the second inning of his first start and benched by the manager.

Dave Danforth

Dave saw very little action during the fateful Black Sox summer, but was kept on the roster until the first week of September, when he was shipped to the Columbus Clippers of the American Association as payment for rookie right-hander Roy Wilkinson.

Danforth was never used properly or even appreciated by White Sox management, and he languished in the minors for the next two seasons. But the St. Louis Browns resurrected him from oblivion in 1922. In fact, they pinned their 1922 title hopes on the spitballing lefty, who won 25 games in 1921, and they richly compensated the Clippers with *11 rostered players* to secure his services. If not a record setter, it stands as one of the most unusual baseball trades of all time.

Dave enjoyed four years of success—as a starting pitcher with a knack for beating the White Sox.

Danks, John

White Sox: 2007–
Pitcher
Birthplace: Austin, Texas

B: April 15, 1985
Bats left, throws left
Ht. 6–2; **Wt.** 210

Danks, John

White Sox	W	L	Pct.	ERA	G	CG	IP	H	BB	K	Sho	Sv
2007	6	13	.316	5.50	26	0	139	160	54	109	0	0
2008	12	9	.571	3.32	33	0	195	182	57	159	0	0
2009	13	11	.542	3.77	32	1	200⅓	184	73	149	0	0
2010	15	11	.576	3.72	32	1	213	189	70	162	1	0
Career	46	44	.511	3.96	123	2	747⅓	715	254	579	1	0

One of the really pleasant surprises of the post–World Series seasons on the South Side was the speedy development of the young southpaw Johnny Danks, a June 2003 first-round draft pick by the Texas Rangers surrendered to the White Sox on December 23, 2006, in a much-maligned trade for pitcher Brandon McCarthy (who did not quite pan out the way everyone had expected him to). But then the White Sox have been frequently guilty of heaping excessive praise with glowing predictions of future MLB stardom on a collection of rookie prospects who ultimately missed the mark. Over the past 25 years, the names Joel Davis, Edwin Correa, Joel Skinner, Rod Bolton, Scott Ruffcorn, Chris Snopek, Jeremy Reed, Joe Borchard, Brian Anderson, and Josh Fields resonated with a lot of hype, but they delivered little in the way of solid performance to back up the optimistic scouting reports and signing bonuses. Inevitably, the best prospects to emerge on the South Side during that time have been plucked from the *other* guy's system, as was the case with Johnny Danks from Round Rock, Texas, who had been ranked as the Rangers' No. 2 prospect in 2004 by *Baseball America.*

Slotted into the starting rotation in 2007, John's rookie year left little for him to crow about. In July and August his confidence appeared to be badly shaken after losing six straight decisions and racking up an inflated 7.42 ERA. Ozzie Guillen asked the media to refrain from asking the kid pointed questions about his status in the starting rotation. But Danks was philosophical: "I'll take the ball whenever they give it to me and hope to get us deeper in the game and hold the lead. My job is to take the ball and work from there."

Over the winter Danks watched tapes of his 2007 games at his parents' home in Round Rock to try to figure out what went wrong. His father, a former University of Texas basketball guard, sat in on those sessions. "I noticed that I got into a pattern where I'd throw change-ups behind in the count or on 3–2 every time," he explained. "I'm really focused on mixing it up and not falling into a pattern as far as the way I pitch." With the help of ex–Sox reliever Kevin Hickey, who served as the team's 2008 batting practice pitcher, Johnny developed a cut fastball to accompany an above average curveball.

The second-year southpaw won six straight games between May 29 and August 6 and finished fifth in the American League in ERA. It was a solid, impressive performance capped off by eight innings of shutout baseball against the Twins in the "Blackout" playoff game on September 30, won by the Sox 1–0. Overall, it was a wonderful breakout year for the sophomore pitcher, highlighted by his victory over Tampa Bay in the American League Division Series and the signing of his brother Jordan to a White Sox minor league contract on August 14. The younger Danks, an outfielder in his college days, was praised by Guillen: "He's got pop. I don't know what the deal is, but I think he has a chance to play in the big leagues. It would be nice to have the two kids play in the big leagues for the same team."

John Danks pitched the Sox into the 2008 playoffs with his win in the "Blackout Game." (Courtesy of the Chicago White Sox)

While Jordan divided the 2009 season between Winston-Salem and Birmingham, brother John and Mark Buehrle became the first pair of Sox lefties to pitch 200 or more innings in a season since Britt Burns and Floyd Bannister in 1985. By making 25 starts in each of his first three seasons, Danks joined Roy "the Boy Wonder" Patterson (1901–1903) and Tommy Thomas (1926–1928) from the distant past as the only Sox pitchers in team history to accomplish this rare feat. As the 2010 season unfolded, Danks seemed to be the "ace apparent," but not until Mark Buerhle's days on the South Side had ended. "He's really a front-line starter," observed Paul Konerko. "He's always had the stuff, but he's showing his nerve out there. He's a great teammate. He's not scared out there. He wants the ball. He's not the ace, but I think in time he could turn into that guy because he has the stuff."

Davis, George

White Sox: 1902; 1904–09
Shortstop, second baseman
Birthplace: Cohoes, New York

B: August 23, 1870
D: October 17, 1940
Batted right and left, threw right
Ht. 5–9; **Wt.** 180

Davis, George

White Sox	G	AB	H	AVG	RBI	R	2B	3B	HR	SA	SB
1902	132	485	145	.299	93	76	27	7	3	.402	31
1904	152	563	142	.252	69	75	27	15	1	.359	32
1905	157	550	153	.278	55	74	29	1	1	.340	31
1906	133	484	134	.277	80	63	26	6	0	.355	27
1907	132	466	111	.238	52	59	16	2	1	.288	15
1908	128	419	91	.217	26	41	14	1	0	.255	22
1909	28	68	9	.132	2	5	1	0	0	.147	4
Career	2,377	9,060	2,688	.297	1,435	1,544	452	167	73	.408	616

A mainstay of the New York Giants for nearly a decade before "jumping" to the White Sox prior to the 1902 season, fancy-fielding George Davis achieved Hall of Fame numbers but until 1998 was overlooked and largely forgotten by the Veterans Committee in the intervening decades. His anti-establishment posturing against baseball's ruling powers late in his career has undoubtedly cost him his chance.

When Giants owner Andrew Freedman demoted George Davis from the manager's chair after the 1901 season, Davis repaid him in kind by accepting Comiskey's surprisingly generous offer to play for the White Sox at a salary of $4,000 per year. According to published newspaper reports, it was the highest salary paid to a baseball player in 1902.

Despite an outstanding season, Davis was unhappy in his new surroundings. Enticed by an even larger sum of money than he was being paid in Chicago, Davis jumped back to the Giants after failing to come to terms with Comiskey over his 1903 salary. The 1903 peace agreement between the two warring leagues returned Davis to Chicago, but the stubborn veteran refused to comply with the edict.

Angered by the duplicity of George Davis and the National League, Comiskey secured an injunction barring his shortstop from continuing in the New York Giants' employ after Davis played four games in Gotham. John Montgomery Ward, the famous baseball lawyer, represented Davis in court in a futile and losing effort to win his freedom. Finally on July 15, 1903, the case was thrown out, and Davis was awarded to Chicago. It was an early and important test of baseball's hallowed reserve clause. Round one in this ancient and bitter struggle was won by Charles Comiskey.

George Davis, the anchor of the 1906 infield, was elected to the Hall of Fame in 1998.

Though his batting average fizzled in the dead-ball era that followed, Davis stabilized the Sox's infield defense. Despite his annual salary holdout, Davis provided leadership and direction to the evolving Hitless Wonder ballclub, and he was the first in a tradition of great shortstops to don the White Sox flannels. Released by Comiskey after the 1909 season, Davis managed the Des Moines club of the Western League the following season, then coached baseball at Amherst College from 1913 to 1918. Thereafter he drifted into limbo—his exact whereabouts were unknown for many years.

George Davis spent his last six years at the Philadelphia State Hospital, where he died from the complications of syphilis. He is buried in an unmarked cemetery plot outside Philadelphia.

Dent, Russell

White Sox: 1973–76
Shortstop
Nickname: Bucky
Birthplace: Savannah, Georgia

B: November 25, 1951
Bats right, throws right
Ht. 5–9; **Wt.** 170

Dent, Russell

White Sox	G	AB	H	AVG	RBI	R	2B	3B	HR	SA	SB
1973	40	117	29	.248	10	17	2	0	0	.265	2
1974	154	496	136	.274	45	55	15	3	5	.347	3
1975	157	602	159	.264	58	52	29	4	3	.341	2
1976	158	562	138	.246	52	44	18	4	2	.302	3
Career	1,392	4,512	1,114	.247	423	451	169	26	40	.321	17

Bucky Dent, born Russell Earl O'Dey, was the first White Sox casualty of baseball's changing economic order in the late 1970s. The imposition of free agency in 1976 allowed the White Sox All-Star shortstop to force Bill Veeck to trade him—or lose him—when it became apparent that the embattled owner could not meet his demand for a three-year package deal worth $420,000.

Dent was originally signed out of Miami-Dade Junior College by White Sox scout Walt Widmayer in 1970. He earned high marks for his fielding work, but was tagged as a "Punch and Judy" singles hitter—.250 material at best.

A rash of player injuries in 1973 hastened Dent's Chicago debut late in the season. The kid shortstop with boyish, crowd-pleasing All-American charm showed great range and agility and a strong throwing arm. His fine fielding in 1974 nearly earned him Rookie of the Year honors. He finished second in the balloting that year to Mike Hargrove, a full-time designated hitter.

The following year, Dent led the AL in fielding with a .981 mark—three points ahead of Mark Belanger of the Baltimore Orioles.

A change in ownership and a managerial switch from Chuck Tanner to the out-of-touch Paul Richards affected Dent's play in 1976. His hitting tailed off after Bill Veeck resodded the infield with natural grass. Astroturf base hits became routine ground-ball outs. Dent was most unhappy and vowed to play out his option. "I was excited at first when Veeck bought the club," he said. "But I was disappointed at the end of the year because I felt he was trying to please the fans more than the players. There were gimmicks on the field all the time. You would have to wade through fire trucks to get to the field."

Bucky Dent and Bill Veeck continued their verbal sparring in the off-season. Veeck countered the criticisms by touting Alan Bannister and Kevin Bell as his shortstops for the future. The long-rumored deal sending Bucky to the Yankees finally materialized on April 5, 1977, when LaMarr Hoyt, Oscar Gamble, Bob Polinsky, and $250,000 cash were pried away from George Steinbrenner. The upshot of all this was that the trade was contingent on Dent coming to terms with the New York Yankees. Bucky obliged—and for a lot less money than he had originally demanded from Veeck.

Bucky Dent, No. 30

Dietrich, Bill

White Sox: 1936–46
Pitcher
Nickname: Bullfrog
Birthplace: Philadelphia, Pennsylvania

B: March 29, 1910
D: June 20, 1978
Batted right, threw right
Ht. 6–0; **Wt.** 185

Dietrich, Bill

White Sox	W	L	Pct	ERA	G	CG	IP	H	BB	K	ShO
1936	4	4	.500	4.68	14	6	82⅔	93	36	39	1
1937	8	10	.444	4.90	29	7	143⅓	162	72	62	1
1938	2	4	.333	5.44	8	1	48	49	31	11	0
1939	7	8	.467	5.22	25	2	127⅔	134	56	43	0
1940	10	6	.625	4.03	23	6	149⅔	154	65	43	1
1941	5	8	.385	5.35	19	4	109⅓	114	50	26	1
1942	6	11	.353	4.89	26	6	160	173	70	39	0
1943	12	10	.545	2.80	26	12	186⅔	180	53	52	2
1944	16	17	.485	3.62	36	15	246	269	68	70	2
1945	7	10	.412	4.19	18	6	122⅓	136	36	43	4
1946	3	3	.500	2.61	11	3	62	63	24	20	0
Career	108	128	.458	4.48	366	92	2,003⅔	2,117	890	660	18

Myopic Bill Dietrich could not see across the room without his glasses, and his control was at times erratic, but this Clark Griffith castoff stuck around the majors for more than a decade after the Senators owner simply gave up on him.

Jimmie Dykes was the only American League manager to stake a claim for Dietrich when Griffith asked waivers on the bespectacled righty. On July 20, 1936, Dykes literally

Bill "Bullfrog" Dietrich was another of Jimmie Dykes' famous reclamation projects.

pulled Bullfrog off an Albany-bound train and redirected him to Chicago, where pitching coach Muddy Ruel was waiting to correct the flaws in his delivery that contributed to his streak of wildness. Ruel found that Dietrich was gripping the ball too tightly. After further refinements, Bill moved into the starting rotation in the closing days of the season.

Possessing the best fastball on the club, Dietrich overcame his control problems and fired a no-hitter at the Browns on June 1, 1937. He did not know that he was about to enter the record books until the last out was recorded and his teammates rushed the mound to congratulate him.

Dietrich flirted with no-hit glory several more times in his White Sox career. He came within one out of firing a second no-hitter in Detroit on April 22, 1941. Hank Greenberg, a thorn in the side of the White Sox for so many years, broke it up in the ninth inning. Again on May 29 Bullfrog held an opponent hitless going into the ninth inning, this time against the Browns in Comiskey Park. Chet Laabs' single with one out ended the suspense.

In later years Bill's control improved, but poor batting support cost him many victories. For his career, he won seven 1–0 complete-game decisions. Dietrich underwent elbow surgery in April 1945 and missed seven weeks of the season. Age and arm miseries finally caught up with him. Sold to the Philadelphia A's in 1946, Dietrich appeared in only a handful of games and retired after the 1948 season.

Dobson, Joe

White Sox: 1951–53
Pitcher
Nickname: Burrhead
Birthplace: Durant, Oklahoma

B: January 20, 1917
D: June 23, 1994
Batted right, threw right
Ht. 6–2; **Wt.** 197

Dobson, Joe

White Sox	W	L	Pct	ERA	G	CG	IP	H	BB	K	ShO	Sv
1951	7	6	.538	3.62	28	6	146⅔	136	51	67	0	3
1952	14	10	.583	2.51	29	11	200⅔	164	60	101	3	1
1953	5	5	.500	3.67	23	3	100⅔	96	37	50	1	1
Career	137	103	.571	3.62	414	112	2,170	2,048	851	992	22	18

The youngest of 14 children reared in the heart of America's dustbowl, Joe Dobson lost his left thumb and forefinger when, at the age of nine, he experimented with dynamite. This childhood mishap did not deter him from pursuing a career in professional baseball. He quit high school to sign his first contract with Cleveland, but was dealt to Boston in 1940. With his good pitching hand, Dobson proved to be a steady and dependable workman for the Red Sox during their glory years in the late 1940s. Several times he came close to winning 20 games with the Bosox, managing to record double-digit victories five straight seasons before coming to the White Sox.

Seeking a veteran presence to solidify his youthful White Sox, general manager Frank Lane took a pass on veteran Yankees relief ace Joe Page to acquire Dobson, outfielder Al Zarilla, and pitcher Dick Littlefield from Boston on December 11, 1950. In return, the Sox sent away Ray Scarborough and Bill Wight, two pitchers who were relentlessly pummeled by American League hitters during their tenure with the White Sox. The deal was a good one for Chicago.

Dobson, considered too old to play for the Red Sox in 1951, collected his first Sox victory over Early Wynn and the Cleveland Indians on May 11 of that year—a near no-hit performance. He went on to record the lowest earned run average of his career with the White Sox in 1952.

Father Time finally caught up with him in 1953. With the rotation bolstered by the acquisition of Mike Fornieles, Virgil Trucks, and Sandy Consuegra, the old veteran no longer figured in Lane's long-range plans. After a mediocre start, Dobson was handed his unconditional release on August 25, 1953, to make room for infielder Connie Ryan, whom Lane had just claimed on waivers from the Phillies. Joe closed out his career with the Red Sox the following season.

Joe Dobson

Donahue, John

White Sox: 1904–09	**B:** July 13, 1879
First baseman	**D:** July 19, 1913
Nickname: Jiggs	**Batted left, threw left**
Birthplace: Springfield, Ohio	**Ht.** 6–1; **Wt.** 178

Donahue, John

White Sox	G	AB	H	AVG	RBI	R	2B	3B	HR	SA	SB
1904	102	367	91	.248	48	46	9	7	1	.319	18
1905	149	533	153	.287	76	71	22	4	1	.349	32
1906	154	556	143	.257	57	70	17	7	1	.318	36
1907	157	609	158	.259	68	75	16	4	0	.299	27
1908	93	304	62	.204	22	22	8	2	0	.243	14
1909	86	287	67	.233	30	13	12	1	0	.282	9
Career	813	2,862	731	.255	327	319	90	31	4	.313	143

A notoriously weak hitter but a defensive virtuoso and one of the main reasons why the Hitless Wonder White Sox upset the powerful Cubs in the 1906 all-Chicago World Series, Jiggs Donahue, remarkably, was one of only three regulars to top the .250 mark in that championship season.

Donahue began playing professionally in Marietta, Ohio, in 1898. He debuted with the Pittsburgh Pirates in 1901 as a catcher, spending a portion of the 1901 season with the Milwaukee Brewers. In 1902 the team was transferred to St. Louis, where it began play as the Browns. Donahue, as the third-string catcher, was returned to Milwaukee (now a member of the American Association) to refine his first-base skills. Charles Comiskey (who recognized a first baseman when he saw one), purchased Donahue's contract for the White Sox in 1903. Jiggs became the everyday player at that position for the next five seasons.

In a May 31, 1908, game played in Detroit, Jiggs recorded 21 putouts in nine innings. Steady, dependable—a player who voiced few complaints and caused no disruptions—Jiggs was one of the hitting stars of the '06 World Series. He batted .333 for the six games, committing only one error. His seventh-inning single in Game 2 broke up Ed Ruelbach's bid to become the first pitcher to throw a no-hitter in a World Series game. It was the only hit the White Sox collected that afternoon.

Playing on the rough, uneven American League fields of the dead-ball era, Donahue paced the circuit in fielding average for first basemen in 1905, 1906, and 1907. He was always ranked among the yearly leaders in putouts and assists.

Sadly, Donahue's skills waned with advancing age. Comiskey traded him to the Washington Senators with Nick Altrock during the White Sox' post–Hitless Wonder rebuilding program begun in 1909. Jiggs played out the string in the minors thereafter. He was a member of Joseph Cantillon's Minneapolis club of the American Association in 1910.

Returning to Chicago, Donahue ran a bowling alley, but he had contracted syphilis during his playing career, and his health was rapidly declining. He died in the Columbus State Hospital a year later, his mind and body ravaged by the deadly disease. He was survived by a brother, Patrick, who played for the Boston Red Sox.

Reflecting back on the golden summer of 1906, students of baseball history evoke the poetry of Franklin P. Adams, who immortalized the Cubs infield of Tinker to Evers to Chance in verse. The real heroes of that summer—ignored by the poets and philosophers—happened to be the unheralded double-play combo of Davis to Isbell...to Jiggs.

Jiggs Donahue was one of the best all-around glove men of the dead-ball era.

Donovan, Dick

White Sox: 1955–60
Pitcher
Birthplace: Quincy, Massachusetts

B: December 7, 1927
D: January 6, 1997
Batted left, threw right
Ht. 6–3; **Wt.** 205

Donovan, Dick

White Sox	W	L	Pct	ERA	G	CG	IP	H	BB	K	ShO
1955	15	9	.625	3.32	29	11	187	186	48	88	5
1956	12	10	.545	3.64	34	14	234⅔	212	59	120	3
1957	16	6	.727	2.77	28	16	220	203	45	88	2
1958	15	14	.517	3.01	34	16	248	240	53	127	4
1959	9	10	.474	3.66	31	5	179⅔	171	58	71	1
1960	6	1	.857	5.38	33	0	78⅔	87	25	30	0
Career	122	99	.552	3.67	345	101	2,017⅓	1,988	495	880	25

Dick Donovan waited a long time for a chance to prove himself in the majors. Down on his luck and resentful toward the Milwaukee Braves ownership who buffeted him around the minor leagues for six years, Donovan was encouraged to hang in there by former Sox pitcher Whitlow Wyatt, who was coaching for the Atlanta Crackers of the Southern Association. Dick was placed in Wyatt's care after the Braves cut him loose in 1953.

Urged on by Whit Wyatt, the tall right-hander with the exaggerated "boardinghouse" windup added a slider pitch to his repertoire, and finally the big leagues beckoned. The Detroit Tigers purchased Dick's contract, but after a month of bench duty they shuttled him back to Atlanta, where he won 18 games for Wyatt, who had taken Gene Mauch's place as manager of the Crackers. Despite Donovan's impressive 1954 campaign, White Sox GM Frank Lane was advised by his scouts that Dick was a bad investment—an aging journeyman with no future and a bleak past. Disregarding these reports, Lane acquired Donovan for the Sox on September 7, 1954.

Dick Donovan and his "boarding house" delivery

He made his first start for the White Sox in Kansas City on April 24, 1955—and it was unimpressive. Haunted by visions of a return trip to the minors, Donovan refused to surrender the ball to manager Marty Marion when he came out to change pitchers. "Come on, Dick; it's one of those things," Marion assured him. "You'll be our starter when your regular turn comes up." The Sox lost the game 5–0, but Donovan settled in for the long haul. He won 13 of his first 17 decisions before an emergency appendectomy ended his season on July 31.

Throughout his White Sox career, Donovan was a model of consistency, though at times he was prone to dry spells, especially in the early months of the season. Under Al Lopez he avoided the spring doldrums to record his finest effort to date in 1957. An intense competitor in the Early Wynn mold, Donovan's wry humor and good-natured disposition vanished on game day. He would drape a towel over the bench of the dugout so no one would sit next to him and distract his attention. Donovan posted a strong 16–6 record, which led the league in percentage. He completed 16 games in 1957, and tossed a pair of one-hitters against Cleveland and Boston.

Hobbled with a sore shoulder during the heat of the 1959 pennant race, Donovan turned the tide of victory in Chicago's favor by blanking Cleveland in Game 2 of the crucial August 28–30 road trip that helped wrap up the flag. In the World Series that year, he preserved Bob Shaw's hard-fought 1–0 shutout in Game 5 by pitching out of an eighth-inning bases-loaded jam.

Left unprotected in the 1960 AL expansion draft, Donovan was picked up by the Washington Senators. He won 20 games for Cleveland in 1962, a high-water mark for his career. In later years Donovan retired to Cohasset, Massachusetts, where he worked as a real estate appraiser.

Dotson, Richard

White Sox: 1979–87; 1989
Pitcher
Birthplace: Cincinnati, Ohio

B: January 10, 1959
Bats right, throws right
Ht. 6–3; **Wt.** 203

Dotson, Richard

White Sox	W	L	Pct	ERA	G	CG	IP	H	BB	K	ShO
1979	2	0	1.000	3.75	5	1	24	28	6	13	1
1980	12	10	.545	4.27	33	8	198	185	87	109	0
1981	9	8	.529	3.77	24	5	141	145	49	73	4
1982	11	15	.423	3.84	34	3	196⅔	219	73	109	1
1983	22	7	.759	3.23	35	8	240	209	106	137	1
1984	14	15	.482	3.59	32	14	245⅔	216	103	120	1
1985	3	4	.428	4.47	9	0	52⅓	53	17	33	0
1986	10	17	.370	5.48	34	3	197	226	69	110	1
1987	11	12	.478	4.17	31	7	211⅓	201	97	114	2
1989	3	7	.300	3.88	17	1	99⅔	112	41	55	0
Career	111	113	.495	4.17	305	55	1,857	1,884	740	973	11

No less of an authority than George "Sparky" Anderson predicted great things for Richard Dotson, the "throw-in"

Arm miseries ruined Richard Dotson's bid for stardom.

pitcher who completed the multiplayer deal with the California Angels that sent Brian Downing, Chris Knapp, and Dave Frost to Anaheim for Bobby Bonds and Thad Bosley on December 7, 1977. "He makes the whole deal for the White Sox," Anderson commented. "He has a tremendous future." Jack Donovan, an Angels farm executive, was even more enthusiastic: "This kid is the next Tom Seaver."

When all was said and done, it boiled down to the two players who made a difference with their new teams: Brian Downing and Richard Dotson. And when the final votes were counted, the Angels with Downing came out ahead, Jack Donovan's prophecy notwithstanding. Dot had only one really big year with the Sox, and that was 1983. He became the youngest White Sox pitcher to win 20 games since Reb Russell in 1913.

Dotson won 16 of his last 18 decisions that year and was unbeatable down the stretch. His success spilled over into the first half of the 1984 season. Between the 1983 and 1984 All-Star Games, Dot was the best pitcher in baseball. His record of 25–6 attests to that fact. After that, Dotson's career fell apart because of a circulatory problem near his right shoulder. His 1985 season ended in June, and whatever hopes he had of becoming another Seaver faded with these setbacks.

Richard Dotson did not miss a turn in 1986, but the zip was gone from his fastball, and his ERA soared. The following year he seemed to regain his confidence and started the season brilliantly. On July 26 he made a heroic bid to become the first White Sox pitcher to hurl a perfect game in Comiskey Park by retiring the first 22 Yankees batters in a row before losing the game 5–2. He was traded to the Yankees on November 13, 1987, with Scott Neilsen for outfielder Dan Pasqua, pitcher Steve Rosenberg, and catcher Mark Salas—the promise and the glory left for another.

Dotson rejoined the White Sox in 2002 as a pitching coach for Bristol. Over the next eight seasons, he worked his way through the minor league system and is currently working with the youngsters at Triple A Charlotte.

Dougherty, Patrick

White Sox: 1906–11
Outfielder
Nickname: Patsy
Birthplace: Andover, New York

B: October 27, 1876
D: April 30, 1940
Batted left, threw right
Ht. 6–2; **Wt.** 190

Dougherty, Patrick

White Sox	G	AB	H	AVG	RBI	R	2B	3B	HR	SA	SB
1906	75	253	59	.233	27	30	9	4	1	.312	11
1907	148	533	144	.270	59	69	17	2	2	.321	33
1908	138	482	134	.278	45	68	11	6	0	.326	47
1909	139	491	140	.285	55	71	23	13	1	.391	36
1910	127	443	110	.248	43	45	8	6	1	.300	22
1911	76	211	61	.289	32	39	10	9	0	.422	19
Career	1,233	4,558	1,294	.284	413	679	138	78	17	.370	261

Pat Dougherty played for the same high school baseball team as Fielder Jones, his future White Sox manager. Jones was already playing professional baseball in the Oregon State

Patsy Dougherty was a valuable addition in 1906.

League when Dougherty enrolled in Bolivar High. But Pat's skills with a baseball bat and glove did not go unnoticed by Fielder Jones, who discovered the young man playing in a sandlot game in Shinglehouse, Pennsylvania.

Jones secured a position for Dougherty in the Eastern League, where he starred for several years before breaking into the majors with the Red Sox in 1902. A year later the brawny Irishman clubbed two home runs in the second game of the 1903 World Series. Pat's feat was not duplicated until Harry Hooper turned the trick against the Phillies in the 1915 Series.

Mindful of Dougherty's excellent range in the outfield, Fielder Jones traveled to Lancaster, Pennsylvania, in early July 1906 to convince Dougherty to join the White Sox for the pennant run. Disgusted over his 1906 contract with New York, Dougherty jumped the team early in the season vowing never to play for the Highlanders again. Jones convinced Dougherty to join the Sox over the objections of Highlander manager Clark Griffith, who filed a protest with AL President Ban Johnson.

Johnson eventually cleared the way for Dougherty to join the Sox on July 16 following completion of a 10-day suspension handed down by the league for playing on an "outlaw" team after leaving the Highlanders.

Dougherty, a slashing line-drive hitter with exceptional speed, stabilized the White Sox muddled outfield situation and helped them win a pennant against seemingly impossible odds. Despite a poor performance in the 1906 World Series, Dougherty settled into the starting lineup as the regular left fielder for the next four seasons. After he retired, Patsy was elected president of the Inter-State League in 1916. At the time of his death, Dougherty was working as the assistant cashier in the State Bank of Bolivar.

Downing, Brian

White Sox: 1973–77
Catcher, infielder, outfielder
Nickname: The Bionic Man
Birthplace: Los Angeles

B: October 9, 1950
Bats right, throws right
Ht. 5–10; **Wt.** 170

Downing, Brian

White Sox	G	AB	H	AVG	RBI	R	2B	3B	HR	SA	SB
1973	34	73	13	.178	4	4	1	0	2	.274	0
1974	108	293	66	.225	39	41	12	1	10	.375	0
1975	138	420	101	.240	41	58	12	1	7	.324	13
1976	104	317	81	.256	30	38	14	0	3	.328	7
1977	69	169	48	.284	25	28	4	2	4	.402	1
Career	2,344	7,853	2,099	.267	1,073	1,188	360	28	275	.425	50

When considering the all-time worst trades in White Sox history, the Brian Downing giveaway should *not* be overlooked. Because it was engineered by the beloved Bill Veeck during his second ownership, however—the height of the Chicago media's love affair with the colorful baseball maverick—very little has been said of this clunker trade, which came back to haunt the ballclub for years to come.

Brian Downing's transformation from utility catcher and part-time outfielder to one of the American League's top performers was a reflection of his sound work ethic and a personal triumph over physical adversity. It was one of the few heart-rending stories of the early free agency era, when the players were assailed for selfishness and greed.

Downing's interest in baseball was sparked by a visit to the Los Angeles Coliseum to see the White Sox and Dodgers do battle in the 1959 World Series. Brian had been a three-sport star at Magnolia High School in Anaheim, California, but he was physically limited, and the big-league scouts turned their back on him in the 1970 draft. It was Bill Lentini, Brian's Junior American Legion manager and a West Coast White Sox bird-dog scout, who recommended Downing to the White Sox when no one else showed interest.

Originally signed as an infielder, Downing was summoned from the White Sox Iowa affiliate on May 29, 1973, to take the place of the injured Ken Henderson. But in his major league debut against the Tigers two days later, Brian tore up his knee diving for a pop foul on the rough, uneven warning-track gravel along third base. Placed on the disabled list before he had registered his first big-league at-bat, Downing was out of action for the next six weeks. Oddly enough, he collected his first hit against Detroit on August 11—an inside-the-park home run off of Tigers ace Mickey Lolich.

Brian Downing

Sox manager Chuck Tanner converted the hard-nosed young infielder to a catcher in 1974. By the time the season ended, Downing had demonstrated proficiency behind the plate, especially when he handled Wilbur Wood's elusive knuckleball. Over the next three seasons, Brian split the catching duties with Ed Herrmann, then later with Jim Essian. He was considered one of the best handlers of pitchers, despite developing soreness in his throwing arm in 1975–76.

Hustle was Downing's trademark, which helped to overcome a subpar batting average. In 1977, his last year with the Sox, Brian showed signs of evolving into a fine natural hitter. Veeck and Roland Hemond packaged Brian with pitchers Chris Knapp and Dave Frost, however, in a six-player swap with the Angels on December 5, 1977, that brought Bobby Bonds, Richard Dotson, and Thad Bosley to Chicago. Dotson was the saving grace of a losing-end trade that seemed very promising at the time.

Over the next 12 years, Downing set career batting marks with the Angels, and he is still ranked near the top in 10 different offensive categories for that team. He set an American League record for consecutive errorless games by an outfielder (244 games, from May 25, 1981, to July 21, 1983).

Downing, a hard-edged player who offered no apologies, made the Sox pay dearly for their miscalculation. "In Chicago I was booed so long it affected how I felt about fans," he said in a 1981 interview. "I don't tip my hat. I don't take bows. If they cheer fine—but I've heard boos too often." At the "Big A" the cascade of boos finally subsided.

Meanwhile, six weeks into the 1978 season, Bobby Bonds was traded to Texas. Thad Bosley did his best work as a pinch-hitter in the National League, and Dotson, despite hopeful predictions that he would evolve into the next Tom Seaver, had only one really productive season in Chicago.

Dropo, Walter

White Sox: 1955–58
First baseman
Nickname: Moose
Birthplace: Moosup, Connecticut

B: January 30, 1923
D: December 18, 2010
Batted right, threw right
Ht. 6–5; **Wt.** 220

Dropo, Walter

White Sox	G	AB	H	AVG	RBI	R	2B	3B	HR	SA	SB
1955	141	453	127	.280	79	55	15	2	19	.448	0
1956	125	361	96	.266	52	42	13	1	8	.374	1
1957	93	223	57	.256	49	24	2	0	13	.439	0
1958	28	52	10	.192	8	3	1	0	2	.327	0
Career	1,288	4,124	1,113	.270	704	478	168	22	152	.432	5

The big Moose from Moosup, Connecticut, embodied an era that passed away all too quickly. Walter Dropo was the archetypal 1950s power hitter cast in the Gus Bell–Wally Post mold. With the coming of the base thieves in the late 1950s and early 1960s, the game began to change, and the Walt Dropos and Gus Bells and all the other slow-footed sluggers not quite up to the standards of excellence set by Mickey

Walt Dropo

Mantle and Henry Aaron were replaced by more versatile performers who blended speed and defensive acumen into their baseball repertoire. Their ice age had come.

But while Walter was in there, this 1950 Rookie of the Year was an important contributor to four American League teams including the White Sox. A three-sport star at the University of Connecticut, the Moose turned down an offer from the Chicago Bears to sign with the Boston Red Sox in 1947. He broke into the big leagues three years later in a spectacular way, crushing 34 homers in his rookie campaign.

Dropo's long-distance power is what most interested Frank Lane when he went to the 1954 winter meetings in search of a big RBI man to drive in Nellie Fox, Chico Carrasquel, and Minnie Minoso. Gimpy Ferris Fain, a bustout with the White Sox in two disappointing seasons, was packaged along with two minor leaguers and sent to Detroit on December 6 for Dropo, outfielder Bob Nieman, and pitcher Ted Gray.

In the second game of the 1955 season, the Moose blasted the first of his four White Sox grand-slam home runs when he teed off on Cleveland Indians relief ace Ray Narleski in a 9–4 rout of the Tribe. Dropo was benched in early May for poor hitting, but put it together later in the month and went on to complete a fine all-around season.

The 1956 season wasn't nearly as personally satisfying for the Moose, but he seemed to have it in for the Cleveland Indians—especially on the bone-chilling second day of the season. His 1955 grand slam was high drama in itself. But a year later he really drove a dagger into the hearts of Cleveland fans after his April 19 eighth-inning single broke up Herb Score's bid for a no-hitter in Comiskey Park. Jack Harshman took care of the rest by holding the Tribe scoreless in a 1–0 Sox victory.

Old No. 8 (Dropo's number in Chicago) never supplied the White Sox with the kind of long-distance power he had shown early on in his career, but then Comiskey Park was never the same home run haven as Tiger Stadium and

Fenway Park, where Walter enjoyed his finest offensive campaigns. By 1958, Dropo's playing time was limited to an occasional spot start and pinch-hitting appearances. He was purchased by the Cincinnati Redlegs for the $20,000 waiver price on June 24, 1958, and used thereafter as a pinch-hitter.

Durham, Ray

White Sox: 1995–2002
Infielder
Birthplace: Charlotte, North Carolina
B: November 30, 1971
Bats both, throws right
Ht. 5–8; **Wt.** 196

Durham, Ray

White Sox	G	AB	H	AVG	RBI	R	2B	3B	HR	SA	SB
1995	125	471	121	.257	51	68	27	6	7	.384	18
1996	156	557	153	.275	65	79	33	5	10	.406	30
1997	155	634	172	.271	53	106	27	5	11	.382	33
1998	158	635	181	.285	67	126	35	8	19	.445	36
1999	153	612	181	.296	60	109	30	8	13	.435	34
2000	151	614	172	.280	75	121	35	9	17	.450	25
2001	152	611	163	.267	65	104	42	10	20	.466	23
2002	96	345	103	.299	48	71	20	2	9	.446	20
Career	1,572	6,076	1,050	.280	666	1,050	354	70	149	.435	248

A lead-off hitter with exceptional power, Ray Durham was an offensive igniter for seven stellar seasons. His name might have been etched into the White Sox all-time honor roll of brilliant second basemen alongside Nellie Fox and Eddie Collins if the economics of modern baseball and free agency had not intervened. Faster than Fox, and possessing greater power than Collins, who played in a distant era, Durham was selected by the Sox in the fifth round of the June 1990 free agent draft. He put up big numbers in five minor league seasons before answering the call on Opening Day 1995, with the dubious task of replacing Joey Cora as the every day second baseman. The loss of Cora to free agency stirred criticism—and inevitable comparison between the veteran and the rookie. Sensitive to the media scrutiny, Durham turned to teammate Ozzie Guillen for encouragement and mentoring. "How I feel about Ozzie is that he told me if I ever needed anything to come to him, and I do," Durham said. Durham adjusted to big-league life and blended into the Sox infield nicely. As a leadoff man he was without peer. Durham is the only player in Sox history to score 100 runs and steal 30 bases three years in a row (1997–99), and is one of seven players since 1950 to record 40 doubles, 10 triples, and 20 home runs in a single season (2001). Although he was among the league leaders in errors every year, Ray was a run-producing machine during his extended White Sox career. In 2000 he joined Fox as the only other Sox second baseman to dent the plate 100 times in four consecutive seasons. He hit 20 leadoff home runs in eight White Sox seasons (a team record), and currently ranks in baseball's all-time top 10 in that category.

Durham's younger brother Chad was an outfielder in the Sox farm system for six seasons, but never made it up to the parent club and was out of the organization not long after Ray departed. Facing another free agency situation, Kenny Williams elected to trade his two-time All-Star second baseman in his option year rather than lose him outright. Durham was earning $6.3 million per year, third highest on the team behind Frank Thomas ($9.93 million) and Magglio Ordonez ($6.5 million), and a luxury the White Sox could ill afford. Besides, the coaches and scouts throughout the organization were raving about Durham's likely successor, minor league infielder Willie Harris, picked up from Baltimore over the winter in exchange for outfielder Chris Singleton. A fire-sale trade with Oakland for right-handed Triple A pitcher Jon Adkins (and cash considerations) went through on July 25, 2002, after the Sox had fallen 14 games out of first and Williams decided it was an appropriate time to restock the farm system with prospects.

Hustle and a lot of heart: "Ray Ray" Durham

Working out of the bullpen as a set-up man, Adkins struggled in his first three seasons in Chicago while Durham lasted just long enough in Oakland to make the postseason before signing a lucrative three-year contract with the Giants estimated to be worth $7.2 million per year. For five years Ray was the cornerstone of the Giants inner defense, putting up solid numbers each year.

Dye, Jermaine

White Sox: 2005–2009
Outfielder
Nickname: J.D.
Birthplace: Vacaville, California

B: January 28, 1974
Bats right, throws right
Ht. 6–5; **Wt.** 245

Dye, Jermaine

White Sox	G	AB	H	AVG	RBI	R	2B	3B	HR	SA	SB
2005	145	529	145	.274	86	74	29	2	31	.512	11
2006	146	539	170	.315	120	103	27	3	44	.622	7
2007	138	508	129	.254	78	68	34	0	28	.486	2
2008	154	590	172	.292	96	96	41	2	34	.541	3
2009	141	503	126	.250	81	78	19	1	27	.453	0
Career	1,763	6,487	1,779	.274	1,072	984	363	25	325	.488	46

The acrimonious free agent departure of Magglio Ordonez after the 2004 season left a gaping hole on the right side of the White Sox outfield—a hole that was promptly filled by the December 9, 2004, free agent signing of Jermaine Dye, the son of a Baptist minister, and a quiet but well-liked and respected teammate, whose most productive years were in a White Sox uniform. A 17th-round pick in the 1993 draft by the Atlanta Braves, Dye homered in his first major league at-bat on May 17, 1996, at Turner Field—the first for a Braves player since Chuck Tanner, of all people, in 1955.

Traded to Kansas City in 1997, Dye was an instant fan favorite—inspiring a chorus of "Dye-no-mite" each time he stepped up to the plate in 1999, his breakout year, when he was named the Royals Player of the Year. A midseason trade to the Oakland A's in 2001 proved to be a mixed blessing. He escaped the bottom-feeding Royals and joined a competitive team, leading the A's to a wild-card berth in the playoffs but was hobbled by injuries for most of the next three years. J.D. then inked a two-year, $10.15 million contract with the White Sox and helped erase the bitter memory of Ordonez's angry slap at Chicago by his solid—and occasionally spectacular—play in right field.

In the 2005 World Series, he copped the Series MVP award on the strength of a .438 average with a home run and three RBIs in the four-game sweep of the Astros, thus becoming the first player to win this award in his first season with the Series champion since Scott Brosius of the Yankees in 1998. The road jersey he wore during the '05 Series now resides in the Hall of Fame. His finest season, far and away, was the memorable 2006 campaign. Dye finished fifth in MVP voting on the strength of 44 home runs—second highest in team history behind Albert Belle's 49 in 1998—and was honored with a Silver Slugger award. Dye was one of four Sox sluggers to record 30 or more dingers that year. Only the 2000 Angels and the 2000 Blue Jays matched the record of four or more 30-plus home run hitters in a single season. In Jermaine's case, his home runs were coming mostly in the clutch—when the game was on the line. The same could not be said for other Sox sluggers.

The future was looking rosy, and J.D. signed a two-year contract extension in 2007, but like the rest of the team, the entire year was a washout. His batting average sagged to its lowest point since 2002—the first half of the season was particularly brutal for Dye before he went on a tear and hit .304 over the last 47 games to salvage a measure of respectability. The every-other-year, up-and-down pattern of success then failure continued into 2008 with another solid, all-around contribution to the division-winning Sox. Dye won the club's Marvin Miller Man of the Year Award and a Roberto Clemente Award; but 2009 was another story. After a decent first-half record of 20 homers and a gaudy .302 average—at that point the media and his teammates prodded the fans to vote J.D. into the All-Star Game—he hit just .179 the rest of the way and looked overmatched at the plate. It was almost as if Dye caught a bad case of the "Steve Blass Syndrome"—a brilliant career suddenly and mysteriously ended.

Kenny Williams and the White Sox brain trust took a hard look at the situation and decided not to pursue a contract extension, buying out his contract and allowing J.D. to enter a rather lean free agent market that simply turned its back on one of the most productive hitters of the decade. Over a five-year span, Dye was first among AL outfielders in home runs

Jermaine Dye studies the action. (Courtesy of Mike McKay)

and second in RBIs, but the free agent offers in 2009–10 were few and far between, even for a Type A player, as Dye was classified. "I want to play everyday," J.D. explained. "Cleveland was interested but never made an offer. Tampa was supposed to call. There have been offers, but like I said, nothing worth it." Toronto made a serious pitch and so did the Cubs, but Dye did not relish playing for an also-ran in the American League East, and he knew his playing time with the Cubs would be limited, so he took a pass.

There were ugly rumors of collusion among the owners to limit free agent spending in a tough economic climate, and the specter of racism was raised by several African American players, but in truth Jermaine, at 36, was getting on in age, and his career seemed to be on the precipitous downgrade. Unwilling or too proud to accept reserve status with another club, he chose instead to reject the available opportunities. "The last few years it is weird to see guys kind of weeded out. It's like, 'You play for us or don't play at all.' For me it's not about money, but the situation also. Yeah, I can go to Toronto, but I want to win and not be in a situation where if I do well I can be traded." Returning to U.S. Cellular Field to celebrate Frank Thomas Day on August 30, 2010, Dye promised to return to active duty in 2011—but it was conceded that it would not be with the White Sox.

Esposito, Sammy

White Sox: 1952; 1955–63
Infielder
Birthplace: Chicago

B: December 15, 1931
Bats right, throws right
Ht. 5–9; **Wt.** 165

Esposito, Sammy

White Sox	G	AB	H	AVG	RBI	R	2B	3B	HR	SA	SB
1952	1	4	1	.250	0	0	0	0	0	.250	0
1955	3	4	0	.000	0	3	0	0	0	.000	0
1956	81	184	42	.228	25	30	8	2	3	.342	1
1957	94	176	36	.205	15	26	3	0	2	.256	5
1958	98	81	20	.247	3	16	0	0	0	.284	1
1959	69	66	11	.167	5	12	1	0	1	.227	0
1960	57	77	14	.182	11	14	5	0	1	.286	0
1961	63	94	16	.170	8	12	5	0	1	.255	0
1962	75	81	19	.235	4	14	1	0	0	.247	0
1963	1	0	0	.000	0	0	0	0	0	.000	0
Career	560	792	164	.207	73	130	27	2	8	.278	7

Hometown hero Sammy Esposito never batted above .247 during his professional career, and he played in fewer than 100 games in each of his 10 White Sox seasons. But he had a lot of heart, and a player of this stature does not remain with an organization for so long a time unless he has something positive to contribute.

"Bantam Sam" was a three-sport prep star at Chicago's Fenger High School, leading the varsity basketball, baseball, and football squads to citywide glory. In his senior year he established a Public League scoring record by putting up 81 points in a 107–32 victory over Carver High in a south sectional senior basketball game on January 23, 1950. Standing

Sammy Esposito, hometown hero

just under 6′ tall, Esposito was a point guard without peer. His exploits on the hardwood were remembered for many years to come—columnist Dave Condon of the *Chicago Tribune* and Bill Gleason of the *Sun-Times* recalled his big game against Carver, his gridiron glory as the Fenger starting quarterback, and his modest contributions to the White Sox in glowing South Side reminiscences through the 1970s. Sammy was draining jump shots for Indiana University when he got the call from Frank Lane and Johnny Rigney, summoning him back home to the South Side. Esposito received a staggering (for the times) $25,000 signing bonus and signed his first pro contract with the Sox on August 29, 1952. A month later he got his first taste of major league action before a throng of family and friends.

Esposito's career was interrupted by military service in 1954. He spent the majority of the 1955 season with the Sox' Memphis affiliate before earning a permanent spot on the roster the following year as a fill-in for Nellie Fox and Chico Carrasquel in the middle of the Sox infield. Sammy accepted his limitations and was never considered a knocker by his teammates.

Neither Sammy nor his South Side admirers will ever forget the evening of September 7, 1960, when he was called upon to start in place of Nellie Fox, thus ending Nell's consecutive game streak at 798. After Esposito booted a cinch double play that opened the floodgates for a four-run Yankees uprising that cost the Sox the game, an enraged fan named Willie Harris jumped the wall and went after Sammy. Before he could land a punch, several off-duty cops rushed to Sammy's rescue.

Esposito, a confirmed bachelor who lived at home with mom and dad throughout his playing career, was placed on waivers by Ed Short on May 9, 1963. He was picked up by the A's on May 25, but lasted only 18 games before retiring. Sammy signed on as head baseball coach of the North Carolina State Wolfpack in 1967, and in his next 21 years at the helm, he never suffered a losing season. As assistant basketball coach at NC State, Sammy helped develop 6′7″ forward Tim Stoddard, who signed a contract with the White Sox on May 28, 1975. Stoddard, a pitching prospect, was only the second rookie to ink a full major league contract with the Sox. Dave DeBusschere, future NBA Hall of Famer, was the first in 1962. But neither DeBusschere nor Stoddard stuck around long enough to make a lasting impression on the South Side. Sammy, however, was a capable bench player in some of the best and most unforgettable seasons of White Sox baseball.

Faber, Urban

White Sox: 1914–33
Pitcher
Nickname: Red
Birthplace: Cascade, Iowa

B: September 6, 1888
D: September 25, 1976
Batted right, threw right
Ht. 6–2; **Wt.** 180

Faber, Urban

White Sox	W	L	Pct	ERA	G	CG	IP	H	BB	K	ShO
1914	10	9	.526	2.68	40	11	181⅓	154	64	88	2
1915	24	14	.632	2.55	50	22	299⅔	264	99	182	3
1916	17	9	.654	2.02	35	15	205⅓	167	61	87	3
1917	16	13	.552	1.92	41	17	248	224	85	84	3
1918	4	1	.800	1.23	11	5	80⅔	70	23	26	1
1919	11	9	.550	3.83	25	9	162⅓	185	45	45	0
1920	23	13	.639	2.99	40	28	319	332	88	108	2
1921	25	15	.625	2.48	43	32	330⅔	293	87	124	4
1922	21	17	.553	2.80	43	31	353	334	83	148	4
1923	14	11	.560	3.41	32	15	232⅓	233	62	91	2
1924	9	11	.450	3.85	21	9	161⅓	173	58	47	0
1925	12	11	.522	3.78	34	16	238	266	59	71	1
1926	15	8	.652	3.56	27	13	184⅔	203	57	65	1
1927	4	7	.364	4.55	18	6	110⅔	131	41	39	0
1928	13	9	.591	3.75	27	16	201⅓	223	68	43	2
1929	13	13	.500	3.88	31	15	234	241	61	68	1
1930	8	13	.381	4.21	29	10	169	188	49	62	0
1931	10	14	.417	3.82	44	5	184	210	57	49	1
1932	2	11	.154	3.74	42	0	106	123	38	26	0
1933	3	4	.429	3.44	36	0	86⅓	92	28	18	0
Career	254	212	.545	3.15	669	275	4,087⅔	4,106	1,213	1,471	30

Red Faber and fellow Hall of Famer Burleigh Grimes were the last of the "legal" spitball pitchers permitted to throw the deadly pitch long after baseball's governing powers outlawed it in 1920. "It was the easiest of all pitches on the arm," Faber recalled. "Take your regular turn, and there was nothing to worry about. There was no reason for ever outlawing the pitch that I could see."

In a long and exemplary 20-year career, Faber played with some of the very best—and worst—White Sox teams. He suffered through 13 seasons of second-division ball, but his winning percentage is a respectable .545. With 254 victories in the ledger, the big redhead from Cascade, Iowa, is the second-winningest pitcher in team history.

Red's dad, Nicholas Faber, was a first-generation immigrant from Luxembourg who owned and operated the only hotel in Cascade—a prairie town that numbered fewer than

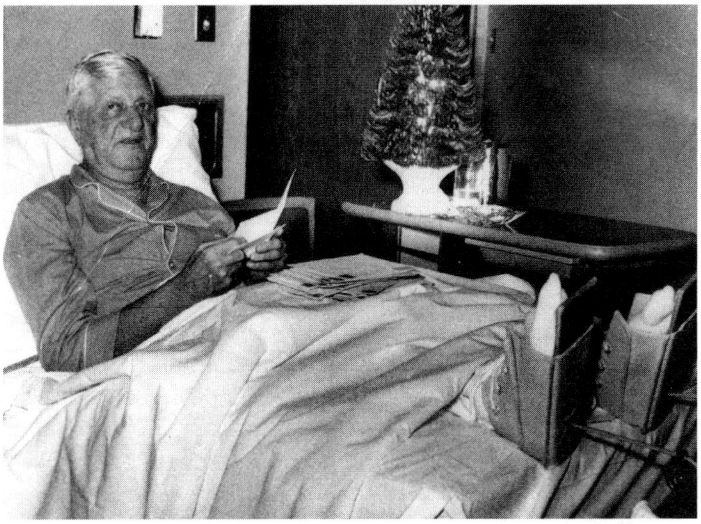

Top: Urban "Red" Faber, 1917; Bottom: Faber, White Sox spitball ace from 1913 to 1933, reads his fan mail while recovering from arthritis treatment at Passavant Hospital in Chicago, December 19, 1966. The old "Redhead" from Cascade, Iowa, won 253 games for the White Sox. He passed away in 1976.

1,500 inhabitants. His brother managed the local billiard parlor where Red worked during the off-season. Baseball held little interest for the family, but Red became an avid fan as a youth.

Faber was studying bookkeeping and playing for the varsity team at St. Joseph's College in Dubuque when he was discovered by future White Sox manager Clarence "Pants" Rowland, who induced him to sign a contract to pitch for the local minor league ballclub.

In the fall of 1909 he was drafted by the Pittsburgh Pirates after tossing a perfect game against the Davenport club of the Three-I League. However, for 1910 Faber was returned to Dubuque, where he won 18 and lost 19. The Pirates offered Faber a spring training tryout in 1911, but the results were disappointing, and the club shipped him to Minneapolis for the remainder of that season. Faber wrenched a tendon in his pitching arm after only six games and was vanquished to Pueblo, Colorado, of the Western League. Traded to the White Sox's Des Moines affiliate in 1912, Faber seemed destined to toil in minor league obscurity until the parent ballclub purchased his contract for $3,500 on August 25, 1913.

Faber had not yet pitched an inning of major league baseball when White Sox owner Charles Comiskey "loaned" him to New York Giants manager John McGraw for the goodwill World Tour of 1913–1914 after Christy Mathewson declined to make the trip. McGraw was so impressed with Faber's work during the exhibition series that he offered to purchase the young right-hander's contract from the Old Roman. Comiskey, a shrewd judge of talent, said no and promoted Faber to the active roster when the team returned to New York in March 1914. The youngster made an impressive debut against the Tigers on June 1 of that season. Faber was brilliant for 13 innings but lost a close 2–1 decision.

Red Faber's peak years followed. He won three games for the White Sox in the 1917 World Series, but an oddball play in the fifth inning of Game 2 involving the old Redhead stands out in baseball folklore. Buck Weaver was perched on third base and focusing on the batter when Faber slid headlong into the bag. To the amazement of the fans Faber had stolen third only to find it occupied by Weaver. "Where the hell do you think you're going?" Weaver snapped. "Right back to pitch," came the reply.

Recurring arm trouble sidelined him for much of the 1919 season. He was on the bench with a bout of the flu during the ill-fated Black Sox World Series that year, but returned to form in 1920 with the first of three consecutive 20-victory seasons.

A great control pitcher, who was very methodical in his approach to the game, Faber was at the center of an enduring White Sox mystery. The veteran ace was resting in his room at the Youree Hotel in Shreveport, Louisiana, on March 9, 1927, when teammate Johnny Mostil knocked on the door, presumably to arrange a card game with some of the other boys. A short time later Mostil left Faber's room. Instead of retrieving a deck of playing cards, he reached for a safety razor blade from the medicine cabinet that he used to slash his arms, chest, and leg. Mostil was saved, but Faber's role in the botched suicide attempt and the young outfielder's motives for trying to end his life when he was about to be married were covered up by the Comiskey family in order to minimize scandal.

After that experience, Faber was never the same formidable pitcher he had been earlier in his career. Advancing age and injuries took their toll. In his farewell Chicago appearance before retirement, Red shutout the Cubs 2–0 in a memorable City Series game played at Wrigley Field, October 5, 1933. Faber was 45 years old at the time.

A familiar figure in Chicago for many years to come, Red opened a bowling alley in suburban Grayslake, northwest of Chicago, after his retirement. Over the years he participated in numerous charity events, celebrity get-togethers, and neighborhood youth programs. At Ted Lyons' insistence, Faber returned to Comiskey Park as a coach from 1946 to 1948. While in his sixties and very robust for his age, Faber took a job as a surveyor for the Cook County Highway Department.

Thanks to a campaign initiated by *Chicago American* sportswriter Warren Brown, the Hall of Fame finally beckoned Faber on February 2, 1964—an anxious time in Red's life because his 15-year-old son Pepper was slowly recovering from a swimming accident that nearly claimed his life. Urban Clarence Faber passed away at his South Side home on September 25, 1976, from the complications of old age.

Falk, Bibb

White Sox: 1920–28
Outfielder
Nickname: Jockey
Birthplace: Austin, Texas

B: January 27, 1899
D: June 8, 1989
Batted left, threw left
Ht. 6–3; **Wt.** 175

Falk, Bibb

White Sox	G	AB	H	AVG	RBI	R	2B	3B	HR	SA	SB
1920	7	17	5	.294	2	1	1	1	0	.471	0
1921	152	585	167	.285	82	62	31	11	5	.402	4
1922	131	483	144	.298	79	58	27	1	12	.433	2
1923	87	274	84	.307	38	44	18	6	5	.471	4
1924	138	526	185	.352	99	77	37	8	6	.487	6
1925	154	602	181	.301	99	80	35	9	4	.409	4
1926	155	566	195	.345	108	86	43	4	8	.477	9
1927	145	535	175	.327	83	76	35	6	9	.465	5
1928	98	286	83	.290	37	42	18	4	1	.392	5
Career	1,354	4,656	1,463	.314	785	656	300	59	69	.448	46

Originally groomed as a pitcher, Bibb Falk replaced Shoeless Joe Jackson in left field after the Black Sox scandal. Batting fifth in the lineup for seven consecutive seasons, Falk was a good contact hitter whose .315 career batting average ranks sixth in the White Sox all-time top 10, and 58th overall in baseball history.

Falk was one of several Texas collegians who impressed White Sox scouts during "pickup games" played between the big-league roster and the university squad when the team headquartered in Waco and Waxahachie during the 1920 and 1921 spring training practice sessions. A versatile performer in several sports, Bibb was an All-Conference tackle and the top-rated pitching prospect for the University of

Bibb "Jockey" Falk

Texas when he received the call to report to Chicago. Manager Kid Gleason was convinced that his value to the organization rested in his hitting, not his pitching. Bibb was switched to the outfield by the Sox skipper, but his glove work was subpar those first few years.

After completing his junior year of college, Falk reported to Chicago in July 1920, sticking around long enough to witness the disintegration of the ballclub as a result of the scandal. Without Jackson standing in the way, Bibb won the starting assignment the next year.

Bibb credited Eddie Collins and Ty Cobb with helping him develop into one of the league's feared batsmen. In 1924 he finished third in the AL batting race with a .352 average. He stroked 43 doubles in 1926, which stood as a single-season club record until Floyd Robinson topped the mark in 1962.

A member of the 1922 big-league all-star team that toured the Far East and Comiskey's 1924 European traveling party that entertained the continent with a set of exhibition games against the New York Giants, Falk was dealt to Cleveland for catcher Marvin Autry on February 28, 1929. The trade was a clunker from a White Sox perspective. Bibb contributed three more .300-plus seasons, including the last two as the league's top pinch-hitter.

After his playing days ended in 1932, Falk managed the Indians' minor league affiliate in Toledo. He coached for the Indians and Red Sox through 1939 before returning to the University of Texas as the head baseball coach. His teams won 20 consecutive conference championships and two national titles.

Felsch, Oscar

White Sox: 1915–20
Outfielder
Nicknames: Happy; Hap
Birthplace: Milwaukee, Wisconsin

B: August 22, 1891
D: August 17, 1964
Batted right, threw right
Ht. 5–10; **Wt.** 175

Felsch, Oscar

White Sox	G	AB	H	AVG	RBI	R	2B	3B	HR	SA	SB
1915	121	427	106	.248	53	65	18	11	3	.363	16
1916	146	546	164	.300	70	73	24	12	7	.427	13
1917	152	575	177	.308	102	75	17	10	6	.403	26
1918	53	206	52	.252	20	16	2	5	1	.325	6
1919	135	502	138	.275	86	68	34	11	7	.428	19
1920	142	556	188	.338	115	88	40	15	14	.540	8
Career	749	2,812	825	.293	446	385	135	64	38	.427	88

A carpenter by trade, a wrestler by inclination, and a ballplayer by profession, Oscar Felsch belonged to the Milwaukee City League when he signed his first pro contract with Fond du Lac of the Wisconsin-Illinois League in 1913. Transferred to his hometown American Association team that same year, Felsch became the property of the White Sox on August 8, 1914, for a $19,000 cash consideration.

Oscar "Happy" Felsch—not always a "most happy fella"

A broad and powerful hitter, Felsch played the game with childish exuberance and was just coming into his own as one of the league's top hitters when the Black Sox scandal permanently ended his career. Oscar hit .300 in three of his six White Sox seasons, and might have made it four in 1918, if not for repeated clashes with teammate Eddie Collins that underscored the deeper divisions within this ballclub that indirectly contributed to the Black Sox scandal. Felsch angrily jumped the team on July 1 and did not return until the following season.

Hap Felsch was one of 12 children born to a dirt-poor German immigrant. He quit school in the sixth grade to take a factory job that paid $10 a week. Lacking the semblance of a formal education, he was outwitted, ridiculed, and often taken advantage of by his teammates. Felsch found friendship and acceptance with Chick Gandil, Lefty Williams, Joe Jackson, Swede Risberg, and Ed Cicotte—the "outcast" clique of players united in their dislike of Comiskey and the so-called Clean Sox faction—Eddie Collins and Ray Schalk. As one of the lowest-paid men on the team, Felsch was easily recruited into the conspiracy. In the World Series of 1919, Hap's batting average was only .192.

Acquitted in a court of law on conspiracy charges but condemned by Commissioner Landis, Felsch avowed his innocence. "I never had anything to do with any conspiracy," he said. Barred for life from organized baseball, Felsch returned to Milwaukee where he raised six children working as a crane operator and tavern proprietor.

Fernandez, Alex

White Sox: 1990–96
Pitcher
Birthplace: Miami Beach, Florida

B: August 13, 1969
Bats right, throws right
Ht. 6–1; **Wt.** 215

Fernandez, Alex

White Sox	W	L	Pct	ERA	G	CG	IP	H	BB	K	ShO
1990	5	5	.500	3.80	13	3	87⅔	89	34	61	0
1991	9	13	.409	4.51	34	2	191⅔	186	88	145	0
1992	8	11	.421	4.27	29	4	187⅔	199	50	95	2
1993	18	9	.667	3.13	34	3	247⅓	221	67	169	1
1994	11	7	.611	3.86	24	4	170⅓	163	50	122	3
1995	12	8	.600	3.80	30	5	203⅔	200	65	159	2
1996	16	10	.615	3.45	35	6	258	248	72	200	1
Career	107	87	.552	3.74	263	33	1,760⅓	1,693	552	1,252	10

Finishing in the nether regions of the American League in the late 1980s had its advantages. The White Sox selected high in the amateur draft, and they chose their players wisely—at least while Larry Himes the "Master Builder" was still in charge. Alex Fernandez was initially selected by the Milwaukee Brewers in the June 1988 draft, but the power-throwing right-hander from Miami's Pace High School chose college over baseball. Alex was a standout player with the Miami Hurricanes and Miami Dade South Community College. He was named the National Junior College Player of the Year in 1990. He won the coveted Golden Spikes Award and was selected by the White Sox in the June draft shortly afterward.

Fernandez rounded out an amazing year by debuting against the Brewers—the team that had staked a claim for Alex's services two years earlier—on August 2, 1990. He pitched well for seven innings but failed to register a decision. Two lackluster seasons followed before Alex blossomed into stardom in the 1993 championship season. His 18 victories were the most by a Sox pitcher age 24 or under since Richard Dotson won 22 games in 1983.

Alex was a model of consistency over the next three seasons. He held the staff together in the dismal days of 1995 and 1996; and in his last start of the '96 campaign, before playing out his option, he became only the fifth White Sox hurler to record 200 strikeouts in a season.

Signed by the free-spending Wayne Huizinga, owner of the Florida Marlins, as a free agent on December 9, 1996, Fernandez won 17 games in the first year of his contract before a series of shoulder injuries curtailed his career. A fully torn rotator cuff forced Fernandez out of postseason play in 1997. He endured two operations and painful rehabilitation while pitching only 193⅓ innings over the last four years. In some respects, his post–White Sox misfortunes provided an eerie parallel to former teammates Wilson Alvarez and Jack McDowell, in the sense that their decision to opt for free agency fell far short of the panacea they otherwise anticipated. At a press conference announcing his retirement at age 32, Fernandez said: "The day has come that I have to move on with my life. It's unfortunate that I had to end my career at such a young age because of the troubles with my arm, but at the same time I feel very fortunate to have played 12 years in the major leagues and won a world championship with the Florida Marlins."

Alex Fernandez

Knuckleball aces Eddie Fisher (left) and Hoyt Wilhelm, 1965

Fisher, Eddie

White Sox: 1962–66; 1972–73
Pitcher
Birthplace: Shreveport, Louisiana

B: July 16, 1936
Bats right, throws right
Ht. 6–2½; **Wt.** 200

Fisher, Eddie

White Sox	W	L	Pct	ERA	G	CG	IP	H	BB	K	ShO	Sv
1962	9	5	.643	3.10	57	2	182⅔	169	45	88	1	5
1963	9	8	.529	3.95	33	2	120⅔	114	28	67	1	0
1964	6	3	.667	3.02	59	0	125	86	32	74	0	9
1965	15	7	.682	2.40	82	0	165⅓	118	43	90	0	24
1966	1	3	.250	2.29	23	0	35⅓	27	17	18	0	6
1972	4	6	.400	3.91	49	0	103⅔	104	40	42	0	0
1973	6	7	.462	4.88	26	2	110⅔	135	38	57	0	0
Career	85	70	.548	3.41	690	7	1,538⅓	1,398	438	812	2	81

Aside from doing a bang-up imitation of the cartoon character Donald Duck, knuckleball specialist Eddie Fisher teamed with Hoyt Wilhelm to provide the White Sox with superior depth in the bullpen during the mid-1960s.

Fisher was originally scouted by Ted Lyons, who came to watch him pitch at the University of Oklahoma. Eddie bypassed the White Sox in favor of the San Francisco Giants, who assigned him to Corpus Christi. He spent much of the 1961 season in Tacoma before receiving word on September 24 that he was ticketed for Chicago after all. Fisher was the front man in another one of Ed Short's "housecleaning" trades that sent away career veterans for younger, unproven players. In this case Billy Pierce was traded to the Giants for Fisher, Dom Zanni, and outfielder Bob Farley.

Manager Al Lopez utilized Fisher as a spot starter and reliever during his first two campaigns. Eddie's rubbery arm made him particularly valuable as an emergency reliever, which became a full-time role for him in 1964. Eddie shattered several records in 1965, en route to a career-best 15–7 mark. His 82 appearances broke a year-old American League mark set by John Wyatt of the Kansas City A's. Fisher easily won Fireman of the Year honors that season. With any other team he might have remained the No. 1 closer for years to come. But the White Sox had pitching to burn during those pennant-contending seasons including Hoyt Wilhelm, the premier knuckleball pitcher of the age, and up-and-coming Bob Locker, who was groomed as Eddie Fisher's replacement when general manager Ed Short began shopping Fisher in the off-season. Eddie was also the Sox's player representative, and in those days it was almost a certainty that he would be traded sooner or later.

Fisher was dealt to Baltimore for infielder Jerry Adair on June 12, 1966, with disappointing results. Eddie remained at the top of his game through the late 1960s. Adair failed to supply the batting punch the Sox so desperately needed and was gone a year later.

Roland Hemond claimed Fisher on waivers from the California Angels on August 17, 1972, at a point when his career was on the downgrade. Chuck Tanner hoped to duplicate his earlier success with Wilbur Wood by converting Eddie to a starting role, but the experiment failed. Eddie retired in 1973 and returned to Oklahoma to pursue a career in the insurance business.

Fisk, Carlton

White Sox: 1981–93
Catcher
Nicknames: Pudge; the Commander
Birthplace: Bellows Falls, Vermont

B: December 26, 1947
Bats right, throws right
Ht. 6–3; **Wt.** 200

Fisk, Carlton

White Sox	G	AB	H	AVG	RBI	R	2B	3B	HR	SA	SB
1981	96	338	89	.263	45	44	12	0	7	.361	3
1982	135	476	127	.267	65	66	17	3	14	.403	17
1983	138	488	141	.289	86	85	26	4	26	.518	9
1984	102	359	83	.231	43	54	20	1	21	.468	6
1985	153	543	129	.238	107	85	23	1	37	.488	17
1986	125	457	101	.221	63	42	11	0	14	.337	2
1987	135	454	116	.256	71	68	22	1	23	.460	1
1988	76	253	70	.277	50	37	8	1	19	.542	0
1989	103	375	110	.293	68	47	25	2	13	.475	1
1990	137	452	129	.285	65	65	21	0	18	.451	7
1991	134	460	111	.241	74	42	25	0	18	.413	1
1992	62	188	43	.229	21	43	4	1	3	.308	3
1993	25	53	10	.189	4	2	0	0	1	.245	0
Career	2,489	8,756	2,356	.269	1,330	1,276	421	47	376	.457	128

A front-office blunder cost the Boston Red Sox the services of their ironclad, gilt-edged New England hero—Carlton Fisk—who came to symbolize a team, a city, and a defining moment of World Series history. By their failure to postmark Fisk's 1981 contract, the Red Sox inadvertently allowed their All-Star catcher to become a free agent. Boston's pain was Chicago's gain.

Eager to establish instant credibility in their first season of ownership, Jerry Reinsdorf and Eddie Einhorn aggressively pursued Fisk through his agent, Jerry Kapstein. The $3 million deal was struck on March 10, 1981. "Pudge" was coming to Chicago to begin his second career in a new city and with a ballclub on the upswing.

In storybook fashion Fisk stroked a game-winning home run against his old teammates in his very first White Sox game. On his last day in a White Sox uniform—June 28, 1993—Fisk was ordered to turn in his equipment and return to Chicago after being given the heave-ho by general manager Ron Schueler. A brilliant beginning and a sad, pathetic fall from grace marked the extremes of the "Fisk decade" in Chicago.

A proud, aloof athlete who was not well-liked by the White Sox front-office personnel for these very reasons, Fisk quarreled with the owners, managers Tony LaRussa and Jim Fregosi, and general manager Ken "Hawk" Harrelson—the latter deciding that it was in Fisk's best interests to switch to left field at a time late in Pudge's career when he was keying in on Bob Boone's record for games caught.

Fisk was one of the affected players caught in the middle of a 1980s "collusion" controversy involving a management conspiracy to drive down salaries by refusing to sign another team's free agents. All throughout his stormy 12-year run in Chicago, Fisk fought to preserve the game's rich tradition while engaging in a constant sniper war with owner Jerry Reinsdorf, who called him a "baby" and a "prima donna." Fisk paid his dues. He believed he was entitled to respect—and some special considerations that management was unwilling to grant.

"I can't say I've been liked by everyone, but I can't say that was my No. 1 objective," he said, reflecting back on his career. "I think I do have the respect of my teammates throughout the years." The "Commander" was tough on lazy veterans

Carlton "Pudge" Fisk in catcher's regalia (left) and shattering the home run mark for catchers (since broken) by hitting his 328th round-tripper in Texas, April 17, 1990.

and young pitchers who ignored his directives. Fisk slapped Greg Hibbard in the face one evening when it appeared that the lefty junk-baller wasn't paying attention. In a 1989 game the curmudgeonly backstop made headlines again after scolding Yankees outfielder Deion Sanders for failing to run out a groundball. "When you think about it, when you think about who the youth in America look to in the game over the years, and then see what personality and what kind of player they will have to settle for, it raises a lot of questions," he flatly stated.

The beat writers resented Fisk's slow, methodical approach to calling his pitches. Sox games dragged on well past the three-hour mark when Pudge crouched behind the plate, but Sox fans in the stands idolized their catcher with the regal bearing and frankly did not care if the boys in the press box were inconvenienced.

In the early months of 1983, when his average dipped to .136, media critics and even his own manager, Tony LaRussa, wondered if he was over the hill at age 33. Fisk finished a strong third in balloting for the Most Valuable Player award that year. Two years later Pudge belted 37 home runs, equalling Dick Allen's 13-year-old team record. Thirty-three of those round-trippers were hit while Fisk toiled behind the plate, thus shattering the single-season standard for catchers set by Lance Parrish in 1982. Yankees pitcher Wade Taylor surrendered Fisk's 200th White Sox home run on August 6, 1991—a seemingly insurmountable milestone that some longtime White Sox observers believed would never be broached.

At age 40, Fisk was the oldest catcher in major league history to hit 20 home runs when he turned the trick in 1987. At the All-Star Game in Toronto four years later, Fisk became the oldest player to record a hit in the midsummer classic. He was an ageless wonder and a model of physical conditioning. As the years rolled by and the front-office magnates drummed their fingers on the desk impatiently waiting for him to retire, Fisk seemed to improve like a fine old wine. He fended off rookie pretenders who would lay claim to his throne—Joel Skinner, Matt Merullo, Don Wakamatsu, and Ron Karkovice.

Already No. 1 on the all-time home run list for catchers and the White Sox team leader in this department, Fisk outdistanced such famous stalwarts as Johnny Bench, Ray Schalk, Gary Carter, and the incumbent record holder Bob Boone when he caught his 2,226th game on June 22, 1993. Jerry Reinsdorf, general manager Ron Schueler, and other top White Sox brass were noticeably absent in pregame ceremonies honoring Fisk on this historic occasion. Carlton thanked his teammates and the fans, but his choice of words left no room for doubt that his differences with management were irreconcilable. The bitter feud had no happy ending. Carlton Fisk played his last major league game that night.

Floyd, Gavin

White Sox: 2007–
Pitcher
Birthplace: Annapolis, Maryland

B: January 27, 1983
Bats right, throws right
Ht. 6–6; **Wt.** 235

Floyd, Gavin

Year	W	L	Pct.	ERA	G	CG	IP	H	BB	K	Sho	Sv
2007	1	5	.167	5.27	16	0	70	85	19	49	0	0
2008	17	8	.680	3.84	33	1	206⅓	190	70	145	0	0
2009	11	11	.500	4.06	30	1	193	178	59	163	0	0
2010	10	13	.434	4.08	31	1	187⅓	199	58	151	0	0
Career	46	42	.523	4.53	123	4	765⅓	777	270	583	1	0

It didn't look like much of a trade at the time, but the December 6, 2006, exchange of Freddy Garcia (coming off his most productive season with the White Sox) for rookie unknowns Gavin Floyd and Gio Gonzalez of the Phillies was one of those deals you can point to down the road as a stroke of genius (or luck)—although sacrificing the success and experience in a battle-tested veteran like Garcia for unproven youth is always a dangerous gamble in baseball and one that doesn't usually set well with the fans.

"We realized that if we're going to have any sort of sustained success, we're going to have to filter in some of the

Gavin Floyd on the mound in Glendale. (Courtesy of Mike McKay)

young players, and we think we've acquired two special ones," explained Sox GM Ken Williams at the 2006 winter meetings. Phillies assistant GM Mike Arbuckle agreed and added, "We were reluctant to give him up, because I think Gavin's going to be a little bit of a late bloomer. I compared him numerous times to Chris Carpenter, who was slow to come around, but when he did, became a good big-league pitcher. I still think that's going to happen."

Selected in the first round (fourth overall) in the June 2001 First-Year Player Draft, Floyd had exhausted the Phillies' patience after three failed attempts and just 19 MLB starts to make the grade in the City of Brotherly Love. He was 4–3 with a 7.29 ERA in 11 starts for the Phillies in 2006 before being optioned to Triple A on June 3 and then showed more inconsistency in the Arizona Fall League. In other words, he was ripe for the taking. Baseball people will tell you that the best trades are those that benefit *both* teams, and there is no pleasure taken when the other side is completely snookered, as were the Phillies in the Garcia-for-Gavin Floyd swap. Don't believe it. Any day you can get something for nothing—you grab it and walk away laughing—just not too loud as to offend the victimized party (in this case, Mike Arbuckle).

Freddy Garcia was 1–5 in his injury-wracked year in Philadelphia. Gavin Floyd, on the other hand, was summoned to Chicago from Triple A Charlotte on July 5, 2007. After a rocky start in the bullpen and as a spot starter with a penchant for surrendering too many long balls to opposing hitters, he settled into the rotation nicely on August 28 and posted a 3.41 ERA in his final six appearances of the season, despite poor run support from the hitters. "I'm pretty impressed with what I've seen the last six starts," opined Ozzie Guillen. "This kid has opened a lot of people's eyes. I feel proud of this kid to do what he did in those outings."

When the bell rang on the 2008 season, Floyd sparkled in his second start of the season—holding the AL champion Detroit Tigers hitless through 7⅓ innings of work. Gavin flirted with no-hit glory again on May 6 against the Twins, carrying the possible no-no into the ninth inning before Joe Mauer doubled with one out. It was the first time a Sox pitcher had lost a no-hitter in the ninth inning since Dennis Lamp surrendered a bloop double to Robin Yount that was just out of the reach of Rusty Kuntz in the ninth inning of a 5–1 Sox win on August 25, 1981, in Milwaukee.

In 2008 White Sox hitters provided much better offensive support, and at season's end Gavin led the staff in wins and had the honor of recording the final victory by an opposing pitcher in old Yankee Stadium on September 16. Awarded a four-year contract extension on March 22, 2009, Gavin turned in a very workman-like performance in '09, after being hobbled by a sore hip that closed him down for the season on September 16. Don Cooper worked patiently with Floyd, and despite stingy offensive support for much of the 2010 season, he was a pillar of consistency. During one 77-inning stretch, he yielded not one opponent home run; he also became something of a "Red Sox killer," sporting a perfect 4–0 career record against the always-fearsome "Carmines." Gavin paid tribute to his coach for his success: "It's breaking it down to basics," he said. "You're a young pitcher; you have a lot thrown at you, you're putting pressure on yourself. Coop helped me strip it down to some of the simplest things and keeping that as my focus."

Forster, Terry

White Sox: 1971–76
Pitcher
Nickname: Trees
Birthplace: Sioux Falls, South Dakota
B: January 14, 1952
Bats left, throws left
Ht. 6–3; **Wt.** 200

Forster, Terry

White Sox	W	L	Pct	ERA	G	CG	IP	H	BB	K	ShO	Sv
1971	2	3	.400	3.96	45	0	50	46	23	48	0	1
1972	6	5	.545	2.25	62	0	100	75	44	104	0	29
1973	6	11	.353	3.23	51	4	172⅔	174	78	120	0	16
1974	7	8	.467	3.63	59	0	134	120	48	105	0	24
1975	3	3	.500	2.19	17	0	37	30	24	32	0	4
1976	2	12	.143	4.38	29	1	111	126	41	70	0	1
Career	54	65	.454	3.23	614	5	1,105	1,034	457	791	0	116

A phenom at age 19—a glutton at 34. By the time Terry Forster's career had ended in 1986, his eating habits had become a national joke among the stand-up comics. David Letterman's mocking reference to Forster as a "big tub of goo" before his nationwide TV audience epitomized the unraveling of a once-promising big-league career.

Terry Forster, a left-handed speed-baller, was signed by the White Sox out of Santana High School, in Santee, California, where he played basketball against Bill Walton. After pitching in just 10 minor league games, Forster received a vote of confidence—and the green light—from Sox pitching coach

Terry Forster

Johnny Sain to move up to Chicago. "From what you have seen of this boy on the mound, would you hesitate to bring him to the big leagues if he were a couple of years older?" Sain asked. The answer was no, of course. "Then why not?"

Summoned to Chicago midway through the 1971 campaign, the 19-year-old lefty was assigned to bullpen duty. In 1972 he set a new team record for saves with 29 (since broken by Ed Farmer, Bob James, Bobby Thigpen, Roberto Hernandez, and Keith Foulke), and he was an effective closer through 1975. From 1971 through 1973, when Chuck Tanner was forced to insert him into the starting rotation because of injuries, Terry hurled 138⅓ innings without surrendering a home run.

An outstanding glove man and an even better hitter (for a pitcher), Forster was named AL Fireman of the Year in 1974. His fastball was clocked at 94.9 miles an hour during a reading taken on September 7 that year, which placed him fifth on the unofficial all-time list behind Bob Feller and Nolan Ryan. Overwork and misuse by Chuck Tanner probably shortened Forster's career. His inattention to physical conditioning may also have been a factor in his slow, almost unavoidable decline. Used as a starter by Paul Richards in 1976, his final White Sox season, Terry played out the string with the Pirates, Dodgers, and Braves following his trade to Pittsburgh on December 10, 1976.

Foulke, Keith

White Sox: 1997–2002
Pitcher
Birthplace: Ellsworth AFB, Rapid City, South Dakota

B: October 19, 1972
Bats right, throws right
Ht. 6–1; **Wt.** 210

Foulke, Keith

White Sox	W	L	Pct	ERA	G	CG	IP	H	BB	K	ShO	Sv
1997	3	0	1.000	3.45	16	0	28⅓	28	5	21	0	3
1998	3	2	.600	4.13	54	0	65⅓	51	20	57	0	1
1999	3	3	.500	2.22	67	0	105⅓	72	21	123	0	9
2000	3	1	.750	2.97	72	0	88	66	22	91	0	34
2001	4	9	.307	2.33	72	0	81	57	22	75	0	42
2002	2	4	.333	2.90	65	0	77⅓	65	13	58	0	11
Career	41	37	.526	3.33	619	0	786⅔	652	194	718	0	191

Keith Foulke

Ranked third on the all-time White Sox saves list with 100 (behind Bobby Thigpen and Roberto Hernandez), Keith Foulke spurned an offer to sign with the Detroit Tigers in the 1993 amateur draft. Chosen by the San Francisco Giants in the ninth round the following year, Foulke was impressive in a starting role in the high minors. But a starting pitcher he was never destined to be. Foulke was converted to the bullpen not long after Ron Schueler acquired his services from the Giants on July 31, 1997—the much maligned "White Flag" trade with the Giants, bringing Foulke, Mike Caruso, Bob Howry, Lorenzo Barcelo, Brian Manning, and Ken Vining to Chicago for Roberto Hernandez, Danny Darwin, and Wilson Alvarez. Though few could have possibly suspected it at the time, Foulke turned out to be the key to the deal. Brought up to the parent club from Triple A Nashville on August 14, the youngster converted three of his first five save opportunities and looked impressive. Relying on a fastball that creeps into the low nineties, the tall right-hander with a "hesitation delivery" added a slow change-up to his repertoire with an occasional slider for even greater effectiveness. He took over the full-time closer role from Bobby Howry in 1999, converting nine of 13 chances. That year he fanned 123 hitters, becoming the first Sox pitcher since "Goose" Gossage in 1975 to lead American League relievers in strikeouts.

In June 2000 he recorded 12 saves for the month—the second highest total in major league history behind Bobby Thigpen's 13 in 1990. Foulke's emergence as one of the game's most dominant closers was a thing of beauty, and it continued the long-standing White Sox tradition of coming up with exciting new bullpen aces, even in the leanest of times. Working the outside part of the plate to perfection, Foulke was a great control pitcher, and his 42 saves in 2001 rank second only to Thigpen's record-setting performance in 1990.

Foulke led the league that year with a .933 save percentage. Despite a low ERA in 2002, his final White Sox season, Foulke was hit hard the first two months and was demoted from the closer role before the All-Star break. He fought his way back and allowed only one earned run over his final 31⅓ innings, but with a year left to go on a two-year contract worth $4 million per annum, Kenny Williams decided the time was right for the Sox and Foulke to part ways.

On December 3 Williams pulled the pin and sent Foulke, catcher Mark Johnson, and minor leaguer Joe Valentine to Oakland for Billy Koch, a hard-throwing right-hander signed through 2004. The trade worked out fine for Oakland, but not so good for the Sox—for the first year. Granted his free-agency after a 2003 season that saw him nail down 43 saves, Foulke signed with the Boston Red Sox. He had a superb season and recorded the final out for the Carmines in the 2004 World Series. Meanwhile, the White Sox nurtured Neal Cotts, their "player to be named later" from Oakland to complete the Foulke trade. The lefty Cotts developed into a strong middle-relief man during the 2005 pennant chase, redeeming a trade that author Michael Lewis mercilessly ridiculed in his 2003 book *Moneyball: The Art of Winning an Unfair Game*, a fawning biography of Oakland general manager Billy Beane, who suddenly didn't look quite like the genius Lewis made him out to be.

Fournier, Jacques

White Sox: 1912–17
First baseman
Birthplace: Au Sable, Michigan

B: September 28, 1892
D: September 5, 1973
Batted left, threw right
Ht. 6–0; **Wt.** 195

Fournier, Jacques

White Sox	G	AB	H	AVG	RBI	R	2B	3B	HR	SA	SB
1912	35	73	14	.192	2	5	5	2	0	.315	1
1913	68	172	40	.233	23	20	8	5	1	.355	9
1914	109	379	118	.311	44	44	14	9	6	.443	10
1915	126	422	136	.322	77	86	20	18	5	.491	21
1916	105	313	75	.240	44	36	13	9	3	.367	19
1917	1	1	0	.000	0	0	0	0	0	.000	0
Career	1,530	5,208	1,631	.313	859	821	252	113	136	.483	145

Jacques Fournier

The dilemma that Clarence Rowland and a half-dozen other big-league managers faced was what to do with lumbering Jack Fournier, a pure hitter who couldn't field worth a lick. Purchased from the Boston Red Sox on May 8, 1912, Fournier frustrated everyone with his fielding ineptitude.

Jacques played sparingly during his first two seasons, but his timely hitting during the 1913 City Series earned the big Frenchman a starting assignment the following spring. But for all his dazzling line-drive doubles into the gap, Fournier surrendered nearly twice as many runs with his stone glove. At the close of the 1915 season, Clarence Rowland dragged Shano Collins in from the outfield to take over for Fournier. The next spring, a weak-hitting Pacific Coast League recruit named Jack Ness supplanted Fournier at first base.

The acquisition of Chick Gandil prior to the 1917 season spelled the end of the line for Jacques Fournier as far as the White Sox were concerned. He drifted into the National League, where he maintained a solid average with the Cardinals. He was traded to the Brooklyn Dodgers on February 15, 1923, and moved easily into a potent offensive unit that included Zack Wheat, Milt Stock, and Zack Taylor.

Hindsight suggests that the White Sox would have been a whole lot better off if they had only exercised a little more patience with Jacques Fournier.

Fox, Jacob Nelson

White Sox: 1950–63
Second baseman
Nicknames: Nellie; Little Nell
Birthplace: St. Thomas, Pennsylvania

B: December 25, 1927
D: December 1, 1975
Batted left, threw right
Ht. 5–9; **Wt.** 160

Fox, Jacob Nelson

White Sox	G	AB	H	AVG	RBI	R	2B	3B	HR	SA	SB
1950	130	457	113	.247	30	45	12	7	0	.304	4
1951	147	604	189	.313	55	93	32	12	4	.425	9
1952	152	648	192	.296	39	76	25	10	0	.366	5
1953	154	624	178	.285	72	92	31	8	3	.375	4
1954	155	631	201	.319	47	111	24	8	2	.391	16
1955	154	636	198	.311	59	100	28	7	6	.406	7
1956	154	649	192	.296	52	109	20	10	4	.376	8
1957	155	619	196	.317	61	110	27	8	6	.415	5
1958	155	623	187	.300	49	82	21	6	0	.353	5
1959	156	624	191	.306	70	84	34	6	2	.389	5
1960	150	605	175	.289	59	85	24	10	2	.372	2
1961	159	606	152	.251	51	67	11	5	2	.295	2
1962	157	621	166	.267	54	79	27	7	2	.343	1
1963	137	539	140	.260	42	54	19	0	2	.343	0
Career	2,367	9,232	2,663	.288	790	1,279	355	112	35	.363	76

In 1989 a well-heeled gathering of Chicago attorneys, judges, and downtown politicians organized the Nellie Fox Society to lobby for the inclusion of their beloved "Mighty Mite" into baseball's Hall of Fame—a mission that was finally accomplished in 1997.

Nellie Fox was an uncommon ballplayer who defined an era and a style of play. Lacking the blazing speed of his sidekick Louie Aparicio and unable to drive the ball deep into the power alleys, he compensated for his lack of physical prowess in more significant ways. Nellie Fox was "Charlie Hustle" long before Pete Rose copyrighted the moniker. Nellie was beloved by Chicago fans because he was an "everyman" ballplayer who played the game with the childish exuberance of a sandlotter.

Fox was only 16 years old when his mom and dad drove him to Frederick, Maryland, to try out for a spot on Connie Mack's Philadelphia A's. With player material at a low ebb because of World War II, Mack agreed to give the elfish-looking youngster a tryout—at first base. "I don't think I was any ball of fire," Fox remembered. "But I was draft-proof for a couple of years, so they decided to keep me."

A first baseman's glove was all that Fox owned at the time. Nellie had his heart set on a baseball career, and his persistence was rewarded when Connie Mack offered him a contract. Fox alternated between first base, the outfield, and second base in his first few years of pro ball. He played a handful of games in 1947 and 1948 as a late-season call-up—nothing to suggest future stardom.

Nellie's arrival in the Windy City had more to do with some clubhouse fisticuffs between Sox manager Jack Onslow and catcher Joe Tipton than the Comiskeys' desire to acquire Fox for his diamond skills. Onslow accused Tipton of failing to cover up his signals to the pitcher in a game against Cleveland. The two men later came to blows over the matter, prompting Tipton's trade to the Philadelphia A's for Fox. The historic date: October 19, 1949.

Still, Fox was just a name on the roster until Frank Lane traded the incumbent second baseman, Cass Michaels, to Washington on Memorial Day 1950. The writers laughed when Lane said that the pint-sized Fox was going to be Michaels' replacement. It took a dose of Lane confidence, fielding refinements from Sox coach Jimmy Adair, and necessary adjustments to Nellie's batting stance made by Sox coach Roger "Doc" Cramer in the spring of 1951 for the young man to blossom into stardom. In May of that year Fox was hitting .370, and suddenly the laughter from the press box ceased.

Thereafter, sprightly Nelson Fox became the "Iron Man" of the White Sox. He played through bone-jarring collisions, spike wounds, a cut eye, minor illness, and fatigue. Only a manager's whim could keep Fox out of the lineup, and that, unfortunately, occurred in Baltimore on August 6, 1955. Fox had already played in 277 consecutive games when manager Marty Marion decided his star needed a rest.

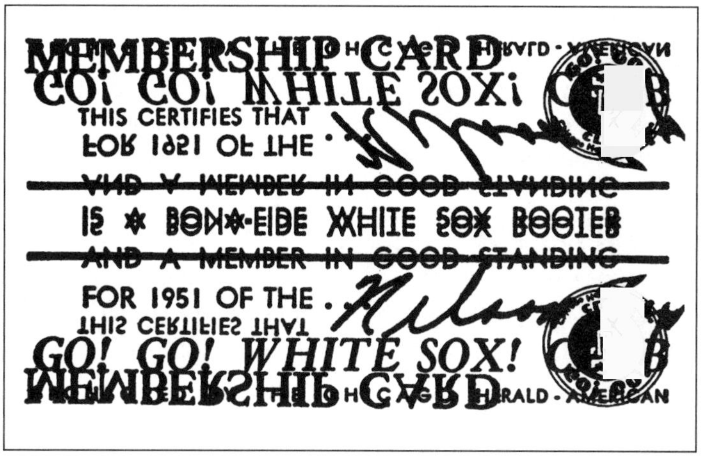

Left: Nellie Fox, heart and soul of the South Side; right: 1951 membership card for the Fox fan club

Nellie and his wife, Joanne, who was sitting in the players' wives' section, were upset by the decision—but could do nothing to influence Marion to the contrary. Nellie began another streak two days later. Fox would play in the next 798 consecutive games—a record for second basemen that came to an end in Chicago on September 3, 1960, because of illness. If not for the 1955 game, Fox would have had a 1,075-game streak to accompany his many other achievements.

In 1958 Fox played in 98 consecutive games without striking out. He led the league 11 times in this category. Nellie was named to the All-Star team 12 times and won three Gold Glove awards. Fox was a brilliant glove man and is a member of the exclusive but unheralded "Defensive Triple Crown Club" of fielders who led the league in fielding percentage, putouts, and assists in the same season. Fox accomplished this three times: 1952, 1956, and 1959.

His Most Valuable Player award, coming in the pennant year, earned Nellie the highest salary ever paid to a White Sox player to that time. He pulled down $47,000 in 1960.

Nellie's infectious enthusiasm for the game never waned. The famous Fox trademarks—the chaw of tobacco tucked inside the left cheek, the bottle bat, and the familiar No. 2 emblazoned on the back of his sleeveless jersey—symbolized an era. But that era ended all too quickly when Ed Short pulled the pin and traded this perennial fan favorite to Houston on December 10, 1963, for pitcher Jim Golden and outfielder Danny Murphy. Fox was reunited with his old boss, Paul Richards, who was calling the shots for the Colt .45s as their general manager. Richards desperately needed Fox to impart his knowledge to young Joe Morgan, an up-and-coming second baseman in the Houston system.

Fox remained with Houston until 1967. He coached for Ted Williams when Williams was managing the Washington Senators/Texas Rangers (1969–1972), but his heart was in Chicago, and in all likelihood Fox would have found employment with Bill Veeck in 1976 if he had not been struck down in the prime of life by skin cancer.

Nellie's death at such an early age undoubtedly hurt his chances for early enshrinement in the Hall of Fame. The Veterans Committee repeatedly failed to muster the required number of votes to open the gates for Fox, until 1997.

Nellie's former manager, Al Lopez, deepened the mystery by remaining tight-lipped and defensive about the committee's reasoning. There are those who believe that it is Lopez, and not the other committee members, who cast the deciding vote to keep Fox out of the Hall.

Gamble, Oscar

White Sox: 1977; 1985
Outfielder, designated hitter
Birthplace: Ramer, Alabama

B: December 20, 1949
Bats left, throws right
Ht. 5–11; **Wt.** 160

Gamble, Oscar

White Sox	G	AB	H	AVG	RBI	R	2B	3B	HR	SA	SB
1977	137	408	121	.297	83	75	22	2	31	.588	1
1985	70	148	30	.203	20	20	5	0	4	.493	0
Career	1,460	4,229	1,142	.270	619	619	181	31	186	.459	46

The joy of the South Side Hitmen summer was clouded by the certain knowledge that Oscar Gamble, the spindle-legged slugger with the big Afro haircut, would not return to Chicago in 1978 unless the Bill Veeck ownership satisfied his demand for a boxcar-sized multiyear contract. And, of course, that did not happen. When it was over, Sox fans were left to ponder the unjust consequences of free agency and the collective memories of a year that ended far too soon.

Oscar Gamble came to Chicago on April 5, 1977, in exchange for Bucky Dent after the Sox failed to satisfy their All-Star shortstop's salary requirements. By acquiring Gamble from the Yankees, Veeck inherited another salary headache. "The only way I'll play for Chicago is if they come up with some money!" Gamble complained. He was obviously upset at going from a pennant winner to a last-place doormat.

Bill Veeck "rented" Oscar Gamble for one year. And what a year it was! Batting in front of Richie Zisk, the 27-year-old Gamble clouted 31 home runs. Most of them landed in the same identical location—hugging the right-field foul pole. Oscar was an improbable power hitter, but his 31 roundtrippers remained a club record for left-handed batters until 1996, when Robin Ventura shattered the mark. Gamble enjoyed a career year in Chicago, and it was unfortunate for the Sox—and Oscar—when he spurned Bill Veeck's final offer and signed with the San Diego Padres on November 29.

Gamble rejoined the Sox as a free agent on March 23, 1985, but his skills had eroded, and he was released on August 12. He never matched his 1977 numbers.

Oscar Gamble

Gandil, Arnold

White Sox: 1910; 1917–19
First baseman
Nickname: Chick
Birthplace: St. Paul, Minnesota

B: January 19, 1887
D: December 13, 1970
Batted right, threw right
Ht. 6–1½; **Wt.** 190

Gandil, Arnold

White Sox	G	AB	H	AVG	RBI	R	2B	3B	HR	SA	SB
1910	77	275	53	.193	21	21	7	3	2	.262	12
1917	149	553	151	.273	57	53	9	7	0	.315	16
1918	114	439	119	.271	55	49	18	4	0	.330	9
1919	115	441	128	.290	60	54	24	7	1	.383	10
Career	1,147	4,245	1,176	.277	557	449	173	78	11	.362	153

Chick Gandil ran away from home at age 17 to play "desert ball" in the rugged border towns straddling the Mexico-Arizona boundary. Later, he picked up a few dollars as a substitute first baseman for a mining team in Cananea, Mexico, of the Cactus League. To survive in this lawless, wide-open territory, Gandil boxed in the local heavyweight division, earning $150 a fight. His baseball salary was $15 a game.

In the fall of 1908, Gandil was sold to the St. Louis Browns, but he refused a minor league assignment in order to play for the Sacramento team of the Pacific Coast League. At the close of the 1909 season he was sold to the White Sox, who were in desperate need of a first baseman to replace Jiggs Donahue. Gandil opened the season at first, but injuries and inconsistent play ruined his chances to remain on the roster until the end of the year. He was sold to Montreal of the Eastern League on September 2, 1910.

Following another year of minor league apprenticeship, Chick was back in the majors in 1912 with the Washington Senators, where he refined his hitting and fielding skills. In the next few years he struck up a friendship with Boston gambler Joseph "Sport" Sullivan, who found it useful for his business to socialize with the ballplayers. Sullivan had rich and influential friends, and luring Gandil into a plot to throw the 1919 World Series was crucial for success.

Gandil's role as the Black Sox ringleader goes unquestioned. He was the "master of ceremonies" who arranged the first meeting between Sullivan and "the boys" at Boston's Buckminster Hotel in late September 1919, according to Ed Cicotte.

Sold to Cleveland on February 15, 1916, and secured by the White Sox exactly a year later for $3,500, Gandil proved to be the missing link who helped turn a pennant contender into a world champion. "Gandil makes plays at first base so that they all look easy," lauded his manager Kid Gleason. "He knows more about shifting his feet than any of them. He'll be in a position to take a bad one with two hands where a lot of others would have to stab it with one."

Gandil never confessed to throwing the 1919 World Series. "My hits won two of the three games against the Reds," he said 50 years later. "If I'd been trying to throw the series, would I have tried to win those games?"

The 1919 season turned out to be Gandil's final major league campaign. Bowing to the wishes of his wife, Chick refused to sign a 1920 contract with Comiskey. He played for an independent team in Idaho that paid him a salary commensurate with the $4,000 he earned from the Old Roman in 1919. Following his banishment from the majors by Judge Landis in 1921, Gandil played many years of semipro and outlaw baseball up and down the West Coast and in Arizona.

Arnold "Chick" Gandil was the ringleader of the 1919 fix.

The roughhousing Chickie took up the plumbing trade in the late 1930s. He worked in the San Francisco Bay area for the next 14 years before retiring in 1952.

Even in his final days Gandil continued to deny his Black Sox guilt. Famed criminal attorney Melvin Belli was approached about representing Gandil in a suit against organized baseball to clear his name, but it never moved past the discussion stage. Wracked by emphysema and heart disease, Chick Gandil passed away at the Calistoga Convalescent Home in California, a bitter and defiant baseball rebel to the end.

Garcia, Freddy

White Sox: 2004–06; 2009–10
Pitcher
Birthplace: Caracas, Venezuela

B: June 10, 1975
Bats right, throws right
Ht. 6–4; **Wt.** 235

Garcia, Freddy

White Sox	W	L	Pct	ERA	G	CG	IP	H	BB	K	ShO	Sv
2004	9	4	.692	4.46	16	16	103	96	32	102	0	0
2005	14	8	.636	3.87	33	2	228	225	60	146	0	0
2006	17	9	.654	4.53	33	1	216⅓	228	48	135	0	0
2009	3	4	.429	4.34	9	0	56	56	12	37	0	0
2010	12	6	.667	4.64	28	0	157	171	45	89	0	0
Career	133	87	.605	4.13	303	12	1,929⅔	1,896	611	1,390	4	0

Freddy Garcia, the major league's winning pitcher from Venezuela

Freddy Garcia is the "great road warrior" of the White Sox. He does his best work pitching away from home, as demonstrated by a gaudy 10–3 record away from U.S. Cellular Field in the championship season. When you get down to it, the best pitchers in the game are those who can master their opponents in hostile surroundings. Others on the staff can easily pick up the slack at home. Garcia is an intense competitor, a real "gamer" who gives his manager innings and holds opponents close.

Freddy was originally signed by the Houston Astros as a non-drafted free agent on October 21, 1993. At the time, the Astros stationed Carl Reiner, a full-time scout in Venezuela to scour the cities and countryside for prospects. He delivered a number of outstanding young players to the Houston farm system, including Freddy Garcia, a converted infielder who languished in the minors for five seasons before the 'Stros executed another of their famous bonehead trades, dealing away Garcia, Carlos Guillen, and John Halama to Seattle for the soon-to-be-free agent Randy Johnson on July 31, 1998.

The next year the young Venezuelan easily transitioned into the M's starting rotation, defeating the White Sox in his major league debut on April 7, rolling on to 17 wins in 1999, his rookie season. Freddy was the first Mariner to win a game in the new Safeco Field on July 17, but when he exhibited a tendency of tiring in the late innings, manager Lou Piniella ordered him to change his eating habits after being informed that Garcia skipped breakfast throughout his minor league career. The rook was told to chow down on pancakes, eggs, ham, and bacon every morning, and wouldn't you know, he grew stronger by the day. A year later, in 2000, he opened the American League Division Series against the Sox, but failed to register a decision. White Sox scouts took note; this was a player the ballclub deeply coveted.

The opportunity to acquire this young man's services came midway through the 2004 season. The Mariners had unraveled at the seams, and the front office was dismantling. White Sox pitching, aside from Mark Buehrle's fine work every four days, was in shambles. Unafraid to wheel and deal his prospects if it meant immediate improvement for the parent club, GM Kenny Williams parted with top outfield prospect Jeremy Reed, catcher Miguel Olivo, and shortstop Michael Morse in return for Garcia and catcher Ben Davis. It was a gamble: Garcia was in his option year, and Reed was ranked the No. 1 prospect in the White Sox farm system by *Baseball America*. Was this to be another frustrating White Sox rent-a-player scheme? Not quite. On July 5 the Sox broke with long-standing tradition and signed Garcia to a three-year contract extension. His close association with manager Ozzie Guillen had a lot to do with it. Garcia is married to Ozzie's niece.

Assessing the trade a year later, it was clear that the Sox had outmaneuvered Seattle. In 2005 the M's cut Miguel Olivo loose while Jeremy Reed was just so-so in his first full season. Meanwhile, Freddy Garcia was looking awfully good in his new Sox pinstripes. On August 23, 2005, he carried a no-hitter into the eighth inning at the Hubert H. Humphrey Metrodome until Jacque Jones led off with a home run to hand the Sox a bitter 1–0 loss. That one hit was all Garcia surrendered to the Twins. Thus he joined Richard Dotson in the team record book as the only other Sox pitcher to lose a one-hitter. While it was true that he did his best pitching in the daytime (39–13 through 2005), Garcia brought to the dance two years of postseason experience with the Mariners—a real plus for the White Sox going into the championship round. After winning the decisive 1–0 clincher, thus sealing the four-game World Series sweep of the team that traded him away in 1998, Freddy Garcia's cap from Game 4 was sent to the Baseball Hall of Fame to be put on display alongside Jermaine Dye's jersey and Joe Crede's glove.

Garcia was the workhorse of the staff in 2006, logging 216 innings—but all that work began to take a painful toll on the veteran right-hander. In this, his best all-around Sox season, "Sweaty Freddy," as he was dubbed by the fans, accomplished the rare feat of allowing opponents just one hit through eight innings—in two consecutive starts on September 13 and 19. Dave Stieb, a notorious White Sox killer from the 1980s, was the last to accomplish it during the 1988 season. Garcia passed Wilson Alvarez for the most wins by a Venezuelan pitcher with 103 on April 28 at Anaheim and was nearly unhittable in the month of September. With so many superlatives, it was hard to imagine Kenny Williams dealing his staff ace for prospects, but that was the genius of the Sox's gambling GM, whose instincts told him it was time to cut bait. Garcia was shipped to Philadelphia on December 6, 2006, for two unknown rookie pitchers, Gavin Floyd and Gio Gonzalez. It was a terrific deal for the Pale Hose, although sadly for Garcia his career after Chicago quickly derailed. Beset by biceps tendinitis and a right shoulder strain, Freddy appeared in only 11 games in 2007. Phillies fans derisively mocked Garcia's only victory in the red pinstripes that year as the "$10 million win." Cut loose in Philadelphia, Freddy was picked up by the Tigers as a free agent on August 14, 2008, but was limited to only three games. With his career in the dumps after failing to make the grade with the Buffalo Bisons, the Mets' Triple A affiliate, Williams gambled again and signed "Big Game" Freddy to a minor league contract on June 8, 2009, after he passed his physical. Summoned to Chicago on August 18, he made seven quality starts and showed improved velocity in his nine appearances—pleasing Ozzie Guillen, who penciled Garcia in as his fifth starter for 2010. In the spring angry Cubs fans dubbed "Big Game" Freddy "Trash Talking" Freddy for certain disparaging remarks he made about the North Siders—but as Garcia correctly pointed out, he was back with the Sox now, and they were signing his checks. The 35th Street faithful didn't expect much of him going into the 2010 season, but they couldn't have been more pleased, especially after he won nine of his first 12 decisions as the fifth starter, and delivered 18 quality starts.

Garland, Jon

White Sox: 2000–07
Pitcher
Birthplace: Valencia, California

B: September 27, 1979
Bats right, throws right
Ht. 6–6; **Wt.** 215

Garland, Jon

White Sox	W	L	Pct	ERA	G	CG	IP	H	BB	K	ShO	Sv
2000	4	8	.333	6.46	15	0	69⅓	82	40	42	0	0
2001	6	7	.462	3.69	35	0	117	123	55	61	0	1
2002	12	12	.500	4.58	33	1	192⅓	188	83	112	1	0
2003	12	13	.480	4.51	32	0	191⅓	188	74	108	0	0
2004	12	11	.522	4.89	34	1	217	223	76	113	0	0
2005	18	10	.643	3.50	32	3	221	212	47	115	3	0
2006	18	7	.720	4.51	33	1	211⅓	247	41	112	1	0
2007	10	13	.435	4.23	32	2	208⅓	219	57	98	1	0
Career	131	114	.535	4.32	344	10	2,029⅓	2,120	680	1,096	6	1

Patience and perseverance finally paid off for the White Sox in 2005 with the emergence of Jon Garland, the tall, lanky "California Kid" who required five seasons of on-the-job training before leaving his mark. Garland was just 20 years old when he made his major league debut with the White Sox on July 4, 2000, in Kansas City—a day he would just as soon forget. The kid allowed seven runs in three innings—he was the youngest player in the big leagues at the time and pretty green. But what potential! At least the Cubs thought so when they claimed him in the first round of the June 1997 free agent draft. But somewhere along the line Garland lost his fastball and the confidence of Cubs general manager Ed Lynch, who dealt him to the White Sox on July 29, 1998, for 32-year-old journeyman reliever Matt Karchner, who was expected to provide the North Siders with bullpen help for the stretch run. Karchner failed to stick with the Cubs, was demoted to the minors, and was gone from the organization after the 2000 season. Also gone that year was Ed Lynch, whose hasty, ill-advised decision to trade youth for experience was undoubtedly a major factor in the Cubs' decision to terminate his services.

Meanwhile, Garland struggled to find consistency and an aggressive attitude. Maybe he brought too much of the laid-back California lifestyle and attitude with him to the big leagues. Kenny Williams traced the problem to a lack of mental toughness. "There's a certain aggression I noticed in type 1 and type 2 pitchers," Williams said in 2002. "Garland doesn't

Taking aim on stardom: Jon Garland

have that yet. I hope he can develop it soon." It would take another three seasons, a rumored trade to the Angels for Darin Erstad that never materialized, and a change of managers for the young pitcher to find himself and live up to his early promise. Part of the problem was Jerry Manuel's low threshold for Garland's early inning struggles. Too often, he was not given much of a chance to work out of tough situations or pitch past the fifth inning. Ozzie Guillen approached things a little differently. He allowed Big Jon the chance to escape jams on his own without summoning bullpen help at the first hint of trouble. And with this important vote of confidence, Garland blossomed into a star in 2005 and worked himself up from fifth starter to first in the rotation until Jose Contreras caught his second wind and carried the ballclub through the final two months of the season.

Garland won his first eight decisions of the season, equaling the earlier accomplishments of John "Porkchops" Whitehead (1935) and Wilson Alvarez (1994). (The club record for most wins to start a season is nine and was set by Claude "Lefty" Williams in 1917.) His back-to-back shutouts against Oakland and Detroit on April 25 and May 1 were the first time a Sox pitcher turned the trick since Jack McDowell in September 1991. In the third game of the American League Championship Series, Garland threw his sinking fastball and change-up to absolute perfection in a 5–2, complete-game victory over the Angels in their home park—just 50 miles from where he grew up. He was pitching on 12 days of rest, but the long layoff certainly did not hurt his effectiveness. In Game 3 of the 2005 World Series, Jon overcame a shaky start and pitched through the seventh inning before giving way to the bullpen. The relief corps held the Astros scoreless the rest of the way.

Blessed with strong offensive support in back of him—the potent White Sox offense averaged 6.39 runs in his 2006 starts—the whimsical Garland became the first Sox hurler to win 18 (or more) in back-to-back seasons since "Black" Jack McDowell in 1992–93. However, Jon's soaring ERA was a more ominous indicator that he still had not taken his career to the next level as the '06 season wore on. In a 14–1 pasting in Cleveland on September 25, 2006, Garland became the first pitcher with a winning record (in a season) to surrender 12 runs in a start since Red Ruffing of the Yankees dropped a 20–4 decision to the Red Sox on September 2, 1939. Jon notched a more satisfying mark of distinction in 2006 when he whacked a two-run homer off of Esteban Yan in Cincinnati's Great American Ballpark on June 18. Garland's mighty blast into the left-field seats broke a homerless drought by White Sox pitchers dating back to September 6, 1971, when right-handed reliever Steve Kealey launched one into the upper deck of old Comiskey Park.

In 2007 Garland lowered his ERA and reduced his hit total, but limped home with a subpar 10–13 mark in a season when the entire team underachieved. Looking to shake things up, Kenny Williams traded his 2005 World Series ace to the Angels for shortstop Orlando Cabrera on November 19, 2007. The deal was unsatisfactory for both teams. Cabrera proved more than capable, but he made waves in his one season in Chicago, and Garland opted for free agency. Both were gone from their respective teams after the '08 season.

Garland signed with the Arizona Diamondbacks in January 2009, but failed to last the year. He was traded to the Dodgers on August 31 but did not appear in L.A.'s extended playoff run. Jon became a free agent for a third straight season when the Dodgers opted not to pick up his option for $10 million for 2010. He was given a $2.25 million buyout and signed with the San Diego Padres, happy to be pitching close to his Southern California home and in a spacious ballpark. "San Diego has one of the last pitcher's parks," said Garland. "Petco Park is a place where I saw myself pitching."

Garr, Ralph

White Sox: 1976–79
Outfielder
Nickname: The Main Man
Birthplace: Monroe, Louisiana

B: December 12, 1945
Bats left, throws right
Ht. 5–11; **Wt.** 185

Garr, Ralph

White Sox	G	AB	H	AVG	RBI	R	2B	3B	HR	SA	SB
1976	136	527	158	.300	36	63	22	6	4	.387	14
1977	134	543	163	.300	54	78	29	7	10	.435	12
1978	118	443	122	.275	29	67	18	9	3	.377	7
1979	102	307	86	.280	39	34	10	2	9	.414	2
Career	1,317	5,108	1,562	.306	408	717	212	64	75	.416	172

Fans of the Atlanta Braves dubbed Ralph Garr the Roadrunner because of his speed and his high-pitched squeaky voice. The marketing firm of Aarner Brothers, Inc., granted him exclusive rights to use the copyrighted name, but the image just did not seem to accurately reflect the quality of the player the White Sox received in exchange for Ken Henderson, Dick Ruthven, and Dan Osborn on December 12, 1975.

As a left fielder who exhibited limited range, diminished speed, and a flair for the unusual, the Roadrunner was billed as the Main Man by the keeper of the White Sox scoreboard, who flashed an inspirational chant to Comiskey Park fans reading the Sox-o-Gram message board each time Garr approached the plate:

"C'mon Main Man! C'mon!"

Ralph Garr lived in terror of the left-field wall. Never had there been a Sox outfielder so poor at cutting off base hits into the corner. Every fly ball was an adventure, and the most routine play became a nail-biting test of endurance.

And yet...Garr approached his job with a certain charisma and determination lacking in the 1970s baseball player. He ignited the Sox offense by batting an identical .300 in 1976 and 1977. Ralph sparred with teammate Francisco Barrios, the hotheaded pitcher often victimized by Garr's fielding mishaps. And who can forget that awful moment on June 24, 1977, when a Garr home run was ruled a single because he charged past a runner on first base who would not move off the bag until he was sure the ball was out of the park? Sox fans who made the seven-hour trek to old Metropolitan Stadium in Bloomington, Minnesota, that night will never forget it.

Ralph Garr: a clubhouse character

Ralph Garr. What made him run? Nobody knew for sure. The strange saga ended on September 20, 1979, when Bill Veeck shed a big salary by selling Ralph to the contending California Angels.

Gossage, Rich

White Sox: 1972–76
Pitcher
Nickname: Goose
Birthplace: Colorado Springs, Colorado

B: July 5, 1951
Bats right, throws right
Ht. 6–3; **Wt.** 180

Gossage, Rich

White Sox	W	L	Pct	ERA	G	CG	IP	H	BB	K	ShO	Sv
1972	7	1	.875	4.28	36	0	80	72	44	57	0	2
1973	0	4	.000	7.43	20	1	49⅔	57	37	33	0	0
1974	4	6	.400	4.15	39	0	89	92	47	64	0	1
1975	9	8	.529	1.84	62	0	141⅔	99	70	130	0	26
1976	9	17	.346	3.94	31	15	224	214	90	135	0	1
Career	124	107	.536	2.96	1,002	16	1,809⅓	1,497	732	1,502	0	310

Just before a player's strike canceled out the 1994 season, Rich Gossage nailed down career save No. 310 in his 1,002nd career appearance. Only two pitchers have appeared in more major league games: Hoyt Wilhelm (1,070) and Kent Tekulve (1,050). Unfortunately for Sox fans, Bill Veeck laid the proverbial egg by trading the Golden Goose to Pittsburgh on December 10, 1976, for Richie Zisk and Silvio Martinez. Gossage enjoyed his most productive seasons after leaving Chicago.

Rich Gossage, a flame-throwing right-hander, was signed by White Sox scout Bill Kimball following his high school graduation in 1970. After being named the Midwest Minor League Player of the Year in 1971, Gossage reported to Comiskey Park in 1972. Slightly bewildered by the big city and its ways, Rich's period of adjustment was rather painful. Despite winning his first seven decisions as one of Chuck Tanner's long-range relievers, the Goose was unable to marshal control over his 90-mph-plus fastball, and he was eminently hittable. Gossage shuttled back and forth between the minors and Comiskey Park through the 1973 and 1974 seasons, showing little improvement each time.

In 1975, however, after Terry Forster was bothered by a bad elbow and sidelined for most of the season, Gossage took over as the No. 1 closer and paced the league with 26 saves. When postseason awards were handed out, Gossage was justly named AL Fireman of the Year—an award the White Sox bullpen aces had come to monopolize in the 1960s up through the early 1970s.

Bill Veeck and Paul Richards converted him to a starting role in 1976 because there just wasn't enough quality talent to go around. The Goose was named to the All-Star squad for the second year in a row, thus becoming the only pitcher to earn an All-Star berth as a reliever and a starter in consecutive seasons. It turned out to be a lost year for Gossage, apart from the accolades of his peers. His record dipped to 9–17, and the unfamiliar role thrust upon him was ill-suited to his real talents. Goose Gossage never started another game again. He emerged as the dominant closer of the late 1970s with one of the finest New York Yankee teams in recent memory. It was a role that Bill Kimball and others in the Sox organization had envisioned for Gossage—but not with George Steinbrenner's ballclub.

Rich "Goose" Gossage in Milwaukee, 1975

The "Goose" was elected to the Hall of Fame on January 8, 2008, in his ninth year on the ballot. He did not go in wearing a White Sox cap, of course, but as a Yankee; his love-hate relationship with the pinstripes lasted through six turbulent seasons of his long and meritorious 22-year career. Gossage said that his signing with the Yankees as a free agent in 1978 was "an out-of-body experience" but candidly admitted that his decision to depart from the "Bronx Zoo" for the serenity of the San Diego Padres in 1984 had everything to do with the endless bickering between his former manager Billy Martin and owner George Steinbrenner. On January 5, 2009, the "son of the Goose"—Todd Gossage, an infielder, no less—signed a minor league contract with the White Sox's Great Falls, Montana, affiliate on the advice of scout J.J. Lally.

Orval Grove

Grove, Orval

White Sox: 1940–49
Pitcher
Birthplace: Mineral, Kansas

B: August 29, 1919
D: April 20, 1992
Batted right, threw right
Ht. 6–3; **Wt.** 196

Grove, Orval

White Sox	W	L	Pct	ERA	G	CG	IP	H	BB	K	ShO
1940	0	0	—	3.00	3	0	6	4	4	1	0
1941	0	0	—	10.29	2	0	7	9	5	5	0
1942	4	6	.400	5.16	12	4	66⅓	77	33	21	0
1943	15	9	.625	2.75	32	18	216⅓	192	72	76	3
1944	14	15	.483	3.72	34	11	234⅔	237	71	105	2
1945	14	12	.538	3.44	33	16	217	233	68	54	4
1946	8	13	.381	3.02	33	10	205⅓	213	78	60	1
1947	6	8	.429	4.44	25	6	135⅔	158	70	33	1
1948	2	10	.167	6.16	32	1	87⅔	110	42	18	0
1949	0	0	—	54.00	1	0	⅔	4	1	1	0
Career	63	73	.463	3.78	207	66	1,176⅔	1,237	444	374	11

Orval Grove was the first pitcher to graduate from the White Sox farm system, put in place by Billy Webb, Bob Tarleton, and Harry Grabiner in 1939. This former prep sensation from Proviso West High School in Maywood, Illinois, had to wait until World War II had just about depleted the White Sox roster before he was given a legitimate shot to win a permanent spot on the roster. Grove was invited to spring training in 1943 with a contract calling for the payment of $1.00—until he could prove to manager Jimmie Dykes that his arm and leg were sound and healthy. A damaged left knee kept him out of the military.

Grove opened the 1943 season in Chicago, but did not start a game until June 6. When he looked good in a no-decision outing against Boston, Dykes kept him in the rotation. From June 10 through July 25, Grove was unbeatable. He won nine straight decisions to open the season, thus equaling a team record originally set by Lefty Williams in 1917 and later matched by LaMarr Hoyt in 1982. Included in this remarkable skein was a near no-hitter against the Yankees on July 8. With two outs in the ninth inning and 31,000 fired-up Sox fans hanging on every pitch, Grove surrendered a bloop double to Joe Gordon that dropped down on the left-field foul line in back of third base—fair by inches.

This game proved to be the high-water mark of Grove's career. He was a wartime replacement who faded away when the returning players were added to the roster in 1946. General manager Frank Lane sold Orval to Sacramento of the PCL on April 29, 1949, ending his up-and-down nine-year run in the big leagues.

Guillen, Ozzie

White Sox: 1985–97
Shortstop
Birthplace: Oculare del Tuy, Venezuela

B: January 20, 1964
Bats left, throws right
Ht. 5–11; **Wt.** 164

Guillen, Ozzie

White Sox	G	AB	H	AVG	RBI	R	2B	3B	HR	SA	SB
1985	150	491	134	.273	33	71	21	9	1	.358	7
1986	159	547	137	.250	57	58	19	4	2	.311	8
1987	149	560	156	.279	51	64	22	7	2	.354	25
1988	156	566	148	.261	39	58	16	7	0	.315	25
1989	155	597	151	.253	54	63	20	8	1	.318	36
1990	160	516	144	.279	58	61	21	4	1	.341	13
1991	154	524	143	.273	49	52	20	3	3	.340	21
1992	12	40	8	.200	7	5	4	0	0	.300	1
1993	134	457	128	.280	50	44	23	4	4	.374	5
1994	100	365	105	.288	39	46	9	5	1	.348	5
1995	122	415	103	.248	41	50	20	3	1	.318	6
1996	150	499	131	.263	45	62	24	8	4	.367	6
1997	142	490	120	.245	52	59	21	6	4	.337	5
Career	1,993	6,686	2,261	.264	619	1,764	275	69	28	.338	169

As a youngster, Oswaldo Guillen idolized Davey Concepcion—a national hero to his countrymen. Concepcion, the great shortstop of Cincinnati's Big Red Machine of the 1970s, set the example for Guillen to follow. After joining the White Sox in 1985, Ozzie asked for uniform No. 13 in honor of his hero.

To White Sox fans who had grown accustomed to witnessing excellence in the Comiskey Park infield, Guillen evoked warm memories of an earlier era—one that started in 1950 when Chico Carrasquel reported to Chicago and continued later in the decade with Luis Aparicio. In the 1990s Ozzie carried on the rich traditions of the "Venezuelan connection."

Guillen was originally signed by the San Diego Padres as a free agent on December 17, 1980, when he was only 16. Despite a composite batting average of .308 in his four minor league campaigns, Ozzie was labeled a good-field, no-hit prospect.

General manager Roland Hemond paid a high price to acquire Guillen on December 6, 1984. He had confidence in his abilities, and the deal was cut with Ozzie in mind. Examining that trade more than a decade later—LaMarr Hoyt and a pair of undistinguished farmhands for Guillen, Tim Lollar, and Bill Long—it was an inconsequential price to pay after all.

Ozzie capped off an outstanding rookie season by winning 1985 AL Rookie of the Year honors from the Baseball Writers of America. He was the fifth White Sox player so honored since the award was first conceived in 1947. Guillen was a free-swinging contact hitter tough to strike out, but almost impossible to walk. His tendency to chase balls in the dirt and outside the strike zone has frustrated his managers and adversely affected his batting average over the years, though few fans took issue with Guillen's dazzling glove work. He won his first Gold Glove Award in 1990 and has cracked the White Sox top 10 fielding list three times.

A freakish collision with teammate Tim Raines on April 21, 1992, prematurely ended Guillen's eighth White Sox season and fueled concerns about his future in baseball. Ozzie underwent a tortuous off-season rehabilitation and was restored to health a year later, but he had lost a few steps on the base paths as a result of his knee surgery.

With the departure of Carlton Fisk in 1993, Ozzie became the senior member of the squad in length of service, and he was acknowledged as the White Sox's field leader—a role the gregarious, talkative shortstop happily accepted. In recognition of Ozzie's enthusiasm for the White Sox and their fans—"I want to be a Chicago player for the rest of my days. I told them that!"—management appointed him cocaptain with Fisk in 1990. "Ozzie's the machine that makes everything happen for us" was how his third manager, Jeff Torborg, summed up his contributions.

Cut loose after the 1997 season, Ozzie was deeply incensed when Ron Schueler filled his roster spot with Benji Gil, a good-field, no-hit shortstop from Texas. "If they want to go with kids, fine," Ozzie snapped. "But don't say Benji is better than me. Who are you kidding?" Embittered, Guillen signed a two-year, $1 million contract with Atlanta, but he fell behind Jose Hernandez and Walt Weiss on the Braves' depth chart and was spending more time on the bench than he would have liked. The end was in sight for the old veteran. Ozzie played out the string with Baltimore and the Tampa Bay Devil Rays before retiring in 2001. He had made it to the World Series with the Braves in 1999 and retired as the all-time leader in fielding among White Sox shortstops with a .974 percentage. Ozzie is second to fellow countryman Luis Aparicio in games played. Although he didn't retire a career White Sox player as he had hoped, Guillen's affection for the ballclub never wavered. Upon the recommendation of Jeff Torborg, he was named the 37th White Sox manager on November 3, 2003, and brought a new winning attitude, enthusiasm, and the elusive World Championship to the South Side.

Ozzie Guillen

Hairston, Jerry

White Sox: 1973–77; 1981–89
Outfielder, pinch-hitter
Nickname: Popeye
Birthplace: Birmingham, Alabama

B: February 16, 1952
Bats both, throws left
Ht. 5–10; **Wt.** 170

Hairston, Jerry

White Sox	G	AB	H	AVG	RBI	R	2B	3B	HR	SA	SB
1973	60	210	57	.271	23	25	11	1	0	.333	0
1974	45	109	25	.229	8	8	7	0	0	.294	0
1975	69	219	62	.283	23	26	8	0	0	.320	1
1976	44	119	27	.227	10	20	2	2	0	.277	1
1977	13	26	8	.308	4	3	2	0	0	.385	0
1981	9	25	7	.280	6	5	1	0	1	.440	0
1982	85	90	21	.233	18	11	5	0	5	.456	0
1983	101	126	37	.294	22	17	9	1	5	.500	0
1984	115	227	59	.260	19	41	13	2	5	.401	2
1985	95	140	34	.243	20	9	8	0	2	.343	0
1986	101	225	61	.271	26	32	15	0	5	.404	0
1987	66	126	29	.230	20	14	8	0	5	.413	0
1988	2	2	0	.000	0	0	0	0	0	.000	0
1989	3	3	1	.333	0	0	0	0	0	.333	0
Career	859	1,699	428	.252	205	216	91	6	30	.371	4

The Hairston family left behind a quiet but noble legacy. Sam Hairston was the first American-born black to shatter the color barrier in Chicago. (Cuban-born Minnie Minoso, who broke in on May 1, 1951, was the Sox's first black player.) Sam was a member of the Indianapolis Clowns barnstorming team when he agreed to terms with the White Sox on July 31, 1950. The stockily built catcher won a Triple Crown playing in the Negro Leagues in 1949 and was one of three highly touted African American players coming up through the Sox's minor league system at that time. Infielder Bobby Boyd and pitcher Connie Johnson were the others.

Hairston appeared in only two games in 1951, but his role in White Sox affairs cannot be discounted. Since 1961, Sam has worked continuously within the organization as an advance scout and minor league instructor. Along with Walt Widmayer, Sam helped sign his son Jerry to a Sox contract. The younger Hairston was a good-hit, no-field outfielder who failed to impress in his first White Sox tour of duty. He was sold to the Pittsburgh Pirates on June 13, 1977. Jerry described it as one of the unhappiest days of his life. He drifted into the Mexican League and had just about abandoned hope of returning to the majors when Roland Hemond journeyed south on a scouting mission to locate a few good men to join the Sox for the stretch run. Impressed with Hairston, the Sox GM purchased his contract on September 10, 1981.

Jerry Hairston

Hairston was a team player who accepted his role as a bench player and substitute. Within a year of his "homecoming," Jerry established himself as the American League's most effective pinch-hitter, reprising an earlier Sox tradition carried on with great skill by Ron Northey in the 1950s and Smoky Burgess a decade later. Hairston, however, easily surpassed them both when he banged out his 51st career pinch hit in Boston's Fenway Park on April 15, 1985. Two years earlier he broke up Milt Wilcox's bid for a perfect game with a ringing base hit with two outs in the ninth inning at old Comiskey Park. Jerry led the league in emergency safeties three years in a row (1983–85), placing him in 14th place on baseball's all-time list in career pinch hits.

The bespectacled left-hander, who always pounded his bat twice on home plate before taking his cuts against an opposing pitcher, retired in 1990 as the all-time White Sox pinch-hit leader with 87.

Hansen, Ron

White Sox: 1963–67; 1968–69
Shortstop
Birthplace: Oxford, Nebraska

B: April 5, 1938
Bats left, throws right
Ht. 6–3; **Wt.** 190

Hansen, Ron

White Sox	G	AB	H	AVG	RBI	R	2B	3B	HR	SA	SB
1963	144	482	109	.226	67	55	17	2	13	.351	1
1964	158	575	150	.261	68	85	25	3	20	.419	1
1965	162	587	138	.235	66	61	23	4	11	.344	1
1966	23	74	13	.176	4	3	1	0	0	.189	0
1967	157	498	116	.233	51	35	20	0	8	.321	0
1968	40	87	20	.230	4	7	3	0	1	.299	0
1969	85	185	48	.259	22	15	6	1	2	.335	2
Career	1,384	4,311	1,007	.234	501	446	156	17	106	.351	9

Long and lanky Ron Hansen was one of the great clutch players of the 1960s. When the game was on the line, Hansen usually came through, even though his batting average never rose above .261 in any one of his seven White Sox seasons.

This former Rookie of the Year award winner was traded by the Baltimore Orioles with Hoyt Wilhelm, Pete Ward, and Dave Nicholson for Louie Aparicio and Al Smith on January 14, 1963. Beset by a nagging back injury and military service that limited his Baltimore playing time to weekends, Hansen's batting average had slipped to .173 in 1962. In

Ron Hansen was always tough in the clutch.

Chicago Ron was under tremendous pressure and constant fan scrutiny as he fought hard to prove himself a worthy successor to Little Louie at shortstop. Hansen's fielding was spectacular from the moment of his arrival. In 1963 Aparicio beat him out by only one percentage point for league honors.

Hansen clouted 20 home runs in 1964, which stood until 2000 as a team record for White Sox shortstops in a single season. The durable, raw-boned shortstop established a major league record on August 29, 1965, by handling 28 chances in a doubleheader against the Red Sox at Comiskey Park. For the third year in a row he was a runner-up to Aparicio in fielding average.

Persistent back problems cut into his playing time in 1966 and limited his fielding range in succeeding years. There was no logic for what happened next. Ed Short, the enigmatic general manager, traded Hansen, with pitchers Dennis Higgins and Steve Jones, to the Washington Senators for weak-hitting Tim Cullen and two pitchers, Buster Narum and Bob Priddy, on February 13, 1968. Ronnie pulled off an unassisted triple play in D.C. and then was *traded back* to Chicago for Tim Cullen on August 2, making them the only two players to be traded for each other twice in the same season. No rational explanation has ever been given to account for these peculiar moves.

A mainstay of the Sox infield through much of the 1960s, Hansen was bitter and upset when general manager Ed Short attempted to impose a maximum 20 percent cut on Ronnie's $38,000 salary as the 1970 spring training sessions commenced. Hansen became a lengthy salary holdout—and as the White Sox player representative (replacing the recently departed Gary Peters), that was the final kiss of death for him in a Chicago uniform. In dealing his sure-fielding veteran shortstop to the Yankees on a conditional basis on February 28, 1970, Short said the trade "had nothing to do with his holding out or that he was player representative." But the penurious reputation of the White Sox front office in the days of the Allyn brothers' stewardship was well-known and notorious. The disgruntled bunch of rookies and veterans who gathered in Sarasota in the bleak winter of 1970 could only chuckle with irony when manager Don Gutteridge reminded them, "We're going to have fun, work hard, and play hard."

Harshman, Jack

White Sox: 1954–57
Pitcher
Birthplace: San Diego, California

B: July 12, 1927
Bats left, throws left
Ht. 6–2; **Wt.** 178

Harshman, Jack

White Sox	W	L	Pct	ERA	G	CG	IP	H	BB	K	ShO
1954	14	8	.636	2.95	35	9	177	157	96	134	4
1955	11	7	.611	3.36	32	9	179⅓	144	97	116	0
1956	15	11	.577	3.10	34	15	226⅔	183	102	143	4
1957	8	8	.500	3.10	30	6	151⅓	142	82	83	0
Career	69	65	.515	3.50	217	61	1,169⅓	1,025	539	741	12

In the space of just 10 days, Jack Harshman etched his name into the White Sox record book ahead of Ed Walsh, Jim Scott, and other luminaries of the past by fanning 16 Red Sox batters on July 25, 1954. The single-game strikeout record has held up all these years, and it represents quite an accomplishment for a 27-year-old National League castoff who had actually opened the 1950 season as the starting first baseman for the New York Giants. Harshman was converted to a pitcher in 1951 by Larry Gilbert, his manager in Nashville. Jack won 23 games for Nashville in 1953 before Sox GM Frank Lane took note and purchased his contract for $15,000 on September 19. It was like money in the bank.

Harshman followed up his strikeout performance with a heroic 16-inning, 1–0 whitewashing of the Tigers on August 13. Jack worked out of several bases-loaded jams before Minnie Minoso tripled home the game winner in the 16th inning. Few of the sportswriters could recall such a cold-blooded job of pitching.

Jack Harshman pries loose Chuck Comiskey's lucky victory hat, April 22, 1957.

Jack was one of Frank Lane's most famous reclamation projects. Relying on a slip pitch taught to him by Paul Richards, Harshman was a reliable member of the vaunted Sox's starting corps through 1957, and he was a valuable "ninth man" in the offense. He clubbed six home runs in 1956, which still stands as a team record for pitchers. His 19 RBIs that season led the league as well.

Sensing that his market value had peaked, Chuck Comiskey and John Rigney engineered a multiplayer trade on December 3, 1957, sending Harshman, Larry Doby, and two minor leaguers named Russ Heman and Jim Marshall to Baltimore for Tito Francona, Ray Moore, and Billy Goodman. The Comiskeys were correct about Harshman. His best days were already behind him.

Hayes, Minter

White Sox: 1932–40
Second baseman
Nickname: Jackie
Birthplace: Clanton, Alabama

B: July 19, 1906
D: February 9, 1983
Batted right, threw right
Ht. 5–10½; **Wt.** 165

Hayes, Minter

White Sox	G	AB	H	AVG	RBI	R	2B	3B	HR	SA	SB
1932	117	475	122	.257	54	53	20	5	2	.333	7
1933	138	535	138	.258	47	65	23	5	2	.331	2
1934	62	226	58	.257	31	19	9	1	1	.319	3
1935	89	329	88	.267	45	45	14	0	4	.347	3
1936	108	417	130	.312	84	53	34	3	5	.444	4
1937	143	573	121	.229	79	63	27	4	2	.300	1
1938	62	238	78	.328	20	40	21	2	1	.445	3
1939	72	269	67	.249	23	34	12	3	0	.316	0
1940	18	41	8	.195	1	2	0	1	0	.244	0
Career	1,091	4,040	1,069	.265	493	494	196	33	20	.344	34

The tragedy that befell Jackie Hayes in the prime of his life tugged at the heartstrings of all Chicagoans. Early in the 1940 spring training sessions, the scrappy second baseman complained of problems with his vision. He thought a speck of coal dust might have lodged in his eye, causing the inflammation. Team doctors advised Hayes that it was probably just a minor infection that would likely clear up in a few days. In truth, the doctors had no clue as to what the affliction could be.

When the problem failed to correct itself by late July, the physicians took a second look and determined that it was a cataract. But how could a cataract cause complete and total loss of eyesight, which is what happened to Jackie Hayes over the winter?

Jackie had aspired to study medicine at the University of Alabama long before he began his baseball career with the Washington Senators in 1927. Forsaking medicine for baseball, Hayes signed with the Nats. He was counted among the top-fielding second basemen of the day when J. Lou Comiskey completed his first trade as a new owner on December 3, 1931. Hayes, Bump Hadley, and Sam Jones came to the Sox from the nation's capital in exchange for Carl Reynolds and Johnny Kerr.

Jackie Hayes, his wife, and their seeing-eye dog, Abano, are met at the train station by former teammate Tony Piet shortly before "Jackie Hayes Night" at Comiskey Park, August 30, 1949.

Never a robust hitter and often plagued by minor injuries throughout his nine-year Sox career, Hayes was a tremendous pivot man on the double play. He formed the nucleus of a fast-moving infield that included Luke Appling at short and Joe Kuhel at first—until the tandem was broken up by Jackie's misfortune. Hayes was a fan favorite, and nearly a decade after his forced retirement, he returned to Chicago to take part in a touching pregame ceremony organized by *Chicago Sun-Times* columnist Gene Kessler, who refused to forget the heroism of the tough little second baseman.

Haynes, Joe

White Sox: 1941–48
Pitcher
Birthplace: Lincolnton, Georgia

B: September 21, 1917
D: January 7, 1967
Batted right, threw right
Ht. 6–2½; **Wt.** 190

Haynes, Joe

White Sox	W	L	Pct	ERA	G	CG	IP	H	BB	K	ShO	Sv
1941	0	0	.000	3.86	8	0	28	30	11	18	0	0
1942	8	5	.615	2.62	40	1	103	88	47	35	0	6
1943	7	2	.778	2.96	35	1	109⅓	114	32	37	0	3
1944	5	6	.455	2.57	33	8	154⅓	148	43	44	0	2
1945	5	5	.500	3.55	14	8	104	92	29	34	1	1
1946	7	9	.438	3.76	32	9	177⅓	203	60	60	0	2
1947	14	6	.700	2.42	29	7	182	174	61	50	0	0
1948	9	10	.474	3.97	27	6	149⅔	167	52	40	0	0
Career	76	82	.481	4.01	379	53	1,581	1,672	620	475	5	21

In a decade of travail at the House of Comiskey, where hard-luck stories abounded, Joe Haynes—no stranger to hardship himself—was one of the few bright spots to emerge in the Sox pitching galaxy of castoffs, retreads, and reclamation projects. Joe Haynes brought a good curveball to the majors after toiling in the Washington Nationals system for three years before the bell finally rang for him in 1939. Haynes was discovered in a South Carolina textile league by a Washington talent scout. The Nats, however, were in search of a new speedballer along the lines of a Walter Johnson. They weren't very impressed with the young man's repertoire of off-speed junk pitches even if he happened to be the owner's son-in-law.

When Haynes' arm went bad in June 1940, the Nats released him to the Sox in return for a meager $3,000 cash payment. Washington owner Clark Griffith desperately wanted to keep Joe in the majors for personal reasons. He even promised the White Sox that he would take Haynes back if he failed to impress Jimmy Dykes and his bullpen professor, pitching coach Harold "Muddy" Ruel. Joe was married to Griffith's adopted daughter Thelma.

White Sox trainer Ad Schacht cured Haynes of the neuritis-like pain in his pitching arm through a regimen of rest and muscle manipulation. Coach Ruel made some minor adjustments with his delivery, and soon the Washington pitcher, sold to the Sox on a lend-lease basis, earned a spot in the White Sox starting rotation after starting the 1942 campaign in the pen.

In many ways, Haynes was regarded as the South Siders' most dependable pitcher during the war years, but like teammate Eddie Smith, Joe suffered from a lack of hitting support and lost more than his share of one-run decisions.

Injuries also curtailed his effectiveness. He was carried off the field on a stretcher after suffering a compound fracture of his right ankle sliding into third base in the fifth inning of a game against the Tigers on June 17, 1945. "It is the worst athletic injury I have ever seen," exclaimed Dr. John D. Claridge of Mercy Hospital in Chicago. But Joe was resilient, and he came back for another go-around the following season.

Clark Griffith was anxious to reacquire Joe after the Sox peddled their sore-armed pitcher to Cleveland on November 22, 1948, for rookie catcher Joe Tipton. Haynes eventually settled into lifetime employment with the Nats, beginning with a coaching job with the team after his playing days ended in 1952. Tipton, as every die-hard fan of the Pale Hose knows, was shuttled off to Philadelphia for Nellie Fox in 1949.

Herbert, Ray

White Sox: 1961–64
Pitcher
Birthplace: Detroit, Michigan

B: December 15, 1929
Bats right, throws right
Ht. 5–11; **Wt.** 185

Herbert, Ray

White Sox	W	L	Pct	ERA	G	CG	IP	H	BB	K	ShO
1961	9	6	.600	4.05	21	4	137⅔	142	36	50	0
1962	20	9	.690	3.27	35	12	236⅔	228	74	115	2
1963	13	10	.565	3.24	33	14	224⅓	230	35	105	7
1964	6	7	.462	3.47	20	1	111⅔	117	17	40	1
Career	104	107	.493	4.01	407	68	1,881	2,000	571	864	13

Until he arrived in Chicago on June 10, 1961, in a multi-player trade that sent Bob Shaw and Gerry Staley to the Kansas City A's, Ray Herbert was another journeyman pitcher on the losing side of the ledger. Then he made the acquaintance of Sox pitching coach Ray Berres, who corrected a serious flaw in his mechanics. "Stand back," Berres advised. "Don't allow your arm to go forward ahead of your body. They must go forward together."

Berres, arguably the finest pitching coach in baseball at that time, turned Herbert's career around.

Ray Herbert played sandlot ball at Detroit's Northwestern Field not far from the Olympia, where the hockey Red Wings played. He was signed to his first pro contract with the Tigers in 1949, but he did not achieve success until he hooked up with Berres.

Herbert became the most recent White Sox 20-game winner in 1962 and bagged a victory in the second All-Star Game played in Wrigley Field that year.

Ray's finest career accomplishment occurred a year later, however, when he pitched four consecutive shutouts. Herbert was flirting with mound glory when he took the hill in Baltimore on May 19. He had reeled off 36 consecutive scoreless innings and was one complete-game shutout away from equaling Doc White's 1904 record. Unfortunately this was Memorial Stadium—a house of horrors—where the Sox had played poorly for many years.

In the third inning Johnny Orsino rapped a questionable home run that struck the railing of the left-field wall. Al Lopez argued unsuccessfully that since the ball had bounced back on to the playing field, it should have been called a ground-rule double. Orsino snapped Ray's streak at 38 innings. The Sox lost the game 4–3, a very typical result for White Sox–Orioles encounters over the years.

Ray Herbert

The veteran Herbert tailed off following this sizzling performance. He was traded to Philadelphia for Danny Cater on November 30, 1964, a deal that would have been fine for the White Sox if only they had managed to hang on to Cater for a few years.

Hernandez, Roberto

White Sox: 1991–97
Pitcher
Birthplace: Santurce, Puerto Rico

B: November 11, 1964
Bats right, throws right
Ht. 6–4; **Wt.** 235

Hernandez, Roberto

White Sox	W	L	Pct	ERA	G	CG	IP	H	BB	K	ShO	Sv
1991	1	0	1.000	7.80	9	0	15	18	7	6	0	0
1992	7	3	.700	1.65	43	0	71	45	20	68	0	12
1993	3	4	.429	2.29	70	0	78⅔	66	20	71	0	38
1994	4	4	.500	4.91	45	0	47⅔	44	19	50	0	14
1995	3	7	.300	3.92	60	0	59⅔	63	28	84	0	32
1996	6	5	.545	1.91	72	0	84⅔	65	38	85	0	38
1997	5	1	.833	2.44	46	0	48	38	24	47	0	27
Career	67	71	.486	3.45	1,010	0	1,071⅓	1,002	462	945	0	326

Roberto Hernandez

Very few bullpen closers maintain their effectiveness over a long period of time. To fully appreciate the achievements of Lee Smith, Goose Gossage, or Dennis Eckersley, who only improved with advancing age, one need only consider the meteoric rise and fall of Bobby Thigpen.

Thigpen's inability to close out the opposition following his record-setting performance in 1990 provided a window of opportunity for Roberto Hernandez, a Puerto Rican fastball pitcher originally signed by the California Angels in 1986. Roberto was acquired by Larry Himes from the Angels on August 3, 1989, for outfielder Mark Davis. The former Sox GM spent his entire career with the Angels before coming to Chicago, and he recognized Roberto's enormous potential.

When Thigpen completely fell apart in 1992, manager Gene Lamont designated Hernandez as his No. 1 closer. Roberto was up to the challenge. In 1993 he became the second-fastest Sox relief ace to reach the 30-save plateau. Between July 26 and September 11, Hernandez recorded 15 consecutive saves in as many appearances. Hernandez has averaged 8.3 strikeouts per nine innings over his career, and his save percentage is 80.0 percent for his first four seasons. His tally of 38 saves recorded in 1993 ranks third behind Thigpen and Keith Foulke.

Roberto Hernandez waited a long time for the opportunity to prove himself in the big leagues, and he made the most of it. But like so many other relief specialists who reach an early pinnacle then tail off, Roberto showed alarming signs in 1994 and into the '95 campaign that he, too, was vulnerable. No longer could a one-run, ninth-inning lead be considered safe and secure with Roberto on the hill. He led the American League with 10 blown saves in 1995. Observing the Hernandez foibles .from his vantage point in the Comiskey Park press box, a noted local baseball commentator dubbed Roberto the "arsonist." Such is the fate that befalls all good closers sooner or later. But in this case, Roberto earned partial vindication in 1996 by lowering his ERA by two runs and saving 38 games. If manager Terry Bevington had not overused Hernandez in the final three months, the numbers might have been more spectacular. Hernandez was gone a year later in the much-maligned "White Flag Trade" with the San Francisco Giants, who ended up losing both Hernandez and Wilson Alvarez to free agency after the 1997 season. Hernandez enjoyed three of his best years with the expansion Tampa Bay Devil Rays, where he shattered Bobby Thigpen's 1990 American League record of saving 60.6 percent of his team's games in a single season. Hernandez saved 62.3 percent of all Devil Rays victories in 1999, becoming one of only four pitchers to accomplish the feat since the statistic was first tracked. After leaving the White Sox, this ace reliever was effective wherever he played, but he had become something of a baseball nomad. He went through free agency five different times, and was signed by the Pittsburgh Pirates on December 8, 2005, at age 41.

Hernandez played out the string with the Mets, the Indians, and the Dodgers—becoming only the 11th pitcher in history to appear in 1,000 major league games when he took the mound on August 16, 2007, against Houston.

Herrmann, Ed

White Sox: 1967; 1969–74
Catcher
Birthplace: San Diego, California

B: August 27, 1946
Bats left, throws right
Ht. 6–1; **Wt.** 195

Herrmann, Ed

White Sox	G	AB	H	AVG	RBI	R	2B	3B	HR	SA	SB
1967	2	3	2	.667	1	1	1	0	0	1.000	0
1969	102	290	67	.231	31	31	8	0	8	.341	0
1970	96	297	84	.283	52	42	9	0	19	.505	0
1971	101	294	63	.214	35	32	6	0	11	.347	2
1972	116	354	88	.249	40	23	9	0	10	.359	0
1973	119	379	85	.224	39	42	17	1	10	.354	2
1974	107	367	95	.259	39	32	13	1	10	.381	1
Career	922	2,729	654	.240	320	247	92	4	80	.364	6

"Sup-Herrmann" (as he was tagged by his teammates and the "Sox Supporters" fan group of the early 1970s) was a fearless backstop who stopped many an on-charging runner with his bulky frame. The image of Bert "Campy" Campaneris barreling headlong into Herrmann, spikes flying, is one of the great photographic images of the 1970s. Ed never wavered. He took the charge and tagged Campy out.

Although he lacked speed, Ed Herrmann was a solid receiver with a strong arm. Originally signed by the Atlanta Braves in 1964, but acquired by the White Sox in the first-year player draft held that year, Herrmann was most effective handling the knuckleball slants of Wilbur Wood. Thanks to Wood, Herrmann led the AL in passed balls four times. Without Ed, his erstwhile roommate on the road, Wilbur would have not have become the pitcher he was in the early 1970s.

Herrmann tied a major league record on July 4, 1972, for most double plays by a catcher in a nine-inning game by throwing out three would-be Minnesota Twins base stealers following a strikeout. Big Ed was also the "pilot" of the "Big White Machine," a smoke-belching, souped-up 1929 Ford that he would drive around the Comiskey Park warning track following those all-too-infrequent White Sox victories in 1970. The Big White Machine was loaned to the Sox by a local Ford dealership after Herrmann came up with the idea of adopting the road machine as a team mascot.

The Big White Machine lasted all of one year. Ed Herrmann, however, remained with the ballclub until April 1, 1975, when he was sold to the New York Yankees after owner John Allyn refused to meet his salary demand. Herrmann asked for $32,000—the financially troubled ballclub simply could not afford to keep him on the roster any longer.

April 8, 1974. Ed Herrmann misses making the tag on the Angels' Lee Stanton. Game time temps that day were 35–40 degrees.

Hodgin, Ralph

White Sox: 1943–44; 1946–48
Outfielder, infielder
Birthplace: Greensboro, North Carolina

B: February 10, 1916
Bats left, throws right
Ht. 5–10; **Wt.** 167

Hodgin, Ralph

White Sox	G	AB	H	AVG	RBI	R	2B	3B	HR	SA	SB
1943	117	407	128	.314	50	52	22	8	1	.415	3
1944	121	465	137	.295	51	56	25	7	1	.385	3
1946	87	258	65	.252	25	32	10	1	0	.298	0
1947	59	180	53	.294	24	26	10	3	1	.400	1
1948	114	331	88	.266	34	28	11	5	1	.388	0
Career	530	1,689	481	.285	188	198	79	24	4	.367	7

White Sox scouts discovered Ralph Hodgin patrolling the San Francisco Seals outfield after seven uneventful years in the minors. His baseball travel itinerary included brief stopovers in Reidsville of the Bi-State League, Charleston, Scranton, Evansville, Hartford, and a cup of coffee with the Boston Braves in 1939.

The sharpest thinkers within the organization regarded this Pacific Coast Leaguer a top prospect based on his .320

Ralph Hodgin

batting average in 1942. Accordingly they drafted him over the winter, promising him a shot at the war-depleted 1943 roster. Hodgin played sparingly in the first half of the 1943 season. Given a chance to start in June, Ralph sizzled at the plate. He elevated his average from a meager .196 to .341 and completed an outstanding freshman campaign with a .314 mark, good for third place among AL hitters—that is, if he had had enough at bats to qualify—which he did not. After Bob Kennedy was lost to the war effort, manager Jimmie Dykes experimented with Hodgin at third base until his draft notice arrived in 1945.

Hodgin returned to the Sox in 1946, but his skills diminished after he suffered a severe concussion when a Hal Newhouser fastball glanced off his skull on April 21, 1947.

After the beaning, he seemed to lose his aggressiveness at the plate. Hodgin was a natural hitter, but he was never quite rugged enough to stand the major league pace or the returning prewar pitching stars. Nor could Ralph's fielding shortcomings be overlooked. Relegated to the bench in the postwar years, Ralph nevertheless made the best of his limited opportunities.

Hodgin compiled an impressive .385 pinch-hitting average in 104 emergency situations spanning five years. Slight of build, he possessed a good work ethic and always maintained perfect physical conditioning. But on January 4, 1949, Sox general manager Frank Lane sold his contract to Sacramento of the Pacific Coast League as a part of his housecleaning. Hodgin never again returned to the majors.

Harry Hooper

Hooper, Harry

White Sox: 1921–25
Outfielder
Birthplace: Bell Station, California

B: August 24, 1887
D: December 18, 1974
Batted left, threw right
Ht. 5–10; **Wt.** 168

Hooper, Harry

White Sox	G	AB	H	AVG	RBI	R	2B	3B	HR	SA	SB
1921	108	419	137	.327	58	74	26	5	8	.470	13
1922	152	602	183	.304	80	111	35	8	11	.444	16
1923	145	576	166	.288	65	87	32	4	10	.481	16
1924	130	476	156	.328	62	107	27	8	10	.481	16
1925	127	442	117	.265	55	62	23	5	6	.380	12
Career	2,308	8,785	2,466	.281	817	1,429	389	160	75	.387	375

Harry Hooper never led the American League in any of the important offensive categories, but he was a major star in the Red Sox galaxy during the World War I period when the team was pennant-caliber. A man of deep religious convictions and high ideals, Hooper expressed his disgust with Boston owner Harry Frazee by holding out for a $15,000 salary in the spring of 1921. Frazee had sold Babe Ruth the year before and was dumping other top Red Sox players in order to finance Broadway shows.

Frazee obliged and dealt Hooper to the White Sox on March 4, 1921, for first baseman Shano Collins, outfielder Nemo Leibold, and a cash consideration. Leibold and Collins were excellent reserve players for Comiskey, but the Old Roman could not pass up the chance to acquire one of the marquee stars of the American League to ease the pain of losing Shoeless Joe Jackson and his Black Sox teammates at the end of the 1920 season.

At first the 12-year veteran, who for years was one of the top leadoff men in the game, balked at coming to Chicago. Hooper finally relented and decided to join the Sox at a salary of $13,750—considerably less than what he had originally demanded from Frazee—but he told the Old Roman this decision was his "goodwill gesture" toward his new employers who were trying to build a new dynasty to replace the old one.

The White Sox outfield trio of Bibb Falk in left, Johnny Mostil in center, and the veteran Harry Hooper playing right was among the most potent in baseball during the five seasons they were together. Hooper chipped in with three outstanding offensive seasons: 1921, 1922, and 1924.

By the time the White Sox had seemingly righted themselves with an influx of new talent, Comiskey reexamined his generosity and reduced Hooper's 1925 salary to $7,000. At the end of that season Harry retired from professional baseball in order to enter the California real estate market. Hooper owned a considerable amount of property on the West Coast and was not dependent on baseball for his continued livelihood.

Harry coached baseball at Princeton University in 1931 and 1932 before retiring to private life as the postmaster of Capitola, California.

Horlen, Joel

White Sox: 1961–71
Pitcher
Birthplace: San Antonio, Texas

B: August 14, 1937
Bats right, throws right
Ht. 6–0; **Wt.** 170

Horlen, Joel

White Sox	W	L	Pct	ERA	G	CG	IP	H	BB	K	ShO
1961	1	3	.250	6.62	5	0	17⅔	25	13	11	0
1962	7	6	.538	4.89	20	5	108⅔	108	43	63	1
1963	11	7	.611	3.27	33	3	124	122	55	61	0
1964	13	9	.591	1.88	32	9	210⅔	142	55	138	2
1965	13	13	.500	2.88	34	7	219	203	39	125	4
1966	10	13	.435	2.43	37	4	211	185	53	124	2
1967	19	7	.731	2.06	35	13	258	188	58	103	6
1968	12	14	.462	2.37	35	4	223⅔	197	70	102	1
1969	13	16	.448	3.78	36	7	235⅔	237	77	121	2
1970	6	16	.273	4.87	28	4	172	198	41	77	0
1971	8	9	.471	4.27	34	3	137	150	30	82	0
Career	116	117	.498	3.11	361	59	2,001⅓	1,829	554	1,065	18

Joel Horlen: a Cy Young Award denied

Joel Horlen gained a reputation early in his White Sox career as a "hard-luck" pitcher who always kept his team in the game but somehow ended up losing 2–1 or 3–2 in the late innings. There is some truth to the old baseball adage that some pitchers are tragically cursed by their very nature. A shortage of batting support cost Horlen many victories in his 10-year stint on the South Side. He also lacked concentration—a flaw detected by pitching coach Ray Berres shortly after the slim Texan was signed out of Oklahoma State University in 1959. "If a pitcher wavers in his concentration when he has to get that one vital out in an inning, then he's going to lose those close ballgames," theorized Eddie Stanky.

Stanky knew what he was talking about. Horlen's first bid for a no-hitter was broken up by Chuck Hinton of the Washington Senators on July 29, 1963. Hinton's seeing-eye single with one out in the ninth inning was followed by a two-run Don Lock homer that sank the White Sox 2–1 and handed Joel the most bitter defeat of his career.

Pitching behind ace lefties Gary Peters and Tommy John in the mid-1960s, Horlen always finished among the league leaders in earned run average—while remaining a .500 pitcher. His breakthrough year came in 1967. Horlen won his first eight decisions en route to a solid 19–7 season that included the long-awaited no-hitter on September 10 against the Tigers in Comiskey Park. His 2.06 ERA led the American League, but the sportswriters bypassed Horlen for Cy Young honors. It was a terrible oversight and reinforced the hard-luck image Joel fought to overcome throughout his career.

Armed with a good curveball, a clever change-up, and a wad of Kleenex that he stuffed into his mouth because tobacco made him sick, Horlen's fortunes faded with the team in 1968. He never again posted a winning season and was released by the White Sox in the spring of 1972. Signed by the Oakland A's as a spot starter, Joel wrapped it up in 1972. His record was a very Horlen-like 116–117.

Horlen experienced some personal tragedies after his playing career ended. His brother was killed in a plane crash, and then Joel went through a painful divorce. But he got back into baseball in 1987 with the New York Mets and worked as a pitching coach for the Phoenix Firebirds. When working with young hurlers, Horlen utilizes the Ray Berres lesson plan taught to him when he was a Sox rookie.

Hoyt, LaMarr

White Sox: 1979–84
Pitcher
Birthplace: Columbia, South Carolina

B: January 1, 1955
Bats left, throws right
Ht. 6–3; **Wt.** 222

Hoyt, LaMarr

White Sox	W	L	Pct	ERA	G	CG	IP	H	BB	K	ShO
1979	0	0	—	0.00	2	0	3	2	0	0	0
1980	9	3	.750	4.58	24	3	112	123	41	55	1
1981	9	3	.750	3.56	43	0	91	80	28	60	0
1982	19	15	.559	3.53	39	14	239⅔	248	48	124	2
1983	24	10	.706	3.66	36	11	260⅔	236	31	148	1
1984	13	18	.419	4.47	34	11	235⅔	244	43	126	1
Career	98	68	.590	3.99	244	48	1,311⅓	1,313	279	681	8

When he was on top of the world, Dewey LaMarr Hoyt was hailed as the greatest right-handed pitcher in the American League. After that world fell apart and he languished

LaMarr Hoyt

inside a jail cell, Hoyt looked back in anger knowing that he had only himself to blame for his troubles.

The burly right-hander was signed by the Yankees in June 1973. He quietly passed through their farm system in the next few years, secure in the belief that he was being groomed by George Steinbrenner to replace Catfish Hunter in New York at some future point. The strategy was abruptly canceled on April 5, 1977, when he was packaged with Oscar Gamble and Bob Polinsky, another obscure Yankees farmhand, and sent to Chicago for Bucky Dent. The trade was universally assailed by White Sox fans who expected much more in return for the personable Dent.

A starter for most of his professional career, Hoyt was advised by Tony LaRussa, his manager at Knoxville, that the quickest path to the majors was as an emergency closer. By the time he arrived in the Windy City (to stay) on June 17, 1980, LaRussa was running the Sox, and Hoyt had honed his skills as a relief pitcher. On and off the field, Hoyt exuded a quiet toughness. "I've never been one to kiss anybody's behinds," he said with no apologies.

LaMarr was a backwoodsman at heart, spending his leisure time tramping around the South Carolina countryside with a fishing pole in hand. On the mound in Chicago, he was all business. Hoyt opened the 1982 season as the No. 1 closer, replacing Ed Farmer, who had signed with Philadelphia over the winter. After he had won his first three seasons, LaRussa moved him into the starting rotation on April 27.

Blessed with marvelous control, Hoyt set a team record for consecutive wins spanning two seasons (14, 1981–1982). In '82 he matched Orval Grove's and Lefty Williams' White Sox record of nine wins to open a season and was the league leader in victories with 19. When the moment arrived to select a Cy Young Award winner, not one vote was cast for Hoyt.

If the world failed to take notice of Hoyt in 1982, there was no mistaking him in 1983. Beyond his Cy Young Award–winning season, LaMarr was an intimidating presence on the mound who was in total control of the strike zone. He walked only 31 batters in 260⅔ innings of work, three shy of the AL record set by Cy Young in 1904. Hoyt won his last 13 decisions of the '83 campaign and opened the playoffs with a brilliant 2–1 victory over the Baltimore Orioles in Memorial Stadium. The consensus of opinion is that the White Sox would have advanced to the World Series that year if his teammates could have extended the playoffs past the fourth game. Hoyt was scheduled to pitch Game 5. "If the series had gone to a fifth game, there's no way we would have lost," Hoyt agreed.

Quite simply, LaMarr Hoyt was at the top of his game. In 1984, however, it was a different story. He suffered his first losing season and yielded the second-highest number of home runs in the American League. The genius of Roland Hemond was knowing when to let go. Sensing that Hoyt's market value had depreciated, Hemond traded the Sox ace and two minor leaguers to San Diego on December 6, 1984, for Ozzie Guillen, Bill Long, and Tim Lollar.

Hoyt started the 1985 All-Star Game for the National League, but his private troubles were already bubbling to the surface. Commissioner Peter Uebberoth suspended the big right-hander for one year in 1987 after he had been stopped at the Mexican border by customs officials who found marijuana cigarettes in his posession. The San Diego front office enrolled Hoyt in a drug and alcohol rehab program in Minnesota following his first scrape with the law. They were hopeful he might be able to resurrect his career with proper guidance. Hoyt was unrepentant.

Let go by the Padres after a second brush with the law, LaMarr was invited back to Chicago in July 1987 at the insistence of Sox chairman Jerry Reinsdorf to try out with the Sox following completion of his 45-day jail term. General manager Larry Himes was dead set against it, but he was overruled by his boss.

Seemingly unfazed by these humiliating setbacks that derailed his career, Hoyt was again taken into custody when police discovered 25 grams of marijuana in his South Carolina apartment. He was sent to the Allenwood Federal Prison in Montgomery, Pennsylvania, to serve a one-year sentence that began in February 1988.

Isbell, Frank

White Sox: 1901–09
Second baseman, first baseman, pitcher
Nicknames: Bald Eagle; Izzy
Birthplace: Delavan, New York
B: August 21, 1875
D: July 15, 1941
Batted left, threw right
Ht. 5–11; **Wt.** 190

Isbell, Frank

White Sox	G	AB	H	AVG	RBI	R	2B	3B	HR	SA	SB
1901	137	556	143	.257	70	93	15	8	3	.329	52
1902	137	520	133	.256	59	65	14	4	4	.321	38
1903	138	546	139	.255	59	52	25	9	2	.344	26
1904	96	314	66	.210	34	27	10	3	1	.271	19
1905	94	.341	101	.296	45	55	21	11	2	.440	15
1906	143	549	153	.279	57	71	21	11	0	.357	37
1907	125	486	118	.243	55	60	22	8	0	.321	22
1908	84	320	79	.247	49	31	15	3	1	.322	18
1909	120	433	97	.224	39	33	17	6	0	.291	23
Career	1,119	4,224	1,066	.252	475	504	164	63	13	.330	253

Tall, bony, and embarrassed about his receding hairline, Frank Isbell was upset with his teammates one afternoon when they sat down to pose for the team portrait without their caps on their heads. Though he was short of hair and sensitive about the subject, "Izzy" was an important figure in early White Sox history. He was the first 10-year man on the South Side. His hitting helped win the 1906 World Series. And as a minor league executive of some renown, Isbell became an important ally of Charles Comiskey in the Western League when his playing days were through.

Izzy broke into pro ball in 1896 as a pitcher for Comiskey's St. Paul Saints of the Western Association—forerunner of the Chicago White Sox. Because of his hitting, Commy later moved him to the outfield and other infield positions. Isbell hit .365 that first season in St. Paul. Two years later he was drafted by the Chicago Cubs, but was returned to St. Paul in August 1898 for pitcher Bill Phyle. Thereafter he was a career White Sox player.

Isbell was a standout first baseman until Jiggs Donahue joined the team in 1904. The balance of his White Sox career was spent at second base, though he was utilized as an emergency relief pitcher, outfielder, and shortstop as situations arose. Batting third in the lineup during the 1906 World Series, Isbell collected only one hit in 15 at bats in the first four games. Berated by manager Fielder Jones for his poor play, Isbell broke out of his slump with four doubles in the fifth game—still a series record—and three more hits in Game 6 after Charles Comiskey suggested that he discard his bottle bat and use a heavier piece of lumber.

Teammate Patsy Dougherty accidentally spiked Isbell in the left hand during some pregame horseplay on August 27, 1907. The injury was severe. Frank Isbell decided it was a good time to ask Comiskey for his release in order to fulfill a wide-ranging ambition to manage the Wichita team of the Western Association. The Old Roman refused. He talked his veteran into remaining on the roster for a few more years because there was just no one to take his place. Izzy finally won

Frank Isbell

his freedom and bid adieu to Chicago on January 20, 1910. He managed in Wichita for the next two seasons before moving on to Des Moines in 1912, where he became president and part owner of team controlled by Charles Comiskey. For the next three years Izzy developed future White Sox stars for the Old Roman, including a young Red Faber.

In his declining years, Frank Isbell was employed by the Wichita recreational department. He ran a local filling station on the side.

Jackson, Joe

White Sox: 1915–20
Outfielder, first baseman
Nickname: Shoeless Joe
Birthplace: Brandon Mills, South Carolina
B: July 16, 1887
D: December 5, 1951
Batted left, threw right
Ht. 6–1; **Wt.** 200

Jackson, Joe

White Sox	G	AB	H	AVG	RBI	R	2B	3B	HR	SA	SB
1915	46	162	43	.265	36	21	4	5	2	.389	6
1916	155	592	202	.341	78	91	40	21	3	.495	24
1917	146	538	162	.301	75	91	20	17	5	.429	13
1918	17	65	23	.354	20	9	2	2	1	.492	3
1919	139	516	181	.351	96	79	31	14	7	.506	9
1920	146	570	218	.382	121	105	42	20	12	.589	9
Career	1,330	4,981	1,774	.356	785	873	307	168	54	.518	202

Shoeless Joe Jackson

As long as the game of baseball is played, Shoeless Joe Jackson will continue to inspire debate, controversy, and remorse—remorse for the greatest natural hitter of his time who was done in by the stupidity, avarice, and greed of his teammates who led him down a path of their own undoing. Jackson's precise role in the 1919 Black Sox Scandal is shrouded in mystery. He batted .375 in the eight-game World Series and fielded flawlessly.

And yet, in Game 5, according to *Reach's 1920 Official Guide,* "Jackson seemed to be daydreaming when [pitcher Hod] Eller's fly was hit in his direction." That hit began a four-run Redleg uprising that ended in a 5–0 Cincinnati rout. The night before, Jackson had accepted $5,000 in bribe money from the gamblers to ensure his continued cooperation in the fix.

Jackson arrived in Chicago at the prime of his career. His arrival had a lot to do with the financial hardships plaguing Cleveland owner Charles W. Somers and the Old Roman's dissatisfaction with his two incumbent first basemen, Anthony "Bunny" Brief and Jacques Fournier, who divided responsibilities in the first two months of the 1915 season. White Sox secretary Harry Grabiner was dispatched to Cleveland to negotiate for outfielder Jackson, who had torn apart AL pitching in 1911 with a .408 average. Grabiner outbid three other teams for Jackson, who was acquired on August 20, 1915, for $31,500 cash (contemporary newspaper accounts peg this amount at only $15,000) and a trio of lesser-known players: Robert "Braggo" Roth, Larry Chappell, and Ed Klepfer. Shoeless Joe played his first White Sox game the next day.

Using a bat that he nicknamed "Black Betsy," Jackson swung the lumber effectively against any kind of pitching. Dutch Ruether, the great Cincinnati pitcher who defeated the Sox in Game 1 of the 1919 World Series, recalled Jackson's deadly swing: "We had bleacher seats in right field at Cincy, about 380 feet away. Nobody ever hit in there, either in a game or batting practice. Jackson stepped to the plate before the first game of the '19 series and put three consecutive pitches not only over that fence but halfway up the stands."

Ty Cobb and Tris Speaker were *made* hitters. They perfected their own styles and studied pitchers. Jackson's skills, however, came naturally.

Joe remained popular with his fans long after Charles Comiskey and members of the media branded him a coward and a slacker for choosing a civilian job in the Delaware Naval Yards over combat duty in France during the war-shortened 1918 season. When he returned to Comiskey Park in April 1919, the "Joe Jackson Rooters" hired a big brass band to properly welcome him back into the fold.

Jackson ranks in the top 10 in numerous single-season White Sox offensive categories. His 21 triples in 1916 set a club record that has gone unchallenged for nearly 100 years. Joe's 336 total bases in 1920 stand at fourth on the list.

This magnificent athlete undoubtedly was underpaid by Comiskey for all that he achieved on the diamond. However, in fairness to the Old Roman, his star outfielder arrived in Chicago already bound to a four-year, ironclad contract. Joe made $6,299 in 1919, and was awarded a slight raise for 1920, which elevated his salary to $8,000 by the time the scandal broke.

Without benefit of legal counsel, Joe Jackson confessed to participating in the 1919 World Series fix. "I got $5,000 and they promised me $20,000," he told the grand jury. "All I got was $5,000 that Lefty Williams handed me in a dirty envelope. I never got the $15,000." Joe's startling confession came as a jolt of reality to a generation of baseball aficionados who had come to believe that the national pastime was the last clean sport in America.

Jackson and his teammates were banned from baseball for life. Even if Landis had ruled in his favor, it is likely that Jackson would have retired after the 1920 season. "I'm through with organized baseball," he told reporters following the Black Sox trial. "At present I'm contemplating taking a position as a coach for a university team in Japan. I've also had an offer to go before the footlights."

He would do neither. Angry and resentful toward Comiskey, Joe sued the White Sox owner for slander and breach of contract in April 1924. Jackson's attorney demanded $119,000 in punitive damages from the Old Roman. But Comiskey's agents produced Joe's confession—missing and presumed stolen since 1920. No one could explain how these documents surfaced after all that time. No one seemed to care, nor did they want to take pity on Jackson. The case against Comiskey collapsed, and Jackson retreated into the shadows.

Using an assumed name, Joe Jackson played sandlot games with "outlaw" teams outside the governance of organized baseball through 1933. He was 45 when he finally hung up the spikes. Later he owned a dry-cleaning business with his wife, Kate, who managed his financial affairs throughout their years together.

Toward the end of his life, Joe's loyal fans and hometown supporters organized a campaign to clear his name. The South Carolina Senate and House of Representatives drafted a resolution on his behalf in February 1951. Joe was invited to appear on Ed Sullivan's *Toast of the Town* television program to relate his side of the story before a national audience in December of that year. However, 10 days before his live appearance was scheduled to air, Joe Jackson suffered a fatal heart attack. The lingering secrets surrounding his involvement with the Black Sox went to the grave, and with them Shoeless Joes's last chance to receive final absolution from the public for the role he played during baseball's darkest hour.

In death, for good or bad, Joe Jackson is today considered by many to be a martyr of the times. In April 2006 the 950-square-foot, red-brick Greenville, South Carolina, home where Jackson lived with his wife from 1940 to 1951 was moved from its original location to 356 Field Street—across from Fluor Field, where the Red Sox Class A affiliate plays. The woodwork, windows, and doors are all original, and the old Shoeless Joe homestead is today a baseball museum and research library. In downtown Greenville, a life-sized bronze statue of Joe stands in "Joe Jackson Plaza." The base of the statue was formed from bricks salvaged from old Comiskey Park. Charles A. Comiskey, who died a bitter and unhappy man as a result of the Black Sox Scandal and the heartbreaking betrayal of his star players, must be rolling over in his grave.

Jackson, Vincent

White Sox: 1991; 1993
Designated hitter, outfielder
Nickname: Bo
Birthplace: Bessemer, Alabama

B: November 30, 1962
Bats right, throws right
Ht. 6–1; **Wt.** 228

Jackson, Bo

White Sox	G	AB	H	AVG	RBI	R	2B	3B	HR	SA	SB
1991	23	71	16	.225	14	8	4	0	3	.408	0
1992	Did not play due to injury										
1993	85	284	66	.232	45	32	9	0	16	.433	0
Career	694	2,393	598	.250	415	341	86	14	141	.474	82

Few athletes rode the crest of glory on the back of adversity better than Bo Jackson, a Heisman Trophy winner out of Auburn University who made the Pro Bowl as a member of the Los Angeles Raiders a year after being named to the American League All-Star team from the Kansas City Royals. But in the end, Bo paid a heavy price for athletic fame. His competitive nature and burning desire to excel at two sports prematurely ended his career before it had reached midpoint.

Against the better judgment of the Royals, the strapping outfielder gifted with abundant speed and above-average power insisted upon playing pro football until he severely injured his left hip in a postseason game with the Cincinnati Bengals on January 13, 1991. After examining the X rays, Kansas City team physicians were convinced that Bo was finished—not only with football but with baseball, as well. After four seasons as a Royal, he was released on March 19, 1991, only to be signed by the White Sox two weeks later.

In the face of rising media skepticism about the team's true motives, general manager Ron Schueler defended the signing as more than just a publicity stunt to capitalize on Bo's undeniable popularity. "We saw star value—but only if he could play," Schueler explained.

Bo's comeback was an admitted long shot, but after spending the entire summer on the disabled list, he was added to the roster on September 2—just in time to face his former teammates before a large crowd at the new Comiskey Park. He collected an RBI in his first appearance—the first of several dramatic "Bo-moments" in a White Sox uniform.

Jackson sat out the entire 1992 season after undergoing reconstructive hip surgery on April 5. But as soon as he was able to, Bo was back on the comeback trail, undergoing a grueling rehab in Phoenix, Arizona. Day and night he fought to regain his strength under the prodding direction of Dr. Mack Newton—all the while contemplating an eventual return to the majors.

His crowning glory occurred on April 9, 1993—the third Opening Day at the new Comiskey. Pinch-hitter Jackson strode to the plate amid a thunderous ovation from 42,775 fans who respected his hard work and determination. They were not prepared for what happened next. Jackson swung hard at Yankees pitcher Neal Heaton's first pitch and drove the ball deep into the right-field stands. It was a riveting, improbable moment among many in White Sox history. Within days vendors were hawking Bo Jackson T-shirts outside the new Comiskey. He was the Windy City's latest marquee attraction, and his popularity translated into ticket sales and a whirlwind of favorable publicity for the ballclub.

That summer he was greeted by hordes of media at scheduled press conferences in each American League city where

Bo Jackson and manager Jeff Torborg, 1991

the Sox played. He was receiving the adulation and fanfare normally reserved for rock stars on tour, and you can be sure Bo savored every second of it.

Jackson divided his time that season between the outfield and designated-hitter assignments. On occasion he was every inch the hitter he had once been in Kansas City, but too often he struck out in the clutch, and his speed and range were of course greatly diminished by the surgery. In the heat of a pennant chase, however, Bo showed his mettle. He provided Sox fans with the thrill of a decade—perhaps of a lifetime—when he clouted a "surprise" three-run homer off of Seattle's Dave Fleming to help wrap up the American League Western Division title on September 27, 1993.

"I thought it was a pop fly," Jackson modestly explained of his elevator-shaft homer. "It kept drifting and drifting.... It must have gotten caught in the jet stream."

After the game had ended, Bo ran a victory lap around the perimeter of the warning track, waving his cap and whipping Sox fans into a frenzy of exultation. "I've said it before and I'll say it again. The man has a flair for the dramatic," Frank Thomas chuckled.

Sadly though, that's where the good times ended. Jackson failed to collect a hit in 10 at bats and struck out six times in the 1993 American League Championship Series, exposing a serious Sox weakness in the designated hitter slot not easily corrected by Bo, who was openly critical of manager Gene Lamont throughout the playoffs. Jackson and teammate Jorge Bell created an air of clubhouse dissension with their constant griping, hastening Bo's exit from Chicago.

The team made only a halfhearted attempt to re-sign Bo after refusing to pick up his option for 1994. Jackson was signed as a free agent by the California Angels on January 31, 1994. He spent the strike-shortened season with the Angels before calling it quits.

Jenks, Bobby

White Sox: 2005–10
Pitcher
Birthplace: Mission Hills, California

B: March 14, 1981
Bats right, throws right
Ht. 6–4; **Wt.** 275

Jenks, Bobby

White Sox	W	L	Pct.	ERA	G	CG	IP	H	BB	K	Sho	Sv
2005	1	1	.500	2.75	32	0	39⅓	34	15	50	0	6
2006	3	4	.429	4.00	67	0	69⅔	66	31	80	0	41
2007	3	5	.375	2.77	66	0	65	45	13	56	0	40
2008	3	1	.750	2.63	57	0	61⅔	51	17	38	0	30
2009	3	4	.429	3.71	52	0	53⅓	52	16	49	0	29
2010	1	3	.250	4.44	55	0	52⅔	54	18	61	0	27
Career	14	18	.438	3.40	329	0	341⅔	302	110	334	0	173

Bobby Jenks' journey from a cabin in the Idaho woods to success in the major leagues was a succession of fits and starts and trips and stumbles before the young man answered his wake-up call to become one of the American League's top closers. Selected by the Los Angeles Angels of Anaheim in the fifth round of the 2000 draft, the teenage Jenks' fastball clocked in at 100-plus mph. He complemented his Nolan Ryan–like velocity with a sharp breaking curveball, a hard slider, and a fair change-up.

Jenks had all the tools of the trade, but it was self-discipline that he lacked. At Timblerlake High School in Spirit Idaho, then later at Inglemoor High in Kenmore, Washington, the kid pitcher was academically ineligible in three of his four years. He began his career at Butte, Montana, in 2000, but struggled with a 1–7 record and an inflated 7.86 ERA. His minor league odyssey encompassed five different whistle-stop towns—with mixed results. Mostly, Jenks' problems stemmed from issues of self-control. He was suspended for participating in a barroom brawl and reportedly showed up for a game in a state of intoxication. *ESPN The Magazine* reported that Jenks torched himself with a lighter and passed out drunk. The Angels were patient, but eventually gave up on him after a series of injuries and Bobby's all-around bad behavior had finally exhausted their patience.

Bobby was claimed on waivers by the White Sox on December 17, 2004, and assigned to Birmingham of the Double A Southern League. There, "Bad Bobby," as he has sometimes been called, was converted to a role in the bullpen. "When I got the opportunity to come to Chicago, it was a wake-up call," Jenks admitted. "I've grown up a lot since I've had issues in the minor leagues." His 19 saves earned him a speedy promotion to the parent ballclub on July 5, 2005, just in time to enjoy the team's roller-coaster ride into the World Series, where Bobby really shined.

Dustin Hermanson was the Sox's closer when Bobby came up, but it was quickly apparent that Jenks was set to inherit the role sooner as opposed to later. During the World Series, manager Ozzie Guillen provoked good-natured humor by signaling for Jenks in the bullpen in an uncustomary manner. As he approached the mound, Ozzie extended his arms in front of his stomach with an exaggerated gesture, as if to say, "Send in the big guy." (Or fat guy!) Jenks became the first rookie pitcher to record a save in a World Series game, and the first rookie hurler to *finish* a championship-clinching game since Larry Sherry of the Dodgers in 1959—the old White Sox Series nemesis.

In 2006 he took over closer duties from Hermanson on a full-time basis and saved 41 games—becoming only the third major league pitcher to hit the elite 40 mark in either his first or second season. Jenks followed up his sophomore success with a lights-out 2007 campaign, chalking up 40 more saves. Bobby is the only Sox pitcher to record back-to-back 40-save seasons. The '07 campaign was noteworthy for Bobby in one other respect. On July 17 in Cleveland, he commenced a remarkable 13-game streak by retiring 41 consecutive hitters, to equal an MLB record first set by Jim Barr of the Giants back in 1972. The streak was ended by Joey Gathright of the Royals on August 20. (Mark Buehrle broke the record in 2009 by setting down 45 batters in a row). The going was a little tougher in the second half of 2008 for Jenks. Bobby's 2009 campaign ended on the disabled list with a sore calf muscle.

As is so often the case with White Sox closers of the recent past, the brilliance of their first couple of years in a Chicago uniform is often marred by setbacks and ineffectiveness by

"Bad" Bobby Jenks saves Game 3 in the 2008 ALDS. (Courtesy of the Chicago White Sox)

the third or fourth year. His six blown saves in 2009 represented a career high, and his save percentage was the lowest of any of his White Sox years. In non-save situations, Jenks was terrible—there's just no polite way to describe it. And with the game on the line, it was white-knuckle time when Jenks strolled out of the pen in the ninth inning to try to preserve a Sox victory. Inevitably in '09, for better or worse, he would walk the leadoff hitter, and for fans in the stands and those watching on TV at home, it was time to cringe. Especially during day games. Bobby's ERA when the sun is out is nearly 1½ runs higher than at night.

Guillen and pitching coach Don Cooper faulted Jenks for his excessive weight and poor conditioning habits for one too many meltdowns—factors that undoubtedly contributed to his injuries—and with it, a war of words ensued. The rumor mill reported that GM Kenny Williams was willing to listen to offers for Jenks as the 2009 winter meetings commenced in Indianapolis, but Williams put them to rest: "He's my closer, and I haven't had one discussion about him. He's one of the game's better closers and people need closers, but so do we." Jenks quit drinking during the off-season and reported to the 2010 spring camp in Arizona 25 pounds lighter.

Two-thousand-nine was his first year of eligibility for salary arbitration, and with so much money at stake, apparently it was a *second* wake-up call. "For me, it was easier to just quit. It was to the point where it was easy for me to lose control," he said. "I got to the point where not for my sake and my family's sake, but everyone's around me, it was just time to back off and live my life not for myself." Only Mariano Rivera, at age 43, was closing games longer for the same team than Jenks, but another shaky start to begin the 2010 campaign caused doubts to be raised about his future role. "I get paid to win games," snapped Guillen after a particularly galling extra-inning loss to the Mariners due to Bobby's poor performance on July 21. "And I'm going to put guys there with the best shot." It was a dip in Jenks' velocity that raised concerns, but after that he seemed to regain his fastball and converted 15 of 15 save opportunities. He saved both ends of a rare White Sox doubleheader sweep in Boston, but for the second year in a row he went down in early September with a nerve problem in his right arm. Without the closer, the bullpen collapsed, and the 2010 division title chase was quickly over.

"That's something we have to evaluate strongly because I've been disappointed on a number of levels," Williams candidly admitted. "And there are certain things that...I'm not going to talk about right now. What I will say is Bobby Jenks has been good for a long time here. He is one of the reasons we've got that [World Series] banner up here and a [20]08 division as well." In reality, there was little chance the Sox would bring Jenks back after his lackluster 2009 campaign, especially after rookie Chris Sale effortlessly transitioned from his college campus into the closer role in the closing weeks of September. Non-tendered by the White Sox, Jenks inked a two-year, $12 million deal with the Red Sox on December 16, 2010.

John, Tommy

White Sox: 1965–71
Pitcher
Birthplace: Terre Haute, Indiana

B: May 22, 1943
Bats right, throws left
Ht. 6–3; **Wt.** 180

John, Tommy

White Sox	W	L	Pct	ERA	G	CG	IP	H	BB	K	ShO
1965	14	7	.667	2.62	39	6	183⅔	162	58	126	1
1966	14	11	.560	2.47	34	10	223	195	57	138	5
1967	10	13	.435	1.98	31	9	178⅓	143	47	110	6
1968	10	5	.667	3.25	25	5	177⅓	135	49	117	1
1969	9	11	.450	3.28	33	6	232⅓	230	90	128	2
1970	12	17	.414	3.62	37	10	269	253	101	138	3
1971	13	16	.448	2.89	38	10	229	244	58	131	3
Career	288	231	.555	3.34	760	162	4,708⅓	4,783	1,259	2,245	46

General manager Ed Short's most successful White Sox trade also sparked the greatest controversy. Determined to acquire a bona fide long-ball threat to insert into a weak-hitting lineup that nearly stole an American League pennant in 1964, Short entered into discussions with Cleveland GM Gabe Paul for the services of John Romano, a solid catcher who was getting on in years. Paul encouraged Short to make an offer, since the Sox were in a position to acquire former AL home run champion Rocky Colavito from Kansas City. The Indians desperately wanted Colavito, a fan favorite along the shores of Lake Erie.

The Sox held the trump card and bargained from a position of strength by first going after Colavito. The three-team deal was announced on January 20, 1965. Outfielders Mike Hershberger and Jim Landis and pitcher Fred Talbot were sent to Kansas City for Colavito. Then Colavito, who was Sox property for about 10 minutes, was dealt to the Tribe for Romano and a pair of rookie unknowns: pitcher Tommy John and outfielder Tommie Agee. The fans were understandably upset after hearing that Short frittered away Colavito for the washed-up Romano. But Short was a patient man, and in a few years he could easily justify the trade.

The Sox had received good scouting reports on John and were encouraged to go after the soft-throwing lefty over a right-hander named Tom Kelly. Manager Al Lopez strongly advised against Kelly, and the rest, as they say, is history.

With a better team behind him and Ray Berres correcting a few minor flaws in his delivery, the Hoosier southpaw bloomed into stardom in 1965 with 14 wins—tops among the starters that year. But the one thing that the Hoosier southpaw was forced to battle year in and year out was arm soreness. It was an issue he had to deal with even in his great White Sox years. John first experienced occasional pain in his throwing arm in 1961 when the Cleveland Indians signed him in the amateur free agent draft. Of course, the doctors of that era could not come up with an adequate remedy until 1974, when Dr. Frank Jobe performed successful ulnar collateral ligament reconstruction—the replacement of a ligament in the medial elbow with a tendon from elsewhere in the body. Although T.J. is not in the Hall of Fame (he deserves to be), he must certainly be in the hall of fame of medicine for what is commonly known today as "Tommy John surgery."

Tommy John was ideally suited to pitching in spacious Comiskey Park. John was a sinker-ball specialist, and the infield grass was kept high and the dirt portions soft and mushy by head groundskeeper Gene Bossard. T.J. led the league in shutouts in 1966 and 1967, and more importantly he was manager Eddie Stanky's kind of pitcher. In 1967 Stanky offered to buy his pitchers a new suit of clothes for every complete game they recorded. John tossed nine complete games—six of them were shutouts.

Weekend duty with the Indiana Air National Guard limited his appearances in 1967 and 1968, but oddly enough, the miserable '68 season was actually Tommy's finest as a member of the White Sox. He won his first seven decisions of the year, but was sidelined for the rest of the year with a shoulder injury after tangling with Dick McAuliffe in a brawl at Tiger Stadium on August 22.

Tommy's value to the Sox was diminished when owner Art Allyn foolishly decided to carpet the Comiskey Park infield with Astroturf in 1969. The sinker-ball grounders that were once slowed by the thick wet grass shot through into the outfield for base hits. John's earned run average ballooned to 3.25—a sharp contrast from his 1.98 ERA a year earlier. Two more losing seasons followed before Roland Hemond, the new director of player personnel, traded John to Los Angeles for Dick Allen on December 2, 1971. It was a short-term trade that helped "save" the White Sox for Chicago, but it proved to be a very costly one down the road. T.J.'s greatest years were still ahead of him.

Tommy John

Johnson, Bart

White Sox: 1969–74; 1976–77
Pitcher
Nickname: Mr. Smoke
Birthplace: Torrance, California

B: January 3, 1950
Bats right, throws right
Ht. 6–5; **Wt.** 190

Johnson, Bart

White Sox	W	L	Pct	ERA	G	CG	IP	H	BB	K	ShO	Sv
1969	1	3	.250	3.22	4	0	22⅓	22	6	18	0	0
1970	4	7	.364	4.80	18	2	90	92	46	71	1	0
1971	12	10	.545	2.93	53	4	178	148	111	153	0	14
1972	0	3	.000	9.22	9	0	13⅔	18	13	9	0	1
1973	3	3	.500	4.13	22	0	80⅔	76	40	56	0	0
1974	10	4	.714	2.73	18	8	122	105	32	76	2	0
1975	Did not play due to injury											
1976	9	16	.360	4.73	32	8	211	231	62	91	3	0
1977	4	5	.444	4.01	29	4	92	114	38	46	0	2
Career	43	51	.457	3.93	185	22	809⅔	806	348	520	6	17

Bart Johnson: As the World Turns

Bart Johnson and his explosive 95 mph fastball victimized American League hitters in 1971 and again in 1974. In between his two outstanding seasons, the string-bean right-hander, who had starred in prep sports at Torrance High School, fought off the injury jinx and his own impulsive nature.

Bart established himself as a future star of the game in 1971 after finishing 24 of the 37 games he appeared in. His 14 saves led the ballclub that year, and an earned run average under 3 ranked him 10th-best in the junior circuit. Bart Johnson, however, was restless and impatient. He yearned for new vistas.

When things weren't going too well for Bart in the middle of the 1972 season, he decided that he would forgo pitching and become an outfielder. He was convinced that his days as a pitcher were over because of a knee injury sustained while playing basketball in the off-season. The White Sox hoped that their future Nolan Ryan would come to his senses, but in the meantime they allowed him to live out his fantasy of becoming the next Babe Ruth in the low minors.

Bart was back on the mound in 1973, but a knee operation curtailed his mound time to only 22 appearances. In the off-season he tried out for a spot with the Seattle Supersonics. Johnson had been a prep star back in Torrance, and he was eager to tee it up with the seven-footers in the NBA, but his tryout lasted only two days.

Hearing that he had been farmed out to Des Moines, Iowa, just before the Sox broke camp to begin the 1974 season, Johnson angrily stormed out of the clubhouse and returned to the Windy City, where he worked as a ticket salesman for the Chicago Fire, the new entry in the World Football League. The Bart Johnson soap opera had taken yet another unusual twist.

The free-spirited Johnson rejoined the White Sox on July 5 and turned in what was probably the finest half season of his career. Bart gave every indication of finally becoming a bona fide star. Before this prophecy was fulfilled, Johnson suffered a back injury, sidelining him for the entire 1975 season. He was never quite the same after that unfortunate occurrence and played out the string with Bill Veeck's wrecks in 1976 and 1977.

Bart was working in the White Sox scouting department in 1985 when general manager Roland Hemond persuaded him to give it one last shot. Nothing came of the attempt, but it was good for a few lines in the morning paper at the very least. For a few years, Johnson served as a special assistant to Sox GM Ron Schueler. In recent years he has served as a special assignment scout for the Washington Nationals.

Johnson, Lamar

White Sox: 1974–81
Infielder
Nickname: Bumper
Birthplace: Bessemer, Alabama

B: September 2, 1950
Bats right, throws right
Ht. 6–2; **Wt.** 225

Johnson, Lamar

White Sox	G	AB	H	AVG	RBI	R	2B	3B	HR	SA	SB
1974	10	29	10	.345	2	1	0	0	0	.345	0
1975	8	30	6	.200	1	2	3	0	1	.400	0
1976	82	222	71	.320	33	29	11	1	4	.432	2
1977	118	374	113	.302	65	52	12	5	18	.505	1
1978	148	498	136	.273	72	52	23	2	8	.376	6
1979	133	479	148	.309	74	60	29	1	12	.449	8
1980	147	541	150	.277	81	51	26	3	13	.409	2
1981	41	134	37	.276	15	10	7	0	1	.351	0
Career	792	2,631	755	.287	381	294	122	12	64	.415	22

Lamar Johnson

Burly Lamar Johnson battered down the fences of minor league parks for nearly eight years before receiving the big league call. The genial giant led the American Association in hitting in 1975. In Denver's thin mountain air Lamar whaled on opposing pitching to a tune of .336. But could he do the job around first base? The White Sox were not so sure.

General manager Roland Hemond prioritized defense and traded for Jim Spencer, a Gold Glove fielder who opened the 1976 season at first base. Lamar Johnson caddied for Spencer through the next two seasons. His biggest day by far was a beautiful sunlit Sunday afternoon at Comiskey Park, June 19, 1977. Lamar exercised his pipes and sang the National Anthem before a crowd of 25,000. He then collected the only three hits garnered by the Sox in the game. Lamar's two homers sank the Oakland A's 2–1.

When Bill Veeck could no longer afford to keep Spencer on the payroll and traded him to the Yankees for farmhands, Lamar took over first base on a full-time basis. Given the opportunity to play every day, Lamar took a step back. He never put up the big offensive numbers expected of him, and his fielding skills were subpar.

The Sox made no effort to re-sign him after the 1981 season. Johnson came to terms with the Texas Rangers as a free agent on January 15, 1982. A year later he announced his retirement.

Johnson, Lance

White Sox: 1988–95
Outfielder
Nickname: The One Dog
Birthplace: Cincinnati, Ohio
B: July 6, 1963
Bats left, throws left
Ht. 5–11; **Wt.** 160

Johnson, Lance

White Sox	G	AB	H	AVG	RBI	R	2B	3B	HR	SA	SB
1988	33	124	23	.185	6	11	4	1	0	.234	6
1989	50	180	54	.300	16	28	8	2	0	.367	16
1990	151	541	154	.285	51	76	18	9	1	.357	36
1991	160	588	161	.274	49	72	14	13	0	.342	26
1992	157	567	158	.279	47	67	15	12	3	.363	41
1993	147	540	168	.311	47	75	18	14	0	.396	35
1994	106	412	114	.277	54	56	11	14	3	.393	26
1995	142	607	186	.306	57	98	18	12	10	.425	40
Career	1,447	5,379	1,565	.291	486	767	175	117	34	.386	352

Like fine wine, Lance Johnson just kept improving with age. "The One Dog"—a nickname given to him by TV announcer Ken Harrelson because of his uniform number—is one of the unheralded stars of baseball. Even though Lance moved on to greener pastures in the National League, he took his place with some of the great White Sox center fielders from the past—Johnny Mostil, Mike Kreevich, Jim Landis, and Ken Berry.

In his near-sensational four-year run as general manager (1986–90), Larry Himes built the foundation of the contending White Sox ballclubs of the 1990s. The acquisition of St. Louis Cardinals farmhand Lance Johnson on February 9, 1988, for pitcher Jose DeLeon was in some respects Larry Himes' single most important player move. Strength up the middle is the hallmark of a team that contends year in and year out. In the years immediately before the speedy Johnson arrived on the scene to anchor the spacious center-field grounds of Comiskey Park, there was Kenny Williams and Dave Gallagher. The plays that Johnson made appear routine in the 1990s had dropped in for singles and doubles with these slower outfielders patrolling the region. Johnson's range was tremendous. The One Dog ranks with the all-time White Sox greats in single-season putouts.

Though he was not known as a big RBI man, Johnson's clutch hitting during the 1993 divisional championship year was one of the big reasons why the Chisox advanced to the playoffs for the first time in 10 years. "Lance is unbelievable," praised teammate Tim Raines. "We always say on the bench, 'If we've got runners on second and third and two out, we've got 'em where we want 'em."

Tough to strike out and brutal in the clutch, Johnson reeled off a 25-game hitting streak in 1992 (July 16 to August 11), which placed him third in Sox history behind Luke Appling and Guy Curtright, a World War II–era outfielder.

Johnson joined the illustrious Minnie Minoso and Shoeless Joe Jackson as the only White Sox players to lead the league in triples more than once. In fact, Lance Johnson became the *only* major leaguer to do it in four consecutive

Lance Johnson: the "One Dog"

seasons (1991–1994). "Lance turns it on when he gets to first base. It's really something to see," noted second baseman Joey Cora, who was no slouch on the base paths himself during those years.

Inserted into the lead-off spot by Terry Bevington in 1995, the One Dog battered opposing pitching to the tune of .343 after the All-Star break. He became the first Sox player since Minnie Minoso in 1960 to lead the league in hits. Lance staged a hitting clinic at the Minnesota Metrodome on September 22, 1995, by collecting six hits in six at bats (including *three* triples) against a trio of arm-dead Twins pitchers. "When you're swinging good, you've got to try to milk it," he explained. He was only the fourth Sox hitter to turn the trick.

Lance missed out on a fifth consecutive-triples title on the last day of the '95 season, but his enormously satisfying campaign established him as one of the all-time Sox greats.

His agent played hardball with Sox owner Jerry Reinsdorf over the winter, however, and the ballclub simply refused to meet his salary demands. Lance was signed by the New York Mets as a free agent on December 14, 1995.

Jolley, Smead

White Sox: 1930–32
Outfielder
Birthplace: Wesson, Arkansas

B: January 14, 1902
D: November 17, 1991
Batted left, threw right
Ht. 6–3½; **Wt.** 210

Jolley, Smead

White Sox	G	AB	H	AVG	RBI	R	2B	3B	HR	SA	SB
1930	152	616	193	.313	114	76	38	12	16	.492	3
1931	54	110	33	.300	28	5	11	0	3	.482	0
1932	12	42	15	.357	7	3	0	0	0	.429	1
Career	473	1,710	521	.305	313	188	111	21	46	.475	5

Smead Powell Jolley's hitting tore up the Pacific Coast League. He led the PCL six times in batting, and his lifetime .366 minor league average is the third-highest in history. As a member of the San Francisco Seals from 1926 to 1929, the big, affable right fielder hit .346, .397, .404, and .387. Smead was touted as the next Babe Ruth. He was certainly capable of driving the ball out of any stadium in America, and that power was the main reason why Charles Comiskey eagerly parted with $50,000 to secure Jolley for the 1930 season.

Unfortunately, the slow-footed Jolley's fielding was far below average. He made the most routine play an adventure, and though there is no evidence to support the folktale that Jolley once committed three errors on one play by allowing a line drive to whiz through his legs, bounce off the right-field wall and sail *back* through the wickets, *then* overthrowing the cutoff man, Jolley's glove work was a cause for concern.

A cartoonish but rather lovable character in the Babe Herman mold, Smead inspired his right-field fans to organize their own fan club called the Jolley Boosters. However, their hero wasn't long for right field—or the White Sox. In an effort to keep Jolley's bat in the lineup and salvage Comiskey's

Smead Jolley

$50,000 investment, manager Lew Fonseca used him as a pinch-hitter then converted him to catcher during the 1932 spring training workouts. The experiment was doomed to failure. Smead was traded to Boston with John Watwood on April 29, 1932, for outfielder John Rothrock and catcher Charlie Berry.

Kaat, Jim

White Sox: 1973–75
Pitcher
Nickname: Kitty
Birthplace: Zeeland, Michigan

B: November 7, 1938
Bats left, throws left
Ht. 6–4½; **Wt.** 205

Kaat, Jim

White Sox	W	L	Pct	ERA	G	CG	IP	H	BB	K	ShO
1973	4	1	.800	4.22	7	3	42⅔	44	4	16	1
1974	21	13	.618	2.92	42	15	277	263	63	142	3
1975	20	14	.588	3.11	43	12	303	321	77	142	1
Career	283	237	.544	3.45	898	180	4,528	4,620	1,083	2,461	31

Jim Kaat notched his 200th career victory as a member of the Sox on June 18, 1974, in Cleveland. His teammates add the numbers to his locker.

Acquired on waivers from the Minnesota Twins, August 14, 1973, after his former employers pronounced the last rites on his 14-year career, Jim Kaat caught his second wind and was restored to winning form by White Sox pitching coach Johnny Sain.

After he lost five straight decisions in May 1974, fresh concerns were raised about Jim's baseball future. A good all-around athlete who was always up to a challenge, Kaat made the most of a bad situation by making use of his time in the White Sox bullpen to correct a few flaws and develop a new gimmick—the quick pitch. Kaat's rapid-fire delivery gained him a competitive edge. Kaat's quick pace kept the opposing hitters off guard, but it also wreaked havoc with the airing of TV commercials between innings. The ads for Falstaff beer and Chevrolet were still running while Kaat was already dealing to enemy hitters to start the next inning. General Roland Hemond told Jim to slow things up—the advertisers were screaming. So, in order to appease the beer company, Kaat eased up. He won all seven of his September decisions, while posting a sizzling 0.31 ERA. For only the second time in his career Kaat surpassed the 20-win mark.

From September 4, 1974, through May 9, 1975, he won 12 straight games to break the old team record of 11 jointly held by Johnny Rigney (1939) and Gary Peters (1963). Kaat continued an uninterrupted streak by winning his 13th and 14th consecutive Gold Glove Awards as a member of the White Sox.

For all of his good work anchoring a ballclub that never recovered from the loss of Dick Allen, Jim Kaat's age and salary were issues that could not be easily overlooked by incoming owner Bill Veeck, who was anxious to rebuild with a younger nucleus. Roland Hemond explained the tough financial position the ballclub was in to Kaat, and said he had three National League teams interested in acquiring his services as the 1975 winter meetings opened. The Cardinals and Phillies had shown the greatest interest, so Hemond offered Jim the choice of where he wanted to play in 1976. The veteran ace said he preferred Philadelphia, and a deal was consummated on December 10, sending Jim to the Phils for infielder Alan Bannister and pitchers Roy Thomas and Dick Ruthven. Although his final White Sox season in '75 was his last big winning year, Kaat completed another eight seasons as a spot starter and bullpen set-up man for the Phils, Yanks, and Cardinals, then served as a Reds pitching coach under Pete Rose. Thereafter, he joined the ranks of television analysts, described Yankees games for a decade, and at present is part of the MLB Network and doing occasional broadcasts. In 2003 he published a memoir of his 24-year major league career titled *Still Pitching: Musings from the Mound and the Microphone.*

Kamm, Willie

White Sox: 1923–31
Third baseman
Birthplace: San Francisco, California

B: February 2, 1900
D: December 24, 1988
Batted right, threw right
Ht. 5–10; **Wt.** 170

Kamm, Willie

White Sox	G	AB	H	AVG	RBI	R	2B	3B	HR	SA	SB
1923	149	544	159	.292	87	57	39	9	6	.430	17
1924	147	528	134	.254	93	58	28	6	6	.364	9
1925	152	509	142	.279	83	82	32	4	6	.393	11
1926	143	480	141	.294	62	63	24	10	0	.385	14
1927	148	540	146	.270	59	85	32	13	0	.378	7
1928	155	552	170	.308	84	70	30	12	1	.411	17
1929	147	523	140	.268	63	72	32	6	3	.369	12
1930	111	331	89	.269	47	49	21	6	3	.396	5
1931	18	59	15	.254	9	9	4	0	0	.322	1
Career	1,692	5,851	1,643	.281	826	802	347	85	29	.384	126

Few rookies attracted as much press attention before they had played their first major league game as Willie Kamm, the "$100,000 San Francisco Beauty." In order to rebuild an infield that had been shattered by the Black Sox scandal, Charles Comiskey scoured the minor leagues for replacement talent but achieved only mixed results until his scouts tipped him off about a 22-year-old kid whose fielding play was the envy of every Pacific Coast League team.

The Old Roman outbid nearly every other big league team for the services of third baseman Kamm, who had played semipro in Golden Gate Park before signing his first professional contract with the San Francisco Seals of the Pacific Coast League in 1920. Comiskey paid $100,000 to Charles Strub, Charlie Graham, and George Putnam, the triumvirate Seals ownership, tossing in pitcher Douglas McWeeney to complete a record-setting deal that had only one parallel from a dollars-and-cents standpoint. And that occurred in January 1920 when Red Sox owner Harry Frazee sold Babe Ruth to the Yankees for $125,000.

Charles Comiskey was beaming when he announced the transaction to members of the press on May 28, 1922. "As far as I know, and I have been in the game as long as any of them, this consideration overshadows any that ever passed from a big-league club for the services of a minor leaguer."

Reticent and very shy by nature, Kamm was under intense pressure to justify Comiskey's faith in his ability—and his own salary—when he reported to camp the following spring. Nevertheless, he quickly established himself as a solid contact hitter and even better glove man. Willie topped the American League in third-base fielding percentage for six straight seasons (1924–29) and rarely missed a game during that whole time.

Kamm replaced Eddie Collins as team captain in 1925. The job carried with it an additional $3,600 a year in salary, which was one reason why baseball players of that era were reluctant to step aside when asked to do so by management. Willie relinquished these duties to Art Shires in 1929, but a permanent rift developed between management and their star third baseman. Kamm was no happier playing under Donie Bush in 1930. He was a preseason holdout after Comiskey refused to raise his salary and Bush denied his request to restore the White Sox captaincy to him.

Willie was benched in June 1930 for lackadaisical play and left at home to contemplate his future when the team began an August road trip. Bush accused Kamm of loafing and indifference. For his part, Willie was sullen and uncommunicative. Attempts were made over the winter to oblige Kamm's request for a trade, but talks with the Cleveland Indians stalled. It wasn't until May 16, 1931, that the long-rumored trade materialized. Willie Kamm was shipped to Cleveland for Lew Fonseca, a natural second baseman who was brought to Chicago to play first.

A telephone operator advised Kamm of the deal. The Comiskeys, who had welcomed Willie with open arms in 1923, never bothered to contact him prior to announcing the trade to the media. It was evident that Kamm had worn out his welcome in Chicago.

Willie benefited from a change of scenery. He enjoyed several more productive seasons along the shores of Lake Erie before hanging up the spikes in 1935. Kamm managed the San Francisco Missions of the Pacific Coast League in 1936 and 1937. He coached for the Indians later in the decade and was instrumental in starting a pension plan for ballplayers.

To a younger generation of fans, the name Willie Kamm means nothing. But in weighing the merits of White Sox third basemen over the years, only four names stand out in a very weak field. Willie Kamm, Bill Melton, Buck Weaver, and Robin Ventura. An informal poll of White Sox fans conducted in 1954 ranked Willie as the greatest third baseman in club history. The passage of four decades has not diminished the honor bestowed upon this flawless workman at the hot corner.

Willie Kamm

Karkovice, Ron

White Sox: 1986–97
Catcher
Birthplace: Union, New Jersey

B: September 16, 1963
Bats right, throws right
Ht. 6–1; **Wt.** 219

Karkovice, Ron

White Sox	G	AB	H	AVG	RBI	R	2B	3B	HR	SA	SB
1986	37	97	24	.247	13	13	7	0	4	.443	1
1987	39	85	6	.071	7	7	0	0	2	.141	3
1988	46	115	20	.174	9	10	4	0	3	.287	4
1989	71	182	48	.264	24	21	9	2	3	.385	0
1990	68	183	45	.246	20	30	10	0	6	.399	2
1991	75	167	41	.246	22	25	13	0	5	.413	0
1992	123	342	81	.237	50	39	12	1	13	.392	10
1993	128	403	92	.228	54	60	17	1	20	.424	2
1994	77	207	44	.213	29	33	9	1	11	.425	0
1995	113	323	70	.223	51	44	14	1	13	.387	2
1996	111	355	78	.220	38	44	22	0	10	.366	0
1997	51	138	25	.181	18	10	3	0	6	.333	0
Career	939	2,597	574	.221	335	336	120	6	96	.383	24

"Karko" played in Carlton Fisk's shadow for six seasons until the White Sox organization pronounced his lengthy apprenticeship over and rudely shoved the old Commander aside.

Signed to his first White Sox contract by Jerry Krause in the June 1982 free agent draft, Karkovice established himself as one of the top three defensive catchers in the American League after taking over for Fisk on a full-time basis in 1992.

Blessed with a powerful and accurate throwing arm, Karkovice has gunned down 41.1 percent of all attempted base stealers in his first seven White Sox seasons. In a poll of major league managers taken in 1993, he was named the best throwing catcher." *Baseball America* named him the best defensive catcher in 1994.

Ron Karkovice (© 1992 Finalshot.com)

To cut down on debilitating injuries from foul tips, Karko has become the league's foremost practitioner of the one-handed catching style. Unfortunately, other injuries sidelined him down through the years. Torn cartilage in the heat of the 1994 pennant race laid him up for nearly a month.

Karko would probably be a Hall of Fame shoo-in if only he could hit like Fisk and provide the same caliber of leadership. Except for the occasional grand-slam homer (he's hit five for sixth place on the Sox all-time list), Karkovice was a chronic .230 banjo hitter (in his *better* years) whose alarming strikeout totals obscured his defensive prowess.

In the division championship season, Ron became only the third Sox catcher (Carlton Fisk and Sherm Lollar are the others) to hit 20 home runs in a single season.

On October 31, 1997, the ballclub announced that it would not exercise their option for 1998, thus ending Karko's professional career. He retired from baseball a career White Sox player, having logged 918 games behind the plate—sixth on the all-time list of Sox catchers for games caught, trailing only Ray Schalk, Sherm Lollar, Carlton Fisk, Billy Sullivan, and Mike Tresh.

Kelly, Pat

White Sox: 1971–76
Outfielder
Birthplace: Philadelphia, Pennsylvania

B: July 30, 1944
D: October 2, 2005
Batted left, threw left
Ht. 6–1; **Wt.** 185

Kelly, Pat

White Sox	G	AB	H	AVG	RBI	R	2B	3B	HR	SA	SB
1971	67	213	62	.291	22	32	6	3	3	.390	14
1972	119	402	105	.261	24	57	14	7	5	.368	32
1973	144	550	154	.280	44	77	24	5	1	.347	22
1974	122	424	119	.281	21	60	16	3	4	.361	18
1975	133	471	129	.274	45	73	21	7	9	.406	18
1976	107	311	79	.254	34	42	20	3	5	.386	15
Career	1,385	4,338	1,147	.264	418	620	189	35	76	.377	250

Why the Royals let Pat Kelly get away after he stole 40 bases in his rookie season—and was named one of the top nine dressers in Kansas City on top of it—has never been explained. "P.K." was originally signed by the Minnesota Twins in 1963, but he did not make it up to the majors until 1969 after being selected in the expansion draft by the Royals.

Roland Hemond acquired Kelly along with pitcher Don O'Riley in exchange for first baseman Gail Hopkins and John Matias on October 13, 1970. It was the kind of sleeper trade that established the soft-spoken Hemond as one of the very best talent judges in baseball.

Pat Kelly opened the 1971 season in the minors, but was called up to the White Sox to stay in midseason. Over the next five seasons he provided stellar defensive play and good offensive numbers as the Sox leadoff man. Kelly's patented drag bunt down the first-base line kept opposing infielders

Pat Kelly, out at the plate

on their toes. In 1973 he was named to the All-Star team in the middle of his best all-around season.

Nicknamed No-Fro by his teammates at a time when the Afro hairstyle was popular in the United States, Kelly was always a good-natured and gregarious presence in the clubhouse. Pat came from an athletic family. His older brother LeRoy Kelly played for the Cleveland Browns.

P.K. had many more hits in his bat when he was traded to Baltimore on November 18, 1976, but it was fire-sale time for the cash-strapped Bill Veeck, who received catcher Dave Duncan in return. At the end of his life, Pat Kelly was a minister in Baltimore.

Kennedy, Bob

White Sox: 1939–42; 1946–48; 1955–56
Infielder, outfielder
Birthplace: Chicago

B: August 18, 1920
D: April 7, 2005
Batted right, threw right
Ht. 6–2; **Wt.** 193

Kennedy, Bob

White Sox	G	AB	H	AVG	RBI	R	2B	3B	HR	SA	SB
1939	3	8	2	.250	1	0	0	0	0	.250	0
1940	154	606	153	.252	52	74	23	3	3	.315	3
1941	76	257	53	.206	29	16	9	3	1	.276	5
1942	113	412	95	.231	38	37	18	5	0	.299	11
1946	113	411	106	.258	34	43	13	5	5	.350	6
1947	115	428	112	.262	48	47	19	3	6	.362	3
1948	30	113	28	.248	14	4	8	1	0	.336	0
1955	83	214	65	.304	43	28	10	2	9	.495	0
1956	8	13	1	.077	0	0	0	0	0	.077	0
Career	1,483	4,624	1,176	.254	514	514	196	41	63	.355	45

June 22, 1937, was the night of the Joe Louis–Jimmy Braddock heavyweight title fight at Comiskey Park. Roaming the stands that night was a 16-year-old Chicago boy trying to earn a few nickels peddling popcorn to the fans. The youngster out of Morgan Park High School returned to Comiskey Park the next day to sign a professional contract with the White Sox.

Bob Kennedy (left), John Rigney, and Ken Silvestri, 1941

Bob Kennedy's 50-year odyssey from the playing fields to the front office began that day. He was one of the first products of the Sox farm system to crack the major leagues on the strength of his powerful throwing arm and above-average skills around the hot corner. Kennedy earned a starting assignment in 1940 after his call-up from Shreveport, Louisiana, and would hold down the job before going off to war in 1943. During the Korean conflict in the early 1950s, Kennedy re-enlisted in the service. In his second tour of duty, he taught Ted Williams how to fly a fighter jet.

A versatile performer who could play the infield and the outfield with the same skill, Kennedy was dealt to Cleveland in 1948 in a poorly thought-out trade that brought Pat Seerey to Chicago. The Tribe came out ahead on the deal—Kennedy helped them win a pennant.

Thereafter he became a baseball nomad but returned to the Sox for another go-around on May 30, 1955. Bob's Chicago homecoming was sensational. He won several crucial games down the stretch with his timely hitting.

Kennedy led the Cubs during their infamous "College of Coaches" period, 1963–65, then took over the A's in 1968 following their move to Oakland. He later served as general manager of the Cubs and Astros.

Kennedy, Lloyd Vernon

White Sox: 1934–37
Pitcher
Nickname: Vern
Birthplace: Kansas City, Missouri

B: March 20, 1907
D: January 28, 1993
Batted left, threw right
Ht. 6–0; **Wt.** 175

Kennedy, Lloyd Vernon

White Sox	W	L	Pct	ERA	G	CG	IP	H	BB	K	ShO
1934	0	2	.000	3.72	3	1	19⅓	21	9	7	0
1935	11	11	.500	3.91	31	16	211⅔	211	95	65	2
1936	21	9	.700	4.63	35	20	274⅓	282	147	99	1
1937	14	13	.519	5.09	32	15	221	238	124	114	1
Career	104	132	.441	4.67	344	126	2,025⅔	2,173	1,049	691	7

Vern Kennedy

Sore-armed Vern Kennedy was one of Jimmie Dykes' most successful rehab projects among many. A former winner of the Penn Relays decathlon while attending Central Missouri Teachers College, Kennedy was fighting for a roster spot on Connie Mack's pitching staff when his arm went bad. He was released in spring training but was purchased by the White Sox from the Oklahoma City club of the Texas League after he had won 18 games in 1934. Vern was a September call-up, but he dropped his first two decisions and was unimpressive.

Starting pitching assignments were up for grabs when Dykes gathered the troops for his first spring training session in 1935. Relying on a curve, a naturally sinking fastball, and an occasional knuckler, Kennedy easily cracked the starting rotation now that his arm was strong and healthy. On August 31 he no-hit the Cleveland Indians in Comiskey Park without realizing it until the last man was out. The following year he won 21 games but led the league in issuing walks. Kennedy reverted back to .500 form in 1937. He seemed to lose his composure on the mound and appeared to be suffering from anxiety attacks. At least that was the diagnosis of Jimmie Dykes and the White Sox brain trust, who traded Vern to Detroit with Dixie Walker and Tony Piet for Marv Owen and Gee Walker on December 2, 1937.

Kerr, Dickie

White Sox: 1919–21; 1925
Pitcher
Birthplace: St. Louis, Missouri

B: July 3, 1893
D: May 4, 1963
Batted left, threw left
Ht. 5–7; **Wt.** 155

Kerr, Dickie

White Sox	W	L	Pct	ERA	G	CG	IP	H	BB	K	ShO
1919	13	7	.650	2.88	39	10	212⅓	208	64	79	1
1920	21	9	.700	3.37	45	20	253⅔	266	72	72	3
1921	19	17	.528	4.72	44	25	308⅔	357	96	80	3
1925	0	1	.000	5.15	12	0	36⅔	45	18	4	0
Career	53	34	.609	3.84	140	55	811⅓	876	250	235	7

Dickie Kerr was a journeyman minor leaguer—not the fresh-faced adolescent portrayed in director John Sayles' 1988 screen adaptation of *Eight Men Out*—when Kid Gleason inserted him into the starting rotation in the spring of 1919. Kerr had bounced around the minor leagues for eight seasons before answering the call in Chicago. His professional career began in 1910 with the Paragould team in the short-lived North Eastern Arkansas League. In the next few years Kerr's baseball safari included stopovers in Cairo in the Kentucky-Indiana League; Paris, Texas; Memphis, Tennessee; Fort Worth, Texas; Milwaukee, Wisconsin; and Cleburne, Texas, in the South Central League.

"Wee Richard Kerr, the world's smallest southpaw," as Ring Lardner aptly described him to his *Tribune* following, was inserted into the starting rotation early in the 1919 season through sheer necessity. Red Faber was sidelined by a lingering arm ailment. Joe Benz had retired, and Reb Russell, who had starred in the 1917 championship season, was gone, providing the long-awaited opportunity for Dickie. Gleason used Kerr both as a starter and as an occasional reliever. He won 13 and lost seven that year as the No. 3 man on the staff.

The little southpaw became a symbol of integrity and honesty by steering clear of the gamblers and pitching his heart out in the 1919 World Series. Just before Kerr took the mound to start Game 3, manager Kid Gleason asked him if he knew what was going on with the boys. "Yes, I do," he replied. "But I can't prove it, and all I can do is pitch my best." Kerr shut out the Reds 3–0 and came back to win Game 6, 5–4 in 10 innings.

Dickie won 21 games the next year, and 19 in 1921. He asked for a modest $500 raise after the 1921 season but was rebuffed by Charles Comiskey. Angry and hurt by the Old Roman's stubborn refusal to reward his yeomanlike work for a seventh-place team stripped of its stars, Kerr jumped the ballclub to play "outlaw" ball with a Chicago sandlot team outside of organized baseball. His action led to a suspension by Commissioner Kenesaw Mountain Landis—one that held for four years.

Judge Landis permitted Kerr to return to the White Sox provided that he agreed to play a full season with an "accredited" minor league team, in this case a ballclub in South Bend, Indiana. Dickie accepted these terms, and the suspension was finally lifted in August 1925. Kerr was warmly received by Sox fans on August 15, the occasion of his triumphant South Side homecoming. However, Dickie was ineffective in 12 appearances and was sold to San Francisco of the Pacific Coast League that year.

Dickie coached baseball at Rice Institute in 1928. He managed in the St. Louis Cardinals farm system, where he convinced a sore-armed pitcher named Stan Musial to forgo early retirement and switch to the outfield. In 1959 a grateful Musial purchased a $20,000 home for Dickie Kerr and remained one of his closest friends right up to the moment when cancer claimed the life of the diminutive lefty who always remained true to his convictions.

Diminutive Dickie Kerr, hero of the 1919 World Series

Kittle, Ron

White Sox: 1982–86; 1989–91
Outfielder, first baseman, designated hitter
Nickname: Kitty
Birthplace: Gary, Indiana

B: January 5, 1958
Bats right, throws right
Ht. 6–3; **Wt.** 195

Kittle, Ron

White Sox	G	AB	H	AVG	RBI	R	2B	3B	HR	SA	SB
1982	20	29	7	.241	7	4	2	0	1	.414	0
1983	145	520	132	.254	100	75	19	2	35	.504	8
1984	139	466	100	.215	74	67	15	0	32	.453	3
1985	116	379	87	.230	58	51	12	0	26	.467	1
1986	86	296	63	.213	48	34	11	0	17	.422	2
1989	51	169	51	.302	11	26	10	0	11	.556	0
1990	83	277	68	.245	43	29	14	0	16	.469	0
1991	17	47	9	.191	7	7	0	0	2	.319	0
Career	843	2,708	648	.239	460	356	100	2	176	.473	16

Ron Kittle was employed as a construction worker back home in Indiana when former White Sox great Billy Pierce invited him to Comiskey Park to audition for Bill Veeck. It was at the tail end of the 1978 season. The White Sox and Kittle were down on their luck. The team languished in fifth place with few prospects of moving up. Kittle had been given his release by the Los Angeles Dodgers after undergoing spinal-fusion surgery over the winter.

Veeck was a sucker for a hard-luck story, but as he watched the Gary strong boy jolt seven of 12 pitches into the distant seats of old Comiskey Park that day, he whispered two words: "Sign him!"

Fully recovered from his surgery, Kitty posted big numbers in the minor leagues. He slugged 50 home runs for the Edmonton Trappers in 1982. The late Steve Bilko had been the last player to top the 50 mark in the minors, and that feat occurred way back in 1957. Ronnie was finally ready for prime time.

A throwback to the hard-as-nails, old-time ballplayer, Kittle poled 35 home runs in 1983, his rookie season. He fell just two homers short of equaling Al Rosen's rookie record. Although Kittle struck out at an often alarming rate, he maintained his batting average in the comfortable .250–.260 range, which helped him garner Rookie of the Year honors.

After that promising beginning, the road got tougher. Kittle's average dropped 40 points in 1984. His tape-measure home runs failed to compensate for his inability to advance runners or make contact with the ball at key points in the game. Plagued by injuries in 1985, Kittle balked at returning to the minors for a rehab assignment. General manager Ken Harrelson traded Ronnie to the Yankees on July 29, 1986, for Ron Hassey and Carlos Martinez. He passed through New York and Cleveland before re-signing with the Sox as a free agent in November 1988. And though he gave every indication of returning to his 1983 award-winning form, Kittle was slowed by a herniated disc that required

Ron Kittle (far right): 1983 home run trot

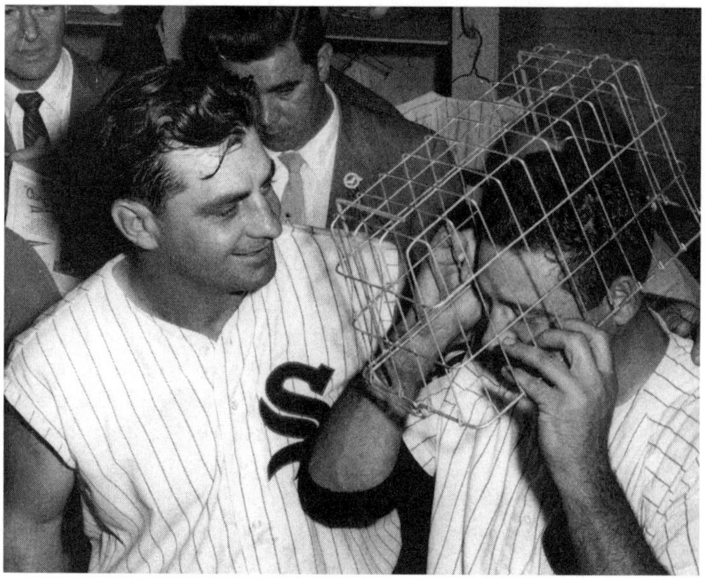

Big Klu makes a "basket case" out of Early Wynn during some 1959 World Series horseplay.

midseason surgery. He opened the 1990 campaign in Chicago but was traded to Baltimore on July 30 for outfielder Phil Bradley.

Kluszewski, Ted

White Sox: 1959–60
Infielder
Nickname: Klu
Birthplace: Argo, Illinois

B: September 10, 1924
D: March 29, 1988
Batted left, threw left
Ht. 6–2; **Wt.** 245

Kluszewski, Ted

White Sox	G	AB	H	AVG	RBI	R	2B	3B	HR	SA	SB
1959	31	101	30	.297	10	11	2	1	2	.396	0
1960	81	181	53	.293	39	20	9	0	5	.425	0
Career	1,718	5,929	1,766	.298	1,028	848	290	29	279	.498	20

Big Klu played less than two seasons with the White Sox, but Chicago fans who savor the memory of the Go-Go era will never forget the hitting clinic that the big man with the bulging biceps put on in Game 1 of the 1959 World Series. Ted Kluszewski powered two home runs and drove in five to lead the Sox to an easy 11–0 rout in Comiskey Park. Klu batted .391 with three homers against Dodgers pitching. His 10 RBIs remain a record for a six-game series.

A former football star at Indiana University, Klu terrorized National League pitchers for nearly a decade before coming to the White Sox in a waiver deal with the Pittsburgh Pirates on August 25, 1959. He wore sleeveless jerseys and was a walking poster boy for Charles Atlas bodybuilding. In his prime, Klu was a formidable power hitter who led the National League in home runs in 1954, topping the century mark in RBIs five consecutive years in the mid-1950s.

Big Ted was playing on borrowed time when the White Sox acquired him as pennant insurance just before they were scheduled to go into Cleveland for a crucial four-game showdown with the second-place Tribe. Klu rapped out 18 singles and was on a torrid hitting pace even before he connected for his first White Sox roundtripper. Though he failed to exhibit the kind of long-ball power that made him famous in the National League, Ted played errorless ball in the field, and the Sox front office had every expectation that he would return to form in 1960. Instead he just got older and was relegated to part-time duty. Left unprotected in the 1961 expansion draft, Klu was drafted by the Los Angeles Angels.

Kolloway, Don

White Sox: 1940–43; 1946–49
Infielder
Nickname: The Blue Island Bird Dog
Birthplace: Posen, Illinois

B: August 4, 1918
D: June 30, 1994
Batted right, threw right
Ht. 6–3; **Wt.** 200

Kolloway, Don

White Sox	G	AB	H	AVG	RBI	R	2B	3B	HR	SA	SB
1940	10	40	9	.225	3	5	1	0	0	.250	1
1941	71	280	76	.271	24	33	8	3	3	.354	11
1942	147	601	164	.273	60	72	40	4	3	.368	16
1943	85	348	75	.216	33	29	14	4	1	.368	16
1946	123	482	135	.280	53	45	23	4	3	.363	14
1947	124	485	135	.278	35	49	25	4	2	.359	11
1948	119	417	114	.273	38	60	14	4	6	.369	2
1949	4	4	0	.000	0	0	0	0	0	.000	0
Career	1,079	3,993	1,081	.271	393	466	180	30	29	.353	76

Don Kolloway was playing American Legion ball and Sunday pickup games in south suburban Blue Island when a scout named John Fitzpatrick discovered and signed the young man for $75. In those days a big-league scout was paid only if his prospect made it to up to the majors. In Kolloway's case, payment was delayed until the September 1940 call-ups when the rosters were expanded. Don's major league debut on September 15 coincided with "Ted Lyons Day" festivities honoring the White Sox great on his 17th season.

Kolloway respected Lyons, but as a boy he had idolized Tigers second baseman Charlie Gehringer, a player he tried to pattern his career after. Nicknamed the Blue Island Bird Dog by Sox radio announcer Bob Elson, Kolloway was shipped to Oklahoma City of the Texas League in the spring of 1940 after losing out to Bob Kennedy for one of the final roster spots. It wasn't until the onset of World War II, when the draft began to deplete the rosters, that Don was able to crack the starting lineup on a permanent basis.

In 1942, his second-best White Sox season, second baseman Kolloway led the league in doubles en route to a .273 average. The fleet-footed Bird Dog was also the last big leaguer to steal second, third, and home in the same inning. He turned the trick in Cleveland on June 28, 1941. Military service interrupted his career in 1943, but he returned to a starting role with the Sox three years later, thus surviving the stigma of being typecast as just another wartime replacement.

Kolloway played well for some very bad White Sox teams in the postwar period, but was shipped to the Detroit Tigers for Earl Rapp on May 7, 1949, as a part of a general housecleaning engineered by new general manager Frank Lane. Kolloway was resentful toward Lane—who had cut his salary from $13,000 to $10,000 and then ordered manager Jack Onslow to play Cass Michaels at second base in 1949. Don was happy to leave the White Sox, but not the city that he called home. After his career ended in 1953, Kolloway returned to Blue Island, where he opened a tavern that became a popular after-hours destination point for visiting major leaguers.

Don Kolloway. Top: the Blue Island Bird Dog; bottom: 1940s aerobics

Konerko, Paul

White Sox: 1999–
Infielder
Birthplace: Providence, Rhode Island

B: March 5, 1976
Bats right, throws right
Ht. 6–3; **Wt.** 205

Konerko, Paul

White Sox	G	AB	H	AVG	RBI	R	2B	3B	HR	SA	SB
1999	142	513	151	.294	81	71	31	4	24	.511	1
2000	143	524	156	.298	97	84	31	1	21	.481	1
2001	156	582	164	.282	99	92	35	0	32	.507	1
2002	151	570	173	.304	104	81	30	0	27	.498	0
2003	137	444	104	.234	65	49	19	0	18	.399	0
2004	155	563	156	.277	117	84	22	0	41	.535	1
2005	158	575	163	.283	100	98	24	0	40	.534	0
2006	152	566	177	.313	113	97	30	0	35	.551	1
2007	151	549	142	.259	90	71	34	0	31	.490	0
2008	122	438	105	.240	62	59	19	1	22	.438	2
2009	152	546	151	.277	88	75	30	1	28	.489	1
2010	149	548	171	.312	111	89	30	0	39	.584	0
Career	1,849	6,642	1,861	.280	1,156	971	339	8	365	.498	8

A White Sox hero for all time and a much-beloved fan favorite, "Paulie" Konerko rose from obscurity to become a clubhouse leader and the catalyst for the team's first championship title run since 1917. "Youthful insurance against an uncertain future" is how *Sun-Times* beat writer Dave Van Dyck described the November 10, 1998, straight-up swap of center fielder Mike Cameron for Konerko, *Baseball America*'s Minor League Player of the Year in 1997, when he was still a Dodgers farm hand showing a lot of promise. The Konerko acquisition was seen as an "insurance policy" at third base, pending Robin Ventura's decision to opt for free agency or remain in Chicago. Ventura was still White Sox property when Paulie came over from Cincinnati, following a disappointing 26-game audition with the Reds in 1998. The other option the Sox considered was moving Konerko to left once Albert Belle was gone, or

Paul Konerko: one of the all-time Sox greats

to position him at first base after Frank Thomas settled in as the full-time designated hitter. In 1998 Greg Norton and Wil Cordero divided time at first, but neither man made a lasting impression. Jerry Manuel needed much more offense on the right side of the infield than the cumulative .253 average they provided. Konerko was the Dodgers' Opening Day first baseman, but he batted only .217 in 75 games and was shipped off to the Reds on July 4 for pitchers Jeff Shaw and Dennys Reyes. After he fared no better in Cincy, the Sox jumped at the chance to reel him in.

"We hate to lose a player with the potential of Mike Cameron, but we feel Konerko is a player who can solidify our lineup for years to come," commented Schueler, who had just pulled off the trade of the decade and arguably one of the best of all time. Manuel tinkered with alternating Konerko between first and third, but scrapped the idea after Paul's successful rookie season in 1999. His rugged good looks made him popular with younger female fans. In recognition, *Chicago Magazine* voted Paulie one of Chicago's "25 Most Eligible Bachelors" for 2000. That year, Konerko led the Sox to a division title and accomplished the rare feat of pounding out two hits in one inning—twice; the first time in Kansas City on July 3, and against the Cardinals on July 15. Making his first All-Star appearance in 2002, Konerko doubled twice in Milwaukee's Miller Park. A disappointing season followed, but Paul earned the *Sporting News* Comeback Player of the Year award in 2004 after narrowly missing out on winning the AL home run title.

When he stroked his 40th home run of the year in the final week of the 2005 season, Konerko joined Frank Thomas as the only other Sox player to wallop 40 or more in a season twice. After the 2005 All-Star break, Paulie took charge and was living large—batting a robust .323 while leading his teammates through a postseason romp of the Red Sox and Angels. Named MVP of the American League Championship Series after slugging two home runs (a total of five for the playoffs and World Series) and driving in seven against Anaheim, Konerko saved his best moment of all for Game 2 of the Series. With his team trailing 4–2 in the seventh inning, and with the bases loaded, Konerko teed off on reliever Chad Qualls's first pitch (a sinker that didn't sink) and deposited the ball in the left-field seats for only the 18th grand slam in World Series history—pandemonium at the Cell on a wet, chilled evening and an unforgettable week for Konerko whose old high school coach, Jerry Dawson, was on hand to see it. Paul and his wife, Jennifer, were celebrating the arrival of their first child, Nicholas, born on the eve of the Series. "It was a rush. It [the grand slam] is the second best feeling I've had all week," he said. "The baby born Tuesday night and that's first for the week; and that [home run] is second. Anybody could have hit it, and it feels like everybody is up there pulling for you and you're pulling for everybody up there. It's hard to explain, other than it's fun. It's kind of an out-of-body thing. But you're looking; it's 4–2 now, it's 6–4, and we can win."

Sadly, the euphoria of a World Series sweep was tempered by the sobering reality of pending free agency and the likelihood of Konerko leaving for greener pastures, as his contract expired with the last out of Game 4. Konerko earned $8.75 million in 2005, the final season of a three-year deal worth $23 million. His electrifying slam was a thrilling moment and a wonderful shot in the arm for pennant-starved Chicago fans who had waited so long and with such great patience. But Konerko's father put a damper on the entire proceeding by telling a reporter that his son's "price just went up," and the White Sox were "no longer eligible for a hometown discount." And so it would be, as another contentious off-season loomed. Paulie was seeking a five-year, $65 million package through his agent, Craig Landis (son of ex-White Sox great Jim Landis), who also represented Jon Garland. He made no promises or guarantees to Reinsdorf regarding his plans for 2006 beyond his expressed desire to "shop the market." In their opening move, the White Sox brain trust (Kenny Williams and Rick Hahn) reportedly offered four years and an estimated $48 million against stronger and more lucrative offers from the deep-pocketed Baltimore Orioles and Los Angeles Angels of Anaheim. However, the drama and suspense ended happily for everyone concerned on November 30, when the Sox trumped the high-bidding Orioles and re-signed Konerko to a five-year, $60 million contract.

"He had a hard time turning down the chance to go back and try to win another championship in Chicago," explained Landis. "He has loyalty to his teammates and to the fans there and feels very wanted, not just by the White Sox organization but by the whole city of Chicago. He felt that that could not be matched in other cities." In a heartwarming gesture that put the finishing touches on an unforgettable season, Konerko presented the chairman with the final-out souvenir ball from Game 4 during the downtown ticker-tape parade on October 28. "Konerko is a superstar, a real superstar," beamed Ozzie Guillen. "He's a superstar because he shows up here every day the same way. He goes by the team rules and is just another guy. That's truly a superstar. He plays the game properly. He plays hard. He doesn't put himself in front of anybody. He's here for the team."

From a point of service, Konerko became the senior member of the team after the departure of Frank Thomas, and with seniority came obligations. Appointed team captain, Paulie was counted on to provide leadership and direction—although he was not quite the same forceful clubhouse presence as Carlton Fisk had been in his 12 years with the club. He accepted this role and became the de facto player spokesman—meeting with the media before nearly every game in front of his locker, patiently answering their questions. Inside the clubhouse his teammates called him "the King"—according him a high level of respect as the senior member of the crew.

In recognition of Konerko's importance to the franchise, White Sox marketing played the intro to "Harvester of Sorrow" by Metallica moments before the start of each game in U.S. Cellular Field. Paulie is a fan of the group. The post-pennant year was his best all-around season, and for the second year in a row he was a runner-up for the prestigious Hank Aaron Award, given to the player with the best all-around performance. With advancing age, his batting average and power numbers tailed off after 2006—but his fielding acumen improved, and steadily Konerko climbed the all-time White Sox charts in nearly every offensive category despite chronic, nagging little injuries and repeated cortisone shots to mend a sore thumb.

There were many fine moments for Paulie's loyal fans to savor in the second half of his White Sox career. On August 14, 2008, Konerko, Jim Thome, Alexei Ramirez, and Juan Uribe tied a major league record by belting four consecutive home runs in one inning during a 9–2 drubbing of the Royals. On April 13, 2009, Konerko and Jermaine Dye went back-to-back in the second inning of a game in Detroit, but here's the kicker: they became the first two players in major league history to clout their 300th career home runs *in the same game.* Konerko was a one-man wrecking crew on July 7, 2009, with three home runs and seven driven in versus Cleveland at U.S. Cellular Field. It was the 12th time a Sox player accomplished the feat—but a first at U.S. Cellular Field. In a long and successful career in Chicago, there were few disappointments for the Sox captain, with the possible exception of one—the failure of the front office to install a Slurpee machine in the Sox clubhouse. "Konerko wanted the Slurpee machine, and that's one of the failures of my career thus far," laughed Brooks Boyer, vice president and chief marketing officer. "I'm sure [White Sox director of conditioning] Allen Thomas appreciates that. We were only going to put diet products in there."

Konerko entered the 2010 season in the final year of his five-year contract and facing free agency. He was 33 years old at this point and slipping past his prime, but the Sox captain was philosophical about advancing age and his future with the club. "They might call tomorrow. They might call in the middle of the season. They might never call. That's very possible," he said. Paulie got out of the gate fast—very uncharacteristic for the veteran slugger through his career. His 11 home runs in April smashed Jim Thome's franchise record of 10, set in 2006, and he went on to post one of his finest seasons—putting up Dick Allen–like numbers and making a strong push for MVP consideration as the burning question of where he would playing loomed ever larger in the final days of the 2010 campaign. The last game of the season was filled with emotion—Paulie received two standing ovations from the crowd. When the game ended, he addressed the throng from the field after 12 seasons of meritorious service to the franchise, but gave no clear indication of his intentions.

Then later, inside the U.S. Cellular Field Conference and Learning Center, he told reporters, "It's kind of one of those things where the door is not shut here by any means. I just want to get that across. I feel almost guilty now. If I was to come back, and this happened a couple of years from now, I feel like no man should get what I got today twice. I felt like, 'Should I buy into it all the way? It's possible, very possible, I could be back.' It's possible I go somewhere else, who knows? I don't walk out of here today going, 'God, I'm done with that city.' I'm totally open to anything, but it has to be right on all accounts."

The King kept his loyal subjects guessing until December 9, when he inked a three-year $37.5 million deal with deferred payments from the Sox. A.J. Pierzynski also reupped but agreed to take less money in order to help his employers clear the decks for a Paulie return. "My goal was to come back when my last contract expired [in 2005]," the Sox captain explained after inking the agreement. "That would give me 10 years plus with one team, and I thought that was really cool, not to mention a chance to win while you're doing it. Now to sit there and say it's going to be 15, that's a nice round number, that's intriguing, as well. I was prepared and had options to do other things. You've got to take all the steps necessary if it goes to the free agent process, and I think I did a pretty good job of that."

Kravec, Ken

White Sox: 1975–80
Pitcher
Birthplace: Cleveland, Ohio
B: July 29, 1951
Bats left, throws left
Ht. 6–2; **Wt.** 185

Kravec, Ken

White Sox	W	L	Pct	ERA	G	CG	IP	H	BB	K	ShO	Sv
1975	0	1	.000	6.23	2	0	4⅓	1	8	1	0	0
1976	1	5	.167	4.86	9	1	50	49	32	38	0	0
1977	11	8	.579	4.10	26	6	167	161	57	125	1	0
1978	11	16	.407	4.08	30	7	203	188	95	154	2	0
1979	15	13	.536	3.74	36	10	250	208	111	132	3	1
1980	3	6	.333	6.91	20	0	82	100	44	37	0	0
Career	43	56	.434	4.46	160	24	859⅓	814	404	557	6	1

For three seasons, Ken Kravec was the best thing going for a pitching-thin White Sox team that at different times was tagged the South Side Hitmen, Veeck's Wrecks, and the Keystone Sox by a cynical, and occasionally amused, Chicago press corps.

In 1980, the downside of the Bill Veeck era, when all of the rent-a-player schemes, bargain basement free agent signings, and nightly promotional gimmickry were adjudged a collective failure and the team was put up for sale, Kravec suggested the Sox were only three players away from turning it around. "They are," the southpaw opined, "the Father, the Son, and the Holy Ghost."

Ken Kravec: top left-hander for Bill Veeck's "Wrecks"

Patience and a good sense of humor were in short supply during these tense, difficult years, and Kravec, an All-American signed out of tiny Ashland College in Ashland, Ohio, in the June 1973 free agency draft by Sox scout Fred Shaffer, represented the best hopes of a decrepit farm system that slipped into a state of chaos and disarray by the time Veeck bought the club from John Allyn in 1975.

In Des Moines, Iowa, where he roomed with teammate Jack Kucek for the better part of two seasons before being called up to Chicago at the end of May 1977, Kravec studied the art of pitching, preparing for his future role in the Sox rotation. When that day came, Ken provided instant pitching relief and was a big factor in the surprising success of the Hitmen. He led the team in strikeouts for the next three years and posted respectable numbers, despite the usual poor fielding of the Keystone Sox.

Kravec was expected to be the No. 1 starter in 1980, but he woke up one morning in spring training complaining of back spasms. He pitched sporadically thereafter, and as the frustrations continued to mount, he said, "I'm not gonna pitch 'til I'm effective, and I'm not going to be effective until I pitch." His peculiar catch-22 logic sent Roland Hemond scurrying to the phones. Kravec was offered as trade bait with the hope of landing an everyday third baseman before the 1980 deadline passed. But the asking price was too steep, and the Tigers, among other teams, took a pass on the left-hander.

Hemond finally found an interested party in the Cubs, who sent the scowling sinkerball pitcher Dennis Lamp to the South Side on March 28, 1981, for Kravec—another vintage, unsung Hemond masterpiece.

Kreevich, Mike

White Sox: 1935–41
Outfielder
Nickname: Iron Mike
Birthplace: Mount Olive, Illinois
B: June 10, 1908
D: April 25, 1994
Batted right, threw right
Ht. 5–7½; **Wt.** 168

Kreevich, Mike

White Sox	G	AB	H	AVG	RBI	R	2B	3B	HR	SA	SB
1935	6	23	10	.435	2	3	2	0	0	.522	1
1936	137	550	169	.307	69	99	32	11	5	.433	10
1937	144	583	176	.302	73	94	29	16	12	.468	10
1938	129	489	145	.297	73	73	26	12	6	.436	13
1939	145	541	175	.323	77	85	30	8	5	.436	23
1940	144	582	154	.265	55	86	27	10	8	.387	15
1941	121	436	101	.255	30	57	19	1	1	.309	7
Career	1,238	4,676	1,321	.283	514	676	221	75	45	.391	115

As a boy growing up in Mount Olive, Illinois, Mike Kreevich accidentally shot off a finger on his left hand in a hunting mishap. Years later, after Mike had established himself as one of the top defensive center fielders in the game, he would often joke about his handicap. After collecting four hits one afternoon, Kreevich held up his three good fingers and a thumb and quipped: I got a handful today. Now four hits for anybody means he got a *Kreevich handful*!

Mike Kreevich

Hardened by his years of shoveling coal into the transport cars deep inside the Mount Olive coal mines, Kreevich fought his way to the major leagues. He appeared in five games for the 1931 Cubs but was returned to the American Association, where he languished at third base for the next four seasons. As a member of the Kansas City Blues, Kreevich pounded Double A pitching at a .345 clip in 1935, which earned him a late-season tryout with the White Sox.

Kreevich was the spotlighted rookie in the 1936 spring training camp. No less an authority than Luke Appling predicted success for the stockily built outfielder who was tabbed to replace Al Simmons: "Boy, this fellow has a lot of power. He's so little, I don't know where he gets it. But he's got it." Kreevich enjoyed a fine rookie season in 1936, batting .307. A year later he paced the junior circuit with 16 triples. Mike became an instant favorite of the Comiskey Park bleacherites, but it was his stellar defensive work that helped land the Sox in the top four for the first time since 1920. With his powerful throwing arm, Mike's bulletlike pegs to Mike Tresh or Luke Sewell nailed some of the league's best runners at the plate. Kreevich collected 18 assists in 1939—a year when he hit a career-high .323.

Unfortunately, Iron Mike could not maintain his average in the 1940s. After a two-year slump, Kreevich and Jack Hallett were traded to the Philadelphia A's for Wally Moses. Harry Grabiner made the swap just 48 hours after Pearl Harbor—December 9, 1941.

Kuhel, Joe

White Sox: 1938–43; 1946–47
First baseman
Birthplace: Cleveland, Ohio

B: June 25, 1906
D: February 26, 1984
Batted left, threw left
Ht. 6–0; **Wt.** 180

Kuhel, Joe

White Sox	G	AB	H	AVG	RBI	R	2B	3B	HR	SA	SB
1938	117	412	110	.267	51	67	27	4	8	.410	9
1939	139	546	164	.300	56	107	24	9	15	.460	18
1940	155	603	169	.280	94	111	28	8	27	.488	12
1941	153	600	150	.250	63	99	39	5	12	.392	20
1942	115	413	103	.249	52	60	14	4	4	.332	22
1943	153	531	113	.213	46	55	21	1	5	.284	14
1946	78	258	68	.264	22	26	9	3	4	.368	4
1947	4	4	0	.000	0	0	0	0	0	.000	0
Career	2,105	7,985	2,212	.277	1,049	1,236	412	111	131	.406	178

In the spring of 1938, Jimmie Dykes' patience with Zeke "the Physique" Bonura had run out. For the fourth year in a row, the power-hitting prima donna held out for $15,000—which was about $3,000 more than the cash-strapped Comiskeys were willing to pay for a first baseman of such limited range. "Get rid of him!" Dykes advised general manager Harry Grabiner. The Sox GM obliged and shipped Bonura to Washington for Joe Kuhel on March 18, 1938. Sox fans were alarmed and outraged. Their beloved "Banana Nose" was gone—in a trade that rang with irony. If Bonura was the worst glove man in the league around first, Kuhel was reputed to be the very best.

Joe Kuhel, fancy fielder

Hobbled by an early season ankle injury in 1938, Kuhel silenced his critics in 1939 with a solid .300 campaign. His manual dexterity around first base won many converts. Not since the days of Jiggs Donahue had there been such an accomplished first baseman on the South Side. He tied for the league lead in fielding during the 1943 season.

Joe Kuhel wasn't all that bad as a hitter, either. He equaled Bonura's record-setting 1934 home run output with 27 roundtrippers in 1940. Kuhel's mark remained a team record until Gus Zernial eclipsed it in 1950. In a July 20, 1941, doubleheader against the Philadelphia A's in Comiskey Park, Kuhel matched a 1905 record held by Hal Chase by recording 17 putouts in the first game and 23 in the second.

Joe was sold to the Washington Senators on November 23, 1943, but was returned to Chicago on June 13, 1946, after manager Ted Lyons put out an emergency call for a first baseman to replace rookie hotshot Murrell Jones, who had suffered a fracture. Kuhel was 40 years old and on his last legs. He closed out his major league career the following April.

Jim Landis' leaping grab of a certain home run in 1962

Landis, Jim

White Sox: 1957–64
Outfielder
Birthplace: Fresno, California

B: March 9, 1934
Bats right, throws right
Ht. 6–1; **Wt.** 180

Landis, Jim

White Sox	G	AB	H	AVG	RBI	R	2B	3B	HR	SA	SB
1957	96	274	58	.212	16	38	11	3	2	.296	14
1958	142	523	145	.277	64	72	23	7	15	.434	19
1959	149	515	140	.272	60	78	26	7	5	.379	20
1960	148	494	125	.253	49	89	25	6	10	.389	23
1961	140	534	151	.283	85	87	18	8	22	.470	19
1962	149	534	122	.228	61	82	21	6	15	.375	19
1963	133	396	89	.225	45	56	6	6	13	.369	8
1964	106	298	62	.208	18	30	8	4	1	.272	5
Career	1,346	4,288	1,061	.247	467	625	169	50	93	.375	139

Graceful as a cat, Jim Landis played center field with style and flair during the second half of the Go-Go era. In the learned opinion of Minnie Minoso, who patrolled left field alongside Jimmy for three of those years, Landis was the very best at his position. He played the center-field bullpen fence in old Comiskey Park like an acrobat and won four Gold Glove awards. His perfectly timed leaps robbed many opposing batters of certain home runs. That is the image of Landis that longtime Sox fans remember best.

Johnny Mostil, who was no stranger to the outfield pastures of Comiskey himself, worked closely with the speedy youngster after Hollis "Sloppy" Thurston, another White Sox 1920s alumnus, inked Landis to his first professional contract in 1952. He received a $2,500 signing bonus and was promised an additional $5,000 if he made it up to the big leagues.

Jim Landis was originally ticketed for third base, but Al Lopez needed a center fielder, and Jimmy seemed to fill the bill. He was a quick learner, but his hitting was another matter. A sucker for outside curves, Landis struggled in the early going. In 1958, his first full season with the Sox, his average hovered below .200, and his strikeout total was alarming, until Nellie Fox advised Jimmy to stop copying his Punch-and-Judy style and concentrate on developing a full, effortless swing. He raised his batting average nearly 100 points in the second half of the '58 campaign and was on his way to a long and productive career.

Jimmy hit a respectable .292 in the 1959 World Series, but he admits that the Sox went into postseason play feeling a little overwhelmed by it all. The Dodgers were a veteran team, seasoned by many World Series appearances. The Sox were just happy to win the pennant. In 1959 Landis received 66 votes from the sportswriters in postseason Most Valuable Player balloting.

Linked in triumph to that unforgettable pennant year, Landis's most satisfying season, ironically, was the otherwise lackluster 1961 campaign when he avoided his usual spring slump to finish with a solid .283 average.

Thereafter things slowly began to unravel. Landis fell out of favor with manager Al Lopez, and was benched in early 1964. Protesting this and other Lopez moves, *Chicago American* sportswriter Bill Gleason sponsored his own "Jim Landis Night" testimonial at Comiskey Park on June 10. Landis fans hung the Sox manager in effigy.

Over the winter Jim's desire to be traded was satisfied when Ed Short dealt him to Kansas City as a part of the big three-team swap that brought Tommy John to Chicago. He was deemed expendable because the Sox had Ken Berry waiting in the wings.

Law, Rudy

White Sox: 1982–85
Outfielder
Nickname: The Lawman
Birthplace: Waco, Texas

B: October 7, 1956
Bats left, throws left
Ht. 6–2; **Wt.** 180

Law, Rudy

White Sox	G	AB	H	AVG	RBI	R	2B	3B	HR	SA	SB
1982	121	336	107	.318	32	55	15	8	3	.438	36
1983	141	501	142	.283	34	95	20	7	3	.369	77
1984	136	487	122	.251	37	68	14	7	6	.345	29
1985	125	390	101	.259	36	62	21	6	4	.374	29
Career	749	2,421	656	.271	198	379	101	37	18	.366	228

Speed at the top and bottom of the lineup was in short supply before Rudy Law and Julio "Juice" Cruz arrived in time to spark the 1983 Winning Ugly title drive. In that storybook season these two speedsters created havoc on the bases, and they set up numerous RBI opportunities for the "big boppers" in the lineup—Carlton Fisk, Greg Luzinski, and Harold Baines.

Rudy Law's boyhood hero was Willie Davis of the Los Angeles Dodgers. When Rudy made his major league debut playing for the Dodgers years later, he wore Davis's No. 3 in honor of the retired outfielder. After joining the White Sox on March 30, 1982, Law was assigned Louie Aparicio's famed No. 11.

It was a portent of things to come because in 1983, Rudy eclipsed Aparicio's 24-year-old team stolen-base record (which Louie shared with Wally Moses), by swiping 77 bases. A share of the credit has to go to Davey Nelson, the White Sox's first-base coach in the early 1980s. "When Rudy first came here, he was getting off with his heels on the ground," Nelson said at the time. "We changed him to the balls of his feet. We've also spread his stance so it's easier for him to rotate on the steal move. Rudy's in full gear by his second step."

Rudy Law

Law, who began his White Sox career as a utility outfielder, broke into the starting lineup in July 1, 1982, and was sensational. His .328 second-half average in the up-and-down 1982 campaign set the stage for the superlatives yet to come.

Rudy shattered Aparicio's stolen-base record in Texas on August 19, 1983—the very same day Rangers manager Doug Rader was quoted in the papers as saying the White Sox were "winning ugly." Propelled by Law's two record-setting thefts, the Sox escaped Texas with a commanding eight-game lead over the rest of the division and never looked back.

Rudy Law led the American League in defense that year, and in the League Championship Series he collected seven hits—more than any other player.

The Sox speedster had regained a large measure of confidence after having it nearly destroyed by his former Dodgers manager, Tommy LaSorda, who put intense pressure on the rookies trying out for a spot on the roster.

As lean and as fast as a whippet when he was healthy, Law's future with the White Sox seemed assured. But in 1984 there occurred a bad omen. The White Sox retired Aparicio's uniform number, forcing Rudy to switch to No. 23, and he was never the same afterward. He pulled a hamstring muscle, lost 32 points on the batting average, and was not the intimidating force on the base paths he had been when the Sox were winning in 1982 and 1983.

The downward slide continued through 1985, another disappointing, injury-riddled season. Rudy played out his option and was picked up by the Kansas City Royals on April 4, 1986. He suffered a cartilage tear and torn ligaments in his right knee early in the season and was out of baseball the following season.

Lee, Carlos

White Sox: 1999–2004
Outfielder
Nickname: El Caballo; C-Lee
Birthplace: Aguadulce, Panama

B: June 20, 1976
Bats right, throws right
Ht. 6–2; **Wt.** 240

Lee, Carlos

White Sox	G	AB	H	AVG	RBI	R	2B	3B	HR	SA	SB
1999	127	492	144	.293	84	66	32	2	16	.463	1
2000	152	572	172	.301	92	107	29	2	24	.484	18
2001	150	558	150	.269	84	75	33	3	24	.468	25
2002	140	492	130	.264	80	82	26	2	26	.484	7
2003	158	623	181	.291	113	100	35	1	31	.499	9
2004	153	591	180	.305	99	103	37	0	31	.525	0
Career	1,797	6,848	1,967	.287	1,192	1,006	404	14	331	.495	118

In six South Side seasons, Carlos Lee did so many things well, supplying consistent power and RBIs to a team that lived and died by the home run. For a big man, he ran the

Carlos Lee: "El Caballo"

bases with surprising skill, and although he was not exactly Gold Glove worthy, El Caballo exhibited good range and was a capable fly chaser in left. In fact, he ran off a streak of 167 errorless games spanning two seasons, 2003–04. Ultimately, what Lee did best was inflict punishment on the Chicago Cubs during the annual interleague showdown with the North Siders. There have been other notable "killers" in Sox history. John Buzhardt was a Yankees killer. Joel Horlen did the same to the Angels throughout the 1960s, and Mark Buehrle is most effective against the Twins. It seemed Carlos May did a number on the Texas Rangers every year. Charlie Maxwell killed the ball on Sundays only, and C-Lee, showing a flair for the dramatic, belted a game-winning grand-slam home run against the Cubbies in the 10th inning of a 7–3 victory on June 8, 2001. It was the first time a player stroked an extra-inning slam in interleague play, including the World Series, and one of two bases-loaded shots he hit against the Cubs during his Sox career. Most of the 46,000 fans (the Sox partisans, at least) jamming U.S. Cellular Field that night were dancing in the aisles. The following season, Lee battered Cubs pitching with three more home runs and a .381 average. For his 2003 encore, his average against the Cubs climbed to .385. Lee's hitting prowess wasn't confined solely to the crosstown series. A year later, in 2004, Carlos shattered Luke Appling's White Sox record 27-game consecutive hitting streak (shared jointly with Albert Belle) with a dramatic 10th-inning double off of Florida's Toby Borland on June 15. It ended at 28 games the next day, but if past history is any indicator, the new team record is likely to withstand the test of time.

Signed through the 2005 season with an option on 2006 that may or may not have been exercised, general manager Kenny Williams was looking to shake up the ballclub when the annual winter meetings convened in Anaheim in December 2004. Ozzie Guillen was not pleased with a perceived lack of aggression on C-Lee's part. The club was looking to improve by shedding salary and an over-reliance on the long-ball in favor of a motion-oriented offense. The fans, fed a daily dose of rumor-mongering by the media, were half-expecting Williams to deliver Randy Johnson to the South Side on a gold plate, but instead the gambling GM traded Lee to the Milwaukee Brewers for second-year man Scott Podsednik, relief pitcher Luis Vizcaino, and rookie throw-in Travis Hinton. The geniuses in the Chicago press corps roasted Williams for "dumping" salary, calling the deal "senseless." *Sun-Times* beat writer Chris De Luca commented: "If Williams doesn't land the front-line starting pitcher he is dreaming of with the sudden riches of losing Lee's contract, this trade could wind up haunting the Sox. Saying Everett, Dye, and Podsednik can replace Lee, Ordonez, and Thomas is laughable." The ultimate Sox basher, Jay Mariotti, tossed this log on the fire: "Oh this makes loads of sense, building a slap-and-tickle team to play 81 games in the most power-friendly ballpark in the majors. Is it me, or is it that crotchety lady in *Major League* running the White Sox?"

Williams knew what he was doing—Mariotti and company did not have a clue. Shedding Lee's $8 million salary freed up the dollars necessary to sign three free agents pivotal to the 2005 championship run: catcher A.J. Pierzynski, outfielder Jermaine Dye, reliever Dustin Hermanson, and a fifth starter in Orlando "El Duque" Hernandez. Essentially, it boiled down to an exchange of Carlos Lee for Podsednik, Vizcaino, Hermanson, Dye, Pierzynski, Hernandez, and a World Series title. C-Lee set the National League on fire in the first half of the 2005 season, then faded. Meanwhile, Scotty Podsednik ignited the White Sox offense by pilfering 59 stolen bases. He was named to the All-Star team on the strength of a write-in campaign organized and sustained by his teammates. Were the White Sox being cheap, according to Mariotti's impossible logic, or was it a case of simply being smarter than their harshest critic?

Lee, Thornton

White Sox: 1937–47
Pitcher
Nickname: Lefty
Birthplace: Sonoma, California

B: September 13, 1906
D: June 9, 1997
Batted left, threw left
Ht. 6–3; **Wt.** 205

Lee, Thornton

White Sox	W	L	Pct	ERA	G	CG	IP	H	BB	K	ShO
1937	12	10	.545	3.52	30	13	204⅔	209	60	80	2
1938	13	12	.520	3.49	33	18	245⅓	252	84	77	1
1939	15	11	.577	4.21	33	15	235	260	70	81	2
1940	12	13	.480	3.47	28	24	228	223	56	87	1
1941	22	11	.667	2.37	35	30	300⅓	258	92	130	3
1942	2	6	.250	3.32	11	6	76	82	31	25	1
1943	5	9	.357	4.18	19	7	127	129	50	35	1
1944	3	9	.250	3.32	11	6	76	82	31	25	0
1945	15	12	.556	2.44	29	19	228⅓	208	76	108	1
1946	2	4	.333	3.53	7	2	43⅓	39	23	23	0
1947	3	7	.300	4.47	21	2	86⅔	86	56	57	1
Career	117	124	.485	3.56	374	155	2,331⅓	2,327	838	937	14

Thornton Lee was a subpar performer for the Cleveland Indians who was getting on in years when Jimmie Dykes and Harry Grabiner expressed an interest in the 31-year-old lefty who traced his run of bad luck to the fact that he had been born on Friday the 13th. The White Sox were in need of a southpaw pitcher, and Lee was available at a bargain-basement price.

To acquire the tall but muscular lefty on December 8, 1936, the Sox traded Jack Salveson, a 21-game winner for the Los Angeles Angels of the Pacific Coast League a year before, to the Washington Senators. Clark Griffith, in turn, dealt veteran Earl Whitehill to Cleveland for the vastly overrated Salveson to complete the trade.

It turned out to be a wonderful deal for both Cleveland and Chicago. Pitching coach Muddy Ruel worked closely with Lee that spring, and he deserves full credit for developing Lefty into one of the premier pitchers of the American League spanning the next four seasons. Jimmie Dykes moved Lee into the starting rotation, where he acquired a reputation as a Yankees killer. In 1937 he beat the Bronx Bombers four times—no small accomplishment in those days. The Yanks won 102 games that year.

Lefty Lee led the American League in complete games and earned run average in 1941, en route to a 22-win season and a $2,500 bonus from the Comiskeys for surpassing 20 victories. Injuries, however, took a toll that seemed to confirm Lefty's old superstitions.

Bone chips in his pitching arm limited him to 19 appearances in 1943. A wrist fracture in July 1944 ended his comeback hopes the next year. In fact, Lee won only 10 games for the Sox in a three-year stretch beginning in 1942. Finally restored to good health in 1945, Lefty won 15 games for the Sox. It was his last really good year before calling it quits in 1948. His son Don Lee broke into the majors with the Detroit Tigers in 1957. Ted Williams claimed the unusual distinction of being the only player to homer off of both father and son.

Thornton Lee

Lemon, Chester

White Sox: 1975–81
Outfielder
Nicknames: Chet; Juice
Birthplace: Jackson, Mississippi

B: February 12, 1955
Bats right, throws right
Ht. 6–0; **Wt.** 190

Lemon, Chester

White Sox	G	AB	H	AVG	RBI	R	2B	3B	HR	SA	SB
1975	9	35	9	.257	1	2	2	0	0	.314	1
1976	132	451	111	.246	38	46	15	5	4	.328	13
1977	150	553	151	.273	67	99	38	4	19	.459	8
1978	105	357	107	.300	55	51	24	6	13	.510	5
1979	148	556	177	.318	86	79	44	2	17	.496	7
1980	147	514	150	.292	51	76	32	6	11	.442	6
1981	94	328	99	.302	50	50	23	6	9	.491	5
Career	1,055	3,721	1,045	.281	469	556	219	35	116	.452	46

Stretching singles into doubles, racing from left field to right to haul down fly balls well out of his range, and of course belly-flopping headlong into first base—Chet Lemon's aggressive style of play was often confused with hot-dogging by the press-box cynics covering the Sox beat during the second Bill Veeck era.

"It's his desire to excel at what he does," Veeck explained, just days after Lemon staged his famous two-day "walkout" in August 1979. "I can't compare Chet to some of the all-time greats like Joe DiMaggio, because frankly he's not there yet. Chet will be one of the great ones when he realizes that he can't throw out every runner at the plate or score the winning run every day."

Chet Lemon was selected by the Oakland A's as their No. 1 draft choice in 1972. His signing represented one of the last great finds of A's owner Charles O. Finley, who built a dynasty and then lost it in a heartbeat.

Chet's infield play was erratic during those first few years, but Sox scouts who charted his progress in the Midwest League were most impressed by his hitting.

The Oakland A's were on the downgrade in 1975, but were still in a position to win a fourth consecutive pennant. The Sox, on the other hand, were unloading their veterans and cutting salaries. These were the circumstances culminating in the June 15, 1975, trade that brought Lemon and pitcher Dave Hamilton to Chicago for Stan Bahnsen and Lee "Skip" Pitlock.

Manager Paul Richards recognized Lemon's intrinsic value as an outfielder. Chet made the switch to center field in the spring of 1976. Under coach Larry Doby's patient instruction, Lemon blossomed into a fine offensive performer a year later. He played an important role in the South Side Hitmen summer of 1977. Chet set new records for chances accepted by an outfielder (524) and for putouts (512), the latter breaking a 1948 record held by Dom DiMaggio of the Red Sox.

Chet Lemon

Lemon was named to the All-Star team in 1978 and 1979. These were his most productive years playing on the South Side. After hitting .300 for the third and final time, Chet was traded to the Detroit Tigers for outfielder Steve Kemp on November 27, 1981—an unfortunate decision by Sox management. Kemp played out his option in 1982 to sign with the Yankees after a so-so season. In the friendly confines of Tiger Stadium Lemon's home run production increased, but his batting average declined.

Loaiza, Esteban

White Sox: 2003–04; 2008
Pitcher
Birthplace: Tijuana, Baja, Mexico

B: December 31, 1971
Bats right, throws right
Ht. 6–4; **Wt.** 190

Loaiza, Esteban

White Sox	W	L	Pct	ERA	G	CG	IP	H	BB	K	ShO	Sv
2003	21	9	.700	2.90	34	1	226⅓	196	56	207	0	0
2004	9	5	.642	4.86	21	2	140⅓	156	71	83	1	0
2008	0	0	.000	3.00	3	0	3	3	0	1	0	0
Career	126	114	.525	4.65	377	14	2,099	2,352	603	1,382	6	1

There is nothing remarkable about Esteban Loaiza's career numbers. He was a journeyman pitcher with a high ERA and a poor hits-to-innings-pitched ratio, who moved around a lot trying to find his groove under a patient manager willing to hand him the ball every four days. The remarkable aspect to the Loaiza story was his wonderful 2003 season under the White Sox sun, when he threw lights-out and narrowly missed out on the Cy Young Award. And then, just like that, he reverted back to the Esteban Loaiza of old, making the rounds from team to team just trying to hang on.

There have been other "flash-in-the-pan" pitchers like this down through the years. Ted Blankenship was the Esteban Loaiza in the pitiful 1920s, but Ted lasted a lot longer on the South Side, whereas Loaiza was gone midway through the second year. A product of the Pittsburgh Pirates organization, the big Mexican right-hander won no more than 11 games in any single season by the time he hooked up with the ballclub as a free agent on January 24, 2003. Written into the starting rotation, Loaiza won the Sox home opener in 2003 and never looked back. He was the first Pale Hose pitcher to lead the league in strikeouts since old Early Wynn back in 1958, and the first since Wynn to start an All-Star Game, this one played in U.S. Cellular Field. On the last day of the season, after Mark Buehrle yielded his final start in order to give his teammate the chance to earn his 21st victory, Loaiza came through and tied Fernando Valenzuela for the most wins by a Mexican pitcher. Loaiza was masterful that day before a silent, but packed house of Royals fans in K.C.'s Kaufmann Stadium. With his cut fastball, he held K.C. hitless through seven and walked off with a 5–1 victory that supplied a happy ending to an entire-career highlight film boiled down to just one season.

Few people in baseball counted on him to match these totals again, and he didn't. His ERA soared to a more familiar

Esteban Loaiza in 2003 form (photo courtesy of Major League Baseball)

range in 2004, and he was no longer counted on as the stopper. The problem seemed to be that the opposing hitters had figured him out the second time through the lineup. Impatient and sensing that Loaiza's 2003 season was one of those baseball aberrations, Kenny Williams did not hesitate to work the angles when the pitching-desperate Yankees called. They offered Jose Contreras—a disappointment in New York—and cash for the veteran Loaiza on July 31, 2004. It was larceny on a grand scale for the White Sox. One of Williams' best all-time trades was quickly finalized. The Yankees were looking to shore up the rotation for the playoff run, but Loaiza couldn't get anyone out. He was wearing a Washington Nationals uniform the following season and Dodgers garb a year after that. Contreras, on the other hand, was World Series–bound.

Locker, Bob

White Sox: 1965–69
Pitcher
Birthplace: George, Iowa

B: March 15, 1938
Bats right, throws right
Ht. 6–3; **Wt.** 200

Locker, Bob

White Sox	W	L	Pct	ERA	G	CG	IP	H	BB	K	ShO	Sv
1965	5	2	.714	3.15	51	0	91⅓	71	30	69	0	2
1966	9	8	.529	2.46	56	0	95	73	23	70	0	12
1967	7	5	.583	209	77	0	124⅔	102	23	80	0	20
1968	5	4	.556	2.29	70	0	90⅓	78	27	62	0	10
1969	2	3	.400	6.55	17	0	22⅓	26	6	15	0	4
Career	57	39	.594	2.76	576	0	878⅔	776	257	577	0	95

Sox GM Ed Short badly miscalculated when he traded sinker-ball specialist Bob Locker to the Seattle Pilots for a washed-up, unconcerned veteran pitcher named Gary "Ding Dong" Bell on June 7, 1969. Locker was coming into his own as one of the American League's top relief pitchers after serving his apprenticeship behind Eddie Fisher and Hoyt Wilhelm in the mid-1960s. His sinker ball was ideally tailored to the contours of old Comiskey—a pitcher's haven. The Locker trade, more than any of the other panic moves Short made during the final years of his fading regime, plunged the Sox deeper into the abyss.

Bob Locker was scouted by Johnny Mostil and signed by the White Sox on June 14, 1960, while he was still enrolled as

Bob Locker

a geology major at Iowa State University. After completing a two-year hitch in the army, Locker settled in as a starting pitcher, but Sox manager Al Lopez recognized that his great sinker ball could be put to better use in the bullpen. Locker's success allowed Short the luxury of trading Eddie Fisher to Baltimore in 1966—a testament to the strength of the White Sox bullpen during those years. In 1967 the lanky Iowan led the AL in appearances. He traced his success to a good work ethic and a daily consumption of bottled honey—nature's essence—which provided him with instant energy.

After leaving Chicago, Bob Locker pitched for the Pilots, Milwaukee Brewers, and Oakland A's before winding up his career with the Cubs in 1975. After baseball, Bob entered the real estate business in Lafayette, California, but he has also devoted much of his time to helping financially strapped old-timers who missed out on the big salaries that came down the road in the late 1970s.

Lollar, John Sherman

White Sox: 1952–63
Catcher
Nickname: Sherm
Birthplace: Durham, Arkansas

B: August 23, 1924
D: September 24, 1977
Batted right, threw right
Ht. 6–0; **Wt.** 185

Lollar, John Sherman

White Sox	G	AB	H	AVG	RBI	R	2B	3B	HR	SA	SB
1952	132	375	90	.240	50	35	15	0	13	.384	1
1953	113	334	96	.287	54	46	19	0	8	.416	1
1954	107	316	77	.244	34	31	13	0	7	.351	0
1955	138	426	111	.261	61	67	13	1	16	.408	2
1956	136	450	132	.293	75	55	28	2	11	.438	2
1957	101	351	90	.256	70	33	11	2	11	.393	2
1958	127	421	115	.273	84	53	16	0	20	.454	2
1959	140	505	134	.265	84	63	22	3	22	.451	4
1960	129	421	106	.252	46	43	23	0	7	.356	2
1961	116	327	95	.282	41	38	10	1	7	.380	0
1962	84	220	59	.268	26	17	12	0	2	.350	1
1963	35	73	17	.233	6	4	4	0	0	.288	0
Career	1,752	5,351	1,415	.264	808	623	244	14	155	.402	20

A large, gentle man from the Missouri Ozarks whose wit and wisdom were a calming influence during the hectic days of the 1959 flag chase, Sherm Lollar is the unsung, forgotten hero of the Go-Go Sox era. Sherm went about his business quietly but with great dignity and precision. He was a slow-footed dead pull hitter on a ballclub that lived and died with a speed-oriented offense. Lollar was a White Sox anomaly.

Unforgiving Sox fans are quick to pin the goat horns on the strapping catcher born in Arkansas for one particular play in Game 2 of the 1959 World Series that turned the tide of victory in favor of the Dodgers. The Sox trailed L.A. 4–2 in the last of the eighth inning. Lollar was perched on first base and representing the tying run when Al Smith drove a Larry Sherry pitch into the left-field gap, easily scoring pinch runner Earl Torgeson, who occupied second at the time. Third-base coach Tony Cuccinello waved Lollar home, but a perfect relay throw from Maury Wills to John Roseboro nailed Sherm by nine feet. He did not even slide. The blame for this baserunning gaffe rested with Cuccinello, not Lollar, who still was forced to take all the heat.

John Sherman Lollar was catching for a company team in Baxter Springs, Kansas, when former White Sox pitcher Tommy Thomas came down to scout the young man for the Baltimore team of the International League. Lollar made the jump from the Kansas sandlots to Baltimore in 1943. He was a standout catcher with the Orioles for three years before Cleveland purchased his contract for $10,000 in 1946. Unable to make suitable use of his skills, Indians owner Bill Veeck traded him to the Yankees in a multiplayer deal. Lollar rode the bench for the next two and a half seasons. After three years in St. Louis as the everyday backstop for the hapless Browns, Lollar was dealt to the White Sox on November 28, 1951, with Al Widmar and Tom Upton for Joe DeMaestri, Gordie Goldsberry, Jim Rivera, Gus Niahros, and Dick Littlefield.

Paul Richards platooned Lollar with a string of second-rate catchers those first few years in Chicago. It wasn't until Marty Marion's arrival in the closing weeks of the 1954 season that Lollar was finally handed a vote of confidence by the incoming manager. Marion told him that he was going to be the White Sox catcher day in and day out.

Named to the American League All-Star team five times in the next six years and awarded the Gold Glove three straight

Sherman Lollar, a big, pleasant man from the Missouri Ozarks

years (1958–1960), Lollar was praised for his mechanical ability, a strong and accurate throwing arm, and his unmatched skill at calling pitches. Sherm paced the AL catchers in fielding in three separate years: 1956, 1960, and 1961. Lollar ranked number 10 on the all-time list for games caught and number one in lifetime fielding percentage (.992), when he was eased into retirement by general manager Ed Short after the 1963 season.

Following his exit from the game as an active player, Lollar managed the Tucson, Arizona, farm team for the Oakland A's. He owned and operated a bowling alley in Springfield, Missouri, when he was struck down by cancer in 1977.

Sherm was an outstanding catcher, and an even finer human being. His baserunning blunder in the 1959 World Series was one of those awful moments in life that very often overshadow the good deeds of the great man.

Lown, Omar

White Sox: 1958–62
Pitcher
Nickname: Turk
Birthplace: Ridgewood, New York

B: May 30, 1924
Bats right, throws right
Ht. 6–0; **Wt.** 185

Lown, Omar

White Sox	W	L	Pct	ERA	G	CG	IP	H	BB	K	ShO	Sv
1958	3	3	.500	3.98	27	0	40⅔	49	28	40	0	8
1959	9	2	.818	2.89	60	0	93⅓	73	42	63	0	15
1960	2	3	.400	3.88	45	0	67⅓	60	34	39	0	5
1961	7	5	.583	2.76	59	0	101	87	35	50	0	11
1962	4	2	.667	3.04	42	0	56⅓	58	25	40	0	6
Career	55	61	.474	4.12	504	10	1,032	933	590	574	1	73

Turk Lown was half of a bullpen dynamic duo that helped nail down the 1959 pennant. The veteran National Leaguer, who was originally signed by the Brooklyn Dodgers in 1941, teamed with Gerry Staley to provide the Sox with the best one-two relief pitching in the league. He answered the call 60 times in 1959 and was nearly as effective as Staley, who set a new team record that year for appearances.

Turk Lown relied on a breaking fastball for much of his career, which included a six-year hitch with the Cubs in the mid-1950s. The rubber-armed Lown was converted to a relief role late in his Cubs career. It was for this reason the Comiskeys expressed an interest in Lown when other teams considered him washed up. The White Sox gambled that Turk had a few good years left in his 34-year-old arm when they purchased his contract from the Cincinnati Reds for $20,000 on June 23, 1958. The first time this ex-Cub faced Mickey Mantle and Ted Williams, he struck them out.

A sore arm reduced his effectiveness in 1960, but Turk rebounded a year later to lead the team in earned run average. After the 1962 season he retired to Pueblo, Colorado, where he worked for the U.S. Postal System as a mail carrier. His eldest son, Craig, pitched in the Sox system for two years but never made it to the big leagues.

Turk Lown

Luzinski, Greg

White Sox: 1981–84
Designated hitter
Nickname: The Bull
Birthplace: Chicago

B: November 22, 1950
Bats right, throws right
Ht. 6–1; **Wt.** 220

Luzinski, Greg

White Sox	G	AB	H	AVG	RBI	R	2B	3B	HR	SA	SB
1981	104	378	100	.265	62	55	15	1	21	.476	0
1982	159	583	170	.292	102	87	37	1	18	.451	1
1983	144	502	128	.255	95	73	26	1	32	.502	2
1984	125	412	98	.238	58	47	13	0	13	.420	5
Career	1,696	6,093	1,697	.279	1,070	833	331	24	294	.485	32

Once an imposing—if plodding—left-field presence for the Philadelphia Phillies during their glory years of the 1970s, Greg Luzinski was a "meat and potatoes" Chicago kind of player whose homecoming was one of the contributing factors that sparked a resurgence of fan interest in the White Sox following the dull 1980 season. The "Bull" was a standout prep athlete at Notre Dame High School in suburban Niles, Illinois, and fit the "working-class" profile Sox fans easily identified with. *Chicago Sun-Times* columnist John

"The Bull" Luzinski, 1981

Schulian wondered if there had ever existed a "bespectacled Polish sumo wrestler."

The power-hitting, overweight Luzinski was sold to the Sox on March 30, 1981, after a falling-out with Phillies management. The designated-hitter role the Sox had in mind for the Bull ideally suited him—and probably prolonged his career. In his first Sox season, Greg broke Oscar Gamble's home run record for designated hitters with 21. Luzinski then shattered his own mark in 1983 by pounding 32 giant-sized home runs—three of which cleared the left-field roof. Only five other Sox players had accomplished the Herculean feat up to that point in time.

Named the AL Designated Hitter of the Year in two of his first three Sox seasons, Luzinski's second-half hitting following a slow start galvanized the offense during the 1983 title run. His overheated, cheerleading exhortations whipped up thousands of Sox fans into a mad frenzy during a downtown pep rally, but they also provided the Baltimore Orioles with bulletin-board material—and added motivation—going into the 1983 playoffs. Luzinski's .133 average in the five-game series compounded the embarrassment. After a disappointing 1984 season, the Bull called it quits.

Lyons, Steve

White Sox: 1986–90
Outfielder, infielder
Nickname: Psycho
Birthplace: Tacoma, Washington

B: June 3, 1960
Bats left, throws left
Ht. 6–3; **Wt.** 190

Lyons, Steve

White Sox	G	AB	H	AVG	RBI	R	2B	3B	HR	SA	SB
1986	42	123	25	.203	6	10	2	1	0	.236	2
1987	76	193	54	.280	19	26	11	1	1	.363	3
1988	146	472	127	.269	45	59	28	3	5	.373	1
1989	140	443	117	.264	50	51	21	3	2	.339	9
1990	94	146	28	.192	11	22	6	1	1	.267	1
Career	853	2,162	545	.252	196	264	100	17	19	.340	42

Nobody is exactly sure which drummer Steve Lyons was marching to during his years with the White Sox. One thing seems certain, looking back on it: life was never dull with the "Psycho" man around to liven up the proceedings.

Voted the most popular player in a citywide poll of Boston Red Sox fans taken during his rookie year in 1985, Lyons impressed Sox GM Ken Harrelson with his hustle and determination. When the time came to accommodate Tom Seaver's desire to finish up his career with an East Coast team, the Hawk negotiated a deal with the Red Sox that landed Lyons in Chicago. The date: June 29, 1986. Things were never quite the same after that in the Sox clubhouse.

Steve Lyons probably wasn't happy about his status as a utility player on a *whole team* of utility players that filled out the Sox roster in the late 1980s, but he made the most of it and always managed to show a good sense of humor. One night Lyons was pulled over by a Chicago police officer on Rush Street. When asked by the officer to produce his home address, Steve listed 324 West 35th Street—Comiskey Park. The cop was not amused, and Lyons received a citation.

Steve Lyons

Then came the infamous night in Detroit when Lyons supplied baseball with one of its most riveting images. Steve slid hard into first base on a close play, then dropped his pants in order to shake the dirt out—before a national television audience. In the midst of all the hype, *Playgirl* magazine offered Steve the chance to pose in a photo spread. Lyons, married with children, graciously declined the offer.

This is how sports fans remember Steve Lyons, but it is not necessarily how Steve Lyons wants to be remembered by the public. He would prefer to be thought of as a versatile utility man and team player who did whatever his manager asked of him, including a two-inning pitching stint against Oakland in 1990. Steve was a hard worker who was the first to show up in the clubhouse on game day and the last one to go home.

Lyons is one of only three players in modern major league history to play all nine positions in games. He continued his antics in Atlanta and then back home in Boston after leaving the White Sox on January 8, 1992.

After retiring from the game in 1993, Psycho was forced to take a job selling hotdogs at the concession stand of an Arizona golf course. He has since launched a more rewarding career as a colorful, sometimes outrageous, commentator on ESPN. Steve authored his autobiography titled—what else?—*Psycho-analysis*.

Lyons, Ted

White Sox: 1923–42; 1946
Pitcher
Nicknames: The Baylor Bearcat; Amar
Birthplace: Lake Charles, Louisiana
B: December 28, 1900
D: July 25, 1986
Batted right and left, threw right
Ht. 5–11; **Wt.** 200

Lyons, Ted

White Sox	W	L	Pct	ERA	G	CG	IP	H	BB	K	ShO
1923	2	1	.667	6.35	9	0	22⅔	30	15	6	0
1924	12	11	.522	4.87	41	12	216⅓	279	72	52	0
1925	21	11	.656	3.26	43	19	262⅔	274	83	45	5
1926	18	16	.529	3.01	39	24	283⅔	268	106	51	3
1927	22	14	.611	2.84	39	30	307⅔	291	67	71	2
1928	15	14	.517	3.98	39	21	240	276	68	60	0
1929	14	20	.412	4.10	37	21	259⅓	276	76	57	1
1930	22	15	.595	3.78	42	29	297⅔	331	57	69	1
1931	4	6	.400	4.01	22	7	101	117	33	16	0
1932	10	15	.400	3.28	33	19	230⅔	243	71	58	1
1933	10	21	.323	4.38	36	14	228	260	74	74	2
1934	11	13	.458	4.87	30	21	205⅓	249	66	53	0
1935	15	8	.652	3.02	23	19	190⅔	194	56	54	3
1936	10	13	.435	5.14	26	15	182	227	45	48	1
1937	12	7	.632	4.15	22	11	169⅓	182	45	45	0
1938	9	11	.450	3.70	23	17	194⅔	238	52	54	1
1939	14	6	.700	2.76	21	16	172⅔	162	26	65	0
1940	12	8	.600	3.24	22	17	186⅓	188	37	72	4
1941	12	10	.545	3.70	22	19	187⅓	199	37	63	2
1942	14	6	.700	2.10	20	20	180⅓	167	26	50	1
1946	1	4	.200	2.32	5	5	42⅔	38	9	10	0
Career	260	230	.531	3.67	594	356	4,161	4,489	1,121	1,073	27

As a unproven college recruit, Ted Lyons pitched to Ty Cobb. In a 23-year, event-filled career, Lyons faced players who spanned the horse-and-buggy era and the jet age. He was a career White Sox player, manager, and scout who might have been recognized as the greatest right-hander of his time if only he had the good fortune of playing with a better ballclub than the post–Black Sox scandal White Sox. His teammates finished in the second division 16 times during Ted's 21 White Sox seasons.

Despite the team's losing ways, Ted Lyons was as graceful in defeat as he was intense in combat. On game day he went into a trancelike meditation. He was a study in self-concentration.

Lyons was enrolled at Baylor University in Waco, Texas, and planning to embark on a legal career when he was thrust into the starting rotation of his college nine. In his first season in the Southwest Conference, Lyons posted a 10–2 record and attracted the attention of Harry Davis, a Philadelphia A's scout sent down by Connie Mack with a generous offer of a tuition-free education at Baylor. Concerned about losing his amateur standing, Lyons politely rebuffed Davis.

Two years passed. "Though my scholastic career was nearing an end and I had decided definitely that I was going into baseball as a business, I hadn't thought about who might sign me until one day Ray 'Cracker' Schalk showed up at our field," Lyons recalled. "I didn't think I showed Cracker much stuff, but several days later when the Sox were playing in San Antonio, I went down and signed a contract."

Ted Lyons

Lyons proceeded directly from the Baylor campus to the big leagues without playing so much as a day of minor league ball. Naive about big-city ways, the young Louisianan paid a St. Louis cabbie $5 for a roundabout 75¢ excursion to the team hotel. He finally caught up with his new teammates the next day—July 2, 1923—making a perfect debut that same afternoon. Lyons retired all three batters in one inning of relief. Two years later Teddy logged the first of three 20-win seasons. Pitching in Washington on September 19, Lyons was one out away from a no-hitter when Bobby Veach laced a hit over first baseman Earl Sheely's head.

A good-hitting pitcher who was often summoned from the bench to swing the lumber in game situations, Lyons became the mainstay of the starting rotation in the mid- to late 1920s. He pitched the only no-hitter of his career against the Boston Red Sox on August 20, 1926, after walking the first two batters of the game. Three years later, on May 24, 1929, he hurled 21 innings of a 6–5 loss to the Tigers. When Ted was plagued by arm miseries for much of the 1931 season, manager Donie Bush pronounced him "arm-dead" and sent him home, his career presumably at an end. Harry Grabiner said nonsense, and ordered him back to Chicago. Teddy would remain an active White Sox player for the next 16 years!

As a result of his brush with early retirement, Lyons added a knuckleball pitch to his repertoire. As the decade wore on, he became an even more effective pitcher—his mound appearances were limited to Sundays only beginning in 1939. The anticipation of seeing Teddy pitch the first game of the traditional Sabbath doubleheader unwittingly bolstered Sox attendance, and it guaranteed a restful afternoon for manager Jimmie Dykes' pitching reserves. In 1942 he completed all 20 of his starting assignments. For his career, Lyons completed 74 percent of all his starts, ranking close behind Walter Johnson and Christy Mathewson in that category. "We were expected to go nine innings whenever we went out there," he said.

Sox management honored Lyons with two testimonial days while he was still an active player, the first coming on August 26, 1933; the second, September 15, 1940. A crowd of 39,191 turned out for the second Lyons Day to celebrate Ted's good fortune. He received a new car and $1,800 in cash—$100 for each of his first 18 seasons. It was a Sunday ...naturally.

After completing a four-year hitch in the U.S. Marine Corps, Lyons returned to the Sox in 1946, winding up a long and meritorious career with his 260th and final White Sox victory on April 28 against St. Louis. It was his 28th complete game in a row.

Ted removed his name from the roster on May 26—hours after replacing Jimmie Dykes as manager of the Sox. Lyons was the popular, sentimental choice of the fans, Mrs. Grace Comiskey, and sportswriter Gene Kessler, but after a flurry of early success, it was clear that the job of building a winning ballclub from a ragtag collection of returning war veterans and untested rookies was beyond his ability. After two disastrous seasons, Lyons resigned in favor of Jack Onslow. Teddy served as a Detroit Tigers pitching coach for the next three years.

Ted Lyons was inducted into baseball's Hall of Fame in 1955, but his role in White Sox affairs was not limited solely to the history books. As a roving scout in the 1950s and 1960s he signed outfielder Ken Berry and pitcher Joel Horlen to White Sox contracts, among many others.

A lifelong bachelor, Ted Lyons retired from baseball in 1966 to manage his sister's Louisiana rice plantation. In his declining years Lyons rarely ventured outside of his home. When Jerry Reinsdorf and Chuck Comiskey tried to persuade him to return to Chicago in 1983 to participate in the festivities of All-Star week, Lyons said no. His eyesight had deteriorated, and he was self-conscious about his impairment. Besides, baseball, and all of its attending glory, was already behind him. Lyons died in a nursing home, all but forgotten on July 25, 1986.

Maltzberger, Gordon

White Sox: 1943–44; 1946–47
Pitcher
Birthplace: Utopia, Texas

B: September 4, 1912
D: December 11, 1974
Batted right, threw right
Ht. 6–0; **Wt.** 170

Maltzberger, Gordon

White Sox	W	L	Pct	ERA	G	CG	IP	H	BB	K	ShO	Sv
1943	7	4	.636	2.46	37	0	98⅔	86	24	48	0	14
1944	10	5	.667	2.96	46	0	91⅓	81	19	49	0	12
1946	2	0	1.000	1.59	19	0	39⅔	30	6	17	0	2
1947	1	4	.200	3.39	33	0	63⅔	61	25	22	0	5
Career	20	13	.606	2.70	135	0	293⅓	258	74	136	0	33

Gordon Maltzberger

There were 14 Maltzberger children but only one made it to the big leagues. That was Gordy, the 13th child born to a Texas farm wife.

The slim, harmonica-playing right-hander knocked around the Texas League and the Pacific Coast League in the mid-1930s with little success.

Gordy moved on to Atlanta, then Knoxville, to New Orleans, next to Jackson, Mississippi, and finally to Dallas in 1941. "I was always being sold in midseason. I guess I am a slow starter," the Texan drawled. Maltzberger finally caught a break when the talent-shorn White Sox purchased his contract from Shreveport, Louisiana, on February 1, 1942, for $6,000. It was another in a long line of Jimmie Dykes' "bargain basement" finds.

Jimmie Dykes sent the rubber-armed righty to the bullpen, where he excelled as the American League's most effective reliever for the next two years. Possessing pinpoint control and a sharp breaking ball, Gordy paced the American League in saves and appearances in 1944 en route to a 10–5 record, which included a string of seven relief wins in a row. The next year he was drafted.

Maltzberger was something of a baseball anomaly in those days. He wore eyeglasses—the result of a 1934 automobile accident that required two stitches to repair one of his eyeballs. There just weren't many players who sported glasses in that era. But the White Sox, not surprisingly, carried three on the roster—Gordy, Bill Dietrich, and Thurman Tucker.

Long after his abbreviated wartime career ended, Maltzberger rejoined the White Sox organization in 1965 as manager of the Double A affiliate in Lynchburg, Virginia. He was the top contender to succeed Don Gutteridge as the next White Sox manager in 1971, but was bypassed at the 11th hour in favor of a younger man—Chuck Tanner.

Martin, J.C.

White Sox: 1959–67
Catcher
Birthplace: Axton, Virginia

B: December 13, 1936
Bats left, throws right
Ht. 6–2; **Wt.** 188

Martin, J. C.

White Sox	G	AB	H	AVG	RBI	R	2B	3B	HR	SA	SB
1959	3	4	1	.250	1	0	0	0	0	.250	0
1960	4	20	2	.100	2	0	1	0	0	.150	0
1961	110	274	63	.230	32	26	8	3	5	.336	1
1962	18	26	2	.077	2	0	0	0	0	.077	0
1963	105	259	53	.205	28	25	11	1	5	.313	0
1964	122	294	58	.197	22	23	10	1	4	.279	0
1965	119	230	60	.261	21	21	12	0	2	.339	2
1966	67	157	40	.255	20	13	5	3	2	.363	0
1967	101	252	59	.234	22	22	12	1	4	.337	4
Career	905	2,189	487	.222	230	189	82	32	32	.315	9

Originally a first baseman when he signed with the White Sox in 1956, J.C. Martin was switched to third because of the desperate need for a reliable glove at the hot corner. Martin's sure hands and agility impressed his minor league coaches at San Diego in 1960. Unfortunately, he could not hit a lick. J.C.'s poor showing convinced the sharpest thinkers in the organization to switch him to catcher. Sherm Lollar was getting on in years. Earl Battey had just been traded to Washington. The big-league ballclub desperately needed a catcher before time ran out, and Martin seemed to be the best bet.

J.C. learned his craft from the very best in the organization. Les Moss taught him the rudimentary skills at Savannah in the Sally League. Sherm Lollar was a great help to him those few years in Chicago, and later on he roomed with Smoky Burgess on the road.

Martin caught the majority of White Sox games from 1963 to 1967, but in the desperate search for a backstop who could also contribute to the offense, manager Al Lopez and his successor Eddie Stanky rotated J.C. with Camilo Carreon, John Romano, Gerry McNertney, and Duane Josephson behind the plate. Martin was the best defensive catcher in the bunch. He set an American League record on June 23, 1963, at Cleveland by participating in three double plays. There was no one better at handling Hoyt Wilhelm's knuckleball than Martin. He imparted his knowledge to rookie Ed Herrmann, who handled Wilbur Wood's knuckler with equal effectiveness a few years later.

J.C. was sent to the Mets as compensation for the acquisition of Ken Boyer in July 1967. He delivered key hits for the "Amazin' Mets" during their charge toward a 1969 championship and was a World Series hero that year. In 1975 Martin teamed with Harry Caray in the White Sox TV broadcast booth, but his slow southern drawl and obvious discomfort behind the microphone doomed the experiment to failure.

J. C. Martin

May, Carlos

White Sox: 1968–76
Outfielder
Birthplace: Birmingham, Alabama

B: May 17, 1948
Bats left, throws right
Ht. 5–11; **Wt.** 200

May, Carlos

White Sox	G	AB	H	AVG	RBI	R	2B	3B	HR	SA	SB
1968	17	67	12	.179	1	4	1	0	0	.194	0
1969	100	367	103	.281	62	62	18	2	18	.488	1
1970	150	555	158	.285	68	83	28	4	12	.414	12
1971	141	500	147	.294	70	64	21	7	7	.406	16
1972	148	523	161	.308	68	83	26	3	12	.438	23
1973	149	553	148	.268	96	61	20	0	20	.412	8
1974	149	551	137	.249	58	66	19	2	8	.334	8
1975	128	454	123	.271	53	55	19	2	8	.374	12
1976	20	63	11	.175	3	7	2	0	0	.206	0
Career	1,165	4,120	1,127	.274	536	544	172	23	90	.392	85

Carlos May is probably the only major leaguer to wear his name and birth date on the back of his uniform—May 17. This little bit of vanity did not diminish May's popularity with the left-field grandstand fans in Comiskey Park, who proclaimed him "King" after the stockily built youngster homered twice against Kansas City pitching on Opening Day, 1969.

May was selected by Walt Widmayer and Sam Hairston as their No. 1 pick in the 1965 draft. He seemed a shoo-in for 1969 Rookie of the Year honors when his season was interrupted by a career-threatening injury. While on duty with the marine reserves in Camp Pendleton, California, May blew off the tip of his right thumb when a mortar unit misfired as he was swabbing it after firing. At the time he was hitting a solid .281 with 18 home runs.

May showed determination through several painful skin-graft operations. After he was released from the military hospital, Carlos spent the off-season regaining his strength at the Illinois Institute of Technology. He made a courageous comeback in 1970, and while never matching the numbers that his older brother Lee posted with the Astros and Reds, Carlos was always a good contact hitter through the mid-1970s—especially against the Texas Rangers. In his 1972 All-Star season, May feasted on Rangers pitching to the tune of .510.

Often criticized for lazy, indifferent outfield play, May was put on the trading block after Wilbur Wood shattered his kneecap a month into the 1976 season. Desperate for pitching help, Roland Hemond dealt Carlos to the Yankees for Ken Brett and outfielder Rich Coggins on May 18, 1976.

Carlos retired from baseball after the 1977 season.

Carlos suffered many personal misfortunes during his professional career. Following the conclusion of one of the annual father-son games played in old Comiskey Park in the early 1970s, his estranged wife exited the ballpark—and permanently walked out of her husband's life with their child in hand. She left no forwarding address or the slightest clue as to her intentions. May engaged private detectives and exhausted his resources over a period of years trying to track them down, but after more than 30 years, he is no closer to finding his son than he was back then. The boy is a grown man now, and Carlos does not even know what he looks like. The setback is compounded by bad business decisions. With only nine years of service in the big leagues (playing in Japan at the end of his career was an ill-advised move and a costly mistake), Carlos is ineligible for pension benefits and has worked as a postal worker at Chicago's downtown branch in order to make ends meet while making occasional celebrity appearances for the White Sox at various charity and fan-related events.

Carlos May

McCraw, Tommy

White Sox: 1963–70
Infielder
Birthplace: Malvern, Arkansas

B: November 21, 1940
Bats left, throws left
Ht. 6–0; **Wt.** 183

McCraw, Tommy

White Sox	G	AB	H	AVG	RBI	R	2B	3B	HR	SA	SB
1963	102	280	71	.254	33	38	11	3	6	.379	15
1964	125	368	96	.261	36	47	11	5	6	.367	15
1965	133	273	65	.238	21	38	12	1	5	.344	12
1966	151	389	89	.229	48	49	16	4	5	.329	20
1967	125	453	107	.236	45	55	18	3	11	.362	24
1968	136	477	112	.235	44	51	16	12	9	.375	20
1969	93	240	62	.258	25	21	12	2	2	.350	1
1970	129	332	73	.220	31	39	11	2	6	.319	12
Career	1,468	3,956	972	.246	404	484	150	42	75	.362	143

Tommy McCraw

By the time Tommy McCraw learned how to a hit a baseball with authority, it was too late to salvage his career. Ted Williams, his 1971 manager in Washington, convinced Tommy his problems were all in his head. What McCraw learned from Williams served him well in the early 1980s as the hitting coach for the Cleveland Indians. Tommy was regarded as one of the finest hitting theoreticians in the game.

Before that time, McCraw was a very ordinary batsman blessed with abundant speed and good range around the first-base bag. He won the 1962 American Association batting title and made the jump to the White Sox on June 4, 1963, after Joe Cunningham shattered his collarbone. Tommy's big-league debut fulfilled a prophecy. In his last game with Indianapolis just before his call-up, a leather-lunged fan in the stands yelled across the field, "C'mon, McCraw! Get a base hit! Cunningham might break his leg!"

Tommy struggled with his batting average for most of his seven seasons in a Chicago uniform. His big moment at the plate occurred against the Minnesota Twins on May 24, 1967, when he homered three consecutive times off Jim Kaat. He narrowly missed a fourth when his long blast backed the Twins' right fielder up to the base of the wall in old Metropolitan Stadium. Had he not bailed out on the pitch, Tommy might have cracked the record books. As it turned out, he made baseball history a year later by committing three errors in one inning against the Yankees on May 3, 1968, to tie a major league record.

Tommy was traded to the Senators on March 29, 1971, for outfielder Ed Stroud. In 2010 McCraw completed his 35th season as a hitting coach—his most recent tour of duty was with the New York Mets' Florida Gulf Coast team at Tradition Field in Port St. Lucie, managed by another former 1960s White Sox player, Sandy Alomar Sr.

McDowell, Jack

White Sox: 1987–88; 1990–94
Pitcher
Nickname: Black Jack
Birthplace: Van Nuys, California

B: January 16, 1966
Bats right, throws right
Ht. 6–5; **Wt.** 188

McDowell, Jack

White Sox	W	L	Pct	ERA	G	CG	IP	H	BB	K	ShO
1987	3	0	1.000	1.93	4	0	28	16	6	15	0
1988	5	10	.333	3.97	26	1	158⅔	147	68	84	0
1990	14	9	.609	3.82	33	4	205	189	77	165	0
1991	17	10	.630	3.41	35	15	253⅔	212	82	191	3
1992	20	10	.667	3.18	34	13	260⅔	247	75	178	1
1993	22	10	.688	3.37	34	10	256⅔	261	69	158	4
1994	10	9	.526	3.73	25	6	181	186	42	127	2
Career	119	77	.607	3.73	251	62	1,753⅓	1,683	564	1,216	13

The White Sox' angriest rebel shed no tears for the fans of Chicago when it was announced on December 14, 1994, that Jack McDowell was on his way to New York for outfielder Lyle Mouton and a minor league pitcher named Keith Heberling. For seven years, "Black Jack" earned the admiration of Chicago's Generation X baseball fans who admired his rebellion against authority and his skill at throwing a baseball.

McDowell was an intimidating presence on the mound who relished a good fight. He battled Sox chairman Jerry Reinsdorf at contract time, and he stared down Dave Stewart when the veteran Oakland pitcher suggested in 1990 that Black Jack wasn't fit to carry his jockstrap.

Jack McDowell was selected by Larry Himes in the first round of the June 1987 free agent draft after leading his Stanford team to the College World Series. He opened his major league career with 13 consecutive scoreless innings, but a strained right hip muscle exiled him to the minors in 1989.

A scowling, gritty competitor, McDowell emerged as the ace of the staff in 1990. In 1991 he became the first Sox pitcher since Billy Pierce to lead the American League in complete games. A year later he finished second to Dave Eckersley for the Cy Young, and again led the league in complete games. The protracted cold war with Reinsdorf began in earnest around this same time, when the Sox refused to reward him with a multiyear contract after Robin Ventura and Frank Thomas were offered long-term arrangements. "I'm all for Frank and Robin," Jack snarled. "They're great players. I hope they get what they deserve. What do I get? More grief!"

There were two sides to the story, of course. Sox management was peeved by McDowell's endless carping to the press and his after-hours antics. Jack was hammered for six runs in a 1991 game against Baltimore a few hours after performing with his grunge rock band V.I.E.W. at a live concert at a Chicago street festival. "My music has no effect on my baseball," he answered.

McDowell won the Cy Young Award in 1993, but he was also involved in a bar fight in New Orleans' French Quarter

Jack McDowell

with his buddy Eddie Vedder of the rock band Pearl Jam. Jack was knocked cold. The same could be said of McDowell's performance in the 1993 American League Championship Series against Toronto.

Before the strike-shortened 1994 season began, McDowell announced to the press that there was absolutely "no chance" that he would return to Chicago in 1995 after an arbitrator ruled in favor of the White Sox in the latest salary showdown with Reinsdorf. It marked the second time in three years that Jack had come up a loser in arbitration.

Sullen and uncommunicative, McDowell dropped seven of his first nine decisions. Just when his market value seemed to be diminishing, the Sox ace turned it around. He lowered his ERA by three runs and won eight of his last 10 to finish the year at 10–9.

McDowell was traded to the Yankees for two minor league prospects on December 14, 1994, eight days before becoming an unrestricted free agent. He played just one year in the Bronx, then signed as a free agent with the Cleveland Indians. Unhappy Jack was content at last on the Lake Erie shoreline.

McMullin, Fred

White Sox: 1916–20
Third baseman
Birthplace: Scammon, Kansas

B: October 13, 1891
D: November 21, 1952
Batted right, threw right
Ht. 5–10; **Wt.** 165

McMullin, Fred

White Sox	G	AB	H	AVG	RBI	R	2B	3B	HR	SA	SB
1916	68	187	48	.257	10	8	3	0	0	.273	9
1917	59	194	46	.237	12	35	2	1	0	.258	9
1918	70	235	65	.277	16	32	7	0	1	.319	7
1919	60	170	50	.294	19	31	8	4	0	.388	4
1920	46	127	25	.197	13	14	1	4	0	.268	1
Career	304	914	234	.256	70	120	21	9	1	.302	30

As a spot starter and reserve infielder from the late teens through the end of the Black Sox period, Fred McMullin provided the Sox with valuable bench help, particularly when the regulars were sidelined by injury. The White Sox purchased Freddie's contract from the Los Angeles Angels of the Pacific Coast League in September 1915. There were few opportunities available to McMullin with this star-studded ballclub, but when the time came, Freddy came through.

At a defining moment late in the 1917 pennant race, Buck Weaver broke his finger in Washington and was sidelined for the balance of the season. McMullin filled in for Weaver through the World Series and could not be dislodged from the hot corner until the following season.

Fred McMullin: guilt by association

McMullin was incidental to the plot to throw the 1919 World Series. He happened to eavesdrop on a locker-room conversation between Chick Gandil and Swede Risberg, and demanded to be let in on the conspiracy. For the Series, McMullin collected one hit in two pinch-hitting appearances—and a $5,000 payoff.

It was curious and rather ironic that McMullin should cast his fate with the gamblers. He had been arrested by the Boston Police on June 16, 1917, with Buck Weaver after the pair engaged in a fistfight with ballpark gamblers who had stormed the field in order to induce umpire Tom Connolly to declare a forfeit.

Melton, Bill

White Sox: 1968–75
Third baseman, outfielder
Birthplace: Gulfport, Mississippi

B: July 7, 1945
Bats right, throws right
Ht. 6–2; **Wt.** 200

Melton, Bill

White Sox	G	AB	H	AVG	RBI	R	2B	3B	HR	SA	SB
1968	34	109	29	.266	16	5	8	0	2	.394	1
1969	157	556	142	.255	87	67	26	2	23	.433	1
1970	141	514	135	.263	96	74	15	1	33	.488	2
1971	150	543	146	.269	86	72	18	2	33	.492	3
1972	57	208	51	.245	30	22	5	0	7	.370	1
1973	152	561	155	.276	87	85	29	1	20	.439	4
1974	136	495	120	.242	63	63	17	0	21	.404	5
1975	149	512	123	.240	70	62	16	0	15	.328	2
Career	1,144	3,972	1,004	.253	591	498	162	9	160	.419	23

Seventy-one seasons passed before the White Sox produced their first American League home run champion. Going into the final day of the 1971 season, Bill Melton was involved in a three-way tie with Reggie Jackson and Norm Cash for the AL home run lead. Each player had 32—an unusually low sum among the league's power-hitting elite.

Manager Chuck Tanner afforded Melton every chance to win the title by batting him first in the lineup against Bill Parsons of the Milwaukee Brewers, a low-ball pitcher. In the third inning the slugging Sox third baseman crushed a line drive toward left-center field. When the ball settled into the lower left-field grandstands, Melton carved his name into the Sox record books. Instead of being rewarded with a much-deserved salary increase or a special cash bonus for this breakthrough moment in team history, Sox GM Roland Hemond presented the Sox slugger with a gold crown to wear on his head—a lighthearted, whimsical gesture to be sure. But, as the American League's new home run king, Melton would have much preferred something a little more substantial than a fake crown as his fair and just reward. The crown was later donated to the White Sox archives, where it was put on display. Bill's achievement erased earlier, more painful memories of the 1970 season when he lost a routine pop fly in the lights of Baltimore's Memorial Stadium and broke his nose. After Bill had committed 10 errors in his first 24 games, manager Don Gutteridge decided that for the good of the team—and Melton's personal safety—he would play right field. Chuck Tanner put him back at third base after taking over for Gutteridge in the waning days of the 1970 season.

Tanner taught Melton a shuffling technique that had helped turn Eddie Mathews into a good-fielding third sacker after Mathews experienced a similar set of problems early in his career. "Melton was sort of glued there at third base," Tanner explained. "He was flat-footed just like Mathews was when he came up with the Braves. They got Mathews to move a little bit as the pitch was delivered, take little steps just barely inching forward. And that's what we got Melton to do." Thereafter, Bill's infield play improved by slow, sometimes painful degrees.

Bill Melton was never in the Brooks Robinson class, but he worked hard at his craft, and he managed to surpass the Hall of Fame Oriole third baseman in fielding percentage for the 1971 season. Unfortunately, Bill seemed to take the sarcastic barbs of TV broadcaster Harry Caray to heart, and his play suffered as a consequence.

Melton was signed by scouts Hollis Thurston and Dock Bennett in 1964 after he had starred in football at Citrus College in California. Summoned to the majors in September 1968, Bill replaced the slumping Pete Ward as the everyday third baseman. Ultimately he became the first bona fide White Sox long-ball hitter since Roy Sievers challenged the team home run record in 1960 and 1961. But it was Melton and not Sievers who finally cracked the seemingly impenetrable 30-home-run plateau in 1970 when he whacked 33 long ones to eclipse the team record of 29 held jointly by Gus Zernial and Eddie Robinson.

Bill's career took an abrupt U-turn in the winter of 1971 when he fell off of the roof of his garage. He underwent surgery for a ruptured disc, forcing him to miss all but 57 games of the 1972 season. The freakish injury probably cost the Sox the division title.

The Sox front office awarded Bill Melton a crown for winning the 1971 home run title. He would have much preferred a raise or a bonus.

The next few years were the down times. The ballclub played poorly. Harry Caray's tell-it-like-he-sees-it repartee made him a bigger star than the players on the field. And Melton, more than of the other players on the team, took exception. The two men nearly came to blows one night in Milwaukee's Marc Plaza Hotel.

Bill Veeck might have kept Bill Melton on the team in 1976, but he could not afford to pay both his salary and Wilbur Wood's. Forced to choose between the two veterans, Veeck dealt Melton and pitcher Steve Dunning to the Angels on December 11, 1975, for Jim Spencer and Morris Nettles. Bill's career ended in Cleveland two years later. Melton was employed in the White Sox marketing and promotions department before launching his broadcasting career in 1996 as a color analyst on the Sox radio and television network.

Hank Bauer slides under Cass Michaels, May 21, 1949.

Michaels, Cass (Casimir Kwietniewski)

White Sox: 1943–50; 1954
Infielder
Birthplace: Detroit, Michigan

B: March 4, 1926
D: November 12, 1982
Batted right, threw right
Ht. 5–11; **Wt.** 175

Michaels, Cass

White Sox	G	AB	H	AVG	RBI	R	2B	3B	HR	SA	SB
1943	2	7	0	.000	0	0	0	0	0	.000	0
1944	27	68	12	.176	5	4	4	1	0	.265	0
1945	129	445	109	.245	54	47	8	5	2	.299	8
1946	91	291	75	.258	22	37	8	0	1	.296	9
1947	110	355	97	.273	34	31	15	4	3	.363	10
1948	145	484	120	.248	56	47	12	6	5	.329	8
1949	154	561	173	.308	83	73	27	9	6	.421	5
1950	36	138	43	.312	19	21	6	3	4	.486	0
1954	101	282	74	.262	44	35	13	2	7	.397	10
Career	1,288	4,367	1,142	.262	501	508	147	46	53	.353	64

Seventeen-year-old rookie hotshot Casimir Eugene Kwietniewski jumped from American Legion ball directly into the big leagues in 1943, on the strength of a blistering .608 batting average. Finding players to fill out a roster during wartime was a problem for every team, but in Kwietniewski the Sox believed they had uncovered a future star—and Luke Appling's replacement at shortstop. As it turned out, Michaels was All-Star material. It just took six years and a lot of maturing in order for him to live up to his potential.

"When he first came up, we had some fellas on the Sox who were don't-give-a-damn guys, and that had an effect on him," coach Bing Miller recalled. Kwietniewski roomed with Luke Appling on the road, and the crusty old veteran taught the kid some valuable lessons in responsibility.

The fair-haired Kwietniewski changed his name *and* his position after the war. Henceforth, *Cass Michaels* was the second baseman after Luke Appling returned from the service to resume his shortstop duties. Michaels played all 154 games in 1949, hit a career-high .308, and made the All-Star team despite frequent run-ins with his manager, Jack Onslow. Michaels was traded to Washington for Eddie Robinson on May 31, 1950, and was replaced at second base by Nellie Fox. It was a daring maneuver on Frank Lane's part, but the Sox GM had every expectation that Nellie could fill the bill, and he did.

After collecting his 1,000th career hit in Comiskey Park on June 11, 1953, as a member of the Philadelphia A's, Cass was reacquired by Lane as bench help on December 8. The well-traveled veteran pulled the pin after the 1954 season in order to accept a job as a White Sox scout.

Minoso, Orestes

White Sox: 1951–57; 1960–61; 1964; 1976; 1980
Outfielder, third baseman, designated hitter
Nicknames: Minnie; the Cuban Comet

Birthplace: Havana, Cuba
B: November 29, 1922
Bats right, throws right
Ht. 5–10; **Wt.** 175

Minoso, Orestes

White Sox	G	AB	H	AVG	RBI	R	2B	3B	HR	SA	SB
1951	138	516	167	.324	74	109	32	14	10	.498	31
1952	147	569	160	.281	61	96	24	9	13	.424	22
1953	157	556	174	.313	104	104	24	8	15	.466	25
1954	153	568	182	.320	116	119	29	18	19	.535	18
1955	139	517	149	.288	70	79	26	7	10	.424	19
1956	151	545	172	.316	88	106	29	11	21	.525	12
1957	153	568	176	.310	103	96	36	5	12	.454	18
1960	154	591	184	.311	105	89	32	4	20	.481	17
1961	152	540	151	.280	82	91	28	3	14	.420	9
1964	30	31	7	.226	5	4	0	0	1	.323	0
1976	3	8	1	.125	0	0	0	0	0	.125	0
1980	2	2	0	.000	0	0	0	0	0	.000	0
Career	1,841	6,579	1,963	.298	1,023	1,136	336	83	186	.459	205

By any other name, Saturnino Orestes Arrieta Armas Minoso is "Mr. White Sox." Jerry Reinsdorf, who was a Dodgers fan growing up in Brooklyn when Minnie Minoso cracked the team color barrier on May 1, 1951, decided that he should be accorded the special honor because no other player symbolizes the spirit of the White Sox better than No. 9. He is baseball's six-decade legend, and there are few White Sox fans who would take issue with Jerry's accolade.

Minnie was the essence of an era of Sox history that passed much too quickly. His entire career represents a triumph over the barriers of language, color, and ethnicity in a nation just coming to grips with the deeper meaning of the civil rights movement.

As a boy growing up in rural Cuba, Orestes Minoso tended to the sugarcane crop alongside men twice his age. He broke into organized ball with a team sponsored by the Ambrosia Candy Company for two dollars a game. He progressed through the Cuban League and up through the Negro League after turning down a generous offer to sidestep the United States and play for Jorge Pasquel's Tampico Club in the Mexican League. "I say no," Minnie recalled. "I say the money is not everything. I say that compared to what you have over there, this is only one penny."

Minnie was willing to risk the inherent hardships of segregation in a foreign country in order to play for the New York Cubans. He joined the team in 1946 and played brilliantly for two seasons until "Reindeer" Bill Killefer, a scout for the Cleveland Indians, recommended him to Bill Veeck. Signed to a minor league contract and assigned to Dayton, Ohio, of the Central League, Minoso broke the color barrier in that city despite the usual harassment coming from some of his white teammates. Minnie looked past it and concentrated on the game between the lines...as was his custom.

The landmark deal that landed Minoso in Chicago was consummated by Frank Lane on April 30, 1951, following a marathon bargaining session with the Indians and Philadelphia A's. Lane traded away Gus Zernial and Dave Philley, two of Chicago's brightest young stars, to secure Minoso. The next night, Minnie made his debut against Vic Raschi and the New York Yankees. He smoked a bullpen home run off the Yankees ace in his first at-bat to properly inaugurate the Go-Go decade of White Sox baseball. In that same game, another rookie of note also hit his first round-tripper. The kid's name was Mickey Mantle.

Minoso was the most exciting player to burst on the Chicago scene in many a year. His speed on the base paths inspired the famous "Go-Go" chant emanating from the grandstand. He could run, he could field, and he could be counted on to hit .300 just about every year. Minoso acquired his famous nickname in 1951 from a Chicago dentist named Dr. Robinson—and not from the cartoon character Minnie Mouse or the popular Cab Calloway song, as is commonly assumed.

For seven thrill-packed seasons he batted third in the Sox lineup and conspired to get on base through whatever means necessary. For six consecutive seasons (1956–1961) he led the AL in getting hit by a pitch—a major league record.

Despite some occasional run-ins with the Sox brass who were not sympathetic to Minnie's visa problems, which inevitably delayed his spring training arrival each year, Minoso never hit lower than .288 in his worst season. That is why he could never understand the logic behind Chuck Comiskey's decision to trade him to Cleveland on December 4, 1957, for Early Wynn and Al Smith.

Minnie missed out on the 1959 World Series, but he was awarded an honorary ring by Bill Veeck, who brought him back to Chicago on December 6, 1959, in a controversial trade that shipped Norm Cash, Bubba Phillips, and John Romano to Cleveland. It was not a good trade for the Sox, but it was certainly a popular one among Chicago fans at the time. Minnie played well through the 1960 and 1961 seasons, though he was considerably slowed by advancing age. After Veeck sold the ballclub in May 1961, Minoso's status became uncertain.

The new regime decided to dump the veteran nucleus and bring forth a younger corps of players who had been marking time in the high minors patiently waiting for their chance. Minnie was traded to St. Louis for Joe Cunningham on November 27, 1961. It was a trade that worked out for the Sox because Minoso was fast approaching the end of the line as far as the American game was concerned.

Injuries curtailed his National League odyssey. Minoso was signed as a free agent by the Sox in April 1964, then released in July by Al Lopez, whom he blamed for all three of his forced departures from the Windy City. Actually, Sox GM Ed Short and Lopez tried to bring Minoso back for the final month of the '64 season, but commissioner Ford Frick ruled Minnie ineligible on the grounds that the team tried to "hide" him from other teams who might have claimed him in waivers.

Through the remainder of the 1960s and on into the next decade, Minoso prolonged his career in the Mexican League as a player/manager. Then Minnie's old friend Bill Veeck persuaded him to return to Chicago as a coach in 1976. In September of that year, Minnie was activated at age 54, thus achieving four-decade status. He collected one hit in eight designated hitter appearances in what many critics viewed as a rather shabby publicity stunt on Veeck's part. Four years later, at the tail end of another losing season, Bill Veeck

Minnie Minoso is out trying to steal home, June 26, 1960.

again allowed Minnie the opportunity of cracking the record books by becoming a *five-decade* man.

Owner Jerry Reinsdorf, after some initial trepidations, gave Minnie the green light to see through his ambition of appearing in a major league game for the sixth decade in September 1993. Reinsdorf and general manager Ron Schueler activated Minoso in time for the final home game of the 1993 season after AL president Bobby Brown signed off on the Sox's request.

The Major League Players Association and whining Jack McDowell, among others, voiced strong objections through union attorneys, forcing an embarrassed Minoso to decline the offer in the interest of preserving team unity on the eve of the playoffs.

There is a happy ending to the story, however. On June 30, 1993, Mike Veeck, the son of the former Sox owner and the president of the St. Paul Saints of the Northern Baseball League had invited Minnie to the Twin Cities to appear in a game against the Thunder Bay Whiskey Jacks. In a pinch-hitting appearance against 19-year-old Yoshi Seo, Minnie waited out two pitches then took his shot at a slider that looked pretty good. He swung hard and chopped the ball back to the mound.

Minnie Minoso was an easy out, but "Mr. White Sox"—the Chisox goodwill ambassador who speaks to thousands of admiring fans every year—added another important milestone to his illustrious and rewarding career.

Mostil, Johnny

White Sox: 1918; 1921–29
Outfielder
Birthplace: Chicago

B: June 1, 1896
D: December 10, 1970
Batted right, threw right
Ht. 5–8½; **Wt.** 168

Mostil, Johnny

White Sox	G	AB	H	AVG	RBI	R	2B	3B	HR	SA	SB
1918	10	33	9	.273	4	4	2	2	0	.455	1
1921	100	326	98	.301	42	43	21	7	3	.436	10
1922	132	458	139	.303	70	74	28	14	7	.472	14
1923	153	546	159	.291	64	91	37	15	3	.430	41
1924	118	385	125	.325	49	75	22	5	4	.439	7
1925	153	605	181	.299	50	135	36	16	2	.421	43
1926	148	600	197	.328	42	120	41	15	4	.467	35
1927	13	16	2	.125	1	3	0	0	0	.125	1
1928	133	503	136	.270	51	69	19	8	0	.340	23
1929	12	35	8	.229	3	4	3	0	0	.314	1
Career	972	3,507	1,054	.301	376	618	209	82	23	.427	176

Johnny Mostil had been trying to catch on with the White Sox for three seasons, but he was an infielder competing against the likes of Buck Weaver and Swede Risberg for a starting berth. Manager Kid Gleason encouraged the Whiting, Indiana, youth to utilize his exceptional speed and convert to the outfield. After the Black Sox scandal decimated this mighty ballclub, Gleason turned to Mostil and asked him if he was ready to open the 1921 season as the everyday center fielder.

Through the 1920s, Mostil provided the Sox with superior outfield play and good depth up the middle. Twice he led the league in stolen bases. He paced the junior circuit in fielding percentage in 1925. And in a spring training game played in Birmingham in 1924, the fleet-footed Mostil snared a foul fly down the left-field line—while playing center. Why then would a young ballplayer in the prime of his life try to kill himself?

It happened in the White Sox spring training hotel in Shreveport, Louisiana, on March 9, 1927. Returning to a hotel room registered to P.J. Prunty, a vacationing Sox fan who was close to Charles Comiskey, Mostil inflicted 13 razor cuts to his wrist, arms, and neck. He hovered near death for several days, then slowly began to recover his strength and the will to live.

Johnny Mostil

The press reported that Mostil complained of neuritis, a painful nerve disease that caused extreme pain to his jaw. This was the official version presented to the reporters by the image-conscious Comiskeys, who rushed Mostil back to Chicago to begin his convalescence. Over the years unsubstantiated rumors involved Mostil in an extramarital affair with the wife of a famous Sox pitcher of the day. Johnny was engaged to an Indiana woman at the time.

Mostil sat out most of the 1927 season but returned to duty the following year. He was sold to the Toledo ballclub after the 1929 season but failed in a comeback bid with the New York Giants that spring.

Johnny rejoined the White Sox in 1949 as a roving talent scout. He worked for the ballclub in this capacity for the next two decades and is responsible for signing many of the fine young players who joined the team in the 1950s and 1960s.

Whatever the true circumstances of his failed suicide attempt, Johnny Mostil was one of the all-time Sox greats. The fans showed their support by voting him the starting center fielder in a 1969 poll to determine the all-time White Sox all-star team. The tragedy that befell Johnny at such a young age is best left to the chroniclers of "Baseball Babylon" to ponder.

Nicholson, Dave

White Sox: 1963–65
Outfielder
Birthplace: St. Louis, Missouri

B: August 29, 1939
Bats right, throws right
Ht. 6–2; **Wt.** 215

Nicholson, Dave

White Sox	G	AB	H	AVG	RBI	R	2B	3B	HR	SA	SB
1963	126	449	103	.229	70	53	11	4	22	.419	2
1964	97	294	60	.204	39	40	6	1	13	.364	0
1965	54	85	13	.153	12	11	2	1	2	.271	0
Career	538	1,419	301	.212	179	184	32	12	61	.381	6

Dave Nicholson may or may not have hit the longest home run in major league history. After three decades, the issue is still open to debate and interpretation.

The last-place Kansas City A's were in town for a twi-night doubleheader the evening of May 6, 1964. Moe Drabowsky was on the mound. It was the fifth inning of Game 1. Big Nick strode to the plate.

Nicholson's blast soared high above the upper-deck roof in left field. When there was no mad scramble to retrieve the ball, everyone knew that it was out of the park. The only question remaining was whether or not the ball bounced on the roof before landing in neighboring Armour Park. If not, then the Nicholson home run traveled 573 feet, eclipsing Mickey Mantle's prodigious 565-foot blast in Griffith Stadium eight years earlier. Several of the upper-deck fans claimed to have heard the dull thud of the ball meeting the roof, but Sox officials contended that their assertion was nonsense. The ball was not even scuffed upon further examination.

Dave Nicholson catching some Sarasota sun

Nicholson's mammoth home run was the saving grace of a disappointing career. When the Baltimore Orioles signed the strapping outfielder for $100,000 in 1959, Paul Richards could scarcely contain his glee. "The greatest swing I've ever seen!" But the swing had trouble making contact with the ball. Nicholson was one of four players traded to the Sox on January 14, 1963, for Louie Aparicio and Al Smith.

Al Lopez and his coaches worked with Nicholson for hours on end to try to get him to meet the ball. But it was a lost cause. Dave set a major league record for strikeouts in 1963 with 175, and he was simply beyond help. For his career, Nick was the easiest batter in big-league history to fan, striking out on the average of once every 2.48 at bats. He was traded to the Houston Astros for pitcher Jack Lamabe on December 1, 1965.

Ordonez, Magglio

White Sox: 1997–2004
Outfielder
Birthplace: Caracas, Venezuela

B: January 28, 1974
Bats right, throws right
Ht. 6–0; **Wt.** 215

Ordonez, Magglio

White Sox	G	AB	H	AVG	RBI	R	2B	3B	HR	SA	SB
1997	21	69	22	.319	11	12	6	0	4	.580	1
1998	145	535	151	.282	65	70	25	2	14	.415	9
1999	157	624	188	.301	117	100	34	3	30	.510	13
2000	153	588	185	.315	126	102	34	3	32	.546	18
2001	160	593	181	.305	113	97	40	1	31	.533	25
2002	153	590	189	.320	135	116	47	1	38	.597	7
2003	160	606	192	.317	99	95	46	3	29	.546	9
2004	52	202	59	.292	37	32	8	2	9	.485	0
Career	1,756	6,649	2,072	.312	1,204	1,043	416	21	289	.511	92

For the better part of eight seasons, the rhythmic chant "O-E-O–Magglio!" echoed through the rafters of U.S. Cellular Field every time Magglio Ordonez approached the plate. The sound byte, emanating from the center-field scoreboard, was borrowed from the march of the flying-monkey army in *The Wizard of Oz*, of course, but it revved up the crowd in anticipation of a ringing double or the next long-distance shot from Maggs, who ranks in the top 10 in nearly every White Sox offensive category. Signed as a minor league free agent on May 18, 1991, Ordonez was an exceptionally disciplined hitter who won the American Association batting title and MVP award in 1997 while with Nashville. Called up to the parent club on August 29, 1997, Ordonez recorded four hits in his first seven at-bats, including his first career home run off of Houston's Jose Lima. Thereafter, he went on an offensive tear, becoming the first player in team history to record 30 homers, 40 doubles, and 100 RBIs in consecutive seasons (2001 and 2002).

Magglio Ordonez: Tigertown bound

Popular with the fans, Magglio Ordonez replica jerseys seemed to outsell that of any other White Sox player. Honored by President George W. Bush during National Hispanic Heritage Month in 2001, it only seemed natural that so fine a player as this, gifted with all the tools, low-key, and unprepossessing, would want to finish his career in Chicago and take his place among the great icons of Windy City sports. But agent Scott Boras, persona non grata in White Sox circles, represented Ordonez, a four-time All-Star, and had other ideas. With his three-year contract expiring in 2004, speculation mounted as to his future plan. He wanted his compensation to equal the salaries of Vladimir Guerrero and Miguel Tejada, with a five- or six-year contract to go with it. "It could be even more if you take into account that the market is going up again," Ordonez said on February 3, 2004. Kenny Williams tugged at his tie and gulped. He asked for "everyone's understanding while we just keep this matter between the two parties."

So would Maggs stay or go? The issue was clouded by a career-threatening knee injury suffered in Cleveland on May 19 of the new season, when Ordonez collided with teammate Willie Harris while chasing a pop fly. He landed on the disabled list May 26 before undergoing surgery at Rush University Medical Center on June 5 to repair a torn meniscus. Returned to active duty in July before the injury had time to heal properly, Ordonez was sidelined again with bone marrow edema in his left knee two weeks later. His season—and his White Sox career—ended unceremoniously on July 22. Kenny Williams thought he had a trade worked out with Toronto that would have sent Maggs to the Blue Jays for slugger Carlos Delgado, but Delgado balked at coming to Chicago, and the deal was canceled. Thereafter, a war of words erupted between Maggs and Ozzie Guillen—at one point Ordonez called Ozzie his "enemy." Guillen, of course, could not let the insult fade away and responded with a few choice words of his own before a shaky truce was called. Labeled as "damaged goods," few teams, including the Cubs and Mets, were willing to mortgage the house on a Type A free agent whose health was called into question. The exception being the Detroit Tigers, whose owner Michael Ilitch signed Ordonez to a five-year, $75 million contract with a

$6 million signing bonus and an option, on February 7, 2005. "I look forward to showing everybody that I'm healthy," said Maggs, who remained secretive and mysterious about the extent of the injury to Sox officials. "A lot of people are talking about my knee. I've got to prove people wrong." As it turned out, the knee wasn't his biggest problem. Ordonez went under the knife with an emergency appendectomy and missed more than half of the 2005 season, foiling the predictions of the crystal-ball gazers deluded into thinking that the Detroit Tigers were strong enough to overtake the White Sox.

Maggs and his Tigers teammates upset the oddsmakers and replaced the White Sox as AL champs in 2006, but Ordonez hit a paltry .105 in the World Series against tough Cardinals pitching. His disappointing performance foreshadowed a brilliant 2007 campaign when the Venezuelan star captured the American League batting title with a blistering .363 average—the highest for a Tigers hitter since Charlie Gehrenger's .371 in 1937 and a painful reminder that an earlier Detroit-bound ex-Sox player, Norm Cash, hit .361 in 1961. The White Sox front office and their fans drew enormous satisfaction in the personal accomplishments of Jermaine Dye, Maggs' steady and sure-handed right-field replacement, but nevertheless the free agent departure of Ordonez was a tragic setback to an otherwise successful first decade of White Sox baseball in the new millennium.

Orta, Jorge

White Sox: 1972–79
Second baseman, third baseman, outfielder
Birthplace: Mazatlán, Mexico

B: November 26, 1950
Bats left, throws right
Ht. 5–10; **Wt.** 170

Orta, Jorge

White Sox	G	AB	H	AVG	RBI	R	2B	3B	HR	SA	SB
1972	51	124	25	.202	11	20	3	1	3	.315	3
1973	128	425	113	.266	40	46	9	10	6	.376	8
1974	139	525	166	.316	67	73	31	2	10	.440	9
1975	140	542	165	.304	83	64	26	10	11	.450	16
1976	158	636	174	.274	72	74	29	8	14	.410	24
1977	144	564	159	.282	84	71	27	8	11	.417	4
1978	117	420	115	.274	53	45	19	21	13	.421	1
1979	113	325	85	.262	46	49	18	3	11	.437	1
Career	1,396	4,740	1,317	.278	600	613	205	53	106	.411	77

Jorge Orta turned down a basketball scholarship from John Wooden of UCLA in order to follow in the baseball footsteps of his dad, Pedro Charolito Orta, who was known in his day as the Babe Ruth of the Mexican League. Jorge's father attained stardom in the 1930s in a long-running career that continued for two decades. Pedro's talented son came to the attention of White Sox general manager Roland Hemond in 1971 when he was playing for San Luis Potosí. Through the intervention of Jesus Carmona and Dr. Alvin Lebrija, Mexican League officials who kept in close contact with Hemond, the White Sox were granted exclusive first rights to Orta.

Jorge was recalled from the minor leagues in time for the home opener in 1972. But his fielding was erratic, and the shy, uncomfortable looking youth who could barely speak a word of English was returned to Knoxville for further seasoning. Orta made it up to stay in 1973 following the departure of Mike Andrews, the incumbent second baseman up to that point.

Orta finished second to Rod Carew in the 1974 AL batting race, drawing favorable comparisons to the Twins perennial All-Star, at least in the learned opinion of announcer Harry Caray. Jorge collected five hits in three separate games that season to come within only one game of tying the major league record shared by Willie Keeler (1897), Ty Cobb (1922), and Stan Musial (1948).

A solid line-drive hitter and key contributor to the offense, Jorge was named to Mexico's baseball Hall of Fame in 1976—a turning point in his White Sox career. Paul Richards experimented with Orta at third base that season with disastrous results. Jorge's shaky glove work cost pitcher Ken Brett a shot at a perfect game on May 26 in Anaheim. Orta missed a slow roller hit by Jerry Remy after Brett had retired the first 26 batters in order. The ball skidded under Orta's glove, but the official scorer, who was kindly disposed to the hometown Angels, ruled the questionable play a hit.

Succeeding managers shuttled Jorge to the outfield and back to second base in an effort to keep his bat in the lineup. But it was useless. Orta was unable to develop consistency at any position and had become a real puzzle to the organization. Jorge was granted free agency in November 1979 and promptly signed with the Cleveland Indians.

Orta concluded his 15-year playing career after the 1987 season and joined the coaching ranks not long after. In his three seasons as manager of the Martinsville team of the Appalachian League, Jorge posted a 114–86 mark and led his team to the championship series in 2003—quite an accomplishment for the shy, introverted young Sox infielder who could barely speak a word of English when he came up. Orta joined the Cincinnati Reds organization in 2006 as a minor league hitting coach after wrapping up nine seasons of coaching young hitters in the Houston Astros system.

Jorge Orta

Owen, Frank

White Sox: 1903–09
Pitcher
Nickname: Yip
Birthplace: Ypsilanti, Michigan

B: December 23, 1879
D: November 24, 1942
Batted left and right, threw right
Ht. 6–1; **Wt.** 175

Owen, Frank

White Sox	W	L	Pct	ERA	G	CG	IP	H	BB	K	ShO
1903	8	12	.400	3.50	26	15	167⅓	167	44	66	1
1904	21	15	.583	1.94	37	34	315	243	61	103	4
1905	21	13	.618	2.10	42	32	334	276	56	125	3
1906	19	12	.613	2.33	42	27	293	289	54	66	7
1907	2	3	.400	2.49	11	2	47	43	13	15	0
1908	6	9	.400	3.41	25	5	140	142	37	48	1
1909	1	1	.500	4.50	3	1	16	19	3	3	0
Career	79	68	.537	2.55	194	119	1,368⅓	1,249	298	443	16

Frank Owen, one of the most capable right-handed pitchers of the dead-ball era, served in the Hospital Corps side by side with his father during the Spanish-American War of 1898. After the war, Owen inherited his dad's medical practice and worked in Ypsilanti as a physician in the off-season.

Owen had begun his baseball career a year earlier while enrolled at the Agricultural College in Lansing, Michigan. He was pitching for Omaha of the Western League in 1902 when Sox manager Clark Griffith arrived in town ostensibly to scout Mordecai "Three Finger" Brown, a promising right-hander destined for stardom with the Cubs.

Unable to secure Brown, who signed with the St. Louis Cardinals, the Sox "settled" for Owen, who had joined the ballclub a year later. He earned a permanent spot in the starting rotation after downing the Cubs three times in the first-ever post-season City Series, in impressive fashion.

Owen was an excellent fielding pitcher and a good cold-weather athlete who posted 20 or more wins in 1904 and 1905. On July 1, 1905, Frank became the first major league pitcher to hurl two complete-game victories in one day, when he limited the St. Louis Browns to only seven hits in a twin bill.

The decline set in after the 1906 season. In an effort to prolong his career, Frank Owen began experimenting with a knuckleball with little success. After his baseball career had ended, he resumed his medical practice.

Frank Owen

Paciorek, Tom

White Sox: 1982–85
Outfielder, infielder
Nickname: Wimpy
Birthplace: Detroit, Michigan

B: November 2, 1946
Bats right, throws right
Ht. 6–4; **Wt.** 205

Paciorek, Tom

White Sox	G	AB	H	AVG	RBI	R	2B	3B	HR	SA	SB
1982	104	382	119	.312	55	49	27	4	11	.490	3
1983	115	420	129	.307	63	65	32	3	9	.462	1
1984	111	363	93	.256	29	35	21	2	4	.358	0
1985	46	122	30	.246	9	14	2	0	0	.262	0
Career	1,392	4,121	1,162	.282	503	494	232	30	80	.415	55

The "Wimperoo," as he is sometimes called by Ken Harrelson, his sidekick and broadcast partner in the White Sox television booth, is one of three Paciorek brothers who played in the major leagues. By far, Tom Paciorek is the most famous of the trio. "Wimpy" was a fifth-round pick in the June 1968 free agent draft after turning down a chance to play football with the Miami Dolphins. He spent portions of six seasons in the Dodgers farm system before cracking the show on a permanent basis in 1973.

Paciorek never got the chance to play regularly until the talent-thin Seattle Mariners installed him in the everyday lineup in 1979. Thereafter "Wimpy" was a solid, consistent performer whose average hovered in the .300 range.

The versatile, easygoing Paciorek came to the White Sox on December 11, 1981, in a trade that sent the forgettable Todd Cruz and outfielder Rod Allen to the Mariners. It was another Roland Hemond masterpiece that helped thrust the Sox over the top in 1983. Tommy alternated between the outfield and the infield in '83, and led the team in batting average. On September 8 he etched his name into the Sox record book by joining Greg Luzinski and Carlton Fisk in a consecutive three-homer parade off Tommy John in Comiskey Park.

Plagued by a series of nagging injuries in 1982, Paciorek was sidelined for an entire month in the 1984 season. While on the DL, he got his first taste of broadcasting. Wimpy provided color commentary and exhibited a good rapport with the listening audience. When he returned to active duty, his average tailed off—and his value to the organization was diminished by advancing age. Hemond traded his veteran first baseman to the New York Mets on July 16, 1985, for outfielder Dave Cochrane.

Paciorek retired after the 1987 season to pursue broadcasting on a full-time basis. He teamed with Ken Harrelson

Tom Paciorek: the "Wimperoo" in '82

on television, providing incisive, sometimes hilarious commentary. In the middle of the 1989 season the Wimperoo went way out on the limb and vowed to shave his head if the last-place Sox won eight games in a row.

Well, after the Sox bagged their eighth straight game on June 21, Paciorek received his buzz cut—right on the field and in front of a throng of fans filing into Comiskey Park during batting practice. In 2000 the White Sox decided to sever ties with the popular and likeable Paciorek—for reasons that remain unclear a decade later. After Chicago, Tom moved around from team to team, beginning with the Tigers in 2000; the Braves from 2001 to 2005; and as Bob Carpenter's color analyst on MASN, the Washington Nationals' network, until November 2006 when he was let go. After that final disappointment, Paciorek flatly stated that he had no further desire to work behind a microphone again. "Hawk" Harrelson's glib sidekick was a great storyteller, and he lent considerable good cheer to the Sox TV booth during his 11 seasons. Not everyone appreciated his particular style of partisanship for the home team, of course, but he always kept it simple, and his insight into the mechanics of hitting was very sound.

Pasqua, Dan

White Sox: 1988–94
Outfielder
Birthplace: Yonkers, New York

B: October 17, 1961
Bats left, throws left
Ht. 6–0; **Wt.** 218

Pasqua, Dan

White Sox	G	AB	H	AVG	RBI	R	2B	3B	HR	SA	SB
1988	129	422	96	.227	50	48	16	2	20	.417	1
1989	73	246	61	.248	47	26	9	1	11	.427	1
1990	112	325	89	.274	58	43	27	3	13	.495	1
1991	134	417	108	.259	66	71	22	5	18	.465	0
1992	93	265	56	.211	33	26	16	1	6	.347	0
1993	78	176	36	.205	20	22	10	1	5	.358	2
1994	11	23	5	.217	4	2	2	0	2	.565	0
Career	905	2,620	638	.244	390	340	129	15	117	.438	7

Danny Pasqua was a worrier by nature, but he also possessed a fair amount of self-confidence, and he placed a high premium on personal goals. When he arrived in Chicago after three up-and-down seasons with the Yankees, he predicted a 30-home-run season for himself if he were able to come to the plate 500 times.

The portly outfielder, who grew up as a Yankees fan, never approached these numbers, and as the strikeouts and frustrations began to mount, he became a target of the Comiskey Park boo birds. "I've got to stop worrying about the numbers and just worry about tomorrow," Pasqua said.

Injuries put him on the shelf for an extended period in 1989 and again in 1992. The unrelenting chorus of boos grew even louder during the 1993 playoffs when Pasqua appeared completely overmatched by superior Toronto Blue Jay pitching. But in the quiet of retirement, Danny can reflect on few a redeeming moments in a White Sox uniform.

The White Sox acquired Pasqua for his left-handed power in a multiplayer deal with the Yankees on November 13, 1987. General manager Larry Himes had his eye on Danny for a long time, and once the Sox had him under contract, management showed great patience waiting for his "breakthrough" year—which never came. He was re-signed to a gilt-edged contract worth $6.75 million in 1991 just before the injuries set in.

Danny was a dead pull hitter when he came to Chicago, and if he had stuck to the formula instead of trying to go to the opposite field, he might have enjoyed far greater success as a member of the Pale Hose.

But until some player can better the mark, Pasqua will always be remembered for hitting the second longest recorded home run in the short history of the new Comiskey Park. According to the IBM Tale of the Tape measurement, Danny's line drive rocket hit off of Yankees pitcher Eric Plunk on April 27, 1991, sailed 484 feet—just shy of the right-field concourse.

His 445-foot blast off of Tigers southpaw Frank Tanana on May 30, 1989, was the second-to-last "roof shot" hit in the old Comiskey Park.

Dan Pasqua

Twice Dan Pasqua spared the White Sox the indignity of being no-hit. His eighth-inning double on August 26, 1992, spelled heartbreak for Toronto pitcher Todd Stottlemyre. Boston's Danny Darwin carried a no-hitter into the eighth inning of a Fenway Park game on August 18, 1993, until Pasqua rifled a triple off the center-field wall. But his failure to deliver in the clutch in too many game situations, together with another stint on the disabled list in 1994, hastened his departure. Pasqua was removed from the roster after being denied salary arbitration on October 21, 1994.

The Sox slugger settled permanently in south suburban Orland Park after his playing days ended and currently is spending time coaching the kids in the Bulls/White Sox Training Camp.

Patterson, Roy

White Sox: 1901–07
Pitcher
Nickname: The Boy Wonder
Birthplace: Stoddard, Wisconsin

B: December 17, 1876
D: April 14, 1953
Batted right, threw right
Ht. 6–0; **Wt.** 185

Roy Patterson

Patterson, Roy

White Sox	W	L	Pct	ERA	G	CG	IP	H	BB	K	ShO
1901	20	16	.556	3.37	41	30	312⅓	345	62	127	4
1902	19	14	.576	3.06	34	26	268	262	67	61	2
1903	16	15	.516	2.70	34	26	293	275	69	89	2
1904	9	8	.529	2.29	22	14	165	148	24	64	4
1905	4	5	.444	1.83	13	7	88⅔	73	16	29	1
1906	10	6	.625	2.09	21	12	142	119	17	45	3
1907	4	6	.400	2.63	19	4	96	105	18	27	1
Career	82	70	.539	2.75	184	119	1,365	1,327	273	442	17

In the closing days of the 1898 season, Charles Comiskey's St. Paul Saints were scheduled to play a pickup game against a sandlot team in Duluth, Minnesota. The Dukes, as they were known to the local fans, pulled off a surprising upset and defeated the heavily favored Saints behind a young pitcher named Roy Patterson, whom Comiskey immediately signed to a professional contract.

If the "Old Roman" Comiskey was the founding father, then Roy Patterson must be regarded as the trailblazing pioneer of early White Sox history. In 1900, when the Saints were transferred to Chicago to begin play as the White Stockings, the "Boy Wonder" was the team's most effective pitcher. Patterson was the starting pitcher in several historic games.

He pitched the first spring exhibition game for the White Sox in their new surroundings on April 2, 1900, downing the University of Illinois varsity team 10–9. A year later, after the American League had declared itself the second major league, free from the shackles of the National Agreement, Patterson entered the record books as the AL's first winning pitcher when he defeated the Cleveland Blues 8–2 at the old 39th Street Grounds on April 24, 1901, in the league's inaugural game. The scheduled eastern games that day had all been canceled because of torrential rains.

After his career ran its course in 1907, Roy returned to Minneapolis, where he played minor league ball for the Millers through the next decade. In 1963 Patterson's widow threw out the first pitch on Opening Day at Comiskey Park.

Perez, Melido

White Sox: 1988–91
Pitcher
Birthplace: San Cristobal, Dominican Republic

B: February 15, 1966
Bats right, throws right
Ht. 6–4; **Wt.** 210

Perez, Melido

White Sox	W	L	Pct	ERA	G	CG	IP	H	BB	K	ShO	Sv
1988	12	10	.545	3.79	32	3	197	186	72	138	1	0
1989	11	14	.440	5.01	31	2	183⅓	187	90	141	0	0
1990	13	14	.481	4.61	35	3	197	177	86	161	3	0
1991	8	7	.533	3.12	49	0	135⅔	111	52	128	0	1
Career	78	85	.478	4.17	243	5	1,354⅔	1,268	551	1,092	5	1

When Larry Himes set out to rebuild a tattered White Sox farm system in the wake of Ken Harrelson's departure as general manager, his first priority was to secure young pitching to carry the ballclub into the 1990s. The disappointing Floyd Bannister and his multimillion-dollar contract were shipped to the Kansas City Royals on December 10, 1987, for four pitching prospects, including Melido Perez, the younger brother of the showboating Pascual Perez of the Atlanta Braves. Floyd was happy to escape Chicago. Melido welcomed the chance to pitch every fourth day.

Melido was not nearly as colorful or controversial as Pascual, nor did he enjoy the same levels of success as his brother. But in his freshman season he finished sixth in American League Rookie of the Year balloting and seemed destined to become, if not the ace of the youthful White Sox staff, then a strong No. 2 starter. Melido raced to a 5–1 start with the woebegone 1988 White Sox, and raised his record to 10–5 by July 27 before losing his concentration and rhythm, a problem that has plagued him throughout his entire career. Despite the second-half slump, Melido became the first Sox rookie to notch double-digit victories since Britt Burns and Richard Dotson in 1980.

During the Jeff Torborg years (1989–91), Perez presented more than the usual problems confronting a manager guiding a talented but inexperienced ballclub. Melido's biggest problem was escaping the first inning. Too many times he was kayoed by the opposition before retiring the first three hitters in the game. His dreadful performance on June 16, 1990, qualifies for the Hall of *Shame*. With first place on the line, the Oakland A's in town, and playing before the largest crowd of the 1990 season—44,176 pumped-up Sox fans—Melido surrendered seven earned runs before his teammates came to bat.

Melido Perez

At other times Perez was brilliant—and unhittable. He made history on July 12, 1990, but because of a rule change, Melido's name will not appear in the record books. On this rain-soaked and dreary night in the Bronx, the Sox righty fired an abbreviated six-inning no-hitter against the Yankees, winning 8–0 before the steady shower washed away the rest of the contest. In the opposing dugout Melido's brother Pascual cheered him on. "I know we lost, but he's my brother. He would have been rooting for me if I was throwing it," Pascual Perez said afterward.

It was the first time since 1958 that the Yankees were no-hit in their own yard, and only the second time in history that a Sox pitcher tossed a less-than-nine-inning no-hitter (Ed Walsh, on May 26, 1907, versus New York was the first), but the commissioner later decreed that these games would no longer qualify for no-hit status, since they were not complete games.

Melido's inconsistency resulted in his demotion to the bullpen on May 29, 1991. He performed brilliantly in long relief but was not happy with his new arrangement and desired a trade.

On-and-off again negotiations with the New York Yankees culminated in a trade that sent Perez and two minor league pitchers to the Yankees for veteran infielder Steve Sax. Eager to dump Sax' $10.9 million, four-year salary, the Yanks sweetened the pot by throwing in $1.6 million.

It was a good-looking trade on paper, but it turned out to be one of Ron Schueler's worst miscalculations as general manager. Sax was past his prime and contributed little to the team's success in the early 1990s. One of the rookie pitchers, Bob Wickman, a second-round pick in the June 1990 draft, was a fine addition to the Yankees bullpen corps, while Melido enjoyed a few redeeming moments in their starting rotation.

Peters, Gary

White Sox: 1959–69
Pitcher
Birthplace: Grove City, Pennsylvania

B: April 21, 1937
Bats left, throws left
Ht. 6–2; **Wt.** 200

Peters, Gary

White Sox	W	L	Pct	ERA	G	CG	IP	H	BB	K	ShO
1959	0	0	—	0.00	2	0	1	2	2	1	0
1960	0	0	—	2.70	2	0	3⅓	4	1	4	0
1961	0	0	—	1.74	3	0	10⅓	10	2	6	0
1962	0	1	.000	5.68	5	0	6⅓	8	1	4	0
1963	19	8	.704	2.33	41	13	243	192	68	189	4
1964	20	8	.714	2.50	37	11	273⅔	217	104	205	3
1965	10	12	.455	3.62	33	1	176⅓	181	63	95	0
1966	12	10	.545	1.98	30	11	204⅔	156	45	129	4
1967	16	11	.593	2.28	38	11	260	187	91	215	3
1968	4	13	.235	3.76	31	6	162⅔	146	60	110	1
1969	10	15	.400	4.53	36	7	218⅔	238	78	140	3
Career	124	103	.546	3.25	359	79	2,081	1,894	706	1,420	23

Gary Peters was tabbed as the Billy Pierce of the 1960s. In some ways his graceful fluid-drive windup and delivery were reminiscent of the Sox great who had left the team two years before Peters hit his stride. For a few years at least, Gary was a worthy successor, but time and circumstances conspired against him.

This tall and rangy southpaw, known for his biting humor and imaginative practical jokes, struggled to crack a veteran-oriented starting rotation. Originally signed as a first baseman by scout Fred Shaffer, Peters languished in Triple A for the better part of seven seasons before manager Al Lopez added him to the Opening Day roster in 1963 after his options had expired.

Gary Peters, stylish lefty

Gary was finally ready to answer the bell, with a tip of his cap to a shatter-proof five-foot mirror supplied to White Sox pitching coach Ray Berres during the 1962–1963 spring training sessions by Danny Litwhiler, a former Boston Brave and a coach at Florida State University. The mirror enabled struggling Sox pitchers like Peters and Herb Score to detect and correct flaws in their delivery as they aimed their pitches at the glass from a distance of 30 feet. By observing his windup and delivery, Berres detected that Gary was failing to conceal the ball before delivery, thus making the grip on his fastball apparent to the opposing hitters. "A hitter could read him like a book," observed coach Don Gutteridge. With further refinements and by no longer easing up on his curveball as he had in the past, Peters was at last ready to make his mark, but he knew he had to pass muster in 1963 or be gone. "This was his last chance," Lopez recalled years later. "If he failed again, we had no other choice but to let him go. I mean out of the organization altogether. We were all out of options on him."

Peters' big break came on May 6 of that year against the team that would have claimed him if he had been sent back to the minors. Juan Pizarro, the White Sox left-handed pitching ace, came down with the flu just before the Sox were to square off against the A's in Kansas City. Instead of a one-way ticket back to the minors, Peters was surprised to receive the starting call from Lopez. Peters not only won the game 5–1 but also slugged a home run off Ted Bowsfield, the first of 19 career roundtrippers.

Lopez and his successor Eddie Stanky often used Peters in pinch-hitting roles. Stanky paid him the highest compliment by batting him No. 6 in the order on May 26, 1968, ahead of Duane Josephson, Tim Cullen, and Louie Aparicio.

Peters was the pitching sensation of 1963. He reeled off 11 straight wins to finish 19–8, clinching Rookie of the Year honors over teammate Pete Ward. The handsome pitcher-slugger was even better in 1964. He won 20 for the only time in his career and paced the AL in victories despite enduring several hard-luck losses to Whitey Ford and the Yankees—a 1960s nemesis who bested Gary five times without sustaining a defeat.

A vexing arm problem sent his career into a tailspin in 1965. But Peters rebounded in 1967 to win 16 games and strike out 215 batters. Tom Bradley and Ed Walsh are the only other White Sox pitchers to fan more than 200 batters in two or more seasons.

A groin injury and a tender elbow spelled the beginning of the end in 1968. Another subpar season followed before Ed Short traded Gary with catcher Don Pavletich to the Boston Red Sox on December 13, 1969, for pitcher Billy Farmer—who refused to report to Chicago. The White Sox acquired infielder Sid O'Brien and Jerry "the Wheat Germ Kid" Janeski as compensation; that is to say, they received no compensation at all.

Peters was in San Juan, Puerto Rico, in his official capacity as player representative when word of the trade reached him. "I expected to be traded," he said, fully aware of the White Sox austerity movement and their desperate attempt to shed veterans with higher salaries in favor of youth. "My relationship with the White Sox was the best, and I will have to admit I really wasn't much help the last two years."

Philley, Dave

White Sox: 1941; 1946–51; 1956–57
Outfielder
Birthplace: Paris, Texas
B: May 16, 1920
Bats both, throws right
Ht. 6–0; **Wt.** 188

Philley, Dave

White Sox	G	AB	H	AVG	RBI	R	2B	3B	HR	SA	SB
1941	7	9	2	.222	0	4	0	0	0	.333	3
1946	17	68	24	.353	17	10	2	3	0	.471	0
1947	143	551	142	.258	45	55	25	11	2	.354	21
1948	137	488	140	.287	42	51	28	3	5	.387	8
1949	146	598	171	.286	44	84	20	8	0	.346	13
1950	156	619	150	.242	80	69	21	5	14	.360	6
1951	7	25	6	.240	2	0	2	0	0	.320	0
1956	86	279	74	.265	47	44	14	2	4	.373	1
1957	22	71	23	.324	9	9	4	0	0	.380	1
Career	1,904	6,296	1,700	.270	729	789	276	72	84	.377	102

In a confident, boyish manner, 21-year-old Dave Philley strode into the White Sox 1941 spring camp and announced to his curmudgeonly manager Jimmie Dykes: "Hell, I can hit as good as Hornsby, and I plan on getting paid for such talents!" Dykes rubbed his chin and smiled. "We'll just see about that, son, we'll see."

Philley played a handful of games in 1941, but he did not make a lasting impression. Then came a two-year apprenticeship in the minor leagues sandwiched around a three-year hitch in the army. Returning to baseball in 1946, Philley enjoyed a banner season with the Milwaukee Brewers of the American Association, earning him a late-season promotion to the White Sox.

Ted Lyons, desperate to rebuild with some new faces, called Philley into his office one afternoon to convey the good news. "I'm going to count on you next season," he said. "There's no reason why you can't win a regular spot." Puffed up with his manager's vote of confidence, Philley decided that it was in his best interests to hold out for a boxcar salary.

After coming to terms with the Comiskeys following some heated contract discussions, the brash young American Association flychaser won a starting assignment in left. In that first full season, Philley waxed hot and cold. During a hot streak in mid-June, Dave pounded out 13 hits in 22 at bats against the Red Sox and Yankees in their respective ballparks. He was on his way to a long and productive 20-year run in the big leagues.

Possessing an above-average throwing arm, good speed, and adequate power from both sides of the plate, the lean Texas cowpoke (he raised cattle in the off-season), patrolled the Sox outfield for the next four years. He led the American League in double plays by outfielders in 1948 and 1950, and he might have lingered in Chicago if only Frank Lane had not mentioned his name during the early stages of trade talks with Cleveland.

Dave Philley (left) with Ted Williams, May 9, 1947

Unfortunately Dave was dealt with Gus Zernial to the Philadelphia A's on April 30, 1951, in a complicated three-cornered deal also involving the Cleveland Indians. The Sox landed Minnie Minoso, but Sox manager Paul Richards was hypercritical of Lane and his willingness to surrender the popular Philley, when Minnie might have been acquired straight up for Zernial if only the Sox GM had played a better hand.

The Comiskeys reacquired Dave from the Baltimore Orioles on May 21, 1956. He was an important contributor for the Sox down the stretch drive, but was gone less than a year later. The well-traveled veteran lasted into the 1960s. He became one of the top pinch-hitters of all-time in the waning years of his career. Dave Philley collected 24 pinch-hits with the Orioles in 1961 to set a new American League record. When his playing days ended, Dave attended to his cattle ranch in Paris, Texas, and was later elected to the local city council.

Pierce, Billy

White Sox: 1949–61
Pitcher
Birthplace: Detroit, Michigan

B: April 2, 1927
Bats left, throws left
Ht. 5–10; **Wt.** 160

Pierce, Billy

White Sox	W	L	Pct	ERA	G	CG	IP	H	BB	K	ShO
1949	7	15	.318	3.88	32	8	171⅔	145	112	95	0
1950	12	16	.429	3.98	33	15	219⅓	189	137	118	1
1951	15	14	.517	3.03	37	18	240⅓	237	73	113	1
1952	15	12	.556	2.57	33	14	255⅓	214	79	144	4
1953	18	12	.600	2.72	40	19	271⅓	216	102	186	7
1954	9	10	.474	3.48	36	12	188⅔	179	86	148	4
1955	15	10	.600	1.97	33	16	205⅔	162	64	157	6
1956	20	9	.690	3.32	35	21	276⅓	261	100	192	1
1957	20	12	.625	3.26	37	16	257	228	71	171	4
1958	17	11	.607	2.68	35	19	245	204	66	144	3
1959	14	15	.483	3.62	34	12	224	217	62	114	2
1960	14	7	.667	3.62	32	8	196⅓	201	46	108	1
1961	10	9	.526	3.80	39	5	180	190	54	106	1
Career	211	169	.555	3.27	585	193	3,306⅔	2,989	1,178	1,999	38

Billy Pierce was the quiet man of the silent generation—a Hall of Fame caliber pitcher who has thus far been overlooked for inclusion among baseball's immortals. There was nothing in his character to qualify him as a showboat or flake. He did not run the bases backward, participate in brawls at popular New York night spots, or perform any of the other colorful antics associated with Jimmy Piersall and other 1950s players who upset baseball's staid decorum.

He was an All-American role model for youngsters, and he never voiced a complaint or lifted a hand in anger. Billy Pierce was a class act from the moment he arrived in Chicago on November 10, 1948. It was Frank Lane's first trade as the new Sox general manager, and it was nothing short of brilliant.

To satisfy the concerns of the Comiskey family, who expected either Dizzy Trout or Ted Gray in return for catcher

Billy Pierce

Aaron Robinson, Lane pried $10,000 out of the Detroit Tigers to clinch the deal.

Pierce first came to the attention of Wish Egan, a Tigers scout who had his eye on the 15-year-old lefty who was already making a solid impression on his coach at Highland Park High School in Detroit. Billy was voted the star of the 1944 Boy's National All-Star Game of 1944, then rejected a college scholarship in order to sign with the Tigers.

Billy's 12-year White Sox career is dotted with superlatives. In those dozen years of wearing the pinstripes Pierce lost 10 decisions to American League opponents by 1–0 and 2–0 scores. In 1955, the year he led the league in earned run average with 1.97, Pierce dropped four heartbreaking 1–0 decisions. He was never a knocker though. After the White Sox pushed across a rare first-inning run, roommate Nellie Fox trotted to the mound while Billy completed his warm-ups. "Okay," Fox chided. "Here's your run, better hold it!"

Thirty-five of Pierce's 38 career shutouts came as a member of the White Sox. Number 30, however, is a bittersweet memory. Pitching against the Washington Senators in Comiskey Park the evening of June 27, 1958, Pierce nursed a perfect game into the ninth inning. Pinch-hitter Ed Fitzgerald, a forgettable bench player, whacked his best curveball down the right-field line just out of the reach of first baseman Ray Boone. In characteristic manner, Billy brushed it off, saying he was just happy to win the game.

The 1950s are remembered as a great pitchers' decade, and when the three top contenders got together—the Indians, the White Sox, and the Yankees—it was a moral certainty that Billy would square off against Whitey Ford or Bob Lemon. Both men are in the Hall of Fame. Yet, in head-to-head competition, Pierce out-decisioned Lemon 7–2, and Ford, the notorious White Sox killer, 8–6.

The youthful White Sox ace started the 1953, 1955, and 1956 All-Star Games. He hurled four-one hitters during his career, and he pitched 39⅔ consecutive scoreless innings in August 1953, ranking him third behind Doc White and Ed Walsh on the all-time Sox list.

Billy's most bitter disappointment, aside from missing out on a perfect game, was Al Lopez's puzzling decision to exile him to the bullpen during the 1959 World Series. Lopez was not pleased with Billy's numbers all season long. And while it was true that Pierce had suffered through an uncharacteristic pitching slump in '59, he was the popular and sentimental choice to open the Series in Chicago. This was not to be the case, and though he has never publicly criticized Lopez, the veteran pitcher was understandably resentful. Fortunately, Billy finally got his chance to start a World Series game—but not in Chicago.

The opportunity presented itself with the San Francisco Giants in 1962, a full year after closing out his White Sox career. Pierce was traded to the Giants on November 30, 1961, as a part of Ed Short's commitment to youth. Billy was not happy to hear the news, but he took it gracefully and without complaint.

When his playing days were over, Billy Pierce settled down in Chicago to begin a separate career with the Continental Envelope Company. He was the color man on the White Sox TV telecast in 1969, but his rather high-pitched voice was ill-suited to television. The White Sox retired Billy's No. 19 in 1987, but the larger tribute—induction into the Hall of Fame—is an unfulfilled dream.

Pierzynski, Anthony John

White Sox: 2005–
Catcher
Nickname: A.J.
Birthplace: Bridgehampton, New York

B: December 30, 1976
Bats left, throws right
Ht. 6–3; **Wt.** 230

Pierzynski, Anthony John

White Sox	G	AB	H	AVG	RBI	R	2B	3B	HR	SA	SB
2005	128	460	118	.257	56	61	21	0	18	.420	0
2006	140	509	150	.295	64	65	24	0	16	.436	1
2007	136	472	124	.263	50	54	24	0	14	.403	1
2008	134	534	150	.281	60	66	31	1	13	.416	1
2009	138	504	151	.300	49	57	22	1	13	.425	1
2010	128	474	128	.270	56	43	29	0	9	.388	3
Career	1,365	5,207	1,379	.284	605	575	285	16	120	.424	13

Who was the real "face of the White Sox" in the winning 2000s? Was it Paul Konerko for his quiet, thoughtful leadership role? Or mound ace Mark Buehrle and his easy-going, bemused persona? After Frank Thomas departed the scene in 2005, that designation seemed to fall to A.J. Pierzynski. A.J. came to symbolize the grit and determination of a style of play called "grinder baseball," as he helped to make it more than a marketing slogan but instead a philosophy the front office wholly embraced and endeavored to impart to the players. Pierzynski, a teammate of Johnny Damon at Dr. Phillips High School in Orlando, Florida, before forsaking an offer to play baseball for the University of Tennessee to accept an offer from the Minnesota Twins, meshed well with the "Twins method" of choosing only intuitive, heads-up players well schooled in the fundamentals of the game. In 2002, after several earlier trials, Pierzynski took over day-to-day catching duties for the Twins and was named to the All-Star team as a reserve. A solid hitter—but possessing limited skill throwing out base thieves—A.J. hit .312 the next season and established himself as a formidable contact hitter.

The game plan soon changed, as it usually does for the Twins, when they drafted blue-chip catcher Joe Mauer in the first round of the 2001 First-Year Player Draft. Suddenly expendable, A.J. was traded to the San Francisco Giants on November 14, 2003, for Joe Nathan, Boof Bonser, and Francisco Liriano—and what a trade that was! Never popular with his Giants teammates, A.J. got off on the wrong foot by allegedly kneeing Giants trainer Stan Conte in the groin during spring training—a charge A.J. hotly denied. "Don't you think if something like that happened, in spring training, you would have heard about it? I would have gotten in some sort of trouble?" he wondered. Throughout the '04 campaign there were whispers from the Giants clubhouse that Pierzynski was a lightning rod who was more interested in what the Twins were doing than his own ballclub. A.J.'s colorful, albeit controversial reputation as baseball's version of "Peck's Bad Boy" was well documented around baseball when Ken Williams signed him to a free agent contract on January 6, 2005. Miguel Olivo and Jaime Burke were found wanting in 2004—in fact the search for a capable everyday catcher who could hit the ball *and* field the position after Carlton Fisk was released had been as elusive of a quest as Ahab's search for the white whale.

But without A.J. behind the plate in 2005—his .999 fielding percentage outpaced every other AL backstop that year—who knows what might have happened? In the championship season (and into the next), he set an AL record with 962 consecutive chances without an error from April 18, 2005, to May 19, 2006, breaking Yogi Berra's mark of 950 set from 1957 to 1959. In the key play of the 2005 ALCS, A.J.'s heads-up sprint to first base after he deceived umpire Doug Eddings into thinking that Angels' catcher (and ex-Sox) Josh Paul dropped the ball after an apparent strikeout shifted momentum and sparked a Sox rally that led to a series rout of the Halos. The "fourth out" rally still inspires the boo-birds of Anaheim every time Pierzynski shows his face at Angel Stadium of Anaheim.

A.J. has a knack for getting under an opponent's skin, evidenced by his altercation with the excitable Cubs catcher Michael Barrett on May 20, 2006—a delightful Saturday afternoon contest with the North Siders won in a whitewash by the Sox 7–0. After barreling into Barrett in a home-plate collision that dazed the Cubs catcher, the brawl of the decade followed. Benches cleared and fists flew. A.J.'s "What did I do?" look of innocence was a classic Chicago sports moment—and inspired the marketing department to conceive the "Punch A.J." campaign to encourage and fire up the fans to send him to the All-Star Game as a write-in candidate. More than 3.6 million fans responded, and Pierzynski made the cuts. The A.J. contretemps established him as one of the most disliked players in the league according to fan polls—but much loved by the Sox faithful, and that's the only thing that mattered. "I'm under the microscope more than any other player besides Barry [Bonds]," Pierzynski reflected. "If I do any little thing that any other player would do, when I do it, they say, 'Oh, that's just him being dumb.' Somebody else does it, and people just look the other way. I think a lot of it is hype." In a 2005 survey, *GQ* magazine ranked Pierzynski No. 9 on a list of the 10 most hated athletes in all of sports. "He's Bill Laimbeer!" commented Paul LoDuca of the New York Mets, drawing a comparison of A.J. to the former Detroit Pistons bad boy.

Nevertheless, the Sox inked A.J. to a two-year $12.5 million contract extension in 2007 despite an off year. As the team's fortunes improved in 2008, A.J.'s batting average soared—proving that as their durable catcher goes, so go the Sox. His 150 hits tied a club record for hits by a catcher—eclipsing such all-time Sox stalwarts as Carlton Fisk, Ray Schalk, and Sherm Lollar. A.J. broke his own record a year later and became the team's first backstop to hit .300 in a season. (In 1970 Duane Josephson hit .316, but in part-time play.) His .998 White Sox fielding average ranks first in team history, but numbers only tell part of the story. Summing up the essence of A.J., Ozzie Guillen correctly noted, "If you play against him, you hate him. If you play with him, you hate him a little less."

Blending intensity with mischief: A.J. Pierzynski

Pizarro, Juan

White Sox: 1961–66
Pitcher
Birthplace: Santurce, Puerto Rico

B: February 7, 1937
Bats left, throws left
Ht. 5–11; **Wt.** 170

Pizarro, Juan

White Sox	W	L	Pct	ERA	G	CG	IP	H	BB	K	ShO
1961	14	7	.667	3.05	39	12	194⅔	164	89	188	1
1962	12	14	.462	3.81	36	9	203⅓	182	97	173	1
1963	16	8	.667	2.39	32	10	214⅔	177	63	163	3
1964	19	9	.679	2.56	33	11	239	193	55	162	4
1965	6	3	.667	3.43	18	2	97	96	37	65	1
1966	8	6	.571	3.76	34	1	88⅔	91	39	42	0
Career	131	105	.555	3.43	488	79	2,034	1,807	888	1,522	17

Enigmatic Juan Pizarro displayed occasional flashes of brilliance during four trials with the Milwaukee Braves in the late 1950s. The hard-throwing lefty, who struggled to learn the English language and to master an explosive curveball, finally wore out the patience of Braves manager Charley Dressen.

Bill Veeck and his scouts were not sure about Pizarro. But they rolled the dice and gambled that Sox pitching coach Ray Berres just might be able to improve Pizarro's control. A tricky, three-way trade involving the Braves, White Sox, and Reds was finalized on December 14, 1960, sending Gene Freese to Cincinnati, with Cal McLish and Pizarro coming to Chicago.

"When we dealt for Pizarro, we gambled that a consistently effective pitcher could be made out of him," Veeck would later boast. "In spring training and for a while thereafter, it looked like a thousand-to-one shot. It certainly doesn't now."

Pizarro opened the 1961 season in the bullpen. He made his first start on June 10 and would not be dislodged from the starting rotation for the next four years. Credit Ray Berres with correcting Juan's mechanics and instilling a large dose of confidence.

Despite recurring arm problems in 1962 and 1963, Pizarro became one of the league's top left-handed strikeout artists. He fanned 14 Washington Senators on July 31, 1964—just two shy of Jack Harshman's single-game Sox record. In 1963 the White Sox tandem of Gary Peters and Juan Pizarro were ranked one-two in American League earned run average. Juan narrowly missed a 20-win season in 1964 but was named to the All-Star team for the second year in a row.

Pizarro went about his business in a quiet, workmanlike manner. At times he was perceived as distant, aloof, and unresponsive—when the real problem was his difficulty with the English language. Sensitive to the criticisms of Al Lopez and Sox GM Ed Short, Juan concealed an arm injury he had sustained in the Puerto Rican Winter League after he reported to Sarasota to begin the 1965 spring workouts. His ERA soared to 7.20 before the ailment was properly diagnosed and the player assigned to the disabled list. When pressed for an explanation, Pizarro sheepishly explained that he did not want to be called a quitter.

A change of managers didn't help his cause either. Eddie Stanky was furious with Pizarro when he showed up in the clubhouse one afternoon in June 1966 with his head bandaged. Juan had been involved in a car accident and said that he could not play because of his headache. "Fine him?" Stanky snarled to reporters. "I'm too nice of a guy!" Instead, general manager Ed Short traded him to Pittsburgh for minor league pitcher Wilbur Wood on October 12, 1966.

Podsednik, Scott

White Sox: 2005–2007; 2009
Outfielder
Nickname: Scotty Pods
Birthplace: West, Texas

B: March 18, 1976
Bats left, throws left
Ht. 6–0; **Wt.** 187

Podsednik, Scott

White Sox	G	AB	H	AVG	RBI	R	2B	3B	HR	SA	SB
2005	129	507	147	.290	25	80	28	1	0	.349	59
2006	139	524	137	.261	45	86	27	6	3	.353	40
2007	62	214	52	.243	11	30	13	4	2	.369	12
2009	132	537	163	.304	48	75	25	6	7	.412	30
Career	1,016	3,707	1,036	.279	300	544	171	41	41	.381	301

Injuries, inconsistencies, and an unforgettable walkoff homer in Game 2 of the 2005 World Series are what White Sox fans remember the most about the Scott Podsednik years on the South Side. Ozzie Guillen candidly assessed Podsednik's situation at the 2007 All-Star break when a strained muscle in the left rib cage sent him to the disabled list following an injury-plagued 2006 campaign. "He's unreliable," the impatient manager complained. "Now he has a different injury. It's not his legs. It's his side. It's important for a ballclub to have a guy like him. But in the meanwhile, if you can't count on a guy one day in and one day out, it makes it hard." Podsednik's history of injuries began in high school when he busted a collarbone playing football in his freshman year.

He quit the gridiron and turned to baseball, but he made it hard for a succession of managers even at the minor league level. Nagging injuries ultimately delayed his arrival in the big leagues for eight years. Drafted out of West High School in the third round (85th overall) in the 1994 Major League Player Draft by the Texas Rangers, Scotty Pods passed through the Rangers' minor league system—Chicago fans got an early preview of his skills and ability as a speed merchant when he was a member of the Kane County Cougars in 1997—but that was short-lived. He signed a minor league contract with the Seattle Mariners in November 2000, and after a spectacular MLB debut with the Mariners in 2002 (he hit a bases-loaded triple in his first at-bat), the Milwaukee Brewers acquired him as a free agent. In 2003 he made the Opening Day roster and the most of his opportunities by impressing manager Ned Yost and the rest of the Brewers organization to the point where they traded center fielder Alex Sanchez to Detroit to open an everyday spot in the lineup for Podsednik. He pilfered 43 bases, hit .314, and finished second in Rookie of the Year balloting.

Scotty Pods

It was a long struggle, and the future appeared bright—that is, until the sophomore hitting slump of 2004 diminished his market value. This made him attractive to Ken Williams, who was desperately seeking a speed burner at the top of the lineup to change the complexion of the team from a collection of power-hitting, grazing water buffaloes into a traditional speed and motion offense. Despite a poor 2004 average, Scotty led the majors in stolen bases, and that superlative alone was the most compelling résumé credential for Williams to go forward and swap Carlos Lee to the Brewers for Podsednik, pitcher Luis Vizcaino, and rookie prospect Travis Hinton on December 14, 2004. The media—mostly the Sox-hating Jay Mariotti—condemned the Sox for making this deal, but it proved to be the mortar between the bricks of the 2005 championship team. Scotty was the igniter—he swiped 59 bases (52 in the first four months of the season) to rank second in the White Sox single-season rankings behind Rudy Law's 77 steals in 1983 until Juan Pierre passed Podsednik up in 2010.

His 39 infield singles and 16 bunt hits led the league—and his first and only home run of the season couldn't have come at a more opportune moment: he struck the winning blow off of Houston's Brad Lidge in Game 2 of the World Series. Some players give you an entire career, others an unforgettable moment. Few would argue the point that Podsednik sealed the controversial Lee deal as a winner in the minds of Sox fans forever when that ball cleared the wall. Sadly, there were few great moments to savor in 2006 and 2007—injuries and mediocrity soured Guillen on his center fielder. With 40 steals in 2006, Scotty became only the fourth player in franchise history to swipe 40 or more in back-to-back seasons, joining Eddie Collins, Luis Aparicio, and Tim Raines. But 40 was *not* the 59 of 2005, and his feat was mostly overshadowed by the injuries. His second-half stats in 2007 were subpar. He went on the disabled list for the second time in two months on July 3 and was hitting a modest .269 with only four stolen bases at the time. Then, in the off-season when his value to the team had plummeted to its lowest ebb, Podsednik went under the knife to repair a sports hernia.

On November 20 the Sox continued a postseason housecleaning by designating Podsednik for assignment—effectively severing all ties with their World Series hero. Signed by the Colorado Rockies as a minor league free agent on April 14, 2008, the injury-jinxed outfielder fractured a finger and was limited to only 93 games. While the '08 Sox prepped for the postseason, Scotty was out of a job and headed home to Dallas, Texas. Forced retirement at age 32 seemed a very real possibility. "I think that being successful is about how you deal with the hard times," he said. "The people who can deal with setbacks are the people who can continue to move forward. I definitely learned what it takes to grind through some of the tough times." And this was one of them.

Cast adrift by the Rockies and sitting on his couch when the 2009 season unfolded, Podsednik waited for a call from his agent with hopeful news that at least one team was in need of a capable leadoff man. That team turned out to be the White Sox, who had opened the campaign with Dewayne Wise penciled in at the top of the lineup. (What *were* they thinking?) But the notoriously weak-hitting Wise blew his last chance to become a big league starter and was sent to the bench after Williams signed Podsednik to a one-year free agent deal on April 14. Scotty said his injuries were a thing of the past and he never felt better. After a 10-game stint in Charlotte, he returned to the South Side on May 1 and delivered a solid, season-long performance. Avoiding the injury bug, he stunned the front office and fans alike by leading all Sox hitters in average, multi-hit games, and stolen bases. However, he was not the same speed-burner he had been in 2005, and his instincts seemed, to most fans, to be below average. Not many among the Sox faithful could remember the last time they saw a runner get picked off of third base, but in one embarrassing moment, Podsednik was easily nailed after straying too far off the bag. Of course, he was also picked off of first and second too many times, and his fielding range and throwing ability were mediocre.

But there was no denying that Scotty showed a lot of heart during the '09 season, and he believed he was entitled to some job security and a two-year contract. But Scotty's agent and Williams were far apart in negotiations because the Sox were not entirely sold on Podsednik as their 2010 leadoff man. After they dealt two minor leaguers for Juan Pierre on December 9, 2009—a personal favorite of Ozzie Guillen's from his Florida Marlin days—it was over for Podsednik on the South Side.

He signed with the Kansas City Royals on January 8, 2010, but with a measure of regret. "It was no secret I wanted to come back here," Scotty said, wistfully. "It didn't work out. I don't want to get into the details of all that went on, but the bottom line was K.C. was the most aggressive at the start of free agency. They made me feel wanted." That is, until they traded him to the Dodgers on July 28.

Quentin, Carlos

White Sox: 2008–
Outfielder
Birthplace: Bellflower, California

B: August 28, 1982
Bats right, throws right
Ht. 6–2; **Wt.** 235

Quentin, Carlos

White Sox	G	AB	H	AVG	RBI	R	2B	3B	HR	SA	SB
2008	130	488	138	.288	100	96	26	1	36	.571	7
2009	99	351	83	.236	56	47	14	0	21	.456	3
2010	131	453	110	.243	87	73	25	2	26	.479	2
Career	498	1,679	422	.251	306	268	94	6	97	.488	15

Looking to add some depth to an inexperienced outfield surrounding Jermaine Dye, the White Sox kicked off the trading sessions at the 2007 winter meetings on December 3 with a trade that would pay them some immediate and long-term dividends. They sent Chris Carter, a Class A infield prospect from their Kannapolis team of the South Atlantic League to the Arizona Diamondbacks for a former Stanford Cardinal and the best defensive outfielder in the D'backs system: Carlos Quentin, who, by the way, was also known to hit the long ball on occasion. On the surface of things, it was not an attention-grabbing kind of trade; in fact it was a real sleeper. Carter's 25 home runs topped all of the Sox minor leaguers, but he was mostly unknown in Chicago. Quentin showed up in 2007 spring training as Arizona's starting right fielder but instead was dogged by nagging injuries. *Baseball America* ranked him as the No. 20 prospect in pro baseball and the best defensive outfielder in the Arizona system, but he had injured his left labrium in spring training and was demoted to Triple A in July. Exacerbating the situation, the former Stanford All-American later injured a hamstring and was left off the playoff roster when the D'backs advanced to the 2007 postseason. Frustrated with Quentin, Arizona was elated to receive Carter.

"It comes down to getting the best return for Carlos, and we felt like this was it. He's got a nice power track record already in the minors," beamed D'backs GM Josh Byrnes. "He's a college-aged junior prospect who's ready to go to High A and continue as a very solid power bat prospect." On the other hand, Quentin appeared to be little more than damaged goods—a down-on-his-luck, but very affordable kind of player the late Bill Veeck would have coveted back in the 1970s. Quentin made the cuts in spring training and earned a starting spot in the lineup in late May after Ozzie Guillen moved him up in the batting order into Jim Thome's customary third spot for one game against the Angels in Anaheim. Quentin delivered a key eighth-inning grand slam, breaking a 1–1 tie, and kicked off a run that saw the White Sox win 10 of 12 games, catapulting them into first place.

There he would remain for the rest of the season. His home runs came in bunches that season, drawing favorable comparisons to Jose Canseco and Luis Gonzalez. Torii Hunter of the Angels likened his pure, raw power to Hulk Hogan: "He's crazy strong." Intensely focused on his batting stance, Quentin amazed teammates and the coaches by the hundreds of "dry swings" (practice swings) he would make in the clubhouse. Carlos was highly motivated, if not driven by a crazy inner fury to attain the highest levels of personal achievement. His 36 homers in 2008 surprised the fans and stunned the front office—but not him. He expected no less out of himself. If not for a season-ending injury—a freakish mishap occurring after he slammed his bat with his wrist in frustration after fouling off a Cliff Lee pitch in Cleveland—he might have hung on and claimed the AL home run crown. He collected a Silver Slugger award instead and finished fifth in the voting for Most Valuable Player. However, Quentin's 2009 drive for personal excellence ended up stuck in reverse, his playing time limited to just 99 games because of plantar fasciitis in his left foot. After a slow start in 2010, the ominous possibility was raised that he might just be a another one-year wonder until his torrid hitting in the month of June and July helped lead the team's astounding 26–5 charge back into the thick of the AL Central Division race. He clouted a franchise record six home runs in the four games leading up to the All-Star break and was simply on fire. "Every time Carlos swings the bat good, we are very dangerous," Ozzie Guillen said. But

The "All-Intensity Team"—Carlos Quentin. (Courtesy of Mike McKay)

after a hot June, his average dipped and the home runs stopped—just like that—although he continued to drive in the runs.

Carlos Quentin was an enigma—he produced runs and was among the league leaders in getting hit by the pitch, but he couldn't lift his batting average over .240. Inside the clubhouse, the media took note of his serious manner and intense demeanor—he was all business, and there was no time for joking around. If anything, Carlos needed to learn to relax and take the pressure off of himself—something he vowed to work on after the 2010 season ended. Meanwhile, the vaunted Chris Carter was passed on to Oakland as part of a trade that brought Dan Haren to Arizona. Carter was a late-season call-up in 2010 and produced in a big way for the A's.

Radcliff, Ray

White Sox: 1934–39
Outfielder
Nickname: Rip
Birthplace: Kiowa, Oklahoma
B: January 19, 1906
D: May 23, 1962
Batted left, threw left
Ht. 5–10; **Wt.** 170

Radcliff, Rip

White Sox	G	AB	H	AVG	RBI	R	2B	3B	HR	SA	SB
1934	14	56	15	.268	5	7	2	1	0	.339	1
1935	146	623	178	.286	68	95	28	8	10	.404	4
1936	138	618	207	.335	82	120	31	7	8	.447	6
1937	144	584	190	.325	79	105	38	10	4	.445	6
1938	129	503	166	.330	81	64	23	6	5	.429	5
1939	113	397	105	.264	53	49	25	2	2	.353	6
Career	1,081	4,074	1,267	.311	532	598	205	50	42	.417	40

Rip Radcliff and Luke Appling provided the Sox with a lethal one-two batting punch that helped lift the ballclub out of its second-division doldrums in the late 1930s. Rip's torrid hitting compensated for his limited range in left field and a weak throwing arm.

Radcliff came to the attention of the Sox in 1930 after he won the Triple Crown in the Southeastern League. He was given a spring training audition at first base in 1931 by manager Donie Bush, but failed to make the grade. Ray was returned to the minors for further development. He hit in sensational style for Dallas and St. Paul for the next few seasons, but his defensive liabilities held him back. The White Sox secured Ray from Louisville in 1934, and finally the veteran minor leaguer was on his way to an abbreviated though rewarding career.

In 1936, his greatest White Sox season, Radcliff nearly stole the batting crown from Appling. The Sox duo ran neck and neck for much of the season, though at times it appeared that Radcliff might pull away. After a 6-for-7 performance against the Philadelphia A's in a July 19 twin bill in the City of Brotherly Love, Rip lifted his average to .383. In a remarkable 12-game stretch that same month, he collected 29 hits.

At other times, however, he couldn't buy a hit. Radcliff's streaky hitting and erratic defensive play were constant concerns to manager Jimmy Dykes and sources of amusement to Cubs GM Jimmy Gallagher, who called Rip the greatest *self-defense* left fielder in the game. That is, self-preservation was always uppermost in Rip's mind as he drew a bead on a descending fly ball.

After a disappointing 1939 campaign, Dykes and Harry Grabiner traded to Rip to the St. Louis Browns for Julius "Moose" Solters on December 8, 1939. It was a bad trade for Chicago, and one of Jimmy Dykes' rare miscalculations. Radcliff hit .342 in 1940 and led the American League in hits.

Raines, Tim

White Sox: 1991–95
Outfielder
Nickname: Rock
Birthplace: Sanford, California
B: September 16, 1959
Bats both, throws left
Ht. 6–5; **Wt.** 275

Raines, Tim

White Sox	G	AB	H	AVG	RBI	R	2B	3B	HR	SA	SB
1991	155	609	163	.268	50	102	20	6	5	.345	51
1992	144	551	162	.294	54	102	22	9	7	.405	45
1993	115	415	127	.306	54	75	16	4	16	.480	21
1994	101	384	102	.266	52	80	15	5	10	.409	13
1995	133	502	143	.285	67	81	25	4	12	.422	13
Career	2,502	8,872	2,605	.294	980	2,605	430	113	170	.425	806

Early in his career Tim Raines entered a drug rehab clinic. He faced some hard choices in life: give it up and go straight, or get out of baseball. Raines was only 22 years old and had just won Rookie of the Year honors with Montreal on the strength of 71 stolen bases and a .304 average. Raines conquered his problems and achieved stardom with the Montreal Expos in the 1980s. Tim won the National League batting title in 1986, and he was always a long-ball threat at the plate.

And yet, Tim's baserunning abilities always seemed to overshadow his skills with a bat and a glove. Raines wanted to be known as the complete player—not just as a burner on the base paths. Eight times in his career, Tim pilfered 50 or more bases. Entering the 1995 season, Raines trailed only Rickey Henderson, Lou Brock, and Ty Cobb on the all-time list. Just don't call him a base thief.

"Call me Rock," he advised the White Sox brass after joining the ballclub on December 24, 1990, in a multiplayer trade that shipped Ivan Calderon and Barry Jones to Montreal. "Rock" Raines swiped his customary 50 in 1991, but his batting average took a dip, and there were concerns that the White Sox had acquired a player well past his prime.

The trade turned out to be a good one for Chicago. In fact, it is probably one of the best White Sox player deals in the last 25 years, though Tim got off to a less than auspicious start.

Raines slowed down in the next few seasons. He was criticized by the TV broadcast crew for being tentative at first base. But when he turned on the after-burners, the Rock was usually successful. He is the all-time leader in stolen base percentage, with an 85.1 percent success ratio. Entering the 1995 season, he was only three bases short of the American

League record of 32 consecutive steals. Raines tied the mark within the first few weeks of the strike-shortened season and set a new record in the seventh inning of a game against the Toronto Blue Jays on June 5. Timmy ran his streak to 40 before it was finally snapped on September 2, 1995.

Raines was a key contributor during the drive toward division championship in 1993 when he returned to .300 form. He became only the second player in team history to homer from both sides of the plate in the same game on August 31 in New York. Tim was perfect in the field and led the league with a 1.000 percentage.

Tim played in two league championship series—one with Montreal, the other with the Sox—but the larger goal of appearing in a World Series evaded him until 1996. "I'd rather hit .200 than .330 if it meant winning the playoffs and World Series," he told sportswriter Scott Gregor. "More than anything else I play to win." After leaving the White Sox on January 23, 1996, to sign a two-year free agent deal with the Yankees, Timmy finally achieved his baseball dream.

In return, the White Sox received Blaise Kozeniewski (the proverbial "player to be named later") who never made it up to the majors. "Rock" had a few more good years left in him and rounded out a superlative 23-year career by playing four games with his son Tim Jr. as a member of the Baltimore Orioles in 2001. The Griffeys, Ken Sr. and Ken Jr., are the only other father-and-son teammates in baseball history. On November 1, 2004, Raines rejoined the White Sox as a first-base coach for Ozzie Guillen. Raines replaced Rafael Santana and served the White Sox as a first-base and running coach for the next two seasons until he was fired by Guillen on October 13, 2006.

Tim Raines

Ramirez, Alexei

White Sox: 2008–
Infielder
Nickname: The Cuban Missile
Birthplace: Pinar del Rio, Cuba

B: September 22, 1981
Bats right, throws right
Ht. 6–2; **Wt.** 170

Ramirez, Alexei

White Sox	G	AB	H	AVG	RBI	R	2B	3B	HR	SA	SB
2008	136	480	139	.290	77	65	22	2	21	.475	13
2009	148	542	150	.277	68	71	14	1	15	.389	14
2010	156	585	165	.282	70	83	29	2	18	.431	13
Career	440	1,667	454	.283	214	219	65	5	54	.430	40

A star of the Cuban League for seven seasons who alternated between shortstop and the outfield for his hometown team in Pinar del Rio, Alexi Ramirez, a dead fastball hitter, impressed U.S. scouts with his strong showing during the 2006 World Baseball Classic, collecting six hits in 16 at-bats. In September 2007 Ramirez, a former Olympian, fled Cuba for the Dominican Republic, where he joined his wife and children in exile and applied for citizenship. At the same time, he advertised his services to Major League Baseball, hoping to catch on as a free agent with a big-league club through his agent, Jaime Torres, who also represented Jose Contreras. After a number of tryouts with various teams, he inked a four-year contract with the White Sox worth $4.75 million on December 21, 2007, thus becoming the 15th native of Cuba to play for the South Side team. Alexei bypassed the minor leagues and reported to the big-league camp in March—surviving the roster cuts and making the team as a second baseman. His rush to the majors was capped off by an outstanding 2008 season—with many clutch hits and the MLB record for most grand slam home runs in a season by a rookie (four). The fourth one, coming off of Detroit's Gary Glover on September 29, catapulted the White Sox into a one-game playoff with the Minnesota Twins for the AL Central Division crown the next day. At season's end, Alexei finished in second place in the voting for American League Rookie of the Year honors, losing out to Evan Longoria of the Tampa Bay Rays. It was a solid, productive year, but changes were in store. The White Sox brain trust made the decision over the winter to shift him to shortstop—Alexei's natural position—but the transition was a rough one, and the entire '09 season was a time of painful readjustment.

Ramirez committed 20 errors (fourth highest among shortstops in both leagues) with a lackluster .969 fielding average, and his batting average and home run total dropped. Dubbed "the Cuban Missile" (not to be confused with Minnie Minoso, the "Cuban Comet") by Hawk Harrelson, Ramirez fielded the last out of Mark Buehrle's perfect game on July 23. Harrelson's famous call up in the broadcast booth—"Alexei!... Yes!"—as Ramirez fielded the ground ball and fired a strike to Josh Fields at first base perfectly captured the excitement and said it all. For 2010 the Sox signed future Hall of Famer Omar Vizquel as a free agent with the intention of working with Ramirez to sharpen his fielding skills.

Alexei Ramirez celebrates another 2008 grand slam. (Courtesy of the Chicago White Sox)

Vizquel noted that Ramirez "needs to move his feet when fielding. He has the tendency to stand still and not move to the ball." Positioning himself properly to tag out would-be base stealers at second base was another problem. Ramirez picked up the bad habit of standing in front of the bag, or to the left of second, thus allowing the would-be stealer to slide around his tag.

Alexei gradually worked through these flaws, with Joey Cora hitting him a steady diet of ground balls during pregame workouts, and blossomed into a fine fielding and occasionally spectacular shortstop in the second half of the 2010 season, while his hitting contributions earned him a Silver Slugger award.

Reynolds, Carl

White Sox: 1927–31
Outfielder
Nickname: Sheeps
Birthplace: LaRue, Texas

B: February 1, 1903
D: May 29, 1978
Batted right, threw right
Ht. 6–0; **Wt.** 194

Reynolds, Carl

White Sox	G	AB	H	AVG	RBI	R	2B	3B	HR	SA	SB
1927	14	42	9	.214	7	5	3	0	1	.357	1
1928	84	291	94	.323	36	51	21	11	2	.491	15
1929	131	517	164	.317	67	81	24	12	11	.474	19
1930	138	563	202	.359	100	103	25	18	22	.584	16
1931	118	462	134	.290	77	71	24	14	6	.442	17
Career	1,222	4,495	1,357	.302	695	672	247	107	80	.458	112

Carl Reynolds was a personal favorite of Charles Comiskey from the moment he joined the White Sox from the campus of Southwestern University in Texas. Reynolds was a refreshing departure from the yearly array of collegiate hopefuls who failed to pass spring training inspection. Carl was a consistent hitter from the moment he debuted with the Sox in September 1927.

Reynolds paid his dues in right field and worked hard to correct his fielding deficiencies. Manager Donie Bush shifted him to left field for the 1930 season, and the change of scenery energized his career. Playing in Yankee Stadium on July 2 of that year, Reynolds became the first Sox player to pole three home runs in one game. The three distance blows occurred in successive innings, tying a record held by George Kelly since 1923.

His .359 batting average tied Babe Ruth for third place in the AL batting race, and it ranks him fifth on the all-time single-season chart for Sox hitters. Carl might have closed to within a few points of the leader, but five potential hits were washed away by rainouts.

Things were a little different in 1931. Carl missed time because of sprained ankles and a pulled leg tendon. Considered temperamental by his manager and quarrelsome with his teammates, Reynolds was traded to the Senators for Bump Hadley, Sam Jones, and Jackie Hayes on December 3, 1931. There must have been some truth to the rap against Reynolds because he was traded five times in the next six years.

Carl Reynolds

John Rigney: from flannels to front office pinstripes

Rigney, Johnny

White Sox: 1937–42; 1946–47
Pitcher
Nickname: Dunc
Birthplace: Oak Park, Illinois

B: October 28, 1914
D: October 21, 1984
Batted right, threw right
Ht. 6–2½; **Wt.** 190

Rigney, Johnny

White Sox	W	L	Pct	ERA	G	CG	IP	H	BB	K	ShO
1937	2	5	.286	4.96	22	1	90⅔	107	46	38	1
1938	9	9	.500	3.56	38	7	167	164	82	84	1
1939	15	8	.652	3.70	35	11	218⅔	208	84	119	2
1940	14	18	.438	3.11	39	19	280⅔	240	90	141	2
1941	13	13	.500	3.84	30	18	237	224	92	119	3
1942	3	3	.500	3.20	7	6	59	40	16	34	0
1946	5	5	.500	4.03	15	3	82⅔	76	35	51	2
1947	2	3	.400	1.95	11	2	50⅔	42	15	19	0
Career	63	64	.496	3.59	197	67	1,186⅓	1,101	450	605	11

On and off the field, John Dungan Rigney was a key player in White Sox affairs for more than two decades.

A tall, lanky right-hander from Chicago's western suburbs, Rigney made his professional debut in 1935 after completing his college studies at St. Thomas College in St. Paul, Minnesota. In his first year of pro ball Dunc played with five different minor league teams; he was selected by the White Sox after posting an 8–4 record with St. Paul in 1936.

Rigney enjoyed his greatest success in 1939. He was on the mound the night the lights went on for the first time in Comiskey Park, whipping the St. Louis Browns 5–2 before a packed house on August 14. It was his seventh win in a string of victories that reached 11 in a row until he bowed to Detroit on September 10.

Two years later, on October 8, 1941, Rigney married Dorothy Comiskey, the eldest daughter of Grace and J. Louis Comiskey. Thus the young pitcher was ensured of a future role in White Sox policy making once his playing career ended.

Drafted into the military in May 1942, Rigney blew out his arm pitching for the navy all-star team in the Pacific theater. He attempted a comeback in 1946, but gave it up a year later in order to move into the front office as director of the White Sox farm system. During the next nine years Rigney retooled the minor league affiliates with marvelous results. He significantly expanded the scouting operation, hired new coaches and managers, and deserves much of the credit for the success the parent club enjoyed throughout the 1950s.

Rigney was elevated to a dual vice presidency with his brother-in-law Chuck Comiskey on November 16, 1955, and remained with the team in this capacity until his wife received the green light from the courts to sell her controlling interest in the ballclub to Bill Veeck in March 1959.

Risberg, Charles

White Sox: 1917–20
Shortstop
Nickname: Swede
Birthplace: San Francisco, California

B: October 13, 1894
D: October 13, 1975
Batted left, threw right
Ht. 6–0; **Wt.** 175

Risberg, Charles

White Sox	G	AB	H	AVG	RBI	R	2B	3B	HR	SA	SB
1917	149	474	96	.203	45	59	20	8	1	.285	16
1918	82	273	70	.256	27	36	12	3	1	.333	5
1919	119	414	106	.256	38	48	19	6	2	.345	19
1920	126	458	122	.266	65	53	21	10	2	.369	12
Career	476	1,619	394	.243	175	196	72	27	6	.332	52

Toughened by a life that included little formal education, fistfights with Ty Cobb, the humility of banishment from professional baseball following the Black Sox scandal, and the loss of his life savings in the stock market crash of 1929, "Swede" Risberg remained unrepentant and a "hard guy" to the very end.

Risberg, the "missing link" who made it possible for the contending but incomplete White Sox ballclub to win two championships, debuted with the Vernon, California, club of the Pacific Coast League in 1912. He was purchased by Comiskey from Vernon after the 1916 season. His range in the field and strong throwing arm won him a starting assignment with the Sox and allowed manager Kid Gleason to shift Buck Weaver back to third base, his natural position.

"Every kid had to pick a favorite player," recalled famed author Nelson Algren, who grew up in Chicago when the Black Sox were making headlines. "No rumors of the fix had yet reached us by midsummer 1920. The White Sox were still white. Swede Risberg was still my favorite player. I began to walk pigeon-toed because Risberg was pigeon-toed."

Risberg fell in with the outcast clique of Sox players, united in their dislike of owner Charles Comiskey and the haughty airs of Swede's keystone partner Eddie Collins. Chick Gandil recruited Swede as his "second lieutenant" during the initial plan to throw the 1919 World Series to the Redlegs. Swede lived up to his end of the bargain by hitting .080—lowest among the regulars. Years later Risberg hotly denied complicity in the fix. "What did they have on me?" he told reporters in 1931. "The records show I made a new mark for shortstops in the World Series by accepting 53 chances and making 31 assists."

In his sworn testimony Shoeless Joe Jackson related a somewhat different version to the grand jury. Afterward he told reporters: "Now Risberg threatens to bump me off if I squawk. That's why I had all the bailiffs with me when I left the grand jury room this afternoon."

After Judge Kenesaw Landis barred him from organized ball in 1921, Swede continued to play the game outside the long shadow cast by the commissioner. In 1925 Risberg and Hap Felsch were teammates in Scobey, Montana, earning $600 a month plus expenses.

Two years after losing his house, his automobile agency, and the family dairy farm in the crash of 1929, Risberg signed on with the Sioux Falls (South Dakota) Canaries of the Northern League as a second baseman. Owner Rex Stucker kicked him off the team in 1932 after Swede tried to foment a revolt among his teammates.

According to Robert Risberg, one of Swede's four children, his dad played in the Negro Leagues in later years and earned more money barnstorming than he received in any single year from Charles Comiskey. Swede carefully disguised his identity by applying shoe polish to his face and hands. Historians can neither confirm nor deny the authenticity of the story, but if true, it would certainly be in line with the character of the man Joe Jackson called a hard guy.

The Swede was a dairy farmer. Here he is in 1927.

Rivera, Manuel

White Sox: 1952–61
Outfielder, first baseman
Nickname: Jungle Jim
Birthplace: New York City

B: July 22, 1922
Bats left, throws right
Ht. 6–0; **Wt.** 196

Rivera, Manuel

White Sox	G	AB	H	AVG	RBI	R	2B	3B	HR	SA	SB
1952	150	537	136	.253	48	72	20	9	7	.363	21
1953	156	567	147	.259	78	79	26	16	11	.420	22
1954	145	490	140	.286	61	62	16	8	13	.431	18
1955	147	454	120	.264	52	71	24	4	10	.401	25
1956	139	491	125	.255	66	76	23	5	12	.395	20
1957	125	402	103	.256	52	51	21	6	14	.443	18
1958	116	276	62	.225	35	37	8	4	9	.380	21
1959	80	177	39	.220	19	18	9	4	4	.384	5
1960	48	17	5	.294	1	17	0	0	1	.471	4
1961	1	0	0	.000	0	0	0	0	0	.000	0
Career	1,171	3,552	911	.256	422	503	155	56	83	.402	160

In an era defined by colorless, long-distance home run hitters, this young Puerto Rican outfielder from the Bronx captured the imagination of Sox fans with his reckless, belly-flopping slides into second base, his colorful and humorous observations on American life, and his infectious enthusiasm for the game, the city of Chicago, and the South Side fans. "He'll do anything to win," commented Marty Marion, his second White Sox manager. "He's one of the most exciting players I've ever seen."

Frank Lane purchased Jim Rivera from the Seattle Rainers on July 1, 1951, after he won the PCL batting title. He was shuttled to the St. Louis Browns on November 28, in a package deal involving a half dozen other players, including Sherm Lollar, who moved into the starting lineup as the No. 1 catcher. Rivera was returned to Chicago by Browns owner Bill Veeck on July 28, 1952, in a straight cash sale. Thereafter, "Jungle Jim" became a Comiskey Park institution in both right and center field. In 1955 he swiped 25 bases—an uncommon feat until Louie Aparicio arrived on the scene to steal his thunder a year later.

Jim never approached the .300 mark during his nine-year run in Chicago, but the fans adored him, and no other player of that era appeared before more church, civic, and youth

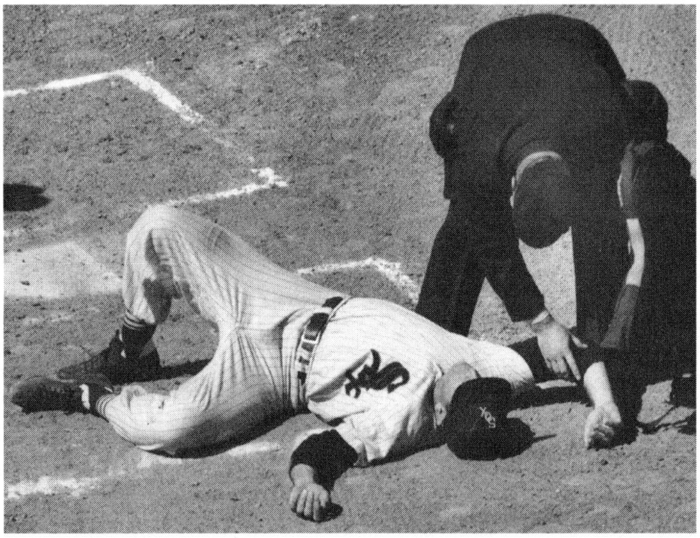

"Jungle Jim" Rivera skulled by Eddie Lopat. He's okay.

groups in the off-season than Rivera. A collection of "Rivera-isms" never made it into book form, but they received wide play in the press:

- To Frank Lane on his decision to resign from the White Sox: "I had you around just for laughs. When you stopped, I had to get rid of you."
- To former first lady Bess Truman in attendance at a Sox-A's game in Kansas City: "I'm sure sorry my homer beat your team, but it was a hell of a wallop, eh, Bess?"
- To manager Al Lopez, who shifted Jim to first base in 1957: "What's all this stuff I've been reading about these guys who are going to play right field? When the bell rings, you will see only one guy in right: Big Jim!"
- To President John F. Kennedy on Opening Day 1961, after receiving an autograph: "What's this? This is just a scribble! I can hardly make it out! You'll have to do better than this, John!"

In the off-season, Jim augmented his income selling season tickets. Personable and gregarious, he was the team's most successful and talented salesman—he drove a White Sox station wagon to the homes of season-ticket holders and businesses all over the South Side to peddle the pasteboards for the upcoming season. "I have a motto," he said. "I tell the fans, 'You come visit us in the summer. Now we're coming to visit you in the winter. Remember," he counseled his more skeptical prospects, "if you buy these tickets, you'll get the same seats for the World Series. And we're gonna be in the World Series, you know, cuz we ain't lost a game yet. You want two good seats near the dugout? I'll do better than that for you. I'll get you two seats *in* the dugout right next to me!" Imagine a modern-day megabillionaire player coming up to *your* door to persuade *you* to reup for the coming season!

The Rivera show had its day, and then quietly expired on June 7, 1961, when the White Sox handed him his unconditional release. In the years to come he amused and delighted the visitors to his Captain's Cabin Restaurant near Angola, Indiana, with colorful reminiscences of his White Sox career.

Robinson, Eddie

White Sox: 1950–52
First baseman
Birthplace: Paris, Texas

B: December 15, 1920
Bats left, throws right
Ht. 6–2½; **Wt.** 210

Robinson, Eddie

White Sox	G	AB	H	AVG	RBI	R	2B	3B	HR	SA	SB
1950	119	428	133	.311	73	62	11	2	20	.486	0
1951	151	564	159	.282	117	85	23	5	29	.495	2
1952	155	594	176	.296	104	79	33	1	22	.466	2
Career	1,314	4,279	1,145	.268	723	545	171	24	172	.439	10

Before he blossomed into stardom in 1949, the kindest thing anyone could say about this granite-jawed first baseman from the Lone Star State was that he bore a striking resemblance to "Jumbo" Joe Stydahar, coach of the NFL's Los Angeles Rams.

After weeks of negotiation, Robby was traded from the Washington Senators to the White Sox with infielder Al Kozar and pitcher Rae Scarborough for Cass Michaels, John Ostrowski, and Bob Kuzava on May 31, 1950. Eddie only had one home run when he joined the team on Memorial Day. After joining the Sox, he slugged 20 home runs to establish himself as one of the league's most productive power hitters, despite the obvious liabilities of playing in spacious Comiskey Park.

In 1951 Robby crushed 29 home runs to tie Gus Zernial's year-old club record. The mark held up until 1970 when Bill Melton came along. Robinson reached peak efficiency with the White Sox in 1951 and 1952. He was an enthusiastic, cheerleading, holler guy and a positive contributor to the offense. However, Eddie was getting on in years, and Frank Lane sensed that it was time to let go while his market value remained high. Lane engineered a trade with the A's on January 28, 1953, sending Robby and Joe DeMaestri to Philadelphia for Ferris Fain, the American League batting champion who was also past his prime. The deal turned out to be a washout for both clubs.

1951 Murderers' Row (left to right): Nellie Fox, Minnie Minoso, and Eddie Robinson

Robinson, Floyd

White Sox: 1960–66
Outfielder
Birthplace: Prescott, Arkansas

B: May 9, 1936
Bats left, throws right
Ht. 5–9; **Wt.** 175

Robinson, Floyd

White Sox	G	AB	H	AVG	RBI	R	2B	3B	HR	SA	SB
1960	22	46	13	.283	1	7	0	0	0	.283	2
1961	132	432	134	.310	59	69	20	7	11	.465	7
1962	156	600	187	.312	109	89	45	10	11	.475	4
1963	146	527	149	.283	71	71	21	6	13	.419	4
1964	141	525	158	.301	59	83	17	3	11	.408	9
1965	156	577	153	.265	66	70	15	6	14	.385	4
1966	127	342	81	.237	35	44	11	2	5	.325	8
Career	1,012	3,284	929	.283	426	458	140	36	67	.409	42

In the latter stages of the Go-Go era, the White Sox farm system yielded an exciting bumper crop of rookies who reached peak performance early and then faded away. Bruce Howard, Camilo Carreon, Mike Hershberger, and Floyd Robinson, a chunky ex-Marine acquired from the minor league San Diego Padres in 1960, immediately come to mind.

Robby burst upon the scene in a blaze of glory in 1961. He hit a solid .310 but missed out on Rookie of the Year honors because he fell 10 at-bats shy of qualifying. Floyd seemed destined for greatness. The following year he banged out a league-leading 45 doubles, which stood as the team record until 1992 when Frank Thomas bettered the mark. Robinson's memorable 1962 campaign also included a 6-for-6 effort (all singles) against the Red Sox in Boston on July 22. Over the winter the Chicago baseball writers at their annual Diamond Dinner named him Player of the Year.

Robinson's situation changed when Eddie Stanky took over the club in 1966. His batting average plummeted in the second half of the season, and a verbal sparring match developed between the two men. Floyd's White Sox career ended on December 15, 1966, when Ed Short traded him to Cincinnati for another fading veteran, Jim O'Toole.

Rogovin, Saul

White Sox: 1951–53
Pitcher
Birthplace: Brooklyn, New York

B: October 10, 1922
D: January 23, 1995
Batted right, threw right
Ht. 6–2; **Wt.** 205

Rogovin, Saul

White Sox	W	L	Pct	ERA	G	CG	IP	H	BB	K	ShO	Sv
1951	11	7	.611	2.48	22	17	192⅔	166	67	77	3	0
1952	14	9	.609	3.85	33	12	231⅔	224	79	121	3	1
1953	7	12	.368	5.22	22	4	131	151	48	62	1	1
Career	48	48	.500	4.06	150	43	883⅔	888	308	388	9	2

Sleepy-eyed Saul Rogovin toiled in a war plant, and he was playing sandlot ball for the company team when he was discovered one Sunday afternoon by umpire Dolly Stark, who procured a tryout for his young charge with Chattanooga of the Southern Association.

Rogovin began his career as a third baseman but made the switch to the pitching mound in 1945, his first year of pro ball. On the last day of the season he asked his manager for a chance to pitch. He shut out the Birmingham Barons on four hits, and from that day forward he was a pitcher. A sore arm limited his playing time with the Detroit Tigers in 1950, his freshman season, but Sox skipper Paul Richards had been favorably impressed by Rogovin's assortment of pitches when Richards was managing Buffalo in 1949 and Saul was his ace hurler. "If I can't win for Richards, I can't win for anybody," Rogovin said in praise of his former boss.

In search of a consistent No. 4 starter, Frank Lane traded Bob Cain, one of his 1950 mainstays, to the Tigers for Rogovin on May 15, 1951. It was an admitted gamble, and the news of the trade stunned White Sox players and fans alike, but the Brooklyn boy came through after Richards helped restore his straight overhand delivery.

Saul pitched consecutive two-hitters against the Browns and Red Sox in late May and early June to cement his place in the rotation, but his finest performance en route to the 1951 American League earned-run-average crown was a

Saul Rogovin

masterful 16-inning job against Boston in the second game of a twi-night doubleheader on July 12. The Sox lost the game in the 17th inning, but his 14-strikeout effort was indicative of the character of the 1951 Go-Go boys.

Pitching a heavier schedule in 1952, Rogovin enjoyed his most productive season. He fanned 14 Red Sox hitters in a memorable 17-inning marathon on September 14, but Luis Aloma picked up the victory in the final frame. Rogovin, who sometimes fell asleep on the bench and complained of chronic soreness in his pitching arm, was not nearly as effective in 1953.

Paul Richards believed Saul's problems were all in his head until physicians at Johns Hopkins University diagnosed bone chips in his elbow. Rogovin was placed on the inactive list and wasn't much use to the team down the stretch. Dissatisfied with his work ethic and in desperate need of a third baseman, Lane dealt Saul to Cincinnati on December 11, for Willard Marshall, who was ticketed for an Opening Day assignment in the outfield in order to free up Minnie Minoso for third-base duties. Minnie lasted only nine games at the hot corner in 1954.

Rohe, George

White Sox: 1905–07
Infielder
Birthplace: Cincinnati, Ohio

B: September 15, 1875
D: June 10, 1957
Batted right, threw right
Ht. 5–9; **Wt.** 165

Rohe, George

White Sox	G	AB	H	AVG	RBI	R	2B	3B	HR	SA	SB
1905	34	113	24	.212	12	14	1	0	1	.248	2
1906	75	225	58	.258	25	14	5	1	0	.289	8
1907	144	494	105	.213	51	46	11	2	2	.255	16
Career	253	868	197	.227	92	81	19	3	3	.266	27

George Rohe was the unheralded utility infielder who became a World Series hero overnight. Otherwise he was a footnote player of the passing scene.

Rohe began playing professionally in 1899 for the Wabash team of the Indiana League. In 1904 he was the team captain for the pennant-winning New Orleans Pelicans of the Southern Association before a yellow fever epidemic broke up the league. White Sox owner Charles Comiskey purchased his contract for the White Sox on August 28, 1905. Strictly bench material, Rohe was pressed into emergency duty on the eve of the 1906 World Series after George Davis sustained an injury.

George Rohe tied Jiggs Donahue for the highest individual batting average in the series—.333. It was an incredible performance—divine intervention beamed toward the happy White Sox fan.

In Game 1 Rohe scored the winning run after breaking for home on a weak tap to the third baseman. He belted a bases-loaded triple to win Game 3. When the Series concluded and the Sox emerged victorious, Comiskey made a foolish promise as he stood in an open automobile addressing the

George Rohe

fans: "Whatever George Rohe may do from now on, he's signed for life with me!"

Rohe played regularly in 1907 but was released at the end of the season. He never played another game of major league ball but is credited with convincing Shoeless Joe Jackson to sign a professional contract with the Cleveland Indians. Rohe later became a commercial photographer.

Rowand, Aaron

White Sox: 2001–05
Outfielder
Birthplace: Portland, Oregon

B: August 29, 1977
Bats right, throws right
Ht. 6–0; **Wt.** 200

Rowand, Aaron

White Sox	G	AB	H	AVG	RBI	R	2B	3B	HR	SA	SB
2001	63	123	36	.293	20	21	5	0	4	.431	5
2002	126	302	78	.258	29	41	16	2	7	.394	0
2003	93	157	45	.287	24	22	8	0	6	.452	0
2004	140	487	151	.310	69	94	38	2	24	.544	17
2005	157	578	156	.270	69	77	30	5	13	.407	16
Career	1,250	4,043	1,116	.276	515	579	245	16	132	.442	65

Credit the Chicago Bears with an assist in bringing Aaron Rowand to the South Side after he turned down an offer to sign with the New York Mets in 1995. Rowand is a passionate fan of the Monsters of the Midway, and the chance to play in their home town, albeit in another sport, was too good to pass up—at least that is what we have come to suspect.

Aaron Rowand: a Jim Landis/Ken Berry player

Selected in the June 1998 First-Year Player Draft, Aaron attended Cal State–Fullerton and was a 35th pick. He was another one of those "sleepers" who escaped the watchful eye of the scouts. Following his June 2001 call-up, Rowand established his value to the team with an aggressive, "I'll play anywhere, just let me play," kind of attitude. He did not relish the tag "utility outfielder," but unfortunately that is what he seemed destined to be. With some players—even a guy like Aaron Rowand with twice as much hustle, heart, and love of the game as some of the overpaid, ego-tripping superstars too proud to sign autographs or participate in team-sponsored charity events—it is impossible to alter perceptions and make the big step up and achieve that next level of success. In Aaron's case, he played himself into the starting lineup through grit and determination, then reached his plateau early. The proverbial road to success was filled with obstacles, both literal and figurative. In November 2002 he was involved in a near-fatal dirt-bike accident and sustained a broken scapula and rib, missing part of the 2003 season.

Under Ozzie Guillen's direction, Rowand enjoyed something of a break-out year in 2004. As a starting center fielder in the Jim Landis–Ken Berry tradition of White Sox center fielders, Aaron crashed into walls, reeled in fly balls that might have sailed over the fence or past lesser outfielders, and mixed his fielding skills with good speed and occasional power at the plate. He hit .310 in what was admittedly an offense-oriented season for baseball. One can only wonder whether the 2004 campaign represented the "real" Aaron Rowand, or if his 2005 numbers were a more realistic and accurate reflection of his capabilities as the team's everyday center fielder. That is not to say his numbers were bad; they were not. And he always found interesting ways to get on base. Aaron was plunked 21 times by opposing pitchers in 2005, two shy of Minnie Minoso's team record of 23 set in 1956. But he fanned an alarming 116 times, and that is not good for a contact hitter setting up scoring situations for Paul Konerko and company. It was his second year in a row with 100-plus strikeouts, so, by the time of the playoffs and World Series, he seemed to be swinging a "tired" bat, but he was razor sharp in the field all year long.

Life is not always fair. It certainly wasn't for Rowand in 2005. His .992 fielding percentage was a strong enough credential for Gold Glove consideration, but he was beaten out by Torii Hunter of the Twins who played only 98 games with a mark of .987. Go figure. Nevertheless, Aaron truly loved playing in Chicago and was particularly close to teammate and buddy Joe Crede. Rowand had signed a two-year, $5.25 million contract extension before the 2005 season and made his intentions widely known that he was in it for the long haul. Aaron had heard the rumors of an impending off-season deal that might send him away. It came as a bitter disappointment when the news of his trade reached him the day before Thanksgiving that he was being shipped off to Philadelphia with minor leaguers Donald Haigwood and Gio Gonzalez for former Sox-killer Jim Thome, the "big bat" missing from the middle of the lineup in 2005. "If we brought back the same team, it would have been difficult to repeat," explained Kenny Williams. "We feel like we need a left-handed presence in the middle of the order." Rowand was disappointed but resigned to his fate. "It's just an ugly reminder about what kind of business this really is," he said. "You end up doing something special and get to share it with so many special people and enjoy it as much as possible. The next thing you know, you're talking about leaving town. It's part of baseball that's not my favorite, but it's something you have to deal with." A solid performer with the Phillies for two seasons, he signed with the Giants in 2008 and played on another world champion club in 2010.

Russell, Ewell

White Sox: 1913–19
Pitcher
Nickname: Reb
Birthplace: Jackson, Mississippi

B: April 12, 1889
D: September 30, 1973
Batted right, threw right
Ht. 5–11; **Wt.** 185

Russell, Ewell

White Sox	W	L	Pct	ERA	G	CG	IP	H	BB	K	ShO
1913	21	17	.553	1.91	51	25	316	249	79	122	8
1914	7	12	.368	2.90	38	8	167⅓	168	33	79	1
1915	11	10	.524	2.59	41	10	229⅓	215	47	90	3
1916	17	11	.607	2.42	56	16	264⅓	207	42	112	5
1917	12	5	.706	1.95	35	11	189⅓	170	32	54	5
1918	6	5	.545	2.60	19	10	124⅔	117	33	38	2
1919	0	0	—	0.00	1	0	—	1	1	0	0
Career	74	60	.552	2.34	241	80	1,291	1,127	267	495	24

Ewell "Reb" Russell

The townspeople of Bonham, Texas—a whistle-stop in the northern corner of the Lone Star State—turned out to bid farewell to Ewell Russell, a local boy who was off to join the White Sox. A brass band and the tearful good wishes of the simple farmers sent him on his way.

Raised on a Bonham farm, Russell aspired to a baseball career in order to see the country beyond the confines of the Texas-Oklahoma border. Drafted by the White Sox from Fort Worth for $1,200, Russell was taught to throw a curveball by coach Kid Gleason. Armed with this new pitch, "Reb" Russell was an immediate sensation. He cracked the starting rotation on May 17, 1913, before a packed house of 35,000 fans who had come to Comiskey Park to celebrate "Frank Chance Day." The kid displayed coolness under fire before such an imposing throng by beating the Yankees 6–3. He led the league in appearances and set a rookie record for Sox pitchers by winning 21 games in 1913.

Russell's arm went bad later in his career, forcing his release in 1919. Reconciled to the fact that his career was over, Russell went to work in an Indianapolis garage. In the middle of the 1920 season, Joe Cantillon of the Minneapolis Millers hired Russell to play the outfield for his ballclub. He hit .339 for the season, and before another two years had passed, Reb was back in the majors with the Pittsburgh Pirates. He hit .368 as a pinch-hitter and reserve outfielder in 1922.

Schalk, Ray

White Sox: 1912–28
Catcher
Nickname: Cracker
Birthplace: Harvey, Illinois

B: August 12, 1892
D: May 19, 1970
Batted right, threw right
Ht. 5–9; **Wt.** 165

Schalk, Ray

White Sox	G	AB	H	AVG	RBI	R	2B	3B	HR	SA	SB
1912	23	63	18	.286	8	7	2	0	0	.317	2
1913	128	401	98	.244	38	38	15	5	1	.314	14
1914	135	392	106	.270	36	30	13	2	0	.314	24
1915	135	413	110	.266	54	46	14	4	1	.327	15
1916	129	410	95	.232	41	36	12	9	0	.305	30
1917	140	424	96	.226	51	48	12	4	3	.295	19
1918	108	333	73	.219	22	35	6	3	0	.255	12
1919	131	394	111	.282	34	57	9	3	0	.320	11
1920	151	485	131	.270	61	64	25	5	1	.348	10
1921	128	416	105	.252	47	32	24	4	0	.329	3
1922	142	442	124	.281	60	57	22	3	4	.371	12
1923	123	382	87	.228	44	42	12	2	1	.277	6
1924	57	153	30	.196	11	15	4	2	1	.268	1
1925	125	343	94	.274	52	44	18	1	0	.332	11
1926	82	226	60	.265	32	26	9	1	0	.314	5
1927	16	26	6	.231	2	2	2	0	0	.308	0
1928	2	1	1	1.000	0	0	0	0	0	1.000	1
Career	1,760	5,306	1,345	.253	594	579	199	48	12	.316	176

Ray Schalk

For 17 seasons—encompassing the best and worst of White Sox history—Ray Schalk offered a daily exhibition of skill, intelligence, nerve, and endurance that was the envy of opponents and a wonder to his teammates. There have been better hitting catchers than Schalk, catchers with better speed and throwing range. Few of the modern-day backstops, though, will ever approach his mental toughness or his rugged approach to the game.

"Too small!" the critics charged, after previewing the spry kid who reported for duty on August 11, 1912, just six days after his transaction was finalized. Schalk began his career with Taylorville of the Illinois-Missouri League in 1911. He was discovered by Sox coach Kid Gleason, who recommended him to Charles Comiskey midway through the 1912 season.

After donning the mask and chest protector that afternoon in Comiskey Park, Schalk was sent out to warm up Ed Walsh. The great Sox pitcher chuckled and called over to the kid: "I'll just toss 'em up easy." Schalk frowned. He would have none of it. But he also knew that if he could handle the deadly spitball, he could handle anyone on the staff. "Never mind me," he replied. "If you have any speed, I'd like to see a little of it now!"

Sixteen years and 1,755 games later "Cracker" Schalk was considered the preeminent catcher of his generation. He passed his first test with flying colors.

Ray Schalk caught 100 or more games for 12 seasons (1913–23; 1925). Before Ray appeared on the scene, it was a rare achievement for any backstop. He made history of a similar bent on July 21, 1925, by appearing in his 1,576th game, thus breaking a record held by Deacon McGuire. Schalk held the iron-man record until crosstown rival Gabby Hartnett shattered the mark a few years later.

Realizing at the outset of his career that his arm was not as strong as it should be for his chosen profession, Ray regularly exercised his shoulder muscles. He would give a runner a long start toward second base and beat him without effort. Ray's lightning quickness and deadly accuracy made it possible. When Eddie Collins joined the Sox in 1915, he was able, with Schalk's assistance, to bring to perfection a unique method of breaking up double steals. Ray's unerring throws simplified the task for Collins, Buck Weaver, and Swede Risberg during the years the quartet worked together. Double steals against Chicago were rare in those days.

Schalk led the league in fielding eight times. His .989 average in 1922 tied an AL record at the time. He is one of only three White Sox players to hit for the cycle (Carlton Fisk and Jack Brohamer were the others), turning the trick against the Tigers in Detroit on June 27, 1922.

Built like a fireplug and known as a dugout motivator, Ray is credited with being the first catcher to back up first and third base, and he had few peers when it came to snaring foul balls outside the grasp of ordinary backstops. He caught a record four no-hitters, including Charlie Robertson's perfect game on April 30, 1922.

During the 1919 World Series, Schalk batted .304, and he showed his crooked teammates no quarter when he suspected the fix was on. Ray nearly came to blows with Lefty Williams. Umpire Billy Evans, who observed Schalk's numerous run-ins with a lazy or uncooperative pitcher, remembered his rage: "When the pitcher appeared to be loafing or getting a bit careless, Schalk proceeded to return the ball with such speed that one begins to wonder who was really doing the pitching."

Ray was an excellent field general, but a poor choice for manager. He was handed the job almost by default on November 11, 1926, but was unable to exercise control over a rebellious corps of veterans who resented his authority. At Comiskey's urging, Schalk submitted his resignation on July 4, 1928. He finished his major league career in 1929 as a player/coach for the New York Giants, then retired to Chicago, where he opened a South Side bowling alley.

In 1945 Ray was signed by Cubs general manager Jim Gallagher to scout the Chicagoland area for the National League ballclub. It was his final baseball excursion before being inducted into the Hall of Fame in 1955 through the generous help of *American* sportswriter Warren Brown, who wielded tremendous clout among the BBWAA members, passing judgment on the game's immortals.

Scott, Jim

White Sox: 1909–17
Pitcher
Nickname: Death Valley
Birthplace: Deadwood, South Dakota

B: April 23, 1888
D: April 7, 1957
Batted right, threw right
Ht. 6–1; **Wt.** 235

Scott, Jim

White Sox	W	L	Pct	ERA	G	CG	IP	H	BB	K	ShO
1909	13	12	.520	2.30	36	19	250⅓	194	93	135	4
1910	9	17	.346	2.43	41	14	229⅔	182	86	135	2
1911	12	11	.522	2.63	39	14	202	195	81	128	3
1912	2	2	.500	2.15	6	2	37⅔	36	15	23	1
1913	20	21	.488	1.90	48	27	312⅓	252	86	158	4
1914	16	18	.471	2.84	43	12	253⅓	228	75	138	2
1915	24	11	.686	2.03	48	23	296⅓	256	78	120	7
1916	9	14	.391	2.72	32	8	165⅓	155	53	71	1
1917	6	7	.462	1.87	24	6	125	126	42	37	2
Career	111	113	.496	2.32	317	125	1,872	1,624	609	945	26

Jim Scott was one of many Wichita players recommended to the White Sox by Frank Isbell, former dead-ball-era second baseman who bought a piece of the minor league franchise when his playing career was over. Glowing press reports submitted from the White Sox 1909 spring training camp described Scott as a "wonder"—the next Ed Walsh, Mordecai Brown, and Cy Young rolled into one.

On any given day, Scott was capable of living up to the advance billing. However, the tall right-hander who relied on a spitball and fade-away pitch was often plagued by spells of wildness. He developed a reputation as a pitcher who could beat the Philadelphia A's, especially in 1915 when he beat the A's seven times, including a 5–0 whitewashing on August 29, played in record time: 68 minutes. At other times, Scott was streaky, inconsistent, and bothered by injuries.

Jim Scott bridged the Hitless Wonder era and the Black Sox.

During his White Sox career, Scott fashioned two one-hitters and a no-hit performance against the Senators on May 14, 1914. He lost the no-hitter when ex-Sox Chick Gandil singled, then lost the game when Gandil was doubled home by Howard Shanks.

Jim Scott bridged the Hitless Wonder and Black Sox eras with mixed results. After his return from military duty in 1918, Scott found work as a minor league umpire. Published reports out of Los Angeles in the 1920s indicated that he had formed a religious sect.

Seerey, Pat

White Sox: 1948–49
Outfielder
Birthplace: Wilburton, Oklahoma

B: March 17, 1923
Bats right, throws right
Ht. 5–10; **Wt.** 200

Seerey, Pat

White Sox	G	AB	H	AVG	RBI	R	2B	3B	HR	SA	SB
1948	95	340	78	.229	64	44	11	0	18	.421	0
1949	4	4	0	.000	0	1	0	0	0	.000	0
Career	561	1,815	406	.224	261	236	73	5	86	.412	3

Pat Seerey

Fat Pat Seerey hit the ball a country mile...when he wasn't striking out. Relegated to bench duty with the Cleveland Indians at the time of his trade to Chicago on June 2, 1948, for Bob Kennedy, Seerey was assigned uniform No. 5 by manager Ted Lyons. He joked to reporters that this was not only Joe DiMaggio's number, but also that of his former manager Lou Boudreau, whose patience he had exhausted.

Seerey, a footnote player in the passing scene, clubbed four mammoth home runs in a July 18, 1948, game in Philadelphia off of Carl Scheib (2), Bob Savage (1), and Lou Brissie (1). Lou Gehrig and Chuck Klein were the only other major leaguers to accomplish this historic feat up to that time.

Pat Seerey's moment of fame was fleeting. He was sold to the Memphis Chicks on October 15, 1949.

Sewell, Luke

White Sox: 1935–38
Catcher
Birthplace: Titus, Alabama

B: January 5, 1901
D: May 14, 1987
Batted right, threw right
Ht. 5–9; **Wt.** 160

Sewell, Luke

White Sox	G	AB	H	AVG	RBI	R	2B	3B	HR	SA	SB
1935	118	421	120	.285	67	52	19	3	2	.359	3
1936	128	451	113	.251	73	59	20	5	5	.350	11
1937	122	412	111	.269	61	51	21	6	1	.357	4
1938	65	211	45	.213	27	23	4	1	0	.242	0
Career	1,630	5,383	1,393	.259	696	653	273	56	20	.341	65

Locating a veteran catcher to work with a talented but unproven quartet of young pitchers topped Jimmie Dykes' list of priorities as he wrapped up his first year at the White Sox helm. The team had crash-landed in the AL cellar for the second time in three years.

Harry Grabiner and Dykes solved the problem on January 22, 1935, when they purchased Luke Sewell, one of the game's outstanding backstops, from the St. Louis Browns. An alumnus of the University of Alabama, Luke was a standout for 14 seasons with the Indians and Senators before joining the Sox.

He was an expert handler of pitchers and was blessed with a powerful throwing arm. During his long career, Sewell caught three no-hitters, including two with the White Sox: Vern Kennedy's whitewashing of the Indians on August 31, 1935, and Bill Dietrich's masterpiece on June 2, 1937, against the Browns.

Sewell was sold to Brooklyn on December 20, 1938, because the Sox were eager to experiment with 23-year-old Mike Tresh behind the plate.

"It was obvious last season that Sewell's usefulness was virtually at an end," Lou Comiskey explained. "We realized that even with Sewell on the team the young fellows would have to do most of the catching anyhow, so we figured we might as well put the full burden on them." Imagine a baseball executive saying such a thing today.

Luke Sewell, iron-man catcher

Shaw, Bob

White Sox: 1958–61
Pitcher
Birthplace: Bronx, New York

B: June 29, 1933
D: September 23, 2010
Batted right, threw right
Ht. 6–2; **Wt.** 195

Shaw, Bob

White Sox	W	L	Pct	ERA	G	CG	IP	H	BB	K	ShO
1958	4	2	.667	4.64	29	0	64	67	28	18	0
1959	18	6	.750	2.69	47	8	230⅔	217	54	89	3
1960	13	13	.500	4.06	36	7	192⅔	221	62	46	1
1961	3	4	.429	3.79	14	3	71⅓	85	20	31	0
Career	108	98	.524	3.52	430	55	1,778	1,837	511	880	14

Bob Shaw wrote the book on pitching. Unfortunately for this athlete turned author, no one bothered reading his instructional manual titled (what else?) *Pitching*. In hindsight, maybe Bob didn't even read the book himself.

Controversy surrounded Shaw. The husky right-hander out of St. Lawrence University in New York was traded to the White Sox by the Detroit Tigers on June 15, 1958, after he refused to report to the Tigers minor league farm club in Charleston. The trade was a mixed blessing for the White Sox, who surrendered a future all-star, Tito Francona, for a pitcher who would win them a pennant and then just kind of fade away.

Bob Shaw

Shaw opened the 1959 season in the bullpen, but was converted to a starting role in mid-May. Given an opportunity by manager Al Lopez, Shaw emerged as the No. 2 starter on the strength of an effective change-up, slider, and curve. He won 18 games and was the hands-down choice of the sportswriters for the American League Sophomore of the Year award.

But Shaw was a flake...and probably ahead of his time in many respects. He waged a season-long protest against the White Sox when they refused to cave in to his 1960 salary demands. Shaw never reconciled his differences and sulked through another tight pennant race. High atop the catwalk outside Comiskey Park one afternoon, Shaw stood over the street, exhorting Sox fans to turn around and go home: "We're not gonna win! Why are you people here?" Or so the story goes.

After another slow start for Shaw in 1961, Hank Greenberg traded him to Kansas City for pitcher Ray Herbert. The deal was a good one for the White Sox and their unhappy pitcher. Shaw had a few good seasons in the National League and a couple not worth mentioning.

Shaw presided over a flourishing real estate empire that included office buildings, orange groves, and a retail company. In his spare time, he coached a generation of young players in American Legion ball at West Palm Beach, where he was remembered for his competitive spirit and good nature. In addition to his first book, *Pitching: The Basic Fundamentals and Mechanics of Successful Pitching,* Shaw penned a sequel. Incredibly, though, his car was stolen, and the only copy of the manuscript was locked inside the trunk. The car was never recovered, and Shaw said, "So much for book writing," and never went back to the project. Wheelchair-bound, he made his last public appearance in Chicago at Sox Fest 2009, joining Billy Pierce and Jim Rivera in a 50-year anniversary fan celebration of the 1959 Go-Go pennant. He passed away at his home in Jupiter, Florida, on September 23, 2010, from the ravages of liver cancer.

Big Earl Sheely was a great Sox first baseman.

Sheely, Earl

White Sox: 1921–27
First baseman
Nickname: Whitey
Birthplace: Bushnell, Illinois

B: February 12, 1893
D: September 16, 1952
Batted right, threw right
Ht. 6–3½; **Wt.** 195

Sheely, Earl

White Sox	G	AB	H	AVG	RBI	R	2B	3B	HR	SA	SB
1921	154	563	171	.304	95	68	25	6	11	.428	4
1922	149	526	167	.317	80	72	37	4	6	.437	4
1923	156	570	169	.296	88	74	25	3	4	.372	5
1924	146	535	171	.320	103	84	34	3	3	.411	7
1925	153	600	189	.315	111	93	43	3	9	.442	3
1926	145	525	157	.299	89	77	40	2	6	.417	3
1927	45	129	27	.209	16	11	3	0	2	.279	1
Career	1,234	4,471	1,340	.300	747	572	244	27	48	.399	33

With his infield blown apart by the Black Sox scandal, Charles Comiskey looked to Salt Lake City for replacements. Earl Sheely, whose blistering .373 average led the Pacific Coast League in 1920, was the key member of a snappy-looking quartet of infielders who reported to the Sox for the 1921 season after the Old Roman agreed on a dollar amount with the Salt Lake City ownership.

Sheely was a powerfully built first baseman who worked hard to overcome fielding deficiencies caused by a left-ankle fracture in 1912 that had never healed properly. Earl's slowness afoot prevented him from becoming one of the all-time greats.

His talent was hitting a baseball. In 1925 he hit 43 doubles, a White Sox single-season record that stood until 1962. Between May 19 and May 21, 1926, a remarkable exhibition of batting skill, he collected nine hits in 13 at-bats. Earl poled six doubles and one home run against the Red Sox in two of these three games.

For a half dozen years, Earl's massive 6′ frame aided and abetted the base thievery of Johnny Mostil, who sped into third base while the hulking Sheely did his best to impair the throwing angle and sight line of the opposing catcher.

Following his retirement, Sheely served as the Sox' West Coast scout and manager of the Sacramento Pacific Coast League affiliate. His son Hollis joined the White Sox in 1951 as a reserve catcher.

Shires, Art

White Sox: 1928–30
Third baseman
Nicknames: Art the Great; Whattaman
Birthplace: Italy, Texas

B: August 13, 1907
D: July 13, 1967
Batted left, threw right
Ht. 6–1; **Wt.** 195

Shires, Art

White Sox	G	AB	H	AVG	RBI	R	2B	3B	HR	SA	SB
1928	33	123	42	.341	11	20	6	1	1	.431	0
1929	100	353	110	.312	41	41	20	7	3	.433	4
1930	37	128	33	.258	18	14	5	1	1	.336	2
Career	290	968	287	.291	119	118	45	12	11	.395	8

There was no controlling Art Shires, a fast-living, hard-drinking embodiment of the wild and woolly 1920s Jazz Age. The youngster from Waco packed a hip flask. He stepped out on the town in tie, tails, and spats, and he bragged of his diamond abilities in silly rhymes he published in the Chicago dailies:

You may brag about Babe,
you may rave about Lou,
why be so snotty,
the Great Shires is good too!

"I'm going to make $250,000 out of baseball before I'm through!" Shires vowed after Charles Comiskey purchased his contract from the Waco team of the Texas League. The outspoken youngster made a splashy debut in Fenway Park against the venerable Red Ruffing on August 20, 1928. He rapped out four hits, including a triple, in his first game. Only 11 other hitters in modern major league history have equaled or surpassed Shires' first-game heroics.

Appointed team captain in 1929, Shires spearheaded a rookie rebellion against manager Lena Blackburne that culminated in a clubhouse fistfight after the cocky youngster refused to discard a red felt hat he wore to the plate during batting practice. In September, two months after being reinstated following his first suspension, Shires tore apart his Philadelphia hotel room in a drunken frenzy. Blackburne's attempts to pacify his troubled player ended in a wild free-for-all involving traveling secretary Lou Barbour, whose thumb was nearly bitten off by Shires in the mêlée. Hotel detectives arrived a few minutes later and put an end to the row.

Comiskey suspended Shires for the balance of the season, but he held out hopes that his talented first baseman would rethink his behavior over the winter and rejoin the Sox with a healthier, more mature outlook on life. As it turned out, Shires squandered all of his money on booze and nightclubs in the off-season. To help pay his bills, he approached Chicago fight promoter Nessie Blumenthal for a loan. Blumenthal obliged—but on the condition that Shires agree to put his considerable pugilistic skills on display before a cash-paying audience at Chicago's White City amusement park. A series of amateur bouts pitting Shires against all comers was hastily arranged.

The "Great" Shires knocked off "Mysterious" Dan Daly in just 21 seconds before 1,000 fans on December 9, 1929. Daly was a ringer. There were a few others before Shires finally met his match in big George Trafton of the Chicago Bears. The two prized athletes squared off at White City amid a media feeding frenzy. Trafton and Shires pounded away at each other for five rounds. Bloodied and beaten, Art refused to go down. The fight was awarded to Trafton on points.

Undaunted by the taste of defeat, Shires agreed to jump in the ring against another "ardent spirit," Hack Wilson of the Cubs. It promised to be the fight of the decade—a crosstown battle for bragging rights—until Commissioner Kenesaw Landis put a stop to all the nonsense. "Art," he

Art "Whattaman" Shires

warned, "I'm the commissioner of baseball. You can either play baseball or fight. You can't do both!"

After due deliberation, Shires abandoned the fight game but decided to squeeze Comiskey for a $25,000 contract as his price for returning to the Sox in 1930. The Old Roman was old and brittle and not in the mood to mollycoddle Shires for another year. The Great One was traded to Washington on June 16 for pitcher Garland Braxton and catcher Bennie Tate.

Years later Shires was implicated in the murder of W.H. Erwin, a former minor league umpire he had beaten to a pulp in a Dallas street brawl. Art was exonerated after a coroner determined that Erwin had died of natural causes, and not of the beating administered by Shires.

Sievers, Roy

White Sox: 1960–61
First baseman
Nickname: Squirrel
Birthplace: St. Louis, Missouri

B: November 18, 1926
Bats right, throws right
Ht. 6–1; **Wt.** 195

Sievers, Roy

White Sox	G	AB	H	AVG	RBI	R	2B	3B	HR	SA	SB
1960	127	444	131	.295	93	87	22	0	28	.534	1
1961	141	492	145	.295	92	76	26	6	27	.537	1
Career	1,887	6,387	1,703	.267	1,147	945	292	42	318	.475	14

Roy Sievers

In the spring of 1959, Bill Veeck pestered manager Al Lopez about Roy Sievers—a power-hitting first baseman for the Washington Nationals whose greatest years were already behind him. Lopez, who had fine-tuned this ballclub with the help of Chuck Comiskey and John Rigney for two years, believed that the acquisition of Sievers was not essential for the Sox' long-range success. The Señor believed that the Sox not only would contend, but also were perfectly capable of winning the 1959 AL flag without Roy Sievers anchoring first base.

Bill Veeck listened, but Al's logic failed to convince him—and not without some justification—that this team would be an "also-ran" unless there was a real home run threat present in the lineup. Sievers had paced the American League in home runs in 1957. He was an outstanding hitter and a good bargaining chip for owner Calvin Griffith and his struggling Washington club. But he was getting on in years, and for a team that struggled to pay its bills, Sievers was a luxury Griffith could hardly afford.

For more than a year Roy's name kept popping up in trade talks between the two clubs. Veeck was fixated on Sievers, and he was prepared to barter the farm system to obtain him.

On April 5, 1960, two weeks before the season opener, Hank Greenberg finalized a deal with Calvin Griffith that sent away catcher Earl Battey and first baseman Don Mincher, as well as a bundle of White Sox money, for the aging, injury-plagued Washington slugger. Chuck Comiskey, who was traveling with the ballclub, was en route to Miami from Puerto Rico when the news of the trade came out. Comiskey had not been consulted by either Veeck or his general manager Hank Greenberg prior to the trade, and he harbored resentment for years to come because he had personally signed Earl to his first White Sox contract.

It was left to young Comiskey to try to console a tearful and distraught Battey at the Miami airport. The young man had labored in the White Sox system for nearly seven years, but everyone knew that sooner or later he would emerge as an all-star White Sox backstop—the heir apparent to Sherm Lollar, whose legs were starting to go. When Comiskey signed Battey out of Jordan High School in Los Angeles, it was with the understanding that he would remain a member of the White Sox. Promises broken. It was a bad deal all around.

Veeck, the Chicago press corps, and even Roy Sievers gloated over Griffith's perceived "misfortune." "I'm grateful for the opportunity to get a grab at some World Series money," Roy exclaimed.

Sievers smashed 29 home runs despite missing 27 games to an injury in 1960 and having to divide playing time with Earl Torgeson and Ted Kluszewski. But sometimes numbers do not tell a complete story. Slow afoot, Roy's presence substantially altered the White Sox game plan. Instead of making things happen through speed and improvisation, the players sat back and waited for Sievers or Gene Freese to unload a home run. The Go-Go Sox were transformed into the Oh-So-Slow Sox, a pattern that continued into 1961, when Roy's right shoulder went bad and Al Lopez increasingly turned to all-purpose J.C. Martin to spell the veteran at first base.

Meanwhile, a young and healthy Earl Battey established himself as one of the American League's most sure-handed catchers. Cal Griffith, who absorbed a lot of heat from the Washington fans for trading the popular Sievers, silenced his critics.

With Veeck out of the picture, Roy Sievers became one of the first casualties of Ed Short's youth movement, which began in earnest after the 1961 season ended. He was traded to Philadelphia for John Buzhardt and Charley Smith on November 28, 1961.

Simmons, Al (Aloysius Szymanski)

White Sox: 1933–35
Outfielder
Nickname: Bucketfoot Al
Birthplace: Milwaukee, Wisconsin

B: May 22, 1902
D: May 26, 1956
Batted right, threw right
Ht. 5–11; **Wt.** 190

Simmons, Al

White Sox	G	AB	H	AVG	RBI	R	2B	3B	HR	SA	SB
1933	146	605	200	.331	119	85	29	10	14	.481	5
1934	138	558	192	.344	104	102	36	7	18	.530	3
1935	128	525	140	.267	79	68	22	7	16	.427	4
Career	2,215	8,761	2,927	.334	1,827	1,507	539	149	307	.535	87

Al Simmons never lived up to the performance standards expected of him by owner J. Louis Comiskey. On the surface at least, it appeared that this Hall of Fame slugger with the unorthodox batting stance (he drew his left foot away the moment he swung the bat) was the same dead-eyed hitter he had been in his formative years with the Philadelphia A's. Simmons batted .315 in his three White Sox seasons, but the relationship between Sox management and their star outfielder was a shaky one.

Born and raised on Mitchell Street in the Polish section of Milwaukee and fiercely proud of his ethnic heritage, Simmons abided by a strong work ethic—up to the moment he was sold to the White Sox by Connie Mack on September 28, 1932, with Mule Haas and Jimmy Dykes, for the sum of $150,000. In the larger scheme of things, the Simmons acquisition was seen as the first step toward building up the drawing power of the weakest team in the nation in the second-largest baseball market. April ticket sales vindicated Comiskey.

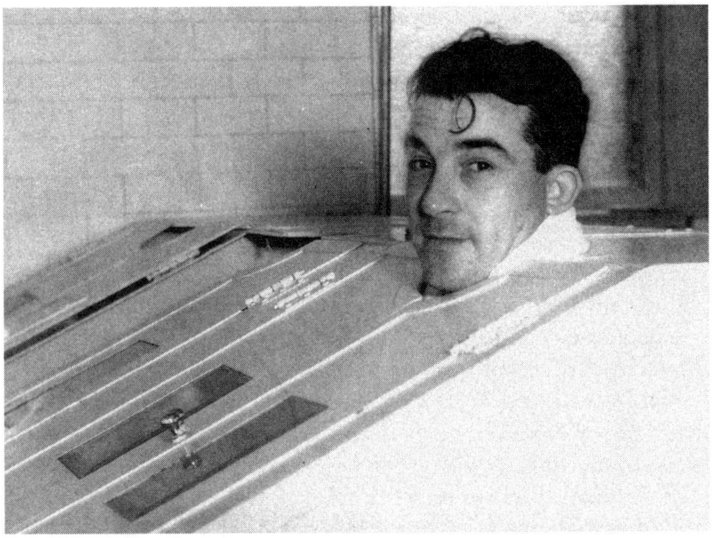

Al Simmons, relaxing in a steam bath during spring training, 1932

Al Simmons was the top vote-getter in fan balloting for the first All-Star Game played in Comiskey Park, July 5, 1933. His torrid hitting keyed a White Sox comeback. His home run production, however, dropped precipitously. Because Comiskey was more interested in home runs that batting average, the owner shortened the foul lines by nine feet and moved home plate 14 feet closer to center field for the 1934 season. Simmons clubbed only 18 home runs, well below his output for the A's.

Al's hefty $33,000 salary, coupled with his unhappiness playing in cavernous Comiskey Park and heated exchanges with Jimmie Dykes, hastened his departure from Chicago. Lou Comiskey tried to recoup his investment loss by holding up the Detroit Tigers for $400,000. Instead, he was forced to settle for $75,000 on December 12, 1935.

Skowron, Bill

White Sox: 1964–67
First baseman
Nickname: Moose
Birthplace: Chicago

B: December 18, 1930
Bats right, throws right
Ht. 5–11; **Wt.** 195

Skowron, Bill

White Sox	G	AB	H	AVG	RBI	R	2B	3B	HR	SA	SB
1964	73	273	80	.293	38	19	11	3	4	.399	0
1965	146	559	153	.274	78	63	24	3	18	.424	1
1966	120	337	84	.249	29	27	15	2	6	.359	1
1967	8	8	0	.000	1	0	0	0	0	.000	0
Career	1,658	5,547	1,566	.282	888	681	243	53	211	.459	16

Even though he spent the productive years of his 14-year run in the big leagues wearing the hated Yankees pinstripes, and far too many of his late-inning hits found the mark against White Sox pitching and broke up close ballgames, Bill Skowron remains a hometown favorite whose big-league career came full circle before it was all over.

The Moose—his grandmother gave him that nickname in "honor" of Italian dictator Benito Mussolini—came to the public's attention in 1947, when he was still attending classes at Weber High School in Chicago. An "Outdoor Show" was being staged at the International Amphitheater, and one of the attractions was the newly invented pitching machine, whose promoters invited visitors to take their chances against the device. The idea was to swing at five pitches and drive the ball into a net on the second floor. The hitter amassing the greatest distance was proclaimed champion by the *Chicago American*—the sponsoring newspaper.

The husky youngster from Weber High stepped up and blasted holes in the net to win the prize easily. Later in his prep career, young Skowron drilled a home run into the left

Bill "Moose" Skowron interviewed by Johnny Morris of WBBM-TV

field of the Polo Grounds in New York during a high school all-star game between the two cities. The major league scouts in attendance that day took note.

Skowron attended Purdue University, where he was coached by Mel Taube and White Sox Hall of Famer Ray Schalk, who recognized a natural hitter—with limited defensive ability. "We tried him at short, second, and third and then moved him to the outfield," Schalk recalled years later. "Regardless of his fielding, we had to use him somewhere. You don't keep .500 hitters on the bench—even in college."

The Moose gave up his promising collegiate football career in order to accept a $40,000 signing bonus from the Yankees. He replaced Joe Collins at first base in 1954 and was integral to the Yankees' success through 1962, when he was dealt to the Los Angeles Dodgers.

Desperate for some hitting punch in the middle of the lineup in order to keep pace with the Yankees, the White Sox acquired Skowron in a waiver deal with the Washington Senators on July 13, 1964, sending away Joe Cunningham and pitcher Frank Kruetzer. After the trade flashed across the wire, a Chicago reporter caught up with Skowron's former Yankees manager, Casey Stengel, who had a few cogent observations on the Moose that he wished to share with Al Lopez: "Al is gonna like my fella' because he's the type who'll hit as well at 44 as he did at 24, and he's only 34 now!"

Moose was excited about his homecoming. He was an instant fan favorite and important contributor down the stretch of the most frenzied pennant race in many years. The old veteran led the team in most of the important offensive categories in 1965—a fine all-around season for the Moose.

A chorus of "Moooose! Moooose!" greeted him from the stands each time he came to bat, but as Jack Brickhouse patiently explained to the listening audience from the Comiskey Park broadcast booth, "No folks, they're not booing him, they're moose-ing him!"

After Eddie Stanky took over for Al Lopez as manager in 1966, several of the veteran players like John Romano and Moose Skowron fell out of favor.

Tommy McCraw, a slick fielder but notoriously weak hitter, took over full-time duties at first base. The Moose did not figure in Stanky's plans after Moose informed his manager that he was no longer an everyday player, and he was traded to the California Angels on May 6, 1967, for a bundle of cash and Charles "Cotton" Nash, a towering 6′6″ All-American who played collegiate basketball at Kentucky.

Seven days later Moose repaid his former teammates in kind by collecting the only hit in nine innings off of Jim O'Toole in his bid to pitch the first White Sox no-hitter since 1957. It was a discouraging moment for the veteran O'Toole, who went on to defeat the Angels 1–0 in extra innings.

Skowron wrapped up his career that same year and returned home to Chicago. Bill is a familiar figure on the Chicago sports banquet circuit these days. He opened a sports bar in suburban Cicero, Illinois, and named the place (what else?) "Call Me Moose" Restaurant and Bar. He is currently employed by the White Sox in a public-relations capacity.

Smith, Alphonse

White Sox: 1958–62
Outfielder, third baseman
Nickname: Fuzzy
Birthplace: Kirkwood, Missouri

B: February 7, 1928
D: January 3, 2002
Batted right, threw right
Ht. 6–½; **Wt.** 189

Smith, Al

White Sox	G	AB	H	AVG	RBI	R	2B	3B	HR	SA	SB
1958	139	480	121	.252	58	61	23	5	12	.396	3
1959	129	472	112	.237	55	65	16	4	17	.396	7
1960	142	536	169	.315	72	80	31	3	12	.451	8
1961	147	532	148	.278	93	88	29	4	28	.506	4
1962	142	511	149	.292	82	62	23	8	16	.462	3
Career	1,517	5,357	1,458	.272	676	843	258	46	164	.429	67

Al Smith provided Sox fans with one of the enduring images of the unforgettable 1950s. It happened in the fifth inning of Game 2 of the 1959 World Series. In his haste to grab Charley Neal's home run, a careless fan sitting in the front row of the left-field grandstand dumped a glass of beer over Al's head.

That's the kind of year this multitalented athlete, who became only the fourth African American in the major leagues when he made his professional debut with the Cleveland Indians in 1953, experienced in the pennant season.

Smitty enjoyed his best years in Cleveland until their manager Kerby Farrell converted him to third base for the 1957 season. Unhappy with this new arrangement, Smith was obliged by Indians management, who traded him to Chicago with Early Wynn for Minnie Minoso and Fred Hatfield on December 4, 1957.

Al was a fine defensive outfielder, but he was plagued by a chronic ailment in his left leg in 1958 and by a ceaseless chorus of boos from the left-field fans who never forgave the Comiskeys for trading their hero, Minnie Minoso. Sensitive to Smitty's plight, Bill Veeck sponsored "Al Smith Night" on August 26, 1959. Any fan who displayed an ID bearing the name Smith, Schmidt, Smythe, or Smithe was admitted for free. Ushers passed out buttons that said: "I'm a Smith and I'm for Al!" On his big night, Smith grounded into a pair of double plays and dropped a routine fly ball, contributing to Boston's winning run. Inside the clubhouse he was consoled by—who else?—Wendell Smith of the *Chicago American.*

Al Smith gets tagged out by Russ Nixon, July 16, 1961.

Al's redemption came at the decisive hour. He belted a home run against the Cleveland Indians that wrapped up the pennant for the South Siders on the shores of Lake Erie, September 22, 1959. A year later he was on the comeback trail, finishing second in the AL batting race with a .315 average—a new career high.

Always a solid performer at the plate, Smith cheerfully adapted to tough circumstances. He switched to right field in 1960 in order to accommodate Minnie Minoso, who returned to Chicago over the winter. But in 1962 Smith balked at making the switch to third base and showed resentment toward the Allyn ownership when they asked him to work as an off-season ticket salesman for the ballclub. Al became a casualty of the Sox youth movement on January 14, 1963, when he was dealt to Baltimore with Louie Aparicio for Hoyt Wilhelm, Ron Hansen, Dave Nicholson, and Pete Ward.

Smith, Edgar

White Sox: 1939–43; 1946–47
Pitcher
Nickname: Gorby
Birthplace: Bordentown, New Jersey

B: December 14, 1913
D: January 2, 1994
Batted right and left, threw left
Ht. 5–10; **Wt.** 174

Smith, Edgar

White Sox	W	L	Pct	ERA	G	CG	IP	H	BB	K	ShO
1939	9	11	.450	3.67	29	7	176⅔	161	90	67	1
1940	14	9	.609	3.21	32	12	207⅓	179	95	119	0
1941	13	17	.433	3.18	34	21	263⅓	243	114	111	1
1942	7	20	.259	3.98	29	18	215	223	86	78	2
1943	11	11	.500	3.69	25	14	187⅔	197	76	66	2
1946	8	11	.421	2.85	24	3	145⅓	135	60	59	1
1947	2	6	.250	7.33	23	0	50⅓	58	42	27	0
Career	73	113	.392	3.82	282	91	1,595⅔	1,554	739	694	8

Do not be deceived by the record. Eddie Smith was really a very good pitcher who suffered the misfortune of being cast into a starting role with the second-division A's and White Sox at a time when both ballclubs struggled to score runs. He was the champion "tough-luck" pitcher of the 1930s and 1940s.

Edgar "Gorby" Smith: a life drowned in alcohol and disappointment

Smith was originally signed by Connie Mack after Roger Cramer scouted the kid left-hander pitching in the Burlington County League. Edgar's won-lost record with the A's was poor—but he always kept his team in the game. And his penchant for knocking off the Yankees at inopportune moments in the pennant race was the main reason why Harry Grabiner and Jimmy Dykes purchased his contract on April 27, 1939.

Eddie pitched his heart out with the White Sox, but was never fully appreciated for his contributions because defeat always seemed to accompany his finest efforts.

It was Smith who was on the losing end of the only Opening Day no-hitter in baseball on April 16, 1940. Eddie yielded only six hits and one run. In defeat he was nearly as effective as his opponent Bob Feller. Among Edgar's other career highlights was a relief win in the 1941 All-Star Game in Detroit. Smith surrendered the first hit to Joe DiMaggio to begin the fabled 56-game streak on May 15, 1941. And yet, Eddie was ignored by Yankees management in 1988 when the Yankee Clipper was honored for his achievement at their annual Old-Timers' Day. Eddie sat in the stands with a few of his New Jersey neighbors who took him to the Bronx to see the game.

In 1942 "Gorby" led the league in losses despite posting a decent 3.98 earned run average. Smith dropped his first 10 decisions that season before picking up his first victory on June 14. Among his 20 losses that year were three 1–0 decisions and two 2–1 defeats. He pitched a two-hitter against the A's on June 9, but still lost 2–0. Then, in 1944, he was drafted into the Army.

Relegated to bullpen duty in 1947, Smith was sold to the Red Sox on August 11 of that year for $10,000—the minimum waiver price.

Eddie Smith's life after baseball was one of misery, alcoholism, and poverty. Separated from his wife and estranged from his grown son, the ex–big leaguer wallowed in self-pity and lived a hand-to-mouth existence in Bordentown, New Jersey, during his final years. A sour, bitter, hard-drinking man up to the very end of his life, Eddie Smith deeply resented the Comiskey family and the baseball establishment for turning their backs on the old-timers in their hour of need.

Smith, Frank

White Sox: 1904–10
Pitcher
Birthplace: Pittsburgh, Pennsylvania

B: October 28, 1879
D: November 3, 1952
Batted right, threw right
Ht. 5–10½; **Wt.** 194

Smith, Frank

White Sox	W	L	Pct	ERA	G	CG	IP	H	BB	K	ShO
1904	16	9	.640	2.09	26	22	202⅓	157	58	107	4
1905	19	13	.594	2.13	39	27	291⅔	215	107	171	4
1906	5	6	.455	3.39	20	8	122	124	37	53	1
1907	22	11	.667	2.47	41	29	310	280	11	139	3
1908	17	16	.515	2.03	41	24	297⅔	213	73	129	3
1909	24	17	.585	1.80	51	37	365	278	70	177	7
1910	4	9	.308	2.03	19	9	128⅔	91	40	50	3
Career	136	112	.548	2.59	354	184	2,273	1,975	676	1,051	27

A malcontent from the very beginning, Frank Smith battled his teammates and manager Fielder Jones while pitching some wonderful baseball for the Hitless Wonder White Sox.

Smith coached at Grove City College in Pennsylvania before launching his playing career in Raleigh, North Carolina. He was transferred to Birmingham of the Southern Association in 1902 and drafted by Charles Comiskey two years later after winning 18 of 31 decisions.

In the midst of his brilliant 1905 season—a year when the big right-hander fashioned a no-hitter against the Detroit Tigers on September 6, as well as a pair of one-hitters—Smith threatened to jump the team in order to play for an outlaw ballclub in the Tri-State League. He did not make good on the threat until 1908, the year in which he threw the second no-hitter of his White Sox career on September 20 against Philadelphia.

Smith, who worked as a piano mover in Pittsburgh during the off-season, jumped the Sox in the middle of the 1908 season after deciding that the weight of a baby grand was far less than the load he had to carry for the fiery Jones, who had publicly berated him for wasting two pitches to a Detroit hitter in a May 30 game. An angry Comiskey accused Smith of habitual boozing and careless practices. But a reconciliation was reached, and the pitcher returned to Chicago on July 27.

Frank Smith

Inconsistency was always a problem with Smith. He fired the only Opening Day one-hitter in White Sox history on April 14, 1910, but lost nine of his next 13 decisions. Seeing no future for Smith with the White Sox, Comiskey traded the troublesome pitcher and infielder Billy Purtell to Boston for Ambrose McConnell and Harry Lord on August 10 after breaking off trade talks with the Detroit Tigers.

"The Sox catchers will not weep a great deal over his departure," commented a *Tribune* sportswriter the next day, "as he has crossed them so many times this year that they were in constant terror of having their heads knocked off."

Soderholm, Eric

White Sox: 1977–79
Third baseman
Birthplace: Cortland, New York

B: September 24, 1948
Bats right, throws right
Ht. 5–11; **Wt.** 187

Soderholm, Eric

White Sox	G	AB	H	AVG	RBI	R	2B	3B	HR	SA	SB
1977	130	460	129	.280	67	77	20	3	25	.500	2
1978	143	457	118	.258	67	57	17	1	20	.431	2
1979	56	210	53	.252	34	31	8	2	6	.395	0
Career	894	2,894	764	.264	383	402	120	14	102	.421	18

In an annual poll conducted by the *Sporting News* after the 1977 season, Eric Soderholm was the hands-down choice for Comeback Player of the Year. It was a most deserved tribute for one of the hardest-working, most dedicated players to grace the Comiskey Park diamond in many a year.

Eric's achievement was a remarkable story. The Twins closed the book on Soderholm's five-year career after Eric fell into a storm sewer on piece of property he had purchased in Minnesota. This mishap broke two ribs and shattered portions of his left leg. Soderholm missed the entire 1976 season after undergoing two operations on his damaged knee. The recovery process was grueling. In Eric's own words: "Sometimes I'd work myself into a state of shock. I'd find myself on the floor, eyes glazed, vomiting. Then I'd get up and work some more."

Released by the Twins after the 1976 season, Eric was selected by Bill Veeck in the November free agency reentry draft. Soderholm refused to admit he was through. Veeck, who was no stranger to these kinds of physical misfortunes, agreed. Eric justified Veeck's confidence and paid immediate dividends as the "bargain-basement find" of the 1977 South Side Hitmen summer.

Sod loved playing for the Sox, and his exuberance was reflected by his unselfish play and team spirit. During the off-hours Eric penned this verse to his teammates, the city, and the fans:

Saga of the 1977 Sox

With every new day a different star was born always
coming in on time;
And if I named them all you know
we'd never finish this rhyme;
But the real stars were you, the great fans. It was
something we'll tell our grandkids about
when we get old and gray;
How in the summer of '77 the pennant somehow
slipped away;
The season went by too quickly and many
of us cried in our beer;
The winter will pass by slowly as we await a new year.

Minus Richie Zisk and Oscar Gamble, the 1978 season was not nearly as much fun for Eric or the fans. Without these two power hitters hitting in back of him, Soderholm lost 22 points on the batting average. He was traded the following year to Texas for Ed Farmer because of the immediate need for a bullpen closer. As it turned out, the deal worked out nicely for Chicago, but Farmer was a poor substitute for Soderholm—the White Sox' answer to Rocky Balboa.

Eric Soderholm: poet laureate of the South Side Hitmen

Squires, Mike

White Sox: 1975; 1977–85
First baseman, third baseman, catcher
Nickname: Spanky
Birthplace: Kalamazoo, Michigan
B: March 5, 1952
Bats left, throws left
Ht. 5–11; **Wt.** 190

Squires, Mike

White Sox	G	AB	H	AVG	RBI	R	2B	3B	HR	SA	SB
1975	20	65	15	.231	4	5	0	0	0	.231	3
1977	3	3	0	.000	0	0	0	0	0	.000	0
1978	46	150	42	.280	19	25	9	2	0	.367	4
1979	122	295	78	.264	22	44	10	1	2	.325	15
1980	131	343	97	.283	33	38	11	3	2	.350	8
1981	92	294	78	.265	25	35	9	0	0	.296	7
1982	116	195	52	.267	21	33	9	3	1	.359	3
1983	143	153	34	.222	11	21	4	1	1	.281	3
1984	104	82	15	.183	6	9	1	0	0	.195	2
1985	2	0	0	.000	1	0	0	0	0	.000	0
Career	779	1,580	411	.260	141	211	53	10	6	.318	45

It was appropriate on the occasion of the White Sox' first-ever divisional championship in 1983 that Mike Squires, the ranking veteran in terms of service to the organization, should be called on to hoist the pennant flag high above Comiskey Park. When the team needed a judge and jury to oversee their "kangaroo court," Mike Squires was appointed. Come to think of it there was very little Spanky couldn't...or wouldn't...do in the 10 years he played for the Sox.

Mike "Spanky" Squires, left-handed catcher in an odd-ball era

Mike was a top-notch first baseman who was assigned backup duty behind Lamar Johnson, Jim Spencer, and others for the duration of his White Sox career. In 1981, the one year when he played his position more or less on a full-time basis, Squires won a Gold Glove Award. At other times he filled in as needed—including catching and playing third base—unfamiliar territory for a left-handed thrower.

Squires became the first left-handed catcher to appear in a major league game since Dale Long in 1958. On May 4 and May 7, 1980, he fielded his position flawlessly. This may or may not have been another Bill Veeck stunt, but not even the master showman could take credit for what happened next. When Mike filled in at third base on August 23, 1983, he became the first left-hander stationed at the hot corner in at least 50 years. The next year he made 13 appearances at third, including one start. If all this seems somewhat far-fetched, consider that in the same year Mike also pitched one-third of an inning.

Mike shared his nickname with Spanky McFarland of *Our Gang* comedy fame. But it was never understood why the Sox just didn't rename the Squires misadventures "Our Game *Is* Comedy," with respect to playing this Gold Glover behind the plate and at third. Mike is still in baseball, working as a professional scout for the Cincinnati Reds.

Staley, Gerry

White Sox: 1956–61
Pitcher
Birthplace: Brush Prairie, Washington
B: August 21, 1920
D: January 2, 2008
Bats right, throws right
Ht. 6–0; **Wt.** 195

Staley, Gerry

White Sox	W	L	Pct	ERA	G	CG	IP	H	BB	K	ShO	Sv
1956	8	3	.727	2.92	26	5	101⅔	98	20	25	0	0
1957	5	1	.833	2.06	47	0	105	95	27	44	0	7
1958	4	5	.444	3.16	50	0	85⅓	81	24	27	0	8
1959	8	5	.615	2.24	67	0	116⅓	111	25	54	0	14
1960	13	8	.619	2.42	64	0	115⅓	94	25	52	0	10
1961	0	3	.000	5.00	16	0	187	17	5	8	0	0
Career	134	111	.547	3.70	640	58	1,981⅔	2,070	529	727	9	61

For most of his career, Gerry Staley was a starting pitcher and a pretty good one at that. But after his won-lost record slipped to 7–13 in 1954, the St. Louis Cardinals traded him to Cincinnati, and then he went to the Yankees for the 1955 stretch drive. Staley, a lumberjack in the Pacific Northwest before he began playing pro ball, had pitched only one-third of an inning for New York when he was purchased by the Sox on May 29, 1956. The veteran hurler was switched to the bullpen by Marty Marion and used exclusively as a closer by Al Lopez thereafter.

Relying on a mixed assortment of pitches, including a knuckleball and a sinker, Staley teamed up with Turk Lown to form the nucleus of an outstanding bullpen that carried the White Sox to their first pennant in 40 years. One pitch—a Staley sinker ball—clinched the pennant for the Sox on

Gerry Staley

September 22, 1959. Entering the game with the bags full in the ninth inning, the 39-year-old relief specialist induced Vic Power of the Indians to hit into a double play that uncorked the champagne for the Sox.

Staley set a new Sox record (since broken) by appearing in 67 games in 1959. He was named *Sporting News* Fireman of the Year in 1960, but was sacrificed a year later when Ed Short commenced his rebuilding program. Gerry was traded to the Kansas City A's on June 10, 1961, with Bob Shaw, Wes Covington, and Stan Johnson for Ray Herbert, Don Larsen, Andy Carey, and Al Pilarcik. After his career ended, Staley returned to Clark County, Washington, where he served as superintendent of parks and recreation.

Stone, Steve

White Sox: 1973; 1977–78
Pitcher
Birthplace: Cleveland, Ohio

B: July 14, 1947
Bats right, throws right
Ht. 5–10; **Wt.** 175

Stone, Steve

White Sox	W	L	Pct	ERA	G	CG	IP	H	BB	K	ShO	Sv
1973	6	11	.353	4.29	36	3	176⅓	163	82	138	0	1
1977	15	12	.556	4.52	31	8	207	228	80	124	0	0
1978	12	12	.500	4.37	30	6	212	196	84	118	1	0
Career	107	93	.535	3.97	320	43	1,789⅓	1,707	716	1,065	7	1

More than any other player who passed through Comiskey Park in the waning years of the second Veeck ownership, Steve Stone came to symbolize the frustrations of the cash-poor ballclubs hopelessly attempting to compete in the high-stakes era of free agency.

Stone's salary demands angered and disappointed Bill Veeck after the Sox owner provided him with a new lease on his faltering pitching career by signing him to a Sox contract on November 24, 1976.

Steve Stone—a gourmet cook, accomplished chess player, published poet, wine connoisseur, investor in Chicago's trendy Lettuce Entertain You restaurant chain, and "Renaissance man"—played for the White Sox on two separate occasions. He was the throw-in player in the 1972 Ken Henderson–for–Tom Bradley swap with the San Francisco Giants, but was subsequently dealt to the Cubs for Ron Santo on December 11, 1973. Steve remained a so-so performer for the North Siders over the next three seasons.

Handicapped by shoulder injuries that kept him on the disabled list during a three-month stretch in 1976, Stone staged a remarkable comeback with the Sox a year later. He emerged as the "ace" of the pitching staff, if such a designation can be applied to a corps of hurlers whose earned run average was a very un–White Sox–like 4.25. He put the 1977 Sox on the winning track by bagging five of six decisions in May.

Stone won his last two 1978 decisions to pull up even with the league, then signed a four-year guaranteed contract with the Baltimore Orioles on November 29, 1978. He became the first player to go through the free agent reentry draft twice after its inception two years earlier. This historical footnote aside, it was a bitter personal blow for Bill Veeck, who simply could not afford to tie up his limited funds in a four-year deal with a .500-caliber pitcher.

"The years were too much for us," Veeck sighed. "We offered Steve a considerable amount of money for one year, but before we could even get to discussing two, the years suddenly jumped up." Greed had supplanted loyalty in baseball's changing order.

Steve Stone, "Stoney," 1973

Stone led the majors and set an Orioles team record with 25 victories en route to a Cy Young Award. That was Stoney's final flourish of success. He retired in June 1982 after suffering elbow and shoulder problems, which had put him on the shelf for much of the 1981 season. He became the color analyst for the Cubs on WGN-TV in 1983.

Stone spent 17 of the next 20 years providing thoughtful analysis and commentary, working side-by-side with Harry Caray, Harry's grandson Chip, Thom Brenamann, and others in the Cubs' cast of characters until he came under fire for certain on-air comments critical of the team's 2004 performance and the managerial strategy employed by Dusty Baker. The former Cy Young Award winner and college roommate of the late Hall of Fame catcher Thurman Munson announced his resignation, but many unhappy fans logically assumed that he had been shown the door by the Cubs brass and WGN. John McDonough, the Cubs senior vice president of marketing and broadcasting, was quick to point out that Stone wasn't fired for his candor—and in fact had been invited back. Steve wasn't buying it, however, and moved on. In 2007 Stoney filled in for Darrin Jackson in the Sox TV broadcast booth for seven games. His style meshed nicely with Ken Harrelson. The Hawk, who loved pinning endearing nicknames on players and colleagues, dubbed his part-time sidekick "Stone Pony," and a fruitful, future partnership took root. In October 2008 Stone inked a six-year contract to provide color analysis on the White Sox television network. Darrin Jackson had already moved over to the radio booth, replacing the departing Chris Singleton, and finally Sox fans could draw a measure of personal satisfaction after Jerry Reinsdorf reeled in a Cubs broadcast superstar in the same fashion as the Cubs pirated away Harry Caray from the South Side back in 1982.

Stratton, Monty

White Sox: 1934–38
Pitcher
Birthplace: Celeste, Texas

B: May 21, 1912
D: September 28, 1982
Batted right, threw right
Ht. 6–5; **Wt.** 180

Stratton, Monty

White Sox	W	L	Pct	ERA	G	CG	IP	H	BB	K	ShO
1934	0	0	—	5.40	1	0	3⅓	4	1	0	0
1935	1	2	.333	4.03	5	2	38	40	9	8	0
1936	5	7	.417	5.21	16	3	95	117	46	37	0
1937	15	5	.750	2.40	22	14	164⅔	142	37	69	5
1938	15	9	.625	4.01	26	17	186⅓	186	56	82	0
Career	36	23	.610	3.71	70	36	487⅓	489	149	196	5

We will never know how far Monty Stratton might have progressed with his baseball career if only he had chosen to remain at home the afternoon of November 27, 1938.

The 25-year-old White Sox pitcher was out for a canter in the woods near his Greenville, Texas, home when he spotted a rabbit hopping through the brush. Monty fired his .32-caliber pistol at the animal, but as he holstered the weapon a bullet discharged into the femoral artery of his right leg.

Top: Monty Stratton, before his terrible accident; bottom: Post-operation Stratton in his new duties as a Sox coach

Stratton crawled to a private road a half mile away, where he called to his wife, Ethel. When the doctors examined the wound, they arrived at the dreadful conclusion that the leg would have to be amputated because of poor blood circulation. After further consultation with White Sox owner J. Louis Comiskey, the physicians proceeded with the operation.

Monty's career was over when it had hardly begun. But while it lasted, he was one of the most promising righthanders of the Depression era. Stratton's baseball career began in the early 1930s when White Sox scouts spotted him while he was pitching for Van Alstyne in a Texas amateur league. His professional career began in Galveston in 1934. Stratton was summoned to Chicago to make his big-league debut on June 2 against the Tigers, but he was ineffective in less than four innings of work. Monty had a big year with St. Paul in 1935, but it wasn't until two years later that he became a valuable contributor to the White Sox cause.

Relying primarily upon a trick pitch called the gander and a good sweeping curveball, Stratton's victory total ran in the double digits in 1937 and 1938. But even before his terrible accident, Monty was beset by injuries and illness. He missed seven weeks in 1937 because of an arm ailment, and another five weeks a year later. These setbacks cost him a shot at becoming a 20-game winner.

Stratton was grimly determined to resume his professional career, wooden leg and all. The White Sox sponsored a fundraising game against the Cubs on May 1, 1939, with $28,000 in proceeds going to Monty and his wife. He took the Comiskey Park mound that afternoon and showed the crowd that he could still get the ball over the plate, but it was obvious that much of the old velocity was gone. Still, Monty had something much more to prove. He spent the 1939 season pitching batting practice to Sox hitters, but this wasn't the kind of baseball job he had in mind.

When the opportunity to manage a Sox minor league affiliate at Lubbock, Texas, surfaced at the 1941 winter meetings, Monty jumped at the chance, even though he would have much preferred active duty over managing. The job lasted only one season.

For the next three years Stratton returned to his 52-acre Greenville ranch, where he heaved baseballs at a painted target on the side of his barn. By 1944 the former Sox ace figured that he had overcome his handicap sufficiently to pitch for a regular team again. He organized a pickup team in Greenville and appointed himself the Sunday pitcher. His ballclub reached the semifinals in a local tournament.

Monty refused any favors or special consideration and never minded when opposing hitters laid down a bunt when he was on the mound. He reasoned that it was all a part of the game and that he would have to work that much harder to overcome the problem. Pitching for Sherman-Dennison of the East Texas League in 1946, Stratton won 18 games. It was around this time that the nation—and Hollywood screenwriters—took note of Monty's quiet but valiant comeback.

A scriptwriter named Douglas Morrow approached the Strattons about the possibility of doing a screenplay. At first Monty and Ethel thought Morrow's notions were far-fetched, but after a while they warmed up to the idea. Morrow convinced them that a screen dramatization would be a real inspiration to returning World War II vets who had lost limbs in combat.

Metro-Goldwyn-Mayer cast Jimmy Stewart in the role of Monty Stratton and June Allyson as Ethel. The film premiered in Monty's hometown in 1949, and suddenly the Strattons basked in the instant glow of celebrity fame. "We rode around in big limousines, and big stars hounded me for autographs," Monty remembered. "You thought we were some sort of celebrities."

Throughout his lifetime Monty experienced the extremes of joy and sorrow. His 23-year-old son Dennis committed suicide in 1964. It was a painful, bitter blow, but Monty moved on with his life.

Fishing and attending to 100 head of cattle kept Stratton busy in his twilight years. Comforted by his memories, Monty passed away in 1982. A few of his baseball artifacts are on display at the Texas Cotton Museum, not far from the family home in Hunt County. *The Stratton Story* remains a classic of late-night TV.

Sullivan, Billy

White Sox: 1901–14
Catcher
Birthplace: Fort Atkinson, Wisconsin

B: February 1, 1875
D: January 28, 1965
Batted right, threw right
Ht. 5–9; **Wt.** 155

Sullivan, Billy

White Sox	G	AB	H	AVG	RBI	R	2B	3B	HR	SA	SB
1901	98	367	90	.245	56	54	15	6	4	.351	12
1902	76	263	64	.243	26	36	12	3	1	.323	11
1903	32	111	21	.189	7	10	4	0	1	.252	3
1904	108	371	85	.229	44	29	18	4	1	.307	11
1905	99	323	65	.201	26	25	10	3	2	.269	14
1906	118	387	83	.214	33	37	18	4	1	.289	10
1907	112	339	59	.174	36	30	8	4	0	.221	6
1908	137	430	82	.191	29	40	8	4	0	.228	15
1909	97	265	43	.162	16	11	3	0	0	.174	9
1910	45	142	26	.183	6	10	4	1	0	.225	0
1911	89	256	55	.215	31	26	9	3	0	.273	1
1912	39	91	19	.209	15	9	2	1	0	.253	0
1914	1	0	0	—	0	0	0	0	0	—	0
Career	1,146	3,657	777	.212	378	363	119	33	20	.279	98

Before Billy Sullivan revolutionized the game, big-league catchers stood 20 feet behind the batter in order to guard against injury. Sullivan is believed to be the first modern-day backstop to crouch right behind the batter.

To reduce the chance of injuries from batted balls and errant deliveries from the mound, Sullivan injected compressed air into a wind pad that he had installed into a chest protector—at that time it was a flat piece of leather ineffective against the serious types of injuries that befell catchers. Billy secured a patent on his device, January 31, 1909, the same year Comiskey awarded him the manager's chair.

Sullivan's lifetime .212 batting average is second-worst among all big-league hitters with 3,000 or more at bats, but

Billy Sullivan

numbers alone do not accurately reflect Billy's contributions to White Sox history in the dead-ball era. He was a steady handler of pitchers who Ty Cobb once described as the best catcher "ever to wear shoe leather."

Billy Sullivan began his professional career at Dubuque in 1897 as a shortstop. He was sold to the Boston Braves in 1899, but was induced to jump to the White Sox in 1901 with the promise of a $2,400 salary. Thereafter he became the everyday catcher except for those frequent occasions when he was sidelined with injuries or illness. The lengthy hospital chronology: a foul tip smashed his throwing hand in 1901. He underwent emergency appendectomy surgery in 1902. Sullivan was knocked unconscious by a pitched ball in 1904. He reinjured his right hand during the 1906 stretch drive. And he stepped on a rusty nail in March 1910, resulting in a case of blood poisoning. Sullivan ignored the advice of his teammates to consult a physician, but instead relied on the word of a quack pharmacist who prescribed a near-lethal dose of turpentine to cure the malady. Sully nearly lost a leg before seeking out competent medical attention.

Despite the injury bug, Sullivan agreed to participate in a crazy publicity stunt at the Washington Monument on August 24, 1910. In the presence of assembled newspaper reporters, government officials, and several teammates, Ed Walsh climbed to the top of the monument with a bag of baseballs in hand. From a distance of 542 feet up in the air, Walsh dropped the balls one at a time to his battery mate, who planted himself on the ground pounding a pancake-sized glove. It was estimated that each ball traveled at the rate of 161 feet a second. On his 23rd try, the ball finally settled into Billy's mitt.

Billy was promised lifetime employment by Comiskey for his years of faithful service as a catcher and playing manager (in 1909), but the guarantee was invalidated on February 15, 1914, when he was handed his unconditional release. "Where can I go? I can still play," Sullivan whispered, fighting back the tears. Billy played one more game for the Sox in 1914, then finished up as a player/coach with the Tigers in 1916. At the end of the season, he retired to his 20-acre fruit farm outside Newberg, Oregon.

His son, Billy Jr., broke in with the Sox in 1931, briefly reprising the famous Walsh-Sullivan battery of yesteryear—but with less than spectacular results.

Tannehill, Lee Ford

White Sox: 1903–12
Shortstop, third baseman
Birthplace: Dayton, Kentucky

B: October 26, 1880
D: February 16, 1938
Batted right, threw right
Ht. 6–1; **Wt.** 175

Tannehill, Lee

White Sox	G	AB	H	AVG	RBI	R	2B	3B	HR	SA	SB
1903	138	503	113	.225	50	48	14	3	2	.276	10
1904	153	547	125	.229	61	50	31	5	0	.303	14
1905	142	480	96	.200	39	38	17	2	0	.244	8
1906	116	378	69	.183	33	26	8	3	0	.220	7
1907	33	108	26	.241	11	9	2	0	0	.259	3
1908	141	482	104	.216	35	44	15	3	0	.259	6
1909	155	531	118	.222	47	39	21	5	0	.281	12
1910	67	230	51	.222	21	17	10	0	1	.278	3
1911	141	516	131	.254	49	60	17	6	0	.310	0
1912	3	3	0	.000	0	0	0	0	0	.000	0
Career	1,089	3,778	833	.220	346	331	135	27	3	.273	63

Lee Tannehill, younger brother of the famous Red Sox pitcher Jesse Tannehill, fit in perfectly with the White Sox' Hitless Wonder image. He couldn't hit worth a lick, but his fielding exploits at the hot corner forced manager Fielder Jones to keep him in the lineup when common sense dictated that owner Charles Comiskey should have traded for an infielder with some batting punch.

Tannehill came up through the Virginia League as a pitcher, but as he completed his minor league apprenticeship in the Western League and American Association, he was forced to alternate between shortstop and third base. The veteran minor leaguer was purchased by Comiskey from Louisville in 1903. "Tanny" filled in for George Davis at shortstop while Davis awaited the outcome of his free agency challenge in 1903. But when Davis was ordered back to Chicago for 1904,

Lee Tannehill

Tannehill was shifted to third base, where he would remain on a more-or-less permanent basis for the next six seasons.

In 1906 Tannehill batted .183, the lowest mark ever achieved by a regular playing 100 or more games. But no matter how pitiful his offensive contributions, Jones could find no one better to take his place. He was always among the league leaders in assists and putouts and is the only shortstop to have executed two unassisted double plays in one game.

Ironically, it was Tannehill who claimed the honor of hitting the first home run in Comiskey Park on July 31, 1910. With the bases full of White Sox, Tannehill drilled a line drive off Tigers ace Wild Bill Donovan that skipped through the wickets of a small fence connecting the left field pavilion to the grandstand. Under the existing ground rules, the play was ruled a home run…and a grand slam at that.

Tannehill lost his starting job to Harry Lord in 1912. He was sold to Kansas City of the American Association on August 5 of that year when manager Jimmy Callahan made the decision to purge the veterans from the roster and go with the kids. The slick-fielding veteran lingered in the minors another two years before retiring in 1914.

Thigpen, Bobby

White Sox: 1986–93
Pitcher
Nickname: Thiggy
Birthplace: Tallahassee, Florida

B: July 17, 1963
Bats right, throws right
Ht. 6–3; **Wt.** 222

Thigpen, Bobby

White Sox	W	L	Pct	ERA	G	CG	IP	H	BB	K	ShO	Sv
1986	2	0	1.000	1.77	20	0	35⅔	26	12	20	0	7
1987	7	5	.583	2.73	51	0	89	86	24	52	0	16
1988	5	8	.385	3.30	68	0	90	96	33	62	0	34
1989	2	6	.250	3.76	61	0	79	62	40	47	0	34
1990	4	6	.400	1.83	77	0	88⅔	60	32	70	0	57
1991	7	5	.583	3.49	67	0	69⅔	63	38	47	0	30
1992	1	3	.250	4.75	55	0	55	58	33	45	0	22
1993	0	0	.000	6.05	17	0	19⅓	23	9	10	0	1
Career	31	34	.476	3.72	441	0	561	525	233	372	0	201

Baseball's sharpest thinkers are at a loss to pinpoint the reasons for a star pitcher's sudden and swift decline in the midst of a brilliant career. Bobby Thigpen recorded career save No. 200 two months shy of his 29th birthday. Not even the great Bruce Sutter matched Thiggy's timetables.

Bobby was rated as the American League's second-most-dominant relief pitcher—with top honors going to Dennis Eckersley, Oakland's mechanical man. And then, just like that, Bobby Thigpen could not retire the batboy. The mere sight of Thigpen, who was unable to find the plate, ignited the Comiskey Park boo birds every time he raced in from the bullpen. The magic was gone, and no one was sure why.

Thiggy was an outfielder for the Mississippi State Bulldogs, a team of future all-stars that included Will Clark, Rafael Palmiero, and Jeff Brantley. After leading the Dogs into the

Bobby Thigpen's fluid drive delivery

College World Series, Thigpen was selected by the White Sox in the fourth round of the June 1985 free agent draft.

Used primarily as a starter in the minor leagues, Bobby was converted to a relief role after being summoned to Chicago on August 6, 1986. He reeled off 28⅓ consecutive scoreless innings his first month in the big leagues, and easily sewed up the No. 1 closer spot for himself in 1987 and beyond.

In 1990, his greatest year, Thiggy smashed Dave Righetti's single-season record by nailing down 57 saves. Righetti's mark of 46 fell on September 3. Bobby was the easy choice for the 1990 *Sporting News* Fireman of the Year and the Rolaids Relief Man Award based on the overwhelming number of saves. Because so many of these saves were ninth-inning mop-up jobs when the Sox's lead was secure, criticisms were leveled at manager Jeff Torborg for playing a numbers game in order to pad Thiggy's season statistics.

Thigpen was never the same after his big year. The American League finally figured out a way to connect with his 90-mph-plus fastball. His ERA ballooned in the next two years, and by the end of the 1992 season, Bobby relinquished his closer role to Roberto Hernandez. As the Sox closed in on a 1993 division title, Thigpen had become the forgotten man in the bullpen. He demanded a trade from general manager Ron Schueler, who was equally anxious to dump Bobby's $3.25-million-per-year contract.

Schueler opened trade talks with Philadelphia, hoping to pry loose Mitch Williams, but when the Phillies said no, the Sox settled for Jose DeLeon on August 10, 1993. It was a good trade for Chicago, but DeLeon was far below the market value Bobby Thigpen commanded in 1990 and 1991 when he sat on top of the world. Failing to last in Philadelphia and Seattle, Thigpen went off to Japan to resurrect his career. He caught on with the Fukuoka Daiei Hawks and attempted a major league comeback in 1996, but the effort was cut short by back problems. He rejoined the Sox organization in 2007, and since 2009 Bobby has served as the pitching coach for the White Sox Class A affiliate, the Winston-Salem Dash. Thigpen's saves record held until 2008, when Francisco "K-Rod" Rodriguez of the Los Angeles Angels of Anaheim broke the mark with 62.

Thomas, Alphonse

White Sox: 1926–32
Pitcher
Nickname: Tommy
Birthplace: Baltimore, Maryland

B: December 23, 1899
D: April 27, 1988
Batted right, threw right
Ht. 5–10; **Wt.** 175

Thomas, Alphonse

White Sox	W	L	Pct	ERA	G	CG	IP	H	BB	K	ShO
1926	15	12	.556	3.80	44	13	249	225	110	127	2
1927	19	16	.543	2.98	40	24	307⅔	271	94	107	3
1928	17	16	.515	3.08	36	24	259⅔	270	76	129	3
1929	14	18	.438	3.19	36	24	259⅔	270	60	62	2
1930	5	13	.278	5.22	34	7	169	229	44	58	0
1931	10	14	.417	4.80	42	11	242	296	69	71	2
1932	3	3	.500	6.18	12	1	43⅔	55	15	11	0
Career	117	128	.478	4.12	397	128	2,173	2,339	712	735	15

Tommy Thomas

Charles Comiskey invested heavily in unproven minor league players throughout the 1920s in the vain hope of building a last great ballclub to cement his legacy. Tommy Thomas was one of the notable success stories during this 11-year litany of failure (1921–31). Comiskey traded outfielder Maurice Archdeacon, another flash-in-the-pan flop, to the Baltimore Orioles of the International League for Thomas on September 12, 1925.

Tommy Thomas was a star-caliber pitcher in the minors. He posted a sensational 32–12 record in 1925, but throughout his White Sox career he gained a reputation as a hard-luck pitcher unable to shut down his opponents after the fifth inning. His roommate, Ted Lyons, helped him master the curveball, and thus Thomas strung together three winning seasons and led the league in starts and innings pitched in 1927 before overwork weakened his throwing arm. He was sold to the Washington Senators on June 11, 1932.

Thomas entered the record books by surrendering the first over-the-roof home run in the newly renovated Comiskey Park. Babe Ruth's mammoth shot on August 16, 1927, defied the architectural experts who declared that such a feat could never be accomplished by mortal man. The new upper deck was just too imposing, or so they believed at the time.

Thomas, Frank

White Sox: 1990–2005
First baseman, designated hitter
Nickname: The Big Hurt
Birthplace: Columbus, Georgia

B: May 27, 1968
Bats right, throws right
Ht. 6–5; **Wt.** 257

Thomas, Frank

White Sox	G	AB	H	AVG	RBI	R	2B	3B	HR	SA	SB
1990	60	191	63	.330	31	39	11	3	7	.529	0
1991	158	559	178	.318	109	104	31	2	32	.553	1
1992	160	573	185	.323	115	108	46	2	24	.536	6
1993	153	549	174	.317	112	106	36	0	41	.607	4
1994	113	399	141	.353	109	106	34	1	38	.729	2
1995	145	493	152	.308	136	102	27	0	40	.606	3
1996	141	527	184	.349	109	110	26	0	40	.626	1
1997	146	530	184	.347	109	110	35	0	35	.611	1
1998	160	585	155	.265	110	109	35	2	29	.480	7
1999	135	486	148	.305	87	74	36	0	15	.471	3
2000	159	582	191	.328	112	115	44	0	43	.625	1
2001	20	68	15	.221	10	8	3	0	4	.441	0
2002	148	523	132	.252	88	77	29	1	28	.472	3
2003	153	546	146	.267	100	87	35	0	42	.562	0
2004	74	240	65	.271	64	53	16	0	18	.562	0
2005	34	105	23	.219	16	19	3	0	12	.590	0
Career	2,322	8,199	2,468	.301	1,704	1,494	495	12	521	.555	32

Comparisons are inevitably drawn among Frank Thomas, Albert Belle, and Ken Griffey Jr.—the brightest stars in the American League in their day. It is hard to speculate who is the greatest ballplayer, because everything they did, they did so well.

Frank's remarkable patience at the plate, his willingness to take a walk down to first rather than chase a pitch outside the zone, is what is unique about this broad-shouldered power hitter.

Frank Thomas is the son of a Baptist deacon who also doubles as a bondsman in Columbus, Georgia. The elder Thomas is Frank's most enthusiastic backer, and he was always there to support him through youth baseball and on into college, where Frank was named Southeastern Conference Most Valuable Player in 1989. As a freshman at Auburn University who played tight end for the football team and first base for the baseball squad, Frank set a new school record with 21 home runs. "If Frank put in his mind to do something, he was going to do it," recalled Frank Thomas Sr.

Frank Jr. was scouted by Tom Calvano, Mark Bernstein, and Mike Rizzo. "He'll be an impact first baseman," Rizzo reported to scouting director Al Goldis. Thomas was the guy, but the White Sox held their breath until they could jump into the draft and claim him for the ballclub.

Baltimore, Philadelphia, Houston, Texas, Seattle, and St. Louis all bypassed Thomas in the June 1989 draft. Their logic was mystifying but fortunate for the Sox, who chose Frank in the seventh round. He was probably ready to play in the big leagues the moment he signed the contract. However, Larry Himes traveled a cautious path with respect to the care and feeding of a budding superstar. Himes made sure that Thomas would play at least a full season in the minors.

Thomas was named *Baseball America*'s Minor League Player of the Year in 1990—an honor that hardly came as a surprise to those who charted his progress at Birmingham. Frank joined the Chicago ballclub in Milwaukee the night of August 2, 1990. He drove in the winning run in his first game and hit a booming triple the next evening to help seal a victory over the Brewers.

In his first four seasons (1991–94), Thomas put up numbers matched by only five players in major league history by driving in 100 runs and walking 100 times. By comparison, Babe Ruth reached this milestone 12 times in his storied 20-year career. Lou Gehrig, Ted Williams, and Ralph Kiner round out the list. In 1995 and 1996 he surpassed them all by becoming the only player in history to bat .300 or better with 20 home runs and 100 RBIs, 100 walks, and 100 runs scored over the course of six straight seasons. Through 1996, Thomas never went more than two games without reaching base.

Thomas was the unanimous choice for the Most Valuable Player Award in 1993. In the strike-shortened season that followed, Frank became the first White Sox player to win baseball's top accolade in back-to-back seasons and the first American Leaguer since Roger Maris (1960–61). It is worth noting that only 11 other players in history have accomplished this singular feat. In 1993 Thomas set a new team home run record by driving 41 balls out of the park. No Sox home run hitter from the past has ever come close to these numbers.

Frank Thomas in full hitting stride

Thomas' stature grew steadily once he arrived in Chicago. With the retirement of Michael Jordan in 1993, the Big Hurt (a nickname given to Frank by announcer Ken Harrelson) slowly evolved into Chicago's most recognizable sports personality. Frank's aura lured a national following in the mid-1990s—no easy feat for White Sox players who have toiled in the shadow of the Cubs for so many years. But then, Frank Thomas was knocking on the door of the kind of immortality reserved for the icons of baseball history—Ruth, Mickey Mantle, Willie Mays, and Ted Williams.

How far could Frank go with his awesome abilities? "I've already fulfilled my ultimate goal, to be financially secure the rest of my life," explains Thomas. "The ultimate goal now would be the Hall of Fame. The goal before that would be winning the World Series." Some thought the Hurt might even give the Baltimore iron man a run for his money before the book was closed. At the close of the 1995 season, Thomas had played in 259 straight games—second among active players to Cal Ripken. The streak might have extended into the next century if not for a stress-fracture injury to Frank's left foot midway through the 1996 season. The Big Hurt's streak was snapped at 345 straight games.

In the middle of the dismal 1995 season, Frank became the first White Sox player to hit a home run in an All-Star Game. The historic White Sox power shortage was never so evident as in All-Star competition down through the years.

The second half of Thomas' Hall of Fame career was one marked by frustration and bitter disappointment. Plagued by recurring injuries that cost him the opportunity to hit 500 home runs in a White Sox uniform, the Big Hurt publicly feuded with Jerry Manuel much of the time Manuel was managing the ballclub. He engaged in fisticuffs with Robin Ventura in the Yankees dugout one night, and his marital problems became a matter of public record. In 2001 David Wells questioned his commitment and asked if his physical ailments were legitimate. The press aired his personal grievances with management over the "diminished skills" clause inserted into his contract by Reinsdorf and company in 2001, prompting Thomas to walk out on a team meeting convened by the brass on February 12 for the purpose of introducing Kenny Williams, the new general manager, to the ballclub. Even the taciturn Paul Konerko called him to task for showing up late for a game. Then he made a clumsy remark about the late Jackie Robinson and left the All-Star Game early.

So who was the real Frank Thomas? The gifted athlete knocking on the door of immortality based on his first seven seasons in a White Sox uniform, when his numbers compared favorably to Ted Williams and Mickey Mantle? Or was he a moody, inner-directed complainer, angry because he was not shown the love and respect he believed he deserved? Perhaps the truth lies halfway in between. Thomas, who heads the list in nine all-time White Sox offensive categories, became only the 36th player in major league history to hit 400 home runs when he teed off on Tampa Bay's Jorge Sosa on July 25, 2003.

Frank's accomplishments drew little local or national attention because he suffered the same fate as the South Side franchise playing in the shadow of the Cubs for so many years. While the Hurt was battering down fences in his most productive years, Sammy Sosa was grabbing all the headlines and warm publicity across town, despite being caught red-handed swinging a corked bat and rumors of steroid abuse swirling around him the last few years he was a Cub. One thing is for sure: Thomas always played four-square and by the rules and never once injected foreign substances into his body to gain a competitive advantage. Thus, he earned his accomplishments honestly but was never recognized or fully appreciated in an era of rampant steroid abuse in baseball.

These omissions are easily rectified when Thomas becomes eligible for Hall of Fame consideration, but there are, of course, the intangibles to consider. Expecting Frank to emerge as the clubhouse leader and spokesman for the ballclub was probably too much to ask of him. Leadership tasks were better suited for Robin Ventura and Jack McDowell, but once they were gone, Thomas, the two-time American League MVP, was expected to step up and assume a role he was never entirely comfortable with.

Frank was sincere in his stated desire to lead the Sox into the World Series—and to exit the game gracefully, on his own terms, and when the time was right. Sadly, he was denied that right. He made small, but significant contributions to help his teammates get to the big show in 2005, but he missed out on the chance to play in the World Series because of a fracture to his left foot—and that was the unkindest and most unfair blow of all. The White Sox bought out the remainder of his contract and cut him loose after the World Series. Like former teammate Carlton Fisk, who should have gauged that the time to leave was at hand, Frank's parting was awkward and unfortunate. As he exited the Wyndham Anatole Hotel in Dallas on December 6, 2005, after the club declined to offer salary arbitration, Thomas registered his disappointment to reporters but vowed to seek out the best situation elsewhere. "The door is closed. The White Sox did what they had to do. I have much respect and love for the city and the fans, but I would have wanted my chapter to end a little bit differently than the way it ended. I think I deserve that. I was forced to move on," he said.

The Big Hurt wasn't through yet—not with the elusive quest for the 500th home run still on his radar. Thomas believed the goal was obtainable and within his reach. He was signed as a free agent by the Oakland A's on January 25, 2006, and with a change of scenery, he overcame years of physical adversity and staged a brilliant comeback despite another stint on the disabled list. He was the catalyst of the A's postseason run, pounding out 39 homers en route to winning the Player's Choice Award as AL Comeback Player of the Year. White Sox faithful will never forget his May 22 homecoming, and his two long-distance shots while wearing the green and gold. The cheers from the fans were genuine. How different his reception was compared to the relentless chorus of boos meted out by Cleveland Indians fans when Jim Thome came up to bat at Progressive Field as a member of the White Sox that same season.

Playing in the 2006 ALDS against Minnesota, Frank became the oldest player in postseason history to clout two home runs in a postseason game. But the cash-strapped A's opted out of free agent bidding, and the Hurt was picked up by the Toronto Blue Jays on November 17, 2006. The culminating moment of his brilliant career arrived on June 28, 2007—appropriately inside the Hubert H. Humphrey Metrodome, when, 16 years and 10 months earlier (to the very day), he had stroked his first home run off of Gary Wayne of the Twins in the same batter's box. Now, 7,583 at-bats later, Frank hit No. 500 off of Carlos Silva, becoming the 21st player to reach the historic plateau. As it turned out, the 2007 season was the last productive year for the big man from Auburn University. The Blue Jays released him on April 20, 2008, after just 16 games following a well-publicized tiff with his manager, John Gibbons, over a lack of playing time. Frank was only a few weeks shy of his 40th birthday and nearing the end, and he knew it, but still chose to keep going. The A's re-signed him four days later, but injuries limited his playing time that year to just 55 games. Thomas did not play in 2009 and delayed a formal retirement announcement until February 12, 2010, with an impromptu press conference at U.S. Cellular Field, where the bitter acrimony of the past was pushed aside and the legendary slugger at last mended his fences with White Sox officials.

"People think we had a rocky relationship, but Jerry [Reinsdorf] was the first one I called to say I was going to retire," Thomas told reporters. "And that conversation was as warm as all the others we had over the years. For some reason, it seems like there is never a happy ending to superstars' careers. They end up playing for other teams but always end up coming back. I'm really proud to be able to retire as a Chicago White Sox player. When players get to a certain level, it's never easy to say good-bye." The Big Hurt's No. 35 was formally retired, and Frank Thomas Day was celebrated in front of a packed house of 39,000 fans on August 29, 2010. "I had a speech written out," Thomas told the media during a press box interview after the on-field ceremony. "The tears started flowing with Hawk [Harrelson]'s introduction and seeing my picture on the [left-field] wall. It is the proudest day of my life. My dad is dead, but he was the biggest motivator in my life," the great star said. The Big Hurt's immediate future—and his place in history—was finally secure with a 2014 induction date into the Hall of Fame looming and a new gig as a postgame color analyst on Comcast SportsNet.

Thome, Jim

White Sox: 2006–2009
Designated Hitter
Birthplace: Peoria, Illinois

B: August 27, 1970
Bats left, throws right
Ht. 6–3; **Wt.** 250

Thome, Jim

White Sox	G	AB	H	AVG	RBI	R	2B	3B	HR	SA	SB
2006	143	490	141	.288	109	108	26	0	42	.598	0
2007	130	432	119	.275	96	79	19	0	35	.563	0
2008	149	503	123	.245	90	93	28	0	34	.503	1
2009	107	345	86	.249	74	55	15	0	23	.493	0
Career	2,392	7,982	2,216	.278	1,624	1,534	428	26	589	.559	19

Crowd pleaser and fan favorite, Big Jim Thome

The jury is still out, and the final verdict yet to be rendered on the Jim Thome–for–Aaron Rowand swap completed on November 25, 2005. Rowand, the kind of player who seemed to personify the "grinder" type of player so highly coveted by the White Sox organization, who insisted on shedding the home run–centric offense in order to remain competitive with the Minnesota Twins (the "Piranhas," in Ozzie Guillen's parlance), was sacrificed for the kind of player who represented the antithesis of the hit-and-run, speed-on-the-base-paths, grinder intensity. Jim Thome is a mortal cinch for the Hall of Fame. In his prime, he was one of the great sluggers of the game, a perfect gentleman on and off the field, and a beloved fan favorite—except perhaps in Cleveland, where angry fans of the Tribe refuse to forgive him for signing with the Phillies as a free agent on December 3, 2002. But by the time the White Sox completed the stunning trade with Philadelphia, Big Jim was on the back end of his long and meritorious career. He could no longer play first base—the Phillies had already primed Ryan Howard as his replacement—and Thome's slowness afoot made him a station-to-station runner on the base paths. His genial, easygoing manner was appreciated by his teammates in the clubhouse and with the media, but did he have the same sense of urgency to win, with the same fire in his belly as the departing Aaron Rowand?

It is a hard question to answer. Sometimes what seems best for a ballclub at a given moment can, over time, backfire. In the first half of the 2006 season, the Rowand trade looked ridiculously lopsided. By July 11, as Guillen prepared to manage the American League All-Star Team to victory in Pittsburgh, Thome was healthy and had already slugged 30 home runs to go along with 77 RBIs. He was putting up Babe Ruth numbers and threatening Albert Belle's team record for home runs in a single season, while Rowand was hitting a measly .264 in Philadelphia. Paul Konerko said Thome was the one player the Sox could not afford to lose. "That's one player we can't replace," Paulie said. "He's just too big of a presence in the lineup to lose." But could he say the same a year later? In the 2006 second-half letdown, Thome hit only 12 homers with 32 RBIs. Belle's record was still safe, but on the strength of his first-half showing, Big Jim claimed the 2006 AL Comeback Player of the Year award following an injury-shortened '05 campaign.

After a hot month of April to open the 2007 campaign, Thome went on the disabled list for two weeks, and his average tailed off the rest of the way. Nineteen of his 34 home runs were solo shots, which underscores a fundamental problem with the Sox's overdependence on the long ball during those years. If the "table setters" could not get on base, it nullified the value of the home run and exposed the glaring weaknesses of power hitters like Thome in general. That is, you can tolerate a high strikeout percentage from your top slugger if the rest of the offense is clicking—but after 2006, this team's ability to play opportunistic baseball withered. Big Jim fanned 147 times in 2006 and 134 times in 2007—but with 58 fewer at-bats in his second year. His 134 whiffs in '07 were a lot more noticeable on a ballclub struggling to score runs than during the 90-win season of 2006. With Thome as the club's full-time DH and unable to play first base, the White Sox's fortunes fell during interleague play in National League parks. Jim had to sit those games out, limiting manager Ozzie Guillen's strategic options. As the 2007 losses mounted, the focus of attention of course shifted to Thome's quest for his 500th career home run.

Frank Thomas had already passed that milestone on June 28 at Minnesota (and how much nicer would it have been to see him accomplish the feat in a Sox uniform?), but Big Jim provided us with one of the decade's greatest thrills by drilling his historic shot at U.S. Cellular Field on September 16 off of Angels hurler Dustin Moseley. The blast was dramatic—a game-winning, walkoff bomb that gave the Sox a 9–7 victory on (believe it or not!) Jim Thome Bobblehead Day. Will Stewart, a visitor from Austin, Texas, caught the historic ball and returned it to Thome, who donated it to the Hall of Fame. Big Jim, just the 23rd player to hit 500 homers in a career, became the first to deliver the historic blow in walkoff fashion. In 2008 the genial Sox DH set his sights on attaining the magical 600 mark as he continued his upward climb on the all-time home run list—moving from 22nd to 14th place, just behind Mike Schmidt, whom he would pass in 2009. He also reached the 1,500 plateau in career walks—a tribute to the respect shown him by American and National League pitchers.

But as the season wore on and the same old offensive problems plagued the Sox as they dashed toward postseason play, advancing age was catching up to Jim Thome, who could no longer get around on a fastball as quickly as he once had. The strikeout total mounted, and his batting average suffered. If the "Pride of Peoria" was to reach the coveted 600 home run threshold, time was running out. It was becoming less certain he would topple the 600 mark in a Sox uniform, even after slugging the game-winning home run to wrap up the 2008 Central Division title off of the Twins' Nick Blackburn, in a dramatic one-game playoff on September 30. His 461-foot missile to dead center in the seventh inning of the "Blackout Game" sunk the Twins' hopes and was a spectacular exclamation point to an exciting season. None of this was too surprising when you think about it because, through 2009, 57 of his career home runs had come against Minnesota pitchers. Although he was signed through the '09 season, it seemed unlikely that the White Sox would be willing to extend the contract of their 38-year-old full-time DH past one year. Thome represented a dilemma for the Sox—his role on the team transcended the field.

Active in the community and a generous supporter of numerous charitable causes, Jim and his wife, Andrea, had pledged $1,000 to the Children's Hospital of the Illinois Neonatal Intensive Care Unit for each of his home runs. There were to be 23 of them in 2009—Jim pushed past Reggie Jackson into 12th place on the all-time list and set a new team record with 14 RBIs over a three-game stretch from July 11 to 17. But the Sox were underachieving again, and the sputtering offense was very lame as the dog days of August rolled on. It was the time of year when the also-rans began shedding salary, and as much as the Ken Williams regime hated to be thrust into that position by the players (Williams said he would rather be the buyer than the seller), eight losses in nine games during a pivotal three-city road trip to Boston, New York, and Minnesota was the decisive factor in cutting loose the veterans. The White Sox sent a memo to various GMs, reportedly offering Thome, Jermaine Dye, and the erratic bullpen set-up man Scott Linebrink to the highest bidders.

The Dodgers, fighting for the postseason, went ahead and made the deal for Thome on August 31, sending to the Sox infielder Justin Fuller—a lowly regarded prospect. Thome waived his no-trade rights and agreed to go to the National League. On the surface of things, it made no sense. "We're not bringing him over here to play first base," explained Dodgers GM Ned Colletti. "We're bringing him here to come off the bench and be a great influence in the clubhouse. He's one of the true great guys in the game. In fact, the night before the deadline he called me. He just said, 'I just want to be honest with you. I'd love to come. I want to help you guys any way I can. But playing first base is not something I'm going to be able to do—maybe in an emergency situation, perhaps.'" L.A. did not go very far in the playoffs, and at season's end, Thome was not tendered a contract. Fans wondered if the team was keen on bringing Jim back for another year.

But at Sox Fest 2010, Ozzie Guillen put to rest rumors that Thome was returning to Chicago. Kenny Williams had left the door open for a Chicago homecoming, but Ozzie squelched that notion during a fan interview session, making it clear there would not be enough bats for Jim in the revamped batting order. Privately, he didn't want him back. For the first time, the Sox seemed serious about changing their persona as a slow, power-hitting team with no other offensive tools beyond the long ball. But Guillen's plan for a "designated hitter by committee" in 2010, featuring outfielder Mark Kotsay, a bench player for most of his career as the left-handed "muscle," backfired. It was a terrible miscalculation, and the Sox paid a heavy price in the thick of a pennant chase. For Jim, with one door shut, another one quickly opened up.

Thome and the Minnesota Twins agreed to a one-year, incentive-laden $1.5 million contract on January 25, 2010. The Twins could not promise him the full-time DH job—but Jim appeared content to accept a part-time, situational role, and he made the best of it. "They were really excited about me coming there, so to me it was a no-brainer," Thome said on a conference call with the Minnesota media. "I've always enjoyed the way they play and how they go about their business. To be a part of that will be a lot of fun to go there and help them win."

Later he spoke of his time in Chicago with fondness. "Chicago, for me, I grew up—that's kind of my home. Growing up in Peoria, and when I went there that time my mom passed, and getting that opportunity to play there as I did, it's always very special. But I cherish my time there for sure. Those guys are like brothers to me, they really are." In consideration of the 2005 trade that looked to be so lopsided in July 2006, let it be said that Aaron Rowand was still productive as a San Francisco Giant in 2010—and with Thome wearing the hated Twin City threads, and contributing in a big way to Minnesota's late-season surge in 2010 once Justin Morneau went down with a season-ending concussion, it can also be said that things have a way of evening out in baseball—and not always as intended...or hoped.

Thornton, Matt

White Sox: 2006–
Pitcher
Birthplace: Three Rivers, Michigan

B: September 15, 1976
Bats left, throws right
Ht. 6–6; **Wt.** 235

Thornton, Matt

White Sox	W	L	Pct.	ERA	G	CG	IP	H	BB	K	Sho	Sv
2006	5	3	.625	3.33	63	0	54	46	21	49	0	2
2007	4	4	.500	4.79	68	0	56⅓	59	26	55	0	2
2008	5	3	.625	2.67	74	0	67⅓	48	19	77	0	1
2009	6	3	.667	2.74	70	0	72⅓	58	20	87	0	4
2010	5	4	.556	2.67	61	0	60⅔	41	20	81	0	8
Career	26	23	.531	3.55	410	0	400⅓	336	173	436	0	17

Baseball executives on the talent procurement side of the ledger like to say that the best trades they make are the ones that benefit all parties to the transaction—the greatest satisfaction comes when value exchanged is for value received. If so, the Seattle Mariners, who were left holding the bag in the lopsided Joe Borchard–for–Matt Thornton trade on March 20, 2006, may never want to do business with the Chicago White Sox again. Borchard, a first-round selection (12th pick overall) in the 2000 amateur draft out of Stanford, was paid a record $5.5 million signing bonus. The player the Sox received for this highly coveted prize was Thornton, chosen 22nd in the June 1998 First-Year Player Draft by Seattle. It was a master stroke and arguably one of Kenny Williams' greatest, albeit most unsung trades in the first 10 years of his tenure as GM. Borchard, a power-hitting outfielder who failed to live up to his press clippings in four separate tryouts with the White Sox between 2002 and 2005, hit the longest home run in U.S. Cellular Field history—a monster 504-foot cannon shot off of Brett Myers of the Phillies to the left-field concourse in 2004. But like Dave Nicholson in an earlier era of Sox history, one mighty blast could not compensate for chronic subpar performance at the plate, especially with expectations riding so high.

The Thornton trade turned out to be larceny on a grand scale, and Williams was guilty as charged. The really hilarious aspect to the whole thing was the public jubilation expressed in the Mariners camp when the deal was consummated. On the USS Mariner, the Seattle Mariners' online blog for news and commentary, one of their excited "analysts" posted the following note on March 20, 2006: "Thornton was, and still is, essentially useless. Yes, he throws 95, but big whoop-de-doo. He's basically pitched well as a pro for all of one season, back in A ball, pre-surgery [he underwent Tommy John surgery in 2002], and been mediocre to bad the rest of his career. He throws straight, without command, and has no real secondary pitches to speak of. He doesn't hide the ball well,

Matt Thornton, stolen away from Seattle. (Courtesy of Mike McKay)

and hitters tee off on his hittable fastball, especially when they're sitting on it 2–0. He didn't deserve to be on the team last year, and he certainly didn't deserve to be on the team this year."

With the White Sox, the mechanical flaws were easily detected, and immediate corrections were made to Matt's delivery and release point by pitching coach Don Cooper—the best South Side pitching coach since Ray Berres for his uncanny ability to turn around the careers of struggling hurlers. "It's not any one thing Coop did that helped necessarily," Thornton said. "But overall he underscores your own strengths as a pitcher and helps pare away the other stuff that gets in the way." Thornton made his first appearance in a Sox uniform on Opening Night of 2006 against Cleveland, and right away he helped shore up a shaky bullpen in a middle relief role. Eventually, he settled in as one of the top three bullpen set-up men in the American League, averaging 60 or more appearances in each of his first four South Side campaigns. He ranks as the club's all-time leader in "holds," a new pitching statistic that came into vogue in the 1990s, and at times his fastball is lights out. In two separate relief appearances on June 1 and June 6, 2009, Matt struck out six consecutive hitters, one shy of Joe Cowley's team record set back in 1986.

During Bobby Jenks' struggles to regain his effectiveness in 2009 and early 2010, there were many who believed that Williams should deal Jenks and allow Thornton to step into the role of team closer, a natural progression, they argued. Joey Cora, acting as interim manager when Ozzie Guillen was attending his son's graduation in 2010, seized the opportunity to audition Matt in the unfamiliar role. Although the short-lived experiment proved successful, Guillen kept him on as the seventh- and eighth-inning set-up man—he was just too valuable setting the table for Jenks. In recognition of his success, and the reputation he established as one of the league's best, Yankees manager Joe Girardi added Matt to the 2010 All-Star squad—a rare distinction for a relief pitcher who is not a closer. Meanwhile, Joe Borchard, this generation's answer to big Ron Jackson, another celebrated "can't-miss" prospect from the late 1950s, lasted barely two months in Seattle before he was cut loose and claimed off waivers by the Florida Marlins. He has not appeared in a big league game since 2007.

Thurston, Hollis

White Sox: 1923–26
Pitcher
Nickname: Sloppy
Birthplace: Fremont, Nebraska

B: June 2, 1899
D: September 14, 1973
Batted right, threw right
Ht. 5–11; **Wt.** 165

Thurston, Hollis

White Sox	W	L	Pct	ERA	G	CG	IP	H	BB	K	ShO
1923	7	8	.467	3.05	44	8	192	223	36	55	0
1924	20	14	.588	3.80	38	28	291	330	60	37	1
1925	10	14	.417	6.17	36	9	175	250	47	35	0
1926	6	8	.429	5.02	31	13	134⅓	164	36	35	1
Career	89	86	.509	4.26	288	95	1,534⅔	1,859	369	306	8

Neat, meticulous—Hollis Thurston was a real dandy dresser of the Jazz Age. That's why he was nicknamed Sloppy by his White Sox teammates and Ted Lyons, whom he shared a room with during their first season with the ballclub.

Thurston was acquired on waivers from the St. Louis Browns on May 12, 1923. He compensated for a below-average fastball by developing a screwball pitch and a double-pump windup. In 1924, his one season of note, Sloppy reeled off a 10-game winning streak and finished up at 20–14 for the last-place Sox. After this brief flourish of mound glory, Thurston became a very ordinary .500 pitcher afflicted by recurring arm troubles. Manager Eddie Collins declared him arm-dead after the 1926 season and traded him to the Washington Senators on January 15, 1927, for shortstop Roger Peckinpaugh.

After retirement, he was a successful scout for the White Sox and other ballclubs, credited with discovering Pittsburgh Pirates slugger Ralph Kiner.

Hollis "Sloppy" Thurston

Tresh, Mike

White Sox: 1938–48
Catcher
Birthplace: Hazleton, Pennsylvania
B: February 23, 1914
D: October 4, 1966
Batted right, threw right
Ht. 5–11; **Wt.** 170

Tresh, Mike

White Sox	G	AB	H	AVG	RBI	R	2B	3B	HR	SA	SB
1938	10	29	7	.241	2	3	2	0	0	.310	0
1939	119	352	91	.259	38	49	5	2	0	.284	3
1940	135	480	135	.281	64	62	15	5	1	.340	3
1941	115	390	98	.251	33	38	10	1	0	.282	1
1942	72	233	54	.232	15	21	8	1	0	.275	2
1943	86	279	60	.215	20	20	3	0	0	.226	2
1944	93	312	81	.260	25	22	8	1	0	.292	0
1945	150	458	114	.249	47	50	11	0	0	.273	6
1946	80	217	47	.217	21	28	5	2	0	.258	0
1947	90	274	66	.241	20	19	6	2	0	.277	2
1948	39	108	27	.250	11	10	1	0	1	.287	0
Career	1,027	3,169	788	.249	297	326	74	14	2	.283	19

Mike Tresh began playing baseball in the Detroit metropolitan area when he was only eight years old. He was voted the Most Valuable Player for the Pittinger Post American Legion team in 1930, a few years before he signed a contract with the hometown Tigers. Tresh was rated a defensive standout behind the plate, but he was very weak offensively and was therefore deemed expendable.

The youthful backstop was a throw-in in the big winter trade with Detroit that brought Marv Owen and Gee Walker to Chicago on December 2, 1937, for Vern Kennedy, Dixie Walker, and Tony Piet. Mike was lost in the shuffle for the moment—but, given a chance to start the 1939 season as the everyday catcher, Tresh came through in a big way. He beat out Buddy Rosar of the New York Yankees for a berth on the All-Star Major Freshman Team.

Mike caught 115 or more games each year from 1939 through 1941, and led the league in putouts in '41. Writers were effusive in their praise for the Sox iron-man catcher, despite his weakness with the bat. "There is not another catcher in the league who is throwing or handling pitchers any better than the Detroit boy who came to Chicago to find baseball glory," commented James Enright in the *Herald Examiner*.

After a decade of loyal and faithful service, Tresh was sold to Cleveland on January 11, 1949. His son Tom was a standout infielder for the Yankees in the early 1960s.

Trucks, Virgil

White Sox: 1953–55
Pitcher
Nickname: Fire
Birthplace: Birmingham, Alabama
B: April 26, 1919
Bats right, throws right
Ht. 5–11; **Wt.** 198

Trucks, Virgil

White Sox	W	L	Pct	ERA	G	CG	IP	H	BB	K	ShO	Sv
1953	15	6	.714	2.86	24	19	176⅓	151	67	102	3	1
1954	19	12	.613	2.79	40	16	264⅓	234	99	149	5	3
1955	13	8	.619	3.96	32	7	175	176	95	152	5	3
Career	177	135	.567	3.39	517	124	2,682⅓	2,416	1,088	1,534	35	30

The success of the White Sox pitching staff in the 1950s owed much to the genius of Frank Lane, and then later Chuck Comiskey. Their uncanny ability to procure veteran talent from other teams when they needed it the most kept the Sox in contention. The big names of that era who kept the South Siders competitive year after year did not come up through the vaunted White Sox farm system, but from opposing teams where they had achieved only marginal success or had worn out their welcome.

In the Lane years, Saul Rogovin, Joe Dobson, Harry Dorish, Mike Fornieles, and Virgil Oliver Trucks were the key acquisitions who caught their second wind in Chicago working under the tutelage of Paul Richards. Later in the decade Turk Lown, Jim Wilson, Early Wynn, Bob Shaw, and Gerry Staley—castoffs all—provided the pitching leadership for Marty Marion and Al Lopez.

Virgil Trucks

Virgil Trucks, a burly Southerner who tossed a pair of no-hitters while with the Detroit Tigers in 1952, was one of the truly remarkable success stories of the Lane era. Trucks was 35 years old and playing out the string for Bill Veeck's pitiful St. Louis Browns when Lane and Veeck got together on the eve of the 1953 trading deadline and cooked up another one of their fabled Missouri-to-Chicago "shuttle bus" deals.

Veeck, eager to unload another expensive veteran's salary, sent Trucks and infielder Bob Elliott to the Sox for pitcher Lou Kretlow, an erratic right-hander plagued by control problems, along with $95,000 in cash and catcher Darrell Johnson. The money helped keep Veeck solvent in St. Louis until the end of the season when he could sell the team to Baltimore interests. Lane believed he had found the missing link at third base in the person of Elliott. The unexpected dividend turned out to be Trucks.

Virgil, one of the great control pitchers of the game who could always be counted on to go at least seven innings per start, brought an unremarkable 5–4 record to the Windy City. But with a better supporting cast behind him, he won his first eight decisions in a Sox uniform until the Yankees ended the streak on August 8 in typical heartbreaking New York fashion. Old Virg was shut out 3–0, but in 1953 he completed the first and only 20-win season of his career and was named Chicago Comeback Player of the Year by the local baseball writers' fraternity at the annual Diamond Dinner.

Trucks kept rolling merrily along in 1954. The big man tossed a pair of one-hitters against the Red Sox and Tigers, and his five shutouts tied Cleveland's Mike Garcia for the league lead. His bid for a second straight 20-win season fell short on the next-to-last day of the season, when Billy O'Dell of the Orioles edged the Sox 2–1 in Baltimore.

Knowing when to let go is another hallmark of a winning team. Virgil lost the zip in his fastball in 1955 when he surrendered a team-high 19 home runs. His won-lost record did not accurately reflect his performance that year. At the winter meetings in Columbus, Ohio, the new front-office tandem of Chuck Comiskey and John Rigney traded the aging pitcher to the Tigers for 25-year-old third baseman Bubba Phillips, one of five contenders for the hot corner in 1956. The deal was completed on November 30, 1955. That very same day, it was announced that the White Sox had purchased the contract of a young shortstop named Luis Aparicio from their Memphis farm club.

Trucks retired in 1958, but within two years he was reduced to near poverty. Virg lost a substantial amount of money through bad investments and then drove himself to the point of near exhaustion by agreeing to barnstorm the country with the legendary Satchel Paige and a collection of Latin American players known as the Caribbean Kings. Paige and Trucks logged 16,000 miles by car, but they barely had enough money left to pay for their meals in restaurants. In desperation, he called Danny Murtaugh and begged the Pirates manager for a job as a batting practice pitcher, which Murtaugh was more than happy to provide after hearing the details of Virgil's recent misfortunes.

Tucker, Thurman

White Sox: 1942–44; 1946–47
Outfielder
Birthplace: Gordon, Texas

B: September 26, 1917
D: May 7, 1993
Batted left, threw right
Ht. 5–10½; **Wt.** 165

Tucker, Thurman

White Sox	G	AB	H	AVG	RBI	R	2B	3B	HR	SA	SB
1942	7	24	3	.125	1	2	0	1	0	.208	0
1943	139	528	124	.235	39	81	15	6	3	.303	29
1944	124	446	128	.287	46	59	15	6	2	.361	13
1946	121	438	126	.288	36	62	20	3	1	.354	9
1947	89	254	60	.236	17	28	9	4	1	.315	10
Career	701	2,331	570	.255	179	325	79	24	9	.325	77

After catching a glimpse of Thurman Tucker, the rookie outfielder who finally made the ballclub after three unsuccessful spring training tryouts, the Chicago press corps posed the logical question to the bespectacled fly chaser: "Say, kid, you don't happen to be any relation to Joe E. Brown, do you?"

Tucker's resemblance to the popular 1940s nightclub comic was striking. Everywhere Thurman went, he was asked the same tiresome question, and each time he smiled politely

Look alikes: Comedian Joe E. Brown (center) and Thurman Tucker confuse Chuck Comiskey.

and shook his head. Sensing his discomfort, the fans began calling him Joe E. Tucker.

Tucker by any other name got off to a sizzling start early in the 1944 campaign. He led the American League in hitting for nearly three months, and his batting average hovered near .400 through June.

Suddenly Thurman was a matinee idol instantly recognizable by his *own* name, which took on greater significance when he was chosen to lead off for the American League in the 1944 All-Star Game.

Shortly after this dazzling display of hitting, Tucker lapsed into an 0–32 slump and was benched by manager Jimmie Dykes.

Thurman, one of the league's fastest players, once ran a footrace against George Case, the league's premier base stealer during the World War II era. Unfortunately Tucker lost the 75-yard dash by three paces. At the end of the 1947 season Thurman was traded to Cleveland for catcher Ralph Weigel, his best years already behind him.

Valentin, Jose

White Sox: 2000–04
Infielder
Birthplace: Manati, Puerto Rico

B: October 12, 1969
Bats both, throws right
Ht. 5–10; **Wt.** 175

Valentin, Jose

White Sox	G	AB	H	AVG	RBI	R	2B	3B	HR	SA	SB
2000	144	568	155	.273	92	107	37	6	25	.491	19
2001	124	438	113	.258	68	74	22	2	28	.509	9
2002	135	474	118	.249	75	70	26	4	25	.479	3
2003	144	503	119	.237	74	79	26	2	28	.463	8
2004	125	450	97	.216	70	73	20	3	30	.473	8
Career	1,490	4,989	1,204	.241	736	798	267	37	228	.447	128

Ron Schueler's last great trade before stepping aside as general manager brought to Chicago veteran shortstop Jose Valentin, a gritty "throwback" type of player who compensated for his fielding deficiencies and alarmingly high strikeout totals with a real "can do" attitude on and off the field. After the Cubs had tried and failed to secure the services of the power-hitting Valentin from the Milwaukee Brewers, where he had become only the seventh shortstop of the 20th century to hit three home runs in a game (April 3, 1998 vs. Florida), Schueler succeeded in moving the troublesome Jaime Navarro, his $5-million-per-year contract, and the equally disappointing John Snyder to the beer city on January 12, 2000. Cal Eldred, recovering from reconstructive surgery to his pitching arm, accompanied Valentin to Chicago, and without these veterans in place for 2000, it is unlikely the youthful White Sox could have won the division title.

The trade was not without some risk. Valentin, originally signed by the San Diego Padres on October 12, 1986, missed more than two months of the 1999 season with ligament damage to his left thumb, but with Mike Caruso written out of the White Sox starting lineup for 2000 because of his erratic fielding, the ex-Brewer became the Opening Day shortstop by default, injury or no injury. The gamble paid off. Despite committing a frightening 36 errors (the worst in the league), Valentin supplied plenty of offensive fireworks in 2000 and, for that matter, in each of his five Sox seasons. His 25 homers shattered Ron Hansen's once-insurmountable team mark of 20 for shortstops set back in 1964. Jose became only the fifth player in Sox history to hit for the cycle when he turned the trick against the Orioles on April 27. He narrowly missed doing it again exactly a month later against Cleveland. On September 30 he joined Ken Henderson, Brian Simmons, and Tim Raines as the only Sox players to smack home runs from both sides of the plate in a 9–1 rout of Kansas City at U.S. Cellular Field. Valentin would accomplish the feat once more, in 2003. Average-wise, the 2000 campaign was Jose's best all-around season, but his glove work was subpar—although he seemed to save the best for

Jose Valentin: The only Sox shortshop to slug 30 homers in a season

the annual Sox showdown against the Cubs. His 12 home runs and 31 RBIs against the North Siders were his best against any NL opponent.

Williams attempted to plug the defensive hole at short by bringing in the fancy-fielding Royce Clayton and shifting Valentin over to third, where he would spend much of the 2001 and 2002 seasons. Clayton did what he had to before moving on, while Jose alternated between third, the outfield, and short—a man without a position. To keep his bat in the lineup, manager Jerry Manuel took a chance and moved him back to short for the 2003 season. "Jose plays to win," Manuel said at the time. "He is exactly what we talk about when we say 'team player.' " Valentin's fielding improved steadily—his 20 miscues were the lowest since the 1997 season—but it was accompanied by a corresponding drop-off in batting average. A free swinger who always seemed to be aiming for the fences regardless of the situation, Valentin slugged 30 homers in 2004 but fanned 139 times. His strikeouts-to-at-bats ratio was alarming, and at age 35, Jose was out of options with the White Sox after Ozzie Guillen evaluated newcomer Juan Uribe, and his ability to go deep into the hole and fire strikes to first base with strength and accuracy. It was changing-of-the-guard time at U.S. Cellular Field. Granted his free agency, Valentin signed for less money with the Los Angeles Dodgers on December 31, 2004. Penciled in as Adrian Beltre's replacement at third, Jose missed most of the 2005 season with a sprained right knee. His .170 batting average in limited play discouraged the Dodgers from offering arbitration, but the Mets countered with a $912,000 contract offer for 2006, and Valentin was signed as a bench reserve.

Robin Ventura

Ventura, Robin

White Sox: 1989–98
Third baseman
Birthplace: Santa Maria, California

B: July 14, 1967
Bats left, throws right
Ht. 6–1; **Wt.** 198

Ventura, Robin

White Sox	G	AB	H	AVG	RBI	R	2B	3B	HR	SA	SB
1989	16	45	8	.178	7	5	3	0	0	.244	0
1990	150	493	123	.249	54	48	17	1	5	.318	1
1991	157	606	172	.284	100	92	25	1	23	.442	2
1992	157	592	167	.282	93	85	38	1	16	.431	2
1993	157	554	145	.262	94	85	27	1	22	.433	1
1994	109	401	113	.282	78	57	15	1	18	.459	3
1995	135	492	145	.295	93	79	22	0	26	.498	4
1996	158	586	168	.287	105	96	31	2	34	.520	1
1997	54	183	48	.262	26	27	10	1	6	.426	0
1998	161	590	155	.263	91	84	31	4	21	.436	1
Career	2,079	7,064	1,885	.267	1,182	1,006	338	14	294	.444	24

The White Sox never expected Robin Ventura to become the next Brooks Robinson at the hot corner. When Larry Himes selected Robin in the June 1988 free agent draft, it was with his hitting abilities in mind and not his glove work, which was considered suspect during the time he played for Oklahoma State.

Ventura was nationally acclaimed in the collegiate ranks for his 58-game hitting streak, which was abruptly ended by Stanford ace Jack McDowell in the 1987 College World Series. Robin won the 1988 Golden Spikes Award, baseball's equivalent of the Heisman Trophy, and was a member of the U.S. Olympic team that year. *Baseball America* named him College Player of the Decade. Then he came to Chicago, where his batting stance was completely turned around and altered by hitting coach Walter Hriniak.

For good or bad, Ventura adopted to the Hriniak "scattergun" offense. Robin never hit the .300 mark with the White Sox, which Himes reasonably expected him to broach every year. But he was critical to the 1990s power-laden offense, and is one of only 11 major league third basemen who have driven in 90 or more runs a year three or more times since the end of World War II. Robin set an individual team record for RBIs by a third basemen in 1991 when he drove home an even 100 runs.

Ventura's fielding excellence was the unexpected dividend. He won three consecutive Rawlings Gold Glove

Awards (1991–93), thus becoming the first White Sox repeat winner since Jim Kaat in the mid-1970s. He added another to his collection in 1996.

It took a lot of courage for a 26-year-old third baseman playing in only his fourth full season to take on grizzled Nolan Ryan—a Texas institution—in a baseball brawl. Ventura sent a powerful message to the future Hall of Fame pitcher, who threw one too many brush-back pitches, by charging the mound in a game played in hostile Arlington Stadium on August 4, 1993. Robin took his licks from the 46-year-old Ryan. He was ordered to sit out a two-game suspension, and was roundly booed by the Texas Rangers fans well into the 1994 season. But as Jack McDowell observed, sometimes a man has got to do what a man has got to do.

Robin permanently silenced his Rangers critics by blasting two consecutive grand slam home runs in the Ballpark at Arlington on September 4, 1995, thus joining Tony Lazzeri, Jim Tabor, Rudy York, Jim Gentile, Tony Cloninger, Jim Northrup, and Frank Robinson as the only players in modern major league history to accomplish the rare hitting miracle of two slammers in one game. A year later Robin shattered Oscar Gamble's team record for most home runs by a left-handed batter when he poled 34 round-trippers. The 1996 campaign, by far, was his best all-around season.

Robin Ventura ranks as one of the greatest Sox third baseman of all time. From the standpoint of longevity, Willie Kamm and Bill Melton also paid their dues. Buck Weaver and Jimmie Dykes must also be included in any discussion of White Sox hot-corner heroes.

Unfortunately, free agency got in the way of the gold watch and the testimonial day. "Rockin" Robin filed after the 1998 season and was grabbed by the New York Mets on December 1 of that year. Losing a four-time Gold Glove third baseman was a terrible setback for the White Sox. Before Ventura's arrival, the position had been a revolving door. You could count on one hand the truly great third basemen who had left their mark on team history, but the White Sox brain trust counted on Joe Crede to fill the void. Not until 2002, when Crede finally settled into the position on a full-time basis, did the White Sox regain the strength they had lost at the hot corner.

Meanwhile, Ventura was traded from the Mets to the Yankees in December 2001 in a cost-cutting measure designed to reduce team payroll. He anchored the Yankees infield with Derek Jeter for less than three seasons before being sent off to the Dodgers on July 31, 2003, for Bubba Crosby and Scott Proctor. Used mostly in a utility role with the Dodgers, Ventura hit two grand slams in 2004—raising his career total to 18 and tying Willie McCovey for the third most in baseball history, behind Lou Gehrig (23) and Eddie Murray (19). Bothered by an arthritic right ankle and with little fanfare, he announced his retirement after 16 years on October 11, 2004. "I'm absolutely positive. I've realized that it's time to go, and that's it," he said.

Walker, Greg

White Sox: 1982–90
First baseman, designated hitter
Birthplace: Douglas, Georgia

B: October 6, 1959
Bats left, throws right
Ht. 6–3; **Wt.** 215

Walker, Greg

White Sox	G	AB	H	AVG	RBI	R	2B	3B	HR	SA	SB
1982	11	17	7	.412	7	3	2	1	2	1.000	0
1983	118	307	83	.270	55	32	16	3	10	.440	2
1984	136	442	130	.294	75	62	29	2	24	.532	8
1985	163	601	155	.258	92	77	38	4	24	.454	5
1986	78	282	78	.277	51	37	10	6	13	.493	1
1987	157	566	145	.256	94	85	33	2	27	.465	2
1988	99	377	93	.247	42	45	22	1	8	.374	0
1989	77	233	49	.210	26	25	14	0	5	.335	0
1990	2	5	1	.200	0	0	0	0	0	.200	0
Career	839	2,825	740	.262	442	366	164	19	113	.449	18

Left unprotected by the Philadelphia Phillies in the December 1979 minor league draft, Greg Walker was spotted by scout Jerry Krause and claimed by the White Sox for the mere sum of $12,000—another Bill Veeck "bargain-basement" find.

Quiet and reticent in his dealings, this handsome Georgian came up to the Sox at the same time as the more flamboyant Ron Kittle. Because it was not in his nature to pop off to the media or say outrageous things, Greg played in Kittle's

Greg Walker

shadow for much of the time the two played together on the South Side. Commented former Sox manager Tony LaRussa: "Everybody sees his swing and knows it's great. But his toughness. Hey, that's something you don't appreciate until you've been around him."

Walker concentrated on his hitting. He fine-tuned his swing through constant practice, learned how to hit the curveball, and enjoyed some very productive seasons in the mid-1980s before injuries set in. Greg was platooned with Tom Paciorek at first base his first few years in Chicago, but took over on a full-time basis in 1984. Walker appeared in 163 games in 1985, equaling Don Buford's 1966 team record, and his 27 home runs in 1987 were the most by a White Sox first baseman since the days of Dick Allen. For his career, Walker slugged 113 home runs, third highest among left-handed hitters behind Harold Baines and Robin Ventura.

Walker's 1988 season was cut short by a life-threatening viral infection to the brain—an ailment that cleared up through quiet recuperation at his Georgia home. However, Greg's 1989 comeback was curtailed by shoulder surgery. He was released on waivers two weeks into the 1990 season.

Jerry Manuel appointed Walker as hitting coach on May 19, 2003, after Greg finished a one-year apprenticeship with the Triple A Charlotte Knights in 2002. Under his tutelage, White Sox hitters established a raft of team home run records during the "power years" of the early new millennium, but "Walk" took a lot of heat from the fans in 2007 for a short-circuiting offense that dropped them into last place overall with a miserable .246 team average. The subpar hitting problems continued in 2008, 2009, and through the early months of the 2010 season. The slow-mo offense and overreliance on the home run ball was not a healthy mix—it was inconsistent with the traditions and history of White Sox baseball. Walker took his lumps for it, but clung to his job when nearly everyone else had written him off. Through the whole thing, Greg maintained a stoic outlook. "Even those years we did underachieve we went about our business the right way," he said after the tough 2009 season. "When they decide it's someone else's turn, then it will be someone else's job." Commenting on the Greg Walker controversy in his online blog, the always-quotable and controversial Jack McDowell noted on June 16, 2009: "Walker's work ethic, expertise, personality are all top-notch when you are looking for an MLB coach. Results need to fall on the players' laps. Coaches will get fired when they have personality clashes with players (or the manager) or when they aren't putting the time and effort into it that is needed to be a top-notch guy."

Walsh, Ed

White Sox: 1904–16
Pitcher
Nicknames: Big Ed; the Big Reel; the Moose
Birthplace: Plains, Pennsylvania
B: May 14, 1881
D: May 26, 1959
Batted right, threw right
Ht. 6–1; **Wt.** 193

Walsh, Ed

White Sox	W	L	Pct	ERA	G	CG	IP	H	BB	K	ShO
1904	6	3	.667	2.60	18	6	110⅔	90	32	57	1
1905	8	3	.727	2.17	22	9	136⅔	121	29	71	1
1906	17	13	.567	1.88	41	24	278⅓	215	58	171	10
1907	24	18	.571	1.60	56	37	422⅓	341	87	206	5
1908	40	15	.727	1.42	66	42	464	343	56	269	12
1909	15	11	.577	1.41	31	20	230⅓	166	50	127	8
1910	18	20	.474	1.27	45	33	369⅔	242	61	258	7
1911	27	18	.600	2.22	56	33	368⅔	327	72	255	5
1912	27	17	.614	2.15	62	32	393	332	94	254	6
1913	8	3	.727	2.58	16	7	97⅔	91	39	34	1
1914	2	3	.400	2.82	8	3	44⅔	33	20	15	1
1915	3	0	1.000	1.33	3	3	27	19	7	12	1
1916	0	1	.000	2.70	2	0	3⅓	4	3	3	0
Career	195	126	.607	1.82	430	250	2,964⅓	2,346	617	1,736	58

The spitball, in order to be effective, requires speed and control. Ed Walsh, one of 13 children born to an impoverished family of Pennsylvania coal miners, became its greatest practitioner.

Ed Walsh, "the Big Reel," modeling his 1910 uniform

Before baseball Walsh worked in the local coal mine driving a mule team to the storage bins. It was hard and mean work, but it was an honest living that paid $1.25 a day. Seeing no future in the grueling, life-shortening work, Walsh turned to baseball for salvation.

He was drafted by the White Sox from the Newark club of the Eastern League in 1904 for the sum of $750, after Comiskey followed up on a tip from the owner of the Boston Red Sox.

The wild and ineffective Walsh was struggling to develop a replacement pitch for a subpar curveball. The tall right-hander with an exaggerated windup had injured his wrist and just could not snap off a curveball with any degree of velocity.

Walsh was taught to throw a spitball in the spring of 1904 by Elmer Stricklett, whom some historians credit with inventing the moist delivery. Stricklett was a teammate of Walsh at Newark in 1903. A year later the two pitchers were reunited in Chicago and vied for a starting berth with the White Sox, but after one disappointing start Elmer Stricklett was cut loose. Ed Walsh, however, embarked on a brilliant career that might have lasted longer than it did if overwork and misuse had not sapped him of his strength.

"Big Ed" made his debut pitching in relief on May 12, 1904. A week later he shut out the Washington Senators on just two hits and was well on his way to big-league stardom.

He moved into the starting rotation on a permanent basis late in the 1905 season after pitching both ends of a doubleheader in Boston on September 26. Walsh won both games, sealing his future role as the "iron man" of the pitching staff. On the average, Ed pitched once every three days in 1908, a season which stands as the single greatest pitching performance in White Sox history. He logged 464 innings as the No. 1 starter...and closer. Walsh was called upon to close 15 games in addition to his 49 starts.

However, there is some lingering doubt about his victory total. Under modern scoring rules it is clear that at least four of Ed's 40 credited 1908 wins would not qualify as victories. The passage of time has not diminished his remarkable accomplishments, whatever the true circumstances of the official scorer's decisions might have been. Ed's heart-rending performance on October 2, 1908, in Cleveland has to be considered his best one-game performance.

In the heat of a torrid three-team pennant race, Ed limited the Naps to just three paltry hits, while fanning 15 batters. His opponent, Addie Joss, hurled a perfect game that afternoon and came up a winner only because catcher Ossee Schreck failed to hang on to a sharply breaking spitter, allowing the winning run to cross the plate.

Owner Charles Comiskey received the play-by-play results from a ticker tape in Chicago's Orchestra Hall. Turning to sportswriter Harvey Woodruff, the Old Roman said of his pitcher: "Walsh pitched wonderfully. He is a big-hearted fellow, always willing to work his arm off, and to lose such a contest! Joss must have been great!"

Comiskey's praise did not ring true the following season when Walsh held out for a $7,500 salary. The owner and his star pitcher were often at odds over salary matters. He missed the first month of the season but still retained his effectiveness. His 1909 ERA was an incomprehensible 1.41. Walsh's career 1.82 ERA is the lowest among all major league pitchers since 1893. Addie Joss, Big Ed's archrival for so many years, is in second place.

The Moose tossed the first Comiskey Park no-hitter on August 27, 1911, defeating Boston 5–0. He led the league in appearances from 1910 through 1912, but the strain of so much wear and tear was ruining his throwing arm. By 1916, Ed's once powerful arm simply gave out. Charles Comiskey privately assured Walsh that the day would come when he would take his turn at managing the Sox. Instead, he released Walsh a few weeks into the 1916 season. Walsh caught on with the Boston Braves in 1917 but was ineffective. He finished his career five victories shy of the 200 mark. "If only my arm had held up a little longer," he used to say.

The closest the great spitball pitcher ever came to managing the White Sox was a three-day stint in 1924, while Comiskey weighed his options after Johnny Evers underwent emergency appendectomy surgery.

Voted into the Hall of Fame in 1946, Walsh remained bitter toward the Old Roman through the remainder of his days. And who could really blame him? Comiskey was always tight with a dollar, and when the fans and some of his teammates staged an Ed Walsh Day just after the 1911 season, the White Sox owner refused to contribute to a pool of money collected to buy Ed a car.

Ed Walsh Jr. pitched briefly for the White Sox in the late 1920s, but the son was nothing like the father. In fact the two were never very close. Walsh Jr. died of rheumatic fever in 1937 at age 32.

Walsh Sr. finally received his long-overdue White Sox tribute when Chuck Comiskey, the grandson of the founder, brought Ed back to the ballpark on June 22, 1958, where he was reunited with his old catcher Ray Schalk and thousands of White Sox fans. Most of them had never even heard of Ed Walsh, and that was unfortunate. Frail and ravaged by cancer, the 77-year-old Sox great was pushed to the Comiskey Park mound in a wheelchair. The venerable old pitcher—the greatest right-hander in White Sox history bar none—seemed embarrassed by all the attention. The acclaim was 40 years overdue.

Ward, Pete

White Sox: 1963–69
Third baseman, first baseman, outfielder
Nickname: Pistol Pete

Birthplace: Montreal, Quebec
B: July 26, 1939
Bats left, throws right
Ht. 6–1; **Wt.** 185

Ward, Pete

White Sox	G	AB	H	AVG	RBI	R	2B	3B	HR	SA	SB
1963	157	600	177	.295	84	80	34	6	22	.482	7
1964	144	539	152	.282	94	61	28	3	23	.473	1
1965	138	507	125	.247	57	62	25	3	10	.367	2
1966	84	251	55	.219	28	22	7	1	3	.291	3
1967	146	467	109	.233	62	49	16	2	18	.392	3
1968	125	399	86	.216	50	43	15	0	15	.366	4
1969	105	199	49	.246	32	22	7	0	6	.372	0
Career	973	3,060	779	.254	539	371	136	17	98	.405	20

If not for Gary Peters' sensational pitching, Pete Ward would have been the unanimous choice for 1963 American League Rookie of the Year. As it turned out, the spotlighted youngster acquired in the big winter trade with the Baltimore Orioles settled for second place in BBWAA balloting, but won the honor from the *Sporting News*.

Pete was thrown into the deal at the insistence of White Sox special assignment scout Charley Metro, who managed Ward when he broke into pro ball in 1958 at Vancouver. The son of National Hockey League star Jimmy Ward, the rangy infielder defied convention by sticking with a strange, herky-jerky batting stance. He pointed his rear foot at home plate and his front foot at the pitcher. You wouldn't recommend Ward's low crouching stance to a Little Leaguer, but he was Chicago's most consistent power threat for five seasons.

Pete slugged three grand-slam home runs in 1964 to set a team record. He avoided the sophomore jinx—but in April 1965 disaster struck. While en route to a Blackhawks hockey game at the Chicago Stadium, Ward, Tommy John, and two White Sox investors were rear-ended by another motorist. A serious neck backlash injury derailed his career, and after that baseball was a struggle.

In the next few seasons, Pete exhibited flashes of his early brilliance. But in his struggle to lose weight, continue his therapy with the osteopaths and chiropractors, and regain his batting eye, Ward relinquished his third-base job to Don Buford in 1966, and thereafter he was shuttled between first base and the outfield by Eddie Stanky and Al Lopez.

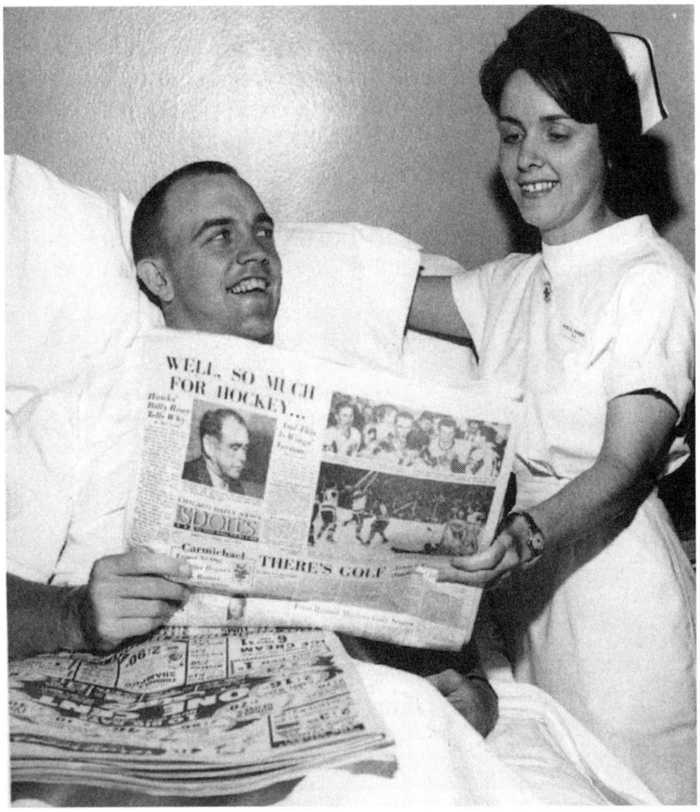

Pete Ward recovers from his injuries at Mercy Hospital. "So much for hockey..."

Hobbled by injuries, Pete never completely regained his old form, but in limited part-time play in 1969, he led the American League with 17 pinch-hits and a .442 on-base percentage. In the weeks leading up to Christmas of that year, Pete was one of a group of major leaguers who accompanied longtime White Sox broadcaster Bob Elson to South Vietnam to meet and greet U.S. soldiers on the frontlines during a goodwill tour. Elson and the players spent 15 days and 15 nights in the war-torn region, making 16 helicopter trips a day. Then on December 18, a few days after returning to his home in Portland, Oregon, Ward received sudden notification that he had been traded to the Yankees for a young German-born pitcher named Ralph "Mickey" Scott and a bundle of cash, desperately needed by the nearly bankrupt John Allyn ownership to keep the ship afloat. Ward accepted the news as best he could. He explained to reporters that he had expected this to happen for nearly three seasons. The trade came just five days after GM Ed Short had swapped Pete's old sidekick Gary Peters to Boston for untried prospects and of course the much-needed "long green" to keep the shaky franchise solvent. The really galling aspect to all of this, apart from losing these respected veterans, was the way Short had tried to cloak these austerity moves as "youth rebuilding." "We are trying to shore up our pitching," he callously explained. "And we want to do it with kids who have a future, not with those who have only a past." Ralph Scott, a teenaged sensation who had quickly faded in the Yankees farm system, never played a day of major league baseball.

Weaver, George

White Sox: 1912–20
Shortstop, third baseman
Nickname: Buck
Birthplace: Pottstown, Pennsylvania
B: August 18, 1890
D: January 31, 1956
Batted right, threw right
Ht. 5–11; **Wt.** 170

Weaver, George

White Sox	G	AB	H	AVG	RBI	R	2B	3B	HR	SA	SB
1912	147	523	117	.224	43	55	21	8	1	.300	12
1913	151	533	145	.272	52	51	17	9	2	.356	20
1914	136	541	133	.246	28	64	20	9	2	.327	14
1915	148	563	151	.268	49	83	18	11	3	.355	24
1916	151	582	132	.227	38	78	27	6	3	.309	22
1917	118	447	127	.284	32	64	16	5	3	.362	19
1918	112	420	126	.300	29	37	12	5	0	.352	20
1919	140	571	169	.296	75	89	33	9	3	.401	22
1920	151	630	210	.333	75	104	35	8	2	.424	19
Career	1,254	4,810	1,310	.272	421	625	199	69	21	.356	172

Decades after the Black Sox scandal had passed into the collective memory of the sportswriters and an aging generation of fans prone to sentimentality, the name "Buck" Weaver evoked only the deepest sorrow and regret. Even Charles Comiskey, the Old Roman, who paid plantation wages to his greatest stars, conceded in a private moment that Weaver deserved a reprieve from baseball's unforgiving establishment. The worst that can be said of George Weaver was that he

Happy-go-lucky Buck Weaver

refused to sell out his friends for the sake of the World Series. Buck's "guilty knowledge" ultimately cost him his career, and with it, his reason for living.

Back in the winter of 1912, Buck Weaver was working at a stock ranch in California. It was rough, physical work, but it helped him get in shape for his approaching tryout with the White Sox. Weaver had toiled in the minors for two seasons when he received the invitation to report to the Sox camp in Waco, Texas. The day he was scheduled to depart California, Buck received word that his mother had passed away. His dad, Daniel Weaver, advised Buck to continue on to Texas. Both father and son realized that the funeral in Pennsylvania would compromise any chance he had of making the team.

So the grieving Weaver showed up in camp, but he kept his family misfortune to himself. Buck kept his chin up and maintained a happy-go-lucky image that was a Weaver trademark in later years. But *Tribune* sportswriter Sam Weller saw him alone in his hotel room in a private, unguarded moment crying his eyes out, as he did for many nights to come. Buck Weaver easily made the ballclub and moved into the lineup as the starting shortstop. He was a better third baseman if the truth be known, but he had to wait until 1917 when Comiskey acquired Swede Risberg before he could resume his natural position.

After Harry Lord jumped the ballclub in 1914, Buck was appointed team captain—his leadership skills and enthusiasm for the game had come to the fore years earlier. Weaver was a solid hitter and a fielder of exceptional ability. Old-timers claimed that Ty Cobb would never lay down a bunt when Buck was stationed at third. "Buck made himself into a fine hitter," recalled teammate Ray Schalk. "He was strictly a right-handed batter for the first five or six years and then made himself over into a left-handed swinger. He was the sort of fellow that keeps a club fired up. Buck had a lot of spirit."

Weaver excelled in postseason play. He batted .333 in the 1917 World Series and .324 in the infamous set of games two years later—figures that tend to belie his guilt in the Black Sox conspiracy. Indeed, Weaver fought his entire life trying to clear his name. He exhausted his life savings on legal appeals. "It hasn't been easy earning a living since I was thrown out of baseball in 1920," he said years later, "but I've been able to live with my conscience."

Buck Weaver was working as a pari-mutuel clerk at the $50 window at Chicago's three racetracks up to the moment of his death in 1956. In all those years he never abandoned his private war against baseball.

In death, he has not been forgotten or abandoned by a sympathetic public, and the fight to clear his name goes on. On November 23, 2005, then-senator Barack Obama of Illinois (with the support of senator Dick Durbin), sent a formal letter of appeal to commissioner Allan H. "Bud" Selig, petitioning for a posthumous reinstatement of Buck Weaver into baseball. "I respectfully request that your office conduct a posthumous investigation and hearing of the claims of Mr. Weaver's family and those interested Chicagoans and others who believe fervently that this honorable man was treated unjustly," implored Obama. There is no question in the minds of baseball historians who are not blinded by sentimentality that Cicotte, Risberg, Gandil, Williams, and "Shoeless" Joe Jackson are culpable for their crimes against baseball (the evidence is damning). But Weaver's case is separate and apart from the transgressions of his teammates. Only time will tell if George Weaver is granted dispensation by the powers that be. The educated guess is that he won't.

White, Guy Harris

White Sox: 1903–13
Pitcher
Nickname: Doc
Birthplace: Washington, D.C.

B: April 9, 1879
D: February 17, 1969
Batted left, threw left
Ht. 6–1; **Wt.** 150

White, Guy Harris

White Sox	W	L	Pct	ERA	G	CG	IP	H	BB	K	ShO
1903	16	15	.516	2.13	37	29	300	258	69	135	3
1904	16	12	.571	1.71	30	23	237	201	68	115	7
1905	18	14	.563	1.76	36	25	260⅓	204	58	120	4
1906	18	6	.750	1.52	28	20	219⅓	160	38	102	7
1907	27	13	.675	2.26	47	24	291	270	38	141	7
1908	19	13	.594	2.55	41	24	296	267	69	126	5
1909	10	9	.526	1.72	24	14	177⅔	149	31	77	3
1910	15	13	.536	2.56	33	20	245⅔	219	50	111	2
1911	10	14	.417	2.98	34	16	214⅓	219	35	72	4
1912	8	10	.444	3.24	32	9	172	172	47	57	1
1913	2	4	.333	3.50	19	2	103	106	39	39	0
Career	189	156	.548	2.38	428	262	3,059	2,743	670	1,412	46

Doc White, and the sheet music to a song he wrote, 1910

Doc White wore many hats during his long and productive life: dentist, evangelist, songwriter, World Series hero. His genius and talents have long been overlooked except by a handful of baseball historians who are in general agreement that White's exclusion from the Hall of Fame is one of the tragic injustices occasionally perpetrated against 19th-century and dead-ball-era players.

After receiving a degree in dental surgery from Georgetown University in 1902, White was signed to a professional contract by Phillies owner John I. Rogers for $1,200. The soft-spoken lefty jumped to the White Sox the following season and quickly established himself as the ace of the vaunted Hitless Wonder teams carefully assembled by Charles Comiskey in the first decade. In a period of 19 days in September 1904, White created a baseball legend that withstood the test of time for the next 64 years by spinning five consecutive shutouts, and a total of six for the month. His 45 consecutive scoreless innings is a team record that will never be broken, in all likelihood.

Doc White downed the Cubs in the final game of the 1906 World Series, limiting the National League champs to seven hits. But it was Hughie Jennings' Detroit Tigers, the three-time AL champions (1907–09), led by Ty Cobb, who could do nothing with White's tricky curveball. Against the powerful Tigers, Doc White won 31 of 46 decisions.

Absolute control was a Doc White trademark. He once held the American League record for consecutive innings without issuing a walk—65 in all. Indeed, White was one of the all-time greats, but there was more to his life story than just baseball. Doc practiced dentistry in the off-season until February 1906, when he closed the office to devote his full-time energies to baseball. White was an accomplished violinist and balladeer who wrote song lyrics in his spare time. With *Chicago Tribune* columnist Ring Lardner supplying the lyrics to White's composition, the pair published "Little Puff of Smoke, Goodnight" in 1910—a best-seller in sheet music.

White purchased a part ownership of the Dallas–Fort Worth ballclub of the Texas League after his retirement from active play in 1916, but he relinquished his interest in the team when the schedule was suspended because of World War I. In later years, Doc reportedly took to the road as an evangelist minister, preaching to the sinners along the Chautauqua Circuit.

When a younger generation of reporters descended on White for an interview after his shutout record had finally been snapped by Don Drysdale in 1968, they were turned away. He was just too old and feeble to come to the phone.

Whitehead, John

White Sox: 1935–39
Pitcher
Nickname: Porkchops
Birthplace: Coleman, Texas

B: April 27, 1909
D: October 20, 1964
Batted right, threw right
Ht. 6–2; **Wt.** 195

Whitehead, John

White Sox	W	L	Pct	ERA	G	CG	IP	H	BB	K	ShO	Sv
1935	13	13	.500	3.72	28	18	222⅓	209	101	72	1	0
1936	13	13	.500	4.64	34	15	230⅔	254	98	70	1	1
1937	11	8	.579	4.07	26	8	165⅔	191	56	45	4	0
1938	10	11	.476	4.76	32	10	183⅓	218	80	38	2	2
1939	0	3	.000	8.16	7	0	32	60	5	9	0	0
Career	49	54	.476	4.60	172	52	944	1,074	372	254	9	4

Johnny Whitehead struggled with his weight—and his control—during his three-plus years on the South Side. If only he had been the master of his own fate and paid closer attention to the pleadings of his manager James J. Dykes and coach Harold "Muddy" Ruel, who tried to instill a better work ethic within him, Whitehead might have eventually become one of the better sinkerball pitchers in the junior circuit.

The portly right-hander, rated one of the top prospects in the Texas League based on 19 victories and a nifty 2.34 earned run average in 1934, was purchased by the White Sox from the Dallas Steers that season. A year later, in his rookie season, big John won his first eight decisions for the rejuvenated White Sox coming out of spring training. The streak was halted in St. Louis by the Browns on June 5, after Whitehead fired nine straight balls to start the game.

John Whitehead

Chronic wildness, his other great problem, was too much to overcome. After posting an 8–0 record to open his major league career, Whitehead lost his next eight decisions and remained in a .500 holding pattern for the balance of his career. As Dykes searched for ways to improve Whitehead's luck, Clark Griffith, owner of the Washington Nationals, expressed the opinion that after the first look at his sinker, John was no great mystery for hitters to solve.

Whitehead, an introvert who rarely communicated his thoughts to reporters or even his teammates, refused to take the game seriously, and he paid the price. Dykes suspended him in 1937 for poor physical conditioning. Dogged by injuries, Whitehead was traded to the Browns for pitcher Johnny Marcum even up in June 1939.

Wilhelm, Hoyt

White Sox: 1963–68
Pitcher
Nicknames: Old Tilt; Dr. Wilhelm
Birthplace: Huntersville, North Carolina

B: July 26, 1923
D: August 23, 2002
Batted right, threw right
Ht. 6–0; **Wt.** 190

Wilhelm, Hoyt

White Sox	W	L	Pct	ERA	G	CG	IP	H	BB	K	ShO	Sv
1963	5	8	.385	2.64	55	0	136⅓	106	30	111	0	21
1964	12	9	.571	1.99	73	0	131⅓	94	30	95	0	27
1965	7	7	.500	1.81	66	0	144	88	32	106	0	20
1966	5	2	.714	1.66	46	0	81⅓	50	17	61	0	6
1967	8	3	.727	1.31	49	0	89	58	34	76	0	12
1968	4	4	.500	1.73	72	0	93⅔	69	24	72	0	12
Career	143	122	.540	2.52	1,070	20	2,254	1,757	778	1,610	5	227

In his final White Sox season, a reporter asked ageless Hoyt Wilhelm about his future baseball plans. "I don't know how long I can go, but I'm not thinking about quitting," he replied. I'd really like to hit a thousand games." Wilhelm, the last World War II veteran still active in baseball in 1968, had just pitched in both ends of a July 24, Comiskey Park doubleheader to break Cy Young's mark of 906 appearances, which had stood since 1911.

The secret of Hoyt Wilhelm's longevity was tied to the knuckleball, which he copied from Emil "Dutch" Leonard of the Washington Senators, whom he had studied while still in high school. Hoyt threw the pitch 85–90 percent of the time. It was his bread-and-butter delivery, and it inspired Paul Richards to introduce an oversized catcher's mitt into the game after his Baltimore Orioles receivers set a modern-day record of 49 passed balls in 1959.

After Wilhelm was traded to the White Sox on January 14, 1963, in a multiplayer swap with the O's, it fell upon J.C. Martin's youthful shoulders to bear the full brunt of the sharp-breaking, unpredictable knuckleball. Martin did a creditable job for five seasons. He passed along his defensive skills to Ed

"Old Tilt" Hoyt Wilhelm (left) demonstrates the knuckleball grip to his protégé, young Wilbur Wood, in 1967.

Herrmann, who in turn caught Wilbur Wood—Hoyt Wilhelm's knuckleballing protégé.

Through the mid- to late 1960s, the taciturn right-hander was the American League's most effective relief pitcher. For five consecutive seasons his earned run average never rose above 2.00. This rubber-armed workhorse was an outstanding fielder who set a record for pitchers by working in 319 consecutive games (beginning May 16, 1963) without committing an error.

The White Sox did not believe that either of the two American League expansion teams would claim 45-year-old Hoyt Wilhelm in the 1968 draft. It was an embarrassing faux pas on the part of Ed Short. The Kansas City Royals selected Wilhelm and then used him in a trade with the Angels. Hoyt finally retired after the 1972 season, having appeared in 1,070 games and holding several other records. In 1985 he became the first full-time relief pitcher to be voted into baseball's Hall of Fame.

Williams, Claude

White Sox: 1916–20
Pitcher
Nickname: Lefty
Birthplace: Aurora, Missouri

B: March 9, 1893
D: November 4, 1959
Batted right, threw left
Ht. 5–9; **Wt.** 160

Williams, Claude

White Sox	W	L	Pct	ERA	G	CG	IP	H	BB	K	ShO
1916	13	7	.650	2.89	43	10	224⅓	220	65	138	2
1917	17	8	.680	2.97	45	8	230	221	81	85	1
1918	6	4	.600	2.73	15	7	105⅔	76	47	30	2
1919	23	11	.676	2.64	41	27	297	265	58	125	5
1920	22	14	.611	3.91	39	26	299	302	90	128	0
Career	82	48	.631	3.13	189	81	1,186	1,121	347	515	10

Lefty Williams emerged as the No. 2 man in the Black Sox's starting rotation after a long and difficult minor league apprenticeship. A quiet, soft-spoken southerner blessed with pinpoint control of an elusive curveball that he threw with great effect in five White Sox seasons, Williams had begun his career with Springfield of the Missouri-Kansas League back in 1911.

After two unsuccessful trials with the Detroit Tigers, Lefty was returned to Sacramento of the PCL on August 14, 1913. Comiskey plucked Williams off the Salt Lake City roster in 1915 after he had struck out 294 batters and won a staggering 33 games. Based on Williams' achievements at the top rung of the minor league ladder, the Old Roman concluded that the young pitcher was at last ready for major league play.

Lefty was a spectacular addition to a formidable pitching staff. He won his first nine decisions in 1917, a team record shared with Orval Grove (1943) and LaMarr Hoyt (1983). In 1918, however, he ran afoul of Comiskey by sidestepping the military draft in order to work in the navy shipyards as a painter. "I don't consider them fit to play on my club," the Old Roman crackled, after hearing that Lefty and teammate Byrd Lynn left the team on June 11.

Both players were welcomed back with open arms in 1919. Lefty hit his peak by posting 23 wins and seemed headed toward a long and brilliant career. It was not to be.

Williams earned only $500 a month playing for Comiskey and was among the lowest-paid players on the team. He was easily drawn into the Black Sox conspiracy and shoulders much of the guilt for what was to follow. Lefty, however, remained wary of the gamblers, and his heart was never really

Claude "Lefty" Williams

in it—even after he divided up $10,000 in bribe money with his roommate, Shoeless Joe Jackson.

Joseph "Sport" Sullivan, the intermediary between New York crime boss Arnold Rothstein and the corrupted Sox players, allegedly threatened the life of Mrs. Williams the night before the eighth and final game on October 9 in Chicago when it appeared that Lefty was about to double-cross the gamblers. Williams yielded four runs in the first inning and was through for the day. The World Series was in the bag…for the gamblers.

In his final season Williams won 22 games and was ranked among the league's finest left-handed starters—for which he was paid $2,800 by Comiskey.

During the subsequent Black Sox trial, it was revealed that the fixing of games was a rather routine practice at all levels of professional baseball. Williams' name kept surfacing as one of the players who allegedly received payoffs in the Pacific Coast League a year before joining the White Sox.

Lefty Williams, who would never play at the major league level following his banishment from the game, remained closemouthed about this and other matters throughout the ordeal. "Did I give Jackson $5,000?" he snapped. "Ask the policeman on the corner. He may tell you something. I'm not talking for publication. I'm not stampeded, either, get me?"

Williams, Walter

White Sox: 1967–72
Outfielder
Nickname: No-Neck
Birthplace: Brownwood, Texas

B: December 19, 1943
Bats right, throws right
Ht. 5–6; **Wt.** 190

Williams, Walter

White Sox	G	AB	H	AVG	RBI	R	2B	3B	HR	SA	SB
1967	104	275	66	.240	15	35	16	3	3	.353	3
1968	63	133	32	.241	8	6	6	0	1	.308	0
1969	135	471	143	.304	32	59	22	1	3	.374	6
1970	110	315	79	.251	15	43	18	1	3	.343	3
1971	114	361	106	.294	35	43	17	3	8	.424	5
1972	77	221	55	.249	11	22	7	1	2	.317	6
Career	842	2,373	640	.270	173	284	106	11	33	.365	34

Effervescent Walt Williams was not your average 1960s ballplayer either in his approach to the game or his mental outlook. Here was a guy in a real hurry. Walt ran down to first base at full speed after drawing a walk. He charged into the dugout or back into the field at a dead run after each inning. His normal gait was all-out acceleration.

Williams was signed to his first pro contract in 1963 by Bill Wight, a Sox pitcher in the early 1950s. Walt won a pair of Texas League and Pacific Coast League batting titles in 1965 and 1966, before he was included in a trade that shipped John Romano to the St. Louis Cardinals on December 14, 1966. The Sox received pitcher Don Dennis and "No-Neck" Williams, whose head seemed to rest on top of his massive shoulders.

Walt was a valuable utility player for Eddie Stanky in his first two White Sox season, but he was considered a long shot to make the ballclub in 1969. His obvious physical limitations placed him at a competitive disadvantage, but his hustle and spirit won him an occasional starting assignment in the outfield despite manager Don Gutteridge's desire to have Bill Melton play right field. White Sox fans took Walt Williams to heart, and they showed their support by wearing "Play No-Neck" buttons to the park in order to prod Gutteridge into action.

Williams' emergence as a hitter began in 1969 when he became the first Sox player since Floyd Robinson in 1964 to top the .300 mark. And even then, he had to battle hard to crack a weak lineup. In a 2010 interview with writer Mark Liptak, Williams, now a recreation center director in Brownwood, Texas, reflected on his shabby treatment by Sox GM Ed Short, when he went to the bargaining table expecting to be rewarded with a nice increase for 1970 following his breakout '69 campaign. "I was making $12,000, and the Sox offered me $14,000," he said. "I didn't sign the contract. Everyone else signed, and by now the newspaper guys like [Jerome] Holtzman and Dave Nightingale were writing, 'Why can't the Sox sign their only .300 hitter?' Ed Short called me in his office and just cursed me out. He called me things you couldn't do today, and to be honest, when I left that meeting I was crying. But I told him I wanted a 100 percent raise on what I made. Short finally said that I had a choice of taking the Sox offer of $14,000 or I could have my 100 percent raise, but he

Walter "No-Neck" Williams: no-neck, but a big heart

promised I wouldn't play a lot, maybe once a week against tough right-handed pitching and that next season he'd cut me the maximum amount, which at that time was 20 percent. I told him I wanted the 100 percent raise. He said fine. I signed the contract, and I didn't play a lot. I wasn't in the lineup much, and it was an unpleasant year."

It was the same old story playing for Chuck Tanner in the early 1970s, but Walt always held up his end of the bargain with exemplary hustle and desire. He was traded to Cleveland on October 19, 1972, for shortstop Eddie Leon. He was in the Cleveland lineup on August 21, 1973, ruining Stan Bahnsen's heroic bid for a no-hitter by chopping a single over Bill Melton's head with two out in the ninth inning.

Wood, Wilbur

White Sox: 1967–78
Pitcher
Birthplace: Cambridge, Massachusetts
B: October 22, 1941
Bats right, throws left
Ht. 6–0; **Wt.** 200

Wood, Wilbur

White Sox	W	L	Pct	ERA	G	CG	IP	H	BB	K	ShO	Sv
1967	4	2	.667	2.45	51	0	95⅓	95	28	47	0	4
1968	13	12	.520	1.87	88	0	159	127	33	74	0	16
1969	10	11	.476	3.01	76	0	119⅔	113	40	73	0	15
1970	9	13	.409	2.80	77	0	122	118	36	85	0	21
1971	22	13	.629	1.91	44	22	334	272	62	210	7	1
1972	24	17	.585	2.51	49	20	376⅔	325	74	193	8	0
1973	24	20	.545	3.46	49	21	359⅓	381	91	199	4	0
1974	20	19	.513	3.60	42	22	320	305	80	169	1	0
1975	16	20	.444	4.11	43	14	291⅓	309	92	140	2	0
1976	4	3	.571	2.25	7	5	56	51	11	31	1	0
1977	7	8	.467	4.98	24	5	123	139	50	42	1	0
1978	10	10	.500	5.20	28	4	168	187	74	69	0	0
Career	164	156	.513	3.24	651	114	2,684	2,582	724	1,411	24	57

Wilbur Wood had a graceful windup and delivery for a big man.

Appearances are deceiving. At first glance, corpulent Wilbur Wood resembled the guy on the bar stool lamenting the "one that got away" between sips of Pabst Blue Ribbon. Wood, a plump left-hander who happened to be one of the top sport fishermen in the major leagues, delivered the knuckleball for the White Sox with deadly effectiveness for more than a decade.

Woody won 163 games for the White Sox during his long career, ranking him No. 5 on the all-time team list behind Ted Lyons, Red Faber, Ed Walsh, and Billy Pierce. And yet few fans count him among the Sox immortals, and that exclusion is a rather sad commentary because Wilbur richly deserves to see his No. 28 retired before much more time passes.

Before launching his pro career in 1960, Wood was one of the top prep pitchers in the Boston area. He experimented with the knuckler as a grade school kid playing catch with his dad on the front lawn of his suburban home, but did not become reacquainted with the pitch until 1967 when Hoyt Wilhelm advised him to forget about the fastball and curve and throw the knuckleball 60–70 percent of the time.

This former Boston Red Sox bonus baby had drifted in and out of the majors for nearly seven seasons and was discouraged by his lack of progress throwing the conventional pitches. He was just another journeyman toiling for the Columbus Clippers of the International League when the Sox acquired his contract in exchange for the fading Juan Pizarro on October 12, 1966. Ed Short's benign interest in Wood turned out to be the best break of Wilbur's career.

The decision to adopt the knuckleball as his bread-and-butter pitch was a leap of faith born out of frustration. But it paid immediate and long-term dividends for Wilbur and the ballclub. Manager Eddie Stanky assigned Wood to bullpen duty in 1967. He emerged as the No. 1 closer of the staff following Wilhelm's departure after the 1968 season. Wood led the league in appearances for three straight seasons (1968–70) and set a single-season record in '68 by answering the call 88 times. The mark has since been broken, but Woody's reputation as a workhorse was already firmly established.

Wood was perfectly content coming out of the bullpen, but when Joel Horlen went down with an injury in the spring of 1971, pitching coach Johnny Sain came upon the idea of converting Wilbur to a starting role. The rubber-armed southpaw logged 334 innings, posted a miserly 1.91 ERA (second in the league to Vida Blue), and won 22 games—the most by a Sox pitcher since 1959. Only Blue stood in the way of Wilbur's winning a Cy Young Award.

And so ended the first of four straight 20-win seasons. Working on only two days' rest, Wood won 13 of his first 16 decisions in 1973...before Memorial Day. Wilbur was the last of the great "iron-men" pitchers in the Ed Walsh mold. Too much work, however, began taking a toll. Chuck Tanner started Wood in both ends of a July 20, 1973, doubleheader in New York, but it was a personally embarrassing setback. The previously unhittable Wood was rocked hard by the Yankees in both games.

The invincible knuckleball began coming in high, and his miniscule earned run average ballooned to 4.11 by the end of the 1975 season. Woody reached the end of the road for all intents and purposes on May 9, 1976, when Ron LeFlore's line drive shattered his left kneecap. The knee was sound in 1977, but the knuckleball had flattened out, and it was finally time to say good-bye—though Wood could not admit it to himself at the time. "The damn thing hypnotizes the guys who throw it as much as it does the hitters," Wood commented. "You really do think you can go on forever even when your body won't permit it."

Bill Veeck had no further use for Wilbur Wood's services. He released him in July 1978 with no personal regrets. The Milwaukee Brewers expressed a mild interest in the portly lefty, but they never tendered a contract offer.

In the years that followed, Wilbur operated a seafood business outside of Boston and more recently has worked for a Massachusetts pharmaceutical company, while longing to get back into the game as a pitching coach. Baseball has thus far shut him out.

Wright, Taft

White Sox: 1940–42; 1946–48
Outfielder
Nickname: Taffy
Birthplace: Tabor City, North Carolina

B: August 10, 1911
D: October 22, 1981
Batted left, threw right
Ht. 5–10; **Wt.** 180

Wright, Taft

White Sox	G	AB	H	AVG	RBI	R	2B	3B	HR	SA	SB
1940	147	581	196	.337	88	79	31	9	5	.448	4
1941	136	513	165	.322	97	71	35	5	10	.468	5
1942	85	300	100	.333	47	43	13	5	0	.410	1
1946	115	422	116	.275	52	46	19	4	7	.389	10
1947	124	401	130	.324	54	48	13	0	4	.387	8
1948	134	455	127	.279	61	50	15	6	4	.365	2
Career	1,029	3,583	1,115	.311	553	465	175	55	38	.423	32

The White Sox brain trust of the late 1930s never imagined that Taffy Wright would linger on the South Side for nearly a decade when they acquired him on December 7, 1939. Wright, a chunky outfielder with limited fielding range, was trade bait in an expanded deal Harry Grabiner had in mind. Outfielder Gee Walker was shipped to Washington for Wright and pitcher Pete Appleton—a deal completed in anticipation of moving Taffy to St. Louis for Moose Solters. It was a lucky break when the Browns decided to take a pass on Wright, who keyed the Sox offense through the war years despite a chronic weight problem that always seemed to place his job in jeopardy.

Wright alternated between right and left field for much of the time he was in Chicago. He was a consistent .300 hitter and good RBI man who drove home six runs against the Browns on August 8, 1941. He was among the first of the Sox players summoned to military service in 1942, after starting out the season batting .333.

Taft Wright

Returning to Chicago in 1946, Wright picked up where he had left off, until advancing age and an influx of younger players squeezed Taffy out of the picture. He was sold to the Philadelphia A's on November 15, 1948, by Frank Lane in an effort to rebuild a last-place team with youth.

Wynn, Early

White Sox: 1958–62
Pitcher
Nickname: Gus
Birthplace: Hartford, Alabama

B: January 6, 1920
D: April 4, 1999
Batted right and left, threw right
Ht. 6–0; **Wt.** 190

Wynn, Early

White Sox	W	L	Pct	ERA	G	CG	IP	H	BB	K	ShO
1958	14	16	.467	4.13	40	11	239⅔	214	104	179	4
1959	22	10	.688	3.17	37	14	255⅔	202	119	179	5
1960	13	12	.520	3.49	36	13	237⅓	220	112	158	4
1961	8	2	.800	3.51	17	5	110⅓	88	47	64	0
1962	7	15	.318	4.46	27	11	167⅔	171	56	91	3
Career	300	244	.551	3.54	691	290	4,564	4,291	1,775	2,334	49

The decision to trade Minnie Minoso to the Cleveland Indians for Early Wynn on December 4, 1957, was never a very popular one with White Sox fans. Like most baseball deals, it was guided by cold-blooded logic and a disregard for sentiment and nostalgia. The Sox needed a veteran pitcher if they hoped to contend for the 1958 flag, and Wynn fit the bill. "I have just traded the White Sox into a pennant," predicted Cleveland general manager Frank Lane. As it turned out, he was correct.

There was truth to the old saying that "Gus" Wynn would knock down his own grandmother if she crowded the plate. Easygoing and fond of a good practical joke, Wynn's demeanor changed when he took the mound. He was the league's top winner by the time he joined the Sox, though it had taken Gus nine full seasons to hit the century mark in career victories.

Wynn struggled in 1958, despite leading the league in strikeouts for the second consecutive year. Some serious concerns were raised over whether his career could survive into the 1960s—which would represent his fourth decade of big league service.

These concerns were brushed aside in 1959 when the husky right-hander won the Cy Young Award, the American League Comeback Player of the Year Award, and a berth on the Major League All-Star Team following a brilliant 22–10 campaign that boosted his team into the World Series for the first time in 40 years. Wynn was simply brilliant. On May 1 he one-hit the Boston Red Sox and accounted for the only run of the White Sox victory by homering in the eighth inning. Early was always a dangerous man with the bat.

Early Wynn: "Ol' Gus"

His 11–0 blanking of the Los Angeles Dodgers in Game 1 of the 1959 World Series was an unforgettable moment for Sox fans. However, things began to unravel after that. Early's legs were weakened by the gout, and he was operating on borrowed time in a personal quest to surpass the 300-victory plateau. "I hope you don't think I'm greedy," he said, "but I want one more than Bob [Lefty] Grove had, and I want it more than ever."

Wynn pursued his goal through 1960, 1961, and 1962—years of transition on the South Side when younger, more agile players were dotting the roster. He only needed eight wins when the 1962 season began, but they were becoming harder and harder to obtain.

September rolled around and he was just two victories short of the coveted 300. That's when Sox management decided on a promotional campaign revolving around Wynn to hype ticket sales. Fans were encouraged to wear "300 Club" buttons to the park. On September 8, Wynn nailed down No. 299 just before the Sox embarked on a week-long road trip. Manager Al Lopez signed off on a plan to hold Wynn back so that the 300th victory could be achieved in Chicago. The press criticized this tacky, exploitive maneuver on the part of Lopez and general manager Ed Short, but they refused to bend to pressure.

Wynn never made it. He lost his final two decisions to the Yankees and ended the season in a holding pattern. On November 21, 1962, Gus was released from his contract, but he was invited to spring training as a nonroster player. His 43-year-old legs just weren't up to the strain, but the old campaigner kept going. Ineffective, Wynn was cut loose on April 2, just as the Sox broke camp. Fortunately the Cleveland Indians had a heart. They added Wynn to the 25-man roster, and in his fifth start of the season on July 13, 1963, he finally won No. 300.

Voted into the Hall of Fame in 1972, Gus was a member of the White Sox radio broadcast team in 1982 and 1983.

Zernial, Gus

White Sox: 1949–51
Outfielder
Nickname: Ozark Ike
Birthplace: Beaumont, Texas

B: June 27, 1923
Bats right, throws right
D: January 20, 2011
Ht. 6–2½; **Wt.** 210

Zernial, Gus

White Sox	G	AB	H	AVG	RBI	R	2B	3B	HR	SA	SB
1949	73	198	63	.318	38	29	17	2	5	.500	0
1950	143	543	152	.280	93	75	16	4	29	.484	0
1951	4	19	2	.105	4	2	0	0	0	.105	0
Career	1,234	4,131	1,093	.265	776	572	159	22	237	.486	15

Brawny, muscle-bound Gus Zernial clouted 40 home runs for the Hollywood Stars of the Pacific Coast League in 1948. Fred Haney, who broadcast the Stars home games that year, nicknamed Gus "Ozark Ike" after the popular cartoon character.

A standout power hitter but only an average fielder, Zernial joined the Sox in the spring of 1949. From the moment

Old No. 6, Gus Zernial, clouts his team record–setting 29th home run in 1950.

he arrived in camp, Big Gus was under tremendous pressure to provide long-ball thrills to reawaken fan interest after the horrendous last-place finish of 1948. To aid Zernial in his quest for 30 or more home runs, general manager Frank Lane strung a five-foot-high chicken-wire fence along the warning track of the Comiskey Park outfield, reducing the distance by 20 feet.

On May 29 disaster struck when Zernial shattered his collarbone. It was a costly injury that sidelined Gus for two-thirds of the season. The wire fence, as you might expect, was torn down after opposing hitters clubbed eight homers in 11 games.

Zernial started slowly in 1950. He lost his job to Johnny Ostrowski after an .067 dry spell in early April. His strikeout ratio was alarming, and for the season he fanned 110 times, shattering Pat Seerey's four-year-old team mark. Zernial redeemed himself in the second half of the season. On October 1, 1950, officially the last day of the season, Zernial slammed three home runs in a doubleheader with St. Louis to end the year with 29 roundtrippers—a new single-season team record that was equaled a year later by Eddie Robinson.

A player of Zernial's obvious abilities was ill-suited to play in spacious Comiskey Park where the lay of the land was more conducive to a hit-and-run, motion offense. With this in mind, Lane engineered a blockbuster trade with the A's and Indians on April 30, 1951, that brought just such a player to Chicago—Orestes "Minnie" Minoso. Zernial enjoyed a long and productive career, and was the fourth most prolific American League home run hitter in the 1950s, trailing only Mickey Mantle, Yogi Berra, and Larry Doby.

Zisk, Richie

White Sox: 1977
Outfielder
Birthplace: Brooklyn, New York

B: February 6, 1949
Bats right, throws right
Ht. 6–1; **Wt.** 208

Zisk, Richie

White Sox	G	AB	H	AVG	RBI	R	2B	3B	HR	SA	SB
1977	141	531	154	.290	101	78	17	6	30	.514	0
Career	1,453	5,144	1,477	.287	792	681	245	26	207	.466	8

A banner strung along the left-field wall during the 1977 South Side Hitmen summer cautioned opponents to "Pitch at Risk to Zisk." For one thrill-packed season, Zisk put a charge into an otherwise dreary period of White Sox history. And then, because of the changing economic climate of baseball in the late 1970s, Zisk forsook his Chicago love affair in order to chase the fast and easy riches available through free agency.

After surveying the wreckage of the 1976 season, owner Bill Veeck realized that in order to lure the fans back to Comiskey Park and refill the empty coffers, he needed a potent hitter in the lineup—a home run threat to liven up the show. Veeck and general manager Roland Hemond mortgaged the future by trading Rich Gossage and Terry Forster to Pittsburgh for Zisk and pitcher Silvio Martinez on December 10, 1976.

Richie Zisk was going into his option year. The Pirates knew they couldn't sign him, so they took what they could get from the White Sox. The price was a high one to pay in retrospect, but the "Polish Prince" helped Veeck achieve his goal of financial solvency, if only on an interim basis.

Richie was an immediate fan favorite among the ethnic Europeans who found much to identify with in this solidly built slugger who wore a gold No. 22 pin around his neck. Zisk cracked a home run his first time up to the plate in the snowy road opener in Toronto, April 7, 1977, to begin his season-long assault on enemy pitching.

The Richie Zisk–Oscar Gamble tandem formed a lethal home run threat. And as their home run output and RBI totals soared through the summer, so too did their market value. Veeck and his investment partners tried to negotiate an equitable salary with Zisk, their "Rent a Player" star, but it was hopeless in the final analysis. On November 7, Zisk signed a multiyear deal with Texas Rangers owner Brad Corbett. The sum seems trifling by current standards—$250,000 per year.

3

All the Team's Men

Since 1901, the year the American League declared its intention to become the second major league, 1,598 men appeared in one or more White Sox games through the 2010 season.

A

Aardsma, David, B: Dec. 27, 1981, Denver, Colo. Pitcher (2007).

Abbott, Jeff, B: Aug. 17, 1972, Atlanta, Ga. Outfielder (1997–2000).

Abbott, Jim, B: Sept. 18, 1967, Flint, Mich. Pitcher (1995).

Abner, Shawn, B: June 17, 1966, Hamilton, Ohio. Outfielder (1992).

Abrams, Cal, B: Mar. 2, 1924, Philadelphia, Pa.; D: Feb. 25, 1997, Ft. Lauderdale, Fla. Outfielder (1956).

Ackley, Fritz, B: Apr. 10, 1937, Howard, Wis; D: May 22, 2002, Duluth, Minn. Pitcher (1963–64).

Acosta, Cy, B: Nov. 22, 1946, Sabino, Mexico. Pitcher (1972–74).

Acosta, Jose, B: Mar. 4, 1891, Havana, Cuba.; D: Nov. 16, 1977, Havana, Cuba. Pitcher (1922).

Adair, Jerry, B: Dec. 17, 1936, Sand Springs, Okla.; D: May 31, 1987, Tulsa, Okla. Infielder (1966–67).

Adams, Bobby, B: Dec. 14, 1921, Tuolumne, Calif.; D: Feb. 13, 1997, Gig Harbor, Wash. Infielder (1955).

Adams, Doug, B: Jan. 27, 1943, Blue River, Wis. Catcher (1969).

Adams, Herb, B: Apr. 14, 1928, Hollywood, Calif. Outfielder (1948–50).

Jim Abbott

Adkins, Grady, B: June 29, 1897, Jacksonville, Ark.; D: Mar. 31, 1966, Little Rock, Ark. Pitcher (1928–29).

Adkins, Jon, B: Aug. 30, 1977, Huntington. W.Va. Pitcher (2003–05).

Agee, Tommie, B: Aug. 9, 1942, Magnolia, Ala; D: Jan. 22, 2001, New York, NY. Outfielder (1965–67).

Agosto, Juan, B: Feb. 23, 1958, Rio Piedras, P.R. Pitcher (1981–86).

Alcock, Scotty, B: Nov. 29, 1885, Wooster, Ohio; D: June 30, 1973, Wooster, Ohio. Infielder (1914).

Allen, Dick, B: Mar. 8, 1942, Wampum, Pa. Infielder (1972–74).

Allen, Hank, B: July 23, 1940, Wampum, Pa. Infielder (1972–73).

Allen, Lloyd, B: May 8, 1950, Merced, Calif. Pitcher (1974–75).

Allen, Neil, B: Jan. 24, 1958, Kansas City, Kan. Pitcher (1986–87).

Almon, Bill, B: Nov. 21, 1952, Providence, R.I. Infielder (1981–82).

Aloma, Luis, B: June 19, 1923, Havana, Cuba; D: Apr. 7, 1997, Park Ridge, Ill. Pitcher (1950–53).

Alomar, Roberto, B: Feb. 5, 1968, Ponce, P.R. Infielder (2003, 2004).

Alomar, Sandy, B: Oct. 19, 1943, Salinas, P.R. Infielder (1967–69).

Alomar, Sandy Jr., B: June 18, 1966, Salinas, P.R. Catcher (2001–04; 2006).

Altizer, Dave, B: Nov. 6, 1876, Pearl, Ill.; D: May 14, 1964, Pleasant Hill, Ill. Outfielder (1909).

Altrock, Nick, B: Sept. 15, 1876, Cincinnati, Ohio; D: Jan. 20, 1965, Washington, D.C. Pitcher (1903–09).

Alvarado, Luis, B: Jan. 15, 1949, LaJas, P.R.; D: Mar. 20, 2001, Lo Jas, P.R. Infielder (1971–74).

Brian Anderson

Alvarez, Wilson, B: Mar. 24, 1970, Maracaibo, Venezuela. Pitcher (1991–97).

Anderson, Brian, B: Mar. 11, 1982, Tucson, Ariz. Outfielder (2005–09).

Anderson, Hal, B: Feb. 10, 1904, St. Louis, Mo.; D: May 1, 1974, St. Louis, Mo. Outfielder (1932).

Anderson, John, B: Dec. 14, 1873, Sarpsborg, Norway; D: July 23, 1949, Worcester, Mass. Outfielder/infielder (1908).

Luis Aparicio, 1969

The "Big Hurt" Frank Thomas studies the pitcher.

Luke Appling

Anderson, Larry, B: Dec. 3, 1952, Maywood, Calif. Pitcher (1977).

Andrews, Mike, B: July 9, 1943, Los Angeles, Calif. Infielder/DH (1971–73).

Andujar, Luis, B: Nov. 22, 1972, Bani, Dominican Republic. Pitcher (1995–96).

Aparicio, Luis, B: Apr. 29, 1934, Maracaibo, Venezuela. Infielder (1956–62, 68–70).

Appleton, Pete, B: May 20, 1904, Terryville, Conn.; D: Jan. 18, 1974, Trenton, N.J. Pitcher (1940–42).

Appling, Luke, B: Apr. 2, 1907, High Point, N.C.; D: Jan. 3, 1991, Cumming, Ga. Infielder (1930–50).

Archdeacon, Maurice, B: Dec. 14, 1898, St. Louis, Mo.; D: Sept. 5, 1954, St. Louis, Mo. Outfielder (1923–25).

Maurice Archdeacon

Arias, Rudy, B: June 6, 1931, Las Villas, Cuba. Pitcher (1959).

Armbruster, Charlie, B: Aug. 30, 1880, Cincinnati, Ohio; D: Oct. 7, 1964, Grant's Pass, Ore. Catcher (1907).

Arrigo, Gerry, B: June 12, 1941, Chicago, Ill. Pitcher (1970).

Ash, Ken, B: Sept. 16, 1901, Anmoore, W.Va.; D: Nov. 15, 1979, Clarksburg, W.Va. Pitcher (1925).

Assenmacher, Paul, B: Dec. 10, 1960, Detroit, Mich. Pitcher (1994).

Atz, Jake (John Zimmerman), B: July 1, 1879, Washington, D.C.; D: May 22, 1945, New Orleans, La. Infielder/outfielder (1907–09).

Autry, Martin, B: Mar. 5, 1903, Martindale, Tex.; D: Jan. 26, 1950, Savannah, Ga. Catcher (1929).

Averill, Earl Jr., B: Sept. 9, 1931, Cleveland, Ohio. Catcher (1960).

B

Bahnsen, Stan, B: Dec. 15, 1944, Council Bluffs, Iowa. Pitcher (1972–75).

Baines, Harold, B: Mar. 15, 1959, St. Michaels, Md. Outfielder/DH (1980–89, 1996–97, 2000–01).

Bajenaru, Jeff, B: Mar. 21, 1978, Pomona, Calif. Pitcher (2004–05).

Baker, Floyd, B: Oct. 10, 1916, Luray, Va.; D: Nov. 17, 2004, Youngstown, Ohio. Infielder (1945–51).

Baker, Howard, B: Mar. 1, 1888, Bridgeport, Conn.; D: Jan. 16, 1964, Bridgeport, Conn. Infielder (1914–15).

Baker, Jesse, B: June 3, 1888, Anderson Island, Wash.; D: Sept. 26, 1972, Tacoma, Wash. Pitcher (1911).

Baldwin, Dave, B: Mar. 30, 1938, Tucson, Ariz. Pitcher (1973).

Baldwin, James, B: July 15, 1977, Southern Pines, N.C. Pitcher (1995–2001).

Bannister, Alan, B: Sept. 3, 1951, Montebello, Calif. Infielder/DH (1976–80).

Bannister, Floyd, B: June 10, 1955, Pierre, S.D. Pitcher (1983–87).

Barcelo, Lorenzo, B: Aug. 10, 1977, San Pedro de Macoris, D.R. Pitcher (2000–02).

Barnabe, Charlie, B: June, 12, 1900, Russell Gulch, Colo.; D: Aug. 16, 1977, Waco, Tex. Pitcher (1927–28).

James Baldwin

Barnes, Bob, B: Jan. 6, 1902, Washburn, Ill.; D: December 8, 1993, Peoria, Ill. Pitcher (1924).

Barnes, Emile "Red," B: Dec. 25, 1903, Suggsville, Ala.; D: July 3, 1959, Mobile, Ala. Outfielder (1930).

Barnes, Rich, B: July 21, 1959, Palm Beach, Fla. Pitcher (1982).

Barojas, Salome, B: June 16, 1957, Cordoba, Mexico. Pitcher (1982–84).

Barrett, Bill, B: May 28, 1900, Cambridge, Mass.; D: Jan. 26, 1951, Cambridge, Mass. Outfielder (1923–29).

Barrios, Francisco, B: June 10, 1953, Hermosillo, Mexico; D: Apr. 9, 1982, Hermosillo, Mexico. Pitcher (1974, 76–81).

Barrows, Roland "Cutie," B: Oct. 20, 1883, Gray, Maine; D: Feb. 10, 1955, Gorham, Maine. Outfielder (1909–12).

Bartholomew, Les, B: Apr. 4, 1903, Madison, Wis.; D: Sept. 19, 1972, Barrington, Ill. Pitcher (1932).

Battey, Earl, B: Jan. 5, 1935, Los Angeles, Calif.; D: Nov. 15, 2003, Ocola, Fla. Catcher (1955–59).

Battle, Jim, B: Mar. 26, 1901, Bailey, Tex.; D: Sept. 30, 1965, Chico, Calif. Infielder (1927).

Batts, Matt, B: Oct. 16, 1921, San Antonio, Tex. Catcher (1954).

Baumann, Frank, B: July 1, 1933, St. Louis, Mo. Pitcher (1960–64).

Gordon Beckham. (Courtesy of Mike McKay)

Baumer, Jim, B: Jan. 29, 1931, Tulsa, Okla.; D: July 8, 1996, Paoli, Pa. Infielder (1949).

Baumgarten, Ross, B: May 27, 1955, Highland Park, Ill. Pitcher (1978–81).

Beall, Johnny, B: Mar. 12, 1882, Beltsville, Md.; D: June 14, 1926, Beltsville, Md. Outfielder (1913).

Beard, Ted, B: Jan. 7, 1921, Woodsboro, Md. Outfielder (1957–58).

Bearden, Gene, B: Sept. 5, 1920, Lexa, Ark.; D: Mar. 1, 2004, Alexander City, Ala. Pitcher (1953).

Beckham, Gordon, B: Sept. 16, 1986, Atlanta, Ga. Infielder (2009–)

Albert Belle

Bejma, Ollie (Alojze Bejma), B: Sept. 12, 1907, South Bend, Ind.; D: Jan. 3, 1995, South Bend, Ind. Infielder (1939).

Beirne, Kevin, B: Jan 1, 1974, Houston, Tex. Pitcher (2000).

Belcher, Tim, B: Oct. 19, 1961, Mount Gilead, Ohio. Pitcher (1993).

Bell, Gary, B: Nov. 17, 1936, San Antonio, Tex. Pitcher (1969).

Bell, George, B: Oct. 21, 1959, San Pedro de Macorís, Dominican Republic. Outfielder/DH (1992–93).

Bell, Kevin, B: July 13, 1955, Los Angeles, Calif. Infielder (1976–80).

Bell, Ralph, B: Nov. 6, 1890, Kohoka, Mo.; D: Oct. 18, 1959, Burlington, Iowa. Pitcher (1912).

Belle, Albert, B: Aug. 25, 1966, Shreveport, La. Outfielder (1997–98).

Beltre, Esteban, B: Dec. 26, 1967, Ingenio Quisqueya, Dominican Republic. Infielder (1991–92).

Bender, Charles "Chief," B: May 5, 1884, Crow Wing County, Minn.; D: May 22, 1954, Philadelphia, Pa. Pitcher (1925).

Bennett, Joseph "Bugs," B: Apr. 19, 1892, Kansas City, Mo.; D: Nov. 21, 1957, Noel, Mo. Pitcher (1921).

Benz, Joe, B: Jan. 21, 1886, New Alsace, Ind.; D: Apr. 22, 1957, Chicago, Ill. Pitcher (1911–19).

Bere, Jason, B: May 26, 1971, Cambridge, Mass. Pitcher (1993–98).

Berg, Moe, B: Mar. 2, 1902, New York, N.Y.; D: May 29, 1972, Belleville, N.J. Catcher (1926–30).

Berger, Joe, B: Dec. 20, 1886, St. Louis, Mo.; D: Mar. 6, 1956, Rock Island, Ill. Infielder (1913–14).

Berger, Louis "Boze," B: May 13, 1910, Baltimore, Md.; D: Nov. 3, 1992, Bethesda, Md. Infielder (1937–38).

Berghammer, Marty, B: June 18, 1888, Elliott, Pa.; D: Dec. 21, 1957, Pittsburgh, Pa. Infielder (1911).

Bernazard, Tony, B: Aug. 24, 1956, Cagus, P.R. Infielder (1981–83).

Berran, Denny, B: Oct. 8, 1887, Merrimac, Mass.; D: Apr. 28, 1943, Boston, Mass. Outfielder (1912).

Berry, Charlie, B: Oct. 18, 1902, Phillipsburg, N.J.; D: Sept. 6, 1972, Evanston, Ill. Catcher (1932–33).

Jason Bere

Berry, Claude, B: Feb. 14, 1880, Losantville, Ind.; D: Feb. 1, 1974, Richmond, Va. Catcher (1904).

Berry, Ken, B: May 10, 1941, Kansas City, Mo. Outfielder (1962–70).

Berry, Neil, B: Jan. 11, 1922, Kalamazoo, Mich. Infielder (1953).

Bertotti, Mike, B: Jan. 18, 1970, Jersey City, N.J. Pitcher (1995–97).

Betemit, Wilson, B: Nov. 2, 1981, Santo Domingo, Dominican Republic. Infielder (2009).

Biddle, Lee "Rocky," B: May 21, 1976, Arcadia, Calif. Pitcher (2000–02).

Biggs, Charlie, B: Sept. 15, 1906, French Lick, Ind.; D: May 24, 1954, French Lick, Ind. Pitcher (1932).

Bischoff, John, B: Oct. 28, 1894, Edwardsville, Ill.; D: Dec. 28, 1981, Granite City, Ill. Catcher (1925).

Kenny "the Bandit" Berry

Lu Blue, Johnny Kerr, Bill Cissell, and Billy Sullivan Jr.

Bithorn, Hi, B: Mar. 18, 1916, Santurce, P.R.; D: Jan. 1, 1952, El Mante, Mexico. Pitcher (1947).

Bittiger, Jeff, B: Apr. 13, 1962, Jersey City, N.J. Pitcher (1988–89).

Black, Bill, B: Aug. 12, 1899, Philadelphia, Pa.; D: Jan. 14, 1968, Philadelphia, Pa. Infielder (1924).

Blackburn, Foster "Babe," B: Jan. 6, 1895, Chicago, Ill.; D: Mar. 9, 1984, New Port Richey, Fla. Pitcher (1921).

Blackburne, Lena, B: Oct. 23, 1886, Clifton Heights, Pa.; D: Feb. 29, 1968, Riverside, N.J. Infielder (1910–12, 1914–15, 1927, 1929).

Bobby Bonds

Blackerby, George, B: Nov. 18, 1903, Luther, Okla.; D: May 30, 1987, Wichita Falls, Tex. Outfielder (1928).

Blanco, Ossie, B: Sept. 8, 1945, Caracas, Venezuela. Infielder/outfielder (1970).

Blankenship, Homer, B: Aug. 4, 1902, Bonham, Tex.; D: June 22, 1974, Longview, Tex. Pitcher (1922–23).

Blankenship, Ted, B: May 10, 1901, Bonham, Tex.; D: Jan. 14, 1945, Atoka, Okla. Pitcher (1922–30).

Block, Bruno, B: Mar. 13, 1885, Wisconsin Rapids, Wis.; D: Aug. 6, 1937, South Milwaukee, Wis. Catcher (1910–12).

Blomberg, Ron, B: Aug. 23, 1948, Atlanta, Ga. DH (1978).

Blue, Lu, B: Mar. 5, 1897, Washington, D.C.; D: July 28, 1958, Alexandria, Va. Infielder (1931–32).

Blum, Geoff, B: Apr. 26, 1973, Redwood City, Calif. Infielder (2005).

Bocek, Milt, B: July 16, 1912, Chicago, Ill.; D: Apr. 29, 2007, Brookfield, Ill. Outfielder (1933–34).

Bodie, Francesco "Ping," B: Oct. 8, 1887, San Francisco, Calif.; D: Dec. 17, 1961, San Francisco, Calif. Outfielder (1911–14).

Boken, Bob, B: Feb. 23, 1908, Maryville, Ill.; D: Oct. 6, 1988, Las Vegas, Nev. Infielder (1934).

Bollo, Greg, B: Nov. 16, 1943, Detroit, Mich. Pitcher (1965–66).

Bolton, Rodney, B: Sept. 23, 1968, Chattanooga, Tenn. Pitcher (1993, 95).

Bonds, Bobby, B: Mar. 15, 1946, Riverside, Calif.; D: Aug. 23, 2003, San Carlos, Calif. Outfielder (1978).

Bonilla, Bobby, B: Feb. 23, 1963, Bronx, N.Y. Infielder/outfielder (1986).

Bonura, Henry "Zeke," B: Sept. 20, 1908, New Orleans, La.; D: Mar. 9, 1987, New Orleans, La. Infielder (1934–37).

Booker, Buddy, B: May 28, 1942, Lynchburg, Va. Catcher (1968).

Boone, Ike, B: Feb. 17, 1897, Samantha, Ala.; D: Aug. 1, 1958, Northport, Ala. Outfielder (1927).

Boone, Ray, B: July 27, 1923, San Diego, Calif.; D: Oct. 17, 2004, San Diego, Calif., Infielder (1958–59).

Borchard, Joe, B: Nov. 25, 1978, Panorama City, Calif. Outfielder (2002–05).

Bordagaray, Stan "Frenchy," B: Jan. 3, 1910, Coalinga, Calif.; D: Apr. 13, 2001, Ventura, Calif. Outfielder (1934).

Borders, Pat, B: May 14, 1963, Columbus, Ohio. Catcher (1996).

Borgmann, Glenn, B: May 25, 1950, Paterson, N.J. Catcher (1980).

Borton, Bill "Babe," B: Aug. 14, 1888, Marion, Ill.; D: July 29, 1954, Berkeley, Calif. Infielder (1912–13).

Bosley, Thad, B: Sept. 17, 1956, Oceanside, Calif. Outfielder/DH (1978–80).

Boston, Daryl, B: Jan. 4, 1963, Cincinnati, Ohio. Outfielder (1984–90).

Bourgeois, Jayson, B: Jan. 4, 1982, Houston, Tex. Infielder (2008).

Bowers, Grover "Billy," B: Mar. 25, 1923, Parkin, Ark.; D: Sept. 17, 1996, Wynne, Ark. Outfielder (1949).

Bowler, Grant, B: Oct. 24, 1907, Denver, Colo.; D: June 25, 1968, Denver, Colo. Pitcher (1931–32).

Bowles, Emmett, B: Aug. 2, 1898, Wanette, Okla.; D: Sept. 3, 1959, Flagstaff, Ariz. Pitcher (1922).

Bowser, Jim "Red," B: Sept. 20, 1881, Freeport, Pa.; D: May 22, 1943, Moundsville, W.Va. Outfielder (1910).

Zeke Bonura

Boyd, Bob, B: Oct. 1, 1925, Potts Camp, Miss.; D: Sept. 7, 2004, Wichita, Kan. Infielder/outfielder (1951, 53–54).

Boyer, Ken, B: May 20, 1931, Liberty, Mo.; D: Sept. 7, 1982, St. Louis, Mo. Infielder (1967–68).

Boyles, Harry, B: Nov. 29, 1911, Granite City, Ill.; D: Jan. 7, 2005, McAllen, Tex. Pitcher (1938–39).

Bradford, Chad, B: Sept. 14, 1974, Jackson, Miss. Pitcher (1998–2000).

Bradford, Charles "Buddy," B: July 25, 1944, Mobile, Ala. Outfielder (1966–70, 72–76).

Joe Borchard

Bradley, Fred, B: July 31, 1920, Parsons, Kan. Outfielder (1948–49).

Bradley, Phil, B: Mar. 11, 1959, Bloomington, Ind. Outfielder/DH (1990).

Bradley, Scott, B: Mar. 22, 1960, Glen Ridge, N.J. Catcher (1986).

Bradley, Tom, B: Mar. 16, 1947, Asheville, N.C. Pitcher (1971–72).

Brady, Doug, B: Nov. 23, 1969, Jacksonville, Fla. Infielder (1995).

Brain, Dave, B: Jan. 24, 1879, Hereford, England; D: May 25, 1959, Los Angeles, Calif. Infielder (1901).

Bratschi, Fritz, B: Jan. 16, 1892, Alliance, Ohio; D: Jan. 10, 1962, Massillon, Ohio. Outfielder (1921).

Bravo, Angel, B: Aug. 4, 1942, Maracaibo, Venezuela. Outfielder (1970).

Braxton, Garland, B: June 10, 1900, Snow Camp, N.C.; D: Feb. 26, 1966, Norfolk, Va. Pitcher (1930–31).

Breazeale, Jim, B: Oct. 3, 1949, Houston, Tex. Infielder/DH (1978).

Brennan, Tom, B: Oct. 30, 1952, Chicago, Ill. Pitcher (1984).

Breton, Jim, B: July 15, 1891, Chicago, Ill.; D: May 30, 1973, Beloit, Wis. Infielder (1913–15).

Brett, Ken, B: Sept. 18, 1948, Brooklyn, N.Y.; D: Nov. 18, 2003, Spokane, Wash. Pitcher (1976–77).

Brice, Alan, B: Oct. 1, 1937, New York, N.Y. Pitcher (1961).

Brideweser, Jim, B: Feb. 13, 1927, Lancaster, Ohio; D: Aug. 25, 1989, El Toro, Calif. Infielder (1955–56).

Brief, Tony "Bunny," B: July 3, 1892, Remus, Mich.; D: Feb. 10, 1963, Milwaukee, Wis. Infielder (1915).

Brinkman, Chuck, B: Sept. 16, 1944, Cincinnati, Ohio. Catcher (1969–74).

Broadway, Lance, B: Aug. 20, 1983, Bryan, Tex. Pitcher (2007–09).

Brohamer, Jack, B: Feb. 26, 1950, Maywood, Calif. Infielder (1976–77).

Brosnan, Jim, B: Oct. 24, 1929, Cincinnati, Ohio. Pitcher (1963).

Brown, Clint, B: July 8, 1903, Blackash, Pa.; D: Dec. 31, 1955, Rocky River, Ohio. Pitcher (1936–40).

Brown, Delos, B: Oct. 4, 1892, Anna, Ill.; D: Dec. 21, 1964, Carbondale, Ill. Pinch-hitter (1914).

Brown, Dick, B: Jan. 17, 1935, Shinnston, W.Va.; D: Apr. 12, 1970, Baltimore, Md. Catcher (1960).

Brown, Hal, B: Dec. 11, 1924, Greensboro, N.C. Pitcher (1951–52).

Brown, Joe, B: July 3, 1900, Little Rock, Ark.; D: Mar. 7, 1950, Los Angeles, Calif. Pitcher (1927).

Browne, George, B: Jan. 12, 1876, Richmond, Va.; D: Dec. 9, 1920, Hyde Park, N.Y. Outfielder (1910).

Bruner, Jack, B: July 1, 1924, Waterloo, Iowa; D: June 24, 2003, Lincoln, Neb., Pitcher (1949–50).

Brusstar, Warren, B: Feb. 2, 1952, Oakland, Calif. Pitcher (1982).

Bubser, Hal, B: Sept. 28, 1895, Chicago, Ill.; D: June 22, 1959, Melrose Park, Ill. Pinch-hitter (1922).

Buehrle, Mark, B: Mar. 23, 1979, St. Charles, Mo. Pitcher (2000–).

Buford, Don, B: Feb. 2, 1937, Linden, Tex. Infielder (1963–67).

Bukvich, Ryan, B: May 13, 1978, Naperville, Ill. Pitcher (2007).

Burgess, Forrest "Smoky," B: Feb. 6, 1927, Caroleen, N.C.; D: Sept. 15, 1991, Asheville, N.C. Catcher/Pinch-hitter (1964–67).

Burke, Jaime, B: Sept. 24, 1971, Roseburg, Ore. Catcher (2003–05).

Burke, Jimmy, B: Oct. 12, 1874, St. Louis, Mo.; D: Mar. 26, 1942, St. Louis, Mo. Infielder (1901).

Burks, Ellis, B: Sept. 11, 1964, Vicksburg, Miss. Outfielder (1993).

Burns, Bill, B: Jan. 29, 1880, San Saba, Tex.; D: June 6, 1953, Ramona, Calif. Pitcher (1909–10).

Burns, Britt, B: June 8, 1959, Houston, Tex. Pitcher (1978–85).

Burns, Joe, B: Feb. 25, 1900, Trenton, N.J.; D: Jan. 7, 1986, Trenton, N.J. Catcher (1924).

Ellis Burks (left) and Tim Raines

Busby, Jim, B: Jan. 8, 1927, Kenedy, Tex.; D: July 8, 1996, Augusta, Ga. Outfielder (1951–52, 55).

Buzhardt, John, B: Aug. 17, 1936, Prosperity, S.C.; D: June 15, 2008, Prosperity, S.C. Pitcher (1962–67).

Byrd, Harry, B: Feb. 3, 1925, Darlington, S.C.; D: May 14, 1985, Darlington, S.C. Pitcher (1955–56).

Byrne, Bobby, B: Dec. 31, 1884, St. Louis, Mo.; D: Dec. 31, 1964, Wayne, Pa. Infielder (1917).

Byrne, Jerry, B: Feb. 2, 1907, Parnell, Mich.; D: Aug. 11, 1955, Lansing, Mich. Pitcher (1929).

Byrne, Tommy, B: Dec. 31, 1919, Baltimore, Md.; D: Dec. 20, 2007, Wake Forest, N.C. Pitcher (1953).

C

Cabrera, Orlando, B: Nov. 12, 1974, Cartagena, Colombia. Infielder (2008).

Cadore, Leon, B: Nov. 20, 1890, Chicago, Ill.; D: Mar. 16, 1958, Spokane, Wash. Pitcher (1923).

Cain, Bob, B: Oct. 16, 1924, Longford, Kan.; D: Apr. 8, 1997, Cleveland, Ohio. Pitcher (1949–50, 54).

Cain, Merritt "Sugar," B: Apr. 5, 1907, Macon, Ga.; D: Apr. 3, 1975, Atlanta, Ga. Pitcher (1936–38).

Caithamer, George, B: July 22, 1910, Chicago, Ill.; D: June 1, 1954, Chicago, Ill. Catcher (1934).

Pat Caraway

Harry Chappas

Calderon, Ivan, B: Mar. 19, 1962, Fajardo, P.R.; D: Dec. 27, 2003, Loiza, P.R. Outfielder (1986–90, 1993).

Caldwell, Earl, B: Apr. 9, 1905, Sparks, Tex.; D: Sept. 15, 1981, Mission, Tex. Pitcher (1945–48).

Callahan, James "Nixey," B: Mar. 18, 1874, Fitchburg, Mass.; D: Oct. 4, 1934, Boston, Mass. Pitcher/outfielder (1901–05, 1911–13).

Callison, Johnny, B: Mar. 12, 1939, Qualls, Okla.; D: Oct. 12, 2006, Abington, Pa. Outfielder (1958–59).

Cameron, Mike, B: Jan. 8, 1973, LaGrange, Ga. Outfielder (1995–98).

Campbell, Bruce, B: Oct. 20, 1909, Chicago, Ill.; D: June 17, 1995, Ft. Myers Beach, Fla. Outfielder (1930–32).

Cangelosi, John, B: Mar. 10, 1963, Brooklyn, N.Y. Outfielder (1985–86).

Canseco, Jose, B: July 2, 1964, Havana, Cuba. Outfielder/DH. (2001).

Caraway, Cecil "Pat," B: Sept. 26, 1905, Erath County, Tex.; D: June 9, 1974, El Paso, Tex. Pitcher (1930–32).

Carey, Andy, B: Oct. 18, 1931, Oakland, Calif. Infielder (1961).

Carlos, Cisco, B: Sept. 17, 1940, Monrovia, Calif. Pitcher (1967–69).

Carlton, Steve, B: Dec. 22, 1944, Miami, Fla. Pitcher (1986).

Carnett, Eddie, B: Oct. 21, 1916, Springfield, Mo. Outfielder/infielder (1944).

Camilo "Cam" Carreon

Carrasco, D.J., B: Apr. 12, 1977, Safford, Ariz. Pitcher (2008–09).

Carrasquel, Alex, B: July 24, 1912, Caracas, Venezuela; D: Aug. 19, 1969, Caracas, Venezuela. Pitcher (1949).

Carrasquel, Alfonso "Chico," B: Jan. 23, 1928, Caracas, Venezuela; D: May 26, 2005, Caracas, Venezuela. Infielder (1950–55).

Carreon, Camilo, B: Aug. 6, 1937, Colton, Calif.; D: Sept. 2, 1987, Tucson, Ariz. Catcher (1959–64).

Carroll, Clay, B: May 2, 1941, Clanton, Ala. Pitcher (1976–77).

Carter, Jeff, B: Dec. 3, 1964, Tampa, Fla. Pitcher (1991).

Caruso, Mike, B: May 27, 1977, Queens, N.Y. Infielder (1998–99).

Cary, Chuck, B: Mar. 3, 1960, Whittier, Calif. Pitcher (1993).

Casanova, Raul, B: Aug. 23, 1972, Ponce, P.R. Catcher (2005).

Cash, Norm, B: Nov. 10, 1934, Justiceburg, Tex.; D: Oct. 12, 1986, Beaver Island, Mich. Infielder (1958–59).

Casian, Larry, B: Oct. 28, 1965, Lynwood, Calif. Pitcher (1998).

Castillo, Carlos, B: Apr. 21, 1975, Boston, Mass. Pitcher (1997–99).

Castillo, Tony, B: Mar. 3, 1963, Lara, Venezuela. Pitcher (1996–98).

Castino, Vince, B: Oct. 11, 1917, Willisville, Ill.; D: Mar. 6, 1967, Sacramento, Calif. Catcher (1943–45).

Hal Chase

Castner, Paul, B: Feb. 16, 1897, St. Paul, Minn.; D: Mar. 3, 1986, St. Paul, Minn. Pitcher (1923).

Castro, Ramon, B: Mar. 1, 1976, Vega Baja, P.R. Catcher (2009–).

Cater, Danny, B: Feb. 25, 1940, Austin, Tex. Outfielder/infielder (1965–66).

Causey, Wayne, B: Dec. 26, 1936, Ruston, La. Infielder (1966–68).

Cavarretta, Phil, B: July 19, 1916, Chicago, Ill.; D: Dec. 19, 2010, Liburn, Ga. Infielder (1954–55).

Cedeno, Domingo, B: Nov. 4, 1968, LaRomana, Dominican Republic. Infielder (1996).

Chakales, Bob, B: Aug. 10, 1927, Asheville, N.C.; D: Feb. 28, 2010, Richmond, Va. Pitcher (1955).

Chamberlain, Bill, B: Apr. 21, 1909, Stoughton, Mass.; D: Feb. 6, 1994, Brockton, Mass. Pitcher (1932).

Chamberlain, Joe, B: May 10, 1910, San Francisco, Calif.; D: Jan. 28, 1983, San Francisco, Calif. Infielder (1934).

Chapman, Ben, B: Dec. 25, 1908, Nashville, Tenn.; D: July 7, 1993, Hoover, Ala. Outfielder (1941).

Chappas, Harry, B: Oct. 26, 1957, Mount Rainier, Md. Infielder (1978–80).

Chappell, Larry, B: Feb. 19, 1890, McClusky, Ill.; D: Nov. 8, 1918, San Francisco, Calif. Outfielder (1913–15).

Chase, Hal, B: Feb. 13, 1883, Los Gatos, Calif.; D: May 18, 1947, Colusa, Calif. Infielder (1913–14).

Chelini, Italo, B: Oct. 10, 1914, San Francisco, Calif.; D: Aug. 25, 1972, San Francisco, Calif. Pitcher (1935–37).

Chouinard, Felix, B: Oct. 5, 1887, Hines, Ill.; D: Apr. 28, 1955, Hines, Ill. Outfielder (1910–11).

Chouneau (Cadreau), Bill "Chief," B: Sept. 2, 1889, Cloquet, Minn.; D: Sept. 17, 1948, Cloquet, Minn. Pitcher (1910).

Christensen, McKay, B: Aug. 14, 1975, Upland, Calif. Outfielder (1999–2001).

Christian, Bob, B: Oct. 17, 1945, Chicago, Ill.; D: Feb. 20, 1974, San Diego, Calif. Outfielder (1969–70).

Christmas, Steve, B: Dec. 9, 1957, Orlando, Fla. Catcher (1984).

Christopher, Lloyd, B: Dec. 31, 1919, Richmond, Calif.; D: Sept. 5, 1991, Richmond, Calif. Outfielder (1947).

Cicotte, Eddie, B: June 19, 1884, Springwells, Mich.; D: May 5, 1969, Detroit, Mich. Pitcher (1912–20).

Cintron, Alex, B: Dec. 17, 1978, Humacao, P.R. Infielder (2006–07).

Cissell, Chalmer "Bill," B: Jan. 3, 1904, Perryville, Mo.; D: Mar. 15, 1949, Chicago, Ill. Infielder (1928–32).

Citarella, Ralph, B: Feb. 7, 1958, East Orange, N.J. Pitcher (1987).

Clancy, John "Bud," B: Sept. 15, 1900, Odell, Ill.; D: Sept. 26, 1968, Ottumwa, Iowa. Infielder (1924–30).

Clark, Allie, B: June 16, 1923, South Amboy, N.J. Outfielder (1953).

Clark, Bryan, B: July 12, 1956, Madera, Calif. Pitcher (1986–87).

Clark, Harry "Pep," B: Mar. 20, 1883, Union City, Ohio; D: June 8, 1965, Milwaukee, Wis. Infielder (1903).

Clarke, Richard "Grey," B: Sept. 26, 1912, Fulton, Ala.; D: Nov. 25, 1993, Kannapolis, N.C. Infielder (1944).

Clayton, Royce, B: Jan. 2, 1970, Burbank, Calif. Infielder (2001–02).

Clemons, Chris, B: Oct. 31, 1972, Baytown, Tex. Pitcher (1997).

Coan, Gil, B: May 18, 1922, Monroe, N.C. Outfielder (1955).

Cochrane, Dave, B: Jan. 31, 1963, Riverside, Calif. Infielder (1986).

Coggins, Rich, B: Dec. 7, 1950, Indianapolis, Ind. Outfielder (1976).

Colavito, Rocky, B: Aug. 10, 1933, New York, N.Y. Outfielder (1967).

John "Jocko" Conlan

Colbern, Mike, B: Apr. 19, 1955, Santa Monica, Calif. Catcher (1978–79).

Cole, Bert, B: July 1, 1896, San Francisco, Calif.; D: May 30, 1975, San Mateo, Calif. Pitcher (1927).

Cole, Willis, B: Jan. 6, 1882, Milton Junction, Wis.; D: Oct. 11, 1965, Madison, Wis. Outfielder (1909–10).

Coleman, Ray, B: June 4, 1922, Dunsmuir, Calif.; D: Sept. 19, 2010, Norman, Okla. Outfielder (1951–52).

Collins, Eddie, B: May 2, 1887, Tarrytown, N.Y.; D: Mar. 25, 1951, Boston, Mass. Infielder (1915–26).

Collins, John "Shano," B: Dec. 4, 1885, Charlestown, Mass.; D: Sept. 10, 1955, Newton, Mass. Outfielder/infielder (1910–20).

Colon, Bartolo, B: May 24, 1973, Puerto Plata, D.R. Pitcher (2003; 2009).

Coluccio, Bob, B: Oct. 2, 1951, Centralla, Wash. Outfielder (1975–77).

Conde, Ramon, B: Dec. 29, 1934, Juana Diaz, P.R. Infielder (1962).

Conlan, John "Jocko," B: Dec. 6, 1899, Chicago, Ill.; D: Apr. 16, 1989, Scottsdale, Ariz. Outfielder (1934–35).

Connally, George "Sarge," B: Aug. 31, 1898, McGregor, Tex.; D: Jan. 27, 1978, Temple, Tex. Pitcher (1921–27).

Connelly, Bill, B: June 29, 1925, Alberta, Va.; D: Nov. 27, 1980, Richmond, Va. Pitcher (1950).

Neal Cotts

Connors, Mervyn, B: Jan. 23, 1914, Berkeley, Calif.; D: Jan. 8, 2006, Berkeley, Calif. Infielder (1937–38).

Conseugra, Sandy, B: Sept. 3, 1920, Potrerillos, Cuba; D: Nov. 18, 2005, Miami, Fla. Pitcher (1953–56).

Contreras, Jose, B: Dec. 6, 1971, La Martinas, Cuba; Pitcher (2004–09).

Contreras, Nardi, B: Sept. 19, 1951, Tampa, Fla. Pitcher (1980).

Cook, Dennis, B: Oct. 4, 1962, La Marque, Tex. Pitcher (1993).

Coombs, Cecil, B: Mar. 18, 1888, Moweaqua, Ill.; D: Nov. 25, 1975, Fort Worth, Tex. Outfielder (1914).

Cora, Joey, B: May 14, 1965, Caguas, P.R. Infielder (1991–94).

Cordero, Wilfredo, B: Oct. 3, 1971, Mayaguez, P.R. Infielder/outfielder (1998).

Corey, Ed (Abraham Cohen), B: July 13, 1899, Chicago, Ill.; D: Sept. 17, 1970, Kenosha, Wis. Pitcher (1918).

Corhan, Roy, B: Oct. 21, 1887, Indianapolis, Ind.; D: Nov. 24, 1958, San Francisco, Calif. Infielder (1911).

Correa, Ed, B: Apr. 29, 1966, Hato Rey, P.R. Pitcher (1985).

Cortazzo, John "Shine," B: Sept. 26, 1904, Wilmerding, Pa.; D: Mar. 4, 1963, Pittsburgh, Pa. Pinch-hitter (1923).

Cotts, Neal, B: Mar. 25, 1980, Belleville, Ill. Pitcher (2003–06).

Courtney, Clint, B: Mar. 16, 1927, Hall Summit, La.; D: June 16, 1975, Rochester, N.Y. Catcher (1955).

Courtney, Henry, B: Nov. 19, 1898, Asheville, N.C.; D: Dec. 11, 1954, Lyme, Calif. Pitcher (1922).

Covington, Wes, B: Mar. 27, 1932, Laurinburg, N.C. Outfielder (1961).

Cowley, Joe, B: Aug. 15, 1958, Lexington, Ky. Pitcher (1986).

Cox, Bill, B: June 23, 1913, Ashmore, Ill.; D: Feb. 16, 1988, Charleston, Ill. Pitcher (1937–38).

Cox, Ernie, B: Feb. 19, 1894, Birmingham, Ala.; D: Apr. 29, 1974, Birmingham, Ala. Pitcher (1922).

Cox, George, B: Nov. 15, 1904, Sherman, Tex.; D: Dec. 17, 1995, Bedford, Tex. Pitcher (1926).

Cox, Les, B: Aug. 14, 1905, Junction, Tex.; D: Oct. 14, 1934, San Angelo, Tex. Pitcher (1926).

Crabb, Jim, B: Aug. 23, 1890, Monticello, Iowa; D: Mar. 30, 1940, Lewistown, Mont. Pitcher (1912).

Craig, Rodney, B: Jan. 12, 1958, Los Angeles, Calif. Outfielder (1986).

Cravath, Gavvy, B: Mar. 23, 1881, Escondido, Calif.; D: May 23, 1963, Laguna Beach, Calif. Outfielder (1909).

Crede, Joe, B: Apr. 26, 1978, Jefferson City, Mo. Infielder (2000–08).

Crider, Jerry, B: Sept. 2, 1941, Sioux Falls, S.D.; D: Apr. 4, 2008, Phoenix, Ariz. Pitcher (1970).

Cron, Chris, B: Mar. 31, 1964, Albuquerque, N.M. Infielder (1992).

Crouse, Clyde "Buck," B: Jan. 6, 1897, Anderson, Ind.; D: Oct. 23, 1983, Muncie, Ind. Catcher (1923–30).

Julio Cruz

Cruz, Henry, B: Feb. 27, 1952, Christiansted, Virgin Islands. Outfielder/DH (1977–78).

Cruz, Julio, B: Dec. 2, 1954, Brooklyn, N.Y. Infielder (1983–86).

Cruz, Nelson, B: Sept. 13, 1972, Puerta Laza, D.R. Pitcher (1997).

Cruz, Todd, B: Nov. 23, 1955, Highland Park, Mich.; D: Sept. 2, 2008, Bullhead City, Ariz. Infielder (1980).

Cruz, Tommy, B: Feb. 15, 1951, Arroyo, P.R. Outfielder (1977).

Cuccinello, Tony, B: Nov. 8, 1907, Long Island City, N.Y.; D: Sept. 21, 1995, Tampa, Fla. Infielder (1943–45).

Cuellar, Charlie, B: Sept. 24, 1917, Ybor City, Fla.; D: Oct. 11, 1994, Tampa, Fla. Pitcher (1950).

Cullen, Tim, B: Feb. 16, 1942, San Francisco, Calif. Infielder (1968).

Culler, Dick, B: Jan. 15, 1915, High Point, N.C.; D: June 16, 1964, Chapel Hill, N.C. Infielder (1943).

Cunningham, Joe, B: Aug. 27, 1931, Paterson, N.J. Infielder (1962–64).

Curtright, Guy, B: Oct. 18, 1912, Holliday, Mo.; D: Aug. 23, 1997, Sun City Center, Fla. Outfielder (1943–46).

Cvengros, Mike, B: Dec. 1, 1901, Pana, Ill.; D: Aug. 2, 1970, Hot Springs, Ark. Pitcher (1923–25).

D

Daglia, Pete, B: Feb. 28, 1906, Napa, Calif.; D: Mar. 11, 1952, Willits, Calif. Pitcher (1932).

Dahlke, Jerry, B: June 8, 1930, Marathon, Wis.; D: Sept. 2, 2006, Batesville, Miss. Pitcher (1956).

Dal Canton, Bruce, B: June 15, 1942, California, Pa.; D: Oct. 7, 2008, Pittsburgh, Pa. Pitcher (1977).

Dalesandro, Mark, B: May 14, 1968, Chicago, Ill. Catcher (2001).

Daly, Tom, B: Feb. 7, 1866, Philadelphia, Pa.; D: Oct. 29, 1938, Brooklyn, N.Y. Infielder (1902–03).

Daly, Tom, B: Dec. 12, 1891, St. John, New Brunswick; D: Nov. 7, 1946, Medford, Mass. Outfielder/catcher (1913–15).

Danforth, Dave, B: Mar. 7, 1890, Granger, Tex.; D: Sept. 19, 1970, Baltimore, Md. Pitcher (1916–19).

Daneker, Pat, B: Jan. 14, 1976, Williamsport, Pa. Pitcher (1999).

John Danks. (Courtesy of Mike McKay)

Danks, John, B: Apr. 15, 1985, Austin, Tex. Pitcher (2007–).

Darensbourg, Vic, B: Nov. 13, 1970, Los Angeles, Calif. Pitcher (2004).

Darwin, Danny, B: Oct. 25, 1955, Bonham, Tex. Pitcher (1997).

Darwin, Jeff, B: July 6, 1969, Sherman, Tex. Pitcher (1996–97).

Dashiell, Wally, B: May 9, 1902, Jewett, Tex.; D: May 20, 1972, Pensacola, Fla. Infielder (1924).

Daubach, Brian, B: Feb. 11, 1972, Belleville, Ill. Infielder/outfielder (2003).

Davenport, Joe, B: Mar. 24, 1976, Chicago, Ill. Pitcher (1999).

Davenport, Joubert "Lum," B: June 27, 1900, Tucson, Ariz.; D: Apr. 21, 1961, Dallas, Tex. Pitcher (1921–24).

Davis, Ben, B: Mar. 10, 1977, Chester, Pa. Catcher (2004).

Davis, Frank "Dixie," B: Oct. 12, 1890, Wilson Mills, N.C.; D: Feb. 4, 1944, Raleigh, N.C. Pitcher (1915).

Ben Davis

Davis, George, B: Aug. 23, 1870, Cohoes, N.Y.; D: Oct. 17, 1940, Philadelphia, Pa. Infielder (1902, 1904–09).

Davis, Ike, B: June 14, 1895, Pueblo, Colo.; D: Apr. 2, 1984, Tucson, Ariz. Infielder (1924–25).

Davis, Joel, B: Jan. 30, 1965, Jacksonville, Fla. Pitcher (1985–88).

Davis, John, B: Jan. 5, 1963, Chicago, Ill. Pitcher (1988–89).

Davis, Tommy, B: Mar. 21, 1939, Brooklyn, N.Y. Outfielder (1968).

Dawley, Bill, B: Feb. 6, 1958, Norwich, Conn. Pitcher (1986).

Day, Dewon, B: Sept. 29, 1980, Jackson, Miss. Pitcher (2007).

De Aza, Alejandro, B: Apr. 11, 1984, Guaymote, Dominican Republic, Outfielder (2010–).

DeBusschere, Dave, B: Oct. 16, 1940, Detroit, Mich.; D: May 14, 2003, New York, N.Y. Pitcher (1962–63).

Degerick, Mike, B: Apr. 1, 1943, New York, N.Y. Pitcher (1961–63).

DeLeon, Jose, B: Dec. 20, 1960, La Vega, Dominican Republic. Pitcher (1986–87, 93–95).

Delhi, Lee "Flame," B: Nov. 5, 1892, Harqua Hala, Ariz.; D: May 9, 1966, San Rafael, Calif. Pitcher (1912).

Dellaero, Jason, B: Dec. 17, 1976, Mount Kisco, N.Y.; D: May 4, 2006, Chesterfield, Mo. Infielder (1999).

Delsing, Jim, B: Nov. 13, 1925, Rudolph, Wis.; D: May 4, 2006, Chesterfield, Mo. Outfielder (1948, 56).

DeMaestri, Joe, B: Dec. 9, 1928, San Francisco, Calif. Infielder (1951).

Demmitt, Ray, B: Feb. 2, 1884, Illiopolis, Ill.; D: Feb. 19, 1956, Glen Ellyn, Ill. Outfielder (1914–15).

Denson, Drew, B: Nov. 16, 1965, Cincinnati, Ohio. Infielder (1993).

Dent, Russell "Bucky," B: Nov. 25, 1951, Savannah, Ga. Infielder (1973–76).

Dente, Sam, B: Apr. 26, 1922, Harrison, N.J.; D: Apr. 21, 2002, Montclair, N.J. Infielder (1952–53).

Derrington, Jim, B: Nov. 29, 1939, Compton, Calif. Pitcher (1956–57).

De Sa, Joe, B: July 27, 1959, Honolulu, Hawaii; D: Dec. 20, 1986, San Juan, P.R. Infielder/DH (1985).

Devereaux, Mike, B: Apr. 10, 1963, Casper, Wy. Outfielder (1995).

Russell "Bucky" Dent

DeViveiros, Bernie, B: Apr. 19, 1901, Oakland, Calif.; D: July 5, 1994, Oakland, Calif. Infielder (1924).

DeVormer, Al, B: Aug. 19, 1891, Grand Rapids, Mich.; D: Aug. 29, 1966, Grand Rapids, Mich. Catcher/outfielder (1924).

Diaz, Felix, B: July 27, 1980, Las Matas De Farfan, D.R. Pitcher (2004).

Diaz, Mike, B: Apr. 15, 1960, San Francisco, Calif. Infielder (1988).

Dibble, Rob, B: Jan. 24, 1964, Bridgeport, Conn. Pitcher (1995).

Dickey, George, B: July 10, 1915, Kensett, Ark.; D: July 16, 1976, DeWitt, Ark. Catcher (1941–42, 1946–47).

Dickshot, Johnny, B: Jan. 24, 1910, Waukegan, Ill.; D: Nov. 4, 1997, Waukegan, Ill. Outfielder (1944–45).

Johnny Dickshot (sliding)

Ray Durham

Dietrich, Bill, B: Mar. 29, 1910, Philadelphia, Pa.; D: June 20, 1978, Philadelphia, Pa. Pitcher (1936–46).

Dillard, Steve, B: Feb. 8, 1951, Memphis, Tenn. Infielder (1982).

Dillinger, Bob, B: Sept. 17, 1918, Glendale, Calif.; D: Nov. 7, 2009, Santa Clarita, Calif. Infielder (1951).

Dilone, Miguel, B: Nov. 1, 1954, Santiago, Dominican Republic. Outfielder (1983).

Dobb, John, B: Nov. 15, 1901, Muskegon, Mich.; D: July 13, 1991, Muskegon, Mich. Pitcher (1924).

Dobernic, Jess, B: Nov. 20, 1917, Mount Olive, Ill.; D: July 16, 1998, St. Louis, Mo. Pitcher (1939).

Dobson, Joe, B: Jan. 20, 1917, Durant, Okla.; D: June 23, 1994, Jacksonville, Fla. Pitcher (1951–53).

Doby, Larry, B: Dec. 13, 1923, Camden, S.C.; D: June 18, 2003, Montclair, N.J. Outfielder (1956–57, '59).

Dolan, Pat "Cozy," B: Dec. 3, 1872, Cambridge, Mass.; D: Mar. 29, 1907, Louisville, Ky. Outfielder (1903).

Donahue, John "Jiggs," B: July 13, 1879, Springfield, Ohio; D: July 19, 1913, Columbus, Ohio. Infielder (1904–09).

Donovan, Dick, B: Dec. 7, 1927, Quincy, Mass.; D: Jan. 6, 1997, Weymouth, Mass. Pitcher (1955–60).

Dorish, Harry, B: July 13, 1921, Swoyersville, Pa.; D: Dec. 31, 2000, Wilkes Barre, Pa. Pitcher (1951–55).

Dorman, Dwight "Charlie," B: Apr. 23, 1898, San Francisco, Calif.; D: Nov. 15, 1928, San Francisco, Calif. Catcher (1923).

Dotel, Octavio, B: Nov. 25, 1973, Santo Domingo, Dominican Republic. Pitcher (2008–09).

Dotson, Rich, B: Jan. 10, 1959, Cincinnati, Ohio. Pitcher (1979–87, '89).

Dougherty, Patsy, B: Oct. 27, 1876, Andover, N.Y.; D: Apr. 30, 1940, Bolivar, N.Y. Outfielder (1906–11).

Dougherty, Tom, B: May 30, 1881, Chicago, Ill.; D: Nov. 6, 1953, Milwaukee, Wis. Pitcher (1904).

Douglas, Phil, B: June 17, 1890, Cedartown, Ga.; D: Aug. 1, 1952, Sequatchie, Valley, Tenn. Pitcher (1912).

Downing, Brian, B: Oct. 9, 1950, Los Angeles, Calif. Catcher/outfielder (1973–77).

Drabek, Doug, B: July 25, 1962, Victoria, Tex. Pitcher (1997).

Drabowsky, Moe, B: July 21, 1935, Ozanna, Poland; D: June 10, 2006, Little Rock, Ark. Pitcher (1972).

Drahman, Brian, B: Nov. 7, 1966, Kenton, Ky. Pitcher (1991, 93).

Dransfeldt, Kelly, B: Apr. 15, 1975, Joliet, Ill. Infielder (2004).

Drees, Tom, B: June 17, 1963, Des Moines, Iowa. Pitcher (1991).

Dropo, Walt, B: Jan. 30, 1923, Moosup, Conn.; D: Dec. 18, 2010, Storrs, Conn. Infielder (1955–58).

Duff, Cecil "Larry," B: May 6, 1895, Radersburg, Mont.; D: Nov. 10, 1969, Bend, Ore. Pitcher (1922).

Dugan, Dan, B: Feb. 22, 1907, Plainfield, N.J.; D: June 25, 1968, Green Brook, N.J. Pitcher (1928–29).

Walt Dropo (left), Minnie Minoso, and Sherm Lollar celebrate a win over the Tribe in 1956.

Jermaine Dye

Dundon, Gus, B: July 10, 1874, Columbus, Ohio; D: Sept. 1, 1940, Pittsburgh, Pa. Infielder (1904–06).

Dunkle, Davey, B: Aug. 30, 1872, Phillipsburg, Pa.; D: Nov. 19, 1941, Lock Haven, Pa. Pitcher (1903).

Dunne, Mike, B: Oct. 27, 1962, South Bend, Ind. Pitcher (1992).

Dupee, Frank, B: Apr. 29, 1877, Monkton, Vt.; D: Aug. 14, 1956, Portland, Maine. Pitcher (1901).

Durham, Ed, B: Aug. 17, 1908, Chester, S.C.; D: Apr. 27, 1976, Chester, S.C. Pitcher (1933).

Durham, Jimmy, B: Oct. 7, 1881, Douglass, Kan.; D: May 7, 1949, Coffeyville, Kan. Pitcher (1902).

Durham, Ray, B: Nov. 30, 1971, Charlotte, N.C. Infielder (1995–2002).

Dybzinski, Jerry, B: July 7, 1955, Cleveland, Ohio. Infielder (1983–84).

Dye, Jermaine, B: Jan. 28, 1974, Vacaville, Calif. Outfielder (2005–09).

Dykes, Jimmy, B: Nov. 10, 1896, Philadelphia, Pa.; D: June 15, 1976, Philadelphia, Pa. Infielder (1933–39).

E

Earnshaw, George, B: Feb. 15, 1900, New York, N.Y.; D: Dec. 1, 1976, Little Rock, Ark. Pitcher (1934–35).

Easterly, Ted, B: Apr. 20, 1885, Lincoln, Neb.; D: July 6, 1951, Clear Lake Highlands, Calif. Catcher (1912–13).

Carl Everett. (© 2005 finalshot.com)

Eaves, Vallie, B: Sept. 6, 1911, Allen, Okla.; D: Apr. 19, 1960, Norman, Okla. Pitcher (1939–40).

Eddy, Don, B: Oct. 25, 1946, Mason City, Iowa. Pitcher (1970–71).

Eden, Mike, B: May 22, 1949, Fort Clayton, Panama Canal Zone. Infielder (1978).

Edmondson, Paul, B: Feb. 12, 1943, Kansas City, Kan.; D: Feb. 13, 1970, Santa Barbara, Calif. Pitcher (1969).

Edwards, Hank, B: Jan. 29, 1919, Elmwood Place, Ohio; D: June 22, 1988, Santa Ana, Calif. Outfielder (1952).

Edwards, Jim Joe, B: Dec. 14, 1894, Banner, Miss.; D: Jan. 19, 1965, Serepta, Miss. Pitcher (1925–26).

Edwards, Wayne, B: Mar. 7, 1964, Burbank, Calif. Pitcher (1989–91).

Egan, Tom, B: June 9, 1946, Los Angeles, Calif. Catcher (1971–72).

Egbert, Jack, B: May 12, 1983, Staten Island, N.Y. Pitcher (2009).

Eichrodt, Fred, B: Jan. 6, 1903, Chicago, Ill.; D: July 14, 1965, Indianapolis, Ind. Outfielder (1931).

Eldred, Cal, B: Nov. 24, 1967, Cedar Rapids, Iowa. Pitcher (2000–01).

Elia, Lee, B: July 16, 1937, Philadelphia, Pa. Infielder (1966).

Elliott, Bob, B: Nov. 26, 1916, San Francisco, Calif.; D: May 4, 1966, San Francisco, Calif. Outfielder (1953).

Ellis, Sammy, B: Feb. 11, 1941, Youngstown, Ohio. Pitcher (1969).

Elsh, Roy, B: Mar. 1, 1892, Pennsgrove, N.J.; D: Nov. 12, 1978, Philadelphia, Pa. Outfielder (1923–25).

Embrey, Charlie "Slim," B: Aug. 17, 1901, Columbia, Tenn.; D: Oct. 10, 1947, Nashville, Tenn. Pitcher (1923).

English, Charlie, B: Apr. 8, 1910, Darlington, S.C.; D: June 25, 1999, Pasadena, Calif. Infielder (1932–33).

Ennis, Delmer, B: Jan. 8, 1925, Philadelphia, Pa.; D: Feb. 8, 1996, Huntingdon Valley, Pa. Outfielder (1959).

Enright, George, B: May 9, 1954, New Britain, Conn. Catcher (1976).

Ens, Anton "Mutz," B: Nov. 8, 1884, St. Louis, Mo.; D: June 28, 1950, St. Louis, Mo. Infielder (1912).

Erautt, Joe, B: Sept. 1, 1921, Vibank, Saskatchewan; D: Oct. 6, 1976, Portland, Ore. Catcher (1950–51).

Erstad, Darin, B: June 4, 1974, Jamestown, N.D. Outfielder (2007).

Escarrega, Ernesto, B: Dec. 27, 1949, Los Mochis, Mexico. Pitcher (1982).

Esposito, Sammy, B: Dec. 15, 1931, Chicago, Ill. Infielder (1952, 55–63).

Esser, Mark, B: Apr. 1, 1956, Erie, Pa. Pitcher (1979).

Essian, Jim, B: Jan. 2, 1951, Detroit, Mich. Catcher (1976–77, 81).

Evans, Russ "Red," B: Nov. 12, 1906, Chicago, Ill.; D: June 14, 1982, Lakeview, Ark. Pitcher (1936).

Evans, William Arthur, B: Aug. 3, 1911, Elvins, Mo.; D: Jan. 8, 1952, Wichita, Kan. Pitcher (1932).

Evans, William Lawrence "Bill," B: Mar. 25, 1919, Quanah, Tex.; D: Nov. 30, 1983, Grand Junction, Colo. Pitcher (1932).

Everett, Carl, B: June 3, 1971, Tampa, Fla. Outfielder (2003–04; 2005).

Evers, Johnny, B: July 21, 1881, Troy, N.Y.; D: Mar. 28, 1947, Albany, N.Y. Infielder (1922).

Ewing, Sam, B: Apr. 9, 1949, Lewisburg, Tenn. Infielder (1973, 76).

Eyre, Scott, B: May 30, 1972, Ingleside, Calif. Pitcher (1997–2000).

F

Faber, Urban "Red," B: Sept. 6, 1888, Cascade, Iowa; D: Sept. 25, 1976, Chicago, Ill. Pitcher (1914–33).

Fabregas, Jorge, B: March 13, 1970, Miami, Fla. Catcher (1997).

Fain, Ferris, B: Mar. 29, 1921, San Antonio, Tex.; D: Oct. 18, 2001, Georgetown, Calif. Infielder (1953–54).

Falk, Bibb, B: Jan. 27, 1899, Austin, Tex.; D: June 8, 1989, Austin, Tex. Outfielder (1920–28).

Fallon, Bob, B: Feb. 18, 1960, Bronx, N.Y. Pitcher (1985).

Farley, Bob, B: Nov. 15, 1937, Watsontown, Pa. Infielder/outfielder (1962).

Farmer, Ed, B: Oct. 18, 1949, Evergreen Park, Ill. Pitcher (1979–81).

Farrell, Kerby, B: Sept. 3, 1913, Leapwood, Tenn.; D: Dec. 17, 1975, Nashville, Tenn. Infielder (1945).

Fautsch, Joe, B: Feb. 28, 1887, Minneapolis, Minn.; D: Mar. 16, 1971, New Hope, Minn. Pinch-hitter (1916).

Fehring, Bill "Dutch," B: May 31, 1912, Columbus, Ind.; D: Apr. 13, 2006, Palo Alto, Calif. Catcher (1934).

Felsch, Oscar "Happy," B: Aug. 22, 1891, Milwaukee, Wis.; D: Aug. 17, 1964, Milwaukee, Wis. Outfielder (1915–20).

Fenner, Horace "Hod," B: July 12, 1897, Martin, Mich.; D: Nov. 20, 1954, Detroit, Mich. Pitcher (1921).

Ferris Fain

Carlton Fisk

Fernandes, Ed, B: Mar. 11, 1918, Oakland, Calif.; D: Nov. 27, 1968, Hayward, Calif. Catcher (1946).

Fernandez, Alex, B: Aug. 13, 1969, Miami Beach, Fla. Pitcher (1990–96).

Ferrarese, Don, B: June 19, 1929, Oakland, Calif. Pitcher (1960).

Fieber, Clarence, B: Sept. 4, 1913, San Francisco, Calif.; D: Aug. 20, 1985, Redwood City, Calif. Pitcher (1932).

Fields, Josh, B: Dec. 14, 1982, Ada, Okla. Infielder (2006–09).

Fiene, Lou, B: Dec. 29, 1884, Fort Dodge, Iowa; D: Dec. 22, 1964, Chicago, Ill. Pitcher (1906–09).

Filson, Pete, B: Sept. 28, 1958, Darby, Pa. Pitcher (1986).

Fireovid, Steve, B: June 6, 1957, Bryan, Ohio. Pitcher (1985).

Fischer, Bill, B: Oct. 11, 1930, Wausau, Wis. Pitcher (1956–58).

Scott Fletcher

Lew Fonseca (left) with Joe Cronin

Fischer, Carl, B: Nov. 5, 1905, Medina, N.Y.; D: Dec. 10, 1963, Medina, N.Y. Pitcher (1935).

Fisher, Eddie, B: July 16, 1936, Shreveport, La. Pitcher (1962–66, '72–73).

Fisher, Jack, B: Mar. 4, 1939, Frostburg, Md. Pitcher (1968).

Fisk, Carlton, B: Dec. 26, 1947, Bellows Falls, Vt. Catcher/outfielder/DH (1981–93).

Flaherty, Patsy, B: June 29, 1876, Mansfield, Pa.; D: Jan. 23, 1968, Alexandria, La. Pitcher (1903–04).

Flanigan, Tom, B: Sept. 6, 1934, Cincinnati, Ohio. Pitcher (1954).

Flannery, John, B: Jan. 25, 1957, Long Beach, Calif. Infielder (1977).

Flaskamper, Ray, B: Oct. 31, 1901, St. Louis, Mo.; D: Feb. 3, 1978, San Antonio, Tex. Infielder (1927).

Fletcher, Scott, B: July 30, 1958, Fort Walton Beach, Fla. Infielder (1983–85, 1989–91).

Flowers, Tyler, B: Jan. 24, 1986, Roswell, Ga. Catcher (2009–).

Floyd, Gavin, B: Jan. 27, 1983, Annapolis, Md. Pitcher (2007–).

Fogg, Josh, B: Dec. 13, 1976, Lynn, Mass. Pitcher (2001).

Foley, Marv, B: Aug. 29, 1953, Stanford, Ky. Catcher (1978–80, 1982).

Fonseca, Lew, B: Jan. 21, 1899, Oakland, Calif.; D: Nov. 26, 1989, Ely, Iowa. Infielder (1931–33).

Fonville, Chad, B: March 5, 1971, Jacksonville, N.C. Infielder/outfielder (1997).

Ford, Gene, B: June 23, 1912, Fort Dodge, Iowa; D: Sept. 7, 1970, Emmetsburg, Iowa. Pitcher (1938).

Fordham, Tom, B: Feb. 20, 1974, San Diego, Calif. Pitcher (1997–98).

Terry Forster

Fordyce, Brook, B: May 7, 1970, New London, Conn. Catcher (1999–2000).

Foreman, August "Happy," B: July 20, 1897, Memphis, Tenn.; D: Feb. 13, 1953, New York, N.Y. Pitcher (1924).

Fornieles, Mike, B: Jan. 18, 1932, Havana, Cuba; D: Feb. 11, 1998, St. Petersburg, Fla. Pitcher (1953–56).

Fortugno, Tim, B: Apr. 11, 1962, Clinton, Mass. Pitcher (1995).

Forster, Terry, B: Jan. 14, 1952, Sioux Falls, S.D. Pitcher (1971–76).

Foster, Clarence "Pop," B: Apr. 8, 1878, New Haven, Conn.; D: Apr. 16, 1944, Princeton, N.J. Outfielder (1901).

Foster, George, B: Dec. 1, 1948, Tuscaloosa, Ala. Outfielder/DH (1986).

Fothergill, Bob, B: Aug. 16, 1897, Massillon, Ohio; D: Mar. 20, 1938, Detroit, Mich. Outfielder (1930–32).

George Foster

Nellie Fox (right) to Luis Aparicio

Foulke, Keith, B: Oct. 19, 1972, Ellsworth AFB, Rapid City, S.D. Pitcher (1997–2002).

Fournier, Jack, B: Sept. 28, 1892, Au Sable, Mich.; D: Sept. 5, 1973, Tacoma, Wash. Infielder (1912–17).

Fox, Nellie, B: Dec. 25, 1927, St. Thomas, Pa.; D: Dec. 1, 1975, Baltimore, Md. Infielder (1950–63).

Frailing, Ken, B: Jan. 19, 1948, Madison, Wis. Pitcher (1972–73).

Franco, Julio, B: Aug. 23, 1958, Hato Mayor, Dominican Republic. Infielder/DH, (1994).

Francona, Tito, B: Nov. 4, 1933, Aliquippa, Pa. Outfielder (1958).

Frasier, Vic, B: Aug. 5, 1904, Ruston, La.; D: Jan. 10, 1977, Jacksonville, Tex. Pitcher (1931–33, 39).

Frazier, Lou, B: Jan. 26, 1965, St. Louis, Mo. Outfielder (1998).

Freeman, Marvin, B: Apr. 10, 1963, Chicago, Ill. Pitcher (1996).

Freese, Gene, B: Jan. 8, 1934, Wheeling, W.Va. Infielder (1960, 65–66).

Freeze, Jake, B: Apr. 25, 1900, Huntington, Ark.; D: Apr. 9, 1983, San Angelo, Tex. Pitcher (1925).

French, Charlie, B: Oct. 12, 1883, Indianapolis, Ind.; D: Mar. 30, 1962, Indianapolis, Ind. Infielder (1910).

French, Ray, B: Jan. 9, 1895, Alameda, Calif.; D: Apr. 3, 1978, Alameda, Calif. Infielder (1924).

Frost, Dave, B: Nov. 17, 1952, Long Beach, Calif. Pitcher (1977).

Funk, Elias "Liz," B: Oct. 28, 1904, La Cygne, Kan.; D: Jan. 16, 1968, Norman, Okla. Pitcher (1932–33).

G

Gabler, Frank, B: Nov. 6, 1911, East Highlands, Calif.; D: Nov. 1, 1967, Long Beach, Calif. Pitcher (1938).

Gallagher, Dave, B: Sept. 20, 1960, Trenton, N.J. Outfielder (1988–90).

Gallivan, Phil, B: May 29, 1907, Seattle, Wash.; D: Nov. 24, 1969, St. Paul, Minn. Pitcher (1932, 34).

Gamble, Oscar, B: Dec. 20, 1949, Ramer, Ala. Outfielder/DH (1977, 1985).

Gandil, Arnold "Chick," B: Jan. 19, 1887, St. Paul, Minn.; D: Dec. 13, 1970, Calistoga, Calif. Infielder (1910, 1917–19).

Garcia, Freddy, B: June 10, 1976, Caracas, Venezuela. Pitcher (2004–06, 2009–10).

Garcia, Mike, B: Nov. 17, 1923, San Gabriel, Calif.; D: Jan. 13, 1986, Fairview Park, Ohio. Pitcher (1960).

Garcia, Ramon, B: Feb. 9, 1969, Guanare, Venezuela. Pitcher (1991).

Garland, Jon, B: Sept. 27, 1979, Valencia, Calif. Pitcher (2000–07).

Garland, Lou, B: July 16, 1905, Archie, Mo.; D: Aug. 30, 1990, Idaho Falls, Idaho. Pitcher (1931).

Garr, Ralph, B: Dec. 12, 1945, Monroe, La. Outfielder (1976–79).

Garrity, Francis "Hank," B: Feb. 4, 1908, Boston, Mass.; D: Sept. 1, 1962, Boston, Mass. Catcher (1931).

Garvin, Virgil "Ned," B: Jan. 1, 1874, Navasota, Tex.; D: June 16, 1908, Fresno, Calif. Pitcher (1901).

Gaston, Milt, B: Jan. 27, 1896, Ridgefield Park, N.J.; D: Apr. 26, 1996, Hyannis, Mass. Pitcher (1932–34).

Gates, Joe, B: Oct. 3, 1954, Gary, Ind.; D: Mar. 28, 2010, Gary, Ind. Infielder (1978–79).

Gebrian, Pete, B: Aug. 10, 1923, Bayonne, N.J.; D: May 6, 2005, Stuart, Fla. Pitcher (1947).

Geddes, Jim, B: Mar. 23, 1949, Columbus, Ohio. Pitcher (1972–73).

Gerlach, Johnny, B: May 11, 1917, Shullsburg, Wis.; D: Aug. 28, 1999, Madison, Wis. Infielder (1938–39).

Gettel, Alan, B: Sept. 17, 1917, Norfolk, Va.; D: Apr. 8, 2005, Norfolk, Va. Pitcher (1948–49).

Getz, Chris, B: Aug. 30, 1983, Southfield, Mich. Infielder (2008–09).

Gick, George, B: Oct. 18, 1915, Dunnington, Ind.; D: Aug. 12, 2008, Lafayette, Ind. Pitcher (1937–38).

Gilbert, Mark, B: Aug. 22, 1956, Atlanta, Ga. Outfielder (1985).

Giles, Brian, B: Apr. 27, 1960, Manhattan, Kan. Infielder (1986).

Gillenwater, Claral, B: May 20, 1900, Sims, Ind.; D: Feb. 26, 1978, Bradenton, Fla. (1923).

Gillespie, Bob, Oct. 8, 1918, Columbus, Ohio; D: Nov. 4, 2001, Winston-Salem, N.C., Pitcher (1947–48).

Ginsberg, Joe, B: Oct. 11, 1926, New York, N.Y. Catcher (1960–61).

Ginter, Matt, B: Dec. 24, 1977, Lexington, Ky. Pitcher (2000–03).

Gleason, William "Kid," B: Oct. 26, 1866, Camden, N.J.; D: Jan. 2, 1933, Philadelphia, Pa. Infielder (1912).

Gleaton, Jerry Don, B: Sept. 14, 1957, Brownwood, Tex. Pitcher (1984–85).

Billy Goodman

Gload, Ross, B: Apr. 5, 1976, Brooklyn, N.Y. Infielder (2004–06).

Glover, Gary, B: Dec. 3, 1976, Cleveland, Ohio. Pitcher (2001–03).

Gobble, Jimmy, B: July 19, 1981, Bristol, Tenn. Pitcher (2009).

Gogolewski, Bill, B: Oct. 26, 1947, Oshkosh, Wis. Pitcher (1975).

Goldsberry, Gordon, B: Aug. 30, 1927, Sacramento, Calif.; D: Feb. 23, 1996, Lake Forest, Calif. Infielder (1949–51).

Goletz, Stan, B: May 21, 1918, Crescent, Ohio; D: June 7, 1997, Bell County, Tex. Pinch-hitter (1941).

Gonzalez, Angel "Andy," B: Dec. 15, 1981, Rio Piedras, P.R. Infielder (2007).

Tony Graffanino. (© 2002 finalshot.com)

Good, Wilbur, B: Sept. 28, 1885, Punxsutawney, Pa.; D: Dec. 30, 1963, Brooksville, Fla. Outfielder (1918).

Goodell, John, B: Apr. 5, 1907, Muskogee, Okla.; D: Sept. 21, 1993, Mesquite, Tex. Pitcher (1928).

Goodman, Billy, B: Mar. 22, 1926, Concord, N.C.; D: Oct. 1, 1984, Sarasota, Fla. Infielder (1958–61).

Goodwin, Jim, B: Aug. 15, 1926, St. Louis, Mo.; D: Apr. 12, 2008, St. Louis, Mo. Pitcher (1948).

Gordon, Tom "Flash," B: Nov. 18, 1967, Sebring, Fla. Pitcher (2004).

Gossage, Rich "Goose," B: July 5, 1951, Colorado Springs, Colo. Pitcher (1972–76).

Grabowski, Johnny, B: Jan. 7, 1900, Ware, Mass.; D: May 23, 1946, Albany, N.Y. Catcher (1924–26).

Graffanino, Tony, B: June 6, 1972, Amityville, N.Y. Infielder (2000–03).

Graham, Roy, B: Feb. 22, 1895, San Francisco, Calif.; D: Apr. 26, 1933, Manila, Philippines. Catcher (1922–23).

Granger, Wayne, B: Mar. 15, 1944, Springfield, Mass. Pitcher (1974).

Grant, Jimmy, B: Oct. 6, 1918, Racine, Wis.; D: July 8, 1970, Rochester, Minn. Infielder (1942–43).

Gray, Lorenzo, B: Mar. 4, 1958, Mound Bayou, Miss. Infielder (1982–83).

Gray, Ted, B: Dec. 31, 1924, Detroit, Mich. Pitcher (1955).

Grebeck, Craig, B: Dec. 29, 1964, Johnstown, Pa. Infielder (1990–95).

Green, Danny, B: Nov. 6, 1876, Burlington, N.J.; D: Nov. 9, 1914, Camden, N.J. Outfielder (1902–05).

Gregory, Paul, B: June 9, 1908, Tomnolen, Miss.; D: Sept. 16, 1999, Southaven, Miss. Pitcher (1932–33).

Griffey, Ken Jr., B: Nov. 21, 1969, Donora, Pa. Outfielder (2008).

Griffith, Clark, B: Nov. 20, 1869, Stringtown, Mo.; D: Oct. 27, 1955, Washington, D.C. Pitcher (1901–02).

Grilli, Jason, B: Nov. 11, 1976, Royal Oak, Mich. Pitcher (2004).

Grimsley, Ross, B: June 4, 1922, Americus, Kan.; D: Feb. 6, 1994, Memphis, Tenn. Pitcher (1951).

Grissom, Marv, B: Mar. 31, 1918, Los Molinas, Calif.; D: Sept. 18, 2005, Red Bluff, Calif. Pitcher (1952).

Groth, Ernest, B: May 3, 1922, Beaver Falls, Pa.; D: Dec. 27, 2004, Beaver, Pa. Oufielder (1949).

Groth, Johnny, B: July 23, 1926, Chicago, Ill. Outfielder (1954–55).

Grove, Orval, B: Aug. 29, 1919, Mineral, Kan.; D: Apr. 20, 1992, Carmichael, Calif. Pitcher (1940–49).

Grube, Frank, B: Jan. 7, 1905, Easton, Pa.; D: July 2, 1945, New York, N.Y. Catcher (1931–33, 1935–36).

Guillen, Ozzie, B: Jan. 20, 1964, Oculare del Tuy, Venezuela. Infielder (1985–97).

Gulley, Tom, B: Dec. 25, 1899, Garner, N.C.; D: Nov. 24, 1966, St. Charles, Ark. Outfielder (1926).

Gumpert, Randy, B: Jan. 23, 1918, Monocacy, Pa.; D: Nov. 25, 2008, Wyomissing, Pa. Pitcher (1948–51).

H

Haas, Bert, B: Feb. 8, 1914, Naperville, Ill.; D: June 23, 1999, Tampa, Fla. Infielder (1951).

Haas, George "Mule," B: Oct. 15, 1903, Montclair, N.J.; D: June 30, 1974, New Orleans, La. Outfielder (1933–37).

Hacker, Warren, B: Nov. 21, 1924, Marissa, Ill.; D: May 22, 2002, Lenzburg, Ill. Pitcher (1961).

Hadley, Irving "Bump," B: July 5, 1904, Lynn, Mass.; D: Feb. 15, 1963, Lynn, Mass. Pitcher (1932).

Haefner, Mickey, B: Oct. 9, 1912, Lenzberg, Ill.; D: Jan. 3, 1995, New Athens, Ill. Pitcher (1949–50).

Haeger, Charlie, B: Sept. 19, 1983, Livonia, Mich. Pitcher (2006–07).

Hafey, Daniel "Bud," B: Aug. 6, 1912, Berkeley, Calif.; D: July 27, 1986, Sacramento, Calif. Outfielder (1935).

Hahn, Ed, B: Aug. 27, 1875, Nevada, Ohio; D: Nov. 29, 1941, Des Moines, Iowa. Outfielder (1906–10).

Haid, Hal, B: Dec. 21, 1897, Barberton, Ohio; D: Aug. 13, 1952, Los Angeles, Calif. Pitcher (1933).

Hairston, Jerry, B: Feb. 16, 1952, Birmingham, Ala. Outfielder/pinch-hitter (1973–77, 1981–90).

Mid-1960s White Sox (left to right): Ron Hansen, Gary Peters, Moose Skowron, coach Tony Cuccinello, J.C. Martin, and Eddie Fisher

Hairston, Sam, B: Jan. 20, 1920, Crawford, Miss.; D: Oct. 31, 1997, Birmingham, Ala. Catcher (1951).

Hajduk, Chet, B: July 21, 1918, Chicago, Ill.; D: July 5, 2006, Chicago, Ill. Pinch-hitter (1941).

Hall, Joe, B: Mar. 6, 1966, Paducah, Ky. Outfielder (1994).

Hall, Toby, B: Oct. 21, 1975, Tacoma, Wash. Catcher (2007–08).

Hallett, Jack, B: Nov. 13, 1914, Toledo, Ohio; D: June 11, 1982, Toledo, Ohio. Pitcher (1940–41).

Hallman, Bill, B: Mar. 15, 1876, Philadelphia, Pa.; D: Apr. 23, 1950, Philadelphia, Pa. Outfielder (1903).

Hamilton, Dave, B: Dec. 13, 1947, Seattle, Wash.; Pitcher (1975–77).

Hamilton, Jack, B: Dec. 25, 1938, Burlington, Iowa. Pitcher (1969).

Hamilton, Steve, B: Nov. 30, 1935, Columbia, Ky.; D: Dec. 2, 1997, Morehead, Ky. Pitcher (1970).

Hammaker, Atlee, B: Jan. 24, 1958, Carmel, Calif. Pitcher (1994–95).

Hamner, Ralph, B: Sept. 12, 1916, Gibsland, La.; D: May 22, 2001, Little Rock, Ark. Pitcher (1946).

Hancock, Fred, B: Mar. 28, 1920, Allenport, Pa.; D: Mar. 12, 1986, Clearwater, Fla. Infielder (1946).

Hansen, Ron, B: Apr. 5, 1938, Oxford, Neb. Infielder (1963–67, 1968–69).

Hanski, Don, B: Feb. 27, 1916, La Porte, Ind.; D: Sept. 2, 1957, Worth, Ill. Infielder (1943–44).

Happenny, John, B: May 18, 1901, Waltham, Mass.; D: Dec. 29, 1988, Coral Springs, Fla. Infielder (1923).

Hardgrove, Pat, B: May 10, 1895, Palmyra, Kan.; D: Jan. 26, 1973, Jackson, Miss. Pinch-hitter (1918).

Hardy, Jack, B: Oct. 8, 1959, St. Petersburg, Fla. Pitcher (1989).

Harrell, Lucas, B: June 3, 1985, Springfield, Mo. Pitcher (2010–).

Harris, Dave, B: July 14, 1900, Summerfield, N.C.; D: Sept. 18, 1973, Atlanta, Ga. Outfielder (1930).

Harris, Spence, B: Aug. 12, 1900, Duluth, Minn.; D: July 3, 1982, Minneapolis, Minn. Outfielder (1925–26).

Harris, Willie, B: June 22, 1978, Cairo, Ga. Infielder (2002–05).

Harrist, Earl, B: Apr. 20, 1919, Dubach, La.; D: Sept. 1, 1998, Sinsboro, La. Pitcher (1947–48, 53).

Harshman, Jack, B: July 12, 1927, San Diego, Calif. Pitcher (1954–57).

Hart, Jim "Hub," B: Feb. 2, 1878, Everett, Mass.; D: Oct. 10, 1960, Fort Wayne, Ind. Catcher (1905–07).

Hartman, Fred, B: Apr. 25, 1868, Allegheny, Pa.; D: Nov. 11, 1938, McKeesport, Pa. Infielder (1901).

Harvey, Ervin, B: Jan. 5, 1879, Saratoga, Calif.; D: June 3, 1954, Santa Monica, Calif. Pitcher (1901).

Hasbrook, Bob "Ziggy," B: Nov. 21, 1893, Grundy Center, Iowa; D: Feb. 9, 1976, Garland, Tex. Infielder (1916–17).

Hassey, Ron, B: Feb. 27, 1953, Tucson, Ariz. Catcher (1986–87).

Hatfield, Fred, B: Mar. 18, 1925, Lanett, Ala. Infielder (1956–57).

Hatton, Grady, B: Oct. 7, 1922, Beaumont, Tex. Infielder (1954).

Hayes, Frankie, B: Oct. 13, 1914, Jamesburg, N.J.; D: June 22, 1955, Point Pleasant, N.J. Catcher (1946).

Hayes, Jackie, B: July 19, 1906, Clanton, Ala.; D: Feb. 9, 1983, Birmingham, Ala. Infielder (1932–40).

Haynes, Joe, B: Sept. 21, 1917, Lincolnton, Ga.; D: Jan. 6, 1967, Hopkins, Minn. Pitcher (1941–48).

Heath, Bill, B: Mar. 10, 1939, Yuba City, Calif. Catcher (1965).

Heath, Spencer, B: Nov. 15, 1894, Chicago, Ill.; D: Jan. 25, 1930, Chicago, Ill. Pitcher (1920).

Heathcott, Mike, B: May 16, 1969, Chicago, Ill. Pitcher (1998).

Heim, Val, B: Nov. 4, 1920, Plymouth, Wis. Outfielder (1942).

Held, Woodie, B: Mar. 25, 1932, Sacramento, Calif.; D: June 11, 2009, Dubois, Wy. Infielder (1968–69).

Hemond, Scott, B: Nov. 18, 1965, Taunton, Mass. Catcher/infielder (1992).

Hemphill, Frank, B: May 13, 1878, Greenville, Mich.; D: Nov. 16, 1950, Chicago, Ill. Outfielder (1906).

Henderson, Joe, B: July 4, 1946, Lake Cormorant, Miss. Pitcher (1974).

Ken Henderson (left) and Ron Santo

Mike Hershberger

Henderson, Ken, B: June 15, 1946, Carroll, Iowa. Outfielder (1973–75).

Henline, Walter "Butch," B: Dec. 20, 1894, Fort Wayne, Ind.; D: Oct. 9, 1957, Sarasota, Fla. Catcher (1930–31).

Henry, Frank "Dutch," B: May 12, 1902, Cleveland, Ohio; D: Aug. 23, 1968, Cleveland, Ohio. Pitcher (1929–30).

Herbert, Ray, B: Dec. 15, 1929, Detroit, Mich. Pitcher (1961–64).

Hermanson, Dustin, B: Dec. 21, 1972, Springfield, Ohio. Pitcher (2005–06).

Hernandez, Orlando "El Duque," B: Oct. 11, 1969, Havana, Cuba. Pitcher (2005).

Hernandez, Roberto, B: Nov. 11, 1964, Santurce, P.R. Pitcher (1991–97).

Hernandez, Rudy, B: Oct. 18, 1951, Enpalme, Mexico. Infielder (1972).

Herring, Art, B: Mar. 10, 1907, Altus, Okla.; D: Dec. 2, 1995, Marion, Ind. Pitcher (1939).

Herrmann, Ed, B: Aug. 27, 1946, San Diego, Calif. Catcher (1967, '69–74).

Hershberger, Mike, B: Oct. 9, 1939, Massillon, Ohio. Outfielder (1961–64, 1971).

Heving, Joe, B: Sept. 2, 1900, Covington, Ky.; D: Apr. 11, 1970, Covington, Ky. Pitcher (1933–34).

Heydon, Mike, B: July 15, 1874, Missouri; D: Oct. 13, 1913, Indianapolis, Ind. Catcher (1904).

Hibbard, Greg, B: Sept. 13, 1964, New Orleans, La. Pitcher (1989–92).

Hickey, Kevin, B: Feb. 25, 1956, Chicago, Ill. Pitcher (1981–83).

Hickman, Charles "Piano Legs," B: May 4, 1876, Taylortown, Pa.; D: Apr. 19, 1934, Morgantown, W.Va. Infielder (1907).

Hicks, Jim, B: May 18, 1940, East Chicago, Ind. Outfielder (1964–66).

Hicks, Joe, B: Apr. 7, 1933, Ivy, Va. Outfielder (1959–60).

Higdon, Bill, B: Apr. 27, 1924, Camp Hill, Ala.; D: Apr. 30, 1986, Pascagouia, Miss. Outfielder (1949).

Higgins, Dennis, B: Aug. 4, 1939, Jefferson City, Mo. Pitcher (1966–67).

Hill, Donnie, B: Nov. 12, 1960, Pomona, Calif. Infielder (1987–88).

Hill, Marc, B: Feb. 18, 1952, Elsberry, Mo. Catcher (1981–86).

Hillegas, Shawn, B: Aug. 21, 1964, Dos Palos, Calif. Pitcher (1988–90).

Hinton, Rich, B: May 22, 1947, Tucson, Ariz. Pitcher (1971, 1975, 1978–79).

Hoag, Myril, B: Mar. 9, 1908, Davis, Calif.; D: July 28, 1971, High Springs, Fla. Outfielder (1941–42, 1944).

Hockett, Oris, B: Sept. 29, 1909, Amboy, Ind.; D: Mar. 23, 1969, Torrance, Calif. Outfielder (1945).

Hodapp, Johnny, B: Sept. 26, 1905, Cincinnati, Ohio; D: June 14, 1980, Cincinnati, Ohio. Outfielder (1932).

Hodge, Clarence "Shovel," B: July 6, 1893, Mount Andrew, Ala.; D: Dec. 31, 1967, Fort Walton Beach, Fla. Pitcher (1920–22).

Hodgin, Ralph, B: Feb. 10, 1916, Greensboro, N.C. Outfielder (1943–44, 1946–48).

Hoffman, Clarence "Dutch," B: Jan. 28, 1904, Freeburg, Ill.; D: Dec. 6, 1962, Belleville, Ill. Outfielder (1929).

Hoffman, Guy, B: July 9, 1956, Ottawa, Ill. Pitcher (1979–80, 1983).

Holcombe, Ken, B: Aug. 23, 1918, Burnsville, N.C.; D: Mar. 15, 2010, Weaverville, N.C. Pitcher (1950–52).

Hollingsworth, Al, B: Feb. 25, 1908, St. Louis, Mo.; D: Apr. 28, 1996, Austin, Tex. Pitcher (1946).

Gail Hopkins

Holmes, James "Ducky," B: Jan. 28, 1869, Des Moines, Iowa; D: Aug. 6, 1932, Truro, Iowa. Outfielder (1903–05).

Hooper, Harry, B: Aug. 24, 1887, Bell Station, Calif.; D: Dec. 18, 1974, Santa Cruz, Calif. Outfielder (1921–25).

Hopkins, Gail, B: Feb. 19, 1943, Tulsa, Okla. Infielder (1968–70).

Hopkins, Marty, B: Feb. 22, 1907, Wolfe City, Tex.; D: Nov. 20, 1963, Dallas, Tex. Infielder (1934–35).

Horlen, Joel, B: Aug. 14, 1937, San Antonio, Tex. Pitcher (1961–71).

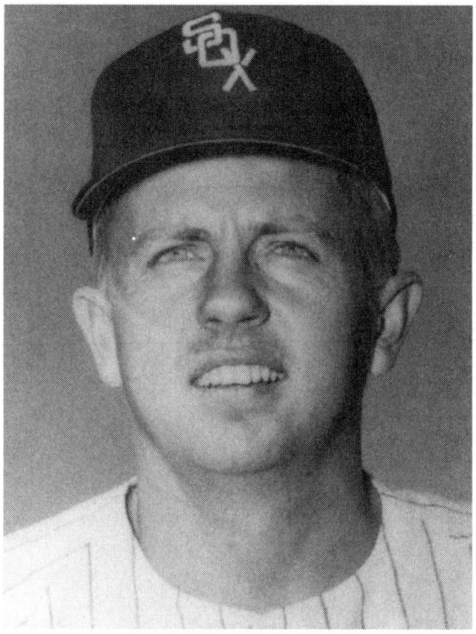

Bruce Howard

Horton, Ricky, B: July 30, 1959, Poughkeepsie, N.Y. Pitcher (1988).

Hottman, Ken, B: May 7, 1948, Stockton, Calif. Outfielder (1971).

Hough, Charlie, B: Jan. 5, 1948, Honolulu, Hawaii. Pitcher (1991–92).

Hovlik, Joe, B: Aug. 16, 1884, Austria-Hungary; D: Nov. 3, 1951, Oxford Junction, Iowa. Pitcher (1911).

Howard, Bruce, B: Mar. 23, 1943, Salisbury, Md. Pitcher (1963–67).

Howard, Chris, B: Nov. 18, 1965, Lynn, Mass. Pitcher (1993).

Howard, Fred, B: Sept. 2, 1956, Portland, Maine. Pitcher (1979).

Howell, Millard "Dixie," B: Jan. 7, 1920, Bowman, Ky.; D: Mar. 18, 1960, Hollywood, Fla. Pitcher (1955–58).

Howitt, Dann, B: Feb. 13, 1964, Battle Creek, Mich. Infielder (1994).

Howry, Bob, B: Aug. 4, 1973, Phoenix, Ariz. Pitcher (1998–2002).

Hoy, William "Dummy," B: May 23, 1862, Houckstown, Ohio; D: Dec. 15, 1961, Cincinnati, Ohio. Outfielder (1901).

Hoyt, LaMarr, B: Jan. 1, 1955, Columbia, S.C. Pitcher (1979–84).

Hudson, Daniel, B: Mar. 9, 1987, Lynchburg, Va. Pitcher (2009–10).

Hudson, Hal, B: May 4, 1927, Grosse Pointe, Mich. Pitcher (1952–53).

Huelsman, Frank, B: June 5, 1874, St. Louis, Mo.; D: June 9, 1959, Afton, Mo. Outfielder (1904).

Millard "Dixie" Howell

John Humphries

Huff, Mike, B: Aug. 11, 1963, Honolulu, Hawaii. Outfielder (1991–93).

Hughes, Ed, B: Oct. 5, 1880, Chicago, Ill.; D: Oct. 11, 1927, McHenry, Ill. Catcher (1902).

Hughes, Jim, B: Mar. 21, 1923, Chicago, Ill.; D: Aug. 12, 2001, Chicago, Ill. Pitcher (1957).

Hulett, Tim, B: Jan. 20, 1960, Springfield, Ill. Infielder (1983–87).

Humphries, John, B: June 23, 1915, Clifton Forge, Va.; D: June 24, 1965, New Orleans, La. Pitcher (1941–45).

Hunnefield, Bill, B: Jan. 5, 1899, Dedham, Mass.; D: Aug. 28, 1976, Nantucket, Mass. Infielder (1926–30).

Huntz, Steve, B: Dec. 3, 1945, Cleveland, Ohio. Infielder (1971).

Hutchinson, Ira, B: Aug. 31, 1910, Chicago, Ill.; D: Aug. 21, 1973, Chicago, Ill. Pitcher (1933).

I

Iguchi, Tadahito, B: Dec. 4, 1974, Tokyo, Japan. Infielder (2005–07).

Infante, Gregory, B: July 10, 1987, Caracas, Venezuela, Pitcher (2010–).

Isbell, Frank, B: Aug. 21, 1875, Delevan, N.Y.; D: July 15, 1941, Wichita, Kan. Pitcher/infielder (1900–09).

Tadahito Iguchi

J

Jackson, Charlie, B: Feb. 7, 1894, Granite City, Ill.; D: May 27, 1968, Radford, Va. Pinch-hitter (1915).

Jackson, Darrin, B: Aug. 22, 1963, Los Angeles, Calif. Outfielder (1994).

Jackson, Edwin, B: Sept. 9, 1983, Neu-Ulm, West Germany. Pitcher (2010–).

Jackson, Joe, B: July 16, 1887, Brandon Mills, S.C.; D: Dec. 5, 1951, Greenville, S.C. Outfielder (1915–20).

Jackson, Mike, B: Dec. 22, 1964, Houston, Tex. Pitcher (2004).

Jackson, Ron, B: Oct. 22, 1933, Kalamazoo, Mich.; D: June 6, 2008, Kalamazoo, Mich. Infielder (1954–59).

Jackson, Vincent "Bo," B: Nov. 30, 1962, Bessemer, Ala. Outfielder/DH (1991–93).

Bo Jackson

Bobby Jenks

Jacobs, Elmer, B: Aug. 10, 1892, Salem, Mo.; D: Feb. 10, 1958, Salem, Mo. Pitcher (1927).

Jacobs, Otto, B: Apr. 19, 1889, Chicago, Ill.; D: Nov. 19, 1955, Chicago, Ill. Catcher (1918).

Jacquez, Pat, B: Apr. 23, 1947, Stockton, Calif. Pitcher (1971).

James, Bill, B: Jan. 20, 1887, Detroit, Mich.; D: May 24, 1942, Venice, Calif. Pitcher (1919).

James, Bob, B: Aug. 18, 1958, Glendale, Calif. Pitcher (1985–87).

Janeski, Gerry, B: Apr. 18, 1946, Pasadena, Calif. Pitcher (1970).

Jasper, Harry "Hi," B: Nov. 15, 1880, St. Louis, Mo.; D: May 22, 1937, St. Louis, Mo. Pitcher (1914–15).

Jefferson, Jesse, B: Mar. 3, 1949, Midlothian, Va. Pitcher (1975–76).

Jeffries, Irv, B: Sept. 10, 1905, Louisville, Ky.; D: June 8, 1982, Louisville, Ky. Infielder (1930–31).

Jenkins, Joe, B: Oct. 12, 1890, Shelbyville, Tenn.; D: June 21, 1974, Fresno, Calif. Catcher (1917, 1919).

Jenkins, John, B: July 7, 1896, Bosworth, Mo.; D: Aug. 3, 1968, Columbia, Mo. Infielder (1922).

Jenks, Bobby, B: Mar. 14, 1981, Mission Hills, Calif. Pitcher (2005–10).

Jeter, John, B: Oct. 24, 1944, Shreveport, La. Outfielder (1973).

Jeter, Shawn, B: June 28, 1966, Shreveport, La. Outfielder (1992).

Jimenez, D'Angelo, B: Dec. 21, 1977, Santo Domingo, Dominican Republic. Infielder (2002–03).

John, Tommy, B: May 22, 1943, Terre Haute, Ind. Pitcher (1965–71).

Johns, Pete, B: Jan. 17, 1889, Cleveland, Ohio; D: Aug. 9, 1964, Cleveland, Ohio. Infielder (1915).

Johnson, Bart, B: Jan. 3, 1950, Torrance, Calif. Pitcher (1969–74, 1976–77).

Johnson, Connie, B: Dec. 27, 1922, Stone Mountain, Ga.; D: Nov. 28, 2004, Kansas City, Mo. Pitcher (1953, 1955–56).

Johnson, Dane, B: Feb. 10, 1963, Coral Gables, Fla. Pitcher (1994).

Johnson, Darrell, B: Aug. 25, 1928, Horace, Neb.; D: May 3, 2004, Fairfield, Calif. Catcher (1952).

Johnson, Deron, B: July 17, 1938, San Diego, Calif.; D: Apr. 23, 1992, Poway, Calif. Infielder (1975).

Johnson, Don, B: Nov. 12, 1926, Portland, Ore. Pitcher (1954).

Johnson, Ellis, B: Dec. 8, 1892, Minneapolis, Minn.; D: Jan. 14, 1965, Minneapolis, Minn. Pitcher (1912, 1915).

Johnson, Ernie, B: Apr. 29, 1888, Chicago, Ill.; D: May 1, 1952, Monrovia, Calif. Infielder 1912, '21–23).

Johnson, Johnny, B: Sept. 29, 1914, Belmore, Ohio; D: June 26, 1991, Iron Mountain, Mich. Pitcher (1945).

Johnson, Lamar, B: Sept. 2, 1950, Bessemer, Ala. Infielder/DH (1974–81).

Johnson, Lance, B: July 6, 1963, Cincinnati, Ohio. Outfielder (1988–95).

Johnson, Larry Doby, B: Aug. 17, 1950, Cleveland, Ohio. Catcher/DH (1978).

Johnson, Mark, B: Sept. 12, 1975, Wheat Ridge, Colo. Catcher (1998–2002).

Johnson, Randall, B: Aug. 15, 1958, Miami, Fla. Outfielder (1980).

Johnson, Stan, B: Feb. 12, 1937, Dallas, Tex. Outfielder (1960).

Johnston, Jimmy, B: Dec. 10, 1889, Cleveland, Tenn.; D: Feb. 14, 1967, Chattanooga, Tenn. Outfielder (1911).

Johnstone, Jay, B: Nov. 20, 1945, Manchester, Conn. Outfielder (1971–72).

Jok, Stan, B: May 3, 1926, Buffalo, N.Y.; D: Mar. 6, 1972, Buffalo, N.Y. Infielder (1954–55).

Jolley, Smead, B: Jan. 14, 1902, Wesson, Ark.; D: Nov. 17, 1991, Alameda, Calif. Outfielder/catcher (1930–32).

Jones, Al, B: Feb. 10, 1959, Charleston, Miss. Pitcher (1983–85).

Jones, Andruw, B: Apr. 23, 1977, Willemstad, Curacao. Outfielder (2010).

Jones, Barry, B: Feb. 15, 1963, Centerville, Ind. Pitcher (1988–90, 1993).

Jones Charles Claude, B: June 2, 1876, Butler, Pa.; D: Apr. 2, 1947, Two Harbors, Minn. Outfielder (1904).

Jones, Cleon, B: Aug. 4, 1942, Plateau, Ala. Outfielder (1976).

Jones, Davy, B: June 30, 1880, Cambria, Wis.; D: Mar. 31, 1972, Mankato, Minn. Outfielder (1913).

Jones, Grover "Deacon," B: Apr. 18, 1934, White Plains, N.Y. Infielder (1962–63, 66).

Jones, Fielder, B: Aug. 13, 1871, Shinglehouse, Pa.; D: Mar. 13, 1934, Portland, Ore. Outfielder (1901–08).

Jones, Jake, B: Nov. 23, 1920, Epps, La.; D: Dec. 13, 2000, Epps, La. Infielder (1941–42, 46–47).

Jay Johnstone

"Sad" Sam Jones

Jones, "Sad" Sam, B: July 26, 1892, Woodsfield, Ohio; D: July 6, 1966, Barnesville, Ohio. Pitcher (1932–35).

Jones, Stacey, B: May 26, 1966, Gadsden, Ala. Pitcher (1996).

Jones, Steve, B: Apr. 22, 1941, Huntington Park, Calif. Pitcher (1967).

Jones, William "Tex," B: Aug. 4, 1885, Marion, Kan.; D: Feb. 26, 1938, Wichita, Kan. Infielder (1911).

Jonnard, Clarence "Bubber," B: Nov. 23, 1897, Nashville, Tenn.; D: Aug. 23, 1977, New York, N.Y. Catcher (1920).

Jordan, Ray "Rip," B: Sept. 28, 1889, Portland, Maine; D: June 5, 1960, Meriden, Conn. Pitcher (1912).

Jordan, Tom, B: Sept. 5, 1919, Lawton, Okla. Catcher (1944, 1946).

Josephson, Duane, B: June 3, 1942, New Hampton, Iowa.; D: Jan. 30, 1997, New Hampton, Iowa. Catcher (1965–70).

Jourdan, Ted, B: Sept. 5, 1895, New Orleans, La.; D: Sept. 23, 1961, New Orleans, La. Infielder (1916–18, 1920).

Joyce, Mike, B: Feb. 12, 1941, Detroit, Mich. Pitcher (1962–63).

Judson, Howie, B: Feb. 16, 1926, Hebron, Ill. Pitcher (1948–52).

Duane Josephson

K

Kaat, Jim, B: Nov. 7, 1938, Zeeland, Mich. Pitcher (1973–75).

Kalin, Frank, B: Oct. 3, 1917, Steubenville, Ohio; D: Jan. 12, 1975, Weirton, W.Va. Pinch-hitter (1943).

Kamm, Willie, B: Feb. 2, 1900, San Francisco, Calif.; D: Dec. 21, 1988, Belmont, Calif. Infielder (1923–31).

Kane, Johnny, B: Feb. 19, 1900, Chicago, Ill.; D: July 25, 1956, Chicago, Ill. Infielder (1925).

Karchner, Matt, B: June 28, 1967, Berwick, Pa. Pitcher (1995–98).

Karkovice, Ron, B: Aug. 8, 1963, Union, N.J. Catcher (1986–97).

Pat Kelly

Katoll, John, B: June 24, 1872, Germany; D: June 18, 1955, Hartland, Ill. Pitcher (1900–02).

Kavanagh, Charlie, B: June 9, 1893, Chicago, Ill.; D: Sept. 6, 1973, Reedsburg, Wis. Pinch-hitter (1914).

Kealey, Steve, B: May 13, 1947, Torrance, Calif. Pitcher (1971–73).

Keedy, Pat, B: Jan. 10, 1958, Birmingham, Ala. Infielder (1987).

Keegan, Bob, B: Aug. 4, 1920, Rochester, N.Y.; D: June 20, 2001, Rochester, N.Y. Pitcher (1953–58).

Kell, George, B: Aug. 23, 1922, Swifton, Ark.; D: Mar. 24, 2009, Swifton, Ark. Infielder (1954–56).

Kelly, Al "Red," B: Nov. 15, 1884, Union, Ill.; D: Feb. 4, 1961, Zepherhills, Fla. Outfielder (1910).

Kelly, Pat, B: July 30, 1944, Philadelphia, Pa.; D: Oct. 2, 2005, Baltimore, Md. Outfielder (1971–76).

Kemmerer, Russ, B: Nov. 1, 1931, Pittsburgh, Pa. Pitcher (1960–62).

Kemp, Steve, B: Aug. 7, 1954, San Angelo, Tex. Outfielder (1982).

Kennedy, Bill, B: Mar. 14, 1921, Carnesville, Ga.; D: Apr. 9, 1983, Seattle, Wash. Pitcher (1952).

Kennedy, Bob, B: Aug. 18, 1920, Chicago, Ill.; D: Apr. 7, 2005, Mesa, Ariz. Infielder (1939–42, 1946–48, 1955–57).

Kennedy, Vern, B: Mar. 20, 1907, Kansas City, Mo.; D: Jan. 28, 1993, Mendon, Mo. Pitcher (1934–37).

Steve Kemp

Don Kessinger

Kenworthy, Dick, B: Apr. 1, 1941, Red Oak, Iowa.; D: Apr. 22, 2010, Kansas City, Mo. Infielder (1962, 1964–68).

Keough, Joe, B: Jan. 7, 1946, Pomona, Calif. Pinch-hitter (1973).

Keriazakos, Gus, B: July 28, 1931, West Orange, N.J.; D: May 4, 1996, Hilton Head, S.C. Pitcher (1950).

Kern, Jim, B: Mar. 15, 1949, Gladwin, Mich. Pitcher (1982–83).

Kerr, Dickie, B: July 3, 1893, St. Louis, Mo.; D: May 4, 1963, Houston, Tex. Pitcher (1919–21, 25).

Kerr, John, B: Nov. 26, 1898, San Francisco, Calif.; D: Oct. 19, 1993, Long Beach, Calif. Infielder (1924–31).

Kessinger, Don, B: July 17, 1942, Forrest City, Ark. Infielder (1977–79).

Keyser, Brian, B: Oct. 31, 1966, Castro Valley, Calif. Pitcher (1995–96).

Kiefer, Joe, B: July 19, 1899, West Leyden, N.Y.; D: July 5, 1975, Utica, N.Y. Pitcher (1920).

Kimm, Bruce, B: June 29, 1951, Cedar Rapids, Iowa. Catcher (1980).

Kimsey, Chad, B: Aug. 6, 1905, Cooperhill, Tenn.; D: Dec. 3, 1942, Pryor, Okla. Pitcher (1932–33).

Kinder, Ellis, B: July 26, 1914, Atkins, Ark.; D: Oct. 16, 1968, Jackson, Tenn. Pitcher (1956–57).

King, Eric, B: Apr. 10, 1964, Oxnard, Calif. Pitcher (1989–90).

King, Jim, B: Aug. 27, 1932, Elkins, Ark. Outfielder (1967).

Kinzy, Harry, B: July 19, 1910, Hallsville, Tex.; D: June 22, 2003, Fort Worth, Tex. Pitcher (1934).

Kirkwood, Don, B: Sept. 24, 1949, Pontiac, Mich. Pitcher (1977).

Kirrene, Joe, B: Oct. 4, 1931, San Francisco, Calif. Infielder (1950, 1954).

Kittle, Ron, B: Jan. 5, 1958, Gary, Ind. Outfielder/infielder (1982–86, 89–90, 91).

Klaerner, Hugo, B: Oct. 15, 1908, Fredericksburg, Tex.; D: Jan. 3, 1982, Fredericksburg, Tex. Pitcher (1934).

Klages, Fred, B: Oct. 31, 1943, Ambridge, Pa. Pitcher (1966–67).

Klepfer, Ed, B: Mar. 17, 1888, Summerville, Pa.; D: Aug. 9, 1950, Tulsa, Okla. Pitcher (1915).

Klieman, Eddie, B: Mar. 21, 1918, Norwood, Ohio; D: Nov. 15, 1979, Homosassa, Fla. Pitcher (1949).

Klinger, Joe, B: Aug. 2, 1902, Cannonsburg, Pa.; D: July 31, 1960, Little Rock, Ark. Catcher (1930).

Kluszewski, Ted, B: Sept. 10, 1924, Argo, Ill.; D: Mar. 29, 1988, Cincinnati, Ohio. Infielder (1959–60).

Knapp, Chris, B: Sept. 16, 1953, Cherry Point, N.C. Pitcher (1975–77).

Billy Koch

Knickerbocker, Bill, B: Dec. 29, 1911, Los Angeles, Calif.; D: Sept. 8, 1963, Sebastopol, Calif. Infielder (1941).

Knoop, Bobby, B: Oct. 18, 1938, Sioux City, Iowa. Infielder (1969–70).

Knott, Jack, B: Mar. 2, 1907, Dallas, Tex.; D: Oct. 13, 1981, Brownwood, Tex. Pitcher (1938–40).

Koch, Billy, B: Dec. 14, 1974, Rockville Center, N.Y. Pitcher (2003–04).

Kolloway, Don, B: Aug. 4, 1918, Posen, Ill.; D: June 30, 1994, Blue Island, Ill. Infielder (1940–43, 1946–49).

Konerko, Paul, B: Mar. 5, 1976, Providence, R.I. Infielder (1999–).

Koosman, Jerry, B: Dec. 23, 1942, Appleton, Minn. Pitcher (1981–83).

Kotsay, Mark, B: Dec. 2, 1975, Whittier, Calif. Infielder/Outfielder (2009–10).

Kowalik, Fabian, B: Apr. 22, 1908, Falls City, Tex.; D: Aug. 14, 1954, Karnes City, Tex. Pitcher (1932).

Kozar, Al, B: July 5, 1921, McKees Rocks, Pa.; D: Sept. 6, 2007, Palm Beach Gardens, Fla. Infielder (1950).

Kravec, Ken, B: July 29, 1951, Cleveland, Ohio. Pitcher (1975–80).

Kreevich, Mike, B: June 10, 1908, Mount Olive, Ill.; D: Apr. 25, 1994, Pana, Ill. Outfielder (1935–41).

Kreitz, Ralph, B: Nov. 13, 1885, Plum Creek, Neb.; D: July 20, 1941, Portland, Ore. Catcher (1911).

Kress, Charlie, B: Dec. 9, 1921, Philadelphia, Pa. Infielder (1949–50).

Don Kolloway

Kress, Ralph "Red," B: Jan. 2, 1907, Columbia, Calif.; D: Nov. 29, 1962, Los Angeles, Calif. Outfielder (1932–33).

Kretlow, Lou, B: June 27, 1921, Apache, Okla.; D: Sept. 12, 2007, Enid, Okla. Pitcher (1950–53).

Kreuter, Chad, B: Aug. 26, 1964, LaQuinta, Calif. Catcher (1996).

Kreutzer, Frank, B: Feb. 7, 1939, Buffalo, N.Y. Pitcher (1962–64).

Krsnich, Rocky, B: Aug. 5, 1927, West Allis, Wis. Infielder (1949, 52–53).

Kruk, John, B: Feb. 9, 1961, Charleston, W.Va. DH (1995).

Kucek, Jack, B: June 8, 1953, Warren, Ohio. Pitcher (1974–78, 79).

Kuhel, Joe, B: June 25, 1906, Cleveland, Ohio; D: Feb. 26, 1984, Kansas City, Kan. Infielder (1938–43, 1946–47).

Kuhn, Walt, B: Feb. 2, 1884, Fresno, Calif.; D: June 14, 1935, Fresno, Calif. Catcher (1912–14).

Kuntz, Rusty, B: Feb. 4, 1955, Orange, Calif. Outfielder (1979–83).

Kusnyer, Art, B: Dec. 19, 1945, Akron, Ohio. Catcher (1970).

Kutzler, Jerry, B: Mar. 25, 1965, Waukegan, Ill. Pitcher (1990).

Kuzava, Bob, B: May 28, 1923, Wyandotte, Mich. Pitcher (1949–50).

L

LaGrow, Lerrin, B: July 8, 1948, Phoenix, Ariz. Pitcher (1977–79).

Lamabe, Jack, B: Oct. 3, 1936, Farmingdale, N.Y.; D: Dec. 21, 2007, Baton Rouge, La. Pitcher (1966–67).

Lamline, Fred, B: Aug. 14, 1887, Port Huron, Mich.; D: Sept. 20, 1970, Port Huron, Mich. Pitcher (1912).

Lamp, Dennis, B: Sept. 23, 1952, Los Angeles, Calif. Pitcher (1981–83).

Lerrin LaGrow

Jim Landis

Landenberger, Ken, B: July 29, 1928, Lyndhurst, Ohio; D: July 28, 1960, Cleveland, Ohio. Infielder (1952).

Landis, Jim, B: Mar. 9, 1934, Fresno, Calif. Outfielder (1957–64).

Landrum, Jesse, B: July 31, 1912, Crockett, Tex.; D: June 27, 1983, Beaumont, Tex. Infielder (1938).

Lane, Dick, B: June 28, 1927, Highland Park, Mich. Outfielder (1949).

Lange, Frank, B: Oct. 28, 1883, Columbia, Wis.; D: Dec. 26, 1945, Madison, Wis. Pitcher (1910–13).

LaPalme, Paul, B: Dec. 14, 1923, Springfield, Mass.; D: Feb 7, 2010, Leominster, Mass. Pitcher (1956–57).

LaPoint, Dave, B: July 29, 1959, Glens Falls, N.Y. Pitcher (1987–88).

Lapp, Jack, B: Sept. 10, 1884, Frazer, Pa.; D: Feb. 6, 1920, Philadelphia, Pa. Catcher (1916).

Larsen, Don, B: Aug. 7, 1929, Michigan City, Ind. Pitcher (1961).

Lary, Frank, B: Apr. 10, 1930, Northport, Ala. Pitcher (1965).

Lathrop, Bill, B: Aug. 12, 1891, Hanover, Wis.; D: Nov. 20, 1958, Janesville, Wis. Pitcher (1913–14).

Latman, Barry, B: May 21, 1936, Los Angeles, Calif. Pitcher (1957–59).

LaValliere, Mike, B: Aug. 18, 1960, Charlotte, N.C. Catcher (1993–95).

Law, Rudy, B: Oct. 7, 1956, Waco, Tex. Outfielder (1982–85).

Carlos Lee

Law, Vance, B: Oct. 1, 1956, Boise, Idaho. Infielder (1982–84).

Lawrence, Bob, B: Dec. 14, 1899, Brooklyn, N.Y.; D: Nov. 6, 1983, Jamaica, N.Y. Pitcher (1924).

Lazar, Danny, B: Nov. 14, 1943, East Chicago, Ind. Pitcher (1968–69).

Leach, Terry, B: Mar. 13, 1954, Selma, Ala. Pitcher (1992–93).

Lee, Carlos, B: June 20, 1976, Aguadulce, Panama. Outfielder (1999–2004).

Lee, Thornton, B: Sept. 13, 1906, Sonoma, Calif.; D: June 9, 1997, Tucson, Ariz. Pitcher (1937–47).

Lees, George, B: Feb. 2, 1895, Bethlehem, Pa.; D: Jan. 2, 1980, Mechanicsburg, Pa. Catcher (1921).

LeFlore, Ron, B: June 16, 1948, Detroit, Mich. Outfielder (1981–82).

Lehner, Paul, B: July 1, 1920, Dolomite, Ala.; D: Dec. 27, 1967, Birmingham, Ala. Outfielder (1951).

Leibold, Harry "Nemo," B: Feb. 17, 1892, Butler, Ind.; D: Feb. 4, 1977, Detroit, Mich. Outfielder (1915–20).

Leifer, Elmer, B: May 23, 1893, Clarington, Ohio; D: Sept. 26, 1948, Everett, Wash. Outfielder (1921).

Leitner, George "Dummy," B: June 19, 1871, Parkton, Md.; D: Feb. 20, 1960, Baltimore, Md. Pitcher (1902).

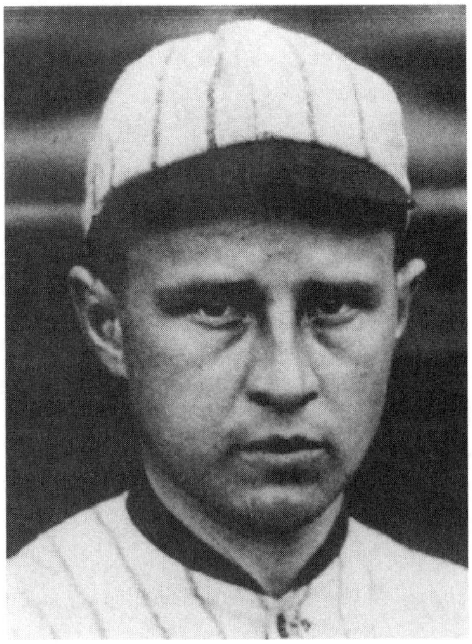

Harry "Nemo" Leibold

Esteban Loaiza

Lemon, Chet, B: Feb. 12, 1955, Jackson, Miss. Outfielder (1975–81).
Lemon, Jim, B: Mar. 23, 1928, Covington, Va.; D: May 14, 2006, Brandon, Miss. Infielder (1963).
Lemonds, Dave, B: July 5, 1948, Charlotte, N.C. Pitcher (1972).
Lenhardt, Don, B: Oct. 4, 1922, Alton, Ill. Outfielder (1951).
Leon, Eddie, B: Aug. 11, 1946, Tucson, Ariz. Infielder (1973–74).
Leopold, Rudy, B: July 27, 1905, Grand Cane, La.; D: Sept. 3, 1965, Baton Rouge, La. Pitcher (1928).

Chet Lemon

Lepcio, Ted, B: July 28, 1930, Utica, N.Y. Infielder (1961).
Leverett, Gorham "Dixie," B: Mar. 29, 1894, Georgetown, Tex.; D: Feb. 20, 1957, Beaverton, Ore. Pitcher (1922–24, 1926).
Levine, Alan, B: May 22, 1968, Park Ridge, Ill. Pitcher (1996–97).
Lewis, Darren, B: Aug. 28, 1967, Berkeley, Calif. Outfielder (1996–97).
Liefer, Jeff, B: Aug. 17, 1974, Fontana, Calif. Outfielder (1999–2002).
Lillibridge, Brent, B: Sept. 18, 1983, Everett, Wash. Infielder (2009–).
Lindsey, Bill, B: Apr. 12, 1960, Staten Island, N.Y. Catcher (1987).
Lindsey, Doug, B: Sept. 22, 1967, Austin, Tex. Catcher (1993).
Lindstrom, Charlie, B: Sept. 7, 1936, Chicago, Ill. Catcher (1958).
Linebrink, Scott, B: Aug. 4, 1976, Austin, Tex. Pitcher (2008–10).
Little, Bryan, B: Oct. 8, 1959, Houston, Tex. Infielder (1985–86).
Littlefield, Dick, B: Mar. 18, 1926, Detroit, Mich.; D: Nov. 20, 1997, Detroit, Mich. Pitcher (1951).
Loaiza, Esteban, B: Dec. 31, 1971, Tijuana, Mexico. Pitcher (2003–04; 2008).
Locker, Bob, B: Mar. 15, 1938, George, Iowa. Pitcher (1965–69).
Lodigiani, Dario, B: July 16, 1916, San Francisco, Calif.; D: Feb. 10, 2008, Napa, Calif. Infielder (1941–42, 1946).
Logan, Boone, B: Aug. 13, 1984, San Antonio, Tex. Pitcher (2006–08).
Lolich, Ron, B: Sept. 19, 1946, Portland, Ore. Outfielder (1971).
Lollar, Sherm, B: Aug. 23, 1924, Durham, Ark.; D: Sept. 24, 1977, Springfield, Mo. Catcher (1952–63).
Lollar, Tim, B: Mar. 17, 1956, Poplar Bluff, Mo. Pitcher (1985).
Long, Bill, B: Feb. 29, 1960, Cincinnati, Ohio. Pitcher (1985, 1987–90).
Long, Jim, B: June 29, 1898, Fort Dodge, Iowa; D: Sept. 14, 1970, Fort Dodge, Iowa. Catcher (1922).
Long, Jeoff, B: Oct. 9, 1941, Covington, Ky. Infielder (1964).
Look, Dean, B: July 23, 1937, Lansing, Mich. Catcher (1961).
Lopat, Ed, B: June 21, 1918, New York, N.Y.; D: June 15, 1992, Darien, Conn. Pitcher (1944–47).
Lopez, Pedro, B: Apr. 28, 1984, Moca, D.R. Infielder (2005).
Lord, Harry, B: Mar. 8, 1882, Porter, Maine; D: Aug. 9, 1948, Westbrook, Maine. Infielder (1910–14).
Lorraine, Andrew, B: Aug. 11, 1972, Los Angeles, Calif. Pitcher (1995).
Lovett, Merritt "Mem," B: June 15, 1912, Chicago, Ill. Pinch-hitter (1933).
Loviglio, Jay, B: May 30, 1956, Freeport, N.Y. Infielder (1981–82).
Lowe, Sean, B: Mar. 29, 1971, Dallas, Tex. Pitcher (1999–2001).
Lowdermilk, Grover, B: Jan. 15, 1885, Sandborn, Ind.; D: Mar. 31, 1968, Odin, Ill. Pitcher (1919–20).
Lown, Omar "Turk," B: May 30, 1924, Ridgewood, N.Y. Pitcher (1958–62).
Lucy, Donny, B: Aug. 8, 1982, Escondido, Calif. Catcher (2007; 2010–).
Lundquist, David, B: June 4, 1973, Beverly, Mass. Pitcher (1999).
Lupien, Ulysses "Tony," B: Apr. 23, 1917, Chelmsford, Mass.; D: July 9, 2004, Norwich, Tex. Infielder (1948).
Luzinski, Greg, B: Nov. 22, 1950, Chicago, Ill. DH (1981–84).
Lyle, Albert "Sparky," B: July 22, 1944, Du Bois, Pa. Pitcher (1982).

Ted Lyons

Lynn, Byrd, B: Mar. 13, 1889, Unionville, Ill.; D: Feb. 5, 1940, Napa, Calif. Catcher (1916–20).

Lyons, Barry, B: June 3, 1960, Biloxi, Miss. Catcher (1995).

Lyons, Steve, B: June 3, 1960, Tacoma, Wash. Infielder/outfielder (1986–91).

Lyons, Ted, B: Dec. 28, 1900, Lake Charles, La.; D: July 25, 1986, Sulphur, La. Pitcher (1923–42, 1946).

Lyttle, Jim, B: May 20, 1946, Hamilton, Ohio. Outfielder (1972).

M

MacDougal, Mike, B: Mar. 5, 1977, Las Vegas, Nev. Pitcher (2006–09).

Machado, Robert, B: June 3, 1973, Caracas, Venezuela. Catcher (1996–98).

Mack, Frank, B: Feb. 2, 1900, Oklahoma City, Okla.; D: July 2, 1971, Clearwater, Fla. Pitcher (1922–23, 1925).

Mackowiak, Rob, B: June 20, 1976, Oak Lawn, Ill. Infielder/outfielder (2006–07).

Madjeski, Ed, B: July 20, 1908, Far Rockaway, N.Y.; D: Nov. 11, 1994, Montgomery, Ohio. Catcher (1934).

Magnuson, Jim, B: Aug. 18, 1946, Marinette, Wis.; D: May 30, 1991, Green Bay, Wis. Pitcher (1970–71).

Magoon, George, B: Mar. 27, 1875, St. Albans, Maine; D: Dec. 6, 1943, Rochester, N.H. Infielder (1903).

Magrane, Joe, B: July 2, 1964, Des Moines, Iowa. Pitcher (1996).

Mahoney, Bob, B: June 20, 1928, Leroy, Minn.; D: Aug. 27, 2000, Lincoln, Neb. Pitcher (1951).

Majeski, Hank, B: Dec. 13, 1916, Staten Island, N.Y.; D: Aug. 9, 1991, Staten Island, N.Y. Infielder (1950–51).

Mallonee, Jule, B: Apr. 4, 1900, Charlotte, N.C.; D: Oct. 26, 1934, Charlotte, N.C. Outfielder (1925).

Malone, Eddie, B: June 16, 1920, Chicago, Ill.; D: June 1, 2006, Laguna Hills, Calif. Catcher (1949–50).

Maltzberger, Gordon, B: Sept. 4, 1912, Utopia, Tex.; D: Dec. 11, 1974, Rialto, Calif. Pitcher (1943–44, 1946–47).

Manda, Carl, B: Nov. 16, 1888, Little River, Kan.; D: Mar. 9, 1983, Artesia, N.Mex. Infielder (1914).

Mangum, Leo, B: May 24, 1896, Durham, N.C.; D: July 9, 1974, Lima, Ohio. Pitcher (1924–25).

Mann, Johnny, B: Feb. 4, 1898, Fontanet, Ind.; D: Mar. 31, 1977, Terre Haute, Ind. Infielder (1928).

Manrique, Fred, B: Nov. 5, 1961, Edo Bolivar, Venezuela. Infielder (1987–89).

Carlos May

Manuel, Mark "Moxie," B: Oct. 16, 1881, Metropolis, Ill.; D: Apr. 26, 1924, Memphis, Tenn. Pitcher (1908).

Manzanillo, Ravelo, B: Oct. 17, 1963, San Pedro de Macorís, Dominican Republic. Pitcher (1988).

Marcum, Johnny, B: Sept. 9, 1909, Cambellsburg, Ky.; D: Sept. 10, 1984, Louisville, Ky. Pitcher (1939).

Marlowe, Dick, B: June 27, 1929, Hickory, N.C.; D: Dec. 30, 1968, Toledo, Ohio. Pitcher (1956).

Marquez, Isidro, B: May 15, 1965, Navoja, Mexico. Pitcher (1995).

Marquez, Jeff, B: Aug. 10, 1984, Vacaville, Calif. Pitcher (2010–).

Marsh, Freddie, B: Jan. 5, 1924, Valley Falls, Kan.; D: Oct. 26, 2006, Corry, Pa. Infielder (1953–54).

Marshall, Willard, B: Feb. 8, 1921, Richmond, Va.; D: Nov. 5, 2000, Norwood, N.J. Outfielder (1954–55).

Marte, Damaso, B: Feb. 14, 1975, Santo Domingo, D.R. Pitcher (2002–05).

Martin, J.C., B: Dec. 13, 1936, Axton, Va. Catcher (1959–67).

Martin, Joe, B: Aug. 28, 1911, Seymour, Mo.; D: Sept. 28, 1960, Buffalo, N.Y. Infielder (1938).

Martin, Morrie, B: Sept. 3, 1922, Dixon, Mo.; D: May 24, 2010, Washington, Mo. Pitcher (1954–56).

Martin, Norberto "Paco," B: Dec. 10, 1966, San Pedro de Macorís, Dominican Republic. Infielder (1993–97).

Brandon McCarthy

Ed McFarland

Martinez, Carlos, B: Aug. 11, 1965, La Guaira, Venezuela.; D: Jan. 24, 2006, Vargas, Venezuela. Outfielder (1988–93).

Martinez, Dave, B: Sept. 26, 1964, Safety Harbor, Fla. Outfielder/infielder (1995–97).

Martinez, Silvio, B: Aug. 19, 1955, Santiago, Dominican Republic. Pitcher (1977).

Martz, Randy, B: May 28, 1956, Harrisburg, Pa. Pitcher (1983).

Masi, Phil, B: Jan. 6, 1916, Chicago, Ill.; D: Mar. 29, 1990, Mount Prospect, Ill. Catcher (1950–52).

Masset, Nick, B: May 17, 1982, St. Petersburg, Fla. Pitcher (2007–08).

Matias, John, B: Aug. 15, 1944, Honolulu, Hawaii. Infielder (1970).

Mattick, Wally, B: Mar. 12, 1887, St. Louis, Mo.; D: Nov. 5, 1968, Los Altos, Calif. Outfielder (1912–13).

Mauldin, Mark, B: Nov. 5, 1914, Atlanta, Ga.; D: Sept. 2, 1990, Union City, Ga. Infielder (1934).

Maxwell, Charlie, B: Apr. 8, 1927, Lawton, Mich. Outfielder (1962–64).

May, Carlos, B: May 17, 1948, Birmingham, Ala. Outfielder/DH (1968–76).

May, Milt, B: Aug. 1, 1950, Gary, Ind. Catcher (1979).

Maye, Lee, B: Dec. 11, 1934, Tuscaloosa, Ala.; D: July 17, 2002, Riverside, Calif. Outfielder (1970–71).

Mayer, Erskine, B: Jan. 16, 1889, Atlanta, Ga.; D: Mar. 10, 1957, Los Angeles, Calif. Pitcher (1919).

Mayer, Wally, B: July 8, 1890, Cincinnati, Ohio; D: Nov. 18, 1951, Minneapolis, Minn. Catcher (1911–12, 1914–15).

McAleese, John, B: Aug. 22, 1878, Sharon, Pa.; D: Nov. 14, 1950, New York, N.Y. Pitcher (1901).

McAnany, Jim, B: Sept. 4, 1936, Los Angeles, Calif. Outfielder (1959–60).

McBee, Pryor, B: June 20, 1901, Blanco, Okla.; D: Apr. 19, 1963, Roseville, Calif. Pitcher (1926).

McBride, Ken, B: Aug. 12, 1935, Huntsville, Ala. Pitcher (1959–60).

McCabe, Dick, B: Feb. 21, 1896, Mamaroneck, N.Y.; D: Apr. 11, 1950, Buffalo, N.Y. Pitcher (1922).

McCall, Brian, B: Jan. 25, 1943, Kentfield, Calif. Outfielder (1962–63).

McCarthy, Brandon, B: July 7, 1983, Colorado Springs, Colo. Pitcher (2005–06).

McCarthy, Tom, B: June 18, 1961, Lundstahl, West Germany. Pitcher (1988–89).

McCaskill, Kirk, B: Apr. 9, 1961, Kapuskasing, Ontario. Pitcher (1992–96).

McClellan, Harvey, B: Dec. 22, 1894, Cynthiana, Ky.; D: Nov. 6, 1925, Cynthiana, Ky. Infielder (1919–24).

McConnell, Amby, B: Apr. 29, 1883, North Powell, Vt.; D: May 20, 1942, Utica, N.Y. Infielder (1910–11).

McCormick, Mike, B: May 6, 1917, Angel's Camp, Calif.; D: Apr. 14, 1976, Ventura, Calif. Outfielder (1950).

McCraw, Tom, B: Nov. 21, 1940, Malvern, Ark. Infielder (1963–70).

McCray, Rodney, B: Sept. 13, 1963, Detroit, Mich. Outfielder (1990–91).

McCurdy, Harry, B: Sept. 15, 1899, Stevens Point, Wis.; D: July 21, 1972, Houston, Tex. Catcher (1926–28).

McDonald, Jim, B: May 17, 1927, Grant's Pass, Ore. Pitcher (1956–58).

McDowell, Jack, B: Jan. 16, 1966, Van Nuys, Calif. Pitcher (1987–88, 1990–94).

McElroy, Chuck, B: Oct. 1, 1967, Port Arthur, Tex. Pitcher (1997).

McFarland, Ed, B: Aug. 3, 1874, Cleveland, Ohio; D: Nov. 28, 1959, Cleveland, Ohio. Catcher (1902–07).

McFarland, Herm, B: Mar. 11, 1870, Des Moines, Iowa; D: Sept. 21, 1935, Richmond, Va. Outfielder (1901–02).

McGhee, Ed, B: Sept. 29, 1924, Perry, Ark.; D: Feb. 13, 1986, Memphis, Tenn. Outfielder (1950, 1954–55).

McGlothen, Lynn, B: Mar. 27, 1950, Monroe, La.; D: Aug. 14, 1984, Dubach, La. Pitcher (1981).

McGlothlin, Jim, B: Oct. 6, 1943, Los Angeles, Calif.; D: Dec. 23, 1975, Union, Ky. Pitcher (1973).

McGuire, Tom, B: Feb. 1, 1892, Chicago, Ill.; D: Dec. 7, 1959, Phoenix, Ariz. Pitcher (1919).

McIlwain, Stover, B: Sept. 22, 1939, Savannah, Ga.; D: Jan. 15, 1966, Buffalo, N.Y. Pitcher (1957–58).

McIntyre, Matty, B: June 12, 1880, Stonington, Conn.; D: Apr. 2, 1920, Detroit, Mich. Outfielder (1911–12).

Eric "Boob" McNair

McKain, Hal, B: July 10, 1906, Logan, Iowa; D: Jan. 24, 1970, Sacramento, Calif. Pitcher (1929–32).

McKeon, Joel, B: Feb. 25, 1963, Covington, Ky. Pitcher (1986–87).

McKinney, Rich, B: Nov. 22, 1946, Piqua, Ohio. Infielder (1970–71).

McLarry, Howard "Polly," B: Mar. 25, 1891, Leonard, Tex.; D: Nov. 4, 1971, Bonham, Tex. Pinch-hitter (1912).

McLish, Cal, B: Dec. 1, 1925, Anadarko, Okla.; D: Aug. 26, 2010, Edmond, Okla. Pitcher (1961).

McMackin, Sam, B: 1872, Cleveland, Ohio; D: Feb. 11, 1903, Columbus, Ohio. Pitcher (1902).

McMahon, Don, B: Jan. 4, 1930, Brooklyn, N.Y.; July 22, 1987, Los Angeles, Calif. Pitcher (1967–68).

McMullin, Fred, B: Oct. 13, 1891, Scammon, Kan.; D: Nov. 21, 1952, Los Angeles, Calif. Infielder (1916–20).

McNair, Eric, B: Apr. 12, 1909, Meridian, Miss.; D: Mar. 11, 1949, Meridian, Miss. Infielder (1939–40).

McNertney, Jerry, B: Aug. 7, 1936, Boone, Iowa. Catcher (1964, 1966–68).

McWeeney, Doug, B: Aug. 17, 1896, Chicago, Ill.; D: Jan. 1, 1953, Melrose Park, Ill. Pitcher (1921–22, 1924).

Mele, Sam, B: Jan. 21, 1923, Astoria, N.Y. Outfielder (1952–53).

Meloan, Paul, B: Aug. 23, 1888, Paynesville, Mo.; D: Feb. 11, 1950, Taft, Calif. Outfielder (1910–11).

Melton, Bill, B: July 7, 1945, Gulfport, Miss. Infielder/DH (1968–75).

Melvin, Bob, B: Oct. 28, 1961, Palo Alto, Calif. Catcher (1994).

Merriman, Lloyd, B: Aug. 2, 1924, Clovis, Calif.; D: Jan. 20, 2004, Fresno, Calif. Outfielder (1955).

Mertes, Sandow, B: Aug. 6, 1872, San Francisco, Calif.; D: Mar. 11, 1945, San Francisco, Calif. Infielder (1901–02).

Merullo, Matt, B: Aug. 4, 1965, Winchester, Mass. Catcher (1989, 1991–93).

Messenger, Bobby, B: Mar. 19, 1884, Bangor, Maine; D: July 10, 1951, Bath, Maine. Outfielder (1909–11).

Metkovich, George "Catfish," B: Oct. 8, 1920, Angel's Camp, Calif.; D: May 17, 1995, Costa Mesa, Calif. Outfielder (1949).

Metzig, Bill, B: Dec. 4, 1918, Fort Dodge, Iowa; D: Mar. 12, 2006, Lubbock, Tex. Infielder (1944).

Metzler, Alex, B: Jan. 4, 1903, Fresno, Calif.; D: Nov. 30, 1973, Fresno, Calif. Outfielder (1927–30).

Meyer, Billy, B: Jan. 14, 1892, Knoxville, Tenn.; D: Mar. 31, 1957, Knoxville, Tenn. Catcher (1913).

Meyer, George, B: Aug. 3, 1909, Chicago, Ill.; D: Jan. 3, 1992, Hoffman Estates, Ill. Infielder (1938).

Michaels, Cass, B: Mar. 4, 1926, Detroit, Mich.; D: Nov. 12, 1982, Grosse Pointe, Mich. Infielder (1943–50, 1954).

Michaelson, John, B: Aug. 12, 1893, Taivalkosi, Finland; D: Apr. 16, 1968, Woodruff, Wis. Pitcher (1921).

Miles, Aaron, Dec. 15, 1976, Pittsburg, Calif. Infielder (2003).

Miller, Abraham "Corky," B: Mar. 18, 1976, Yucaipa, Calif. Catcher (2009).

Miller, Bob, B: Feb. 18, 1939, St. Louis, Mo.; D: Aug. 6, 1993, Rancho Bernardo, Calif. Pitcher (1970).

Miller, Frank, B: May 13, 1886, Allegan, Mich.; D: Feb. 19, 1974, Allegan, Mich. Pitcher (1913).

Miller, Walter "Jake," B: Feb. 28, 1898, Wagram, Ohio; D: Aug. 20, 1975, Venice, Fla. Pitcher (1933).

Minoso, Minnie, B: Nov. 29, 1922, Havana, Cuba. Outfielder/infielder (1951–57, 1961–62, '64, '76, '80).

Miranda, Willie, B: May 24, 1926, Velasco, Cuba. D: Sept. 7, 1996, Baltimore, Md. Infielder (1952).

Mitchell, Roy, B: Apr. 19, 1885, Belton, Tex.; D: Sept. 8, 1959, Temple, Tex. Pitcher (1918).

Mogridge, George, B: Feb. 18, 1889, Rochester, N.Y.; D: Mar. 4, 1962, Rochester, N.Y. Pitcher (1911–12).

Molina, Gustavo, B: Aug. 24, 1983, La Guaira, Venezuela. Catcher (2007).

Molinaro, Bob, B: May 21, 1950, Newark, N.J. Outfielder/DH (1977–78, 1980–81).

Moloney, Rich, B: June 7, 1950, Brookline, Mass. Pitcher (1970).

Monroe, Larry, B: June 20, 1956, Detroit, Mich. Pitcher (1976).

Monteagudo, Aurelio, B: Nov. 19, 1943, Calbarien, Cuba; D: Nov. 10, 1990, Saltillo, Mexico. Pitcher (1967).

Montero, Agustin, B: Aug. 26, 1977, San Pedro de Macoris, Dominican Republic. Pitcher (2006).

Moore, Alvin "Junior," B: Jan. 25, 1953, Waskom, Tex. Outfielder (1978–80).

Moore, Barry, B: Apr. 3, 1943, Statesville, N.C. Pitcher (1970).

Willie Miranda

Don Mossi

Moore, Jim, B: Dec. 14, 1903, Prescott, Ark.; D: May 19, 1973, Seattle, Wash. Outfielder (1930).

Moore, Jimmy, B: Apr. 24, 1903, Paris, Tenn.; D: Mar. 7, 1986, Memphis, Tenn. Pitcher (1930–32).

Moore, Randy, B: June 21, 1906, Naples, Tex.; D: June 12, 1992, Mount Pleasant, Tex. Outfielder (1927–28).

Moore, Ray, B: June 1, 1926, Meadows, Md.; D: Mar. 2, 1995, Clinton, Md. Pitcher (1958–60).

Morales, Rich, B: Sept. 20, 1943, San Francisco, Calif. Infielder (1967–73).

Moran, Carl, B: Sept. 26, 1950, Portsmouth, Va. Pitcher (1974).

Morehart, Ray, B: Dec. 2, 1899, Abner, Tex.; D: Jan. 13, 1989, Dallas, Tex. Infielder (1924, 1926).

Morel, Brent, B: Apr. 21, 1987, Bakersfield, Calif. Infielder (2010–).

Moriarty, George, B: June 7, 1884, Chicago, Ill.; D: Apr. 8, 1964, Miami, Fla. Infielder (1916).

Morman, Russ, B: Apr. 28, 1962, Independence, Mo. Infielder/DH (1986, 1988–89).

Morrison, Jim, B: Sept. 23, 1952, Pensacola, Fla. Infielder (1979–82).

Morrissey, Joseph "Jo Jo," B: Jan. 16, 1904, Warren, R.I.; D: May 2, 1950, Worcester, Mass. Infielder (1936).

Moses, Gerry, B: Aug. 9, 1946, Yazoo City, Miss. Catcher (1975).

Moses, Wally, B: Oct. 8, 1910, Uvalda, Ga.; D: Oct. 10, 1990, Vidalia, Ga. Outfielder (1942–46).

Moss, Les, B: May 14, 1925, Tulsa, Okla. Catcher (1955–58).

Mossi, Don, B: Jan. 11, 1929, St. Helena, Calif. Pitcher (1964).

Mostil, Johnny, B: June 1, 1896, Chicago, Ill.; D: Dec. 10, 1970, Midlothian, Ill. Outfielder (1918, 1921–29).

Moulder, Glen, B: Sept. 28, 1917, Cleveland, Okla.; D: Nov. 27, 1994, Decatur, Ga. Pitcher (1948).

Mouton, Lyle, B: May 13, 1969, Lafayette, La. Outfielder (1995–97).

Mueller, Bill, B: Nov. 9, 1920, Bay City, Mich.; D: Oct. 24, 2001, Wheeling, Ill. Outfielder (1942, 1945).

Mueller, Don, B: Apr. 14, 1927, St. Louis, Mo. Outfielder (1958–59).

Mulleavy, Greg, B: Sept. 25, 1905, Detroit, Mich.; D: Feb. 1, 1980, Arcadia, Calif. Infielder (1930, 1932).

Mullen, Charlie, B: Mar. 15, 1889, Seattle, Wash.; D: June 6, 1963, Seattle, Wash. Infielder (1910–11).

Mulligan, Eddie, B: Aug. 27, 1894, St. Louis, Mo.; D: Mar. 15, 1982, San Rafael, Calif. Infielder (1921–22).

Mullins, Fran, B: May 14, 1957, Oakland, Calif. Infielder (1980).

Mulrenan, Dominic, B: Dec. 18, 1893, Woburn, Mass.; D: July 27, 1964, Melrose, Mass. Pitcher (1921).

Munoz, Arnie, B: June 21, 1982, Mao, D.R. Pitcher (2004).

Munoz, Jose, B: Nov. 11, 1967, Chicago, Ill. Infielder (1996).

Mura, Steve, B: Feb. 12, 1955, New Orleans, La. Pitcher (1983).

Murphy, Danny, B: Aug. 23, 1942, Beverly, Mass. Pitcher (1969–70).

Murphy, Eddie, B: Oct. 2, 1891, Hancock, N.Y.; D: Feb. 21, 1969, Dunmore, Pa, Outfielder/DH (1915–21).

Murray, George, B: Sept. 23, 1898, Charlotte, N.C.; D: Oct. 18, 1955, Memphis, Tenn. Pitcher (1933).

Muser, Tony, B: Aug. 1, 1947, Van Nuys, Calif. Infielder/DH (1971–75).

Myers, Mike, B: June 26, 1969, Arlington Heights, Ill. Pitcher (2007).

Myette, Aaron, B: Sept. 26, 1977, New Westminster, B.C., Canada. Pitcher (1999–2000).

N

Nagel, Bill, B: Aug. 19, 1915, Memphis, Tenn.; D: Oct. 8, 1981, Freehold, N.J. Infielder (1945).

Nahorodny, Bill, B: Aug. 31, 1953, Hamtramck, Mich. Catcher (1977–79).

Naleway, Frank, B: July 5, 1902, Chicago, Ill.; D: Jan. 28, 1949, Chicago, Ill. Infielder (1924).

Nash, Charles "Cotton," B: July 24, 1942, Jersey City, N.J. Infielder (1967).

Navarro, Jaime, B: Mar. 27, 1968, Bayamon, P.R. Pitcher (1997–98).

Neis, Bernie, B: Sept. 26, 1895, Bloomington, Ill.; D: Nov. 29, 1972, Inverness, Fla. Outfielder (1927).

Nelson, Andy, B: Nov. 30, 1884, St. Paul, Minn.; D: Unknown. Pitcher (1908).

Nelson, Gene, B: Dec. 3, 1960, Tampa, Fla. Pitcher (1984–86).

Nelson, Glenn "Rocky," B: Nov. 18, 1924, Portsmouth, Ohio; D: Oct. 31, 2006, Portsmouth, Ohio. Infielder (1951).

Nelson, Jeff, B: Nov. 16, 1966, Baltimore, Md. Pitcher (2006).

Nelson, Roger, B: June 7, 1944, Altadena, Calif. Pitcher (1967).

Ness, Jack, B: Nov. 11, 1885, Chicago, Ill.; D: Dec. 3, 1957, DeLand, Fla. Infielder (1916).

Neumeier, Dan, B: Mar. 9, 1948, Shawano, Wis. Pitcher (1972).

Newson, Warren, B: July 3, 1964, Newman, Ga. Outfielder/pinch-hitter (1991–95).

Niahros, Gus, B: Dec. 6, 1920, Birmingham, Ala.; D: Dec. 29, 2004, Harrisonburg, Va. Catcher (1950–51).

Nicholas, Don, B: Oct. 30, 1930, Phoenix, Ariz.; D: Oct. 23, 2007, Garden Grove, Calif. Outfielder (1952, 1954).

Nichols, Reid, B: Aug. 5, 1958, Ocala, Fla. Outfielder (1985–86).

Nicholson, Dave, B: Aug. 29, 1939, St. Louis, Mo. Outfielder(1963–65).

Nielsen, Scott, B: Dec. 18, 1958, Salt Lake City, Utah. Pitcher (1987).

Nieman, Bob, B: Jan. 26, 1927, Cincinnati, Ohio; D: Mar. 10, 1985, Corona, Calif. Outfielder (1955–56).

Niemann, Randy, B: Nov. 15, 1955, Scotia, Calif. Pitcher (1984).

Nix, Jayson, B: Aug. 26, 1982, Dallas, Tex. Infielder (2009–10).

Nordbrook, Tim, B: July 7, 1949, Baltimore, Md. Infielder (1977).

Nordhagen, Wayne, B: July 4, 1948, Thief River Falls, Minn. Outfielder/DH (1976–81).

Norman, Bill, B: July 16, 1910, St. Louis, Mo.; D: Apr. 21, 1962, Milwaukee, Wis. Outfielder (1931–32).

Northey, Ron, B: Apr. 26, 1920, Mahonoy City, Pa.; D: Apr. 16, 1971, Pittsburgh, Pa. Outfielder/pinch-hitter (1955–57).

Norton, Greg, B: July 6, 1972, San Leandro, Calif. Infielder (1996–2000).

Noyes, Wynn, B: June 16, 1889, Pleasanton, Neb.; D: Apr. 8, 1969, Cashmere, Wash. Pitcher (1919).

Nunez, Jhonny, B: Nov. 26, 1985, San Jose de las Matas, Dominican Republic. Pitcher (2009–).

Nyman, Chris, B: June 6, 1955, Pomona, Calif. Infielder (1982–83).

Nyman, Gerry, B: Nov. 23, 1942, Logan, Utah. Pitcher (1968–69).

Nyman, Nyls, B: Mar. 7, 1954, Detroit, Mich. Outfielder (1974–77).

O

O'Brien, Charlie, B: May 1, 1961, Tulsa, Okla. Catcher (1998).

O'Brien, Syd, B: Dec. 18, 1944, Compton, Calif. Infielder (1970).

O'Brien, Thomas "Buck," B: May 9, 1882, Brockton, Mass.; D: July 25, 1959, Boston, Mass. Pitcher (1913).

Odom, John "Blue Moon," B: May 29, 1945, Macon, Ga. Pitcher (1976).

Olivo, Miguel, B: July 15, 1978, Villa Vasquez, D.R. Catcher (2002–04).

Olmstead, Fred, B: July 3, 1881, Grand Rapids, Mich.; D: Oct. 22, 1936, Muskogee, Okla. Pitcher (1908–11).

O'Malley, Tom, B: Dec. 25, 1960, Orange, N.J. Infielder (1984).

O'Neill, Bill, B: Jan. 22, 1880, St. John, New Brunswick; D: July 20, 1920, Woodhaven, N.Y. Outfielder (1906).

O'Neill, Emmett, B: Jan. 13, 1918, San Mateo, Calif.; D: Oct. 11, 1993, Sparks, Nev. Pitcher (1946).

Ordonez, Magglio, B: Jan. 28, 1974, Caracas, Venezuela. Outfielder (1997–2004).

Orengo, Joe, B: Nov. 29, 1914, San Francisco, Calif.; D: July 24, 1988, San Francisco, Calif. Infielder (1945).

Orta, Jorge, B: Nov. 26, 1950, Mazatián, Mexico. Infielder/DH (1972–79).

Ortiz, Jose, B: June 25, 1947, Ponce, P.R. Outfielder (1969–70).

Osborn, Danny, B: June 19, 1946, Springfield, Mo. Pitcher (1975).

Osinski, Dan, B: Nov. 17, 1933, Chicago, Ill. Pitcher (1969).

Osteen, Claude, B: Aug. 9, 1939, Caney Springs, Tenn. Pitcher (1975).

Ostergard, Ray "Red," B: May 16, 1896, Denmark, Wis.; D: Jan. 13, 1977, Hemet, Calif. Infielder (1921).

Ostrowski, John, B: Oct. 17, 1917, Chicago, Ill.; D: Nov. 13, 1992, Chicago, Ill. Outfielder (1949–50).

Osuna, Antonio, B: Apr. 12, 1973, Sinaloa, Mexico. Pitcher (2001–02).

Jorge Orta

Jim O'Toole

O'Toole, Denny, B: Mar. 13, 1949, Chicago, Ill. Pitcher (1969–73).

O'Toole, Jim, B: Jan. 10, 1937, Chicago, Ill. Pitcher (1967).

Otten, Jim, B: July 1, 1951, Lewiston, Mont. Pitcher (1974–76).

Owen, Frank, B: Dec. 23, 1879, Ypsilanti, Mich.; D: Nov. 24, 1942, Dearborn, Mich. Pitcher (1903–09).

Owen, Marv, B: Mar. 22, 1906, Agnew, Calif.; D: June 22, 1991, Mountain View, Calif. Infielder (1938–39).

Owens, Frank, B: Jan. 26, 1886, Toronto, Ontario, Canada; D: July 2, 1958, Minneapolis, Minn. Catcher (1909).

Marv Owen

Owens, Jerry, B: Feb. 16, 1981, Hollywood, Calif. Outfielder (2006–09).

Ozuna, Pablo, B: Aug. 25, 1974, Santo Domingo, D.R. Outfielder (2005–08).

P

Paciorek, Tom, B: Nov. 2, 1946, Detroit, Mich. Infielder/outfielder (1982–85).

Paddock, Del, B: June 8, 1887, Volga, S.D.; D: Feb. 6, 1952, Remer, Minn. Infielder (1912).

Pall, Donn, B: Jan. 11, 1962, Chicago, Ill. Pitcher (1988–93).

Paniagua, Jose, B: Apr. 4, 1996, San Jose De Ocoa, D.R. Pitcher (2004).

Papai, Al, B: May 7, 1919, Divemon, Ill.; D: Sept. 7, 1995, Springfield, Ill. Pitcher (1955).

Papish, Frank, B: Oct. 21, 1917, Pueblo, Colo.; D: Aug. 30, 1965, Pueblo, Colo. Pitcher (1945–48).

Parent, Freddy, B: Nov. 25, 1875, Biddeford, Maine; D: Nov. 2, 1972, Sanford, Maine. Infielder (1908–11).

Paris, Kelly, B: Oct. 17, 1957, Encino, Calif. Infielder (1988).

Parque, Jim, B: Feb. 8, 1976, Norwalk, Calif. Pitcher (1998–2002).

Parsons, Casey, B: Apr. 14, 1954, Wenatchee, Wash. Outfielder (1983–84).

Pasek, Johnny, B: June 25, 1905, Niagara Falls, N.Y.; D: Mar. 13, 1976, Niagara Falls, N.Y. Catcher (1934).

Frank Papish

Dan Pasqua

Pasqua, Dan, B: Oct. 17, 1961, Yonkers, N.Y. Outfielder/infielder (1988–94).

Patterson, Ham, B: Oct. 13, 1877, Belleville, Ill.; D: Nov. 25, 1945, East St. Louis, Ill. Outfielder (1909).

Patterson, Ken, B: July 8, 1964, Costa Mesa, Calif. Pitcher (1988–91).

Patterson, Reggie, B: Nov. 7, 1958, Birmingham, Ala. Pitcher (1981).

Patterson, Roy, B: Dec. 17, 1876, Stoddard, Wis.; D: Apr. 14, 1953, St. Croix Falls, Wis. Pitcher (1900–07).

Paul, Josh, B: May 19, 1975, Evanston, Ill. Catcher (1999–2003).

Pavletich, Don, B: July 13, 1938, Milwaukee, Wis. Catcher (1969).

Pawlowski, John, B: Sept. 6, 1963, Johnson City, N.Y. Pitcher (1987–88).

Payne, Fred, B: Sept. 2, 1880, Camden, N.Y.; D: Jan. 16, 1954, Camden, N.Y. Catcher (1909–11).

Payne, George, B: May 23, 1890, Mount Vernon, Ky.; D: Jan. 24, 1959, Bellflower, Calif. Pitcher (1920).

Pearson, Ike, B: Mar. 1, 1917, Grenada, Miss.; D: Mar. 17, 1985, Sarasota, Fla. Pitcher (1948).

Peavy, Jake, B: May 31, 1981, Mobile, Ala. Pitcher (2009–).

Peckinpaugh, Roger, B: Feb. 5, 1891, Wooster, Ohio; D: Nov. 17, 1977, Cleveland, Ohio. Infielder (1927).

Pena, Jesus, B: Mar. 8, 1975, Santo Domingo, D.R. Pitcher (1999–2000).

Pena, Tony, B: June 4, 1957, Monte Cristi, D.R. Catcher (1997).

Pena, Tony, B: Jan. 9, 1982, Santo Domingo, Dominican Republic. Pitcher (2009–).

Pence, Elmer, B: Aug. 17, 1900, Valley Springs, Calif.; D: Sept. 17, 1968, San Francisco, Calif. Outfielder (1922).

Pence, Russ, B: Mar. 11, 1900, Marine, Ill.; D: Aug. 11, 1971, Hot Springs, Ark. Pitcher (1921).

Perconte, Jack, B: Aug. 31, 1954, Joliet, Ill. Infielder (1986).

Perez, Melido, B: Feb. 15, 1966, San Cristóbal, Dominican Republic. Pitcher (1988–91).

Perez, Timo, B: Apr. 8, 1975, Juan Baron Palenque, D.R. Outfielder (2004–05).

Perkovich, John, B: Mar. 10, 1924, Chicago, Ill. Pitcher (1950).

Perme, Len, B: Nov. 25, 1917, Cleveland, Ohio; D: Jan. 24, 2009, Hayward, Calif. Pitcher (1942, 46).

Perry, Herbert, B: Sept. 15, 1969, Live Oak, Fla. Infielder (2000–01).

Perzanowski, Stan, B: Aug. 25, 1950, East Chicago, Ind. Pitcher (1971, 1974).

John "Bubba" Phillips

A.J. Pierzynski

Peters, Gary, B: Apr. 21, 1937, Grove City, Pa. Pitcher (1959–69).

Peters, Oscar "Rube," B: Mar. 15, 1885, Grantfork, Ill.; D: Feb. 7, 1965, Pequannock, N.J. Pitcher (1912).

Peterson, Adam, B: Dec. 11, 1965, Long Beach, Calif. Pitcher (1987–90).

Peterson, Carl "Buddy," B: Apr. 23, 1925, Portland, Ore.; D: Sept. 19, 2006, Sacramento, Calif. Infielder (1955).

Phelps, Ray, B: Dec. 11, 1903, Dunlap, Tenn.; D: July 7, 1971, Fort Pierce, Fla. Pitcher (1935–36).

Philley, Dave, B: May 16, 1920, Paris, Tex. Outfielder (1941, 1946–51, 1956–57).

Phillips, Heath, B: Mar. 24, 1982, Evansville, Ind. Pitcher (2007).

Phillips, John "Bubba," B: Feb. 24, 1928, West Point, Miss.; D: June 22, 1993, Hattiesburg, Miss. Infielder (1956–59).

Phillips, Paul, B: Apr. 15, 1977, Demopolis, Ala. Catcher (2008).

Phillips, Taylor, B: June 18, 1933, Atlanta, Ga. Pitcher (1963).

Phillips, Tony, B: Apr. 25, 1959, Atlanta, Ga. Outfielder (1996–97).

Piatt, Wiley, B: July 13, 1874, Blue Creek, Ohio; D: Sept. 20, 1946, Cincinnati, Ohio. Pitcher (1901–02).

Pierce, Billy, B: Apr. 2, 1927, Detroit, Mich. Pitcher (1949–61).

Pieretti, Marino, B: Sept. 23, 1920, Luccia, Italy; D: Jan. 30, 1981, San Francisco, Calif. Pitcher (1948–49).

Pierre, Juan, B: Aug. 14, 1977, Mobile, Ala. Outfielder (2010–).

Pierzynski, Anthony John "A.J." B: Dec. 30, 1976, Bridgehampton, N.Y. Catcher (2005–).

Piet, Tony, B: Dec. 7, 1906, Berwick, Pa.; D: Dec. 1, 1981, Hinsdale, Ill. Infielder (1935–37).

Pilarcik, Al, B: July 3, 1930, Whiting, Ind.; D: Sept. 20, 2010, Schererville, Ind. Outfielder (1961).

Pinelli, Ralph "Babe," B: Oct. 18, 1895, San Francisco, Calif.; D: Oct. 22, 1984, Daly City, Calif. Outfielder (1918).

Pitlock, Lee "Skip," B: Nov. 6, 1947, Hillside, Ill. Pitcher (1974–75).

Pizarro, Juan, B: Feb. 7, 1937, Santurce, P.R. Pitcher (1961–66).

Platt, Mizel "Whitey," B: Aug. 21, 1920, West Palm Beach, Fla.; D: July 27, 1970, West Palm Beach, Fla. Outfielder (1946).

Podsednik, Scott, B: Mar. 18, 1976, West, Tex. Outfielder (2005–07; 2009).

Politte, Cliff, B: Feb. 27, 1974, St. Louis, Mo. Pitcher (2004–06).

Tony Piet

Scott Podsednik

Pollet, Howie, B: June 26, 1921, New Orleans, La.; D: Aug. 8, 1974, Houston, Tex. Pitcher (1956).

Pomorski, John, B: Dec. 30, 1905, Brooklyn, N.Y.; D: Dec. 6, 1977, Brampton, Ontario. Pitcher (1934).

Poreda, Aaron, B: Oct. 1, 1986, Walnut Creek, Calif. Pitcher (2009).

Porter, Irv, B: May 17, 1888, Lynn, Mass.; D: Feb. 20, 1971, Lynn, Mass. Outfielder (1914).

Porzio, Mike, B: Aug. 20, 1972, Waterbury, Conn. Pitcher (2002–03).

Poser, Bob, B: Mar. 16, 1910, Columbus, Wis.; D: May 21, 2002, Columbus, Wis. Pitcher (1932).

Pratt, Frank, B: Aug. 24, 1897, Blocton, Ala.; D: Mar. 8, 1974, Centreville, Ala. Pinch-hitter (1921).

Priddy, Bob, B: Dec. 10, 1939, Pittsburgh, Pa. Pitcher (1968–69).

Prinz, Brett, B: June 15, 1977, Chicago Heights, Ill. Pitcher (2007).

Proctor, Noah "Red," B: Oct. 27, 1900, Williamsburg, Va.; D: Dec. 17, 1954, Richmond, Va. Pitcher (1923).

Proly, Mike, B: Dec. 15, 1950, Jamaica, N.Y. Pitcher (1978–80).

Pruitt, Ron, B: Oct. 21, 1951, Flint, Mich. Outfielder/infielder (1980).

Pryor, Greg, B: Oct. 2, 1949, Marietta, Ohio. Infielder (1978–81).

Purdy, Everett "Pid," B: June 15, 1904, Beatrice, Neb.; D: Jan. 16, 1951, Beatrice, Neb. Outfielder (1926).

Purtell, Billy, B: Jan. 6, 1886, Columbus, Ohio; D: Mar. 17, 1962, Bradenton, Fla. Infielder (1908–10).

Putz, Joseph Jason, "J.J.," B: Feb. 22, 1977, Trenton, Mich. Pitcher (2010).

Q

Qualls, Jimmy, B: Oct. 9, 1946, Exeter, Calif. Outfielder (1972).

Qualters, Tom, B: Apr. 1, 1935, McKeesport, Pa. Pitcher (1958).

Quentin, Carlos, B: Aug. 28, 1982, Bellflower, Calif. Outfielder (2008–).

Quillen, Lee, B: May 5, 1882, North Branch, Minn.; D: May 14, 1965, White Bear Lake, Minn. Infielder (1906–07).

Quinlan, Tom "Finners," B: Oct. 21, 1887, Scranton, Pa.; D: Feb. 17, 1966, Scranton, Pa. Outfielder (1915).

Quinn, Jack, B: July 5, 1883, Janesville, Pa.; D: Apr. 17, 1946, Pottsville, Pa. Pitcher (1918).

Quirk, Jamie, B: Oct. 22, 1954, Whittier, Calif. Infielder/catcher (1984).

R

Radcliff, Ray "Rip," B: Jan. 19, 1906, Kiowa, Okla.; D: May 23, 1962, Enid, Okla. Outfielder (1934–39).

Rader, Don, B: Sept. 5, 1893, Wolcott, Ind.; D: June 26, 1983, Walla Walla, Wash. Outfielder (1913).

Radinsky, Scott, B: Mar. 3, 1968, Glendale, Calif. Pitcher (1990–95).

Ragan, Pat, B: Nov. 15, 1888, Blanchard, Iowa; D: Sept. 4, 1956, Los Angeles, Calif. Pitcher (1919).

Raines, Tim, B: Sept. 16, 1959, Sanford, Fla. Outfielder (1991–95).

Ramirez, Alexei, B: Sept. 22, 1981, Pinar del Rio, Cuba. Infielder (2008–).

Ramirez, Horacio, B: Nov. 24, 1979, Carson, Calif. Pitcher (2008).

Ramirez, Julio, B: Aug. 10, 1977, San Juan de Maguana, D.R. Outfielder (2001).

Ramirez, Manny, B: May 30, 1972, Santo Domingo, D.R. Outfielder (2010).

Randall, Jim "Sap," B: Aug. 19, 1960, Mobile, Ala. Infielder (1988).

Rapp, Earl, B: May 20, 1921, Corunna, Mich.; D: Feb. 13, 1992, Swedesboro, N.J. Outfielder (1949).

Rath, Fred, B: Sept. 1, 1943, Little Rock, Ark. Pitcher (1968–69).

Rath, Morrie, B: Dec. 25, 1886, Mobeetie, Tex.; D: Nov. 18, 1945, Upper Darby, Pa. Infielder (1912–13).

Rauch, Jon, B: Sept. 27, 1978, Louisville, Ky. Pitcher (2002, 2004).

Raymond, Claude, B: May 7, 1937, St. Jean, Quebec, Canada. Pitcher (1959).

Redfern, George "Buck," B: Apr. 7, 1902, Asheville, N.C.; D: Sept. 8, 1964, Asheville, N.C. Infielder (1928–29).

Redus, Gary, B: Nov. 1, 1956, Tanner, Ala. Outfielder (1987–88).

Reed, Ron, B: Nov. 2, 1942, La Porte, Ind. Pitcher (1984).

Regan, Phil, B: Apr. 6, 1937, Otsego, Mich. Pitcher (1972).

Reichardt, Rick, B: Mar. 16, 1943, Madison, Wis. Outfielder (1971–73).

Reilly, Barney, B: Feb. 7, 1884, Brockton, Mass.; D: Nov. 15, 1934, St. Joseph, Mo. Infielder (1909).

Renko, Steve, B: Dec. 10, 1944, Kansas City, Kan. Pitcher (1977).

Rensa, Tony, B: Sept. 29, 1901, Parsons, Pa.; D: Jan. 4, 1987, Wilkes-Barre, Pa. Catcher (1937–39).

Reuss, Jerry, B: June 19, 1949, St. Louis, Mo. Pitcher (1988–89).

Reynolds, Carl, B: Feb. 1, 1903, La Rue, Tex.; D: May 29, 1978, Houston, Tex. Outfielder (1927–31).

Reynolds, Danny, B: Nov. 27, 1919, Stony Point, N.C. Infielder (1945).

Rhawn, Bobby, B: Feb. 13, 1919, Catawissa, Pa.; D: June 9, 1984, Danville, Pa. Infielder (1949).

Rhyne, Hal, B: Mar. 30, 1899, Paso Robles, Calif.; D: Jan. 7, 1971, Orangeville, Calif. Infielder (1933).

Ribant, Dennis, B: Sept. 20, 1941, Detroit, Mich. Pitcher (1968).

Richar, Danny, B: June 9, 1983, La Romana, Dominican Republic, Infielder (2007).

Richard, Clayton, B: Sept. 12, 1983, Lafayette, Ind. Pitcher (2008–09).

Richard, Lee, B: Sept. 18, 1948, Lafayette, La. Infielder (1971–72, 1974–75).

Rickert, Marv, B: Jan. 8, 1921, Long Branch, Wash.; D: June 3, 1978, Oakville, Wash. Outfielder (1950).

Alexei Ramirez

Riddle, Johnny, B: Oct. 3, 1905, Clinton, S.C.; D: Dec. 15, 1998, Indianapolis, Ind. Catcher (1930).

Righetti, Dave, B: Nov. 28, 1958, San Jose, Calif. Pitcher (1995).

Rigney, Johnny, B: Oct. 28, 1914, Oak Park, Ill.; D: Oct. 21, 1984, Lombard, Ill. Pitcher (1937–42, '46–47).

Rios, Alex, B: Feb. 18, 1981, Coffee, Ala. Outfielder (2009–).

Rios, Armando, B: Sept. 13, 1971, Santurce, P.R. Outfielder (2003).

Risberg, Charles "Swede," B: Oct. 13, 1894, San Francisco, Calif.; D: Oct. 13, 1975, Red Bluff, Calif. Infielder (1917–20).

Riske, David, B: Oct. 23, 1976, Renton, Wash. Pitcher (2006).

Ritchie, Todd, B: Nov. 7, 1971, Portsmouth, Va. Pitcher (2002).

Rivera, Jim, B: July 22, 1922, New York, N.Y. Outfielder (1952–61).

Riviere, Arthur "Tink," B: Aug. 2, 1899, Liberty, Tex.; D: Sept. 27, 1965, Liberty, Tex. Pitcher (1925).

Rizzo, Todd, B: May 24, 1971, Clifton Heights, Pa. Pitcher (1998–99).

Roberge, Bert, B: Oct. 3, 1954, Lewiston, Maine. Pitcher (1984).

Robertson, Charlie, B: Jan. 31, 1896, Dexter, Tex.; D: Aug. 23, 1984, Fort Worth, Tex. Pitcher (1919, 1922–25).

Robertson, Mike, B: Oct. 9, 1970, Norwalk, Conn. Infielder (1996).

Robidoux, Billy Jo, B: Jan. 13, 1964, Ware, Mass. Infielder (1989).

Robinson, Aaron, B: June 23, 1915, Lancaster, S.C.; D: Mar. 9, 1966, Lancaster, S.C. Catcher (1948).

Robinson, Dewey, B: Apr. 28, 1955, Evanston, Ill. Pitcher (1979–81).

Robinson, Eddie, B: Dec. 15, 1920, Paris, Tex. Outfielder (1950–52).

Robinson, Floyd, B: May 9, 1936, Prescott, Ark. Outfielder (1960–66).

Rock, Les, B: Aug. 19, 1912, Springfield, Minn.; D: Sept. 9, 1991, Davis, Calif. Infielder (1936).

Rodriguez, Aurelio, B: Dec. 28, 1947, Cananea, Mexico; D: Sept. 23, 2000, Detroit, Mich. Infielder (1982, 1983).

Rodriguez, Hec, B: June, 13, 1920, Alquizar, Cuba. Infielder (1952).

Rick Reichardt (right)

Rodriguez, Liu, B: Nov. 5, 1976, Caracas, Venezuela. Infielder (1999).

Rogovin, Saul, B: Oct. 10, 1923, Brooklyn, N.Y.; D: Jan. 23, 1995, New York, N.Y. Pitcher (1951–53).

Rohe, George, B: Sept. 15, 1875, Cincinnati, Ohio; D: June 10, 1957, Cincinnati, Ohio. Infielder (1905–07).

Romano, Johnny, B: Aug. 23, 1934, Hoboken, N.J. Catcher (1958–59, 1965–66).

Romo, Vincente, B: Apr. 12, 1943, Santa Rosalia, Mexico. Pitcher (1971–72).

Rondon, Gil, B: Nov. 18, 1953, Bronx, N.Y. Pitcher (1979).

Roof, Phil, B: Mar. 5, 1941, Paducah, Ky. Catcher (1976).

Roselli, Bob, B: Dec. 10, 1931, San Francisco, Calif.; D: Nov. 5, 2009, Rocklin, Calif. Catcher (1961–62).

Rosenberg, Lou, B: Mar. 5, 1904, San Francisco, Calif.; D: Sept. 8, 1991, Daly City, Calif. Infielder (1923).

Rosenberg, Steve, B: Oct. 31, 1964, Brooklyn, N.Y. Pitcher (1988–90).

Rosenthal, Larry, B: May 21, 1910, St. Paul, Minn.; D: Mar. 4, 1992, Woodbury, Minn. Outfielder (1936–41).

Ross, Lee "Buck," B: Feb. 2, 1915, Norwood, N.C.; D: Nov. 23, 1978, Charlotte, N.C. Pitcher (1941–45).

Rotblatt, Marv, B: Oct. 18, 1927, Chicago, Ill. Pitcher (1948, 1950–51).

Roth, Frank, B: Oct. 11, 1878, Chicago, Ill.; D: Mar. 27, 1955, Burlington, Wis. Catcher (1906).

Roth, Robert "Braggo," B: Aug. 28, 1892, Burlington, Wis.; D: Sept. 11, 1936, Chicago, Ill. Outfielder (1914–15).

Rothrock, Jack, B: Mar. 14, 1905, Long Beach, Calif.; D: Feb. 2, 1980, San Bernardino, Calif. Outfielder (1932).

Rounsaville, Virle, B: Sept. 27, 1944, Konawa, Okla. Pitcher (1970).

Roush, Edd, B: May 8, 1893, Oakland City, Ind.; D: Mar. 21, 1988, Bradenton, Fla. Outfielder (1913).

Rowand, Aaron, B: Aug. 29, 1977, Portland, Ore. Outfielder (2001–05).

Royster, Jerry, B: Oct. 18, 1952, Sacramento, Calif. Infielder (1987).

Rudolph, Don, B: Aug. 16, 1931, Baltimore, Md.; D: Sept. 12, 1968, Granada Hills, Calif. Pitcher (1957–59).

Ruel, Harold "Muddy," B: Feb. 20, 1896, St. Louis, Mo.; D: Nov. 13, 1963, Palo Alto, Calif. Catcher (1934).

Ruffcorn, Scott, B: Dec. 29, 1969, New Braunfels, Tex. Pitcher (1993–96).

Ruffing, Charles "Red," B: May 3, 1904, Granville, Ill.; D: Feb. 17, 1986, Mayfield Heights, Ohio. Pitcher (1947).

Rush, Bob, B: Dec. 21, 1925, Battle Creek, Mich. Pitcher (1960).

Russell, Adam, B: Apr. 14, 1983, North Olmsted, Ohio. Pitcher (2008).

Russell, Ewell "Reb," B: Apr. 12, 1889, Jackson, Miss.; D: Sept. 30, 1973, Indianapolis, Ind. Pitcher (1913–19).

Russell, John, B: Oct. 20, 1895, San Mateo, Calif.; D: Nov. 20, 1930, Ely, Nev. Pitcher (1921–22).

Ryal, Mark, B: Aug. 28, 1960, Henryetta, Okla. Outfielder (1985).

Ryan, Connie, B: Feb. 27, 1920, New Orleans, La.; D: Jan. 3, 1996, Metairie, La. Infielder (1953).

Ryan, John "Blondy," B: Jan. 4, 1906, Lynn, Mass.; D: Nov. 28, 1959, Swampscott, Mass. Infielder (1930).

S

Sabo, Chris, B: Sept. 19, 1962, Detroit, Mich. Outfielder (1995).

Sadowski, Bob, B: Jan. 15, 1937, St. Louis, Mo. Infielder (1962).

Saenz, Olmedo, B: Oct. 8, 1970, Chitre Herrera, Panama. Infielder (1994).

Salas, Mark, B: Mar. 8, 1961, Montebello, Calif. Catcher (1988).

Salazar, Luis, B: May 19, 1956, Barcelona, Venezuela. Infielder (1985–86).

Sale, Chris, B: Mar. 30, 1989, Lakeland, Fla. Pitcher (2010–).

Salkeid, Bill, B: Mar. 8, 1917, Pocatello, Idaho; D: Apr. 22, 1967, Los Angeles, Calif. Catcher (1950).

Salveson, Jack, B: Jan. 5, 1914, Fullerton, Calif.; D: Dec. 28, 1974, Norwalk, Calif. Pitcher (1935).

Sanders, David, B: Aug. 29, 1979, Oklahoma City, Okla. Pitcher (2003, 2005).

Sanderson, Scott, B: July 22, 1956, Dearborn, Mich. Pitcher (1994).

Santo, Ron, B: Feb. 25, 1940, Seattle, Wash.; D: Dec. 2, 2010, Phoenix, Ariz. Infielder/DH (1974).

Santos, Sergio, B: July 4, 1983, Bellflower, Calif. Pitcher (2010–).

Chris Sale

Santovenia, Nelson, B: July 27, 1961, Pinar del Río, Cuba. Catcher (1992).

Sauveur, Rich, B: Nov. 23, 1963, Falls Church, Va. Pitcher (1996).

Sawatski, Carl, B: Nov. 4, 1927, Shickshinny, Pa.; D: Nov. 24, 1991, Little Rock, Ark. Catcher (1954).

Sax, Steve, B: Jan. 29, 1960, Sacramento, Calif. Infielder (1992–93).

Scala, Jerry, B: Sept. 27, 1926, Bayonne, N.J.; D: Dec. 14, 1993, Fallston, Md. Outfielder (1948–50).

Scarbery, Randy, B: June 22, 1952, Fresno, Calif. Pitcher (1979–80).

Scarborough, Ray, B: July 23, 1917, Mount Gilead, N.C.; D: July 1, 1982, Mount Olive, N.C. Pitcher (1950).

Schaefer, Jeff, B: May 31, 1960, Patchogue, N.Y. Infielder (1989).

Schaffer, Jimmie, B: Apr. 5, 1936, Limeport, Pa. Catcher (1965).

Schalk, Leroy, B: Nov. 9, 1908, Chicago, Ill.; D: Mar. 11, 1990, Gainesville, Tex. Infielder (1944–45).

Schalk, Ray, B: Aug. 12, 1892, Harvey, Ill.; D: May 19, 1970, Chicago, Ill. Catcher (1912–28).

Schaller, Walter "Biff," B: Sept. 23, 1889, Chicago, Ill.; D: Oct. 9, 1939, Emeryville, Calif. Outfielder (1913).

Schlueter, Norm, B: Sept. 25, 1916, Belleville, Ill.; D: Oct. 6, 2004, Belleville, Ill. Catcher (1938–39).

Schmidt, Dave, B: Apr. 22, 1957, Niles, Mich. Pitcher (1986).

Schoeneweis, Scott, B: Oct. 2, 1973, Long Branch, N.J. Pitcher (2003–04).

Schreckengost, Ossee, B: Apr. 11, 1875, New Bethlehem, Pa.; D: July 9, 1914, Philadelphia, Pa. Catcher (1908).

Schreiber, Hank, B: July 12, 1891, Cleveland, Ohio; D: Feb. 23, 1968, Indianapolis, Ind. Outfielder (1914).

Schueler, Ron, B: Apr. 14, 1948, Catherine, Kan. Pitcher (1978–79).

Schultz, Webb, B: Jan. 31, 1898, Wautoma, Wis.; D: July 26, 1986, Delevan, Wis. Pitcher (1924).

Schupp, Ferdie, B: Jan. 16, 1891, Louisville, Ky.; D: Dec. 16, 1971, Los Angeles, Calif. Pitcher (1922).

Schwarz, Jeff, B: May 20, 1964, Fort Pierce, Fla. Pitcher (1993–94).

Scoggins, Jim, B: July 19, 1891, Killeen, Tex.; D: Aug. 16, 1923, Columbia, S.C. Pitcher (1913).

Score, Herb, B: June 7, 1933, Rosedale, N.Y.; D: Nov. 11, 2008, Rocky River, Ohio. Pitcher (1960–62).

Scott, Everett, B: Nov. 19, 1892, Bluffton, Ind.; D: Nov. 2, 1960, Fort Wayne, Ind. Infielder (1926).

Scott, Jim, B: Apr. 23, 1888, Deadwood, S.D.; D: Apr. 7, 1957, Jacumba, Calif. Pitcher (1909–17).

Searage, Ray, B: May 1, 1955, Freeport, N.Y. Pitcher (1986–87).

Seaver, Tom, B: Nov. 17, 1944, Fresno, Calif. Pitcher (1984–86).

Secrist, Don, B: Feb. 26, 1944, Seattle, Wash. Pitcher (1969–70).

Seeds, Bob, B: Feb. 24, 1907, Ringgold, Tex.; D: Oct. 28, 1993, Erick, Okla. Outfielder (1932).

Seerey, Pat, B: Mar. 17, 1923, Wilburton, Okla.; D: Apr. 28, 1986, Jennings, Mo. Outfielder (1948–49).

Segura, Jose, B: Jan. 26, 1963, Fundación, Dominican Republic. Pitcher (1988–89).

Seilheimer, Rick, B: Aug. 30, 1960, Brenham, Tex. Catcher (1980).

Selph, Carey, B: Dec. 5, 1901, Donaldson, Ark.; D: Feb. 24, 1976, Houston, Tex. Infielder (1932).

Sewell, Luke, B: Jan. 5, 1901, Titus, Ala.; D: May 14, 1987, Akron, Ohio. Catcher (1935–38).

Sharp, Bill, B: Jan. 18, 1950, Lima, Ohio. Outfielder (1973–75).

Shaw, Al, B: Oct. 3, 1874, Burslem, England; D: Mar. 25, 1958, Uhrichsville, Ohio. Catcher (1908).

Shaw, Bob, B: June 29, 1933, Bronx, N.Y.; D: Sept. 23, 2010, Jupiter, Fla. Pitcher (1958–61).

Shaw, Jeff, B: July 7, 1966, Washington Courthouse, Ohio. Pitcher (1995).

Shea, Merv, B: Sept. 5, 1900, San Francisco, Calif.; D: Jan. 27, 1953, Sacramento, Calif. Catcher (1934–37).

Herb Score

Sheely, Earl, B: Feb. 12, 1893, Bushnell, Ill.; D: Sept. 16, 1952, Seattle, Wash. Infielder (1921–27).

Sheely, Hollis "Bud," B: Nov. 26, 1920, Spokane, Wash.; D: Oct. 17, 1985, Sacramento, Calif. Catcher (1951–53).

Shellenback, Frank, B: Dec. 16, 1898, Joplin, Mo.; D: Aug. 17, 1969, Newton, Mass. Pitcher (1918–19).

Shipley, Joe, B: May 9, 1935, Morristown, Tenn. Pitcher (1963).

Shires, Art, B: Aug. 13, 1907, Italy, Tex.; D: July 13, 1967, Italy, Tex. Infielder (1928–30).

Shook, Ray, B: Nov. 18, 1889, Perry, Ohio; D: Sept. 16, 1970, South Bend, Ind. Pinch-hitter (1916).

Shores, Bill, B: May 26, 1904, Abilene, Tex.; D: Feb. 19, 1984, Purcell, Okla. Pitcher (1936).

Short, Dave, B: May 11, 1917, Magnolia, Ark.; D: Nov. 22, 1983, Shreveport, La. Outfielder (1940–41).

Shoun, Clyde, B: Mar. 20, 1912, Mountain City, Tenn.; D: Mar. 20, 1968, Mountain Home, Tenn. Pitcher (1949).

Shugarts, Frank, B: Dec. 10, 1866, Luthersburg, Pa.; D: Sept. 9, 1944, Clearfield, Pa. Infielder (1901).

Sierra, Ruben, B: Oct. 6, 1965, Rio Piedras, P.R. Outfielder/DH (1998).

Sievers, Roy, B: Nov. 18, 1926, St. Louis, Mo. Infielder (1960–61).

Sigafoos, Frank, B: Mar. 21, 1904, Easton, Pa.; D: Apr. 12, 1968, Indianapolis, Ind. Infielder (1929).

Silvestri, Ken, B: May 3, 1916, Chicago, Ill.; D: Mar. 31, 1992, Tallahassee, Fla. Catcher (1939–40).

Sima, Al, B: Oct. 7, 1921, Mahwah, N.J.; D: Aug. 17, 1993, Suffern, N.Y. Pitcher (1954).

Simas, Billy, B: Nov. 28, 1971, Hanford, Calif. Pitcher (1995–2001).

Simmons, Al, B: May 22, 1902, Milwaukee, Wis.; D: May 26, 1956, Milwaukee, Wis. Outfielder (1933–35).

Simmons, Brian, B: Nov. 4, 1973, Lebanon, Pa. Outfielder (1998–99).

Simons, Mel, B: July 1, 1900, Carlyle, Ill.; D: Nov. 10, 1974, Paducah, Ky. Outfielder (1931–32).

Simpson, Harry, B: Dec. 3, 1925, Atlanta, Ga.; D: Apr. 3, 1979, Akron, Ohio. Outfielder (1959).

Singleton, Chris, B: Aug. 15, 1972, Martinez, Calif. Outfielder (1999–2001).

Sirotka, Mike, B: May 13, 1971, Chicago, Ill. Pitcher (1995–2000).

Sisco, Andrew, B: Jan. 13, 1983, Steamboat Springs, Colo. Pitcher (2007).

Sisk, Tommie, B: Apr. 12, 1942, Ardmore, Okla. Pitcher (1970).

Siwy, Jim, B: Sept. 20, 1958, Pawtucket, R.I. Pitcher (1982–84).

Sketchley, Harry "Bud," B: Mar. 30, 1919, Virden, Manitoba; D: Dec. 19, 1979, Los Angeles, Calif. Outfielder (1942).

Skinner, Joel, B: Feb. 21, 1961, La Jolla, Calif. Catcher (1983–86).

Skizas, Lou, B: June 2, 1932, Chicago, Ill. Outfielder (1959).

Skopec, John, B: May 8, 1880, Chicago, Ill.; D: Oct. 20, 1912, Chicago, Ill. Pitcher (1901).

Skowron, Bill "Moose," B: Dec. 18, 1930, Chicago, Ill. Infielder (1964–67).

Slattery, Jack, B: Jan. 6, 1878, South Boston, Mass.; D: July 17, 1949, Boston, Mass. Catcher (1903).

Slaught, Don, B: Sept. 11, 1958, Long Beach, Calif. Catcher (1996).

Smalley, Roy, B: Oct. 25, 1952, Los Angeles, Calif. Infielder (1984).

Smaza, Joe, B: July 7, 1923, Detroit, Mich.; D: May 30, 1979, Royal Oak, Mich. Outfielder (1946).

Smith, Al, B: Feb. 7, 1928, Kirkwood, Mo.; D: Jan. 3, 2002, Chicago, Ill. Outfielder (1958–62).

Smith, Art, B: June 21, 1906, Boston, Mass.; D: Nov. 22, 1995, Norwalk, Conn. Pitcher (1932).

Smith, Bob, B: July 20, 1890, Woodbury, Vt.; D: Dec. 27, 1965, West Los Angeles, Calif. Pitcher (1913).

Smith, Charley, B: Sept. 15, 1937, Charleston, S.C.; D: Nov. 29, 1994, Reno, Nev. Infielder (1962–64).

Smith, Clarence "Pop Boy," B: May 23, 1892, Newport, Tenn.; D: Feb. 16, 1924, Sweetwater, Tex. Pitcher (1913).

Smith, Eddie, B: Dec. 14, 1913, Bordentown, N.J.; D: Jan. 2, 1994, Willingboro, N.J. Pitcher (1939–43, 1946–47).

Smith, Ernie, B: Oct. 11, 1899, Totowa, N.J.; D: Apr. 6, 1973, Brooklyn, N.Y. Infielder (1930).

Smith, Frank, B: Oct. 28, 1879, Pittsburgh, Pa.; D: Nov. 3, 1952, Pittsburgh, Pa. Pitcher (1904–10).

Smith, Harry, B: Aug. 15, 1889, Union, Neb.; D: July 26, 1964, Dunbar, Neb. Pitcher (1912).

Snipes, Wyatt "Roxy," B: Oct. 28, 1896, Marion, S.C.; D: May 1, 1941, Fayetteville, N.C. Pinch-hitter (1923).

Snopek, Chris, B: Sept. 20, 1970, Cynthiana, Ky. Infielder (1995–98).

Snyder, Cory, B: Nov. 11, 1962, Inglewood, Calif. Outfielder/DH (1991).

Snyder, John, B: Aug. 16, 1974, Southfield, Mich., Pitcher (1998–99).

Snyder, Russ, B: June 22, 1934, Oak, Neb. Outfielder (1968).

Soderholm, Eric, B: Sept. 24, 1948, Cortland, N.Y. Infielder (1977–79).

Solomon, Eddie, B: Feb. 9, 1951, Perry, Ga.; D: Jan. 12, 1986, Macon, Ga. Pitcher (1982).

Solters, Julius "Moose," B: Mar. 22, 1906, Pittsburgh, Pa.; D: Sept. 28, 1975, Pittsburgh, Pa. Outfielder (1940–41, 1943).

Steve Stone

Sosa, Sammy, B: Nov. 10, 1968, San Pedro de Macorís, Dominican Republic. Outfielder (1989–91).

Souchock, Steve, Mar. 3, 1919, Yatesboro, Pa.; D: July 28, 2002, Westland, Mich. Outfielder (1949).

Speer, Floyd, B: Jan. 27, 1913, Booneville, Ark.; D: Mar. 22, 1969, Little Rock, Ark. Pitcher (1943–44).

Spence, Bob, B: Feb. 10, 1946, San Diego, Calif. Infielder (1969–71).

Spencer, Jim, B: July 30, 1946, Hanover, Pa.; D: Feb. 10, 2002, Ft. Lauderdale, Fla. Infielder (1976–77).

Spencer, Tom, B: Feb. 28, 1951, Gallipolis, Ohio. Outfielder (1978).

Spiezio, Ed, B: Oct. 31, 1941, Joliet, Ill. Infielder (1972).

Spillner, Dan, B: Nov. 27, 1951, Casper, Wy. Pitcher (1984–85).

Squires, Mike, B: Mar. 5, 1952, Kalamazoo, Mich. Infielder/catcher (1975, 1977–85).

Staehle, Marv, B: Mar. 13, 1942, Oak Park, Ill. Infielder (1964–67).

Staley, Gerry, B: Aug. 21, 1920, Brush Prairie, Wash.; D: Jan. 2, 2008, Vancouver, Wash. Pitcher (1956–61).

Stange, Lee, B: Oct. 27, 1936, Chicago, Ill. Pitcher (1970).

Stanka, Joe, B: July 23, 1931, Hammon, Okla. Pitcher (1959).

Stanton, Mike, B: Sept. 25, 1952, Phenix City, Ala. Pitcher (1985).

Stark, Matt, B: Jan. 21, 1965, Whittier, Calif. DH (1990).

Steengrafe, Milt, B: May 26, 1900, San Francisco, Calif.; D: June 2, 1977, Oklahoma City, Okla. Pitcher (1924–26).

Stegman, Dave, B: Jan. 30, 1954, Inglewood, Calif. Outfielder (1983–84).

Stein, Bill, B: Jan. 21, 1947, Battle Creek, Mich. Infielder (1974–76).

Steinbacher, Hank, B: Mar. 22, 1913, Sacramento, Calif.; D: Apr. 30, 1977, Sacramento, Calif. Outfielder (1937–39).

Stephens, Gene, B: Jan. 20, 1933, Gravette, Ark. Outfielder (1963–64).

Stephens, Vern, B: Oct. 23, 1920, McAllister, N.Mex.; D: Nov. 3, 1968, Long Beach, Calif. Infielder (1953, 1955).

Stephenson, Joe, B: June 30, 1921, Detroit, Mich.; D: Sept. 20, 2001, Detroit, Mich. Catcher (1947).

Stewart, Chris, B: Feb. 19, 1982, Fontana, Calif. Catcher (2006).

Stewart, Eddie "Bud," B: June 15, 1916, Sacramento, Calif.; D: June 21, 2000, Palo Alto, Calif. Outfielder (1951–54).

Stewart, Frank, B: Sept. 8, 1906, Minneapolis, Minn.; D: Apr. 30, 2001, Stillwater, Minn. Pitcher (1927).

Stewart, Jimmy, B: June 11, 1939, Opelika, Ala. Infielder (1967).

Stewart, Josh, B: Dec. 5, 1978, Paducah, Ky. Pitcher (2003–04).

Stieb, Dave, B: July 22, 1957, Santa Ana, Calif. Pitcher (1993).

Stillman, Royle, B: Jan. 2, 1951, Santa Monica, Calif. Outfielder (1977).

Stine, Lee, B: Nov.17, 1913, Stillwater, Okla.; D: May 6, 2005, Hemet, Calif. Pitcher (1934–35).

Stobbs, Chuck, B: July 2, 1929, Wheeling, W.Va.; D: July 7, 2008, Sarasota, Fla. Pitcher (1952).

Stoddard, Tim, B: Jan. 24, 1953, East Chicago, Ind. Pitcher (1975).

Stone, Dean, B: Sept. 1, 1930, Moline, Ill. Pitcher (1962).

Stone, Steve, B: July 14, 1947, Euclid, Ohio. Pitcher (1973, 77–78).

Stoneham, John, B: Nov. 8, 1908, Wood River, Ill.; D: Jan. 1, 2004, Owosso, Okla. Outfielder (1933).

Strahs, Dick, B: Dec. 4, 1923, Evanston, Ill.; D: May 26, 1988, Las Vegas, Nev. Pitcher (1954).

Strang, Sammy, B: Dec. 16, 1876, Chattanooga, Tenn.; D: Mar. 13, 1932, Chattanooga, Tenn. Infielder (1902).

Stratton, Monty, B: May 21, 1912, Celeste, Tex.; D: Sept. 28, 1982, Greenville, Tex. Pitcher (1934–38).

Stricklett, Elmer, B: Aug. 29, 1876, Glasco, Kan.; D: June 7, 1964, Santa Cruz, Calif. Pitcher (1904).

Striker, Jake, B: Oct. 23, 1933, New Washington, Ohio. Pitcher (1960).

Stroud, Ed, B: Oct. 31, 1939, Lapine, Ala. Outfielder (1966–67, 71).

Strunk, Amos, B: Jan. 22, 1889, Philadelphia, Pa.; D: July 22, 1979, Llanerch, Pa. Outfielder (1920–24).

Stumpf, George, B: Dec. 15, 1910, New Orleans, La.; D: Mar. 6, 1993, Metairie, La. Outfielder (1936).

Sturtze, Tanyon, B: Oct. 12, 1970, Worcester, Mass. Pitcher (1999–2000).

Sugden, Joe, B: July 31, 1870, Philadelphia, Pa.; D: June 28, 1959, Philadelphia, Pa. Catcher (1900–01).

Sullivan, Billy, B: Feb. 1, 1875, Fort Atkinson, Wis.; D: Jan. 28, 1965, Newberg, Ore. Catcher (1901–12, 14).

Sullivan, Billy Jr., B: Oct. 23, 1910, Chicago, Ill.; D: Jan. 4, 1994, Sarasota, Fla. Catcher/infielder (1931–33).

Sullivan, John, B: May 31, 1894, Chicago, Ill.; D: July 7, 1958, Chicago, Ill. Pitcher (1919).

Sullivan, Scott, B: Mar. 13, 1971, Tuscaloosa, Ala. Pitcher (2003).

Surkont, Max, B: June 16, 1922, Central Falls, R.I.; D: Oct. 8, 1986, Largo, Fla. Pitcher (1949).

Suter, Harry "Rube," B: Sept. 15, 1887, Independence, Mo.; D: July 24, 1971, Topeka, Kan. Pitcher (1909).

Joe Sugden (left) and Billy Sullivan

Sutherland, Leo, B: Apr. 6, 1958, Santiago, Cuba. Infielder (1980–81).

Sveum, Dale, B: Nov. 23, 1963, Richmond, Calif. Infielder (1992).

Swanson, Evar, B: Oct. 15, 1902, DeKalb, Ill.; D: July 17, 1973, Galesburg, Ill. Outfielder (1932–34).

Swanson, Karl, B: Dec. 17, 1903, North Henderson, Ill.; D: Apr. 3, 2002, Moline, Ill. Infielder (1928–29).

Sweeney, Ryan, B: Feb. 20, 1985, Ceder Rapids, Iowa. Outfielder (2006–07).

Swentor, Augie, B: Nov. 21, 1899, Seymour, Conn.; D: Nov. 10, 1969, Waterbury, Conn. Catcher (1922).

Swift, Bill, B: Jan. 10, 1908, Elmira, N.Y.; D: Feb. 23, 1969, Bartow, Fla. Pitcher (1943).

Swisher, Nick, B: Nov. 25, 1980, Columbus, Ohio. Outfielder (2008).

T

Taitt, Doug, B: Aug. 3, 1902, Bay City, Mich.; D: Dec. 12, 1970, Portland, Ore. Outfielder (1929).

Takatsu, Shingo, B: Nov. 25, 1968, Hiroshima, Japan. Pitcher (2004–05).

Talbot, Fred, B: June 28, 1941, Washington, D.C. Pitcher (1963–64).

Tankersley, Leo, B: June 8, 1901, Terrell, Tex.; D: Sept. 18, 1980, Dallas, Tex. Catcher (1925).

Tannehill, Lee, B: Oct. 26, 1880, Dayton, Ky.; D: Feb. 16, 1938, Live Oak, Fla. Infielder (1903–12).

Tanner, Bruce, B: Dec. 9, 1961, New Castle, Pa. Pitcher (1985).

Tapani, Kevin, B: Feb. 18, 1964, Des Moines, Iowa. Pitcher (1996).

Tartabull, Danny, B: Oct. 30, 1962, Miami, Fla. Outfielder (1996).

Tate, Bennie, B: Dec. 3, 1901, Whitwell, Tenn.; D: Oct. 27, 1973, West Frankfort, Ill. Catcher (1930–32).

Tatum, Ken, B: Apr. 25, 1944, Alexandria, La. Pitcher (1974).

Tauby, Fred, B: Mar. 27, 1906, Canton, Ohio; D: Nov. 23, 1955, Concordia, Calif. Outfielder (1935).

Taylor, Leo, B: May 13, 1901, Walla Walla, Wash.; D: May 20, 1982, Seattle, Wash. Pinch-hitter (1923).

Taylor, Wiley, B: Mar. 18, 1888, Wamego, Kan.; D: July 8, 1954, Westmoreland, Kan. Pitcher (1912).

Teahen, Mark, B: Sept. 6, 1981, Redlands, Calif. Infielder (2010–).

Terrero, Luis, B: May 18, 1980. Barahona, Dominican Republic. Outfielder (2007).

Terry, Zeb, B: June 17, 1891, Denison, Tex.; D: Mar. 14, 1988, Los Angeles, Calif. Infielder (1916–17).

Thigpen, Bobby, B: July 17, 1963, Tallahassee, Fla. Pitcher (1986–93).

Thomas, Frank, B: May 27, 1968, Columbus, Ga. Infielder/DH (1990–2005).

Frank Thomas

Thomas, Larry, B: Oct. 25, 1969, Miami, Fla. Pitcher (1995–97).

Thomas, Leo, B: July 26, 1923, Turlock, Calif.; D: Mar. 5, 2001, Concord, Pa. Infielder (1952).

Thomas, Tommy, B: Dec. 23, 1899, Baltimore, Md.; D: Apr. 27, 1988, Dallastown, Pa. Pitcher (1926–32).

Thome, Jim, B: Aug. 27, 1979, Peoria, Ill. DH (2006–09).

Thompson, Lee, B: Feb. 26, 1898, Smithfield, Utah; D: Feb. 17, 1963, Santa Barbara, Calif. Pitcher (1921).

Jim Thome

Thompson, Tommy, B: May 19, 1910, Elkhart, Ill.; D: May 24, 1971, Auburn, Calif. Pitcher (1926–32).

Thornton, Matt, B: Sept. 15, 1976, Three Rivers, Mich. Pitcher (2006–).

Threets, Erick, B: Nov. 4, 1981, Hayward, Calif. Pitcher (2010).

Thurston, Hollis "Sloppy," B: June 2, 1899, Fremont, Neb.; D: Sept. 14, 1973, Los Angeles, Calif. Pitcher (1923–26).

Tidrow, Dick, B: May 14, 1947, San Francisco, Calif. Pitcher (1983).

Thurman Tucker

Tiefenthaler, Verle, B: July 11, 1937, Brenda, Iowa. Pitcher (1962).

Tietje, Les, B: Sept. 11, 1911, Sumner, Iowa.; D: Oct. 2, 1996, Rochester, Minn. Pitcher (1933–36).

Tingley, Ron, B: May 27, 1959, Presque Isle, Maine. Catcher (1994).

Tipton, Joe, B: Feb. 18, 1922, McCaysville, Ga.; D: Mar. 1, 1994, Birmingham, Ala. Catcher (1949).

Tolleson, Wayne, B: Nov. 22, 1955, Spartanburg, S.C. Infielder (1986).

Torgeson, Earl, B: Jan. 1, 1924, Snohomish, Wash.; D: Nov. 8, 1990, Everett, Wash. Infielder (1957–61).

Torrealba, Pablo, B: Apr. 28, 1948, Barquisimento, Venezuela. Pitcher (1978–79).

Torres, Carlos, B: Oct. 22, 1982, Santa Cruz, Calif. Pitcher (2009–).

Torres, Rusty, B: Sept. 30, 1948, Aquadilla, P.R. Outfielder (1978–79).

Touchstone, Clay, B: Jan. 24, 1903, Moore, Pa.; D: Apr. 28, 1949, Beaumont, Tex. Pitcher (1945).

Towne, Jay "Babe," B: Mar. 12, 1880, Coon Rapids, Iowa; D: Oct. 29, 1938, Des Moines, Iowa. Catcher (1906).

Tracey, Sean, B: Nov. 14, 1980, Upland, Calif. Pitcher (2006).

Tremie, Chris, B: Oct. 17, 1969, Houston, Tex. Catcher (1995).

Tresh, Mike, B: Feb. 23, 1914, Hazleton, Pa.; D: Oct. 4, 1966, Detroit, Mich. Catcher (1938–48).

Trosky, Hal Jr., B: Sept. 29, 1936, Cleveland, Ohio. Pitcher (1958).

Trosky, Hal Sr., B: Nov. 11, 1912, Norway, Iowa; D: June 18, 1979, Cedar Rapids, Iowa. Infielder (1944, 1946).

Trout, Steve, B: July 30, 1957, Detroit, Mich. Pitcher (1978–82).

Trucks, Virgil, B: Apr. 26, 1917, Birmingham, Ala. Pitcher (1953–55).

Tucker, Thurman, B: Sept. 26, 1917, Gordon, Tex.; D: May 7, 1993, Oklahoma City, Okla. Outfielder (1942–44, 46–47).

Turner, Jerry, B: Jan. 17, 1954, Texarkana, Ark. Outfielder (1981).

Turner, Tom, B: Sept. 8, 1916, Custer, Okla.; D: May 14, 1986, Kennewick, Wash. Catcher (1940–41).

Twombly, Cy, B: June 15, 1897, Groveland, Mass.; D: Dec. 3, 1974, Savannah, Ga. Pitcher (1921).

Juan Uribe

U

Uhalt, Bernie "Frenchy," B; Apr. 27, 1910, Bakersfield, Calif.; D: Sept. 3, 2004, Rossmor, Calif. Outfielder (1934).

Uhl, Bob, B: Sept. 17, 1913, San Francisco, Calif.; D: Aug. 21, 1990, Santa Rosa, Calif. Pitcher (1938).

Uhlir, Charlie, B: July 30, 1912, Chicago, Ill.; D: July 9, 1984, Spirit Lake, Iowa. Outfielder (1934).

Upshaw, Cecil, B: Oct. 22, 1942, Spearsville, La.; D: Feb. 7, 1995, Lawrenceville, Ga. Pitcher (1975).

Uribe, Juan, B: Mar. 22, 1979, D.R. Infielder (2004–08).

V

Valdez, Mario, B: Nov. 19, 1974, Ciudad Obregon, Mexico. Infielder (1997).

Valdez, Wilson, B: May 20, 1978, Bani, D.R. Infielder (2004).

Art Veltman

Robin Ventura

Valentin, Jose, B: Oct. 12, 1969, Manati, P.R. Infielder (2000–04).

Valentinetti, Vito, B: Sept. 16, 1928, West New York, N.J. Pitcher (1954).

Vance, Joe, B: Sept. 16, 1905, Devine, Tex.; D: July 4, 1978, Devine, Tex. Pitcher (1935).

Varney, Pete, B: Apr. 10, 1949, Roxbury, Mass. Catcher (1973–75, '76).

Vazquez, Javier, B: June 25, 1976, Ponce, P.R. Pitcher (2006–08).

Veltman, Art, B: Mar. 24, 1906, Mobile, Ala.; D: Oct. 1, 1980, San Antonio, Tex. Infielder (1926).

Omar Vizquel

Ventura, Robin, B: July 14, 1967, Santa Maria, Calif. Infielder (1989–98).

Verhoeven, John, B: July 3, 1953, Long Beach, Calif. Pitcher (1977).

Viciedo, Dayan, B: Mar. 10, 1989, Remedios, Cuba. Infielder (2010–).

Vining, Ken, B: Dec. 5, 1974, Decatur, Ga. Pitcher (2001).

Vinson, Ernie "Rube," B: Mar. 20, 1879, Dover, Del.; D: Oct. 12, 1951, Chester, Pa. Outfielder (1906).

Vizcaino, Luis, B: Aug. 6, 1974, Bani, Dominican Republic. Pitcher (2005).

Vizquel, Omar, B: Apr. 24, 1967, Caracas, Venezuela. Infielder (2010–).

Von Kolnitz, Alfred "Fritz," B: May 20, 1893, Charleston, S.C.; D: Mar. 18, 1948, Mount Pleasant, S.C. Infielder (1916).

Voss, Bill, B: Oct. 31, 1943, Glendale, Calif. Outfielder (1965–68).

Vuckovich, Pete, B: Oct. 27, 1952, Johnstown, Pa. Pitcher (1975–76).

W

Wade, Jake, B: Apr. 1, 1912, Morehead City, N.C.; D: February 1, 2006, Wildwood, N.C. Pitcher (1942–44).

Wagner, Leon, B: May 13, 1934, Chattanooga, Tenn.; D: Jan. 3, 2004, Los Angeles, Calif. Outfielder (1968).

Wakamatsu, Don, B: Feb. 22, 1963, Hood River, Ore. Catcher (1991).

Walker, Fred "Dixie," B: Sept. 24, 1910, Villa Rica, Ga.; D: May 17, 1982, Birmingham, Ala. Outfielder (1936–37).

Walker, Gerry "Gee," B: Mar. 19, 1908, Gulfport, Miss.; D: Mar. 20, 1981, Jackson, Miss. Outfielder (1938–39).

Walker, Greg, B: Oct. 6, 1959, Douglas, Ga. Infielder (1982–90).

Walker, Kevin, B: Sept. 20, 1976, Irving, Tex. Pitcher (2005).

Wallaesa, Jack, B: Aug. 31, 1919, Easton, Pa.; D: Dec. 27, 1986, Easton, Pa. Infielder (1947–48).

Walsh, Ed Jr., B: Feb. 11, 1905, Meriden, Conn.; D: Oct. 31, 1937, Meriden, Conn. Pitcher (1928–30, 32).

Walsh, Ed Sr., B: May 14, 1881, Plains, Pa.; D: May 26, 1959, Pompano Beach, Fla. Pitcher (1904–16).

Wapnick, Steve, B: Sept. 25, 1965, Panorama City, Calif. Pitcher (1991).

Ward, Aaron, B: Aug. 28, 1896, Booneville, Ark.; D: Jan. 30, 1961, New Orleans, La. Infielder (1927).

Ward, Bryan, B: Jan. 25, 1972, Bristol, Pa., Pitcher (1998–99).

Ward, Pete, B: July 26, 1939, Montreal, Quebec, Canada. Infielder/outfielder (1963–69).

Washington, Claudell, B: Aug. 31, 1954, Los Angeles, Calif. Outfielder (1978–80).

Washington, Sloane "George," B: June 4, 1907, Linden, Tex.; D: Feb. 17, 1985, Linden, Tex. Outfielder (1935–36).

Wassermann, Ehren, B: Dec. 6, 1980, Sylacuaga, Ala. Pitcher (2007–08).

Watwood, John "Cliff," B: Aug. 17, 1905, Alexander City, Ala.; D: Mar. 1, 1980, Goodwater, Ala. Outfielder (1929–32).

Way, Bob, B: Apr. 2, 1906, Elmenton, Pa.; D: June 20, 1974, Pittsburgh, Pa. Infielder (1927).

Weaver, Art, B: Apr. 7, 1879, Wichita, Kan.; D: Mar. 23, 1917, Denver, Colo. Catcher (1908).

Weaver, Floyd, B: May 12, 1941, Ben Franklin, Tex.; D: Nov. 17, 2008, Powderly, Tex. Pitcher (1970).

Weaver, George "Buck," B: Aug. 18, 1890, Pottstown, Pa.; D: Jan. 31, 1956, Chicago, Ill. Infielder (1912–20).

Gerald "Gee" Walker

Webb, Earl, B: Sept. 17, 1897, Bon Air, Tenn.; D: May 23, 1965, Jamestown, Tenn. Outfielder (1933).

Webb, Jim "Skeeter," B: Nov. 4, 1909, Meridian, Miss.; July 8, 1986, Meridian, Miss. Infielder (1940–44).

Wehde, Wilbur "Biggs," B: Nov. 23, 1906, Holstein, Iowa; D: Sept. 21, 1970, Sioux Falls, S.D. Pitcher (1930–31).

Wehrmeister, Dave, B: Nov. 9, 1952, Berwyn, Ill. Pitcher (1985).

Weigel, Ralph, B: Oct. 2, 1921, Coldwater, Ohio; D: Apr. 15, 1992, Memphis, Tenn. Catcher (1948).

Weiland, Bob, B: Dec. 14, 1905, Chicago, Ill.; D: Nov. 9, 1988, Chicago, Ill. Pitcher (1928–31).

Weiland, Ed, B: Nov. 26, 1914, Evanston, Ill.; D: July 12, 1971, Chicago, Ill. Pitcher (1940, 42).

Weis, Al, B: Apr. 2, 1938, Franklin Square, N.Y. Infielder (1962–67).

Welday, Mike, B: Dec. 19, 1879, Conway, Iowa; D: May 28, 1942, Leavenworth, Kan. Outfielder (1907–09).

Wells, David "Boomer," B: May 20, 1963, Torrance, Calif. Pitcher (2001).

Al Weis

Wells, Leo, B: July 18, 1917, Kansas City, Kan.; D: June 23, 2006, St. Paul, Minn. Infielder (1942, 1946).

Wells, Robert "Kip," B: Apr. 21, 1977, Houston, Tex. Pitcher (1999–2001).

West, Sammy, B: Oct. 5, 1904, Longview, Tex.; D: Nov. 23, 1985, Lubbock, Tex. Outfielder (1942).

Wheeler, Don, B: Sept. 29, 1922, Minneapolis, Minn.; D: Dec. 10, 2003, Bloomington, Minn. Catcher (1949).

Whisler, Wes, B: Apr. 7, 1983, Indianapolis, Ind. Pitcher (2009).

White, Ed, B: Apr. 6, 1926, Anniston, Ala.; D: Sept. 28, 1982, Lakeland, Fla. Outfielder (1955).

White, Guy "Doc," B: Apr. 9, 1879, Washington, D.C.; D: Feb. 19, 1969, Silver Spring, Md. Pitcher (1903–13).

White, Rick, B: Dec. 23, 1968, Springfield, Ohio. Pitcher (2003).

Whitehead, John, B: Apr. 27, 1909, Coleman, Tex.; D: Oct. 20, 1964, Bonham, Tex. Pitcher (1935–39).

Whitman, Frank, B: Aug. 15, 1924, Marengo, Ind.; D: Feb. 6, 1994, Maryville, Ill. Infielder (1946, 48).

Widger, Chris, B: May 21, 1971, Wilmington, Del. Catcher (2005–06).

Widmar, Al, B: Mar. 20, 1925, Cleveland, Ohio. Pitcher (1952).

Wieneke, Jack, B: Mar. 10, 1894, Saltsburg, Pa.; D: Mar. 16, 1933, Pleasant Ridge, Mich. Pitcher (1921).

Wight, Bill, B: Apr. 12, 1922, Rio Vista, Calif.; D: May 17, 2007, Mount Shasta, Calif. Pitcher (1948–50).

Wiles, Randy, B: Sept. 10, 1951, Fort Belvoir, Va. Pitcher (1977).

Wilhelm, Hoyt, B: July 26, 1923, Huntersville, N.C.; D: Aug. 23, 2002, Sarasota, Fla. Pitcher (1963–68).

Wilkinson, Roy, B: May 8, 1894, Canandaigua, N.Y.; D: July 2, 1956, Louisville, Ky. Pitcher (1919–22).

Willard, Jerry, B: Mar. 14, 1960, Oxnard, Calif. Infielder (1990).

Williams, Claude "Lefty," B: Mar. 9, 1893, Aurora, Mo.; D: Nov. 4, 1959, Laguna Beach, Calif. Pitcher (1917–20).

Williams, Eddie, B: Nov. 1, 1964, Shreveport, La. Infielder (1989).

Williams, Kenny, B: Apr. 6, 1964, Berkeley, Calif. Outfielder/infielder (1986–88).

Williams, Randy, B: Sept. 18, 1975, Harlingen, Tex. Pitcher (2009–10).

Williams, Walt, B: Dec. 19, 1943, Brownwood, Tex. Outfielder (1967–72).

Williamson, Al, B: Feb. 20, 1900, Buckville, Ark.; D: Nov. 29, 1978, Hot Springs, Ark. Pitcher (1928).

Willingham, Hugh, B: May 30, 1906, Dalhart, Tex.; D: June 15, 1988, El Reno, Okla. Infielder (1930).

Willis, Carl, B: Dec. 28, 1960, Danville, Va. Pitcher (1988).

Willoughby, Jim, B: Jan. 31, 1949, Salinas, Calif. Pitcher (1978).

Wills, Ted, B: Feb. 9, 1934, Fresno, Calif. Pitcher (1965).

Willson, Frank "Kid," B: Nov. 3, 1895, Bloomington, Neb.; D: Apr. 17, 1964, Union Gap, Wash. Outfielder (1918, 1927).

Wilson, Bill, B: Nov. 6, 1928, Central City, Neb. Outfielder (1950, 1953–54).

Wilson, Bob "Red," B: Mar. 7, 1929, Milwaukee, Wis. Catcher (1951–54).

Wilson, Craig, B: Sept. 3, 1970, Chicago, Ill. Infielder (1998–2000).

Wilson, Jim, B: Feb. 20, 1922, San Diego, Calif.; D: Sept. 2, 1986, Newport Beach, Calif. Pitcher (1956–58).

Wilson, Roy, B: Sept. 13, 1896, Foster, Iowa; D: Dec. 3, 1969, Clarion, Iowa. Pitcher (1928).

Wilson, Ted, B: Aug. 30, 1925, Cherryville, N.C.; D: Oct. 29, 1974, Gastonia, N.C. Outfielder (1952).

Winn, Jim, B: Sept. 23, 1959, Stockton, Calif. Pitcher (1987).

Wirts, Elwood "Kettle," B: Oct. 31, 1897, Consumnes, Calif.; D: July 12, 1968, Sacramento, Calif. Catcher (1924).

Wise, Archie, B: July 31, 1912, Waxahachie, Tex.; D: Feb. 2, 1978, Dallas, Tex. Pitcher (1923).

Wise, DeWayne, B: Feb. 24, 1978, Columbia, S.C., Outfielder (2008–09).

Wolfe, Roy "Polly," B: Sept. 1, 1888, Knoxville, Ill.; D: Nov. 21, 1938, Morris, Ill. Outfielder (1912, '14).

Wolfgang, Mellie, B: Mar. 20, 1890, Albany, N.Y.; D: June 30, 1947, Albany, N.Y. Pitcher (1914–18).

Wood, Wilbur, B: Oct. 22, 1941, Cambridge, Mass. Pitcher (1967–78).

Wilbur Wood

Woodard, Mike, B: Mar. 2, 1960, Melrose Park, Ill. Infielder (1988).

Woodward, Frank, B: May 17, 1894, New Haven, Conn.; D: June 11, 1961, New Haven, Conn. Pitcher (1923).

Wortham, Rich "Tex," B: Oct. 22, 1953, Odessa, Tex. Pitcher (1978–80).

Worthington, Al, B: Feb. 5, 1929, Birmingham, Ala. Pitcher (1960).

Wright, Dan, B: Dec. 14, 1977, Longview, Tex. Pitcher (2001–04).

Wright, Ed "Ceylon," B: Aug. 16, 1893, Minneapolis, Minn.; D: Nov. 7, 1947, Hines, Ill. Infielder (1916).

Wright, Glenn, B: Feb. 6, 1901, Archie, Mo.; D: Apr. 6, 1984, Olathe, Kan. Infielder (1935).

Wright, Taffy, B: Aug. 10, 1911, Tabor City, N.C.; D: Oct. 22, 1981, Orlando, Fla. Outfielder (1940–42, 1946–48).

Wright, Tom, B: Sept. 22, 1923, Shelby, N.C. Outfielder (1952–53).

Wrona, Rick, B: Dec. 10, 1963, Tulsa, Okla. Catcher (1993).

Wunsch, Kelly, B: July 12, 1972, Houston, Tex. Pitcher (2000–04).

Wyatt, Whitlow, B: Sept. 27, 1907, Kensington, Ga.; D: July 16, 1999, Carrolton, Ga. Pitcher (1933–36).

Wynn, Early, B: Jan. 6, 1920, Hartford, Ala.; D: Apr. 4, 1999, Venice, Fla. Pitcher (1958–62).

Wynne, Billy, B: July 31, 1943, Williamston, N.C. Pitcher (1968–70).

Y

Yancy, Hugh, B: Oct. 16, 1950, Sarasota, Fla. Infielder (1972, 1974, 1976).

Yankowski, George, B: Nov. 19, 1922, Cambridge, Mass. Catcher (1949).

Yaryan, Clarence "Yam," B: Nov. 5, 1892, Knowlton, Iowa; D: Nov. 16, 1964, Birmingham, Ala. Catcher (1921–22).

York, Rudy, B: Aug. 17, 1913, Ragland, Ala.; D: Feb. 5, 1970, Rome, Ga. Infielder (1947).

Young, Irv, B: July 21, 1877, Columbia Falls, Maine; D: Jan. 14, 1935, Brewer, Maine. Pitcher (1910–11).

Z

Zanni, Dom, B: Mar. 1, 1932, Bronx, N.Y. Pitcher (1962–63).

Zarilla, Al, B: May 1, 1919, Los Angeles, Calif.; D: Sept. 4, 1996, Honolulu, Hawaii. Outfielder (1951–52).

Zeider, Rollie, B: Nov. 16, 1883, Auburn, Ind.; D: Sept. 12, 1967, Garrett, Ind. Infielder (1910–13).

Zernial, Gus, B: June 27, 1923, Beaumont, Tex.; D: Jan. 20, 2011, Fresno Calif. Outfielder (1949–51).

Zisk, Richie, B: Feb. 6, 1949, Brooklyn, N.Y. Outfielder (1977).

Zupcic, Bob, B: Aug. 18, 1966, Pittsburgh, Pa. Infielder/outfielder (1994).

Zwilling, Ed "Dutch," B: Nov. 2, 1888, St. Louis, Mo.; D: Mar. 27, 1978, La Crescenta, Calif. Outfielder (1910).

Rollie Zeider

4

The Strategists

Thirty-five men took their turn at managing the Chicago White Sox—34 if you peek into the team archives or examine the ninth edition of the *Macmillan Baseball Encyclopedia.* They seem to have completely forgotten or ignored George "Mule" Haas, who opened the 1946 season as the interim skipper while Jimmie Dykes recovered from gallstone surgery.

So far, there have really only been six truly outstanding managers who altered the course of Sox history through their motivational skills, leadership, or dazzling bits of strategy at a decisive moment in a game. Heading this list is Fielder Allison Jones, a brilliant motivator and relentless tactician who won the 1906 pennant and World Series with the barest amount of talent of any team in this century. Jimmie Dykes, Al Lopez, Paul Richards, Tony LaRussa, and Ozzie Guillen must also be included in this all-star assembly, though won-and-lost records alone may not accurately reflect their lasting contributions to the well-being of the franchise during their respective eras.

Only seven White Sox managers can truthfully say that they walked away from the job before they could be fired—Clark Griffith, Fielder Jones, Billy Sullivan, Kid Gleason, Donie Bush, Paul Richards, and Al Lopez. The other unlucky 28 were discharged or forced to resign for the usual stated reasons: incompetency, quarrels with the front office, salary disagreements, and generational conflicts with the players. Of course, the real reason often was the marginal talent these men were counted on to lead to the promised land.

The average tenure for a White Sox manager is only 2.6 years. Only Jimmy Callahan, Kid Gleason, Jimmie Dykes, Paul Richards, Al Lopez, Chuck Tanner, Tony LaRussa, Jerry Manuel, and Ozzie Guillen survived through five or more hectic White Sox seasons. Lopez led the Sox to nine winning seasons—the most for any Sox manager—followed by Dykes, with five, and Guillen, also with five (through the 2010 season).

Going by the numbers, Clark Griffith was the most successful of all Sox managers (.581 winning percentage), but he lasted only two seasons. Lew Fonseca (.380 percentage) is at the bottom of the list for managers who logged one or more seasons. Jimmie Dykes enjoyed the longest tenure (13 seasons), Doug Rader the shortest (two games).

Paul Richards, who began his second go-around in 1976 at age 68, was the oldest White Sox manager. Twenty-nine-year-old Jimmy Callahan, promoted from the playing ranks in 1903, was the youngest.

In the early years of the 20th century, Charles Comiskey hired his veteran players to manage the ballclub. By World War I, playing managers gradually began to disappear from baseball.

Comiskey searched for the right combinations to rebuild his shattered team from the ashes of the Black Sox scandal. Nothing seemed to work. The team was adrift and in a state of confusion. Gradually, despair gave way to complacency, and until the great revival of 1951, getting by was good enough. Then Paul Richards arrived, and for the first time in many years optimism reigned on the South Side.

In 2005 the unlikely Sox, under Ozzie Guillen, were finally back in the national spotlight. The optimism of the 1950s has, for the moment, finally returned. It had been a long time coming.

The longest-serving Sox manager was James J. Dykes—tough, uncompromising, and a fierce enemy of the umpires. He's shown here in spring training, using microphones to get his point across.

Manager Profiles

1900

Comiskey, Charles

Record: 82–53 (.607)
Birthplace: Chicago, Illinois
B: August 15, 1859
D: October 26, 1931

Comiskey, Charles

	W	L	T	Pct
1900	82	53	2	.607
White Sox	82	53	2	.607
Career	839	542	29	.608*

*Does not include 1900 season. The American League was not designated as a bona fide major league at the time.

The inaugural season of White Sox baseball coincided with Charles Comiskey's retirement as a field manager. The rigors of directing the ballclub from both the dugout and swivel chair proved to be a bit too much, even for the tireless Old Roman, who had promised to deliver an exciting team to Chicago baseball fans months before the governing powers signed off on his request to move from St. Paul to Chicago.

Comiskey spent a busy winter examining the National League waiver lists for veteran players to fill out his roster. Up until a week before the scheduled start of the 1900 season, the composition of the team remained in doubt. Under the terms of the 1900 National Agreement, the Old Roman and the other American League owners were not permitted to negotiate with players under contract.

Two key acquisitions sparked the 1900 title drive. Comiskey purchased infielder Dick Padden from the Washington Senators on March 20, and outfielder Dummy Hoy three weeks later, after Louisville refused to renew the contract of baseball's most famous deaf-mute.

Charles Comiskey was involved in all phases of the game—a habit that transcended the playing field and one that annoyed every manager he hired thereafter—over the next 30 years. He was the only Sox manager who wore street clothes in the dugout.

Whatever else one may say about Comiskey's dealings in the latter stages of his life, the Old Roman's yeoman work in 1900 built the foundation of White Sox history. In less than a year's time he saw through an ambitious plan to relocate his team to Chicago's South Side. He named the team the White Stockings, acquired a veteran corps of players in the span of three months, erected a ballpark on a weed patch in 90 days, and then guided this ensemble cast to a championship season.

It is quite an achievement by anyone's standards, and the main reason why Charles Comiskey, as a builder of baseball, was voted into the Hall of Fame in 1939.

1901–02

Griffith, Clark

Record: 157–113 (.581)
Birthplace: Stringtown, Missouri
B: November 20, 1869
D: October 27, 1955

Griffith, Clark

	W	L	T	Pct
1901	83	53	1	.610
1902	74	60	4	.552
White Sox	157	113	5	.581
Career	1,491	1,367	58	.522

Clark Griffith anchored the starting rotation of the Chicago Colts (later Cubs) through the 1890s. In stardom, he remained restless and discontented with the National League power structure that conspired to drive down salaries and keep players in servitude. As president of the Protective Players Association, he threatened to call baseball's first strike in 1900. There was great irony to all of this, because as the owner of the Washington Senators, Griffith jealously

Clark Griffith

guarded his checkbook during salary negotiations with his unhappy players.

Unable to come to terms with National League president Nicholas Young at baseball's 1900 winter meetings over a demand calling for a minimum yearly salary of $3,000, Griffith jumped to the White Sox in March 1901 at a substantially higher salary and a promise of stock ownership in the team. With vengeance in his heart, Griffith convinced teammates Sandow Mertes and Jimmy Callahan to join him on the South Side.

Clark Griffith, the "Old Fox," was a fiery manager and a staunch defender of his players. With a strong ballclub bolstered by the addition of four National League stars, Griffith's task of repeating was made simple. To the dismay of Comiskey and AL president Ban Johnson, however, Griffith refused to back down from supporting several of his players who physically assaulted umpires.

In late August 1901, Griffith threatened a team walkout after Johnson suspended pitcher Jack Katoll and infielder Frank Shugarts after they had engaged in a fistfight with umpire Jack Haskell. "Let them jump back to the National League!" Johnson snorted. "Inexperienced playing managers have made all the trouble this year!" with reference to the conduct of the Sox freshman manager.

The play of the 1902 Sox mirrored Griffith's growing distractions. The team got off to a fine start but withered in early August when the rumors first circulated concerning his impending departure to New York. The league was contemplating a transfer of the Baltimore franchise to Gotham, and Johnson needed a forceful presence to counter John McGraw of the New York Giants, who intrigued against the American League in 1902. Griffith, who held McGraw in low esteem, was sacrificed for the good of the league with Comiskey's blessings.

1903–04; 1912–14

Callahan, James

Record: 308–329 (.484)
Birthplace: Fitchburg, Massachusetts
B: March 18, 1874
D: October 4, 1934

Callahan, James

	W	L	T	Pct
1903	60	77	1	.438
1904	22	18	1	.550
1912	78	76	4	.506
1913	78	74	1	.513
1914	70	84	3	.455
White Sox	308	329	10	.484
Career	393	458	14	.462

Hard-drinking, undisciplined "Nixey" Callahan seemed an unlikely choice to manage the White Sox—and at so young of an age. Callahan was two days shy of his 29th birthday when Charles Comiskey tabbed him to manage the Sox on March 16, 1903. He was one of three unhappy and underpaid Colt (later Cubs) contract jumpers who joined the Sox in 1901 at the urging of former teammate Clark Griffith. Callahan was a pitcher before he became an outfielder, and he authored the first White Sox no-hitter on September 20, 1902.

James Callahan

Comiskey went out on a limb by hiring such a young and inexperienced man. But the Old Roman was confident of his protégé, saying, "He has the ability, and all he needs is the developing…the right way."

Nothing went right in 1903. The team was a loser, and some of the older players resented taking orders from a man several years their junior. Callahan voluntarily stepped down on June 4, 1904, in order to concentrate on his play, which had suffered as a result of his divided responsibilities.

After a falling-out with Comiskey in 1905 over his excessive drinking and weight problems, Callahan quit the White Sox in order to take over the front-office duties of the Logan Squares, a famous Chicago semipro team with a tremendous neighborhood following in the years after the turn of the century. His 1906 team defeated both the Cubs and the Sox in a post–World Series exhibition series the old-timers talked about for years to come.

Convinced that this side of the game had reached its peak, and unable to pay the escalating park rentals, Callahan severed his ties to amateur baseball and petitioned Comiskey and the National Commission for reinstatement into the pro game. He was turned down in 1908, but finally was admitted back into the lodge prior to the 1911 season. Given a choice between playing for the St. Louis Browns or the White Sox, Callahan chose Chicago, where he took up full-time outfield duties.

Comiskey reappointed him manager on October 23, 1911, partially out of his personal fondness for Cal, but he also desired to have a full-time manager living in Chicago. Callahan's predecessor, Hugh Duffy, resided in Massachusetts.

It wasn't much of a ballclub that Callahan took over in the spring of 1912. The team was in a rebuilding mode and never gained the competitive edge it had enjoyed under Fielder Jones' stewardship. Callahan was always at Comiskey's side. He was a faithful and loyal employee in his second Sox go-around, and he always was counted among the traveling party who made the yearly hegira up to Comiskey's Wisconsin hunting lodge at the conclusion of each season.

After a disappointing second-division finish in 1914, Callahan was summarily fired and handed his unconditional release a week before Christmas. He was rumored to be headed to New York as the next Yankees manager, but talks collapsed. Callahan managed the Pirates in 1916 and 1917, with poor results.

Fielder Jones

1904–08

Jones, Fielder

Record: 427–293 (.593)
Birthplace: Shinglehouse, Pennsylvania
B: August 13, 1874
D: March 13, 1934

Jones, Fielder

	W	L	T	Pct
1904	67	47	2	.588
1905	92	60	5	.605
1906	93	58	3	.616
1907	87	64	6	.576
1908	88	64	4	.579
White Sox	427	293	20	.593
Career	685	582	32	.541

Fielder Jones, the greatest of all White Sox managers, ignored the advice of his mother, who offered him a land deed worth $1,000 if he would give up baseball and pursue a more satisfactory career in business. Jones signed a contract with Brooklyn instead, where he remained until Comiskey and Clark Griffith encouraged him to bolt the National League and join the White Sox as a contract jumper in 1901.

After Jones had spent three seasons as the starting White Sox center fielder, Comiskey appointed him field manager on June 4, 1904. It was something of a coincidence, because the man whose job he claimed had begun his baseball career playing side by side with Jones for Springfield, Massachusetts, of the Eastern League in 1895. Jimmy Callahan was a pitcher, and Fielder Jones backed him up in center field. There were no hard feelings between the two. Callahan welcomed the change and pledged to support his new boss.

Quiet in manner but possessing a fiery temper when provoked by an umpire, Jones would race in from center field to plead his case. Very often the Sox manager would kick the umpire in the shins, or have to be physically restrained from commiting further acts of violence by his players. Such exploits resulted in frequent fines, suspensions, and reprimands from AL president Ban Johnson, who always supported his umpires regardless of any mitigating circumstances.

Jones was a stern disciplinarian who showed zero tolerance for overweight, lazy, and out-of-condition players. Star players like Frank Smith were exiled to the bench when they crossed the line. But Jones was also an early champion of player rights and argued passionately against the inherent injustices of the reserve clause. "I am practically a slave," he once said. "We are human chattel in the sense that we cannot sell our ability—the only asset on which we can realize contracts of a satisfactory nature—in any market to which we may elect to take that commodity."

Jones was a baseball innovator who was never afraid to experiment with some new piece of strategy or a secret play to give his team an edge. He is credited with devising the "motion" infield to thwart hit-and-run plays and drag bunts down the third-base line with men on base. As the third baseman broke toward home plate to field the ball, Jones would have the other infielders maneuver around the infield and cover the bases in a manner similar to a well-choreographed dance routine. He invented the "body twist" slide for his base stealers after deciding that the runner lost a second or two sliding head-first into the bag.

Fielder Jones will always be remembered for leading a collection of featherweight hitters into the 1906 World Series against the mighty Chicago Cubs, then standing the baseball world on its ear by staging one of the greatest upsets the game has ever seen. His "Hitless Wonder" ballclub was beset by season-long injuries, dissension, and a shortage of talent. But his sheer genius and abiding faith in their abilities was the key to the whole thing. Jones was a brilliant tactician and motivator. His White Sox teams remained in pennant contention up until the last few days of the season in each of the five years he guided the ballclub. No other White Sox manager has come close to duplicating the feat.

His nearly flawless run as manager ended on a sour note. Jones lost the final game of the 1908 season—and the American League pennant—after starting arm-weary Doc White against the Detroit Tigers in the decisive showdown. Frank Smith was well rested and the logical choice to pitch for the White Sox, but he was permanently exiled to Jones' doghouse and was powerless to escape.

Jones called it quits after 1908. His heart was no longer in the game, and he desired to return to his home in Portland, Oregon, where he owned acres of prime, undeveloped timberland with his brother Willard and White Sox teammate Billy Sullivan. All winter long, Comiskey tried to convince Jones to return to Chicago in 1909, believing that no died-in-the-wool baseball man could simply walk away from the game. At the urging of the White Sox owner, *Chicago Tribune* sportswriter Harvey Woodruff was dispatched to Portland in a last-ditch effort to convince Jones to change his mind.

Woodruff discovered that Fielder was sincere in his desire to quit the game but that he would entertain a notion of a comeback only if Comiskey would agree to sell him stock in the ballclub. The Old Roman replied that he would pay Jones any salary within reason, but he no longer desired to take on a business partner.

Fielder Jones ran his timber business for the next few years, but he was lured back into baseball after Federal League promoters offered him a sizable contract to manage the St. Louis entry. His 1915 team finished within one percentage point of the pennant-winning Chicago Whales, proving that the old magic had not entirely abandoned him.

1909

Sullivan, Billy

Record: 78–74 (.513)
Birthplace: Fort Atkinson, Wisconsin
B: February 1, 1875
D: January 28, 1965

Sullivan, Billy

	W	L	T	Pct
1909	78	74	7	.513
White Sox	78	74	7	.513
Career	78	74	7	.513

Fielder Jones served formal notice on February 21, 1909, that he would not be returning to manage the Sox. And yet Charles Comiskey chose to wait until April 12, just two days before the scheduled 1909 opener, before naming Jones' business partner and former White Sox roommate Billy Sullivan as the new manager.

Following in the successful footsteps of Fielder Jones was just too much to ask of Sully. His appointment was born out of Comiskey's panic and desperation. The Old Roman, to no one's great surprise, found Billy's leadership skills wanting.

By midseason Sullivan and Comiskey pretty much agreed that a change of managers was in order for 1910. The veteran catcher agreed to stick it out until the end of the season or until another man could be hired. Comiskey unveiled Hugh Duffy as his choice for the new skipper on October 19, 1909. The owner added to the indelicacy of the whole situation by taking a parting shot at Sullivan, who agreed to remain on the roster as a full-time player: "I selected him [Duffy] because he is a fighting manager with brains, and that is what the White Sox have needed during the past season."

1910–11

Duffy, Hugh

Record: 145–159 (.477)
Birthplace: Cranston, Rhode Island
B: November 26, 1866
D: October 19, 1954

Duffy, Hugh

	W	L	T	Pct
1910	68	85	3	.444
1911	77	74	3	.510
White Sox	145	159	6	.477
Career	535	671	15	.444

Before deciding on Billy Sullivan's replacement, Charles Comiskey again prevailed on Fielder Jones to return to the White Sox for 1910. The fruitless effort compelled Comiskey to look outside the organization for an experienced manager.

Hugh Duffy

A series of back-and-forth negotiations conducted through long-distance telephone hookup and a salary described by Hugh Duffy as "enough to make me give up the management of the Providence club" brought one of the greatest stars of the 1890s to Chicago. Diminutive in size, Duffy was the owner of the highest single-season batting average in the history of the game (.438 in 1894). Charles Comiskey made Duffy's acquaintance in 1890 when the two men bolted the National League to play for the Chicago team in the Brotherhood (Players) League. Comiskey played and managed the ballclub during its brief one-year history. Duffy was the left fielder.

Comiskey believed that Duffy's three years at the Philadelphia Phillies' helm provided him the level of managerial experience at the major league level he needed to resurrect the Sox from slipping into the second division. But the Old Roman did not give Duffy much to work with in 1910, despite promises to the contrary.

After two disappointing seasons, the Old Roman replaced Duffy with a Chicago resident—Jimmy Callahan—someone he could remain in close contact with during the winter months. "This thing of bidding good-bye to a manager after a season is over and not seeing him again until the day the team starts away on the spring training trip belongs to other days," Comiskey told the press. "I want a man that can help arrange the spring trip, attend to the scheduling of exhibition games on that trip, and look out for trades during the winter months, as well as handle the team on the ballfield."

In essence, Comiskey expected his manager to function as traveling secretary, general manager, and ticket salesman all rolled into one, which of course Duffy was not willing to do.

1915–18

Rowland, Clarence

Record: 339–247 (.578)
Birthplace: Platteville, Wisconsin
B: February 12, 1879
D: May 17, 1969

Rowland, Clarence

	W	L	T	Pct
1915	93	61	1	.604
1916	89	65	1	.578
1917	100	54	2	.649
1918	57	67	0	.460
White Sox	339	247	4	.578
Career	339	247	4	.578

Clarence "Pants" Rowland, the Iowa "busher" summoned from obscurity by Charles Comiskey on December 17, 1914, was the first manager to win a pennant and a World Series in the 20th century without any prior big-league playing experience.

Rowland was a reserve catcher and a successful manager in the Three-I League before coming to Chicago. His Peoria team won a Three-I pennant in 1914, and several of his prized pupils, including Red Faber, were advanced to the majors on his advice.

Clarence "Pants" Rowland

Rowland's age and inexperience—and the nickname "Pants," which he had acquired years earlier from semipro teammates in Dubuque, Iowa, who ridiculed him for wearing his dad's blue knickers to the ballfield one afternoon—came back to haunt him in Chicago. He was never made to feel welcome by either his veteran players or the press corps.

The 1917 championship, coming after a decade-long pennant drought on the South Side, did little to enhance his reputation as a strategist, because much of the behind-the-scenes direction was provided by Comiskey and coach Kid Gleason, whose driving temperament contrasted to Rowland's evenhanded approach to management. Always the gentleman, manager Rowland extended his hand in friendship to Giants manager John McGraw following the last out of the 1917 World Series. "Mr. McGraw, I'm glad we won, but I'm sorry you had to be the one to lose."

McGraw frowned and replied, "Get away from me, you damned busher!" Such was the level of respect.

"Pants" Rowland directed his team from the third-base coaching box. He appeared to be in firm control of the game, but Rowland was diplomatic to the extreme in the handling of his players. Directives often took the form of fatherly advice and well-meaning suggestions. Seldom would he compromise his calm judgments with angry histrionics.

The Sox manager deserved a lot more credit for his accomplishments than Comiskey or the writers were willing to concede. A disappointing sixth-place finish in 1918, caused by the loss of his star players to the war effort, contributed to his long-rumored dismissal on New Year's Eve.

Rowland took it hard, and the timing was poor—but the youthful Sox manager went on to complete a long and rewarding career as an American League umpire (1923–27), president of the Pacific Coast League, and executive vice president of the Cubs, a two-year appointment that ended in 1956.

William "Kid" Gleason

1919–23

Gleason, William

Record: 392–364 (.519)
Birthplace: Camden, New Jersey
B: October 26, 1866
D: January 2, 1933

Gleason, William

	W	L	T	Pct
1919	88	52	0	.629
1920	96	58	0	.623
1921	62	92	0	.403
1922	77	77	1	.500
1923	69	85	2	.448
White Sox	392	364	3	.519
Career	392	364	3	.519

There was a hardly a player in the White Sox camp who would have been willing to mix it up with coach "Kid" Gleason, a hard-boiled Irishman who played second base for Wilbert Robinson's Baltimore Orioles in the 1890s.

Hired as a coach by Comiskey in 1912, Gleason was tough on discipline but a warm-hearted man who earned the respect and unflagging loyalty of his players. They called him "Pop" as a gesture of respect for his years of experience and standards of fairness. He served under two White Sox managers, Jimmy Callahan and Clarence Rowland, but some writers were of the opinion the real Sox boss was Gleason. He was enormously popular among the members of the fourth estate.

Chicago Tribune columnist Ring Lardner, a regular visitor to the White Sox spring training camps during those years, observed Gleason conducting his practice sessions and was amused by his rugged and often sharp repartee with the young players. The wit and wisdom of the Kid was written into the character of the grizzled but kind-hearted manager portrayed in Lardner's nationally syndicated *Jack Keefe—You Know Me, Al* columns.

Although he had not played in a game since 1907, Gleason volunteered for emergency duty in Fenway Park on August 26, 1912, after Morrie Rath and Buck Weaver were tossed out by umpire Silk O'Laughlin. Turning to Callahan, Gleason said, "Say, Cal, you know I played second base once." The partisan Boston Red Sox fans gave the 46-year-old Gleason a thunderous ovation when he trotted out to second base. The Kid booted an easy grounder, but quickly atoned by collecting one hit in two official at-bats.

Acting under Comiskey's strident orders, secretary Harry Grabiner fired Gleason in January 1915, but the veteran coach was recalled in 1917 when the owner decided that Rowland was not capable of bringing the team across the finish line. Gleason decided not to return to Chicago in 1918 after a falling-out with the owner, but the wartime collapse convinced Comiskey that he needed Gleason more than the Kid needed him. His appointment as Sox manager was announced on December 31, 1918.

Kid Gleason managed the White Sox through their darkest hour. The ordeal of the Black Sox scandal took a terrible toll on his health and shattered his outlook on life.

Gleason knew the fix was on from the very first pitch delivered by Ed Cicotte in Game 1 of the 1919 World Series, but he had no proof to offer Comiskey. On a rainy Sunday afternoon in the middle of the World Series, Gleason sat in his office quietly contemplating the unfolding events while some of Comiskey's Woodland Bard cronies sipped their highballs and devoured free food provided by the owner. "I don't know what's the matter," Gleason sighed. "But I know my club isn't playing ball and the best club is losing this World Series." The idea seemed so fantastic that Gleason could not admit to himself that his players had been bought off—while in the saloons of Chicago the fans were singing chorus after chorus of "I'm Forever Blowing Ball Games," composed by the Kid's friend and admirer from days past, Ring Lardner.

Gleason defended his men in open court, even after the full details of the conspiracy were aired to the press. It was a mark of the great man that he would stand by his "boys" when the chips were down.

The Kid valiantly tried to rebuild the shattered ballclub with younger players, but he was just not up to the task. He resigned as White Sox manager moments after winning the 1923 City Series. Gleason retired to his home to mull over the cruel hand of fate. Suffering from chronic depression and unable to eat, Gleason's health steadily declined.

In the fall of 1924, after an eclipse of two years, the Kid was spotted in Pittsburgh at the World Series by Connie Mack and offered a coaching job with the A's. Gleason wasn't sure he was up to the task, but Mack asked him to come on board and work with Joe Hauser, a rookie slugger trying out with the A's.

Gleason reluctantly agreed, and as it turned out, Mack's baseball therapy was the ticket that restored the Kid to robust health.

1924

Chance, Frank

Record: 0–0 (.000)
Birthplace: Fresno, California
B: September 9, 1877
D: September 15, 1924

Through the tireless efforts of Larry Graver, the Boston Red Sox team secretary, the White Sox were able to persuade former Cubs manager Frank Chance to return to Chicago to manage the White Sox for 1924. Charles Comiskey was excited by the possibilities. Chance was still a big name in Chicago, and good box office, presumably.

At the winter meetings held in Chicago the following December, Chance contracted a cold that developed into bronchial pneumonia over a period of weeks. Unable to fulfill his contractual obligations, Chance submitted his resignation on February 16, 1924. Comiskey, however, refused to accept it and urged him to join the club after regaining his health.

Frank Chance climbed out of his sickbed ahead of schedule and arrived in Chicago to resume his duties in early April. He managed the White Sox in only one game—a meaningless 2–1 preseason exhibition victory over the New York Giants in Comiskey Park on April 12 that ultimately cost him his life. The following week the former "Peerless Leader" of the Cubs underwent emergency surgery at Chicago's Mercy Hospital. Five months later he was dead, and all of baseball mourned his passing. Frank Chance was only 47 years old.

On April 12, 1924, following the World Tour, the New York Giants played an exhibition game in Comiskey Park. For Frank Chance (right), the "Peerless Leader," it would be the only game he ever managed with the Sox, as his pneumonia worsened shortly after. With Chance are Giants manager John McGraw (left), and Sox coach Johnny Evers (center).

1924

Evers, Johnny

Record: 51–72 (.415)
Birthplace: Troy, New York
B: July 12, 1881
D: March 28, 1947

Evers, Johnny

	W	L	T	Pct
1924	51	72	1	.415
White Sox	51	72	1	.415
Career	101	193	3	.343

Ex-Cubs great Johnny Evers was signed as a coach by Frank Chance at the 1923 winter meetings in Chicago. When his old friend and former infield mate was unable to report to spring training because of his bronchial condition, Evers was placed in charge of the ballclub by Comiskey, with Eddie Collins and Ed Walsh designated as field assistants.

The slight-of-frame, temperamental Evers, who was nicknamed the Crab by his former Cubs teammates, took over a bad ballclub made worse by a series of devastating injuries and illness. The Sox had gotten off to an 8–15 start and were preparing to open a series in Boston on May 14 when Evers was stricken with a stomach ailment he first thought might be ptomaine poisoning. Evers immediately departed the ballclub for his home in Troy, New York, where his physician diagnosed the problem as acute appendicitis. Johnny returned weeks later, but the White Sox were well out of the race and plummeting toward the AL cellar.

Comiskey had no intention of bringing the Crab back for another year anyway. Evers was replaced by Eddie Collins on December 11. "I have always liked Johnny Evers," explained the Old Roman. "I feel he had a bad break last year when he was sick himself and when we were in need of a shortstop following the illness to [Harvey] McClellan. But I don't think he was seriously anxious to take the job another time."

Johnny Evers

1924

Walsh, Ed

Record: 1–2 (.333)
Birthplace: Plains, Pennsylvania
B: May 14, 1881
D: May 26, 1959

Walsh, Ed

	W	L	T	Pct
1924	1	2	0	.333
White Sox	1	2	0	.333
Career	1	2	0	.333

From the moment he retired from the game in 1917, Ed Walsh yearned to come back to Chicago and manage the Sox. Charles Comiskey never lived up to his halfhearted promises to appoint Walsh skipper until 1923, when the "Moose" was hired as a base-line coach and assistant to Frank Chance.

The death of Chance and Johnny Evers' appendectomy early in the 1924 season finally provided Walsh a rare window of opportunity. Before Evers went under the knife in a New York hospital, he appointed Walsh interim manager on May 15. But when Sox outfielder Roy Elsh was victimized by the

Ed Walsh

hidden-ball trick two days later, Comiskey reconsidered the situation. He decided that Walsh was probably better suited to coaching duties than running the team on a day-to-day basis.

Walsh was standing in the third-base coaching box several feet away from the runner Elsh when the kid was caught off base by Red Sox third baseman Danny Clark. No one knows how far Commy might have gone with Walsh if the embarrassing mental lapse had not occurred when it did. Eddie Collins took over as the new interim manager on May 19, permanently ending Big Ed's dream.

1924–26

Collins, Eddie

Record: 174–160 (.521)
Birthplace: Tarrytown, New York
B: May 2, 1887
D: March 25, 1951

Collins, Eddie

	W	L	T	Pct
1924	14	13	0	.518
1925	79	75	0	.513
1926	81	72	2	.529
White Sox	174	160	2	.521
Career	174	160	2	.521

Eddie Collins

Charles Comiskey recognized a natural-born leader in Eddie Collins, White Sox team captain since 1915. Collins, like Walsh, harbored a strong desire to manage at the major league level. As far back as 1914, when he was still a member of the Philadelphia A's, Eddie approached Connie Mack about the possibility of going to the New York Yankees as a player/manager when Mack indicated that he was going to sell his top stars at auction. Collins changed his mind about New York and accepted the transfer to Chicago when he realized that the Yankees situation was filled with uncertainties.

A full decade would pass before Comiskey turned over the ballclub to Collins on a permanent basis. The Old Roman was generally pleased with Eddie's work as an interim manager in 1924, and he recognized that Collins also had a tremendous fan following. "There are some very good ballplayers among the Sox, and while I realize that it is a tough job to develop a winner in a short time, we may surprise some people," Collins said.

The White Sox played their best ball of the woeful 1920s under Collins' leadership. The team climbed three notches in the standings in 1925, and narrowly missed a first-division finish a year later. As long as Eddie's 38-year-old legs held up and he was able to continue his second-base duties, Comiskey was satisfied. The Old Roman reasoned that the fans came to see Eddie play—not manage. But when playing every day became an impossibility for Collins and he simply could not go on, the owner had no further use for him.

Without extending the courtesy of placing a phone call or sending a telegram to Collins, Comiskey placed him on waivers and named Ray Schalk manager on November 11, 1926. "I have not received any word from Comiskey and have not talked to him since the close of the baseball season," Collins said. "I have nothing to say and will not talk until I am officially notified by the club."

1927–28

Schalk, Ray

Record: 102–125 (.449)
Birthplace: Harvey, Illinois
B: August 12, 1892
D: May 19, 1970

Schalk, Ray

	W	L	T	Pct
1927	70	83	0	.458
1928	32	42	1	.432
White Sox	102	125	1	.449
Career	102	125	1	.449

It is hard to say whether or not Ray "Cracker" Schalk actively campaigned to unseat Eddie Collins or if this was another one of Charles Comiskey's poorly-thought-out snap decisions. Schalk's appointment on November 11, 1926, caught the media off guard and left the fans guessing. "I feel we have a pretty good ballclub as it is," Schalk ventured. "But of course we will try to build it up even stronger. I can see where we need some building up on the infield and perhaps on the pitching staff, but those things will be taken up later."

If anything, Schalk's poor performance as manager spoke volumes about Eddie Collins' fine work the previous two seasons. Always an aggressive, heads-up player, the veteran catcher's disposition seemed to change as a manager. He became cautious in his dealings and was inclined to be overly lenient with his players, particularly veterans who took advantage of his good nature. Some of them talked back while he gave orders to the squad; others openly ridiculed him. Morale collapsed. The Sox dropped into the cellar early in the 1928 campaign. Ray Schalk accepted full blame for the team's collective failures and offered his resignation in a letter to Comiskey dated July 4, 1928.

Schalk hoped that Comiskey would want to keep him on the roster as an active player, but he recognized that time was not on his side. "If I received an offer from another club, I don't think the Sox would block me," he said, "but after 16 years in the majors I don't expect there will be any great clamor for my services." Schalk was given a brief trial with the Giants in 1929, before retiring to his South Side bowling alley.

1928–29

Blackburne, Russell "Lena"

Record: 99–133 (.427)
Birthplace: Clifton Heights, Pennsylvania
B: October 23, 1886
D: February 29, 1969

Blackburne, Russell "Lena"

	W	L	T	Pct
1928	40	40	0	.500
1929	59	93	0	.388
White Sox	99	133	0	.427
Career	99	133	0	.427

The success or failure of a major league manager is seldom judged by the care and handling of one player, but in the case of Russell Blackburne, his tenure as Sox skipper was sabotaged by Art Shires, the Texas wild man who took over first-base duties in August 1928.

Comiskey hired Blackburne to instill discipline among a rebellious faction of veterans and younger players who took advantage of Ray Schalk's better nature. Blackburne was a hard-boiled scrapper and a throwback to the rough-and-tumble era of baseball. Through hard work and the threat of $50 fines hanging over the heads of players who defied his edicts, Blackburne hoped to transform the ballclub into a contender. He did not count on Shires' volatile disruptions.

Blackburne was recommended to the Sox by Hugh Duffy in the fall of 1909. Acting on the tip, Comiskey exchanged $3,500, infielder Jakie Atz, and outfielder Mike Welday to secure the player from the Providence, Rhode Island, club. In his two tours of duty with the Sox, Blackburne never hit above .222. By the time he was called back to Chicago to coach for Ray Schalk, Lena (he claimed the nickname was given to him because of a lean and trim physique) was playing semipro games in Palmyra, New Jersey.

Russell "Lena" Blackburne

Things went generally well for Russ after he relieved Schalk as manager on July 4, 1928. The team played .500 ball through the remainder of the season, and the media praised him for his efforts. The real trouble began in the spring of 1929 after Blackburne sent Shires back to Chicago to have his head examined for irregularities following several drunken episodes in the clubhouse. Comiskey refused to pay any doctor's consulting fees and ordered the player back to Dallas, Texas, to work things out with Blackburne. A truce was agreed upon, but the peace ended on May 15 after the manager objected to Shires wearing a red felt hat as he stepped up to the plate. Blackburne coldcocked Shires in the clubhouse and dared him to stand up. Teary-eyed, Shires crawled away, vowing to have Blackburne fired.

This wasn't the end of it, however. During the Sox's final 1929 visit to Philadelphia, Shires ran wild in his hotel room one night and began pounding away at Blackburne and traveling secretary Lou Barbour, whose finger was nearly bitten off in the mêlée. The story was retold in baseball locker rooms and the press box for many years to come, and each time with a different twist. In one version, Barbour bit his own finger.

Blackburne was permitted to finish out the season, but after this latest row, the ailing and infirm Comiskey, who read about these alarming accounts in his morning newspaper while regaining his health at his Wisconsin summer home, ordered Grabiner to locate and hire a new man forthwith.

Though he never managed at the big-league level again, Blackburne was hired to coach the Philadelphia A's in 1933. Meanwhile, Lena developed a profitable side business bottling and selling mud from the Delaware River in New Jersey to the American, National, and International leagues. It was used by the umpires to remove the high gloss from new baseballs prior to game time.

1930–31

Bush, Donie

Record: 118–189 (.384)
Birthplace: Indianapolis, Indiana
B: October 8, 1888
D: March 28, 1972

Bush, Donie

	W	L	T	Pct
1930	62	92	1	.403
1931	56	97	3	.366
White Sox	118	189	4	.384
Career	497	539	9	.480

The vindictiveness of Donie Bush cost him his job managing the Pittsburgh Pirates, and his heartless treatment of Sox pitcher Pat Caraway during a very rough period in the young man's career illustrated the crude manner by which some big-league pilots operated their ballclubs in the old days.

Bush was let go by Pirates owner Barney Dreyfuss on August 28, 1929, and hired by Harry Grabiner September 30—a few hours ahead of an offer to manage the Yankees submitted by Ed Barrow, their general manager. Bush was sorely tempted to break his agreement with the Sox and accept the high-profile position with the Yanks, but he was gently reminded of his obligations by AL president Ernest Barnard, who was looking after Comiskey's interests during the period of the Old Roman's convalescence.

Owen "Donie" Bush (left) and an ailing Charles Comiskey confer at a spring training exhibition game, March 17, 1931.

Donie Bush was impatient for success, but the White Sox team he took over had just about hit rock bottom talent-wise. Because he preferred working with veteran players, the youngsters in the camp were often ignored. Bush quickly became embroiled in petty feuds and jealousies with Willie Kamm and Ted Lyons, two of the stars remaining on the roster. Kamm was traded to Cleveland. Lyons was sent home a year later after Bush decided he was all washed up.

His treatment of rookie pitcher Pat Caraway bordered on the criminal. The nervous and shaky rookie's confidence was totally destroyed in a game played in Boston on July 21, 1930. For reasons known only to Bush, he kept Caraway in the game after he had surrendered a dozen runs in less than five innings. When the Sox came to bat, Bush could be seen standing in the dugout scolding and berating the shamefaced young pitcher. All in all, Donie Bush's two-year run was a fiasco start to finish.

Bush tossed in the crying towel on October 9, 1931, saying he no longer wanted to manage a team as bad as the White Sox. He feared jeopardizing his managerial career, or what was left of it.

Donie Bush returned to the Hoosier state, where he managed the Indianapolis Indians and acquired part ownership of the team. The minor league stadium where the team played, which in later years was named after Bush, was the set locale for John Sayles' 1988 film *Eight Men Out,* based on the Black Sox scandal.

1932–34

Fonseca, Lew

Record: 120–196 (.380)
Birthplace: Oakland, California
B: January 21, 1899
D: November 26, 1989

Fonseca, Lew

	W	L	T	Pct
1932	49	102	1	.325
1933	67	83	1	.447
1934	4	11	0	.266
White Sox	120	196	2	.380
Career	120	196	2	.380

Former American League batting champion Lew Fonseca was acquired in a trade with the Cleveland Indians that sent away star third baseman Willie Kamm. Lew was an expensive if rather useless acquisition as a player, but he seemed to possess a manic kind of energy and enthusiasm that warranted a second look from the Comiskeys.

Fonseca cheerfully accepted his appointment as manager on October 12, 1931, and vowed to remain in the lineup. "I'll

Lew Fonseca demonstrates batting technique in this spring training photo from 1932.

play left field as I did last year, and I won't even try that if I think I have a better man for the job!" he said.

Lew was a man of action, and nobody could fault him for trying to improve a bad situation. He hired Johnny "Trolley Line" Butler to serve exclusively as an infield coach. Bill Cunningham, a defensive specialist from his years in the National League, was brought in to work with the outfielders. Fonseca converted Smead Jolley to a catcher. He considered shifting Luke Appling to third base, and he took a long look at the rookies in camp. "Sox supporters are going to see a lot of new faces if I don't get results fast," he vowed. "They better hit or get out!" His April trades, discussed in Chapters 1 and 12, failed to achieve the desired results, and the team sank to lower depths than even Donie Bush could have imagined.

Fonseca's moment of infamy occurred in Cleveland on May 30, 1932, when his flying fists landed umpire George Moriarity in a local hospital. The arbiter had baited several Sox players as they walked back to their dressing room following a discouraging doubleheader loss to the Tribe. Milt Gaston and Charley Berry made a move toward the burly Moriarity, who assumed the fighting stance. Moriarity knocked Gaston to the floor, bringing Fonseca and catcher Frank Grube out of the locker room. The battling Sox manager, who was several years younger and faster on his feet, made short work of Moriarity, who was suspended by the league for his troubles.

The team improved in 1933, thanks to the addition of Al Simmons and Jimmie Dykes, but they took another tumble early into the next season. A disastrous eastern road trip, when the White Sox played some of their worst baseball of the 1930s, convinced Lou Comiskey to sever Fonseca from the organization on May 8, 1934. Lew took the news gracefully and parted company with the Comiskeys on fine terms.

After leaving the White Sox, Fonseca accepted appointment as director of promotions for Major League Baseball. Ever since he appeared in a walk-on role in the 1927 comedy *Slide, Kelly, Slide,* Fonseca had always had a yen to integrate the medium of film with baseball. In later years, Fonseca and his cameramen shot the yearly World Series and All-Star Game films—very often the only surviving footage of some of the most important and historic games.

1934–46

Dykes, Jimmie

Record: 894–933 (.489)
Birthplace: Philadelphia, Pennsylvania
B: November 10, 1896
D: June 15, 1976

Dykes, Jimmie

	W	L	T	Pct
1934	49	88	1	.357
1935	74	78	1	.487
1936	81	70	2	.536
1937	86	68	0	.558
1938	65	83	1	.439
1939	85	69	0	.552
1940	82	72	0	.532
1941	77	77	2	.500
1942	66	82	0	.446
1943	82	72	1	.532
1944	71	83	0	.461
1945	71	78	1	.477
1946	5	13	0	.277
White Sox	894	933	9	.489
Career	1,402	1,533	13	.477

Lou Comiskey, the invalid son of the White Sox founder, understood the subtleties of baseball as well as any executive in the majors, and probably better than most. Once, when one of his cronies from the sporting world kidded him about the poor return on his $150,000 investment in Al Simmons, Jimmie Dykes, and Mule Haas, Comiskey answered back: "Well, I got the best manager in baseball, didn't I? You can't pick up guys like Dykes on street corners!"

Jimmie Dykes was a metaphor of White Sox baseball in the Depression era and World War II. He puffed round, fat cigars. He was a student of temperament and personalities, and he always managed to make do with the meager talent made available to him by the Comiskeys and Harry Grabiner in the leanest of times.

The real genius of Dykes was his uncanny skill at perusing the league waiver list and securing for the Sox the players who had outlasted their usefulness in other organizations but would make significant contributions for the minimal cash outlay. Luke Sewell, Bill Dietrich, Edgar Smith, Clint Brown, Thornton Lee, and Taft Wright were among the more notable success stories. The entire roster of players in any given year was a reflection of Jimmie's rummage-sale shopping sprees.

Dykes was 37 years old and past his prime as a player when Lou Comiskey asked him to take over the Sox on May 9, 1934. He was a hustling old-time ballplayer who was well respected by his teammates and rival managers. He had no illusions about improving the team overnight, but was confident that he could get the job done with a little bit of patience from the Comiskeys. Within a year, the tree began to bear fruit.

Jimmie evolved into one of the league's best managers, though in large measure his two coaches, Harold "Muddy" Ruel and George "Mule" Haas, must also share the credit. Ruel was an expert handler of pitchers who was in his element working with down-on-their-luck, injury-prone veterans trying to hang on to what was left of their fading careers.

Dykes managed the ballclub for a longer period of time than any White Sox skipper before or since. A whole generation

Left: Jimmie Dykes tips his hat in Wrigley Field to the boss lady, Grace Comiskey (in glasses and feathered hat), and her offspring—Charley, Dorothy, Gracie Lou. Right: Dykes searches the AL waiver lists for help, while Cubs general manager Jim Gallagher is "bearish." (*Chicago Sun*)

of fans came of age on the South Side secure in the belief that Franklin D. Roosevelt would always be the president and Jimmie Dykes the White Sox manager.

With his left foot firmly planted on the top step, his cap perched low over his forehead, and observing the proceedings intently from his familiar perch in the left-hand corner of the third-base dugout, Jimmie was a study in self-absorbed concentration. He was a salty-tongued bench jockey whose fearsome tirades directed against American League umpires became something of a legend around the league.

The usual fine and suspension accompanied each explosive outburst. "No manager is bigger than the league," snapped AL president Will Harridge, after suspending Jimmie on July 6, 1941, for obscene and abusive language directed at umpire Steve Basil. "For years Dykes has tried to promote himself at the expense of the league and the president's office. His tactics are in delaying our games and attempting to bulldoze and browbeat umpires while filing protests which have no basis in fact or justification."

Dykes could be equally tough on his own players. He refused to nominate Ted Lyons to the 1941 All-Star Game, but pitched him in an exhibition game instead. In 1942 Jimmie benched his entire starting infield and threatened to activate his coaches unless there was immediate improvement.

Jimmie's White Sox teams finished in the first division six times—but never a pennant. And though his record leans toward the losing side of the ledger, Dykes always maintained a biting sense of humor. Ted Williams remembers the day when Dykes and several of his cohorts showed up in the Sox dugout attired in raincoats and firemen's regalia. The Red Sox slugger had expressed a desire to quit baseball and become a firefighter.

It was Dykes who called Joe McCarthy of the Yankees a "push-button" manager and the 1940 Cleveland Indians the "Wubber Dowy Boys" after they complained to the ownership about their manager, Oscar Vitt.

Grace Comiskey allowed Dykes a free hand to manage as he saw fit in the years following her husband's death. But as the years passed, the White Sox matriarch became increasingly perturbed over Jimmie's obstinacy at contract time. He would haggle over dollars and cents and the length of the contract before affixing his signature to a contract. Such tactics wore thin by the spring of 1946, when Dykes was unable to accompany the team back to Chicago to begin the season. His 15-cigar-a-day habit had landed him in the hospital with an attack of gallstones. Mrs. Comiskey reasoned that Dykes should have had the problem attended to in October, and not in April.

Rumors of Dykes' dismissal percolated for months until the shoe finally dropped on May 24, 1946, after 12 years and 13 days at the Sox helm. The testy, "star-chamber" conference between Dykes and Mrs. Comiskey yielded a new manager in Ted Lyons and the usual jest from Jimmie.

"I knew the handwriting was on the wall then, and it wouldn't be long," Dykes said. "I simply told her that I wasn't sick in October. And that people didn't go around having operations just because it was a slack month."

Mrs. Comiskey paid him his full 1946 salary (worth $25,000), and sent him away in a mood of discord. Jimmie traveled to California, where he took over as manager of the Hollywood Stars in the Pacific Coast League for the next few years. He returned to the majors in 1951, succeeding Connie Mack as manager of the Philadelphia A's.

1946

Haas, George

Record: 5–7 (.417)
Birthplace: Montclair, New Jersey
B: October 15, 1903
D: June 30, 1974

Haas, George

	W	L	T	Pct
1946	5	7	0	.417
White Sox	5	7	0	.417
Career	5	7	0	.417

"Mule" Haas was a sharp-tongued bench jockey who was reunited with Jimmie Dykes as a coach in 1940. Haas was originally included in the $150,000 cash purchase that brought Al Simmons and Dykes to Chicago in the fall of 1932. The Mule bowed out as an active player in 1938. He tried his hand at managing in the minor leagues before returning to Chicago, where he tutored the White Sox outfielders for the next six seasons.

George "Mule" Haas

Jimmie Dykes' gallstone attack before the 1946 spring training wrap-up unintentionally thrust Haas into the spotlight as interim manager—a fact overlooked and forgotten by baseball historians who have neglected to list him on the all-time roster of major league managers.

Haas guided the team to a 5–7 record before Dykes temporarily resumed his duties on April 30. Less than a month later Jimmie stepped down as manager, but Haas was never given serious consideration as a replacement. He remained on as a coach, serving under Ted Lyons until the end of the season.

1946–48

Lyons, Ted

Record: 185–245 (.430)
Birthplace: Lake Charles, Louisiana
B: December 28, 1900
D: July 25, 1986

Lyons, Ted

	W	L	T	Pct
1946	64	60	1	.516
1947	70	84	1	.455
1948	51	101	2	.336
White Sox	185	245	4	.430
Career	185	245	4	.430

Grace Comiskey selected Ted Lyons as the new field leader six months ahead of the scheduled start of the 1946 season. She delayed her showdown with Dykes until he had completely recovered from stomach surgery, and then moved the ball forthrightly and with a sense of urgency.

Lyons' appointment on May 24, 1946, was greeted with warm enthusiasm by the media, particularly *Chicago Sun-Times* columnist Gene Kessler, who lobbied hard for the old veteran during the "hot-stove" season. "I'm going to be a bench manager…no more pitching, Sundays or otherwise," Lyons vowed.

Red Faber was brought out of retirement to replace Muddy Ruel as pitching coach. Lyons seemed to push all the right buttons, and a very weak ballclub won 64 and lost 60 through the remainder of the 1946 season.

Things appeared to be on an upswing, but the improvement was only illusory. General manager Leslie O'Connor was not a "baseball man" in the strict sense of the word, and he attached far too much significance to Teddy's second-half success. As a result, Lyons was rewarded with a two-year contract extension in the spring of 1947.

Ted Lyons was the victim of an austerity program, even as postwar attendance began to boom on the South Side. Mrs. Comiskey and Les O'Connor eliminated bonus contracts, and a general belt-tightening within the organization affected the development of younger players.

With the talent shorn at all levels, the Sox crash-landed in the cellar in 1948. Part of the problem might have been Ted's leadership skills—he was no Dykes in personality and temperament. Nor did he receive the proper support from the front office. Lyons resigned before he could be fired on October 3, 1948.

Ted Lyons (left) welcomes rookie Al Albosta to camp, March 11, 1947. The kid never made it.

1949–50

Onslow, Jack

Record: 71–113 (.386)
Birthplace: Scottdale, Pennsylvania
B: October 13, 1888
D: December 22, 1960

Onslow, Jack

	W	L	T	Pct
1949	63	91	0	.409
1950	8	22	0	.267
White Sox	71	113	0	.386
Career	71	113	0	.386

The stage was set for a fresh, new beginning with Frank Lane installed as general manager and young Chuck Comiskey assuming a significant front-office role following the 1948 debacle. Before that future could be realized, however, Sox fans suffered through the Jack Onslow follies and more losing baseball.

"Honest" Jack Onslow spent a lifetime in baseball as a catcher, coach, manager, and talent scout. As a base-line coach back in the 1920s, he served under Bill McKechnie at Pittsburgh and Bucky Harris in Washington, earning favorable reviews. Considered to be something of an expert at developing younger players for the majors, Onslow supplanted Johnny Mostil as manager of the White Sox affiliate at Waterloo, Iowa, in June 1947. He led the team to a Three-I League pennant that year, and Memphis to a successful second-place finish in the Southern Association in 1948.

Chuck Comiskey, the 22-year-old heir to the throne who was completing his baseball apprenticeship in the minor leagues around the same time, lobbied hard for Onslow's appointment as Sox manager. Against Frank Lane's better judgment, Grace Comiskey endorsed her son's selection, and Onslow was hired for two years at $20,000 per season. "I'm going to be there for a long time!" Onslow chirped.

The bubble burst very quickly after rookie power hitter Gus Zernial broke his collarbone in the spring of 1949. Onslow was ill-suited to manage under the circumstances thrust upon him. He was too old and way out of touch with the players, and he bristled every time Frank Lane poked his head into the clubhouse to second-guess one of his recent managerial decisions. Privately, Lane berated Onslow as a "lousy manager," and on several occasions the two men engaged in shouting matches easily overheard by snooping reporters.

Comiskey tried to act as peacemaker, but he soon agreed with Frank Lane that Onslow was the wrong man for the job. But when Lane put it up to Mrs. Comiskey to fire "Honest Jack" at the end of the 1949 season, she demurred, deciding that if her son wanted Onslow's ouster, he would have to say so publicly. The young and painfully inexperienced Comiskey ruled in favor of the grandfatherly manager and invited him back for 1950.

Lane and Onslow valiantly tried to patch things up, but the Sox lost 20 of their first 28 games, prompting an angry Chuck Comiskey to threaten to resign unless the manager was replaced. Mrs. Comiskey settled matters by cutting the strings binding Onslow to the Sox. He was fired on May 26, 1950, but was paid off until the end of the season. Jack Onslow said it was a pleasure to leave the Sox in the hands of Red Corriden, adding a classic parting shot: "They won't second-guess me anymore. As far as I'm concerned, Lane can manage the Sox, and Comiskey can coach at third base or any place he likes!"

"Honest" Jack Onslow. Right: Onslow makes his point to Umpire Cal Hubard.

1950

Corriden, John "Red"

Record: 52–72 (.419)
Birthplace: Logansport, Indiana
B: September 4, 1887
D: September 28, 1959

Corriden, John "Red"

	W	L	T	Pct
1950	52	72	2	.419
White Sox	52	72	2	.419
Career	52	72	2	.419

Frank Lane kept insisting that 62-year-old Red Corriden was not just an interim manager but would be given equal consideration in the hunt for a new manager after the 1950 season.

There was little chance of such an occurrence. Lane had kept Paul Richards waiting in the wings since October 1949 and was already preparing to unveil him after the season. Corriden, who joined the organization in 1950, was already well known to Chicago baseball fans for his North Side tour of duty, as a part-time player, as a bird-dog scout, and then as the Cubs' third-base coach spanning the Depression years, 1931–40.

As a member of the Louisville infield in 1916, Corriden and his teammates played through 168 consecutive innings without missing an inning—the highlight of an otherwise undistinguished career.

John "Red" Corriden

1951–54; 1976

Richards, Paul

Record: 406–362 (.529)
Birthplace: Waxahachie, Texas
B: November 21, 1908
D: May 4, 1986

Richards, Paul

	W	L	T	Pct
1951	81	73	1	.526
1952	81	73	2	.526
1953	89	65	2	.578
1954	91	54	1	.628
1976	64	97	0	.398
White Sox	406	362	6	.529
Career	923	901	12	.506

Success in major league baseball is a subjective kind of thing, but the historical rendering on Paul Rapier Richards reflects so many superlatives that it is surprising he hasn't been given much consideration for the Hall of Fame by the Veterans Committee.

Paul Richards never won a pennant as a field manager, nor in later years as a general manager who courted controversy wherever he hung his hat. But he was one of baseball's most brilliant and creative strategists and an expert on pitching technique—the mechanics of gripping a baseball and pitch selection. His bold and imaginative strokes were later copied by Dick Williams, Joe Torre, and Whitey Herzog—students of the Richards method of management.

Richards, an ambidextrous pitcher and third baseman for his high school team, caught the attention of White Sox manager Eddie Collins when the ballclub passed through Dallas in the winter of 1926. Collins told Paul to contact him after he left school, but a Brooklyn scout under orders from Dodgers manager Wilbert Robinson voided the request by signing Richards first.

Richards was reunited with the Sox nearly a quarter century later when he flew to Chicago in October 1949 at Frank Lane's urging. The Sox general manager became acquainted with Richards while directing the Cincinnati Reds farm system for Larry McPhail. Richards was managing Atlanta at the time. "Considering him my discovery, I followed Paul closely thereafter and finally made up my mind after he had gone to Detroit as a coach in 1945 and wound up catching at the age of 36, that if I ever had to hire a manager, Richards was my man," Lane recalled. "I guess the things which impressed me most were his insistence on speed and aggressiveness." Paul Richards had every expectation of replacing Jack Onslow, but left Chicago empty-handed after Grace Comiskey handed her embattled manager a stay of execution for 1950.

Richards returned to Seattle, where his Rainiers finished sixth in the Pacific Coast League. It was his only notable failure during a nine-year run of success in minor league ball that

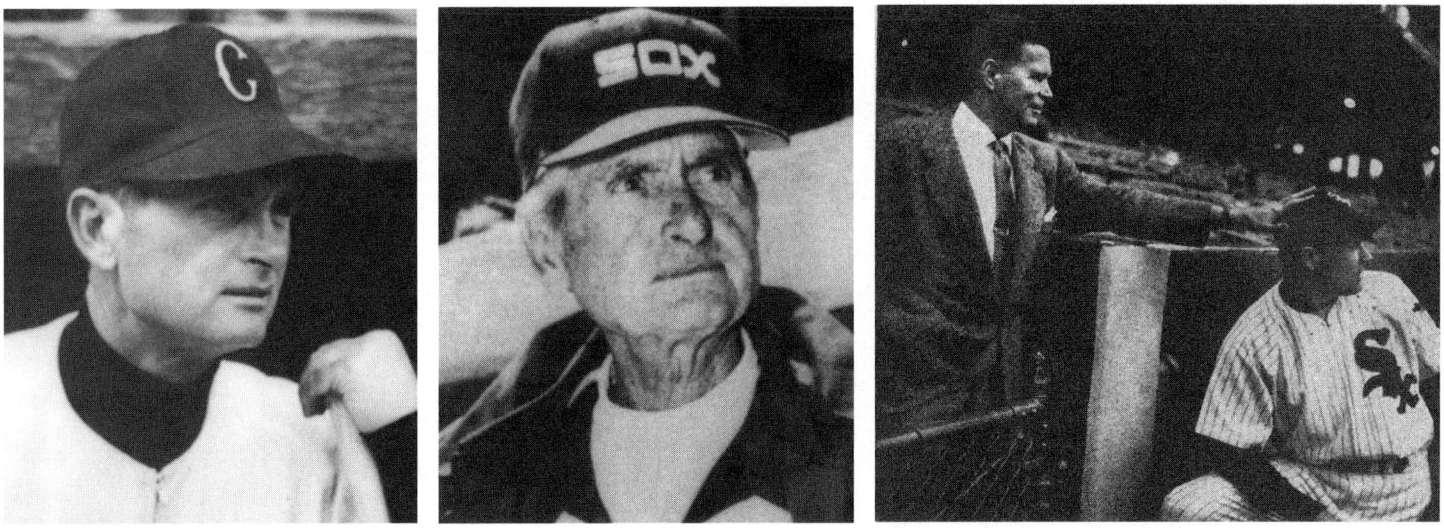

Paul Richards as rookie manager in 1951 (left), and 25 years later in 1976 (center); Frank Lane and Paul Richards (right)—the relationship wasn't always amicable.

brought him two Southern Association pennants in Atlanta and another at Buffalo in the Triple A International League.

Despite a no-comment stance emanating from the front office, Richards was the inside choice for 1951. Lane finally achieved his objective October 15, 1950. The reed-thin Texan was awarded a two-year contract with his salary money linked to attendance bonuses. This linkage later became a serious bone of contention between Richards and the Comiskeys.

A quiet but commanding presence in the dugout, Richards stressed fundamentals but encouraged a daring hit-and-run style offense revolving around a walk, a stolen base, and a timely base hit. The long-dormant franchise awoke from its 30-year slumber in 1951. Most remarkable was the freshman manager's unorthodox strategy—in a May 15 game he moved pitcher Harry Dorish to third base for one batter in order to have Billy Pierce come in from the bullpen to pitch to Ted Williams, who popped the ball up. Such tactics raised the eyebrows of the baseball world. Richards inaugurated the "Go-Go" era of White Sox baseball and returned the franchise to its historic dead-ball-era roots. Only Fielder Jones, Jimmie Dykes, Al Lopez, Tony LaRussa, and Kid Gleason had a greater long-term impact on Sox history.

"Satisfy yourself as to what you are doing and at the same time satisfy your men that you're getting the most out of them," was Paul's management credo.

This simple logic did not extend upstairs, where Richards encountered difficulties with "Frantic" Frank Lane, the second-guessing general manager, whose meddling led to a permanent schism—and Paul's hasty exit from Chicago on September 14, 1954. When the Baltimore Orioles approached him with a three-year offer to pilot the Orioles and supervise the baseball operation as their new general manager, Richards received Chuck Comiskey's permission to be let out of his contract, which had more than a month left to go. Their parting was otherwise amicable. Richards wished the Sox good luck and was on his way, not fully realizing that the mysterious hand of fate would guide him back to Chicago more than two decades later.

At a time when most men gear up for a quiet retirement or afternoons on the golf course, 68-year-old Paul Richards accepted Bill Veeck's offer to manage the 1976 White Sox. The public relations value of the Richards name was enough motivation for Veeck to recycle the once-popular manager. However, the younger players on the squad could not relate to the aging, rather austere figure in the dugout, and the Sox were shut out 21 times en route to a last-place finish.

Bill Veeck liked to refer to the 1976 reunion of Richards, Minnie Minoso, and his long-time business partner Rudy Schaffer as the "last hurrah of the Over-the-Hill Gang." It was sad to comprehend that for these baseball legends, their time had already passed.

1954–56

Marion, Marty

Record: 179–138 (.565)
Birthplace: Richburg, South Carolina
B: December 1, 1917

Marion, Marty

	W	L	T	Pct
1954	3	6	0	.333
1955	91	63	1	.591
1956	85	69	0	.552
White Sox	179	138	1	.565
Career	356	373	3	.488

With a year left to go on his contract, Marty Marion was fired as a manager of the St. Louis Browns by Bill Veeck because he was just too honest. In a frank and revealing statement, Marion said that it wasn't much of a club that the good people of Baltimore were to receive when the Browns moved there in 1954.

Marty Marion (left) with his crosstown counterpart, Stan Hack, before the 1956 Boys' Benefit game.

Known in his National League playing days as Mr. Shortstop, Marion signed on as a White Sox coach after the 1953 season. He was a man of boundless energy and Paul Richards' ablest assistant during spring training, though at times he sharply disagreed with some of Richards' decisions.

Marty Marion played the waiting game his first year in Chicago. He steered clear of the sound and fury between Richards and Lane, knowing that sooner or later one or both of these singular-minded men would likely depart, leaving a vacancy he was all too eager to fill. Marion did not have to wait long. He was appointed the new Sox manager on September 14, 1954.

New controversies flared up in 1955—the "year of rising expectations" on the South Side. A third-place finish was just not good enough to satisfy either Lane or Chuck Comiskey. The front office expected Marion to bring the horses across the finish line ahead of the Yankees and Indians for a change, but the Sox faded down the stretch and ended in their usual third-place holding pattern. The outspoken manager criticized his pitching staff and demanded an infusion of new players for 1956. "Let's put it this way," Marion said. "Even now I have definite ideas of what I would like to do. Whether I will be able to do any or all of these things, I can't say just now."

Relations between Marion and Comiskey fell apart in 1956. Another third-place finish and Marty's absentee style of management—he commuted to his St. Louis home on off-days—convinced Comiskey to make a change. Marion offered his resignation on October 24, after learning that Comiskey was negotiating for the services of Cleveland Indians manager Al Lopez. "In my heart I know I did a good job," Marion said. "Other people didn't think so, and that is why I resigned."

1957–65; 1968–69

Lopez, Al

Record: 840–650 (.564)
Birthplace: Tampa, Florida
B: August 20, 1908
D: October 30, 2005

Lopez, Al

	W	L	T	Pct
1957	90	64	1	.584
1958	82	72	1	.532
1959	94	60	2	.610
1960	87	67	0	.565
1961	86	76	1	.531
1962	85	77	0	.525
1963	94	68	0	.580
1964	98	64	0	.605
1965	95	67	0	.586
1968	21	26	0	.446
1969	8	9	0	.470
White Sox	840	650	5	.564
Career	1,410	1,004	11	.584

Al Lopez was a catcher by profession and a manager *by reputation.* In his first 12 years of managing in the American League, his teams never finished lower than second. Lopez is the only AL skipper to wrest the pennant away from Casey Stengel during the era of Yankees dominance, 1949–64. He did it twice; once with Cleveland in 1954, and again in 1959 as the manager of the Go-Go White Sox.

The genial "Señor" grew up in the Ybor City neighborhood of Tampa. He was a catcher almost from the moment he set foot on a diamond, and as a big leaguer, he logged 1,918 games behind the plate in a 19-year career with the Dodgers, Braves, Pirates, and Indians. Lopez held the major league record for games caught until the 1980s.

As a manager, he offered honest objectivity to the media. Steady in a dignified kind of way, Lopez was never prone to shrieking tirades against either his players or umpires, and he was a very gentle man by all outward appearances. "A manager's main job is inspiring his players and handling the pitchers," he liked to say. Only in recent years has history begun to alter this image.

Al Lopez (right) relaxes with Yogi Berra, 1964.

With the publication of Larry Doby's biography *Pride Against Prejudice* by Joseph Moore, a more complex picture of Lopez begins to emerge—we learn of his spiteful side in his dealings with Doby. In Chicago, Minnie Minoso, Billy Pierce, Nellie Fox, and Jim Landis experienced similar problems getting along with Lopez, though their beef was a private matter and was never aired in the press. Baseball insiders have long believed that Lopez, as a past voting member of the Hall of Fame Veterans Committee, consistently vetoed Nellie Fox's inclusion at Cooperstown for reasons we can only surmise.

Al Lopez could not be all things to all people, of course, and he had his detractors in the local media. *Chicago American* columnist Bill Gleason was his toughest critic, and after the bitter disappointment of losing the AL pennant in the final week of the 1964 season, the reporter noted: "It has been written before that Lopez is a good manager. It also has been written here that he is not a great one. Lopez obviously believes that a team can be managed to a pennant. History has always refuted a belief in managerial legerdemain and it is my hope that that what happened this year may convince the White Sox manager that he has been wrong."

Veteran baseball men did not share Gleason's opinions. At Cleveland, Lopez was considered something of a genius. And once general manager Hank Greenberg had trespassed on Lopez's rights as manager and it was clear that he would not offer Al the opportunity to return for another year, Chuck Comiskey and John Rigney were the first to pay the Señor a courtesy call. Al's interest in the Sox was reciprocal, and a one-year contract was hastily drawn up for Lopez on October 29, 1956.

Al Lopez was hired to lead the Sox into the World Series. He was voted UPI AL Manager of the Year in 1957 as a tune-up before accomplishing the stated objective two years later. Lopez won the 1959 pennant with a ballclub tailored along the traditional lines of pitching, speed, and defense. The pitching staff lacked the dominance of his vaunted Cleveland teams of the early 1950s, and there were gaping holes at first and third bases. But Lopez, the seventh son of a seventh son, possessed a strange sixth sense about the 1959 season.

He alone believed the Sox were strong enough to finally pass the Yankees after years of frustration. He kept encouraging a jittery Bill Veeck to sit back and enjoy the ride after the new Sox owner threatened to mortgage the future by trading away half the team for Roy Sievers, the aging Washington Senators first baseman.

After the 1959 miracle, Lopez could have negotiated a lifetime contract with the White Sox, if that had been his pleasure. Following the retirement of his nemesis, Casey Stengel, no one but Lopez could rightfully be called the "dean" of American League managers. He appreciated the honor, but the strain of managing a ballclub in a rebuilding phase began to take its toll. The transitional White Sox teams of the early to mid-1960s would not have finished nearly as high with any other manager. There is no doubt.

The rumors of Al's retirement circulated for several years until he finally severed the cord on November 4, 1965, because of his heartfelt desire to spend more time with his family. Owner Art Allyn kept Lopez in the organization as a "special assignment" vice president and used him as a sounding board in the selection of the next White Sox manager—Eddie Stanky.

Lopez probably did not expect to resume his duties as field manager, but Art Allyn badgered him into returning after Stanky was fired on July 12, 1968.

A cloud of tension was lifted by Lopez. The players appreciated Al's calm, rational way of running a ball game compared to the frenzied, overheated Stanky approach. But nine days into the new regime, Lopez suffered an attack of appendicitis and was hospitalized for several weeks. His stomach troubles never completely cleared up, and because of these, coupled with the daily grind of travel, Lopez simply had enough. He resigned on May 2, 1969, and this time it was for good. Al retired to his Florida home, where he contented himself with rounds of golf and gin rummy games with Tony Cuccinello, his neighbor and his sidekick through so many Sox seasons.

1966–68

Stanky, Eddie

Record: 206–197 (.511)
Birthplace: Philadelphia, Pennsylvania
B: September 3, 1916
D: June 6, 1999

Stanky, Eddie

	W	L	T	Pct
1966	83	79	1	.512
1967	89	73	0	.549
1968	34	45	0	.430
White Sox	206	197	1	.511
Career	467	435	4	.518

Eddie Stanky. He was the last of a fearless breed. Leo Durocher knew exactly what he was talking about when he delivered his "nice guys finish last" speech. Pointing to the New York Giants dugout one afternoon, the Lip sent a message to all of the "nice guys" of the world: "Look at Mel Ott over there. He's a nice guy and he finishes second. Now look at the Brat [Stanky's famous nickname]. He can't hit, can't run, can't field. He's no nice guy, but all the SOB can do is win."

Stanky and Durocher. For more than two emotional seasons these hell-bent-for-leather brawlers guided the destiny of Chicago's teams. It was a colorful and sometimes outlandish era of Chicago baseball. You just never knew what was going to happen next with Eddie and Leo exchanging crosstown barbs.

"This may raise a few eyebrows," Stanky said. "But the best manager I ever played for was Leo Durocher. Anytime you're around Leo you learn something."

Always a kidder, Eddie Stanky holds up a fake headline suggesting that he wrestled and defeated Pete Ward on the mats, September 5, 1967.

The Brat was hired by Arthur Allyn on December 14, 1965—the same day Paul Richards was fired as general manager of the Houston Astros because he had granted the White Sox permission to talk to Grady Hatton, one of his minor league managers, about the vacated Chicago job.

Eddie's appointment was laced with irony. The Sox completely broke with their recent history by hiring a man who was the exact opposite of the introspective Al Lopez. Stanky was a man possessed by the furies. His day was not complete without first insulting a rival manager or calling Carl Yastrzemski an "all-star from the neck down." He accused his pitchers of treachery and betrayal when they refused to throw at a rival player's head. He recruited White Sox groundskeeper Gene Bossard into a sinister conspiracy to freeze baseballs in order to provide his pitchers with a competitive advantage every time they took the mound. The Brat managed to make news despite himself.

Stanky was barely into his third week as manager when he staged his famous "striptease" for the benefit of Watson Spoelstra, a writer for the *Detroit News* who dared to ask the Sox potentate what pitch Bob Locker threw to Gates Brown in a game situation. Stanky was changing into his street clothes at the time, but the innocuous question triggered a wild frenzy. The Sox manager ripped his jersey to shreds and threw his spiked shoes into the wall of the Tigers clubhouse as the bewildered reporter stood aghast.

In 1967, an unforgettable year when the punchless White Sox nearly stole a pennant, Stanky was in rare form. "This is a better team than we had last year," he said, "because we don't have to rely on individuals. Everyone is playing a part. All of them are aroused. Last year, we had some players who didn't care whether we won or lost, just so they had a good game." Stanky purged the troublemakers—John Romano and Floyd Robinson—over the winter. There were others.

To keep his players on their toes, Stanky punished the laggards with fines and rewarded his top performers with new clothes, free shoes, and other gifts to get them to play better. If Pete Ward missed a sign, Stanky collected $50. If Tommy John pitched a complete game, Tommy got a new suit. Stanky's variation of Mark Twain's fence-painting trick in *Tom Sawyer* had its supporters and detractors. One thing though, this was a team well versed in the fundamentals. Stanky had made sure of it.

The sizzling 1967 pennant race was settled in the closing days. The White Sox regulars, wound tighter than piano wire all season long by Stanky, choked down the stretch. The crushing doubleheader loss to Charley Finley's last-place A's on September 27 not only knocked them out of the four-team race, but also signaled the end of 17 years of first-division occupancy for the White Sox—an end to an era. "I guess I'll remember Kansas City for a long time to come," Stanky sighed, his voice almost a whisper. "All year long the elephants feared the mouse."

Stanky's team lost their first 10 games of the 1968 season. Personal conflicts between the manager and the players, a carryover from 1967, were magnified by the team's inability to win games. Angry and frustrated, the manager barred reporters from entering the clubhouse to interview the players after the game. The situation was threatening to spiral out of control when, finally, Stanky offered his resignation on July 12. "I'm sorry if it's me," he said. "But that's the way I am, and that's the way I do things. I'm not the sort to change my ways."

1968

Moss, Les

Record: 12–24 (.333)
Birthplace: Tulsa, Oklahoma
B: May 14, 1925

Moss, Les

	W	L	T	Pct
1968	12	24	0	.333
White Sox	12	24	0	.333
Career	39	50	0	.438

Les Moss, a utility catcher the White Sox acquired from the Baltimore Orioles in exchange for Harry Dorish on June 6, 1955, remained with the organization as a bullpen catcher for two years following his retirement in 1958. He managed in the minor leagues for several years in the 1960s prior to joining Eddie Stanky as a coach in 1967.

Moss was placed in charge of the ballclub following Stanky's resignation on July 12, 1968. He managed the Sox for two games until Al Lopez collected his bearings and was able to take over the ballclub on a full-time basis. Then, when Lopez was hospitalized with an attack of appendicitis after only nine days on the job, Les Moss again assumed command until the Señor was strong enough to resume his duties.

Les Moss

1969–70

Gutteridge, Don

Record: 109–172 (.388)
Birthplace: Pittsburg, Kansas
B: June 19, 1912
D: September 7, 2008

Gutteridge, Don

	W	L	T	Pct
1969	60	85	0	.414
1970	49	87	0	.360
White Sox	109	172	0	.388
Career	109	172	0	.388

Though not necessarily the worst manager to lead a White Sox team into battle, Don Gutteridge absorbed much of the blame for the disastrous 1970 season. The White Sox lost a record 106 games, and as the frustrations began to mount, the fans and the front office found a convenient scapegoat in their easygoing manager.

In his playing days with the St. Louis Browns and several other clubs, Gutteridge overcame the handicap of a small physique with a fierce competitive desire. He was a take-charge infielder, and then a very competent first-base coach with the White Sox from 1955 to 1966, until he was replaced by Grover Resinger in 1967.

Reassigned to the Sox's Indianapolis affiliate by Art Allyn, Gutteridge began his second tour of duty as a White Sox Triple A manager. At the end of the season he joined the expansion Kansas City Royals as a scout. But he was unhappy with these arrangements and jumped at the chance to return to Chicago with Al Lopez when the Señor emerged from retirement in July 1968. He did not count on taking Al's job, however.

For health reasons, Lopez resigned on May 4, 1969. "I was in Kansas City," Gutteridge recalled. "Ed Short called me and said the club would like to have me as the manager. Al told me to take it. I was happy and didn't want to manage as long as Lopez was managing. I didn't care a thing about it."

Gutteridge tried hard to improve the ballclub. But with few exceptions he allowed the players to walk all over him, and he was unable to light a fire underneath a ballclub that came to accept defeat with startling equanimity. One glaring incident that embarrassed the entire organization involved 15 Sox players who were told to attend a memorial dinner at the California home of Paul Edmondson, a rookie pitcher who was killed in a tragic automobile accident outside Santa Barbara on February 13, 1970. Only six players bothered to show up. They knew there would be no reprisals coming from Gutteridge.

The problems were deep and pervasive, and they went far beyond Don Gutteridge, who resigned before he could be

Don Gutteridge (center) flanked by owner John Allyn (left) and GM Ed Short

fired on September 2, 1970. He left the organization for good after declining a consolation job in the minor league system.

Don Gutteridge died at the ripe old age of 96 on September 7, 2008, in his hometown of Pittsburg, Kansas, after contracting pneumonia. At the time of his passing, Gutteridge was the oldest living former manager or coach in Major League Baseball and the last living member of the St. Louis Browns who played in the 1944 World Series. Beginning in 2006, on the anniversary of his June 19 birth date, the town of Pittsburg honors their native son with Don Gutteridge Day ceremonies.

1970

Adair, Billy

Record: 4–6 (.400)
Birthplace: Mobile, Alabama
B: February 10, 1916
D: June 18, 2002

Adair, Billy

	W	L	T	Pct
1970	4	6	0	.400
White Sox	4	6	0	.400
Career	4	6	0	.400

Third-base coach Billy Adair served as interim manager until Chuck Tanner flew into Chicago to take control of the ballclub on September 13, 1970.

Adair had been added to the coaching staff by Don Gutteridge in September 1969, following the conclusion of the Pacific Coast League season. He was in charge of the Sox's Tucson affiliate and had managed at all levels of the minor leagues for 19 years through 1969. After the 1970 season, Adair was dumped by Tanner.

Billy Adair

1970–75

Tanner, Chuck

Record: 401–414 (.492)
Birthplace: New Castle, Pennsylvania
B: July 4, 1928
D: February 11, 2011

Tanner, Chuck

	W	L	T	Pct
1970	3	13	0	.188
1971	79	83	0	.488
1972	87	67	0	.565
1973	77	85	0	.475
1974	80	80	3	.531
1975	75	86	0	.466
White Sox	401	414	3	.492
Career	1,352	1,381	5	.495

Chuck Tanner welcomes Dick Allen into the Sox family in February 1972—just as the players were preparing to walk off and strike the camps.

White Sox owner John Allyn signaled his intention to wipe the slate clean and begin the decade of the 1970s with fresh faces, an interesting new uniform, and a spirited attitude that would relegate losing to the dustheap of Sox history. The man he chose to accomplish this important task had never managed in the majors but had already won awards in the Texas League and Pacific Coast League for managerial excellence.

"New blood is coming into baseball," commented Frank Lucchese of the Philadelphia Phillies upon hearing the news of Tanner's appointment. "Guys like Earl Weaver, Sparky Anderson, and Dave Bristol. It's a different era now, and baseball people are not just hiring the same old people over and over, or going for former stars."

Tanner represented the best of the new generation. He was considered a player's manager—relevant to the times and in touch with the changing realities of baseball. In his first year at the helm, he elevated a shoddy, last-place ballclub to a surprising third-place finish through experimentation, innovation, and an abiding faith in his younger players. Tanner's enthusiasm was infectious. The team could at last look to the future with confidence.

The arrival of Dick Allen in 1972 sabotaged the rebuilding program, nearly drove John Allyn into bankruptcy, and created a cloud of dissension filtering down from the front office to the locker room. Dick Allen's MVP season helped Tanner win the Associated Press and *Sporting News* Manager of the Year awards for 1972 and artificially inflated expectations for 1973 and beyond. The team simply was not that good, and the special favors and privileges Tanner granted his temperamental star set a dangerous precedent that led to the resignation of executive vice president Stu Holcomb on July 27, 1973.

Holcomb quarreled with his two subordinates over the dubious decision to curry Dick Allen's favor by adding his older brother, Hank, to the roster in order for him to qualify for the major league pension. John Allyn personally flew to Boston to assure Tanner that Holcomb had agreed to an early retirement, just in case the Sox manager entertained a notion of leaving the organization because of this power struggle.

After the Holcomb episode was played out, the wheels fell off the cart. The team struggled to win games. Tanner traded verbal shots with TV announcer Harry Caray, who criticized the ballclub for listless, indifferent play. All the while, the Sox manager presented a cheerful outlook amid the turmoil on the field and rumors of the team's impending sale to Seattle interests. Tanner's bubbly optimism flew in the face of hard reality. The fans sided with Caray and refused to come out to Comiskey Park to watch a losing ballclub minus Dick Allen.

Bill Veeck assumed command on December 16, 1975, and had already settled on a new manager. With three years left on his $70,000-per-year contract, Chuck Tanner was replaced by Paul Richards. As usual, Tanner exited smiling.

Chuck Tanner managed in the big leagues for 19 seasons, garnering one championship ring along the way with the 1979 Pittsburgh Pirates—but his career record was lackluster at 1,352–1,381. After being replaced by Russ Nixon as manager of the Atlanta Braves on May 22, 1988, the affable Tanner went to work as a scout for the Cleveland Indians, continuing through the 1991 season. For the next 11 years after that, he was a special assistant to the Milwaukee Brewers' general manager before the Pennsylvania native was hired by Pirates general manager Neal Huntington as senior advisor on November 9, 2007—a mostly ceremonial public relations position. Tanner passed away in 2011 at age 82.

Bob Lemon (left) and Bill Veeck

1977–78

Lemon, Bob

Record: 124–112 (.525)
Birthplace: San Bernardino, California
B: September 22, 1920
D: January 12, 2000

Lemon, Bob

	W	L	T	Pct
1977	90	72	0	.556
1978	34	40	0	.459
White Sox	124	112	0	.525
Career	430	403	0	.516

Bob Lemon was the perfect antidote for what ailed the Sox in the second year of the Bill Veeck regime. The former Cleveland ace had spent 38 years in professional baseball going into the 1977 season. He patterned his managerial style after his baseball mentor Al Lopez, who had been his manager during the glory years of the early 1950s, when the Tribe was still the big story in Cleveland. Elected to the Hall of Fame in 1976, Bob Lemon agreed to terms with Veeck on November 16 of that year and braced for the worst. Managing is often a thankless process with only one certainty: you will be fired eventually.

It is not exactly clear why Lemon agreed to manage the worst team in the American League—one that had been asleep at the switch under Paul Richards all through the 1976 season. The Sox were expected to lose 100 games in 1977 with little or no pitching and few prospects worth mentioning in the minor leagues.

But Lemon, a hard-drinking man with a reserved, philosophical nature, surprised the baseball world—and probably himself—by directing these misfits to a strong third-place finish. The "South Side Hitmen" provided Sox fans with thrills galore in the most unforgettable summer of baseball since the 1959 pennant year. Credit for this miracle in the making rested with the thoughtful, low-key Lemon and his hitting coach Larry Doby, who sharpened the skills of some of the fringe players surrounding Richie Zisk and Oscar Gamble—the big guns in the lineup.

The 1977 season was a joy. The following year things were a little different. The 1978 edition stumbled all over themselves the first month of the season. Lamar Johnson and Steve Stone—pivotal to the Sox' success a year earlier—second-guessed Lemon and were vocal in their criticisms of his managerial competency.

Bill Veeck's frustration and impatience mounted with each loss. In June American League president Leland MacPhail, acting as George Steinbrenner's emissary, suggested to Veeck that the Sox and Yankees might improve their luck by "trading" managers—Bob Lemon for Billy Martin. Veeck, always the consummate showman, was intrigued by the possibility, but he wanted a Yankees player included in the deal.

George Steinbrenner patched things up with Martin for the moment and was no longer interested in making a trade—not when he could bide his time and hire Lemon at a cheaper price later on.

Bob Lemon's position became untenable in Chicago. Veeck made his move on June 30 when the team was visiting Minneapolis and sliding further and further down in the standings. Lemon was out. Larry Doby, a friend of Veeck's since the 1940s, was in. The change, Veeck explained rather mysteriously, "was not meant as a commentary on Lemon's ability, but rather as a result of unusual circumstances which seemed to make a change necessary."

Bob Lemon deserved a second chance. The White Sox situation demanded a little patience from Veeck, but the owner was desperate to stimulate attendance by hiring Doby, baseball's second African American manager. It was a calculated move that misfired. Meanwhile, Bob Lemon replaced Billy Martin later that season and guided the Yankees into a World Series. But not even a world championship could save Lemon from George Steinbrenner's chopping block. Lemon was replaced by Billy Martin a year later.

Larry Doby

1978

Doby, Larry

Record: 37–50 (.425)
Birthplace: Camden, South Carolina
B: December 13, 1923
D: June 18, 2003

Doby, Larry

	W	L	T	Pct
1978	37	50	0	.425
White Sox	37	50	0	.425
Career	37	50	0	.425

Larry Doby, a nervous and shy 23-year-old rookie, broke the American League color barrier in Comiskey Park on July 5, 1947. Doby's impact upon baseball at the dawn of the Civil Rights era in America is profound and enduring, though in many respects he missed out on the greater glory surrounding Jackie Robinson.

Doby also played a large role in White Sox affairs as a player and as baseball's second black manager. He was traded to the Sox by Cleveland on October 25, 1955, for Chico Carrasquel and Jim Busby, and enjoyed some productive seasons playing under Marty Marion, a manager he respected and admired. His long-standing differences with Al Lopez caused problems in 1957 and indirectly led to his departure from Chicago at the end of that season.

Larry was out of baseball for eight years following his retirement in 1960. He was hired as a hitting instructor by the Montreal Expos beginning in 1969, and he earned high marks for his work with the youngsters. He joined the White Sox in 1977 at Bill Veeck's invitation and continued to earn respect as a batting coach. Doby improved the hitting stroke of Alan Bannister and Eric Soderholm among others.

Doby did not campaign for Bob Lemon's job. It was Lemon's suggestion to Veeck that elevated Larry into the hot seat on July 1, 1978. Out of respect to his pal Bob Lemon, he would not have taken the job as Sox manager unless all parties were in agreement.

Larry Doby probably sensed that his appointment was a publicity stunt on Veeck's part to jack up attendance and garner publicity, but he did not seem to care. He just wanted to prove himself before the baseball world. Doby was warmly received by a clique of Sox players who considered the outgoing Lemon "soft" and out of touch. By comparison, Doby was a fiery, aggressive type of manager who argued with umpires on his players' behalf. Lemon rarely questioned an official's decision.

Though his abbreviated term as manager failed to reverse the losing pattern or fill the grandstands as Veeck might have hoped, Larry Doby was responsible for bringing minor league manager Tony LaRussa to Chicago as the new first-base coach on July 4. Otherwise, there was little else to celebrate.

Upon conclusion of the 1978 season, Veeck informed Doby that he would not be retained for the following year. The announcement of a successor was delayed until October 19. Larry Doby, being the gentleman he is, accepted the news without rancor or ill-feeling toward Bill Veeck. He thanked Veeck for giving him the chance to manage and hoped that he might return to the big leagues at some future point, but he was never given that opportunity.

1979

Kessinger, Don

Record: 46–60 (.434)
Birthplace: Forest City, Arkansas
B: July 17, 1942

Kessinger, Don

	W	L	T	Pct
1979	46	60	0	.434
White Sox	46	60	0	.434
Career	46	60	0	.434

Bill Veeck's standard reply to reporters who second-guessed his decision to hire the likable, down-home Don Kessinger as the franchise's first player/manager since Jimmie Dykes ran along these lines: "I am in the business of selling tickets." Winning baseball games and building something of consequence for the future were always secondary to this equation.

Don Kessinger, one of Chicago's most popular, easygoing players, was acquired for the stretch drive on August 20, 1977. Kess was at the tail end of a brilliant career. But he had

Mounting frustrations. Left to right: Don Kessinger, Bill Veeck, and general manager Roland Hemond in 1979

enough life in his 36-year-old legs to unseat Alan Bannister as the starting shortstop in 1978.

Veeck recognized a box-office appeal in Kessinger that simply failed to materialize under Larry Doby. A crowd of 30,270 fans jammed Comiskey Park on September 8, 1978, to celebrate Don Kessinger Night at Comiskey Park. The evening was an unexpected success, and it became the impetus for naming Kessinger the next Sox manager on October 19. After all, Veeck was in the business of selling tickets and had said so. "I think you can be a nice guy and manage," Kessinger announced, tipping off the media as to what they could expect of him in 1979. "A lot of guys scream and holler, but I've yet to see them win an argument."

Kessinger presided over a curious circus sideshow—not a baseball team. In the spring all of the attention centered on 5′3″ Harry Chappas, the slight-of-frame shortstop whose presence on the roster was another promotional stunt to capture the imagination of the fans. By midseason Chappas was back in the minors.

The job was beyond Kessinger's capabilities. He did the best he could under adverse circumstances—the death of pitching coach Freddie Martin was an unexpected setback—but to satisfy Veeck, he graciously agreed to step down on August 2. "I just wanted to sit down with him for a good heart-to-heart talk and share my feelings," Kess admitted. "When he sort of agreed a change would be a good move, I had no alternative."

Veeck replaced Kessinger with 35-year-old Tony LaRussa, manager of the Triple A Iowa Oaks. For the moment, the gimmicks and sideshows were over on the South Side. It was time to get down to serious business.

1979–86

LaRussa, Tony

Record: 522–510 (.506)
Birthplace: Tampa, Florida
B: October 4, 1944

LaRussa, Tony

	W	L	T	Pct
1979	27	27	0	.500
1980	70	90	2	.438
1981	54	52	0	.509
1982	87	75	0	.537
1983	99	63	0	.612
1984	74	88	0	.457
1985	85	77	1	.525
1986	26	38	0	.406
White Sox	522	510	3	.506
Career	2,638	2,293	3	.535

South Side fans never warmed up to Tony LaRussa, arguably the finest manager to pace the White Sox dugout since the days of Al Lopez. He was perceived by the fans as rather cold and aloof, and he was held accountable for the loss of Harry Caray and Jimmy Piersall by the fans. LaRussa was no fan of Harry's candid and often outrageous announcing style. But Tony was a winner, and that was more important than worrying about the bruised egos of the broadcasters.

"I think we're going to find out that he is one of the really outstanding managers before he's through," Veeck predicted in the spring of 1980, days before LaRussa began his first full season as Sox skipper. "In baseball, the better managers usually weren't outstanding players. All the star has to do is go up and hit the ball out of the park. What does he care

Above: Jerry Reinsdorf (left), Tony LaRussa, and Sox vice president Eddie Einhorn. Right: LaRussa looks on from the dugout.

about the finer points of the game? But when you're a scuffler like Tony was—up and down, trying to stick with limited talent—then you have to learn the nuances that give you a little bit of an advantage."

Eighteen-year-old Tony LaRussa signed a contract with the Kansas City A's the night of his high school graduation in 1962. A career .199 hitter, Tony bounced around the A's minor league affiliates for nine years with little success. Between baseball seasons, LaRussa attended Florida State University Law School. He was admitted to the Florida bar in the winter of 1979–80. "I realized I wasn't as good as I thought...that I'd never make any real money in baseball and would only bounce around," LaRussa explained.

The 1976 spring training lockout was the turning point of LaRussa's uninspired 14-year playing career. Bill Veeck opened the camp in defiance of the owners' edicts and invited minor leaguers and several veteran players who had been recently released from their former teams. Loren Babe, manager of the Sox' Triple A affiliate at Des Moines, pointed out this kid LaRussa to general manager Roland Hemond. "Keep an eye on him," Babe advised. "He's got potential."

Tony served under Loren Babe as a player/coach at Iowa before taking over the Knoxville club of the Southern Association in 1978. The team won a first-half championship behind the hitting of Harold Baines and the pitching of Steve Trout—the two top prospects in the system at that time.

After Kessinger bowed out on August 2, 1979, LaRussa took over a ballclub going through the motions, and immediately things improved. The Sox played .500 ball the rest of the way. LaRussa stressed the fundamentals. He had a lot of personal contact with the players, and he instilled an aggressive, winning attitude among a group of players accustomed to losing.

LaRussa stood his ground against the criticisms of Caray, Piersall, and several rebellious players like Steve Trout and Ross Baumgarten who tried to undermine his authority. Tony had the ability to communicate, and as the team improved in the early 1980s, he was accorded a grudging respect among his older peers. With the fans it was an entirely different story. "All I'd like is a fair shot from the fans," LaRussa commented. "They can boo anything they want, but I'm going to take shots at winning wherever it makes sense. I'm not going to skip a trip to the mound to avoid one boo."

In 1983 he guided the Sox to their first Western Division title. He was voted Manager of the Year by the Baseball Writers Association, the *Sporting News,* and the Associated Press—a well-deserved honor. The old guard remained cautious in their praise, however. Detroit Tiger coach Dick Tracewski sarcastically referred to Tony as a "minor league punk manager." Tracewski did not know what he was talking about. In head-to-head competition versus the managers considered the "deans" of the American League, LaRussa's record was well over .500—at least in the early 1980s when Jerry Reinsdorf's ownership sailed a unified course, free of the acrimony that characterized the ballclub and front office later in the decade.

LaRussa was absolutely loyal to general manager Roland Hemond through several rugged seasons that accompanied the 1983 championship. Tony never warmed up to Ken "Hawk" Harrelson, Roland Hemond's successor, nor did he work very hard to make the relationship work.

The Hawk perceived that LaRussa was treating the players he acquired during the off-season poorly, and as the season dragged on, Harrelson took steps to rid himself of Tony by first approaching Billy Martin with an offer to pilot the Sox. Against his better judgment Jerry Reinsdorf sided with Harrelson in this front-office power struggle.

Tony LaRussa was let go by the Sox ownership on June 19, 1986, with more than the usual misgivings. Reinsdorf respected LaRussa's abilities and would later admit that the decision to fire Tony was a "great tragedy."

LaRussa managed the Oakland A's to four divisional titles and two American League pennants in a five-year period

(1988–92). After a disappointing finish to the 1995 post-strike year, LaRussa moved over to the Cardinals on October 23 of that year to begin a long and successful run in St. Louis, surpassing Red Schoendienst as the longest-tenured Redbirds manager (15 seasons through 2010). He led St. Louis to eight division titles, two National League pennants, and a 2006 World Series championship. If there was still any lingering doubt on the part of the Comiskey Park boo-birds of the early 1980s that this quiet, taciturn leader who champions animal rights as his personal cause is not one of the game's greatest baseball tacticians, his all-time record should finally silence the naysayers. LaRussa ranks third all-time in wins as a manager, trailing only the venerable Connie Mack, who led the Philadelphia A's for 50 years, and John McGraw, the Hall of Fame "bulldog" who guided his teams to 2,763 victories. Only Joe Torre and Bobby Cox have more postseason wins to their name than Tony. And he is one of only five licensed attorneys to ever manage a major league baseball team—joining Monte Ward, Hughie Jennings, Miller Huggins, and Branch Rickey—all of them enshrined in the Hall of Fame, where LaRussa's plaque will eventually be displayed.

Jerry Reinsdorf has candidly admitted that the poorly thought-out move to allow "Hawk" Harrelson to fire Tony in the 1986 campaign was the worst business decision he ever made during his ownership. But is it possible that mistake could be amended? LaRussa is on a one-year contract arrangement in St. Louis. His affection for the city of Chicago and his friendship for Jerry Reinsdorf endures. There is a growing school of thought among baseball insiders that Tony will someday return to the White Sox in a managerial or executive capacity.

1986

Rader, Doug

Record: 1–1 (.500)
Birthplace: Chicago, Illinois
B: July 30, 1944

Rader, Doug

	W	L	T	Pct
1986	1	1	0	.500
White Sox	1	1	0	.500
Career	388	417	2	.482

As manager of the Texas Rangers in 1983, Doug Rader accused the Sox of "winning ugly." His off-the-cuff remarks to a Dallas reporter provided Tony LaRussa's club with the motivation to go on and claim the AL Western Division. Three years later Rader found himself working for LaRussa as a third-base coach, replacing Jim Leyland. The colorful and quotable "Rooster" managed the ballclub for two games (June 20–21) until Jim Fregosi arrived in town to take over as LaRussa's full-time replacement.

Doug Rader

1986–88

Fregosi, Jim

Record: 193–226 (.461)
Birthplace: San Francisco, California
B: April 4, 1942

Fregosi, Jim

	W	L	T	Pct
1986	45	51	0	.468
1987	77	85	0	.475
1988	71	90	0	.441
White Sox	193	226	0	.461
Career	861	937	0	.479

Jim Fregosi, a six-time All-Star and Gold Glove winner, managed the White Sox through a tumultuous period of their history. The larger controversies surrounding the proposed appropriation of state money to build a new Comiskey Park often obscured the game on the field—not that anyone really cared or was even watching.

The former Angels shortstop had not managed in the big leagues since 1981. But in three full seasons piloting the Louisville Cardinals, Fregosi won two American Association championships and was regarded as the top managerial prospect in baseball. Ken Harrelson, the White Sox vice president of baseball operations, was convinced that Fregosi was the ideal candidate to replace Tony LaRussa. The Hawk traveled to Louisville to negotiate a three-year contract with Fregosi, who had spurned an earlier offer to manage the Seattle Pilots.

If Jim Fregosi believed he was coming into an optimum situation, he was badly mistaken. A faction of the players still loyal to LaRussa made his task an uphill battle. But as long as Harrelson was around to protect him, Fregosi's opinions carried weight in the organization. As the Hawk's situation became less certain in the closing weeks of the 1986 season, he

Jim Fregosi

deferred to Fregosi on a number of personnel matters. The manager had his own ideas about managing, which he voiced to the front office.

Fregosi was opposed to signing expensive free agents at the cost of a top draft choice, but some of his decisions were perplexing. He completely shattered the confidence of rookie outfielder Kenny Williams by forcing the young man to play third base in 1988. The players sensed devisiveness and front-office uncertainty, and they missed the clubhouse unity that characterized the LaRussa years.

If one of his men missed a signal or blew a routine play, Fregosi would make disparaging remarks to the other players seated on the bench but would not confront the player directly when he returned to the dugout. Under these circumstances, the morale of the talent-thin White Sox suffered.

The arrival of Larry Himes as the new general manager spelled the end of the Fregosi regime. Their private disagreements were aired in the press, but it was the general manager's prerogative to place his own man in charge. Fregosi was fired on October 7, 1988. "Jim did a fine job of managing...with the talent he had," Himes said.

1989–91

Torborg, Jeff

Record: 250–235 (.515)
Birthplace: Westfield, New Jersey
B: November 26, 1941

Torborg, Jeff

	W	L	T	Pct
1989	69	92	0	.429
1990	94	68	0	.580
1991	87	75	0	.537
White Sox	250	235	0	.515
Career	492	551	0	.471

Jeff Torborg beat out six other candidates, including Bucky Dent and Gene Lamont, in a nationwide talent search for a new Sox manager. Larry Himes was genuinely pleased when he announced the selection of Torborg on November 3, 1988. "I don't know if it was his experience or age, but I felt that the veteran players would receive him very well," Himes said. "I felt that with our young pitching staff, it was very important to have someone with a pitching background. That's the main strength Jeff has."

As a member of the Los Angeles Dodgers and the Angels, Torborg caught three no-hitters during his playing career, one short of Ray Schalk's major league record. Quiet, reflective, and something of a scholar, Jeff authored a graduate thesis discussing the effects of platooning in baseball. But he knew it would take more than academic theory or magic formulas to turn the Sox around. Torborg accepted the job with his eyes wide open. "This job is altogether different," he said. "This club has outstanding pitching."

The first year was a struggle. A rash of injuries to key contributors and youthful inexperience doomed the Sox to a last-place finish. In 1990, the final season in old Comiskey Park, the "Cinderella" White Sox improved by 25 games. The incredible turnaround earned Torborg a clean sweep of the American League Manager of the Year awards from the *Sporting News,* Associated Press, United Press International, and Baseball Writers Association. At the moment of Jeff's greatest success, however, the seeds of his own undoing were being sown by the front office. Larry Himes was fired as general manager and replaced by Ron Schueler before the ink was even dry on the history of the 1990 season.

An inherited manager is never a bankable commodity, and despite good intentions and a proven track record, Torborg became a target. Schueler criticized Torborg for his preferential treatment of catcher Carlton Fisk—who had fallen out of favor with the front office. He didn't care much for the idea of Torborg employing two pitching coaches—Dave LaRoche in the bullpen and Sammy Ellis on the bench

Jeff Torborg

for counsel and advice. And finally, Jeff was not aggressive enough to suit Schueler.

Torborg was not fired in the usual sense of the word. Instead, he was "encouraged" by Schueler to consider an offer from the New York Mets, who were just as puzzled by the White Sox's actions as the media and fans in Chicago. "Why were the White Sox willing to let him be talked to?" wondered Al Harazin, general manager of the Mets. "I can't explain it other than to accept at face value what they've said. You try to size up a situation, and we thought it was worth a phone call."

Torborg cited a desire to be closer to his family in New Jersey as his reason for accepting the Mets job. The halfhearted explanation just did not ring true.

Gene Lamont (left) and Walt Hriniak

1992–95

Lamont, Gene

Record: 258–210 (.551)
Birthplace: Rockford, Illinois
B: December 25, 1946

Lamont, Gene

	W	L	T	Pct
1992	86	76	0	.429
1993	94	68	0	.580
1994	67	46	0	.593
1995	11	20	0	.355
White Sox	258	210	0	.551
Career	553	562	0	.496

It is not often that a team on the brink of a championship decides to change managers. But after two consecutive second-place finishes, Ron Schueler handed over the reins to Gene Lamont, a third-base coach for the Pittsburgh Pirates the previous six seasons leading up to his appointment on November 26, 1991.

Neither Schueler nor Sox chairman Jerry Reinsdorf was interested in recycling an old and familiar face. They wanted a new man for the job, and they solicited the opinions of Jim Leyland, a Sox alumnus from the Tony LaRussa regime and an old friend who managed the Pittsburgh Pirates to three straight division titles in the early 1990s.

Leyland recommended Lamont to Schueler, and it was on his word that the Sox front office decided to take a pass on Larry Bowa, Bill Russell, and Rene Lachemann, who were also considered to be in the running.

The players adjusted slowly to Lamont's passivity. Gene is a quiet, no-frills family man who prefers a seat at the end of the bench to public appearances and the harsh glare of publicity. It was something new for the veteran players, who had become accustomed to Jeff Torborg's daily briefings and one-on-one involvement in their lives.

The 1992 season provided Lamont with valuable on-the-job training, but Sox fans were becoming increasingly impatient. Lamont was not the kind of manager to engage in theatrical shouting matches with umpires. In fact, it was suggested by a radio talk show host that the only way to dislodge the Sox manager from the bench was to light a bonfire under him.

A strong second-half finish in 1993 culminating in a Western Division title silenced Lamont's media critics for the moment and earned him AL Manager of the Year honors from the Baseball Writers Association. Gene Lamont's .565 winning percentage in his first three seasons is fourth highest in White Sox history. Only Clark Griffith, Clarence Rowland, and Fielder Jones surpassed Gene's ratio of success.

For all of his early success, however, the jury was still out on Gene Lamont as the 1995 season finally got under way. Ron Schueler offered Lamont a modest one-year contract extension following the strike-shortened 1994 season. This was not quite the resounding vote of confidence Gene hoped for when he first approached Schueler about a multiyear deal, but he agreed to the terms anyway, explaining that he would be "crazy" not to, given the uncertain times in Major League Baseball.

The White Sox floundered in the early going. The players were not ready to begin the season, and a listless, don't-give-a-damn attitude seemed to permeate the clubhouse, which the impatient Schueler blamed on Lamont after the team dropped 20 of its first 31 games. A four-game sweep at the hands of the inspired Cleveland Indians sealed Gene Lamont's fate on June 2.

At a press conference announcing Lamont's firing, Schueler was candid about the need for a change. "If they can't get up for a series like the Cleveland series, I can't let it go any further. I'm not going to ask our owner to put out good money for a team nine or 10 games under .500. Are we good enough to win?" Schueler asked rhetorically. "I think we are."

Thirty-eight-year-old third-base coach Terry Bevington, a successful manager at all three levels of minor league baseball, was named interim manager for the remainder of the 1995 season. "I'll be harder on myself than they'll ever be on me," Bevington told the press. "I'm going to look at this as my shot, and it's the only shot I'll ever have. That's some pressure, isn't it?"

In 1997 new Pirates owner Kevin McClatchy slashed the team's $23 million payroll, and a disgusted Jim Leyland asked to be released from his contract, ending his 11-year tenure as manager. Leyland sidekick Gene Lamont was ushered in as his replacement, but the former Sox skipper remembered by many as the player chosen by Detroit *ahead* of Johnny Bench in the June 1965 free agent draft, proved he was no miracle worker either, directing a bedraggled small-market, revenue-sharing bottom-feeder. Gene was let go after the 2000 season. He moved on to Boston, then Houston, before catching on with the Tigers on October 11, 2005, as a third-base coach for, you guessed it...Jim Leyland.

1993, 1995

Nossek, Joe

Record: 3–2 (.600)
Birthplace: Cleveland, Ohio
B: November 8, 1940

Nossek, Joe

	W	L	T	Pct
1993	1	0	0	1.000
1995	2	2	0	.500
White Sox	3	2	0	.600
Career	3	2	0	.600

Joe Nossek was strictly bench material during a forgettable nine-year playing career with the Minnesota Twins and other teams in the 1960s. But as a coach with the White Sox through two tours of duty (1984–86 and 1990–95), Nossek earned a reputation as a crafty sign stealer. During the 1990 season he was dispatched to the upper deck to align the defense and perhaps pilfer an opponent's sign or two as the White Sox' very own "Eye in the Sky."

Nossek filled in for Gene Lamont for one game during the 1993 season and was Terry Bevington's stand-in during the four-game suspension meted out by the American League, August 1–4, 1995. After splitting the four games with the Royals and Indians, Joe reported that he was happy to return to the coaching sidelines.

Terry Bevington: tough love

1995–1997

Bevington, Terry

Record: 222–214 (.509)
Birthplace: Akron, Ohio
B: July 27, 1956

Bevington, Terry

	W	L	T	Pct
1995	55	54	1	.505
1996	85	77	0	.525
1997	80	81	0	.497
White Sox	222	214	1	.509
Career	222	214	1	.509

From the moment he stepped to the podium to greet the media as the new White Sox manager, Terry Bevington fell into disfavor with the members of the fourth estate who were already contemplating a likely successor before he even handed in his first lineup card. He just never escaped the perception of being an interim manager, filling in until someone better came along.

Bevington's peevish, short-circuiting answers to straightforward questions during postgame question-and-answer sessions won him few converts among the Chicago press corps. He was the complete antithesis of the closemouthed Gene Lamont and a throwback to the old-fashioned brawlers of yesteryear who disdained fraternization with opposing players. The new Sox manager drew four ejections during his first *half* season.

Bevington earned a four-game suspension in 1995 for skirmishing with Milwaukee Brewers manager Phil Garner in Comiskey Park in the heat of combat, but management looked past the altercation because he took over a team in total disarray and guided it to a respectable .505 record (excluding the four games managed by Joe Nossek) after the Gene Lamont disaster.

Awarded a two-year contract extension and a shaky vote of confidence from Ron Schueler on the final day of the 1995 season, Bevington began his first full season vowing to teach the fundamentals to a revamped lineup featuring several high-priced free agents acquired over the winter.

The combative Sox manager scrapped his controversial and much-maligned "Bevington Rule," whereby the manager promised to deliver the quick hook to any starter or reliever walking two batters in an inning who came around to score. There was no need for the "Rule" to begin with, because in 1996, Terry Bevington removed his starting pitchers with impunity. Sometimes his managerial moves bordered on the mystifying. Rookie right-hander James Baldwin carried a one-hit shutout into the eighth inning and was cruising along toward a certain victory when suddenly Bevington popped out of the dugout and called for a new pitcher. The results of such misguided strategies were apparent by midseason when the talented young bullpen hurlers fell apart from exhaustion and overwork.

Off the field, Terry Bevington resumed where he left off in 1995. Fisticuffs with American League umpire Richie Garcia at a downtown Chicago steak house stirred comment among the press. Such actions were inconsistent with Jerry Reinsdorf's intention to promote his product as a wholesome, fan-friendly attraction. Sensitivity training for this disgruntled bunch of athletes and their manager was strongly encouraged.

The White Sox were coming apart at the seams at the most critical juncture. As the season wore on and as the team surrendered its wild-card advantage to the onrushing Baltimore Orioles in the final weeks, Bevington was greeted with a chorus of boos every time he stepped out of the dugout. Several frustrated Sox veterans were of the opinion that their manager would be job hunting during the off-season. And as it turned out, Terry very nearly joined the ranks of the unemployed.

The day after the disappointing 1996 campaign ended, Reinsdorf flew off on a secret mission to Pittsburgh in an futile attempt to lure Jim Leyland back to Chicago, where he had launched his career as one of Tony LaRussa's coaches in the early 1980s. Leyland said he was flattered by Reinsdorf's "generous offer," but he chose the Florida Marlins instead. Many observers believe that Leyland decided to forgo the White Sox's offer only because of the unfortunate way in which management had treated his friend, Gene Lamont, in 1995.

Meanwhile, Terry Bevington's status remained very much in doubt, but he showed a measure of class by distancing himself from the fray and just riding out the storm. "I take a lot of pride in the things I do, but I'm not a big ego guy," the embattled manager told speculating reporters who waited for the other shoe to drop. But the shoe never dropped. After a few more days of artful suspense, and with no new Tony LaRussas or Jim Leylands appearing over the horizon, Ron Schueler awarded Bevington a contract extension through 1998.

"I don't believe in letting players dictate who the manager will be," Schueler commented. "That's my decision. I don't hire any of them to manage. They all think they can manage. They all think they can play, too."

Jerry Manuel—columnist Jay Mariotti called him "Manager Ghandi."

1998–2003

Manuel, Jerry

Record: 500–471 (.515)
Birthplace: Hahira, Georgia
B: December 23, 1953

Manuel, Jerry

	W	L	T	Pct
1998	80	82	0	.494
1999	75	86	1	.466
2000	95	67	0	.586
2001	83	79	0	.512
2002	81	81	0	.500
2003	86	76	0	.531
White Sox	500	471	1	.515
Career	704	684	2	.507

A career .150 hitter with three different teams, Jerry Manuel was selected from a pool of 14 candidates to succeed Terry Bevington as manager on December 4, 1997, becoming the first African American to be hired as a manager or coach in Chicago sports history (Larry Doby was an interim Sox manager in 1978). "I'm convinced we have the right man, and believe me, there were some good candidates out there," (one was former Sox shortstop Bucky Dent) beamed general manager Ron Schueler, who considered Manuel's coaching apprenticeship under such fine mentors as Felipe Alou in Montreal and Jim Leyland in Florida as adequate preparation for the tasks ahead. Manuel was a finalist for the Tampa Bay Devil Rays job when this former switch-hitting infielder, who had played briefly for minor league teams on both sides of town, accepted a multi-year offer from Messrs. Schueler and Reinsdorf. He said that he made his decision after "three days of fasting and prayer." A deeply religious man whose father was a church deacon, Manuel practiced Hinduism and studied the Islamic faith. He said that God "had given him a plan." The plan, whatever it was, must have left a deep and abiding impression on the Sox's ruling cadre. In a series of job interviews that followed, the soft-spoken Manuel won over Schueler by stressing his reliance on fundamentals—"The way they should be." His low-key demeanor on and off the field was another important consideration following three fractious seasons of Terry Bevington. More important, ownership believed Jerry was the right guy to "relate" to their moody superstar Albert Belle. "I want to sit down with [Belle]," said Manuel, "and pick his brain and ask him, 'Did [you] come here to win a world championship?'" Good question. Manuel exercised the utmost diplomacy with the sensitive slugger in 1998, their only season together. Following one angry and emotional temper tantrum coming from Belle inside the White Sox lunchroom, Manuel pulled him aside and warned him: "That's not going to happen anymore, or you're not going to play. That's it. It's up to you. I don't care about any fine. You're just not going to play. If you want to try me, go ahead, tear it up!"

Manuel had no further issues with Belle but was frequently at loggerheads with Frank Thomas over his playing time at first base. The Big Hurt wanted to be the DH, not a full-time position player, and this tried the manager's patience. "I love him like a son. If I spank my son, it doesn't mean I don't love him," he said following a heated altercation in Texas. "I love Frank Thomas, but when you draw a line in the sand and have it kicked on you, it upset me at the time."

Jerry's first two seasons were disappointing, but he earned a pass—the sub-.500 records were chalked up to the inexperience of youth and the pains of rebuilding. Easily out-distancing Art Howe of Oakland, Manuel was named Major League Manager of the Year by the Associated Press, the *Sporting News*, and the Baseball Writers' Association of America (BBWAA) on the strength of a surprising division title in 2000. In the All-Century Team poll conducted that same year, the fans of Chicago voted Manuel the third-best manager in team history behind Al Lopez and Tony LaRussa. Polls of this nature are entirely subjective, of course, and the fans tend to vote for individuals within their own span of memory. It was a flattering statement, but surely Manuel's accomplishments cannot be held in the same brilliant light as Fielder Jones—arguably the most brilliant strategist in White Sox history—or Jimmie Dykes, with the greatest longevity of any Sox manager.

The success of the 2000 White Sox was premature—the team was far from championship caliber. But the trip to the playoffs whetted ownership's appetite for more of the same, and it raised the bar on expectations. Thus, after another mediocre performance in 2001, the media and fans began finding fault with Jerry's laid-back, easygoing, Zen-like style, although he exhibited occasional fire with umpires and had his fair share of ejections. Manuel, an avid reader in his spare time, was derisively mocked as "Manager Ghandi" because he cited the works of Mohandas K. Ghandi and the Rev. Dr. Martin Luther King Jr. But all the peace, love, and harmony in the world counted for little if the White Sox were incapable of reaching "Point C." Given a ballclub in 2003 believed strong enough to finally shoot past the small-market Minnesota Twins, the manager was let go for much the same reasons as Marty Marion back in 1956—being the perennial second- or third-place finisher was no longer good enough. In 1997 Jerry said, "Commitment means change, and sometimes change is uncomfortable." And it was just as uncomfortable in 2003 when Manuel was shown the door.

He hooked up with the New York Mets as a bench coach in 2006 and was appointed interim manager on June 17, 2008, replacing Willie Randolph. Manuel enjoyed a brief burst of success managing a chronically underachieving team that scored a 55–38 (.591) record for him in 2008—good enough to earn him a two-year contract extension in the off-season. But success was fleeting. The Mets were an also-ran in 2009 and a flop in 2010, despite a sky-high payroll and the presence of veteran superstars Carlos Beltran and Johan Santana acquired at great cost. Mets fans were disgusted and impatient, and the tough New York media had already penciled in Brooklyn native Joe Torre as Manuel's likely replacement in 2011—weeks before the season ended and Jerry's inevitable departure. As usual, Jerry, in his Zen-like way, was philosophical and took the rumors in stride. "That's part of life in New York," he said. "You expect to hear that."

2004–

Guillen, Ozzie

Record: 600–535 (.529)
Birthplace: Ocumare del Tuy, Venezuela
B: January 20, 1964

Guillen, Ozzie

	W	L	T	Pct
2004	83	79	0	.512
2005	99	63	0	.612
2006	90	72	0	.556
2007	72	90	0	.444
2008	89	74	0	.546
2009	79	83	0	.488
2010	88	74	0	.543
White Sox	600	535	0	.529
Career	600	535	0	.529

A national hero in his native land as a result of his masterful job of leading an underdog White Sox team devoid of superstar talent into the 2005 World Series, Ozzie Guillen was the unlikely "Point C" manager to transform a contending team into a champion. Outspoken, opinionated, saying what's on his mind regardless of consequence, Ozzie is a throwback manager—a latter-day Eddie Stanky (minus Stanky's mean-spiritedness) for his uncanny ability to stir controversy and upset the status quo.

Jerry Reinsdorf and Kenny Williams understood the risks going in when the former Sox shortstop was hired to succeed Jerry Manuel on November 3, 2003. Knowing his temperament, his unbridled enthusiasm for the game, and his off-handed—and occasionally off-color—commentary and prickly analogies, the Sox chairman tagged Ozzie the "Hispanic Jackie

Ozzie Guillen greets Sox fans in a Sox Fest autograph line, 2009. (Courtesy of the Chicago White Sox)

Mason," while urging his general manager, Kenny Williams, to bypass a more seasoned manager in Cito Gaston and give Guillen the strongest consideration during the screening process. This, despite a frank admission from Ozzie that he went into his job interview with a hangover after celebrating the Marlins' World Series triumph the night before. (In contrast, Jerry Manuel had fasted and prayed.) Guillen is the first native of Venezuela to manage in the big leagues and the 16th former Sox player to pilot the ship. For all of his success in 2005, the question arises: could the White Sox have won a World Series without Ozzie Guillen? It is doubtful any of his immediate predecessors could have exerted so much positive energy and put forth the last full measure of effort as the "Wizard of Oz." His team capitalized on their opponent's every weakness. The Sox were 35–19 in one-run games and 26–15 in two-run decisions. Taught the finer points of the game by Jeff Torborg in Chicago and by Bobby Cox in Atlanta, Ozzie joined Frank Robinson and Lou Piniella as the only two former players to garner both Rookie of the Year honors and the Manager of the Year award. In 2005 Guillen became the fifth White Sox Manager of the Year recipient, polling 105 votes from the Baseball Writers' Association of America (BBWAA). Cleveland's Eric Wedge, the Central Division's other wunderkind, finished a distant second.

"This is the most fun year for me and my team, but it was the hardest year I've ever had," said Guillen, who at one point in the campaign said of his team that "we flat out stink," then later threatened to quit if the Sox won the World Series because of his disgust over incessant press negativity. "Winning's tough because all of a sudden you've got to keep winning and winning and winning. I want to be like Michael Jordan, have rings all over the place." He says he'll never retire until the Maker waves him home one last time. "I'm going to die doing this. I'm going to die on the field. I hope the day I die I just like, go to the field and am gone. Game's over. Tomorrow's the funeral." Guillen has traveled a long way in life since December 6, 1984, when he came over to the White Sox as an unknown rookie in a trade with the San Diego Padres that sent away La Marr Hoyt and two minor leaguers.

"That was my trade," recalled Roland Hemond. "With the blessings of our ownership, we made the trade at the Hotel Anatole in Dallas. It goes back to our scouts, Jerry Krause and Duane Shaffer, who highly recommended Ozzie. It didn't take long to find out he had leadership qualities. Tom Seaver was talking to me last fall about how he got a kick out of Ozzie. He was a rookie shortstop coming to the mound repeatedly making suggestions to Tom Seaver. Others told me when he was in the minor leagues he took charge of the infield and the outfield as an 18- to 19-year-old shortstop."

Guillen had many mentors praising his abilities as he moved up through the ranks. If Bobby Cox taught him the mechanics of skippering a ballclub, it was Jeff Torborg who transitioned him from the playing field into the coach's box. In 2001, the year he was hired to manage the Montreal Expos, Torborg convinced Guillen to take over as his third base coach despite having no formal training. Torborg was soon fired, and Ozzie moved down to Florida with owner Jeffrey Loria, who swapped the pathetic Expos for the upstart Marlins in a nifty bit of baseball carpetbagging. After the Marlins knocked off the Cubs in the 2003 NLCS and drove the heavily favored Yankees to the wall in the World Series, Torborg, remembering his former protégé, picked up the phone and dialed Jerry Reinsdorf. "He's ready," Torborg said, and the chairman listened. "I know how he feels about me and my kids," Ozzie said of Torborg. "Our relationship is way beyond baseball. He's the guy who is responsible for me being here. He had faith in me and what I could do."

As the World Series pandemonium subsided, much of the media focus in the post-pennant years shifted from the games and players on the field to the words and actions of their volatile manager. Guillen's off-color vocabulary and penchant for saying whatever happened to be on his mind at any moment of the day led to many anxious moments in the front office at 35th and Shields. Not since the days of Eddie Stanky in the late 1960s and Jimmie Dykes during the years of the Great Depression and World War II had there been a Sox manager of such great candor, raw language, and utter unpredictability who stirred as much continuous controversy and consternation as the South Side's Wizard of Oz.

When he wasn't battling the umpires—24 ejections and counting through 2010 with a few random, choice words for his archnemesis, Joe West, during a 2010 game in Cleveland thrown in: "He's a [bleeping bleep], that's what he is!"—Ozzie was attacking the Chicago media for their pro-Cubs bias. "We won it a couple of years ago, and we're horse [bleep]! The Cubs haven't won in 120 years and they're the [bleeping] best! We are the bitch of Chicago!" The brutal play of the 2007 team was particularly hard on the Ozeroo: "They're killing me! They're killing my family! They're killing my coaching staff! Kill the White Sox fans! They kill the owner! They kill everyone!"

Even baseball's greatest stars were not exempt from censure. Before the 2006 season unfolded, Guillen had this to say about A-Rod participating in the World Baseball Classic. "Alex [Rodriguez] was kissing Latino people's asses.... He knew he wasn't going to play for the Dominicans. He's not a Dominican! It's the same thing with [Nomar] Garciaparra playing for Mexico. Garciaparra only knows Cancun because he went to visit." Guillen had no love for former Texas Rangers manager Buck Showalter, either. In 2004 Ozzie said, "Showalter never even smelled a jock in the big leagues. He didn't even know how the clubhouse in the big leagues was when he got his first job. 'Mr. Baseball' never even got a hit in Triple A. He was a backup catcher or a first baseman. Now all of a sudden he's the best manager in baseball!"

As his 2010 team made great strides and captured first place in the heat of the Central Division race, Oz turned his attention to the issue of the translators Major League Baseball provided to Japanese and Korean players and wondered why Latinos were not accorded the same consideration. "Don't take this wrong, but they take advantage of us," he complained. "We bring a Japanese player, and they are very good and they bring all these privileges to them. We bring a Dominican kid [and say], '[Bleep] you, you go to the minor leagues, good luck. And it's always going to be like that. It's never going to change. But that's the way it is." The club took issue and issued an immediate statement: "Ozzie certainly has his own experiences as a player, coach, and manager, and is entitled to his own opinions, but the Chicago White Sox believe his views are incorrect."

After a news report of a berserk bull charging into the stands during a Spanish bullfight, the Sox manager told his players that unlike deer or duck hunting south of the border, bullfights were the genuine article and the sport of hunting was strictly for sissies. "That's a *real* sport," Guillen told his off-season nimrods. "Not! 'Oh, here comes a deer! How big are his horns?' Let's shoot it and take a picture of it!"

His sarcastic taunts against opposing players was strangely reminiscent of 1967, when Stanky called Carl Yastrzemski an All-Star from "the neck down," and the late Bill Rigney a "television manager."

Owner Arthur Allyn eventually silenced Stanky by firing him. General manager Kenny Williams was more inclined to forgive and forget, even after the many heated exchanges between the two in 2010 that threatened to tear asunder a previously amicable relationship. "Are there some times where you wish he would shut his mouth? Yeah," Williams admitted in the first episode of *The Club*, the television reality series featuring an insider's unvarnished look at the White Sox operation that premiered in the MLB Network in July 2010 and ran for six episodes.

Opening segments of the series were filmed amid a spring training flap over Guillen's social media blog on Twitter—and some embarrassing, ill-chosen comments posted to the blog by Guillen's son, 24-year-old Oney, concerning a trio of front-office executives and the young man offering unsolicited advice to the club about re-signing free-agent-to-be A.J. Pierzynski. Worse, the Chicago restaurant, Market, owned by Williams, was panned by the younger Guillen—although, according to Williams, the young man had eaten there 21 times. Ozzie's plan to launch his own website was immediately nixed by the front office, and bitter feelings continued until Oney, who had been drafted in 2007 by the White Sox but washed out a year later, opted to resign from his full-time position in the team's video department rather than simply give up his blogging.

Could this marriage be saved? The fans and the media wondered what other bumps in the road awaited Guillen and Williams, even as the "Twitter in a Teapot Tempest" finally ended. They didn't have long to wait. A heated argument in early June over Williams' decision not to draft another Guillen son—Ozney—until the 22nd round of the selection process rankled the manager and led to a closed door session with Jerry Reinsdorf. Ozzie and the GM were told to work it out for the sake of the club. Reportedly, Reinsdorf had ordered Williams not to travel on road trips to avoid any future confrontations with his manager. When it was over, Guillen was contrite, if not philosophical about the whole thing.

"We're all where we are and respect Jerry more than anything," Ozzie said. "Kenny loves Jerry, and I love Jerry. I want to do this thing for him. My greatest moment in my career in 2005 was when I won the World Series for him. I separate my problems on the field and off the field. It's the only way this thing is going to work—and if we pull from the same end of the rope, and we do. Even if we don't agree with each other, at the end of the day we do pull from the same rope."

During the early months of the 2010 season when the Sox foundered, Phil Rogers of the *Tribune* postulated that Guillen might be managing elsewhere when 2011 rolled around, although he was signed by the club through 2012. Nothing seemed further from the truth than for Guillen to voluntarily hang it up, although he expressed a thinly veiled threat that he would not rule out managing the Cubs if he felt unloved on the South Side and was cut loose. But that was Ozzie being Ozzie, no more, no less. Guillen has made it clear all along that he would remain with the White Sox for as long as they wanted him. Long after the media and the fans had written off the 2010 edition as a sub-.500 loser, only Ozzie Guillen continued to believe—and Guillen's faith transcended negative predictions and unsubstantiated speculation by Rogers and the beat writers.

Ozzie grew up with the White Sox and will remain the White Sox manager until such time when fate or circumstances (an ill-chosen remark, perhaps?) or his decision to step aside intervene. After notching his 523rd victory early in the 2010 season, he is now ranked third on the all-time list of wins for a Sox manager, trailing only Jimmie Dykes and the venerable "Señor," Al Lopez. In fact, only Lopez has more winning seasons in the service of the White Sox than Ozzie. Despite the silliness of the Twitter-gate fiasco, his rants and tirades about this and that, and a checkered vocabulary that would make a longshoreman blush, Guillen has served notice that he is one of the canniest and most intuitive managers in the game.

5

The Front Office

The Owners

1900–31

Charles A. Comiskey

"I'd been with the St. Louis club about two or three weeks in the 1902 season when we went to Chicago to play the White Sox. It was a rainy Saturday, and as we sat on the bench waiting for the game to begin, somebody pointed out Mr. Comiskey, the owner of the White Sox. He was out there in the infield with his pants rolled up, soaking up water with a couple of sponges and wringing them into a pail, trying to get the diamond in shape to play. That was my first sight of Charles A. Comiskey," recalled infielder Davey Jones.

Baseball historians who study the national pastime have long considered Charles Comiskey a tightfisted misanthrope whose shabby treatment of his eight underpaid players on the 1919 squad was the catalyst of the Black Sox scandal. Comiskey's notoriety for penurious treatment of the players who conspired to throw the 1919 World Series to the Cincinnati Redlegs tarnished an otherwise exemplary career in professional baseball.

What is overlooked and forgotten is the warm affection and high level of regard accorded the White Sox owner during his lifetime. Nicknamed the "Noblest Roman of the Baseball Field" (later shortened to the "Old Roman") because of his prominent gladiatorial stance as a first baseman during his playing days, and as a token of respect by his peers, Charles Comiskey was a highly regarded civic figure, philanthropist, and sportsman during his lifetime. It was only after the publication of Eliot Asinof's 1963 book *Eight Men Out* that the Sox founder was recast into the role of baseball's consummate villain.

Comiskey commanded the unflagging loyalty of the media and of Chicago's South Side Irish constituency, which adopted the neighborhood baseball park bearing the owner's name as the focal point of community life. An affluent clientele of politicians, business leaders, and show business figures enjoyed Comiskey's hospitality in a private clubroom setting at the ballpark. In 1907 Chicago attorney Robert Emmet Cantwell and songwriter Joseph Farrell organized these fans into a cheering club known as the White Sox Rooters Association. Around 1912 the name was changed to the Woodland Bards because of their love of the great outdoors, reciting Shakespearean verse, and of course, White Sox baseball.

Following the conclusion of each baseball season, Comiskey escorted the Bards to his northern Wisconsin hunting resort, where they would cavort through the forest like small boys on a holiday. These were the happy, carefree days... before the Black Sox scandal shattered Charles Comiskey's world.

The White Sox founder was the son of one of Chicago's most recognizable 19th-century political leaders: Alderman John Comiskey, who represented the Irish 10th ward in the city council for 13 years. Charley Comiskey answered the calling of sport early in life and gravitated toward baseball while serving as the catcher for the varsity team at St. Mary's College in Kansas, in 1873.

Comiskey, a fair-complected six-footer with a regal bearing, aspired to become a pitcher but attained baseball fame as a first baseman whom historians credit with inventing the defensive technique of fielding ground balls while playing off the bag. Others are uncertain whether it was Comiskey or Cap Anson of the Cubs who perfected this play.

The Old Roman tries his hand at Cricket, Sydney, Australia, World Tour, 1914.

Charles Comiskey, the Old Roman, or "Noblest Roman," at the apex of his 50-year career in baseball

Ted Sullivan, a long-forgotten star of the 19th century, encouraged Comiskey to pursue baseball as a career while they attended classes together at St. Mary's. Sullivan organized the Dubuque Rabbits of the Northwestern League in 1879, and hired Comiskey to play first base at a salary of $125 a month. During off-days, Comiskey was required to sell refreshments and newspapers to Illinois Central rail passengers commuting between Chicago and Dubuque.

The Northwestern League collapsed after only three years. However, Comiskey's formidable skills caught the attention of several St. Louis baseball promoters who organized a team to compete in the newly formed American Association, a challenger to the National League's trade monopoly.

Appointed team manager in 1885 by the Browns' eccentric owner Christian Von der Ahe, whose special flair for promotion and hucksterism set him apart from other owners of the day, Charles Comiskey guided St. Louis to four consecutive American Association titles spanning 1885 to 1888. His upset victory over the powerful Chicago White Stockings (now the Cubs) in the forerunner of the modern World Series in 1886 established the Old Roman as a national figure in the sporting world.

Because Comiskey was considered to be something of a management-oriented player, it came as a surprise when he bolted the American Association in 1890 to play for the Chicago "Brotherhood" team in the short-lived Players League. But, as Comiskey later explained, he had to do so in order to "remain square with the boys."

Comiskey wound up his playing career with the Cincinnati Redlegs in 1894 to seek new vistas with Byron Bancroft Johnson, a local sportswriter who envisioned the formation of a new baseball league. With Comiskey's encouragement, Johnson abandoned his newspaper duties to serve as president of the Western League, organized in the fall of 1893. A year later, when Comiskey's contract with Redlegs owner John T. Brush expired, the Old Roman pooled his life savings and purchased the struggling Sioux City, Iowa, team.

He moved the team to St. Paul, Minnesota, and piloted the Twin Cities ballclub until 1899, when Johnson drew up an ambitious plan to transform their minor league into a bona fide challenger to the National League. The key to the plan was the transfer of Comiskey's St. Paul team to Chicago—a major-market city that would put the Western League on the map. Despite considerable vocal opposition coming from the National League, the move was completed in October 1899. The rechristened American League opened for business the following season.

Comiskey reaped the harvest of favorable press—strong attendance figures—and he expended large sums of money to build an exciting, winning ballclub. With his surprise victory over the Cubs in the 1906 World Series, the Old Roman established himself as the Windy City's most beloved sports figure—an image that held up in the minds of the fans years after his death in 1931.

In 1910, with the opening of the new Comiskey Park, baseball's third concrete and steel stadium, the owner arrived at the pinnacle of his career. A celebrated global goodwill tour to Europe and the Orient followed in 1913. The White Sox owner garnered favorable acclaim for his statesmanship abroad, but it was to be the last hurrah for Comiskey, who built the greatest White Sox team of them all only to see it decimated in the autumn of 1920 when the charges of crookedness against the eight Black Sox players were finally confirmed by a Cook County grand jury.

Charles Comiskey paid his athletes what the market would bear. Other owners, like Connie Mack and Clark Griffith, also forced their players to labor under a "plantation" system that required them to launder their own uniforms and accept substandard pay. Comiskey was a 19th-century man whose values were shaped by the principles of thrift, hard work, self-reliance, and entrepreneurship. By the same token, he could be surprisingly generous with his younger players by doling out bonus money to motivate them to play better.

Sadly, the Old Roman also had a petty, venal side that baseball historians dwell upon almost exclusively these days. Time after time Comiskey broke his word to his most loyal employees. George Rohe, hero of the 1906 World Series, was promised lifetime employment in the organization—before the Old Roman cast him into the unemployment line a year later.

Comiskey's coldhearted release of Billy Sullivan and Eddie Collins at the end of their long and meritorious careers bordered on the criminal.

The White Sox players deeply resented Comiskey's generosity toward his well-heeled patrons in the Woodland Bards social club and the baseball beat writers. The yearly hunting trips and lavish buffet tables prepared for them on game day earned Charles Comiskey favorable press, and it was an important conduit to the city power brokers. When Comiskey required a zoning change in order to complete construction on his new ballpark, the aldermen were more than eager to accommodate their benefactor by pushing through an ordinance in the City Council.

Comiskey, however, was as much a victim of the Black Sox scandal as the players and fans and cannot be held entirely at fault for the tragedy that transpired in the fall of 1920. The owners had done very little to eliminate the presence of gamblers from their stadiums over the years. In this sense the Black Sox scandal had been simmering beneath the surface for many years, and it was Comiskey's great misfortune that this tragedy should occur when it did.

The scandal had a jarring effect on Comiskey's outlook on life and his physical health. The White Sox relinquished their position as the "cornerstone" franchise of the American League to the New York Yankees. They became a doormat in the 1920s and a local laughingstock for many years thereafter. Nancy Comiskey, the Old Roman's devoted wife, passed away in 1922, and increasingly Comiskey distanced himself from his friends and acquaintances, preferring the seclusion of his Eagle River, Wisconsin, hunting lodge. Through the 1920s, Comiskey allowed his trusted associate, Harry Grabiner, to spend the family fortune on unproven minor league prospects in the vain hope of rebuilding a championship ballclub.

The Old Roman would never see his dream fulfilled. He died in Eagle River, some say of a broken heart, on October 26,

1931. He left behind a sizable estate valued at $1,529,707, real estate properties in Chicago and Wisconsin, membership in several prestigious country clubs, and control of the ballclub to his frail and sickly son John Louis Comiskey.

For his many contributions to the game as a player, manager, owner, and cofounder of the American League, Charles Comiskey was voted into the Hall of Fame in 1939.

1931–39

John Louis Comiskey

The only son of Charles Comiskey was a shy, reclusive man who toiled quietly in the shadow of his flamboyant father. "Uncle Lou," as he was known to his small circle of acquaintances, carefully sidestepped publicity and personal acclaim, which he viewed as threats to the quiet home life he cherished.

Lou Comiskey was born in Dubuque in 1885. He was a likable youngster who showed tremendous athletic promise while attending classes at DeLaSalle Institute, just a few blocks east of the stadium bearing his family name. He was captain and tackle of the high school football team, and he counted on a full and rewarding career in sports administration until he contracted a malignant case of scarlet fever when he was only 27.

Lou Comiskey never shook off the aftereffects of the terrible disease. For years to come he carried a portable oxygen mask around with him, while maintaining a suite of rooms at St. Luke's Hospital for all-too-frequent medical emergencies. He was a big man who weighed in at more than 300 pounds. A battery of medical specialists tried to help Lou control his weight through the prescription of fad diets, Turkish baths, sanatorium treatments, and daily regimens of physical therapy that might have broken the spirits of most other men. It was his remarkable vitality, good sense of humor, and optimistic nature that allowed him to carry on through the trying years that were to follow.

Lou Comiskey was a frail but compassionate man.

When Comiskey Park opened on July 1, 1910, the Old Roman placed his son in charge of the concessions and bottling plant underneath the stands. In his small office far removed from his dad and all of the Woodland Bard camp followers, Lou began his baseball apprenticeship supervising the manufacture and bottling of orange soda pop that was peddled by strolling vendors in the stands.

Brusque in manner but possessing a deeper compassion that his father seemed to lack at times, Lou Comiskey fed an army of homeless tramps who lined up outside the park during the worst days of the Depression. Lou passed out the unsold sandwich meats and bread from the previous day's game. "Give the other guy a break, and he'll give you one," was the way J. Lou Comiskey chose to conduct his business—and his life.

Despite the physical limitations imposed by his illness and unable to travel with his ballclub on the road, Lou Comiskey conceived an ambitious plan to rebuild the tattered remains of the White Sox following his dad's death in 1931. Tired of losing games with such stunning regularity, Comiskey drew up the blueprints for the White Sox's minor league system, which began operation in 1939 after nearly a decade of planning and negotiation.

Comiskey borrowed against the equity of the ballclub in order to finance the purchase of Al Simmons, Mule Haas, and Jimmie Dykes in 1932. The move was made to bring some excitement back to the South Side after years of costly failure. Al Simmons failed to deliver the kind of spectacular results Lou hoped for, but Dykes made it all worthwhile in the end.

Lou Comiskey exhibited greater degrees of professionalism and fairness dealing with the players at contract time than his nickel-and-diming father. Lou was no soft touch, but invariably the men received the salary they were looking for. There were never any serious holdouts come Opening Day on the South Side.

It was Comiskey's heartfelt desire that his only son Charles assume command of the White Sox as soon as he was old enough to see it through. However, the lad was only 13 years old when the complications of the debilitating disease caught up with Lou on July 18, 1939—a month before the first scheduled night game at Comiskey Park.

Lou's death at age 54 was a terrible blow. Under his firm, guiding hand, the White Sox were well on the road to recovery. Afterward, the rebuilding program ground to a halt. Worse, the language of Comiskey's will was deliberately vague as to Charley's right of succession.

The legal loophole that ultimately split apart the Comiskey family and paved the way for outside interests to purchase the ballclub was "if circumstances arise after my death, which in the opinion of the trustees would render a sale prudent and desirable." There is no doubt that Lou Comiskey intended for his son to run the White Sox someday, but he did not specify his wishes with clear conviction, and therein lay the tragedy of White Sox baseball in the next two decades.

1939–56

Grace Reidy Comiskey

Grace Elizabeth Reidy, born and raised on the West Side of Chicago, was married to John Louis Comiskey on September 29, 1913. The "grand matriarch" of White Sox baseball bore her husband three children. Each of them assumed an active role in the day-to-day affairs of the ballclub: Dorothy, the eldest; Gracie Lou, a young woman of fragile health; and Charley, the heir apparent to the baseball throne.

Grace Comiskey respected her late husband's wishes concerning the right of succession—to a point. "There must always be a Comiskey at the head of the White Sox," she said. "My son Charley, grandson of the founder of the White Sox, will be fully fitted to operate the franchise when he reaches the proper age." Her later actions belied these earlier public statements.

After the 1939 season, Mrs. Comiskey was confronted with an immediate crisis that imperiled her family's continuing ownership of the ballclub. The First National Bank, a partner in White Sox affairs since 1900, continued on as executor of Lou Comiskey's will. In January 1940 bank trustee John S. Gleason made known his intention to solicit outside bids after revealing that the ballclub had lost $675,029 in an 11-year period. Operating the White Sox, he argued, was a "hazardous enterprise."

To counteract the bank's sudden and capricious move, Grace Comiskey renounced her dower rights to one-third of her husband's estate and asked for her dower rights under Illinois law. A second petition was filed by Grace's eldest daughter, 23-year-old Dorothy Comiskey, who asked the court for 413 shares of White Sox stock. Mrs. Comiskey and her daughter went to court with public opinion running high in their favor. Probate Judge John F. O'Connell denied the bank's petition on February 29, 1940, claiming that the trustee's sole function was to preserve the estate, not dissolve it. Family attorneys argued convincingly that the White Sox would satisfy every outstanding debt now that night baseball had proven to be a financial salvation for the cash-strapped team.

Peace was restored for the moment. Grace was formally elected team president on March 4, 1941, commencing the third era of Comiskey ownership.

Having recovered the White Sox against tough odds, Mrs. Comiskey was viewed as a genuine heroine to the members of the fourth estate who understood and sympathized with the family's continuous struggles dating back to the Black Sox scandal. There was another side to the story, however. Grace was a tough, uncompromising dowager who ruled the ballclub—and her family—with a velvet fist. She alienated and drove away Harry Grabiner, the faithful and loyal general manager whose employment with the White Sox dated back to 1905, and she made it all but impossible for Jimmie Dykes to continue on as White Sox manager after 12 years at the helm.

Grabiner quit in 1945 after 40 years of unbroken service to the organization because Mrs. Comiskey mistrusted his motives. She replaced him with Leslie O'Connor, a competent assistant to commissioner Kenesaw Landis, but woefully inexperienced in the day-to-day operation of a big-league club. Grace studied the *Sporting News* and surrounded herself with veteran baseball men to proffer advice and counsel. They enjoyed job security just so long as they did not overstep their authority.

During the war years Mrs. Comiskey and her attorneys operated the ballclub under the misguided assumption that everything would be all right "once the boys returned" from service. Breaking even, which meant drawing 500,000 fans at

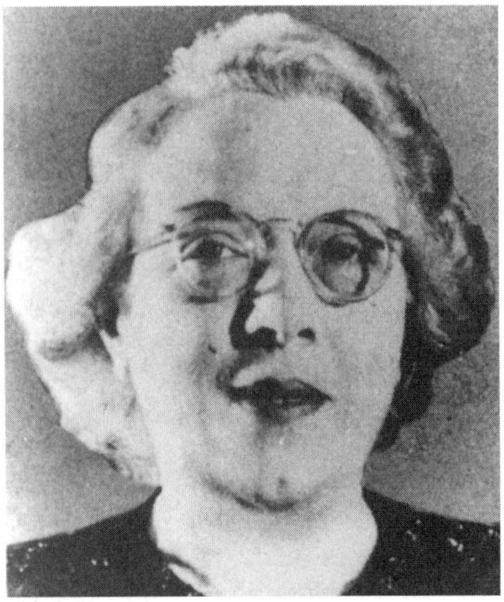

Left: Grace Reidy Comiskey; right: Mrs. Comiskey (in the veil), her daughter Gracie Lou, and young Charley (on the far right) with friends and well-wishers, c.1938

home and another 500,000 on the road, became her obsession. Little effort was made to bolster the farm system during these lean years or to secure quality replacement players. Mrs. Comiskey's frugality when it came to spending money to build a winner left her open to much criticism from the fans, and it hamstrung the sincere efforts of Grabiner, Dykes, and O'Connor to improve the team's fortunes.

If Grace Comiskey was biding her time until she could turn the ballclub over to her son Charles, then she went about it the wrong way. Charley, the youngest of her three children, joined the organization in an executive capacity in 1948. His precise role was vague, and his mother's instructions were contradictory. On the one hand, Charley was vested with the authority to hire Frank Lane as the new general manager, but on the other hand, she kept pulling in the reins on the young man and always treated him like a 14-year-old schoolboy.

Comiskey routinely worked 14 hours a day and reasonably expected to be fairly compensated for his service. Grace promised him a modest raise, then went back on her word at a January 18, 1952, board meeting. Charley quit the organization in a huff, but was taken back several months later when a broadcast venture he got into failed to work out. Time and again the mother cruelly ridiculed the son to the press. "Charles just talks too much," Grace snapped. "When he was smaller I could tell him to keep his mouth shut, but after all he's 29 now."

Dorothy and her mother presented a united front to the media, and they succeeded in making Charley appear ridiculous because of his youthful demeanor and rash decisions. In gratitude for her daughter's loyalty and "responsible" behavior, Grace awarded 3,975 shares (54 percent) of the team stock to Dorothy, but only 3,475 shares (46 percent) to Charley, thereby assuring a vicious ownership fight that would allow the ballclub to slip away from the family after nearly 60 years of Comiskey ownership. It was tragic, senseless, and a completely unintended outcome of Lou Comiskey's murky and deliberately vague will.

Grace Comiskey, who suffered from a drinking problem that may have clouded her judgment in her final years, succumbed to a fatal heart attack at her Lake Shore Drive apartment on December 10, 1956. The "First Lady" of Chicago sports was eulogized throughout the baseball world as a wise and benevolent owner, though the historical record suggests otherwise.

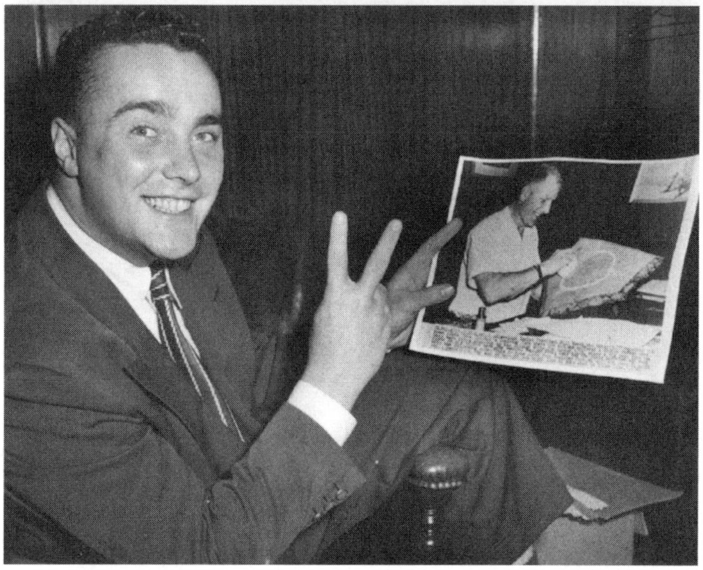

Top: John Rigney, Dorothy Comiskey Rigney, and their two daughters, Christmas, 1956. Bottom: Charley Comiskey signals "victory" after the White Sox whitewashed Bill Veeck's Cleveland Indians twice in a May 1949 doubleheader. Veeck is shown holding the Comiskey Park home plate, which Charley had mailed to him as a souvenir.

1956–59

Charles Comiskey II and Dorothy Comiskey Rigney

The namesake of the Old Roman was only six years old when his famous grandfather died in 1931. But Charley Comiskey vividly remembered the White Sox founder in his declining years taking him to the ballpark and spinning stories of baseball's bygone days across the family dinner table when the old man came to live with his only son, J. Lou. From the time he was in knee britches, Charley Comiskey was told by his elders that the day would come when he would inherit the White Sox and carry on the rich family traditions. At the decisive hour, the promise was broken and Comiskey's dream shattered. Charley paid the ultimate price for his youthful indiscretions, and the future history of the ballclub was rewritten as a result.

His older sister Dorothy majored in economics at Northwestern University. Like her brother, Dorothy grew up in a baseball household and was encouraged to take on a role in the organization. While attending classes at the Lake Shore campus in 1937, Dorothy approached her dad, J. Lou Comiskey, about a job with the team. "That's fine, but remember in the baseball business we have regular hours and no running off to the beach or up to the lakes on Sundays

The Old Roman's grandson, Charley Comiskey, age 15, receiving some sound advice from Jimmie Dykes, April 1, 1941.

either," Lou replied. Dorothy served as her dad's secretary and proved to be a diligent employee. In fact, Comiskey was so pleased with her performance that he called her his "general manager."

Dorothy was married to White Sox pitcher John Rigney on October 8, 1941. During the war years, following the death of Lou Comiskey, Dorothy faithfully served her mother as vice president and treasurer, and later in the decade as team secretary. The White Sox matriarchy failed to deliver a winner to the South Side fans, but they succeeded in keeping the franchise afloat during some rigorous and strenuous times.

Charley kept faith with the Comiskey timetables by launching his baseball career in 1947, following a two-year hitch in the navy and a short enrollment at St. Thomas College in Pennsylvania. He alternated between the White Sox's farm clubs at Waterloo, Iowa, and Hot Springs, Arkansas, that season. As president of the Waterloo White Hawks, Comiskey's promotional skills helped set a daily attendance record in 1948. It was the perfect preparatory education for the larger role his father had in mind for the young man.

Charley Comiskey arrived in Chicago in October 1948 to frame a policy for running the Sox and to restore the health of the franchise. As his first order of business, he placed the entire team on waivers. Only one player was claimed: pitcher Howie Judson, who lost 14 straight games the next season. Comiskey selected Frank Lane, former president of the American Association, to replace Les O'Connor as general manager. The Old Roman's grandson persuaded Lane to join the White Sox, then had to convince his mother to sign off on the appointment. Nothing of consequence could be done without first checking in with Grace.

Frank Lane wheeled and dealed. Charley Comiskey worked around the clock building, promoting, and dreaming of ways to improve the club. Then in 1951 the tree bore its fruit, and the White Sox emerged from a three-decade slumber. Under Lane and Comiskey the value of the franchise doubled in the early 1950s. But amid the excitement of a contending ballclub, favorable press, and an old stadium filled to the rafters, tensions boiled over in the house of Comiskey.

Charley resigned his position on January 18, 1952, after his mother and the two family attorneys turned down his modest request for a salary increase. Comiskey stalked off in anger and went to work for the Liberty Broadcasting System in Texas, but the short-lived venture ended in failure. Charley was taken back by his mother and his title restored, but a climate of maternal mistrust and suspicion lingered.

Grace Comiskey pinned the blame for Frank Lane's defection to St. Louis on her son. Charley took his licks, but the public airing of the Comiskey dirty laundry further eroded his credibility in the media. Following Grace Comiskey's passing in December 1956, control of the ballclub passed to Dorothy, who shunned the public spotlight at all costs. Mrs. Rigney desired to retreat behind the walls of her River Forest, Illinois, estate to raise her two daughters and attend to her horses.

Beginning in November 1957, Comiskey sought legal redress from the courts in order to force his sister to distribute

Charley revisits the old park on its last day in 1990.

the 2,582 shares of remaining stock held in trust by their mother's estate. It was the opening salvo of a messy two-year court battle for control of the White Sox pitting the Rigneys of River Forest and their loyal family attorneys, Roy Egan and Tom Sheehan, against the Comiskeys of the neighboring suburb of Hinsdale, together with Charley's father-in-law, Frank Curran.

The lengthy court proceedings and name-calling attracted considerable press attention—much of it unfavorable to Charley, who was unfairly cast as the spoiled and pouting "Crown Prince." His youthful overzealousness cost him the support of the media, and it invited interested outside parties in through the back door. Chicago insurance magnate Charles O. Finley and a group headed by showman Bill Veeck submitted bids for Dorothy's controlling 54 percent.

Dorothy initially preferred to deal directly with Charley, but she demanded from him fair market value for her stock. Comiskey, citing the wishes of his late father, felt that Dorothy should have reduced the price.

Before matters were resolved, Charley came in with a higher bid than either Veeck or Finley. By this time, however, Dorothy Rigney granted the Veeck partners a 60-day, $100 option to buy her stock. Under fire from all sides, Comiskey returned to court in a vain attempt to forestall the impending sale, but Judge Robert Dunne ruled against him on March 5, 1959, paving the way for Veeck to buy controlling interest in the ballclub.

After leaving baseball, Mrs. Rigney and her husband indulged their interest in the thoroughbreds by racing two prize-winning steeds at Arlington Park. One of the Rigney horses, Fast Hilarious, captured the 1969 American Derby.

Dorothy's sudden passing on January 22, 1971, at age 54, closed an unfortunate chapter of White Sox history.

Bill Veeck made a conciliatory gesture to Charley Comiskey, but his front-office status was greatly diminished, and Charley was constantly at loggerheads with Hank Greenberg, Veeck's choice for general manager.

Charley Comiskey lingered in the organization until May 5, 1962, when he sold his 46 percent to Arthur Allyn Jr. after failing in a countermove to buy out Allyn, who stubbornly refused to negotiate with the Crown Prince. Art Allyn was a Bill Veeck ally, and he bought Veeck's stock in June 1961, partly to checkmate the ambitions of Comiskey.

It was a bitter outcome for Comiskey, who still managed to walk away from the battlefield with his head held high. In the ensuing decades, Charley plunged into the real estate market. He financed a community theater venture, but in the back of his mind he kept alive the fading dream of returning to the game he loved so well.

That day never came, of course, but in the 1980s White Sox owner Jerry Reinsdorf frequently turned to Comiskey for counsel. The former Crown Prince in waiting had come full circle and was accorded the well-earned status of a respected tribal elder by the current regime.

Two years after seeing his team win the World Series, Charley Comiskey—he always preferred to be addressed as Charley and not Chuck—died in his sleep at age 81 on August 26, 2007. The grandson of the Old Roman had left an indelible mark on the franchise in many ways. He was survived by four children, seven grandchildren, and his devoted wife of 57 years, Donna Jo Curran. Charley never fulfilled his life's earliest dream of becoming a star first baseman like his illustrious grandfather, but he did so much more for the city of Chicago by restoring the pride, the tradition, and the luster of winning baseball to the South Side after so many dark and depressing years.

1959–61; 1976–80

Bill Veeck

Bill Veeck, a baseball visionary, was a man well ahead of his time in every facet of life. There was much more to this consummate baseball showman than midgets and fireworks. Throughout his lifetime Veeck fought hard for civil rights. He integrated the American League in 1947, and he marched alongside Dr. Martin Luther King Jr. in Selma, Alabama, during the tense days of the southern civil rights crusade.

Veeck was a champion of the common man who never took himself or the role he was destined to play in the national pastime very seriously. There was a sense of whimsy to the man that often obscured a deeper, reflective nature. He had a passion for baseball and all life had to offer. Bill Veeck was many things to many people—though it must also be said that his skills at promotion far outweighed his ability to deliver a winning ballclub to the South Side.

Bill Veeck soared the heights with his pennant-winning ballclub in 1959, only to see his methods repudiated in his second ownership by such embarrassing stunts as the 1979 Disco Demolition riot at Comiskey Park. Critics charged that Veeck was out of touch and a relic of a passing era.

He was a larger-than-life figure and a prodding voice against the status quo in baseball. Veeck recognized that free agency was just over the horizon, and he urged his fellow owners to head off the coming labor problems by instituting a salary structure patterned after the Hollywood studio system. He was ignored.

Bill Veeck followed in the baseball footsteps of his illustrious father, William Veeck Sr., a *Chicago American* sportswriter who authored his game stories and commentary under the nom de plume "Bill Bailey" in the first decade of the 20th century. Later, the elder Veeck was welcomed into Charles Comiskey's inner circle of Woodland Bards. As an executive with the Chicago Cubs in the 1930s, Veeck Sr. employed his son in the marketing and promotions department. The once and future king of baseball promotions showed his genius by coming up with the idea to plant vines on the outfield walls of Wrigley Field.

By the time Bill Veeck purchased controlling interest in the White Sox from Dorothy Comiskey in 1958, he was a seasoned campaigner and a national celebrity because of his well-publicized gimmicks and headline-grabbing stunts. As the embattled owner of the comical St. Louis Browns, Veeck sent a midget up to the plate.

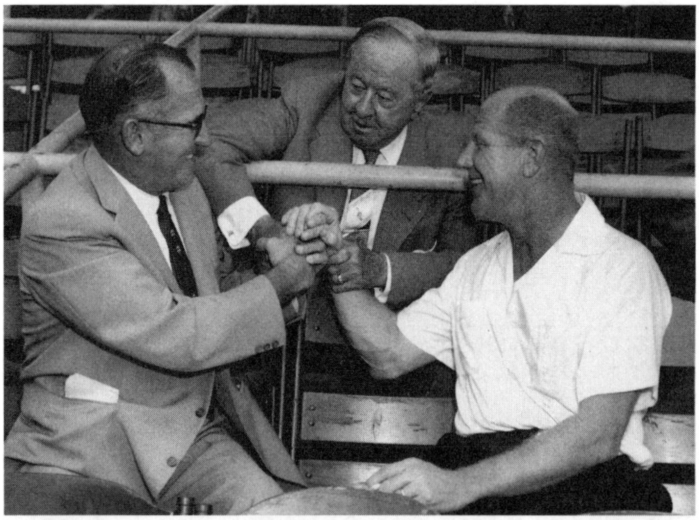

Top: Three Sox legends gather, circa 1959: Al Lopez; Clarence "Pants" Rowland, who managed the 1917 Sox; and Bill Veeck. Middle: Veeck hoists a stein with one of his favorite little people, Herve Villechaize. Bottom: Bill Veeck and Mayor Richard J. Daley inaugurate Opening Day of the second Veeck regime in 1976.

After he returned from military duty in the Pacific theater (minus his right leg), Veeck was rebuffed in his first attempt to purchase the White Sox from the Comiskey family. He purchased the Cleveland Indians in 1946 and with a few adjustments helped lead that team to a world championship in 1948. He divested his holdings two years later. He acquired the White Sox in 1959 after a protracted legal fight with Charley Comiskey, who failed to block the sale in probate court.

In recent years an interesting new theory has surfaced—whether it is rumor or fact cannot be fully ascertained—that Bill Veeck harbored a secret plan to acquire the White Sox and transfer the team to Los Angeles, in order to be the first to open up the lucrative Southern California market to the American League. Such a plan never took flight, of course. The unexpected 1959 pennant got in the way—and the institutional opposition among the fraternity of owners to his operational methods would have likely checkmated the scheme had he in fact tried to go through with it. There was a historic precedent for a West Coast move, of course. Los Angeles was high on his list of cities for relocating the St. Louis Browns to after the Boston Braves beat him to Milwaukee in 1953. The L.A. move did not materialize because the American League owners believed it would be too difficult to schedule games due to the vast distance teams would be required to travel by train in those years before transcontinental jet travel became de rigueur. Bitter and vindictive, Veeck finally sold the unwanted lame-duck Browns to Baltimore attorney Clarence Miles, but only after the league had voted him down twice. Still the question remains: what would have happened if the Sox had not won the pennant in 1959? Would he have written Chicago off as a one-team town and pushed the league moguls on the issue of franchise relocation? In 1960 the AL expanded into Los Angeles, and in June 1961—less than a year later—Veeck disposed of his ownership interests in the White Sox. Was that just a coincidence? Could be, but then again, who really knows?

Bill Veeck inherited a ballclub poised on the threshold of a pennant. Whether or not the Sox could have won the 1959 flag without Veeck is impossible to say. The main components of the team had already been put in place by Comiskey, Frank Lane, and John Rigney. But Veeck's showmanship went a long way toward building an esprit de corps on and off the field. The fans sensed a new attitude, and the players responded.

In the memorable summer of 1959, Veeck unveiled a dazzling array of promotions, including cow-milking contests, midget "Martians" descending on the Comiskey Park infield from a hovering helicopter, and any number of special giveaways. A year later Veeck threw baseball's old guard another curve by stitching the names of the players on the backs of their jerseys—another first for the grand old game. The "exploding" scoreboard, dubbed the Monster because of its whistles, sirens, bells, and rocketry accompanying each White Sox home run, was installed in center field prior to the 1960 season.

Unfortunately, the 1959 World Series loss convinced Veeck to make wholesale personnel changes for 1960 in a futile effort to win back-to-back pennants. Bill Veeck mortgaged the future by trading away the brightest young stars in the farm system—Norm Cash, John Romano, Earl Battey,

Don Mincher, and Johnny Callison. The fading veterans he received in return finished far off the pace in 1960 and 1961. By gutting the farm system, Veeck jeopardized the franchise for years to come.

A serious illness sidelined Veeck in the spring of 1961, and it kept him away from the team and a busy schedule of personal appearances while he recovered his health at the Mayo Clinic. "The doctors tell me that I'm likely to be out of action for six or seven months, and I know you can't run a ballclub in absentia," he said.

Veeck decided to put his 54 percent of the stock up for sale. He spurned an offer from Chicago attorney (and future mayoral candidate) Bernard Epton, who was acting in concert with Charley Comiskey, in order to sell his parcel of stock to Arthur Allyn Jr., son of his former business partner. The sale was finalized on June 10, 1961, at a price pegged at $3.25 million.

In his memoirs published a year later, Bill Veeck promised that he would be back someday to rescue a franchise down on its luck, and one that nobody particularly wanted. "And then Ole Will will come wandering along to laugh some more," he wrote.

The self-fulfilling prophecy came to pass on December 10, 1975, when the American League owners reluctantly signed off on his purchase of the White Sox from John Allyn, who had fended off a serious bid from a Seattle investment group in order to keep this dispirited and financially troubled team rooted in Chicago.

The league objected to Veeck's method of financing, and they gave him exactly seven days to raise $1.2 million of investment capital to solidify the purchase. Against impossible odds, Veeck scraped together the money and returned to the owners' table, where he was approved by a 10–2 vote.

Events on the playing field did not quite match up to the excitement of his first ownership or of the tense days leading up to the moment he received final league approval to buy the team. Veeck was hampered by free agency and not fully versed on the tax breaks available to him as an owner; as a result, the White Sox finished dead last in 1976 with a Triple A roster of players.

Unable to compete with the cash-rich teams like the Yankees for the services of expensive free agents, Veeck chose instead to "rent" Richie Zisk and Oscar Gamble for the 1977 season, and he was named UPI Executive of the Year after the rejuvenated ballclub finished a surprising third. The team set a new attendance record that year, and things appeared to be on an upswing. Hopes for long-term success were immediately shattered by the loss of Zisk and Gamble in 1978.

The White Sox never recovered their competitive advantage, and as the team sank lower in the standings, Veeck resorted to nightly giveaways, ethnic festivals, belly dancers, animal acts, breakfast matinees, treasure hunts, beer-case stacking contests, and on and on to lure fans to the park. Attendance declined after 1977, but the drop was not all that severe, given the quality of talent on the field. There were more subtle reasons for his desire to make a permanent break with the game.

Bill Veeck scolded the media for their biased and preferential coverage of the Cubs. He arrived at the weary conclusion that his ballclub would never receive an even break from the press in Chicago's volatile two-team market, and he commenced negotiations with oil magnate Marvin Davis to transfer the franchise to Denver before the 1981 season.

Davis expressed some initial interest but backed out of the deal, leaving Veeck to ponder his fate. Edward DeBartolo of Youngstown, Ohio, stepped forward with an offer to buy the White Sox, renovate Comiskey Park, and bolster the caliber of talent with an infusion of free agents. The league, however, took a dim view of DeBartolo's racetrack interests, his veiled threat to move the team to New Orleans, and the prospect of another absentee ownership. The owners twice voted down Veeck's proposed sale to DeBartolo before he threw in the towel on December 11, 1980. Despite resounding support for the sale coming from the White Sox board of directors, commissioner Bowie Kuhn refused to be swayed by their arguments.

Angry and showing visible signs of strain, Bill Veeck next turned to Jerry Reinsdorf and Eddie Einhorn, who were acceptable to Kuhn and the American League owners. On January 29, 1981, the sale of the White Sox for the sum of $19 million was finalized. Angered by some ill-chosen remarks made by Eddie Einhorn during the negotiations, Veeck turned his back on the new ownership and lived out the remainder of his days in silent protest over the directions the club was taking. Jerry Reinsdorf extended the olive branch of friendship and did everything he could to pay tribute to Veeck, but the maverick owner would have none of it, and that refusal was very tragic, because it exposed a rather petty side to the man that had never been apparent in his earlier dealings.

In his final years, Bill Veeck, sans shirt, was a familiar figure in the Wrigley Field bleachers where he sipped beer, swapped stories, and enjoyed the company of the fans. Bill Veeck survived a bout of cancer, the loss of a leg in combat, and a lifetime of pain and illness. That is why his passing on January 2, 1986, came as such a shock to his many admirers in the media who considered this old veteran indestructible. "He was the spirit of Chicago—a lot of gusto and verve and vigor, an emancipated man," commented Mayor Harold Washington.

1961–69

Arthur C. Allyn Jr.

Art Allyn, a rather bland and unassuming figure who wore black horn-rimmed glasses to complement a marine-style butch crew cut, had attended only two baseball games in his life before purchasing the White Sox from Bill Veeck on June 10, 1961. Collecting butterflies, conducting scientific research, and managing the LaSalle Street securities and investments firm he and his younger brother John had inherited from their father in 1960 were more to Art's liking than the rough-and-tumble world of baseball.

Art Allyn was a baseball novice, but he persevered with a farm system that had been stripped of its top-flight talent by Bill Veeck. Arthur was a stubborn man, and though baseball might not have been his cup of tea to begin with, he adamantly refused to sell his White Sox stock to Charley Comiskey or anyone else flashing a bankroll. Allyn realized he had four to six years of tax breaks to capitalize on, so he plunged into unfamiliar waters as a baseball mogul.

Allyn promoted Edwin Short, the former White Sox publicity director, to general manager. Short wheeled and dealed as he saw fit while Art tried to force himself upon the league power brokers. But he made few friends within the American League's inner circle during his eight years as Sox owner. He had a churlish, contrary nature, evidenced by his attempt to block the CBS television network from purchasing the New York Yankees in 1964. Leaving no doubt as to where he stood, the Sox owner blasted AL president Joe Cronin for not consulting with him first. "I know Joe Cronin is put out with me because I told him so," Allyn crackled. "He can get mad all he wants because I'm just a little madder."

On the plus side of the ledger, Arthur purchased the Sarasota Motor Hotel in 1962 in order to save his black players the indignity of locating separate lodging miles away from the spring-training compound. Allyn struck a blow for civil rights and sent a wake-up call to baseball—one they could no longer continue to ignore. He also bought a private jetliner for his team and opened a boys' camp in Wisconsin. Dwindling public interest closed the summer resort a decade later, and prohibitive costs grounded the jet in the mid-1960s.

Art Allyn was brimming with ideas, but unfortunately most of them never escaped the White Sox boardroom. For two years (1967–69) Art jousted with Mayor Richard J. Daley and the Chicago City Council over his proposal to build a privately financed stadium in the rail yards south of downtown Chicago. Allyn alienated the mayor by his stubborn refusal to commit the White Sox to Daley's plan for a multipurpose stadium housing the Sox, Cubs, Bears, and Blackhawks.

Mayor Richard J. Daley (right) usually attended every Sox opener. Here he meets and greets Art Allyn.

Allyn was an impatient man who quickly lost interest in his team once it became clear that Daley would never sign off on a White Sox–only facility. After the team fell out of contention in 1968 and the tax breaks dried up, Arthur turned over the management of the ballclub to his five vice presidents in order to research lucrative new markets for the Sox. Allyn scheduled a series of "home games" in Milwaukee's County Stadium in 1968 and 1969. His purpose, he explained, was to "help" Bud Selig and his Teams Inc. organization land a tenant for County Stadium.

The White Sox's situation became increasingly desperate in 1969. The ballclub lost $500,000, forcing Allyn into a corner. Secret negotiations to transfer the White Sox to Milwaukee were conducted through the summer months. Selig offered Arthur $13 million for the franchise, an offer that Allyn was prepared to accept when his brother John interceded at the 11th hour. The younger Allyn countered Selig's proposition with an offer to split off the Artnell Corporation (holding company of the White Sox), assume all outstanding debt, and take over the White Sox. The sale was finalized on September 24, 1969, leaving Bud Selig out in the cold in his bid for a baseball team.

Arthur took his money and retired to Sarasota, Florida, where he founded the Allyn Museum of Entomology, a scientific research facility housing his world-class collection of butterflies. He died on March 23, 1985, virtually forgotten by younger White Sox fans who often confused him with his kid brother John.

1969–75

John W. Allyn

John Allyn, a quiet, pipe-smoking sportsman, was better prepared to run the White Sox than his argumentative older brother. By the terms of the 1961 sale agreement with Bill Veeck, however, John was relegated to the role of minority investor. He devoted much of his time to managing the affairs of the family's brokerage firm, the Francis I. DuPont Corporation.

An ardent golfer, photography buff, and gun collector, Allyn remained deeply behind the scenes through the 1960s, though he was listed in the corporate masthead as a team vice president. His actual role in the sports world was limited to his involvement with the Chicago Mustangs of the United Soccer Association, who played their home games in Comiskey Park. The league collapsed after only two seasons.

The Allyn brothers were never very close to begin with. Sibling rivalries and differences in temperament and business outlook contributed to a permanent falling-out shortly after John convinced his brother to sell him the White Sox in September 1969.

Nevertheless, John Allyn is one of the unsung heroes of White Sox history, who saved the team from a certain demise in 1969—and again in 1975 when he fended off a syndicate of would-be buyers from Seattle in order to sell to Bill Veeck at a greatly reduced price.

John Allyn

Allyn looked to the future with confidence and was never dismayed by poor home attendance and record-setting losses during his first full year as owner in 1970. He hired a team of specialists to rebuild the farm system, improve the public image of the ballclub, and bring in a new group of players to replace fading and unproductive veterans.

Allyn did not mind spending money on the team because, unlike his brother Arthur, John loved the action and the competitive challenge of running a big-league ballclub. Outfitted in his custom-tailored White Sox uniform, the owner was often spotted wandering the field during spring training workouts and filming his players with a handheld home movie camera.

The rebuilding program was judged a success at the end of the 1972 season. Chuck Tanner, Roland Hemond, and Stu Holcomb molded a contending ballclub revolving around slugger Dick Allen. Unfortunately for John Allyn, his namesake Dick Allen, who was so instrumental to the stunning 1972 success, sold him out two years later by announcing his retirement.

Dick Allen left behind a void that was impossible to fill. Announcer Harry Caray's on-air harangues contributed to a morale problem, and another dose of losing baseball in 1975 returned the Sox to their familiar post-1968 losing patterns.

John Allyn traced the blame to Caray and fired him on October 1, 1975. The fans sided with Caray in this latest White Sox row, not comprehending the desperation of Allyn's situation. The beleaguered owner confronted the grim possibility of missing his final payroll of the season. If he had, every one of the players could have become an unrestricted free agent.

Arthur Allyn compounded the problem by introducing a lawsuit alleging that John had withheld certain monies due him from the original sale in 1969. John Allyn was besieged from all sides, but he gamely held on while Bill Veeck assembled his syndicate and raised the financing to purchase the struggling franchise. The league would have favored Charley Finley's plan to transfer the Sox to Seattle and move his Oakland A's to Chicago, but after Veeck satisfied the owners' demand for additional investor money, the sale was grudgingly approved on December 10, 1975.

Allyn remained a stockholder in the White Sox operation up until the moment of his death on April 29, 1979. "It was John Allyn's determination, really selflessness, that saved the White Sox for the city of Chicago," commented Bill Veeck.

1981–

Jerry Reinsdorf and Edward M. Einhorn

Jerry Reinsdorf's media portrayal as the influential anti-union hardliner who stood in the way of ending baseball's longest and most costly work stoppage in 1994–95 is at odds with the private persona of an owner who would prefer to quietly recede into the background and allow his players to reap the harvest of media publicity.

Unfortunately for Jerry Reinsdorf, he has never been able to shed his reputation as baseball's top power broker, and he finds the image personally troubling. "The only owner in baseball who has any power since I've been around is Bud Selig," Reinsdorf replies. "He's the only one who can call people on the phone and say, 'I've got to have your vote on this.' I can't do that. I'm on a lot of committees. I speak up if I can make a good argument. If I can convince people of the correctness of my position, I can get their vote. I don't consider that being powerful. I consider that being smart... maybe."

The *Sporting News* would disagree. It consistently ranks the Sox chairman among the 100 most powerful sports figures in the nation. "I've gone from fourth to eighth to 13th, but I won't be satisfied until I'm behind the guy who's 100th," Jerry adds.

Since coming into the league as a new owner on January 29, 1981, Reinsdorf has preached fiscal responsibility to his fellow owners. As a member of the prestigious Executive Council of Major League Baseball, Reinsdorf cautioned against awarding long-term multi-million-dollar contracts to average or below-average journeymen players. This is where the salary structure spiraled out of control, he argued. Sometimes they listened to him; most of the time they did not.

On the eve of the 1994 player's strike Reinsdorf told the Chicago media that up until the moment the players walked

Top: A modest office space reflects the low-key management style of Jerry Reinsdorf. Bottom left: Reinsdorf's dugout communications. Bottom right: Eddie Einhorn

out, he was counted among the baseball "doves," the small faction of owners who were willing to drop the salary cap and preserve the status quo in order to head off a strike. After the walkout Jerry became a self-described hawk. However: "I have no interest in being a leader in this industry because I don't want to do the work that's necessary to create a power base."

Born in Brooklyn and raised as a loyal Dodgers fan, Jerry Reinsdorf received his law degree from Northwestern University. In the late 1950s he struck up a friendship with his future business partner, Eddie Einhorn.

Jerry was part of a syndicate that tried to purchase the New York Mets in the mid-1970s, but when the deal collapsed, Reinsdorf kept his eyes open and waited for the right opportunity to break into baseball.

Jerry made his fortune in Chicago real estate as chairman of the board and chief executive officer of Balcor/American Express, Inc. With investments totaling $3.5 billion, Balcor, before its merger with American Express, ranked as one of the largest real estate investment firms in the United States. Reinsdorf, as the founder of Balcor, was a recognized expert on securities.

Einhorn, his imaginative partner, was the executive producer of the *CBS Sports Spectacular* in the 1970s. While completing his law studies at Northwestern, Eddie worked as a part-time hot dog vendor at Comiskey Park during the 1959 World Series. That was his only connection to the White Sox until Reinsdorf assembled his syndicate in 1980 to bid for the ballclub.

The Reinsdorf group waited patiently until the American League twice voted down Edward DeBartolo before receiving the nod from Bill Veeck. The ink on the sales agreement was still drying when Einhorn made some ill-chosen remarks about running a "class operation." Veeck was bitter to begin with, and he took it as a slap to his administration. Einhorn was looking to the future and had not intended to demean Bill Veeck in any way, but that is how it was taken.

Though they had gotten off on the wrong foot, Jerry and Eddie made instant amends to the fans by signing Carlton Fisk and Greg Luzinski to White Sox contracts. The relationship between the fans and new ownership soured by the mid-1980s. The perception that Jerry Reinsdorf and his Sox investors only cared about his corporate skybox holders was an emotional, angry reaction coming from the traditional blue-collar South Side fan base.

But in order for the Sox to compete in a volatile two-team market where the Cubs had enjoyed a competitive advantage for so many years, Sox marketing strategists decided that it was essential for the team's long-term survival to capture a larger share of the Chicago market by promoting the product as wholesome, family-oriented entertainment.

During the last years of the Veeck regime, Comiskey Park had acquired a sinister reputation as the "world's largest outdoor saloon" because of many incidences of drunken rowdyism, particularly on Friday nights. Sales of hard alcohol in the park were halted, and costumed mascots were hired to entertain the kiddies between innings.

Jerry Reinsdorf's problems deepened in 1986 when he convened a hasty press conference to announce his intention to build a new stadium in Chicago's western suburbs because old Comiskey Park was in such bad physical shape and could no longer produce the revenue to pay for its constant upkeep. The team floundered in the standings. The media, the fans, and the politicians mistrusted the motives of the two men they had tagged the Sunshine Boys. And as the months counted down, increasingly it began to appear that the White Sox were ticketed to St. Petersburg, Florida, unless the state of Illinois appropriated the necessary funds to finance the construction of the new Comiskey Park.

Jerry never intended to move the Sox out of Chicago unless he was left with no other alternative. Because certain White Sox marketing executives were tired of competing with the Cubs and actually hoped that the team would relocate to the Sun Belt, the media were left to ponder for themselves just what this ownership was *really* up to.

It took three years of nail-biting negotiation, broken promises, and political bickering before the Illinois General Assembly appropriated $137 million in state money to build a new Comiskey Park directly across the street from the old one. The stadium crisis, resolved satisfactorily on July 1, 1988, was another black eye for the ownership.

Jerry Reinsdorf's popularity sank to new lows. Public relations consultants advised Eddie Einhorn to assume a lower profile and to refrain from issuing statements likely to antagonize the fans. Not even the presence of Michael Jordan playing for Jerry Reinsdorf's other team, the Chicago Bulls, spared him the customary torrent of boos every time he was introduced or had to appear before the fans in a public setting.

The fans' misguided loyalty to the late Bill Veeck hurt the new ownership. Following Veeck was a tough challenge for anyone, let alone an introspective ex–New Yorker like Jerry Reinsdorf who had shrugged off much of the personal criticism in order to remain focused on building a winning, exciting ballclub for White Sox fans. Not all of Jerry Reinsdorf's decisions have worked out—firing Tony LaRussa was a mistake by Jerry's own admission.

Other decisions were laden with controversy and puzzling even to the sharpest observers. Larry Himes did a creditable job as general manager and laid the groundwork for the team's success in the 1990s by drafting star-quality players, but he was fired because he could not get along with Jerry or anyone else in the organization. Reinsdorf's pay-for-performance contract proposals alienated Jack McDowell and ultimately drove him out of the organization. Through Jack Gould, his senior vice president for baseball operations, Reinsdorf acquired a reputation as a tough, unbending negotiator during contract talks with players and agents.

Players' union boss Don Fehr and others have gone so far as to suggest that Jerry Reinsdorf is baseball's de facto commissioner, or at the very least a powerful behind-the-scenes operative who calls the shots through commissioner Bud Selig.

Whatever the final rendering may be about this enigmatic and controversial owner, Reinsdorf's top priority is for his White Sox to win. "I would rather win and break even than finish second and make $20 million," he has said. And he delivered. With six NBA championships and a World Series victory in his pocket, Reinsdorf is the most successful professional sports mogul in Chicago history, with the possible lone exception of the late George Halas. Even more importantly, he restored financial solvency to a ballclub that had operated far too long on a candy-store budget.

With the passing of George Steinbrenner in 2010, Jerry became the longest-tenured owner in Major League Baseball. In 2011 he will have equaled the Old Roman, Charles Comiskey, in the number of years of running the White Sox—31. Recalling the farcical prediction of the late sportswriter Bill Gleason that Reinsdorf would keep the Sox just long enough to receive his tax breaks then quickly cash out, Jerry soldiers on—outlasting his two harshest media critics. Gleason, a South Sider and self-professed Sox fan, took many cheap shots at Jerry in the 1980s as he tried to torpedo plans to build the new ballpark through a series of hostile and uninformed opinions expressed in his weekly column. A decade later the editorial vitriol of that other *Sun-Times* man, Jay Mariotti, breached journalistic objectivity and proper business ethics until, to the enormous relief of just about every sports fan in Chicago, he finally moved on, taking his poison pen with him out to Los Angeles to torment other figures in the sports world.

Reinsdorf showed dignity and class by not publicly responding to the scatter-shot attacks of either writer, focusing instead on improving his two teams and working for the public good. These days he devotes much of his energy and resources to building up Chicago White Sox Charities and his pro basketball foundation, CharitaBulls. His legacy is profound, not only on the White Sox franchise, which boasts the fourth-best won-lost record in baseball since his first year of ownership in 1981, but also in civic matters. In building the new United Center for his Bulls, Reinsdorf's efforts helped redevelop and reenergize the blighted West Side community adjacent to the Madison Street arena.

In 2009 Jerry the builder was largely responsible for the opening of the new Camelback Ranch in Glendale, Arizona, where the White Sox and Dodgers share spring training headquarters. In 2008, in recognition of his many long years of service to Major League Baseball, Reinsdorf was asked to serve on the board of the Baseball Hall of Fame. It is not beyond the realm of possibility that the Sox chairman will one day join Charles Comiskey in the founders and builders wing of the Hall.

The General Managers

1915–45

Harry M. Grabiner

It must have come as a bitter, bitter, disappointment for Harry Mitchell Grabiner to depart the White Sox after nearly 40 years of loyal and faithful service to the Comiskey family and the Chicago White Sox organization. In 1945, after Grace Comiskey had made it all but impossible for him to continue his duties with the ballclub, Harry went to work for Bill Veeck, the youthful owner of the Cleveland Indians who understood that loyalty was a two-way street. If Mrs. Comiskey mistrusted Grabiner's motives after four decades, young Veeck shrewdly recognized that Harry was an executive of exceptional ability and an asset to any baseball organization.

Grabiner climbed the ladder of baseball from the ground up. The year was 1905. Fourteen-year-old Harry Grabiner and his brother Joe lingered outside the portals of the old 39th Street Grounds after every game, until Comiskey finally relented and gave them both a job sweeping out the grandstand and selling scorecards. Harry sold tickets and peanuts and assisted the customers to their seats. There was no task beneath his dignity or beyond his capabilities. He was baseball's Horatio Alger in the flesh.

The Old Roman rewarded Grabiner's hard work and cheerful disposition with a promotion to the front office as a clerical assistant. The unexpected death in 1915 of Charles Fredericks, a nephew of Comiskey who had presided as traveling secretary and keeper of the records for more than a decade, provided an opportunity for Harry. Comiskey elevated Grabiner to team secretary and vice president—a position analogous to that of the modern general manager.

Harry supervised the team's financial affairs. He negotiated salary contracts with the players. He acted as team spokesman, organized the yearly spring training junket, screened the callers, maintained the Old Roman's busy schedule, and shielded Comiskey from the prying eyes of the press. He was the perfect assistant in a bygone era when the owners maintained a staff of less than a half dozen front-office employees. In the years of Comiskey's Wisconsin "exile" following the heartbreak of the Black Sox scandal, Harry virtually ran the ballclub.

Grabiner was more than just a good business manager. He was also a genuine fan, and he refused to give in to negativity. When asked by the writers on Opening Day what the fans of Chicago could reasonably expect from the White Sox, Harry would flash a big grin and reply: "Boys, this is the year we'll win the pennant!" He never gave up, and he dreamed of the day when his White Sox could be counted among the American League elite. That day never came, of course, but he took his raps without complaint. Harry was always careful to shield Mrs. Comiskey from direct criticism, even though her penny-pinching policies never allowed him to fulfill the Old Roman's legacy by bringing the World Series back to the South Side.

Harry Grabiner and John Louis Comiskey at the back of a Pullman car in December 1927.

Harry Grabiner liked to play the ponies, and he dabbled in the stock market. He was a human computer whose remarkable command of numbers undoubtedly helped keep the franchise solvent through the lean Depression years. Though introverted by nature, he enjoyed the company of Hollywood celebrities and was well-known in 1940s cafe society through his only daughter, June Travis, who starred in a number of low-grade Warner Brothers motion pictures during that period.

After Lou Comiskey died in 1939, Harry's precise role with the Sox was less certain. By the terms of Lou's will, Harry was guaranteed 10 more years of employment with the White Sox—if he chose to remain in the organization. In an ideal world this would have been a happy ending to the story. But Harry was an outsider by birth, and Mrs. Comiskey did not share her husband's faith in Grabiner's methods. Nor did she appreciate Harry's connivance with Bill Veeck when Veeck returned from combat duty in the South Pacific and tried to buy the White Sox.

With five years left to go on his "guaranteed" contract, Grabiner retired on December 15, 1945, after releasing pitcher Lee "Buck" Ross—his last official act after four decades as a White Sox executive. Harry never demanded recompense from Mrs. Comiskey for the five years remaining on his contract. He was entitled to the money, but he bore no malice toward his employer and only desired to make a clean break. A few months later he joined Veeck in Cleveland, where he would live just long enough to experience the glory of another pennant-winning ballclub.

Ravaged by brain cancer, Harry died in Chicago on October 24, 1948. Only the venerable Connie Mack and Clark Griffith had logged more years in the American League than Harry Grabiner at the time of his death. His legion of friends and admirers in the baseball world mourned the passing of one of the great gentlemen of the game.

1946–48

Leslie M. O'Connor

For 24 years, Leslie O'Connor toiled in the shadow of commissioner Kenesaw Mountain Landis as his trusted secretary and treasurer. A graduate of Chicago's Kent College of Law, O'Connor impressed Landis while trying a case in his federal courtroom. He recognized in O'Connor the same sterling qualities that Comiskey valued most in Harry Grabiner: unquestioned loyalty, a willingness to subordinate his personal life to his career, and a strong Puritan work ethic.

The boyish-looking Chicago attorney beat out 22 other applicants for the job, and he would remain at Landis's side until his death in 1944. O'Connor agreed to serve as interim commissioner, but was bypassed for promotion in April 1945 by an owner's faction led by Lee MacPhail. Kentucky Senator A.B. "Happy" Chandler was named commissioner, and for the first time in a quarter century, O'Connor was out of work.

Les O'Connor replaced Harry Grabiner as vice president and general manager because Mrs. Comiskey preferred to surround herself with men rich in baseball experience. There is little doubt that O'Connor understood administration, but his skill in player procurement was an entirely different matter.

During his brief tenure as Sox GM, O'Connor attempted to rejuvenate the farm system and bring into the organization big-name (but over-the-hill) players like Rudy York and Red Ruffing to spur fan interest. But York and Ruffing were not the answer, and O'Connor's efforts were thwarted by Grace Comiskey's belt-tightening policies. Building a winner required an expenditure of cash, and though the Sox made money in the postwar boom period (1946–47), Grace was unwilling to part with these added revenues.

O'Connor crossed swords with commissioner Chandler in October 1947 after the Sox GM defied a major league edict by signing a prep pitcher whose team belonged to the National Federation of State Athletic Associations (NFSAA). O'Connor paid pitching sensation George Zoeterman a $2,000 signing bonus and dared Chandler to act in an arbitrary manner. Believing he had the law on his side, O'Connor stood his ground and refused to withdraw the original contract offer. The Comiskeys were caught in an embarrassing faux pas when Chandler suspended the White Sox from the league on October 28. O'Connor counted on Grace Comiskey's support, but he was let down with a dull sickening thud. Charley Comiskey quietly paid the fine.

Fed up with the direction the franchise seemed to be taking and undermined by his employers, Les O'Connor submitted his resignation in writing on October 8, 1948.

1948–55

Frank C. Lane

For seven emotional seasons, "Frantic" Frank Lane was the White Sox' man in motion. He was a bundle of raw energy—outspoken, controversial, and brimming with ideas. In large measure, the success the White Sox enjoyed in the early 1950s was a reflection of his strategies as general manager.

Born and raised in Cincinnati, Lane went to work for Larry MacPhail, the brilliant tactician who was in charge of the hometown Reds. MacPhail hired Lane as the team's traveling

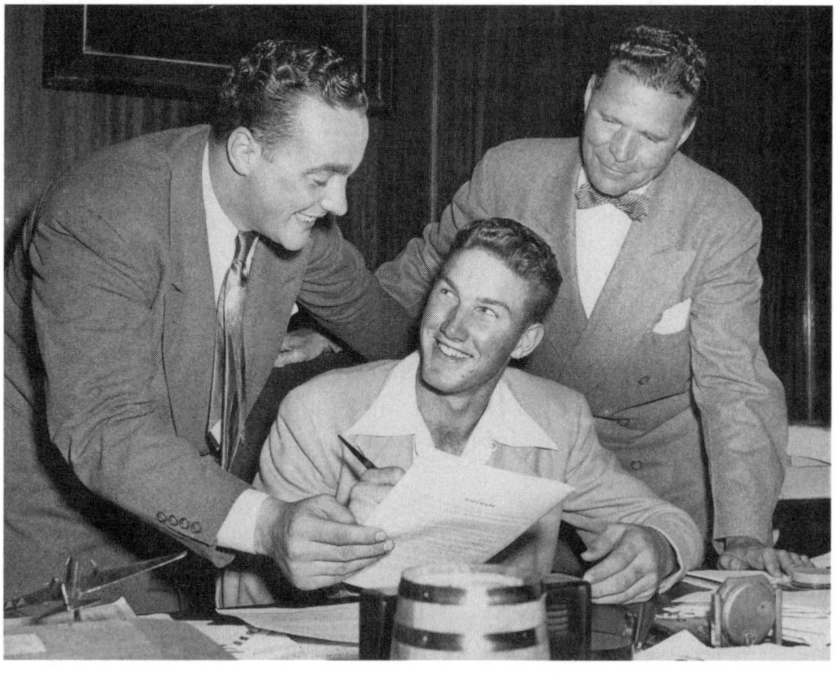

Shortshop Jim Baumer, the pride of Broken Arrow, Oklahoma, is all smiles after accepting a $50,000 signing bonus from Charley Comiskey (left) and Frank Lane (right) on June 3, 1949. In his first game at Yankee Stadium later that year, he allegedly fainted from excitement or shock after glimpsing the House that Ruth Built.

Top left: Frank Lane (in the bowtie) with pitcher Saul Rogovin. Bottom left: Frank Lane's trades give the Sox new life in 1951. (Courtesy of the *Chicago American*)

secretary, then advanced him to general manager of the Reds' Durham, North Carolina, affiliate. Lane eventually took over the Reds' farm system.

After serving a hitch in the navy during World War II, Lane moved on to New York, where he was reunited with MacPhail. After serving as general manager of the Yankees' affiliate in Kansas City, Lane was appointed president of the American Association in 1946.

Frank Lane's firsthand knowledge of the young players passing through the league served him well when he set out to rebuild the White Sox from the ground up.

Ironically, it was Les O'Connor, the outgoing general manager, who introduced Charley Comiskey to Lane at the 1948 All-Star Game in St. Louis. A year later Lane replaced O'Connor as the Sox GM after Comiskey convinced his mother that Frank was the right guy to turn things around.

A bear for physical fitness who completed a daily regimen of 50 to 75 push-ups, Lane jumped into his new job with the same gusto that guided him in every other baseball assignment he had held, going back 25 years. Lane asked for waivers on the entire 1949 team. Finding no takers, he turned over the roster in entire lots.

Between October 1948, when he joined the White Sox, and February 1953, Lane completed 155 player transactions involving 220 players. During the seven years he was involved with the ballclub, 353 players packaged in 241 separate trades were shuttled in and out of Chicago.

Many of these trades were inconsequential. One of them even bordered on the ridiculous. Utility infielder Willie Miranda was dealt to Bill Veeck's St. Louis Browns on June 15, 1952, in a four-player trade. Thirteen days later Miranda returned to the White Sox for the waiver price. Then on October 16, Miranda was traded *back* to St. Louis for Tommy Byrne. At this point Veeck suggested to Lane that they should pool their resources and open a farm team in Mattoon, Illinois—halfway between Chicago and St. Louis—so Miranda would have somewhere to spend the night between his bus trips.

Nevertheless, if it were not for Frank Lane, who also traded for Billy Pierce, Nellie Fox, Minnie Minoso, and Chico Carrasquel, the White Sox would never have enjoyed the levels of success they enjoyed in the 1950s.

Paul Richards, who was hired by Lane after the 1950 season, simply called his high-strung boss Frantic. Richards and Lane were opposite in temperament, and many times petty clubhouse disagreements boiled over into angry shouting matches between these two strong-willed men. Paul Richards' decision to abandon the White Sox in September 1954 was partly a reflection of this bickering state of affairs.

Frank Lane followed Richards out the door a year later after Charley Comiskey scolded him for comments unbecoming to umpire Larry Napp. The Lane-Comiskey imbroglio flared up on August 30, 1955, after Sherm Lollar was kicked out of the game for bench-jockeying Napp. When Lollar got the thumb, Lane rushed into the private box occupied by American League president Will Harridge and supervisor of umpires Cal Hubbard. "What the f— kind of umpiring is that?" Lane screamed.

Commissioner Ford Frick assessed Lane a $500 fine and ordered him to issue a public apology to Harridge. Comiskey threw salt into the wound by agreeing with Harridge that Lane was way out of line in this instance. "I wish it were possible for me to spend the rest of my life in Chicago, but there's no chance of that now," Lane told reporters as the rumors of his resignation began to fly. "Chuck, either by design or accident, has made it impossible for me to continue. His act of belittling me was the last straw."

Frank Lane resigned on September 21, 1955. Thereafter he became a baseball nomad, unable to replicate his early and impressive White Sox success with a succession of teams, including the Cardinals, Indians, Athletics, and Brewers. He will forever be remembered as the man who singlehandedly destroyed the Cleveland Indians by trading away Rocky Colavito and Roger Maris.

1956–58

Charles Comiskey II and John D. Rigney

Elevated to a dual vice presidency on November 16, 1955, Charley Comiskey and John Rigney collaborated on all player trades and personnel moves within the organization until majority control of the ballclub passed into the hands of Bill Veeck early in 1959. By all accounts the Rigney-Comiskey alliance, though tinged with a hint of uneasiness, was a successful one. Their decision to trade Chico Carrasquel and Jim Busby to Cleveland for Larry Doby undoubtedly clinched third place for the Sox in 1956.

Their faith in Louie Aparicio's ability to replace Carrasquel at shortstop was justified by Rookie of the Year honors. The acquisition of Early Wynn prior to the 1958 season all but sewed up the 1959 flag—but to the victors go the spoils. Bill Veeck, coming into the organization with the fanfare of a 100-piece brass band, received much of the credit for what Comiskey and Rigney laid in place during their regime.

1959–61

Henry B. Greenberg

Shortly after Hank Greenberg was released by the Pittsburgh Pirates at the end of the 1947 season, Bill Veeck hired the former Tigers slugger to serve as general manager of the Cleveland Indians. In the early 1950s Greenberg earned a reputation as an astute judge of playing talent. While Frank Lane was performing a few miracles of his own in Chicago, Greenberg was molding the Indians into a champion.

There exists an interesting parallel between the two men. Greenberg was successful in Cleveland, but earned only mixed reviews in Chicago. Cleveland fans are quick to blame Frank Lane for their 36-year litany of failure, while Sox fans have only warm memories of his years on the South Side.

Hank Greenberg breezed into town with Bill Veeck in 1959, after selling his stock in the Indians for $400 a share. He was named vice president and worked in concert with Veeck on all personnel moves made during the two and a half years they operated the ballclub.

To assuage the bruised ego of Charley Comiskey, Bill Veeck promised Charley that he would have equal say when it came time to make a roster move. This was not the case. Greenberg undercut young Comiskey's authority and froze him out at the bargaining table. Charley was coming back from Puerto Rico when he learned that Greenberg had just traded away catcher Earl Battey, who was destined for stardom with the Minnesota Twins.

Comiskey would never have sanctioned this trade. When Battey was signed to a White Sox contract in the early 1950s, Comiskey provided assurances to the young man's mother that he would remain in the organization through his career. Earl was in tears when he heard the news. There was little Comiskey could say except to wish him well and send him on his way. "The organization has changed," he told Battey.

Hank Greenberg's trades devastated the farm system for years to come. Then, after Bill Veeck signaled his intention to dispose of his White Sox stock because of poor health and other considerations, Greenberg personally blocked a proposed sale to a syndicate headed by Chicago attorney Bernard Epton and entertainer Danny Thomas. He correctly sensed that Charley Comiskey was Epton's silent partner. Greenberg's personal animosity toward the Old Roman's grandson was the main reason why he "queered" the deal.

Greenberg stayed on in the organization after Arthur Allyn Jr. assumed control on June 10, 1961. He reluctantly agreed to Allyn's request that he take over the duties of general manager until a younger man could be hired on a more permanent basis. "I never wanted to be the big boss or the man who had to make the abrupt decisions as Veeck did," Greenberg explained. "But I will fill the job until I can find someone else who can do it."

Unable to find such a man outside the organization and anxious to pursue some business opportunities in New York, Greenberg submitted his resignation on August 26, 1961. In a move that caught many fans off guard, Art Allyn replaced Greenberg with Ed Short, the longtime White Sox publicity director and traveling secretary.

Hank Greenberg

1961–70

Edwin G. Short

Among the bewildering changes that overtook the White Sox organization in the late 1950s and on into the "New Frontier" of the early '60s was the appointment of Ed Short, a roly-poly promotions man and radio executive, to vice president and general manager. Art Allyn bypassed Frank Lane and other rumored candidates after Short voiced an interest in the vacated position.

Ed Short was a died-in-the-wool Chicagoan who grew up in the same Northwest Side neighborhood as comedian George Gobel. He joined a Chicago advertising agency after World War II, then moved over to WJJD radio as a sports director and part-time assistant to White Sox play-by-play announcer Bob Elson. Short was hired as a public relations director by Frank Lane and Charley Comiskey in November 1950.

He quickly settled into a comfortable job charting White Sox statistics, providing the media with up-to-the-minute information, and coordinating promotional campaigns which had been virtually nonexistent prior to the advent of the Go-Go era. He was one of the best in the business, working side-by-side all those years with Don Unferth. During spring training sessions he was the man in charge—without question, the hardest worker in the organization.

Short was a self-made man with a strong work ethic and a biting sense of humor that was not always readily apparent to the members of the fourth estate, who found him churlish and uncommunicative, particularly in the last few years when the team dropped into the second division.

His promotion to general manager was more than a dream come true. It was *his life.* "I have Mr. Allyn's word that the job is mine and that's good enough for me," he said. "I think I can do the job. If I can't, then I'll step out of the picture."

With the help of farm director Glen C. Miller and his assistant C.V. Davis, who provided him with a crash course on the status of the White Sox minor league system, Short embarked on a rebuilding program aimed at purging the aging veterans from the big-league roster in favor of younger players.

Short bit the bullet and traded away Nellie Fox, Billy Pierce, Jim Landis, and Minnie Minoso, knowing that he would take his knocks from the fans for doing so. Maybe it was a cold-blooded thing to do to these players in the twilight of their careers, but Short honestly believed that he had to churn the organization top to bottom if the Sox were to maintain their grip on the first division. His strategies were validated, as the historical record shows.

Tommy John, Pete Ward, Hoyt Wilhelm, Smoky Burgess, and Tommie Agee were key Ed Short acquisitions who kept the Sox in the thick of the AL race through the hectic 1967 season. His best move by far was the purchase of left-hander Wilbur Wood on October 12, 1966, for $25,000 and an unhappy Juan Pizarro.

Then things began to slip away. Short's skills at the bargaining table seemed to abandon him after the Sox dropped to eighth place in 1968. He traded away Gary Peters, Bob Locker, Don Buford, and other players critical to the Sox' success in the mid-1960s, but did not receive commensurate value in return. Panic moves turned into desperation, as Short was powerless to stem the tide. His job was in peril for much of the 1970 season after John Allyn replaced his brother as owner and took a long look at the situation. Short never enjoyed the same confidence levels with John Allyn, and he was unceremoniously fired by the new regime on September 1.

It was a bitter, shocking blow, and he took it personally. The White Sox were Eddie's whole world, and he never completely recovered from the humiliation and disappointment. He lived out the remainder of his days in his north suburban home and was rarely seen by his former White Sox colleagues. Ed Short passed away on July 16, 1984.

And he cuts hair, too! Ed Short receives a trim from Chuck Gorney. A rookie prospect out of East Chicago, Indiana, Gorney had just signed to a minor league contract in December 1961. The young man decided he wanted to become a barber/stylist just in case things didn't work out in baseball, which they didn't.

1970–85

Roland O. Hemond

With one foot in Milwaukee and the other in the grave, the Chicago White Sox franchise desperately needed new direction if it was to survive past 1969. Matters only got worse in 1970 when John Allyn's embattled ballclub lost a record 106 games and home attendance fell below 500,000. During the tedious summer months of that long and difficult year, the name most frequently mentioned to replace Ed Short was Gordon Maltzberger, a war-era pitcher who managed the White Sox' Tucson affiliate of the Pacific Coast League in the late 1960s.

Instead, John Allyn and executive vice president Stuart K. Holcomb looked outside the system to Roland Hemond, who developed such players as Clyde Wright and Jim Spencer while serving as farm director of the California Angels.

Roland Hemond launched his administrative career with the Boston Braves in 1952 before following the team to Milwaukee a year later. He joined the expansion Los Angeles Angels in December 1960, serving as farm director under his former boss in Milwaukee, Fred Haney.

Hemond, named by the White Sox to the newly created position of director of player personnel, moved 16 players in less than 18 hours at the 1970 winter meetings in Los Angeles. His whirlwind activity brought Mike Andrews, Pat Kelly, Tom Egan, Jay Johnstone, Vincente Romo, Tom Bradley, and Steve Kealey to Chicago, but that was just a tune-up. Then, after a couple of months had passed, Hemond sent pitcher Jerry Janeski to Washington for slugger Rick Reichardt—one of the great unsung trades in White Sox history.

These moves restored the White Sox to respectability in 1971 as the team posted a remarkable 23-game improvement over the 1970 results. "We didn't have a five-year plan like a lot of other clubs have when new people take over," he recalled. "We just said we'd give it our best every day, 24 hours a day. We decided to trade value just to change things around. After you lose 106 ballgames, you need new personnel—you need new faces."

He was gifted with the Midas touch those first few years in Chicago, or seemed to be. Roland was named the 1972 UPI Executive of the Year, largely because of the contributions of one Richard Anthony Allen, who came to Chicago in exchange for Tommy John. It was Roland's most controversial trade. Dick Allen provided short-term salvation. "He was the savior of our franchise," Hemond liked to say—an exaggeration to be sure, because the White Sox were on the upswing *before* Allen's arrival.

A front-office power struggle pitting Chuck Tanner and Roland Hemond against 60-year-old Stu Holcomb, who had coached Purdue football for nine years before joining the Sox, was resolved in favor of Hemond on July 27, 1973, when John Allyn promoted him to vice president and general manager. Holcomb had been listed in the directory as GM, but it was really Hemond who had been performing these duties without benefit of the title.

Wilbur Wood (left) and Roland Hemond (center) welcome Chuck Tanner as the new Sox manager, September 1970.

Roland was a baseball survivor who hung on to his job through three White Sox ownerships—John Allyn, Bill Veeck, and Jerry Reinsdorf. He worked quietly but with great effectiveness, and his lengthy tenure in the organization is a reflection of his skills. Hemond was the principal architect of the 1977 Hitless Wonder team and the 1983 Winning Ugly division champs. In recognition of his '83 accomplishments, Roland was awarded his second Major League Executive of the Year award by United Press International.

The night the White Sox clinched the 1983 Western Division crown, Roland was saturated with champagne in the wild clubhouse celebration that accompanied the final out. The rumpled gray suit he was wearing that evening was retrieved for posterity, placed in a glass display case, and put on permanent display outside the media dining room in old Comiskey Park.

Roland Hemond added a new wrinkle to Leo Durocher's old adage about nice guys finishing last. He is one of the true gentlemen of the game, well liked and respected by his peers. But in the volatile world of front-office politics where success is measured on a year-to-year basis, Roland Hemond was cast into baseball limbo after the Sox finished the 1985 season in third place. During the year Roland absorbed a lot of criticism from announcers Ken Harrelson and Don Drysdale after failing to come up with a suitable replacement for pitcher Richard Dotson, who went down with a season-ending injury. Commented Harrelson: "Dotson goes down. Goddamn, you gotta do something." Maybe so, but Roland did not deserve the shot.

Jerry Reinsdorf named Harrelson general manager on October 2 after bumping Hemond into a meaningless front-office assignment that was tantamount to being fired. Roland lingered in the organization until the following May when he joined the commissioner's office. He replaced Hank Peters as the general manager of the Baltimore Orioles on November 10, 1987. Two years later he captured his third Executive of the Year award after masterminding the O's remarkable 32-game turnaround in 1989.

1985–86

Ken "the Hawk" Harrelson

For sheer style and personal charisma, Ken Harrelson has few peers. The colorful antiestablishment slugger, who had helped make the Red Sox' 1967 "Impossible Dream" come true, teamed up with Don Drysdale in 1982 to provide lively, incisive commentary in the White Sox television broadcast booth for the next four seasons.

Though less critical in their judgments than Harry Caray and Jimmy Piersall had been during their South Side heyday, the Hawk's well-timed criticisms against Roland Hemond in the 1985 season carried weight with the White Sox front office. The Reinsdorf ownership registered growing alarm over declining attendance, the improved marketing posture of the crosstown Cubs, and a feeling of complacency that seemed to permeate the whole organization.

Ken Harrelson submitted a blueprint for success, calling for a revamping of the entire farm system, the recruitment of "specialists" to instruct the players in all phases of the game, and two pitching coaches on the major league level, one for the starters and one for the relievers.

Harrelson did not actively campaign for Roland Hemond's job. It was offered to him on October 2, 1985, because he was a high-profile guy with the courage of his convictions. Meanwhile, the marketing department cooked up a slick promotional package for 1986 revolving solely around Harrelson. The preseason advertisements urged the season-ticket holders to reup because "The Hawk Wants You!"

Ken "the Hawk" Harrelson: cowboy hats and sunglasses

Harrelson's sincere desire to do a competent job was at odds with his down-home image as a wisecracking ex-jock in a cowboy hat, blue jeans, and shades. Countering this image became a problem.

The indelicate firing of Tony LaRussa midway through the season was damaging to Ken's credibility. There was strong opposition within the White Sox organization to Alvin Dark, a lifelong friend of Harrelson's who was brought in to replace the popular and respected Dave Dombrowski as the director of the minor leagues.

As the season wore down and the losses mounted, Harrelson withdrew from the limelight. His blueprint for success was ridiculed and deemed a failure, and the press sparred with him over technicalities. The shoe finally dropped on September 25, when the Hawk submitted his resignation. Job pressure had taken a physical and emotional toll on the ex-announcer, who returned to his true calling and accepted the New York Yankees play-by-play job on Sports Channel. Harrelson covered the Yanks for two seasons before returning to the White Sox airwaves in 1990 after reconciling with Reinsdorf.

1986–90

Larry Himes

After 14 years in the California Angels system as a scout and director of player development, 46-year-old Larry Himes joined the White Sox on October 29, 1986, as vice president and general manager. The public image of the ballclub had taken a real beating in the press for the LaRussa firing and the failed Harrelson experiment. Jerry Reinsdorf's intention was to restore normality and stability to the organization with a new baseball chief who had earned high marks for drafting Wally Joyner, Kirk McCaskill, Chuck Finley, and other youthful stars processed through the Angels farm system. Using the Angels' mold, Himes outlined an ambitious plan to rebuild the club through minor league development and judicious trades. "I don't plan on doing it overnight," he said. "I'll go very slowly, trying to put together something for a long time."

Larry Himes hired Al Goldis, his longtime associate in the Angels system, to oversee minor league development for the Sox. Through their efforts, the White Sox struck pay dirt by drafting Jack McDowell, Robin Ventura, Frank Thomas, and Alex Fernandez in consecutive years. The results speak for themselves.

Never before had the White Sox tapped into the major league draft with such stunning success. Perhaps it will never happen again. Himes completely reorganized the club's player development and scouting departments, moving these two operations to the White Sox's spring training

Billy Pierce (left) and Larry Himes

home base in Sarasota, Florida, where work could continue throughout the year. Larry's innovative work earned him a promotion to senior vice president in December 1987.

In other areas of the organization, however, Himes stirred controversy. The Sox GM banned liquor consumption in the clubhouse and on the team plane—a move that caught the players by surprise.

Himes took heat for trading Harold Baines to the Texas Rangers for Scott Fletcher, Sammy Sosa, and Wilson Alvarez. Manager Jeff Torborg, who replaced the ousted Jim Fregosi, was not informed of the trade beforehand. The Baines trade turned out to be an outstanding one—for the future.

The rap against Himes—and the main reason he was fired on September 15, 1990—was his difficulty getting along with White Sox officials and league executives, according to Jerry Reinsdorf's public statements: "There are an awful lot of general managers who wouldn't talk to Larry Himes because they didn't like him and didn't like his style. This is a man with a severe personality problem." Reinsdorf's brutally frank comments to Chicago sports commentator Chet Coppock do not accurately reflect Himes' contributions in his four-year tenure as general manager. He laid the foundation of the 1993 division title and the string of winning seasons the ballclub enjoyed in the coming decade.

Larry's career took some abrupt U-turns after he left the White Sox. He accused Reinsdorf of blackballing him when employment offers from other major league teams failed to materialize. Himes spent a year scouting for three American League teams before accepting an offer from Chicago Cubs chairman Stanton Cook to replace Jim Frey as general manager of the ballclub.

Larry Himes never duplicated his early White Sox success and was roundly criticized by legions of Cubs fans after the National League ballclub crashed into the cellar in 1994. He was reassigned to Mesa, Arizona, to oversee construction of the Cubs' spring training facility, while the new general manager, Andy MacPhail, tried to figure out just what had gone wrong.

1990–2000

Ron Schueler

Ron Schueler concluded an undistinguished eight-year, injury-plagued pitching career with the White Sox in 1979. The burly right-hander—one of Bill Veeck's original "bargain-basement" free agent finds—was signed to his first White Sox contract on November 17, 1977. He remained in the organization as a pitching coach, serving under Don Kessinger and Tony LaRussa before moving on to Oakland in 1982.

Schueler was eager to escape field duty and launch a front-office career. He was eventually named special assistant to Sandy Alderson, the vice president of baseball operations for the Oakland A's. In the mid-1980s, Schueler intensified their scouting efforts, which resulted in the acquisition of All-Stars Jose Canseco, Mark McGwire, and Walt Weiss.

Mindful of Ron Schueler's growing status in the American League, Jerry Reinsdorf initiated preliminary discussions with Schueler during a scouting trip to Chicago in the

Ron Schueler, a Sox pitcher in 1979 (left) and general manager in 1993 (right)

closing weeks of the 1990 season. After the Oakland A's clinched the pennant, Reinsdorf contacted Schueler about the possibility of coming to Chicago as Larry Himes' replacement. Ron wasn't sure whether he wanted to leave Oakland after hearing the sad news that his wife was suffering from leukemia. But Maureen Schueler convinced him to accept the offer and move ahead.

Schueler was hired in November 1990 and handed a stiff mandate from Reinsdorf: deliver the White Sox from "Point B" (contention) to the elusive "Point C" (title). In other words, the Sox chairman expected something more than a second- or third-place finish for his money. In return came Reinsdorf's promise of lifetime employment for Schueler.

The new Sox GM traveled a cautious path by sidestepping expensive free agents demanding long-term contracts. He preferred to build from within and trade prudently. However, the acquisition of infielder Steve Sax from the Yankees on January 10, 1992, for Melido Perez and a pair of promising youngsters—Bob Wickman and Domingo Jean—was probably the worst White Sox trade in a decade. Schueler countered media criticism by pointing to the depth in the farm system—the fruit of Larry Himes' labors.

Schueler balanced the ledger by picking up veteran Tim Raines from the Montreal Expos for Ivan Calderon and Barry Jones. After a slow start, Raines blended nicely into the offense as the leadoff man.

As the Sox inched ever closer to championship caliber, Schu decided to test the free agent market and sign Ellis Burks, Julio Franco, and Darrin Jackson to contracts—only to lose them after only one season. However, Burks was a catalyst for the 1993 title run, and Franco and Jackson were valuable contributors in the strike-shortened 1994 campaign.

Schueler's toughest challenge—one that undoubtedly tugged at his conscience and left him open for further attack from members of the media who recalled his days as the White Sox union representative—was to assemble a team of replacement players to open the 1995 season. "In 1976 we were fighting for a pension, for medical benefits," Schueler patiently explained. "We were fighting for the future of the game, but for ourselves, too. Today, it is an entirely different world."

2000–

Kenny Williams

Claimed by the White Sox out of high school in the June 1982 free agent draft, Kenny Williams was a second-team wide receiver for Stanford University (and a teammate of John Elway's), unsure of whether or not he wanted to play baseball or football—or both—until Jerry Reinsdorf personally visited the young man at his home in San Jose to effect a compromise plan allowing him to pursue both options. Williams chose wisely and abandoned football after his freshman year to devote full energy to a baseball career. A September 1986 call-up,

Kenny Williams as a young, up-and-coming player

the young man failed to distinguish himself in the crowded White Sox outfield and was moved to third base—then back to center field in 1987—his best all-around season. A career highlight came on June 9 of that year, when he collected the only hit off of Oakland's Curt Young, ruining a no-hitter in the making with an eighth-inning homer. Following a disappointing 1988 campaign, Williams was traded to Detroit for Eric King—some much-needed pitching help—on March 23, 1989. At the time, Kenny had struck up a close friendship with Ozzie Guillen, who broke the news of the trade to a dazed Williams in spring training. "Ozzie was crying," Williams recalled. "It took him a while to convince me I really was traded because I didn't think I would be hearing that from Ozzie Guillen. I thought I should be hearing it from [former general manager] Larry Himes. But that was that."

Calling it quits after the 1991 season, Williams rejoined the White Sox as a special scout assigned to the inner cities. Two years later he was appointed special assistant to Chairman Reinsdorf, then vice president of player development in 1997. At the 1999 winter meetings, Williams represented Ron Schueler in absentia, fueling speculation that the incumbent GM was about to step down, but Schueler agreed to come back for the 2000 season, applying the finishing touches to a 35-year baseball career. Williams, just 36, was anointed the 11th White Sox general manager on October 24, 2000. "We didn't just pluck Kenny out of thin air. We knew him and what a great job he'd done with the farm system," Reinsdorf said. "He wasn't a risk at all. He was the logical one." Bypassed for promotion, the personable Danny Evans, who had spent nearly half his life working in a variety of assignments in the White Sox front office, left the organization disappointed, but with a fresh opportunity with the Los Angeles Dodgers as their new GM. Meanwhile, Williams made a brash promise to Sox fans. "If we do not bring a world championship to Chicago, I will have failed. We are about to embark on a four- or five-year window where we are going to be pretty darn competitive," he vowed, adding a tantalizing caveat. The Sox would "consider" signing free agent Alex Rodriguez. That never happened, of course, but eyebrows were raised nevertheless.

Williams was confident, upbeat, and candid with the media. When asked about the significance of becoming only the third African American GM in baseball, following Bill Lucas with Atlanta in 1979 and Bob Watson in Houston and New York, Williams said: "I hope someone out there is watching and gets inspired by it. It's not every day you can make history of some sort. I'm proud of that. I look forward to being proud of that as a world champion."

An old gray head of the baseball establishment offered the young GM what he considered to be a sage piece of advice: don't trade the fan favorites, because the fans and the front office won't like it. "I forgot that advice the minute I walked through the door," he recalled. "You are either going for it or you're not. And if you're not, you should hand the reins over to someone else. You have to risk looking like an idiot. That doesn't mean you are an idiot." Williams is an aggressive general manager, unafraid to wheel and deal and trade away the sacred cows if it means improving the club. Moving a fan favorite like Aaron Rowand to Philadelphia for the burly slugger Jim Thome less than a month after the World Series was a gamble, but one Williams believed was worth taking if the Sox had any hope of cashing in on their 2005 success in 2006. In every respect, he is the new Frank Lane—but with greater compassion and common sense. Under his watch, the baseball operation enhanced and supported the scouting system with a team-designed database supplemented with digital video of minor league prospects, uploaded to the team intranet. Minus the Yankees-sized payroll, the White Sox made do with what they had to work with, and that often meant dipping into the farm system for trade bait. Williams is a risk-taker. He traded 25 high-ranking prospects in his first five years at the helm—16 of them never made it up to Chicago before being dealt away. But only two out of that entire bunch, pitcher Frankie Francisco and outfielder Jeremy Reed, have exhibited big-league promise. At other times, he showed no qualms about dumping veterans and their high salaries if the team fell out of contention. In July 2002 Bobby Howry, Ray Durham, Kenny Lofton, and Sandy Alomar Jr. were all gone within a whirlwind 10-day period as Williams attempted to restock the farm system. Trades for veteran players like Todd Ritchie, Billy Koch, and David Wells flopped. Better results were achieved with key pickups Antonio Osuna, Damaso Marte, Juan Uribe, Freddy Garcia, Carl Everett, Neal Cotts, Scott Podsednik, and Jose Contreras.

But front-office machinations can only go so far toward building a winner. It takes a manager to raise a team up. Looking into his heart, but relying more on his gut instinct, Williams hired his buddy and former teammate Ozzie Guillen to lead the Sox after Jerry Manuel demonstrated he was not a "Point C" manager. Cito Gaston, architect of so many successful Toronto teams in the early 1990s, was briefly considered, but after Guillen told Williams to "go to hell" during the job interview and threatened to walk out, Williams knew he had a man of refreshing candor. A new era began, and a partnership jelled. "You're talking about a guy [Guillen] who can go from tough as nails to displaying a sensitivity that you don't see from many men in his position. He is a unique man," Williams said. Working as a team, they are both uniquely qualified men.

Ozzie Guillen and Kenny Williams are baseball's answer to *The Odd Couple*. It is a long-playing soap opera that grows more interesting and amusing with each passing year. Williams is a button-down, close-to-the-vest baseball executive of regular habits who lives with his wife, Jessica, and their family in button-down Naperville. He once told an interviewer that he has eaten a peanut butter and jelly sandwich for lunch every day for the past nine years. Guillen, on the other hand, stirs controversy by just being Ozzie Guillen. And like Felix and Oscar, the relationship between the two White Sox leaders is fraught with tension, bickering, and reconciliation. William winces every time the flamboyant Ozzie opens his mouth, and he would prefer that the dirty laundry remain private—in the Sox laundry room—and not in the media, out in cyberspace, or open to public scrutiny on sports talk radio. That, of course, is too much to expect from Ozzie.

As a GM, however, Kenny, with Ozzie's help, has kept the Sox in the thick of the flag chase nearly every season they have been here. The team does not have the luxury of launching into five-year rebuilding programs to grow and nurture the farm system through high draft picks while down at the Cell the product on the field atrophies and falls below the .500 mark in multiple seasons. White Sox fans will not stand for it—and attendance in this tough, two-team market where the Cubs are the media kingpins will sink like a stone in water. The economics of the Sox's situation forces Ken Williams to do his rebuilding (reshuffling, for lack of a better word) on the fly. In the first decade of his stewardship (October 2000 to October 2009), Williams completed 63 trades involving 161 players. Not since the days of Lane in the

General manager Kenny Williams had plenty to smile about in the summer of 2005. (White Sox photo by Ron Vesely)

The 2005 World Champs built by general manager Kenny Williams, shown in the second row, center. (White Sox photo by Ron Vesely)

1940s and 1950s had a White Sox GM expended this much energy changing the complexion of a roster to produce immediate results.

Kenny's August 2009 acquisition of All-Star outfielder Alex Rios and his hefty $61.6 million contract on a waiver claim from Toronto was one of his vintage under-the-radar moves that inspired Gordon Edes of Yahoo Sports to describe Williams as the "stealth bomber" among baseball's general managers. Getting former Cy Young Award–winner Jake Peavy after Peavy said no to the Sox the first time was another end-around move that raised eyebrows and caught everyone off guard. A National League scout put it this way: "Ken Williams is cold-blooded. If this was a biggest-balls contest, he's the winner."

While Theo Epstein in Boston and Billy Beane of Oakland and *Moneyball* fame garnered greater attention in the 2000s, Williams' task in some ways was far more daunting than theirs. Epstein sits on owner John Henry's huge money pile and does not have to play the *Moneyball* game like Beane, but then Oakland A's fans and the Bay Area media do not have the same low tolerance for failure as in Chicago. In recent years the Billy Beane formula for success has wilted and is no longer the same blueprint for success as before, especially after the A's fell on hard times. Commenting on Beane's lower profile, Monte Poole of the *Oakland Tribune* noted in July 2010, "Without a contending team to fortify, he has become an architect more concerned with construction than completion."

Kenny, on the other hand, is always under the microscope in Chicago—the skepticism (bordering on open hostility) of the Cubs-leaning press in this town spells enormous pressure on the front office to win year in and year out. If he trades youth for veterans, he is criticized for selling out the future. The departure of prospects Clayton Richard, Chris Young, Aaron Poreda, John Ely, Chris Carter, and Daniel Hudson in recent years were excoriated by the *Tribune* baseball columnists as short-sighted, risky, and unwise; but by the same token, if he does not make the effort to improve his team in the thick of a pennant race, he is accused of "standing by and doing nothing" by these same self-styled press box "experts." In other words, you're damned if you do and damned if you don't.

A bad start, a string of losses in April and May, and the columnists and beat writers are spouting dire warnings and unfounded predictions of an eminent break-up of the team—despite all the evidence to the contrary proving that Williams is not in the business of gutting his ballclub or backing up the truck to economize on salary. If anything, he has made it abundantly clear that winning is the first priority, but the press just doesn't get it. The frustrations of running the White Sox baseball organization and his high-strung manager took a toll on Williams—and as the possibilities of a return to the playoffs in 2010 fizzled, the GM candidly admitted that if an offer to join the Oakland Raiders (his favorite team as a kid) was to come through he would jump at the chance. Managing baseball operations from the C-suite can often be the toughest job in baseball.

The Support Staff

For more than 50 years, baseball on the South Side was a family affair. The White Sox were a Comiskey enterprise, and the family jealously protected its interests from the intrusions of outsiders. From the earliest days Charles Comiskey refused to take on a partner, and this policy cost him the services of manager Fielder Jones, who envisioned a larger role in the organization that never materialized.

The Old Roman groomed his sickly and frail son, John Louis, for a future role as owner of the White Sox. The younger Comiskey in turn designated his only son, Charley, as his successor. Events beyond Charley's control, however, ended the dream in 1959.

Other family members outside the immediate circle of Comiskeys were also provided front-office employment down through the years. Charles Fredericks, a nephew of the founding Comiskey, served as traveling secretary from 1900 up until his death in 1915. Fredericks was the Old Roman's right-hand man who coordinated the annual spring training junket to the West Coast, Texas, and Mexico—wherever the four winds took the ballclub in the first decade. Charley Fredericks supervised the books, made the daily bank deposit, and oversaw the maintenance of the ballpark up until the moment of his death.

Walter Clark, whom we know very little about, replaced Fredericks. Clark held the position until 1921, when he resigned in order to pursue a private business venture. Comiskey hired a former infielder named Lou Barbour as Clark's replacement in March 1921. Barbour was a Western League recruit who was invited to the White Sox training camp in 1914. He retired from the game after failing to win a spot on the roster, but served as the White Sox traveling secretary until 1931. Barbour is best remembered for his violent encounter with Art Shires in a Philadelphia hotel room in 1929. In a fit of rage, the drunken Shires nearly bit off Lou's finger as the two men punched, kicked, and scratched at each other until the Philadelphia police dragged the incorrigible infielder away.

Joseph T. Barry, who married Grace Comiskey's sister, Irene Reidy, in 1909, was appointed the new traveling secretary in 1931. Barry, known to every baseball writer in Chicago as Uncle Joe, was a noted Chicago police detective for nearly 14 years. At various times this famous gumshoe of yesteryear served as a bodyguard to Presidents William McKinley, Theodore Roosevelt, William Howard Taft, and Woodrow Wilson. Barry continued through the war years and was succeeded in later years by Frank McMahon, Bernie Snyderworth, Ed Short, Howie Roberts, Don Unferth, and Glen Rosenbaum.

Unferth and Rosenbaum were Chicago White Sox mainstays who handled the enormous job pressures associated with ferrying a baseball team from city to city with great skill and aplomb. Don Unferth, a kindly and gentle man, joined the White Sox as assistant farm director to John Rigney in 1948. Over the course of the next 32 years in the organization, Don cheerfully accepted any assignment thrown his way, including publicity and media relations. The attending ego perks of working in an executive capacity for the Comiskeys, Veeck, and the Allyns never led him to arrogantly deny press credentials to the little guys from rural communities. He was a a Comiskey Park treasure and a walking encyclopedia of White Sox trivia, statistics, and folklore.

A native of Fond du Lac, Wisconsin, Unferth had entered a contest sponsored by the *Sporting News* in 1939, asking readers to correctly pick the starting lineups of the All-Star Game.

Lou Barbour

Joe Barry (left) and Lew Fonseca

Don Unferth: versatile and good-hearted

Christine O'Reilly, senior director of community relations and executive director of White Sox Charities

Don was a first-place winner and was awarded an all-expenses paid trip to New York to see the game. "That's how I got my start in baseball," Don would chuckle. The truth is, he broke into the game without the usual family connections or boost coming from friends in high places. Don Unferth *earned* his success, and everyone who knew him mourned his passing in 1989.

Glen Rosenbaum, who served as traveling secretary for more than 20 years, began his career as a pitcher in the White Sox farm system back in 1955. Though he never appeared in a major league game, Glen has probably logged more "unofficial" innings than any pitcher since Cy Young. From 1968 through the 1980s, Rosenbaum supplemented his other duties by pitching batting practice to White Sox hitters. Tendinitis ended this phase of his career.

Before Frank Lane came up with the idea, little consideration was ever given to hiring a public relations expert to polish the team's image in the media. Lane stepped in and hired his friend Earl Flora, who handled public relations for the American Association prior to joining the Sox. Flora proved to be a valuable asset—attendance perked up in 1949. But he quit the team after the 1950 season to become the editor of a Columbus, Ohio, newspaper.

Versatile general manager Eddie Short handled the dual function of promotions, publicity, and media relations through 1961. Howie Roberts and Don Unferth continued the job in the 1960s and 1970s. Before Jerry Reinsdorf and Eddie Einhorn reorganized the front office and created departments where none had existed before, the entire White Sox payroll numbered only 175 employees during the second Bill Veeck ownership. Of this group, 120 were rostered players.

Under Reinsdorf, the payroll easily doubled, and the marketing function was divorced from media relations. Skilled sports information directors like Chuck Shriver, Ken Valdiserri, Paul Jensen, Chuck Adams, Doug Abel, Scott Reifert, and Bob Beghtol coordinated a public relations staff that also dispensed statistics, press releases, and information to the media through the 2000s.

Named vice president of communications in April 2004, the personable Reifert has logged 16 seasons with the ballclub and is an important liaison to the fans and media, while overseeing many philanthropic initiatives as president of White Sox Charities. Under his leadership, White Sox Charities has sponsored celebrity appearances, organized outreach programs to aid a variety of worthy causes, and has donated baseball equipment and millions of dollars. In 2005, through his leadership (and $1 million donated to the Chicago Park District), the team established Miracle Field in the Mt. Greenwood neighborhood of Chicago's Southwest Side for special-needs athletes. Jeff Szynal is another "behind-the-scenes" front-office veteran who, like Reifert, has contributed to the day-to-day operations in significant ways for more than a decade. Szynal is the manager of scoreboard operations and in-game entertainment, but he is also very appreciative of team history and has assembled a fine collection of memorabilia for the White Sox Museum located behind home plate. Christine O'Reilly, senior director of community relations, interfaces with the public on a constant basis. With Julie Taylor, and many other White Sox colleagues

Brooks Boyer, vice president of marketing and idea man

Scott Reifert, vice president of communications and a Sox professional since 1991

working tirelessly in a support function, O'Reilly does much to ensure the yearly success of SoxFest, the team's annual fan convention in January, and the comfort and enjoyment of the fans and visitors to U.S. Cellular Field throughout the year.

Marketing and broadcasting were consolidated under Mike McClure in the 1980s. McClure, who earned high marks with the Houston Oilers and the Chicago Bulls in the 1970s, substantially increased season-ticket sales through increased television and radio advertising. McClure, however, favored a move to St. Petersburg, Florida, where the team could enjoy a monopoly over press, radio, and TV. After the stadium appropriations bill passed through the Illinois General Assembly in July 1988 and the Sox recommitted to Chicago, McClure left the organization and was replaced by Rob Gallas, a former sportswriter for the suburban Arlington Heights *Daily Herald*. Gallas continued to expand White Sox visibility in the marketplace. New attendance records were set in the 1990s. Sales of team paraphernalia zoomed to number one in 1991 after the team reverted to its classic 1950s pinstripes and Old English logo.

After Rob Gallas resigned his position, Brooks Boyer was anointed vice president of marketing on April 25, 2004. Boyer had spent the previous 10 years directing advertising and sponsorship activity for the Chicago Bulls during some of their greatest seasons. Stepping into his new role, this Notre Dame grad immediately beefed up the size of the White Sox sales staff. In 2004 he came up with a "Sox Pride" theme—one that rolled over nicely into 2005. It complemented the "Win or Die Trying" advertising campaign, which was so effective in generating publicity, exposure, and branding for a team that had passively accepted its role as the "second team in the second city" for far too many years. Boyer also oversees the relationship between the team and its broadcast partners on radio and pubic and cable television, identifying and signing up new corporate sponsorships. He was instrumental in the startup of Silver Chalice Ventures (SCV), a new White Sox revenue stream and a medium for integrating non-baseball events and new media with the sports/entertainment world. Under his watch, White Sox attendance surpassed 2 million in six consecutive seasons—2005 to 2010—a new team record.

The White Sox were one of the first teams to hire a physical conditioning specialist. When injuries threatened to derail the 1906 pennant run, Charles Comiskey brought in Hiram "Doc" Connibear from the University of Chicago to work with the team. Connibear remained with the team until September, when he accepted an offer to join the University of Washington. He is credited with inventing a new kind of stroke that revolutionized competitive swimming in the United States.

William Buckner was the Sox's trainer during the 1920s—the "revolving door" era of White Sox history when dozens of eager young hopefuls showed up in spring training each year

Billy Webb (left) with coach Pepper Austin

Danny Evans

to vie for a spot on this woeful second-division ballclub. "They are all alike, these rookies," Billy observed in 1928. "They want to show the world they're champs, but ol' Buck knows they're only chumps."

Dr. A.F. Schacht rubbed the liniment in the 1930s. Ed "Packy" Schwartz kept the boys in shape during the World War II era. Myron "Mush" Esler took over as trainer in 1951. Eddie Froelich succeeded Esler and remained with the ballclub through the 1960s. Froelich was the best in the business; he had broken in with the Cubs in 1926 under Dr. Andy Lotshaw, a legend in sports medicine.

Trainer Ad Schacht (center) with Ted Lyons (left) and George Earnshaw

To combat pain and misfortune on the field, Froelich packed his black bag with the daily necessities: penicillin (infections), Pro-Banthine (ulcers), Analdein (pain), Colchicine Decadron (gout), antihistamine (allergies), Phenolax (laxatives), morphine tablets (pain), Chloromycetin (infections), Varidase (bruises), Kaopectate (stomach problems), Triaminic (colds), Acromycin (viruses), Seconal (sleeping pills), Dramamine (motion sickness), and elastic adhesives. "If there weren't a lot of laughs in this business to compensate for the long hours and hard work, I wouldn't be in it," Froelich said. "I'd find some other job."

When the laughs ended, Charley Saad stepped in and remained the Sox's No. 1 trainer until Herman Schneider came over from the Yankees in 1978. Born in the Netherlands, Hermie operates the finest training facility in the majors. He was the trainer for the 1988 All-Star Team on tour in Japan and during the 1983 All-Star Game festivities in Chicago.

Since the 1950s, three familiar voices have announced the lineups and manned the White Sox public address system, although, until Gene Honda took over microphone duties in 1991, the job was more multifaceted in the old days than it is now. Tates Johnson, who was an usher at both Wrigley Field and Comiskey Park in the 1940s and 1950s, divided his workload by doubling as a "field announcer" (as the PA guy was then known) at both ballparks. Johnson's familiar, expressive South Side monotone echoed across the enormous expanse of the old ballpark through the great years of the 1950s and '60s. "For the White Sox...No. 2... Nellie Fox!" Baby boomers never forgot him. After Johnson

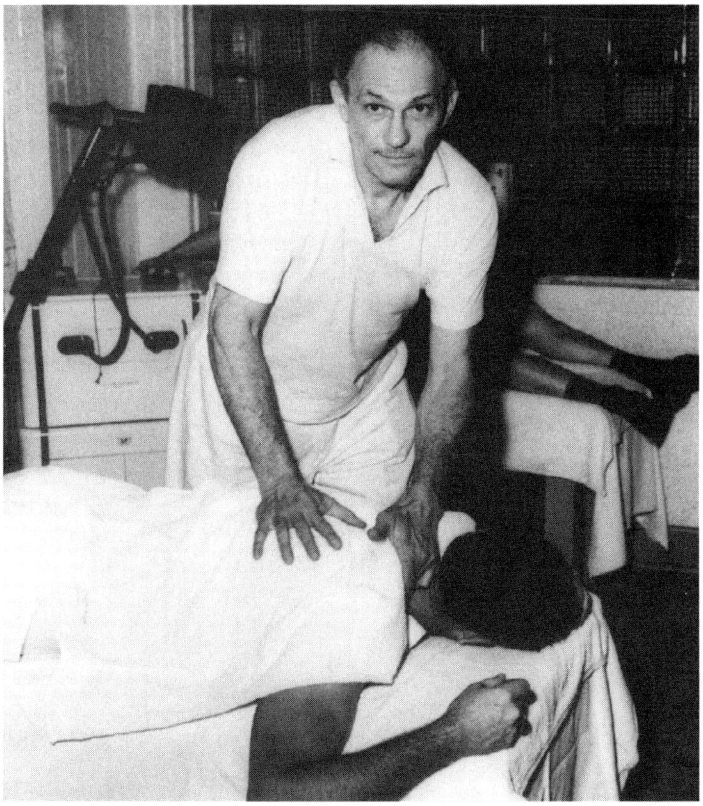

Ed Froelich rubs 'em down.

exited the scene, genteel Bob Finnegan, with the debonair, formalized style of announcing and who had briefly called the CBS *Game of the Week* from 1959 to 1961 before joining Bob Elson in the broadcast booth in 1966, took over as PA man and pulled double duty as the press box usher—assisting Joe Pinotti, a Bridgeport guy who for many years was the smiling face assisting local and visiting reporters. After more than two decades of service, Finnegan retired after the final game in old Comiskey Park in September 1990, giving way to the savvy and charismatic Gene Honda, the voice of WLIT Radio promos, the Big Ten Network, and WTTW-Channel 11 in Chicago, and the only person to have announced at the World Series, the MLB All-Star Game, the NHL Stanley Cup Playoffs, the NCAA Final Four, and a World Class Marathon.

Bill Veeck installed Comiskey Park's first in-house organ in the center-field bleachers—some 420 feet from home plate—in 1960. Shay Torrent became the first of only three organists to be employed by the ballclub in four decades. Shay left his mark on Sox history by playing the first White Sox "fight song" in 1962—a rather lame ditty composed by Marvin Frank of the W.B. Doner Advertising Company:

The White Sox are playing a game today
Come on and get out in the air
You'll forget your troubles watching singles and doubles
As the Sox hit the ball from everywhere

Concession stand at old Comiskey, 1950s

And it's a wonderful way to get away from it all
When the umpire yells play ball
There's plenty of action—the crowd is tense
There goes a long one over the fence
So go-go-go-go—Go you White Sox
Let's have another win today
They're all in that ballgame
Come out and watch your White Sox play!

The real White Sox fight song—imitated by amateur and professional teams in every stadium across the United States—was popularized by Nancy Faust, the White Sox music lady who was hired by Stuart Holcomb in 1970 as a replacement for Bob Creed, the second Comiskey Park organist. Charismatic, blond-haired Nancy Faust was barely out of her teens when she took her place in the organist's booth. Over the years she developed a loyal and devoted fan following through the good and bad of White Sox baseball. At times she was the best thing the ballclub had going.

In the memorable South Side Hitmen season of 1977, Nancy adapted a forgotten rock standard originally composed by the group Steam to her Comiskey Park routines. Her rendition of "Na Na Hey Hey Kiss Him Goodbye" inspired thousands of fans to join in a loud, boozy chorus every time an opposing pitcher was driven off the mound. Nancy's automobile license plate reads (what else?), "Na Na Hey Hey."

Pretty and popular Nancy Faust served as the White Sox organist for four incredible decades before announcing her retirement near the end of the 2010 season, after 3,000 games sitting in front of the Hammond. She was only the third White Sox organist to entertain the fans—succeeding Shay Torrent, a Californian who was a regular on the popular 1950s Chicago television program *Polka Party* before Bill Veeck hired him in 1959, and Bob Creed. Torrent serenaded Sox fans until he packed it up in May 1966 to accept an offer to pound the keys closer to home—at Anaheim Stadium for the Angels. Bob Creed, a nightclub performer at Ray Colomb's South Side

Clockwise from top left: Nancy Faust, the Comiskey Park organist from 1970 to 2010, in her center-field bleacher perch in 1972 (courtesy of Len Maybaum); Faust, early in her career, surrounded by the admiring Bill Melton and Wilbur Wood; Faust on her last day as Sox organist (courtesy of the Chicago White Sox); Faust honored outside of her performance room at U.S. Cellular Field, September 18, 2010 (courtesy of the Chicago White Sox).

Sharkey Colledge was the Sox equipment manager for 50 years.

supper club, took over as organist in 1966 and was Nancy's immediate predecessor.

General Manager Stu Holcomb hired Nancy after hearing her perform at a luncheon. She was only 23 at the time, but no stranger to live performance. Her mother, Jackie, was a member of the Jenny, Joy, and Jean trio on the old WLS *Barn Dance* in the early 1940s, and she already shed any lingering stage fright at a tender age. Borrowing from Shay Torrent's old songbook, which he passed down to her, Nancy played before a mostly empty stadium that first year—the South Siders drew only 495,000 fans in 1970, but she quickly caught on and became a bona fide ballpark celebrity, especially after Harry Caray began singing her praises up in the broadcast booth.

But as the philosophy of in-park entertainment changed in the mid-1990s, and loud, canned rock lyrics aimed at teenagers and children curtailed her playing time until she was limited to just working day games, Nancy correctly sensed that it was time to move on. "It's my choice, based on my role at the park," she said, just as plans for Nancy Faust Appreciation Day were announced for September 18, 2010. "I feel very proud to be a long-term team player. Never in my wildest dreams did I think they'd keep me around this long. They never told me to take a hike. Never. I'm using my best judgment and I feel it's right. I feel this is the best time, with the way things are going and the fact that I just play day games," she added. "The job has been whittled down quite a bit, because they do a wonderful job of entertaining the fans, I don't have more time to play complete songs. I find myself doing smaller and smaller sound bites."

In terms of job longevity, Ephraim "Sharkey" Colledge had no peer within the organization. The White Sox clubhouse equipment manager retired in 1966 after logging *60 years* in the organization. Sharkey, an 11-year-old neighborhood boy, was hired by Charles Comiskey in 1906 to sell peanuts and sweep up empty bottles from the 39th Street Grounds. In 1922 trainer William Buckner promoted Sharkey to the clubhouse, where he would serve as valet to more baseball players than any other man in history.

Traditions in baseball run very deep. The Bossard family of groundskeepers offers another example of the multi-generational aspects we still find in the game, amid the constant turnover of players and executive personnel. Gene Bossard took over as the Comiskey Park groundskeeper in 1940. He attended to the playing surfaces until 1983 when he handed down the job to his son, Roger—whose grandfather, Emil, and two uncles, Marshall and Harold, took care of the Cleveland field at Municipal Stadium from 1936 to 1973.

"Between Grandpa and Dad, I was able to follow in their footsteps and pick their brains," Roger said. At age 19, Roger Bossard watched his dad and Sox manager Eddie Stanky cook up a new scheme to give the pitchers an edge. Bossard and Stanky placed game balls in a room equipped with a humidifier. Over the course of the next 12 days, the balls absorbed up to two ounces of moisture, which cut the distance of a ball as much as 15 feet upon impact.

Two generations of groundskeepers: Roger Bossard (left) and father Gene (center) honored by Sox vice president Howard Pizer

The younger Bossard cannot take credit for this bit of larceny, but he has good reason to be proud of his own accomplishments. Roger has grown grass in the Arabian desert for envious Middle Eastern sheikhs, and painstakingly transported the original infield dirt from old Comiskey Park across the street into the new ballpark, where he continues a family tradition.

6

The Ballparks

1900–10

39th Street Grounds

The White Sox inaugurated the American League in a tiny, cramped wooden structure located near the corner of 39th Street and Princeton Avenue, four blocks south of the present Comiskey Park. The 39th Street Grounds were the fourth baseball facility to open south of Madison Street, the traditional dividing line separating the North Side of Chicago from the South Side.

The original playing field opened around the time of the 1893 World's Fair for a professional cricket team known as the Chicago Wanderers. By 1900, the year Charles Comiskey moved his St. Paul Saints to Chicago, the field had long since been abandoned, and the lot was overgrown with weeds and strewn with debris. Neighborhood boys played rounders and kick the can on the jagged, uneven surface.

By the terms of the transfer agreement with the Chicago National League ballclub, Comiskey was forbidden to build a stadium north of 35th Street. The American League had not yet declared itself a professional association and was therefore subject to the will of the National League through the sacrosanct National Agreement. James Hart, owner of the West Side Colts (now Cubs), was opposed to the move to begin with, and in order to secure his permission it was necessary for Comiskey to accede to his rather harsh and dictatorial terms.

The South Side had the reputation of being a baseball graveyard. Several 19th-century teams had failed to make a go of it, but Comiskey was up to the challenge and was determined to prove to Hart that he could prosper in the Irish Bridgeport setting where the 39th Street Grounds were situated.

The field was ideally located in a light industrial area easily accessible from the Wentworth Avenue streetcar and the South Side elevated trains. Immediate surroundings included St. George's church, a factory, a greenhouse, several saloons, including the original McCuddy's Tap, and an Irish youth club. Nearby lived thousands of first- and second-generation Irish immigrants who quickly adopted the White Sox as the focal point of their community social life.

The Old Roman secured loans from the First National Bank of Chicago to build a wooden grandstand enclosure and to pay for the whitewashing of the exterior. Up to the very moment the first pitch was delivered to the first batter on April 21, 1900, construction crews labored around the clock, applying the finishing touches.

Wooden support posts extended from first to third base. The distance to the left-field wall was 355 feet, 450 feet to dead center, and 400 feet to left-center. The spacious contours reflected the low-scoring, dead-ball-era style of play Comiskey preferred. Home runs were few and far between. Pitching, speed, and defense were the order of the day.

The South Side Grounds, c. 1905

During the first two years of the White Sox tenancy, the seating capacity numbered less than 5,000. In 1902 Comiskey modernized the plant by encircling the outfield with an exposed bleacher section. In order for the fans situated in the center-field section to enjoy an unobstructed view of the field, it was necessary for them to climb up a dozen rows of wooden risers.

To recoup his renovation costs, Comiskey raised the price of his grandstand seats from 50 cents to 75 cents, and the cost of a bleacher ticket doubled from a quarter to 50 cents. The sudden increase was shocking to many longtime baseball fans who came to view the infant American League as an inferior product compared to the National League. Nevertheless, Comiskey was confident that the popularity of the Sox would increase over time, and history has shown his judgment to be sound.

By 1904 the White Sox were a contending ballclub, and the demand for tickets far outweighed the seating capacity of the park. The 39th Street Grounds accommodated only 6,600 patrons after 1902, and the ballpark was inadequate for the crush of fans who turned out to watch the Sox. A single-game attendance record was set on October 2, 1904, when 30,084 fans were shoehorned into the park to witness Doc

The red brick exterior of the main gate of old Comiskey Park in 1941. Charley Comiskey, age 17, strolls by the stadium his grandfather built.

Two views of the 39th Street Grounds: Looking toward the infield from left field (top), and from home plate (bottom)

White extend his consecutive scoreless streak to 45 innings. The overflow crowd stood in roped-off sections in the outfield within close proximity to the players.

The configuration of the 39th Street Grounds allowed close interaction between players and fans that sometimes placed the umpires and opposing athletes at great risk. Very often, unruly fans exchanged insults with the umpires or hurled empty soda pop bottles in their direction. A runway leading through the left-field stands was the only access to and from the ballpark for players of both teams. It was the custom of the time for the players to change into their street clothes at their hotels, and as a result they had to run a gauntlet of fans along the way. It was not an uncommon occurrence in those days for players, fans, and umpires to slug it out long after the game had ended.

For these reasons Charles Comiskey decided to build a new stadium that would provide easier access for the players, seating comfort for his fans, and a modernistic steel and concrete façade to alleviate any chance of fire, which was always a threat in the heyday of the antique wooden ballparks. Site selection for the new Comiskey Park began in 1903. But it wasn't until 1908, when the Old Roman purchased a plot of land four blocks north of the 39th Street Grounds, that his ambitious dream took root.

The White Sox played their final game at the 39th Street Grounds on June 27, 1910, suffering a 7–2 loss at the hands of the Cleveland Naps.

After the new Comiskey Park opened for business on July 1, 1910, the Old Roman leased the 39th Street Grounds to John Schorling, a South Side tavern owner and president of the Chicago American Giants, a Negro League team managed by the legendary Andrew "Rube" Foster. Schorling, for unknown reasons, actually reduced the seating capacity of the park to 4,500.

The venerable and historic 39th Street Grounds hosted Negro League baseball for the next 40 years. As the popularity of black baseball waned in the late 1940s, the City of Chicago redeveloped the site for low-income housing. The Stateway Gardens now stand on the same hallowed ground where the White Sox captured the only all-Chicago World Series, played in 1906.

Left: Charles Comiskey is looking for a new home (*Chicago Tribune,* 1908). Right: a rare photo of old Comiskey Park under construction, 1910 (courtesy of Chicago History Museum, SDN – 008787, *Chicago Daily News*).

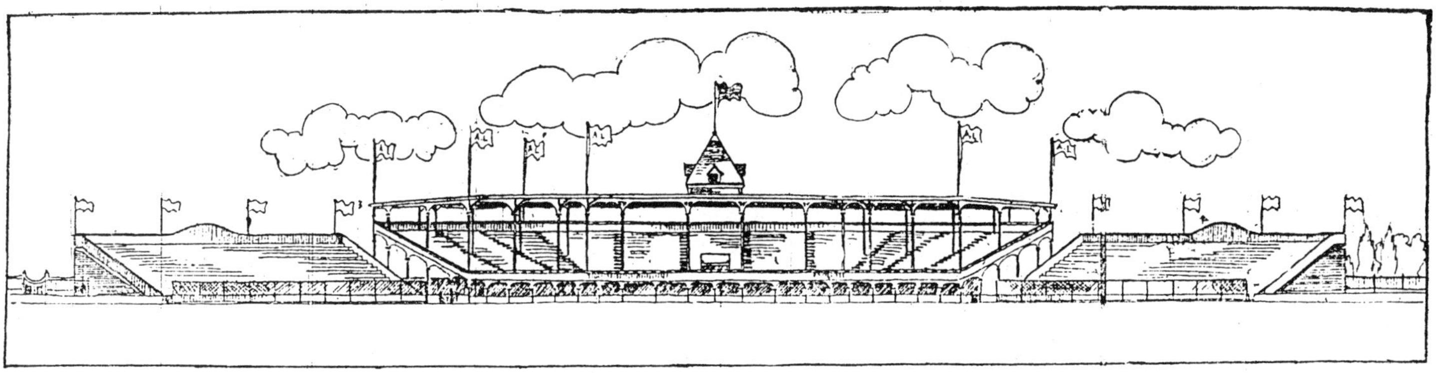

A 1900 schematic drawing of the 39th Street grounds

1910–90

Comiskey Park

After months of delicate negotiation, Charles Comiskey purchased a vacant tract of land in the Canal Trustees Subdivision on January 19, 1909, from Roxanna A. Bowen, granddaughter of John Wentworth, Chicago's colorful and outlandish Civil War–era mayor. Comiskey paid Mrs. Bowen the sum of $100,000 for 600 acres fronting the Wentworth Avenue streetcar line.

As a young ballplayer in 1890, Comiskey played first base for the Chicago Players League team in a small enclosure that stood only a few hundred feet east of 35th and Shields, where the Old Roman would soon erect a pioneering new stadium bearing his family name. After the Players League expired at the conclusion of the 1890 season, the grandstand circling the field where Comiskey played was razed, and the property evolved into a community dumping ground and truck farm. In this pastoral urban setting, an Italian named Scavudo peddled home-grown cabbage and produce from the back of his horse wagon.

To build the "Baseball Palace of the World," Comiskey hired a young architect named Zachary Taylor Davis, who built Wrigley Field (then called Weeghman Park) four years later. Davis submitted his preliminary design on October 6, 1909, after touring other American stadiums in the company of Sox pitcher Ed Walsh and architect Karl Vitzhum, who was attached to Daniel Burnham's staff. Burnham, a nationally known architect and city planner, oversaw the development of the 1893 World's Fair, held in Chicago.

Davis recommended adaptation of a classical design embodying the best features of Philadelphia's Shibe Park, a Beaux Arts masterpiece unique for the time. The technology of the era would have allowed Davis to construct a cantilevered grandstand free of bothersome, obstructing posts for an additional cost of $350,000. Comiskey rejected this idea for reasons that are unclear today. His well-known passion for economy may be the most compelling reason offered. Instead, the Sox owner ordered that construction

Comiskey Park as it appeared in 1910

proceed with the vertical posts and none of the classical ornamentation that made Shibe Park such a delight to behold.

Comiskey's token concession to artistic expression was more a reflection of his own vanity. The park would be built with common pressed brick with the letter "C" set in bas-relief along the exterior walls. It was the only unique characteristic distinguishing the baseball plant from any number of factories and warehouses in the surrounding Bridgeport neighborhood.

Official ground-breaking ceremonies took place on March 17, 1910, when Davis laid in place a "lucky" Irish green brick before a solemn but happy throng of local residents. To assure that the ballpark would open on July 1, Comiskey reportedly paid off officials in the construction industry for scab workers after a strike of the structural steel workers set the project back by five weeks. The infield sod was planted less than two weeks before the first game. In all, the whole project required only four months to complete, and the final price tag was pegged between $500,000 and $750,000. Not a dime of the money came out of the taxpayers' pockets.

Comiskey Park, baseball's third concrete and steel stadium, opened on time and to rave reviews. It was a day of gala celebration on the South Side, and the new plant was hailed as a marvel of modern technology and a tribute to the vision of its owner. Brass bands, an elaborate downtown parade, and the good wishes of many local dignitaries highlighted the calendar of events. With big Ed Walsh on the mound, the Sox dropped a close 2–0 decision to the St. Louis Browns before a crowd estimated to be between 28,000 and 32,000. Comiskey, aware of his loyal working-class following, had seen to it that a generous mix of cheap

From the third-base grandstand, 1910

Fans in the stands, c. 1913

seats were available for purchase at 25 cents apiece. The Old Roman was always mindful of the needs of the little guy.

The notable feature of Comiskey Park—upper-decked from first to third base with two detached grandstand sections in right and left—was its massive size. The stadium was compared to the ancient Roman Coliseum, a comparison that suited Chicago's Old Roman to a tee. The original dimensions were 363 feet down the foul lines and 420 to dead center, where an immense wooden scoreboard loomed over the field.

The first night game to be played in a major league stadium was staged in Comiskey Park during the inaugural season. Nineteen specially installed arc lights were strung along the perimeter of the field, and 3,500 curious fans turned out on August 27, 1910, to watch Jimmy Callahan's semipro team, the Logan Squares, do battle with the Rogers Parkers.

Charles Comiskey had long been intrigued with the possibilities of night baseball. Several years earlier some consideration had been given to installing light towers in the old 39th Street Grounds, but it was determined that the rickety wooden grandstand would not have been able to support the massive beams necessary to project light onto the playing surface. After the 1910 exhibition game between the

Early 1950s: the Chesterfield scoreboard is behind center field.

Photo diagram of the new shortened dimensions of Comiskey Park in 1934—done to accommodate slugger Al Simmons

two Chicago semipro clubs, plans for night baseball were scrapped.

The coming decade brought success and more overflow crowds. The fans were permitted to stand behind roped-off sections of the outfield during the big events like title fights or testimonial days for the ballplayers. Comiskey was understandably concerned about the insurance liability. A section of temporary grandstand collapsed on May 17, 1913, during Frank Chance Day festivities, injuring three people. A standing-room-only crowd swarmed past the restraining ropes on April 26, 1925, forcing the umpires to declare a forfeit.

Comiskey, who fretted over these kinds of security mishaps, addressed the urgency of the situation by ordering construction of an outfield upper deck during the winter of 1926–27. With Zachary Taylor Davis supervising the renovation, the existing detached outfield pavilions were connected to the baseline grandstand seats for the first time, and an elevated bleacher section replaced the field-level scoreboard

Comiskey Park, mid-1960s

in center field. Manually operated scoreboards were built into the outfield walls as Comiskey Park took on a familiar appearance that would last up until the moment of demolition in 1991.

The net effect of the $600,000 remodeling was to make the "Baseball Palace of the World" even more cavernous and imposing than before. Seating capacity increased to 52,000. Double-decking of the outfield pavilions enhanced Comiskey Park's reputation as a pitcher's haven at a time when baseball fans seemed to prefer high-scoring games with a lot of home runs. Comiskey's decision to add an upper deck to the outfield misfired. Between 1927 and 1951, the stadium was filled to capacity only a dozen times; mostly for Sunday doubleheaders with the Yankees. During those long and difficult years, the plaintive cry of "C'mon Luke!" rang through the empty upper-deck stands as Sox fans cheered on their one bona fide hitting star—Luke Appling.

Ironically, the upper deck was better suited to football than baseball. Fans were afforded a better view of the field watching the Chicago Cardinals, who played in Comiskey Park in 1922, 1925, 1929–30, and continuously from 1939 to 1958. In 1947 the Cards won their only NFL title playing on the frozen grounds of old Comiskey.

Numerous cosmetic improvements were made to the park after 1927, but the serious structural problems that began to set in as the building got older ultimately forced Jerry Reinsdorf to seek state funding for a new stadium. These concerns were never properly addressed by the succeeding Comiskeys, Bill Veeck, or the Allyns. A public address system and distance markings were added in 1935. Anchored seats were in place for the 1941 season. Lou Comiskey ordered the light towers installed for night baseball in 1939.

The first electronic scoreboard was built over the centerfield bleachers in 1951. The famous Chesterfield advertisement would light up each time a Sox player connected for a base hit.

Bill Veeck decided that the "Chesterfield! It's a Hit!" message was a bit too sedate for his tastes. With advertiser money paying the freight, Veeck built baseball's first "exploding" scoreboard in 1960. The "Monster" fired its rockets and belched smoke after every White Sox home run for the next 21 years, until it was replaced by a Diamond Vision board in 1982.

At various times the owners altered the spacious dimensions of the park. Chicken-wire fencing was strung along the perimeter of the warning track in 1949 and again in 1969. The infield was moved closer to the outfield walls in 1934 and 1983, with disappointing results for the home team.

Art Allyn changed the name of the stadium to White Sox Park in 1969 and carpeted the infield with Astroturf or "Sox Sod." It was a first for the American League, but when artificial grass fell out of favor in the mid-1970s, Bill Veeck ordered its removal shortly after he bought the club from John Allyn. In token respect to the memory of the founder, Veeck changed the name back to Comiskey Park.

The picnic area, built under the left-field stands in 1960, was another Veeckian innovation. For the first time since the 1920s when the fans were still allowed on the field for the big events, Comiskey Park patrons could observe the proceedings from the same angle as the left fielder while munching on hot dogs and other ballpark snacks.

The color schemes of the park changed as frequently as the ownerships. In 1959 Veeck whitewashed the red brick exterior. During his second ownership, the maverick Sox owner painted an unusual multicolored pattern in a section of the upper deck in left field. No reason was ever given, but it gave the fans something to ponder during slow periods of the game. What could this mean? To this day no one knows for sure.

Bill Veeck's famous center-field shower

An agreement is signed to build a new Comiskey Park. Eddie Einhorn (seated, far left) and Jerry Reinsdorf (far right) flank Governor James Thompson (second from left) and Chicago Mayor Eugene Sawyer, 1988.

Crazy banners, blaring horns, and a thumbs down to the umpires, the Sox Supporters led by Len Maybaum (front row, holding the banner to the right), were a fixture of ballpark life from the early 1970s through the end of the decade. This true-blue South Side answer to the rowdy Bleacher Bums of Wrigley Field carried their colors deep into enemy territory: Fenway Park, Yankee Stadium, Tiger Stadium, and Milwaukee County Stadium, much to the consternation of the locals.

Front gate of old Comiskey on its 75th anniversary in 1985

A happy group of White Sox fans are about to depart Union Station on July 27, 1951, to see the Sox play in New York—where they would lose three straight.

New dugouts, skyboxes (a first for Chicago), wider aisles, and a more luxurious executive office suite were added by Jerry Reinsdorf's regime over three seasons, 1982–84.

When all was said and done, Comiskey Park was a rather jumbled patchwork quilt of ideas reflecting the personality and temperament of its various ownerships.

By the time Comiskey Park celebrated its diamond anniversary, marking its uninterrupted 75-year reign and its status as the oldest baseball stadium in the United States, plans were already afoot to relocate the team to newer, more up-to-date headquarters. The masonry and infrastructure required yearly reinforcement. It was a financial drain on a team that was already in decline following a convincing 1983 divisional championship. By 1988 the Reinsdorf ownership had already invested $20 million in repairs to the park with no end in sight. A structural survey commissioned by the owners stated that Comiskey Park "was nearing the end of its useful life."

Historical preservationists, community groups, and baseball purists rallied to the defense of old Comiskey, conveniently ignoring the larger economic issues the owners were forced to address. The stadium was a crumbling relic of a bygone era, and it was never architecturally significant. Nor did it ever evolve into a popular tourist destination that lured out-of-town visitors or the peripheral fan, the way Wrigley Field was able to.

In the late 1960s racial unrest in the African American neighborhoods to the south and west of the ballpark frightened away many fans who perceived that the area was crime-ridden and dangerous. The misconception that Comiskey Park was an unsafe place to go to with the family lingered for many years, and the two Allyn owners who were most affected by declining attendance were unable to counter the argument effectively.

Yearly police statistics suggested that Bridgeport was still a stable, residential community with a lower crime rate than the neighborhood surrounding Wrigley Field, but old ideas die hard. And it wasn't until the late 1970s when Comiskey Park home attendance finally began to stabilize.

The dead-ball style of play mandated by the imposing size of symmetrical Comiskey Park prevented the White Sox from developing an exciting, offense-oriented ballclub that might have stirred the imagination of the fans and allowed the Sox to better compete with the Cubs for the loyalty of the fans. Instead, the team suffered through one moribund season after another. Even in the winning years, the feeling persisted that if only the Sox played in Wrigley Field they might have shed off their "second banana" image and claimed the entire city as their fan base.

During the hot, sticky months of July and August, the smoky haze of 5,000 cigarettes formed a lingering cloud over the infield. Underneath the splintery stands, the pillars of concrete and the uneven stone floors were damp and reeking from Chicago humidity. Worse yet were the poor sight lines in the left-field and right-field corners and the ever-present iron girders to obstruct the big play.

Jerry Reinsdorf commissioned a marketing survey, which determined that the White Sox's best interests would be served by a move to Chicago's western suburbs, accurately reflecting the demographic shift of fans from the South Side and the heavy exodus of industry from these once-viable blue-collar communities. When this option was rejected in a public referendum by the voters of Addison, Illinois, where the new ballpark was to be built, state politicians rallied to the cause to save the Sox from a certain exodus to the Sun Coast Dome already under construction in St. Petersburg, Florida.

Sox fans gather in the Illinois State Capitol to lobby Governor Thompson and the legislature to pass the Stadium funding bill, June 1988.

The final appropriation to build a new Comiskey Park directly across the street from the old one was approved in the midnight session of the Illinois General Assembly on July 1, 1988. It was the desire of the late Chicago Mayor Harold Washington that the team remain in its ancestral South Side home. Despite some natural misgivings, Jerry Reinsdorf and his investors signed off on the lease package drawn up by the Illinois Sports Facilities Authority and recommitted their resources to building a winner for Chicago in the new stadium towering high above the old one.

Comiskey Park closed its doors for the last time on Sunday, September 30, 1990, ending with a 2–1 victory over the Seattle Mariners. A boisterous but respectful gathering of 42,849 fans jammed the aisles to take one last look around and say farewell. Banners were unfurled in the stands recalling the late, great days—and the moments of infamy. "Shoeless Joe Jackson in the Hall of Fame, Say It Ain't So Joe!" Another one read, "Good-bye Old Friend, R.I.P."

When it was over, the Sox players ran a victory lap around the perimeter of the field to salute the fans and the passing of another Chicago institution. "This is the end of an era," sighed Mayor Richard M. Daley, who had attended so many Sox games in the company of his illustrious father back in the 1950s. The Daley family resided in a modest Bridgeport bungalow on Lowe Avenue, less than a half mile from the ballpark. They were White Sox fans, first, last, and always.

Though tinged with sadness and regret, the historic and memorable afternoon featuring a closely fought come-from-

The walls come tumbling down, May 1991.

behind victory was an appropriate dead-ball sendoff for the grande dame of American stadiums.

For all of its architectural flaws, there is no denying that great deeds happened here. Therein lies the historical significance of Comiskey Park, the South Side "baseball factory." Within the confines of its expansive field, the American League color barrier was broken on July 5, 1947, when rookie outfielder Larry Doby stepped up as a pinch-hitter for the Cleveland Indians. Sox pitcher Earl Harrist struck him out.

The first baseball All-Star Game was played on July 6, 1933. The Joe Louis–Jimmy Braddock fight and a half dozen other famous title bouts were staged in the center of the diamond. Over the years, the park hosted religious revivals, Notre Dame football, auto polo, the annual East-West Negro League All-Star Game, high school prep games, four World Series showdowns (1917; 1918—Cubs versus Red Sox; 1919; and 1959), the Beatles, and numerous rock concerts. It managed to survive a trade unionist pipe bomb that exploded harmlessly outside the main gate in 1923, a fire in the main concession commissary on June 7, 1974, that sent 3,000 fans scurrying to safety in the center of the diamond, and the infamous Disco Demolition riot coming five years later on July 12, 1979.

In its 80-year existence, 72,801,381 hearty souls braved the elements, the hardships of losing baseball, and poor sight lines to watch the White Sox play at the Grand Old Lady at 35th and Shields.

This is the legacy of Comiskey Park—a place for the fans, but also a flawed, imperfect monument to a man whose vision was impaired by his unwillingness to spend a nickel to make a buck. Charles Comiskey's business decisions in 1910 had an unforeseen, negative impact on the team of the late 1980s. The stadium might have become a cherished old landmark ranked on equal footing with Fenway Park in Boston, Tiger Stadium in Detroit, and Wrigley Field. But sadly, it was never mentioned in the same breath with these other baseball landmarks. Comiskey Park stood for a long period of time. But ultimately it failed to withstand the *test* of time.

A COMISKEY PARK EULOGY

by Terrye Cortesi and the membership of Sox Fans on Deck

March 17, 1910–April 3, 1991...Old Comiskey Park, née the "Baseball Palace of the World," aka the Great Lady, beloved daughter of Charles "the Old Roman" Comiskey, died today after a lingering illness, the effect of old age and neglect. In her active life from July 1, 1910, to her formal retirement on September 30, 1990, she has played hostess to many of baseball's greats: Ed Walsh, Ray Schalk, Eddie Collins, Joe Jackson, Luke Appling, Ted Lyons, Billy Pierce, Minnie Minoso, Nellie Fox, Luis Aparicio, Joel Horlen, Gary Peters, Wilbur Wood, Bill Melton, Carlos May, Carlton Fisk, Harold Baines, Tom Seaver, Ozzie Guillen, Robin Ventura, Bobby Thigpen, and Frank Thomas. She was preceded in death by her lamented sisters: the Polo Grounds, Forbes Field, Crosley Field, Ebbets Field, and Connie Mack Stadium. She is survived by three cherished sisters: Fenway Park of Boston, Wrigley Field of Chicago, and Tiger Stadium of Detroit.

Old Comiskey Park distinguished herself among her sisters by giving birth to two beloved offspring: the Negro Leagues' East-West All-Star Game and Major League Baseball's All-Star Game.

No formal ceremonies are planned. South Side breezes will carry her dust over Lake Michigan. In lieu of flowers, mourners are requested to make donations in her name to Chisox Club Charities.

She will be sorely missed and long remembered by her loving friends. *Requiescat in pace.*

Old Comiskey Park Firsts

- **Game**—July 1, 1910 vs. St. Louis Browns
- **Attendance**—28,000–32,000 (estimated)
- **Pitcher**—Ed Walsh, White Sox (7/1/10)
- **Batter**—George Stone, St. Louis (7/1/10)
- **Plate umpire**—Tom Connally
- **Pitch**—Called a ball
- **Winning pitcher**—Barney Pelty, St. Louis Browns (7/1/10)
- **Losing pitcher**—Ed Walsh, vs. Browns (7/1/10)
- **Hit**—George Stone, St. Louis, first inning (7/1/10)
- **First Sox hit**—Lena Blackburne, single, second inning (7/1/10)
- **Run**—Frank Truesdale, St. Louis, third inning (7/1/10)
- **First Sox run**—Patrick Dougherty, third inning (7/2/10)
- **Double**—George Stone, St. Louis (7/1/10)
- **Triple**—Patrick Dougherty, White Sox, seventh inning (7/1/10)
- **Home run**—Lee Ford Tannehill, fourth inning (7/31/10), off of Bill Donovan, Detroit Tigers
- **Opponent home run**—Ty Cobb, Detroit Tigers, fifth inning (7/31/10), off of Ed Walsh
- **Two-run home run**—Arnold "Chick" Gandil, White Sox, fourth inning (9/18/10), off of Ben Hunt, Boston Red Sox
- **Three-run home run**—John "Shano" Collins, White Sox fourth inning (5/23/11), off of Russ Ford, New York Highlanders
- **Grand slam home run**—Lee Ford Tannehill, White Sox (7/31/10), off of Bill Donovan, Detroit Tigers
- **RBI**—George Stone, St. Louis (7/1/10)
- **Putout**—Arnold "Chick" Gandil, White Sox (first inning, 7/1/10)
- **Assist**—Billy Purtell, White Sox (first inning, 7/1/10)
- **Error**—Billy Sullivan, White Sox catcher (7/1/10)
- **Stolen base**—John "Shano" Collins, White Sox, first inning (7/1/10)
- **Double steal**—Al Schweitzer and Pat Newnam, St. Louis (second game, 7/4/10)
- **Steal of home**—Felix Chouinard, White Sox, vs. Boston (first inning, 9/17/10)
- **Caught stealing**—Arnold "Chick" Gandil, White Sox (second inning, 7/1/10)
- **Sacrifice**—Roy Hartzell, St. Louis (7/1/10)
- **Shutout**—Barney Pelty, St. Louis (7/1/10)
- **First Sox shutout**—Ed Walsh, vs. Washington (8/7/10)
- **Complete game**—Barney Pelty, St. Louis Browns (7/1/10)
- **First Sox complete-game victory**—Doc White, vs. St. Louis (7/2/10)
- **Walk**—John "Shano" Collins, White Sox (7/1/10)
- **Strikeout**—Al Schweitzer, St. Louis (7/1/10)
- **Pinch hit**—Freddy Payne, White Sox, vs. St. Louis, second game (7/3/10)
- **Double play**—turned by the White Sox against Bobby Wallace of the St. Louis Browns (Zeider-Sullivan-Purtell-Blackburne), first inning (7/1/10)
- **Triple play**—Turned by the White Sox against Billy Purtell of the Boston Red Sox (Parent-Zeider-Gandil), second inning (9/18/10)
- **Balk**—Doc White, White Sox, vs. Boston (8/9/10)
- **Hit by pitch**—Frank Truesdale, St. Louis (by Frank Smith, second game) (7/4/10)
- **Wild pitch**—Joe Lake, St. Louis (7/5/10)
- **Passed ball**—Billy Sullivan, White Sox (7/4/10)
- **Ejection**—Ed Walsh, White Sox, sixth inning against Detroit (7/31/10)
- **Extra-inning game**—White Sox vs. St. Louis, 10 innings, lose 6–5 (7/5/10)
- **Doubleheader**—White Sox vs. St. Louis (split) (7/3/10)
- **Twi-night doubleheader**—White Sox vs. New York (sweep) (7/29/42)
- **Rainout**—vs. St. Louis (9/12/10)
- **Night game**—White Sox vs. St. Louis (8/14/39)
- **No-hitter** (9 innings)—Ed Walsh, vs. Boston (8/27/11)
- **One-hitter**—Ed Summers, Detroit, vs. White Sox (7/29/10)
- **Two-hitter**—Frank Lange and Jim Scott (combined), White Sox, vs. St. Louis (7/4/10)

The new park under construction, June 1990

1991–

U.S. Cellular Field (Formerly Comiskey Park II)

The new Comiskey Park, blending hi-tech Space Age technology, a spacious food concourse, and unobstructed sight lines, opened for business on time and under budget on April 18, 1991. Recalling the words of the late, great sportswriter Warren Brown, who always said that if the impossible were likely to occur, it would surely involve the White Sox, the ballclub was blown out 16–0 in the inaugural tilt against the Detroit Tigers before Vice President Dan Quayle and 42,191 chilled fans.

As the Tigers runners raced around the bases, the wrecker's ball laid waste to old Comiskey Park standing forlorn and abandoned across the street. Opening Day of year one was a civic embarrassment and a discouraging start to what was hailed as the beginning of a bright new era of baseball on the South Side. "This crowd loves the stadium, but I'm not sure they love the game," Quayle observed, as he ran for the cover of his motorcade after the Tigers' lead ballooned to 12–0.

Fortunately, the White Sox quickly adjusted to their new surroundings and delivered solid, competitive baseball to the fans of Chicago over the next four years.

"What's happening in baseball architecture is what you see here today," commented Richard deFlon, cofounder of a design firm that merged with Hellmuth, Obata & Kassabaum (HOK), the Kansas City–based company that drew up the plans for the new Comiskey Park. "This is the first of the new single-purpose stadiums. Baltimore's next, then Cleveland. There is a return to the intimacy and the character of the old park."

The desire to recapture the glorious traditions of baseball's golden age is a notable feature of Baltimore's Camden Yards and Jacobs Field in Cleveland, but the purists would argue that these features are absent in the design of the new Comiskey Park.

The ballpark enjoyed an abbreviated honeymoon with the fans of Chicago before the muted praise gave way to a chorus of complaints about the steepness of the bowl-shaped upper deck. The intimacy that deFlon spoke of was absent in the new facility. The first row of seats in the upper deck, pitched at 35 degrees, is farther away from home plate than the last row of seats in old Comiskey Park. It was a startling change for Chicago fans who were unaccustomed to the look and feel of new stadiums. The Chicago Stadium, opened for the Blackhawks in 1929, was the last sports arena to be erected inside the city limits before Comiskey Park II opened for business.

Rick deFlon designed the new Comiskey Park with considerable input coming from the members of the Illinois Sports Facilities Authority and Terry Savarise, vice president of stadium operations for the White Sox. Choices had to be made

Robin Ventura (left) and Carlton Fisk in their "Turn Back the Clock" uniforms preview the unfinished ballpark, 1990.

between the look and feel of a vintage stadium like Fenway Park or a more contemporary setting accenting fan convenience, unobstructed sight lines, 118 luxury sky suites, a Jumbotron scoreboard, a White Sox museum, and a montage of souvenir shops and food stands.

The ISFA came down on the side of modern amenities, arguing that where else but in Chicago could baseball fans experience the best of *both* worlds? "Frankly Camden Yards was not around as a model. But to me this looks like a modern baseball stadium. That's what I was after," argues former Illinois Governor James R. Thompson, whose robust support in the General Assembly went a long way toward saving the White Sox for Chicago when the franchise was imperiled.

After nearly four years of emotionally heated debate and political wrangling, ground was finally broken for the new Comiskey Park on May 7, 1989. "It was a long hard-fought battle, but in the end the White Sox, the City of Chicago, and the people of Illinois prevailed," Thompson told a throng of invited dignitaries and fans who came to celebrate this victory over impossible odds. "The rich tradition of American League baseball, which began in Chicago back in 1901, will now continue for generations."

Over the next 22 months executive director Peter C. Bynoe and his capable assistant, Timothy D. Romani of the ISFA, oversaw a construction project on an almost superhuman scale. The ISFA secured a no-strike promise from the trade unions who would build the park. Once the first spade of dirt was turned, there was no looking back. The stadium had to be delivered to the White Sox by April 18, 1991, or the fragile lease agreement binding the team to Chicago for the next 20 years was off.

Bynoe and Romani fulfilled their obligations, but few people outside the inner circle of investors, team executives, and industry insiders fully appreciated their yeomanlike efforts on behalf of Chicago fans. The final price tag for the stadium came in at $119 million. Their careful adherence to the bottom line resulted in a savings to the taxpayers of $18 million from the state-allocated funding.

Even though Comiskey Park has been roundly criticized in some quarters as a cold, impersonal structure that is a monument to yuppie greed and corporate arrogance, the change in locales has helped the White Sox shed their hangdog, loser

The view from the distant upper deck in right field

The "new and improved" U.S. Cellular Field (left). Chopped and lowered (above). The upper deck at U.S. Cellular Field took on a more traditional appearance in 2004, when the canopy-styled roof was replaced with decorative trusses.

U.S. Cellular Field, main gate on 35th Street (left), and "Southpaw" (above, right) the new millennium mascot at the Cell. (Courtesy of the Chicago White Sox)

The "Commander," Carlton Fisk, honored with the unveiling of his statue in 2005.

On the 100th anniversary of the opening of old Comiskey Park (July 1, 1910), Illinois State Representative Patricia R. Bellock from the west suburban 47th District (second from right), who is the great-great-granddaughter of Sox founder Charles A. Comiskey, poses with several Comiskey descendents next to the center-field concourse statue of the "Old Roman" following pregame ceremonies.

Minnie Minoso, "Mr. White Sox," strikes a pose next to his bronze likeness.

Above: Charley Comiskey (left) poses with the statue of his grandfather, Charles the "Old Roman" Comiskey, moments after the unveiling in center field, with Chairman Reinsdorf.
Left: The Champions Plaza and monument outside of Gate No. 4 opened in 2008.

Photos courtesy of the Chicago White Sox

White Sox players lend assistance with the unveiling of Champions Plaza, April 11, 2008. (Courtesy of the Chicago White Sox)

image—one that was steeped in the folklore and traditions of old Comiskey Park.

Ten million fans paid their way into the park in the first five seasons, but public tastes quickly shifted after the 1994 strike. The new Comiskey Park was criticized as a rather bland, sterile place to watch a ballgame after the unveiling of Camden Yards, Jacobs Field, and the other traditional "urban design" ballparks.

By the late 1990s, fan complaints about the steepness of the upper deck, the "mall-like" appearance of the spacious concourse, the absence of a "Wrigleyville" kind of nightlife, after-hours amenities, and saloons in the surrounding Bridgeport neighborhood clogged the airwaves of the 24-hour sports talk shows in Chicago. The fortunes of the team, on and off the field, took a beating. Endless fan harangues about the distant upper-deck seats, which were rarely populated in the first place, seemed to be on everyone's mind. Jerry Reinsdorf patiently reminded the critical fans that there were 25,000 perfectly good seats available in the lower deck on most days, offering unobstructed sightlines. They could be easily obtained for just about any game since home attendance had sagged in the post-strike years. In 1999 the Sox drew 1.3 million fans, unsatisfactory by any standard of comparison, especially when the sixth-place Cubs surpassed 2.8 million. Of course, the resentment toward ownership ran deep after the 1994 work stoppage. Many White Sox fans pinned the complex labor problems on Jerry, which was not only unfair but terribly naïve. They looked at Camden Yards, Comerica Park, Coors Field, and other postmodern HOK wonders with envy, and wondered why Chicago was denied the chance to experience its own urban retro styled stadium, even though so very few of these fans had ever followed their favorite team on road trips to actually preview these parks first-hand (and realize that upper-deck steepness and mall-like concourses were de rigueur everywhere). Nevertheless, the disenchantment with the park had to be addressed sooner or later if the Sox were going to survive and prosper in this major market. With no public funding forthcoming from the state, the White Sox had to first figure out what they could do and, more importantly, find the means to pay for costly renovation through private initiatives. Fan focus groups and discussions with season-ticket holders confirmed levels of dissatisfaction. The club decided to move forward. In 2001 phase one of an ambitious five-year plan to improve the look and feel of the park was unveiled. Over the next three seasons, $69 million was budgeted to HKS of Dallas to design a center-field "terraced" fan deck, shift the bullpens to more visible positioning, and shave off the objectionable eight rows of upper-deck seating while adding decorative trusses and a flat roof to eliminate the "flying saucer" look of the old canopy. "I think what we did was take a look at a whole bunch of options with those seats," explained Terry Savarise, vice president of operations, who was instrumental in the original HOK design planning. "We decided if we can't fix them, then just get rid of them. Get rid of the seats the people hated the most."

In January 2003 stadium naming rights were sold to U.S. Cellular, a Chicago-based wireless provider, hence U.S. Cellular Field, or more colloquially, "the Cell." U.S. Cellular CEO John Rooney promised Sox fans "a new experience." "Fans will love the park when they come back in here in large numbers," said Rooney, an enthusiastic civic booster and fan of the home team. The infusion of cash helped pay for some nice finishing touches: a left-field FUNdamentals skills area for kids to play in and seat replacement with a more appropriate forest-green color scheme demanded by the public. By the start of the 2006 season, the old/new Comiskey Park had been dramatically altered to better integrate with the blue-

Base of the sculpture in Champions Plaza

collar industrial landscape of the city's historic South Side. From the exterior, the flattened roof and new translucent screens, designed to repel the swirling spring and autumn winds and keep the crowd noise inside, added an element of attractive urban functionalism.

Each year thereafter, the Illinois Sports Facilities Authority and the White Sox continued to modify and improve the infrastructure of U.S. Cellular Field—some of the improvements that were made were less visible to the public than others, but all were designed to enhance the baseball experience for the fans. In 2007 the press box was relocated from the 200 level behind home plate and moved to the fourth level upstairs, overlooking the first-base line. Next the Home Plate Club, a deluxe private seating area and restaurant, was carved out of the old press room that had previously afforded the media the most panoramic views of the entire playing field.

TBD, an outdoor beer garden, was unveiled on the north side of 35th Street in 2010, and future plans call for the construction of a White Sox–themed restaurant across the street, on the site of the old Comiskey Park—stirring memories of Art Allyn's ill-fated and long-forgotten attempt to build the Coach & Nine dining club on Shields Avenue in 1961–1963—a project that never got off the drawing board.

Champions Plaza, a lasting tribute and recognition of the great moments in Sox history, culminating in the 2005 World Series, was unveiled outside of Gate 4 at 35th and Shields on April 11, 2008. A bronze frieze and granite monument designed by the Fine Art Studio of Rotblatt and Amrany overlooks a historic timeline of pivotal events in team history dating back to 1900. Each of the 200-plus great moments (supplied by the author, Richard Lindberg), is sequentially inlaid in a series of bricks forming the shape of a baseball diamond and surrounded by an expanse of "legacy plaza" bricks, each bearing a personalized inscription and message from individual fans, players, team officials, and other loyal supporters of ChiSox baseball who had paid the subscription fee. Similar legacy plazas have been added to a number of other stadiums across America, including the renovated Kauffmann Stadium in Kansas City and Comerica Park in Detroit.

It is curious, and rather ironic, that so little of the baseball history occurring in old Comiskey Park was preserved and celebrated by succeeding ownership groups *during* the latter stages of its long 80-year life. How strange no lasting shrine or tribute was ever paid to the past during those defining eight decades. In the 1960s metal markers were affixed to the

World Series game day at 35th and Shields

upper-deck façade indicating where the longest hit home run balls had landed. A mural of newspaper graphics depicting the 1959 flag chase was pasted into the wall behind the old Dugout Café in back of home plate, and a collection of oversized photographs of a handful of players was framed overhead, visible to the fans as they streamed into the park from 35th and Shields. And that was that.

But in the first decade of the new millennium, the new U.S. Cellular Field became a living museum to its predecessor, the games, and the men who had gone before. But will that *finally* assuage the hostility of the many "gloom and doom" community activists, the "Save Our Sox" contingent, and historic preservationists who fought hard to oppose its construction in the mistaken belief that a new stadium could never do justice to the traditions of the past? Beginning in 2004, a "monument park" took shape in the center-field concourse with the unveiling of the Charles Comiskey statue in 2004, followed in the next few years by bronze likenesses of Minnie Minoso, Carlton Fisk, Luis Aparicio and Nellie Fox, Billy Pierce, and Harold Baines.

Let us hope that some equally deserving figures from the more distant past—Ted Lyons, Ray Schalk, Urban "Red" Faber, Luke Appling, Doc White, the great Ed Walsh, and more recently Wilbur Wood—an unheralded and overlooked star of the 1970s—will eventually be honored in this fashion. Their wonderful accomplishments should never be forgotten—or diminished by the passing of time.

The gentrification of tough city neighborhoods to the east and south of the ballpark took root later than what city officials envisioned or could have possibly anticipated back in 1988 when the original stadium-enabling legislation passed, but steady improvements to the housing stock in Bridgeport to the north; the rebirth of the historic Bronzeville neighborhood, the Gap, and Douglas to the east; the final demolition of the last of the derelict, crime-infested Robert Taylor Homes on federal land facing the ballpark east of the Dan Ryan Expressway; and the addition of safe, gated communities, townhomes, and new storefront businesses on 35th Street, serving lower-income residents that have arisen in their place, are hopeful indicators that the *modern legacy* envisioned for the U.S. Cellular Field environs by urban planners has at last become a self-fulfilling prophecy. In 2010 work began on a new Metra Rock Island commuter railroad stop east of the Ryan on 35th Street that will make it much easier for fans coming from the distant South Suburbs to travel to the game without having to fight traffic. The last time a commuter rail line made a scheduled stop at Comiskey Park was way back in 1964 when the Chicago Wabash and Indiana line ended their passenger service. A decaying wooden shack east of Shields Avenue adjacent to the viaduct nearest the park is all that remains from that time. With the return of rail service to augment the rapidly gentrifying neighborhood, the future of the mid–South Side is bright.

For the White Sox, U.S. Cellular Field has given them a true home-field advantage they never really enjoyed while playing at old Comiskey. From 1991 to 2010, the team endured only two losing home seasons (1999, 38–42; and 2007, 38–43). The decision to bring in the outfield fences in 2000 ushered in a new and different era for long-suffering Sox fans who were unaccustomed to seeing so many balls flying into the outfield stands at old Comiskey. In eight of the next 10 seasons, Sox teams slugged 200 or more home runs as they intimidated opposing pitching staffs and indeed "put it on the board" in record numbers. Any reasonably hit fly ball had a chance to go, depending on the prevailing wind currents. In so many years of dead-ball baseball in the 1910s, 1920s, 1930s, 1940s, 1950s, and through the end of the 1960s at old Comiskey, this was the refreshingly new offensive approach to the game the fans asked for and seemed to crave—and now they finally had it.

Apart from White Sox baseball, there have been many other notable happenings at the new South Side shrine. The Rolling Stones played the first rock concert in stadium history on September 13, 2002. Bruce Springsteen and the E Street Band also played here. Scenes from three Hollywood movies—*Little League, Major League Two,* and *My Best Friend's Wedding*—were filmed at the Cell. The All-Star Game returned to the South Side in 2003, and commercials for the PGA Tour, Reebok, the Boys & Girls Clubs of America, and Nike were all shot on location here. On January 20, 2009, the White Sox displayed a banner outside of Gate 6 to honor their First Fan, Barack Obama, on the occasion of his presidential inauguration.

The opening of U.S. Cellular Field in 1991 kicked into high gear a wave of new stadium building across the country. Following the precedent set by the White Sox in their quest to secure public-sector funding to pay for the cost of the facility, nearly every other city hosting a major league baseball team leveraged their own resources, and one after another the enabling legislation was passed and new stadiums were christened while older structures in Anaheim, Boston, Kansas City, and Oakland were significantly remodeled and upgraded. By 2010 U.S. Cellular Field had already become the eighth oldest park in the majors.

White Sox Home Records at Each Stadium

Park	Years	W	L	T	Pct
39th Street Grounds	1900–10	491	276	22	.640
Comiskey Park	1910–90	3,012	2,910	30	.509
U.S. Cellular Field*	1991–	896	688	1	.565
Totals		4,399	3,874	53	.531

* Through 2010 season

Comiskey Park II/U.S. Cellular Field Firsts

- **Game**—April 18, 1991, vs. Detroit Tigers
- **Attendance**—42,191, vs. Detroit Tigers (4/18/91)
- **Pitcher**—Jack McDowell, White Sox, vs. Detroit Tigers (4/18/91)
- **Batter**—Tony Phillips, Detroit Tigers (4/18/91)
- **Plate umpire**—Steve Palermo (4/18/91)
- **Pitch**—Fastball, called a ball (4/18/91)
- **Winning pitcher**—Frank Tanana, Detroit Tigers (4/18/91)
- **Losing pitcher**—Jack McDowell, White Sox, vs. Detroit Tigers (4/18/91)
- **Save**—Jerry Don Gleaton, Detroit Tigers (4/20/91)
- **Hit**—Alan Trammell, Detroit Tigers (first inning, 4/18/91)
- **Run**—Travis Fryman, Detroit Tigers (third inning, 4/18/91)
- **Single**—Alan Trammell, Detroit Tigers, off Jack McDowell, White Sox (first inning, 4/18/91)
- **Double**—John Shelby, Detroit Tigers, off Brian Drahman, White Sox (third inning, 4/18/91)
- **Triple**—Tony Phillips, Detroit Tigers, off Ken Patterson, White Sox (fourth inning, 4/18/91)
- **Home run**—Cecil Fielder, Detroit Tigers, off Jack McDowell, White Sox (third inning, 4/18/91)
- **RBI**—Alan Trammell, Detroit Tigers (third inning, 4/18/91)
- **Putout**—Cory Snyder, White Sox (first inning, 4/18/91)
- **Assist**—Robin Ventura, White Sox (second inning, 4/18/91)
- **Error**—Robin Ventura, White Sox (fourth inning, 4/18/91)

In 2004 the Florida Marlins played two make-up games in U.S. Cellular Field with the Montreal Expos after Gulf Coast hurricanes washed away their home field. The few White Sox fans in attendance rooted hard for the Marlins, who were battling the Cubs for a wild-card berth. The Marlins won.

- **Stolen base**—Lou Whitaker, Detroit Tigers (first inning, 4/18/91)
- **Double steal**—Joey Cora and Tim Raines, White Sox (eighth inning, 6/18/91)
- **Caught stealing**—Tony Phillips, Detroit Tigers (third inning, 4/20/91)
- **Two-run home run**—Rob Deer, Detroit Tigers, off Jack McDowell, White Sox (third inning, 4/18/91)
- **Three-run home run**—Cecil Fielder, Detroit Tigers, off Jack McDowell, White Sox (third inning, 4/18/91)
- **Grand slam**—Mike Gallego, Oakland Athletics, off Ramon Garcia, White Sox (second inning, 5/31/91)
- **Sacrifice bunt**—Joey Cora, White Sox vs. Detroit Tigers (10th inning, 4/20/91)
- **Sacrifice fly**—Matt Merullo, White Sox vs. New York Yankees (third inning, 4/27/91)
- **Shutout**—Frank Tanana, Detroit Tigers (4/18/91)
- **Complete game**—Frank Tanana, Detroit Tigers (4/18/91)
- **Walk**—Travis Fryman, Detroit Tigers, by Jack McDowell, White Sox (third inning, 4/18/91)
- **Intentional walk**—Dan Pasqua, White Sox, by Mike Henneman, Detroit Tigers (ninth inning, 4/20/91)
- **Strikeout**—Tim Raines, White Sox, vs. Detroit Tigers (first inning, 4/18/91)
- **Hit into double play**—Tim Raines, White Sox, vs. Detroit Tigers (eighth inning, 4/18/91)
- **Balk**—Bryan Harvey, California Angels (ninth inning, 5/28/91)
- **Wild pitch**—Melido Perez, White Sox, vs. Detroit Tigers (second inning, 4/20/91)
- **Hit by pitch**—Carlton Fisk, White Sox, by Dave Johnson, Baltimore Orioles (second inning, 4/23/91)
- **Night game**—White Sox vs. Baltimore (4/22/91)
- **Ejection**—Glenallen Hill, Toronto Blue Jays (ninth inning, 5/17/91)
- **Protested game**—Buck Rodgers, California Angels (eighth inning, 9/21/91)

The 1940s Sox logo inlaid on the washroom floor at old Comiskey Park

- **Extra-inning game**—White Sox vs. Detroit Tigers (4/20/91)
- **Rainout**—White Sox vs. Minnesota Twins (10/2/91)
- **Doubleheader**—White Sox vs. Minnesota Twins (10/3/91)
- **One-hitter**—Alex Fernandez, vs. Milwaukee Brewers (5/4/92)
- **Hitting for the Cycle**—Chris Singleton, White Sox, vs. Kansas City (7/6/99)
- **Hit into triple play**—Bengie Molina, Anaheim Angels vs. White Sox (sixth inning, 7/4/04)
- **Hosting**—Due to the threat of Hurricane Ivan, the Florida Marlins and Montreal Expos play the first two games of their five-game series at the home of the White Sox (9/13/04 and 9/14/04).
- **No-hitter**—Mark Buehrle vs. Texas Rangers (4/18/07)
- **Perfect Game**—Mark Buehrle vs. Tampa Bay Rays (7/23/09)

7

The Hall of Famers

Thirty-one former White Sox players and executives are enshrined in the National Baseball Hall of Fame. Old injustices and exclusions were finally addressed by the Veterans Committee, with their vote to admit Nellie Fox on March 5, 1997. But what about Billy Pierce and Minnie "Mr. White Sox" Minoso, or, for that matter, Guy Harris "Doc" White, a player from a much earlier era? White should head the list, based on his superlative pitching in the dead-ball era, but of these three former White Sox greats, Minoso likely stands the best chance of gaining admission because of his past service in the Negro Leagues, his personal charisma, and public visibility as a "good will ambassador" for the ballclub. The key for Minnie will undoubtedly be his Negro League connections. With just a little more than 10 productive major league seasons, the conventional wisdom is that he has not logged enough time in the big show to merit inclusion.

On the other hand, Bill Pierce appeared in two World Series and was a perennial league leader in all of the major pitching categories for a dozen years before winding it up with the Giants. Modest, self-effacing, and unwilling to engage in self-promotion, Pierce does not make an issue of it, and there is no one around to champion his cause or lead a campaign to get him elected into the Hall—but there should be, now, before it's too late. The Nellie Fox Society accomplished its decade-long mission but has not been heard from for quite some time. The time is at hand for them to jump-start efforts and launch a Billy Pierce Society.

There are, of course, other deserving Chisox alums spanning the various eras of team history to consider: Jim Kaat, Wilbur Wood, Tommy John, Ted Kluszewski, Frank Thomas, and "Dummy" Hoy are worthy contenders. In time, at least several of these names will be added to baseball's shrine.

Fourteen White Sox Hall of Famers played for Chicago five seasons or more—Luis Aparicio, Ray Schalk, Nellie Fox, Ted Lyons, Hoyt Wilhelm, Luke Appling, Harry Hooper, Red Faber, Eddie Collins, Carlton Fisk, Rich "Goose" Gossage, Ed Walsh, Early Wynn, and George Davis.

Appling, Faber, and Lyons are the only White Sox players who spent their entire careers with the White Sox. Ed Walsh and Ray Schalk might have fit into this category but were picked up by National League teams at the tail end of their playing careers. Jocko Conlon was elected as an umpire. Frank Chance worked for the ballclub, but illness prevented him from assuming his managerial duties in 1924. Hank Greenberg, Bill Veeck, and Charles Comiskey served in a front-office capacity. The other White Sox inductees included in this grouping played in one or more games with the team.

Ray Schalk proudly displays his 1917 jersey during his 1955 visit to the Hall of Fame.

Luis Ernesto Aparicio

Shortstop
White Sox: 1956–62, 1968–70
Major leagues: 1956–73
Elected: 1984
Birthplace: Maracaibo, Venezuela
B: April 29, 1934
Bats right, throws right

	G	AB	H	AVG	RBI	R	2B	3B	HR	SA	SB
White Sox	1,511	5,856	1,576	.269	464	791	223	54	43	.348	318
Career	2,599	10,230	2,677	.262	791	1,335	394	92	83	.343	506

"Little Louie" Aparicio's impact upon baseball in the 1950s was immediate and far-reaching. In an era defined by slow-footed, long-distance home run hitters, Aparicio and his fellow Go-Go White Sox speedsters brought the stolen-base, hit-and-run offense back into vogue. Louie was a defensive specialist on the left-hand side of the diamond who possessed tremendous range and was gifted with a strong arm. He established numerous records in his career, including the most consecutive years leading the league in stolen bases (nine, 1956–64), most years leading the league in chances accepted, most double plays by a shortstop (1,553), most games by a shortstop (2,581), most assists by a shortstop (8,016), most years leading the league in games played by a shortstop (five), most putouts by a shortstop (4,548), and most chances accepted (12,564).

Lucius Benjamin Appling

Shortstop
White Sox: 1930–50
Major leagues: 1930–50
Elected: 1964
Birthplace: High Point, North Carolina
B: April 2, 1907
D: January 3, 1991
Batted right, threw right

	G	AB	H	AVG	RBI	R	2B	3B	HR	SA	SB
White Sox	2,422	8,857	2,749	.310	1,302	1,319	440	102	45	.398	179
Career	2,422	8,857	2,749	.310	1,302	1,319	440	102	45	.398	179

The "greatest White Sox Player of all time" (as determined by Chicago fans in two separate polls, one in 1949 and one in baseball's centennial year of 1969) held numerous longevity records by the time he retired in 1950. Luke Appling recorded 4,348 putouts and 7,218 assists and played in 2,422 games. These stood as American League records until Luis Aparicio eclipsed "Old Aches and Pains" in the 1970s. Luke led American League shortstops in double plays in 1936, 1937, and 1946, and possesses the league record for the highest batting average recorded by a shortstop playing in 100 or more games (.388, 1936). He was the first White Sox player to win a batting title, and he truly exemplified the spirit of the White Sox for two decades.

Charles Albert Bender

Pitcher
White Sox: 1925
Major leagues: 1903–17, 1925
Elected: 1953
Birthplace: Brainerd, Minnesota
B: May 5, 1883
D: May 22, 1954
Batted right, threw right

	W	L	Pct	ERA	G	CG	IP	H	BB	K	ShO
White Sox	0	0	.000	18.00	1	0	1	1	1	1	0
Career	210	128	.621	2.45	459	261	3,028	2,645	712	1,711	41

"Chief" Bender never appreciated the nickname given to him by his teammates and would always sign his autographs *Charley* Bender. Bender was half German, half Chippewa, and every inch a Hall of Fame pitcher whose greatest years were spent in Philadelphia playing for Connie Mack's pennant-winning ballclubs of the dead-ball era. Bender authored two no-hitters and twice won 20 games. He was hired as a White Sox coach in 1925 by former teammate Eddie Collins and remained with the ballclub through the end of the 1926 season.

The 42-year-old pitching coach was activated by Collins on July 21, 1925, because of a heavy schedule of barnstorming games the Sox were required to play on their off-days. Before World War II, it was common practice for major league owners to stage exhibition games against local sandlot teams in backwater locales during extended road trips. As a tune-up for upcoming games in Battle Creek and Saginaw, Michigan, Bender took the mound in Comiskey Park on July 21 against the Boston Red Sox. He pitched his final major league inning, allowing a walk and a home run.

Steven Norman Carlton

Pitcher
White Sox: 1986
Major leagues: 1965–88
Elected: 1994
Birthplace: Miami, Florida
B: December 22, 1944
Bats left, throws left

	W	L	Pct	ERA	G	CG	IP	H	BB	K	ShO
White Sox	4	3	.571	3.69	10	0	63⅓	58	25	40	0
Career	329	244	.574	3.22	741	254	5,216⅔	4,672	1,833	4,136	55

"Lefty" Carlton was claimed off of the waiver list by general manager Ken Harrelson on August 12, 1986. Three days later the enigmatic "Hawk" acquired George Foster, another aging National Leaguer, through interleague waivers. Both players were fast approaching the end of their long and distinguished careers. And in light of Harrelson's determination to trade Tom Seaver to an East Coast team in order to promote a younger player to the roster, it was curious that he would stake a claim for the veteran hurler at the tail end of a losing season when there was virtually no chance of moving up in the standings. Steve Carlton lost his first American League game the same day he reported to the ballclub. However, Lefty showed flashes of his former brilliance in his first AL win on August 17 against the Milwaukee Brewers. In that same game, Carlton pitched in his 5,000th major league inning.

Steve Carlton was released at the end of the season when the front office decided to recommit its resources to building up the depleted farm system.

Frank LeRoy Chance

First baseman
White Sox: 1924
Major leagues: 1898–1914
Elected: 1946
Birthplace: Fresno, California
B: September 9, 1877
D: September 15, 1924
Batted left, threw right

	G	AB	H	AVG	RBI	R	2B	3B	HR	SA	SB
Career	1,286	4,293	1,271	.296	596	798	200	79	20	.393	405

Frank Chance never officially managed the White Sox in a regular season game, but he was a salaried employee from December 1923 until April 1924 during his long period of convalescence.

The "Peerless Leader" was only 27 years old when he was hired to manage the Cubs in 1905, replacing Frank Selee. As player/manager and the first baseman immortalized in Franklin P. Adams' verse "Tinker to Evers to Chance," he guided the Chicago National League ballclub to four World Series appearances in 1906–08 and 1910.

Edward Trowbridge Collins

Second baseman
White Sox: 1914–26
Major leagues: 1906–30
Elected: 1939
Birthplace: Tarrytown, New York
B: May 2, 1887
D: March 25, 1951
Batted left, threw right

	G	AB	H	AVG	RBI	R	2B	3B	HR	SA	SB
White Sox	1,670	6,064	2,005	.331	803	1,063	265	102	31	.423	366
Career	2,826	9,949	3,311	.333	1,299	1,818	437	187	47	.428	743

Playing under the alias "Sullivan," Eddie Collins made his big-league debut with the Philadelphia A's at the old 39th Street Grounds in 1906. Collins was arguably the greatest second baseman of all time—certainly in White Sox history. He won the Chalmers Award (forerunner of the Most Valuable Player) in 1914, and he held several distinguished records for second basemen, including most games (2,651), most putouts (6,527), most assists (7,629), most chances accepted (14,156), and most years leading the American League in fielding (9). Collins logged 25 years in the American League—a record for longevity in the junior circuit.

Charles Albert Comiskey

First baseman
White Sox: 1900–1931
Major leagues: 1882–94
Elected: 1939
Birthplace: Chicago
B: August 15, 1859
D: October 26, 1931
Batted right, threw right

	G	AB	H	AVG	RBI	R	2B	3B	HR	SA	SB
Career	1,390	5,796	1,531	.264	467	994	206	68	29	.338	378

Charles Comiskey was one of the early inductees into baseball's Hall of Fame. He was welcomed into the lodge on June 12, 1939, because of his contributions to the game as a first baseman who revolutionized infield play, as a manager who guided his St. Louis Browns to four American Association pennants (1885, 1886, 1887, and 1888), and as a cofounder of the American League who overcame impossible odds to anchor his team on the South Side of Chicago.

In their haste to portray the Old Roman as a miserly villain for his mistreatment of the eight Black Sox players who were banned from baseball for life, latter-day historians are unable to justify in their own minds Comiskey's well-deserved inclusion in baseball's Hall of Fame. Nowhere was this unflattering view more evident than in Ken Burns' documentary history of the national pastime, aired nationwide on Public Broadcasting in the fall of 1994. Burns identified for his viewers all but one member of the 1939 Hall of Fame class—Charles Comiskey.

The simplistic, overstated stereotype of the Old Roman as a parsimonious despot ignores the high levels of respect shown him by the citizens of Chicago during his lifetime.

Separated by two generations, Charles Comiskey and Bill Veeck had much in common. The Sox founder and the maverick owner were sired by wealthy and prominent Chicago men who were already well-known public figures when their sons were born. And yet the accomplishments of Charles Comiskey and Bill Veeck far exceeded the work of their fathers. Each man introduced radical new elements to the game of baseball. Throughout their lifetimes, these pioneering rebels strove to provide first-class accommodations to the fans. They both experienced the extremes of success and failure—and remained too long in the game they loved, unaware that baseball had simply passed them by.

History regards Veeck as the hero and Comiskey as the bad guy. But without Charles A. Comiskey to provide the bedrock foundation, one can only wonder where this great game would be today.

John Bertrand Conlan

Outfielder
White Sox: 1934–35
Major leagues: 1934–35
Elected: 1974
Birthplace: Chicago
B: December 6, 1899
D: April 16, 1989
Batted left, threw left

	G	AB	H	AVG	RBI	R	2B	3B	HR	SA	SB
White Sox	128	365	96	.263	31	55	18	4	0	.334	5
Career	128	365	96	.263	31	55	18	4	0	.334	5

"Jocko" Conlan was voted into the Hall of Fame because of his contributions as an umpire who officiated National League games from 1941 to 1964. He sported a polka-dot tie and an outside chest protector, and was respected for his personal integrity, knowledge of the rule book, and defense of the honorable profession he had chosen after his playing career.

Conlan broke in with Wichita of the Western League in 1920 and logged many years in the minors before he joined the Sox as a reserve outfielder in 1934. He got his first taste of umpiring in 1935 when Red Ormsby was overcome with heat exhaustion during a White Sox–Browns game. With no other official present that afternoon, Conlan, with Jimmie Dykes' blessing, volunteered his services. He formally launched his umpiring career in 1936 in the New York–Pennsylvania League.

George Stacey Davis

Infield
White Sox: 1902, 1904–1909
Major Leagues: 1890–1909
Elected: 1998
Birthplace: Cohoes, New York
B: August 23, 1870
D: October 17, 1940
Batted left and right, threw right

	G	AB	H	AVG	RBI	R	2B	3B	HR	SA	SB
White Sox	856	3,035	785	.259	377	393	140	32	6	.332	162
Career	2,372	9,045	2,665	.295	1,440	1,545	453	163	73	.405	619

History had all but forgotten this slick-fielding shortstop from the dead-ball era when the Veterans Committee gave the nod to George Davis and elected him to the Hall of Fame—89 years after he retired and 58 years from the time of his death. Supporters of William Ellsworth "Dummy" Hoy, another ex–National Leaguer and ex–White Sox outfielder from that same period, were bitterly disappointed at the selection of Davis on March 3, 1998, over their favorite. Hoy was a deaf mute who accomplished much despite his handicap. But Davis was equally deserving, if not more so. In a long and meritorious 20-year career, Davis compiled 2,665 hits, a .295 batting average, and 619 stolen bases. Davis, who batted from both sides of the plate, spent much of his career in the employ of two ballclubs: the New York Giants and the White Sox. At a time when big offensive numbers were in general decline, Davis hit over .300 nine consecutive years and reeled off a then-record 33-game hitting streak in 1893 while with the Giants. On June 14 of that year, he became the first player in big-league history to hit a home run and a triple in the same inning.

He joined the White Sox under a dark cloud in 1902 but played well and led the league in fielding percentage. Challenging baseball's reserve clause, which bound a player to whatever team he played for or happened to be traded to, Davis refused to report to the White Sox in 1903, hoping to rejoin the Giants for more money. The matter went to court, and Davis lost. He accepted his fate, rejoined Comiskey's team, and again led all American League shortstops in fielding in 1905. His experience and skills were important factors in the memorable 1906 Hitless Wonder season and a stunning World Series triumph over the Cubs that fall. In that memorable showdown, he hit .308 and became only the second of 12 players to ever steal home in a World Series game. He retired after the 1909 season as the all-time leader in games played, assists, and total chances by a shortstop. In 1910 Davis managed the Des Moines team of the Western League—the Old Roman, Charles Comiskey, held a stake in the club. From 1913 through 1918 Davis coached baseball at Amherst College before disappearing from the public eye. Decades later, researchers discovered that this once brilliant shortstop had died in anonymity in a Philadelphia nursing home in 1940.

Lawrence Eugene Doby

Outfield
White Sox: 1956–1957, 1959, Manager 1978
Major Leagues: 1947–1959
Elected: 1998
Birthplace: Camden, South Carolina
B: December 13, 1924
D: June 18, 2003
Batted left, threw right

	G	AB	H	AVG	RBI	R	2B	3B	HR	SA	SB
White Sox	280	978	269	.275	190	147	50	6	38	.455	3
Career	1,533	5,348	1,515	.283	970	960	243	52	253	.490	47

Although Larry Doby joined the White Sox late in his career, he was deeply connected to Chicago in many ways and was a very close friend of the late Bill Veeck, who arranged Doby's major league debut in Comiskey Park the afternoon of July 5, 1947. Thus, Doby made history by becoming the first African American player to appear in the American League, although he was overshadowed for much of his career by Jackie Robinson. "The only difference [was] that Jackie Robinson got all of the publicity," Doby said in later interviews. "You didn't hear much about what I was going through because the media didn't want to repeat the same story."

Doby contributed mightily to the great Cleveland ballclubs of the late 1940s and early 1950s after starring with the Newark Eagles of the Negro Leagues for four seasons, where he played alongside Monte Irvin. A seven-time All-Star, Doby led the American League twice in homers and was a member of the White Sox on two separate occasions, (1956–1957 and 1959). Acquired from Cleveland on October 25, 1955, for Chico Carrasquel and Jim Busby, Doby was hampered by groin injuries his first year, but supplied much-needed power from the left-hand side of the plate and a brilliant right hook delivered to the jaw of Yankees pitcher Art Ditmar in one of the most famous baseball brawls ever, on June 13, 1957, at Comiskey Park. No one could ever recall seeing a black man engage in fisticuffs with a white player in a big-league game. Correspondent Shirley Povich of the *Sporting News* called it the "complete emancipation of the America Negro in America's National Game." Traded to Baltimore on December 3, 1957, for Ray Moore, Tito Francona, and Billy Goodman, he returned to the Sox two years later, but only briefly following his release by the Detroit Tigers early in the season. In a terrible, one-sided swap, Cleveland had sent Doby to Detroit for Francona, who went on to hit .363 for the Tribe in 1959.

With his stateside career all but ended, Doby joined Don Newcombe in Japan in 1962. They were the first former big-leaguers to play for a Japanese professional team, the Chunichi Dragons. He later coached for the Expos, Indians, and White Sox. In 1978 Veeck hired old No. 14 to manage the Sox in the second half of the season—but it was a short-lived, failed publicity stunt. In 1998 the Hall of Fame opened its doors, and Doby stepped inside. Five years later he was gone from our midst. Hearing the news of Larry Doby's passing in 2003, his former manager Al Lopez noted: "We became good friends in Chicago. He was also close to Al Rosen and really close to Joe Gordon. Since I spoke Spanish, I used to read him his mail that came in from the general manager of one of the winter league teams in the islands that wanted him to play there. It's a sad day today."

Hugh Duffy

Outfielder
White Sox: 1910–11
Major leagues: 1888–1906
Elected: 1945
Birthplace: Cranston, Rhode Island
B: November 26, 1866
D: October 19, 1954
Batted right, threw right

	G	AB	H	AVG	RBI	R	2B	3B	HR	SA	SB
Career	1,736	7,043	2,283	1,324	1,299	1,551	324	116	105	.448	583

Sprightly Hugh Duffy won baseball's first Triple Crown and achieved the highest single-season batting average of all time (.438 in 1894). Duffy broke in with the Chicago White Stockings (Cubs) of the National League in 1888 as Billy Sunday's replacement in right field, and he was one of the top five stars of the 1890s.

Duffy's career as a manager never quite matched the success he enjoyed as a player. He guided the Phillies, Red Sox, White Sox, Braves, and teams in the International League, American Association, and New England League, achieving only meager results. In his eight years of managing at the major league level, Duffy finished over .500 only twice, and never higher than fourth. Two of those years were spent with the White Sox. His 1911 team finished in fourth place with a 77–74 record, but trailed the leader by 24 games. Duffy was voted into the Hall of Fame in 1945 by the Veterans Committee.

John Joseph Evers

Second baseman
White Sox: 1924
Major leagues: 1902–29
Elected: 1956
Birthplace: Troy, New York
B: July 21, 1881
D: March 28, 1947
Batted left, threw right

	G	AB	H	AVG	RBI	R	2B	3B	HR	SA	SB
White Sox	1	3	0	.000	1	0	0	0	0	.000	0
Career	1,783	6,134	1,658	.270	538	919	216	70	12	.334	324

Johnny Evers was the last surviving member of the famous Chicago Cubs double-play combination celebrated in the verse of Franklin P. Adams. The "Trojan," as he was called in his playing days, joined the Cubs in 1902 and was the middle man in the Tinker to Evers to Chance combination. He won a Chalmers Award (MVP) in 1914, and he managed the Cubs in 1913 and 1921. Evers was hired as a White Sox coach at baseball's annual winter meeting in December 1923. He took over the ballclub the next season when his boss Frank Chance was hospitalized with a life-threatening bronchial ailment. Evers never expected to manage the Sox, nor was it a task particularly to his liking. An attack of appendicitis took him away from the ballclub in midseason, by which time the Sox had claimed the American League cellar.

Urban Clarence Faber

Pitcher
White Sox: 1914–33
Major leagues: 1914–33
Elected: 1964
Birthplace: Cascade, Iowa
B: September 6, 1888
D: September 25, 1976
Batted left and right, threw right

	W	L	Pct	ERA	G	CG	IP	H	BB	K	ShO
White Sox	254	212	.545	3.15	669	275	4,087⅓	4,106	1,213	1,471	30
Career	254	212	.545	3.15	669	275	4,087⅓	4,106	1,213	1,471	30

The old redhead from the Iowa cornfields would have easily won 300 games playing for another ballclub. Faber made the best of a tough situation, though at times he bitterly complained about a lack of fielding support behind him that cost him many close decisions. Red Faber won 20 or more games four times in his career—three of them coming in succession (1920–22). He was the last of the legal spitballers, and though he was notoriously weak as a hitter (.134 career average), he swung the bat from both sides of the plate. During one stretch in 1915 he drew seven consecutive walks.

Faber coached for Ted Lyons in 1946 through 1948, and in later years he made numerous appearances on behalf of the ballclub at old-timer gatherings with his former battery mate Ray Schalk.

Carlton Ernest Fisk

Catcher-DH
White Sox: 1981–1993
Major Leagues: 1969–1993
Elected: 2000
Birthplace: Bellows Falls, Vermont
B: December 26, 1947
Bats right, throws right

	G	AB	H	AVG	RBI	R	2B	3B	HR	SA	SB
White Sox	1,421	4,896	1,259	.257	762	649	214	14	214	.438	67
Career	2,499	8,756	2,356	.269	1,330	1,276	421	47	376	.457	128

Carlton Fisk spent a lot of time brooding and boycotting U.S. Cellular Field following his unceremonious release in 1993. It was a painful eulogy to a proud player's remarkable career. He lived in south suburban Lockport, Illinois, coached youth baseball, and appeared at various baseball card shows to sign autographs, but he was rarely seen in the vicinity of 35th and Shields until an inevitable thaw occurred in the frosty relationship between Fisk and his former employer. In 2000 Fisk was named to the White Sox's All-Century Team, along with Harold Baines and Ozzie Guillen, representing the decade of the 1980s. The honor coincided with his election into the Hall of Fame in just his second year of eligibility. The years of rancor melted away; the contract hassles with Jerry Reinsdorf, the embarrassing decision to move Carlton to left field when he was chasing records for catching longevity, battling injuries, and missing out on the chance at the really big money in the collusion year when the owners conspired not to sign each other's top free agents.

"You know, it seems that throughout my entire career, nobody has ever said, 'We like you. We need you. We want you.' Why? Because it takes the hammer away from them," Fisk bitterly reflected. However, rapprochement was a sweet thing. Fisk was honored by the ballclub and threw out the ceremonial first pitch to former teammate Harold Baines. "I don't know if it's a long time in coming," he said. "I don't know if it needs to be considered that way. But this is fairly comfortable being at the ballpark. I like it."

Carlton Fisk received 397 votes (79.6 percent)—well above the required 75 percent required for admission into the Hall of Fame. He said it was a difficult decision for him as to which team's headgear he would be wearing in the induction ceremony, but it was academic. He had played more games in Chicago than in Boston, but that didn't count for much in the scheme of things. Fisk was a native New Englander, and his dramatic arm-waving "shot" in the 1975 World Series was one of those rare historic moments that cemented the player to the team and the birth of a modern legend. Moreover, he had gone to work for Boston general manager Dan Duquette as a special assistant and had repaired his relationship with the Bosox since retiring from the game. It was disappointing to his Chicago fans but less than a surprise when Fisk ascended the dais wearing his Red Sox hat.

Meanwhile, Jerry Reinsdorf and his staff never stopped trying to mend the fences with Carlton Fisk. His number was retired, and on August 7, 2005, a life-sized statue of the Hall of Fame catcher was unveiled in the new Monument Park area of the center-field fan deck concourse, next to previous honorees Minnie Minoso and Charles Comiskey. Was this latest olive branch extended by Reinsdorf and company enough to engender Carlton's future goodwill toward team management and fans, or was his bruised sensitivity over a perceived lack of respect still the burning issue? Only Fisk can answer that question.

Jacob Nelson Fox

Infield
White Sox: 1950–1963
Major Leagues: 1947–1965
Elected: 1997
Birthplace: St. Thomas, Pennsylvania
B: December 25, 1927
D: December 1, 1975
Batted left, threw right

	G	AB	H	AVG	RBI	R	2B	3B	HR	SA	SB
White Sox	2,115	8,486	2,470	.291	740	1,187	335	104	35	.367	73
Career	2,367	9,232	2,663	.288	790	1,279	355	112	35	.363	76

Just when the fans of Chicago were about ready to abandon all hope, the Veterans Committee relented and voted Nellie into the Hall of Fame. On August 3, 1997, he took his rightful place in baseball's Valhalla with fellow inductees Phil Niekro, Tommy Lasorda, and Negro Leagues star Willie Wells. In other years, he had fallen short by an eyelash. In January 1985, for example, Nellie Fox was named on 295 of the 395 baseball writers' ballots (74.7 percent), but the Hall of Fame decided not to round the number up to the required

75 percent, despite strong protests from his many fans and veteran *Chicago Tribune* sportswriter Jerome Holtzman.

A decade later, in March 1996, Fox received the necessary 75 percent of the committee's vote, but the rules allowed just one modern player elected, and that honor went to ex-Tiger and ex-Phillie Jim Bunning, who had more votes. Recognizing the lingering injustice of the situation, a group of prominent attorneys and business leaders in Chicago formed The Nellie Fox Society for the purpose of initiating a letter-writing campaign and to whip up public support in the belief that if Fox had played in New York for much of his career instead of Chicago, his induction would have been pro forma many years earlier.

Of course, there are many old-time players in this situation whose time had passed and were beyond the memory of the current generation of writers and, for that matter, the Veterans Committee. Complicating matters was the rumored disaffection of Al Lopez, who had allegedly blackballed Fox for reasons that remain unclear today, although it may have had something to do with issues of temperament, personality, self-discipline, and demeanor. Fox was more free-spirited than his best pal and roomie, Billy Pierce, and this may have been a contributing factor. In the baseball world, still waters run deep, and no one is talking. Nevertheless, it was a joyous day for Nellie's widow, Joanne, and their two daughters when word came down that he had at last made it in. The White Sox marked the occasion with a second Nellie Fox Day on August 16, 1997, and invited the old gang—Jim Landis, Al Smith, Gary Peters, Ken McBride, Chuck Comiskey, Minnie Minoso, Mrs. Fox, and others to take part in pregame festivities before a rare Comiskey Park sellout.

The little man from St. Thomas, Pennsylvania, who holds the record for most consecutive years leading the league in singles (seven, 1954–1960), would have been very touched by the honor. Everyone, it seems, is a Fox fan. In a 1950s fan poll, the late Mayor Richard J. Daley chimed in with his preference: "I'll have to say Fox is my favorite because he is energetic, hard-working, and an enthusiastic ballplayer. Fox symbolizes what you like to see not only in a ballplayer but in government, in business, and in family life. He hustles all the time and he plays with his heart, as well as with his hand and mind." The late Paul Richards, who helped develop Nellie into a star, once said of his pupil: "I've never seen anybody who wanted to play more than Fox did. In spring training, you had to run him off the field to get him to rest, and I mean literally run him off."

Richard Michael Gossage

Pitcher
White Sox: 1972–1976
Major Leagues: 1972–1994
Elected: 2008
Birthplace: Colorado Springs, Colorado
B: July 5, 1951
Bats right, throws right

	W	L	Pct	ERA	G	CG	IP	H	BB	K	ShO
White Sox	29	36	.446	3.60	188	16	584⅔	534	288	419	0
Career	124	107	.537	3.01	1,002	16	1,809⅓	1,497	732	1,502	0

In the early 1970s three outstanding pitching prospects throwing 90-plus mph dominated the Midwest League, the White Sox's longtime Class A affiliate. Bart Johnson, Terry Forster, and Rich "Goose" Gossage seemed ticketed for stardom. In the parlance of baseball, they could "really bring it." Powder River—aspirin chuckers each. Johnson, who had designs on becoming an outfielder, was 16–4 for the Appleton Foxes in 1969 and was expected to become the next South Side ace, ranked ahead of both Forster and Gossage. "Trees" Forster was the first to break through as a star reliever for Chuck Tanner's White Sox in 1972, while Gossage, putting up an amazing 18–2 record at Appleton in 1971, did not progress to the major leagues as quickly as his two fire-balling teammates.

Chicago fans glimpsed the Goose for the first time on June 24, 1971, when the youngster was summoned from Appleton to pitch in the 22nd Annual Boy's Benefit Game against the Cubs in Wrigley Field. But, of the three top prospects, only Gossage fulfilled the expectations of super scout Bill Kimball, who had charted the kid's progress at Wasson High School and Southern Colorado State College in Colorado Springs, before he was drafted by Chicago in the ninth round of the 1970 amateur draft. "He has a fine fastball and is developing a change-up," commented Tanner, his first big-league manager in June 1971, who personally traveled to Cedar Rapids that summer to watch Gossage pitch. After the game, he instructed Gossage on the mechanics of delivering an effective change-up. "Our scouts are extremely high on him." And with good reason.

The Goose enjoyed a breakout season in 1975, leading the American League in saves, while yielding only three home runs and 99 hits in 142 innings. It was a preview of his future greatness—attained only after he was traded by Bill Veeck and Roland Hemond to Pittsburgh with Forster in an 11th hour deal for the one-year "rent-a-player" Richie Zisk. It was another monumental and embarrassing Veeck blunder.

The Goose played 22 seasons, from 1972 to 1994, for nine different teams, racked up 310 career saves and attained his greatest glory as a New York Yankee, although, by the end of his career, his final save total had dropped to fourth place all-time. On August 4, 1994, Gossage became the third pitcher in major league history to appear in 1,000 games. It took a while for the Goose to obtain the necessary 75 percent voting threshold to gain admission to the Hall of Fame—and he was openly critical of the process. Refreshingly outspoken and opinionated, Gossage was candid in his sharp statements concerning many baseball-related issues. He insisted that Mark McGwire and other steroid users should be barred from HOF induction—not an unreasonable viewpoint. He accused his former manager Billy Martin of mishandling pitching staffs and questioned the validity of awarding the one-inning save. In the days of the Goose, the closer earned his save the hard way—two, sometimes three, innings of work to nail it down. In 1995 the city of Colorado Springs dedicated the Rich "Goose" Gossage Youth Sports Complex, which features five fields for youth baseball and softball competition.

Henry Benjamin Greenberg

Outfielder
White Sox: 1959–63
Major leagues: 1930–47
Elected: 1956
Birthplace: New York City
B: January 1, 1911
D: September 4, 1986
Batted right and left, threw right

	G	AB	H	AVG	RBI	R	2B	3B	HR	SA	SB
Career	1,394	5,193	1,628	.313	1,276	1,051	379	71	331	.605	16

Burly Hank Greenberg tied an American League record for most home runs in a season by a right-handed hitter when he clubbed 58 round-trippers in 1938. Greenberg was one of the most feared sluggers of his era. He won the Most Valuable Player award in 1935 and again in 1940 when he powered the Detroit Tigers to a near pennant. Greenberg moved from the playing field to the front office with Bill Veeck in 1948. He served as general manager of the Indians until 1957, joining the White Sox as a vice president two years later. Greenberg added the title of general manager to his other duties in 1961 at Art Allyn's insistence, but bowed out of the day-to-day affairs of the ballclub later that summer. He remained in the organization as an officer until 1963.

Clark Calvin Griffith

Pitcher
White Sox: 1901–02
Major leagues: 1891–1914
Elected: 1946
Birthplace: Stringtown, Missouri
B: November 20, 1869
D: October 27, 1955
Batted right, threw right

	W	L	Pct	ERA	G	CG	IP	H	BB	K	ShO
White Sox	39	16	.709	3.34	63	46	479⅔	522	97	118	8
Career	237	146	.619	3.31	453	337	3,385⅔	3,670	774	955	22

Clark Griffith attained stardom playing for the crosstown Cubbies (then known as the Colts) in the 1890s. He was a strenuous advocate of player rights who organized a strike of Pacific Coast League players in 1893 after the owner of the Oakland Oaks refused to award his players their back pay. Griffith walked out on the ballclub and found employment as a vaudeville entertainer along San Francisco's Barbary Coast.

The rangy right-hander won 20 or more games six years in a row as a member of the Colts. But in 1901 he led a revolt of unhappy, underpaid National Leaguers who bolted their teams in order to accept generous pay raises from Ban Johnson's fledgling American League. Griffith was hired by Comiskey as a player/manager, and he succeeded in convincing fellow teammates Sandow Mertes and Jimmy Callahan to join him on the South Side. Griffith won 24 games to help the Sox capture the first official American League pennant in a closely contested race against the Boston Puritans. At the conclusion of the 1902 season, Griffith moved to New York where he spent six seasons managing the New York Highlanders.

Griffith piloted the Cincinnati Redlegs (1909–11) before taking over in Washington. He moved into the front office in an executive capacity, serving as president of the Washington Senators from 1920 until his death in 1955. Griffith's life was a series of endless contradictions. His early militancy on behalf of player rights was at odds with his reputation as a notorious pinchpenny owner who was reputed to be even closer with a buck than his former boss, Charles Comiskey.

Harry Bartholomew Hooper

Outfielder
White Sox: 1921–25
Major leagues: 1909–25
Elected: 1971
Birthplace: Bell Station, California
B: August 24, 1887
D: December 18, 1974
Batted left, threw right

	G	AB	H	AVG	RBI	R	2B	3B	HR	SA	SB
White Sox	662	2,515	759	.302	320	441	143	30	45	.436	75
Career	2,308	8,785	2,466	.281	1,136	1,429	389	160	75	.387	375

In the years leading up to World War I, Harry Hooper anchored Boston's "Million Dollar Outfield," which also included Duffy Lewis and Tris Speaker. Hooper was a fine defensive outfielder and excellent leadoff man who always maintained a decent batting average. His .403 on-base leadoff percentage during a 12-year period (1909–20) reflects his value to their organization.

Hooper was acquired in a trade with the Red Sox on March 4, 1921, for Shano Collins and Nemo Leibold. As a member of the White Sox he led the league in double plays three years running, 1922–24. When Harry was flanked by Johnny Mostil and Bibb Falk for five seasons, the White Sox sported (at the very least) a "*Half* Million Dollar Outfield."

George Clyde Kell

Third baseman
White Sox: 1954–56
Major leagues: 1943–57
Elected: 1983
Birthplace: Swifton, Arkansas
B: August 23, 1922
D: March 24, 2009
Batted right, threw right

	G	AB	H	AVG	RBI	R	2B	3B	HR	SA	SB
White Sox	220	742	225	.303	140	76	39	1	14	.415	3
Career	1,795	6,702	2,054	.306	870	881	385	50	78	.414	51

The search for a third baseman who could blend hitting and fielding continued through the 1950s. The hot corner had been a perennial Achilles' heel since Jimmie Dykes retired from active duty. The expensive acquisition of George Kell on May 23, 1954, proved to be only a short-term solution to the problem, however.

Kell, a husky redhead who came up with the Detroit Tigers as a wartime replacement, won the American League batting championship in 1949 with a glittering .343 average. He was a good contact hitter and fair glove man who was suffering from the aftereffects of a sacroiliac condition in 1954 when Red Sox owner Tom Yawkey agreed to sell him to Chicago for $100,000 and infielder Grady Hatton. It was the first time during Yawkey's ownership that he sold one of his star players, but Kell was considered damaged goods and beyond his prime.

Injuries limited Kell's playing time in 1954 and again in 1955. But he outpaced all other White Sox hitters in 1955 with a .312 average—the ninth time in 10 years he surpassed the .300 mark. The old veteran was traded to Baltimore with Mike Fornieles, Bob Nieman, and Connie Johnson for outfielder Dave Philley and pitcher Jim Wilson on May 21, 1956.

Robert Granville Lemon

Pitcher
White Sox: 1977–78
Major leagues: 1941–58
Elected: 1976
Birthplace: San Bernardino, California
B: September 22, 1920
D: January 12, 2000
Batted right, threw right

	W	L	Pct	ERA	G	CG	IP	H	BB	K	ShO
Career	207	128	.618	3.23	460	188	2,850	2,559	1,251	1,277	31

Bob Lemon won 20 or more games seven times during his tour of duty with the Cleveland Indians. He was also one of the best hitting pitchers of his era, compiling a .284 lifetime batting average.

Lemon was named Minor League Manager of the Year in 1966 after his Seattle ballclub won a Pacific Coast League title. He managed the expansion Kansas City Royals to a respectable showing from 1970 to 1972 before agreeing to terms with Bill Veeck after the 1976 season. Bob Lemon was at the controls during the 1977 South Side Hitmen season and certainly did not deserve to be fired. Veeck was impatient and seemed more concerned about his short-term attendance problems than building a winner behind a manager with a proven track record of success. Lemon enjoyed the last laugh by taking the 1978 Yankees all the way to a world championship after being fired by Veeck on June 30.

Alfonso Ramon Lopez

Catcher
White Sox: 1957–65, 1968–69
Major leagues: 1928–47
Elected: 1977
Birthplace: Tampa, Florida
B: August 20, 1908
D: October 30, 2005
Batted right, threw right

	G	AB	H	AVG	RBI	R	2B	3B	HR	SA	SB
Career	1,950	5,916	1,547	.261	652	613	206	42	52	.337	46

Al Lopez probably would not have been elected to the Hall of Fame if his playing record had been the sole criterion for inclusion. The "Señor" from Tampa attained his greatest fame as manager of the Cleveland Indians and Chicago White Sox over a 16-year period (1949–64) when the New York Yankees appeared in the World Series every year except 1954 and 1959 when Lopez-led teams stole their thunder, if only briefly.

Al Lopez held several records in his lengthy catching career for the Boston Braves and other teams. He shared the record for most years catching 100 or more games (12) with Gabby Hartnett of the Cubs, and until the 1980s he topped all major league catchers with 1,918 appearances behind the plate.

In 1948, following his retirement from active duty, Lopez took over as manager of the Cleveland Indians' Triple A affiliate at Indianapolis. He was promoted to the parent club in 1951 and remained in charge of the Tribe until the conclusion of the 1956 season when he was lured to Chicago by Chuck Comiskey and John Rigney.

Lopez remained with the Sox as a manager and vice president for close to a decade. Only Jimmie Dykes enjoyed greater managerial longevity on the South Side.

Theodore Amar Lyons

Pitcher
White Sox: 1923–46
Major leagues: 1923–46
Elected: 1955
Birthplace: Lake Charles, Louisiana
B: December 28,1900
D: July 25, 1986
Batted right and left, threw right

	W	L	Pct	ERA	G	CG	IP	H	BB	K	ShO
White Sox	260	230	.531	3.67	594	356	4,161	4,489	1,121	1,073	27
Career	260	230	.531	3.67	594	356	4,161	4,489	1,121	1,073	27

Teddy Lyons was one of the great gentlemen of the game who deserved a better fate than playing for a perennial loser. Exiled to the South Side at a time when the ballclub's fortunes were at their lowest ebb, Lyons quietly went about the business of baseball and rolled up a career victory total unequaled in team history. The "Baylor Bearcat" led the league in victories in 1925 and 1927. In 1939 he tossed 42 consecutive innings without yielding a base on balls. The streak began on June 11 and ended on June 23. Late in Teddy's career, Jimmie Dykes confined his mound work to Sundays only. His effectiveness on the Sabbath day was measured by his ability to go the route. Lyons completed all 20 of his 1942 starting assignments.

The knuckleballing Sox ace was also a decent hitter from both sides of the plate. He tied an American League record in St. Louis on July 28, 1935, by banging out two doubles in the same inning. Always a Comiskey Park favorite, Lyons was voted the greatest right-handed pitcher in White Sox history in a poll of the fans conducted in 1969.

Edd J. Roush

Outfielder
White Sox: 1913
Major leagues: 1913–31
Elected: 1962
Birthplace: Oakland City, Indiana
B: May 8, 1893
D: March 21, 1988
Batted left, threw left

	G	AB	H	AVG	RBI	R	2B	3B	HR	SA	SB
White Sox	9	10	1	.100	0	2	0	0	0	.100	2
Career	1,967	7,363	2,376	.323	981	1,099	339	183	67	.446	268

Edd Roush broke in with Evansville in 1912. He was purchased from the Lincoln club of the Western League and brought to Chicago as a reserve outfielder and pinch-hitter in August 1913. A year later he jumped to the Federal League, and thus a future Hall of Fame outfielder who went on to claim two National League batting titles (1917, 1919) was gone for good. The loss of Eddie Roush was Charles Comiskey's worst personnel miscalculation in the first two decades of his ownership and the first warning sign that the Old Roman's glory days were slipping away.

Charles Herbert Ruffing

Pitcher
White Sox: 1947
Major leagues: 1924–47
Elected: 1967
Birthplace: Granville, Illinois
B: May 3, 1904
D: February 17, 1986
Batted right, threw right

	W	L	Pct	ERA	G	CG	IP	H	BB	K	ShO
White Sox	3	5	.375	6.11	9	1	53	63	16	11	0
Career	273	225	.548	3.80	624	335	4,344	4,294	1,541	1,987	48

Charley Ruffing was a dismal failure with the Boston Red Sox, but a change of scenery had an uplifting effect on his sagging pitching career. He joined the New York Yankees in 1930 and went on to complete a long and successful run with the Bronx Bombers, despite a crippling disability that prevented him from running with any degree of authority. When he was a boy, Red Ruffing lost four toes on his left foot. He played in pain for much of his career.

Ruffing was released by the Yankees on September 20, 1946, and was signed as a free agent by Les O'Connor on December 6 of that year. The Sox were interested in acquiring bench help. In addition to his mound skills, Ruffing was one of the league's outstanding pinch-hitters. He collected 58 hits in 228 pinch-hitting appearances (.254) over the course of his career, but unfortunately only one of them came in a White Sox uniform. Red pitched sparingly in 1947 and was gone by the end of the year.

Raymond William Schalk

Catcher
White Sox: 1912–28
Major leagues: 1912–29
Elected: 1955
Birthplace: Harvey, Illinois
B: August 12, 1892
D: May 19, 1970
Batted right, threw right

	G	AB	H	AVG	RBI	R	2B	3B	HR	SA	SB
White Sox	1,755	5,304	1,345	.254	594	579	199	48	12	.316	176
Career	1,760	5,306	1,345	.253	595	579	199	48	12	.316	176

Ray "Cracker" Schalk was a brilliant backstop for 16 years, during which time the ballclub soared to the peaks and plummeted to the depths of despair. Through these extremes of success and failure, Schalk was a model of consistency. He held the major league record for most years leading the league in fielding his position (eight), most years leading catchers in putouts (nine), and most assists by a catcher in one league (1,810). He tied a major league record by making three assists in one inning on September 30, 1921, against Cleveland. Schalk caught four no-hitters in his career (Jim Scott, May 14, 1914, versus Washington; Joe Benz, May 31, 1914, versus Cleveland; Ed Cicotte, April 14, 1917, versus St. Louis; and Charlie Robertson's perfect game against Detroit on April 30, 1922). Ray led all American League catchers in double plays in 1923. After completing his stint as manager of the White Sox in 1928, he piloted teams in the International League and the American Association before retiring to the Chicago area, where he operated a bowling alley.

George Thomas Seaver

Pitcher
White Sox: 1984–86
Major leagues: 1967–86
Elected: 1992
Birthplace: Fresno, California
B: November 17, 1944
Bats right, throws right

	W	L	Pct	ERA	G	CG	IP	H	BB	K	ShO
White Sox	33	28	.540	3.66	81	17	547⅓	505	157	296	5
Career	311	205	.603	2.86	656	231	4,782⅔	3,971	1,390	3,640	61

White Sox general manager Roland Hemond stunned the baseball world when he announced the acquisition of Tom Seaver, one of the game's true immortals, on January 23, 1984. Seaver joined the Sox after the New York Mets inadvertently left him unprotected in the compensation draft after the Toronto Blue Jays signed reliever Dennis Lamp as a "Type A" free agent. With this three-time Cy Young Award winner on board for the 1984 season, the White Sox appeared to be a mortal cinch to repeat as divisional champs with a formidable starting rotation that also included LaMarr Hoyt, Richard Dotson, and Floyd Bannister.

Tom Seaver kept his end of the bargain by leading the staff in victories and shutouts. The crafty old veteran could not carry the ballclub alone, however, and his contributions were largely negated by the poor showing of his teammates. Seaver's 1985 season was full of milestones. He recorded his 300th career victory in fairy-tale fashion before a standing-room-only throng in Yankee Stadium on August 4. Yankees fans turned out to celebrate Phil Rizzuto Day, but all eyes were on Seaver in his first attempt to bag No. 300. The classy 39-year-old right-hander did not disappoint. Thousands of Yankees-hating Mets fans cheered Seaver's every delivery as he tossed a complete-game 4–1 victory. Five days later he fanned Milwaukee's Paul Molitor for career strikeout No. 3,500.

It was a season of superlatives for the future Hall of Famer, but at year's end he expressed the desire to be traded to an East Coast ballclub in order to be closer to his family. Ken Harrelson obliged Seaver on June 29, 1986, by trading him to the Boston Red Sox, where he would close out his career, for outfielder Steve "Psycho" Lyons.

Aloysius Harry Simmons

Outfield
White Sox: 1933–35
Major leagues: 1924–44
Elected: 1953
Birthplace: Milwaukee, Wisconsin
B: May 22, 1902
D: May 26, 1956
Batted right, threw right

	G	AB	H	AVG	RBI	R	2B	3B	HR	SA	SB
White Sox	412	1,688	532	.315	302	255	87	24	48	.480	12
Career	2,215	8,761	2,927	.334	1,827	1,507	539	149	307	.535	87

Al Simmons was a proud, intense competitor gifted with a splendid batting eye, despite a rather unusual "bucket-foot" stance at the plate. The Polish slugger from Milwaukee was the only player from all of the great A's teams of the late 1920s whose picture adorned the wall of old Connie Mack's office at Shibe Park. Simmons won the American League Most Valuable Player award in 1929 and league batting titles the following two seasons. He was sold to the White Sox with Jimmie Dykes and Mule Haas during the 1932 World Series, but never put up the same impressive numbers with Chicago, despite being the top vote-getter in 1933 All-Star balloting. Late in his career, Simmons set his sights on 3,000 career hits but came up short by only 73 safeties. He blamed his misfortune on himself and wondered what had possessed him to skip games earlier in his career.

William Louis Veeck Jr.

Owner
White Sox: 1959–61, 1976–80
Major leagues: 1933–80
Elected: 1993
Birthplace: Hinsdale, Illinois
B: February 9, 1914
D: January 2, 1986

Baseball's beloved showman dropped out of college in 1933 to launch his long and meritorious career in baseball. Bill Veeck went to work for his father's team, the Chicago Cubs, as an office boy, vendor, groundskeeper, and treasurer. In the 1930s he planted the fabled vines along the outfield walls of Wrigley Field but still toiled in the shadow of his illustrious dad, William Veeck Sr., who had been a popular sports columnist in Chicago until he joined the Cubs' front-office staff during the World War I period.

The son broke the mold to become a nationally renowned sports celebrity in his own right in the 1940s and 1950s, largely because of his whimsical and innovative style of sports entrepreneurship. Bill Veeck owned four baseball teams during his event-filled life: the Milwaukee Brewers of the American Association, the Cleveland Indians, the St. Louis Browns, and the White Sox. Veeck-owned teams won pennants in 1948 and 1959, but his election to the Hall of Fame had more to do with his genius for promotion, his identification with the common man, and his clear vision of baseball's future.

Veeck foresaw the coming labor struggles between the players and management in the late 1940s, and recommended to his fellow owners adaptation of the "Hollywood Studio system" of negotiated contracts that would have allowed the athletes limited free agency after seven years with one organization. Leslie O'Connor, secretary to commissioner Kenesaw Mountain Landis, advised Veeck in writing that "a little knowledge is a dangerous thing."

In the early 1950s Bill Veeck tried to expand baseball to the West Coast but was dismissed as a heretic until Walter O'Malley took credit for the idea later in the decade.

Bill Veeck was a Chicago original—an informed social critic of the American scene who was gifted with a fine sense of humor and appreciation for arts, music, and literature. He was the author of three acclaimed books: *Veeck as in Wreck, Thirty Tons a Day,* and *The Hustler's Handbook.*

Edward Augustine Walsh

Pitcher
White Sox: 1904–16
Major leagues: 1904–17
Elected: 1946
Birthplace: Plains, Pennsylvania
B: May 14, 1881
D: May 26, 1959
Batted right, threw right

	W	L	Pct	ERA	G	CG	IP	H	BB	K	ShO
White Sox	195	125	.609	1.81	426	249	2,946⅓	2,324	608	1,732	58
Career	195	126	.607	1.82	430	250	2,964⅓	2,346	617	1,736	58

The fans selected Ted Lyons as the greatest right-handed pitcher in a poll of White Sox supporters taken in 1969, but sadly they forgot Ed Walsh, whose exploits in the first decade of the century will never be duplicated. The big Irishman from the Pennsylvania coalfields broke in with the ballclub in 1904. In 1908, his greatest year, Walsh won 40 games (though the actual record suggests that "only" 36 victories were legitimate). He tied the American League record that season for most complete games pitched in succession (three)—a September 29 doubleheader sweep of the Boston Red Sox and the famous October 2, Cleveland showdown won by Addie Joss on the strength of a 1–0 perfect game.

The indestructible Walsh led the American League in appearances in 1907–08 and 1910–12. Though he never fulfilled his personal ambition of managing the Sox through a complete season, he got his taste of running a ballclub in 1920 on a full-time basis when he guided the Bridgeport, Connecticut, club of the Eastern League. Walsh umpired in the American League during the 1922 season before rejoining the White Sox as a coach in 1923. Ed left Chicago in 1926 to accept a one-year assignment coaching Notre Dame baseball before returning to the Sox in 1928.

His son, Ed Jr., a sickly boy plagued by rheumatic fever, appeared briefly with the Sox from 1928 to 1932. The singular highlight of Walsh Jr.'s abbreviated career occurred on July 26, 1933, when he fanned Joe DiMaggio in a Pacific Coast League game, ending Joltin Joe's 61-game hitting streak.

James Hoyt Wilhelm

Pitcher
White Sox: 1963–68
Major leagues: 1952–72
Elected: 1985
Birthplace: Huntersville, North Carolina
B: July 26, 1923
D: August 23, 2002
Batted right, threw right

	W	L	Pct	ERA	G	CG	IP	H	BB	K	ShO
White Sox	41	33	.554	1.92	361	0	675⅔	465	167	521	0
Career	143	122	.540	2.52	1,070	20	2,254	1,757	778	1,610	5

Hoyt Wilhelm was the first pitcher to be inducted into the Hall of Fame possessing fewer than 150 career victories. The knuckleballing relief specialist, who made his major league debut at age 28 with the New York Giants in 1952, set individual records for most innings in relief (1,870), relief wins (123), and games finished by a pitcher (651). Wilhelm first learned about the knuckleball while in high school. He read an article about Dutch Leonard of the Washington Senators who attained stardom by relying exclusively on the trick pitch. The acquisition of Wilhelm in January 1963 was a masterstroke on the part of Sox general manager Edwin Short. Hoyt recorded some of his most productive seasons coming out of the bullpen as the No. 1 closer. His 27 saves in 1964 marked a personal career high. From 1964 through 1968, his earned run average never rose above 1.99 in any year.

"Dr." Wilhelm, as radio announcer Bob Elson affectionately referred to him, was the last World War II veteran to pitch in the big leagues. Hoyt won a Purple Heart at the Battle of the Bulge.

Early Wynn

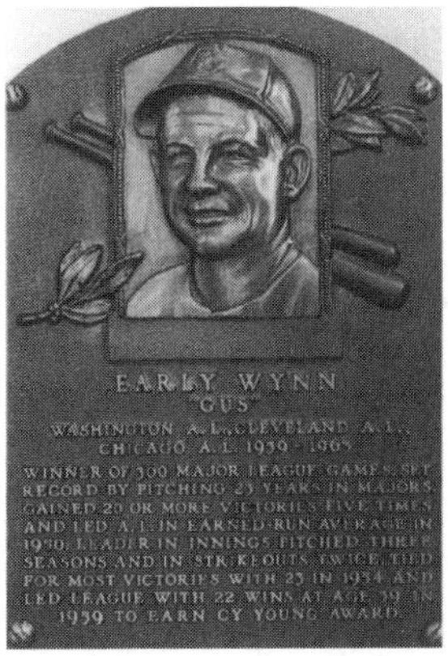

Pitcher
White Sox: 1958–62
Major leagues: 1939–63
Elected: 1972
Birthplace: Hartford, Alabama
B: January 6, 1920
D: April 4, 1999
Batted right, threw right

	W	L	Pct	ERA	G	CG	IP	H	BB	K	ShO
White Sox	64	55	.538	3.72	157	54	1,010⅔	895	438	671	16
Career	300	244	.551	3.54	691	290	4,564	4,291	1,775	2,334	49

Gus Wynn's approach to the game was methodical and intense. He called the pitching mound his office, and he would have brushed back his own mother if she stood too close to the plate—or so the story goes. Wynn holds the major league record for most years as a pitcher (23), and over the course of this long journey he walked 1,775 men, which also stands as a major league record. Early was the 14th major league pitcher to win 300 games, though his chances were placed in serious jeopardy by the White Sox when they released him during the 1963 spring training sessions. Wynn had been stuck on 299 during the final month of the 1962 season. His tired old legs were no longer up to the challenge. Afflicted by the gout, he gamely hung on and crossed the historic threshold on July 13, 1963, after his former ballclub, the Cleveland Indians, agreed to take him on. Gus defeated the Kansas City A's and retired from active duty shortly afterward.

Chicago Media in the Hall of Fame

J.G. Taylor Spink Award	Year Inducted
Ring Lardner	1963
Hugh S. Fullerton	1964
Charles Dryden	1965
Warren Brown	1973
John P. Carmichael	1974
Edgar Munzel	1977
Jerome Holtzman	1989
Wendell Smith	1993

Ford Frick Award	Year Inducted
Bob Elson	1979
Russ Hodges	1980
Jack Brickhouse	1983
Harry Caray	1989
Milo Hamilton	1992

Seven morning and afternoon newspapers, each engaging in fierce circulation wars, supplied local sports fans with all the dope on their local heroes during the first Golden Age of Chicago journalism—a 20-year swing from 1900 culminating in the Black Sox scandal of 1920. Many legends of the press box were as identifiable by their timely observations and acerbic wit as the players they were assigned to cover.

Ring Lardner: *In the Wake of the News*

The finest reporters of the day gravitated to the *Chicago Tribune,* a morning paper that covered baseball in greater detail than its poorer competitors. The *Trib* accorded celebrity status to its top writers by attaching bylines to game summaries and reserving space for sports opinion columns such as *In the Wake of the News,* a Chicago institution that has survived over a century of changing social mores and popular tastes.

Charles Dryden, Hugh Fullerton, Ring Lardner, and Irving S. Sanborn were the top baseball writers of the day, serving under sports editor Harvey Woodruff. Dryden (1869–1931), began his career with the *San Francisco Chronicle,* moved on to the *New York American* and the *Philadelphia North American* before quitting the Hearst papers in order to join the *Tribune* staff. Charley Dryden is believed to be the first reporter to tag the 1906 White Sox the "Hitless Wonders," though Hugh Fullerton can also legitimately claim authorship of the moniker. Dryden may or may not have been the first reporter to refer to Charles Comiskey as the "Old Roman," though it seems fairly certain that this nickname predated Comiskey's arrival in Chicago in 1900.

Hughie Fullerton correctly predicted the precise outcome of the 1906 World Series, though for self-serving reasons he withheld his prognosis until after the games were complete because he feared ridicule from his colleagues and readership. Who would have imagined the Hitless Wonders upsetting the powerful Cubs?

Fullerton began his career in Cincinnati, but joined the staff of the *Chicago Record* in 1896 before moving over to the *Tribune.* Fullerton's Sunday baseball column provided fascinating glimpses of life in the spring training camps to bone-chilled Chicagoans who rarely journeyed to these remote destinations.

Fullerton suspected that the fix was in place long before the final out of the 1919 World Series was recorded, and he said so (in somewhat cryptic terms) in his postseries wrap-up. Hughie left for New York to write for *Liberty Magazine* in the 1920s, and he was one of the founding fathers of the Baseball Writers Association of America (BBWAA).

Ringold Lardner maintained proprietorship of the *In the Wake of the News* column in the second decade of the century. Lardner made few bones about his support for the White Sox and his long-standing friendship with Comiskey. During spring training this cynical and outspoken social critic, possessing a whimsical and farcical side, donned a White Sox uniform and worked out with the players. Many of his legendary *You Know Me, Al* columns written during the Black Sox era revolved around his encounters with Kid Gleason, Ping Bodie, and other White Sox mainstays he socialized with during the long train trips between American League cities. Lardner was a member in good standing of Comiskey's Woodland Bard entourage and would maintain his affection for the ballclub through the Black Sox disgrace.

Warren Brown and John Carmichael joined the staff of the *Chicago Herald and Examiner* in the 1920s, and they would

Warren Brown covered the beat from the '20 to the '60s.

Bob Elson: the voice of midwestern baseball

continue to be prodding voices in local journalism through the 1960s. Carmichael was born in Madison, Wisconsin, and after making an advantageous career switch to the *Chicago Daily News* in 1932, he hosted the *Barber Shop*, a lively and entertaining forum of opinion and observation on American sport. Carmichael was a Chicago raconteur, a witty after-dinner toastmaster, and an unabashed White Sox loyalist whose amusing debates with fellow *Daily News* writer and Cubs fan Lloyd Lewis made for lively reading through the 1930s. Carmichael's column appeared in the *Daily News* after his formal retirement in 1972. After leaving the *News*, he accepted a job with the Sox that year as a public speaker and community relations representative. It was said of Carmichael that he was "a gentleman who always had a good anecdote or corkscrew when the occasion arose."

Warren Brown never dabbled in the gin spirits. He was a teetotaler first, last, and always, but he shared a treasure trove of sports lore with his readers in his famous *So They Tell Me* column, which appeared in the pages of the *Herald and Examiner* through the Depression and war years. Brown was an associate of Grantland Rice, Damon Runyon, Westbrook Pegler, and all the big names on and off the playing field. It was in Comiskey Park, shortly after his arrival in the Windy City, that Brown attended his first major league game.

"I covered my first World Series in 1920," he said in a 1964 interview. "I've covered every one since." As a cub reporter working for the *San Francisco Call Post*, he played first base for a semipro outfit called the Telegraph Hill Boys. Future White Sox Charles "Swede" Risberg was the pitcher in one of the games that Brown played in. Warren Brown was also the author of the first White Sox team history, an anecdotal, breezy collection of stories published in hardcover by G.P. Putnam's in 1952.

Toward the end of his journalistic career, Brown was named chairman of the Veterans Committee of the Hall of

Jack Brickhouse

John Carmichael, a White Sox guy all the way, interviews Early Wynn.

Harry Caray (left) and Jimmy Piersall enjoy a relaxing moment in the press box at old Comiskey Park.

Fame. "It isn't all coincidence that at the first meeting at which I was chairman, Ray Schalk was voted in unanimously," he recalled. "Of living former major leaguers, I have known Dutch Ruether and Schalk the longest."

Edgar Munzel was an alumnus of the *Chicago Sun-Times,* a hybrid of the old *Chicago Sun* and the *Chicago Times,* which merged in 1948. The late Jerome Holtzman began his baseball odyssey in 1943 with the *Chicago Times* and was assigned to the Cubs-Sox beat in the 1950s. Considered the "dean" of the Chicago press corps, Holtzman is credited with inventing the modern baseball save rule and is the author of *No Cheering in the Press Box,* a classic of sports publishing.

Jerome was a throwback to the old days of sportswriting when reporters relied on highly placed sources to provide the grist for a story that a rewrite man assigned to the desk would prepare for publication the following day. He was a respected elder statesman of the profession who continued his baseball commentary for the *Chicago Tribune* until 1998, before being hired as baseball's official historian. He died in 2008. Wendell Smith, the most recent inductee, covered the sports beat for the *Chicago American* in the 1950s and '60s. The crusading African American journalist was instrumental in convincing Sox owner Art Allyn to provide integrated housing for black ballplayers during spring training in Sarasota.

Harry Caray and his famous fishnet—a live remote from the old center-field bleachers with the young ladies, c.1972

Harry Caray in the bleachers at old Comiskey in 1971

In the realm of broadcasting, Bob Elson, Jack Brickhouse, and Harry Caray tower above the profession. Elson set the standards by which all others who followed were to be judged. He began as a staff announcer with WGN Radio in 1930 after a brief stint in St. Louis, where he had won a contest sponsored by station KWK. The station owners were seeking a fresh on-air personality, and Elson's name was drawn from a pool of applicants. After gravitating to Chicago a year later, Elson was assigned broadcast duties for both the Cubs and Sox over four local stations.

To thousands of youngsters growing up in the midwestern heartland during the 1940s and 1950s, Bob Elson was synonymous with White Sox baseball. He was the radio voice of a generation—a skilled interviewer, newsman, expert gin rummy player, and the most effective spokesman for White Owl cigars, Oldsmobile, General Finance Corporation, and other White Sox sponsors of the day.

Bob Elson, a laconic, laid-back figure, hosted a radio program from Chicago's famed Pump Room restaurant that brought him into close contact with visiting Hollywood celebrities, politicians, world leaders, and the captains of commerce and industry. Elson's cool, matter-of-fact style of interviewing the great and near-great was closely studied by younger broadcasters hoping to break into the business.

But it is his close association with the White Sox spanning nearly 40 years for which Bob Elson is remembered today. He remained the Sox's No. 1 announcer until the close of the 1970 season when a younger, more up-tempo play-by-play man—Harry Caray—was hired by John Allyn, who considered the old veteran out of sync with a younger audience demanding color and drama from the on-air personality.

Bob Elson, a true radio pioneer, became the third announcer to be elected to the Hall of Fame, following in the footsteps of Mel Allen and Red Barber. "Barber and Allen could never carry his microphone," commented Jack Brickhouse, who broke in under Elson.

Jack Brickhouse was best known as the voice of Cubs baseball. But until November 10, 1966, when the White Sox severed their bonds with WGN television in order to jump to a local UHF affiliate promising wider, more extensive coverage of road games and home night games, Jack doubled as the Sox's play-by-play man when the team played in Comiskey Park. Brickhouse got his start at station WMBD in the early 1940s, but moved over to WGN and Mutual as a staff specialist and sports announcer, largely through Elson's intervention and help. A framed telegram sent from Elson hung on a wall in Jack's apartment. It read: "Expect call from WGN as a staff announcer and sports assistant. Remember, if asked, you know all about baseball. Best of luck, Bob Elson."

Jack Brickhouse, an enthusiastic, cheerleading baseball purist, was the man behind the mike when the first telecast from Comiskey Park was aired over WGN-TV in April 1948. He plugged the sponsor's beer, rooted for the home team, and otherwise presented a positive image of the game to young fans who were lured to the ballpark by his descriptive phrases, colorful imagery of the stadium, the green grass, the fans in the stands, and a familiar "Back...back...back.... Hey! Hey!" chant each time a White Sox or Cubs home run cleared the outfield wall.

Harry Caray (born Harry Carabina in a tough section of St. Louis) joined the Sox broadcast team in 1971 after a quarter-century broadcasting St. Louis Cardinals baseball and one unhappy year spent in Oakland laboring under Charles O. Finley. Colorful, outrageous, and always to the point in his pronouncements, Caray was the antithesis of gentle Jack Brickhouse, who found very little to criticize and always kept negative thoughts bottled up inside, lest they cast an unfavorable light on the players and the front office.

Harry was popular from the moment he donned the headphones in Comiskey Park, and must share some of the credit for the resurgence of fan interest on the South Side following the dim 1970 season. Caray snared foul balls with an oversized fish net he dangled from the upper-deck TV booth. He quaffed the sponsor's beer with the fans during those rare afternoons when he moved the broadcast equipment into the center-field bleachers. And always, he never minced words when a White Sox player failed to give it his best effort.

Harry Caray, with his "man of the people" image, was often at odds with the front-office personnel, who bristled over criticisms aimed at complacent, nonproductive athletes who appeared to be just going through the motions. He was constantly in trouble with John Allyn in the early 1970s, tolerated by Bill Veeck, who recognized his enormous marketing value to the organization, and despised by Jerry Reinsdorf and Eddie Einhorn. Indeed, Harry Caray and his tempestuous sidekick, Jimmy Piersall, who joined him in the booth in 1977, could put their listening audience in shock.

Following the 1981 season, Caray and the White Sox parted company after the organization committed to a cable-television future. Harry realized that his exposure would be severely curtailed under the new pay-per-view arrangements,

Ken "Hawk" Harrelson is honored by the White Sox for 25 years of outstanding work behind the microphone on June 8, 2010. (Courtesy of the Chicago White Sox)

and therefore he decided to cast his lot with the Cubs after Jack Brickhouse announced his retirement.

The Harry Caray–Cubs union worked out fine for both parties, though it must be pointed out the "tell-it-like-it-is" style that made Caray a legend among baseball announcers disappeared. The Harry Caray of the 1980s and 1990s was not the same "Holy Cow! What a bonehead play *that* was!" play-by-play critic Chicago fans had become accustomed to in the 1970s. And that was regrettable.

Amid frequent reshuffling of on-air personalities in order to achieve the ideal blend of talent to improve ratings, Ken "Hawk" Harrelson endures as the White Sox's anchor and the real face of the franchise night in and night out, spanning more than a quarter-century. He is as much of a Chicago broadcasting legend as Caray, Elson, and Brickhouse ever were in their respective eras, and he seems destined to join them in the broadcaster wing of the Baseball Hall of Fame. Ken Harrelson has certainly earned the honor of a Ford Frick Award, and it is long overdue.

Hawk has been an integral part of the White Sox scene for a much longer period of time than Harry. He has provided Sox fans with solid game commentary, an ex-player's perspective, and he does it each night with a greater style and flair than the featureless, monotone descriptions of Bob Elson or the occasionally mean-spirited sarcasm of Caray. In many respects, he is a more enthusiastic and devoted supporter of Sox baseball than Brickhouse, whose final 16 years were spent up on the North Side.

Long before Hawk arrived in Chicago in 1982 to team up with Drysdale behind the microphone, GM Edwin Short of the White Sox front office negotiated for his services as a long-ball threat after Harrelson was released by the Kansas City A's on August 25, 1967, and declared a free agent. Desperately in need of some firepower to bolster the middle of a weak-hitting lineup that struggled to scratch out barely three runs a game to support a superlative starting pitching corps, Short failed to entice the Hawk to join the ballclub. Instead he joined the Red Sox three days later and helped them steal a pennant away from the South Side. The reason was simple. For a power-hitting, right-handed batter of Harrelson's strength and ability, the left-field wall in Fenway was just too inviting a target.

So Hawk's arrival in the Windy City had to be put off until 1982, when the departure of Harry Caray necessitated a changing of the guard in the broadcast booth. Harrelson had some big shoes to fill, and he knew it. But fill them he did, despite some first-year fan criticisms that the two new announcers kept referring to the team not in familiar terms as the Sox, but as "Chicago"—just as a network guy might do in a game of the week telecast. In other words, they were not Sox partisans, at least not yet.

But as the years passed, Ken Harrelson's affection for the team grew steadily. He suffered along with the rest of Sox Nation in the lean years of the 1980s and exulted in the team's successful rebuilding efforts and 1993 division title. As cable television spread across the land, and the fans of other teams in distant cities (or Cubs fans) listened in and became acquainted with our down-home guy from Savannah, Georgia, negative comments occasionally appeared on websites or in letters to the network expressing displeasure over Hawk's zealous home-town style of announcing. But that was *their* problem and not Harrelson's, who took it in stride as he should. Hawk is the fan's advocate and champion, and his observations and predictions are usually on the mark. Teaming with Drysdale, Tom Paciorek, Darrin Jackson, and Steve Stone, younger fans learned some of the history and traditions of the era in which he played. They learned strategy, nuance, and gained tremendous insight from a veteran master. Older fans who grew up in the baby boom era easily relate to the famous and forgotten players he knew intimately; sharing priceless anecdotes about the faces from our 1964 Topps baseball cards he brought back to life.

And we came to know the enduring Hawk Harrelson baseball clichés. The following is our practical guide to understanding "Hawk Talk" essentials:

Cliché	Translation
That's a hang wiff 'em!	A vicious liner, or a solidly hit fly ball snared by the fielder.
That's a can of corn!	Lazy, easily playable fly-ball out.
That's a little ducksnort!	Texas League single just out of reach of the fielder.
Don't stop now, boys!	Spoken after a big hit to keep a White Sox rally going.
Ball four/base hit!	Urging a Sox hitter on with a three-and-two count.
Dad gum it!	A great catch by an opponent, a warning track out, or a ball hit by a Sox player that is foul by inches.
Be a good two-strike hitter.	Words of advice to a Sox hitter in the hole.
Sit back, relax, and strap it down!	Welcoming in the viewers to the telecast.
You can cancel the postgame show.	No-hitter just broken up.
Cinch it up and hunker down!	We need you to come through. Be tough.
Stretch!	Fly ball with home run distance.
Pick to click.	The Hawk and the crew choosing the Sox player likely to click that night.
Ducks on the pond.	Men on base.
He got a cookie there!	A hittable pitch fouled off or missed by the batter.
Gas! He gone!	Opponent strikes out on a 90-mph fastball.
He's got the catbird seat!	Batter has a 2–0 count.
Right size, wrong shape.	A long, foul-ball.
Rack 'em up!	Routine infield double play.
Big hack no cattle!	A big swing and a miss.
That's a Hazel May!	A timely hit.
Mercy!	A moment of great excitement.
A little humpback liner!	An off-the-end-of-the-bat line drive.
You can put it on the board...!!!	Yes!!

Harrelson's tenure behind the mike was interrupted by that one unhappy year as White Sox general manager in 1986. He inherited a team with few bargaining chips in the minor leagues, and a big-league unit on the downgrade. "There had to be a bit of a turnaround in 1986 with the White Sox, and the organization didn't have much at the minor league level," the Hawk told an interviewer. "Somebody had to come in and clean things out. When you do that, you gotta shovel some stuff around, and it's not gonna be fun."

After one year at the helm, Hawk moved on to New York, where he resumed his broadcast career as play-by-play man for SportsChannel New York in 1987–1988 before Jerry Reinsdorf brought him back to the White Sox in 1989.

With two decades behind him, Harrelson has become the dean of Chicago broadcasters—a certain Hall of Famer and all-around good guy. To those who resent his hometown boosterism, well, this is Chicago, so get used to it. To others who deride his slogans and clichés, what is baseball if not history, tradition, nicknames, and pet phrases?

In recognition of his silver anniversary with the ballclub, Kenny was honored with his own testimonial day on June 8, 2010. In a revealing interview, he admitted that his Hawk persona is an alter-ego, but one that elevated a career .239 hitter to prominence and respect.

"I've talked to some psychiatrists about it, and they said it's very common. We all have alter egos, and I recall playing in Fenway Park and we were trying to win a pennant, and 'Yaz' [Hall of Fame teammate Carl Yastrzemski] would be at the plate and there would be someone at third base with nobody out or one out, and Yaz would pop up or something, and I'd be in the on-deck circle, and I'd say, 'Okay, Kenny, get out of Hawk's way and let him go.' I would actually say that to myself."

8

Great Moments

In a 1976 survey commissioned by commissioner Bowie Kuhn and Major League Baseball, fans across the country were given an opportunity to select their favorite team's "most memorable moment." A poll of this nature is purely subjective, and the final results typically reflected the historical events within the span of memory of the fans who cast ballots.

White Sox fans agreed that their finest moment occurred in Cleveland the night of September 22, 1959, when the ballclub clinched its first pennant in 40 years. Because of the long drought between championship seasons, the choice was inevitable.

The real glory days of White Sox baseball—the Hitless Wonder era and the exploits of the great Black Sox teams of the World War I period that followed—were all but forgotten by 1976.

Therefore, it is incumbent upon the baseball historian to bring these earlier events back to life for younger fans whose sights are almost always locked on the modern era.

Unfortunately for the White Sox, a team stigmatized by the Black Sox scandal and three consecutive decades of second-division baseball, there are few prized moments to cherish. There is no electrifying ninth-inning pennant-winner akin to Bobby Thomson's 1951 "Shot Heard Round the World."

Nevertheless, this is a team steeped in tradition, and the game stories, box scores, and anecdotes presented in this chapter are high points of White Sox history down through the years. It is impossible to attach greater weight to one event than to another. Certainly a White Sox fan who was around in 1917 would argue that the pennant clincher in Boston's Fenway Park that year was a more vivid moment than the 1959 winner in Cleveland. Fans of the Go-Go Sox would beg to differ.

The selection of a "greatest moment" must be deferred to the fans, and with the passing of each decade, it will likely continue to change.

Doc White Pitches Fifth Consecutive Shutout

The Hitless Wonder era of White Sox baseball was born in 1904. Under the brilliant direction of Fielder Jones, who took over as manager of the ballclub on June 5, the White Sox climbed into the four-team American League pennant race in early August.

The acclaimed Hitless Wonder pitching staff was overwhelming down the stretch. In a 10-game swing between September 18 and 30, Sox starters limited the opposition to only eight runs. In winning nine of these 10 games, the pitchers shut out their opponents six times.

Doc White, the stylish left-hander who worked as a dentist during the off-season, keyed the belated pennant push. He began his remarkable shutout streak on September 12, when he blanked the Cleveland Naps 1–0 at the 39th Street Grounds. Four days later he one-hit the Browns in St. Louis by an identical 1–0 score. On September 19, he whitewashed the Detroit Tigers 3–0. The Philadelphia A's fell victim by a 4–0 count six days later, setting the stage for a first-place showdown with the New York Highlanders.

New York arrived in town on September 30, leading the White Sox by three games. Doc White, gunning for his fifth straight shutout, opened this climactic series for Chicago.

Manager Clark Griffith selected his spitballing ace Jack Chesbro to oppose White. Chicago jumped all over Chesbro in the third inning and drove him from the game with a pair of doubles by Danny Green and Jimmy Callahan, an infield hit coming from George Davis, and Chesbro's throwing error.

Meanwhile, Doc White had no problem mowing down the Highlander hitters. He yielded only three harmless safeties in separate innings. Not one opposing batter reached third base all afternoon.

A Ladies' Day crowd of just under 7,000 roared their approval. When the final out had been recorded, the White Sox had pulled to within two games of the leaders.

Handshakes all around at Midway Airport, hours after the Sox clinched the 1959 American League pennant in Cleveland on September 22. Mayor Richard J. Daley (right) shakes hands with manager Al Lopez, along with Charley Comiskey, Bill Veeck (in his customary white sport shirt), and Mrs. Daley.

Doc White's scoreless streak was extended to 45 consecutive innings. The ace lefty surrendered only 17 hits during this remarkable skein, which stood as the major league record until 1968, when Don Drysdale of the Dodgers finally eclipsed the mark. Because it occurred so long ago, few fans had ever heard of Doc White when his name surfaced during Drysdale's 58-inning scoreless run.

But in September 1904 Doctor White was the man of the hour in Chicago. More than 30,000 fans jammed the 39th Street Grounds on October 2 to see if he could work his magic one more time on just two days' rest. "The human mass was surcharged with enthusiasm and anxiety, which found vent in almost continuous cheering," commented a poetic *Tribune* sportswriter in his postgame account.

The Highlanders tallied a run in the very first inning to snap the steak, but White shut them out the rest of the way and bagged a 7–1 complete game victory. Only one other White Sox pitcher has ever come close to duplicating White's streak. In 1963 veteran Ray Herbert tossed four straight shutouts before his string of 38 scoreless innings was snapped in Baltimore on May 19.

New York at Chicago, September 30, 1904

New York	AB	R	H
Keeler, rf	4	0	2
Conroy, 3b	3	0	0
Fultz, cf	3	0	0
Elberfeld, ss	4	0	0
Williams, 2b	4	0	0
Anderson, lf	4	0	1
Ganzel, 1b	2	0	0
McGuire, c	3	0	0
Chesbro, p	1	0	0
Puttman, p	2	0	0
	30	0	3

Chicago	AB	R	H
Green, rf	3	1	1
Jones, cf	4	1	1
Callahan, lf	4	1	1
Davis, ss	4	0	1
Donahue, 1b	4	1	1
Tannehill, 3b	4	0	0
Isbell, 2b	4	0	0
Sullivan, c	2	0	1
Heydon, c	1	0	0
White, p	2	0	0
	32	4	6

New York	0	0	0	0	0	0	0	0—0
Chicago	0	1	3	0	0	0	0	x—4

2B—Anderson, Green, Callahan. 3B—Sullivan, Donohue. DP—Williams, Elberfeld, Ganzil. SB—Jones. LOB—Chicago 7, New York 6. Umpire—Jack Sheridan. Time—1:55. Attendance—6,840.

New York	IP	K	BB	H
Chesbro (L)	3	1	0	4
Puttman	5	4	4	2

Chicago	IP	K	BB	H
White (W)	9	7	3	3

Doc White held the record for consecutive scoreless innings until 1968.

White Sox Win 19th Straight—Set Major League Mark

Manager Fielder Jones entrusted veteran hurler Roy Patterson with the task of prolonging a winning streak that had become the talk of the sports world. Going into an afternoon contest with the Washington Senators in the nation's capital on August 23, 1906, the Hitless Wonder White Sox had reeled off 18 consecutive victories, equaling a record established by the New York Giants two years earlier, in 1904.

"Their run of games won is the most remarkable thing I have ever heard of," lauded manager James McAleer of the St. Louis Browns. "It's nothing short of phenomenal, and Fielder Jones and Charles Comiskey deserve a world of credit for the performance."

Roy Patterson was shaky early in the game. He surrendered five hits in the first four innings and was about to be removed from the contest when he begged his manager for a second chance. Jones relented and allowed Patterson to remain on the hill. From the fifth inning on, Roy allowed the Senators only two scratch hits.

The game was won in the fifth inning after Jones singled and Frank Isbell advanced him to third with a base hit to left. George Davis smashed a sharp grounder in the direction of first baseman Jack Stahl. The ball struck a pebble and bounded into right field, with Jones scoring. Jiggs Donahue popped up to the first baseman in foul territory. Proving again that he was the most innovative and daring manager in the game, Jones signaled Davis to break for second in order to draw a throw from Stahl. The Washington first baseman heaved the ball wildly, and Frank Isbell scored easily.

This is the how the Hitless Wonder White Sox played the game during the Fielder Jones era. It was a daring, imaginative ballclub that exploited an opponent's every weakness. Whatever the Sox lacked in physical talent, they more than compensated through desire and hustle. The improbable 19-game win streak, which ended in Washington the next afternoon, and the surprise World Series upset over the Cubs stand as testament to the abilities of this grossly underrated ballclub.

Chicago at Washington, August 23, 1906

Chicago	H	R	A
Hahn, rf	1	1	0
F. Jones, cf	1	0	6
Isbell, 2b	3	1	3
Davis, ss	1	0	3
Donahue, 1b	0	1	10
Dougherty, lf	0	1	0
Sullivan, c	1	0	0
Tannehill, 3b	1	0	2
Patterson, p	0	0	2
	8	4	26

Washington	H	R	A
Nill, 2b	0	0	1
C. Jones,cf	0	0	0
Altizer, ss	1	0	3
Cross, 3b	1	0	3
Anderson, lf	0	0	2
Hickman, rf	3	1	0
Stahl, 1b	1	0	13
Warner, c	0	0	3
Falkenberg, p	1	0	0
Wakefield, ph	0	0	0
	7	1	16

Chicago	0	0	0	1	2	0	1	0	0—4
Washington	0	0	0	1	0	0	0	0	0—1

2B—Tannehill, Falkenberg, Hickman. 3B—Stahl. Sac—Dougherty. SB—Isbell. LOB—Washington, 7, Chicago 6. PB—Warner. E—Cross. Umpire—Silk O'Loughlin. Time—1:40.

Chicago	IP	K	BB
Patterson (L)	9	4	0

Washington	IP	K	BB
Falkenberg (W)	9	5	4

The Game of Their Lives: Ed Walsh versus Addie Joss

For sheer drama, emotion, and the beauty of sport, the Ed Walsh–Addie Joss showdown in Cleveland on October 2, 1908, stands as one of the greatest regular season games ever played, despite an unfavorable verdict dealt the visiting team.

In the final days of the most heated American League pennant race in the first quarter of the century, the White Sox, Detroit Tigers, and Cleveland Naps battled for supremacy. In early August the Sox found themselves trailing the leader by seven games. By the end of the following month, the deficit had been whittled to just one game.

Ed Walsh was the heart and soul of this great Hitless Wonder club. He won 40 games that year pitching on a steady diet of two days' rest—sometimes even less than that. The team was built around this one amazing spitball pitcher who won three games against the Boston Red Sox on two consecutive days, September 27 and 28.

Fielder Jones' ballclub went into Cleveland on October 2 trailing the Naps by just one game. Again, the Sox manager called on Walsh to take the mound against an old nemesis: Naps right-hander Adrian Joss.

Big Ed took the full measure of Joss—as much as it is possible to outduel a pitcher about to work a *perfect* game. But the White Sox ace was masterful. In eight innings of work he struck out 15 batters, yielding only four hits and a scratchy run that was the difference between victory and defeat. Cleveland scored the only run of the game when catcher Ossee Schreckengost failed to hang on to one of Walsh's sharply breaking spitters. Joe Birmingham trotted across the plate in the third inning on a passed ball. So overwhelming was the pitch that Schreck broke his hand on the play.

In Chicago, fans of the White Sox joined owner Charles Comiskey at Orchestra Hall to watch the drama unfold on an electronic scoreboard erected on the stage. The twinkling green lights indicated the position of the runners, the number of outs, and the ball and strike count.

Comiskey offered no comment as the Sox entered the ninth inning still hitless. Finally he leaned over and whispered to American League president Ban Johnson, "We're not beaten yet. We've got three more men to be put out." But in his heart the Old Roman knew it was not their day. Jiggs Donahue fanned, and utility outfielder John Anderson rolled to first to end the game.

Walsh and Joss. When the two great pitchers met each other hours later in their downtown hotel, Big Ed graciously offered his hand and congratulated his opponent. It was the game of their lives—perhaps one for the century.

Chicago at Cleveland, October 2, 1908

Chicago	AB	R	H	PO	A
Hahn, rf	3	0	0	1	0
Jones, cf	3	0	0	0	0
Isbell, 1b	3	0	0	0	1
Dougherty, lf	3	0	0	0	0
Davis, 2b	3	0	0	0	0
Parent, ss	3	0	0	1	2
Schreck, c	2	0	0	13	0
Shaw, c	0	0	0	2	0
White, ph	1	0	0	0	0
Tannehill, 3b	2	0	0	0	0
Donohue, ph	1	0	0	0	0
Walsh, p	2	0	0	1	3
Anderson, ph	1	0	0	0	0
	27	0	0	18	6

Cleveland	AB	R	H	PO	A
Goode, rf	4	0	0	1	0
Bradley, 3b	4	0	0	0	1
Hinchman, lf	3	0	0	3	0
Lajoie, 2b	3	0	1	2	2
Stovall, 1b	3	0	0	13	0
Clarke, c	3	0	0	4	1
Birmingham, cf	3	1	2	0	0
Perring, ss	2	0	1	1	1
Joss, p	3	0	0	0	0
	28	1	4	24	5

Chicago	0	0	0	0	0	0	0	0	0—0
Cleveland	0	0	1	0	0	0	0	0	x—1

E—Isbell. SB—Lajoie. Sac—none. PB—Schreck (2). Umpires—Connally and O'Laughlin. Time—1:33.

Chicago	IP	R	ER	K	BB
Walsh (L)	8	1	0	15	1

Cleveland	IP	R	ER	K	BB
Joss (W)	9	0	0	3	0

A Double Play Sews Up the 1917 Pennant

All season long in 1917 the Boston Red Sox had taken personal satisfaction every time they managed to defeat the White Sox. A paper-thin partition separating the visitor's dressing room from the home-team locker room in Fenway Park forced the White Sox to endure a torrent of verbal jockeying and insults coming from the Red Sox players. The Sox of white dressed quietly and said nothing. They refused to engage in a war of words with the *second-best* team in the American League.

Minutes after pounding the final nail in the Red Sox's coffin, the White Sox staged a little celebration of their own in the visitor's clubhouse. They returned the compliment by pounding on the partition until it nearly collapsed. Clarence Rowland's boys jeered Babe Ruth, but the future Sultan of Swat had nothing more to say. Chicago was going to the World Series. The second-place Red Sox, who trailed Chicago by eight and a half games going into the decisive game on September 21, would have to wait another year before they too could again sip the champagne.

The Red Sox put up a good fight against Red Faber, who wasn't feeling well during pregame practice. Manager Clarence Rowland had tabbed Reb Russell to open against Dutch Leonard, but Faber went to his skipper minutes before the game was scheduled to start and told him that he could pitch after all.

Leonard, while good, was not nearly as strong as the old redhead this particular afternoon. Faber was perfect for six innings. He had retired every Red Sox hitter in order and was flirting with a perfect game when Harry Hooper ended the suspense with a booming triple to right-center field to open the seventh inning.

The White Sox had taken the lead in the fourth inning, and nursed it along until Jack Barry delivered the game-tying single a moment later.

Red Faber nailed down the 1917 flag for Chicago.

In the 10th inning Ray Schalk drilled a double to the base of the left-center-field wall. Faber, a terrible hitter, struck out after failing to lay down a sacrifice bunt. Shano Collins, a dependable outfielder and first baseman for nearly a decade, stepped up to the plate and delivered the game winner. His line-drive single over the third baseman's head easily scored Schalk.

But in the bottom of the 10th, the Red Sox mounted a final charge. Duffy Lewis and Larry Gardner singled. With one out, Babe Ruth was sent in to pinch hit for shortstop Everett Scott. The Babe chopped a grounder to Eddie Collins at second, who fielded the ball cleanly. The Sox captain flipped to

Buck Weaver, who was playing shortstop. Buck kicked the bag and fired the ball to Chick Gandil who received the throw a split second before the lumbering Ruth could cross the bag. The tiny crowd filed out of the stadium, silent and dejected.

Charles Comiskey received the happy news over the ticker-tape machine installed in the Bards Room of the stadium bearing his family name. Shaken and barely able to speak, he turned to his son, Lou, and a handful of reporters. He recalled the near misses of years past. "Twice I had the pennant all ready to nail on the pole, and both times they snatched it away from my hands," he said. "This one is mine, though. And after 11 years!"

Chicago at Boston, September 21, 1917

Chicago	AB	R	H
J. Collins, rf	5	0	2
McMullin, 3b	4	0	1
E. Collins, 2b	4	0	1
Jackson, lf	5	0	0
Felsch, cf	4	1	1
Gandil, 1b	4	0	0
Weaver, ss	2	0	1
Schalk, c	4	1	2
Faber, p	3	0	0
	35	2	8

Boston	AB	R	H
Hooper, rf	4	1	1
Barry, 2b	4	0	2
Hoblitzel, 1b	4	0	0
Lewis, lf	4	0	0
Shorten, cf	4	0	1
Gardner, 3b	3	0	1
Scott, ss	2	0	0
Thomas, c	3	0	0
Leonard, p	3	0	0
Ruth, ph	1	0	0
	32	1	5

Chicago	0	0	0	1	0	0	0	0	0	1—2
Boston	0	0	0	0	0	0	1	0	0	0—1

2B—Schalk. 3B—Hooper. E—Gardner. HBP—Weaver (by Leonard), Gardner (by Faber). DP—Chicago, 1. Umpires—Hildebrand and Dinneen. Time: 1:48. Attendance—5,000 (est.).

Chicago	IP	BB	K	H
Faber (W)	10	0	1	5

Boston	IP	BB	K	H
Leonard (L)	10	3	4	8

White Sox Clinch the 1919 Pennant

What dark thoughts crossed Ed Cicotte's mind as he took the mound in old Comiskey Park knowing that it was in his power to clinch an American League pennant he and seven of his teammates had already sworn to dishonor?

The "fixing" of the 1919 World Series was already a foregone conclusion when the Sox set their sights on nailing down their second American League pennant in three years. The eight "Black Sox" players had made their bones with the gamblers on the recently concluded eastern road trip, and they were about to make history of a different sort amid the jubilation of a championship.

The sixth-place St. Louis Browns provided the opposition the afternoon of September 24, 1919. The White Sox enjoyed a five-game bulge with five more games left on the schedule.

Even though the clinching was pro forma by this late date, the Sox-Browns contest provided more than the usual share of thrills and drama.

Ed Cicotte was rattled around pretty badly through seven innings. Not until the fifth inning were the White Sox able to dent the plate against Alan Sothoron, who, like Cicotte, threw a shine ball. Kid Gleason's team battled back from a four-run deficit and might have knotted the game in the seventh if not for a questionable call at the plate. Eddie Collins was ruled out at home on a close play by umpire George Hildebrand, who immediately ejected the fuming White Sox captain from the game after he kicked Hildy in the shins.

Dickie Kerr, who replaced Cicotte on the mound, led the victorious assault in the bottom of the ninth by opening with a single. Nemo Leibold's base hit to center sent Kerr to third when Baby Doll Jacobson bobbled the ball. Fred McMullin, who had replaced Collins at second base, drew an intentional pass.

Up stepped Buck Weaver—the least culpable of the eight conspiring Black Sox—and his sacrifice fly to center field drove in Kerr with the tying run. Shoeless Joe Jackson was next, and he delivered the goods as he had so often during this memorable season with a vicious drive that fell into the gap in right-center field. The Sox were in—and all of Chicago celebrated.

The fans, the writers, and most of the Sox players—who were unaware of the dangerous intrigue afoot—looked to the coming World Series with supreme confidence. Who could stop them now?

St. Louis at Chicago, September 24, 1919

Chicago	AB	H	R
Leibold, rf	5	3	2
E. Collins, 2b	4	1	0
McMullin, 2b	0	0	0
Weaver, 3b	4	2	0
Jackson, lf	5	2	0
Felsch, cf	4	1	0
J. Collins, 1b	4	0	0
Risberg, ss	4	1	1
Schalk, c	3	2	1
Cicotte, p	1	1	0
Kerr, p	1	1	1
Murphy, ph	1	0	0
	36	14	5

St. Louis	AB	H	R
Austin, 3b	4	2	2
Gedeon, 2b	5	2	0
Jacobson, cf	5	3	2
Sisler, 1b	4	1	1
Tobin, lf	4	2	0
Demmitt, rf	4	1	0
Severeid, c	4	1	0
Gerber, ss	4	0	0
Sothoron, p	4	0	0
	38	12	5

St. Louis	3	0	1	0	0	0	1	0	0—5
Chicago	0	0	0	0	2	0	2	0	2—6

2B—Sisler, Jacobson, Risberg, Leibold, Felsch. 3B—Austin, Jacobson. E—Collins, Austin. DP—Gideon-Sisler. Sac—Cicotte, Weaver. Umpires—Hildebrand and Evans.

St. Louis	IP	H	BB	K
Sothoron (L)	9	14	2	3

Chicago	IP	H	BB	K
Cicotte	7	10	1	4
Kerr (W)	2	2	0	1

The Perfect 27: Charlie Robertson's One Day of Glory

Kid pitcher Charlie Robertson finally made the White Sox 1922 opening-day roster after two earlier, unsuccessful tries in 1917 and 1918. The struggling right-hander was purchased from the Sherman club of the Texas League for the sum of $1,750, and he was making only his second start of the season when he took the mound on April 30 before a sellout crowd of 25,000 Tigers partisans in Detroit's cramped Navin Field.

From the opening pitch of the game the Tigers fans howled and booed young Robertson after Harry Heilmann complained to umpire Billy Evans that the Sox pitcher was doctoring the ball with an illegal substance. Ty Cobb personally inspected every inch of Robertson's uniform but could find no trace of grease or any other foreign matter.

"There were a lot of things about Robertson's perfect game I'll never forget," reminisced catcher Ray Schalk 42 years later. "That particular day there was a crowd on the field—as there used to be in the old days—and mounted police kept them in check. I mention this because the only ball any of the Tigers hit really hard, Johnny Mostil nailed while fighting off both spectators and mounted police. Johnny, if you notice from the box score, was a left fielder for that game. He was to become one of the great center fielders later on."

The Sox scored their two runs in the second inning off of Herman Pillette. Harry Hooper walked. Johnny Mostil laid down a perfect bunt and was safe at first. Amos Strunk sacrificed the runners to second and third before Earl Sheely drove a hard grounder into left field, plating both runners.

Robertson relied on a fastball and a slider. He didn't have much of a curveball, and that shortcoming doomed him to an otherwise mediocre career. His four-year record with the Sox was 39–56. He was claimed on waivers by the St. Louis Browns after the 1925 season and was out of baseball three years later.

That afternoon, however, Charlie was in a class by himself. Only seven Tigers batters managed to rap the ball on the ground, and none with any great authority. When it was over and the sixth major league perfect game was entered into the history book, the hostile Detroit fans accorded the Sox pitcher a standing ovation.

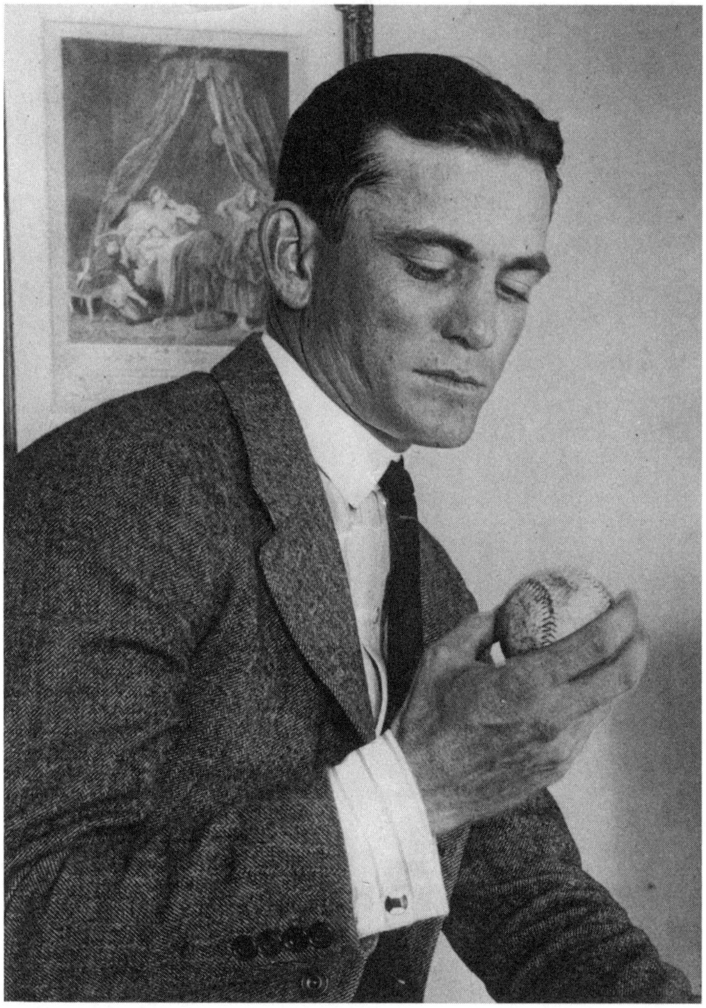

Charlie Robertson displays the game ball he threw in his perfect game against the Tigers. The sore losers accused him of doctoring the ball with a foreign substance.

Chicago at Detroit, April 30, 1922

Chicago	AB	R	H	RBI
Mulligan, ss	4	0	1	0
McClellan, 3b	3	0	1	0
E. Collins, 2b	3	0	1	0
Hooper, rf	3	1	0	0
Mostil, lf	4	1	1	0
Strunk, cf	3	0	0	0
Sheely, 1b	4	0	2	2
Schalk, c	4	0	1	0
Robertson, p	4	0	0	0
	32	2	7	2

Detroit	AB	R	H	RBI
Blue, 1b	3	0	0	0
Cutshaw, 2b	3	0	0	0
Cobb, cf	3	0	0	0
Veach, lf	3	0	0	0
Heilmann, rf	3	0	0	0
Jones, 3b	3	0	0	0
Rigney, ss	2	0	0	0
Manion, c	3	0	0	0
Pillette, p	2	0	0	0
Clark, ph	1	0	0	0
Bassler, ph	1	0	0	0
	27	0	0	0

Chicago	0	2	0	0	0	0	0	0	0—2
Detroit	0	0	0	0	0	0	0	0	0—0

2B—Mulligan, Sheely. SO—Robertson, 6; Pillette, 5. E—Blue. Sac—McClellan, Strunk, Collins. Umpires—Nallin and Evans. Time—1:55. Attendance—25,000.

Thirteen Runs in One Inning

In the closing weeks of the war-torn 1943 season, the crew of replacement players that Jimmie Dykes directed caught fire and won 15 of 19 decisions. When asked by New York sportswriter Dan Daniel how he accomplished this singular feat, Dykes puffed his cigar a moment and replied, "Why, with mirrors of course!"

World War II exacted a heavy toll on the White Sox roster. Luke Appling was still around, however, and about to clinch his second batting crown. His 36-year-old legs pilfered 27 bases that year. In fact, the entire Sox team had become so adept at the motion offense that the writers around town called them the Wild West Boys.

The Sox rolled into Griffith Stadium to play a Sunday doubleheader with the Senators, with "hard-luck" Edgar Smith slated to pitch against young Early Wynn, who was struggling to find the mark in his budding career.

In the fourth inning of Game 1, the Sox pushed across 13 runs, which remains a club record to this day. At the time, the White Sox' single-inning run output was second only to the New York Yankees' 14-run bombardment of the Senators in a 1922 game, which stood as the American League record.

Gus Wynn retired only one White Sox batter in the dizzy fourth. The Sox pounded out 10 hits in the frame against Wynn and two hapless relievers, Jim Mertz and Bill Lefebvre. The highlight of this surprising display of offensive prowess was a perfectly executed triple steal by Thurman Tucker, Guy Curtright, and Luke Appling. Tucker, a dead ringer for comedian Joe E. Brown, slid across the plate in a cloud of dust after taking note of Lefebvre's slow, awkward windup.

There have been other pitchers in Sox history who suffered through prolonged dry spells. Joel Horlen comes to mind. But Eddie Smith was the hard-luck loser of all time. Only with the White Sox could a pitcher of his caliber manage to lose 20 games (1942) and still be named to the All-Star team in the same season. But on one early autumn afternoon in 1943, fate smiled kindly on the portly southpaw. Smith even contributed a home run and two singles to the festivities, proving that sometimes you just have to look after things yourself.

Chicago at Washington, September 26, 1943, Game 1

Chicago	AB	R	H	RBI
Moses, rf	2	1	0	0
Solters, rf	2	0	0	0
Tucker, cf	5	1	2	1
Curtright, lf	5	1	0	1
Appling, ss	4	1	0	1
Culler, ss	1	0	0	0
Hodgin, 3b	4	3	3	2
Cuccinello, 3b	1	0	0	0
Kuhel, 1b	4	3	4	1
Webb, 2b	5	1	3	4
Tresh, c	5	2	2	2
Smith, p	5	2	3	2
	43	15	17	14

Washington	AB	R	H	RBI
Case, lf	4	2	2	0
Vernon, 1b	3	0	0	0
Butka, 1b	1	0	1	1
Ortiz, rf	4	0	1	0
Powell, cf	4	0	1	1
Johnson, 3b	3	0	0	0
Priddy, 2b	4	1	3	0
Sullivan, ss	4	0	1	0
Guillant, c	4	0	2	1
Wynn, p	1	0	1	0
Mertz, p	0	0	0	0
Lefebvre, p	2	0	0	0
Roberts, ph	1	0	0	0
	35	3	12	3

Chicago	0	0	0	13	0	2	0	0	0—15
Washington	0	0	0	0	0	1	1	1	0— 3

E—Johnson (2), Priddy, Guillant (2), Wynn. 2B—Hodgin, Webb, Case, Priddy, Butka. 3B—Hodgin, Kuhel. HR—Smith. SB—Webb, Tucker, Curtright, Appling. DP—Priddy-Sullivan-Vernon, Appling and Kuhel, Sullivan-Priddy-Vernon, Appling-Kuhel, Sullivan-Priddy-Vernon. LOB—Chicago 7, Washington 6. Umpires—Rommel and Grieve. Time—2:00.

Chicago	IP	H	ER	K	BB
Smith (W)	9	12	3	2	1

Washington	IP	H	ER	K	BB
Wynn (L)	3⅓	6	6	0	2
Mertz	0	1	4	0	3
Lefebvre	5⅔	10	2	1	1

Pat Seerey Clouts Four Home Runs in One Game

Pat Seerey was a one-man wrecking crew...for exactly one game. The portly ex-Indian is the only White Sox player to belt four home runs in one game, and he accomplished the feat in the unlikely 1948 season when the ballclub finished dead last and looked very bad losing 101 games.

The White Sox opened a five-game series against the improved Philadelphia A's in Shibe Park on July 18. The team was mired in last place and going absolutely nowhere. Manager Ted Lyons selected Frank Papish to open Game 1 of the doubleheader.

Papish took a hammering—but was rescued from defeat by Seerey, who dented the roof in left field twice, cleared it once, and concluded the assault with a game-winning blow into the upper deck in the 11th: four home runs in all. Carl Scheib was Pat's first victim. His first pitch to Seerey in the fourth inning cleared the left-field pavilion—a feat rarely accomplished in old Shibe Park. In the fifth Seerey teed off on Scheib again. Bob Savage was on the mound for the A's in the sixth when Pat picked on a 2–2 pitch for his third long-distance clout of the day.

The game was knotted at 11 in the 11th when cleanup man Seerey delivered the goods a final time. He stroked a game-winning homer off Lou Brissie to become only the fourth major leaguer in history to accomplish this unique feat. Pat Seerey, whose entire career spanned only 561 games, joined Bobby Lowe (1894), Ed Delahanty (1896), Lou Gehrig (1932), and Chuck Klein (1936) in the record books.

Pat Seerey was gone four games into the 1949 season. He was a one-dimensional strikeout artist, but for one afternoon in Shibe Park, "Fat Pat" was king.

Chicago at Philadelphia, July 18, 1948

Chicago	AB	R	H
Kolloway, 2b	7	2	5
Lupien, 1b	7	1	1
Appling, 3b	7	1	3
Seerey, lf	6	4	4
Robinson, c	6	0	3
Wright, rf	6	0	2
Philley, cf	6	1	2
Michaels, ss	6	3	4
Papish, p	0	0	0
Moulder, p	1	0	0
Hodgin, ph	1	0	0
Caldwell, p	0	0	0
Baker, ph	1	0	0
Judson, p	5	0	0
Pieretti, p	0	0	0
	59	12	24

Philadelphia	AB	R	H
Joost, ss	7	4	4
McCosky, lf	2	2	1
White, cf	4	1	2
Brissie, p	0	0	0
Chapman, ph	0	0	0
Fain, 1b	5	0	0
Majeski, 3b	5	0	1
Valo, rf	3	0	1
Rosar, c	3	0	0
Guerra, c	3	0	0
Suder, 2b	5	2	1
Scheib, p	1	1	0
Savage, p	1	0	0
Harris, p	1	1	1
J. Coleman, p	0	0	0
R. Coleman, cf-ph	2	0	1
DeMars, pr	0	0	0
	42	11	12

Chicago	0	0	1	1	2	5	2	0	0	0	1—12
Philadelphia	1	4	0	1	1	0	4	0	0	0	0—11

RBIs—Kolloway (3), Appling, Seerey (7), Baker, Joost (5), McCosky, Fain (2), Majeski. 2B—Robinson, Wright, Kolloway, Philley, Joost (2), Majeski. 3B—Kolloway. HR—Seerey (4), Joost. DP—McCosky, Rosar; Kolloway, Michaels, Lupien. LOB—Chicago 15, Philadelphia 14. HBP—Valo (by Papish). WP—Papish, Moulder, Savage. Balk—Judson. Umpires—Hurley, Berry, and Grieve. Time—3:44. Attendance—17,296.

Chicago	IP	BB	K	H
Papish	1	4	0	3
Moulder	2	1	1	0
Caldwell	2	1	1	4
Judson (W)	5⅔	7	2	5
Pieretti	⅓	0	0	0

Philadelphia	IP	BB	K	H
Scheib	4⅔	1	2	9
Savage	1	1	0	5
Harris	1⅓	0	0	4
Coleman	1⅔	1	1	3
Brissie (L)	2	0	1	3

Pat Seerey crosses home plate after clouting the third of four home runs on July 18, 1948. Luke Appling (No. 4) and Tony Lupien (No. 8) congratulate him.

End of an Era: Luke Appling's Final Game

Few people suspected that a season-ending doubleheader pitting the sixth-place White Sox against the seventh-place Browns would be anything more than two tailenders playing out the string.

The 1950 season was a disappointing one for the Comiskeys. High expectations quickly gave way to front-office discord and much name-calling. Jack Onslow was fired in May, and his successor, Red Corriden, did little to reverse the losing pattern. The uncertainty of the White Sox' situation was reflected in the day-to-day status of shortstop Luke Appling, who kept the fans and the front office guessing as to his future plans.

"Old Aches and Pains" was wrapping up his 20th season in the White Sox flannels and was looking toward a future role as a Sox manager. Neither Frank Lane nor Chuck Comiskey envisioned Appling in this role, however. They were more anxious for him to retire in order to open up the shortstop position for Chico Carrasquel on a full-time basis.

Appling remained guarded concerning his retirement plans, and as he took the field against the Browns for the

Sunday afternoon twin bill at Comiskey Park, much of the talk in the stands revolved around the prospects for the coming season. Who would manage? Was the kid pitcher Constantine "Gus" Keriazakos, who was scheduled to pitch the second game of the doubleheader, worth the hefty $67,000 bonus paid by the Comiskeys?

The White Sox won the first game 4–3 behind lefty Bill Wight, who went the distance. Appling opened the game at short and collected one hit in three at bats in an otherwise humdrum kind of game. Game 2 was a slugfest between Stubby Overmire and Keriazakos, the $67,000 bust who endured a four-run mauling in the second inning and was excused in the third after loading the bases.

Gus Zernial, the most dangerous White Sox home run threat since Zeke Bonura, slugged his 26th long-distance shot in the first game to draw within one of the team record held jointly by Bonura and Joe Kuhel. In the nightcap he lit up two Brownie pitchers for three more to set a new team record that would stand until 1970, when Bill Melton finally cracked the 30–home run mark.

Luke Appling rapped a harmless single off of Stubby Overmire for the final hit of his star-studded career. And while Gus Keriazakos's entire White Sox career lasted just this one game, Luke's 20-year odyssey spanned 2,422 games. He was voted the greatest player in Sox history by the fans—a deserved honor that has thus far withstood the test of time.

Luke Appling

St. Louis at Chicago, October 1, 1950, Game 2

St. Louis	AB	R	H
Wood, rf	4	0	1
Coleman, cf	4	0	2
Moss, c	3	0	0
Kokos, lf	3	1	1
Lenhardt, 3b	4	3	2
Arft, 1b	2	2	2
Friend, 3b	2	2	2
Upton, ss	5	0	3
DeMars, ss	0	0	0
Sommers, 2b	4	1	1
Overmire, p	3	1	0
Bruner, p	2	0	0
	36	10	14

Chicago	AB	R	H
Fox, 2b	6	1	2
McGhee, rf	5	0	1
Philley, cf	1	0	0
Ostrowski, cf	4	1	2
Robinson, 1b	1	0	0
Goldsberry, 1b	4	1	1
Zernial, lf	4	3	3
Kirrene, 3b	4	0	1
Appling, ss	4	0	1
Erautt, c	4	0	2
Keriazakos, p	1	0	1
Rotblatt, p	2	0	0
	40	6	14

St. Louis	0	4	1	1	0	0	2	0	3—10
Chicago	0	1	3	0	0	0	0	2	0— 6

2B—McGhee. HR—Zernial (3), Kokos, Friend. SB—Upton. E—Goldsberry. DP—Fox to Appling to Goldsberry. LOB—Chicago 7, St. Louis 9. Umpires—Honochick, Soar. Time—2:00. Attendance—4,548.

St. Louis	IP	BB	K	H
Overmire (W)	5	0	2	9
Bruner	4	0	3	4

Chicago	IP	BB	K	H
Keriazakos (L)	$2\frac{1}{3}$	4	2	7
Rotblatt	$6\frac{2}{3}$	4	2	9

A Historic Debut: Minnie Minoso Shatters the Chicago Color Barrier

In 1949 Branch Rickey offered general manager Frank Lane the services of Sam Jethroe, a 27-year-old African American outfielder who was busting down the fences in Montreal. Branch Rickey wanted $100,000 for Jethroe, but Lane demurred. It was too steep a price to pay to the Dodgers, and Jethroe's actual age was questioned. The Chicago color line would remain intact until May 1, 1951.

When Orestes "Minnie" Minoso took the field that night to begin his White Sox career, he broke down a towering barrier that Sam Hairston and Bobby Boyd had been trying to crack for several years. Manager Paul Richards, sensing the potential for trouble, warned several of his players that he would not tolerate any "nonsense" from them in their treatment of Minoso. As it turned out, the warnings were unnecessary. Minnie's teammates welcomed him into the fold with minimal tension.

A shirtsleeve crowd of 14,776 fans turned out to watch Minnie's debut against the Yankees in Comiskey Park. Casey Stengel's team was without the services of Joe DiMaggio, their aging superstar who was out of the lineup with a sore neck. In his place, Stengel penciled in the name of an Oklahoma rookie—Mickey Charles Mantle.

Minnie Minoso, rookie pose

Fans in the stands roar their approval as Minnie Minoso and the rags-to-riches White Sox stir excitement in the baseball world, 1951.

Paul Lehner, acquired in the same trade that brought Minoso to Chicago 24 hours earlier, opened the Sox half of the first inning with a single. Minnie stepped to the plate and coolly belted Vic Raschi's second offering into the center-field bullpen. A southeast wind aided and abetted Minnie's 415-foot shot. It was a pretty fair poke with or without the wind gust.

In the second inning, the jittery Minoso bobbled Phil Rizzuto's sharp grounder, which cost the Sox a pair of runs. "I felt badly," Minoso recalled in his 1994 memoir *Just Call Me Minnie.* "I never liked making errors. I promised myself to show the club the next day that I wasn't a defensive liability." Minnie was playing out of position. After Paul Richards moved him into the outfield, he made good on his promise and established himself as a defensive specialist in left field.

Bob Cain, who started the game for the Sox, was replaced by Randy Gumpert in the sixth inning. The ex-Yankees hurler, who was in the twilight of a very average career, assured his place in history by surrendering a home run to the kid Mantle—a prodigious blast that traveled into the lower right-field stands behind the visitor's bullpen. It was the first of 536 home runs hit by Mantle, but the fan who caught the ball was not interested in receiving the rookie's autograph. He insisted on receiving a replica autographed ball—the kind commonly sold at the concession stands.

New York at Chicago, May 1, 1951

New York	AB	R	H	RBI
Mantle, rf	4	1	1	3
Mapes, rf	1	0	0	1
Coleman 2b	5	0	1	1
McDougald, 3b	4	0	1	0
Woodling, lf	4	0	0	0
Berra, c	2	2	1	1
Silvera, c	1	0	0	0
Jensen, cf	4	0	0	0
Collins, 1b	3	2	1	0
Rizzuto, ss	3	2	2	0
Raschi, p	1	1	1	0
Mize, ph	1	0	1	1
Martin, pr	0	0	0	0
Ferrick, p	0	0	0	0
	33	8	9	7

Chicago	AB	R	H	RBI
Carrasquel, ss	5	0	2	1
Lehner, lf	4	1	1	0
Minoso, 3b	4	1	2	2
Robinson, 1b	4	0	0	0
Zarilla, rf	3	0	0	0
Busby, cf	4	0	0	0
Fox, 2b	4	0	0	0
Niarhos, c	4	1	2	0
Cain, p	1	0	0	0
Stewart, ph	1	0	1	0
Gumpert, p	0	0	0	0
Goldsberry, ph	1	0	0	0
Rotblatt, p	0	0	0	0
Baker, ph	1	0	1	0
	36	3	9	3

New York	0	2	0	2	1	2	0	1	0—8
Chicago	2	0	0	0	1	0	0	0	0—3

New York	IP	H	R	ER	BB	K
Raschi	7	6	3	3	1	4
Ferrick	2	3	0	0	0	1

Chicago	IP	H	R	ER	BB	K
Cain	5	6	5	3	1	1
Gumpert	2	2	2	2	1	1
Rotblatt	2	1	1	1	1	2

Winning pitcher—Raschi (3–1). Losing pitcher—Cain (0–2).

E—Minoso, Rizzuto. 2B—McDougald, Raschi. HR—Minoso, Berra, Mantle. SB—Coleman. Sac—Lehner, Raschi, Rizzuto. DP—Minoso-Fox-Robinson. LOB—White Sox 8, Yankees 5. HBP—Berra and McDougald (by Cain). WP—Cain. Umpires: Berry, Hurley, Napp, Passerella. Time—2:18. Attendance—14,776.

Jack the Whiffer: Harshman Strikes Out 16, Sets Team Record

Relying on a pitch taught to him by Paul Richards, 27-year-old southpaw Jack Harshman fanned 16 Red Sox batters in Fenway Park to eclipse Ed Walsh's single-game record of 15, which had stood since October 2, 1908.

Credit Richards for the development of Harshman's deadly palm ball—a slip pitch he simply called "the thing." Frank Lane acquired this former first baseman from Nashville for the sum of $15,000. In 1954 he was added to an outstanding starting rotation that included Virgil Trucks, Billy Pierce, Bob Keegan, and Sandy Consuegra.

The White Sox were finishing up a disappointing eastern road trip when they arrived in Fenway for a Sunday doubleheader on July 25. Paul Richards' team trailed the Cleveland Indians by seven and a half games and were slipping further away.

Harshman squared off against Willard Nixon in Game 1. The Sox relied on their usual nip-and-tuck offense to grab an early lead against Nixon. Chico Carrasquel, Nellie Fox, and Minnie Minoso peppered the Red Sox starter for three singles and two runs in the fifth. A walk to Fox in the seventh, accompanied by consecutive hits from Minoso and Phil Cavarretta, rounded out the Sox scoring.

Meanwhile Harshman retired the Bosox with alacrity. Three times he struck out four men in a row. Everyone in their lineup, including the great Ted Williams, fanned at least once. Harshman, as you might expect, was oblivious to his own accomplishments. "I didn't know until the seventh inning that I had a chance for a record," he said. "Minnie Minoso told me on the bench. The kid operating the scoreboard in left field was keeping Minnie posted."

Sox catcher Matt Batts shared in Harshman's good fortune. He equaled the modern record of 18 putouts for a catcher.

By the eighth inning, the Red Sox faithful were applauding the Chicago pitcher. His singular achievement that afternoon was the highest strikeout total by an American League pitcher since Bob Feller's 18 Ks on October 2, 1938. Jack Harshman finished the year with a 14–8 record and four shutouts.

Jack "the Whiffer" Harshman

Chicago at Boston, July 25, 1954, Game 1

Chicago	AB	R	H	RBI
Carrasquel, ss	4	2	1	0
Fox, 2b	4	1	2	0
Minoso, lf	5	1	2	1
Cavarretta, 1b	3	0	2	1
Rivera, rf	3	0	0	2
Batts, c	3	1	0	0
Michaels, 3b	4	0	1	0
Groth, cf	4	0	1	1
Harshman, p	4	0	0	0
	34	5	9	5

Boston	AB	R	H	RBI
Consolo, 3b	4	0	0	0
Piersall, rf	4	1	2	0
Williams, lf	3	1	1	0
Agganis, 1b	3	0	0	0
Jensen, cf	3	0	1	0
Wilber, c	4	0	1	2
Lepcio, 2b	3	0	0	0
Bolling, ss	2	0	0	0
Lenhardt, ph	1	0	0	0
Olson, ph	1	0	0	0
Nixon, p	3	0	0	0
	31	2	5	2

Chicago	0	1	0	0	2	0	2	0	0—5
Boston	0	0	0	2	0	0	0	0	0—2

E—Consolo. 2B—Wilber. Sac—Rivera. DP—Michaels-Carrasquel-Cavarreta, Bolling-Lepcio-Agganis. LOB—White Sox 7, Red Sox 7. Umpires—Honochick, McGowan, McKinley, Flaherty. Time—2:28. Attendance—26,068.

Chicago	IP	R	ER	K	BB
Harshman	9	2	2	16	5

Boston	IP	R	ER	K	BB
Nixon	9	5	5	5	4

Winning pitcher—Harshman (7–4). Losing pitcher—Nixon (8–8).

The Kansas City Massacre: Sox Score 29 Runs In One Game

It was a weekend of firsts for Marty Marion's White Sox. The three-game series played in Kansas City April 22–24, 1955, marked the first meeting between the transplanted Philadelphia A's in their new home on Brooklyn Avenue and the contending Sox. When the White Sox boarded their charter flight in Detroit for the short hop to K.C., it was a historic turning point in baseball, for this was the first time the team had flown from one American League city to another. And it was the first (and last) time the Sox plated 29 runs in a game.

The offensive deluge shattered every White Sox scoring record. Sherman Lollar enjoyed the biggest day of his illustrious career by whacking two home runs and three singles. He became only the third player in history to collect two hits in one inning. It came in the visitors' riotous sixth frame. White Sox sluggers, playing in the misty drizzle of old Municipal Stadium, belted seven home runs, one short of a record.

The threatening weather conditions were a constant worry to "Frantic" Frank Lane, who paced the press box nervously glancing up at the skies. It was only the fourth inning, and the score stood at 14–5. "I wasn't thinking about records then," Lane said. "I was hoping the White Sox would strike out."

The Sox were aided by a strong, galelike wind whipping from right to left as the juggernaut rolled on. The Comiskeys piled up 55 total bases—five short of another major league record. Lollar and Chico Carrasquel collected five hits apiece. Bob Nieman, a reserve outfielder, drove in seven runs for the biggest day of his career.

All in all it was quite a showing for a ballclub that lived and died by the walk, stolen base, and well-timed single. Not even the powerful Yankees in their heyday matched the White Sox accomplishment. The Red Sox were the only other team to score 29 runs in a game. They defeated the St. Louis Browns 29–4 on June 8, 1950. The losing pitcher that day was Harry Dorish—who wrapped up the Kansas City Massacre for Jack Harshman.

Chicago at Kansas City, April 23, 1955

Chicago	AB	R	H	RBI
Carrasquel, ss	6	5	5	0
Fox, 2b	5	2	1	1
Minoso, lf	6	5	4	5
Kell, 3b	5	2	2	2
Jok, 3b	1	1	0	0
Nieman, rf	4	3	3	7
Dropo, 1b	7	3	3	7
Rivera, cf	7	1	3	2
Lollar, c	6	4	5	5
Harshman, p	5	2	3	2
Dorish, p	1	0	0	0
McGhee, cf	1	1	0	0
	54	29	29	28

Kansas City	AB	R	H	RBI
Power, 1b	5	1	1	1
Jacobs, 2b	3	2	0	0
Finigan, 1b	4	2	2	1
Zernial, lf	4	0	0	0
Renna, rf	3	1	2	4
Wilson, cf	3	0	0	0
DeMaestri, ss	3	0	0	0
Littrell, ss	1	0	0	0
Astroth, c	3	0	1	0
MacKenzie, c	1	0	0	0
Shantz, p	0	0	0	0
Wheat, p	0	0	0	0
Stewart, ph	1	0	0	0
Trice, p	0	0	0	0
Burtschy, p	1	0	0	0
Spicer, p	1	0	0	0
VanBrabant, p	0	0	0	0
Valo, ph	1	0	0	0
	34	6	6	6

Chicago	4	7	3	2	0	6	3	4	0—29
Kansas City	3	0	2	0	1	0	0	0	0— 6

Chicago	IP	H	R	ER	BB	K
Harshman	7	6	6	5	2	7
Dorish	2	0	0	0	1	2

Kansas City	IP	H	R	ER	BB	K
Shantz	1⅔	7	9	8	1	0
Wheat	⅓	3	2	2	1	0
Trice	1⅓	5	5	4	0	0
Burtshcy	2⅓	7	6	6	1	1
Spicer	1⅔	4	5	5	2	2
VanBrabant	1⅔	3	2	2	1	1

Winning pitcher—Harshman (2–0). Losing pitcher—Shantz (0–2).

E—Finigan, Zernial, Wilson, Kell. 2B—Finigan (2), Rivera (2), Kell, Astroth, Fox. HR—Nieman (2), Lollar (2), Renna, Dropo, Power, Minoso, Harshman. Sac—Fox, Jok. HBP—Fox (by Spicer). WP—Shantz. LOB—Chicago 7, Kansas City 5. Attendance—18,338.

A Hitless Wonder: Sox Score 11 Runs on Just One Hit

In the spring of 1959, Bill Veeck decided that his Go-Go Sox had to have a power hitter if there was any hope at all for a pennant. The Yankees were plagued by injuries and holdouts, leaving the Indians as the Sox' closest competitor in a weakened league. Despite assurances from Al Lopez that the Sox had the horses to go all the way, Veeck kept after Senators owner Clark Griffith, who was shopping slugger Roy Sievers.

Proving once and for all that it was possible to score runs without the benefit of hits, the Sox revisited Kansas City, site of the famous 1955 massacre, where on April 22 they put a new spin on the old Hitless Wonder moniker. On the mound for K.C. was Ned Garver, an old Sox nemesis. He had not lost to the Sox in more than two years and appeared to be well on his way to another win after the A's staked him to an early five-run lead.

But in the seventh inning the Sox staged one of the most bizarre rallies in baseball history. They stood at the plate with their bats planted on their shoulders. The inning dragged on for a full 45 minutes. When it was over, the Sox had scored 11 runs on 10 walks, a base hit, a hit batsman, and three errors. It went like this:

Tom Gorman came in to pitch for the A's. Ray Boone was safe when Joe DeMaestri fielded his grounder but threw wide of first. Al Smith sacrificed Boone to second but was safe when catcher Hal Smith fumbled the ball. Johnny Callison singled to right for the only hit. Boone scored. When Roger Maris fumbled the ball, Smith scored with Callison taking third. Luis Aparicio walked and stole second. Bob Shaw walked to fill the bases. Mark Freeman came in to pitch for the A's. Earl Torgeson walked, forcing in Callison. Nellie Fox walked, forcing in Aparicio. Jim Landis bounced one back to Freeman, who threw to the plate forcing Shaw. Sherm Lollar walked, forcing in Torgeson. George Brunet relieved Freeman. Boone walked, forcing in Fox. Smith walked, forcing in Landis. Callison was hit by a pitch, scoring Lollar. Lou Skizas ran for Callison. Aparicio struck out. Bubba Phillips hit for Torgeson and drew a walk, scoring Smith. Fox walked, forcing in Skizas. Landis grounded to Brunet. Eleven runs, one hit, three errors.

Chicago at Kansas City, April 22, 1959

Chicago	AB	R	H	RBI
Goodman, 3b	3	1	2	0
Esposito, 3b	0	1	0	0
Torgeson, ph	0	1	0	1
Phillips, 3b	1	0	0	1
Fox, 2b	5	1	4	5
Landis, cf	4	1	1	0
Lollar, c	3	2	2	1
Cash, 1b	2	2	0	2
Boone, 1b	2	2	0	2
Rivera, rf	2	1	2	1
A. Smith, rf	2	2	0	1
Callison, lf	4	1	1	2
Skizas, lf	1	1	0	0
Aparicio, ss	4	4	3	4
Wynn, p	0	0	0	0
Shaw, p	4	0	1	0
	37	20	16	20

Kansas City	AB	R	H	RBI
Tuttle, cf	4	1	1	0
Herzog, lf	4	1	1	1
Lopez, 2b	5	0	2	1
Maris, rf	5	1	2	3
Hadley, 1b	3	0	0	0
H. Smith, 3b	4	0	0	0
House, c	3	1	0	0
DeMaestri, ss	4	1	1	0
Garver, p	1	1	1	1
Daley, p	1	0	0	0
Meyer, p	0	0	0	0
Ward, ph	1	0	1	0
Gorman, p	0	0	0	0
Freeman, p	0	0	0	0
Brunet, p	0	0	0	0
	36	6	9	6

Chicago	0	1	1	3	1	2	11	0	1	—20
Kansas City	1	5	0	0	0	0	0	0	0	— 6

Chicago	IP	H	R	ER	BB	K
Wynn	1⅔	6	6	6	2	2
Shaw	7⅓	3	0	0	2	6

Kansas City	IP	H	R	ER	BB	K
Garver	3⅔	6	5	5	1	0
Daley	1⅔	5	3	3	2	0
Meyer	⅔	0	0	0	0	1
Gorman	0	1	6	2	3	0
Freeman	⅓	0	2	0	2	0
Brunet	2⅔	4	4	1	5	4

Winning pitcher—Shaw (1–0). Losing pitcher—Daley (0–2).

E—Lopez, Maris, H. Smith, DeMaestri. 2B—Lollar (2), Rivera, Goodman, Fox, Maris, Ward. HR—Maris, Aparicio. SB—Tuttle, Aparicio. Sac—Landis, A. Smith, Shaw. LOB—Kansas City 7, Chicago 11. HBP—Brunet (Callison). Umpires—Rice, Rommel, Napp, Stevens. Time—3:42. Attendance—7,446.

The Night of the Long Sirens: Sox Clinch the 1959 Flag

Panic, amid the excitement of the first White Sox pennant in 40 years, roused thousands of Chicagoans from their easy chairs at precisely 9:45 PM CDT when the city air-raid sirens sounded a happy alarm. Those who were not nearly as enamored with the White Sox or the game of baseball as an exultant Mayor Richard Daley believed that the Russians had launched their ICBMs at Chicago. Daley had ordered fire commissioner Robert J. Quinn to activate the system in the mistaken belief that everyone was a White Sox fan, at least that evening. Not since Orson Welles' *War of the Worlds* broadcast in 1938 had there been such panic over a staged event in Chicago.

The sirens wailed for nearly five minutes in celebration of the remarkable Go-Go White Sox, who had wrapped up a hectic pennant race on the shores of Lake Erie against their closest pursuers, the Cleveland Indians. It was a moment to savor.

With a crowd of 54,293 feverish Indian fans hanging on every pitch—praying for a ninth-inning miracle to prolong

CHICAGO SUN-TIMES, Wed., Sept. 23, 1959

Sirens For Sox Anger City

Raid Alarms Panic Residents

Jubilant as double play ends ball game at Cleveland and clinches American League pennant for the White Sox, Chicago players race from dugout onto the field. Coach Don Gutteridge (left) grabs manager Al Lopez.

Many thousands of Chicagoans were panic-stricken Tuesday night when air raid sirens were sounded to celebrate winning of the American League pennant by the White Sox.

It was reported that Mayor Daley ordered Fire Comr. Robert J. Quinn, who is also the city's civil defense director, to sound the sirens at 10:30 p.m. if the Sox won.

But the sirens, which continued sounding for some five minutes, brought anything but the joyful reaction that city officials apparently had expected.

Television and radio shows were interrupted to tell Chicagoans that there was no air raid.

Sent By Alarm System

The Illinois Bell Telephone Co. said it handled the heaviest deluge of calls since the death of President Franklin D. Roosevelt.

But the mayor tried to sidestep reporters' questions about the terror-spreading air raid signal when he showed up at Midway Airport early Wednesday to great the victorious Sox.

"The City Council passed a resolution decreeing that there should be hiliarity in the streets and shouting and celebration," Daley said. He declined further comment.

Fire Comr. Quinn also went to the airport. He too, quoted the City Council celebration resolution as the excuse for the sirens.

My Decision: Quinn

But he said the actual decision to set off the sirens was his own and that he notified Mayor Daley of his plan.

Quinn contended that not many Chicagoans paid attention to the sirens.

When a reporter told him that many thouands of persons had been terrified, he commented:

"There should have been 5,000,000 people frightened."

100,000 Welcome Champs

Left: Headline from the *Sun-Times*, 1959; right: Scalping the magic number off the Cleveland Indian (*Chicago American*, September 1959)

their fading title hopes—Sox relief ace Gerry Staley coolly served up a sinker-ball pitch to Vic Power, who rapped into a bases-loaded game-ending double play.

The climactic outcome could not have been more perfect for the legions of pennant-starved White Sox fans.

Staley was the last of three pitchers who frantically clung to a razor-thin two-run lead. Starting pitcher Early Wynn survived a second-inning uprising after Al Smith, one of the unsung heroes of '59, threw a perfect strike to catcher John Romano to double up Minnie Minoso at the plate after he tried to score on Rocky Colavito's foul fly out. "It might have been a different game if Smitty hadn't made that throw," Al Lopez said later. "But what the heck—he's been throwing guys out all season."

In the top of the third the Sox bunched three hits and a fly ball to push across their first two runs. Consecutive home runs from Al Smith and Jungle Jim Rivera in the sixth inning put the game out of reach.

Cleveland manager Joe Gordon, who was in jeopardy of losing his job if the Tribe failed to pull his team out of the fire, utilized his entire bench. The Indians chipped away at the Sox' lead, forcing Lopez to bring in young Bob Shaw, who had emerged as the No. 2 starter on the staff in his sophomore season. Shaw wiggled out of trouble in the seventh inning and again in the eighth, setting the stage for the thrilling finish.

Consecutive singles by Jim Baxes, Jack Harshman, and Jimmy Piersall after one out in the ninth drove Shaw from the mound. Lopez then called on Staley to close things out. The sinker-ball ace delivered only one pitch to Power. He punched a sharp grounder toward Luis Aparicio, who had shaded the Cleveland hitter toward second base. Louie fielded the ball flawlessly, kicked second, and flipped to Ted Kluszewski to complete the twin killing that ended the longest pennant drought in the majors up to that point in time.

Sox fans celebrated their achievement long into the night. An estimated 100,000 fans, swept up in the euphoria of the moment, jammed Midway Airport to welcome their heroes home at 1:30 in the morning. Heading the delegation was Mayor Richard Daley, who was all smiles as he touted his favorite team to the newspaper and radio reporters. "A Chicago finish!" he gushed. "Now for the World Series. We'll win it in four straight!"

Alas...

Chicago at Cleveland, September 22, 1959

Chicago	AB	R	H	RBI
Aparicio, ss	5	1	2	1
Fox, 2b	4	0	0	0
Goodman, 3b	4	0	2	1
Landis, cf	0	0	0	0
Kluszewski, 1b	3	0	0	0
Romano, c	3	0	0	0
Battey, c	0	0	0	0
Lollar, c	1	0	0	0
Smith, lf	4	1	1	1
Rivera, rf	3	1	2	1
Phillips, cf-3b	4	1	2	0
Wynn, p	3	0	0	0
Shaw, p	1	0	0	0
Staley, p	0	0	0	0
	35	4	9	4

Cleveland	AB	R	H	RBI
Piersall, cf	5	0	3	1
Power, 2b	5	0	1	0
Francona, 1b	4	1	1	0
Minoso, lf	3	0	1	0
Nixon, c	4	0	2	0
Colavito, rf	3	0	0	1
Held, ss	3	1	0	0
Strickland, 3b	0	0	0	0
Tanner, ph	1	0	0	0
Leek, 3b	0	0	0	0
Valo, ph	1	0	0	0
Baxes, 3b	1	0	1	0
Webster, pr	0	0	0	0
Perry, p	1	0	0	0
Coleman, ph	1	0	1	0
Grant, p	0	0	0	0
Bell, p	0	0	0	0
Harshman, p	2	0	1	0
Hardy, pr	0	0	0	0
	34	2	11	2

Chicago	0	0	2	0	0	2	0	0	0—4
Cleveland	0	0	0	0	1	1	0	0	0—2

LOB: White Sox, 7; Cleveland, 9. 2B—Aparicio, Goodman. HR—A. Smith, Rivera. Sac—Colavito. DP—Sox, 4; Cleveland, 0. E—Aparicio. HBP—by Wynn (Minoso). Attendance—54,293. Time: 2:43. Umpires: Summers, McKinley, Soar, Chylak.

Chicago	IP	K	BB	ER
Wynn (W, 21–10)	5⅔	2	2	2
Shaw	2⅔	0	0	0
Staley (Save)	⅔	0	0	0

Cleveland	IP	K	BB	ER
Perry (L, 12–10)	5	1	2	2
Grant	1	0	0	2
Bell	1	0	0	0
Harshman	2	1	0	0

Bill Melton Wins AL Home Run Crown on the Last Day of the Season

For most of the 1971 season, Bill Melton ran neck and neck with Reggie Jackson and Norm Cash for a home run crown no one seemed to really want. Going into the last day of the season, the three AL sluggers were tied with 32 apiece. The figure represented the smallest total for a home run champion since 1965.

The burly White Sox third baseman, whose matinee-idol good looks made him a favorite of many female fans at Comiskey Park, had already shattered the team home-run record. In 1970 Melton became the first Sox player to breach the 30–home run mark.

Melton had been pressing. He stroked 12 homers in the month of June to set a new team record, but tailed off in July and August. In order for him to equal his 1970 total of 33, it was necessary to hit three home runs in the last two days of the season. It was a tall order for anyone, but Melton came through in a big way against his favorite patsies—the Milwaukee Brewers. Bill had slugged five home runs off of Brewer pitching in 1971, and he added to this total on the evening of September 29, when he touched Jim Slaton for two more.

Only 2,814 fans showed up for a matinee contest in Comiskey Park the following afternoon. Chuck Tanner juggled his

Bill Melton lines a home run into the left-field seats on the last day of the 1971 season to win the American League home run crown with 33. The catcher is the Brewers' Darryl Porter.

lineup and inserted Melton into the leadoff spot in order to provide him with an extra at-bat if he needed it. In the third inning Brewers pitcher Bill Parsons tried to cross Melton up by throwing a breaking ball. The pitch floated up to the plate, and Bill promptly deposited the ball into the first few rows of the left-field grandstand. With it came the American League home run championship—a first for Melton and for the Chicago White Sox franchise in its storied 71-year existence.

Melton tossed his batting helmet to the fans as a souvenir while Andy Frain, ushers, and park security personnel scoured the stands to retrieve the historic ball. Melton eventually paid the fan $50 for the ball. "He told me it was the 499th ball he caught at the ballpark over the years," Melton said. "I asked him if he ever works."

It was a satisfying outcome, despite the empty grandstands. But as humorist (and Sox fan) Jean Shepherd observed, "Everyman's great moment on the Sox comes when nobody is watching."

Chuck Tanner pops the champagne all over Bill Melton, moments after Melton won the AL home run crown.

Milwaukee at Chicago, September 30, 1971

Milwaukee	AB	R	H	RBI
Harper, lf	2	0	0	0
Auerbach, ss	4	0	0	0
Cardenal, rf	4	1	1	0
Briggs, 1b	3	0	0	0
D. May, cf	3	0	0	0
Theobold, 3b	2	0	1	0
Schofield, 2b	1	0	0	0
Kosco, ph	1	0	0	0
Porter, c	3	0	0	1
Heise, 3b	2	0	0	0
Ratliff, ph	1	0	0	0
Matchick, 3b	1	0	0	0
Parsons, p	2	0	0	0
Krausse, p	0	0	0	0
Tepedino, ph	0	0	0	0
Sanders, p	0	0	0	0
Pena, ph	1	0	0	0
Morris, p	0	0	0	0
	30	1	2	1

Chicago	AB	R	H	RBI
Melton, 3b	2	1	1	1
Williams, rf	1	0	1	0
Kelly, cf	3	0	1	0
McKinney, 2b	4	0	0	0
Hottman, lf	4	0	1	0
Johnstone, cf	3	0	1	0
Morales, 3b	1	0	0	0
Muser, 1b	4	1	2	0
Richard, ss	3	0	0	0
Brinkman, c	2	0	1	1
Magnuson, p	0	0	0	0
Huntz, ph	1	0	0	0
Hinton, p	0	0	0	0
Eddy, p	1	0	1	0
C. May, ph	0	0	0	0
Reichardt, ph	1	0	0	0
O'Toole, p	0	0	0	0
Perzanowski, p	0	0	0	0
	30	2	9	2

Milwaukee	0	0	0	0	0	0	0	0	1—1
Chicago	0	1	1	0	0	0	0	0	x—1

Milwaukee	IP	H	R	ER	BB	K
Parsons	5⅔	8	2	2	2	6
Morris	1	0	0	0	1	1
Krausse	⅓	0	0	0	0	1
Sanders	1	1	0	0	0	0

Chicago	IP	H	R	ER	BB	K
Magnuson	2	0	0	0	0	0
Hinton	2	0	0	0	0	1
Eddy	2	1	0	0	3	1
O'Toole	2	0	0	0	1	2
Perzanowski	1	1	1	0	1	1

Winning pitcher—Hinton (3–4). Losing pitcher—Parsons (13–17). Save—Perzanowski.

E—Heise, Muser. 3B—Muser. HR—Melton (33). SB—Harper (2). 2B—Eddy. Sac—Richard. LOB—Milwaukee 8, Chicago 8. DP—Milwaukee. Time—2:27. Attendance—2,814.

White Sox Clinch 1983 Western Division Title

"Think about it. Just think about it. We are the champions. Not New York. Not Los Angeles. Chicago." Not even White Sox manager Tony LaRussa could fully grasp the magnitude of his words. A Chicago baseball team was advancing to postseason play for the first time since 1959.

LaRussa, a Floridian by birth, understood better than most out-of-towners the frustrations felt by Chicago sports fans who had waited so long for something more than just the end of another losing season to celebrate. This victory had not come easy. The Seattle Mariners battled back from a 3–1 deficit in the ninth inning to tie the score and set the stage for a piece of drama never to be forgotten by the 45,646 fans who filled old Comiskey Park to witness history in the making.

The (near) "Miracle on 35th Street" was almost canceled out by the weathermen. There were scattered rainstorms throughout the Cook County region that evening, but curiously, the inclement weather did not interfere with the progress of the White Sox game. A 38-minute downpour delayed the start of the contest, but after the first pitch was thrown not another drop of rain fell on Comiskey Park, though periodic bolts of lightning were observed in the distance.

The standing-room-only crowd was treated to a daring blend of patented "Winning Ugly" baseball. In the fourth inning, third baseman Vance Law snapped a 1–1 tie by laying down a suicide squeeze bunt that scored ex-Mariner Tom Paciorek.

Harold Baines hammered his 18th home run of the season in the eighth inning to build upon the lead. At this point, things appeared to be under control. Forty-year-old Jerry Koosman, who had been acquired from the Minnesota Twins for three farmhands in 1981, was cruising along in effortless fashion. He had pitched scoreless ball since surrendering an unearned run in the first inning. However, the M's knotted the score against reliever Dennis Lamp following an infield single to ex-Sox Tony Bernazard, a single to Al Cowens, and a bases-clearing double to pinch hitter Ricky Nelson.

In the home half of the ninth, successive walks to Julio Cruz, Rudy Law, and Carlton Fisk from reliever Bill Caudill filled the bases. Harold Baines, who had set a major league record in 1983 with 22 game-winning hits, drove Caudill's first pitch into the air. The towering fly ball settled into Phil Bradley's glove in center field. But it was enough to send the speedy Julio Cruz scurrying across the plate with the game-winning run—and an unforgettable moment of jubilation never before experienced by a generation of younger fans who had no prior memories of 1959 or of the Chicago Bears championship still two years off.

It was the White Sox' 16th straight victory in the friendly Comiskey confines.

General manager Roland Hemond wept openly. He had waited 13 years to see his labors finally bear some fruit. "I never regretted a minute of this," he said. "Not a minute. I worked during some times when the money wasn't there, but—and please don't take this to sound cocky—there was fun in that too. It was like David and Goliath."

In the riotous clubhouse celebration that followed, Roland was drenched in victory champagne. The players and the ownership appreciated his quiet dignified manner, his thoughtfulness, and most of all, his even-handed temperament through some difficult days. This was a victory to savor for Roland Hemond—and for the long-suffering Sox fans who supported this (at times) jinxed ballclub through 24 dry seasons.

Seattle at Chicago, September 17, 1983

Seattle	AB	R	H	RBI
Owen, ss	4	0	1	0
P. Bradley, cf	3	1	0	0
Bernazard, 2b	4	0	3	0
Reynolds, 2b	0	1	0	0
Cowens, dh	4	1	1	0
S. Hendersn, lf	4	0	0	0
Moses, lf	0	0	0	0
D. Henderson, rf	3	0	1	0
R. Nelson, rf	1	0	1	2
Putnam, 1b	2	0	0	0
R. Roenicke, 1b	1	0	0	0
Coles, 3b	4	0	1	0
Mercado, c	4	0	0	0
	34	3	8	2

Chicago	AB	R	H	RBI
R. Law, cf	4	0	1	0
Fisk, c	3	0	1	0
Baines, rf	4	1	1	3
Luzinski, dh	3	0	1	0
Nyman, pr	0	0	0	0
Paciorek, 1b	4	1	2	0
Squires, 1b	0	0	0	0
Kittle, lf	3	0	0	0
V. Law, 3b	3	0	0	1
Fletcher, ss	2	0	0	0
Hairston, ph	1	0	0	0
J. Cruz, 2b	2	2	0	0
	29	4	6	4

Seattle	1	0	0	0	0	0	0	0	2—3
Chicago	0	0	1	1	0	0	0	1	1—4

Two out when winning run scored.

GW RBI—Baines (19). E—J. Cruz, Mercado. DP—Seattle 1, White Sox 1. LOB—Seattle 6, White Sox 9. 2B—Coles, Paciorek, R. Nelson. HR—Baines (18). SB—R. Law (71), Fletcher (5), Nyman (2). J. Cruz (53). S—V. Law. SF—Baines. Time—2:47. Attendance—45,646.

Seattle	IP	H	R	ER	BB	K
Beattle	8	6	3	3	5	5
Caudill (L, 2–8)	⅓	0	1	1	3	0
Vandeberg	⅓	0	0	0	0	0

Chicago	IP	H	R	ER	BB	K
Koosman	8	6	2	1	1	5
Lamp (W, 7–7)	1	2	1	1	1	1

Koosman pitched to one batter in 9th.

White Sox Win Longest Game In AL History—25 Innings

Like two punch-drunk fighters staggering under their own weight, the White Sox and Milwaukee Brewers battled each other for 25 innings, spanning two nights, May 8 and 9, 1984. In all, 44 players from both sides entered the game before Harold Baines drilled the 753rd pitch of the game deep into the center-field bullpen to deliver a victory to Tom Seaver, who was making his first relief appearance since 1976.

"My adrenaline was pumping in the 25th inning, but I could feel I wasn't in total control," Seaver said. "I treated it like I was coming back from a rain delay. I had no other reference point."

The game was suspended on Tuesday night, May 8, after the two ballclubs played to a 17-inning, 3–3 standoff. The White Sox pressed into duty every player on the roster except LaMarr Hoyt, and they refused to concede a victory to Milwaukee even after the Brewers scored three times in the 21st inning. The Sox knotted the score at six apiece in the bottom of the 21st.

Rudy Law was safe at second after third baseman Randy Ready's throw from across the diamond sailed over the first baseman's head. Carlton Fisk, who set a new major league record by catching all 25 innings, singled. Marc Hill followed with another base hit and suddenly the Sox were back in business. Tom Paciorek's single drove in the tying runs to prolong the marathon.

Harold Baines' game-winning, 420-foot home run off Chuck Porter ended the drama just one-inning shy of the major league record set by the Brooklyn Dodgers and Boston Braves, who played to a 26-inning, 1–1 tie back in 1920. The Dodgers-Braves contest required only 3 hours and 50 minutes to complete. This one consumed 8:06, which broke the all-time mark established by the San Francisco Giants and New York Mets on May 31, 1964.

Tom Paciorek slides safely ahead of Robin Yount's tag in the 18th inning of the longest American League game on record.

Milwaukee at Chicago, May 8–9, 1984

Milwaukee	AB	R	H	RBI
Ready, 3b	8	1	1	0
Sundberg, c	4	0	3	0
Romero, pr	0	0	0	0
Schroeder, c	4	0	2	0
Yount, ss	10	1	3	1
Cooper, dh	11	1	2	0
Simmons, 1b	7	2	1	0
Oglivie, lf	10	1	2	4
Clark, cf	2	0	1	0
Manning, cf	6	0	2	0
Moore, rf	2	0	0	0
James, rf	2	0	0	0
Brouhard, rf	4	0	1	0
Gantner, 2b	10	0	2	0
	80	6	20	5

Chicago	AB	R	H	RBI
R. Law, cf	11	1	4	1
Fisk, c	11	1	3	1
Walker, 1b	4	1	2	0
Squires, 1b	2	0	0	0
Hill, 1b	4	0	2	0
Reed, p	1	0	0	0
Dotson, pr	0	1	0	0
Bannister, p	1	0	0	0
Seaver, p	0	0	0	0
Luzinski, dh	2	0	0	0
Stegman, lf	8	0	1	0
Baines, rf	10	1	2	1
Kittle, lf	1	0	0	0
Paciorek, lf	9	1	5	3
V. Law, 3b	10	0	1	0
Fletcher, ss	3	0	0	0
Hairston, ph	1	0	0	0
Dybzinski, ss	6	0	2	0
Cruz, 2b	11	1	1	1
	95	7	23	7

Milw.	000	000	102	000	000	000	003	000	0—6
Chi.	000	001	002	000	000	000	003	000	1—7

One out when winning run scored.
GW RBI—Baines (2). E—Ready 2, Fisk, Moore. DP—Milwaukee 1, White Sox 6. LOB—Milwaukee 13, White Sox 24. 2B—Yount, Cruz, Baines, Hill, Ready, Fisk. HR—Oglivie (2), Baines (2). SB—Walker (1), Yount (3), Manning (3). S—Moore, Ready, Brouhard, V. Law, Dybzinski. Time—8:06. Attendance—14,754.

Milwaukee	IP	H	R	ER	BB	K
Sutton	7	4	1	0	3	6
Ladd	1	0	0	0	1	0
Fingers	2	2	2	0	0	2
Tellmann	3⅓	3	0	0	1	1
Waits	3⅔	3	0	0	0	3
Porter (L, 2–1)	7⅓	11	4	3	2	5

Chicago	IP	H	R	ER	BB	K
Fallon	6	1	1	1	3	4
Barojas	0	2	0	0	0	0
Burns	3	3	2	2	3	3
Jones	4	4	0	0	1	4
Agosto	7	5	0	0	2	1
Reed	2⅔	3	3	3	2	3
Bannister	1⅓	1	0	0	0	1
Seaver (W, 2–2)	1	1	0	0	0	0

Fallon pitched to 1 batter in 7th; Barojos pitched to 2 batters in 7th.
WP—Burns, Jones.

Another Hitless Wonder: No-Hit by the Yankees, Sox Win 4–0

It was a season of surprises on the South Side. In the final year of play at old Comiskey Park, the White Sox climbed into contention following a gloomy last-place finish in 1989. Jeff Torborg's youthful ballclub challenged Tony LaRussa's A's for the division title in 1990 and were only a game behind the leaders when play began on July 1.

Coincidental with the strange developments about to tran - spire on the Comiskey playing field was the 80th-anniversary celebration of the opening of the "Baseball Palace of the World." This little bit of irony brings to mind Warren Brown's observation that if the unlikely were to occur—it would surely happen to the White Sox.

And it did.

Twenty-nine-year-old Andy Hawkins started the game for the once-proud New Yorkers, a tattered collection of castoffs and utility players masquerading as Yankees. Hawkins entered the game with a 1–4 record and a towering 6.49 ERA. But for one afternoon, he was nearly perfect. Locked in a pitcher's duel with the little "Bulldog" Greg Hibbard, the Yankees right-hander had the best of it for seven innings. He retired the first 14 Sox batters before issuing the first of five walks.

In the decisive eighth inning Hawkins retired the first two batters before Sammy Sosa reached first base on an error by third baseman Mike Blowers. Ozzie Guillen and Lance Johnson walked to fill the bases. Then Robin Ventura lifted a lazy fly ball to left field that was completely misjudged by rookie Jim Leyritz, an infielder by trade who had been inserted into the lineup by manager Stump Merrill. The ball thudded off of Leyritz's glove, sending Sosa and Guillen across the plate with the first two runs of the game. Ventura was on second when Ivan Calderon's fly ball to right was dropped by Jesse Barfield.

The fourth run had crossed the plate, and still the Sox had failed to collect a base hit.

Hawkins retired the White Sox in the eighth inning to become only the 13th major league pitcher to lose a no-hitter. (Although MLB later ruled that this was *not* an official no-hitter as Hawkins did not pitch nine innings.) "Anytime you sit down and dream about a no-hitter, the specter of a loss never crosses your mind," he told reporters after the game. "You expect to walk off that field and shake everybody's hand like we've seen this last week with Fernando Valenzuela and Davey Stewart [who won their no-hitters]."

This was not the first time the White Sox pinned a loss on a no-hit pitcher. On May 9, 1901, in Cleveland, pitcher Earl Moore held the South Siders hitless through nine innings, only to lose the game 4–2 in the 10th inning after infielder Sandow Mertes lined a single past shortstop Danny Shay. Twenty-one-year-old Earl Moore completely fell apart and surrendered four runs after the White Sox bench jockeys taunted him from the dugout. It was the American League's first official no-hitter.

New York at Chicago, July 1, 1990

New York	AB	R	H	RBI
Kelly, cf	4	0	0	0
Sax, 2b	4	0	0	0
Mattingly, 1b	4	0	0	0
Balboni, dh	4	0	0	0
Tolleson, pr	0	0	0	0
JeBarfield, rf	4	0	1	0
Leyritz, lf	3	0	1	0
Blowers, 3b	3	0	0	0
Geran, c	3	0	1	0
Espinoza, ss	2	0	1	0
	31	0	4	0

Chicago	AB	R	H	RBI
L. Johnson, cf	3	1	0	0
Ventura, 3b	4	1	0	0
Calderon, dh	3	0	0	0
Pasqua, lf	4	0	0	0
Kittle, 1b	3	0	0	0
Lyons, 1b	0	0	0	0
Karkovice, c	2	0	0	0
Fletcher, 2b	2	0	0	0
Sosa, rf	3	1	0	0
Guillan, ss	2	1	0	0
	26	4	0	0

New York	0	0	0	0	0	0	0	0	0—0
Chicago	0	0	0	0	0	0	0	4	x—4

E—Ventura (2). Blowers, Leyritz, JeBarfield. DP—White Sox 1. LOB—New York 5, White Sox 3. SB—Sosa (14). S—Espinoza. PB—Geran. Umpires—Home, Scott; First, Voltaggio; Second, Reilly; Third, Meriwether. Time—2:34. Attendance—30,642.

New York	IP	H	R	ER	BB	K
Hawkins (L, 1–5)	8	0	4	0	5	3

Chicago	IP	H	R	ER	BB	K
Hibbard	7	4	0	0	0	4
B. Jones (W, 10–1)	1	0	0	0	0	1
Radinsky	1	0	0	0	0	0

White Sox Clinch 1993 Western Division Title

Under a full moon when the improbable often becomes possible, a White Sox team constructed by Larry Himes and Ron Schueler and nurtured under laid-back Gene Lamont won its second American League Western Division crown. It was a night of magic—magic supplied by one Vincent "Bo" Jackson.

Exactly 10 years and 10 days following the last Comiskey Park clinching party, the Seattle Mariners again provided the opposition. The White Sox were expected to win the 1993 divisional crown. This was a strong ballclub built around Larry Himes' shrewd draft choices, along with several key acquisitions made by Ron Schueler since he came on board in 1991.

The stars of this show were Frank Thomas, Robin Ventura, and Jack McDowell, but for much of the year media attention centered on the comeback of Bo Jackson, who was signed as a free agent on April 3, 1991, after the Kansas City Royals pronounced his career over.

Jackson had suffered a career-threatening football injury that cost him the use of his left hip. After missing all of the 1992 season, Bo returned to the Sox in 1993 determined to play baseball with a replacement hip. The tireless efforts of trainer Herman Schneider helped pave the way for Bo's comeback. And even though his offensive contributions as a full-time designated hitter were minimal, Jackson demonstrated a flair for the dramatic. Call it the "Bo moment."

Young Wilson Alvarez, who was in the midst of a scoreless streak that would reach 30 innings before the Mariners pushed across two runs in the eighth inning, turned in another dazzling pitching performance. The Sox were unable to dent the plate against Mariner left-hander Dave Fleming. But in the sixth inning, Bo and the White Sox finally broke through against the Seattle ace.

Ellis Burks, a free agent pickup from the Boston Red Sox, singled and went to second on a bunt single by Craig Grebeck. After retiring the next two batters, Fleming worked the count to 3–0 on Jackson before Bo lofted a towering fly ball to left-center that was aided and abetted by a westerly 9 mph wind.

The ball soared further and further back. Left fielder Brian Turang seemed to draw a bead on the ball, then watched helplessly as it sailed into the stands for a surprise three-run homer.

Jackson was the man of the hour, and after the Mariners had been retired in the ninth inning by Kirk McCaskill, "Bionic" Bo ran a victory lap around the perimeter of the warning track, doffing his cap to the 42,116 sock-waving fans who had borrowed a page from the supporters of the Minnesota Twins. In the late 1980s Twins fans had popularized the "homer hanky" frenzy.

Jerry Reinsdorf, who had been through this once before, was far more subdued in victory than he had been in 1983. "The first time we won it was special," noted the Sox chairman. "But waiting so long to do it again makes this one special too. I'll keep replaying Bo's homer over and over. Bo has to be the comeback player of the century."

On November 5, scarcely a month after the American League playoffs had ended, the ballclub declined to renew its option on Bo Jackson, who was eventually signed as a free agent by the California Angels.

Seattle at Chicago, September 27, 1993

Seattle	AB	R	H	RBI	BB	K
Turang, lf	3	0	1	0	1	0
Amaral, dh	2	0	0	1	0	0
Griffey Jr, cf	4	0	1	0	0	0
Buhner, rf	3	0	1	1	1	1
Blowers, 3b	4	0	0	0	0	3
Boone, 2b	4	0	0	0	0	2
Litton, 1b	2	0	0	0	1	0
a—Magadan, ph	1	0	0	0	0	0
Valle, c	4	1	1	0	0	1
Vizquel, ss	2	1	0	0	1	1
	29	2	4	2	4	8

Chicago	AB	R	H	RBI	BB	K
Burks, rf	3	1	2	1	0	0
Grebeck, 2b	3	1	2	0	1	0
Thomas, 1b	4	0	1	0	0	0
Pasqua, 1b	0	0	0	0	0	0
G. Bell, dh	3	0	0	0	1	1
B. Jackson, lf	3	1	1	3	0	0
Huff, lf	1	0	0	0	0	1
Ventura, 3b	3	0	0	0	1	1
L. Johnson, cf	4	1	2	0	0	0
Karkovice, c	2	0	0	0	0	1
Guillen, ss	3	0	0	0	0	0
	29	4	8	4	3	4

Seattle	0	0	0	0	0	0	0	2	0—2	4	0
Chicago	0	0	0	0	0	3	1	0	x—4	8	0

a—grounded out for Litton in the 9th.

LOB—Seattle 6, White Sox 6. 2B—Thomas (35). HR—B. Jackson (15) off Fleming. RBIs—Amaral (43), Buhner (91), Burks (74), B. Jackson 3 (43). CS—Burks (9). S—Amaral. SF—Amaral, Burks. GIDP—Guillen.
Runners left in scoring position—Seattle 3 (Buhner, Blowers, Litton); White Sox 3 (Thomas, Ventura 2).
Runners moved up—Boone, Guillen.
DP—Seattle 1 (Vizquel, Boone, and Litton).

Seattle	IP	H	R	ER	BB	K	NP
Fleming (L, 11–5)	6⅓	8	4	4	1	3	85
J. Nelson	1⅓	0	0	0	1	1	19
Plantenberg	⅓	0	0	0	1	0	5

Chicago	IP	H	R	ER	BB	K	NP
Alvarez (W, 15–8)	7⅔	4	2	2	4	6	117
McCaskill S, 2	1⅓	0	0	0	0	2	8

Inherited runners–scored—J. Nelson 1–1, McCaskill 2–0.
IBB—off Fleming (G. Bell) 1. HBP—by Fleming (Karkovice).
Umpires—Home, Reilly; First, Roe; Second, Scott; Third, Phillips. Time—2:41, Attendance—42,116.

White Sox Clinch the 2005 Division Title—Prelude to the 2005 World Series

Fearing the worst possible ending to a dream season that saw the South Siders build up a seemingly insurmountable 15-game lead on August 1, only to have it whittled down to a scant one-and-a-half-game lead by September 22, the White Sox embarked on their final road trip of the year with only one thought in mind: "Win or Die Trying." The 2005 marketing slogan had taken on added meaning in the tense, final days of the flag chase as the rampaging Cleveland Indians played with the self-assured belief that they could not—and would not—lose another game, let alone the chance to advance to the postseason. The White Sox dropped the first two games of a four-game set at Comerica Park on September 26 and 27, scoring only five runs off of Jason Johnson and Nate Robertson of the Tigers, two pitchers unlikely to draw comparisons to Cy Young and Walter Johnson. For the better part of two decades, the White Sox took care of business against the toothless Tigers, losing only one season series in the previous 14 years. If the Tigers presented such a formidable challenge this late in the season, what could the fans reasonably expect of the Sox in the playoffs, that is, if they made the playoffs? Fortunately, the Indians went into a tailspin at the same time, losing key home games to the woebegone Tampa Bay Devil Rays. The Sox clung to their precarious two-game lead in the Central Division and extended it to three the night of September 28, as Jose Contreras easily won his final start of the year 8–2. This set the stage for a Thursday afternoon showdown in the empty grandstands of the Tigers' den on Woodward Avenue. Ozzie Guillen juggled his lineup, giving the slumping second baseman Tadahito Iguchi a much-needed rest, with the title hopes pinned on Freddy Garcia, a big-game pitcher who seemed to thrive in the daytime. "All my career, I've been looking for the chance to pitch in that one game to clinch," Garcia said. "I never had that chance before in Seattle." Relying on his change-up, Garcia admitted he didn't have his best stuff, but he limited Tigers batters to just two runs and eight hits in seven innings of work. Carl Everett's two-run triple in the first inning got things going for the Sox. Paul Konerko drilled a mammoth drive into the left-field bullpen in the sixth off of ex-Sox Jason Grilli. It was Paulie's 40th homer of the year, and he matched Frank Thomas as the only other Sox player to clout 40 or more twice in his career. The Tigers did not dent the plate until the seventh inning, by which time Garcia had things well in hand and was cruising along with a 4–0 lead. Bobby Jenks, the portly rookie reliever with the 95 mph fastball, closed out the Tigers in the ninth, and the White Sox were division champs for the first time since 2000. A contingency of front-office people, Chairman Reinsdorf, and a handful of Sox fans who had taken the day off and driven to the Motor City to witness this latest bit of history, celebrated with the players on the field. In 2000 the Sox wrapped up the division in Minnesota with a battered, injury-prone pitching staff and a collection of young players. This time, there were greater expectations. "I got the feeling in 2000 that the division was enough," said Konerko, who was the only holdover left from that season in 2005. "I don't get that feeling with this team. I get the feeling, especially with what happened with Boston last year that this team wants to be more special than that." Konerko could add to his credentials one other designation for 2005: "Paulie the Prophet."

Chicago at Detroit, September 29, 2005

Chicago	AB	R	H	RBI
Podsednik, lf	4	0	1	1
Ozuna, 3b	4	0	2	0
Crede, 3b	1	0	0	0
Dye, rf	4	1	1	0
Konerko, 1b	2	2	2	1
Everett, dh	4	0	3	2
Rowand, cf	4	0	0	0
Pierzynski, c	3	1	1	0
Uribe, ss	4	2	2	1
Harris 2b	2	0	0	0
	30	4	10	4

Detroit	AB	R	H	RBI
Granderson, cf	5	0	5	0
Polanco, 2b	5	1	2	0
Shelton, dh	4	0	1	0
Ordonez, rf	4	0	1	1
Pena, lb	4	0	1	0
Monroe, lf	4	1	1	0
Inge, 3b	4	0	4	0
Wilson, c	4	0	0	0
Infante, ss	3	0	0	0
Young, ph	1	0	0	0
	38	2	10	1

Chicago	2	1	0	0	0	1	0	0	0—4
Detroit	0	0	0	0	0	0	1	1	0—2

E—Crede DP—Detroit 2. LOB—Chicago 7, Detroit 9. 2B—Dye, Pierzynski, Ordonez. 3B—Everett. HR—Konerko. Sac—Uribe. SF—Podsednik. GDP—Dye, Rowand. CS—Ozuna. Umpires—Marvin Hudson, Eric Cooper, Fieldin Culbreth, Larry Young. Time—2:22. Attendance—13,494.

Chicago	IP	H	R	ER	BB	K	Pit	ERA
Garcia	7	8	2	2	0	5	90	3.87
Politte	⅓	1	0	0	0	0	8	2.06
Cotts	⅓	0	0	0	0	1	6	1.97
Jenks	⅓	1	0	0	0	2	17	2.65

Detroit	IP	H	R	ER	BB	K	Pit	ERA
Grilli	7	8	4	4	2	0	83	3.38
Spurling	1	1	0	0	1	0	13	3.20
Rodney	1	1	0	0	1	0	13	2.72

Winning pitcher—Garcia (14–8). Losing pitcher—Grilli (1–1). Save—Jenks (4). HBP—Pierzynski (by Rodney). WP—Garcia, Jenks.

Jim Thome's Walkoff 500th Career Home Run

Inside a jubilant White Sox clubhouse after the game, Ozzie Guillen just couldn't restrain himself. Like everyone else in attendance at U.S. Cellular Field on Jim Thome Bobblehead Day (September 15, 2007), the Sox skipper was caught up in the magic of an unbelievable moment—not the souvenir figurine given to the fans entering the park, but the real deal—Jim's landmark home run. "Even when we won the World Series, I don't think we got so excited," he said. "I was jumping, and [during] the World Series I was calm. All of the sudden we see all of those guys on the field celebrating that, it was real neat."

Jim Thome had just connected on a fastball delivered by Angels reliever Dustin Moseley in the bottom of the ninth inning to snatch a victory away from L.A., who held a commanding 7–1 lead going into the bottom of the seventh inning before Sox hitters inflicted some damage. With Darin Erstad aboard, Big Jim worked a full count off of Moseley before depositing the ball in the left-center-field bleachers—a mighty 426-foot blast to seal a remarkable 9–7 comeback victory and a career milestone likely to ensure Thome's magical ride into the Baseball Hall of Fame.

Thome etched his name into the record book as the 23rd player to record 500 home runs in a career, but he was the first to strike the big blow in walkoff fashion. "Just can't believe it, I really can't," he stammered, his voice cracking with emotion after three curtain calls from the 29,010 Sox fans in attendance. Earlier in the season, Frank Thomas had launched his 500th home run against Minnesota, but the "Big Hurt" was wearing the uniform of the Toronto Blue Jays at the time.

Although two-thirds of his home runs were hit as a member of the Cleveland Indians, this moment was reserved for White Sox fans, deprived as they were of Frank's milestone home run to savor. Two thousand and seven had been a season-long struggle, but the fans showed their support and were 100 percent behind Thome, the Peoria native with humble midwestern charm who had emerged as their new personal favorite.

"The crowd and just the way they hung in there all weekend long, kind of the downs, they had a lot of downs all weekend," Thome said. "I would never have imagined doing that as a walkoff. It's just amazing to see your teammates standing there. It's like a movie script. It really is." Thome was locked in. During the nine-game homestand, he had slugged five home runs, reaching this historic plateau in the fourth-fewest at-bats in history. Thome's famous 500th shot came in his 6,809th at-bat, putting him behind only Mark McGwire (5,487), Babe Ruth (5,800), and Harmon Killebrew (6,671).

"Big" Jim Thome delivers the game-winning blow—his 500th career homer off of Dustin Moseley of the Angels. (Courtesy of the Chicago White Sox)

The historic home run ball was grabbed by 28-year-old Will Stewart of Austin, Texas, who had flown into Chicago early Sunday morning to attend an accounting conference. On a whim he decided to take in a game at the Cell. "I feel it is a part of Chicago baseball history," the man said after handing the ball back to the White Sox slugger to keep as a family heirloom.

Thome, who had won the American League Comeback Player of the Year Award with the White Sox in 2006, seemed awestruck. "When you see your teammates at home plate and then they pick you up like that, and along with probably the greatest fans in sports, in Chicago, what a great, great feeling. You couldn't have written it any better."

Jim Thome punched his ticket to the Hall of Fame with his 500th career home run—a walkoff shot. (Courtesy of the Chicago White Sox)

Los Angeles at Chicago, September 16, 2007

Los Angeles	AB	R	H	RBI
Willits, cf	5	1	1	0
Cabrera, ss	4	0	2	0
Guerrero, dh	4	2	1	1
Quinlan, 1b	4	1	1	1
Kotchman, ph-1b	1	0	1	0
Izturis, 3b	5	1	1	0
Kendrick, 2b	5	1	3	1
Rivera, lf	4	1	2	2
Aybar, ph-lf	1	0	0	0
Napoli, c	2	0	2	1
Evans, rf	3	0	0	0
Morales, ph	1	0	0	0
Haynes, rf	1	0	0	0
	40	7	15	6

Chicago	AB	R	H	RBI
Owens, cf	4	1	1	1
Fields, lf	4	1	2	3
Erstad, lf	1	1	1	0
Thome, dh	5	1	1	2
Konerko, 1b	3	0	1	0
Dye, rf	3	0	0	0
Uribe, ss	3	1	0	0
Richar, 2b	3	3	2	2
Gonzalez, 3b	4	1	1	0
Hall, c	2	0	1	1
	33	9	10	9

Los Angeles	1	0	0	2	0	0	4	0	0—7
Chicago	0	0	0	0	1	0	4	2	2—9

None out when winning run scored. E—Willets, Gonzalez. DP—Chicago, 2. LOB—Chicago 6, Los Angeles 11. 2B—Willits, Kotchman, Fields, Konerko. HR—Guerrero, Rivera, Fields, Thome, Richar. Sac—Cabrera. GDP—Guerrero, Aybar. SB—Owens. CS—Owens. Umpires—Mike Reilly, Jeff Kellogg, Eric Cooper, Andy Fletcher. Time—3:06. Attendance—29,010.

L.A.	IP	H	R	ER	BB	K	Pit	ERA
Saunders	6	2	1	1	5	7	106	3.82
Bootcheck	⅓	4	4	4	0	0	18	4.70
Speier	⅔	1	0	0	0	1	11	3.07
Shields	1	1	2	2	1	1	25	3.93
Moseley	0	2	2	2	0	0	9	4.60

Chicago	IP	H	R	ER	BB	K	Pit	ERA
Buehrle	6⅓	11	7	6	2	3	106	3.55
Bukvich	0	1	0	0	1	0	9	5.05
Thornton	0⅔	0	0	0	0	1	11	5.05
MacDougal	2	3	0	0	1	0	25	6.35

Winning pitcher—MacDougal (2–5). Losing pitcher—Moseley (4–3). Moseley pitched to two batters in the ninth.

Thome's "Blackout Game" Homer Seals the 2008 Division Title in Game No. 163

On August 12, 2008, as the AL Central Division race tightened in the second half of the season, Ozzie Guillen sounded a prophetic warning: "We have to pitch. If we don't, we have a lot of problems. If we don't pitch, we don't win the division."After the All-Star break, Sox pitchers struggled, and with inconsistent pitching the team could not shake loose the Minnesota Twins, who remained within three games (or less) of first-place Chicago through the climactic final games in Chicago, September 28–30.

A week earlier the Sox held what seemed to be a secure 2½-game lead over their archrivals, going into a three-game series at the Metrodome. But the Twins swept the series, coming from five runs down in the last game to win in 10 innings, and that put the White Sox a half-game behind. After taking care of business against Cleveland on September 28, Detroit arrived in Chicago to make up a rainout the next night. Alexei Ramirez was the star of the game, establishing a rookie record with his fourth grand slam of the season to seal the deal for Ozzie's men.The Sox easily conquered Detroit 8–2, forcing a one-game tiebreaker against Minnesota for the AL Central title.

Earlier in the month, the Twins had lost a coin toss to determine home-field advantage for what was to become the eighth one-game playoff in major league history. Minnesota flew to Chicago for the September 30 winner-take-all finale to face John Danks, starting on three days' rest against their own Nick Blackburn, who took the place of the injured Kevin Slowey. "Tomorrow, 162 games mean nothing. It's only about one game, and that's great," Guillen said, hopefully. "A good feeling."

The two Central Division rivals were evenly matched, with identical records at home (53–28), on the road (35–46), and in their division (43–29). A playoff was therefore not only necessary but fitting.

The pressure was squarely on Danks. He had struggled since late August and had posted a 4.91 ERA over his previous seven starts. Of even greater concern, he was just 1–1 with a 7.91 ERA in four previous starts against Minnesota in 2008.

The one-game playoff was billed the "Blackout Game." The White Sox urged their fans to "black out" the stadium by wearing black shirts and wave black towels. They were very much into it—all 40,354 in attendance that night. It was the largest crowd to witness a game at the Cell since August 4, 2003, when 43,922 turned out for a contest against Kansas City, but that was before the seating capacity in the upper deck was reduced. "The Blackout was tremendous," Jim Thome said. "I know we felt the vibe."

Big Jim certainly had his own vibe going. The man with the flair for dramatics supplied all the offense that was needed. His 461-foot solo shot off of Blackburn, who had retired 13 of 14 hitters, cleared the shrubs in center field and

The fans celebrate Jim Thome's game-winning home run in the "Blackout Game." (Courtesy of the Chicago White Sox)

Ken Griffey's throw nails Michael Cuddyer at the plate to preserve the tense 1–0 division-clinching win, as A.J. Pierzynski applies the tag. (Courtesy of the Chicago White Sox)

broke the 0–0 tie. Danks and the defense took care of the rest. Ken Griffey gunned down Michael Cuddyer in the fifth inning, after Cuddyer tried to score from third on a fly ball to center. With the force of a locomotive, Cuddyer barreled into A.J. Pierzynski, but the White Sox's iron-man catcher held on and tagged out the runner. "That play, all I had to do was make a good throw," Griffey explained in the postgame. "The credit is all A.J. I put a two-hopper in there, and he was able to get it and block the plate. That's the key there. He put his body on the line for us."

Danks yielded just two hits in his eight innings of work before yielding to Bobby Jenks, who worked a perfect ninth for his 30th save. The final out came on center fielder Brian Anderson's diving catch of a fast-sinking liner hit by Alexi Casilla. The Sox were back in the playoffs after a three-year hiatus, but more important, the victory really established young Johnny Danks as a pitching star of the American League. The champagne and hugs followed. "I can't put it into words," Danks said. "I'm still shaking right now."

Commenting on the satisfaction of beating the smug Twins at their own game, Ozzie Guillen said, "That's a battle between friends. We just got the last laugh."

The Sox celebrate their 1–0 "Blackout" win to clinch the 2008 Central Division title, September 30, 2008. (Courtesy of the Chicago White Sox)

Minnesota at Chicago, September 30, 2008

Minnesota	AB	R	H	RBI
Span, rf	2	0	0	0
Casilla, 2b	4	0	0	0
Mauer, c	3	0	0	0
Morneau, 1b	3	0	0	0
Cuddyer, dh	3	0	1	0
Young, lf	3	0	0	0
Harris, 3b	3	0	1	0
Tolbert, pr-3b	0	0	0	0
Punto, ss	2	0	0	0
Gomez, cf	2	0	0	0
Kubel, ph	1	0	0	0
	26	0	2	0

Chicago	AB	R	H	RBI
Cabrera, ss	4	0	1	0
Wise, lf	4	0	0	0
Dye, rf	4	0	2	0
Thome, dh	5	1	1	1
Konerko, 1b	3	0	0	0
Swisher, 1b	0	0	0	0
Griffey Jr., cf	3	0	1	0
Anderson, pr-cf	0	0	0	0
Ramirez, 2b	1	0	0	0
Pierzynski, c	3	0	0	0
Uribe, 3b	3	0	0	0
	28	1	5	1

Minnesota	IP	H	R	ER	BB	K	Pit	ERA
Blackburn	6⅓	4	1	1	3	3	89	4.05
Mijares	1⅓	0	0	0	0	0	14	0.87
Nathan	⅓	1	0	0	0	0	8	1.33

Chicago	IP	H	R	ER	BB	K	Pit	ERA
Danks	8	2	0	0	3	4	103	3.32
Jenks	1	0	0	0	0	1	8	2.63

Winning pitcher—Danks (12–9). Losing pitcher—Blackburn (11–11). Save—Jenks (30).

Minnesota	0	0	0	0	0	0	0	0	0—0
Chicago	0	0	0	0	0	0	1	0	x—1

DP—Chicago, 3, Minnesota, 1. LOB—Minnesota 2, Chicago, 6. 2B—Cuddyer, Griffey Jr. HR—Thome. Umpires—Tim McClelland, Derryl Cousins, Gary Cederstrom, Jerry Meals, Ted Barrett, Mike Everett. Time—2:20. Attendance—40,354.

Another Perfect 27: Mark Buehrle Dazzles the Rays

Long after the celebration ended and the White Sox's charter flight was winging its way to Detroit for the next series, Mark Buehrle, Jim Thome, and Paul Konerko passed the time calculating the percentage of baseball games that were perfect. With a little help from baseball-reference.com, it was determined that a perfect game is thrown once every 43,284 opportunities.

From a historical perspective, 87 years had passed since Charlie Robertson, the unsung rookie pitcher the Sox had acquired from the Sherman, Texas, minor league club for the sum of $1,750, neutered Ty Cobb's Tigers in the last White Sox perfect game on April 30, 1922. The beauty of a perfect game is just how unexpected and how unlikely the hero (*Charlie Robertson?!*)—until the unbelievable happens.

Facing a twinight doubleheader in Detroit the following evening, and having played a night game previously, the White Sox assembled for an afternoon contest against the Tampa Bay Rays on July 23, 2009, needing some rest. Ozzie Guillen's lineup was a patchwork quilt of substitutes—almost a split-squad affair. Josh Fields filled in for Paul Konerko at first, and backup catcher Ramon Castro, acquired from the Mets in May to spell A.J. Pierzynski, was behind the plate. He had never caught Buehrle before and had to quickly run through the signs with Mark before the game began. The Tampa Bay lineup featured four home-grown All-Stars—the transformation of this team from a perennial doormat playing in an empty stadium all those years into an AL East contender overnight was a remarkable story in its own right, but the game

Dewayne Wise's sensational catch saved Buehrle's perfect game.

and the glory on this particular day belonged to the fast-working, no-nonsense Sox ace who put down the Rays with the greatest of ease, throwing just 10 pitches in the first inning.

Relying mostly on change-ups and fastballs, Mark dominated the tempo of the game, as is his custom when he finds his rhythm and is locked in. His actual time on the mound was just 32 minutes. Meanwhile, the game was put out of reach by the light-hitting Josh Fields in the second inning, when the former Oklahoma State quarterback filling in for Konerko drilled a grand-slam home run off Scott Kazmir. The Sox lead was insurmountable at this point. There was only one threat. Ex-Twin Jason Bartlett worked a full count off Buehrle in the sixth, but Mark went after the hitter and threw strikes, inducing a harmless ground-out. Excitement mounted after Buehrle breezed through the seventh and eighth.

Up in the broadcast booth, Hawk Harrelson implored his listeners to, "Call your sons! Call your daughters! Call your friends! Call your neighbors!" The mood of the crowd was electric. Could a perfect game be possible? Outfielder Dewayne Wise, a frequent target of U.S. Cellular Field boo-birds because of his poor hitting, was working out in the weight room downstairs when he was summoned by Guillen to be a defensive replacement in the ninth inning—as Scott Podsednik shifted over to left field. Wise was barely settled in when Gabe Kapler drilled Buehrle's 105th pitch of the game to deep left-center field—it looked like a goner. Wise was playing a shallow center field as he was known to do, but he raced back following the flight of the ball, measuring it and timing his last-second leap. If he missed, it was a home run, and Tony Pena stood ready to come in and relieve a dejected Buehrle. Wise collided with the wall, snared the drive, and tumbled to the ground with the ball lodged in his glove, but just barely.

The 18th perfect game in major league history was accomplished moments later on a soft grounder fielded cleanly by Alexei Ramirez. It was time to pop the champagne corks to celebrate a stunning accomplishment. Now the national media was finally forced to pay some attention to a pitcher who had previously garnered little notice outside of Chicago despite four All-Star Game appearances and a 2007 no-hitter.

Because Mark Buerhle was not a Yankee, a Red Sox, an Angel, a Met, a Phillie, a Dodger, or even a Cub, he had toiled in the shadows of obscurity for most of his career. The East Coast/West Coast–centric national media and ESPN consider the White Sox and other heartland teams also-rans or at best "table setters"—relevant only in the nightly wrap-up of game results or within the context of their interaction with the "Big Seven" teams they devote their coverage to.

The coastal bias was even more apparent in Ken Burns' documentary history of the national pastime airing on PBS some years before. Midwestern teams were short-changed and rarely mentioned in the same breath as the Yankees, Dodgers, and Red Sox. There is simply no way to overcome national media partiality of this magnitude, but at least for one full day in July 2009, the sun was shining and Buehrle occupied the national stage. Illinois Governor Pat Quinn joined fellow Sox fan and President Barack Obama in placing congratulatory calls. David Letterman asked Mark to read his nightly Top 10 list, and *Sports Illustrated* made him their cover boy for the August 3 issue. In hindsight, maybe the *Sports Illustrated* cover wasn't such a good idea after all If there is truth to the rumors of an *SI* curse, Mark's 2–7 record after the perfect game seemed to offer convincing proof of it.

Tampa Bay at Chicago, July 23, 2009

Tampa Bay	AB	R	H	RBI
Upton, cf	3	0	0	0
Crawford, lf	3	0	0	0
Longoria, 3b	3	0	0	0
Pena, 1b	3	0	0	0
Zobrist, 2b	3	0	0	0
Burrell, dh	3	0	0	0
Kapler, rf	3	0	0	0
Hernandez, c	3	0	0	0
Bartlett, ss	3	0	0	0
	27	0	0	0

Tampa Bay	0	0	0	0	0	0	0	0	0—0
Chicago	0	4	0	0	1	0	0	0	x—5

Chicago	AB	R	H	RBI
Podsednik, cf-lf	4	1	1	0
Ramirez, ss	3	0	2	1
Dye, rf	4	0	0	0
Konerko, dh	4	1	1	0
Quentin, lf	3	1	0	0
Wise, cf	0	0	0	0
Beckham, 3b	4	0	0	0
Nix, 2b	3	0	0	0
Castro, c	2	1	1	0
Fields, 1b	3	1	1	4
	30	5	6	5

LOB—Chicago, 5. 2B—Podsednik, Ramirez. HR—Fields. HBP—Nix (by Kazmir). Umpires—Mike Reilly, Eric Cooper, Chuck Merriwether, Laz Diaz. Time—2:03. Attendance—28,036.

Tampa Bay	IP	H	R	ER	BB	K	Pit	ERA
Kazmir	6	5	5	5	3	5	98	6.69
Cormier	1	1	0	0	0	0	20	2.65
Thayer	1	0	0	0	0	1	10	4.26

Chicago	IP	H	R	ER	BB	K	Pit	ERA
Buehrle	9	0	0	0	0	6	116	3.28

Winning pitcher—Buehrle (11–3). Losing pitcher—Kazmir (4–6).

White Sox No-Hitters

There have been 17 complete nine-inning no-hit games thrown by White Sox pitchers from 1901 to 2010—ranking the South Siders third all-time behind the Los Angeles Dodgers (20) and the Boston Red Sox (19).

Jimmy Callahan, a future Sox manager whom many of the fans in that era derided as a has-been, tossed the first official no-hitter, a feat accomplished on Amateur Day at the 39th Street Grounds, September 20, 1902. It was the first game of a scheduled doubleheader with Detroit. In the middle of the seventh inning, the contest was halted to allow 200 players from Chicago's amateur leagues, led by Cap Anson and accompanied by a brass band, to parade into the grandstand. Afterward, they presented Charles Comiskey with a new fishing outfit and his wife with a large bouquet of American Beauty roses. Things were done a little differently in the old days, wouldn't you say?

Unfazed by the interruption, Callahan completed his chores and returned home to his wife, who asked if he had been knocked out in the first inning. "You're home so early, dear," she said at the time.

Mark Buehrle and Frank Smith are the only two White Sox pitchers to throw two no-hitters. Smith, the temperamental Pittsburgh piano mover, relied on his deadly "drop ball" pitch and polished off the Detroit Tigers in the second game of a doubleheader in Detroit on September 6, 1905, before 3,500. Only three men reached base all afternoon. Three years later, Smithy joined Cy Young as the only other American League hurler up to that point to author two no-hitters in a career when he defeated the great Eddie Plank of the Philadelphia A's by a 1–0 count on September 20, 1908, at the 39th Street Gounds. Smith's masterpiece was all the more remarkable because the little finger on his pitching hand was badly injured by an opponent's line drive during his previous start. Today such an injury would have landed him on the disabled list.

Bob Keegan (left) celebrates his August 20, 1957, no-hitter with Sherm Lollar.

Smiling Joe enjoys the no-hit glory in the Sox clubhouse, September 10, 1967.

Ed Walsh pitched a five-inning, rain-shortened no-hitter against the New York Highlanders on May 26, 1907, at the 39th Street Grounds. Such games are not considered "legitimate" no-hitters by baseball's governing powers, but Walsh atoned four years later when he blanked the Red Sox on August 27, 1911. It was the first no-hitter to be thrown at Comiskey Park.

Joe Benz, Jim Scott, and Ed Cicotte pitched no-hitters in the second decade. "Death Valley" Scott is the only White Sox no-hit artist to lose his game. Future Black Soxer Chick Gandil scored the winning run in the 10th inning for the Washington Senators on May 14, 1914, after the White Sox blew an excellent scoring opportunity in their half of the frame. Scott received a standing ovation from the partisan Senator fans.

Teddy Lyons pitched a no-hitter in Fenway Park on August 21, 1926, a year after losing a no-hit bid with two outs in the ninth inning at Washington when Bobby Veach singled.

Vern Kennedy and Bill Dietrich fashioned Comiskey Park no-hitters in the 1930s. Kennedy never knew he was flirting with immortality on August 31, 1935, until the game was over. Al Simmons preserved Kennedy's no-hitter with a sensational diving grab of Milt Galatzer's sinking liner in the ninth inning.

Bullfrog Dietrich retired the first 15 Brownie batters in a row before issuing two walks in the sixth inning of his no-hitter on June 1, 1937. "That's the ambition of every fellow who comes to the major leagues," he said. "I feel I had all the luck in the world."

Another 20 years passed between White Sox no-hitters. Hounded by injuries and illness for nearly two seasons, 36-year-old Yankees castoff Bob Keegan whitewashed the Senators in the second game of a twinight doubleheader in Comiskey Park on August 20, 1957. Keegan's no-hitter was never seriously threatened. In the sixth inning Minnie Minoso hauled in a long drive headed for the gap in left-center.

A slower outfielder might not have caught up with the ball, but it was just another routine play for Minnie.

Young Sox fans who grew up in the TV generation undoubtedly remember Joel Horlen's Comiskey Park virtuoso performance on September 10, 1967. The Sunday doubleheader against the Detroit Tigers was telecast over WGN-TV, with Jack Brickhouse doing the play by play. Horlen opened game one for Eddie Stanky's team, and was brilliant. Only two Tigers batters reached base—Bill Freehan was hit by a pitch in the third, and Eddie Mathews reached base in the fifth on an error. In the second game, a rookie flash-in-the-pan named Cisco Carlos spun a 4–0 shutout to compound the Bengals' growing misery.

John "Blue Moon" Odom and Francisco Barrios, a veteran and a youngster on the fringe of the White Sox pitching staff, hurled a combined no-hitter in Oakland on July 28, 1976. It was one of the wildest affairs in baseball no-hit history. Odom walked nine batters in five innings before manager Paul Richards had enough and replaced him with Barrios, an excitable young Mexican who passed away before his 30th birthday. Frankie managed to hold the A's in check while Odom cowered in the White Sox clubhouse. "I couldn't take it, man," he said later. "I was in here pacing the floor." The unlikely pair walked *11 batters,* but still won the game 2–1.

Joe Cowley's no-hitter in Anaheim on September 19, 1986, brought to mind the Odom-Barrios game a decade earlier. The erratic right-hander, who had been acquired in an off-season trade with the Yankees, walked seven Angels batters but managed to hold them hitless through nine innings. Another flawed masterpiece.

Melido Perez pitched the second rain-shortened no-hitter in White Sox history on July 12, 1990, at Yankee Stadium. The Sox prevailed by an 8–0 count after play was halted at the end of the sixth inning.

The Sox's final road trip to old Memorial Stadium in Baltimore featured a stellar no-hit performance from Wilson Alvarez, who was making only his second major league start. Wilson became the eighth-youngest pitcher in history to accomplish the singular feat. It was an appropriate White Sox send-off to a ballpark that was an enduring house of horrors for so many seasons.

Wilson Alvarez and Ron Karkovice celebrate his no-no on August 11, 1991.

April 18, 2007, was a bitterly cold, fog-shrouded night for the 25,390 hearty souls who braved the elements and turned out at U.S. Cellular Field to witness history. That night, Mark Buehrle was nearly perfect in his 6–0 no-hit effort against the Texas Rangers. In the fifth inning, the Sox ace walked Sammy Sosa—then promptly picked him off. Sosa was the only Texas base runner that night. Jermaine Dye's grand-slam home run in the fifth inning salted away the no-hit victory. "Never in a million years did I think this could happen," the Sox ace said. Buehrle and his fans did not have to wait for a million years before another no-hitter—only two, and the next one he threw would be perfect.

White Sox pitchers have recorded 63 one-hitters, beginning on August 1, 1901, when Jimmy Callahan blanked the Tigers 4–0 at the 39th Street Grounds. Ed Walsh and Doc White share the leadership in this overlooked category with five one-hitters apiece. Billy Pierce (four), Frank Smith (three), Ed Cicotte (three), Red Faber (three), Jim Scott (two), Virgil Trucks (two), Dick Donovan (two), and Gary Peters (two) are the only other Sox pitchers who have thrown more than one one-hitter with the ballclub.

Frank Smith, one of the terribly underrated players in history, pitched the only White Sox Opening Day one-hitter on April 14, 1910, against the St. Louis Browns at the 39th Street Grounds.

NO-HIT GAMES BY WHITE SOX

James Callahan, September 20, 1902, Detroit at Chicago

Detroit	AB	R	H	PO
Harley, lf	4	0	0	2
Elberfeld, ss	3	0	0	3
Barrett, cf	4	0	0	1
McAlister, 3b	3	0	0	0
Yeager, 2b	2	0	0	3
Lepine, rf	3	0	0	0
O'Connell, 1b	3	0	0	12
McGuire, c	3	0	0	3
Egan, p	3	0	0	0
	28	0	0	24

Chicago	AB	R	H	PO
Strang, 3b	4	1	2	2
Jones, cf	4	0	0	4
Green, rf	3	1	1	2
Davis, ss	3	1	2	0
Mertes, lf	4	0	0	2
Daly, 2b	4	0	1	1
Isbell, 1b	3	0	1	13
McFarland, c	3	0	1	2
Callahan, p	3	0	0	1
	31	3	8	27

Detroit	0	0	0	0	0	0	0	0	0—0
Chicago	3	0	0	0	0	0	0	0	x—0

E—Davis, Elberfeld (2), McAlister. LOB—Detroit 3, Chicago 6. 2B—Davis. Passed ball—McFarland. Sac—Isbell. SB—Strang, Green. DP—Detroit, 1. Umpires, Caruthers and Sheridan. Time—1:20.

Detroit	IP	K	BB
Egan (L)	8	0	2

Chicago	IP	K	BB
Callahan (W)	9	2	2

Frank Smith's First No-Hitter, September 6, 1905, Game 2, Chicago at Detroit

Detroit	R	H	A
McIntyre, lf	0	0	0
Lindsay, 1b	0	0	2
Schaefer, 2b	0	0	1
Lowe, 2b	0	0	1
Crawford, rf	0	0	0
Cobb, cf	0	0	0
Coughlin, 3b	0	0	3
O'Leary, ss	0	0	4
Warner, c	0	0	0
Doran, c	0	0	0
Wiggs, p	0	0	1
Disch, p	0	0	2
	0	0	14

Chicago	R	H	A
Green, rf	3	1	0
Isbell, cf	2	2	0
Davis, ss	0	0	1
Callahan, lf	1	2	0
Donohue, 1b	1	1	1
McFarland, c	2	2	0
Rohe, 2b	1	1	3
Tannehill, 3b	2	1	1
Smith, p	3	2	0

White Sox	8	1	0	0	1	0	5	0	0—15
Detroit	0	0	0	0	0	0	0	0	0—0

2B—McFarland, Smith, Green. 3B—Callahan. Sac—Davis. SB—Isbell. HBP—Disch (1). LOB—Detroit 3, Chicago 7. Umpires—O'Laughlin and McCarthy. Time—1:43. Attendance—3,500.

Chicago	IP	BB	K	H
Smith (W)	9	3	8	0

Detroit	IP	BB	K	H
Wiggs (L)	1	5	2	1
Disch	8	1	2	11

Frank Smith's Second No-Hitter, September 20, 1908, Philadelphia at Chicago

Philadelphia	AB	R	H
Nichols, ss	4	0	0
Oldring, lf	4	0	0
Murphy, 1b	3	0	0
Coombs, cf	3	0	0
Seybold, rf	3	0	0
Manusch, 3b	2	0	0
Barry, 2b	3	0	0
Lapp, c	3	0	0
Plank, p	3	0	0
	28	0	0

Chicago	AB	R	H
Hahn, rf	4	0	1
Jones, cf	4	0	0
Isbell, 1b	3	1	2
Anderson, lf	4	0	0
Davis, 2b	3	0	0
Parent, ss	4	0	0
Sullivan, c	3	0	1
Tannehill, 3b	3	0	0
Smith, p	3	0	0
	31	1	4

Philadelphia	0	0	0	0	0	0	0	0	0—0
White Sox	0	0	0	0	0	0	0	0	1—1

DP—Murphy (unassisted). HBP—by Plank (Isbell). PB—Lapp. SB—Isbell, Davis. E—Manusch, Barry, Isbell. Umpires—Egan and O'Loughlin. Time—1:30.

Philadelphia	IP	BB	K	R	H
Plank (L)	8⅔	1	4	1	4

Chicago	IP	BB	K	R	H
Smith (W)	9	1	2	0	0

Ed Walsh, August 27, 1911, Boston at Chicago

Boston	AB	H	PO	A
Henrickson, rf	1	0	0	0
Riggert, rf	3	0	0	0
Speaker, cf	1	0	0	0
Williams, 1b	2	0	6	0
Engle, 1b–cf	2	0	4	1
Lewis, lf	3	0	3	0
Gardner, 3b	3	0	1	5
Carrigan, c	3	0	4	0
Wagner, 2b	3	0	1	0
Yerkes, ss	3	0	4	3
Collins, p	2	0	1	1
Nunamaker, ph	1	0	0	0
	37	0	24	10

Chicago	AB	H	PO	A
McIntyre, rf	5	1	3	0
Lord, 3b	3	1	0	3
Callahan, lf	4	1	0	0
Bodie, cf	4	2	1	0
McConnell, 2b	4	1	0	5
Tannehill, ss	4	2	0	3
Mullen, 1b	3	0	17	0
Block, c	4	2	6	4
Walsh, p	4	1	0	2
	35	11	27	17

Boston	0	0	0	0	0	0	0	0	0—0
Chicago	3	0	0	0	0	0	1	1	x—5

E—Williams, Engle. 2B—McConnell, Lord, Tannehill. 3B—McIntyre, Tannenhill. Wild pitch—Collins. Umpires—Evans and Mullen.

Boston	IP	BB	K
Collins (L)	8	0	1

Chicago	IP	BB	K
Walsh (W)	9	1	8

Jim Scott Loses in 10th Inning, May 14, 1914, Chicago at Washington

Chicago	AB	R	H	E
Demmitt, rf	4	0	1	0
Berger, ss	4	0	0	0
Chase, 1b	4	0	1	0
J. Collins, lf	4	0	0	0
Bodie, cf	4	0	1	0
Alcock, 2b	3	0	0	0
Blackburne, ph-2b	4	0	0	2
Schalk, c	3	0	0	0
Scott, p	3	0	0	0
	33	0	3	2

Washington	AB	R	H	E
Moeller, rf	4	0	0	0
Foster, 3b	4	0	0	1
Milan, cf	4	0	0	0
Gandil, 1b	4	1	1	0
Shanks, lf	4	0	1	0
Morgan, 2b	3	0	0	1
McBride, ss	2	0	0	0
Henry, c	2	0	0	0
Ayers, p	3	0	0	0
	30	1	2	2

Chicago	0	0	0	0	0	0	0	0	0	0—0
Washington	0	0	0	0	0	0	0	0	0	1—1

2B—Shanks. 3B—Chase. SB—Collins. DP—Morgan, McBride, Gandil. Umpires—Dinneen and Connally. Time—2:00.

Chicago	IP	BB	K	H
Scott (L)	9⅔	2	2	2

Washington	IP	BB	K	H
Ayers (W)	10	1	1	3

Joe Benz, May 31, 1914, Cleveland at Chicago

Chicago	AB	R	H	E
Weaver, ss	4	1	3	1
Chase, 1b	3	3	1	0
Demmitt, lf	4	2	3	0
J. Collins, rf	3	0	2	0
Bodie, cf	4	0	1	0
Schalk, c	4	0	1	0
Alcock, 3b	4	0	1	1
Berger, 2b	4	0	1	1
Benz, p	4	0	0	0
	34	6	13	3

Cleveland	AB	R	H	E
Wood, 1b	3	1	0	0
Bisland, ss	4	0	0	2
Graney, lf	2	0	0	1
Jackson, rf	3	0	0	0
Lajoie, 2b	3	0	0	0
Turner, 3b	3	0	0	0
Birmingham, cf	3	0	0	0
O'Neill, c	3	0	0	0
Bowman, p	1	0	0	0
Blanding, p	1	0	0	0
Lelivelt, ph	1	0	0	0
	27	1	0	3

Cleveland	0	0	0	1	0	0	0	0	0—1
Chicago	1	0	2	0	0	0	3	0	x—1

2B—Collins, Berger, Chase. DP—Bowman, Turner, Wood; Berger, Chase; Weaver, Chase. SB—Demmitt, Collins. Umpires—Egan and Evans. Time—1:45.

Cleveland	IP	K	BB	H
Bowman (L)	3	1	2	4
Blanding	5	2	0	9

Chicago	IP	K	BB	H
Benz (W)	9	3	2	0

Ed Cicotte, April 14, 1917, Chicago at St. Louis

Chicago	AB	R	H
Leibold, rf	4	2	1
Risberg, ss	5	2	2
E. Collins, 2b	3	3	2
Jackson, lf	4	1	1
Gandil, 1b	3	0	2
Felsch, cf	4	0	0
Weaver, 3b	4	1	0
Schalk, c	4	1	1
Cicotte, p	3	1	1
	34	11	10

St. Louis	AB	R	H
Shotton, lf	2	0	0
Miller, rf	3	0	0
Sisler, 1b	4	0	0
Pratt, 2b	4	0	0
Marsans, cf	3	0	0
Austin, 3b	3	0	0
Lavan, ss	2	0	0
Hale, c	2	0	0
Paulette, ph	1	0	0
Hartley, c	0	0	0
Hamilton, p	0	0	0
Park, p	0	0	0
Rogers, p	2	0	0
Jacobson, ph	1	0	0
Pennington, p	0	0	0
	27	0	0

Chicago	1	7	0	1	0	2	0	0	0—11
St. Louis	0	0	0	0	0	0	0	0	0— 0

E—Felsch, Sisler, Lavan (2), Rogers. 2B—Risberg, Schalk, Jackson. SB—Shotton, Felsch. Sac—Gandil, Felsch, Cicotte, Gandil. DP—Collins, Risberg, Gandil. LOB—Chicago 6, St. Louis 4. HBP—by Hamilton (Weaver); Cicotte (Lavan). Wild pitch—Park. Umpires—O'Loughlin and Hildebrand. Time—2:03.

Chicago	IP	BB	K	H
Cicotte (W)	9	3	5	0

St. Louis	IP	BB	K	H
Hamilton (L)	1	1	0	3
Park	0	0	0	4
Rogers	7	4	1	2
Pennington	1	0	0	1

Ted Lyons, August 21, 1926, Chicago at Boston

Chicago	AB	R	H	PO
Mostil, cf	5	1	4	2
Morehart, 2b	3	1	1	0
Sheely, 1b	4	1	2	9
Falk, lf	3	0	0	1
Barrett, rf	5	0	2	5
Hunnefield, ss	4	0	1	4
Kamm, 3b	4	2	2	2
Grabowski, c	3	1	0	2
Lyons, p	4	0	1	2
	35	6	13	27

Boston	AB	R	H	PO
Tobin, rf	3	0	0	2
Rigney, ss	3	0	0	3
Jacobson, cf	3	0	0	2
Rosenthal, lf	3	0	0	3
Regan, 2b	3	0	0	3
Todt, 1b	3	0	0	8
Haney, 3b	3	0	0	1
Gaston, c	2	0	0	5
Bratchi, ph	1	0	0	0
Stokes, c	0	0	0	0
Harris, p	1	0	0	0
Shaner, ph	1	0	0	0
Russell, p	0	0	0	0
Bischoff, ph	1	0	0	0
	27	0	0	27

Chicago	0	1	0	0	2	2	1	0	0—6
Boston	0	0	0	0	0	0	0	0	0—0

E—Hunnefield, Rosenthal, Regan. LOB—Chicago 9, Boston 2. 2B—Barrett, Mostil. SB—Mostil, Hunnefield. Sac—Morehart, Rigney, Sheely, Hunnefield. Wild pitch—Harris. Umpires—Connolly, Rowland. Umpire-in-chief—McGowan. Time—1:50. Attendance—7,000.

Chicago	IP	BB	K
Lyons (W)	9	3	2

Boston	IP	BB	K
Harris (L)	6	3	2
Russell	3	3	2

Vern Kenendy, August 31, 1935, Cleveland at Chicago

Cleveland	AB	R	H
Galatzer, rf	4	0	0
Averill, cf	3	0	0
Vosmik, lf	3	0	0
Trosky, 1b	3	0	0
Hale, 3b	3	0	0
Knickerbocker, ss	3	0	0
Phillips, c	2	0	0
Hughes, 2b	2	0	0
Hudlin, p	2	0	0
Carson, ph	1	0	0
	26	0	0

Chicago	AB	R	H
Conlon, cf	5	1	1
Simmons, lf	4	0	1
Piet, 2b	4	0	0
Appling, ss	3	0	1
Bonura, 1b	4	2	3
Dykes, 3b	4	1	2
Washington, rf	4	0	1
Sewell, c	1	1	0
Kennedy, p	4	0	1
	33	5	10

Cleveland	0	0	0	0	0	0	0	0	0—0
Chicago	1	0	0	1	0	3	0	0	x—5

E—Phillips. RBI—Appling, Dykes, Kennedy (3). 2B—Bonura. 3B—Kennedy. SB—Hughes. LOB—Cleveland 3, Chicago 3. DP—Chicago 2, Cleveland 1. Umpire—Owens. Time—1:41. Attendance—6,000.

Cleveland	IP	BB	K	H	R
Hudlin (L)	8	4	0	10	5

Chicago	IP	BB	K	H	R
Kennedy (W)	9	4	5	0	0

Bill Dietrich, June 1, 1937, St. Louis at Chicago

St. Louis	AB	R	H
Davis, 1b	4	0	0
West, cf	4	0	0
Vosmik, lf	3	0	0
Bell, rf	3	0	0
Clift, 3b	3	0	0
Knickerbocker, ss	3	0	0
Hemsley, c	2	0	0
Carey, 2b	3	0	0
Hogsett, p	0	0	0
Van Atta, p	1	0	0
Bottomley, ph	1	0	0
	27	0	0

Chicago	AB	R	H
Radcliff, lf	2	1	0
Kreevich, cf	5	2	3
Walker, rf	4	2	2
Bonura, 1b	4	0	1
Appling, ss	4	0	2
Hayes, 2b	4	0	0
Piet, 3b	3	0	1
Sewell, c	2	2	1
Dietrich, p	3	1	0
	31	8	10

St. Louis	0	0	0	0	0	0	0	0	0—0
Chicago	3	0	0	2	0	0	0	3	x—8

2B—Kreevich, Walker, Sewell. SB—Piet, Kreevich. Sac—Dietrich, Radcliff. DP—White Sox 1, St. Louis 1. LOB—St. Louis 2, White Sox 10. Wild pitch—Van Atta. E—Piet. Umpires—Hubbard, Dinneen, Quinn. Time—1:48. Attendance—1,500 (est.).

St. Louis	IP	BB	K	H	R
Hogsett (L)	1	5	0	2	3
Van Atta	7	4	6	8	5

Chicago	IP	BB	K	H	R
Dietrich (W)	9	2	5	0	0

Bob Keegan, August 20, 1957, Washington at Chicago

Washington	AB	R	H	RBI
Yost, 3b	4	0	0	0
Plews, 2b	3	0	0	0
Sievers, lf	3	0	0	0
Schult, rf	3	0	0	0
Runnels, 1b	3	0	0	0
Berberet, c	2	0	0	0
Usher, cf	3	0	0	0
Bridges, ss	2	0	0	0
Stobbs, p	1	0	0	0
Throneberry, ph	0	0	0	0
Lemon, ph	1	0	0	0
Becquer, ph	1	0	0	0
Black, p	0	0	0	0
	26	0	0	0

Chicago	AB	R	H	RBI
Aparicio, ss	5	1	2	0
Fox, 2b	4	1	2	0
Minoso, lf	5	1	2	2
Dropo, 1b	3	1	2	1
Doby, cf	4	1	1	2
Lollar, c	5	0	2	0
Rivera, rf	3	0	0	0
Phillips, 3b	4	1	2	0
Keegan, p	4	0	1	1
	37	6	14	6

Washington	0	0	0	0	0	0	0	0	0—0
Chicago	0	0	5	0	1	0	0	0	x—6

DP—Sox 1. LOB—Sox 12, Washington 1. 2B—Minoso (2), Lollar, Phillips. HR—Doby. HBP, by Stobbs (Fox). Umpires—Stevens, Napp, Rice, Rommel. Time—1:55. Attendance—22,815.

Washington	IP	R	ER	BB	K
Stobbs (L, 5–16)	5	6	6	3	1
Black	3	0	0	1	0

Chicago	IP	R	ER	BB	K
Keegan (W, 8–6)	9	0	0	2	1

Joel Horlen, September 10, 1967, Game 1, Detroit at Chicago

Detroit	AB	R	H	RBI
McAuliffe, ss	4	0	0	0
Cash, 1b	3	0	0	0
Kaline, rf	3	0	0	0
Horton, lf	3	0	0	0
Mathews, 3b	3	0	0	0
Northrup, cf	3	0	0	0
Freehan, c	1	0	0	0
Dobson, p	0	0	0	0
Brown, ph	1	0	0	0
Marshall, p	0	0	0	0
Lumpe, 2b	3	0	0	0
Sparma, p	0	0	0	0
Podres, p	0	0	0	0
Matchick, ph	1	0	0	0
Wickersham, p	0	0	0	0
Heath, c	2	0	0	0
	27	0	0	0

Chicago	AB	R	H	RBI
Agee, cf	3	1	1	0
Buford, 3b	3	0	1	0
Voss, rf	4	1	0	0
Boyer, 1b	4	1	1	0
Nash, 1b	0	0	0	0
Ward, lf	3	1	1	1
Bradford, lf	1	0	0	0
Causey, 2b	4	2	2	2
Martin, c	4	0	1	1
Hansen, ss	3	0	0	0
Horlen, p	2	0	1	1
	31	6	8	5

Detroit	0	0	0	0	0	0	0	0	0—0
Chicago	5	0	0	0	0	0	0	1	x—6

E—Sparma, Boyer. DP—Detroit 1, Chicago 1. LOB—Detroit 1, Chicago 5. 3B—Causey. SB—Agee 2, Buford. HBP—Freehan (by Horlen), Horlen (by Wickersham). Wild pitch—Dobson. PB—Heath. Time—2:17. Attendance—23,625.

Detroit	IP	H	R	ER	BB	K
Sparma	⅓	4	5	3	0	1
Podres	1⅔	1	0	0	1	0
Wickersham	3	1	0	0	0	0
Dobson	2	0	0	0	2	2
Marshall	1	2	1	0	0	0

Chicago	IP	H	R	ER	BB	K
Horlen	9	0	0	0	0	4

Winning pitcher—Horlen (16–6). Losing pitcher—Sparma (14–9).

Blue Moon Odom and Francisco Barrios, July 28, 1976, Chicago at Oakland

Chicago	AB	R	H	RBI
Hairston, rf	3	0	2	0
Nordhagen, rf	2	0	0	0
Garr, cf	4	0	2	0
Orta, lf	3	0	0	0
Kelly, dh	2	0	0	0
Johnson, dh	1	0	0	0
Stein, 3b	4	0	2	0
Spencer, 1b	3	2	2	1
Brohamer, 2b	4	0	1	0
Dent, ss	4	0	1	1
Essian, c	4	0	0	0
Odom, p	0	0	0	0
Barrios, p	0	0	0	0
	34	2	10	2

Oakland	AB	R	H	RBI
North, cf	3	0	0	0
Campaneris, ss	2	0	0	0
Rudi, lf	3	0	0	0
Williams, dh	1	1	0	0
Lintz, pr	0	0	0	0
Baylor, dh	1	0	0	0
Bando, 3b	2	0	0	0
Tenace, c	3	0	0	0
Washington, rf	3	0	0	0
McMullen, 1b	3	0	0	0
Garner, 2b	3	0	0	0
Torrez, p	0	0	0	0
Lindblad, p	0	0	0	0
Fingers, p	0	0	0	0
	24	1	0	0

White Sox	0	1	0	0	0	1	0	0	0—2
Oakland	0	0	0	1	0	0	0	0	0—1

Chicago	IP	R	ER	BB	K
Odom (W, 2–0)	5	1	0	9	3
Barrios (S, 2)	4	0	0	2	2

Oakland	IP	R	ER	BB	K
Torrez	5	1	1	1	2
Lindblad (L, 4–3)	2⅓	1	1	0	0
Fingers	1⅔	0	0	1	2

E—Essian, Bando. DP—Sox 3, Oakland 2. LOB—Sox 8, Oakland 7. 2B—Spencer, Brohamer. HR—Spencer (7). SB—Kelly, North, Washington, Lintz. Sac—Orta. Time—2:31. Attendance—3,367.

Joe Cowley, September 19, 1986, Chicago at California

Chicago	AB	R	H	RBI
Boston, cf	4	1	2	1
Lyons, lf	3	1	1	0
Nichols, lf	0	1	0	0
Baines, rf	4	0	1	1
Hassey, dh	4	1	2	1
Mormon, 1b	4	0	1	2
Guillen, ss	4	0	0	0
Hulett, 3b	4	1	1	0
Perconti, 2b	4	0	0	0
Karkovice, c	3	2	1	1
	34	7	9	6

California	AB	R	H	RBI
Pettis, cf	3	0	0	0
Joyner, 1b	2	0	0	0
Downing, lf	3	0	0	0
R. Jackson, dh	3	0	0	1
DeCinces, 3b	4	0	0	0
Grich, 2b	3	0	0	0
White, rf	3	0	0	0
Schofield, ss	2	0	0	0
Boone, c	1	1	0	0
	24	1	0	1

White Sox	0	0	0	2	1	0	0	3	1—7
California	0	0	0	0	0	1	0	0	0—1

Chicago	IP	H	R	ER	BB	K
Cowley (W, 11–9)	9	0	1	1	7	8

California	IP	H	R	ER	BB	K
McCaskill (L, 16–9)	7⅓	6	4	4	1	6
Finley	0	0	1	1	1	0
Forster	⅓	2	1	1	0	1
Ruhle	1	1	1	1	0	0

2B—Boston. HR—Karkovice (2). SB—Hulett. Sac—Boston. Sac fly—R. Jackson. DP—White Sox 1, California 1. LOB—White Sox 3, California 4. PB—Karkovice. E—Boone, White, 2. Game-winning RBI—Baines. Umpires—Reed, Kosc, Garcia, Ford. Time—2:42. Attendance—28,647.

Wilson Alvarez, August 11, 1991, Chicago at Baltimore

Chicago	AB	R	H	RBI
Raines, lf	5	1	1	2
Ventura, 3b	4	2	3	1
Thomas, dh	5	1	3	3
Pasqua, 1b	4	0	2	1
Newson, rf	4	0	1	0
Huff, rf	1	0	0	0
Johnson, cf	4	0	1	0
Karkovice, c	3	1	1	0
Cora, 2b	3	0	0	0
Guillen, ss	3	2	2	0
	36	7	14	7

Baltimore	AB	R	H	RBI
Devereaux, cf	4	0	0	0
J. Bell, 2b	4	0	0	0
Ripken, ss	3	0	0	0
Evans, rf	2	0	0	0
Milligan, 1b	3	0	0	0
Segui, lf	3	0	0	0
Hoiles, dh	3	0	0	0
Gomez, 3b	2	0	0	0
Melvin, c	3	0	0	0
	27	0	0	0

Chicago	2	2	0	0	0	3	0	0	0—7
Baltimore	0	0	0	0	0	0	0	0	0—0

E—Karkovice. LOB—Baltimore 5, White Sox 7. 2B—Raines, Thomas, Guillen. HR—Thomas. CS—Guillen. Sac—Cora. DP—White Sox, 1; Baltimore, 3. HBP—by Frohwirth (Pasqua). Umpires—Denkinger, McCoy, Merrill, McClelland. Time—2:45. Attendance—40,455.

Chicago	IP	H	R	ER	BB	K
Alvarez	9	0	0	0	5	7

Baltimore	IP	H	R	ER	BB	K
Johnson	1⅓	8	4	4	1	3
Frohwirth	4	3	3	3	2	3
Poole	2⅔	2	0	0	0	2
Olson	1	1	0	0	0	0

Winning pitcher—Alvarez (1–0). Losing pitcher—Johnson (2–4).

Mark Buehrle, April 18, 2007, Texas at Chicago

Texas	AB	R	H	RBI
Lofton, cf	3	0	0	0
Kinzler, 2b	3	0	0	0
Young, ss	3	0	0	0
Texiera, 1b	3	0	0	0
Sosa, dh	2	0	0	0
Blalock, 3b	3	0	0	0
Hairston Jr., lf	1	0	0	0
Kata, lf	2	0	0	0
Cruz, rf	3	0	0	0
Laird, c	3	0	0	0
	26	0	0	0

Chicago	AB	R	H	RBI
Erstad, cf	4	0	0	0
Iguchi, 2b	4	1	2	0
Thome, dh	2	3	2	2
Konerko, 1b	3	1	0	0
Dye, rf	4	1	1	4
Pierzynski, c	4	0	1	0
Crede, 3b	4	0	1	0
Mackowiak, lf	3	0	0	0
Anderson, lf	0	0	0	0
Uribe, ss	3	0	0	0
	31	6	7	6

Texas	0	0	0	0	0	0	0	0	0—0
Chicago	0	0	1	0	4	0	1	0	x—6

E—Lofton, Laird. LOB—Chicago, 6. DP—Texas (1). HR—Thome, Dye. SB—Iguchi, Makowiak. Umpires—James Hoye, Eric Cooper, Mike Reilly, Jeff Kellogg. Time—2:03. Attendance—25,390.

Texas	IP	H	R	ER	BB	K	Pit	ERA
Millwood	5	5	5	5	4	3	94	4.91
Wilson	1	0	0	0	0	0	9	5.79
Benoit	1	1	1	1	0	0	14	3.18
Gagne	1	1	0	0	1	0	14	0.00

Chicago	IP	H	R	ER	BB	K	Pit	ERA
Buehrle	9	0	0	0	1	9	106	2.08

Winning pitcher—Buehrle (1–0). Losing pitcher—Millwood (2–2).

Box Scores of Other Noteworthy Games

First White Sox Game (AL Designated as Minor League)

Milwaukee at Chicago, April 21, 1900

Milwaukee	AB	R	H
Waldron, rf	5	0	0
Garry, cf	4	0	1
Fultz, 2b	5	1	1
Anderson, lf	5	0	2
Clark, 1b	5	1	1
Conroy, ss	4	0	2
Smith, c	4	1	2
Burke, 3b	4	1	2
Dowling, p	4	1	2
	40	5	13

Chicago	AB	R	H
Hoy, cf	3	1	0
McFarland, rf	5	0	2
Lally, lf	4	1	3
Hartman, 3b	5	0	2
Shugarts, ss	5	0	1
Padden, 2b	4	0	0
Isbell, 1b	4	0	1
Buckley, c	0	0	0
Sugden, c	4	1	2
Katoll, p	5	1	0
	39	4	11

Milwaukee	0	0	1	0	0	0	2	1	0	1—5
Chicago	0	0	1	0	0	0	3	0	0	0—4

2B—Hartman, Shugarts, Anderson, Clark, Smith, Burke (2). Sac—Shugarts. SB—Conroy (2). DP—Katoll-Padden-Isbell; Shugarts-Padden-Isbell. Wild pitch—Katoll. PB—Smith. LOB—Chicago 10, Milwaukee 7. Umpire—Sheridan. Attendance—6,000 (est.).

Milwaukee	IP	ER	H	BB	K
Dowling (W)	10	1	11	8	7

Chicago	IP	ER	H	BB	K
Katoll (L)	10	2	13	2	4

White Sox Clinch 1900 Pennant

Cleveland at Chicago, September 12, 1900

Cleveland	R	H	P	A
Pickering, cf	0	1	3	0
Genins, lf	0	0	1	1
Jones, rf	1	1	1	1
Cross, 1b	1	1	12	0
Crisham, c	1	1	2	1
Flood, 2b	1	2	2	3
Shea, ss	0	1	1	3
Martin, 3b	0	0	2	3
Braggins, p	0	0	0	2
	4	7	24	14

Chicago	R	H	P	A
Hoy, cf	3	1	1	1
Padden, 2b	2	3	3	5
Wood, c	3	3	8	1
McFarland, rf	0	1	0	0
Isbell, 1b	0	2	1	0
Shugarts, ss	0	1	1	2
Dillard, lf	2	1	1	0
Brain, 3b	1	2	2	2
Patterson, p	1	1	0	2
	12	15	27	13

Cleveland	0	0	0	0	0	0	1	0	3— 4
Chicago	3	0	0	5	0	1	3	0	x—12

3B—Jones, Shea. Sac—McFarland. SB—Dillard, Wood. DP—Brain-Padden-Isbell; Shugarts-Padden-Isbell; Jones-Crisham-Shea; Brain-Isbell. HBP—Wood. Wild pitch—Patterson. PPB—Crisham. Umpire—Dwyer. Time—1:45. Attendance—1,200.

Cleveland	IP	H	R	BB	K
Braggins (L)	8	15	12	6	0

Chicago	IP	H	R	BB	K
Patterson (W)	9	7	4	3	6

First "Official" White Sox Game Is Also the American League's Inaugural Contest

Cleveland at Chicago, April 24, 1901

Cleveland	R	H	P	A
Pickering, rf	0	1	0	0
McCarthy, lf	0	2	4	0
Genins, cf	0	0	1	1
LaChance, 1b	1	1	12	0
Bradley, 3b	0	0	2	6
Beck, 2b	0	2	1	3
Hallman, ss	1	0	1	3
Wood, c	0	1	2	1
Hoffer, p	0	0	1	0
	2	7	24	14

Chicago	R	H	P	A
Hoy, cf	0	1	3	0
Jones, rf	2	1	4	0
Mertes, lf	2	1	4	0
Shugarts, ss	2	0	4	4
Isbell, 1b	1	2	8	0
Hartman, 3b	0	1	0	6
Brain, 2b	0	0	1	3
Sullivan, c	1	2	2	0
Patterson, p	0	0	1	1
	8	8	27	14

Cleveland	0	0	0	1	0	0	1	0	0—2
Chicago	2	5	0	0	0	0	1	0	x—8

2B—Beck. Sac—Shugarts. SB—Hoy. DP—Hoffer-Hallman-LaChance; Brain-Shugarts-Isbell. Wild pitch—Hoffer. Umpire—Connally. Time—1:30. Attendance—10,073.

Cleveland	IP	BB	K	H
Hoffer (L)	8	6	1	8

Chicago	IP	BB	K	H
Patterson (W)	9	2	0	7

White Sox Clinch 1901 Pennant, but Lose

Chicago at Philadelphia, September 21, 1901

Chicago	R	H	P	A
Hoy, cf	0	1	1	0
Jones, rf	0	1	0	0
Mertes, 2b	0	1	3	2
Hartman, 3b	0	1	0	3
McFarland, lf	0	1	1	0
Isbell, 1b	1	1	7	0
Shugarts, ss	1	2	0	1
Sullivan, c	1	2	11	4
Patterson, p	0	0	1	3
Foster, ph	1	1	0	0
Katoll, p	0	0	0	1
	4	11	24	14

Philadelphia	R	H	P	A
Fultz, 2b	1	1	2	5
Davis, 1b	1	4	13	1
Lajoie, ss	2	2	2	5
Seybold, cf	1	2	1	0
McIntyre, lf	2	1	3	0
Steelman, rf	1	2	1	0
Power, c	1	2	0	1
Dolan, 3b	0	1	4	2
Bernhard, p	0	0	1	4
	10	15	27	16

Chicago	0	0	0	0	0	2	2	0	0— 4
Philadelphia	0	1	2	1	4	0	0	2	x—10

2B—Dolan, Seybold, Powers, Hoy. Sac—Dolan (2), McIntyre. SB—McIntyre, Seybold, Davis, Isbell. LOB—Chicago 6, Philadelphia 7. HBP—Fultz. Wild pitch—Patterson. Umpire—Sheridan. Time—1:40. Attendance—4,464.

Chicago	IP	BB	K
Patterson (L)	6	2	3
Katoll	2	2	2

Philadelphia	IP	BB	K
Bernhard (W)	9	0	1

Frank Owen's Two Complete-Game Wins in a Doubleheader

Chicago at St. Louis, July 1, 1905

Game 1

Chicago	R	H	P	A
Jones, cf	1	1	0	0
Holmes, lf	1	1	1	0
Davis, ss	0	2	3	5
Donohue, 1b	0	1	2	1
Isbell, rf	1	0	0	0
Sullivan, c	0	0	3	1
Dundon, 2b	0	1	3	3
Tannehill, 3b	0	1	4	4
Owen, p	0	0	1	3
	3	7	27	17

St. Louis	R	H	P	A
Rockenfeld, 2b	1	0	2	3
Stone, lf	0	1	5	0
Van Zandt, rf	0	0	3	0
Koehler, cf	1	1	3	0
Wallace, ss	0	1	2	1
Gleason, 3b	0	1	0	1
Sugden, 1b	0	0	9	0
Weaver, c	0	0	3	1
Buchanan, p	0	0	0	0
Frisk, ph	0	0	0	0
	2	4	27	6

Chicago	0	0	0	0	0	2	0	0	1—3
St. Louis	1	0	0	0	0	1	0	0	0—2

2B—Jones, Stone. Sac—Rockenfeld, Stone, Gleason. SB—Davis. LOB—Chicago 4, St. Louis 6. HBP—Donohue. Wild pitch—Owen. DP—Davis-Tannehill; Davis-Dundon-Donohue. Umpire—Sheridan. Time—1:35.

Chicago	IP	R	H	BB	K
Owen (W)	9	2	4	3	3

St. Louis	IP	R	H	BB	K
Buchanan (L)	9	3	7	0	2

Game 2

Chicago	R	H	P	A
Jones, cf	0	1	1	0
Holmes, lf	0	2	4	0
Davis, ss	0	0	1	4
Donohue, 1b	0	0	15	0
Isbell, rf	0	1	4	0
Sullivan, c	0	0	1	0
Dundon, 2b	1	1	0	4
Tannehill, 3b	0	2	1	4
Owen, p	1	3	0	4
	2	10	27	16

St. Louis	R	H	P	A
Rockenfeld, 2b	0	0	1	2
Stone, lf	0	0	2	0
Frisk, rf	0	1	2	1
Koehler, cf	0	0	3	0
Wallace, ss	0	1	3	7
Gleason, 3b	0	1	1	1
Sugden, 1b	0	0	13	1
Weaver, c	0	0	1	2
Glade, p	0	0	1	4
	0	3	27	18

Chicago	0	0	1	0	1	0	0	0	0—2
St. Louis	0	0	0	0	0	0	0	0	0—0

2B—Gleason. Sac—Tannehill, Isbell. LOB—Chicago 8, St. Louis 3. E—Glade. Umpire—Sheridan. Time—1:20.

Chicago	IP	R	H	BB	K
Owen (W)	9	0	3	0	0

St. Louis	IP	R	H	BB	K
Glade (L)	9	2	10	2	1

Ed Walsh's Two Complete-Game Victories in One Day

Chicago at Boston, September 26, 1905

Game 1

Chicago	R	H	P	A	E
Jones, cf	3	4	2	0	0
Isbell, 2b	3	4	1	2	0
Davis, ss	3	2	2	4	1
Callahan, lf	0	0	2	1	1
Donohue, 1b	0	2	14	1	0
Green, rf	0	1	1	0	0
Rohe, 3b	0	0	0	2	0
Sullivan, c	0	2	5	2	0
White, p	0	0	0	0	0
Walsh, p	1	1	0	4	0
	10	16	27	16	2

Boston	R	H	P	A	E
Parent, ss	1	2	2	1	0
Stahl, cf	1	2	2	0	1
Unglaub, 3b	1	1	3	1	1
Burkett, lf	0	0	1	0	1
Freeman, 1b	1	1	8	0	2
Selbach, rf	1	0	5	1	1
Ferris, 2b	0	2	4	3	0
Armbruster, c	0	1	2	3	0
Winter, p	0	0	0	4	0
	5	9	27	13	6

Chicago	1	0	3	0	4	0	0	0	2—10
Boston	5	0	0	0	0	0	0	0	0— 5

2B—Donohue. 3B—Davis. HR—Isbell (1). Sac—Callahan (2). SB—Callahan (2). DP—Parent-Ferris-Freeman, Selbach-Winter-Freeman. Umpire—Connor. Time—1:52.

Boston	IP	BB	K
Winter (L)	9	3	2

Chicago	IP	BB	K
White	0	0	0
Walsh (W)	9	5	5

Game 2

Chicago	R	H	P	A	E
Jones, cf	0	0	0	0	0
Isbell, 2b	0	1	2	1	0
Davis, ss	2	1	4	3	0
Callahan, lf	1	1	3	0	0
Donohue, 1b	0	1	7	1	0
Green, rf	0	1	1	0	1
Rohe, 3b	0	0	1	1	0
Sullivan, c	0	1	6	2	1
Walsh, p	0	1	0	2	1
	3	7	24	10	3

Boston	R	H	P	A	E
Parent, ss	0	1	1	2	0
Stahl, cf	0	0	0	0	0
Unglaub, 3b	0	0	1	4	4
Burkett, lf	0	1	1	1	0
Freeman, 1b	0	0	13	0	0
Selbach, rf	0	1	2	0	0
Ferris, 2b	0	0	3	4	0
Criger, c	1	1	2	1	0
Harris, p	0	1	1	2	0
	1	5	24	14	1

Chicago	1	0	0	0	0	0	0	2—3
Boston	0	0	1	0	0	0	0	0—1

3B—Parent. Sac—Donohue. SB—Davis, Selbach, Criger. DP—Davis-Donohue. PB—Criger. Wild pitch—Walsh (2). Umpire—Sheridan. Time—1:49. Attendance—3,486.

Frank Owen tossed two complete-game victories in one day: July 1, 1905.

Boston	IP	BB	K
Harris (L)	8	5	1

Chicago	IP	BB	K
Walsh (W)	8	4	5

First Game Played in Old Comiskey Park

St. Louis at Chicago, July 1, 1910

St. Louis	R	H	P	A
Stone, lf	1	3	0	0
Hartzell, 3b	0	0	2	3
Wallace, ss	0	1	2	3
Newnam, 1b	0	1	1	0
Schweitzer, cf	0	1	0	0
Hoffman, rf	0	0	1	0
Truesdale, 2b	1	1	5	2
Killifer, c	0	0	6	4
Pelty, p	0	0	0	5
	2	7	27	17

Chicago	R	H	P	A
Zeider, 2b	0	0	0	1
French, 2b	0	0	1	0
Browne, cf	0	1	3	0
Collins, rf	0	0	2	1
Block, c	0	0	1	1
Dougherty, lf	0	1	6	0
Gandil, 1b	0	0	1	1
Purtell, 3b	0	0	2	1
Blackburne, ss	0	2	2	2
Sullivan, c	0	0	8	3
Payne, rf	0	0	0	0
Walsh, p	0	1	2	4
	0	7	27	17

St. Louis	0	0	2	0	0	0	0	0	0—2
Chicago	0	0	0	0	0	0	0	0	0—0

E—Newnam, Killifer, Sullivan. 2B—Stone. 3B—Stone, Dougherty. Sac—Hartzell. SB—Collins, Truesdale, Stone (2), Hartzell, French. DP—Zeider-Sullivan-Purtell-Blackburne. LOB—Chicago 6, St. Louis 10. Time—1:35. Umpires—Connally and Dinneen. Attendance—32,000 (est.).

St. Louis	IP	BB	K	H
Pelty (W)	9	2	4	7

Chicago	IP	BB	K	H
Walsh (L)	9	1	6	7

First Sox Victory in Old Comiskey Park

St. Louis at Chicago, July 2, 1910

St. Louis	AB	R	H	RBI
Stone, lf	4	0	0	0
Hartzell, 3b	4	0	1	0
Wallace, ss	4	0	0	0
Newnam, 1b	4	1	1	0
Schweitzer, cf	3	1	1	0
Griggs, rf	3	0	0	0
Truesdale, 2b	3	0	1	2
Stephens, c	3	0	2	0
Lake, p	3	0	0	0
	31	2	6	2

Chicago	AB	R	H	RBI
French, 2b	3	0	0	0
Browne, cf, rf	3	1	1	0
Collins, rf	2	0	1	0
Parent, cf	2	0	1	0
Dougherty, lf	3	1	2	0
Gandil, 1b	2	0	1	0
Mullen, 1b	2	1	0	0
Purtell, 3b	4	0	1	1
Blackburne, ss	4	0	1	0
Payne, c	2	0	1	0
White, p	4	0	0	0
	33	3	9	1

St. Louis	0	0	0	0	2	0	0	0	0—2
Chicago	0	0	2	0	0	0	1	0	x—3

E—Mullen, Wallace, Stephens, Lake. 3B—Browne. SB—Parent (2), Mullen. DP—Stephens-Hartzell, White-Blackburne-Mullen, Payne-Mullen. Time—1:40. Umpires—Dineen, Connally.

St. Louis	IP	ER	K	BB
Lake (L)	8	0	8	2

Chicago	IP	ER	K	BB
White (W)	9	1	1	0

White Sox Steal 11 Bases in One Game with Three Steals of Home and Three Double Steals

St. Louis at Chicago, July 2, 1909

St. Louis	AB	R	H
Hartzell, rf	4	1	2
Hoffman, cf	2	0	0
McAleese, cf	3	0	1
Griggs, lf	4	0	3
Ferris, 3b	4	0	1
Wallace, ss	5	0	1
Jones, 1b	4	0	0
Williams, 2b	4	0	1
Criger, c	0	0	0
Smith, c	4	1	1
Graham, p	0	0	0
Criss, p	1	0	1
Howell, p	3	1	1
	38	3	12

Chicago	AB	R	H
Hahn, rf	3	3	1
Welday, rf	1	0	1
Parent, cf	6	3	3
Altizer, 1b	6	2	3
Dougherty, lf	4	1	0
Purtell, 3b	3	2	2
Tannehill, ss	4	1	2
Atz, 2b	2	0	0
Reilly, 2b	1	1	0
Payne, c	4	1	1
Walsh, p	5	1	1
	39	14	14

St. Louis	0	0	0	0	3	0	0	0	0— 3
Chicago	5	0	0	5	2	3	0	0	x—15

2B—Criss, Purtell, Walsh. 3B—Tannehill. SB—Altizer, Dougherty (2), Parent, Reilly, Hahn, Atz, Walsh, Purtell (3), Hartzell. DP—Atz-Tannehill-Altizer; Hartzell-Jones-Wallace. E—Reilly, Wallace (2), Jones. HBP—Reilly (by Howell). PB—Criger. Sac—Ferris, Dougherty. Umpire—Evans. Time—2:03.

Stealing Home—Walsh, Purtell, Parent

St. Louis	IP	BB	K	H	R
Graham (L)	1	1	2	5	5
Criss	2⅓	3	4	2	4
Howell	5⅓	3	0	5	6

Chicago	IP	BB	K	H	R
Walsh (W)	9	2	1	12	3

Shortest Game in White Sox History: 68 Minutes

Philadelphia at Chicago, August 29, 1915

Philadelphia	AB	R	H	RBI
Kopf, ss	4	0	0	0
Walsh, rf	4	0	0	0
Strunk, 1b	3	0	0	0
Lajoie, 2b	3	0	1	0
Oldring, lf	3	0	1	0
Schang, 3b	3	0	0	0
Davies, cf	3	0	0	0
Lapp, c	3	0	1	0
Sheehan, p	3	0	0	0
	29	0	3	0

Chicago	AB	R	H	RBI
Murphy, rf	4	1	2	1
J. Collins, 1b	4	1	1	0
E. Collins, 2b	3	1	1	0
Jackson, cf	3	1	2	2
Felsch, lf	3	0	1	2
Weaver, ss	3	0	0	0
Johns, 3b	3	0	0	0
Schalk, c	3	1	1	0
Scott, p	2	0	0	0
	28	5	8	5

Philadelphia	0	0	0	0	0	0	0	0	0—0
Chicago	0	0	5	0	0	0	0	0	x—5

E—Davis. 2B—Lapp. SB—Murphy, Schalk. DP—Scott-Weaver, J. Collins. Sac—Scott. Umpires—Dineen, Nallin. Time— :68.

Philadelphia	IP	R	ER	BB	K
Sheehan (L)	8	5	4	4	0

Chicago	IP	R	ER	BB	K
Scott (W)	9	0	0	1	6

Babe Ruth's First Comiskey Park Home Run

Boston at Chicago, July 12, 1919 (Third Inning, off Dave Danforth)

Boston	AB	R	H	SAC
Lamar, cf	4	2	2	0
Vitt, 3b	5	1	2	0
Hooper, rf	5	2	2	0
Ruth, lf	4	2	3	0
McInnis, 1b	5	1	4	0
Schang, c	5	0	1	0
Scott, ss	4	1	3	0
McNally, ss	0	0	0	0
Shannon, 2b	4	1	0	0
Pennock, p	2	2	1	1
	38	12	17	1

Chicago	AB	R	H	SAC
J. Collins, rf	4	0	1	0
E. Collins, 2b	4	0	1	0
Weaver, ss	2	1	1	0
Jackson, lf	4	1	1	0
Felsch, cf	4	0	1	0
Gandil, 1b	4	1	1	0
McMullin, 3b	4	1	2	0
Schalk, c	2	0	1	0
Lynn, c	2	0	0	0
Kerr, p	1	0	1	0
Danforth, p	2	0	0	0
Jenkins, ph	1	0	0	0
	34	4	10	0

Boston	0	1	4	2	0	2	0	0	3—12
Chicago	2	1	0	0	0	0	0	0	1— 4

2B—Ruth, Kerr, Hooper (2), Vitt. 3B—Jackson, Lamar, McInnis. HR—Ruth. DP—McInnis (unassisted). HBP—Weaver (by Pennock). Umpires—Moriarity and Hildebrand.

Boston	IP	R	BB	K
Pennock (W)	9	4	1	2

Chicago	IP	R	BB	K
Kerr (L)	2⅓	4	1	0
Danforth	6⅔	8	3	4

Eddie Collins' 3,000th Career Hit

Chicago at Washington, June 6, 1925 (Ninth Inning Double off Walter Johnson)

Chicago	AB	R	H
Mostil, cf	4	0	0
Davis, ss	3	1	0
Collins, 2b	4	0	2
Sheely, 1b	4	0	0
Falk, lf	4	0	1
Hooper, rf	4	0	0
Kamm, 3b	3	0	1
Crouse, c	3	0	1
Robertson, p	3	0	0
	32	1	5

Washington	AB	R	H
Leibold, cf	4	1	1
Harris, 2b	4	1	2
Rice, rf	3	0	0
Goslin, lf	4	0	1
Judge, 1b	3	1	1
Peckinpaugh, ss	1	0	0
McNally, 3b	2	0	0
Ruel, c	3	1	3
Johnson, p	3	0	0
	31	4	10

	1	2	3	4	5	6	7	8	9
Chicago	1	0	0	0	0	0	0	0	0—1
Washington	0	0	2	0	0	0	0	2	x—4

2B—Collins (2), Leibold, Crouse, Judge. E—Kamm, Peckinpaugh. Stolen base—Rice. Umpires—Rowland and Owens. Time—1:40.

Chicago	IP	R	H	BB	K
Robertson (L)	8	4	10	1	0

Washington	IP	R	H	BB	K
Johnson (W)	9	1	5	1	4

Ted Lyons' 21-Inning Complete-Game Loss

Detroit at Chicago, May 24, 1929

Detroit	AB	R	H	RBI
Johnson, lf	9	1	4	1
Rice, cf-rf	9	0	2	1
Gehringer, 2b	9	1	3	1
Heilmann, lf-1b	10	0	3	0
Stone, lf	0	0	0	0
Alexander, 1b	7	2	4	1
McManus, 3b-ss	8	0	1	0
Phillips, c	8	1	2	1
Schuble, ss	6	0	1	1
Richardson, ss	0	0	0	0
Sigafoos, 3b	0	0	0	0
Uhle, p	9	1	4	0
Stoner, p	0	0	0	0
Fothergill, ph	1	0	0	0
Hargraves, ph	1	0	0	0
Harris, pr	0	0	0	0
Yde, pr	0	0	0	0
	77	6	24	6

Chicago	AB	R	H	RBI
Metzler, lf	9	1	1	0
Hunnefield, 2b	9	1	1	1
Kamm, 3b	8	1	4	1
Clancy, 1b	9	1	1	0
Reynolds, rf	9	1	2	1
Hoffman, cf	9	0	2	0
Cissell, ss	7	0	3	1
Crouse, c	5	0	2	1
Berg, c	2	0	0	0
Lyons, p	6	0	1	0
Watwood, ph	1	0	1	0
Kerr, pr	0	0	0	0
	74	5	18	5

Detroit	031	000	100	000	000	000	001—6
Chicago	200	030	000	000	000	000	000—5

E—McManus, Cissell. 2B—Rice, Schuble, Heilmann. 3B—Metzler, Kamm, Alexander. SB—Hoffman, Crouse. Sac—Schuble, Cissell, Crouse, Alexander, Lyons (2), Rice, Metzler, McManus, Gehringer. DP—Uhle-Schuble-Alexander; Lyons-Clancy. Wild pitch—Uhle. LOB—Detroit 19, Chicago 14. Time— 3:31. Umpires—Van Graflan, McGowan, Connally.

Detroit	IP	R	ER	BB	K
Uhle (W)	20	5	4	3	4
Stoner	1	0	0	0	0

Chicago	IP	R	ER	BB	K
Lyons (L)	21	6	6	2	4

Save—Stoner.

Carl Reynolds' Three Home Runs in One Game—A Sox First

Chicago at New York, July 2, 1930

Chicago	AB	R	H
Jeffries, ss	5	1	3
Watwood, cf	4	1	1
Reynolds, lf	6	4	5
Jolley, rf	0	1	2
Kerr, 2b	3	2	2
Clancy, 1b	4	0	0
Kamm, 3b	3	3	3
Berg, c	5	1	2
McKain, p	1	2	1
Caraway, p	2	0	0
	39	15	19

New York	AB	R	H
Combs, lf	4	1	1
Reese, 2b	5	1	1
Ruth, rf	1	0	0
Cooke, rf	1	1	0
Byrd, rf	2	0	0
Lazzeri, ss	4	1	1
Gehrig, 1b	3	0	0
Rice, cf	4	0	1
Dickey, c	3	0	1
Chapman, 3b	4	0	0
Ruffing, p	0	0	0
Holloway, p	1	0	0
Gomez, p	1	0	0
Henderson, p	1	0	1
	35	4	6

	1	2	3	4	5	6	7	8	9
Chicago	3	4	4	1	0	1	2	0	0—15
New York	1	0	3	0	0	0	0	0	0— 4

2B—Jolley, Combs, Kamm, Reese, Berg. 3B—McKain. HR—Reynolds (3), Kerr. SB—Watwood, Reynolds. Sac—Jeffries, Clancy, Dickey, Watwood, Kerr. DP—Lazzeri-Reese-Gehrig. HBP—Kerr (by Gomez). E—Jeffries (2), Kerr, Rice, Chapman. Umpires—Moriarity, McGowan, Owens. Time—2:31.

Chicago	IP	H	BB	K
McKain (W)	2⅔	5	3	2
Caraway	6⅓	1	4	1

New York	IP	H	BB	K
Ruffing (L)	1⅔	7	1	1
Holloway	1	5	1	0
Gomez	3⅓	4	2	0
Henderson	3	3	1	0

Rip Radcliff Becomes First Sox Player to Collect Six Hits in One Game

Chicago at Philadelphia, July 18, 1936

Chicago	AB	R	H	RBI
Radcliff, lf	7	4	6	4
Rosenthal, cf	6	3	2	4
Haas, rf	6	3	2	2
Bonura, 1b	5	1	1	1
Appling, ss	5	3	3	3
Hayes, 2b	5	1	3	2
Dykes, 3b	5	2	1	2
Grube, c	4	3	1	1
Whitehead, p	2	1	1	0
Brown, p	0	1	0	0
	45	21	20	19

Philadelphia	AB	R	H	RBI
Finney, lf	4	2	2	1
Dean, 1b	6	1	2	3
Moses, cf	6	1	1	3
Puccinelli, rf	5	1	3	0
Higgins, 3b	5	1	1	0
Johnson, 2b	5	2	3	3
Hayes, c	4	3	4	1
Newsome, ss	5	2	3	3
Ross, p	2	0	0	0
Gumpert, p	0	0	0	0
Naktenis, p	1	0	0	0
Flythe, p	0	0	0	0
Moss, ph	1	1	1	0
Peters, ph	1	0	0	0
	45	14	20	14

	1	2	3	4	5	6	7	8	9
Chicago	3	1	1	0	7	2	0	3	4—21
Philadelphia	3	0	0	3	2	0	0	0	6—14

2B—Bonura, Hayes, Radcliff (2), F. Hayes (2), Dykes, Grube, Rosenthal (2). 3B—Dean, Johnson. HR—Appling, Johnson. Sac—Brown (2). DP—Philadelphia 1, Chicago 1, LOB—Philadelphia 7, Chicago 11. HBP—Appling (by Naktenis), Finney, F. Hayes (by Brown). Wild pitch—Flythe (3). Umpires—Quinn, McGowan, and Owens.

Chicago	IP	H	BB	K
Whitehead	4	13	0	2
Brown (W)	4	7	1	1

Philadelphia	IP	H	BB	K
Ross (L)	4⅓	12	1	1
Gumpert	0	3	1	0
Naktenis	2⅔	1	1	1
Flythe	2	4	1	1

Hank Steinbacher Becomes Second Sox Player to Collect Six Hits in Six At-Bats

Washington at Chicago, June 22, 1938

Washington	AB	R	H	RBI
Myer, 2b	4	1	1	0
West, cf	4	0	2	1
Lewis, 3b	4	1	1	0
Simmons, lf	4	1	2	2
Travis, ss	4	0	2	0
Bonura, 1b	4	0	0	0
Goslin, rf	4	0	0	0
R. Ferrell, c	2	0	0	0
Giuliani, c	2	0	0	0
W. Ferrell, p	0	0	0	0
Weaver, p	1	0	0	0
Hogsett, p	0	0	0	0
Wasdell, ph	1	0	0	0
	34	3	8	3

Chicago	AB	R	H	RBI
Hayes, 2b	4	4	3	1
Steinbacher, rf	6	3	6	2
Kreevich, cf	4	2	0	1
Radcliff, lf	5	0	4	6
Owen, 3b	3	1	0	0
Rensa, c	5	1	1	1
Kuhel, 1b	4	0	0	1
Berger, ss	4	2	0	1
Stratton, p	6	3	3	2
	41	16	17	15

	1	2	3	4	5	6	7	8	9
Washington	0	0	0	0	0	1	0	0	2— 3
Chicago	1	3	1	2	1	3	5	0	x—16

2B-Myer, West, Lewis, Steinbacher, Radcliff, Rensa, Stratton. E-Myer (2), Lewis. 3B—Radcliff. HR—Simmons. Stolen base-Travis. DP—Lewis to Myer to Bonura; Berger to Kuhel. LOB—Washington 5, Chicago 14, Wild pitches—Weaver (2). Umpires—McGowan, Basil, Quinn. Time—2:16. Attendance—500 (estimated).

Washington	IP	R	H	K	BB
Ferrell (L)	2	4	6	0	3
Weaver	3	4	3	0	6
Hogsett	3	8	8	2	4

Chicago	IP	R	H	K	BB
Stratton (W)	9	5	8	1	1

First Night Game at Comiskey Park

St. Louis at Chicago, August 14, 1939

St. Louis	AB	R	H	RBI
Berardino, 2b	3	0	1	1
Heffner, ph-2b	1	0	1	0
Grace, cf	4	0	0	0
McQuinn, 1b	4	0	0	1
Solters, lf	4	0	0	0
Clift, 3b	4	0	0	0
Laabs, rf	4	0	1	0
Glenn, c	2	0	0	0
Christman, ss	3	1	0	0
Trotter, p	1	0	0	0
Sullivan, ph	1	0	0	0
Harris, pr	0	1	0	0
Lawson, p	0	0	0	0
Hoag, cf-ph	1	0	0	0
Whitehead, p	0	0	0	0
	32	2	3	2

Chicago	AB	R	H	RBI
Hayes, 2b	5	0	1	0
Kuhel, 1b	5	2	2	0
Kreevich, cf	4	0	2	0
Walker, lf	3	0	1	1
Appling, ss	4	1	0	1
Radcliff, rf	3	1	1	0
Rosenthal, rf	0	0	0	0
McNair, 3b	4	1	2	1
Tresh, c	3	0	2	2
Rigney, p	4	0	2	0
	35	5	13	5

	1	2	3	4	5	6	7	8	9
St. Louis	0	0	0	0	0	2	0	0	0—2
Chicago	0	1	0	1	1	0	0	2	x—5

E—Appling (2). 2B—Hayes, Kreevich, McNair. SB—Kuhel, Kreevich, Radcliff. Umpires—Hubbard, Kells, Ormsby, Moriarity. HBP—Appling (by Trotter).

St. Louis	IP	K	BB	ER
Trotter (L)	5	1	1	3
Lawson	2	0	2	2
Whitehead	1	0	0	0

Chicago	IP	K	BB	ER
Rigney (W)	9	10	1	1

A Double One-Hitter, Won by the White Sox

Baltimore at Chicago, June 21, 1956

Baltimore	AB	R	H	RBI
Gardner, 2b	4	0	0	0
Evers, rf	3	0	0	0
Kell, 3b	3	0	0	0
Nieman, lf	4	0	0	0
Triandos, 1b	3	0	1	0
Smith, c	2	0	0	0
Pyburn, cf	3	0	0	0
Miranda, ss	3	0	0	0
Johnson, p	2	0	0	0
Hale, ph	1	0	0	0
Zuverink, p	0	0	0	0
	28	0	1	0

Chicago	AB	R	H	RBI
Rivera, rf	2	1	0	0
Fox, 2b	3	0	1	0
Doby, cf	3	0	0	0
Philley, lf	3	0	0	0
Dropo, 1b	3	0	0	0
Hatfield, 3b	3	0	0	0
Moss, c	3	0	0	0
Aparicio, ss	3	0	0	0
Harshman, p	3	0	0	0
	26	1	1	1

Baltimore	0	0	0	0	0	0	0	0	0—0
Chicago	1	0	0	0	0	0	0	0	x—1

Baltimore	IP	H	R	ER	BB	K
Johnson	7	1	1	1	3	7
Zuverink	1	0	0	0	0	0

Chicago	IP	H	R	ER	BB	K
Harshman	9	1	0	0	4	4

Winning pitcher—Harshman (4–4). Losing pitcher—Johnson (2–4).

E—Aparicio, Triandos. 2B—Fox, Triandos. SB—Rivera, Hatfield. LOB—Baltimore 5, Chicago 5. DP—Hatfield to Fox to Dropo. HBP—Zuverink (Fox). Umpires—Tabacchi, Stevens, Runge, Rommel. Time—2:12. Attendance—4,581 (paid).

Bill Pierce Foiled in Bid for Perfect Game (Pinch-Hitter Ed Fitzgerald Doubles with Two Out in Ninth)

Washington at Chicago, June 27, 1958

Washington	AB	R	H	RBI
Pearson, cf	4	0	0	0
Bridges, ss	3	0	0	0
Sievers, lf	3	0	0	0
Lemon, rf	3	0	0	0
Yost, 3b	3	0	0	0
Zauchin, 1b	3	0	0	0
Aspromonte, 2b	3	0	0	0
Korcheck, c	3	0	0	0
Kemmerer, p	2	0	0	0
FitzGerald, ph	1	0	1	0
	28	0	1	0

Chicago	AB	R	H	RBI
Landis, cf	4	1	3	1
Fox, 2b	3	0	0	0
Goodman, 3b	3	0	1	0
Esposito, 2b	0	1	0	0
Boone, 1b	4	0	0	0
Lollar, c	4	0	1	2
Smith, rf	4	0	0	0
Rivera, lf	3	0	1	0
Aparicio, ss	3	0	1	0
Pierce, p	3	1	1	0
	31	3	8	3

Washington	0	0	0	0	0	0	0	0	0—0
Chicago	0	0	1	0	0	0	0	2	x—3

Washington	IP	H	R	ER	BB	K
Kemmerer	8	8	3	3	1	3

Chicago	IP	H	R	ER	BB	K
Pierce	9	1	0	0	0	9

Winning pitcher—Pierce (7–5). SB—Landis (2), Esposito. Sac—Fox. LOB—White Sox 6, Washington 1. Umpires—Chylak, Berry, Flaherty, McKinley. Time—1:46. Attendance—11,300.

Floyd Robinson Becomes Third Sox Player to Collect Six Hits in a Game

Chicago at Boston, July 22, 1962

Chicago	AB	R	H	RBI
Aparicio, ss	6	2	2	1
Cunningham, 1b	4	1	1	0
Robinson, lf-rf	6	1	6	1
Maxwell, lf	5	1	2	1
Landis, cf	1	0	0	0
Smith, 3b	5	0	2	2
Esposito, 3b	1	0	0	0
Fox, 2b	4	0	1	1
Hershberger, cf-rf	4	1	1	0
Carreon, c	3	1	1	0
Herbert, p	2	0	0	0
Baumann, p	2	0	1	1
	43	7	17	7

Boston	AB	R	H	RBI
Bressoud, ss	5	1	2	0
Geiger, cf	4	0	0	0
Yastrzemski, lf	4	1	2	1
Malzone, 3b	4	0	0	0
Runnels, 1b	4	0	1	1
Clinton, rf	4	0	1	0
Pagliaroni, c	3	1	2	1
Schilling, 2b	4	0	0	0
Monboquette, p	1	0	0	0
Fornieles, p	0	0	0	0
Nixon, ph	0	0	0	0
Tillman, ph	1	0	0	0
Kolstad, p	0	0	0	0
Cisco, p	0	0	0	0
Hardy, ph	1	0	0	0
Radatz, p	0	0	0	0
Green, ph	1	0	1	0
	36	3	9	3

Chicago	0	0	3	1	3	0	0	0	0—7
Boston	2	1	0	0	0	0	0	0	0—3

2B—Bressoud, Yastrzemski, Runnels, Smith, Carreon. HR—Pagliaroni. Sac—Cunningham. SF—Fox. LOB—Chicago 16, Boston 7. DP—Aparicio-Cunningham. E—Yastrezemski. Passed ball—Carreon. Time—3:11. Attendance—15,621.

Chicago	IP	H	R	BB	K
Herbert	3⅓	5	3	1	4
Baumann (W)	5⅔	4	0	0	3

Boston	IP	H	R	BB	K
Monboquette	2⅔	7	3	1	1
Fornieles (L)	1⅓	3	1	1	1
Kolstad	1⅔	4	3	2	0
Cisco	1⅓	1	0	1	0
Radatz	2	2	0	0	4

Ray Herbert's Fourth Consecutive Shutout

Detroit at Chicago, May 14, 1963

Detroit	AB	R	H	RBI
Wood, 2b	4	0	1	0
Bruton, cf	4	0	2	0
Herzog, rf	4	0	0	0
Cash, 1b	4	0	0	0
Triandos, c	4	0	1	0
Colavito, lf	3	0	1	0
McAuliffe, ss	3	0	0	0
Phillips, 3b	2	0	0	0
Kostro, 2b	1	0	1	0
Bunning, p	2	0	0	0
Egan, p	0	0	0	0
Freehan, ph	1	0	0	0
	32	0	6	0

Chicago	AB	R	H	RBI
Landis, cf	4	1	2	3
Fox, 2b	4	0	0	0
Ward, 3b	3	0	0	0
Robinson, rf	3	0	0	0
Maxwell, 1b	3	0	0	0
Nicholson, lf	3	1	1	0
Hansen, ss	2	0	0	0
Martin, c	2	1	0	0
Herbert, p	3	0	1	0
	27	3	4	3

Detroit	0	0	0	0	0	0	0	0	0—0
Chicago	1	0	0	0	2	0	0	0	x—3

2B—Bruton. HR—Landis. Stolen base—Wood. Sac—Hansen. DP—Ward-Fox-Maxwell (Wood). LOB—Chicago 2, Detroit 5. Time—1:57. Umpires—Stevens, Napp, Umont, Kinneman. Attendance—13,147.

Detroit	IP	H	R	BB	K
Bunning (L)	7	3	3	1	8
Egan	1	1	0	0	0

Chicago	IP	H	R	BB	K
Herbert (W)	9	6	0	0	7

Nellie Fox's 2,500th Hit

Chicago at Baltimore, July 28, 1963

Chicago	AB	R	H	RBI
Landis, cf	5	0	1	1
Fox, 2b	5	1	1	0
Nicholson, lf	4	1	1	1
Lemon, 1b	2	0	1	1
McGraw, 1b	1	0	1	0
Robinson, rf	3	1	1	0
Hansen, ss	4	0	1	0
Ward, 3b	4	0	1	0
Carreon, c	3	1	2	1
Peters, p	3	0	0	0
	34	4	10	4

Baltimore	AB	R	H	RBI
Aparicio, ss	4	0	0	0
Snyder, rf	4	0	1	1
Johnson, 1b	4	0	1	0
Orsino, c	3	0	1	0
Gaines, lf	4	0	2	0
B. Robinson, 3b	4	0	2	0
Brandt, cf	3	0	0	0
Miller, p	0	0	0	0
Adair, 2b	4	1	1	0
McNally, p	1	0	0	0
Saverine, cf	1	0	0	0
Smith, ph	1	0	0	0
	33	1	8	1

Chicago	1	0	0	0	0	1	1	1	0—4
Baltimore	0	0	0	0	1	0	0	0	0—1

2B—Landis. HR—Nicholson. Sac—McNally, F. Robinson, Peters. DP—Peters-Fox-McCraw (Smith). LOB—Chicago 8, Baltimore 7. Time—2:20. Umpires— Chylak, Rice, Valentine, McKinley. Attendance—5,811.

Chicago	IP	H	R	BB	K
Peters (W)	9	8	1	1	4

Baltimore	IP	H	R	BB	K
McNally (L)	6⅓	5	3	3	1
Miller	2⅔	5	1	0	1

The Boston Massacre: Sox Score 22 Runs, Their Second-Highest Single-Game Total

Chicago at Boston, May 31, 1970

Chicago	AB	R	H	RBI
Williams, rf	7	5	5	2
Aparicio, ss	5	2	5	2
O'Brien, ss	1	1	1	1
Blanco, 1b	5	1	2	3
May, lf	5	2	2	1
Matias, 1b	1	0	0	0
Josephson, c	6	1	3	2
Melton, 3b	6	2	3	4
Bradford, cf	4	2	0	0
Knoop, 2b	6	3	2	1
Janeski, p	3	0	1	1
Weaver, p	2	1	0	0
	51	22	24	18

Boston	AB	R	H	RBI
Andrews, 2b	4	2	3	1
Derrick, lf	4	2	2	2
Yastrzemski, cf	4	1	2	2
Petrocelli, 3b	4	1	1	0
Scott, 1b	4	2	2	1
B. Conigliaro, rf	5	1	2	1
Fiore, ph	1	0	1	1
Alvarado, ss	4	1	1	1
Satriano, c	4	3	3	3
Peters, p	0	0	0	0
Stange, p	1	0	0	0
Brett, p	0	0	0	0
Santiago, p	1	0	0	0
Lyle, p	0	0	0	0
Lee, p	0	0	0	0
	40	13	17	13

Chicago	6	0	1	3	1	7	0	4	0—22
Boston	2	0	0	4	1	2	1	1	2—13

2B—Williams, Josephson (2), Scott (2), Melton, Knoop, Andrews, Derrick, O'Brien, Satriano. 3B—Satriano, Aparicio. HR—Yastrzemski, Melton, Andrews. Stolen base—Williams. Sac—Weaver. SF—Scott, Alvarado. Wild pitches—Brett, Weaver. Time—3:36. Umpires—Umont, O'Donnell, Maloney, Honochick. Attendance—21,952.

Chicago	IP	H	R	BB	K
Janeski	4	7	7	3	1
Weaver (W)	5	10	6	2	2

Boston	IP	H	R	BB	K
Peters (L)	⅔	5	6	1	2
Stange	2⅔	5	4	1	1
Brett	⅔	0	0	0	1
Lee	1	5	5	1	2
Santiago	2	4	3	0	1
Lyle	2	5	4	0	1

Wilbur Wood Wins 21-Inning Game, Then Pitches Nine-Inning Shutout

Cleveland at Chicago, May 26–28, 1973 (Suspended Game)

Cleveland	AB	R	H	RBI
Bell, 3b	9	0	2	0
Lowenstein, rf	3	1	1	0
Torres, rf	5	0	1	0
Chambliss, 1b	8	0	0	0
Spikes, lf	8	1	0	0
Duncan, c	8	0	3	1
Gamble, dh	5	0	1	0
Williams, dh	4	0	2	1
Hendrick, cf	9	0	1	0
Ragland, 2b	8	1	1	0
Duffy, ss	7	0	2	1
Perry, p	0	0	0	0
Johnson, p	0	0	0	0
Wilcox, p	0	0	0	0
Hilgendorf, p	0	0	0	0
Farmer, p	0	0	0	0
	74	3	14	3

Chicago	AB	R	H	RBI
Kelly, rf	8	1	3	0
Sharp, cf	2	0	0	0
May, ph	1	0	0	0
Jeter, cf	4	1	0	0
Allen, 1b-2b	8	1	3	3
Melton, 3b	7	1	1	1
Reichardt, lf	9	0	1	0
Andrews, dh	8	0	0	0
Herrmann, c	3	0	1	0
Alvarado, 2b	2	0	0	0
Muser, 1b	4	1	2	0
Orta, 2b	3	0	2	0
Stone, pr	0	0	0	0
Brinkman, c	4	0	0	0
Leon, ss	8	1	4	2
Bahnson, p	0	0	0	0
Forster, p	0	0	0	0
Wood, p	0	0	0	0
	71	6	17	6

Cleveland	000	000	110	000	000	000	00	1—3
Chicago	000	010	010	000	000	000	00	4—6

Cleveland	IP	H	R	ER	BB	K
Perry	13	10	2	2	5	8
Johnson	3	2	0	0	1	4
Wilcox	4⅓	3	2	2	2	1
Hilgendorf	0	1	1	1	0	0
Farmer	⅓	1	1	1	0	0

Chicago	IP	H	R	ER	BB	K
Bahnson	13	9	2	2	3	4
Forster	3	3	0	0	1	2
Wood	5	2	1	0	1	5

Winning pitcher—Wood (12–3). Losing pitcher—Wilcox (3–1).

E—Bell, Leon. DP—Cleveland 1, Chicago 2. LOB—Cleveland 13, Chicago 16. 2B—Kelly, Lowenstein, Duffy, Gamble, Muser. 3B—Bell. HR—Melton (9), Allen (10). Sac—Melton, Leon, Allen, Jeter, Brinkman. WP—Perry, Wilcox 2. Time—6:03. Attendance—19,486.

Cleveland at Chicago, May 28, 1973

(Wood's Second Victory)

Cleveland	AB	R	H	RBI
Bell, 3b	4	0	0	0
Ragland, 2b	4	0	2	0
Chambliss, 1b	4	0	0	0
Spikes, lf	3	0	0	0
Duncan, c	4	0	0	0
Williams, dh	4	0	1	0
Hendrick, cf	3	0	0	0
Torres, rf	3	0	1	0
Duffy, ss	2	0	0	0
Tidrow, p	0	0	0	0
Hilgendorf, p	0	0	0	0
	31	0	4	0

Chicago	AB	R	H	RBI
Kelly, rf	4	0	1	1
Sharp, cf	3	0	2	0
Allen, 1b	3	1	0	0
Melton, 3b	4	1	1	1
Reichardt, lf	4	0	2	1
May, dh	3	1	1	0
Andrews, 2b	4	0	0	0
Herrmann, c	3	1	0	0
Leon, ss	3	0	2	1
Wood, p	0	0	0	0
	31	4	9	4

Cleveland	0	0	0	0	0	0	0	0	0—0
Chicago	2	0	0	0	0	2	0	0	x—4

2B—Melton. 3B—Sharp. Stolen base—May. E—Melton, Spikes. DP—Cleveland 1, Chicago 1. Time—1:57. Attendance—17,419.

Cleveland	IP	H	R	BB	K
Tidrow (L)	5⅔	7	4	4	5
Hilgendorf	2⅓	2	0	0	0

Chicago	IP	H	R	BB	K
Wood (W)	9	4	0	2	4

An Amazing Comeback: Sox Overcome 9–0 Deficit

Cleveland at Chicago, June 13, 1978

Cleveland	AB	R	H	RBI
Dade, rf	5	2	2	0
Veryzer, ss	5	2	2	2
Bell, 3b	1	2	1	1
Blanks, 3b	3	0	1	0
Thornton, 1b	4	2	3	1
Horton, dh	4	0	2	2
Grubb, lf	5	0	1	2
Pruitt, c	3	0	1	0
Manning, ph	1	0	0	0
Kuiper, 2b	5	0	1	0
Speed, cf	4	1	1	0
Norris, ph	1	0	0	0
	41	9	15	8

Chicago	AB	R	H	RBI
Garr, lf	4	2	2	1
Bannister, cf	1	1	0	0
H. Cruz, cf	2	1	0	0
Lemon, dh	2	1	0	0
Nordhagen, rf	5	2	3	3
Molinaro, rf	0	0	0	0
Johnson, 1b	5	1	2	2
Nahorodny, c	5	1	1	1
Orta, 2b	3	0	1	2
Kessinger, ss	4	0	0	0
Pryor, 3b	3	1	1	0
	34	10	10	9

Cleveland	4	4	1	0	0	0	0	0	0— 9
Chicago	0	0	6	4	0	0	0	0	x—10

Cleveland	IP	H	R	ER	BB	K
Monge	3	5	8	3	4	0
Fitzmorris	0	1	2	2	1	0
Kinney	5	4	0	0	1	1

Chicago	IP	H	R	ER	BB	K
Wood	0	3	4	4	1	0
Torrealba	1⅓	6	4	4	3	0
Hinton	6⅓	5	1	1	0	1
LaGrow	1⅓	1	0	0	0	0

Winning pitcher—Hinton (1–0). Losing pitcher—Fitzmorris (0–1). Save—LaGrow.

E—Pryor, Grubb, Veryzer (2). DP—Chicago 1. LOB—Cleveland 9, Chicago 8. 2B—Thornton, Dade, Kuiper. 3B—Veryzer, Garr. SB—Molinaro. Sac—Garr. SF—Orta. WP—Wood. Time—2:59. Attendance—12,000.

Tom Seaver Wins His 300th Game

Chicago at New York, August 4, 1985

Chicago	AB	R	H	RBI
Law, lf	3	0	2	0
Nichols, lf	1	0	1	0
Little, 2b	2	0	1	2
Fletcher, 2b	1	0	0	0
Baines, rf	5	0	2	0
Walker, 1b	3	0	1	0
Fisk, c	5	1	1	0
Gamble, dh	2	1	1	0
Kittle, ph	1	0	0	0
Hulett, 3b	4	1	2	1
Guillen, ss	4	0	1	1
Salazar, cf	4	1	1	0
	35	4	13	4

New York	AB	R	H	RBI
R. Henderson, cf	4	0	0	0
Griffey, dh	4	0	1	1
Mattingly, 1b	4	0	2	0
Winfield, rf	4	0	0	0
Pasqua, lf	4	0	1	0
Hassey, c	4	0	0	0
Randolph, 2b	3	0	0	0
Pagliarulo, 3b	3	1	1	0
Meacham, ss	3	0	1	0
Baylor, ph	1	0	0	0
	34	1	6	1

Chicago	0	0	0	0	0	4	0	0	0—4
New York	0	0	1	0	0	0	0	0	0—1

E—Hulett. DP—New York 1. LOB—Chicago 10, New York 8. 2B—Salazar, Hulett, Fisk. Game-winning RBI—Guillen. HBP—Randolph (by Seaver). Time—3:20. Attendance—54,032.

Chicago	IP	H	R	BB	K
Seaver (W)	9	6	1	1	7

New York	IP	H	R	BB	K
Cowley (L)	5⅓	7	2	5	2
Fisher	⅔	4	2	1	0
Shirley	2	2	0	0	2
Allen	1	0	0	0	1

Final Game in Old Comiskey Park

Seattle at Chicago, September 30, 1990

Seattle	AB	R	H	BI
Reynlds, 2b	5	0	1	0
Griffey Sr, lf	4	0	0	0
Griffey Jr, cf	4	1	2	0
Cotto, cf	0	0	0	0
A. Davis, dh	4	0	1	0
Briley, pr	0	0	0	0
T. Mrtnz, 1b	4	0	0	0
Buhner, rf	4	0	1	0
Valle, c	3	0	2	0
S. Brdly, ph	1	0	1	0
Vizquel, ss	4	0	3	0
Schaefr, 3b	2	0	0	0
O'Brien, ph	1	0	0	0
Totals	36	1	11	0

Chicago	AB	R	H	BI
Caldern, lf	3	0	1	0
L. Johnson, cf	4	1	3	0
Fisk, c	4	0	0	0
Thomas, 1b	4	1	2	1
Lyons, 1b	0	0	0	0
Pasqua, dh	4	0	1	1
Ventura, 3b	4	0	0	0
Sosa, rf	3	0	0	0
Fletchr, 2b	2	0	1	0
Guillen, ss	2	0	1	0
Totals	30	2	9	2

Seattle	0	0	0	0	0	1	0	0	0—1
Chicago	0	0	0	0	0	2	0	0	x—2

DP—Seattle 1. LOB—Seattle 9, Chicago 7. 2B—Valle, A. Davis. 3B—Griffey Jr, L. Johnson, Pasqua. S—Guillen.

Seattle	IP	H	R	ER	BB	K
Delucia L, 1–2	8	9	2	2	2	4

Chicago	IP	H	R	ER	BB	K
McDwll W, 14–9	8	10	1	1	1	7
Thigpen S, 57	1	1	0	0	0	0

WP—McDowell.
Umpires—Home, Brinkman; First, Cousins; Second, Reed; Third, Cooney. Time—2:43. Attendance—42,849.

First Game in New Comiskey Park

Detroit at Chicago, April 18, 1991

Detroit	AB	R	H	BI
Phillips, dh	6	2	4	3
Tramml, ss	5	3	4	2
Tanana, p	1	0	0	0
Whitakr, 2b	3	2	3	0
Bernzrd, 2b	2	0	1	0
Fielder, 1b	3	2	2	4
Bergmn, 1b	2	0	0	0
Incvglia, lf	3	0	0	1
Cuyler, cf	2	0	1	0
Tettleton, c	6	2	1	2
Deer, rf	5	2	2	4
Allanson, c	0	0	0	0
Shelby, cf	5	1	1	0
Frymn, 3b	1	2	0	0
disSnts, 3b	2	0	0	0
Totals	46	16	19	16

Chicago	AB	R	H	BI
Raines, dh	4	0	1	0
L. Johnsn, cf	4	0	1	0
Ventura, 3b	4	0	2	0
Thomas, 1b	4	0	1	0
Fisk, c	2	0	1	0
Merullo, c	2	0	0	0
Sosa, rf	4	0	0	0
Snyder, lf	3	0	0	0
Guillen, ss	1	0	0	0
Grebck, ss	2	0	0	0
Fletchr, 2b	1	0	0	0
Cora, 2b	2	0	1	0
Totals	33	0	7	0

Detroit	0	0	6	(10)	0	0	0	0	0—16
Chicago	0	0	0	0	0	0	0	0	0— 0

E—Ventura. DP—Detroit 1, Chicago 1. LOB—Detroit 8, Chicago 6. 2B—Shelby, Whitaker. 3B—Phillips. HR—Fielder (1), Deer 2 (2), Phillips (2). SB—Whitaker (1), Fryman (2), Trammell (2), Raines (2).

Detroit	IP	H	R	ER	BB	K
Tanana W, 1–1	9	7	0	0	0	3

Chicago	IP	H	R	ER	BB	K
McDwll L, 2–1	2⅔	5	6	6	3	0
Drahman	⅓	5	5	5	1	0
Patterson	2⅔	7	5	4	1	2
Radinsky	1	1	0	0	0	2
Pall	1	1	0	0	0	2
Thigpen	1	0	0	0	0	0

PB—Merullo 2.
Umpires—Home, Palermo; First, Reilly; Second, Young; Third, Garcia. Time—3:11. Attendance—42,191.

Frank Thomas Becomes First Sox Player to Hit 40 Home Runs

Chicago at Detroit, September 5, 1993

Chicago	AB	R	H	BI	BB	K
Raines, lf	4	0	0	0	1	0
Cora, 2b	4	0	1	0	0	0
Thomas, 1b	4	1	1	2	1	0
Ventura, 3b	3	1	1	0	2	1
G. Bell, dh	5	1	3	2	0	0
Burks, rf	4	0	1	0	0	1
L. Johnson, cf	4	0	1	0	0	1
Karkovice, c	3	1	1	0	1	2
Guillen, ss	4	1	2	0	0	0
Totals	35	5	11	4	5	5

Detroit	AB	R	H	BI	BB	K
Gladden, lf	5	1	2	1	0	1
Barnes, rf	3	0	0	0	0	2
a-Philps, ph-rf	1	0	1	0	0	0
Fryman, 3b	3	0	1	0	1	0
Fielder, 1b	4	0	0	0	0	2
E. Davis, cf	4	1	2	0	0	1
Trammell, ss	3	1	1	1	1	0
Rowland, dh	3	0	0	0	0	2
b-Livingstone, ph	1	0	1	1	0	0
1-Thurman, pr	0	0	0	0	0	0
Kreuter, c	3	0	0	0	0	1
c-Tettleton, ph	0	0	0	0	1	0
C. Gomez, 2b	2	0	0	0	1	0
d-Whitaker, ph	1	0	0	0	0	0
Totals	33	3	8	3	4	9

Chicago	1	0	1	0	0	2	1	0	0—5	11	0
Detroit	0	0	0	1	0	0	1	0	1—3	8	0

a-singled for Barnes in the 8th. b-singled for Rowland in the 9th. c-walked for Kreuter in the 9th. d-lined out for C. Gomez in the 9th.

1-ran for Livingstone in the 9th.

LOB—Chicago 9, Detroit 7. HR—Gladden (12) off Alvarez, Trammell (9) off Alvarez, Thomas (40) off Moore, G. Bell (10) off Moore. RBIs—Thomas 2 (120). G. Bell 2 (55), Gladden (47), Trammell (51), Livingstone (37). SB—Cora (14). CS—Gladden (5). GIDP—Raines, Fielder.

Runners left in scoring position—Chicago 3 (Ventura, G. Bell, Guillen); Detroit 5 (Gladden, Barnes, Fielder, Rowland 2).

Runners moved up—Cora, Thomas, Trammell.

DP—Chicago 1 (Guillen, Cora and Thomas): Detroit 1 (C. Gomez, Trammell and Fielder).

Chicago	IP	H	R	ER	BB	K	NP
Alvarez W, 11–8	7	5	2	2	2	8	104
DeLeon	1	1	0	0	1	1	22
Hernandez S, 33	1	2	1	1	1	0	19

Detroit	IP	H	R	ER	BB	K	NP
Moore L, 11–8	6⅔	10	5	5	2	5	122
Gardiner	1⅓	1	0	0	1	0	22
Henneman	1	0	0	0	2	0	18

Inherited runners-scored—Gardiner 2–0. IBB—off Henneman (Ventura) 1. HBP—by Moore (Cora). WP—Moore, Gardiner. Umpires—Home, Kosc; First, Morrison; Second, Clark; Third, Barnett. Time—2:58. Attendance—26,434.

Robin Ventura's Two Grand Slam Home Runs in Consecutive Innings

Chicago at Texas, September 4, 1995

Chicago	AB	R	H	BI	BB	K
L. Johnson, cf	6	2	2	2	0	0
Raines, lf	4	3	3	0	0	1
Cameron, rf	2	0	0	0	0	2
DaMartinez, 1b	5	1	1	0	1	0
Thomas, dh	2	2	0	0	2	2
a-Lyons, ph-dh	2	0	1	0	0	0
Ventura, 3b	5	3	3	8	1	0
Mouton, rf-lf	3	2	3	1	1	0
Durham, 2b	5	0	2	1	0	0
LaValliere, c	5	0	2	1	0	0
Guillen, ss	5	1	1	1	0	0
Totals	44	14	18	14	5	5

Texas	AB	R	H	BI	BB	SO
Nixon, cf	1	1	0	0	3	0
Marzano, c	1	0	0	0	0	0
McLemore, 2b-lf	4	0	0	0	0	2
W. Clark, 1b	2	1	0	0	1	0
Frye, 2b	1	0	0	0	0	0
J. Gonzalez, dh	3	1	2	2	0	1
b-L. Ortiz, ph-dh	1	0	0	0	0	0
Tettleton, rf	3	0	0	0	0	2
Frazier, cf	1	0	0	0	0	0
I. Rodriguez, c	2	0	0	1	0	0
Valle, 1b	1	0	1	0	0	0
Greer, lf-rf	4	0	1	0	0	0
Pagliarulo, 3b	4	0	0	0	0	1
Gil, ss	3	0	0	0	0	0
c-Horn, ph	0	0	0	0	1	0
Totals	31	3	4	3	5	6

Chicago	1	1	1	6	4	0	0	1	0—14	18	2
Texas	2	0	0	1	0	0	0	0	0— 3	4	0

a-flied out for F. Thomas in the 7th. b-popped out for Gonzalez in the 8th. c-Walked for Gil in the 9th.

E: Raines (3), Durham (14). LOB—Chicago 9, Texas 7. 2B—Ventura (18), Mouton 2 (8), LaValliere (5). 3B—Durham (6), Guillen (3). HR—J. Gonzalez (21) off Bere; L. Johnson (9) off KeGross; Ventura 2 (25) off Cook, Darwin. RBI—L. Johnson 2 (46), Ventura 8 (87), Mouton (18), Durham (46), LaValliere (15), Guillen (33), J. Gonzalez 2 (60), I. Rodriguez (55). SB—Nixon (36). CS—Nixon (17). SF—I. Rodriguez.

Runners left in scoring position—Chicago 6 (L. Johnson 2, Ventura, Durham 2, LaValliere); Texas 3 (Marzano, J. Gonzalez 2). Runners moved up—DaMaritnez, LaValliere, Guillen 2. DP—Texas 1 (Valle).

Chicago	IP	H	R	ER	BB	K	NP	ERA
Bere W	6	3	3	2	4	5	120	6.85
Radinsky	2	0	0	0	0	1	22	5.91
Bolton R	1	1	0	0	1	0	15	7.71

Texas	IP	H	R	ER	BB	K	NP	ERA
KeGross L	3⅔	8	7	7	3	3	85	6.02
Cook	⅓	3	2	2	0	0	18	4.47
Darwin	4	6	5	5	1	1	62	7.67
Brandenburg	1	1	0	0	1	1	11	5.79

Winning pitcher—Bere (7–11). Losing pitcher—Kevin Gross (7–14).

Inherited runners-scored—Cook 3–3.

HBP—Mouton (by Darwin). Umpires—Home, McClelland; First, Roe; Second, Phillips; Third, Cederstrom. Time—3:11. Attendance—18,036.

Lance Johnson Becomes Fourth Player to Record Six Hits in One Game and First to Stroke Three Triples in One Game

Chicago at Minnesota, September 23, 1995

Chicago	AB	R	H	BI	BB	K
L. Johnson, cf	6	4	6	4	0	0
Raines, lf	2	1	0	1	2	1
Cameron, rf	1	0	0	0	0	0
DaMartinez, 1b	4	1	0	2	1	0
Thomas, dh	5	0	2	2	0	1
Tremie, ph-dh	1	0	0	0	0	1
Ventura, 3b	6	1	5	1	0	0
Mouton, rf-lf	4	1	1	0	2	0
Snopek, ss	6	3	3	2	0	0
Karkovice, c	5	0	1	0	0	1
Brady, 2b	5	3	2	1	0	1
Totals	45	14	20	13	5	5

Minnesota	AB	R	H	BI	BB	K
Knoblauch, 2b	3	0	1	1	0	0
Raabe, 2b	1	0	0	1	0	0
Meares, ss-cf	4	0	0	1	0	1
Puckett, dh	3	0	0	0	0	1
A. Cole, ph-dh	1	0	0	0	0	0
P. Munoz, rf	3	0	0	0	1	0
Cordova, lf	3	0	1	0	0	0
Lawton, lf	1	0	0	0	0	1
Coomer, 1b	4	1	1	0	0	1
Walbeck, c	4	1	3	1	0	0
Reboulet, 3b-ss	2	2	1	0	2	0
Becker, cf	1	0	0	0	0	1
Leius ph-3b	3	0	0	0	0	0
Totals	33	4	7	4	3	5

Chicago	2	3	0	0	0	3	3	3	0—14	20	1
Minnesota	0	0	1	0	0	0	0	2	1—4	7	3

E—Ventura (19), P. Munoz (5), Leius (14), Parra (2). 2B—Ventura 3 (21), Snopek 2 (2), Knoblauch (32), Coomer (2), Walbeck (17), Reboulet (11). 3B—L. Johnson 3 (11), Cordova (4).

Chicago	IP	H	R	ER	BB	K	NP	ERA
Alvarez W	9	7	4	3	3	5	141	4.31

Minnesota	IP	H	R	ER	BB	K	NP	ERA
Parra L	5⅔	11	8	7	3	4	108	7.94
Schullstrom	1⅓	4	3	3	1	0	34	7.00
Munoz O	2	5	3	3	1	1	38	6.46

Winning pitcher—Alvarez (8–10). Losing pitcher—Parra (1–5).

Umpires—Home, Shulock; First, Tschida; Second, Craft; Third, Cederstrom. Time—3:04. Attendance—21,007.

First All-Star Game in Comiskey Park

July 6, 1933

National League	AB	R	H	RBI
Martin, 3b	4	0	0	1
Frisch, 2b	4	1	2	1
Klein, rf	4	0	1	0
P. Waner, rf	4	0	1	0
Hafey, lf	4	0	1	0
Terry, 1b	4	0	2	0
Berger, cf	4	0	0	0
Bartell, ss	2	0	0	0
Traynor, ph	1	0	1	0
Hubbell, p	0	0	0	0
Cuccinello, ph	1	0	0	0
Wilson, c	1	0	0	0
O'Doul, p	1	0	0	0
Hartnett, c	1	0	0	0
Hallahan, p	1	0	0	0
Warneke, p	1	1	1	0
English, ss	1	0	0	0
	34	2	8	2

American League	AB	R	H	RBI
Chapman, lf-cf	5	0	1	0
Gehringer, 2b	3	1	0	0
Ruth, rf	4	1	2	2
West, cf	0	0	0	0
Gehrig, 1b	2	0	0	0
Simmons, cf-lf	4	0	1	0
Dykes, 3b	3	1	2	0
Cronin, ss	3	1	1	0
R. Ferrell, c	3	0	0	0
Gomez, p	1	0	1	1
Crowder, p	1	0	0	0
Averill, ph	1	0	1	1
Grove, p	1	0	0	0
	31	4	9	4

Nationals	0	0	0	0	0	2	0	0	0—2
Americans	0	1	2	0	0	1	0	0	x—4

2B—Traynor. 3B—Warneke. HR—Ruth, Frisch. SB—Gehringer. Sac—R. Ferrell. DP—Bartell-Frisch-Terry; Dykes-Gehrig. LOB—National League 5, American League 2. Time—2:05. Umpires—Dinneen, Rigler, McGowan, Klem. Attendance—43,000.

Nationals	IP	BB	K	H
Hallahan (L)	2	5	1	2
Warneke	4	0	2	6
Hubbell	2	1	1	1

Americans	IP	BB	K	H
Gomez (W)	3	0	1	2
Crowder	3	0	0	3
Grove	3	0	3	3

Second All-Star Game at Comiskey Park

July 11, 1950

National League	AB	R	H	RBI
Jones, 3b	7	0	1	0
Kiner, lf	6	1	2	1
Musial, 1b	5	0	0	0
Robinson, 2b	4	1	1	0
Wyrostek, rf	2	0	0	0
Slaughter, cf-rf	4	1	2	1
Schoendienst, 2b	1	1	1	1
Sauer, rf	3	0	0	1
Pafko, cf	4	0	2	0
Campanella, c	6	0	0	0
Marion, ss	2	0	0	0
Konstanty, p	0	0	0	0
Jansen, p	2	0	0	0
Blackwell, p	1	0	0	0
Roberts, p	1	0	0	0
Newcombe, p	0	0	0	0
Sisler, ph	1	0	1	0
Reese, ss	3	0	0	0
	52	4	10	4

American League	AB	R	H	RBI
Rizzuto, ss	6	0	2	0
Doby, cf	6	1	2	0
Kell, 3b	6	0	0	2
Williams, lf	4	0	1	1
D. DiMaggio, lf	2	0	0	0
Dropo, 1b	3	0	1	0
Fain, 1b	3	0	1	0
Evers, rf	2	0	0	0
J. DiMaggio, rf	3	0	0	0
Berra, c	2	0	0	0
Hegan, c	3	0	0	0
Doerr, 2b	3	0	0	0
Coleman, 2b	2	0	0	0
Raschi, p	0	0	0	0
Michaels, ph	1	1	1	0
Lemon, p	0	1	0	0
Houtteman, p	1	0	0	0
Reynolds, p	1	0	0	0
Gray, p	0	0	0	0
Feller, p	0	0	0	0
	49	3	8	3

Nationals	0	2	0	0	0	0	0	0	1	0	0	0	0	1—4
Americans	0	0	1	0	2	0	0	0	0	0	0	0	0	0—3

E—Coleman. 2B—Michaels, Doby, Kiner. 3B—Slaughter, Dropo. HR—Kiner, Schoendienst. DP—Rizzuto=Doerr-Dropo; Jones-Schoendienst-Musial. LOB—Nationals 9, Americans 6. Time—3:19. Umpires—McGowan, Pinelli, Rommel, Conlan. Attendance—46,127.

Nationals	IP	R	H	K	BB
Roberts	3	1	3	1	1
Newcombe	2	2	3	1	1
Konstanty	1	0	0	2	0
Jansen	5	0	1	6	0
Blackwell (W)	3	0	1	2	0

The American League All-Stars at Comiskey Park, July 6, 1933

Americans	IP	R	H	K	BB
Raschi	3	2	2	1	0
Lemon	3	0	1	2	0
Houtteman	3	1	3	0	1
Reynolds	3	0	1	2	1
Gray (L)	1⅓	1	3	1	0
Feller	⅔	0	0	1	1

Fiftieth Anniversary All-Star Game at Comiskey Park

July 6, 1983

National League	AB	R	H	RBI
Sax, 2b	3	1	1	1
Hubbard, 2b	1	0	1	0
Raines, lf	3	0	0	0
Madlock, 3b	1	0	0	0
Dawson, cf	3	0	0	0
Dravecky, p	0	0	0	0
Perez, p	0	0	0	0
Orosco, p	0	0	0	0
Bench, ph	1	0	0	0
L. Smith, p	0	0	0	0
Oliver, 1b	2	1	1	0
Evans, 1b	1	0	0	0
Murphy, rf	3	0	1	1
Guerrero, 3b	1	0	0	0
Schmidt, 3b	2	0	0	0
Benedict, c	2	0	1	0
Carter, c	2	0	0	0
Durham, rf	2	0	0	0
O. Smith, ss	2	1	1	0
McGee, cf	2	0	1	0
Soto, p	1	0	0	0
Hammaker, p	0	0	0	0
Dawley, p	0	0	0	0
Thon, ss	3	0	1	0
	35	3	8	2

American League	AB	R	H	RBI
Carew, 1b	3	2	2	1
Murray, 1b	2	0	0	0
Yount, ss	2	1	0	1
Ripken, ss	0	0	0	0
Lynn, cf	3	1	1	4
Wilson, cf	1	0	1	1
Rice, lf	4	1	2	1
Oglivie, rf	1	0	0	0
Young, p	0	0	0	0
Quisenberry, p	0	0	0	0
Brett, 3b	4	2	2	1
Simmons, c	2	0	0	0
Parrish, c	2	0	0	0
Cooper, ph	1	1	1	0
Boone, c	0	0	0	0
Winfield, rf	3	2	3	1
Kittle, lf	2	1	1	0
Trillo, 2b	3	1	1	0
Whitaker, 2b	1	1	1	2
Stieb, p	0	0	0	0
DeCinces, ph	1	0	0	0
Honeycutt, p	0	0	0	0
Ward, ph	1	0	0	0
Stanley, p	0	0	0	0
Yastrzemski, ph	1	0	0	0
Henderson, lf	1	0	0	1
	38	13	15	13

Nationals	1	0	0	1	1	0	0	0	0—3
Americans	1	1	7	0	0	0	2	2	x—13

E—Steib, Carew, Schmidt, Sax, Guerrero. DP—American League, 2. LOB—Nationals 6, Americans 9. 2B—Winfield, Oliver, Wilson, Brett. 3B—Brett, Whitaker. HR—Rice, Lynn. SB—Sax, Raines. Sac—Steib. Sac. flies—Brett, Yount, Whitaker. Passed ball—Benedict. Time—3:05. Attendance—43,801.

National League	IP	H	R	BB	K
Soto (L)	2	2	2	2	2
Hammaker	⅔	6	7	1	0
Dawley	1⅓	1	0	0	1
Dravecky	2⅔	3	2	0	2
Perez	⅔	3	2	1	1
Orosco	⅓	0	0	0	1
L. Smith	1	2	2	0	1

American League	IP	H	R	BB	K
Stieb (W)	3	0	1	1	4
Honeycutt	2	5	2	0	0
Stanley	2	2	0	0	0
Young	1	0	0	0	1
Quisenberry	1	1	0	0	1

First All-Star Game at U.S. Cellular Field

July 15, 2003

National League	AB	R	H	RBI
Renteria, ss	2	0	0	0
Furcal, ss	3	1	1	0
Edmonds, cf	2	0	1	0
Jones, ph-cf	3	2	2	3
Pujols, lf	1	0	1	1
Gonzalez, lf	3	0	1	0
Bonds, dh	1	0	0	0
White, ph-dh	1	0	0	0
Sheffield, rf	2	1	0	0
Wilson, rf	2	0	1	0
Helton, 1b	2	1	1	2
Sexson, 1b	2	0	0	0
Rolen, 3b	1	1	1	0
Lowell, 3b	1	0	1	0
Boone, ph-3b	2	0	0	0
Lopez, c	2	0	0	0
LoDuca, ph-c	2	0	1	0
Vidro, 2b	2	0	0	0
Castillo, 2b	2	0	0	0
	36	6	11	6

American League	AB	R	H	RBI
Suzuki, rf	1	1	0	0
Ordonez, ph-rf	1	0	0	0
Soriano, 2b	3	0	0	0
Giambi, 1b	1	1	1	1
Delgado, 1b	3	0	1	1
Hernandez, c	1	0	0	0
Rodriguez, ss	3	1	1	0
Garciaparra, ss	1	0	0	0
Anderson, lf	4	1	3	2
Mora, pr-lf	0	1	0	0
Martinez, dh	2	0	0	0
Everett, ph-dh	1	0	0	0
Matsui, cf	2	0	1	0
Wells, pr-cf	2	1	1	1
Glaus, 3b	3	0	0	0
Blalock, ph-3b	1	1	1	2
Posada, c	2	0	0	0
Boone, 2b	2	0	0	0
	33	7	9	7

Nationals	0	0	0	0	5	0	1	0	0—6
Americans	0	0	1	0	0	2	1	3	x—7

National League	IP	R	H	K	BB
Schmidt	2	0	1	3	0
Wolf	1	1	1	2	1
Wood	1	0	1	2	0
Ortiz	1	2	2	1	0
W. Williams	1	2	2	0	0
Wagner	1	1	1	0	0
Gagne	1	3	3	1	0

American League	IP	R	H	K	BB
Loaiza	2	0	1	1	0
Clemens	1	0	0	2	0
Moyer	1	0	0	1	0
Hasegawa	⅔	4	3	1	1
Guardado	⅓	1	2	0	0
Mulder	2	1	5	1	0
Donnelley	1	0	0	1	0
Foulke	1	0	0	0	0

Winning Pitcher—Donnelly. Losing Pitcher—Gagne. Save—Foulke. 2B,—Jones, Lowell, Anderson, Wells. HR—Jones, Helton, Giambi, Anderson, Blalock.

Double Plays—Americans, 2. E—Furcal. Hit by Pitch—Martinez by Schmidt. Wild Pitch—Wolf. Time—2:38. Umpires—McClelland, Young, Darling, Cedarstrom, Carlson, Welke. Attendance—47,609.

Two Grand Slams in One Game: "Dummy" Hoy and Herm McFarland Sink Tigers

Detroit at Chicago, May 1, 1901

Detroit	R	H	P	A	E
Casey, 3b	1	2	3	3	2
Barrett, cf	1	0	1	0	0
Gleason, 2b	1	1	3	3	1
Holmes, rf	0	0	1	0	1
Dillon, 1b	1	2	7	3	1
Elberfeld, ss	2	3	2	1	3
Nance, lf	1	2	2	1	0
McAllister, c	2	2	3	0	2
Yeager, p	0	2	0	1	0
Siever, p	0	0	2	1	0
Frisk, ph	0	0	0	0	0
	9	14	24	13	10

Chicago	R	H	P	A	E
Hoy, cf	4	3	5	0	0
Jones, rf	3	2	1	0	1
Mertes, 2b	2	1	2	1	2
Isbell, 1b	1	1	10	0	0
Hartman, 3b	0	1	0	0	1
Shugarts, ss	2	2	2	5	0
McFarland, lf	1	2	3	0	0
Sullivan, c	2	2	4	1	0
Harvey, p	2	0	0	3	0
Patterson, p	2	1	0	1	0
	19	15	27	11	4

Detroit	1	0	5	0	1	0	0	1	1—9
Chicago	2	8	4	1	4	0	0	0	x—19

2B—Hartman, Nance, Hoy, Gleason. 3B—Casey, Sullivan. HR—Hoy, McFarland. SB—Isbell. DP—Gleason-Dillon. HBP—Hoy (by Yeager). Wild pitch—Harvey. Total bases—Chicago 25, Detroit 18. Sac—Mertes, Holmes, Hartman. Umpire—Connally. Time—2:26. Attendance—1,768.

Detroit	IP	H	R	BB	K
Yeager	1⅓	7	7	3	1
Siever	7⅔	8	12	4	0

Chicago	IP	H	R	BB	K
Harvey	2	4	1	3	0
Patterson	7	10	7	4	1

Winning pitcher—Patterson. Losing pitcher—Yeager

Frank Smith's Opening-Day One-Hitter

St. Louis at Chicago, April 14, 1910

St. Louis	AB	R	H	PO	A	E
Stone, lf	4	0	0	0	0	0
Wallace, 3b	2	0	0	0	3	0
Hoffman, cf	3	0	0	0	0	0
Griggs, 2b	3	0	0	3	4	0
Hartzell, ss	3	0	0	2	3	0
Abstein, 1b	2	0	0	13	0	1
Demmitt, rf	3	0	1	3	0	0
Stephens, c	2	0	0	3	2	0
Graham, p	2	0	0	0	1	1
Lake, p	0	0	0	0	0	0
Criss, ph	1	0	0	0	0	0
	25	0	1	24	13	2

Chicago	AB	R	H	PO	A	E
Hahn, rf	3	1	0	3	0	0
Zeider, 2b	3	0	1	0	3	0
Parent, cf	3	0	0	4	0	0
Dougherty, lf	4	2	1	0	0	0
Gandil, 1b	2	0	1	10	3	0
Purtell, 3b	3	0	1	0	3	0
Blackburne, ss	4	0	0	3	2	0
Payne, c	3	0	1	5	1	0
Smith, p	3	0	0	2	2	0
	28	3	5	27	14	0

St. Louis	0	0	0	0	0	0	0	0	0—0
Chicago	0	0	0	0	1	1	0	1	x—3

2B—Dougherty. HBP—Gandil (by Graham). Time—1:41. Umpires—O'Laughlin & Perrins. Attendance—20,000 (est.).

St. Louis	IP	H	R	BB	K
Graham	5⅓	3	2	3	0
Lake	2⅔	2	1	1	2

Chicago	IP	H	R	BB	K
Smith	9	1	0	2	5

Winning pitcher—Smith. Losing pitcher—Graham.

White Sox Win 100th Game of the Season—A Team Record

Chicago at New York, September 29, 1917

Chicago	AB	R	H	TB
J. Collins, lf	4	0	0	0
McMullin, 3b	4	1	0	0
E. Collins, 2b	4	0	1	1
Jackson, rf	4	0	1	1
Felsch, cf	4	1	1	1
Gandil, 1b	3	1	2	2
Weaver, ss	4	0	2	2
Schalk, c	3	0	0	0
Lynn, c	1	0	1	1
Cicotte, p	3	0	1	1
Murphy, ph	1	0	0	0
	35	3	9	9

New York	AB	R	H	TB
Miller, cf	4	1	2	4
Ward, ss	4	0	1	0
Baker, 3b	3	0	0	1
Pipp, 1b	4	0	1	1
Lamar, lf	4	0	1	1
Vick, rf	4	0	1	2
Fewster, 2b	4	0	2	2
Walters, c	3	0	1	1
Thormahlen, p	2	0	0	0
Brady, p	0	0	0	0
Hendryx, ph	1	0	0	0
	37	1	8	10

Chicago	0	0	0	0	0	2	1	0	0—3
New York	1	0	0	0	0	0	0	0	0—1

Chicago	IP	H	R	BB	K
Cicotte	9	8	1	1	8

New York	IP	H	R	BB	K
Thormahlen	8	9	3	4	3
Brady	1	0	0	0	0

2B—Vick. 3B—Miller. DP—Gandil-Schalk; Collins-Weaver-Gandil. E—E. Collins, Cicotte, Vick, Walters, Thormahlen. Time—1:45. Winning pitcher—Cicotte. Losing pitcher—Thormahlen.

Ray Schalk Is the First Sox Player to Hit for the Cycle

Chicago at Detroit, June 27, 1922

Chicago	AB	R	H	TB
Johnson, ss	5	1	1	2
Mulligan, 3b	4	0	0	0
Collins, 2b	4	2	2	2
Hooper, rf	3	1	0	0
Mostil, cf	5	1	2	5
Falk, lf	5	1	2	3
Sheely, 1b	4	0	0	0
Schalk, c	4	2	4	10
Schupp, p	0	0	0	0
Hodge, p	4	1	1	1
	38	9	12	23

Detroit	AB	R	H	TB
Blue, 1b	4	1	2	3
Haney, 3b	3	0	0	0
Cobb, cf	3	1	0	0
Veach, lf	5	1	2	2
Cutshaw, 2b	3	1	0	0
Flagstead, rf	4	1	2	5
Rigney, ss	3	0	1	1
Bassler, c	4	0	1	1
Ehmke, p	1	0	0	0
Cole, p	2	0	0	0
Clark, ph	1	0	1	1
Gagnon, ph	1	0	0	0
	34	5	9	13

Chicago	0	1	1	3	0	0	0	1	3—9
Detroit	4	0	1	0	0	0	0	0	0—5

2B—Blue, Falk, Schalk, Johnson. 3B—Schalk. HR—Schalk. DP—Collins-Johnson-Sheely. SB—Mostil. Sac—Mulligan. Time—2:00. Umpires—Evans and Owens.

Chicago	IP	H	R	BB	K
Hodge	8	6	5	4	3
Schupp	1	3	0	2	3

Detroit	IP	H	R	BB	K
Cole	5	8	5	2	1
Ehmke	4	4	4	1	2

Winning pitcher—Hodge. Losing pitcher—Cole.

Ted Lyons' Major League Debut

Chicago at St. Louis, July 2, 1923

Chicago	AB	R	H	TB
Hooper, rf	5	0	0	0
McClellan, ss	4	0	1	1
Collins, 2b	3	0	0	0
Happenny, 2b	1	0	0	0
Mostil, cf	4	1	2	3
Sheely, 1b	4	1	2	2
Falk, lf	4	0	1	1
Kamm, 3b	4	0	1	1
Schalk, c	2	0	1	1
Graham, c	2	0	1	1
Leverett, p	0	0	0	0
Mack, p	1	0	0	0
Lyons, p	0	0	0	0
Elsh, ph	1	0	1	1
	36	2	10	11

St. Louis	AB	R	H	TB
Tobin, rf	5	0	0	0
Robertson, 3b	3	2	1	2
Williams, lf	4	1	1	1
Jacobson, cf	3	2	3	3
McManus, 2b	2	0	1	1
Gerber, ss	3	0	1	1
Severeid, c	3	0	1	3
Schliebner, 1b	3	0	0	0
Shocker, p	3	2	1	1
	29	7	9	12

Chicago	0	0	0	0	0	0	0	0	2—2
St. Louis	0	1	2	1	1	2	0	0	x—7

2B—Mostil, Robertson. 3B—Severeid. E—Mostil. Sac—Leverett, Jacobson, McManus (2), Gerber. LOB—Chicago 3, St Louis 7. Time—1:46. Umpires—Moriarity, Holman, and Nallin.

Chicago	IP	H	R	BB	K
Leverett	3	5	4	4	4
Mack	4	4	3	1	2
Lyons	1	0	0	0	0

St. Louis	IP	H	R	BB	K
Shocker	9	10	2	0	5

Winning pitcher—Shocker. Losing pitcher—Leverett.

First Baseman Bud Clancy Records *No* Putouts in a Nine-Inning Game

Chicago at St. Louis, April 27, 1930

Chicago	AB	R	H	P	A
Cissell, 2b	5	1	2	4	1
Reynolds, cf	5	1	1	5	0
Clancy, 1b	4	0	1	0	0
Jolley, rf	3	0	2	0	0
Watwood, rf	0	0	0	0	0
Kamm, 3b	4	0	1	3	0
Moore, lf	4	0	0	2	0
Smith, ss	3	0	1	4	1
Autry, c	4	0	1	3	1
Thomas, p	3	0	0	1	0
McKain, p	1	0	0	0	0
	36	2	10	27	3

St. Louis	AB	R	H	P	A
Blue, 1b	2	0	0	7	0
O'Rourke, 3b	3	0	0	2	2
Hale, 3b	1	0	0	0	0
Badgro, lf	4	0	0	4	1
Kress, ss	4	0	2	2	3
Schulte, cf	4	0	0	0	0
Melillo, 2b	3	1	0	5	5
Gullic, rf	4	0	1	0	0
Ferrell, c	3	0	2	6	1
Kimsey, p	1	0	0	0	0
Gray, p	2	0	0	0	0
Manush, ph	0	0	0	1	1
	32	1	5	27	13

Chicago	0	0	1	0	1	0	0	0	0—2
St. Louis	0	0	0	0	0	0	0	1	0—1

E—Cissell, Gray. 2B—Cissell (2), Kress. HR—Reynolds. DP—Badgro-Melillo-Blue; Ferrell-Melillo. Umpires—Geisel, Dinneen, and Nallin. Time—1:59.

Chicago	IP	H	R	BB	K
Thomas	6⅓	2	0	1	4
McKain	2⅓	3	1	2	4

St. Louis	IP	H	R	BB	K
Gray	8	9	2	2	5
Kimsey	1	1	0	0	1

Winning pitcher—Thomas. Losing pitcher—Gray.

Luke Appling's Major League Debut

Boston at Chicago, September 10, 1930

Boston	AB	R	H	P	A
Oliver, cf	5	1	1	3	0
Scarritt, lf	5	1	2	1	0
Regan, 2b	3	2	1	1	3
Webb, rf	4	1	2	4	0
Reeves, 3b	4	0	0	0	3
Todt, 1b	5	1	3	11	2
Warstler, ss	4	0	1	3	3
Heving, c	3	0	1	2	1
MacFayden, p	4	0	1	2	2
	37	6	12	27	14

Chicago	AB	R	H	P	A
Cissell, 2b-3b	4	0	1	0	2
Watwood, 1b	3	1	1	9	0
Reynolds, lf	3	0	1	2	0
Jolley, rf	4	0	2	2	1
Barnes, cf	4	0	0	1	0
Appling, ss	4	0	1	3	2
Kamm, 3b	2	0	0	1	1
Clancy, ph	1	0	0	0	0
Mulleavy, 2b	1	0	0	0	1
Crouse, c	3	0	0	8	1
Faber, p	1	0	0	0	3
Moore, p	1	0	0	0	1
Fothergill, ph	0	1	0	0	0
Walsh, p	0	0	0	0	1
	31	2	6	27	13

Boston	0	1	0	1	3	1	0	0	0—6
Chicago	1	0	0	0	0	0	0	1	0—2

E—Watwood, Kamm. HR—Webb, Regan. SB—Scarritt. Sac—Reeves, Heving. DP—MacFayden-Warstler. HBP—Fothergill (by MacFayden).

Boston	IP	H	R	BB	K
MacFayden	9	6	2	2	1

Chicago	IP	H	R	BB	K
Faber	4⅓	7	5	1	2
Moore	3⅔	5	1	0	5
Walsh	1	0	0	2	1

Winning pitcher—MacFayden. Losing pitcher—Faber.

Boze Berger and Mike Kreevich Lead Off the Game with Back-to-Back Home Runs

Boston at Chicago, September 2, 1937

Boston	AB	R	H	RBI
Melillo, 2b	4	0	0	1
Cramer, cf	4	0	0	0
Cronin, ss	3	1	1	0
Foxx, 1b	4	0	0	0
Higgins, 3b	3	0	2	0
Mills, lf	4	0	1	1
Chapman, rf	3	1	0	0
Berg, c	2	0	0	0
Marcum, p	0	0	0	0
Gonzalez, p	2	0	0	0
	30	2	4	2

Chicago	AB	R	H	RBI
Berger, 3b	4	2	2	2
Kreevich, cf	4	1	1	1
Walker, rf	4	1	1	1
Radcliff, lf	4	0	2	0
Appling, ss	3	0	0	0
Dykes, 3b	4	0	1	0
Piet, 2b	2	0	0	0
Sewell, c	3	0	0	0
Lee, p	3	0	1	0
	31	4	8	4

Boston	0	0	1	0	0	1	0	0	0—2
Chicago	2	0	2	0	0	0	0	0	x—4

2B—Radcliff. HR—Berger (2), Kreevich, Walker. Sac—Marcum. DP—Appling-Piet-Dykes. LOB—Boston 5, Chicago 5. HBP—Piet (by Marcum). Umpires—Johnston, Dinneen, and Hubbard. Time—1:45. Attendance—7,000 (est.).

Boston	IP	H	R	BB	K
Marcum	2⅓	5	4	0	1
Gonzalez	5⅔	3	0	2	2

Chicago	IP	H	R	BB	K
Lee	9	4	2	3	1

Winning pitcher—Lee. Losing pitcher—Marcum.

White Sox Score a Run in Every Inning

Boston at Chicago, May 11, 1949

Boston	AB	R	H	RBI
DiMaggio, cf	4	2	2	2
Pesky, 3b	3	1	1	0
Williams, lf	5	1	1	2
Stephens, ss	5	0	2	1
Doerr, 2b	4	1	0	0
O'Brien, rf	3	1	2	0
Hitchcock, 1b	5	1	2	0
Tebbetts, c	5	1	1	2
Hughson, p	1	0	1	0
Robinson, p	0	0	0	0
McCall, p	0	0	0	0
Dorish, p	0	0	0	0
	38	8	12	7

Chicago	AB	R	H	RBI
Scala, cf	5	1	1	0
Goldsberry, 1b	5	1	2	1
Appling, ss	5	1	2	0
Zernial, lf	4	3	3	2
Philley, rf	4	1	0	0
Michaels, 2b	4	3	3	3
Baker, 3b	4	2	3	2
Wheeler, c	5	0	1	1
Wight, p	3	0	0	0
Judson, p	2	0	0	0
	41	12	15	9

Boston	0	0	0	5	0	1	0	2	0— 8
Chicago	1	1	2	1	2	1	1	3	x—12

E—Doerr (3), Tebbetts, Appling. Sac—Hughson. 2B—Appling, Zernial, Wheeler. 3B—Scala, DiMaggio, Baker, Zernial, Michaels. HR—Williams. DP—Appling-Goldsberry. LOB—Boston 10, Chicago 10. Wild pitch—Wight, McCall. Balk—Robinson. Umpires—McGowan, Jones, and Hurley. Time—2:33. Attendance—3,203.

Boston	IP	H	R	ER	BB	K
Hughson	5	11	7	5	1	1
Robinson	1	1	1	1	1	0
McCall	1	1	1	0	4	0
Dorish	1	2	3	2	0	1

Chicago	IP	H	R	ER	BB	K
Wight	5⅔	9	6	6	5	5
Judson	3⅓	3	2	2	1	1

Winning pitcher—Wight. Losing pitcher—Hughson.

Go-Go White Sox Win Their 14th Game in a Row—Second Longest in Team History

St. Louis at Chicago, May 30, 1951

St. Louis	AB	R	H	RBI
Marsh, 3b	3	0	1	1
Young, 2b	3	0	1	0
Coleman, rf	4	0	0	0
Lenhardt, lf	4	0	1	0
Delsing, cf	4	0	0	0
Batts, c	3	0	1	0
Arft, 1b	3	0	0	0
Bero, ss	3	1	1	0
Widmar, p	1	0	0	0
Pillette,pr	0	0	0	0
Lollar, ph	1	0	0	0
Sievers, ph	1	0	0	0
Starr, p	0	0	0	0
Fannin, p	0	0	0	0
	30	1	5	1

Chicago	AB	R	H	RBI
Fox, 2b	4	0	2	1
Stewart, lf	4	0	1	0
Minoso, 3b	5	1	1	1
Robinson, 1b	2	3	1	1
Zarilla, rf	4	1	2	0
Busby, cf	1	1	0	0
Carrasquel, ss	4	0	0	0
Lehner, cf-rf	5	0	0	0
Niarhos, c	1	2	1	0
Gumpert, p	3	0	2	2
	33	8	10	5

St. Louis	0	0	1	0	0	0	0	0	0—1
Chicago	0	2	0	1	1	0	3	1	x—8

2B—Zarilla. HR—Minoso, Robinson. SB—Robinson. Sac—Young, Carrasquel, Widmar. LOB—St. Louis 7, Chicago 11. Time—2:07. Umpires—Soar, McGowan, McKinley, and Honochick. Attendance—34,856.

St. Louis	IP	H	R	BB	K
Widmar	6	8	4	4	1
Starr	1	1	4	4	0
Fannin	1	1	0	0	2

Chicago	IP	H	R	BB	K
Gumpert	9	5	1	5	2

Winning pitcher—Gumpert (3–0). Losing pitcher—Widmar (3–4).

Pitcher Tommy Byrne's Ninth-Inning Pinch-Hit Grand Slam Homer Sinks the Yankees

Chicago at New York, May 16, 1953

Chicago	AB	R	H	RBI
Fox, 2b	4	0	1	0
Fain, 1b	2	0	0	0
Minoso, lf	4	1	0	0
Wright, rf	3	1	1	1
Mele, rf	0	0	0	0
Rivera, cf	3	1	1	0
Stephens, 3b	3	0	0	0
Byrne, ph	1	1	1	4
Krsnich, 3b	0	0	0	0
Lollar, c	3	0	0	0
Carrasquel, ss	4	0	0	0
Pierce, p	2	0	0	0
Aloma, p	0	0	0	0
Sheely, ph	1	0	1	0
Marsh, pr	0	1	0	0
Dorish, p	0	0	0	0
	30	5	5	5

New York	AB	R	H	RBI
Rizzuto, ss	2	0	0	0
Collins, ph	1	0	0	0
Bollweg, 1b	5	0	1	0
Bauer, rf	4	1	0	0
Mantle, cf	4	0	1	0
McDougald, 3b	4	0	1	1
Renna, lf	3	1	1	0
Noren, ph, lf	0	0	0	0
Martin, 2b	4	1	1	0
Silvera, c	2	0	2	0
Mize, ph	1	0	0	1
Ford, pr	0	0	0	0
Houk, c	1	0	0	0
Raschi, p	3	0	1	1
Blackwell, p	0	0	0	0
Kuzava, p	0	0	0	0
Woodling, ph	1	0	1	0
Carey, pr	0	0	0	0
	35	3	10	3

Chicago	0	0	0	0	0	0	0	0	5—5
New York	0	0	0	0	0	0	2	1	0—3

Chicago	IP	H	R	ER	BB	K
Pierce	7	9	3	3	2	8
Aloma	1	0	0	0	1	0
Dorish	1	1	0	0	0	1

New York	IP	H	R	ER	BB	K
Raschi	8⅔	4	4	4	3	5
Blackwell	1	1	1	1	1	0
Kuzava	⅓	0	0	0	0	1

Winning pitcher—Aloma (1–0). Losing pitcher—Raschi (2–3). Save—Dorish.

E—McDougald. HR—Byrne. DP—Rizzuto-Martin-Bollweg, McDougald-Martin-Bollweg. Sac—Fain, Rizzuto. LOB—Chicago 3, New York 9. Umpires—Robb, Froese, Summers, and Stevens. Time—3:16. Attendance—22,966.

Early Wynn Strikes Out 14 Red Sox, Pitches a One-Hitter, Then Hits a Game-Winning Home Run

Boston at Chicago, May 1, 1959

Boston	AB	R	H	RBI
Buddin, ss	3	0	0	0
Runnels, 2b-1b	3	0	1	0
Stephens, cf	4	0	0	0
Lepcio, 2b	1	0	0	0
Wertz, 1b	0	0	0	0
Gernert, 1b	2	0	0	0
Jensen, rf	4	0	0	0
Malzone, 3b	4	0	0	0
Renna, lf	2	0	0	0
White, c	1	0	0	0
Brewer, p	3	0	0	0
	27	0	1	0

Chicago	AB	R	H	RBI
Aparicio, ss	3	0	0	0
Fox, 2b	4	0	1	0
Goodman, 3b	4	0	0	0
Esposito, 3b	0	0	0	0
Lollar, c	3	0	0	0
Cash, 1b	3	0	0	0
Smith, rf	3	0	2	0
Phillips, lf	3	0	0	0
Landis, cf	3	0	0	0
Wynn, p	3	1	2	1
	29	1	5	1

Boston 0	0	0	0	0	0	0	0	0—0
Chicago	0	0	0	0	0	0	0	1—1

2B—Wynn. HR—Wynn. SB—Gernert, Brewer. LOB—Boston 7, White Sox 5. Wild pitch—Wynn. Passed ball—Lollar. Umpires—McKinley, Soar, and Chylak. Time—2:46. Attendance—13,022.

Boston	IP	H	R	ER	BB	K
Brewer	8	5	1	1	1	1

Chicago	IP	H	R	ER	BB	K
Wynn	9	1	0	0	7	14

Winning pitcher—Wynn (3–1). Losing pitcher—Brewer (1–2).

Frank Baumann and Sherm Lollar Become the Third Pitcher-Catcher Duo to Hit Back-to-Back Home Runs (Fifth Inning)

New York at Chicago, July 13, 1961

New York	AB	R	H	RBI
Richardson, 2b	5	2	2	0
Kubek, ss	4	1	1	1
Maris, rf	5	1	3	2
Mantle, cf	5	1	3	2
Berra, lf	4	1	0	0
Howard, c	4	0	1	0
Cerv, 1b	3	0	0	0
Torgeson, 1b	0	0	0	0
Boyer, 3b	4	0	2	1
Stafford, p	3	0	1	0
Arroyo, p	1	0	0	0
	38	6	13	6

Chicago	AB	R	H	RBI
Aparicio, ss	4	0	1	0
Fox, 2b	3	0	0	0
Landis, cf	4	0	1	0
Minoso, lf	3	0	0	0
Smith, rf	4	0	2	0
Martin, 1b	3	0	0	0
Carey, 3b	3	0	0	0
Lollar, c	4	1	1	1
Baumann, p	2	1	1	1
Wynn, p	0	0	0	0
Robinson, ph	0	0	0	0
Hacker, p	0	0	0	0
Sievers, ph	1	0	0	0
	31	2	6	2

New York	4	0	0	0	0	0	0	0	2—6
Chicago	0	0	0	0	2	0	0	0	0—2

2B—Maris, Richardson, Kubek. 3B—Boyer, Smith. HR—Maris, Mantle, Lollar, Baumann. Sac—Kubek. DP—Kubek-Cerv-Kubek; Fox-Aparicio-Martin; Torgeson (unassisted). LOB—Chicago 7, New York 8. HBP—Martin (by Arroyo). Umpires—Schwartz, Napp, Stevens, and Rice. Time—2:28. Attendance—43,960.

New York	IP	H	R	ER	BB	K
Stafford	6	5	2	2	3	2
Arroyo	3	1	0	0	1	1

Chicago	IP	H	R	ER	BB	K
Wynn	⅔	4	4	4	2	0
Baumann	6⅓	6	2	2	2	1
Hacker	2	3	0	2	0	1

Winning pitcher—Stafford (8–4). Losing pitcher—Wynn (7–2).

Black Wednesday in Kansas City: Sox Lose Doubleheader to Drop Out of a Four-Team Pennant Race. Go-Go Era Closed Out after 17 Consecutive First-Division Finishes

Chicago at Kansas City, September 27, 1967

Game 1

Chicago	AB	R	H	RBI
Agee, cf	4	1	1	0
Buford, 2b	4	0	0	0
McCraw, 1b	3	1	0	0
Boyer, 3b	3	0	0	0
Ward, lf	1	0	0	0
Berry, lf	1	0	0	0
Burgess, ph	0	0	0	0
Bradford, ph	0	0	0	0
Colavito, rf	4	0	1	1
Alomar, pr	0	0	0	0
Martin, c	2	0	0	0
Wilhelm, p	0	0	0	0
Nelson, p	0	0	0	0
Hansen, ss	4	0	0	0
Peters, p	1	0	1	0
Wood, p	0	0	0	0
McMahon, p	0	0	0	0
Josephson, ph	1	0	0	0
	31	2	4	2

Kansas City	AB	R	H	RBI
Kubiak, ss	5	0	0	0
Donaldson, 2b	4	0	0	0
Rudi, 1b	4	1	1	0
Hershberger, rf	4	2	1	0
Monday, cf	2	2	1	1
Bando, 3b	3	0	2	1
Gosger, lf	4	0	3	3
Duncan, c	3	0	0	0
Dobson, p	3	0	1	0
Krausse, p	0	0	0	0
Lindblad, p	0	0	0	0
	32	5	9	5

Chicago	0	0	0	0	0	0	0	0	2—2
Kansas City	0	1	0	0	0	2	0	2	x—5

2B—Hershberger, Rudi. 3B—Agee. SB—Hershberger. DP—Buford-McGraw-Hansen. LOB—White Sox 6, Kansas City 8. Wild pitch—McMahon, Dobson, Krausse. Passed ball—Martin. Umpires—Umont, Valentine, Kinamon, and Napp. Time—2:51.

Chicago	IP	H	R	ER	BB	K
Peters	5⅔	4	3	3	1	10
McMahon	0	0	0	0	1	0
Wood	1⅓	2	0	0	0	1
Wilhelm	⅓	3	2	2	1	0
Nelson	⅔	0	0	0	1	0

Kansas City	IP	H	R	ER	BB	K
Dobson	8⅓	3	2	2	2	5
Krausse	0	1	0	0	2	0
Lindblad	⅔	0	0	0	0	0

Winning pitcher-Dobson (10–10). Losing pitcher—Peters (16–10).

Game 2

Chicago	AB	R	H	RBI
Berry, rf	3	0	0	0
Buford, 2b	3	0	1	0
Agee, cf	4	0	0	0
Boyer, 3b	4	0	0	0
McCraw, 1b	4	0	1	0
Colavito, lf	3	0	0	0
Hansen, ss	3	0	1	0
Josephson, c	2	0	0	0
Martin, c	1	0	0	0
Horlen, p	2	0	0	0
Wood, p	0	0	0	0
Locker, p	0	0	0	0
McMahon, p	0	0	0	0
Causey, ph	1	0	0	0
	30	0	3	0

Kansas City	AB	R	H	RBI
Kubiak, ss	4	1	1	0
Donaldson, 2b	4	1	1	1
Hershberger, rf	4	0	0	0
Webster, 1b	4	0	2	2
Monday, cf	4	1	1	0
Gosger, lf	4	0	2	0
Bando, 3b	3	0	0	0
Roof, c	3	0	0	0
Hunter, p	3	1	2	0
	33	4	9	3

Chicago	0	0	0	0	0	0	0	0	0—0
Kansas City	0	0	0	0	0	4	0	0	x—4

2B—Webster, McCraw. LOB—Chicago 5, Kansas City 6. Passed ball—Martin. Umpires—Valentine, Kinnamon, Napp, and Umont. Time—2:17. Attendance—5,325.

Chicago	IP	H	R	ER	BB	K
Horlen	5⅓	6	3	3	0	1
Wood	⅓	1	1	0	0	0
Locker	1⅓	0	0	0	1	0
McMahon	1	2	0	0	0	2

Kansas City	IP	H	R	ER	BB	K
Hunter	9	3	0	0	2	1

Winning pitcher—Hunter (13–16). Losing pitcher—Horlen (19–7).

Pitcher Gary Peters Bats Sixth in the Lineup to Generate Offense

Chicago at New York, May 26, 1968

Chicago	AB	R	H	RBI
Berry, cf	4	0	2	1
Voss, rf	4	0	0	0
Ward, 3b	2	0	0	0
McCraw, 1b	4	0	1	0
Davis, lf	4	0	1	0
Peters, p	2	0	0	0
Fisher, p	0	0	0	0
Snyder, ph	1	0	0	0
Priddy, p	0	0	0	0
Causey, ph	1	0	0	0
Josephson, c	2	0	0	0
Alomar, pr	0	1	0	0
Booker, c	0	0	0	0
Aparicio, ss	2	0	0	0
Cullen, 2b	3	0	0	0
	29	1	4	1

New York	AB	H	H	RBI
Clarke, 2b	4	2	2	0
White, lf	2	0	0	0
Tresh, ss	4	1	1	2
Kosco, rf	4	0	1	1
Pepitone, 1b	4	0	1	0
Cox, 3b	2	1	1	1
Robinson, rf	2	0	1	0
Rodriguez, c	3	0	0	0
Stottlemyre, p	3	1	1	0
	31	5	8	4

Chicago	0	0	0	0	0	0	0	1	0—1
New York	2	1	0	0	2	0	0	0	x—5

2B—Robinson. HR—Tresh, Cox. DP—Chicago 1. E—Voss. LOB—Chicago 5, New York 4. HBP—Ward (by Stottlemyre), Cox (by Fisher), White (by Priddy). Time—2:05. Attendance—23,966.

Chicago	IP	H	R	ER	BB	K
Peters	3⅔	5	3	3	0	1
Fisher	2⅓	3	2	2	0	0
Priddy	2	0	0	0	0	1

New York	IP	H	R	ER	BB	K
Stottlemyre	9	4	1	1	3	4

Winning pitcher—Stottlemyre (6–3). Losing pitcher—Peters (2–5).

Sox Score 11 Runs in the Ninth Inning

Chicago at Boston, August 19, 1970

Chicago	AB	R	H	RBI
O'Brien, 3b	5	0	0	0
May, lf	4	1	0	0
Melton, rf	5	3	3	1
Herrman, c	5	3	2	2
Blanco, 1b	4	1	1	2
Berry, cf	5	1	4	2
Knoop, 2b	4	2	1	1
Morales, ss	3	0	0	0
Hopkins, ph	0	0	0	0
Aparicio, ph-ss	2	1	2	3
John, p	2	0	0	0
Wood, p	2	1	1	2
	42	13	14	13

Boston	AB	R	H	RBI
Andrews, 2b	5	1	2	1
Smith, cf	4	1	2	1
B. Conigliaro, lf	4	1	2	0
T. Conigliaro, rf	3	1	1	2
Thomas, lf	1	0	1	0
Petrocelli, ss	4	0	1	1
Scott, 3b	4	0	1	0
Pavletich, 1b	2	1	1	0
Yastrzemski, ph	1	0	0	0
Moses, c	3	0	0	0
Culp, p	4	0	0	0
Wagner, p	0	0	0	0
Lyle, p	0	0	0	0
Hartenstein, p	0	0	0	0
Phillips, p	0	0	0	0
	36	5	11	5

Chicago	1	0	0	0	0	0	1	0	1 1—13
Boston	1	0	0	0	2	2	0	0	0 0— 5

2B—T. Conigliaro, Andrews, Herrmann, Aparicio. HR—Melton. E—Scott, B. Conigliaro. SB—Smith. SF—Blanco, T. Conigliaro. DP—Morales-Knoop-Blanco (Pavletich). LOB—Chicago 4, Boston 9. HBP—B. Conigliaro (by John). Wild pitch—John. Umpires—Flaherty, Anthony, Stewart, and Luciano. Time—2:31. Attendance—17,113.

Chicago	IP	H	R	ER	BB	K
John	7	9	5	5	3	3
Wood	2	2	0	0	0	1

Boston	IP	H	R	ER	BB	K
Culp	8	7	6	6	1	8
Wagner	0	0	1	0	0	0
Lyle	0	2	2	2	0	0
Hartenstein	⅓	2	3	3	1	1
Phillips	⅔	3	1	1	0	0

Winning pitcher—Wood. Losing pitcher—Culp.

Dick Allen Hits Two Inside-the-Park Home Runs

Chicago at Minnesota, July 31, 1972

Chicago	AB	R	H	RBI
Kelly, rf	3	2	1	0
Bradford, cf	1	0	0	0
Alvarado, ss	5	2	2	1
Allen, 1b	4	2	2	5
Muser, 1b	1	1	0	0
Johnstone, rf	4	0	0	0
Spiezio, 3b	4	0	0	0
Herrmann, c	3	1	2	1
Morales, ss	0	0	0	0
Andrews, 2b	4	0	0	0
Bahnsen, p	3	0	0	0
	36	8	9	8

Minnesota	AB	R	H	RBI
Tovar, rf	4	0	0	0
Thompson, ss	4	0	1	0
Braun, 2b	4	0	0	0
Killebrew, lb	4	0	1	0
Reese, lf	4	0	1	0
Darwin, cf	4	1	1	0
Soderholm, 3b	3	0	0	0
Blyleven, p	1	0	0	0
Strickland, p	0	0	0	0
Nettles, ph	1	0	1	1
Gehard, p	0	0	0	0
Brye, ph	1	0	0	0
Goltz, p	0	0	0	0
	33	1	6	1

Chicago	3	0	0	0	3	1	1	0	0—8
Minnesota	0	0	0	0	1	0	0	0	0—1

2B—Kelly, May. HR—Allen 2, Herrmann. SB—May. Sac—Bahnsen. E—Alvarado, Thompson, Darwin. LOB—Chicago 5, Minnesota 5. Time—2:17. Attendance—13,652.

Chicago	IP	H	R	ER	BB	K
Bahnsen	9	6	1	0	0	6

Minnesota	IP	H	R	ER	BB	K
Blyleven	4⅓	5	6	6	3	3
Strickland	⅔	1	0	0	0	0
Gebhard	3	3	2	1	0	1
Goltz	1	0	0	0	0	0

Winning pitcher—Bahnsen (13–11). Losing pitcher—Blyleven (9–14).

South Side Hitmen Clout Six Homers in a Game

Seattle at Chicago, August 9, 1977

Seattle	AB	R	H	RBI
Collins, lf	5	1	2	0
Baez, 2b	5	0	1	0
Meyer, 1b	4	1	2	2
Stanton, dh	4	0	0	0
R. Jones, cf	4	0	1	0
Stein, 3b	4	4	4	0
Lopez, rf	4	0	1	0
Stinson, c	2	0	1	1
Reynolds, ss	4	0	2	0
	36	3	11	3

Chicago	AB	R	H	RBI
Bannister, ss	4	0	0	0
Orta, 2b	4	1	0	0
Zisk, rf	3	1	0	0
Nordhagen, rf	2	0	1	0
Gamble, dh	2	3	2	3
Downing, dh	2	0	0	0
Lemon, cf	4	3	3	3
Stillman, lf	4	1	2	2
Soderholm, 3b	4	2	2	4
Essian, c	4	1	1	1
	37	13	12	13

Seattle	2	0	0	0	0	1	0	0	0— 3
Chicago	5	0	4	0	2	0	2	0	x—13

E—Stein. DP—Chicago (1). LOB—Seattle 8, Chicago 4. 2B—Collins, Lemon. 3B—Meyer. HR—Meyer, Lemon, Gamble, Soderholm (2), Essian, Stillman. Wild pitch—Stone. HBP—Gamble (by Laxton). Time—2:44. Attendance—12,294.

Seattle	IP	H	R	ER	BB	K
Wheelock	⅓	2	5	4	2	0
Montague	2⅔	5	4	4	0	0
Laxton	3	1	2	2	1	1
Segui	1	2	2	2	0	1
Kekich	1	2	0	0	0	1

Chicago	IP	H	R	ER	BB	K
Stone	7	11	3	3	1	2
LaGrow	2	0	0	0	1	2

Winning pitcher—Stone (12–7). Losing pitcher-Wheelock (6–8).

Jack Brohamer Hits for the Cycle—Second Sox Player to Do So

Chicago at Seattle, September 24, 1977

Chicago	AB	R	H	RBI
Garr, lf	4	1	3	0
T. Cruz, lf	1	0	0	0
Lemon, cf	4	1	1	0
Stillman, dh	4	0	0	0
Gamble, rf	5	2	2	1
H. Cruz, rf	0	0	0	0
Soderholm, 3b	5	0	0	0
Spencer, 1b	4	2	2	0
Brohamer, 2b	5	2	5	4
Kessinger, ss	3	0	0	0
Nahorodny, c	4	0	1	2
	39	8	14	7

Seattle	AB	R	H	RBI
Collins, lf	3	0	1	2
Cruz, 2b	4	0	1	0
Braun, ph	1	0	0	0
Fosse, c	4	0	0	0
Stanton, lf	5	0	1	0
Jones, cf	4	0	1	0
Stein, 3b	3	0	1	0
Meyer, 1b	4	1	1	0
Bernhardt, dh	4	1	2	0
Reynolds, ss	4	1	2	1
	36	3	10	3

Chicago	5	0	0	0	1	1	0	0	1—8
Seattle	0	1	0	0	0	0	0	0	2—3

2B—Lemon, Gamble, Brohamer (2), Garr, Cruz, Collins. 3B—Brohamer, Reynolds. HR—Brohamer. SF—Nahorodny. E—Jones. LOB—Chicago 11, Seattle 11. DP—Chicago 1, Seattle 1. Wild pitch—Segui. HBP—Collins (by Kravec). Time—2:45. Attendance—17,636.

Chicago	IP	H	R	ER	BB	K
Kravec	8	10	3	3	3	3
Verhoeven	1	0	0	0	1	0

Seattle	IP	H	R	ER	BB	K
Segui	⅓	3	3	3	0	1
Erardi	4	5	3	3	4	1
Galasso	4⅔	6	2	2	2	1

Winning pitcher—Kravec (10–8). Losing pitcher—Segui (0–7).

Carlton Fisk Hits for the Cycle

Kansas City at Chicago, May 16, 1984

Kansas City	AB	R	H	RBI
Wilson, cf	3	1	1	0
Motley, rf	5	0	1	0
White, 2b	3	0	0	0
McRae, dh	5	1	2	0
Balboni, 1b	5	1	0	0
Roberts, lf	4	1	2	2
Jones, rf	0	0	0	0
Wathan, c	3	2	1	0
Pryor, 3b	4	1	2	2
Washington, ss	3	0	1	2
	35	7	10	6

Chicago	AB	R	H	RBI
Dybzinski, ss	4	0	0	0
Hairston, ph	1	0	0	0
Fisk, c	5	2	4	2
Paciorek, 1b	3	0	0	0
Luzinski, dh	4	0	0	0
Kittle, lf	4	1	2	1
Baines, rf	4	0	0	0
Stegman, cf	2	2	2	3
R. Law, cf	2	0	1	0
V. Law, 3b	3	1	1	0
Walker, ph	1	0	0	0
Fletcher, ss	0	0	0	0
Cruz, 2b	4	0	1	0
	37	6	11	6

Kansas City	1	0	0	3	0	2	1	0	0—7
Chicago	1	2	2	1	0	0	0	0	0—6

2B—Fisk, Roberts, Pryor (2). 3B—Roberts, Fisk. HR—Stegman (2), Fisk. SB—Wilson, R. Law. E—Cruz, Kittle. SF—Washington. LOB—Kansas City 7, Chicago 5. DP—Kansas City 1, Chicago 1. Time—3:08. Attendance—21,669.

Kansas City	IP	H	R	ER	BB	K
Gura	3	7	5	5	1	1
Beckwith	3	2	1	1	0	4
Quisenberry	3	2	0	0	0	2

Chicago	IP	H	R	ER	BB	K
Bannister	5⅓	6	6	4	4	6
Barojas	2⅔	4	1	1	1	1
Reed	1	0	0	0	0	3

Winning pitcher—Beckwith. Losing pitcher—Barojas. Save—Quisenberry. Wild pitch—Bannister.

Joe Cowley Strikes Out the First Seven Batters in the Game, but Loses

Chicago at Texas, May 28, 1986

Chicago	AB	R	H	RBI
Tolleson, 3b	3	2	1	0
Bradley, dh	4	1	2	0
Baines, rf	4	0	1	1
Walker, 1b	4	0	0	0
Fisk, c	3	0	0	0
Bonilla, cf	4	0	1	0
Kittle, lf	4	0	0	0
Hulett, 2b	4	0	1	0
Guillen, ss	3	0	1	0
Nichols, ph	1	0	0	0
	34	3	7	1

Texas	AB	R	H	RBI
McDowell, cf	4	0	0	0
Fletcher, ss	3	1	1	0
O'Brien, 1b	4	1	1	2
Incaviglia, dh	4	1	2	1
Ward, lf	4	1	2	1
Wright, rf	4	0	0	0
Buechele, 3b	4	1	2	1
Mercado, c	4	0	1	0
Wilkerson, 2b	3	1	2	0
	34	6	11	5

E—Wilkerson (2), Fisk, Cowley. 2B—Incaviglia, O'Brien. 3B—Hulett. HR—Buechele. SB—Fisk, Bonilla, Wilkerson. LOB—Chicago 7, Texas 5. Wild pitch—Cowley. Passed ball—Mercado, Fisk. Umpires—Kosc, Reed, Ford, and Garcia. Time—3:02. Attendance—25,028.

Chicago	0	0	1	0	2	0	0	0	0—3
Texas	0	0	0	2	4	0	0	0	x—6

Chicago	IP	H	R	ER	BB	K
Cowley	4⅔	6	6	5	1	8
Nelson	1⅔	3	0	0	0	1
McKeon	⅓	0	0	0	0	0
Dawley	1⅓	2	0	0	0	0

Texas	IP	H	R	ER	BB	K
Correa	6⅔	6	3	1	3	8
Williams	2⅓	1	0	0	0	0

Winning pitcher—Correa (3–3). Losing pitcher—Cowley (1–2).

Frank Thomas' Major League Debut: Three No. 1 Draft Picks Play Together for the First Time (Thomas, Ventura, Fernandez)

Chicago at Milwaukee, August 2, 1990

Chicago	AB	R	H	RBI
Bradley, lf	4	0	1	0
Ventura, 3b	4	1	1	0
Calderon, dh	4	2	2	2
Fisk, c	4	1	2	1
Thomas, 1b	4	0	0	1
Lyons, 2b	0	0	0	0
Sosa, rf	4	0	0	0
Johnson, cf	3	0	1	0
Grebeck, 2b	3	0	0	0
Pasqua, ph	0	0	0	0
Martinez, 1b	1	0	0	0
Guillen, ss	3	0	0	0
	34	4	7	4

Milwaukee	AB	R	H	RBI
Gantner, 2b	4	0	0	0
Yount, cf	1	2	1	0
Sheffield, 3b	3	1	1	2
Parker, dh	3	0	0	1
Vaughn, lf	4	0	0	0
Brock, 1b	4	0	1	0
Deer, rf	4	0	1	0
Surhoff, c	2	0	0	0
Felder, pr	0	0	0	0
Spiers, ss	3	0	1	0
Molitor, ph	1	0	0	0
	29	3	5	3

Chicago	0	0	0	3	0	0	0	0	1—4
Milwaukee	0	0	0	0	2	0	0	1	0—3

LOB—Chicago 4, Milwaukee 6. HR—Calderon (9), Fisk (11), Sheffield (8). SB—Yount. Sac—Sheffield. SF—Parker. HBP—Yount (by Fernandez). Wild pitch—Veres. Umpires—McClelland, Denkinger, Shulock, and Merrill. Time—3:09. Attendance—25,022.

Chicago	IP	H	R	ER	BB	K
Fernandez	7	5	2	2	2	4
Jones	1	0	1	1	1	0
Thigpen	1	0	0	0	1	2

Milwaukee	IP	H	R	ER	BB	K
Higuera	8	6	3	3	0	5
Veres	⅔	1	1	1	1	0
Plesac	⅓	0	0	0	0	0

Winning pitcher—Jones (11–1). Losing pitcher—Veres (0–3). Save—Thigpen.

Two Grand Slams in a Game; Darren Lewis and Robin Ventura Bomb Tigers

Chicago at Detroit, May 19, 1996

Chicago	AB	R	H	RBI
Phillips, lf	6	3	3	2
Martinez, cf	3	1	2	0
Lewis, cf	3	1	1	4
Thomas, 1b	4	1	1	1
Baines, dh	4	1	2	1
Ventura, 3b	5	2	2	4
Munoz, 3b	0	0	0	0
Tartabull, rf	4	1	1	0
Karkovice, c	4	1	0	0
Durham, 2b	5	1	3	0
Guillen, ss	5	2	2	2
	43	14	17	14

Detroit	AB	R	H	RBI
Curtis, lf	3	1	0	0
Trammel, ss	4	1	3	0
Fryman, 3b	3	1	0	0
Nieves, rf	1	0	0	0
Bautista, ph-rf	2	0	0	0
Williams, dh	2	0	0	0
Pride, ph-dh	2	0	1	1
Lewis, 2b	4	0	1	0
Flaherty, c	4	0	0	0
Bartee, cf	3	0	1	0
Singleton, ph	1	0	0	0
Fielder, 1b	3	0	1	1
	32	3	7	2

Chicago	0	0	5	0	0	3	0	0	6—14
Detroit	1	0	0	0	0	2	0	0	0— 3

2B—Baines, Durham, Fielder. 3B—Phillips. HR—D. Lewis, Ventura. SB—Martinez. SF—Thomas. DP—Detroit 1, Chicago 2. E—Bartee. LOB—Chicago 7, Detroit 7. Wild pitch—Keyser. Umpires—McClelland, Tachida, Hickox, and Shulock. Time—3:09. Attendance—9,709.

Chicago	IP	H	R	ER	BB	K
Alvarez	5⅓	4	3	3	4	4
Karchner	1⅔	1	0	0	0	1
Keyser	2	2	0	0	1	1

Detroit	IP	H	R	ER	BB	K
Gohr	4	7	5	5	2	2
Lima	4	6	3	3	0	1
Olson	⅔	4	6	6	2	1
Myers	⅓	0	0	0	0	0

Winning pitcher—Alvarez (4–3). Losing pitcher—Gohr (2–6).

Four Home Runs in an Inning—First Time in Sox History: Frank Thomas, Harold Baines, Robin Ventura, and Chad Kreuter Connect in the Ninth

Milwaukee at Chicago, May 26, 1996

Milwaukee	AB	R	H	RBI
Vina, 2b	4	1	1	0
Seitzer, dh	4	0	1	1
Valentin, ss	3	0	0	0
Vaughn, lf	4	0	0	0
Nilsson, 1b	4	0	2	0
Mieske, rf	4	0	0	0
Cirillo, 3b	3	0	1	0
Hulse, cf	3	0	0	0
Matheny, c	4	0	2	0
	33	1	7	1

Chicago	AB	R	H	RBI
Phillips, lf	6	3	3	0
Lewis, cf	5	3	2	1
Thomas, 1b	4	2	2	3
Snopek, 3b	0	0	0	0
Baines, dh	3	1	2	2
Ventura, 3b-1b	5	2	3	3
Mouton, rf	4	1	2	0
Kreuter, c	4	1	1	2
Durham, 2b	4	0	0	1
Guillen, ss	5	0	1	0
	40	12	17	12

Milwaukee	1	0	0	0	0	0	0	0	0— 1
Chicago	1	0	1	0	3	0	0	7	x—12

2B—Seitzer, Phillips, Ventura, Mouton. HR—Thomas, Baines, Ventura, Kreuter. SB—Lewis. Sac—Valentin. SF—Baines. LOB—Milwaukee 8, Chicago 10. Balk—Potts. Umpires—Young, Coble, and Reed. Time—3:03. Attendance—21,151.

Milwaukee	IP	H	R	ER	BB	K
McDonald	5⅔	8	5	5	5	6
Potts	1⅔	7	6	6	0	1
Garcia	⅔	2	1	1	0	1

Chicago	IP	H	R	ER	BB	K
Tapani	9	7	1	1	2	7

Winning pitcher—Tapani (5–3). Losing pitcher—McDonald (4–2).

Frank Thomas Hits Three Home Runs in One Game and Breaks Carlton Fisk's All-Time Career Record

Chicago at Boston, September 15, 1996

Chicago	AB	R	H	RBI
Phillips, lf	5	1	1	0
DaMartinez, cf-rf	4	0	0	0
F. Thomas, 1b	4	4	3	3
Ventura, 3b	4	1	1	1
Tartabull, rf	3	1	1	1
1-D. Lewis, pr-cf	1	1	1	0
Baines, dh	5	0	1	1
Durham, 2b	4	0	0	0
Borders, c	4	0	1	0
Norton, ss	2	0	0	0
	36	8	9	6

Boston	AB	R	H	RBI
Bragg, cf	4	1	1	0
Frye, 2b	5	0	0	0
Jefferson, dh	4	2	1	0
M. Vaughn, 1b	5	3	3	5
Greenwell, lf	4	0	1	0
2-Tinsley, pr	0	1	0	0
Jn. Valentin, 3b	4	2	3	3
O'Leary, rf	4	0	1	1
N. Garciaparra, ss	4	0	0	0
Haselman, c	3	0	1	0
	37	9	11	9

Chicago	1	0	2	0	2	0	3	0	0—8
Boston	3	0	0	1	2	0	2	0	1—9

Two outs when winning run scored. 1-ran for Tartabull in the 7th. 2-ran for Greenwell in the 9th.

E—Jn Valentin (17), Lacy (1). LOB—Chicago 7, Boston 8. 2B—Phillips (27), Baines (27), Bragg (21). HR—M. Vaughn 2 (41) off Tapani 2; Jn Valentin 2 (13) off Tapani, Simas; F. Thomas 3 (35) off Wakefield 3; Ventura (33) off Wakefield; Tartabull (25) off Wakefield.

Chicago	IP	H	R	ER	BB	K
Tapani	4⅔	6	6	6	5	2
Darwin	1⅔	1	1	1	0	1
Bertotti	⅓	0	0	0	0	0
Simas	⅓	1	1	1	0	0
Levine	⅓	0	0	0	1	0
R. Hernandez (L)	1⅓	3	1	1	0	2

Boston	IP	H	R	ER	BB	K
Wakefield	6	6	5	5	2	6
Eshelman	⅔	1	2	2	1	0
Lacy	⅓	1	1	1	1	0
Mahomes	⅔	0	0	0	1	0
Slocumb (W)	1⅓	1	0	0	1	2

Winning pitcher—Slocum (4–5). Losing pitcher—R. Hernandez (6–4). Passed ball—Borders. Time—2:59. Attendance—32,452.

White Sox Clinch the American League Central Division Title in Minnesota Despite Losing 6–5 in 10 Innings

Chicago at Minnesota, September 24, 2000

Chicago	AB	R	H	RBI
Valentin, ss	5	0	0	0
Graffanino, 2b	5	0	1	0
Thomas, dh	5	0	2	0
Ordonez, rf	5	0	1	0
Lee, lf	4	1	1	0
Konerko, 1b	4	1	1	0
Perry, 3b	2	0	2	0
Norton, pr-3b	1	2	1	1
Wilson, ph-3b	1	0	0	0
Singleton, cf	2	1	1	0
Abbott, ph	1	0	0	0
Christensen, cf	0	0	0	0
C. Johnson, c	4	0	0	3
	39	5	12	4

Minnesota	AB	R	H	RBI
Jones, lf	3	0	0	0
Hunter, ph-lf	2	1	1	0
Hocking, ss-1b	5	0	2	1
Lawton, rf	5	2	3	1
Coomer, 1b	3	0	0	0
Rivas, ss	1	0	0	0
Ortiz, dh	3	0	0	0
Koskie, 3b	4	1	1	1
Canizaro, 2b	4	1	1	0
Pierzynski, c	4	1	2	3
Barnes, cf	3	0	0	0
	37	6	10	6

Chicago	0	0	0	0	1	0	4	0	0	0—3
Minnesota	0	0	0	0	0	0	4	0	0	1—5

Sac.—Singleton. Left on Base—Chicago 5, Minnesota 4. 2B—Johnson, Lawton, Canizaro. 3B—Hunter. HR—Pierzynski (2), Lawton (13). Double Plays—Minnesota, 2. Hit by Pitch—Barnes by Lowe. Wild Pitch—Lowe. Passed Ball—Pierzynski. Time—3:06 Umpires—Roe, Runge, Shulock, Lamplugh. Attendance—9,716.

Chicago	IP	R	H	K	BB
Lowe	6	0	1	4	1
Buehrle	⅔	2	2	0	0
Barcelo	⅓	2	2	0	0
Wunsch	0	1	2	0	0
Howry	2	0	1	1	0
Beirne	⅔	1	1	0	0

Minnesota	IP	R	H	K	BB
Mays	6	5	10	2	0
B. Wells	2	0	1	0	0
Guardado	2	0	1	3	0

Winning Pitcher – Guardado (6-3). Losing Pitcher – Beirne (1-2).

2005 World Series MVP Jermaine Dye

9

White Sox Yarns

At a time in our lives when baseball was at the center of our universe, we appreciated the rich folklore of the game and offbeat tales of the diamond from long ago. Though we were too young to have seen Babe Ruth, Lou Gehrig, or of course Shoeless Joe Jackson, we knew who these great players were because the chroniclers of the game kept their memories alive in print and through the emerging medium of television.

Like a curator of fine old heirlooms tucked away in the dim recesses of the hall closet or the attic trunk, broadcaster Jack Brickhouse shared with his audience many colorful stories of baseball's past and the game's inner workings on his *Tenth Inning* interview program aired over WGN following White Sox and Cub games. *The Tenth Inning* was a delight because Brickhouse introduced to his younger listeners the biggest names in baseball, be it Leo Durocher, Ray Schalk, or Red Faber. Sponsored locally by the Danley Lumber Company or Household Finance, *The Tenth Inning* was a real treat, and it kindled our earliest interest in baseball's bygone eras.

Along these same lines, the ballclub published a quarterly team newsletter for many years, which they called *White Sox Yarns*. The logo on the masthead featured a winged stocking foot, and the newsletter itself was crammed with interesting little tidbits about the farm system, upcoming home stands, promotions, feature stories about the players' lives on and off the field, and historical treasures supplied by statistician and publicist extraordinaire Don Unferth.

In the spirit of those earlier times, we present our own collection of White Sox yarns that we have pulled down from the top shelf of that same hall closet and dusted off one more time. Enjoy.

The White Sox Help Put an End to Racial Segregation in the Spring Training Camps

If you were a professional baseball player and African American in the1950s, segregated living facilities in the Florida spring training camps were a painful reminder of lingering racial injustice in the U.S. The Sox provided accommodations for their white players at the Sarasota Terrace hotel, their spring training headquarters, while their black teammates were forced to live in a segregated facility a mile away from Payne Park. The African American players ate their meals family-style and were given no choice of food selection. In the Jim Crow South at the dawn of the Civil Rights Era, that's the way things were despite strong objections coming from White Sox owner Bill Veeck and Dan Topping of the Yankees, who urged full and equal rights at all of the Florida camps. At that time only the Dodgers operated a fully integrated facility in Vero Beach—but only after they had acquired title to the property in 1948.

On January 23, 1961, in a story published in the *Chicago American*, sportswriter Wendell Smith drew attention to the second-class treatment endured by black players, thus sending an important wake-up call not only to the White Sox, but to all 14 teams training in Florida facilities. Smith's demand for immediate action prompted White Sox owner Arthur C. Allyn to purchase the 10-story Sarasota Terrace Hotel for the sum of $500,000 on November 10, 1961. By the time the team reported for spring training in 1962, all Sox players were living under one roof and enjoying the swimming pool, a cabana, Mrs. O'Leary's Restaurant owned by a transplanted Chicagoan, and a recreation area—amenities previously unavailable to African American players at the other place. "We are very happy," commented outfielder and ex-Marine Floyd Robinson, one of four black players on the roster. "It is a lot better than last year. In the first place, we now feel that we truly belong. Secondly, we can eat in the hotel restaurant and get a decent meal. Moreover, we can do so without other occupants regarding us as some kind of curiosities."

Smith's article had far-reaching implications. By 1962 only Detroit, Pittsburgh, Minnesota, Washington, and Kansas City maintained segregated facilities, but all of that was about to change. The Allyns later added a second motel in back of the property, but by the early 1970s, John Allyn decided it was too much of a financial drain on the resources of the ballclub. He sold the white-brick, pink-roofed old hotel to the county. The county then closed the landmark hostelry and put it up for sale.

The familiar winged stocking-foot logo adorned White Sox publications and promotional materials through the 1950s and '60s.

You Can't Steal First...Or Can You?

For sheer daffiness, Herman "Germany" Schaefer of the Washington Senators led the procession way back in 1911. Schaefer was a speedy first baseman and a fair hitter.

After his 17-year career ended, Schaefer teamed up with former Sox pitcher Nick Altrock, and together these two baseball clowns toured the American vaudeville circuit performing their comic routines.

According to a popular legend that has made the rounds over the years, Germany Schaefer once stole first base against the White Sox. Fact and fiction often blend together in the retelling of baseball's myths and legends. This one, however, happens to be true.

The unusual bit of history occurred in Washington on August 4, 1911, during one of the typical late-summer heat waves that always seemed to drain the energy out of visiting American League teams.

The Sox were well out of the race at this point. They trailed the Philadelphia A's by a dozen games and were content to play out the string. Manager Hugh Duffy selected his veteran lefty Doc White to open Game 1 of a doubleheader against the great Walter Johnson, who was completing his fourth major league season.

The two teams were knotted up in a scoreless tie going into the bottom of the ninth inning when the comedy began. Clyde Milan opened the home half of the inning with a double. Germany Schaefer laid down a sacrifice bunt. A play was made at third, but Milan beat the throw, putting runners on first and third. Kid Elberfeld, the Washington second baseman, popped up. Schaefer then broke for second and was safe without drawing a throw. Doc Gessler, one of only 25 players to hit into a triple play against the White Sox, struck out. There were two outs and runners on second and third.

Germany Schaefer took a wide lead off the bag...but in the wrong direction. The big Dutchman was leaning toward *first.* Doc White peered in at his catcher, Freddie Payne, completely ignoring Schaefer, who startled everyone in the park when he ran full-steam to first base.

Sox manager Hugh Duffy bolted out of the dugout to protest Schaefer's peculiar baserunning to the umpire, whose name was Parker. Duffy was livid. He jumped up and down, and directed a steady stream of profanities at Parker. With the argument raging, Schaefer decided it was a good time to steal second again. Catcher Freddy Payne fired a strike down to second baseman Ambrose McConnell, who had Schaefer hung up between first and second. Clyde Milan suddenly broke for the plate, but was a dead duck after first baseman "Shano" Collins fired a bullet back to Payne, who nailed the runner in a close play.

A swarm of angry Washington Senators surrounded umpire Tom Connolly. They claimed that the play was voided because Hugh Duffy was the 10th man on the field when the odd-ball play transpired. The immortal Connolly rubbed his chin and thought about it for a moment. Finally, he ruled that since the Senators started the play, the outcome of their actions would stand.

Maybe it wasn't the best call in the world, but then, no one had ever tried to steal first base before. The Sox' reprieve was only momentary. They lost the game 1–0 in the 11th inning after Clyde Milan raced across the plate on a failed double-play attempt.

Sixty-Seven Pitches—Game Over

Jim Scott pitched the shortest game in White Sox history—a 68-minute, 5–0 whitewashing of the Philadelphia A's on August 29, 1915. On May 12 of that same season Red Faber dusted off the Washington Senators in the nation's capital, throwing only 67 pitches. The old redhead was magnificent that long-ago afternoon. He limited the Senators to only three scratchy hits in a 4–1 victory.

The scoreboard operator who recorded the balls and strikes at National Park was keeping track of Faber's record-setting pace. After the game ended, he telegraphed the *Chicago Tribune* sports desk to advise them that Faber had just set a new major league record by throwing 67 pitches—50 strikes and 17 balls.

According to his rather detailed recordkeeping, Faber eclipsed a record originally set by Christy Mathewson several years earlier. Red required five less pitches than the great Mathewson to put down the Senators, and in the third and fifth innings, Red retired the six men he faced on only six pitches.

The Hunchback of Comiskey Park

Eddie Bennett, a 15-year-old hunchback, was the greatest good-luck charm in the history of baseball. Crippled at birth, Eddie resided in the Flatbush section of Brooklyn. Despite his debilitating condition, Eddie loved baseball and was one of the hangers-on at the Polo Grounds waiting to catch a glimpse of the ballplayers or an autograph long after the game had ended.

Bennett was spotted one afternoon by Happy Felsch prior to a Sox-Yankees game at the Polo Grounds, just as the players filed into their dressing rooms. Hap was superstitious by nature, and you know what they say about hunchbacks. The Sox outfielder rubbed his back once for good luck, then proceeded to tear the cover off the ball against the Yankees. The next day Felsch invited Eddie into the White Sox clubhouse, where the same procedure was repeated. This time Felsch's White Sox teammates also rubbed his back for good luck, and once again the ballclub prevailed over the Yankees.

After that, Eddie was hired as the new batboy and mascot. The Sox won pennants in 1917 and 1919—with a large share of the credit going to Bennett, the Chisox' good-luck charm.

The Black Sox scandal followed, and Eddie was devastated. He began to doubt his abilities at a time when Charles Comiskey no longer could afford the luxury of a mascot—especially one he believed rained bad luck on his championship team. Eddie went to work for the Brooklyn Dodgers, a broken-down veteran ballclub that suddenly blossomed into a World Series team in 1920.

By now Eddie was hot property. He was hired by the Yankees the following season just as their fabled dynasty was about to commence. With Eddie supplying the main ingredients, the Yankees won six pennants and three World Series between 1921 and 1932. However, the story has an unhappy ending. In 1932 Eddie Bennett was struck by a car and was unable to resume his clubhouse duties at Yankee Stadium. His world was shattered, and he became a recluse in a shabby rooming house on West 84th Street. He was found dead the evening of January 16, 1935. Babe Ruth, who played catch with Eddie before every Yankees game, and his "Murderer's Row" teammates mourned the passing of the heroic hunchback gifted with magical powers.

"Those Players Today Have it Too Good!" Mostil Remembers Spring Training 1919

Johnny Mostil, the speedy White Sox fly-chaser who tried to end his life with a razor blade during the 1927 spring training sessions, must have *really* hated the entire preseason warmups. In March 1966 Mostil, who had recovered from his suicide attempt all those years earlier, was employed as a White Sox scout and was on hand in Sarasota to wax nostalgic about the spring training hardships he endured when he broke in as an untried rookie prospect in 1919. Conditions were pretty tough. The newbies in camp were relegated to second-class status by the veterans and had to prove themselves in order to shake off the sarcastic label of "Goofs" or "Yanigans." Those were the descriptive terms the beat writers gave to the rookies in their dispatches to the newspaper readers back home as the youngsters were put through the grueling paces.

Entrance to Payne Park in Sarasota, Florida, where the Sox played their spring training games from 1960 to 1998. (Courtesy of Len Maybaum)

Mostil remembered the rain-soaked sessions as if it were only yesterday. "My first training camp was in Mineral Wells, Texas, in 1919," he said. "We stayed at a hotel and got our grub there on the American plan. I really have no beefs on the food. But I didn't like livin' on a train for two weeks when the Sox made their way back to Chicago. Those farmhands today live here in the Sarasota Motor Inn, a first-rate hotel. When I first went to spring training, we had to ring a bell to get the hotel keeper to open the door at night. We practiced in front of a pasture that had no fences. Today the minor leaguers have almost perfect conditions. They have four diamonds out at Arthur Allyn Field. When Kid Gleason managed the White Sox, we walked three miles to the pasture and we walked back. There was an automatic fine if we got an automobile ride. The kids in this camp still have to walk to Arthur Allyn Field, but it isn't as far away, as they're walking to better conditions. We never heard of vitamin pills when I first went to camp. It was several years before we began taking salt pills. The first whirlpool bath I ever saw was after Harry Hooper joined the White Sox. He'd sit in an old whisky barrel with a hose pouring water into it. That was our whirlpool bath."

What would the grizzled Mostil have to say about things now, if only he had had lived long enough to behold the wonders of Camelback Ranch in Glendale, Arizona, described by all who have seen it as a 141-acre "baseball paradise" that is more campus than camp; featuring "Dodger Dogs," a two-acre lake system, and an orange grove? Probably not much.

The Comiskey Park Bombing Case

Thomas Healey, a former Chicago police officer who was moonlighting as a night watchman at Comiskey Park on April 22, 1923, was dozing in the stadium offices just above the main entrance at 35th Street and Shields Avenue when he was thrown out of his chair by the detonation of a pipe bomb.

Squads of police detectives descended on the park in the dead of night to search for clues. They found the windows in the upstairs offices blown out by the concussion. A portable hot dog stand at street level was demolished, but there was no significant structural damage to the fortresslike ballpark, and no one had been injured. Who would commit such a dastardly deed? At first Chicago gamblers were suspected. The police had been active at Comiskey Park and Wrigley Field in an all-out effort to bring a halt to bookmaking in the grandstands. Harry Grabiner, secretary of the White Sox, blamed trade unionists. Comiskey Park had recently been painted by nonunion workmen—in accord with a directive that came from the office of commissioner Kenesaw Mountain Landis. It was believed that recent picketing at Wrigley Field over a similar set of grievances by organized labor was tied in with the attempt to blow up the home of the White Sox.

No suspects in Chicago's first "drive-by" bombing were ever identified. Comiskey Park would stand safe and secure for another seven decades.

Myths, Lies, and Legends

There is no truth to the famous "Say it ain't so, Joe" quote associated with Shoeless Joe Jackson in the darkest days of the Black Sox scandal. The great Sox outfielder, whose career and reputation were permanently ruined by the revelations of wrongdoing in the 1919 World Series, said many things without benefit of legal counsel. What he said to the grand jury is by now well documented. "I got in there and I said: 'I got $5,000 and they promised me $20,000. All I got was $5,000 that Lefty Williams handed me in a dirty envelope. I never got the other $15,000.' I told that to Judge MacDonald. He said he didn't care what I got, that if I got what he thought I'd ought to get for crabbing the game of the kids, I wouldn't be telling him my story. I don't think the judge likes me. I never got that $15,000 that was coming to me."

Johnny Mostil, the fleet-footed center fielder who rates consideration for any White Sox all-time all-star team, never caught a foul fly hugging the left-field line while on the dead run from his position in right-center, either in a regular season game or spring training exhibition.

Smead Jolley

Smead Powell Jolley experienced many fielding misfortunes during the two and a half years he haphazardly patrolled the Comiskey Park outfield. But he never committed three errors on one play as baseball chroniclers so often charge. The oft-repeated folktale goes something like this: Jolley was stationed in right field at Comiskey Park one afternoon when a low sinking line drive sailed through his legs and rolled to the wall for error No. 1. Smead chased the ball, but as it rebounded off the bricks it squirted through his wickets a second time for error No. 2. Then he overthrew the cutoff man.

A game-by-game examination of the box scores from 1930 to 1932 exonerates old Smead, who can rest in peace knowing that he was probably not as bad with a glove as is commonly assumed.

Jimmie Dykes versus Master Charles Comiskey II

Chuck Comiskey probably doesn't remember the incident, or he may be too embarrassed to admit the truth of the matter—but the heir to the White Sox throne was fined $10 for breaking training rules during a road trip to Detroit in August 1938.

The 12-year-old lad, who frequently donned White Sox apparel in order to work out with the ballplayers before the game, was caught munching on a sandwich inside the White Sox clubhouse one afternoon. Charley had violated one of Dykes' cardinal mandates, and he had to pay the toll for his indiscretion. The trouble was, Chuck's allowance money was slow in arriving from the folks back home. So he had to wait until the team settled into its Cleveland hotel a few days later in order to settle his score with Jimmie.

Charley Comiskey was never afraid of the cantankerous Dykes, or for that matter, any of the American League umpires. John Quinn was calling balls and strikes the afternoon of July 26, 1942, at Comiskey Park when young Comiskey was tossed out of the game for arguing a close call. The row started when Don Kolloway swung at a pitch that resulted in a tap in front of the plate. Quinn ruled that the Sox second baseman had run into the ball in fair territory and was out.

Dykes roared out of the dugout, followed closely by 16-year-old Chuck Comiskey, who was in uniform and sitting on the bench.

"You called it foul!" Dykes screamed.

"I called him out!" came the reply.

Charley crowded Quinn and had to be restrained by Eddie Rommel, one of the base umpires. It ended poorly for Dykes and his young protégé. They were both bounced out of the game, but the Sox won anyway, defeating the Philadelphia A's 2–1 behind another one of Teddy Lyons' patented Sunday pitching gems.

White Sox Testimonial Days

It is far less common today, but in years past career players, hometown heroes, and the legends of baseball were honored by management with their own special day at the ballpark. Gifts, speeches, parades, a gold watch, and the undying gratitude of the fans, which counted for a lot more than it does today, highlighted these eagerly anticipated player days that helped cement the game's special place in American culture.

The White Sox have honored dozens of players and baseball officials over the years beginning in the very first decade of the team's existence. On September 21, 1906, Charles Comiskey hosted what may or may not have been the first Old-Timers' Day, when members of the Dreadnaughts and Chicago's other legendary amateur teams of the 1870s were introduced to the fans at the old 39th Street Grounds. Jimmy Ryan and Tony Mullane, who starred in the National League for many years, were two of the 19th-century stars who participated in the festivities that afternoon.

Some of the other notables feted by Sox management down through the years follow in chronological order:

Early testimonial day at the 39th Street Grounds, c. 1909. The chubby White Sox mascot is on the far right.

Player	Affiliation	Date
Frank Chance	New York Highlanders	May 17, 1913
Ray Schalk	White Sox	July 1, 1920
John "Shano" Collins	White Sox	September 11, 1920
Dickie Kerr	White Sox	September 29, 1921
Eddie Collins	White Sox	June 19, 1926
Red Faber	White Sox	August 20, 1929
Joe McCarthy	New York Yankees	May 9, 1931
Ted Lyons	White Sox	August 26, 1933
Jocko Conlan	White Sox	August 12, 1934
Tony Piet	White Sox	September 2, 1935
John Rigney	White Sox	June 12, 1937
Billy Webb	White Sox	June 25, 1940
Ted Lyons	White Sox	September 15, 1940
Connie Mack	Philadelphia A's	June 4, 1941
Luke Appling	White Sox	June 8, 1947
Jackie Hayes	White Sox	August 30, 1949
Phil Cavarretta	White Sox	September 14, 1954
Ed Walsh	Retired	June 22, 1958
Nellie Fox	White Sox	August 21, 1959
Al Smith	White Sox	August 26, 1959
Hoyt Wilhelm	White Sox	July 24, 1968
Luis Aparicio	White Sox	July 19, 1970
Bill Veeck	White Sox	September 25, 1976
Don Kessinger	White Sox	September 8, 1978
Bill Veeck	White Sox	September 30, 1980
Harold Baines	White Sox	August 20, 1989
Carlton Fisk	White Sox	June 22, 1993
Nellie Fox	Hall of Fame Commemoration	August 16, 1997
Ken "Hawk" Harrelson	White Sox	June 8, 2010
Frank Thomas	White Sox	August 29, 2010
Nancy Faust	White Sox Organist	September 18, 2010

Ted Lyons Day at Comiskey Park, September 15, 1940

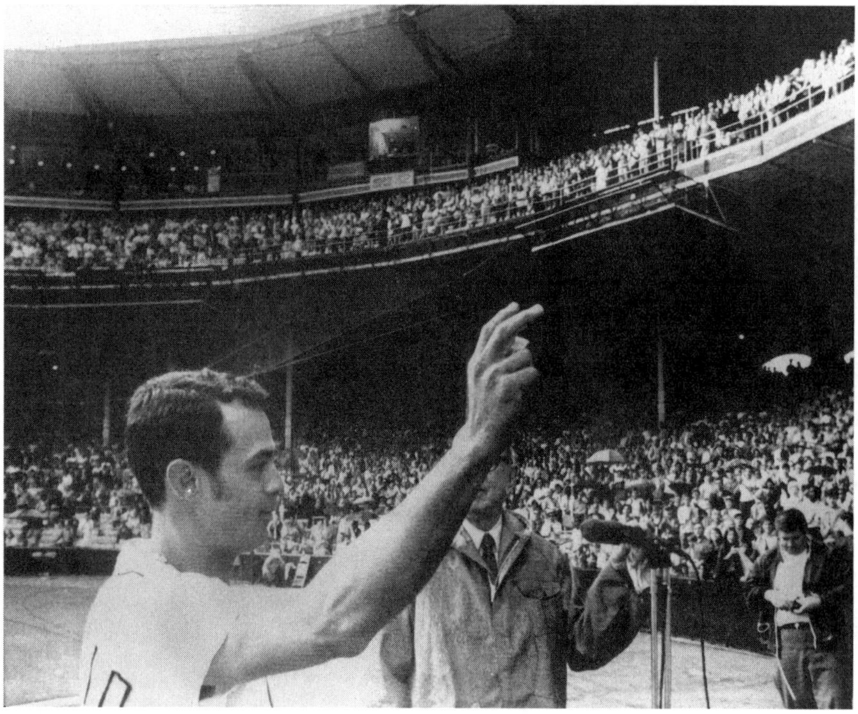

Luis Aparicio acknowledges the crowd on his own special day, July 19, 1970.

Nellie Fox (right) interviewed by Bob Elson on his special night, August 21, 1959

Hoyt Wilhelm and his family are honored on his special night in July 24, 1968. However, the Sox lost both games of a doubleheader to the A's.

Carlton Fisk welcomed back to U.S. Cellular Field as the next "goodwill ambassador."

Frank Thomas Day at U.S. Cellular Field, August 29, 2010. (Courtesy of the Chicago White Sox)

Carlton Fisk Night, June 22, 1993

Ballpark Promotions and Giveaways

Part of the joy of attending baseball games at Comiskey Park over the years was the certain knowledge that a gift item or some unusual bit of between-games entertainment on doubleheader day awaited the Sox fans passing through the turnstiles.

The fun and games really began during Bill Veeck's first ownership when an army of midgets dressed up as "Martians" and led by Eddie Gaedel were lowered by helicopter onto the Sox infield, where they took Louie Aparicio and Nellie Fox prisoner. "Do you want me to take you to my leader?" asked Fox. "No, thanks, I already met him," replied Gaedel, baseball's most famous midget.

Veeck adored midgets. An army of them were pressed into duty as roving beer vendors on Opening Day 1961, after the Sox owner received a number of complaints from Comiskey Park patrons whose view of the game was obstructed by annoying concessionaires transacting business in the aisles.

In the 1960s S&H Green Stamp Day, featuring parade floats, leggy models in bathing suits, and free trading stamps handed out at the main entrance, was popular with the fans. From time to time the jet-propelled "Rocket Man" would fly over the left-field roof and land in the center of the diamond—courtesy of White Owl cigars.

The Indianapolis Clowns, baseball's version of the Harlem Globetrotters, put in a yearly appearance. Mindful of the popularity of folk music, the White Sox staged their own version of a "hootenanny" in the final doubleheader of the 1963 season.

The annual Homecoming Day featured a return of the Sox old-timers. Wilson Ball Day, Bat Day, Banner Day, Seat Cushion Day, Camera Day, and Friday-evening Teen Nights (featuring local rock bands and dance contests), were annual attractions.

The second coming of Bill Veeck in 1976 introduced a dazzling array of wacky promotions. Shrine Night, Diamond Night, Mexican Fiesta Day, beer-case stacking contests, Jersey Day, the King and His Court, Antisuperstition Night, Oktoberfest, McDonald's Breakfast Game—the first matinee contest ever played in Comiskey Park on July 4, 1976—and (gulp!) Disco Demolition.

In contrast to the aggressive marketing strategies employed by the Comiskeys, Veeck, the Allyns, and Jerry Reinsdorf, the Cubs rarely offered their loyal following much more than the game itself. Organ music was considered too radical for the conservative Wrigley family, who did not include the National Anthem in their repertoire until the late 1960s.

Since the advent of the Reinsdorf ownership in 1981, much of the extracurricular promotional campaigns have been linked in one way or another toward raising funds for various charitable and life-changing causes. Since the inception of White Sox Charities, the ballclub has raised more than $16 million for non-profit agencies fighting breast and prostate cancer, with significant funding earmarked for the Greater Chicago Food Depository, Inner City Youth Baseball, civic health programs, the fight against homelessness, youth education, scholarships, and education programs. Family Field Day & Garage Sale, Picnic in the Park, the Celebrity Bowling Classic, the Double Duty Classic, named in honor of the late Ted "Double Duty" Radlciffe, a former Negro Leagues catcher who died in 2005, highlighted ballpark fund-raising efforts in the first decade of the new millennium. In-park entertainment events included Dog Day Afternoon, when the fans were admitted to the grandstands with their mutts; Flying Elvis; and Mullet Night, which were among the best-loved stadium promotions and featured entertainment attractions.

Astonished White Sox players contemplate Bill Veeck's latest stunt—Martians in Comiskey Park, May 26, 1959.

Terry Bevington and Jenna, winner of the 1996 "Future Sox" contest

The Sox's 1966 snowmobile transports a relief pitcher to the mound.

Bat Day, 1972. (Courtesy of Len Maybaum)

Finalists (above) in the 1981 Design the Next Sox Uniform Contest

Harold Baines making his annual Sox Fest appearance in 2009. (Courtesy of the Chicago White Sox)

Fans looking over game-used bats for sale at the 2010 Sox Fest. (Courtesy of the Chicago White Sox)

Kid's Day at U.S. Cellular Field. (Courtesy of the Chicago White Sox)

Remembering the Mascots

Must we? Okay, we'll concede that major league mascots are here to stay—they are a part of the "total" baseball experience; family-oriented comic mop-tops prancing on the dugout and behind the foul lines for the amusement and enjoyment of the kiddies (the future ticket buyers) and to the eternal chagrin of the middle-aged purist of the national pastime.

Since the 1994 player strike, more and more of these obtuse fuzzy creatures have turned up in American ballparks to illustrate that our grand old game is after all really for and about the kids. Before mascots, each stadium had its own certifiable "characters," although not necessarily sanctioned by management. For years, "Wild Bill" Hagy was a fixture atop the Orioles dugout every seventh inning. Can you spell O-R-I-O-L-E-S? Wild Bill helped you out during the stretch. There was Hilda Chester, the Brooklyn bell-ringer, "Woo Woo" Wickers at Wrigley Field, and (bless 'im) Andy Rozdilsky, aka "Andy the Clown," first entertained the Sox faithful in 1961 at old Comiskey Park. The zanies and eccentrics like Hilda and Andy provided plenty of local color, otherwise absent from the pre-mascot days.

And then a new day in ballpark entertainment dawned, and it had nothing to do with Bill Veeck. Jerry Reinsdorf and Eddie Einhorn hired Ribbie and Roobarb, designed by the firm of Harrison/Erickson of New York City. They made their inglorious debut at Comiskey Park in September 1981 in the belief that it was necessary to recast the image of the team and the park into a wholesome family-oriented attraction after years of security problems brought on by the beer-guzzling Friday night fighters occupying the cheap seats. Ribbie, the purple anteater, and his cross-eyed sidekick Roobarb, the strange yellow creature, were universally reviled and often the target of liquored-up hecklers during their eight-year run (1981–1988). Security guards had to keep a watchful eye on the pair as they meandered through the lower box seats. Both mascots were frequently assaulted by fans with punches and side swipes, which the security detail did not take kindly to.

Two dyed-in-the-wool Sox fans from Kankakee show up in their homemade mascot uniforms to inaugurate the 1979 home season at old Comiskey Park. It might be argued that the 1979 Sox comprised an entire team of mascots.

Andy the Clown, the Sox mascot the fans loved best, never worked for the team and never drew a day's pay for entertaining the crowds.

In the early 1990s "Waldo the White Sox Wolf" put in a brief appearance, but the animated cartoon character drawn by artist Will Faust of Cioni Artworks in Chicago was the spokesman for the "White Sox Silver and Black Pack" serving the kiddies, and was confined to the Jumbotron scoreboard in center field. Waldo quietly disappeared, and the park was free of mascots until the arrival of the fuzzy green Southpaw on June 13, 2004, the ever-present mop-top with large disbelieving eyes and a Jimmy Durante schnozz. Southpaw makes personal appearances at all kinds of charitable events and enjoys the distinction of being the only baseball mascot to ride on a presidential float—during the inaugural parade of President Barack Obama in January 2009. Southpaw proudly joined with the Illinois delegation—at President Obama's request.

The San Diego Chicken visits the White Sox for an impromptu "rock concert" with the White Sox on September 5, 1983.

"Ribbie," the 1980s mascot

Southpaw—the latest White Sox mascot—greets fans at the 2009 Sox Fest. (Courtesy of the Chicago White Sox)

Take Me Out to the Brawl Game

In the words of Jack Brickhouse, who witnessed more than one baseball fight during his celebrated announcing career, this one was a real "Pier Six donnybrook." The White Sox were playing the Browns in the second of a two-game set at Sportsman's Park in St. Louis the afternoon of June 20, 1945.

The trouble began in the third inning when Brownie pitcher George Caster was removed from the game by his manager Luke Sewell. Caster stared intently at the White Sox dugout as he slowly exited the field. He did not appreciate the unflattering remarks directed toward him by White Sox batting practice pitcher Karl Scheel, a 23-year-old ex-Marine. Suddenly the peevish Caster hurled the game ball directly at Scheel, who bobbed and weaved in the dugout trying to avoid being hit.

Jimmie Dykes protested the incident to umpire Art Passarella, who curtly told the Sox manager to shut up and sit down. "Play ball…let's go!" the ump roared. Before the game resumed, a contingency of Browns led by Luke Sewell, Ellis Clary, Myron Hayworth, and Sid Jakucki charged the White Sox dugout. Intent upon inflicting bodily harm, the St. Louis players collared the bewildered young Scheel and inflicted a beating that Jimmie Dykes described as the "most brutal thing" he had ever witnessed in baseball. Quite a statement coming from a manager who was no stranger to fisticuffs himself.

A squad of St. Louis police officers separated the combatants, but the young man was already beaten to a pulp. When the dust cleared and the offending players were led away, the Sox sent the remaining Browns down to defeat, 4–1. Later, after all of the evidence had been presented to Commissioner A.B. "Happy" Chandler, Caster, Jakucki, and Clary were assessed $100 fines. Manager Luke Sewell was ordered to pay $250.

The Sox do battle with the Browns, June 20, 1945.

Who's Minding the Store?

Twice in the 1940s the White Sox batted out of order in a regular season game. The ballclub was wrapping up an abbreviated two-game home stand against the Cleveland Indians on April 26, 1942, when outfielder Bud Sketchley, a wartime replacement, lingered in the on-deck circle. Sketchley was due to bat, but Bob Kennedy stepped up to the plate instead. Cleveland manager Lou Boudreau was aware of the mix-up, but since Kennedy was easily retired, he said nothing about it to the umpire. In the third inning, Sketchley again batted out of order. Catcher Tom Turner was scheduled to hit, but Sketchley's mind was obviously not on baseball.

Sketch was retired, but Turner drilled a double, prompting a swift protest from Boudreau. The umpire examined the lineup card and concurred. Turner's double was canceled—end of rally. Despite a well-pitched game from John Rigney, the Sox lost 3–2.

The White Sox were playing in St. Louis on September 15, 1944, when Eddie Carnett and Guy Curtright batted out of order, thus costing the Sox a victory. The mix-up occurred in the first inning with Sox runners on first and third and two out. Outfielder Curtright was due to bat, but the public address man got it wrong and announced Eddie Carnett, who sauntered to the plate and promptly delivered an RBI single. Browns manager Luke Sewell produced the lineup card. Carnett was called out, and the Sox went on to lose 5–1.

Jimmie Dykes could only shake his head and wonder. War is hell…in more ways than one.

Fourteen Sox Players Ejected by "Meathead"

Umpire Red Jones set an unofficial record of sorts when he chased 14 White Sox bench jockeys in a game played at Boston's Fenway Park on July 19, 1946. It happened in the third inning after Jones issued a verbal warning to Sox pitcher Joe Haynes who fired a high hard one at Red Sox slugger Ted Williams.

It was Ladies Day at Fenway, and the White Sox players were convinced that Jones was courting the favor of the fairer sex with decisions that were consistently going to the home team. "Hey, Meathead, what kind of call is *that?*" With his patience exhausted, Jones stormed the Sox dugout. He gave the heave-ho to Ralph Hodgin, Dario Lodigiani, Edgar Smith, Mike Tresh, John Rigney, Mizell Platt, Leo Wells, Hal Trosky, Guy Curtright, Ed Lopat, Wally Moses, Frank Whitman, coach Bing Miller, and batting practice pitcher Glen Liebhardt.

Manager Ted Lyons escaped banishment but was left with only 10 players to finish the game. The tattered Hose of White, as you might expect, lost the game 7–2.

The Old Brawl Game, Part II

Dyed-in-the-wool White Sox fans make no bones about their intense dislike for the New York Yankees. Year in and year out, the American League pennant race had been an exercise in futility. Even after the Sox attained respectability in 1951, they still couldn't beat the Yankees. From 1926 until 1959, Chicago did not capture a season series. Way back in 1925, Eddie Collins' crew had won 13 of 22 decisions.

In June 1957 Al Lopez's White Sox gave every indication of breaking with their past litany of failure. When the Yankees arrived in town on June 11 for a three-game set, Chicago enjoyed a comfortable four-and-a-half-game first-place lead. After the rivals had divided the first two games of the series, Billy Pierce squared off against Art Ditmar in an effort to win the rubber match on June 13.

Ditmar had two strikes on Larry Doby in the first inning when he fired a head-hunting fastball to the veteran Sox slugger that sent him sprawling to the ground. The brushback incident continued a nasty test of wills between the two contending ballclubs. The night before, Yankees pitcher Al Cicotte nearly skulled the normally easygoing Minnie Minoso, who charged the mound seeking retaliation.

Art Ditmar then uncorked a wild pitch to Doby and rushed home to cover the plate in case the runner on second entertained a notion of trying to score. Doby stepped aside, muttering to himself. "If you ever do that again, I'll stick a knife in your back," he reportedly warned the Yankees pitcher.

Ditmar's unprintable four-letter-word reply ignited the brawl—the most famous baseball scuffle of the decade. Doby threw a left hook, sparking a bench-clearing fistfight that took the police and the umpires 30 minutes to end. At various times Whitey Ford, Casey Stengel, Jim Rivera, and Enos Slaughter were in the thick of the mêlée. Slaughter's jersey was torn to shreds, and the image of the ex-Cardinal walking away from the field is one of the classic sports photos of the 1950s. When Ditmar advised his hotheaded teammate Billy Martin of what had happened, the Yankees second baseman blindsided Doby. Two days later, Martin was traded to Kansas City. His antics were just too much for Yankees GM George Weiss.

When order was finally restored, Walt Dropo, Larry Doby, and Enos Slaughter were ejected. Ditmar, however, was allowed to remain in the game, sparking a howl of protest from the Sox dugout.

League fines were handed down the next day. Doby was ordered to pay $150; Dropo, $100. "The Yankees have been bullying their opponents long enough," commented John Rigney from the executive suite. "I'm glad it happened." Unfortunately, Ditmar bagged a 4–3 victory, and a large measure of smug Yankees satisfaction to go along with it.

Baltimore (High) Jinx

The Orioles' move into spacious Camden Yards in 1992 could not have come soon enough for battle-scarred Sox fans who vividly recall so many nightmarish losses in old Memorial Stadium dating back to April 15, 1954, when Chicago helped reintroduce American League baseball in the land of the crab cake by losing to the O's 3–1.

Nestled into a pleasant tree-lined neighborhood not far from Johns Hopkins University, the egg-shaped ballpark was a test of endurance for succeeding White Sox managers.

Al Lopez was 30 seconds away from victory the night of May 18, 1957, when disaster struck.

The Sox were scheduled to catch a midnight train to Boston, so the Orioles management reluctantly agreed to halt the game at 10:20 regardless of the outcome. The visitors were trailing 3–0 in the top of the seventh when the surging White Sox—winners of six straight games—rallied to take the lead 4–3 in their half of the inning. To protect this lead, Lopez summoned southpaw Paul LaPalme to hold them in the ninth inning.

The Sox could have easily won this game by stalling until 10:20, since the existing league rules did not allow for a suspension. LaPalme, however, was unaware of the time. With a man on board, he delivered a pitch to Orioles outfielder Dick Williams, who drilled the ball into the left-field seats for a game-winning home run. If he had only held on to the ball 30 seconds longer, the Sox would have walked away with an easy victory and preserved their momentum.

Curfew, rain, and other assorted acts of God worked to the disadvantage of the Sox for decades to come. In the heat of the torrid 1960 pennant race, a home run denied had disastrous implications for the veteran White Sox, who appeared to be on course for a repeat appearance in the World Series.

The White Sox engaged the contending Orioles on their home grounds the night of August 28, 1960, trailing the first-place Yankees by two and a half games. Opposing Early Wynn that night was young Milt Pappas, one of the prize pupils of the Baltimore "Kiddie Corps." Pappas shut down the Sox attack for seven innings while his teammates built a seemingly insurmountable 3–0 lead. In the visitor's half of the eighth, Louie Aparicio, Nellie Fox, and Roy Sievers lined consecutive singles after Floyd Robinson and Earl Torgeson had been retired.

Big Ted Kluszewski was sent in to hit for Minnie Minoso, and the sleeveless one from Argo, Illinois, came through. He launched a cannon shot into the right-field seats. Klu went into his home-run trot, but stopped dead in his tracks when umpire Ed Hurley ruled no play. The umpire had called time, but neither Pappas nor the other players on the field were paying attention. On his next swing, following a lengthy argument, Klu meekly flied out to right. The Sox lost the game, and probably the 1960 pennant. The demoralized ballclub played only .500 ball the rest of the way.

The Baltimore road trips were fatal poison through the 1970s and 1980s. Chuck Tanner's ballclub dropped a horrific game to the O's on August 26, 1971, after rallying from a huge deficit to claim the lead in the ninth inning. The Sox were still batting when the skies opened up. It rained buckets until the umpires called the game off. Under the existing rules of the day, the score reverted back to the prior inning—O's 8, Sox 7—meaning that another Memorial Stadium defeat had been snatched from the jaws of victory.

Richard Dotson will never forget his 1983 Memorial Stadium nightmare. On May 18 in that championship season, "Dot" was nursing a no-hitter into the eighth inning when suddenly and without warning "Disco" Dan Ford clouted a home run to right field for the only Orioles hit of the game. But it was enough to defeat the White Sox 1–0. In his return engagement on August 14, Dotson yielded only three hits to the Orioles lineup but was charged with a 2–1 loss.

Was there ever a team so tragically cursed in a foreign field as the White Sox playing along the banks of Chesapeake Bay? Perhaps we can blame all of this on Bill Veeck. It was "Barnum Bill" who sold the lovable St. Louis Browns to Baltimore, where they became the decidedly unfriendly birds.

The 1.000 Career Hitter

Catcher Chuck Lindstrom is the only White Sox player to complete his major league career with a perfect 1.000 batting average. Chuck was the son of Freddie Lindstrom, a former Northwestern University coach and a standout infielder in the National League for 12 seasons. Freddie was signed by the White Sox on June 18, 1957, and optioned to Colorado Springs of the Western League, where he batted only .222 in 198 at bats. He was called up to the parent ballclub in the closing weeks of the 1958 season and was inserted into the starting lineup for the final game of the year against the Kansas City A's on September 28 at Comiskey Park. In two plate appearances Lindstrom tripled off the face of the left-field wall and drew a walk. He never appeared in another major league game, and retired with a perfect 1.000 average and a 3.000 slugging average.

They Said It

Another less-than-worthy batting performance at Memorial Stadium was turned in by rookie outfielder Jim Landis on July 28, 1957, when he was fanned four times by Orioles pitcher Billy O'Dell and once by ex–White Sox Connie Johnson to complete a fruitless 0-for-5 day that equalled the major league record for consecutive strikeouts by a batter in one game.

Afterward an unnamed Sox player said of the Baltimore Orioles: "If these guys played everybody else like they do against us, they'd be nine games in front!" White Sox coach Don Gutteridge, overhearing the complaint, replied: "If we played against these guys like we do against everybody else, *we* would be nine games in front!"

Lou Brock: Over the Roof of Old Comiskey

Lou Brock, the big fish that got away from the friendly confines of Wrigley Field in 1964 when the Cubs traded him to the St. Louis Cardinals, launched a mammoth home run over the left-field roof at old Comiskey Park two years before beginning his Hall of Fame career. Lou was a member of the U.S. baseball team playing in the 1959 Pan American Games, held in Chicago the first week of September. His long-distance shot off of a Cuban pitcher occurred during one of the international games played on the Sox's home field.

Jimmy Piersall Having the Time of His Life

The fabled "Monster," baseball's first exploding scoreboard, was built high above the center-field bleachers by Bill Veeck and a generous infusion of Spencer Advertising Agency money. The new board, inspired by the whirring, whistling pinball machine in William Saroyan's *The Time of Your Life,* debuted on Opening Day in 1960. Unfortunately for Veeck, but consistent with the Comiskey "curse," the automatic tape recording featuring a shattering crescendo of two trains colliding, a machine gun burst, a cavalry charge, and a woman screaming "Fireman! Save My Child!" failed to go off on cue after Minnie Minoso hit the first of two home runs in his return engagement as a new member of the White Sox.

"The darned thing never does the same thing twice," lamented Veeck, who absorbed a lot of good-natured ribbing over his $350,000 mechanical marvel that first season. One night Casey Stengel and his players marched up and down in the visitors' dugout waving sparklers after Clete Boyer hit a home run. The Monster, you see, never applauded an opponent's home run, so old Case took matters into his own hands with the assistance of Yankees PR man Bob Fishel.

Then, in a madcap frenzy, Jimmy Piersall of the Cleveland Indians tried to single-handedly destroy the board on May 30. The agitated Piersall was having a bad day all around. He completely emptied the Indians dugout of bats, towels, and helmets to protest an umpire's call. It took the clubhouse attendants a full 10 minutes to clean up the mess.

Jimmy was stationed in center field stewing over past injustices when Minnie Minoso lined a double over his head. Piersall didn't even move. He made no attempt to retrieve the ball, and myopic Ed Short therefore came to the conclusion that the ball had cleared the fence for a home run, which was not the case. The Sox GM pushed the button signaling home run, and the scoreboard rockets blared a lively tune.

That cinched it for Piersall. He picked up the ball and fired it at the Monster, shattering a light bulb or two. It turned out to be a costly temper tantrum. The league slapped a $250 fine on Jimmy. And worse, the Sox won both ends of the doubleheader that day.

Look Back in Anger...Charles A. Comiskey Reflects on the Black Sox

Following the revelations that eight White Sox players had tossed the 1919 World Series to an otherwise inferior Cincinnati Redlegs team for the cheap payoff of several thousand dollars per man, a broken-hearted, physically drained, and ailing Charles Comiskey entered a long period of self-imposed exile and convalescence at his forest retreat and hunting lodge outside of Mercer, Wisconsin. Through much of the 1920s the Old Roman monitored events at 35th and Shields from afar as he fought to regain his once robust health. Comiskey was in his sixties now, and the shock and humiliation of the ordeal had taken an awful physical toll. Through the long summers, he was content to spend the afternoons fly-casting in Northern Wisconsin's abundant streams, entertaining his young grandson, Charles II, and the boy's school chums coming up from Chicago. In the evenings he read or socialized with his woodland neighbors living in the Eagle River vicinity while one rebuilding program after another fizzled back in Chicago and the Sox settled uncomfortably into the second division.

By 1929 there were fears that the sickly Sox owner would never make it back to the city of his birth, let alone gear up for one last fight to craft a pennant-winning ballclub. In September of that year, just 12 days shy of the official 10-year anniversary of the Cook County grand jury indictment handed down against the Black Sox players who had sold him and the fans of Chicago out, Comiskey vowed to return to fight another day. He confided his true feelings to sportswriter Ed Burns of the *Tribune,* as the two men sipped beer in the cozy confines of the Home Plate hunting lodge. The owner was still very bitter, and understandably so. "Ten years ago this fall, my ballclub, the greatest club that was ever assembled, insofar as playing ability was concerned, brought Chicago its last pennant," Comiskey said. "That team, or the eight crooks that were on it, gave me the worst shock that ever a man suffered in baseball. I don't think the public realizes what a crushing blow those Black Sox gave to the proudest owner that ever built up a ballclub. The years haven't healed the wounds completely, and when I recall the reaction to my 'pride' of just 10 years ago... [his voice trailed off].... But I've suffered long enough. I'm coming back to Chicago to start in on a lot of new happiness. I'll live to see my ballclub up there again. I have no illusions about their shortcomings. It's a hard job to build up a pennant winner, but I've done it many times before, and since God has spared me, I'm going to do it again. I am the sole owner of the White Sox and will be as long as I'm on this earth."

Sadly, for this misunderstood old baseball pioneer whose otherwise stellar reputation as a sportsman, philanthropist, and civic leader was slandered as a mean-spirited misanthrope by Eliot Asinof in his quasi-novel *Eight Men Out,* the dream of building a championship team in the image of the 1906 and 1917 World Series winners was beyond Commy's grasp. Charles Comiskey lived exactly two more years. Throughout the 1920s he spent lavishly trying to procure the best young talent on the market, but the returns were minimal, and it would take another two decades and the genius of the young grandson who spent his boyhood summers up at Eagle River to mold a winner in the "hit-and-run, Go-Go" image of the great Comiskey teams of the early years.

Look Back *Not* in Anger

Clarence "Pants" Rowland, who had managed the Sox to their last world championship, was nearing his 80th birthday on the eve of the 1959 World Series. The grizzled old "Iowa Busher" who was unfairly dismissed from his duties by Charles Comiskey after the war-torn 1918 season, was asked to compare the strengths of the Go-Go White Sox of 1959 against his 1917 champions, who set a team record with 100 victories.

Rowland, who was employed by the Cubs as a vice president in 1959, had no doubts as to the team he considered the absolute best. "It's a little unfair to compare them to the 1917 White Sox because you're matching them against the greatest team of all time," commented the Busher. "In my estimation not even the murderous 1927 Yankees—the year Babe Ruth hit his 60 homers—would be a match for them."

The 1917 champions breezed through the New York Giants in a six-game World Series dominated by Red Faber, who won three of the games for Chicago. "Most important probably was the superb spirit and supreme confidence of the team," Rowland added. "Many a time when the 1917 players were behind, they'd come back and say, 'Don't worry, Teach [Rowland's other nickname], we'll get three or four runs for you and win it.' And they'd go ahead and do it."

Rowland stopped short of predicting a 1959 World Series victory for Chicago. He harbored too many old and painful memories of his dealings with the Old Roman. "The World Series?" he smiled. "There I'll have to beg off. After all, I'm a National Leaguer now."

Tribune or *Cub-une*?

The Tribune honchos covering the sports beat bristle every time they hear an angry Sox fan accuse them of media bias, or worse, verbally denigrating the newspaper as the house organ of the Chicago National League team by calling it the *Cub-une.* It is believed that former Sox postgame talk show host Dave Wills, who moved on to join the Tampa Bay Rays broadcast team, coined the nickname after arriving at the same weary conclusion as every man, woman, and child (even Bill Veeck back in the late 1970s) professing allegiance to the White Sox—that is, the "World's Greatest Newspaper" devotes more column inches and story coverage to the Cubs than the Sox. It is undeniable. It is inescapable. It is no illusion. And it has been that way for many years. Even after the Tribune Company divested its holdings to the Ricketts family in 2010, more often than not the Cubs are still the lead story and usually above the fold on page 1. Back in the 1970s, Veeck was measuring column inches in both major dailies and concluded that the Sox were not getting their fair shake in the press and likely never would. That was the main reason why he toyed with the notion of moving the club to Denver in 1980. Author and journalist George Castle put this question to a *Sun-Times* sports editor, who later migrated over to the *Tribune,* and was told quite bluntly, "Why wouldn't we? There are more Cub fans out there than Sox fans." Okay. But if that is true (and it probably is, we must concede), how does that justify blatant journalistic bias for one team over the other? For Sox fans smarting from years of second-class treatment in the second city, let me just add this.... *Cub-une, Cub-une, Cub-une, Cub-une, Cub-une...*

Opening Day and a Horseshoe of Flowers for Good Luck

In the last two years of his life, White Sox founder Charles A. Comiskey lived in a fashionable Hyde Park apartment house that still stands at 5555 S. Everett Avenue. It was from this address that the funeral procession for the Old Roman commenced October 29, 1931, days after his passing in Eagle River, Wisconsin. The funeral was a lavish affair—attended by 275 honorary pallbearers, including a number of Chicago aldermen, the soon-to-become Illinois Governor Henry Horner, police officers, firefighters, and many former and current White Sox players who marched with the casket in silent procession to St. Thomas the Apostle Church at 55th Street and Kimbark for the Requiem High Mass, and then on to Calvary Cemetery in Evanston for final interment.

Archie Spencer, a well-liked Chicago florist and sportsman who operated his business at 1313 W. Randolph Street on the Near West Side, was one of the many friends of Comiskey chosen to serve as a pallbearer. He also supplied all of the floral arrangements to honor the passing of his old friend. Spencer had made it a yearly custom to deliver a personally designed horseshoe of flowers—a symbol of good luck—to the incumbent White Sox manager on each and every Opening Day at Comiskey Park. Through a dozen different managers spanning six decades, Spencer's floral tribute arrived on time every year—until the last one was sent to Don Gutteridge on Opening Day 1970, when this great old tradition was ended by the passing of time.

Charlie Maxwell: never on Saturday

Ed Short was a funny guy...when he wanted to be.

Sunday Fun at the "Maxwell House"

Outfielder Charlie Maxwell lingered in the big leagues for nearly 14 seasons. He was only a .264 career hitter, but if every day were Sunday, Charlie would surely be enshrined in the Hall of Fame today.

Maxwell was acquired from the Detroit Tigers for rookie outfielder Bob Farley in order to shore up the White Sox bench on June 25, 1962. Charlie was hitting only .194 at the time, but everyone knew that if he were turned loose on Sundays and left at home the rest of the week, he would turn his numbers around very quickly.

So it was written. And so it was done.

Old "Paw Paw" went to work on that batting average. He clouted three home runs against the Yankees in a July 29 Sunday doubleheader at New York.

In a Sabbath twin bill against his old teammates in Comiskey Park on August 19, Charlie drove in six runs in the first game, including a grand-slam home run and a double. It was S&H Green Stamp Day at the ballpark, and Charlie won 49 books of free stamps—naturally.

Legalize the Spitball?

There was never a "*Short*-age" of ideas emanating out of the White Sox front office during the years when butterfly collector Arthur Allyn Jr. owned the ballclub, and general manager Edwin Short articulated his viewpoints at the annual winter meetings. With Arthur's blessing, Eddie submitted a written proposal to Charles M. Sager, chairman of the playing rules committee, asking baseball's governing powers to legalize the spitball beginning in 1964. Short requested the change to "eliminate the accusations and suspicions leveled at a number of pitchers in the past years." Short went on to say that if baseball refused to go along with the request, he would demand implementation of a rule to prohibit a pitcher from touching his mouth, forehead, or "any part of his body where moisture might accumulate." The idea died in committee, as most of the Allyn-Short proposals did, but we must ask ourselves, who among those 1960s pitchers was loading up the ball? Hmmmmm?

More Shortcomings

Jack Brickhouse recalls the night Eddie Short gathered together 20 members of the media to play a little joke on the laconic Bob Elson, radio voice of the White Sox heard over station WJJD. "He gambled Elson would show up late, and of course he did," Brickhouse told Jerome Holtzman. "As soon as Elson started his show, all 20 of us walked into the studio. Then the stripper—I don't know where Short found her, but she was a well-endowed woman of Japanese-Hawaiian descent—jumped on Elson's desk. She took off everything but her toenail polish. Elson almost swallowed his mike. But he didn't break up, not completely. The only mention Elson made was 'Well folks, Tokyo Rose has joined us tonight.' I don't think Elson was ever late again."

Disco Demolition and Other Forfeits

White Sox fans are still trying to live down the embarrassment of "Disco Demolition"—the 1979 fiasco that resulted in a forfeit loss to the Detroit Tigers. But there have actually been three other occasions in White Sox history when the umpires were forced to declare a forfeit when circumstances made it impossible to continue the game.

The American League (as a major league entity) was barely two weeks old when the White Sox tested the patience of umpire Tom Connolly and ended up forfeiting a game to the Tigers at the 39th Street Grounds. Clark Griffith's team nursed a 5–2 lead into the ninth inning of a late afternoon game on May 2, 1901, when darkness and rain threatened to cut short the proceedings. However, the Tigers had already erupted for six runs when the first drops began to fall. Knowing that the score would revert back to the eighth inning unless the Sox batted in the their half of the ninth, Griffith's players stalled until Connolly had about enough and declared a forfeit in Detroit's favor.

Bill Veeck and Rudie Schaffer try to figure out a way to restore calm.

The fans riot on Disco Demolition Night.

With the score tied at three apiece in the 10th inning of a September 9, 1917, game against the Cleveland Indians at Comiskey Park, umpire Brick Owens forfeited the contest to the White Sox after left fielder Jack Graney was called out at third on a close play by Owens. The Tribe took the field in a dilatory manner in the last half of the 10th. The Cleveland players protested Owens' decision by hurling their gloves in the air, and two or three of them rolled around in the dirt to express their displeasure. After Cleveland catcher Steve O'Neill deliberately threw a ball into center, Owens ripped off his mask and declared, "Game off! Sox win!" That was the only time the White Sox ever came out ahead in a forfeit.

The Tribe again provided the opposition on April 26, 1925, when 44,000 fans jammed into Comiskey Park to set a new single-game attendance record. Because there were no additional seats available, Charles Comiskey allowed several thousand of them to stand in a roped-off section of the outfield near the left- and right-field walls.

With two outs in the ninth inning and the Sox trailing 7–2, the restless throng in the outfield suddenly broke past the restraining ropes and swarmed the field, thinking that the game had already ended. Unable to restore order, the trio of umpires headed by former Sox manager Clarence Rowland ruled a forfeit.

The growing popularity of White Sox baseball in the era of Babe Ruth and the surprising number of standing-room-only crowds convinced Comiskey to move ahead with his plans to add an outfield upper deck—which was completed in time for the 1927 season.

Nobody knows for certain how many kids turned out for a twi-night doubleheader with the Detroit Tigers on July 12, 1979. The main attraction was not baseball, but a between-games "Disco Demolition" orchestrated by disc jockey Steve Dahl of WLUP-FM, a heavy-metal, razor rock station with an enormous adolescent following. Dahl and his legion of disco-hating fans were to blow up stacks of Donna Summer and Bee Gees records between games as a protest against this kind of music. Mike Veeck, who was working for his dad in the White Sox promotions department, conceived of the idea. But not even the master showman could have conceived of such an outpouring of support for Dahl.

The crowd was estimated to be in the range of 49,000—but by all accounts, there were many more people in attendance that night than the ticket takers could account for.

Throughout Game 1, there were ominous rumblings of trouble. Disco records were hurled through the stands like Frisbees, and no one seemed to be paying very much attention to the Sox, who were quietly bowing to the Tigers by a 4–1 count.

After the first game had ended, Dahl, wearing an army helmet, mounted a specially constructed wooden perch in center field, where he blew up the records on cue to the chant "Disco Sucks!" Then all hell broke loose. The kids ran wild through the outfield and refused to return to their seats. Mayhem and pandemonium reigned. Then Bill Veeck, accompanied by Harry Caray, trudged down to the field with a microphone to plead for order. They were ignored.

In Sox history, only one other incident matched the destructive potential of Disco Demolition. On July 14, 1930, more than 3,000 students from Crane Tech High School stormed the gates, expecting free admission to a Sox-Yankees game. A newspaper promotion had advertised free tickets and Babe Ruth's autograph to youngsters holding special coupon tickets, but the block of prized tickets promised to the Crane students had not been properly endorsed by Charles Comiskey when they were handed over to Chicago alderman T.J. Bowler for distribution. More than 50 mounted police officers were called out to quell the disturbance. Matters were resolved peacefully, however, after the Old Roman ordered the gates thrown open for the students.

But on Disco Demolition night, the playing field was trashed. The forfeit was entered into the books, and the franchise was reduced to an embarrassing new low. Not even Cleveland's 1974 nickel-beer riot compared to this. The Sox had become the laughingstock of baseball, and Veeck an anachronism in a changing time.

Years later Steve Dahl—older and mellowed by his experiences—composed a touching farewell verse to old Comiskey Park in which he apologized for all the trouble he had caused. His tune "At the Old Comiskey" was aired nationally. The shock jock of 1970s FM radio had become—of all things—a White Sox fan.

The First Forfeited Game
Detroit at Chicago, May 2, 1901

Detroit	R	H	P	A
Casey, 3b	1	0	2	3
Barrett, cf	3	3	2	1
Gleason, 2b	1	0	2	2
Holmes, rf	0	1	1	0
Dillon, 1b	1	1	9	1
Elberfeld, ss	0	0	2	2
Nance, lf	0	0	3	0
Buelow, c	1	0	2	2
Frisk, p	1	2	1	3
	8	7	24	14

Chicago	R	H	P	A
Hoy, cf	2	3	2	0
Jones, rf	0	0	0	0
Mertes, 2b	1	0	2	5
Isbell, 1b	1	1	15	0
Hartman, 3b	0	0	0	3
Shugarts, ss	0	1	1	4
McFarland, lf	0	2	0	1
Sullivan, c	0	0	4	1
Griffith, p	1	0	0	3
	5	7	26	16

Detroit	101	000	006—8
Chicago	002	000	30x—5

x—Two outs in the inning when game was forfeited to Detroit

2B—Hoy, Holmes, Frisk. 3B—Barrett. HR—Barrett. Sac—Jones, Gleason. SB—Gleason (2). E—Mertes (2), Isbell, Hartman, McFarland, Casey (2), Gleason, Elberfeld (2), Frisk. LOB—Detroit 6, Chicago 7. PB—Sullivan. Umpire—Connolly. Time—2:10. Attendance—1,000.

Detroit	IP	BB	K
Frisk (W)	8⅔	6	1

Chicago	IP	BB	K
Griffith (L)	9	2	2

The Second Forfeited Game
Cleveland at Chicago, September 9, 1917

Cleveland	AB	R	H	P	A
Graney, lf	4	1	3	0	0
Chapman, ss	3	0	1	3	4
Speaker, cf	5	1	2	1	0
Roth, rf	5	1	0	5	0
Harris, 1b	4	0	0	11	2
Evans, 3b	4	0	0	0	2
Howard, 2b	0	0	0	0	0
Turner, 2b	4	0	1	5	1
Wambsganss, 2b	0	0	0	0	0
O'Neill, c	4	0	1	3	3
Coveleskie, p	0	0	0	0	0
Coumbe, p	4	0	1	0	7
	37	3	9	28	19

Chicago	AB	R	H	P	A
Leibold, rf	0	1	0	1	0
J. Collins, rf	3	0	0	4	0
McMullin, 3b	4	2	1	2	2
E. Collins, 2b	1	0	0	2	4
Jackson, lf	4	0	3	2	1
Felsch, cf	4	0	0	2	0
Gandil, 1b	4	0	0	9	0
Risberg, ss	4	0	1	4	3
Schalk, c	4	0	1	4	1
Russell, p	1	0	0	0	0
Faber, p	0	0	0	0	0
Danforth, p	1	0	0	0	0
Murphy, ph	0	0	0	0	0
	30	3	6	30	12

Cleveland	100	002	000	0—3
Chicago	200	001	000	x—3

x—One out when game was forfeited to Chicago

2B—Speaker (2). SB—Roth. Sac—Chapman, E. Collins (2), Murphy. DP—Jackson-Schalk; E. Collins-Risberg-Gandil. LOB—Cleveland 8, Chicago 5. E—Schalk (2), Faber, Coumbe. Umpires—Owens, Evans. Time—2:05.

Cleveland	IP	H	R	BB	K
Coumbe	9⅓	6	3	2	3
Coveleskie (L)	0	0	0	0	0

Chicago	IP	H	R	BB	K
Russell	2	3	1	1	0
Faber	5	4	2	1	2
Danforth (W)	3	2	0	1	1

The Third Forfeited Game
Cleveland at Chicago, April 26, 1925

Cleveland	AB	R	H
Jamieson, lf	4	0	1
Spurgeon, 3b	5	1	3
Speaker, cf	4	1	1
J. Sewell, ss	2	2	2
Myatt, c	5	1	3
Stephenson, rf	4	0	1
Goode, 1b	5	0	1
Fewster, 2b	4	1	1
Smith, p	4	1	1
	37	7	14

Chicago	AB	R	H
Mostil, cf	4	0	1
Davis, ss	4	1	1
Collins, 2b	4	0	1
Sheely, 1b	3	1	1
Falk, lf	4	0	3
Elsh, rf	4	0	1
Kamm, 3b	4	0	0
Schalk, c	3	0	1
Thurston, p	1	0	0
Connally, p	2	0	0
	33	2	9

Cleveland	011	130	001—7
Chicago	000	100	01x—2

x—Two outs in the ninth inning when the game was forfeited to Cleveland

2B—Fewster, Sheely, Spurgeon. DP—Chicago 1, Cleveland 4. E—Davis, Collins, Stephenson, Goode. Umpires—Evans, Rowland, Hildebrand. Time—2:12. Attendance—44,000 (est.).

Cleveland	IP	BB	K
Smith (W)	8⅔	1	1

Chicago	IP	BB	K
Thurston (L)	4⅓	1	4
Connally	4⅔	2	5

The Disco Demolition Game (Game 2 Forfeited before Starting)
Detroit at Chicago, July 12, 1979

Detroit	AB	R	H	RBI
LeFlore, cf	5	0	2	0
Whitaker, 2b	4	1	0	0
Staub, dh	3	1	1	0
Thompson, 1b	4	0	0	0
Summers, rf	2	1	2	0
Morales, lf	4	1	2	1
Parrish, c	4	0	1	1
Brookens, 3b	4	0	1	1
Trammell, ss	4	0	0	0
	35	4	9	3

Chicago	AB	R	H	RBI
Bannister, 2b	4	0	1	0
Moore, lf	4	0	1	0
Lemon, cf	3	0	1	0
Johnson, 1b	3	0	0	0
Nordhagen, dh	3	0	0	0
Orta, ph	1	0	0	0
Torres, rf	3	1	1	0
Washington, ph	1	0	0	0
Morrison, 3b	4	0	0	0
Pryor, ss	3	0	1	1
Colbern, c	3	0	0	0
	32	1	5	1

Detroit	111	001	000—4
Chicago	010	000	000—1

2B—Bannister, Pryor, Moore. 3B—Brookens. SB—LeFlore (2), Staub, Morales, Summers. DP—Chicago 2. LOB—Detroit 7, Chicago 6. E—Colbern, Morrison. Time—2:38. Attendance—49,000 (est.).

Detroit	IP	H	R	BB	K
Underwood (W)	7⅔	5	1	2	3
Lopez	1⅓	0	0	0	2

Chicago	IP	H	R	BB	K
Howard (L)	4⅓	6	4	2	3
Farmer	4⅔	3	0	1	1

Rusty Torres Attends Veeck-stock and Other Weird 1970s Baseball Riots

White Sox outfielder Rusty Torres was in the lineup the night of July 12, 1979, for Veeck-stock—otherwise remembered as "Disco Demolition," the hair-brained, ill-conceived, and embarrassing marketing stunt that went awry and resulted in the third "baseball riot" of the lamentable 1970s. Torres, an unspectacular outfielder who played for five different teams from 1971 to 1980, posting a career .212 batting average, provides a remarkable footnote to three sorry affairs: the September 30, 1971, Washington Senators forfeit to the New York Yankees during the last game in franchise history before the team moved down to Texas; the Cleveland "10-Cent Beer Riot" on June 4, 1974—also a forfeit resulting from a stupid marketing promotion; and our own moment of shame, Disco Demolition. Torres was in the ballpark and in the lineup for *all three games.* As a rookie in 1971, he hit a home run for the Yankees in the final-game fiasco; and he was stationed in right field during the Sox's 4–1 loss to the Tigers prior to Steve Dahl's Disco Demolition stunt, which was the featured between-games attraction of the scheduled doubleheader.

Coming nearly 10 years after Woodstock, the celebrated 1969 "Aquarian Exposition," Disco Demolition was an ugly reflection of the excesses of the so-called "Me Decade." Bill Veeck and his front-office team had promised a 96¢ admission to the park to witness the destruction of a pile of disco records by deejay Dahl. However, Veeck, the old showman, failed to anticipate the response as 50,000 teenagers jammed their way in—climbing over the security fence behind the left-field walls and rudely shoving aside ushers and security blocking their way. "We were trying to hold the main gate closed," said one usher. "But the kids forced it open, and the ushers got beat up. We just couldn't control them." Lieutenant Robert Reilly of the Chicago Police said, "It's as bad as the night the Beatles were here."

Surveying his destroyed baseball field hours later, a stunned and disheartened Bill Veeck could only mumble, "These weren't real baseball fans. All I know is, we'll make certain we don't try anything like this again. I was amazed. I wish I wasn't." Russ James of WLUP Radio, the event sponsor, was amazed at Veeck's cupidity. "Tonight was like the Toyota commercial," he said. "You asked for it, you got it. What did Veeck expect? He sanctioned this." Indeed he did. As for Rusty Torres, the Sox 1979 player union representative who went 1-for-3 and committed a base-running gaffe that cost him a double in the second inning, the journeyman outfielder took his third riot of the decade in stride: "This wasn't as bad. In Cleveland they were throwing lighters and bottles." Days after the Disco Demolition disaster, White Sox head groundskeeper Gene Bossard discovered to his horror marijuana plants sprouting in center field. Disco rioters had planted seeds of the evil weed in the same patch of grass where Chet Lemon patrolled!

The Bare Essentials: April 5, 1974

Opening Day in frigid Comiskey Park pitted Wilbur Wood against Nolan Ryan of the California Angels. A frozen crowd of 30,041 spectators who braved 35-degree temperatures and a brisk wind howling off Lake Michigan were treated to the added attraction of streakers at the old ballpark. The fun began in the upper deck when several young ladies, emboldened by too many Falstaff beers, shed their brassieres. Then a young man, wearing nothing more than a red White Sox batting helmet, "streaked" across left field. He completed several ballet leaps and lunges before off-duty Chicago police officers could haul him away to the 35th Street lockup. Manager Chuck Tanner, who was not at all pleased with his team's 8–2 drubbing at the hands of the "Ryan Express," said of the streaker, "I wasn't impressed."

More Bare Essentials—X-Rated Antics out at Second Base

The late *Tribune* columnist David Condon—the man who invented the "Curse of the Billy Goat" to explain away the historic misfortunes of Chicago's North Side ballclub—called this next Sox yarn one of his "thrills to remember." It happened in 1950 when "Honest" Jack Onslow, a grim, humorless, old cuss saddled with a terrible ballclub, was calling the shots from the 35th Street dugout. Onslow had vented great disdain to general manager Frank Lane about the candlepower of the lighting system at old Comiskey Park. His boys weren't picking up the ball very well during night games, and in his opinion poor illumination was the main reason for the team's erratic fielding. According to Condon, who was covering the beat in 1950, Onslow said the Comiskey Park illumination was "horseshit."

Lane defended the park lighting and demanded that Onslow prove his point, so, on an off-night, the park engineer was summoned to pull the light switch in what was presumably an empty Comiskey Park. From up in the press box, the lights snapped on, and the old park was aglow. But at that inopportune moment, Onslow nearly swallowed his tobacco chaw as the manager and the GM gaped at an incredible exhibition that Dave Condon euphemistically described as "coeducational calisthenics." A White Sox player who shall go nameless was engaged in sex with his girlfriend out at second base—tossing up the dust on the same spot where, on most other evenings, Nellie Fox routinely fielded ground balls. Needless to say, this was one episode that never made it into the season highlight reel.

A Reporter's Combat Duty at Comiskey

From the moment he donned the headphones as Harry Caray's sidekick in the radio and TV broadcast booth, Jimmy Piersall boiled in a pot of hot water of his own making. Piersall's troubles stemmed from the fact that he simply couldn't control himself. His private thoughts spewed out of his mouth like hot lava.

The outspoken and refreshingly honest commentator, who had tried to sabotage the center-field scoreboard in his playing days, once described White Sox players' wives as "horny broads that wanted to get married, and they wanted a little money, a little security, and a big strong ballplayer. I traveled. I played. I got a load of those broads, too." Those offhand remarks delivered on a local TV talk show cost Jimmy his job in 1981.

A year earlier—on July 2, 1980, to be exact—Piersall had stalked into the White Sox clubhouse in search of Rob Gallas, a baseball beat writer who had covered the team for the *Daily Herald,* a northwest suburban newspaper, since 1976. Piersall was angered by the reporter's secondhand speculation as to why Bill Veeck had relieved him of his part-time coaching duties. "If you have something to ask me, ask me!" ranted Piersall, moments before he grabbed Gallas around the neck and began choking him.

Fortunately the players were able to separate Piersall from his intended victim before he could inflict serious bodily harm. Later, several unnamed White Sox players covered Piersall's locker with masking tape and a copy of a *Chicago Sun-Times* poster asking readers to decide Jimmy's fate in a fan poll. The players left no room for doubt as to where they stood on the issue.

The Sox players taped Jimmy Piersall's locker after he tried to strangle reporter Rob Gallas.

Piersall was suspended from his broadcast duties for two weeks, but an emotional outpouring of cards and letters showing support for the embattled announcer forced Bill Veeck to reinstate him on July 15, after the radio station determined he was fit to return to work.

Rob Gallas, meanwhile, retired from the newspaper business in the mid-1980s. He was hired by the White Sox in September 1989 as vice president of marketing and broadcasting. Since then, Gallas has received much of the credit for the team's remarkable resurgence in the early 1990s through imaginative promotions like "Turn Back the Clock Day," a tribute to baseball's Negro Leagues, White Sox Day at the Taste of Chicago Festival, and far greater exposure in the local media than the team had become accustomed to in the 1970s.

The Seven-Hour Rain Delay

A daylong downpour in Chicago triggered a nasty battle of wills between the White Sox and Texas Rangers on August 12, 1990. The Sox were scheduled to play the concluding game of a three-game set at the new Comiskey Park when the weatherman intervened. Because the Rangers refused to return to Chicago to play a makeup game later in the week, Jerry Reinsdorf, general manager Larry Himes, and manager Jeff Torborg decided to wait out the rain delay rather than face the prospect of playing a doubleheader in Arlington, Texas.

The game was scheduled to begin at 1:35 PM, but it wasn't until 8:58—seven hours and 23 minutes later—that the ball-club relented and allowed the disgruntled umpiring crew headed by Larry Barnett to call the game off. "Whoever was responsible for this should be slapped," complained Jack Daugherty of the Rangers. "They're all jerks," chimed in Julio Franco, who would don the White Sox pinstripes as a free agent in 1994.

The makeup game was played five days later at Arlington Stadium. The Sox divided the doubleheader, losing the first game 1–0 in 13 innings, but capturing the nightcap 4–2.

The seven-hour rain delay is believed to be the longest in major league history.

From the American League to the Humane League

In the heat of the 1960 pennant chase, general manager Hank Greenberg acquired journeyman relief pitcher Al Worthington from the Minneapolis Millers. A deeply religious man who answered his calling after attending a Billy Graham rally in 1958, Worthington was dropped from the Giants roster after protesting the dishonesty of sign stealing. On religious grounds, he boldly informed his manager Bill Rigney that such larceny was cheating and an affront to God. As a member of the White Sox two years later, he made an impressive debut: a win and a save in his first week with the club. But one night he overheard his teammates discussing sign stealing. In a Kansas City hotel lobby, Worthington voiced his objections to manager Al Lopez, who said: "Show me the rule books where it's wrong." The troubled pitcher went to Greenberg and told him that he "couldn't play for a team that's cheating. How can I be a follower of Christ and go along with something that's dishonest?" Greenberg thought for a moment and replied: "Baseball is a game where you try to get away with anything you can." Worthington shook his head, packed his bags and went home to Birmingham, Alabama, mindful that jumping a ballclub could mean permanent banishment. "I was scared," he admitted. The next year he was given a second chance and assigned to the White Sox minor league affiliate in San Diego. In 1962 the new Sox general manager Ed Short tried to sell him to the talent-poor Mets and Colt .45s, but they were more interested in escaping the National League cellar than receiving their salvation. In 1963 Al was given another chance by the Reds. He played another six years, and he did his best work for the Twins in the late 1960s. This humble man of the cloth is a retired lay preacher in his home state of Alabama, still spreading the good word among fans, players, and the townspeople of Sterrett. Said the late Rogers Hornsby: "Worthington should be pitching in the Humane League."

Trivia, Tidbits, Oddities, Records, Historical Firsts, and Little-Known Facts

- Infielder Frank Shugarts stroked the very first White Sox home run off Detroit Tigers pitcher Frank Owen. The shot came in the fifth inning of the fifth game of the 1901 season, played at the South Side Grounds on April 29. Pitcher John Skopec hit the second roundtripper for the infant White Stockings the next afternoon.
- The first home run in old Comiskey Park was a grand-slam shot, hit by infielder Lee Tannehill off Tigers pitcher Wild Bill Donovan on July 31, 1910. The ball touched down in fair territory and rolled through a small picket fence separating the left-field pavilion from the third base grandstand. It was a freak home run that would only be a ground-rule double under modern-day scoring rules.
- The first home run in new Comiskey Park again involved the team from Detroit. Cecil Fielder connected off Jack McDowell in the third inning of the first game, April 18, 1991. The first White Sox home run was a fifth-inning shot by Frank Thomas against the Baltimore Orioles on April 22.
- Lena Blackburne, a utility infielder for the White Sox in 1910, collected the first White Sox hit in the inaugural game at Comiskey Park. He would take over as manager of the ballclub in 1928.
- Ed Walsh pitched the first shutout in old Comiskey Park, a 4–0 whitewashing of the Washington Senators on August 7, 1910. Jack McDowell blanked the Seattle Mariners 4–0 on

Spring training flooding in West Baden, Indiana, 1943

June 25, 1991, for the first White Sox shutout in the new Comiskey Park. McDowell carried a no-hitter into the eighth inning.

- John "Blondy" Ryan, an infielder out of Holy Cross College, became the first player in team history to hit a home run in his first major league at bat—a solo shot delivered against the Philadelphia A's at Comiskey Park on July 17, 1930.
- The White Sox were the first team to lead off a game with two home runs in the first inning, when Louis "Boze" Berger and Mike Kreevich turned the trick against Boston Red Sox pitcher Johnny Marcum on September 2, 1937, at Comiskey Park. The Sox of White downed Boston 4–2.
- In the 25 City Series played between the Sox and Cubs from 1904 to 1942, the Hose held a commanding 18–6–1 advantage. In recent years, the Sox have continued the domination of their North Side rivals by posting an 8–0–2 record in the Crosstown Classic Series, with two ties over an 11-year period (1985–95).
- The White Sox established a team record for most stolen bases in a game when they pilfered 11 against the Browns at Comiskey Park on July 2, 1909. The base thieves included Dave Altizer, Patsy Dougherty (two), Freddy Parent, Barney Reilly, Eddie Hahn, Jackie Atz, Ed Walsh, and Billy Purtell (three).
- The all *K* infield of the 1946 White Sox included Bob Kennedy (3B), Don Kolloway (2B), Joe Kuhel (1B), and Casimir Kwietniewski (SS), who later changed his name to the more familiar Cass Michaels.
- During his illustrious 23-year career, Ted Lyons contributed to Babe Ruth's 1927 home run record *and* Joe DiMaggio's 56-game hitting streak in 1941.
- Old Comiskey Park was the last standing ballpark in America where the immortal Cy Young once pitched. Less than a year before calling it quits, Cy Young was defeated by the Sox 4–0 in Comiskey on June 25, 1910—his final decision against Chicago.
- The White Sox and the Washington Senators share the AL record for fewest errors in one game. Both clubs battled through a grueling six-hour-38-minute, 22-inning marathon at Griffith Stadium on June 12, 1967, without either team committing an error. The Sox lost the game 6–5, prompting an angry Eddie Stanky to demand implementation of a league curfew. The club was drained both mentally and physically. The game-time temperature was 90 degrees.
- Hall of Fame catcher Ray Schalk once picked three Cleveland runners off first base in one inning: Charlie Jamieson, Joe Wood, and Elmer Smith. The game was played in Chicago on September 30, 1921, but the Sox lost, anyway, by a 3–2 score.
- On September 10, 1977, Wilbur Wood tied an AL record by beaning three successive California Angels batters to start a game.
- The 1934 White Sox played the entire season without using one left-handed pitcher. They also lost 99 games that year and finished dead last.
- The millionaire changed his will. He also bought a professional baseball team named the Chicago White Sox...only to die suddenly. And then a shocked world discovered that he had willed his entire fortune, including the White Sox, to Soviet Russia. So begins *Sun-Times* columnist Paul Malloy's acclaimed 1964 novel *A Pennant for the Kremlin.*
- The first twinight doubleheader ever played in Comiskey Park was won by the White Sox, 7–5 and 7–2, over the hated New York Yankees before 27,553 paying customers on July 29, 1942. The wartime promotion became a popular Comiskey attraction in the next three decades.
- On August 14, 1910, a month after the inaugural game in Comiskey Park, 32,498 fans paid their way in to watch the Sox split a doubleheader with the New York Highlanders. At the time it was one of the largest crowds to witness a baseball game in Chicago, and it was also the first White Sox sellout in their new ballpark.
- Prior to a June 19, 1977, encounter with Oakland, first baseman Lamar Johnson sang the National Anthem, then clouted two home runs to beat the A's 2–1. Johnson's three hits were the only ones collected by White Sox batters all afternoon.
- In the 12th inning of a tie game with the Philadelphia A's on August 22, 1923, Sox pitcher Hollis "Sloppy" Thurston struck out three batters on nine pitches. However, he lost the game to Ed Rommel in the 13th inning, 3–2.
- Sherm Lollar and Frank Baumann became only the third pitcher-catcher duo in baseball history to hit back-to-back home runs. Pitcher Baumann and catcher Lollar accomplished this feat against the Yankees in Chicago on July 13, 1961, but the Sox lost the game 6–2. Jim Hegan and Gene Bearden of the Indians had last done it in 1948.
- In a game played at Comiskey Park on June 9, 1947, an angry fan held up play for nearly an hour while he argued a point with an umpire. The Sox went on to defeat the Yankees 9–8 in 10 innings.
- "Marvelous" Marv Rotblatt, a footnote player in Sox history, enjoys the distinction of being the first relief pitcher to be driven to the mound from the center-field bullpen in an automobile. Marv was chauffeured to the Comiskey Park pitcher's mound in style on June 7, 1951. In the 1960s the "Tee-Birdie" golf cart was the preferred mode of transportation from the bullpen.
- During World War II, several fund-raising games were played at Comiskey Park. The first of the war relief games took place on July 1, 1942, between the sailors of Great Lakes against the army team from Chanute Field. The

Comiskey family raised $33,352, which was donated to the armed forces.

- White Sox fan promotions 1901 style: Railway Day for the passenger train workers (July 27), National Union Day (August 3), and Ladies Day (every Wednesday).

- A baseball superstition: Jimmie Dykes was in the habit of collecting hairpins. For every base hit, Dykes threw away one hairpin.

- White Sox slugger Al Simmons garnered 346,291 votes in fan balloting to select the starting nine for baseball's first All-Star Game, played in Chicago on July 6, 1933. Simmons outdistanced Babe Ruth by 26,000 votes.

- Entering the 1995 season, Tim "Rock" Raines was only three stolen bases shy of equaling the American League record for consecutive steals held by Willie Wilson of the Kansas City Royals and Julio Cruz of the Seattle Mariners. Tim's 29 straight steals dated back to 1993. He shattered the old mark on July 18, 1995, in New York and ran the string to 40 before he was nabbed by Toronto catcher Randy Knorr on September 2.

- On August 31, 1993, in New York, Tim Raines became only the second White Sox player to homer from both sides of the plate in the same game. Outfielder Ken Henderson was the first. He connected off of Baltimore left-hander Ross Grimsley and right-hander Wayne Garland on August 29, 1975, in (where else?) Memorial Stadium.

- In their first four years of occupancy at the new Comiskey Park (1991–94), the White Sox drew 9,893,799 fans. The Sox drew their 10 millionth fan on May 8, 1995, in a game against Minnesota. The 10 millionth fan was 11-year-old Dennis Smith of Orland Park, Illinois.

- The White Sox scored in every inning of a 12–8 victory over the Boston Red Sox played at Comiskey Park on May 11, 1949. Chicago scored solo runs in the first, second, fourth, sixth, and seventh; two runs in the third and fifth; and three runs in the eighth. A crowd of only 3,023 witnessed the unusual game, won by Bill Wight.

- Doc White, overlooked and forgotten by the Hall of Fame Veterans Committee, posted the most consecutive seasons of double-figure wins by a Sox pitcher—nine—from 1903 to 1911.

- White Sox pitching staffs have recorded 20-win seasons 49 times during franchise history. They are second only to the Cleveland Indians, who have posted 55.

- The hard-hitting trio of Zeke Bonura (138), Jackie Hayes (84), and Luke Appling (128) combined for 350 RBIs in 1935, the most in franchise history by three players.

- Sox outfielder Taft Wright holds the team record for consecutive games registering an RBI. Taffy collected RBIs in 13 straight games from May 4 to 20, 1941.

- Edgar Smith surrendered the 55th hit—a double—to Joe DiMaggio as he continued his record-setting 56-game hitting streak on July 15, 1941, at Comiskey Park. Exactly two months earlier on May 15, Smith yielded the first hit to the "Yankee Clipper" in a game played in New York.

- The White Sox denied Lefty Grove his 300th career victory on July 18, 1941, when Luke Appling's 10th-inning single drove in Bill Knickerbocker with the winning run. Sox 4, Boston 3.

- Richard Dotson is tied with Jim Scott for most victories by a Sox pitcher under the age of 25. Both men won 56 games before reaching the quarter-century mark.

- First baseman John "Bud" Clancy played an entire nine-inning game in St. Louis on April 27, 1930, without recording a putout or assist. He shares the record with Oakland's Gene Tenace. More importantly, the Sox won the game 2–1.

- The White Sox Boys' Camp, located 15 miles north of Fond du Lac, Wisconsin, on picturesque Lake Winnebago, officially opened for business on June 28, 1964, for young men aged 10 to 16. Conceived by White Sox farm director Glen C. Miller in 1962 and financed with $225,000 of Arthur Allyn's money, the camp was an instant hit with Chicago area families and then faded away in the mid-1970s—a casualty of changing popular tastes. Radio sportscaster Bill Motluck, who was lucky enough to attend one of the summer sessions, recalls that the highlight of the camp was the annual batting clinic held by one of the Sox players—usually Dave Nicholson. It is curious that Nicholson should have been designated for this important assignment, since he holds the club record for strikeouts in a season—175.

- In direct violation of a 1794 Philadelphia statute, the White Sox and A's played the first Sunday game in that city's long history on August 22, 1926. Lefty Grove prevailed for Philadelphia in a 3–2 decision. To add insult to injury, the Philadelphia police attempted to arrest players from both teams before the proper injunction could be filed.

- Unofficially, the White Sox have worn 41 different home and road uniforms since 1901.

- When Joe Cowley struck out the first seven Texas Rangers batters he faced in a game played at Arlington Stadium on May 28, 1986, he broke a long-standing team record shared by Jim Scott and Howard Kolls Judson, the luckless right-hander who lost 14 straight games in 1949. Scott fanned six straight batters in a 2–0 loss to the St. Louis Browns on June 22, 1913. Judson fared no better on August 27, 1949, when he struck out six consecutive hitters but still lost the game to the Red Sox 7–2.

- Even though it is not listed in official American League records, Winford Kellum pitched the first American League no-hitter on June 16, 1900. The Indianapolis pitcher defeated the Sox 16–0.

- Jungle Jim Rivera wowed a $12.50-a-head audience at the 1958 Chicago Baseball Writers' Dinner by showing up

Bud Clancy

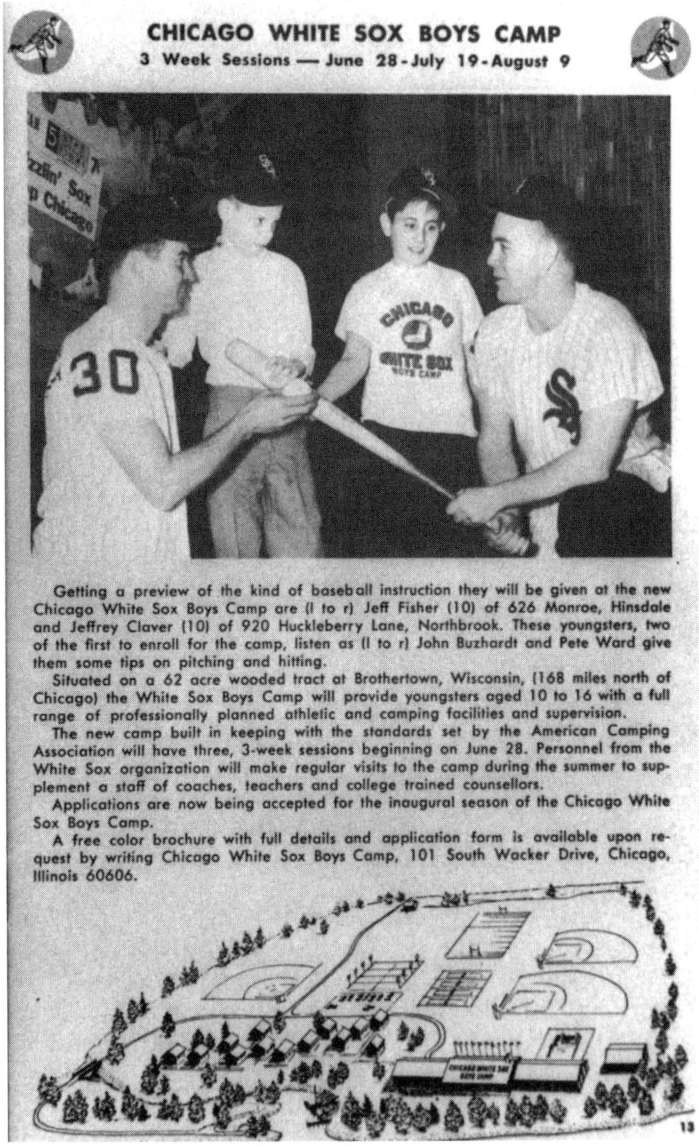

CHICAGO WHITE SOX BOYS CAMP

3 Week Sessions — June 28 - July 19 - August 9

Getting a preview of the kind of baseball instruction they will be given at the new Chicago White Sox Boys Camp are (l to r) Jeff Fisher (10) of 626 Monroe, Hinsdale and Jeffrey Claver (10) of 920 Huckleberry Lane, Northbrook. These youngsters, two of the first to enroll for the camp, listen as (l to r) John Buzhardt and Pete Ward give them some tips on pitching and hitting.

Situated on a 62 acre wooded tract at Brothertown, Wisconsin, (168 miles north of Chicago) the White Sox Boys Camp will provide youngsters aged 10 to 16 with a full range of professionally planned athletic and camping facilities and supervision.

The new camp built in keeping with the standards set by the American Camping Association will have three, 3-week sessions beginning on June 28. Personnel from the White Sox organization will make regular visits to the camp during the summer to supplement a staff of coaches, teachers and college trained counsellors.

Applications are now being accepted for the inaugural season of the Chicago White Sox Boys Camp.

A free color brochure with full details and application form is available upon request by writing Chicago White Sox Boys Camp, 101 South Wacker Drive, Chicago, Illinois 60606.

13

1964 Advertisement for the Sox Boys' Camp

in ambassadorial raiment, including a 12-inch cigar and phony diamond stick pin.

- Soft-spoken Bill Barrett began his career as a shortstop but was a defensive liability and had to switch to the outfield. On May 1, 1924, at Cleveland, Barrett stole home twice in the same game—once in the first inning and again in the ninth.
- Ed Walsh is tied with Roy Patterson for the club lead for most pitching records, but Patterson attained his marks because he was the first Sox pitcher to remain with the club for seven seasons.
- The White Sox established an unusual American League record on July 1, 1962, when pitcher Juan Pizarro, second baseman Nellie Fox, and left fielder Al Smith stroked three consecutive sacrifice flies in the fifth inning of the second game of a doubleheader against the Cleveland Indians, won by the Sox by a 7–6 score.
- Nellie Fox played in all 154 games for seven consecutive years (1953–59). The dynamo of the 1959 AL champions was the toughest American League hitter to fan for 11 years running—1951–62. Nellie collected his 2,000th career hit at Yankee Stadium on July 24, 1960, before 60,002 fans in a 6–3 Sox victory.
- Robin Ventura became only the 11th third baseman since 1945 to register 90 or more RBIs in three or more consecutive seasons (1991–93). Ron Santo heads the list (1963–70).
- A crowd of 52,712 fans jammed old Comiskey Park on June 25, 1964, to watch the White Sox crush the Cubs 11–1 in the annual Boys' Benefit Game played for charity. It marked the last time that Chicago fans were permitted to stand in roped-off sections of the outfield playing areas while a game was in progress.
- Don Rudolph, a 20-game *loser* in the American Association shortly before the White Sox called him up to the big leagues in September 1957, was married to an exotic dancer. The comely Mrs. Rudolph's stage name was "Patti Waggin."
- Playing in Yankee Stadium on September 22, 1966, Joel Horlen and the White Sox downed the Bronx Bombers 4–1. More significantly, only 413 fans paid their way in. It is believed to be the smallest crowd ever to attend a game at the House That Ruth Built.
- The White Sox helped inaugurate major league baseball in three different cities by providing the opening-day opposition in Baltimore (1954), Seattle (1969), and Toronto

Luckless Howie Judson

(1977). The Sox graciously dropped all three games by scores of 3–1, 7–0, and 9–5. On the other hand they gave the Browns a proper sendoff by sweeping the last three American League games played in St. Louis, September 25–27, 1953.

- First baseman Jim Spencer was the first Sox player to drive in eight runs in one game *twice* in the same season. The slick-fielding Spencer collected eight RBIs in an 18–2 drubbing administered to the Cleveland Indians on McDonald's Breakfast Day, May 14, 1977. He duplicated the feat on July 2 against the Minnesota Twins in a 13–8 shootout that temporarily thrust the Sox into first place.
- Steve Kealey was the last White Sox pitcher to hit a home run before implementation of the designated hitter rule in 1973. Kealey connected against Ray Corbin of the Minnesota Twins at Comiskey Park on September 6, 1971. Kealey's upper-deck, three-run shot, coming in the eighth inning, won the game for Bart Johnson. It was the last time a Sox pitcher hit a home run in a regular season game.
- Mike Andrews was the first White Sox designated hitter under the new system that went into effect in 1973. Andrews batted sixth in the opening-day lineup when the Sox squared off against the Texas Rangers on April 7, 1973.
- The White Sox pulled off a rare triple steal in Boston on June 3, 1943, when Joe Kuhel, Luke Appling, and Don Kolloway victimized the Red Sox in the ninth inning.
- Branch Rickey, the Hall of Fame baseball executive who introduced the "chain store" farm system to baseball and helped shatter the color barrier by signing Jackie Robinson to a Dodgers contract, was once White Sox property. A catcher by trade, Rickey was drafted from the Dallas club of the Texas League in 1905. He was traded to the St. Louis Browns for catcher Frank Roth before he played a game in Chicago. Rickey's career spanned 119 games. His lifetime batting average was .239.
- Who *was* on third? A roll call of White Sox third basemen from 1957 until Robin Ventura's arrival in 1989: (1) Fred Hatfield, (2) Sammy Esposito, (3) Billy Goodman, (4) Bubba Phillips, (5) Al Smith, (6) Gene Freese, (7) Andy Carey, (8) J. C. Martin, (9) Charlie Smith, (10) Bob Sadowski, (11) Pete Ward, (12) Don Buford, (13) Ken Boyer, (14) Dick Kenworthy, (15) Ron Hansen, (16) Bill Melton, (17) Rich Morales, (18) Dick Allen, (19) Walt Williams, (20) Ed Spiezio, (21) Bee-Bee Richard, (22) Ron Santo, (23) Luis Alvarado, (24) Mike Andrews, (25) Jorge Orta, (26) Bill Stein, (27) Kevin Bell, (28) Eric Soderholm,

Steve Kealey

Jim Rivera models "Sox Shorts."

(29) Greg Pryor, (30) Jim Morrison, (31) Fran Mullins, (32) Junior Moore, (33) Lorenzo Gray, (34) Aurelio Rodriguez, (35) Vance Law, (36) Tim Hulett, (37) Mike Squires, (38) Jerry Dybzinski, (39) Tom O'Malley, (40) Roy Smalley, (41) Luis Salazar, (42) Russ Morman, (43) Steve Lyons, (44) Dave Cochrane, (45) Donnie Hill, (46) Kenny Williams, (47) Fred Manrique, (48) Eddie Williams, (49) Carlos Martinez, (50) Tracy Woodson, and (51) Carlton Fisk.

- Rookie third baseman Russ Morman logged three hits in his first three major league at-bats following his call-up from the minors on August 3, 1986. Morman tied Billy Martin's major league record by collecting two hits in one inning in his debut. Russ led off the fourth inning with a home run and later followed it up with a single in a 10–1 rout of the Detroit Tigers. The Martin record had stood since April 18, 1950, but was equaled a second time by Sox rookie infielder Greg Norton, who collected two hits in the ninth inning of his debut game on August 9, 1996, in Detroit.
- Among Dick Allen's breathtaking 37 home runs in 1972 were a pair of inside-the-park jobs against the Minnesota Twins on July 31 at Metropolitan Stadium. Allen connected off Twins ace Bert Blyleven in the first and fifth innings. Both homers traveled to the base of the center-field wall. For the day, the "Big Bopper" accounted for five runs batted in, in an 8–1 Sox victory.
- Bill Veeck introduced "Sox shorts" to the baseball world in July 1976, just in time for America's bicentennial celebration. The players expressed the usual "What is this goofy guy going to do next?" reaction to Veeck's latest promotional gimmick. "They don't have to get a pair for me," quipped Bart Johnson. "I'll just use Jack Brohamer's regular pants, and they'll look like shorts." Brohamer chimed in: "I don't think what Bart said is very funny. I'm not going to wear short pants unless they let me wear a halter top, too."
- The cost of a full season ticket to 77 White Sox games in 1953 was $157.50. General admission prices that year were $1.25. Bleacher seats could be purchased for 60 cents apiece.
- The 1979 White Sox established an unofficial record with an all-left-handed pitching rotation: Ken Kravec (15–13), Rich Wortham (14–14), Ross Baumgarten (13–8), and Steve Trout (11–8).
- After the Sox committed 21 errors in the first six games of the 1995 season, the fans had to be asking themselves if there had ever been a sorrier exhibition of fielding by a White Sox ballclub. Take heart, Sox fans. The 1903 ballclub committed a ghastly 297 errors, including 12 in one game. The shabbily played contest took place in Detroit on May 5, 1903. "Truth to tell, it was not a ballgame," the *Tribune* reported. "In fact it was nothing more than a comedy of errors." Despite the 12 errors, the Sox pulled a 10–9 victory out of the fire because the Tigers were just as bad in the field. They committed six errors and lost the game in the ninth inning because of "some of the wildest and weirdest fielding ever perpetrated on any diamond."
- Sox third baseman Billy Purtell was the first major leaguer to strike out twice in the same inning. Purtell went down against the mighty Walter Johnson in the sixth inning of a 10–3 victory over the Senators at the 39th Street Grounds on May 10, 1910. The Sox batted around against the Washington speed-baller, and Billy's two Ks were lost in the euphoria. It wasn't often that Sox hitters swatted Walter Johnson around the park.
- Jim Derrington was only 16 years old when he took the mound in Kansas City to begin his major league career on the last day of the 1956 season. The teenaged left-hander, signed to a sizable bonus contract by Hollis Thurston and Doc Bennett, lasted only 21 innings in the big leagues. Career record: 0–2. He was the youngest player to ever appear in a Sox uniform.
- Five White Sox pitchers claimed victory in baseball's annual All-Star Game. Edgar Smith won the 1941 midseason

classic at Detroit. Early Wynn won in Baltimore in 1958. Ray Herbert pitched three scoreless innings in the second 1962 game played at Wrigley Field to knock down a victory, and Jack McDowell came away with a win in the 1993 game at Baltimore. James Baldwin won in 2000.

- In 1994 Frank Thomas became the 52nd multiple Most Valuable Player award winner in the history of the four major sports—baseball, basketball, football, and hockey. Only five other professional athletes have won three or more consecutive MVP awards, but no one in baseball…yet.

- Albert Belle stirred many controversies in his brief two-year stint with the White Sox, but there was no denying the man could hit. Over a seven-day period, July 9–17, 1998, Belle smacked nine home runs, joining Frank Howard, Shawn Green, Babe Ruth, Hank Greenberg, Sammy Sosa, and Barry Bonds as the only players to accomplish this rare feat.

- John L. Sullivan headed the Comiskey Park police detail for 14 event-filled seasons. This former Chicago Police lieutenant accepted a White Sox retirement job in 1948 and held on to it for the next 14 years. The great John L. never transcribed his memoirs, and that's too bad. By the time he retired in 1962, he had collected enough anecdotes, memories, folklore, and colorful stories to fill a volume. One of his favorite recollections involved a well-known city pickpocket who declared his love for the White Sox and merely desired to gain admittance to the 1959 World Series. "He promised to wear boxing gloves if we let him into the games," Sullivan remembered. "We obliged." On another occasion, Sullivan dragged a drunken Sox fan off of the field after the man interrupted the game with a show-stopping head-first slide into second base. "The judge fined him $10 and said, 'I'm a Sox fan myself. It'd be $100 and costs if this had happened at the Cubs.'"

- A sad ending for a former White Sox great. On July 4, 1933, James J. Callahan, deadball era pitcher/outfielder, ex-manager, and, in retirement, the president of the Logan Squares semipro team in Chicago, was arrested by the police at his home on Kenwood Avenue after he smashed the windows of his residence with a cane. When the cops showed up, the 59-year-old Callahan warned them to come no closer. He said that he "had them covered." The Chicago Police lobbed tear-gas canisters into the house, forcing the alcoholic ex–Sox manager out into the street. He explained that he had "been drinking too much," an affliction he had suffered since his earliest playing days on the South Side. Callahan, something of a prodigal son to the Old Roman, died less than 15 months after this embarrassing incident.

- Mario Valdez and Jeff Abbott, two White Sox rookie hopefuls, hit their first career home runs in the same game on September 15, 1997. Valdez connected off of Milwaukee Brewers right-hander (and future Sox) Cal Eldred in the fifth. Abbott followed up with a two-run blast in the sixth. The only other time in White Sox history that a pair of rookies touched all bases in the same game was back on July 6, 1912, when outfielder Wally Mattick and infielder George "Buck" Weaver went deep against the Detroit Tigers in old Comiskey Park.

- McCuddy's Tap is gone now, but its beer-soaked walls will never be forgotten by generations of fans who passed through its doors to drink their Meister Brau and feast on "Ma" Frances McCuddy's hot dogs and burgers. If it is true that our most important history happened in the everyday kinds of places, then the squat little saloon standing opposite Comiskey Park at 247 West 35th Street from 1910 until 1989 is as important an icon of South Side baseball as Luke Appling or Billy Pierce. The Old Roman, Charles Comiskey, was a friend of Johnny McCuddy, who operated a saloon on 39th Street near old St. George Parish and the South Side Grounds. In 1909 Comiskey tipped off his pal. He let him know he intended to move the club four blocks north into a new stadium bearing his name. McCuddy heeded the advice and opened his second public house bearing the family name. Johnny was a member in good stead of Comiskey's Woodland Bards social group and, in fact, was a founding member of the famed dining and drinking club. Broken-hearted by the Black Sox scandal, Johnny passed away on September 4, 1921. But the family carried on as best they could over the next 68 years, with daughter Frances running the kitchen and keeping an eye on all of the big lugs, like Babe Ruth, who was in the habit of crossing 35th Street for a between-innings quaff of the suds (true story). In 1963 Luke Sanfilippo opened a new establishment next door. He christened the place "Danny O'Brien's," figuring that an Irish trade name was good for business in old Bridgeport, the historic settlement for the sons and daughters of Erin. Frances McCuddy didn't mind the competition. She couldn't possibly shoehorn all of the thirsty fans into her little taproom if she tried. With the building of U.S. Cellular Field (née: Comiskey Park II), the two Comiskeyville sample rooms were forced to close their doors, despite a valiant but failed attempt on the part of Governor James R. Thompson to rescue McCuddy's from its date with the wrecker's ball. The governor paced up and down the streets of old Bridgeport in his official capacity, trying to find an available acre for Frances and her family to move to, but by his own admission, nothing suitable could be secured near the park. The ghost of the Old Roman in all his glory might have done far better for the McCuddys.

- About that nickname: by now everyone knows that broadcaster Ken Harrelson dubbed Frank Thomas "the Big Hurt"—the Hawk has bestowed endearing nicknames on many players. But where did he come up with Frank's now famous moniker? Likely it is borrowed from the title of a forgotten rock ballad by Miss Toni Fisher, a top 10 nationally charted hit in the spring of 1960, but actually released in December 1959—the year the Sox won the pennant. With lyrics by Wayne Shanklin, "The Big Hurt" was Miss Toni's biggest and most memorable hit recording.

- A crazy publicity stunt not even Bill Veeck could top: on May 11, 1925, future Hall of Famer Ray "Cracker" Schalk caught a baseball dropped from the top of the new Tribune Tower—a drop of over 460 feet. The ball had the velocity of a cannon shot by the time it settled in Ray's glove on Michigan Avenue. Three balls were flung off of the suspended scaffold before Schalk snared one, much to the delight of an estimated ten thousand spectators who lined the boulevard. Traffic was suspended for more than 20 minutes. What was the point to all of this? In 1910 Billy Sullivan, another famous White Sox catcher, snagged a ball dropped from the top of the Washington Monument—550 feet up—just to see if it could be done, of course.

- A remarkable season in so many ways. After recording their third eight-game winning streak of the championship season, from June 15 to 24, 2005, the White Sox became one of only five teams in the major leagues since 1900 to accomplish the rare feat before July 1. They share the record with the 2001 Seattle Mariners, the 1998 New York Yankees, the 1978 Boston Red Sox, and the 1912 New York Giants.

- Ex-Sox Mike Cameron was a one-man wrecking crew as he and his Mariners teammates exacted vengeance upon the South Siders for the 1998 trade that sent him to Cincinnati for Paul Konerko. On May 2, 2002, the M's routed the White Sox by a score of 15–4, while Cameron became only the 13th player in baseball history to slug four home runs in a single game, all of them solo shots. Cameron was struck by a pitch and narrowly missed a fifth homer with a deep fly-ball out to right later in the game. Cameron and Bret Boone became the first teammates in history to hit back-to-back home runs twice in the same inning in Seattle's 10-run first inning. To complete a day of humiliation and misery for the Chicago faithful, another Sox alumnus, James Baldwin, earned the win with seven innings pitched. There had only been 39 previous occasions of a player hitting two home runs in an inning, according to the Elias Sports Bureau. Eric Karros was last to do it on August 22, 2000, for Los Angeles. Mark McGwire was the previous American Leaguer on September 22, 1996, for Oakland. May such a thing never happen again to the White Sox.

- The 2000 White Sox established a new major league record for the most runs scored in the month of April: 181.

- Norton, you're the greatest! On May 14, 1998, Greg Norton became only the fifth player to hit two home runs off of "the Big Unit," Randy Johnson, in one game. He turned the trick in the third and sixth innings in a 5–3 win over the Seattle Mariners in Comiskey Park.

- Seventh sons and the Sox. In a song performed in *The Charlatan*, a long-forgotten, old-time musical from the turn of the last century, there is a little verse that went something like this: "For I am the seventh son of a seventh son; in magic I excel." Old superstitions never completely fade away, and in White Sox history two famous names separated by 50 years—pitcher Guy Harris "Doc" White and manager Al Lopez—were seventh sons of seventh sons. Each played important roles in White Sox championship seasons and supplied the requisite magic in two memorable South Side eras. Lopez, the genial "Señor," lived just long enough to see the White Sox win the 2005 World Series. He passed away just two days later.

- The White Sox were the last visiting team to win a game in old Yankee Stadium before the old barn closed its doors. Gavin Floyd put down the Bombers and Andy Pettite 6–2 on September 16, 2008, before 52,558.

- Did you know? On May 13, 1957, Billy Pierce became the first White Sox player to appear on the cover of *Sports Illustrated.* The caption read: "Pride of Chicago: Billy Pierce."

- Did you know? As of June 2010, the oldest living White Sox player was former outfielder Ralph Hodgin from Greensboro, North Carolina, who was born February 10, 1915. Hodgin played 530 games in his career, all of them with the White Sox, from 1943 to 1948 (he missed 1945). He was a terrific pinch-hitter, but his career was derailed in 1947 after he was beaned on the skull by Hal Newhouser of the Tigers. Ralph suffered a concussion. Later, after baseball, he worked for a Greensboro trucking company for 30 years, rising to terminal manager.

- Sherm Lollar, the great Sox backstop of the 1950s, tied a major league record held by Mel Ott, Frank Chance, and two others on June 8, 1956, by getting hit by the pitcher three times in one game. The pitcher was Willard Nixon of the Boston Red Sox, and to add insult to injury, the White Sox lost the game 5–3 in Fenway.

- It's a family affair. Let it not be said that the White Sox run their operation as anything less than a family-oriented business. The sons of Harold Baines, Ozzie Guillen, Rich Gossage, and Kenny Williams have all passed through the farm system one time or another, but you have to wonder what the front office was *really* thinking when they drafted Carey Schueler, the 18-year-old *daughter* of former White Sox GM Ron Schueler in the 1993 major league draft. Ms. Schueler, a pitcher at Campolindo High School in Moragaica, California, was the 1,208th pick overall that year and the first woman ever selected in the MLB Draft. It was an interesting publicity stunt nevertheless and was good for a laugh or two—but if the White Sox had not wasted the pick they could have landed Frank Menechino, later a starting second basemen with the Oakland A's.

- A great trade…that was never made. According to former Sox manager Jeff Torborg, in an interview with Sox aficionado Mark Liptak just before the 1990 season kicked off, the White Sox passed up on a chance to acquire Bernie Williams and Hal Morris from the Yankees in return for pitcher Eric King, who was through in 1992, and journeyman outfielder Steve "Psycho" Lyons, who called it quits after the 1993 season. How different would the 1990s have been if Bernie Williams, a career .297 hitter who clubbed 287 homers, had patrolled the Sox outfield? But Sox GM Larry Himes said no, and a new Yankees dynasty unfolded.

- In 2006 Jermaine Dye (117 RBIs), Paul Konerko (113 RBIs), and Jim Thome (109 RBIs) became only the second trio of White Sox hitters in a single season to drive in 100-plus runs. A decade earlier, in 1996, Frank Thomas (134), Robin Ventura (105), and Danny Tartabull (101) were the first ever to accomplish this rare feat. Also in '06, Thome (44 homers) and Dye (42) became the first Sox duo—ever—to record 40 or more home runs in a season. The 1990s and 2000s will always be remembered as great home run hitting decades on the South Side.

- The 2000–06 White Sox joined the New York Yankees as one of only two teams in major league history to clout 200 or more home runs in seven consecutive seasons. They fell short of extending the mark in 2007 with "just" 190.

- Back-to-back-to-back-to-back. The homer-happy White Sox achieved another significant long-ball milestone on August 14, 2008, when they became only the sixth team in major league history to drill *four* consecutive home runs in an inning. Jim Thome, Paul Konerko, Alexi Ramirez, and Juan Uribe went deep against the Kansas City Royals in the sixth inning during a 9–2 thumping of their Central Division foes at U.S. Cellular Field. Thome, Konerko, and Ramirez struck their blows against Joel Peralta. Juan Uribe hit his blast off of Robinson Tejada. After four Milwaukee Braves hitters turned the trick for the first time back on June 8, 1961, at Cincinnati, baseball experts predicted that such a rare feat as this could never occur again. But the 1963 Indians, the 1964 Twins, the 2006 Dodgers, and the 2007 Red Sox proved the skeptics wrong before the White Sox "lit up the Royals" at the Cell. Through 2010 the White Sox have poled four home runs (non-consecutive) in one inning six times.

- Three times in team history the Pale Hose swatted two grand-slam home runs in one game: the first coming on September 4, 1995, when Robin Ventura hit both of the grand salamis at the Ballpark in Arlington; then on May 19, 1996, at Detroit, Darren Lewis and Ventura; and for the third time on April 13, 2008, against Detroit, Paul Konerko and Joe Crede.

- The 1956 White Sox set an American League record for most home runs hit by a *pitching staff* with 12. Jack Harshman, a converted first baseman, led the way with six round-trippers that year. Only the 1887 National League White Stocking pitchers (forerunners of the Cubs) had more in one year with 16.

- A home run rarity. When Andruw Jones and Alex Rios slugged walkoff homers to seal back-to-back White Sox victories over Seattle on April 23–24, 2010, at U.S. Cellular Field, it marked the first time since July 25, 1967, when longballs by J.C. Martin and Ken Berry downed the Cleveland Indians in a thrill-packed, old-fashioned twinight doubleheader at Comiskey Park won by the Sox 3–1 and 6–5. The second game was a 16-inning marathon that ended happily at 2:15 AM with Berry's bomb off of the upper-deck façade in left field. By then about 50 people of the original crowd of 18,000-plus were on hand to witness it.

- To the delight of Cubs fans everywhere, the White Sox inflicted a mighty whuppin' on the St. Louis Cardinals June 20–21, 2006. In that remarkable two-game span in U.S. Cellular Field, they scored a cumulative 33 runs (20–6 and 13–5 victories, respectively)—one short of the team record of 34—established by the otherwise light-hitting Go-Go Sox on April 22–23, 1955, when they plated 34 runs against the hapless Kansas City A's (5–3 on the 22nd and 29–6 on the 23rd).

- Greatest defensive team ever? The 2006 edition finished the season with a .9852 fielding percentage, shading the defensive prowess of the '05 World Series champs and their .9848 mark.

- In two separate seasons, 1945 and 1960, four White Sox players were ranked among the top 10 hitters for the year. In 1945 Tony Cuccinello (.308), Johnny Dickshot (.302), Wally Moses (.295), and Oris Hockett (.293) finished second, third, sixth, and eighth, respectively. Fifteen years later, Al Smith (.315), Minnie Minoso (.311), Roy Sievers (.295), and Nellie Fox (.288) duplicated the mark by ending the season ranked second, third, sixth and ninth. To give you an idea how rare this is, it has only happened 23 times in major league history.

- The White Sox are only one of nine teams to start a season 10–0 at home. They did it twice at old Comiskey Park, in 1935 and 1960.

- Indian givers and Tribe takers. Since the early 1950s the White Sox have collected ex–Cleveland Indians players in the same fashion a 10-year-old boy hordes the baseball cards of his favorite team. It is remarkable just how many former Tribesmen have donned the White Sox pinstripes after their time had ended along the shores of Lake Erie. The issue surfaced following the 2010 pickup of former Indians bad boy Manny Ramirez for the September stretch run. It was pointed out that seven of nine key players from the 1999 Cleveland roster had passed through Chicago in the first decade of the new millennium: Ramirez; Sandy Alomar Jr., Roberto Alomar, Omar Vizquel, Jim Thome, Kenny Lofton, Bartolo Colon, and Michael Jackson—and this grouping doesn't even include that other problem child, Albert Belle, from their 1995 World Series team! But the "Tribe Trend" really started way back in 1951 with the arrival of Cleveland rookie Minnie Minoso. Over the next two decades a parade of ex-Indians followed, beginning with Allie Clark, Fred Marsh, and manager Al Lopez. Then came Al Smith, Larry Doby, Early Wynn, Harry "Suitcase" Simpson, Dick Brown, Don Ferrarese, Mike Garcia, Joe Ginsberg, Herb Score, Cal McLish, Don Mossi, Tommy John, Tommie Agee, Don McMahon, Rocky Colavito, Leon Wagner, Woodie Held, and Gary Bell, who followed a well-beaten path into Chicago via the trade route or waiver wire. In the 1970s and 1980s and into the early 1990s, there were many more unforgettable "Sons of Chief Wahoo" who exchanged their feathers for socks: Lee Stange, Floyd Weaver, Vincente Romo, Eddie Leon, Jack Brohamer, Rusty Torres, Ron Pruitt, Jim Kern, Dick Tidrow, Ron Hassey, Dan Spillner, Bryan Clark, Rodney Craig, Jerry Willard, Cory Snyder, and Julio Franco. About the only Cleveland import left to acquire is the goof who bangs on his tom-toms from his left-field perch in Progressive Field.

- White Sox fans all agree that losing to the Minnesota Twins—particularly on the artificial sod of the old Humphrey Metrodome—has been maddening, if not galling. Former Bears head coach Mike Ditka was really on to something when he called the old barn a "Roller Dome." Indeed. But amid years of frustrating encounters with the Twins going back to the pre-1982 days at their old rattle-trap Metropolitan Stadium in suburban Bloomington, Minnesota, the cursed Dome, and finally in Chi-town, there have been a few sanguine moments for us to savor. September 7, 2007, was one of them. In the top of the ninth inning, the Twins sent across six runs to break a 4–4 deadlock at U.S. Cellular Field—many of the Sox faithful were scurrying to the exits at this point. But wait! The good guys in black were not done yet. For the first time in franchise history, the club rallied from a six-run deficit against an opponent in the final frame. They knotted the score at 10–10 to send the game into extra innings, but the contest was significant in one other way. It marked the first time in modern major league history that two teams had scored six runs in the ninth inning when the score was tied, according to the Elias Sports Bureau. The Sox and Minnesota battled on until ex-Twin A.J. Pierzynski drove across the winning run in the 13th inning to make a winner out of rookie pitcher Heath Phillips before what was left of the original 34,104 in attendance at the Cell. Satisfaction *was* guaranteed, ye, who had such little faith.

- The 2008 White Sox achieved a rare baseball milestone by becoming the first team in major league history to play three different opponents on consecutive days and winning all three games to end a season. They took care of business by first shutting down the Cleveland Indians 5–1 behind Mark Buehrle on September 28, downing the Detroit Tigers the next night by an 8–2 count, and wresting away the Central Division crown from the Twins in the thrilling "Blackout Game" behind John Danks' brilliant 1–0 victory on September 30.

- The White Sox were participants in two of the first three Civil Rights Games, paying homage to a historical era and the role of professional baseball in breaking down the color barrier. In the second game, held March 29, 2008, they dropped a 3–2 decision to the Mets—but the contest was an exhibition game played at AutoZone Park in Memphis—a neutral site. The June 20, 2009, Civil Rights Game counted in the standings, and Cincinnati provided the opposition at the Great American Ballpark on the banks of the Ohio River, very close to the National Underground Railroad Freedom Center where part of the weekend ceremonies were held. Before a packed house of more than 42,000, the White Sox—wearing commemorative 1964 road uniforms—staged a brilliant comeback from a five-run deficit to win 10–8.

- National League or the Little League? Since interleague play began in 1997, the White Sox have absolutely mauled their NL opponents. During that 14-year span (1997–2010), the Sox have gone 143–104 (.579) against the weak sisters of the senior circuit: 76–46 at home and 67–58 on the road. Only the Yankees (144–102) have a better winning percentage (.585) against the NL than the slugging White Sox during the first 14 years of interleague play. In 2010 the South Siders wracked up an almost unbelievable 15–3 season mark—the best in all of baseball that year. Commenting on the success of his team, Ozzie Guillen offered to trade places with the Cubs and move over to the National League Central, where the Sox could feast on the patsy Pirates, the awful Astros, mediocre Milwaukee, so-so Cincinnati, and the other two so-called "contenders"—you know who they are—but there were no takers, of course.

Hot Hitters

- Earl Sheely, the lumbering first baseman who replaced Chick Gandil in the 1921 lineup, collected seven consecutive extra-base hits in a sizzling two-day period, May 20–21, 1926, to equal the major league mark originally established by Elmer Smith of the Cleveland Indians on September 4 and 5, 1921. Sheely rapped out a home run and six doubles in a pair of games against the Browns in St. Louis.
- On September 2, 1918, Buck Weaver collected eight hits in 10 at-bats in a season-ending doubleheader at Detroit. The 1918 season ended early because of wartime constraints.
- Veteran outfielder George "Mule" Haas reeled off eight hits in 12 at-bats in a doubleheader sweep of the St. Louis Browns on July 30, 1933. Teammate Al Simmons chipped in with seven hits to lift his batting average to .367.
- Ray Morehart (career batting average .269) stole Earl Sheely's thunder by pounding out nine hits in 10 at-bats in a doubleheader against the Tigers at Detroit's Navin Field, August 31, 1926. The weak-hitting Morehart, who caddied at second base for his manager Eddie Collins for much of the season, collected five hits in six at bats in Game 1, and achieved a perfect 4-for-4 performance in the nightcap. The White Sox ran all over the Bengals by a score of 19–2 in the first game, but lost the second 7–6.
- Utility infielder Hal Rhyne played less than one full season with the White Sox in 1933. He hit .265 in only 39 games, but in a two-game set with the Detroit Tigers played at Comiskey Park on August 12 and 13, the little-known substitute caught fire and banged out nine hits in 10 at bats to match Ray Morehart's 1926 heroics. Rhyne collected only 13 more hits *for the entire season.*
- Luke Appling was sensational during the final month of the 1936 season with the American League batting championship on the line. Old Luke fought off a strong challenge from Earl Averill of the Cleveland Indians and his own teammate Rip Radcliff to win the crown going away. In the month of September, Appling collected 42 hits in 88 at-bats for a blistering .477 average. He drove in 23 runs that month, to cap off a perfect year. For the season Luke hit .388. No other Sox player has come close to matching Luke's totals.
- Sam Mele and his White Sox teammates administered a 15–4 pulverizing to the Philadelphia A's on June 10, 1952. In the fourth inning Sox batters crossed the plate 12 times. It was the second-highest run total in a single inning in White Sox history. But what made all this doubly unusual was the hitting of Mele, an outfielder acquired from Washington earlier in the year at great expense. In order to obtain Mele from the Senators, the Sox parted company with Jim Busby, one of the spark plugs of the 1951 Go-Go boys. Mele enjoyed his one day in the sun by driving in six runs during the madcap fourth inning at Shibe Park. In his first plate appearance, Mele belted a three-run homer off Harry Byrd. Later in the inning, after the Sox had batted around, Sam came up with the bases loaded and drilled a triple off Ed Wright, driving in three more runs. Six RBIs in one inning remains a White Sox team record. Unfortunately Sam Mele wasn't of much use to the White Sox after that day. He was sold to Baltimore on February 5, 1954.

In the 1917 World Series, during the first year of American involvement in World War I, the future Black Sox expressed their patriotism by donning star-spangled uniforms. (Courtesy of the Amateur Athletic Foundation of Los Angeles)

10

The Postseason

by Biart Williams

The White Sox have made five World Series appearances, winning three Series (1906, 1917, 2005) and losing two Series (1919, 1959). They also won pennants in 1900 and 1901.

In the Sox's inaugural season (1900), they were champs of the fledgling American League, which was considered a minor league circuit. The next season, the American League became baseball's second major league. Charles Comiskey, raiding the National League for players, put together a strong club that won the AL title. The baseball wars prevented a Chicago-Pittsburgh World Series. Instead, the Sox barnstormed with the Nap Lajoie All-Stars, splitting four games.

The early Sox teams had top-notch pitching staffs, but their lineups were riddled with banjo hitters. The Hitless Wonders scrapped their way to the pennant in 1906. In baseball's first World Series upset, the Sox handily beat the mighty Cubs in six games.

Baseball's second decade was the Sox Golden Age. Charles Comiskey assembled a great club featuring some of the best players in Sox history: Eddie Collins, Ed Cicotte, Ray Schalk, Joe Jackson. But they would capture only two pennants. The work-or-fight edict of World War I temporarily broke up the 1917 championship club. The 1919 White Sox became the notorious Black Sox in the World Series. In 1920 the bad-boy clique cost the Sox the flag as they fixed games right up to their suspension from baseball.

The Sox started the 1921 season as a veritable expansion team. In place of a Sox dynasty, Babe Ruth's Yankees became baseball's most successful franchise. Over the next 15 years the Sox floundered in the second division. They started coming out of it with the addition of Al Simmons, Jimmie Dykes, and Luke Appling. But the Yankees, now led by star Joe DiMaggio, continued to dominate the league.

The postwar Go-Go Sox under Frank Lane were of championship caliber. But it was the Damn Yankees again! Though averaging 90 wins a season, the Sox always seemed to end up bridesmaids to the New Yorkers.

The Go-Go Sox won the 1959 title, ending a 40-year drought. They lost the Series to the Dodgers, prompting owner Bill Veeck to trade for power. But the Yankees one-upped Veeck with the acquisition of slugger Roger Maris and returned to the top in 1960. In 1964 an aging Yankees ballclub squeaked by the White Sox to gain the last title of their vaunted era.

After the Yankees' demise, no dominant team emerged, and a scrappy Eddie Stanky club almost captured a flag in 1967.

With the new division format of 1969, the White Sox had to take that extra step to secure a flag. With division realignment in 1994, another rung was added to the series quest with the extra playoff series.

Maury Wills evades Louie Aparicio's tag and swipes second in Game 4 of the 1959 World Series.

1906 World Series: White Sox versus Cubs

The Sox' first World Series appearance was fittingly against the archrival Cubs. It was labeled the Trolley Car Series, but it could just as well have been called the rich man–poor man games. The Cubs were the darlings of the Michigan Avenue carriage set; the Sox, who were located in the dingy stockyard area of old Bridgeport, were the workingmen's heroes.

The mighty Cubs won a major league–record 116 games (116–36). Their legendary Joe Tinker, Johnny Evers, and Frank Chance infield lent itself to verse. Jimmy Sheckard, Wildfire Schulte, and Jimmy Slagle formed the *S* outfield. Mordecai "Three-Finger" Brown was the National League's premier hurler.

The Hitless Wonder White Sox (93–58) had scratched their way to the top. Posting a league-low .230 batting average, they were shut out 16 times. They had but seven roundtrippers, the same number amassed by Frank Schulte. The Sox, playing with their brains first then their hands and feet, as *Chicago Tribune* sportswriter Hugh Fullerton aptly put it (as opposed to the Cubs who used their hands and feet), relied on walks, stolen bases, and sacrifice bunts for their offense. Given a couple of runs, Sox pitchers did the job. They shut out their opponents 32 times. Ed Walsh had a league-high 10 blank jobs. Doc White and Yip Owen had seven apiece.

The Cubs won the coin toss and enjoyed what is commonly referred to as the home-field advantage. All seat prices were doubled. Circus seats were added in the outfields of both ballparks—which many of the fans would vacate anyway. Instead, they gathered around the outfield retaining rope to be closer to the action.

Two additional downtown viewing arenas were secured by the *Chicago Tribune* for the baseball bugs: the Auditorium, capacity 4,000, and the First Regiment Armory, capacity 5,000.

A 20-foot baseball diamond was erected on each stage. Balls and strikes were indicated by light bulbs. The batter's names were illuminated, as were the on-deck hitters'. Bulbs at first, second, and third designated base runners. An announcer, using a megaphone, called the play as it came over the wire.

Cubs fans were already declaring it no contest. The betting line had the Cubs as three-to-one favorites. Hugh Fullerton disagreed. His analytic baseball report had the Sox winning the Series in six games. (His editor, afraid of the public's reaction, refused to print the article until after the Series.)

Managers Frank Chance of the Cubs and Fielder Jones (in the white cap) of the Sox confer with the umpire prior to the first pitch of Game 1.

Fullerton had it right. The White Sox erupted for 16 runs in the final two contests, breaking a two-game stalemate. Fullerton correctly pointed out that curveballer Mordecai Brown (1–2) was the kind of guy the play-for-a-run Sox could beat. He also noted that the Cubs had problems with spitballers, such as Ed Walsh (2–0), and lefties, such as Doc White (1–1, 1 save). Foremost, Fullerton felt the Cubs were too confident. The Sox, having been through a tough pennant race, were ready for more battle.

Brains over brawn, team play over individual ability—it was the classic Sox style of play. The Series victory gave their followers bragging rights that they still hold today.

Game 1

Amid snow flurries, the World Series started at West Side Park on October 9. The cold weather held the crowd down to 12,693, half the park's capacity.

Bearskin coats and wool blankets were de rigueur for the chilled fans. Many warmed their juices with spirits from flasks hidden in their bulky apparel. The players, sitting on the exposed benches, were buttoned up in long-sleeved crewneck sweaters.

In the more comfortable indoor arenas, the fans shed their topcoats and derbies, loosened their starched collars, lit up stogies, and enjoyed the game even if it was a reproduction.

The freezing temperatures forced Sox manager Fielder Jones to change his lineup. George Davis, the Sox's best hitter, was ailing, so Lee Tannehill took over at short. Reserve infielder George Rohe handled Tannehill's third-base chores. Because Doc White was bothered by the cold and Ed

Walsh's saliva was freezing on the ball, Jones elected to start the dapper Nick Altrock.

Opening ceremonies featured the presentation of loving cups to both teams. Then the fans stood and sang "Auld Lang Syne."

Neither team mounted a threat over the first four innings. With one down in the fifth, George Rohe sent a dart to left past Jimmy Sheckard, through the retaining rope, and into the crowd. Patsy Dougherty bit on a Brown curve and chopped it in front of the plate. Brown scooped the ball up and tossed it home as Rohe, seemingly trapped, dashed down the line. But catcher Johnny Kling, trying to catch the ball and make the tag, muffed the toss, and Rohe slid in safely. The Sox added another run in the sixth on singles by Fielder Jones and Frank Isbell.

The Cubs, in their half, moved two men into scoring position. Altrock wild-pitched one home. But the Cubs couldn't bring the tying run the final 90 feet. Tannehill nabbed Jimmy Sheckard's pop fly in left. Rohe pegged out Schulte, with Jiggs Donahue at first base making a game-saving stretch to gather in Rohe's low throw.

The Sox held on and won the game 2–1. The final out, a towering fly ball, was gathered in by center fielder Fielder Jones, who did an impromptu dance before securing it.

Sox fans dashed onto the field. Nick Altrock and George Rohe were given a police escort lest they be mobbed by the joyous rooters. Observing the wild scene, Cubs owner Charles Murphy smugly remarked, "One swallow does not make a summer."

Game 2

Game 2 was played at South Side Park. Another less-than-expected crowd gathered on another bone-chilling day. South Side Park was a wooden structure similar to the Cubs' west-side plant but not as well-manicured. Mounds and gullies made the outfield a hazardous area, particularly after a rain. The track condition in the icy October weather was "lumpy."

In the bottom of the first, play was halted when Sox manager Fielder Jones came to the plate. Jones was presented with a complete silver set in a costly bound chest of polished wood, a gift from his players and owner Charles Comiskey.

In a Cubs 7–1 rout, Jones would take the collar against curveball artist Ed Reulbach, who opened the six hitless innings, yielding an unearned run in the fifth. Jiggs Donahue's one-out, seventh-inning single spoiled the no-hitter. Reulbach ended up with a one-hitter, but it was hardly a masterpiece as he walked six and hit a batter.

Sox starter Doc White, still bothered by the cold, lasted only three innings. On the day, the Cubs had 10 hits off White and Yip Owen. Three were by Harry Steinfeldt, the corner man of the Tinker to Evers to Chance infield.

The Cubs were aggressive on the base paths, hit-and-running and stealing bases. Bothered by all the movement, two jittery Sox infielders, third baseman George Rohe and second baseman Frank Isbell, committed costly errors in a Cubs three-run second. Speedsters Frank Chance and Joe Tinker tallied the game's final four runs. Before reporting home, they swiped two bases each against pitchers Doc White and Yip Owen and catcher Billy Sullivan.

During the game, Sox fans got even by keeping the balls hit into the stands. At West Side Park, the more refined Cubs rooters had kept with the custom of the day and thrown the balls back to the field for later use. After the final out, the Cubs players were harassed by Sox fans, and police helped them get to their carriages. Also, Cubs fans had to walk gingerly out of Sox park.

Game 3

In Game 3, Ed Walsh tossed a brilliant, 3–0, two-hit shutout. George Rohe's triple busted the game wide open. Walsh fanned 12 Cubs. Shielding his salivary glands with his glove, he occasionally pretended to juice the ball then zipped a curve or fastball by the batter. In one at bat, Joe Tinker stepped forward to put the squeeze on a juicer only to get hooked by a curveball.

Jack Pfeister's snaky curve erased nine White Sox players. He allowed but four hits, two in a Sox three-run sixth. Lee Tannehill opened the winning sixth with a hit just past Harry Steinfeldt's outstretched hands. Pfeister, trying to prevent Walsh from sacrificing, was too careful and issued a walk. Challenging Ed Hahn, he uncorked an inside heater flush on Hahn's face, breaking his nose. The traditional "Is there a doctor in the house?" plea fortunately brought forth a physician. A dressing-muzzled Hahn was rushed to the hospital. Bill O'Neill ran for him.

The next two batters were retired. It looked like Pfeister was going to escape the bases-loaded mess. But Rohe, on the first pitch, drilled a ball to left which, hugging the foul line, skipped past Jimmy Sheckard and into the crowd, clearing the bases.

Rohe was mobbed at third base by his teammates. Sox fans attending the game let out a roar. At the indoor locations across town, Cubs fans, assuming the weak-hitting Rohe would be retired, thought the delayed tape mistakenly read "triple" instead of "third out." Finding out it was correct, they collapsed unhappily into their seats.

The Cubs' two hits were gathered consecutively in the first inning. Solly Hofman singled but was caught stealing. Wildfire Schulte's ensuing double was wasted. Schulte split the air in his next three trips—his final strikeout ending the contest.

Game 4

The next day at South Side Park the Sox lost 1–0. In a rematch of the first game's pitchers, Three-Finger Brown, with a two-hitter, bested Nick Altrock.

The Cubs' only run borrowed a page from the Hitless Wonder script. Leading off the seventh, Frank Chance sent a low fly to right that outfielder Ed Hahn lost in the sun, or in the splint and adhesive tape anchoring his wounded beak. Sacrifice bunts by Harry Steinfeldt and Joe Tinker moved Chance around to third. He scored on Johnny Evers' screamer over short.

The contest was played under ideal conditions—a bright sun, temperatures in the 60s. The 39th Street grounds were jammed. Those who couldn't gain admittance were filled in on the action by the foghorn spectators sitting in the last row of the grandstand.

The warmer weather allowed George Davis to return to the lineup. But Davis's layoff was evident: 0-for-3, a strikeout, an error, caught stealing once.

George Rohe continued his fine play at third base. Series hero Rohe was on deck when a Sox two-out, ninth-inning threat ended abruptly. With Fielder Jones (who had walked and advanced on a passed ball) perched on second, Frank Isbell sent a shot to the mound upending Brown, who recovered in time to make the play at first.

Game 5

The pivotal fifth game went to the Sox, 8–6. The Sox exploded for 12 hits, eight of them for two bases. (Usually, for the Hitless Wonders, a double meant a walk and a sacrifice bunt.) Frank Isbell, punching out four doubles, accounted for over half the Sox runs. George Davis, finding his batting eye, banged out two doubles and KO'd two Cubs hurlers. George Rohe kept it going with three base hits.

Before the contest, two fans paraded snarling bear cubs around West Side Park. They stopped at the Sox bench and allowed the players to examine the animals' incisors close up.

In the first inning of an error-strewn contest, second baseman Frank Isbell's throwing gaffe sent two Bruins home. Jiggs Donahue then dropped a toss at first for another score. Isbell made amends leading off the third with a ground-rule double to left. The switch-hitting Davis, batting from the port side, next poked a ground-ruler to right, ending starter Ed Ruelbach's chores. While Jack Pfeister was settling in, Davis and Patsy Dougherty (who reached on a fielder's choice) performed a Sox specialty—a double steal—for another score.

In the Sox' four-run fourth, back-to-back doubles by Isbell and Davis, batting right-handed, brought Orval Overall scurrying in from the pen. Jiggs Donahue doubled to make it a 7–3 game. George Rohe came through with an RBI single in the sixth inning after his throwing error had given the Cubs a run in the fourth. Helped out by another Rohe muff, the Cubs moved within two, 8–6, in the home sixth. Harry Steinfeldt's leadoff double in the seventh finished Ed Walsh. Doc White rescued the great spitballer and preserved the victory.

First baseman Jiggs Donahue ended a final Cubs threat in the eighth. After taking Lee Tannehill's late throw on Frank Schulte's squibbler, he fired a strike across the infield to George Davis, covering third, who tagged out Jimmy Sheckard trying for an extra base.

The Sox (at bat) taking full measure of Cubs pitching in the 1906 Series

The Sox on enemy turf: Game 3 at West Side Park, the home lair of the Cubs

Game 6

In the Series finale, the surging Sox pounded Three-Finger Brown 8–3. Brown was pitching on only one day's rest. Sox starter Doc White was coming off a relief appearance in Game 5. Both went to the rubber without any pampering from ham-fisted managers Frank Chance and Fielder Jones.

The Cubs started well with a tally in the first on Wildfire Schulte's RBI double. But Schulte was erased at third on Chance's chopper to the mound, preventing a bigger inning. Schulte then became involved in a rhubarb in the Sox half. He claimed fan interference when he couldn't flag down George Davis's bases-loaded double near the throng of fans in right. Just as Schulte prepared to catch the ball, a Sox rooter reached over the outfield rope and pushed the Cubs fielder from behind. The ball dropped, and two runs scored. The umpires, missing the flagrant infraction, allowed the play to stand. Then Donahue laced a double to left for two more runs.

The Sox put the game out of reach in a four-run second. With two men retired, Ed Hahn stroked the second of his

Billy Sullivan draws a bead on Cub pitching. The catcher is Johnny Kling.

An overflow crowd for the final game at South Side Park, October 14, 1906

four hits. Fielder Jones drew a walk. Frank Isbell, George Davis, and the omnipresent George Rohe followed with hits. The Pale Hose then added two more on a Joe Tinker–Johnny Evers mishap and a Brown pass.

Jimmy Sheckard, remaining hitless (0-for-21) for the Series, drove in the Cubs' second run with a grounder in the fifth. The Cubs managed to load the bases with a run in and two out in the ninth, but Schulte grounded to Donahue, clinching the World Series for Charles Comiskey.

After the final out, Sox fans stormed onto the field. The celebration lasted well into the night. Bonfires lit up the South Side. Fans went to the players' homes and offered their heroes a piggyback ride around the block. Cubs fans were harassed, and the bets were settled. Two Cubs rooters were seen hitched to a buggy pulling two laughing White Sox fans down Milwaukee Avenue. Two unfortunate boobs covered their bets by jumping in icy Lake Michigan in December.

Frank Chance, after praising the Sox' efforts, stated: "But there is one thing I will never believe, and that is the White Sox are a better ballclub than the Cubs. We did not play our game, and that's all there is to it."

The Sox triumph was no fluke. Be it the 1906 World Series or the yearly City Series showdown, the Sox would *always* have the Cubs' number.

MONDAY MORNING, OCTOBER 15, 1906. PRICE TWO CENTS.

WHITE SOX CAPTURE BASEBALL CHAMPIONSHIP OF WORLD BY AGAIN DEFEATING THE CUBS

South Siders' Fourth Victory Won by 8 to 3 Score Before Crowd of Nearly 20,000.

MINER BROWN TO THE BENCH

Comiskey Presents Team With $15,000 Check—Crowd Breaks Down Fences in Order to See Game—Dr. White Holds the Sluggers.

THE CHAMPIONSHIP SERIES.

Score of Final Game—White Sox, 8; Giant Killers, 3.

Games Won and Lost—White Sox, won 4, lost 2; Giant Killers, won 2, lost 4

Attendance yesterday... [illegible]
Receipts yesterday ..... [illegible]
Total attendance (six days) ..... [illegible]
Total receipts (six days) ..... [illegible]
Players' Share—
Sox (each) ..... [illegible]
Killers (each) ..... [illegible]
Comiskey's present to Sox 15,000.00
Total for each Sox..... [illegible]

SERIES BATTING AND FIELDING.

Batting. [illegible]

Fielding. [illegible]

President Charles A. Comiskey of the

World Champions! (*Chicago Inter Ocean*)

Game 1

October 9, at West Side Grounds

White Sox	AB	R	H	RBI	PO	A
Hahn, rf	3	0	0	0	1	0
Jones, cf	4	1	1	0	3	0
Isbell, 2b	4	0	1	1	0	1
Rohe, 3b	4	1	1	0	1	2
Donahue, 1b	4	0	0	0	12	2
Dougherty, 1f	3	0	0	0	1	0
Sullivan, c	3	0	0	0	5	2
Tannehill, ss	3	0	0	0	1	4
Altrock, p	2	0	1	0	3	3
	30	2	4	1	27	14

Cubs	AB	R	H	RBI	PO	A
Hofman, cf	3	0	0	0	1	1
Sheckard, lf	3	0	0	0	1	0
a—Moran	1	0	0	0	0	0
Schulte, rf	4	0	1	0	1	0
Chance, 1b	4	0	1	0	11	0
Steinfeldt, 3b	4	0	0	0	0	2
Tinker, ss	3	0	0	0	2	3
Evers, 2b	3	0	0	0	1	3
Kling, c	2	1	1	0	9	1
Brown, p	2	0	1	0	1	6
	29	1	4	0	27	16

White Sox	0	0	0	0	1	1	0	0	0—2
Cubs	0	0	0	0	0	1	0	0	0—1

Sox	IP	H	R	ER	W	K
Altrock (W)	9	4	1	1	1	3

Cubs	IP	H	R	ER	W	K
Brown (L)	9	4	2	0	1	7

a—Flied out for Sheckard in ninth. E—Isbell, Kling, Brown. LOB—Sox 3, Cubs 4. 3B—Rohe. SB—Isbell, Dougherty. SH—Hahn, Hofman, Brown. WP—Brown, Altrock. PB—Kling 2. Umpires—Johnstone (NL), O'Loughlin (AL). Time—1:45. Attendance—12,693.

Game 2

October 10, at South Side Park

Cubs	AB	R	H	RBI	PO	A
Hofman, cf	4	0	1	1	2	0
Sheckard, lf	4	0	0	0	3	1
Schulte, rf	4	0	1	0	1	0
Chance, 1b	5	2	1	0	12	0
Steinfeldt, 3b	3	1	3	1	0	2
Tinker, ss	3	3	2	1	0	3
Evers, 2b	4	1	1	0	4	6
Kling, c	2	0	1	0	5	1
Reulbach, p	3	0	0	1	0	2
	32	7	10	4	27	15

White Sox	AB	R	H	RBI	PO	A
Hahn, rf	3	0	0	0	0	0
Jones, cf	3	0	0	0	1	0
Isbell, 2b	4	0	0	0	6	2
Rohe, 3b	2	0	0	0	0	3
Donahue, 1b	3	0	1	0	10	1
Dougherty, lf	2	1	0	0	1	0
Sullivan, c	4	0	0	0	8	2
Tannehill, ss	3	0	0	0	0	3
White, p	0	0	0	0	0	1
a—Towne	1	0	0	0	0	0
Owen, p	2	0	0	0	1	4
	27	1	1	0	27	16

Cubs	0	3	1	0	0	1	0	2	0—7
White Sox	0	0	0	0	1	0	0	0	0—1

Cubs	IP	H	R	ER	BB	K
Reulbach(W)	9	1	1	0	6	3

Sox	IP	H	R	ER	BB	K
White (L)	3	4	4	0	2	1
Owen	6	6	3	2	3	2

a—Flied out for White in third. E—Tinker, Evers, Isbell, Sullivan. DP—Cubs 2. LOB—Sox 6, Cubs 6. 2B—Kling. SB—Chance 2, Tinker 2, Evers. SH—Sheckard, Steinfeldt, Reulbach. WP—Reulbach, Owen. HBP—by Reulbach (Rohe). Umpires—O'Loughlin (AL), Johnstone, (NL). Time—1:58. Attendance—12,595.

Game 3

October 11, at West Side Grounds

White Sox	AB	R	H	RBI	PO	A
Hahn, rf	2	0	0	0	0	0
a—O'Neill, rf	1	1	0	0	1	0
Jones, cf	4	0	0	0	1	0
Isbell, 2b	4	0	0	0	1	4
Rohe, 3b	3	0	1	3	0	1
Donahue, 1b	3	0	2	0	14	0
Dougherty, lf	4	0	0	0	0	0
Sullivan, c	3	0	0	0	10	2
Tannehill, ss	3	1	1	0	0	5
Walsh, p	2	1	0	0	0	3
	29	3	4	3	27	15

Cubs	AB	R	H	RBI	PO	A
Hofman, cf	4	0	1	0	1	0
Sheckard, lf	4	0	0	0	2	0
Schulte, rf	4	0	1	0	1	0
Chance, 1b	2	0	0	0	7	1
Steinfeldt, 3b	3	0	0	0	1	2
Tinker, ss	3	0	0	0	3	2
Evers, 2b	3	0	0	0	1	2
Kling, c	3	0	0	0	11	3
Pfeister, p	2	0	0	0	0	2
b—Gessler	1	0	0	0	0	0
	29	0	2	0	27	12

White Sox	0	0	0	0	0	3	0	0	0—3
Cubs	0	0	0	0	0	0	0	0	0—0

Sox	IP	H	R	ER	BB	K
Walsh (W)	9	2	0	0	1	12

Cubs	IP	H	R	ER	BB	K
Pfeister (L)	9	4	3	3	2	9

a—Ran for Hahn in sixth. b—Reached first on error for Pfeister in ninth. E—Isbell, Tinker, Pfeister. LOB—Sox 4, Cubs 3. 2B—Schulte. 3B—Donahue, Rohe. SB—Rohe. SH—Donahue, Sullivan. WP—Walsh. HBP—by Pfeister (Hahn). Umpires—Johnstone (NL), O'Loughlin (AL). Time—2:10. Attendance—13,667.

Game 4

October 12, at South Side Park

Cubs	AB	R	H	RBI	PO	A
Hofman, cf	4	0	2	0	1	0
Sheckard, lf	3	0	0	0	1	0
Schulte, rf	4	0	0	0	1	0
Chance, 1b	4	1	2	0	13	1
Steinfeldt, 3b	2	0	1	0	1	1
Tinker, ss	1	0	0	0	1	4
Evers, 2b	3	0	1	1	2	4
Kling, c	3	0	0	0	6	3
Brown, p	3	0	1	0	1	5
	27	1	7	1	27	18

White Sox	AB	R	H	RBI	PO	A
Hahn, rf	4	0	1	0	1	0
Jones, cf	3	0	0	0	0	0
Isbell, 2b	4	0	0	0	1	3
Rohe, 3b	3	0	0	0	0	4
Donahue, 1b	1	0	0	0	13	2
Dougherty, lf	3	0	1	0	2	0
Davis, ss	3	0	0	0	4	2
Sullivan, c	3	0	0	0	3	1
Altrock, p	2	0	0	0	3	8
a—McFarland	1	0	0	0	0	0
	27	0	2	0	27	20

Cubs	0	0	0	0	0	0	1	0	0—1
White Sox	0	0	0	0	0	0	0	0	0—0

Cubs	IP	H	R	ER	BB	K
Brown (W)	9	2	0	0	2	5

Sox	IP	H	R	ER	BB	K
Altrock (L)	9	7	1	1	1	2

a—Grounded out for Altrock in ninth. E—Steinfeldt, Davis. DP—Cubs 1, Sox 1. LOB—Cubs 5, Sox 3. 2B—Hofman. SB—Sheckard. SH—Donahue, Steinfeldt 2, Tinker 3. PB—Kling. Umpires—O'Loughlin (AL), Johnstone (NL). Time—1:36. Attendance—18,385.

Game 5

October 13, at West Side Grounds

White Sox	AB	R	H	RBI	PO	A
Hahn, rf	5	2	1	0	1	0
Jones, cf	4	1	1	0	1	0
Isbell, 2b	5	3	4	2	2	2
Davis, ss	5	2	2	3	2	8
Rohe, 3b	4	0	3	1	0	2
Donahue, 1b	3	0	1	1	15	2
Dougherty, lf	5	0	0	0	0	0
Sullivan, c	4	0	0	0	6	2
Walsh, p	2	0	0	0	0	2
White, p	0	0	0	0	0	0
	37	8	12	7	27	18

Cubs	AB	R	H	RBI	PO	A
Hofman, cf	3	2	1	0	2	0
Sheckard, lf	4	0	0	0	1	0
Schulte, rf	5	1	3	2	2	1
Chance, 1b	4	0	1	0	8	0
Steinfeldt, 3b	5	1	1	1	1	2
Tinker, ss	4	1	0	0	2	2
Evers, 2b	3	0	0	0	2	5
a—Moran	1	0	0	0	0	0
Kling, c	3	0	0	0	9	0
Reulbach, p	0	0	0	0	0	2
Pfeister, p	0	0	0	0	0	0
Overall, p	2	1	0	0	0	1
	34	6	6	3	27	13

White Sox	1	0	2	4	0	1	0	0	0—8
Cubs	3	0	0	1	0	2	0	0	0—6

Sox	IP	H	R	ER	BB	K
Walsh (W)	6	5	6	3	5	5
White (S)	3	1	0	0	1	0

Cubs	IP	H	R	ER	BB	K
Reulbach	2	5	3	3	2	1
Pfeister (L)	1⅓	3	4	4	1	2
Overall	5⅔	4	1	1	1	5

a—Forced runner for Evers in ninth. E—Isbell 2, Davis, Rohe 2, Walsh. DP—Cubs. LOB—Sox 8, Cubs 10. 2B—Isbell 4, Rohe, Davis 2, Donahue, Chance, Schulte, Steinfeldt. SB—Dougherty, Davis, Tinker, Evers. SH—Jones, Sheckard, Reulbach. WP—Overall. HBP—by Walsh (Chance), by Pfeister (Donahue). PB—Sullivan. Umpires—Johnstone (NL), O'Loughlin (AL) Time—2:40. Attendance—23,257.

Game 6

October 14, at South Side Park

Cubs	AB	R	H	RBI	PO	A
Hofman, cf	5	1	2	1	3	0
Sheckard, lf	3	0	0	1	2	0
Schulte, rf	5	0	1	1	0	0
Chance, 1b	2	0	0	0	9	0
Steinfeldt, 3b	3	0	0	0	0	0
Tinker, ss	4	0	1	0	2	6
Evers, 2b	4	1	1	0	2	0
Kling, c	4	1	1	0	6	2
Brown, p	1	0	0	0	0	1
Overall, p	2	0	1	0	0	1
a—Gessler	0	0	0	0	0	0
	33	3	7	3	24	10

White Sox	AB	R	H	RBI	PO	A
Hahn, rf	5	2	4	0	0	0
Jones, cf	3	2	0	0	3	0
Isbell, 2b	5	1	3	1	1	4
Davis, ss	5	2	2	3	1	4
Rohe, 3b	5	1	2	0	3	4
Donahue, 1b	4	0	2	3	15	1
Dougherty, lf	3	0	1	1	0	0
Sullivan, c	4	0	0	0	3	1
White, p	3	0	0	0	1	2
	37	8	14	8	27	16

Cubs	1	0	0	0	1	0	0	0	1—3
White Sox	3	4	0	0	0	0	0	1	x—8

Cubs	IP	H	R	ER	BB	K
Brown (L)	1⅔	8	7	7	1	0
Overall	6⅓	6	1	1	2	3

Sox	IP	H	R	ER	BB	K
White (W)	9	7	3	3	4	2

a—Batted for Overall in ninth. E—Rohe, Donahue, Dougherty. DP—Sox 1. LOB—Sox 9, Cubs 9. 2B—Schulte, Overall, Evers, Davis, Donahue. SB—Rohe. SH—Sheckard, Jones. HBP—by White (Chance). Umpires—O'Loughlin (AL), Johnstone (NL). Time—1:55. Attendance—19,249.

1917 World Series: White Sox versus New York Giants

Opposing managers John McGraw (left) and Clarence "Pants" Rowland, shaking hands on the eve of the 1917 Series.

The White Sox' second championship season coincided with America's entry into World War I. The United States had declared war on the Kaiser shortly before the baseball season started. American combat divisions arrived in France in June 1917, preparing for their first big engagement in October. In the spirit of patriotism, the Sox looked their star-spangled best, donning red, white, and blue–striped uniforms down to their socks. The scribes dubbed them the Red, White, and Blue Sox.

Eleven years had lapsed between world titles. Piece by piece, the Hitless Wonders had been put to rest. Rebuilding with stronger rungs—Eddie Collins, Joe Jackson, Ed Cicotte, Ray Schalk—the Sox climbed their way back up the pennant ladder.

Rookie shortstop Swede Risberg and veteran first baseman Chick Gandil carried the Sox to the top. After Gandil's acquisition, a *Chicago Tribune* writer astutely noted, "You might as well buy your World Series tickets." (Risberg, bothered by a boil, saw little Series duty. Fred McMullen, who had substituted for an injured Buck Weaver at third, played shortstop. Weaver returned to the hot corner.)

Clarence Rowland, a career minor league player and skipper, managed the Sox. During the Series, the busher Rowland outmanaged the master tactician John McGraw. Rowland crossed up the Little Napoleon, mixing his sacrifices and hit-and-runs, and he utilized his bench and juggled his staff better than McGraw.

McGraw had resurrected his club following the Christy Mathewson–Rube Marquard era. He assembled a new infield crafted in his image, featuring hotheads Buck Herzog at second and Artie Fletcher at shortstop, along with an irascible ex-Cub, Henie Zimmerman, playing third. McGraw acquired two good southpaw hurlers: Slim Sallee and Rube Benton. Two-time Federal League batting champ Benny Kauff, an outfielder, came over from the defunct Brooklyn club.

The Sox and Giants were well familiar with each other, having recently completed a world tour. During the trip, league rivalries came to the fore. A near bench-clearing brawl occurred in Cairo, Egypt, before a bewildered group of spectators. The language barrier and the unusual set of exhibition games hardly disguised the teams' contempt for each other. Grudges remained, and the Series was highlighted by some fierce bench jockeying, hard tags, and flying spikes.

This is not to say that the Sox were a united happy bunch. The future Black Sox rogues—Chick Gandil, Swede Risberg, Hap Felsch—had formed their own clique, opposed to a more refined group led by Ray Schalk and Eddie Collins. But the Sox were "of one mind" and played outstanding ball against New York.

Game 1

The World Series bunting at Comiskey Park reflected the country's wartime resolve. Red Cross volunteers roamed the park asking for contributions. A military band played patriotic tunes. Two thousand doughboys marched into the park, then made their way single file to the grandstand section.

Underneath the stands, Charles Comiskey gave the boys a pep talk in the clubhouse. Whether it was Comiskey's speech or the large gate receipts that acted as an incentive, the White Sox, behind Ed Cicotte, defeated the Giants 2–1. Afterward, Comiskey, tears in his eyes, grasped Cicotte's hand in gratitude.

John McGraw selected southpaw Slim Sallee as his opening-game hurler to neutralize port-siders Joe Jackson and Eddie Collins. The Sox stars were contained, but right-handed batters Happy Felsch and Shano Collins were afforded a better view of Sallee's motion. Felsch drove a Sallee fastball six rows into the Comiskey Park bleachers for the Sox' first home run in Series play. Collins had three hits on the day and scored the Sox' first run.

During practice, Giant hurler "Spitball" Fred Anderson had simulated Cicotte's shine ball for the benefit of the hitters. But Cicotte's shine ball was more of a ploy for his dipsy-doodle knuckler. The New York batters constantly bit on the tempting balloon but, catching the hop, popped it up. The Giants, unfamiliar with Cicotte's motion, had two runners picked off base, both times ending innings.

Down 2–0, the Giants tallied in the fifth on catcher Lew McCarty's triple and his battery mate Slim Sallee's hit. But McGraw, who was never a proponent of the sacrifice bunt, had the next man hit away, and the Sox turned a snappy double play.

Though hitless, Joe Jackson made a game-saving grab in left field in the seventh. With one on, he dived headfirst at a liner, skimming his belly on the outfield grass as he made the play.

During the contest, the Giants bench jockeys dished out the raspberries. But the Sox were unusually quiet. In a pregame meeting, they had decided to ignore the taunts and save their yapping for the opportune moment. The Sox fans gave the Giants an earful, particularly ex-Cub Henie Zimmerman, whom they had razzed incessantly during his City Series days.

Al Jolson presented the victorious Sox with a $50 liberty bond. Game hero Felsch received two of Jolson's bonds and some wardrobe gratuities: two suits and dozens of pairs of socks.

Game 2

Red Faber, just three years removed from the cornfields of Cascade, Iowa, hurled the Sox past the city slicker Metropolitans 7–2. Rowland chose Faber after observing Reb Russell's poor performance on the sidelines. McGraw watched "Pol" Perritt and Ferdie Schupp warm up. McGraw chose Schupp over the more seasoned Perritt, perhaps for sentimental reasons, as Schupp's family had come up from Kentucky for the game. However, Schupp seemed rattled by the hostile Chicago crowd and couldn't get past the second inning.

Faber survived a shaky start, yielding two runs in the second inning. After that, he took command of the game and yielded four harmless safeties. Mr. McGraw's Giants were familiar with the lanky spitballer. As a rookie, Faber had accompanied the Sox on the 1914 world tour. When the situation demanded, he donned a Giants uniform. McGraw coveted him and dangled $50,000 in front of Charles Comiskey, who wisely turned him down.

Faber suffered a defensive lapse in the Giants second when he forgot to back up home plate on a hit, allowing a run to score as Joe Jackson's peg skipped away from catcher Ray Schalk. And after the game was safely tucked away, Faber had a brain cramp on the bases. Perched on second base, he tried to pilfer third base, which happened to be occupied by Buck Weaver. Weaver, a teammate but not a friend, gruffly asked Faber where the hell he was going. Faber replied, "Going back to pitch."

Buck Weaver and Joe Jackson paced the Sox with three singles apiece. Buck Weaver's hit, the Sox' fourth straight of the frame, knotted the game in the second inning. Leading off the fourth against Fred Anderson, Weaver started a six-hit, five-run barrage that was capped by Jackson's two-run single.

Oscar "Hap" Felsch (left) and Benny Kauff of the Giants. Both players were later banned from baseball.

After the game it was on to New York. Three trains steamed out of Chicago: one for each club and one carrying Charles Comiskey's Woodland Bards fan group.

World-class infield (left to right): Buck Weaver, Swede Risberg, Eddie Collins, and Chick Gandil

Game 3

Broadway had no patience with losers. So there was no brass band to greet the Giants upon their arrival on the Great White Way. A rain postponement made things even drearier. But the White Sox' dormant offense improved the spirit of New York fans. Not one Sox player would cross home plate in the two games, starting with a 2–0 shutout loss.

McGraw threw his third straight southpaw, Rube Benton, at the White Sox. The Sox flailed away at Benton's mystifying hooks. Only two Chicagoans got as far as second base.

Ed Cicotte pitched out of tough jams in the first three innings. Eddie caught a bad break in the fourth and was tagged for two runs. Joe Jackson slipped and fell trying to retrieve Dave Robertson's triple. Shano Collins attempted a shoestring catch on Walter Holke's drive, but the ball skipped past him for a double. Then McGraw, for the first time in the Series, ordered a sacrifice. Holke moved to third and scored on Cicotte's wild peg to first on George Burns' roller. Cicotte allowed only two hits the rest of the way, but the Sox just couldn't touch Benton.

Game 4

McGraw demanded two straight victories in New York. They accomplished the goal, sending the Series back to Chicago tied, and the Woodland Bards an estimated $50,000 poorer. Besting Red Faber, Ferdie Schupp scattered seven hits and shut out the Sox 5–0. Schupp also contributed an RBI single.

Benny Kauff, known as the Ty Cobb of the Federal League, had a peach of a game, socking two homers good for three runs. In the fourth inning Kauff ended a 0-for-13 drought by driving one past Happy Felsch to the center-field wall. The ball settled under a tarp. Felsch, while glancing back and forth at the infield, repeatedly snatched at the ball before grasping it. Meanwhile, Kauff rounded the bases. A local scorer generously gave him a home run. Kauff's second blast was another gift. Benny lifted a Dave Danforth pitch into the front-row seats of the short porch in right field—a fly ball in Comiskey Park but a war bond blast at the Polo Grounds.

Game 5

After the two embarrassing shutouts in New York, the Sox finally woke up and played real ball. Buck Weaver scattered the Giants players with some batted balls during practice. McGraw's boys weren't about to back down, and the pivotal fifth game was a fiercely fought contest, the White Sox eventually rallying for an 8–5 win.

Reb Russell started for the Pale Hose but was lifted after failing to retire the first three batters. Russell's presence had convinced McGraw to insert Olympic star Jim Thorpe in the lineup. But his hasty departure removed Thorpe from the lineup before he got an at-bat. Dave Robertson took Thorpe's place at the plate and banged out three hits—a performance Thorpe (.193), baseball's "tin medalist," probably could not have duplicated.

Things quickly heated up in the frigid, overcoat weather of Chicago. Walter Holke took exception to Felsch's hand slide in the fifth inning. In the sixth, Weaver, rounding second base, barged through Artie Fletcher and Buck Herzog to reach third base. Fletcher and Clarence Rowland nearly came to blows on the field after Fletcher thumped out Hap Felsch in the eighth.

The Sox tied it at five with three runs in the seventh, two coming home on Gandil's double. Then in the winning eighth inning, the Sox were helped along by Heinie Zimmerman's sloppy play. After staying back on a play at third base, Zimmerman heaved the ball into right field. McGraw unwisely let his tiring starter, Slim Sallee, pitch into the eighth inning. Rowland made all the right calls. Swede Risberg successfully pinch-hit for middle reliever Ed Cicotte in the sixth. Red Faber picked up the win in relief, retiring the New Yorkers in order over the final two innings.

Game 6

In his fourth appearance of the series, Red Faber delivered the world championship to Chicago, 4–2. New York miscues, particularly a costly Heinie Zimmerman blunder, accounted for all four Chicago runs.

Precipitating a three-run fourth, Zimmerman lost a footrace with Eddie Collins in a mad dash toward an unguarded home plate. Collins was Zimmerman's man to begin with, having reached base on Heinie's error. A muff by right fielder Dave Robertson put runners at the corners. Felsch bounded one to Rube Benton on the mound. Collins was moving down the line and caught off the bag. Accepting his fate, Collins hand-signaled the others to advance before he could be tagged out. Benton ran him back toward third and tossed the ball to Zimmerman. Instead of tightening the noose, Zim ignored his catcher and tore after Collins. Collins crossed home plate with the Series flag in his back pocket, just out of reach of Zimmerman's extended fist. The other runners advanced into scoring position, where they scored on Gandil's hit. Gandil was out trying for second, receiving a two-handed beaning from Artie Fletcher.

Later, Zimmerman was to remark, "Who the hell was I going to throw the ball to? [Umpire Bill] Klem?"

The Sox picked up an insurance run on Benny Kauff's muff in the ninth. Artie Fletcher and Buck Weaver, jockeying for position, did some bumping at second base and had to be separated.

Faber plunked Robertson leading off the ninth, then retired the Giants in order to wrap up the Sox' second world title. McGraw rushed out to congratulate Faber and Weaver, but he had no time for pleasantries with Clarence Rowland. Brushing past Rowland, McGraw barked, "Get away from me, you damned busher."

Game 1
October 6, at Chicago

New York	AB	R	H	RBI	PO	A
Burns, lf	3	0	1	0	2	0
Herzog, 2b	4	0	1	0	3	1
Kauff, cf	4	0	0	0	0	0
Zimmerman, 3b	4	0	0	0	1	3
Fletcher, ss	4	0	0	0	2	3
Robertson, rf	4	0	1	0	0	1
Holke, 1b	3	0	2	0	14	0
McCarty, c	3	1	1	0	2	1
Sallee, p	3	0	1	1	0	6
	32	1	7	1	24	15

Chicago	AB	R	H	RBI	PO	A
J. Collins, rf	4	1	3	0	1	0
McMullin, 3b	3	0	1	1	0	3
E. Collins, 2b	3	0	0	0	2	1
Jackson, lf	3	0	0	0	5	0
Felsch, cf	3	1	1	1	4	0
Gandil, 1b	3	0	1	10	0	1
Weaver, ss	3	0	0	0	2	1
Schalk, c	3	0	0	0	3	0
Cicotte, p	3	0	1	0	0	4
	28	2	7	2	27	10

New York	0	0	0	0	1	0	0	0	0—1
Chicago	0	0	1	1	0	0	0	0	x—2

New York	IP	H	R	ER	BB	K
Sallee (L)	8	7	2	2	0	2

Chicago	IP	H	R	ER	BB	K
Cicotte (W)	9	7	1	1	1	2

E—McCarty, Weaver. LOB—Sox 3, Giants 5. 2B—McMullin, J. Collins, Robertson. 3B—McCarty. HR—Felsch. SB—Burns, Gandil. SH—McMullin. Umpires—O'Loughlin (AL), Klem (NL), Rigler (NL), Evans (AL). Time—1:48. Attendance—32,000.

Game 2
October 7, at Chicago

New York	AB	R	H	RBI	PO	A
Burns, lf	3	0	1	0	0	0
Herzog, 2b	4	0	0	0	3	0
Kauff, cf	4	0	0	0	2	0
Zimmerman, 3b	4	0	0	0	4	2
Fletcher, ss	4	0	1	0	2	2
Robertson, rf	3	1	2	0	2	0
Holke, 1b	3	1	1	0	5	0
McCarty, c	1	0	1	1	5	0
Rariden, c	2	0	1	0	1	3
Schupp, p	1	0	0	0	0	1
Anderson, p	0	0	0	0	0	1
Perritt, p	1	0	1	0	0	0
b—Wilhot, p	1	0	0	0	0	0
Tesreau, p	0	0	0	0	0	0
	31	2	8	1	24	9

Chicago	AB	R	H	RBI	PO	A
J. Collins, rf	1	0	0	0	0	1
a—Leibold, rf	3	1	1	1	0	0
McMullin, 3b	5	1	1	1	0	3
E. Collins, 2b	4	1	2	1	4	2
Jackson, lf	3	1	3	2	0	1
Felsch, 3b	4	1	1	0	2	1
Gandil, 1b	4	0	1	1	12	1
Weaver, ss	4	1	3	1	7	6
Schalk, c	4	1	1	0	1	2
Faber, p	3	0	1	0	1	4
	35	7	14	7	27	21

New York	0	2	0	0	0	0	0	0	0—2
Chicago	0	2	0	5	0	0	0	0	x—7

New York	IP	H	R	ER	BB	K
Schupp	1⅓	4	2	2	1	2
Anderson(L)	2	5	4	4	0	3
Perritt	3⅔	5	1	1	1	0
Tesreau	1	0	0	0	1	1

Chicago	IP	H	R	ER	BB	K
Faber (W)	9	8	2	2	1	1

a—Struck out for J. Collins in second. b—Lined into double play for Perritt in eighth. E—Fletcher, Schalk. DP—Giants 1, Sox 3. LOB—Giants 3, Sox 7. SB—E. Collins 2, Jackson. PB—McCarty. Umpires—Evans (AL), Rigler (NL), Klem (NL), O'Loughlin (AL). Time—2:13. Attendance—32,000.

Game 3
October 10, at New York

Chicago	AB	R	H	RBI	PO	A
J. Collins, rf	4	0	0	0	1	0
McMullin, 3b	4	0	0	0	0	1
E. Collins, 2b	4	0	2	0	3	2
Jackson, lf	4	0	0	0	0	0
Felsch, cf	3	0	1	0	5	0
Gandil, 1b	3	0	0	0	6	0
Weaver, ss	3	0	2	0	0	2
Schalk, c	3	0	0	0	9	0
Cicotte, p	3	0	0	0	0	1
	31	0	5	0	24	6

New York	AB	R	H	RBI	PO	A
Burns, lf	4	0	1	1	1	0
Herzog, 2b	4	0	1	0	1	1
Kauff, cf	4	0	0	0	0	0
Zimmerman, 3b	4	0	1	0	0	3
Fletcher, ss	4	0	0	0	1	4
Robertson, rf	4	1	3	0	1	0
Holke, 1b	4	1	1	1	15	0
Rariden, c	2	0	1	0	7	4
Benton, p	3	0	0	0	1	2
	33	2	8	2	27	14

Chicago	0	0	0	0	0	0	0	0	0—0
New York	0	0	0	2	0	0	0	0	x—2

Chicago	IP	H	R	ER	BB	K
Cicotte (L)	8	8	2	2	0	8

New York	IP	H	R	ER	BB	K
Benton (W)	9	5	0	0	0	5

E—J. Collins 2, Cicotte, Fletcher, Holke. DP—Giants 1. LOB—Sox 4, Giants 8. 2B—Holke, Weaver. 3B—Robertson. SB—Robertson. SH—Rariden. Umpires—Klem (NL), O'Loughlin (AL), Evans (AL), Rigler (NL). Time—1:55. Attendance—33,616.

Game 4
October 11, at New York

Chicago	AB	R	H	RBI	PO	A
J. Collins, rf	4	0	2	0	0	0
McMullin, 3b	4	0	1	0	1	2
E. Collins, 2b	3	0	1	0	0	6
Jackson, lf	4	0	0	0	0	0
Felsch, cf	4	0	0	0	2	1
Gandil, 1b	4	0	1	0	15	0
Weaver, ss	3	0	0	0	0	1
Schalk, c	3	0	2	0	6	3
Faber, p	2	0	0	0	0	4
a—Risberg	1	0	0	0	0	0
Danforth, p	0	0	0	0	0	1
	32	0	7	0	24	18

New York	AB	R	H	RBI	PO	A
Burns, lf	4	0	1	0	2	0
Herzog, 2b	3	1	1	0	3	4
Kauff, cf	4	2	2	3	1	0
Zimmerman, 3b	4	0	1	0	2	2
Fletcher, ss	4	1	2	0	1	3
Robertson, rf	3	1	1	0	1	0
Holke, 1b	2	0	1	0	9	0
Rariden, c	3	0	0	1	7	1
Schupp, p	3	0	1	1	1	3
	30	5	10	5	27	13

Chicago	0	0	0	0	0	0	0	0	0—0
New York	0	0	0	1	1	0	1	2	x—5

Chicago	IP	H	R	ER	BB	K
Faber (L)	7	7	3	3	0	3

New York	IP	H	R	ER	BB	K
Schupp (W)	9	7	0	0	1	7

a—Flied out for Faber in ninth. E—Herzog. DP—Giants 1, Sox 1. LOB—Sox 6, Giants 3. 2B—E. Collins. 3B—Zimmerman. HR—Kauff 2. SB—E. Collins. SH—Herzog. WP—Faber. HBP—by Faber (Holke). Umpires—Rigler (NL), Evans (AL), O'Loughlin (AL), Klem (NL). Time—2:09. Attendance—27,746.

Game 5
October 13, at Chicago

New York	AB	R	H	RBI	PO	A
Burns, lf	4	2	1	1	3	0
Herzog, 2b	5	0	1	0	0	1
Kauff, cf	5	0	2	2	2	0
Zimmerman, 3b	5	1	1	0	1	2
Fletcher, ss	5	1	1	0	2	3
Thorpe, rf	0	0	0	0	0	0
a—Robertson, rf	5	0	3	1	2	0
Holke, 1b	5	0	0	0	11	0
Rariden, c	3	1	3	1	3	1
Sallee, p	3	0	0	0	0	2
Perritt, p	0	0	0	0	0	0
	40	5	12	5	24	9

Chicago	AB	R	H	RBI	PO	A
J. Collins, rf	5	1	1	0	1	0
McMullin, 3b	3	0	0	0	1	4
E. Collins, 2b	4	2	3	1	1	4
Jackson, lf	5	2	3	0	3	0
Felsch, cf	5	1	3	2	0	0
Gandil, 1b	5	1	1	2	10	2
Weaver, ss	4	1	1	0	2	2
Schalk, c	3	0	1	0	9	0
Russell, p	0	0	0	0	0	0
Cicotte, p	1	0	0	0	0	2
b—Risberg	1	0	1	1	0	0
Williams, p	0	0	0	0	0	0
c—Lynn	1	0	0	0	0	0
Faber, p	0	0	0	0	0	1
	37	8	14	6	27	15

New York	2	0	0	2	0	0	1	0	0—5
Chicago	0	0	1	0	0	1	3	3	x—8

New York	IP	H	R	ER	BB	K
Sallee (L)	7⅓	13	8	7	4	2
Perritt	⅔	1	0	0	0	0

Chicago	IP	H	R	ER	BB	K
Russell	0	2	1	1	1	0
Cicotte	6	8	3	2	1	3
Williams	1	2	1	1	0	3
Faber (W)	2	0	0	0	0	1

a—Singled for Thorpe in first. b—Singled for Cicotte in sixth. c—Struck out for Williams in seventh. E—Herzog, Zimmerman, Fletcher, J. Collins, Gandil, Weaver 3, Williams. DP—Sox 2. LOB—Giants 11, Sox 10. 2B—Kauff, Felsch, Fletcher, Gandil. SB—Kauff, Robertson, Schalk. SH—Sallee, McMullin. Umpires—O'Loughlin (AL), Klem (NL), Rigler (NL), Evans (AL). Time—2:37. Attendance—27,323.

Game 6
October 15, at New York

Chicago	AB	R	H	RBI	PO	A
J. Collins, rf	3	0	0	0	1	0
b—Leibold	2	0	1	1	1	0
McMullin, 3b	5	0	0	0	0	1
E. Collins, 2b	4	1	1	0	1	8
Jackson, lf	4	1	1	0	1	0
Felsch, cf	3	1	0	0	3	0
Gandil, 1b	4	0	2	2	14	0
Weaver, ss	4	1	1	0	2	2
Schalk, c	3	0	1	0	4	1
Faber, p	2	0	0	0	0	0
	34	4	7	3	27	12

New York	AB	R	H	RBI	PO	A
Burns, lf	4	1	0	0	2	0
Herzog, 2b	4	0	2	2	2	5
Kauff, cf	4	0	0	0	2	0
Zimmerman, 3b	4	0	0	0	1	2
Fletcher, ss	4	0	1	0	1	2
Robertson, rf	3	0	1	0	0	1
Holke, 1b	4	0	1	0	12	0
Rariden, c	3	1	0	0	7	1
Benton, p	1	0	0	0	0	0
a—Wilhoit	0	0	0	0	0	0
Perritt, p	1	0	1	0	0	1
c—McCarty	1	0	0	0	0	0
	33	2	6	2	27	12

Chicago	0	0	0	3	0	0	0	0	1—4
New York	0	0	0	0	2	0	0	0	0—2

Chicago	IP	H	R	ER	BB	K
Faber (W)	9	6	2	2	2	4

New York	IP	H	R	ER	BB	K
Benton (L)	5	4	3	0	1	3
Perritt	4	3	1	1	2	3

a—Walked for Benton in fifth. b—Popped out for J. Collins in seventh. c—Grounded out for Perritt in ninth. E—Schalk, Kauff, Zimmerman, Robertson. LOB—Sox 7, Giants 7. 2B—Holke. 3B—Herzog. SH—Faber. HBP—by Faber (Robertson). PB—Schalk. Umpires—Klem (NL), O'Loughlin (AL), Evans (AL), Rigler (NL). Time—2:18. Attendance—33,969.

1919 World Series: White Sox versus Cincinnati Reds

In order to capitalize on baseball's postwar prosperity, the World Series was expanded to nine games. The world championship was lost not for lack of talent or breaks but for lack of effort as eight White Sox players agreed to throw the Series to the Cincinnati Redlegs for a gambling payoff.

The 1919 Sox were essentially the same crew that had handily won the title in 1917. The Sox led the majors in batting, runs, and stolen bases. Joe Jackson posted a .351 mark. Eddie Collins (.319) topped the league in steals (33). Lefty Williams (23–11) and Ed Cicotte (29–7) combined for more than half of the Sox' victories.

Cincinnati was toasting its first pennant since the days of the touring 1869 Red Stockings. But these Redlegs weren't nearly as good a ballclub as the White Sox. Two members of their lineup had once donned the Pale Hose flannels: second baseman Morrie Rath and outfielder Edd Roush. One starting pitcher, Hod Eller, had failed in an earlier Chicago tryout. Another hurler, Slim Sallee, as a member of the New York Giants, had been roughed up twice by the Sox in the 1917 Series.

Sox first baseman Chick Gandil, an angry malcontent, sought out the gamblers. Gandil's coconspirators comprised the "bad-boy clique": outfielders Joe Jackson and Happy Felsch, third baseman Buck Weaver, shortstop Swede Risberg, pitchers Ed Cicotte and Lefty Williams, and infielder Fred McMullen. The fix was justified as long-overdue retaliation against skinflint owner Charles Comiskey.

The ballplayers ended up working the fix with two sets of gamblers, both underwritten by New York gambling boss Arnold Rothstein. The players were not given all the money they were promised. They were told by Joseph "Sport" Sullivan and Abe Attell that all of it was out on bets.

The little money siphoned their way kept the players off their toes. Feeling betrayed, they started doing some double-crossing of their own. Down four games to one, with no dirty money forthcoming, the Sox took the next two contests. But a hoodlum, the night before the eighth game, warned Lefty Williams that his wife would be physically harmed if he did not fall into line. Williams was blasted in the Series finale.

Comiskey subsequently did some behind-the-door maneuvering of his own in a futile effort to save his team. But his reputation would permanently be soiled in a grand jury investigation. Commissioner Kenesaw Mountain Landis tossed the Black Sox players out of baseball…forever.

Even Buck Weaver, whose only crime was "guilty knowledge," was banned, this despite a sharp Series (.324). Petition after petition on Weaver's behalf would not change Landis' mind. Efforts were also unsuccessful to clear Joe Jackson. Jackson, who was the Series' leading hitter (.375), went along with the fix against his better judgment.

The stench emanating from the Black Sox scandal nearly ruined baseball and sent the White Sox into a 30-year tailspin that almost wrecked the franchise.

The city was gripped with World Series fever.

Game 1

On the eve of the Series, there were rumors that Ed Cicotte had a sore arm. Cicotte was flat in his last three regular season assignments. The Sox, the early favorites, were now listed as 6–5 underdogs. Informed that the odds had dropped, the Black Sox conspirators received only $10,000. Balking at a smaller share, Cicotte was given the entire amount. He sewed the greenbacks into the lining of his suit coat. Cicotte signaled that the fix was on by hitting the first batter of the game—it was all downhill after that.

Doubts about Cicotte's arm would linger after he was shelled in a Reds 9–1 win. A sloppily played, five-run fourth drove Cicotte off the mound. Working in tandem, Cicotte and shortstop Swede Risberg bungled an inning-ending double play. Cicotte, after grabbing Larry Kopf's crack, wheeled around then stopped. Risberg was slow coming to the bag. Instead of a lead throw, Cicotte waited till Risberg reached second base. Risberg then stumbled across the bag and stood upright before making the throw, allowing Kopf to beat the relay.

Then, the usually sure-handed Risberg failed to come up with Greasy Neale's bounder behind second base—the kind of ball he had easily handled all summer. Four hits followed, including a triple by pitcher Dutch Ruether, chasing Cicotte. The next inning, as if to make up for the error, Risberg cleanly handled a grounder.

White Sox breakdowns canceled scoring opportunities in the first two innings. Buck Weaver missed the ball on a hit-and-run play, allowing Eddie Collins to be thrown out at second base. In the next frame, Risberg swung through a pitch, leaving Chick Gandil out to dry. Joe Jackson and Hap Felsch failed with two aboard in the sixth. A Chick Gandil error helped the Reds wrap things up in a two-run seventh.

The Chicago press noted the Sox were playing on their heels. "Overconfident" was also a word bantered about that day. Afterward, Sox manager Kid Gleason lamented, "These kind of losses are good for the White Sox."

Sportswriter Ring Lardner more keenly observed, "I don't like what these old owl eyes are seeing."

Shano Collins opens Game 1 in Cincinnati with a single to center.

Game 2

Game 2 went pretty much the same as Game 1: a big inning decided the issue for Cincinnati. Three fourth-inning walks blossomed into three runs in the Reds' 4–2 triumph. Lefty Williams' strong suit was his control. He had walked only 58 hitters in 300 innings during the regular season, but he couldn't locate the plate in Game 2.

The Sox outhit the Reds 10 to four. Bad breaks was the best excuse offered for this latest failure. The Sox should have taken an early 2–0 lead but for Chick Gandil. Twice he failed to produce a fly ball with runners on third and less than two out. Instead, he slapped down feeble grounders.

The Reds batters waited out Williams in the fourth. Intermixed with the free passes, Edd Roush delivered an RBI single and Larry Kopf a two-run triple. Roush accepted another Williams walk in the sixth, then scooted in on Greasy Neale's hit.

Neale's errant throw on Schalk's double allowed the Sox to tally two in the seventh. Hap Felsch and pinch-hitter Fred McMullen, representing the tying run at the plate in the eighth and ninth innings, failed to connect.

Chick Gandil is out at second in Game 2.

The Black Sox had been promised $40,000: Game 1 and Game 2's payment. Instead, they were shortchanged again by the gamblers. Gandil pocketed $10,000 for himself.

Cincinnati baseball fans celebrated the triumph hoisting a dummy figure of Lefty Williams around town in a torch-light parade. The night before, the dummy's placard had read, "Cicotte."

Game 3

After registering cakewalks against the Sox' two best hurlers, the Reds were shut out 3–0 on a three-hitter by rookie southpaw Dickie Kerr. Manager Kid Gleason, viewing the diminutive Kerr (5'7", 155 lb.) in spring training, remarked, "Why do they send me these samples?" But Kerr, a former bantamweight pugilist, proved to be a fighter and replaced the injured Red Faber as the starter in Game 3. One Comiskey Park Series patron, heavyweight champ Jack Dempsey, was to remark, "It's too bad the kid didn't stay in the ring; he packs an awful wallop in that left mitt."

Chick Gandil, who had no respect for the busher Kerr, doubled home two runs in the second. But, after the hit, Gandil took the Sox out of what could have been a bigger inning. Gandil took his sweet time going to third base on a sacrifice bunt. In the sixth, Joe Jackson and Hap Felsch reached base, then were promptly caught stealing.

Swede Risberg recorded 10 successful chances, including a couple of magnificent plays on slow rollers. One of Risberg's two Series hits—a triple in the fourth—resulted in a run. Back home, the fighting spirit that Gleason said was missing in Cincinnati, returned. The Sox weren't about to get beat this time.

Eddie Collins and the Reds' venom-tongued bench jockey Jimmy Smith got into a row. Joe Jackson, upset by a tight one from Reds hurler Ray Fisher, purposely laid down a bunt toward first base, hoping to draw the pitcher to the baseline. Even the normally reserved Nemo Leibold took exception to some bench razzing.

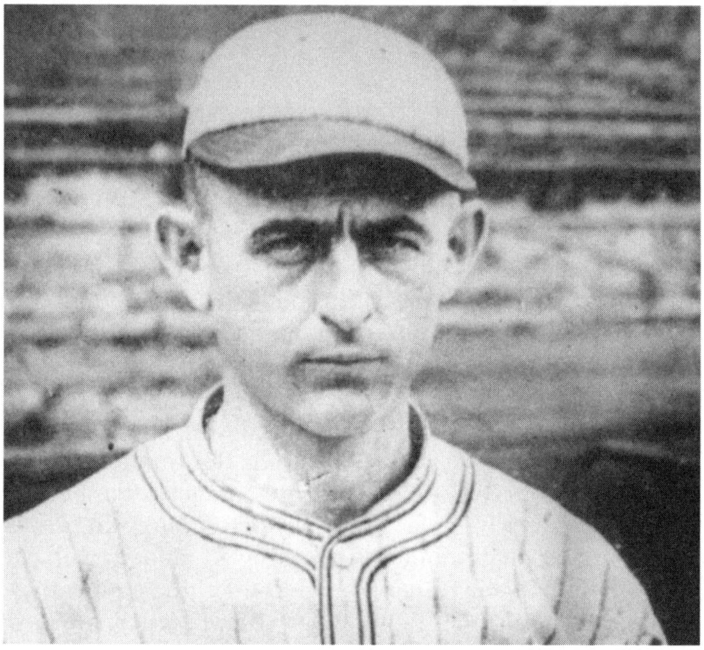

Dickie Kerr was the hero of Game 3.

Kerr finished off the Reds, retiring the last 15 batters. The confidence, optimism, and enthusiasm for this ballclub returned.

Game 4

Comiskey Park was a cacophony of sounds. South Side fans carried pots and pans for noisemakers. The Cincinnati band, who arrived by train from the Queen City, battled Chicago's ensemble for musical honors. The fans, using megaphones, provided the harmonizing, blaring forth the popular tunes of the day. But the enthusiasm in the stands failed to spur the Sox on as they dropped a 2–0 decision, giving the Reds a commanding three-games-to-one lead.

Jimmy Ring, the Reds' fourth pitcher of the Series, tossed a three-hitter. Ed Cicotte, pitching better than in the opener, completed the assignment on five hits, but his two fifth-inning fielding blunders handed the Reds the ballgame.

As usual, the Sox were unable to cash in on an early inning threat. Cicotte flew out, ending a bases-loaded threat in the second. Hap Felsch stranded two runners in the third. The Reds' fifth was Cicotte's undoing. With one out, he threw Pat Duncan's bounder past Chick Gandil for a two-base error. Larry Kopf followed with a hit to left. Joe Jackson fielded it quickly and fired home. But Cicotte tried to cut the ball off. It caromed off his glove past catcher Ray Schalk to the grandstand. Duncan trotted home. Larry Kopf, who had no intention of taking the extra base, moved to second. Greasy Neale then blooped one just past Jackson's outstretched glove, scoring Kopf.

Cicotte committed only three errors all season. Kid Gleason defended his pitcher's errant ways by pointing out Cicotte had rated the Reds too high, noting that Kopf had no more intention of going to second base "than I have of jumping in the lake."

That evening, Chicago saloon patrons were spraying the froth and singing Ring Lardner's latest doggerel, "I'm Forever Blowing Ball Games."

Game 5

Kid Gleason was saddened and angered with his team's poor showing after the Sox suffered their second straight shutout loss at home, 5–0. Cincinnati's youthful ace, Hod Eller, breezed through the Sox lineup, striking out nine. He fanned six in succession over the second and third innings: Chick Gandil, Swede Risberg, Ray Schalk, Lefty Williams, Nemo Leibold, and Eddie Collins. His achievement stands scrutiny because half of the victims were members of the so-called Clean Sox. Eller, who had been labeled a big boob by Kid Gleason during a spring tryout with the Sox some years earlier, was favoring a sore elbow. He claimed to have skidded on a piece of gum in his hotel room and bumped his arm on the wall.

While Eller was stretching his wing in the first inning, the Sox mounted their only threat, placing runners at the corners with one out. Nothing came of it: Jackson hit an infield pop-up; Hap Felsch sent a lazy fly to left.

The Reds managed only one hit off Lefty Williams over the first five innings. But Williams was rocked for four runs in the sixth. Two of the three hits should have been handled. Hod Eller sailed one over Hap Felsch's and Joe Jackson's heads, and, when Swede Risberg mishandled the relay, Eller made third. A hit and walk followed. Edd Roush lifted a long drive to center. A backtracking Felsch appeared to have corralled the sphere, but he dropped it for a triple. On the play, Ray Schalk thought he had nabbed Heinie Groh at the plate. Schalk pawed the umpire with his catcher's mitt and was tossed from the game. Schalk's replacement, Byrd Lynn, mishandled Joe Jackson's throw on Pat Duncan's liner, and Roush slid home with the fourth run.

Fans in Washington watch the results of the 1919 World Series game come in via telegraph and get posted to a storefront tote board.

Buck Weaver turns up the afterburners.

Game 6

The Reds, looking to put a quick end to the Series, grabbed an early 4–0 lead. But the Sox weren't finished. The Black Sox clique, tired of losing and angered by the gamblers' betrayal, were now playing heads-up ball. Dickie Kerr settled down, allowing his teammates to rally for a 5–4 victory. Chick Gandil won his second game on Kerr's behalf, singling home Buck Weaver with the winning run in the tenth inning.

Swede Risberg, however, continued his shabby play. At the plate he was 0-for-4. His errant throw on a play at third base in the fourth inning hit the runner in the back, allowing the Reds to score their fourth run.

The Sox tied it up in the sixth, ending Dutch Ruether's stint. Buck Weaver and Hap Felsch sandwiched doubles around a single by Joe Jackson, who finally got a hit in the clutch. Two outs later, Ray Schalk's base hit sent Felsch in.

The inning before, the Sox finally had gotten on the scoreboard on Eddie Collins' sacrifice fly. On the same play, Kerr (à la Red Faber 1917) tore for second base only to find it occupied by Ray Schalk, who had waved his hands in desperation. The Sox could do nothing right, it seemed.

Joe Jackson approaches home plate after hitting a home run in Game 8.

Game 7

The real Ed Cicotte put on a good show in Game 7. The cool, composed right-hander scattered seven hits for a Sox 4–1 win. His "shine ball" had the Reds so off balance they accused him of doctoring the ball. The whining Reds stopped play numerous times to have the umpire inspect the ball for a greasy substance.

Redland Field was only half filled. Scalpers bought up most of the tickets but couldn't sell them. The Sox' sixth-game comeback victory combined with the lengthy best-of-nine Series caused waning interest in the games.

Shano Collins took over center-field duty. At Redland Field it was considered the worst sun field in either league. Hap Felsch, who was having a poor defensive Series, was switched to right field. Shano singled and scored in the first and third innings. He was driven in each time on base hits by Joe Jackson. His namesake, Eddie Collins, moved him up both times with a sacrifice bunt and a hit-and-run.

Eddie Collins sparked a two-run fifth with a hit. The Sox were finally getting some breaks. Reds infielders made two errors, filling the bases for Hap Felsch, who stroked a single to center.

Afterward, Gleason predicted his club would take the next two games. The Sox were coming on strong now, or so it appeared. They had staged similar rallies against the Cubs in the last City Series.

The Black Sox are confident as they await their 1921 trial, but the judgment of history was against them.

Game 8

Back in Chicago, the dream of a White Sox comeback was shattered early in a four-run Cincinnati first inning. A gamblers' henchman had reached Lefty Williams and threatened to harm him and his family unless Williams pitched poorly. Williams wanted to duplicate Cicotte's fine work in Game 8, but his concern now was for the safety of his wife in the stands. He retired the first batter, then gave up two singles and two doubles before being lifted.

The Reds steadily built up their lead as the Comiskey Park patrons filed out of the gloomy stadium. It became an 8–1 game in the eighth before the Sox made a desperate late run. Joe Jackson, following a solo homer in the third, doubled home two in a four-run eighth inning. Chick Gandil had an RBI triple—his only extra-base hit of the Series.

Cincinnati went on to win the game 10–5 to take the Series. Hod Eller went the distance, working out of a final jam in the ninth. Prior to the game, Eller had been approached in his hotel lobby and offered money for a poor outing. Eller reported the incident to his manager. Gamblers were trying to work both sides of the street, apparently.

For the third time in the Series, Gleason alibied to the press that Williams didn't have his stuff. Would Dickie Kerr or fifth starter Bill James have been a better choice, or were they doomed from the start, too?

In the 1988 film adaptation of *Eight Men Out*, John Cusack (left), D.B. Sweeney, and Charlie Sheen played Buck Weaver, Shoeless Joe Jackson, and Happy Felsch.

Gleason said the Reds had no business beating his Sox. He was right. The Sox played championship ball in only three of the eight games. This tragically cursed ballclub was about to be relegated to the ash heap of history.

Game 1
October 1, at Cincinnati

Chicago	AB	R	H	RBI	PO	A
J. Collins, rf	4	0	1	0	0	0
E. Collins, 2b	4	0	1	0	3	3
Weaver, 3b	4	0	1	0	0	1
Jackson, lf	4	1	0	0	3	0
Felsch, cf	3	0	0	0	4	0
Gandil, 1b	4	0	2	1	7	0
Risberg, ss	2	0	0	0	5	6
Schalk, c	3	0	0	0	2	2
Cicotte, p	1	0	0	0	0	3
Wilkinson, p	1	0	0	0	0	0
a—McMullin	1	0	1	0	0	0
Lowdermilk, p	0	0	0	0	0	1
	31	1	6	1	24	16

Cincinnati	AB	R	H	RBI	PO	A
Rath, 2b	3	2	1	1	4	2
Daubert, 1b	4	1	3	1	9	0
Groh, 3b	3	1	1	2	0	3
Roush, cf	3	0	0	0	8	0
Duncan, 1f	4	0	2	1	1	0
Kopf, ss	4	1	0	0	1	3
Neale, rf	4	2	3	0	3	0
Wingo, c	3	1	1	1	1	2
Ruether, p	3	1	3	3	0	2
	31	9	14	9	27	12

Chicago	0	1	0	0	0	0	0	0	0—1
Cincinnati	1	0	0	5	0	0	2	1	x—9

Chicago	IP	H	R	ER	BB	K
Cicotte (L)	3⅔	7	6	6	2	1
Wilkinson	3⅓	5	2	1	0	1
Lowdermilk	1	2	1	1	1	0

Cincinnati	IP	H	R	ER	BB	K
Ruether (W)	9	6	1	0	1	1

a—Singled for Wilkinson in eighth. E—Gandil, Kopf. DP—Sox 2. LOB—Sox 5, Reds 7. 2B—Rath. 3B—Ruether 2, Daubert. SB—Roush. SH—Felsch, Rath, Roush, Wingo. SF—Groh. HBP—by Cicotte (Rath), by Lowdermilk (Daubert). Umpires—Rigler (NL), Evans (AL), Nallin (AL), Quigly (NL). Time—1:42. Attendance—30,511.

Game 2
October 2, at Cincinnati

Chicago	AB	R	H	RBI	PO	A
J. Collins, rf	4	0	0	0	2	0
E. Collins, 2b	3	0	0	0	2	3
Weaver, 3b	4	0	2	0	3	0
Jackson, lf	4	0	3	0	1	0
Felsch, cf	2	0	0	0	5	1
Gandil, 1b	4	0	1	0	7	0
Risberg, ss	4	1	1	0	2	2
Schalk, c	4	1	2	0	2	2
Williams, p	3	0	1	0	0	2
a—McMullin	1	0	0	0	0	0
	33	2	10	0	24	10

Cincinnati	AB	R	H	RBI	PO	A
Rath, 2b	3	1	0	0	1	2
Daubert, 1b	3	0	0	0	12	2
Groh, 3b	2	1	0	0	0	1
Roush, cf	2	1	1	1	5	0
Duncan, lf	1	1	0	0	1	0
Kopf, ss	3	0	1	2	3	6
Neale, rf	3	0	1	1	1	0
Rariden, c	3	0	1	0	3	0
Sallee, p	3	0	0	0	1	3
	23	4	4	4	27	14

Chicago	0	0	0	0	0	0	2	0	0—2
Cincinnati	0	0	0	3	0	1	0	0	x—4

Chicago	IP	H	R	ER	BB	K
Williams (L)	8	4	4	4	6	1

Cincinnati	IP	H	R	ER	BB	K
Sallee (W)	9	10	2	0	1	2

a—Grounded out for Williams in ninth. E—Risberg, Daubert, Neale. DP—Sox 2, Reds 2. LOB—Sox 7, Reds 3. 2B—Jackson, Weaver. 3B—Kopf. SB—Gandil. SH—Felsch, Daubert, Duncan. Balk—Sallee. Umpires—Evans (AL), Quigley (NL). Nallin (AL), Rigler (NL). Time—1:42. Attendance—29,690.

Game 3
October 3, at Chicago

Cincinnati	AB	R	H	RBI	PO	A
Rath, 2b	4	0	0	0	3	3
Daubert, 1b	4	0	0	0	14	1
Groh, 3b	3	0	0	0	2	5
Roush, cf	3	0	0	0	0	0
Duncan, lf	3	0	1	0	0	0
Kopf, ss	3	0	1	0	1	1
Neale, rf	3	0	0	0	1	0
Rariden, c	3	0	0	0	2	3
Fisher, p	2	0	1	0	0	5
a—Magee	1	0	0	0	0	0
Luque, p	0	0	0	0	1	0
	29	0	3	0	24	18

Chicago	AB	R	H	RBI	PO	A
Leibold, rf	4	0	0	0	2	0
E. Collins, 2b	4	0	1	0	1	5
Weaver, 3b	4	0	1	0	0	4
Jackson, lf	3	1	2	0	1	0
Felsch, cf	2	1	0	0	1	0
Gandil, 1b	3	0	1	2	14	1
Risberg, ss	2	1	1	0	4	6
Schalk, c	3	0	1	1	4	0
Kerr, p	3	0	0	0	0	0
	28	3	7	3	27	16

Cincinnati	0	0	0	0	0	0	0	0	0—0
Chicago	0	2	0	1	0	0	0	0	—3

Cincinnati	IP	H	R	ER	BB	K
Fisher (L)	7	7	3	2	2	1
Luque	1	0	0	0	0	1

Chicago	IP	H	R	ER	BB	K
Kerr (W)	9	3	0	0	1	4

a—Flied out for Fisher in eighth. E—Fisher. DP—Sox 1, Reds 1. LOB—Sox 3, Reds 3. 3B—Risberg. Umpires—Quigley (NL), Nallin (AL), Rigler (NL), Evans (AL). Time—1:30. Attendance—29,126.

Game 4

October 4, at Chicago

Cincinnati	AB	R	H	RBI	PO	A
Rath, 2b	4	0	1	0	5	1
Daubert, 1b	4	0	0	0	9	1
Groh, 3b	4	0	0	0	2	3
Roush, cf	3	0	0	0	2	0
Duncan, lf	3	1	0	0	1	0
Kopf, ss	3	1	1	1	1	1
Neale, rf	3	0	1	1	4	0
Wingo, c	3	0	2	0	2	0
Ring, p	3	0	0	0	1	2
	30	2	5	2	27	8

Chicago	AB	R	H	RBI	PO	A
Leibold, rf	5	0	0	0	0	0
E. Collins, 2b	3	0	0	0	3	5
Weaver, 3b	4	0	0	0	0	3
Jackson, lf	4	0	1	0	3	0
Felsch, cf	3	0	1	0	0	0
Gandil, 1b	4	0	1	0	14	0
Risberg, ss	3	0	0	0	3	4
Schalk, c	1	0	0	0	4	3
Cicotte, p	3	0	0	0	0	2
a—Murphy	1	0	0	0	0	0
	31	0	3	0	27	17

Cincinnati	0	0	0	0	2	0	0	0	0	—2
Chicago	0	0	0	0	0	0	0	0	0	—0

Cincinnati	IP	H	R	ER	BB	K
Ring (W)	9	3	0	0	3	2

Chicago	IP	H	R	ER	BB	K
Cicotte (L)	9	5	2	0	0	2

a—Flied out for Cicotte in ninth. E—Rath, Groh, Cicotte 2. DP—Sox 2. LOB—Sox 10, Reds 1. 2B—Jackson, Neale. SB—Risberg. SH—Felsch. HBP—by Ring (E. Collins, Schalk). Umpires—Nallin (AL), Rigler (NL), Evans (AL), Quigley (NL). Time—1:37. Attendance—34,363.

Game 5

October 6, at Chicago

Cincinnati	AB	R	H	RBI	PO	A
Rath, 2b	3	1	1	1	0	3
Daubert, 1b	2	0	0	0	11	0
Groh, 3b	3	1	0	0	1	2
Roush, cf	4	2	1	2	2	0
Duncan, lf	2	0	0	1	2	0
Kopf, ss	3	0	1	0	0	4
Neale, ss	4	0	0	1	1	0
Rariden, c	4	0	0	0	10	0
Eller, p	3	1	1	0	0	2
	28	5	4	5	27	11

Chicago	AB	R	H	RBI	PO	A
Leibold, rf	3	0	0	0	1	0
E. Collins, 2b	4	0	0	0	1	2
Weaver, 3b	4	0	2	0	1	2
Jackson, lf	4	0	0	0	3	0
Felsch, cf	3	0	0	0	7	0
Gandil, 1b	3	0	0	0	8	1
Risberg, ss	3	0	0	0	1	2
Schalk, c	2	0	1	0	3	2
Lynn, c	1	0	0	0	1	0
Williams, p	2	0	0	0	1	0
a—Murphy	1	0	0	0	0	0
Mayer, p	0	0	0	0	0	0
	30	0	3	0	27	9

Cincinnati	0	0	0	0	0	4	0	0	1	—5
Chicago	0	0	0	0	0	0	0	0	0	—0

Cincinnati	IP	H	R	ER	BB	K
Eller (W)	9	3	0	0	1	9

Chicago	IP	H	R	ER	BB	K
Williams (L)	8	4	4	4	2	3
Mayer	1	0	1	0	1	0

a—Struck out for Williams in eighth. E—E. Collins, Felsch, Risberg. LOB—Sox 4, Reds 3. 2B-Eller. 3B—Roush, Weaver. SB—Roush. SH—Daubert 2, Kopf. SF—Duncan. PB—Schalk. Umpires—Rigler (NL), Evans (AL), Quigley (NL), Nallin (AL). Time—1:45. Attendance—34,379.

Game 6

October 7, at Cincinnati

Chicago	AB	R	H	RBI	PO	A
J. Collins, rf	3	0	0	0	2	0
a—Leibold, rf	1	0	0	0	0	0
E. Collins, 2b	4	0	0	1	4	6
Weaver, 3b	5	2	3	0	2	1
Jackson, lf	4	1	2	1	1	1
Felsch, cf	5	1	2	1	2	0
Gandil, 1b	4	0	1	1	11	0
Risberg, ss	4	1	0	0	3	5
Schalk, c	2	0	1	1	4	2
Kerr, p	3	0	1	0	1	4
	35	5	10	5	30	19

Cincinnati	AB	R	H	RBI	PO	A
Rath, 2b	5	0	1	0	4	1
Daubert, 1b	4	1	2	0	8	0
Groh, 3b	4	0	1	0	2	2
Roush, cf	4	1	1	0	7	2
Duncan, lf	5	0	1	2	2	0
Kopf, ss	4	0	0	0	1	5
Neale, rf	4	1	3	0	3	0
Rariden, c	4	0	1	0	3	0
Ruether, p	2	1	1	1	0	0
Ring, p	2	0	0	0	0	1
	38	4	11	3	30	11

Chicago	0	0	0	0	1	3	0	0	0	1	—5
Cincinnati	0	0	2	2	0	0	0	0	0	0	—4

Chicago	IP	H	R	ER	BB	K
Kerr (W)	10	11	4	3	2	2

Cincinnati	IP	H	R	ER	BB	K
Ruether	5	6	4	4	3	0
Ring (L)	5	4	1	1	3	2

a—Grounded out for J. Collins in seventh. E—Felsch, Risberg 2. DP—Sox 2, Reds 3. LOB—Sox 8, Reds 8. 2B—Groh, Duncan, Ruether, Weaver 2, Felsch. 3B—Neale. SB—Leibold, Schalk, Rath, Daubert. SH—Daubert, Kerr. SF—E. Collins. HBP—by Kerr (Roush). Umpires—Evans (AL), Quigley (NL), Nallin (AL), Rigler (NL). Time—2:06. Attendance—32,006.

Game 7

October 8, at Cincinnati

Chicago	AB	R	H	RBI	PO	A
J. Collins, cf-rf	5	2	3	0	1	0
E. Collins, 2b	4	1	2	0	3	6
Weaver, 3b	4	1	0	0	2	2
Jackson, lf	4	0	2	2	3	0
Felsch, rf-cf	4	0	2	2	2	0
Gandil, 1b	4	0	0	0	9	0
Risberg, ss	4	0	0	0	3	2
Schalk, c	4	0	1	0	4	1
Cicotte, p	4	0	0	0	0	2
	37	4	10	4	27	13

Cincinnati	AB	R	H	RBI	PO	A
Rath, 2b	5	0	1	0	3	3
Daubert, 1b	4	0	0	0	10	1
Groh, 3b	4	1	1	0	0	2
Roush, cf	4	0	0	0	3	1
Duncan, lf	4	0	1	1	1	1
Kopf, ss	4	0	1	0	2	5
Neale, rf	4	0	1	0	3	0
Wingo, c	1	0	1	0	5	1
Sallee, p	1	0	0	0	0	1
Fisher, p	0	0	0	0	0	1
a—Ruether	1	0	0	0	0	0
Luque, p	1	0	0	0	0	0
b—Magee	1	0	1	0	0	0
c—Smith	0	0	0	0	0	0
	34	1	7	1	27	16

Chicago	1	0	1	0	2	0	0	0	0	—4
Cincinnati	0	0	0	0	0	1	0	0	0	—1

Chicago	IP	H	R	ER	BB	K
Cicotte (W)	9	7	1	1	3	4

Cincinnati	IP	H	R	ER	BB	K
Sallee (L)	4 1/3	9	4	2	0	0
Fisher	2/3	0	0	0	0	1
Luque	4	1	0	0	0	5

a—Fouled out for Fisher in fifth. b—singled for Luque in ninth. c—Ran for Magee in ninth. E—E. Collins, Rath, Daubert, Groh, Roush. DP—Reds 1. LOB—Sox 7, Reds 9. 2B—J. Collins, Groh. SH—E. Collins. Umpires—Quigley (NL), Nallin (AL), Rigler (NL), Evans (AL), Time—1:47. Attendance—13,923.

Game 8

October 9, at Chicago

Cincinnati	AB	R	H	RBI	PO	A
Rath, 2b	4	1	2	0	2	2
Daubert, 1b	4	2	2	0	8	0
Groh, 3b	6	2	2	0	1	1
Roush, cf	5	2	3	4	3	0
Duncan, lf	4	1	2	3	1	0
Kopf, ss	3	1	1	0	1	3
Neale, rf	3	0	1	1	4	0
Rariden, c	5	0	2	2	7	0
Eller, p	4	1	1	0	0	0
	38	10	16	10	27	6

Chicago	AB	R	H	RBI	PO	A
Leibold, cf	5	0	1	0	2	2
E. Collins, 2b	5	1	3	0	4	1
Weaver, 3b	5	1	2	0	1	5
Jackson, lf	5	2	2	3	1	0
Felsch, cf	4	0	0	0	2	0
Gandil, 1b	4	1	1	1	9	0
Risberg, ss	3	0	0	0	2	3
Schalk, c	4	0	1	0	6	3
Williams, p	0	0	0	0	0	0
James, p	2	0	0	0	0	0
Wilkinson, p	1	0	0	0	0	2
a—Murphy	0	0	0	0	0	0
	38	5	10	4	27	16

Cincinnati	4	1	0	0	1	3	0	1	0	—10
Chicago	0	0	1	0	0	0	0	4	0	— 5

Cincinnati	IP	H	R	ER	BB	K
Eller (W)	9	10	5	4	1	6

Chicago	IP	H	R	ER	BB	K
Williams (L)	1/3	4	4	4	0	0
James	4 2/3	8	4	3	3	2
Wilkinson	4	4	2	0	4	2

a—Hit by pitch for Wilkinson in ninth. E—Roush, Rariden, Schalk. LOB—Sox 8, Reds 12. 2B—Roush 2, E. Collins, Duncan, Weaver, Jackson. 3B-Kopf, Gandil. HR—Jackson. SB-Neale, Rath, Rariden, E. Collins. SH—Duncan, Daubert. HBP—by James (Eller), by Wilkinson (Roush), by Eller (Murphy). Umpires—Nallin (AL), Rigler (NL), Evans (AL), Quigley (NL). Time—2:27. Attendance—32,930.

1959 World Series: White Sox versus Los Angeles Dodgers

In Chicago in the summer of '59 it was penny loafers, hula hoops, rock and roll, and the White Sox. Under new owner Bill Veeck, the Go-Go Sox of Frank Lane and Charles Comiskey had finally reached the World Series.

The Windy City was in the grip of a baseball frenzy. The Chicago public schools allowed radios in the classrooms; some principals simply let the students go home early. People crowded around the display windows of department stores to view the games on television. Others simply roamed around town with a transistor radio protruding from a shirt pocket and a wire running up to their ear.

The Go-Go Sox resembled their Hitless Wonder ancestors of 1906. The Sox (.250) were outhit by five other American League clubs. They socked the league's fewest homers (97). But, like the '06 bunch, they relied on strong pitching, a tight defense, and speed on the bases.

Bill Veeck despised the Go-Go style and tried all season to add power to the lineup. Unable to pry slugger Roy Sievers from Washington, he acquired Ted Kluszewski in late August. Big Klu led all Sox hitters with a .391 World Series average. His record-setting two homers and five RBIs powered the Sox to an 11–0 whitewash in the opener over the Los Angeles Dodgers.

L.A. rebounded, winning four of the next five games to take the Series. Rookie hurler Larry Sherry turned in a clutch relief performance in each Dodgers victory to earn the Series Most Valuable Player award.

Bill Veeck flashing a stack of World Series tickets. "Who needs tickets? Step right up, boys!"

Ted Kluszewski signs an autograph for a young fan after the first game of the World Series, October 1, 1959.

The Sox, with a break or two, could have won the championship despite Sherry. And with a little more shade from the sun, the Sox could have wrapped things up in California.

The Dodgers' home base was the mammoth Los Angeles Coliseum. In the oval-shaped Olympic stadium, a wire fence was erected to create an outfield. Something had to give in the makeshift ballyard, and it was left field, a mere 250 feet away from home plate, bordered by a 40-foot-high fence.

Home-field advantage was never such an advantage as in the 1959 World Series. The Sox appeared disoriented and lost in the three contests played in the Coliseum. The Sox batters couldn't ignore the tempting Chinese Wall in left field. The fielders had a hard time tracking down the baseball amid the sea of white shirts in the sun-baked stadium.

Easing the Sox loss somewhat, the three 90,000-plus crowds in California set Series records for winner's share ($11,231) and loser's share ($7,275).

Game 1

In the Series opener at Comiskey Park, the Go-Go Sox surprised their fans and shocked their Cy Young Award starting pitcher, Early Wynn, with an 11–0 drubbing of the Dodgers. The rout featured a seven-run third inning that seemed to symbolize the release of the frustrations of 40 title-less years.

In pregame festivities, the old spitballer Red Faber went to the mound and threw the ceremonial first pitch to his 1919 battery mate, Ray Schalk.

Playing in his first World Series, Ted Kluszewski's Popeye biceps were pumped up. Swatting two home runs and a single, he drove in a record-tying five runs. Jim Landis, with three singles on the day, was on base each time Klu connected. In the two-run first inning, Kluszewski singled in Nelson Fox, who had walked, for the Sox's first run. That hit moved Landis around to third in scoring position for a Sherman Lollar sacrifice fly. In the third inning, Fox doubled, and Landis singled him home. Then Klu parked one in the lower right-field stands, KO'ing Roger Craig (11–5, 2.06), the National League ERA champ.

The Sox weren't finished. Aided by three Dodgers errors, they added four more runs in the frame. Outfielders Duke Snider and Wally Moon pulled an Alphonse-Gaston act on Lollar's lazy fly. Billy Goodman singled. Snider missed the relay man on Al Smith's double. On Jim Rivera's grounder, second baseman Charley Neal threw the ball past home plate. A huffing and puffing Early Wynn closed the scoring with an RBI double to right.

In the fourth inning, Kluszewski chased L.A. reliever Chuck Churn with a mammoth drive that vibrated the façade of the upper deck.

Big Ted Kluszewski is congratulated by Jim Landis and Sherm Lollar after the first of two Game 1 World Series home runs.

Wynn's elbow stiffened up in the seventh inning. He signaled the Sox bench to get somebody warmed up. Another elder statesman, 39-year-old Gerry Staley, mopped up for the Sox.

Speedster Luis Aparicio (0-for-5) didn't participate in the rout. Little Louie's on-base tactics just might have slowed down the proceedings.

Game 2

The Series was evened at a game apiece in a tough 4–3 Sox loss. The fans had anticipated a repeat of Game 1's rout as the Sox scored two quick runs in the first inning. Luis Aparicio opened the frame with a double down the right-field line. He moved to third on Nellie Fox's fly ball. Jim Landis walked. Aparicio registered on Ted Kluszewski's grounder; Landis scooted home on Sherman Lollar's infield squibbler.

Charley Neal sliced the lead in half in the fifth inning, when he laced a Bob Shaw letter-high slider into the lower left-field stands. As the ball sailed over the wall, left fielder Al Smith looked up and was doused by a stream of beer from a fan who had accidently tipped his cup off the ledge of the wall while lunging for the ball.

With two gone in the L.A. seventh, former Stanford halfback Chuck Essegian, hitting for starter Johnny Podres, sent a ball into the upper deck of the left-field stands, tying the contest.

The next batter, Jim Gilliam, drew Bob Shaw's first free pass of the game. Charley Neal then drove a belt-high fastball into the Sox bullpen in dead-away center field, giving L.A. a 4–2 lead. Turk Lown then replaced Shaw and held the Dodgers in check the rest of the way.

Smitty's cold beer shower

The turning point of the game and perhaps the entire Series occurred in the eighth inning when the Sox ran themselves out of a comeback bid. Kluszewski and Lollar opened with base hits off Larry Sherry. Sox manager Al Lopez sent Earl Torgeson out to run for Klu, but he didn't provide a pinch runner for the slow-footed Lollar. Al Smith bounced a ball off the left-field wall. Wally Moon grabbed it on one hop and fired it to the cutoff man, Maury Wills, who pegged it home. Lollar, who had paused momentarily at second base, was 10 feet up the line when the ball arrived. He tried to wiggle his way past catcher Johnny Roseboro's tag but was easily tagged out. (If third-base coach Tony Cuccinello had held Lollar up at third base, there would have been runners at second and third, nobody out, and the Sox down by a run.) Smith made third on the play. But Sherry fanned Billy Goodman, and Jim Rivera fouled out. Sherry then put the Sox down quietly in the ninth.

The play that turned the tide: Sherm Lollar is tagged out at home in Game 2.

Game 3

The Dodgers squeaked by the Sox 3–1 in the first of a crazy three-game set in Los Angeles. In the revamped Coliseum, Sox manager Al Lopez advised his players to ignore the short porch in left field. Still, Lopez had to weigh the advantages of stocking the lineup with right-handed hitters.

Right-handed pitching was another important factor. For this reason, Lopez chose Dick Donovan over southpaw Bill Pierce as his starting pitcher. Dodgers manager Walter Alston countered with right-handed sidewinder Don Drysdale.

A record crowd (93,394) attended the match under a sun-baked sky. In the open-air and shadow-free Coliseum, the backdrop of coolie hats and white shirts made it hard to pick up batted balls. There was a hint of trouble in the second inning when left fielder Al Smith lost Gil Hodges' fly ball in the vanilla background. After that mishap, the White Sox infielders and outfielders pointed out the ball location for the benefit of the other fielders.

Drysdale had a poor outing, yielding 11 hits and four walks in seven-plus innings of work. But the Sox couldn't get anything going. All the White Sox hits were singles, five landing against the left-field screen.

The Sox tried blending in their running game. Dodgers catcher Johnny Roseboro knew it was coming, and he won the battle. Three runners were thrown out trying to pilfer

The Sox and Dodgers at the L.A. Coliseum prior to the start of Game 3

bases; twice Roseboro ended innings throwing out would-be base stealers.

Donovan had given up just one hit (to Hodges), but he lost his shutout in the seventh. Charley Neal's "screeno" and two walks filled the bases. Gerry Staley came in from the pen. Veteran Carl Furillo, pinch-hitting for Don Demeter, slapped a ball toward short. Aparicio momentarily lost the ball in the white shirts, and it skipped by him on the rock-hard infield. Two runs crossed the plate.

The Sox came right back in the top of the eighth. Ted Kluszewski and Sherman Lollar singled, ending Drysdale's stint. Larry Sherry hit Billy Goodman, loading the bases. An Al Smith double play put the Sox on the board but helped the Dodgers ease out of the inning with only one run scoring. In their half of the eighth, Los Angeles added an insurance run on Charley Neal's RBI double. It was another snowball that caromed off Sammy Esposito's glove at third base.

Game 4

There were more camouflaged balls and funny bounces in a Sox 5–4 loss at the sun-baked Coliseum. Another record crowd (92,650) attended the match. Unlike the baseball-crazy fans of Chicago, the laid-back California fans required a blair of a bugle to wake them up.

Game 4 featured a rematch of Game 1's pitchers, Early Wynn and Roger Craig. Los Angeles chased Wynn in a four-run third. The Dodgers struck after two were retired. L.A. reeled off five consecutive hits. Two of the safeties dropped in front of temporarily blinded Sox outfielders. Another ball came too quickly upon Louie Aparicio at short.

After stranding eight runners in the first six innings, the Sox cleaned the bases in a four-run seventh. Nelson Fox kept the inning alive with his fifth-straight Series hit. Sherman Lollar capped the scoring with a three-run homer over the Chinese Wall, knotting the contest at 4. Lollar was bound to lift one over the short porch in left sooner or later. In the pregame analysis, it had been noted that he was an upper-cut hitter, as was Jim Landis. The Sox' other right-handed power man, Al Smith, was considered more of a line-drive-type batter.

An inning later, Gil Hodges, enjoying a great series (.391), broke the tie. He sent a towering fly ball over the left-field screen off Gerry Staley. Hodges' home run, like Lollar's four-bagger, traveled a scant 300 feet.

Larry Sherry, making his third straight relief appearance, retired the Sox but for a walk over the final two innings. Afterward, in the L.A. locker room, Dodgers manager Walter Alston's picture was taken next to a placard reading, "One to Go-Go-Go."

Game 5

In a surprising pitchers' duel in the L.A. bandbox, the Sox narrowly avoided elimination with a 1–0 victory. A third record-setting crowd attended the game on another bright sunny day. Fifty-six more fans squeezed themselves onto the Coliseum's wooden benches, some as far as a fifth of a mile away from the action in the cavernous stadium built for track-and-field events.

Bob Shaw squared off against fireballer Sandy Koufax. Koufax, in a regular season game, had fanned 18 batters to tie a major league record. The Sox's run in the fourth inning turned out to be the game winner. Nelson Fox and Jim Landis opened the frame with base hits. The lumbering Sherman Lollar then hit into a double play. The Dodgers conceded the run.

Sherm Lollar's double-play ball in Game 5 drove in Nellie Fox for the only run of the game.

Jungle Jim Rivera's game-saving, over-the-shoulder catch of Charlie Neal's long drive preserved a Sox victory in Game 5.

The lead stood up through some hand-wringing Dodgers uprisings in the seventh and eighth innings. In the seventh, the Dodgers had runners at second and third with two outs. Indirectly, Al Lopez made a brilliant defensive move. With right-handed hitting Charley Neal at the plate, Lopez removed rookie Jim McAnany from the game and moved Al Smith from right to left field. Lopez figured Smith by now was more used to the 40-foot screen. Jim Rivera took over Smith's slot in right field. Neal drilled a shot to right. Rivera, his back to the infield, made a great over-the-shoulder catch just in front of the fence. The ball would have surely eluded right-handers Smith or McAnany.

The eighth inning was another nail-biter. Wally Moon's sinking liner slipped out of Jim Landis' glove. One out later, Gil Hodges arched a pop fly to right just beyond Nellie Fox's reach. Landis' peg to third base was late. Hodges took second on the throw. Al Lopez and Walter Alston then began a baseball battle of righty-lefty percentages. Bob Shaw was lifted. Billy Pierce intentionally walked pinch-hitter Rip Repulski. Dick Donovan came in and retired pinch-hitter Carl Furillo and Don Zimmer, taking the Sox out of the jam.

The Bums, having run out of pinch-hitters, sent in Larry Sherry to pinch-hit for the pitcher in the ninth inning. But there was no storybook ending as Sherry grounded out. Donovan disposed of the next two hitters, and the Sox bade a thankful farewell to the Chinese Wall.

Game 6

After the California nightmare, the Sox felt pretty good about their chances with the final two games to be played at home. Comiskey Park and the surrounding stockyards area may not have been as glitzy as Southern California, but the neighborhood had its own unique flavor. A local supper club chanteuse, Vivienne Chiesa, sang the National Anthem. During the pregame drills, a 53-year-old lady entertained the early arrivals with a twirl around the bases. In the old Windy City scam game, 600 people presenting counterfeit tickets at the gate were denied admittance.

The home-field advantage never materialized, as Los Angeles scored eight runs over the first four innings on their way to a 9–3 Series-clinching win. In the third inning, Duke Snider lined a two-run homer into the left-field stands that would only have rattled the Coliseum screen. Sox starter Early Wynn was chased in the L.A. six-run fourth. Wynn gave up two singles as well as a double to pitcher Johnny Podres. Reliever Dick Donovan issued a walk, a two-run double to Charley Neal, and a homer to Wally Moon.

Ted Kluszewski remained hot, clubbing a three-run, upper-deck homer in the Sox fourth. That blast gave Klu a record 10 RBIs for a six-game Series.

Ending any thoughts of a Sox comeback, Larry Sherry took over for Podres in the fourth inning. Sherry finished up and was credited with the win, his second of the Series, to go along with two saves. In the ninth inning, Chuck Essegian, pinch-hitting for Snider, ran his pigskin dash around the bases with a shot off Ray Moore.

It started raining in the latter innings, and the Comiskey Park lights were turned on amid the cheers of a contingency of Dodgers fans. The dreary atmosphere seemed to signal the end of the Go-Go era. During the off-season, Bill Veeck would change the character of the club. This owner installed an exploding scoreboard in center field. Power hitters were needed to ignite it.

Game 1

October 1, at Chicago

Los Angeles	AB	R	H	RBI	PO	A
Gilliam, 3b	4	0	1	0	0	1
Neal, 2b	4	0	2	0	0	3
Moon, lf	4	0	1	0	2	0
Snider, cf	2	0	0	0	2	0
Demeter, cf	1	0	0	0	0	0
Larker, rf	4	0	1	0	4	0
Hodges, 1b	4	0	2	0	10	0
Roseboro, c	4	0	0	0	5	0
Wills, ss	3	0	1	0	1	2
c—Furillo	1	0	0	0	0	0
Craig, p	1	0	0	0	0	1
Churn, p	0	0	0	0	0	1
Labine, p	0	0	0	0	0	0
a—Essegian	1	0	0	0	0	0
Koufax, p	0	0	0	0	0	0
b—Fairly	1	0	0	0	0	0
Klippstein, p	0	0	0	0	0	1
	34	0	8	0	24	9

Chicago	AB	R	H	RBI	PO	A
Aparicio, ss	5	0	0	0	3	3
Fox, 2b	4	2	1	0	2	2
Landis, cf	4	3	3	1	1	0
Kluszewski, 1b	4	2	3	5	8	2
Lollar, c	3	1	0	1	7	0
Goodman, 3b	2	1	1	1	0	0
Esposito, 3b	2	0	0	0	1	0
Smith, lf	4	1	2	0	2	0
Rivera, rf	4	1	0	0	2	0
Wynn, p	3	0	1	1	1	1
Staley, p	1	0	0	0	0	1
	36	11	11	9	27	9

Los Angeles	0	0	0	0	0	0	0	0	0—	0
Chicago	2	0	7	2	0	0	0	0	x—	11

Los Angeles	IP	H	R	ER	BB	K
Craig (L)	2⅓	5	5	5	1	1
Churn	⅔	5	6	2	0	0
Labine	1	0	0	0	0	1
Koufax	2	0	0	0	0	1
Klippstein	2	1	0	0	0	2

Chicago	IP	H	R	ER	BB	K
Wynn (W)	7	6	0	0	1	6
Staley (S)	2	2	0	0	0	1

a—Struck out for Labine in fifth. b—Grounded out for Koufax in seventh. c—Flied out for Wills in ninth. E—Neal, Snider 2. DP—Sox 1. LOB—Sox 3, Dodgers 8. 2B—Fox, Smith 2, Wynn. HR—Kluszewski 2. SB—Neal. SF—Lollar. Umpires—Summers (AL), Dascoli (NL), Hurley (AL), Secory (NL), Rice (AL), Dixon (NL). Time—2:35. Attendance—48,013.

Game 2

October 2, at Chicago

Los Angeles	AB	R	H	RBI	PO	A
Gilliam, 3b	4	1	1	0	1	1
Neal, 2b	5	2	2	3	2	4
Moon, lf	3	0	1	0	1	1
Snider, cf	4	0	1	0	1	0
Demeter, cf	0	0	0	0	0	0
Larker, rf	3	0	0	0	4	0
Sherry, p	1	0	0	0	1	1
Hodges, 1b	4	0	0	0	10	1
Roseboro, c	4	0	1	0	6	0
Wills, ss	4	0	1	0	1	6
Podres, p	2	0	1	0	0	0
a—Essegian	1	1	1	1	0	0
Fairly, rf	1	0	0	0	0	0
	36	4	9	4	27	14

Chicago	AB	R	H	RBI	PO	A
Aparicio, ss	5	1	2	0	3	1
Fox, 2b	4	0	0	0	0	5
Landis, cf	3	1	0	0	2	0
Kluszewski, 1b	4	0	1	1	9	0
b—Torgeson, 1b	0	1	0	0	0	0
Lollar, c	4	0	2	1	4	0
Smith, lf	3	0	1	1	2	0
Phillips, 3b	3	0	1	0	2	0
c—Goodman, 3b	1	0	0	0	0	0
McAnany, rf	3	0	0	0	3	0
Rivera, rf	1	0	0	0	2	0
Shaw, p	3	0	1	0	0	1
Lown, p	0	0	0	0	0	0
d—Cash	1	0	0	0	0	0
	35	3	8	3	27	7

Los Angeles	0	0	0	0	1	0	3	0	0—	4
Chicago	2	0	0	0	0	0	0	1	0—	3

Los Angeles	IP	H	R	ER	BB	K
Podres (W)	6	5	2	2	3	3
Sherry (S)	3	3	1	1	0	1

Chicago	IP	H	R	ER	BB	K
Shaw (L)	6⅔	8	4	4	1	1
Lown	2⅓	1	0	0	1	3

a—Hit home run for Podres in seventh. b—Ran For Kluszewski in eighth. c—Struck out for Phillips in eighth. d—Grounded out for Lown in ninth. E—Wills. LOB—Sox 8, Dodgers 7. 2B—Aparicio, Phillips, Smith. HR—Neal 2, Essegian. SB—Moon, Gilliam, Neal. Umpires—Dascoli (NL), Hurley (AL), Secory (NL), Summers (AL), Rice (AL), Dixon (NL). Time—2:21. Attendance—47,368.

Game 3

October 4, at Los Angeles

Chicago	AB	R	H	RBI	PO	A
Aparicio, ss	4	0	2	0	0	3
Fox, 2b	4	0	3	0	3	6
Landis, cf	5	0	1	0	2	0
Kluszewski, 1b	3	1	1	0	11	1
Lollar, c	4	0	2	0	5	1
Goodman, 3b	3	0	2	0	1	1
c—Esposito, 3b	0	0	0	0	0	0
Smith, lf	4	0	0	0	0	0
Rivera, rf	3	0	0	0	1	0
Donovan, p	3	0	1	0	1	1
Staley, p	0	0	0	0	0	0
d—Cash	1	0	0	0	0	0
	34	1	12	0	24	13

Los Angeles	AB	R	H	RBI	PO	A
Gilliam, 3b	4	0	0	0	3	2
Neal, 2b	4	1	2	1	3	2
Moon, rf	4	0	0	0	1	0
Larker, lf	2	1	0	0	1	0
Hodges, 1b	2	0	1	0	6	1
Demeter, cf	2	0	0	0	0	0
a—Furillo	1	0	1	2	0	0
b—Fairly, cf	0	0	0	0	0	0
Roseboro, c	3	0	0	0	9	3
Wills, ss	3	1	1	0	3	2
Drysdale, p	2	0	0	0	1	1
Sherry, p	0	0	0	0	0	0
	27	3	5	3	27	11

Chicago	0	0	0	0	0	0	0	1	0—	1
Los Angeles	0	0	0	0	0	0	2	1	x—	3

Chicago	IP	H	R	ER	BB	K
Donovan (L)	6⅔	2	2	2	2	5
Staley	1⅓	3	1	1	0	0

Los Angeles	IP	H	R	ER	BB	K
Drysdale (W)	7	11	1	1	4	5
Sherry (S)	2	1	0	0	0	3

a—Singled for Demeter in seventh. b—Ran for Furillo in seventh. c—Ran for Goodman in seventh. d—Struck out for Staley in ninth. DP—Sox 1, Dodgers 3. LOB—Sox 11, Dodgers 3. 2B—Neal. SB—Landis. SH—Sherry. HBP—by Sherry (Goodman). Umpires—Hurley (AL), Secory (NL), Summers (AL), Dascoli (NL), Dixon (NL), Rice (AL). Time—2:33. Attendance—92,394.

Game 4
October 5, at Los Angeles

Chicago	AB	R	H	RBI	PO	A
Landis, cf	5	1	1	0	0	0
Aparicio, ss	3	0	1	0	0	2
Fox, 2b	5	1	3	0	3	4
Kluszewski, 1b	4	1	2	1	9	0
Lollar, c	4	1	1	3	6	2
Goodman, 3b	4	0	0	0	0	0
Smith, lf	3	0	2	0	3	0
Rivera, rf	3	0	0	0	3	1
Wynn, p	1	0	0	0	0	1
Lown, p	0	0	0	0	0	0
a—Cash	1	0	0	0	0	0
Pierce, p	0	0	0	0	0	0
c—Torgeson	1	0	0	0	0	0
Staley, p	0	0	0	0	0	0
	34	4	10	4	24	10

Los Angeles	AB	R	H	RBI	PO	A
Gilliam, 3b	4	0	0	0	0	1
Neal, 2b	4	0	0	0	4	4
Moon, rf-lf	4	1	2	0	3	0
Larker, lf	2	1	1	0	0	0
b—Furillo, rf	1	0	0	0	0	0
Fairly, rf	1	0	0	0	0	0
Hodges, 1b	4	2	2	2	10	0
Demeter, cf	3	1	2	0	1	0
Roseboro, c	3	0	1	1	7	0
Wills, ss	4	0	1	0	2	6
Craig, p	2	0	0	0	0	1
Sherry, p	0	0	0	0	0	0
	32	5	9	3	27	12

Chicago	0	0	0	0	0	0	4	0	0—4
Los Angeles	0	0	4	0	0	0	0	1	x—5

Chicago	IP	H	R	ER	BB	K
Wynn	2⅔	8	4	3	0	2
Lown	⅓	0	0	0	0	0
Pierce	3	0	0	0	1	2
Staley (L)	2	1	1	1	0	2

Los Angeles	IP	H	R	ER	BB	K
Craig	7	10	4	4	4	7
Sherry (W)	2	0	0	0	1	0

a—Struck out for Lown in fourth. b—Struck out for Larker in fifth. c—Grounded out for Pierce in seventh. E—Landis, Aparicio, Pierce. DP—Sox 2. LOB—Sox 9, Dodgers 6. 2B—Fox. HR—Lollar, Hodges. SB—Aparicio, Wills. Umpires—Secory (NL), Summers (AL), Dascoli (NL), Hurley (AL), Dixon (NL). Rice (AL), Time—2:30. Attendance—92,650.

Game 5
October 6, at Los Angeles

Chicago	AB	R	H	RBI	PO	A
Aparicio, ss	4	0	2	0	3	5
Fox, 2b	3	1	1	0	4	4
Landis, cf	4	0	1	0	2	0
Lollar, c	4	0	0	0	1	0
Kluszewski, 1b	4	0	0	0	12	0
Smith, rf-lf	4	0	0	0	1	0
Phillips, 3b	3	0	1	0	1	2
McAnany, 1f	1	0	0	0	1	0
Rivera, rf	0	0	0	0	2	0
Shaw, p	1	0	0	0	0	3
Pierce, p	0	0	0	0	0	0
Donovan, p	0	0	0	0	0	0
	28	1	5	0	27	14

Los Angeles	AB	R	H	RBI	PO	A
Gilliam, 3b	5	0	4	0	0	3
Neal, 2b	5	0	1	0	5	2
Moon, rf-cf	4	0	1	0	0	0
Larker, lf	4	0	0	0	3	1
Hodges, 1b	4	0	3	0	7	1
Demeter, cf	3	0	0	0	4	0
e—Fairly	0	0	0	0	0	0
f—Repulski	0	0	0	0	0	0
Roseboro, c	3	0	0	0	6	1
g—Furillo	1	0	0	0	0	0
Pignatano, c	0	0	0	0	1	0
Wills, ss	2	0	0	0	1	2
a—Essegian	0	0	0	0	0	0
b—Zimmer	1	0	0	0	0	1
Koufax, p	2	0	0	0	0	0
c—Snider	1	0	0	0	0	0
d—Podres	0	0	0	0	0	0
Williams, p	0	0	0	0	0	0
h-Sherry	1	0	0	0	0	0
	36	0	9	0	27	11

Chicago	0	0	0	1	0	0	0	0	0—1
Los Angeles	0	0	0	0	0	0	0	0	0—0

Chicago	I	H	R	ER	BB	K
Shaw (W)	7⅓	9	0	0	1	1
Pierce	0	0	0	0	1	0
Donovan(S)	1⅔	0	0	0	0	0

Los Angeles	IP	H	R	ER	BB	K
Koufax (L)	7	5	1	1	1	6
Williams	2	0	0	0	2	1

a—Walked for Wills in seventh. b—Ran for Essegian in seventh. c—Hit into force for Koufax in seventh. d—Ran for Snider in seventh. e—Announced for Demeter in eighth. f—Walked for Fairly in eighth. g—Popped out for Roseboro in eighth. h—Grounded out for Williams in ninth. DP—Dodgers 1. LOB—Sox 5, Dodgers 11. 3B—Hodges. SB—Gilliam. SH-Shaw 2. WP—Shaw. Umpires—Summers (AL), Dascoli (NL),
Hurley (AL), Secory (NL) Dixon (NL), Rice (AL). Time—2:28. Attendance—92,706.

Game 6
October 8, at Chicago

Los Angeles	AB	R	H	RBI	PO	A
Gilliam, 3b	4	1	0	0	0	2
Neal, 2b	5	1	3	2	4	4
Moon, 1f	4	2	1	2	3	0
Snider, cf-rf	3	1	1	2	2	0
e—Essegian	1	1	1	1	0	0
Fairly, rf	0	0	0	0	0	0
Hodges, 1b	5	0	1	0	10	0
Larker, rf	1	0	1	0	0	0
a—Demeter, cf	3	1	1	0	4	0
Roseboro, c	4	0	0	0	2	0
Wills, ss	4	1	1	1	2	3
Podres, p	2	1	1	1	0	1
Sherry, p	2	0	2	0	0	2
	38	9	13	9	27	12

Chicago	AB	R	H	RBI	PO	A
Aparicio, ss	5	0	1	0	1	2
Fox, 2b	4	0	1	0	2	2
Landis, cf	3	1	1	0	2	0
Lollar, c	3	1	0	0	5	2
Kluszewski, 1b	4	1	2	3	10	0
Smith, lf	2	0	0	0	2	0
Phillips, 3b-rf	4	0	1	0	3	1
McAnany, rf	1	0	0	0	1	0
b—Goodman, 3b	3	0	0	0	0	1
Wynn, p	1	0	0	0	0	1
Donovan, p	0	0	0	0	0	0
Lown, p	0	0	0	0	0	0
c—Torgeson	0	0	0	0	0	0
Staley, p	0	0	0	0	1	0
d—Romano	1	0	0	0	0	0
Pierce, p	0	0	0	0	0	0
Moore, p	0	0	0	0	0	0
f—Cash	1	0	0	0	0	0
	32	3	6	3	27	9

Los Angeles	0	0	2	6	0	0	0	0	1—9
Chicago	0	0	0	3	0	0	0	0	0—3

Los Angeles	IP	H	R	ER	BB	K
Podres	3⅓	2	3	3	3	1
Sherry (W)	5⅔	4	0	0	1	1

Chicago	IP	H	R	ER	BB	K
Wynn (L)	3⅓	5	5	5	3	2
Donovan	0	2	3	3	0	0
Lown	⅔	1	0	0	0	0
Staley	3	2	0	0	0	0
Pierce	1	2	0	0	1	0
Moore	1	1	1	1	1	0

a—Ran for Larker in fourth. b—Struck out for McAnany in fourth. c—Walked for Lown in fourth. d—Grounded out for Staley in seventh. e—Homered for Snider in ninth. f—Flied out for Moore in ninth. E—Aparicio. DP—Dodgers 1. LOB—Sox 7, Dodgers 7. 2B—Podres, Neal, Fox, Kluszewski. HR—Snider, Moon, Kluszewski, Essegian. SH—Roseboro, HBP—by Podres (Landis). Umpires—Dascoli (NL), Hurley (AL), Secory (NL), Summers (AL), Rice (AL), Dixon (NL). Time—2:33. Attendance—47,653.

The Playoff Era

The introduction of the playoff format in 1969 coincided with some of the worst seasons in Sox history. The 1969 club lost 94 games (68–94); the 1970 club passed the century mark in losses (56–106).

The stronger Pale Hose clubs of the early 1970s found themselves contending against baseball's toughest team, the Oakland A's, who won five straight Western Division titles (1970–75) and three world championships (1972–74).

Shortly after Bill Veeck took control of the Sox, the reserve clause was overturned by the courts, and the era of free agency began. During Veeck's economy-size operation, the Sox, except for the '77 Southside Hit Men season, never seriously challenged for a title.

In 1977 the American League added two new teams, creating two seven-team divisions. One of the original expansion teams, the Kansas City Royals, started their own mini-dynasty, winning four titles over a five-year period (1976–80).

Under the new ownership tandem of Eddie Einhorn and Jerry Reinsdorf, the Sox became instant contenders. They reached the pinnacle in 1983, running away with the flag in a weak Western Division. But in the playoffs they met their old nemesis, the Eastern Division champion Baltimore Orioles. The Sox were beaten in four games.

An overconfident Sox squad failed to repeat in '84. After five more disappointing seasons, the Sox front office soured on free agency and finally began to invest in a good farm system.

In 1993 the Sox youth corps brought them back to the postseason games. But, in an expanded best-of-seven match, the Sox lost in six games to a more experienced Toronto squad.

Clinching the Western Division, September 17, 1983

Baseball expanded to three divisions in 1994, and a wild-card slot was added to the playoff scheme. The Sox were situated in the Central Division, which included their old Kansas City rivals and a feisty Cleveland ballclub.

On August 12 in the shortened '94 season, the Sox held a slim, one-game lead over Cleveland. At the same time, they were one of four teams vying for the league wild-card. Baseball's longest strike ensued, ending whatever hope the Sox had for their first repeat title since 1900–1901.

1983 ALCS: White Sox versus Baltimore Orioles

In 1983 the "Winning Ugly" White Sox won their first Western Division title. The Sox (99–63) romped to the flag, taking 59 of their last 85 games. The majors' winningest pitchers, LaMarr Hoyt (24–10) and Richard Dotson (22–7), combined for a 23-game winning streak down the stretch. Carlton Fisk (.289, 26 HR), one of four Sox players in double figures in home runs, hit .329 from mid-June to the end of the season. Tom Pacorieck (.307) hit a cool .400 in September. Midseason acquisition Julio Cruz (.251, 24 SB) was the catalyst of most big innings.

The White Sox's opponents in the best-of-five-game American League Championship Series were the Eastern Division powerhouse Baltimore Orioles. It was the Orioles' seventh fall series since the playoff format began in 1969. The 1983 ALCS and not the World Series was considered to be the battle between baseball's two best teams. The Orioles (98–64) won one less game than the Sox, and they lost baseball's offense crown to the White Sox by a single run (800–799). Eddie Murray (.306, 33 HR, 111 RBIs) and Cal Ripken (.318, 27 HR, 102 RBIs) could be found at the top of most offensive categories. The Eastern Division's best staff featured outstanding performances from Scott McGregor (18–7, 3.18), Storm Davis (13–7, 3.59), Mike Boddicker (16–8, 2.77), and reliever Tippy Martinez (9–3, 2.35, 21 saves).

Baltimore was the only club to give the Winning Ugly Sox a battle in 1983. The Orioles took the season series seven games to five. The Sox were particularly mindful of one contest, a Baltimore 5–4 victory (August 5), in which the Orioles got five straight two-out, ninth-inning hits for a comeback win.

In baseball parlance, the Sox's "momentum" was expected to carry them through the playoffs. But, after they took the opener, the Sox's drive abruptly stopped. They scored only one run over the final three contests and lost the series.

White Sox hitters left 35 runners on base in the four games. They garnered only four hits in 30 opportunities with runners in scoring position. The middle three batters in the order—Harold Baines (.125), Carlton Fisk (.176), and Bull Luzinski (.133)—had a particularly bad series.

Baltimore went on to manhandle the National League's best team, the Philadelphia Phillies, in five games.

Game 1

At Baltimore's Memorial Stadium, always a tough venue for White Sox teams over the years, the Sox made a good start as LaMarr Hoyt ran his winning streak to 14 games (13 regular season wins) with a snappy 2–1 decision. Hoyt held the Orioles to five hits, fanned four, and walked nobody. His only bad inning was the ninth, when, after two were retired, Disco Dan Ford doubled and Cal Ripken singled for a run. Eddie Murray, representing the winning run, was the next batter, prompting pitching coach Dave Duncan to make a quick visit to the mound. Murray then sent a skimmer through Hoyt's tree-trunk legs to shortstop Scott Fletcher, who stepped on second for the force, ending the game.

Leadoff man Rudy Law chipped in two singles and a double on the day. The book on Law did not support his fine performance. Manager Tony LaRussa's computer spat out a tape that revealed Law was 2-for-36 against Orioles pitching.

The No. 3 batter, first baseman Tom Paciorek, showed nothing but digits (2-for-4, 1 run, 1 RBI) alongside his name in the box score. He lent a hand in both Sox runs. In the third inning, following base hits by Law and Carlton Fisk, Paciorek sent a wicked grounder past third baseman Julio Cruz for an RBI single. Paciorek led off the sixth with a walk, scooted to third when Murray couldn't come up with Bull Luzinski's ball in back of first base, then registered while Ron Kittle was grounding into a double play.

A 42-minute rain delay in the bottom of the fourth seemed to work in the Sox's favor. The skies opened up after shortstop Cal Ripken had leaped high for Fletcher's liner and second baseman Rich Dauer made a nifty backhand stab of Harold Baines' grounder. Instead of carrying the momentum over to their half, spurred on by their fans, the Orioles went to the clubhouse, sat down, and played cards.

Game 2

Mike Boddicker, the American League shutout leader (five), blanked the Sox 4–0 to give the Orioles a split at home. Boddicker, who threw a lot of change-of-speed junk, tossed a five-hitter and fanned an ALCS-record-tying 14 batters. It was Boddicker's second 1983 shutout over the Sox. He tossed the first one at the Comiskeys on May 17, two weeks after being called up from Rochester (Triple A) to replace the injured Jim Palmer in the rotation.

Sox nemesis Gary Roenicke (1983: 4 HR, 12 RBIs) accounted for all the Orioles runs. During the regular season, Roenicke had been platooned in left field with port-sider John Lowenstein. Together they had accounted for 35 homers and 129 RBIs. With southpaw Floyd Bannister on the mound for the Sox, Roenicke got the nod.

After Bannister struck out the side in the first inning, Roenicke opened the second with a double to left. He scored when Vance Law, after knocking down Ken Singleton's bullet, threw the ball past first base.

Gary Roenicke and Ken Singleton teamed up for another score in the fourth. Roenicke walked, then came in when Singleton's hit rattled around a temporary box-seat fence in left field and away from Ron Kittle. Roenicke clinched the contest for the O's in the sixth inning by socking a home run with Cal Ripken aboard. On Roenicke's blast, a bleacher fan dumped his beer on left fielder Ron Kittle, bringing back memories of Al Smith's dousing in the 1959 World Series. But, unlike Smith, Kittle wasn't amused about the shower.

Boddicker experienced control problems throughout the game. He walked three batters and hit two others. Over the first eight innings the Sox twice had two men on and one out but couldn't produce.

The Sox loaded the bases with two down in the ninth. Julio Cruz whipped a shot down the line that just turned foul. Boddicker then reached back and spun a breaking ball past Cruz, fanning him for the third time.

Upended in Baltimore, Game 2

Game 3

In the first postseason contest in 24 years at Comiskey Park, the Sox were routed 11–1 in a brawl-filled game. Signaling a rough night ahead for Richard Dotson and the Sox, Eddie Murray, ending an 0-for-29 postseason slump, walloped a three-run, upper-deck homer in the first inning before all the fans were in their seats.

Ron Kittle and Al Bumbry exchanged run-producing doubles in the second inning. In Kittle's next at bat, he was hit on the right knee by a pitch from Orioles hurler Mike Flanagan. The bruised knee would keep him out of action the rest of the series. After the brushback pitch, the plate umpire had to step between Kittle and Flanagan. Protecting his pitcher, catcher Rick Dempsey stuck his neck in the squabble. Sox manager Tony LaRussa bounded out of the dugout to defend Kittle.

Dotson was ordered to retaliate. In the fifth inning, he pluncked Ripken, who smugly took his base. Dotson's next pitch was an inside heater to Murray. Murray pointed his bat at Dotson, and both benches emptied. There was some pushing and shoving around home plate. LaRussa and Murray had to be separated. Cal Ripken Sr. and LaRussa also entered the row. When play resumed, Murray walked. John Lowenstein then stepped up and swatted a double to right, making it a 6–1 ballgame.

The Orioles rubbed it in in the ninth inning. Dennis Lamp relieved Jerry Koosman with the bags loaded. Gary Roenicke, pinching for Lowenstein, drew a walk, forcing one in. Roenicke then followed the lead runners home a base at a time on two sacrifice flies and a Jerry Hairston error.

Pregame ceremonies in Comiskey Park

Game 4

The Orioles made it three straight wins, blanking the White Sox 4–0 in 10 innings to take the league series. It was a bitter, heartbreaking loss on a dreary autumn afternoon in old Comiskey Park. Sox starter Britt Burns made a heroic effort, tossing nine shutout innings. With no bat support from his teammates, he eventually tired. On Burns' 150th pitch of the afternoon he gave up a one-out, 10th-inning homer to reserve outfielder Tito Landrum. Baltimore, on three singles and a sacrifice fly, added two more runs against relievers Salome Barojas and Juan Agosto.

Storm Davis and Tippy Martinez split the pitching chores for Baltimore. Martinez got credit for the win in relief.

The Sox had 10 hits in the game. They stranded 11 men, leaving someone on base in every inning but the first. Baltimore also squandered numerous opportunities, leaving 10 runners on base in the nail-biting affair.

The Sox's best scoring chance gone awry would earn a niche in the baseball Hall of Blunders, resplendent with a bronze of Jerry Dybzinski, his head down, tearing around second base. "The Dibber" had reached base in the seventh inning on a terrible sacrifice bunt attempt. The ball bounced straight off the plate, allowing catcher Rick Dempsey to get a force at third base. The next batter, Julio Cruz, hit a sharp single to left. Outfielder Gary Roenicke made a clean stab of the ball and quickly relayed it to infielder Rich Dauer. The lead runner, Vance Law, was halted at third base by coach Jim Leyland. But Dybzinski kept coming! Rounding second base, he suddenly realized Law was standing at third. Between stations, Dybzinski was trapped in a rundown. Leyland now had no choice but to send Law home, hoping to draw an Orioles mistake. Law, in a jarring collision with Dempsey, was tagged

Mayor Harold Washington and Carlton Fisk

out at the plate. On the throw home, Dybzinski retreated safely to second base. Dybzinski managed to make third on a balk. But Rudy Law, the Sox's leading hitter (.389) of the series, fanned. Dybzinski had been given the start at shortstop by manager Tony LaRussa to provide a spark, not to snuff it out. Jerry almost redeemed himself by singling with two gone in the ninth. Julio Cruz followed with a hit. But Law fanned again.

Tito Landrum and the Orioles popped the champagne cork in the 10th inning. The somber gathering filed out of the park, knowing that if the Sox had pulled this one out, LaMarr Hoyt would have pitched them into the World Series the next day.

Game 1

October 5, at Baltimore

Chicago	AB	R	H	RBI	PO	A
R. Law, cf	5	1	3	0	3	0
Fisk, c	5	0	1	0	5	0
Paciorek, 1b-lf	4	1	2	1	9	2
Luzinski, dh	3	0	1	0	0	0
Kittle, lf	3	0	0	0	1	0
Squires, 1b	1	0	0	0	2	0
Baines, rf	4	0	0	0	2	0
V. Law, 3b	3	0	0	0	0	2
Fletcher, ss	2	0	0	0	2	2
J. Cruz, 2b	2	0	0	0	1	6
Hoyt, p	0	0	0	0	2	1
	32	2	7	1	27	13

Baltimore	AB	R	H	RBI	PO	A
Bumbry, cf	4	0	0	0	0	0
Ford, rf	4	0	1	0	1	0
Landrum, pr	0	1	0	0	0	0
Ripken, ss	4	0	1	1	2	2
Murray, 1b	4	0	0	0	10	1
Lowenstein lf	3	0	0	0	1	0
Singleton, dh	3	0	1	0	0	0
Dauer, 2b	3	0	0	0	5	3
T. Cruz, 3b	3	0	1	0	3	6
Dempsey, c	2	0	1	0	4	2
Dwyer, ph	1	0	0	0	0	0
McGregor, p	0	0	0	0	1	1
Stewart, p	0	0	0	0	0	0
T. Martinez, p	0	0	0	0	0	1
	31	1	5	1	27	16

Chicago	0	0	1	0	0	1	0	0	0—2
Baltimore	0	0	0	0	0	0	0	0	1—1

Chicago	IP	H	R	ER	BB	K
Hoyt (W)	9	5	1	1	0	4

Baltimore	IP	H	R	ER	BB	K
McGregor (L)	6⅔	6	2	1	3	2
Stewart	⅓	1	0	0	1	1
T. Martinez	2	0	0	0	2	1

E—Murray. DP—Sox 1, Orioles 1. LOB—Sox 10, Orioles 3. 2B—Luzinski, Singleton, R. Law, Ford. SH—Fletcher. WP—T. Martinez. Balk—McGregor. Umpires—McKean, Merrill, Bremigan, Evans, Phillips, Reilly. Time—2:38. Attendance—51,289.

Game 2

October 6, at Baltimore

Chicago	AB	R	H	RBI	PO	A
R. Law, cf	4	0	2	0	2	0
Fisk, c	3	0	0	0	6	0
Baines, rf	4	0	0	0	1	0
Dybzinski, ss	0	0	0	0	1	1
Luzinski, dh	3	0	0	0	0	0
Paciorek, 1b-1f	3	0	1	0	9	0
Kittle, lf	3	0	1	0	2	0
V. Law, 3b	2	0	0	0	0	3
Walker, ph	1	0	0	0	0	0
Rodriguez, 3b	0	0	0	0	0	0
Squires, ph	1	0	0	0	0	0
Fletcher, ss	2	0	0	0	1	3
Hairston, ph-rf	1	0	0	0	0	0
J. Cruz, 2b	4	0	1	0	2	1
Bannister, p	0	0	0	0	0	0
Barojas, p	0	0	0	0	0	1
Lamp, p	0	0	0	0	0	0
	31	0	5	0	24	9

Baltimore	AB	R	H	RBI	PO	A
Shelby, cf	4	0	1	0	0	0
Landrum, rf	4	0	0	0	2	0
Ripken, ss	4	1	2	0	0	0
Murray, 1b	4	0	0	0	6	0
Roenicke, lf	2	3	2	2	1	0
Singleton, dh	4	0	1	1	0	0
Dauer, 2b	3	0	0	0	2	3
T. Cruz, 3b	3	0	0	0	1	3
Dempsey, c	3	0	0	0	15	1
Boddicker, p	0	0	0	0	0	1
	31	4	6	3	27	8

Chicago	0	0	0	0	0	0	0	0	0—0
Baltimore	0	1	0	1	0	2	0	0	—4

Chicago	IP	H	R	ER	BB	K
Bannister (L)	6	5	4	3	1	5
Barojas	1	1	0	0	0	0
Lamp	1	0	0	0	1	0

Baltimore	IP	H	R	ER	BB	K
Boddicker (W)	9	5	0	0	3	14

E—V. Law, Rodriguez. DP—Sox 1, Orioles 1. LOB—Sox 9, Orioles 5. 2B—Roenicke, Singleton, Ripken. HR—Roenicke. SB—R. Law, Shelby. HBP—by Boddicker (Paciorek, Luzinski). Umpires—Merrill, Bremigan, Evans, Phillips, Reilly, McKean. Time—2:51. Attendance—52,347.

Game 3

October 7, at Chicago

Baltimore	AB	R	H	RBI	PO	A
Bumbry, cf	4	0	1	1	3	0
Shelby, ph-cf	0	1	0	0	0	0
Dwyer, rf	3	1	1	0	4	0
Landrum, ph-rf	1	0	0	0	2	0
Ripken, ss	4	3	2	0	2	4
Murray, 1b	2	4	1	3	7	2
Lowenstein, lf	3	0	1	2	3	0
Roenicke, ph-lf	0	1	0	1	0	0
Singleton, dh	3	0	1	0	0	0
Palmer, pr	0	0	0	0	0	0
Nolan, ph	0	0	0	1	0	0
Dauer, 2b	4	0	0	1	1	4
T. Cruz, 3b	5	0	1	1	1	1
Dempsey, c	3	1	0	0	2	0
Flanagan, p	0	0	0	0	0	0
Stewart, p	0	0	0	0	2	0
	32	11	8	10	27	11

Chicago	AB	R	H	RBI	PO	A
R. Law, cf	4	0	2	0	3	0
Fisk, c	4	0	1	0	8	2
Paciorek, 1b	4	0	0	0	11	1
Luzinski, dh	4	0	1	0	0	0
Kittle, lf	1	1	1	0	0	0
Hairston, ph-lf	2	0	0	0	0	0
Baines, rf	4	0	0	0	2	1
V. Law, 3b	2	0	1	1	1	1
Squires, ph	1	0	0	0	0	0
Rodriguez, 3b	0	0	0	0	0	0
Fletcher, ss	3	0	0	0	0	3
J. Cruz, 2b	3	0	0	0	1	5
Dotson, p	0	0	0	0	1	1
Tidrow, p	0	0	0	0	0	0
Koosman, p	0	0	0	0	0	0
Lamp, p	0	0	0	0	0	0
	32	1	6	1	27	14

Baltimore	3	1	0	0	2	0	0	1	4—11
Chicago	0	1	0	0	0	0	0	0	0—1

Baltimore	IP	H	R	ER	BB	K
Flanagan (W)	5	5	1	1	0	1
Stewart (S)	4	1	0	0	0	1

Chicago	IP	H	R	ER	BB	K
Dotson (L)	5	6	6	6	3	3
Tidrow	3	1	1	1	3	3
Koosman	⅓	1	3	2	2	0
Lamp	⅔	0	1	0	1	1

E—Dempsey, Hairston. DP—Sox 1, Orioles 1. LOB—Sox 5, Orioles 6. 2B—Dwyer, Bumbry, Kittle, Fisk, Lowenstein, Ripken. HR—Murray. SB—Murray. SF-Nolan, Dauer. HBP—by Flanagan (Kittle), by Dotson (Ripken). Umpires—Bremigan, Evans, Phillips, Reilly, McKean, Merrill. Time—2:58. Attendance—46,635.

Game 4

October 8, at Chicago

Baltimore	AB	R	H	RBI	PO	A
Shelby, cf	5	0	1	0	3	0
Landrum, rf	5	1	2	1	1	0
Ripken, ss	3	1	1	0	3	5
Murray, 1b	5	1	3	0	11	0
Roenicke, 1f	2	0	1	1	3	1
Singleton, dh	2	0	0	0	0	0
Bumbry, pr	0	0	0	0	0	0
Ford, ph	1	0	0	0	0	0
Lowenstein, ph	0	0	0	0	0	0
Ayala, ph	0	0	0	1	0	0
Dauer, 2b	4	0	0	0	0	2
T. Cruz, 3b	4	0	0	0	1	3
Dempsey, c	4	0	1	0	8	2
Davis, p	0	0	0	0	0	0
T. Martinez, p	0	0	0	0	0	1
	35	3	9	3	30	14

Chicago	AB	R	H	RBI	PO	A
R. Law, cf	5	0	0	0	2	0
Fisk, c	5	0	1	0	8	1
Baines, rf	4	0	2	0	0	0
Luzinski, dh	5	0	0	0	0	0
Paciorek, lf	5	0	1	0	1	0
Walker, 1b	2	0	1	0	7	1
Squires, ph-1b	1	0	0	0	4	0
V. Law, 3b	4	0	1	0	0	3
Dybzinski, ss	4	0	1	0	2	7
J. Cruz, 2b	3	0	3	0	6	2
Burns, p	0	0	0	0	0	1
Barojas, p	0	0	0	0	0	0
Agosto, p	0	0	0	0	0	0
Lamp, p	0	0	0	0	0	0
	38	0	10	0	30	15

Baltimore	0	0	0	0	0	0	0	0	0	3—3
Chicago	0	0	0	0	0	0	0	0	0	0—0

Baltimore	IP	H	R	ER	BB	K
Davis	6	5	0	0	2	2
T. Martinez (W)	4	5	0	0	1	4

Chicago	IP	H	R	ER	BB	K
Burns (L)	9⅓	6	1	1	5	8
Barojas	0	3	2	2	0	0
Agosto	⅓	0	0	0	0	0
Lamp	⅓	0	0	0	0	0

DP—Sox 1, Orioles 2. LOB—Sox 11, Orioles 10. HR—Landrum. SB—J. Cruz 2. SH—Dauer. SF—Ayala. HBP—by Burns (Roenicke). Balk—T. Martinez. Umpires—Evans, Phillips, Reilly, McKean, Merrill, Bremigan. Time—3:41. Attendance—45,477.

1993 ALCS: White Sox versus Toronto Blue Jays

Ten years after the Winning Ugly flag, the White Sox finally returned to postseason play. Not one member of the 1983 crew was still around. Nor was the ballpark. A fresh gathering of Olympic and collegiate recruits—Frank Thomas, Robin Ventura, Jack McDowell—performed to rave reviews in the brand-new Comiskey Park.

The 1993 crew, like their Winning Ugly predecessors, captured their division rather easily, jumping into the top spot for good in late June. They also closed strong by winning 14 of their final 19 games to post a major league–best eight-game margin.

America's championship cup was being held in Canada by a star-studded Toronto Blue Jays squad: Roberto Alomar, John Olerud, Joe Carter, Juan Guzman, Paul Molitor. The Jays had finished atop the Eastern Division four of the last five seasons and were gunning for their second straight world championship.

Still, the short series seemed to favor the stronger-pitching White Sox (Sox ERA 3.70, Jays 4.21) against the more formidable Blue Jays lineup (Jays .279, 170 SB; Sox .268, 106 SB).

But experience was also a factor. Only eight Pale Hose players had postseason experience, and of those eight, only two hurlers, Tim Belcher and Kirk McCaskill, had been in the October spotlight, whereas the nine members of the Toronto starting lineup had been involved in 142 postseason contests, and the Jays' four-man rotation had made 27 playoff appearances.

Unfortunately, outside distractions also entered the equation. Prior to Game 2, basketball superstar Michael Jordan, who worked for Sox owner Jerry Reinsdorf's other team, the Bulls, announced his retirement, sending a buzz through the crowd. To the players' disgust, Jordan became the prominent Chicago story, not the Sox pennant quest.

Gene Lamont, embraced by Sox owner Jerry Reinsdorf after clinching the West

Other players voiced a different gripe. Because slugger Frank Thomas was favoring a sore elbow, he became the designated hitter over the first two games. Manager Gene Lamont put Dan Pasqua at first base. Passed-over players George Bell and Bo Jackson would have plenty to say to the press about the oversight, particularly in light of Pasqua's poor performance.

After two ugly losses in Chicago, the Sox regrouped and grabbed two straight wins in Canada. But, in the end, there was just too much Canadian lumber. Benefiting from the explosive Toronto attack, Juan Guzman (2–0) and Dave Stewart (2–0) won Game 5 and 6 to carry the Jays to the flag.

Game 1

Game 1 was played on a bone-chilling autumn evening before a record crowd of 46,246 at Comiskey Park II. The bundled-up fans waved their souvenir white socks to show support for the "Good Guys in Black" and to warm their extremities.

Sox stopper Jack McDowell (22–10) faced off against Toronto's best hurler, Juan Guzman (14–3). Neither pitcher was very sharp. McDowell gave up a season-high 13 hits in losing 7–3. Guzman managed to escape threats, mostly of his own doing—eight walks, hit batter, three wild pitches—by not allowing the Sox any hits at key spots of the game.

The Jays weren't going to let an injured Frank Thomas beat them, and they pitched around him all night. With two out and nobody on in the first inning, Thomas looked at four straight pitches out of the strike zone. He even received a free pass leading off the ninth. Altogether, Thomas walked four times. But the Toronto strategy worked to perfection, in that the next four batters—Robin Ventura, Ellis Burks, Dan Pasqua, and Lance Johnson—were a combined 1-for-15.

A victory cigar for Robin Ventura

McDowell, looking for his first win over Toronto in two years, had problems finishing off an inning. With two on and two out in the fourth, Ed Sprague drilled a liner just out of a diving Ellis Burks' grasp for three bases, giving Toronto an early 2–0 lead.

The Sox came right back on Ozzie Guillen's two-run single. Guillen then stole second and was driven home on Tim Raines' base hit. A wild pitch, Frank Thomas' obligatory walk, and an intentional pass to Robin Ventura loaded the bases. But Guzman got Ellis Burks on a harmless fly ball to right.

The Sox lead lasted only during the change of bats. Devon White poked a one-out single. Roberto Alomar slapped a double-play grounder to shortstop Ozzie Guillen. But White's hard slide caused second baseman Joey Cora to throw the relay into the dugout. Three straight hits by the heart of the Jays order—Joe Carter (single), John Olerud (double), and Paul Molitor (single)—put them on top for good.

After two were gone in the seventh inning, the Jays retired McDowell. John Olerud singled. Paul Molitor, garnering his fourth hit of the evening, homered.

Guzman was lifted after six long frames of pitching from the stretch. He had provided the Sox with 13 base runners, 11 of whom were stranded. The Toronto pen shut down the Sox the rest of the way on one hit, as the Jordan retirement rumors began to fly around the stadium.

Game 2

At home, the White Sox surrendered the home-field advantage as the Blue Jays, on two unearned runs, took the second match 3–1. Veteran Dave Stewart went six innings for the victory to remain undefeated (7–0) in ALCS competition. Past his prime, Stewart (12–8, 4.44) had benefited from the Jays' strong bats during the regular season. He was 2–0 against the Sox in 1993.

Sox hurler Alex Fernandez, who had a 4–2 career mark against Toronto, received no support at the plate or in the field. The accommodating Sox left 10 runners on base. White Sox mistakes figured in two of the Jays' three runs.

Both teams' leadoff men reached and scored in the first inning. Rickey Henderson was safe when first baseman Dan Pasqua dropped second baseman Joey Cora's throw. Henderson subsequently tallied on Roberto Alomar's fielder's choice. In the Sox half, Tim Raines, drawing the first of three passes in the frame, scored on a wild pitch.

A two-run fourth won it for Toronto. Paul Molitor bounced a ground-rule double into the stands, his sixth straight series hit. Tony Fernandez singled Molitor in and took second on the throw home. Ed Sprague received an intentional walk. Pat Borders' hot grounder deflected off Alex Fernandez's glove to Joey Cora, whose low, wide throw sent Dan Pasqua dancing off the bag, Fernandez scoring. Cora received a questionable error on the play.

The Sox threatened to bust the game open in the sixth inning, loading the bases on two hits and a walk. But Stewart, keeping his composure, retired Dan Pasqua and Lance Johnson on weak pop-ups. Then, after falling behind 3–0 on pinch-hitter Warren Newson and getting the count back to 3–2, Stewart stabbed Newson's chopper to the right of the mound and made the putout at first base unassisted.

In the ninth inning, the Sox brought the tying run to the plate in the person of Joey Cora. The fans booed when Cora took his bat. The fans were actually calling for Bo—Bo Jackson. Sox manager Gene Lamont stuck with Cora, who popped out. Later, in the clubhouse, Jackson remarked, "The Sox were playing the game a man short"—an obvious reference to Pasqua.

Robin Ventura takes aim against Dave Stewart in Game 2, October 6, 1993.

The other forgotten man, George Bell, uttered some rubbish about an impending team insurrection against skipper Gene Lamont. Because of that tirade, Bell would not see any postseason play, and, shortly after the series, he was released.

Wilson Alvarez's fine pitching carried the day for the Sox in Game 3.

Game 3

Going into Game 3 at Toronto, it didn't look good for the White Sox. No team in ALCS play had ever come back to win the series after dropping the first two games at home. Furthermore, there had been boo birds at Chicago and dissension in the clubhouse. Given all that, the Sox went out and handily beat the Blue Jays 6–1.

Wilson Alvarez, who had won seven straight games since returning from an August tune-up in the minor leagues, scattered seven hits in a distance performance. He bested 19-game winner Pat Hentgen.

After two were retired in the third inning, the Sox sent 10 men to the plate, scoring five runs. In the big play of the frame, third sacker Ed Sprague was unable to corral Frank Thomas' bullet with two on. Ellis Burks and Lance Johnson then swatted two-run singles. A spectator to the event, catcher Ron Karkovice opened and closed the inning with strikeouts.

The Sox took advantage of another Jays blunder in the fourth inning. Ozzie Guillen, after singling, was caught leaning toward second base by Hentgen. But, in the ensuing rundown, a high throw from shortstop Tony Fernandez to first baseman John Olerud allowed Guillen to get back safely. He would later score on Robin Ventura's fly ball.

Seven Blue Jays reached base in the first four innings. A White Sox double play took Alvarez out of a first-and-third-base jam in the second inning. In the third inning, after Devon White singled home the Jays' only run, Alvarez picked him off base, retiring the side. With the bags loaded in the fourth inning, Alvarez bore down, fanning Tony Fernandez on three pitches and inducing Ed Sprague to fly out.

The Blue Jays were given no more chances. Over the final five innings Alvarez allowed but two base runners.

Frank Thomas returned to first base. Dan Pasqua was benched. Bo Jackson got his chance at the DH job. He was 0-for-4 with three strikeouts.

Game 4

The White Sox stunned the Toronto Sky Dome fans with a power-laden 7–4 victory to even the series at two games apiece. The Blue Jays, as the Sox had done in Chicago, lost the home-field advantage while at home. The series was now a best-of-three match with the final two games set for Comiskey Park.

One of the Sox smurfs, Lance Johnson, was the hero of the day. His two-run homer in the second inning off Todd Stottlemyre put the Sox up 2–0. For the diminutive Johnson, it was his first homer in 689 at-bats, going back to August 1992.

Johnson then lifted the Sox into the lead for good in a three-run sixth inning. A one-out Frank Thomas homer, his 42nd of the year, knotted the contest at three. One out later, Ellis Burks and Bo Jackson walked. Toronto manager Cito Gaston, perhaps staying with starter Todd Stottlemyre one too many batters, let him face Johnson, who socked a triple just past Devon White's outstretched glove in center field.

Jason Bere, who, like Wilson Alvarez, had a seven-game winning streak, started for the Sox. He had never faced the Blue Jays before in his career. The Jays KO'd Bere in a three-run third. Tim Belcher, a late-season pickup, rescued Bere. Ironically, the rookie Bere had replaced the veteran Belcher in the starting rotation in August. Belcher came in with the bags loaded and a 1–0 count on Tony Fernandez. Belcher ran the count to 3–1 before fanning Fernandez. He then got Ed Sprague on a fielder's choice to retire the side.

Belcher held the Jays to one run in 3⅔ innings, improving his playoff record to 4–0. Gene Lamont's bullpen then finished up the game in order: long reliever Kirk McCaskill, setup man Scott Radinsky, closer Roberto Hernandez.

Tim Raines had three hits, giving him 10 for the series. One of Raines' hits, a double leading off the third inning, took a comical turn. After arriving safely at second base, Raines had his foot lifted off the bag by shortstop Tony Hernandez and was tagged out. The umpire bought Fernandez's ploy and ruled that Raines' forward motion had carried him off the bag. Raines lost that one, but he got even by throwing out Roberto Alomar at home plate, thwarting a Jays rally in the sixth inning.

Game 5

The Sox needed a good outing from Jack McDowell to move ahead in the series. But McDowell, in a rematch with Juan Guzman, was even worse than he had been in Game 1 as the Jays opened with a run an inning over the first four frames on their way to a 5–3 victory.

Rickey Henderson doubled in the first. Pacing back and forth off the bag, he occupied McDowell's attention. Two throws went to second base. The third attempt went awry as Henderson, seemingly picked off, took off for third base. He kept going all the way home.

Ellis Burks dented the right-field wall making a great catch to end the first inning. In the second inning, another spectacular stab by Burks, a diving lunge at the foul line, resulted in a run-scoring sacrifice fly.

McDowell was removed in the third inning following a John Olerud RBI single and a walk to Paul Molitor. Jose DeLeon closed out the inning, but, after fanning the first two Jays in the fourth, he gave up a double to Devon White and a single to Roberto Alomar.

Guzman remained undefeated in ALCS play (5–0). He retired the first 13 Sox players. Burks spoiled the perfect game with a one-out, fifth-inning homer. Guzman made it through a touchy seventh inning, his last frame, by fanning Bo Jackson, who represented the tying run.

Toronto built the lead to 5–1. But there was a glimmer of hope in the Sox ninth. Robin Ventura slugged a two-out, two-run homer off Duane Ward. Burks was hit by a pitch. But Bo Jackson, hitless in the series, struck out for the sixth time, lunging after a Ward slider to end the game.

Catcher Ron Karkovice also experienced a poor-hitting series (0-for-15). And, defensively, he had a bad fifth game. The Jays, with only one stolen base over the first four games, pilfered six bases in Game 5.

Game 6

Back home at Comiskey Park the Sox lost the sixth game 6–3 and another chance at the World Series. The pressure man, Dave Stewart, went 7⅓ innings for his second series win. He was voted the series' Most Valuable Player.

Trying to spark the Sox offense, Gene Lamont inserted designated hitter Warren Newson and catcher Mike LaValliere into the lineup. But, as in Game 2, hurler Alex Fernandez received little support from the Sox hitters.

The Jays took a 2–0 lead in the second inning on Pat Borders' bases-loaded single. An inning later, the White Sox loaded the bases with one out. But, as had been the case all series, they couldn't manufacture a big inning. Stewart wisely gave Frank Thomas an unintentional, intentional base on balls, forcing a run in. Robin Ventura's fielder's choice knotted the game at 2. But Ellis Burks' dribbler to third ended the threat.

Again, Sox infielders made some inopportune errors. Starting the fourth inning, Robin Ventura bobbled Paul Molitor's sharp grounder. One out later, Ed Sprague singled. Pat Borders grounded to Ozzie Guillen, who flipped the ball to Joey Cora, who, nudged by a sliding Sprague, bounced the relay past Thomas at first base, Molitor scoring the go-ahead run.

It remained a one-run game, Jays 3, Sox 2, till the Jays opened it up in a painful three-run ninth inning. It was a case of too many Jays bats eventually wearing down the Sox staff.

Devon White socked a solo home run off reliever Scott Radinsky, who had just entered the game. Against Roberto Hernandez, Paul Molitor tripled home two of Radinsky's base runners.

Warren "the Deacon" Newson clubbed a solo homer in the ninth inning, forcing the exiting fans to pause momentarily. It was the White Sox's first hit of the series coming from the designated hitter spot (sans Frank Thomas).

Game 1
October 5, at Chicago

Toronto	AB	R	H	RBI	PO	A
Henderson, lf	6	0	0	0	3	0
White, cf	5	0	2	0	2	0
Alomar, 2b	4	1	0	0	4	4
Carter, rf	5	1	2	0	2	0
Olerud, 1b	4	3	3	2	7	0
Molitor, dh	5	2	4	3	0	0
T. Fernandez, ss	5	0	1	0	2	2
Sprague, 3b	5	0	4	2	0	0
Borders, c	5	0	1	0	7	1
Guzman, p	0	0	0	0	0	4
Cox, p	0	0	0	0	0	0
Ward, p	0	0	0	0	0	0
	44	7	17	7	27	11

Chicago	AB	R	H	RBI	PO	A
Raines, lf	5	0	2	1	1	0
Cora, 2b	3	0	0	0	4	0
Thomas, dh	1	0	1	0	0	0
Ventura, 3b	3	0	0	0	0	3
Burks, rf	5	0	1	0	3	0
Pasqua, 1b	3	1	0	0	6	1
Johnson, cf	4	1	0	0	3	0
Karkovice, c	3	0	0	0	8	1
Guillen, ss	4	1	2	2	2	4
McDowell, p	0	0	0	0	0	0
DeLeon, p	0	0	0	0	0	0
Radinsky, p	0	0	0	0	0	0
McCaskill, p	0	0	0	0	0	0
	31	3	6	3	27	9

Toronto	0	0	0	2	3	0	2	0	0—7
Chicago	3	0	0	0	0	0	0	0	0—3

Toronto	IP	H	R	ER	BB	K
Guzman (W)	6	5	3	2	8	3
Cox	2	1	0	0	0	2
Ward	1	0	0	0	2	2

Chicago	IP	H	R	ER	BB	K
McDowell (L)	6⅔	13	7	7	2	4
DeLeon	1	2	0	0	0	1
Radinsky	⅓	0	0	0	0	1
McCaskill	1	2	0	0	0	2

E—Olerud, Cora. DP—Toronto 1. LOB—Sox 13, Jays 12. 2B—Burks, Olerud. 3B—Sprague. HR—Molitor. SB—Guillen, Raines. SH—Karkovice. WP—Guzman 3. HBP—by Guzman (Pasqua). Umpires—Evans, Kosc, Shulock, Hendry, Tschida, Kaiser. Time—3:38. Attendance—46,246.

Game 2
October 6, at Chicago

Toronto	AB	R	H	RBI	PO	A
Henderson, lf	3	1	0	0	3	0
White, cf	4	0	2	0	3	0
Alomar, 2b	4	0	0	1	2	1
Carter, rf	4	0	1	0	1	0
Olerud, 1b	4	0	1	0	4	3
Molitor, dh	4	1	2	0	0	0
T. Fernandez, ss	3	1	1	1	3	1
Sprague, 3b	3	0	0	0	2	1
Borders, c	4	0	1	0	7	0
Stewart, p	0	0	0	0	2	0
Leiter, p	0	0	0	0	0	0
Ward, p	0	0	0	0	0	0
	33	3	8	2	27	6

Chicago	AB	R	H	RBI	PO	A
Raines, 1f	4	1	1	0	0	1
Cora, 2b	5	0	0	0	2	9
Thomas, dh	3	0	2	0	0	0
Ventura, 3b-1b	3	0	1	0	4	0
Burks, rf	2	0	0	0	1	0
Pasqua, 1b	3	0	0	0	7	1
Grebeck, ph-3b	1	0	1	0	0	0
Johnson, cf	4	0	1	0	3	0
Karkovice, c	1	0	0	0	3	0
Newson, ph	1	0	0	0	0	0
LaValliere, c	1	0	1	0	2	0
Guillen, ss	4	0	0	0	4	5
A. Fernandez, p	0	0	0	0	1	0
Hernandez, p	0	0	0	0	0	0
	32	1	7	0	27	16

Toronto	1	0	0	2	0	0	0	0	0—3
Chicago	1	0	0	0	0	0	0	0	0—1

Toronto	IP	H	R	ER	BB	K
Stewart (W)	6	4	1	1	4	5
Leiter	2	2	0	0	1	2
Ward (S)	1	1	0	0	0	0

Chicago	IP	H	R	ER	BB	K
A. Fernandez (L)	8	8	3	1	3	5
Hernandez	1	0	0	0	0	0

E—Pasqua, Cora. DP—Sox 2, Jays, 1. LOB—Sox 10, Jays 6. 2B—Johnson, Molitor. SH—Karkovice. WP—Stewart, Umpires—Kosc, Shulock, Hendry, Tschida, Kaiser, Evans. Time—3:00. Attendance—46,101.

Game 3
October 8, at Toronto

Chicago	AB	R	H	RBI	PO	A
Raines, lf	5	1	4	0	4	0
Cora, 2b	3	1	2	0	3	3
Thomas, 1b	3	1	1	1	7	1
Ventura, 3b	2	1	0	1	0	0
Burks, rf	5	1	2	2	4	0
Jackson, dh	4	0	0	0	0	0
Johnson, cf	5	0	2	2	1	0
Karkovice, c	4	0	0	0	6	0
Guillen, ss	4	1	1	0	2	1
Alvarez, p	0	0	0	0	0	2
	35	6	12	6	27	7

Toronto	AB	R	H	RBI	PO	A
Henderson, lf	3	1	1	0	0	0
White, cf	4	0	1	1	3	0
Molitor, dh	4	0	1	0	0	0
Carter, rf	4	0	0	0	1	0
Olerud, 1b	4	0	2	0	14	1
Alomar, 2b	3	0	1	0	0	4
T. Fernandez, ss	3	0	1	0	2	1
Sprague, 3b	3	0	0	0	0	4
Borders, c	3	0	0	0	6	3
Hentgen, p	0	0	0	0	1	0
Cox, p	0	0	0	0	0	1
Eichhorn, p	0	0	0	0	0	0
Castillo, p	0	0	0	0	0	1
	31	1	7	1	27	15

Chicago	0	0	5	1	0	0	0	0	0—6
Toronto	0	0	1	0	0	0	0	0	0—1

Chicago	IP	H	R	ER	BB	K
Alvarez (W)	9	7	1	1	2	6

Toronto	IP	H	R	ER	BB	K
Hentgen (L)	3	9	6	6	2	3
Cox	3	2	0	0	2	3
Eichhorn	2	1	0	0	1	1
Castillo	1	0	0	0	0	1

E—Henderson. DP—Sox 2, Jays 1. LOB—Sox 10, Jays 5. 2B—Raines 2, Henderson. SB—Johnson, Henderson. SH—Cora 2. SF—Ventura. Umpires—Shulock, Hendry, Tschida, Kaiser, Evans, Kosc. Time—2:56. Attendance—51,783.

Game 4

October 9, at Toronto

Chicago	AB	R	H	RBI	PO	A
Raines, lf	5	1	3	0	3	1
Cora, 2b	5	0	1	1	2	3
Thomas, 1b	3	1	1	1	7	0
Ventura, 3b	5	0	2	1	2	2
Burks, rf	4	2	1	0	3	0
Jackson, dh	2	1	0	0	0	0
Johnson, cf	4	1	2	4	3	0
Karkovice, c	4	0	0	0	6	0
Guillen, ss	4	1	1	0	0	1
Bere, p	0	0	0	0	1	1
McCaskill, p	0	0	0	0	0	0
Radinsky, p	0	0	0	0	0	0
Hernandez, p	0	0	0	0	0	0
	36	7	11	7	27	8

Toronto	AB	R	H	RBI	PO	A
Henderson, lf	3	1	0	0	1	0
White, cf	4	1	2	0	3	0
Alomar, 2b	5	1	2	2	4	2
Carter, rf	4	0	2	2	2	1
Olerud, 1b	4	0	0	0	7	2
Molitor, dh	4	0	0	0	0	0
T. Fernandez, ss	3	0	2	0	1	3
Sprague, 3b	4	0	0	0	0	2
Borders, c	4	1	1	0	6	0
Stottlemyre, p	0	0	0	0	2	0
Leiter, p	0	0	0	0	0	0
Timlin, p	0	0	0	0	1	1
	35	4	9	4	27	11

Chicago	0	2	0	0	0	3	1	0	1—7
Toronto	0	0	3	0	0	1	0	0	—4

Chicago	IP	H	R	ER	BB	K
Bere (W)	2⅓	5	3	3	2	3
Belcher	3⅔	3	1	1	3	1
McCaskill	1⅓	1	0	0	1	1
Radinsky	⅔	0	0	0	0	0
Hernandez (S)	1	0	0	0	0	0

Toronto	IP	H	R	ER	BB	K
Stottlemyre (L)	6	6	5	5	4	4
Leiter	⅔	2	1	1	1	0
Timlin	2⅓	3	1	1	0	2

DP—Jays 1. LOB—Sox 7, Jays 11. 2B—Alomar. 3B—Johnson, White. HR—Thomas, Johnson. HBP—by Bere (Olerud). WP—Belcher. Bald—Stottlemyre. Umpires—Hendry, Tschida, Kaiser, Evans, Kosc, Shulock. Time—3:30. Attendance—51,889.

Game 5

October 10, at Toronto

Chicago	AB	R	H	RBI	PO	A
Raines, lf	4	1	1	0	3	0
Cora, 2b	3	0	0	0	2	2
Thomas, 1b	4	0	0	0	5	1
Ventura, 3b	4	1	1	2	1	1
Burks, rf	3	1	2	1	2	0
Jackson, dh	4	0	0	0	0	0
Johnson, cf	3	0	0	0	0	0
Karkovice, c	2	0	0	0	7	1
Guillen, ss	3	0	1	0	4	1
McDowell, p	0	0	0	0	0	1
DeLeon, p	0	0	0	0	0	0
Radinsky, p	0	0	0	0	0	0
Hernandez, p	0	0	0	0	0	0
	30	3	5	3	24	7

Toronto	AB	R	H	RBI	PO	A
Henderson, lf	5	1	2	0	0	0
White, cf	5	1	2	0	3	0
Alomar, 2b	3	1	3	1	2	4
Carter, rf	5	0	1	0	2	0
Olerud, 1b	3	0	1	1	8	2
Molitor, dh	3	2	1	0	0	0
T. Fernandez, ss	4	0	2	0	2	1
Sprague, 3b	3	0	1	2	1	0
Borders, c	4	0	1	0	9	0
Guzman, p	0	0	0	0	0	0
Castillo, p	0	0	0	0	0	0
Ward, p	0	0	0	0	0	0
	35	5	14	4	27	7

Chicago	0	0	0	0	1	0	0	0	2—3
Toronto	1	1	1	1	0	0	1	0	—5

Chicago	IP	H	R	ER	BB	K
McDowell (L)	2⅓	5	3	3	3	1
DeLeon	3⅔	5	1	1	1	5
Radinsky	⅓	1	1	1	1	0
Hernandez	1⅔	3	0	0	0	1

Toronto	IP	H	R	ER	BB	K
Guzman (W)	7	3	1	1	1	6
Castillo	1	0	0	0	1	0
Ward	1	2	2	2	0	3

E—McDowell. DP—Sox 1, Jays 2. LOB—Sox 3, Jays 12. 2B—Henderson, White, Molitor. HR—Burks, Ventura. SB—Henderson, Alomar 3, Borders. SF—Sprague. HBP—by Ward (Burks). WP—McDowell. Umpires—Tschida, Kaiser, Evans, Kosc, Shulock, Hendry. Time—3:09. Attendance—51,375.

Game 6

October 12, at Chicago

Toronto	AB	R	H	RBI	PO	A
Henderson, lf	5	0	0	0	2	0
White, cf	5	1	3	1	1	0
Alomar, 2b	5	0	1	0	2	4
Carter, rf	5	1	1	0	4	0
Olerud, 1b	4	2	1	0	8	1
Molitor, dh	3	2	1	2	0	0
T. Fernandez, ss	4	0	0	0	2	0
Sprague, 3b	3	0	1	0	2	2
Borders, c	4	0	2	3	6	0
Stewart, p	0	0	0	0	0	0
Ward, p	0	0	0	0	0	0
	38	6	10	6	27	7

Chicago	AB	R	H	RBI	PO	A
Raines, lf	4	1	1	0	1	0
Cora, 2b	3	0	0	0	5	3
Thomas, 1b	3	0	1	1	5	1
Ventura, 3b	3	0	0	1	2	0
Burks, rf	4	0	1	0	2	0
Newson, dh	4	1	1	1	0	0
Johnson, cf	3	0	0	0	5	0
LaValliere, c	2	0	0	0	6	0
Karkovice, c	1	0	0	0	0	0
Guillen, ss	3	1	1	0	0	2
A. Fernandez, p	0	0	0	0	1	1
McCaskill, p	0	0	0	0	0	2
Radinsky, p	0	0	0	0	0	0
Hernandez, p	0	0	0	0	1	1
	30	3	5	3	27	9

Toronto	0	2	0	1	0	0	0	0	3—6
Chicago	0	0	2	0	0	0	0	0	1—3

Toronto	IP	H	R	ER	BB	K
Stewart (W)	7⅓	4	2	2	4	3
Ward (S)	1⅔	1	1	1	1	3

Chicago	IP	H	R	ER	BB	K
A. Fernandez (L)	7	7	3	2	3	5
McCaskill	1⅓	0	0	0	0	0
Radinsky	⅓	2	3	1	0	0
Hernandez	⅓	1	0	0	0	0

E—Cora, Ventura, Radinsky. DP—Jays 1. LOB—Sox 7, Jays 10. 2B-Borders, Guillen. 3B—Molitor. HR—White. SB—Alomar. SH—T. Fernandez, Guillen. HBP—by Stewart (Cora), by A. Fernandez (Molitor). WP—Stewart. Umpires—Kaiser, Evans, Kosc, Shulock, Hendry, Tschida. Time—3:31. Attendance—45,527.

2000 ALDS: White Sox versus Seattle Mariners

The White Sox (95–67) bolted to an unexpected division title, setting club records for runs (978), doubles (325), and homers (216), and then with equal surprise the club went down quietly, three games to none, in the first round of the playoffs against the wild-card Seattle Mariners.

The 2000 Sox version of "murderer's row" compared well with the 1927 Yanks: Frank Thomas (43 HRs, 143 RBIs), Magglio Ordonez (32 HRs), Carlos Lee (24 HRs), and second-year man Paul Konerko (21 HRs). Middle infielders Ray Durham, Jose Valentin, and center fielder Chris Singleton set the table for the big thumpers. Offsetting his erratic play at shortstop (36 errors), Valentin also put up some big offensive numbers (25 HRs, 92 RBIs).

The Lou Piniella–led Mariners boasted some firepower of their own: Alex Rodriguez (41 HRs), Edgar Martinez (37 HRs), Jay Buhner (26 HRs), and ex-Sox Mike Cameron (19 HRs). In a slugfest season series (125 runs scored), the Sox enjoyed a 7–5 game edge against the M's, socking 20 homers while compiling a nifty .285 team batting average. Going into the series, Sox pitching was questionable. The fragile Cal Eldred's season ended in July. Mike Sirotka was nursing a tender elbow. Reliever Sean Lowe had a sore shoulder. Pitching in pain, James Baldwin needed cortisone shots to prop up his tired arm.

General manager Ron Schueler was optimistic that his young arms could withstand any pressure, especially under the guidance of "Zen manager" Jerry Manuel. ("We might be sending out Gideon's army, but I'll take that army anytime!") Instead, Schueler had opted for more power for the stretch run, acquiring veteran backstop Charlie Johnson and reacquiring the popular Harold Baines.

As it turned out, the White Sox showed none of their firepower in the series. The Sox scored only seven runs in the three-game series, none after the third inning, and none against the M's bullpen (13⅓ innings, 0 runs, 3 hits). Drawing a "playoff ugly" comparison to the '83 Sox, the 2000 Sox's middle hitters mustered a dismal 4-for-42 against Seattle pitching. The three-game sweep made it eight straight playoff losses for the White Sox, and still no single postseason victory in Chicago since 1959. Seattle went on to lose to the Yankees in the American League Championship Series.

Game 1

A four-hour, 12-minute marathon was abruptly decided in the 10th inning as Seattle poked back-to-back homers off Keith Foulke, who was working his second inning of relief. The Sox stranded 10 runners, including five at third base. The 10-inning affair ended with Carlos Lee perched at third base after a leadoff double. Erasing an early Mariners 3–0 lead, the Sox tallied two in the second on a walk, a Chris Singleton triple, and a wild pitch. In the third, Ray Durham's solo homer and Magglio Ordonez's RBI triple pushed the Sox in front 4–3. Brett Tomko, the first of five Mariners relievers, bailed starter Freddy Garcia out of a one-out, bases-loaded jam in the fourth. Sox hitters managed only three hits the rest of the game. Lefty Jim Parque settled down after a shaky start, retiring 10 in a row. Mike Cameron's RBI single off reliever Chad Bradford knotted the game at four in the seventh, forcing overtime.

Cameron, a bust with the Sox who had "found" himself in Seattle, singled leading off the Seattle 10th. After the dangerous Alex Rodriguez was retired, Cameron stole second, one pitch after Jerry Manuel had called for a pitchout. Sox catcher Josh Paul, the pride of Buffalo Grove, Illinois, telegraphed his intentions to Cameron by lining up outside the batter's box. Martinez then lined a 2–1 pitch into the left-field stands. A nemesis from the 1993 series, John Olerud, added an insurance blast, putting Seattle up 7–4. After Lee's two-bagger raised hopes in the 10th, Seattle closer Kazuhiro Sasaki retired Paul Konerko on a grounder, then fanned Herbert Perry and Chris Singleton.

Game 2

The Sox ignominiously surrendered home-field advantage in the short best-of-five series, losing 5–2.

Again the bats were silent. The big guns—Frank Thomas, Magglio Ordonez, Carlos Lee, and Paul Konerko—failed to get a hit. Frank Thomas stranded five runners, making it nine lost souls in two games. Ray Durham and Jose Valentin greeted Seattle starter Paul Abbott with doubles on consecutive pitches. Valentin stole third base, the Sox "cold corner," where he "froze" as Thomas, Lee, and Konerko again failed to deliver in the clutch. Mike Sirotka, making his first start since hyper-extending his elbow in his last regular season start, gave up four runs in 5⅔ innings.

A Valentin error, which was more like a brain cramp, led to a two-run second inning for Seattle. With runners on first and second, Jay Buhner hit a chopper to Valentin's right. Instead of trying for the lead runner, Jose spun around and threw the ball wide of second base, loading the bases. A single and a sacrifice fly gave the Mariners a 2–1 lead.

In the Sox third, Valentin made amends, scooting around the bases on a bunt single, a stolen base, an infield play, and a sacrifice fly, knotting the game at two. The Sox managed only two more hits the rest of the way, both by third baseman Herbert Perry, "the Milkman." One Perry hit helped mount a Sox two-out, two-man threat in the seventh. The rally ended when the hard-luck Valentin was called out at second on a grounder that glanced off the pitcher's glove to second sacker Mark McLemore, who flipped the ball to shortstop Alex Rodriguez for the force-out.

Jay Buhner's fourth-inning homer put the M's on top to stay. In the fifth, Seattle hitters assisted speedster Rickey Henderson on one of his patented roundtrippers: walk, sacrifice bunt, stolen base, infield grounder. Mike Cameron's base hit in the ninth made it a 5–2 game, salting away a Seattle victory.

Kazuhiro Sasaki earned his second straight save with three strikeouts in the ninth, picking up from Jose Mesa, who had fanned the last two White Sox batters in the eighth inning. It was on to Seattle, to do or die.

Game 3

Sox hurlers welcomed spacious Safeco Field, but for the hitters it was a recipe for disaster. They managed only one run on three hits off starter Aaron Sele and company, in a stunning, ninth-inning 2–1 loss to the Mariners. Manager Jerry Manuel had shaken up the Sox lineup, benching Paul Konerko, putting Frank Thomas at first base, and inserting Harold Baines in the designated hitter's spot. Baines came through with a double leading off the sixth and came around to score on Herbert Perry's deep fly. Konerko pinch-hit in the eighth and killed a Sox threat, grounding into an inning-ending double play. Frank Thomas remained hitless for the series (0-for-9) but drew two walks.

Withering in pain, sore-armed James Baldwin pitched six solid innings, yielding one fluky run after a bad-hop grounder whistled past Ray Durham for an RBI single. Relief pitcher Kelly Wunsch's throwing error led to the winning run. Leading off the Seattle ninth, John Olerud drilled a ball back to the mound off Wunsch's chest, upending the Sox lefty who then fired the ball to first base while on one knee. The ball sailed over Thomas's head and down the first-base line. Olerud ended up at second on the errant throw. Wunsch later admitted he should have eaten the ball.

Keith Foulke came in. Rickey Henderson ran for Olerud. Stan Javier's sacrifice bunt moved Henderson to third. Foulke walked David Bell. But manager Jerry Manuel elected not to load the bases with another walk. Pinch-hitter Carlos Guillen then placed a suicide-squeeze bunt down the first-base line. Thomas, who had been inching forward in anticipation of a bunt, dove head-first for the ball. It trickled past him as Henderson scooted home with the series winner.

Afterward in the Sox clubhouse, Jerry Manuel said, "We all lost it. They out-hit us, they outplayed us, and they outmanaged us." He seemed to be right on all three counts.

Game 1
October 3, at Chicago

Seattle	AB	R	H	RBI	BB	SO
Henderson, lf	3	1	1	0	0	0
a—Javier, if	2	0	0	0	0	1
Cameron, cf	4	2	2	1	0	0
Rodriguez, ss	5	0	3	1	0	0
Martinez, dh	5	1	2	2	0	0
Olerud, 1b	5	1	1	2	0	1
Buhner, rf	1	0	0	0	2	0
b—Ibanez pr-rf	2	1	1	0	0	0
Bell, 3b	4	0	1	0	1	1
Oliver, c	2	1	1	1	0	0
c—Martin, ph	1	0	0	0	0	0
Wilson, c	2	0	0	0	0	2
McLemore, 2b	3	0	1	0	1	0
	39	7	13	7	4	5

Chicago	AB	R	H	RBI	BB	SO
Duhram, 2b	3	1	1	1	1	1
Valentin, ss	4	1	1	0	1	0
Thomas dh	3	0	0	0	2	0
Ordonez, rf	5	0	1	1	0	1
Lee, lf	5	0	1	0	0	2
Konerko, 1b	4	1	0	0	1	0
Perry, 3b	4	0	1	0	1	1
Singleton, cf	5	1	1	1	0	1
Johnson, c	4	0	3	0	0	0
d—Paul pr-c	0	0	0	0	0	0
	37	4	9	3	6	6

a—struck out for Henderson in the seventh. b—ran for J. Buhner in the seventh. c—grounded out for Oliver in the seventh. d—ran for Johnson in the ninth.

Seattle	2	1	0	0	0	0	1	0	0	3—7
Chicago	0	2	2	0	0	0	0	0	0	0—4

Seattle	IP	H	R	ER	BB	SO
Garcia	3⅓	6	4	4	3	2
Tomko	2⅔	1	0	0	1	0
Paniagua	2	1	0	0	1	2
Rhodes	⅔	0	0	0	0	0
Mesa (W)	⅓	0	0	0	1	0
Sasaki (S)	1	1	0	0	0	2

Chicago	IP	H	R	ER	BB	SO
Parque	6	6	3	3	1	2
Howry	⅔	1	1	1	2	1
Bradford	⅔	2	0	0	0	0
Wunsch	⅓	1	0	0	0	0
Simas	⅓	0	0	0	0	0
Foulke (L)	2	3	3	3	1	2

DP—Seattle 1, Chicago 2. LOB—Seattle 7, White Sox 10. 2B—DaBell, Valentin, Lee. 3B—Ordonez, Singleton. HR—Olerud, Martinez, Durham, Oliver. SB—Cameron, Valentin. WP—Garcia, Tomko. HBP—Cameron. Umpires—Reliford, Danley, Reily, Winter, Reed, Eddings. Time—4:12. Attendance—45,290.

Game 2
October 4, at Chicago

Seattle	AB	R	H	RBI	BB	SO
Henderson, lf	2	1	1	0	1	0
Ibanez, lf-rf	2	0	1	0	0	0
Cameron, cf	4	0	1	1	0	0
Rodriguez, ss	5	0	1	1	0	1
Martinez, dh	3	1	1	0	1	0
Olerud, 1b	3	1	1	0	0	0
Buhner, rf	4	1	1	1	0	0
Oliver, c	0	0	0	0	0	0
Bell, 3b	4	0	2	1	0	1
Wilson, c	1	0	0	1	1	0
Javier, if	1	0	0	0	0	1
McLemore, 2b	3	1	0	0	1	0
	32	5	9	5	4	3

Chicago	AB	R	H	RBI	BB	SO
Durham, 2b	4	1	1	0	1	1
Valentin, ss	3	1	2	1	1	0
Thomas, dh	4	0	0	0	0	0
Ordonez, rf	2	0	0	0	2	0
Lee, lf	3	0	0	1	0	0
Konerko, 1b	4	0	0	0	0	1
Perry, 3b	4	0	2	0	0	1
Singleton, cf	2	0	0	0	0	1
a—Abbott, ph-cf	1	0	0	0	0	0
b—Baines, ph	1	0	0	0	0	1
Johnson, c	2	0	0	0	1	1
	30	2	5	2	5	6

a—Abbott flew out for Singleton in the sixth. b—Baines struck out for Abbott in the ninth.

Seattle	0	2	0	1	1	0	0	0	1—5
Chicago	1	0	1	0	0	0	0	0	0—2

Seattle	IP	H	R	ER	BB	SO
Abbott (W)	5⅔	5	2	1	3	1
Rhodes	⅔	0	0	0	2	0
Mesa	1⅔	0	0	0	0	2
Sasaki (S)	1	0	0	0	0	3

Chicago	IP	H	R	ER	BB	SO
Sirotka (L)	5⅔	7	4	3	2	0
Barcelo	1⅔	0	0	0	1	0
Wunsch	⅓	0	0	0	0	0
Simas	1	0	1	1	1	2
Buehrle	⅓	2	0	0	0	1

E—Valentin, Wilson. DP—Seattle 1, Sox 3. LOB—Seattle 7, Sox 8. 2B—Martinez, Durham, Valentin (2), Perry. HR—Buhner. SB—Henderson, Valentin (2), Ordonez. SH—Cameron. SF—Wilson, Lee. HBP—by Sirotka (Olerud), Johnson (Abbott). Umpires—Reliford, Danley, Reily, Winter, Reed, Eddings. Time—4:12. Attendance—45,290.

Game 3
October 6, at Seattle

Chicago	AB	R	H	RBI	BB	SO
Durham, 2b	3	0	0	0	1	1
Valentin, ss	3	0	0	0	0	2
Thomas, 1b	2	0	0	0	2	0
Ordonez, rf	4	0	0	0	0	1
Baines, dh	3	1	1	0	0	0
Johnson, c	3	0	0	0	0	0
Perry, 3b	1	0	1	1	1	0
a—Graffanino pr-3b	0	0	0	0	0	0
Lee, lf	3	0	0	0	0	0
Singleton, cf	2	0	0	0	0	0
b—Konerko, ph	1	0	0	0	0	0
Christensen, cf	0	0	0	0	0	0
	25	1	3	1	4	4

Seattle	AB	R	H	RBI	BB	SO
Cameron, cf	4	0	0	0	0	0
Ibanez, lf	4	1	1	0	0	0
Rodriguez, ss	3	0	0	0	0	1
Martinez, dh	3	0	1	0	1	1
Olerud, 1b	2	0	1	0	2	0
c—Henderson, pr	0	1	0	0	0	0
Javier, lf	3	0	1	1	0	1
DaBell, 3b	3	0	1	0	1	0
Oliver c	2	0	0	0	0	1
d—Guillen, ph	1	0	1	1	0	0
McLemore, 2b	3	0	0	0	0	1
	28	2	6	2	4	5

a—ran for Perry in the eighth. b—grounded into double play for Singleton in the eighth. c—ran for Olerud in the ninth. d—singled for Oliver in the ninth.

Chicago	0	1	0	0	0	0	0	0	0—1
Seattle	0	0	0	1	0	0	0	0	1—2

Chicago	IP	H	R	ER	BB	SO
Baldwin	6	3	1	1	3	2
Howry	2	1	0	0	0	3
Wunsch (L)	0	1	1	0	0	0
Foulke	1/3	1	0	0	1	0

Seattle	IP	H	R	ER	BB	SO
Sele	7 1/3	3	1	1	3	1
Rhodes	1 1/3	0	0	0	0	2
Paniagua	1/3	0	0	0	1	1

E—Wunsch. DP—Seattle 3. LOB—Sox 3, Seattle 8. 2B—Baines. SH—Valentin, Rodriguez, Javier, Oliver. SF—Perry. Umpires—Reliford, Danley, Reily, Winter, Reed, Eddings. Time—4:12. Attendance—45,290.

2005 ALDS: White Sox versus Boston Red Sox

In the American League Division Series, the White Sox were looking to steal the rabbit's foot from the Boston Red Sox, who in 2004 had won their first title in 86 years. The White Sox had their own world championship drought to contend with, dating back to 1917. Whereas Ozzie Guillen's team (99–63) romped to the title and a home-field advantage throughout the playoffs, the Red Sox (95–67) had to settle for a wild-card position after finishing behind the hated Yankees in the American League East.

Befitting the close quarters of Fenway Park—and the state of their woeful pitching staff (4.71 ERA)—the Red Sox looked for the big inning behind sluggers David Ortiz (47 HRs, 148 RBIs) and Manny Ramirez (45 HRs, 144 RBIs), and table-setter Johnny Damon (.316).

The White Sox relied on their familiar Go-Go style of seasons past: speed, top-notch pitching, and proper execution. This exciting fundamental brand of baseball, dubbed "small ball" in 2005, featured speedster Scott Podsednik; bat-control artists Tadahito Iguchi and Aaron Rowand; and long-distance hitters Carl Everett, Jermaine Dye, Paul Konerko, and Joe Crede. The Sox played 95 games decided by two runs or less, winning 61 of them. Still, the revamped South Siders were not lacking in the power department, out-homering the Red Sox 200–199. Slugger Frank Thomas' season ended in late July because of a fractured bone in his left ankle. Sox general manager Kenny Williams wanted to acquire an extra bat for the postseason, but manager Ozzie Guillen preferred to stand pat and not mess with the key ingredient of small ball—team chemistry.

The series proved Ozzie right. The White Sox combined small-ball hustle with some long-ball power to score 24 runs in a surprising three-game sweep.

Sox hurlers held up their share of the small-ball approach, particularly the bullpen artists who stopped Boston cold in the final two contests, just when it appeared the Red Sox were going to forge ahead.

The clutch pitching and timely hitting shown by the White Sox during the Boston series indicated to a skeptical baseball establishment something that White Sox fans had sensed all along: this team was something special.

Game 1

In a contest so reminiscent of the 11–0 thrashing of the Dodgers in Game 1 of the 1959 World Series, the small-ball White Sox brought their big lumber to U.S. Cellular Field, bashing Boston 14–2. The White Sox slugged five homers, resulting in five curtain calls.

Catcher A.J. Pierzynski, tipped his hat twice to the fans.

The home-field rout of the defending champs was the Sox's first postseason win in Chicago since that memorable 1959 opener, and it snapped Boston's eight-game postseason win streak. Jose Contreras, who, in seven previous appearances against Boston, had been roughed up pretty good (2–4, 11.67), allowed two runs and eight hits in 7 2/3 innings of work. Boston's big three—Johnny Damon, Manny Ramirez, and David Ortiz—collected two harmless hits against the Sox's nasty-throwing Cuban right-hander.

Contreras set the tone in the very first inning. After a one-out double by Edgar Renteria, he fanned Ortiz, then splintered Ramirez's bat with an inside heater, resulting in a weak grounder to third base. Ramirez stranded two more runners in the third.

The Sox opened with a five-spot in the first inning against ex-Cubs hurler Matt Clement. The small-ball script featured two hit batsmen, a stolen base, a sacrifice bunt, a sacrifice fly, and a fielder's choice. Things got interesting after that: Carl Everett and Jermaine Dye whacked base hits; A.J. Pierzynski slammed a three-run homer.

Shortstop Juan Uribe's two-run homer in the fourth ended Clement's disastrous stint. Sox fans let the old Cubs hurler have it, adding some extra raspberries to the refrain of "Na Na Hey Hey Kiss Him Goodbye."

Leadoff man Scott Podsednik contributed a three-run blast in the sixth. Pushed up the steps by his teammates, he made a reluctant curtain call. Used to a few accolades of his own, sidelined slugger Frank Thomas tossed out the ceremonial first pitch, then sat back and enjoyed the rout.

Game 2

The White Sox rallied to win 5–4 to take a 2–0 lead in the best-of-five series.

Forty-two-year-old David Wells (15–7, 4.45 ERA), his age reflecting his waist size, took the mound for the Red Sox against his old White Sox team. Wells, who was hampered by a bad back while serving on the White Sox in 2001, faced off against ex-teammate Mark Buehrle, whom Wells had mentored both on and off the field.

The Red Sox started out as if it was their turn for a laugher. The first two men in the lineup, Johnny Damon and Edgar Renteria, stroked base hits. Both scored on a one-out single by Manny Ramirez. Two more Bosox runners crossed the plate in the third.

Meanwhile, Wells kept the Sox hitters off balance with slow curveballs and an occasional heater. The second time around the order, the Sox hitters found their timing. In the fifth, Carl Everett singled. Then Aaron Rowand blooped an RBI double down the left-field line. After A.J. Pierzynski grounded out, Joe Crede cracked a single up the middle, making it a 4–2 game. Juan Uribe then punched a grounder to second baseman Tony Graffanino, who, moving to his right to start an inning-ending double play, momentarily took his eye off the ball. It zipped through his legs for an error, putting runners on second and third. Scott Podsednik fouled out. But Tadahito Iguchi, who was hitless in Game 1, crushed a 1–1 pitch into the left-field stands, giving the Sox a 5–4 lead.

After the third inning, Buehrle retired 12 of 14 batters before giving way to fire-balling rookie Bobby Jenks.

Boston stranded a runner in the eighth, then threatened again in the ninth. With one down, Graffanino hustled a gapper into a double. Jenks retired Johnny Damon on a pop foul and, with David Ortiz waiting on deck, induced Renteria to bounce out to short, ending the game.

Game 3

The Sox were mindful that Boston had rallied from a three-game deficit against the Yankees in the 2004 playoffs. They were understandably anxious to wrap things up in Bean Town as quickly as possible.

In the first two games of the series, the Sox hitters, in baseball parlance, had "stepped up" to do a job. This time, Orlando "El Duque" Hernandez provided the heroics as the Sox advanced to the American League Championship Series, defeating the Bosox 5–3.

Hernandez, shaky for much of the season, claimed to be 38, but some people suspected he was already past 40. He had joined the White Sox in January after an up-and-down career with the Yankees. An impressive postseason record (9–3, 2.65 ERA) and two solid relief appearances against Cleveland late in the season convinced manager Ozzie Guillen to add him to the roster, ahead of rookie sensation Brandon McCarthy.

El Duque entered in the sixth after starter Freddy Garcia gave up a towering homer to Manny Ramirez, cutting the Sox lead to 4–3, and reliever Damaso Marte had loaded the bases on a single and two walks. Hernandez got catcher Jason Varitek to foul out to first baseman Paul Konerko. After a 10-pitch battle, Tony Graffanino popped up meekly to Juan Uribe at short. Johnny Damon fanned on a checked swing.

Hernandez, the unlikely hero of the ALDS, pitched two scoreless innings. Reliever Bobby Jenks finished off Boston on 10 pitches in the ninth to earn his second save of the series.

Boston starter, knuckleball artist Tim Wakefield, was rocked for two runs in the third inning on doubles by Juan Uribe and Scott Podsednik, and a Tadahito Iguchi base hit. With one aboard in the sixth, Paul Konerko took measure of a Wakefield knuckler and drove it up and over the Green Monster, breaking the two-run tie. The White Sox gave the Boston faithful a small-ball sendoff, adding an insurance run in the ninth on a suicide squeeze by Uribe, allowing A.J. Pierzynski to rumble home from third.

After a subdued clubhouse celebration, the Sox flew back to Chicago to await the winner of the Yankees-Angels series, thus giving the players a well-deserved rest and Ozzie Guillen the luxury of arranging his pitching staff to his liking for the next series.

Game 1
October 4, at Chicago

Boston	AB	R	H	RBI	BB	SO
Damon, cf	4	0	0	0	0	2
Cora, ss	0	0	0	0	0	0
Renteria, ss	4	0	1	0	0	0
Hyzdu, cf	0	0	0	0	0	0
Ortiz, dh	4	0	2	0	0	1
Ramirez, lf	4	0	0	0	0	0
Nixon, rf	4	1	2	0	0	0
Varitek, c	4	1	1	0	0	1
Millar, 1b	3	0	1	1	0	1
a—Olerud, ph	1	0	1	0	0	1
Mueller, 3b	4	0	0	0	0	1
Graffanino, 2b	4	0	1	0	0	0
	36	2	9	1	0	6

Chicago	AB	R	H	RBI	BB	SO
Podsednik, lf	3	2	2	3	1	0
Iguchi, 2b	3	0	0	0	0	1
b—Harris, ph-2b	1	0	1	1	0	1
Dye, rf	3	0	0	0	0	0
c—Perez, ph-rf	1	0	0	0	0	0
Konerko, 1b	4	2	1	2	0	0
d—Blum, ph-1b	1	0	0	0	0	0
Everett, dh	4	1	1	0	0	0
Rowand, cf	3	2	1	1	1	0
Pierzynski, c	3	4	3	4	0	0
Crede, 3b	3	1	0	0	1	0
Uribe, ss	4	2	2	3	0	1
	33	14	11	14	3	2

Boston	0	0	0	2	0	0	0	0	0—2
Chicago	5	0	1	2	0	4	0	2	x—14

a—doubled for Miller in the ninth. b—singled for Iguchi in the eighth. c—flied out for Dye in the eighth. d—popped out for Konerko in the eighth.

Boston	IP	H	R	ER	BB	SO
Clement (L)	3⅓	7	8	8	0	0
Bradford	1⅓	0	0	0	0	1
Gonzalez	2⅓	2	4	4	1	0
Arroyo	1	2	2	2	2	1

Chicago	IP	H	R	ER	BB	SO
Contreras (W)	7⅔	8	2	2	0	6
Cotts	⅓	0	0	0	0	4
Politte	1	1	0	0	0	0

E—Crede. LOB—Boston 7, Chicago 2. 2B—Renteria, Ortiz, Millar, Olerud, Graffaninio, Pierzynski. HR—Pierzynski 2, Podsednik, Uribe, Konerko, SB—Podsednik. WP—Contreras. HBP—by Gonzalez (Pierzynski), by Clement (Podsednik). Umpires—Hirschbeck, Miller, Wegner, Carlson, Everitt, Iassogna. Time—2:56, Attendance—40,717.

Game 2
October 5, at Chicago

Boston	AB	R	H	RBI	BB	SO
Damon, cf	5	2	2	0	0	0
Renteria, ss	5	1	2	0	0	0
Ortiz, dh	4	1	1	0	0	1
Ramirez, lf	3	0	1	2	1	0
Varitek, c	4	0	2	1	0	0
Nixon, rf	3	0	0	1	1	0
Mueller 3b	4	0	0	0	0	1
Olerud, 1b	4	0	0	0	0	0
Graffanino, 2b	4	0	1	0	0	0
	36	4	9	4	2	2

Chicago	AB	R	H	RBI	BB	SO
Podsednik, lf	4	0	0	0	0	0
Iguchi, 2b	4	1	2	3	0	0
Dye, rf	4	0	1	0	0	1
Konerko, 1b	4	0	1	0	0	0
Everett, dh	4	1	2	0	0	0
Rowand, cf	3	1	1	1	0	0
Pierzynski, c	3	0	0	0	0	0
Crede, 3b	3	1	1	1	0	1
Uribe, ss	3	1	1	0	0	0
	32	5	9	5	0	2

Boston	2	0	2	0	0	0	0	0	0—4
Chicago	0	0	0	0	5	0	0	0	0—5

Boston	IP	H	R	ER	BB	SO
Wells (L)	6⅔	7	5	2	0	2
Papelbon	1⅓	2	0	0	0	0

Chicago	IP	H	R	ER	BB	SO
Buehrle (W)	7	8	5	2	0	2
Jenks (S)	2	1	0	0	1	0

E—Graffaninio. DP—Boston 2. LOB—Boston 7, Chicago 3. 2B—Renteria, Ortiz, Graffanino, Rowand. HR—Iguchi. Umpires—Hirschbeck, Miller, Wegner, Scott, Everitt, Iassogna. Time—2:56, Attendance—40,717

Game 3
October 7, at Boston

Chicago	AB	R	H	RBI	BB	SO
Podsednik, lf	4	1	1	1	0	1
Iguchi, 2b	5	0	1	1	0	2
Dye rf	3	1	1	0	1	1
Konerko, 1b	4	1	1	2	0	1
Everett, dh	3	0	0	0	0	0
Rowand, cf	4	0	2	0	0	1
Pierzynski, c	3	1	1	0	1	0
Crede, 3b	3	0	0	0	0	0
Uribe, ss	3	1	1	1	0	1
	32	5	8	5	2	7

Boston	AB	R	H	RBI	BB	SO
Damon, cf	4	0	1	0	1	2
Renteria, ss	4	0	0	0	1	1
Ortiz, dh	4	1	1	1	0	1
Ramirez, lf	3	2	2	2	1	0
Nixon, rf	4	0	1	0	0	1
Mueller 3b	3	0	0	0	1	0
Olerud, 1b	2	0	1	0	2	0
a—Machado, pr	0	0	0	0	0	0
Millar, 1b	0	0	0	0	0	0
Mirabelli, c	2	0	0	0	0	0
b—Varitek ph-c	2	0	0	0	0	0
Graffanino, 2b	4	0	1	0	0	0
	32	3	7	3	6	6

Chicago	0	0	2	0	0	2	0	0	1—5
Boston	0	0	0	2	0	1	0	0	0—3

a—ran for J. Olerud in the eighth. b—fouled out for D. Mirabelli in the sixth.

Chicago	IP	H	R	ER	BB	SO
Garcia (W)	5	5	3	3	4	1
Marte	0	1	0	0	2	0
Hernandez	3	1	0	0	0	4
Jenks (S)	1	0	0	0	0	1

Boston	IP	H	R	ER	BB	SO
Wakefield (L)	5⅓	6	4	4	1	4
Bradford	0	1	0	0	0	0
Myers	0	0	0	0	1	0
Papelbon	2⅔	0	0	0	0	2
Timlin	1	1	1	1	0	1

E—Timlin. DP—Chicago 2, Boston 1. LOB—Chicago 6, Boston 8. 2B—Podsednik, Rowand, Pierzynski, Uribe, Damon. HR—Konerko, Ramirez 2, Ortiz. SB—Rowand, Pierzynski. HBP—by Wakefield (Everett). Umpires—Hirschbeck, Miller, Wegner, Scott, Everitt, Iassogna. Time—2:56, Attendance—40,717.

2005 ALCS: White Sox versus Los Angeles Angels

After disposing of the aging and weakened Boston Red Sox in the Division Series, the White Sox moved on to the American League Championship Series to battle the Los Angeles Angels, who, because of a legal entanglement, were officially known as the Los Angeles Angels of Anaheim.

The Sox were riding the crest of an eight-game win streak going back to the regular season. Los Angeles was just as hot, winning 14 of their last 16 regular season games to capture the Western Division title. Pesky leadoff hitter Chone Figgins (62 SBs) was the small-ball counterpart to Scott Podsednik. Garret Anderson (.283, 17 HRs) and Vladimir Guerrero (.317, 32 HRs), the 2004 American League Most Valuable Player, were the main power threats. Shortstop Orlando Cabrera and second sacker Adam Kennedy gave the Angels strength up the middle.

The Angels and White Sox both share a second-city complex. The Sox faithful feel terribly snubbed by the media in Cubville; the Angels are perceived as the Dodgers' poorer distant cousin out in Orange County.

The Angels whipped the New York Yankees in a division series that went the distance due to a rain cancellation. At New York, the Yankees knotted the series at two games apiece. Twenty-four hours later, the Angels won the rubber match in California. The Angels then flew back to Chicago for the White Sox opener, accumulating 5,000 frequent-flyer miles in 30 hours.

The Angels captured the season series six games to four, including a three-game sweep at Chicago during a Sox late-September slump. But a different L.A. ballclub arrived in Chicago. Bartolo Colon (21–8), the Halos' ace pitcher, was out for the series with a sore shoulder. The other star hurler, lefty Jarrod Washburn, had a throat infection that kept him quarantined from his teammates. Because of the injuries and the extended New York series, manager Mike Scioscia juggled his staff and picked veteran hurler Paul Byrd (12–11, 3.74 ERA) for the opener.

For the well-rested White Sox, Ozzie Guillen went with his hot hurler, Jose Contreras, in Game 1, saving Jon Garland (18–10), the Sox' top winner in 2005 (who didn't pitch in the Boston series), for Game 3.

The tired Angels surprised the Sox in the opener. But the Sox caught the Angels catnapping to steal Game 2. They finished off the pesky Halos in Southern California to earn their first pennant taste since 1959.

Game 1

The travel-weary Angels defeated the well-rested Sox 3–2 in the ALCS opener. A sellout crowd (40,659) packed U.S. Cellular Field on a cool autumn night. Rooting the Sox on, Mayor Richard M. Daley, who had attended the '59 World Series games with his father, Richard J. Daley, sat behind the Sox dugout.

Taking the red-eye flight from California, L.A. had arrived at their hotel in time for a quick nap (6:30 AM). Later, after snapping the Sox' eight-game winning streak, one spaced-out Angels player remarked, "We were more delirious then tired."

Stop-gap hurler Paul Byrd turned in a clutch performance, giving up two runs on five hits in six-plus innings. Jose Contreras, who had won 11 of his last 13 decisions and was working on six days rest, performed well (8⅓ innings, 7 hits) after a shaky start.

Garret Anderson began the second inning by drawing a bead on a Contreras 2–0 pitch and hammering it over the right-field wall. A bleacher bum threw the ball back onto the field amid cheers.

In the third inning, the eight and nine hitters, Steve Finley and Adam Kennedy, opened with singles. After Chone Figgins laid down a sacrifice bunt, Finley scored when third baseman Joe Crede couldn't come up with Orlando Cabrera's roller. Kennedy tallied when second sacker Tadahito Iguchi was upended at second base and threw the ball away on a possible 1-4-3 double play. Contreras probably should have thrown the ball home.

The Sox seemed to be mounting a comeback as they cut the lead to 3–2 on Joe Crede's solo homer in the third and an A.J. Pierzynski single in the fourth. But the team was not patient, and the small-ball attack was out of sync all evening. Scott Podsednik was caught stealing on a pitchout in the fifth; he then capped a miserable night with a failed bunt attempt in his next at-bat.

Leading off the sixth, Jermaine Dye popped out on a bunt. Another wasted opportunity occurred in the seventh when Pierzynski was thrown out trying to steal second on what he believed was a hit-and-run play.

The Angels let the Sox seal their own misery in the ninth. After Carl Everett reached base on an error, Aaron Rowand bunted the ball to Figgins at third who got a force-out at second base. Pierzynski lined out, and Crede fanned. The Angels could now take the time to nod off.

In the postgame press conference, Ozzie offered no excuses, but singled out his pitcher for praise. "Before the game, I don't believe they [the Angels] would be tired. We didn't execute well. They played better than we did. We'll come back and play hard," he vowed. "Great job by Jose [Contreras]. The home run by Anderson was the only legit ball hit by them."

Game 2

The Sox started out with a run in the first, fiddled around for eight innings, stranding seven, and then won it in the ninth on a controversial play that would go down in baseball annals as "A.J.'s reprieve" or, to angry Angels fans, the "fourth-out win."

The Sox's first-inning run was a hitless wonder. Scott Podsednik was safe at second on Jarrod Washburn's throwing error. Tadahito Iguchi sacrificed. Podsednik scooted home on Jermaine Dye's grounder.

In the Angels fifth, Robb Quinlan slugged a leadoff homer to left field, knotting the contest at one. With two down in the Sox ninth and extra innings looming, cat burglar A.J. Pierzynski picked the Angels pocket clean. Pierzynski struck out swinging on a low heater from reliever Kelvim Escobar. Ex-Sox backstop Josh Paul matter-of-factly rolled the ball to the mound. A.J. took a step toward the Sox dugout before dropping his bat and charging up the first-base line.

Home-plate umpire Doug Eddings called A.J. safe. Angels manager Mike Scioscia reminded the umpire that he had originally called the batter out with his right hand. Furthermore, Paul claimed he had caught the ball. Eddings said his shaky right-hand call was his swinging-strike mechanic, indicating that the ball was in play. The other umpires agreed with Eddings that the ball had changed directions and skimmed the ground.

Television replays were inconclusive. The play stood. Call it offsetting penalties or contributory negligence, the call went to the Sox. But the national television broadcast team would not let it go. They fixated on every play that went against the Angels—a continuous pattern through the ALCS, much to the disgust of viewers and fans in Chicago. Nevertheless, A.J. was the man of the hour, just as pesky and scrappy as he had been in his years at Minnesota.

Given new life, the Sox went on the offense. Pinch runner Pablo Ozuna promptly stole second base. Joe Crede then slammed the ball off the left-field wall, allowing Ozuna to romp home. And just like that, the Sox had evened up the series at a game apiece.

Lost in all the hullabaloo was Mark Buehrle's stellar performance—a complete-game five-hitter. But for A.J.'s antics, Buehrle would have willingly taken the mound in the 10th inning.

Game 3

The Sox, reminded of their perennial poor play during their regular season western road trips, bore down and took a 5–2 win in the California opener.

The Angels started the always-tough John Lackey (14–5, 2.38 ERA), winner of eight of his last nine decisions. Ozzie Guillen bypassed Freddy Garcia and countered with the well-rested Jon Garland, who had been tossing simulated games during his 12-day layoff.

The Sox struck for three in the first, capped by Paul Konerko's two-run bomb, in effect taking the Angels fans out of the game before they even took their seats. Tadahito Iguchi propelled the Sox to a 5–0 advantage, singling and scoring in the third, and crossing home after doubling in the fifth. All the damage inflicted on the Angels this night came from the top of the lineup.

As the game progressed, the Thunder Stix–waving Angels fans took out their frustrations on umpire Doug Eddings who patrolled the right-field line. One disgruntled surfer tossed a beach ball at Eddings' feet. Another fan held up a sign reminding the Sox that they were still fixing games after 86 years.

Garland, relying on his four-seam sinker, a change-up, and his fastball, scattered four hits and walked only one batter in his complete-game performance. He faced just 30 batters in the game. Orlando Cabrera slugged a two-run homer into the lower-left-field seats in the sixth. After that poke, Garland retired the last 10 batters in a row. The Angels were ice-cold at the plate.

After the game, manager Ozzie Guillen said, "Anytime we score first early in the game, we seem to play better baseball." Especially with native California boy Jon Garland on the mound. "We haven't had much success out west," commented Garland, talking about the team's record of poor performance in California dating back seven seasons. "But to go out there and do it for my team was pretty exciting. This year I had some luck on my side."

Game 4

Same script, different game as "Paulie" Konerko, blasted a three-run homer (on a full count) to cap a three-run first inning, propelling the Sox to an 8–2 victory and a commanding three-games-to-one lead in the ALCS. The 2005 Sox were deadly when they scored first. For the season, they had the biggest run differential in the first inning in the big leagues.

Proud new papa Freddy Garcia, who was pitching on seven days' rest, threw first-pitch strikes and stifled the Angels hitters the entire way. The playoffs-experienced Garcia (2–1 with the Seattle Mariners in 2000–01) retired 16 of the last 18 batters, and joined the other Sox hurlers in keeping the Angels speedy leadoff man Chone Figgins and slugger Vladimir Guerrero in check throughout the ALCS.

Spot starter Ervin Santana, who had shut out the Sox early in the season, took the mound for L.A. The 22-year-old, fastball-slider pitcher turned in a sparkling relief performance against the Yankees, saving the Angels from elimination in the ALDS, but he had nothing from the get-go against the Sox, helping them along with a walk and a hit batsman before Konerko's mighty blast. With his fourth homer of the postseason, Paulie shattered Ted Kluszewski's 46-year-old team record for roundtrippers.

Battered and weary, the L.A. Angels tallied a scratch run in the second on a walk and an infield hit, a Garcia throwing error, and a Bengie Molina single. It could have been a bigger inning, but Steve Finley hit into an inning-ending double play. On the swing, his bat clipped A.J. Pierzynski's mitt. The plate umpire missed the infraction. Finley, waving his arms and screaming catcher's interference as he ran up the line, was nipped at the bag. A.J., baseball's version of the 1950s sitcom bad boy Eddie Haskell, quickly fled the scene as the umpires sorted things out in the Sox's favor. Up in the TV booth, Tim McCarver and Lou Piniella would not let up on the umpires or the notion that the Sox were somehow "lucky" to get the calls. With 99 wins in the book and dominant pitching thus far in the playoffs, luck had nothing to do with it.

The Sox then pulled away, scoring solo runs in the third, fourth, and fifth innings. Pierzynski hit a 450-foot, tape-measure-shot home run in the fourth. Carl Everett helped account for the other runs with clutch base hits. Joe Crede's two-run single off of an Esteban Yan hanging splitter in the eighth rounded out the Sox scoring.

Freddy Garcia's nine-inning performance marked the first time in ALCS history that three starting pitchers tossed three consecutive complete games. The tandem of Tom Seaver, Jon Matlack, and Jerry Koosman of the New York Mets were the only other trio of pitchers to accomplish the rare feat, and that was back in the 1973 NLCS. A.J. Pierzynski, who caught all three complete games, deflected personal credit but praised the starters. "They're getting the first strike over, getting ahead, and using all their pitches," he said. "Once they get ahead, we feel pretty good about putting guys away. I'm lucky I can catch these guys."

After 46 years, the Chicago White Sox stood on the brink of the World Series. Ozzie Guillen called upcoming Game 5 "the most important game in Sox history."

Game 5

The Sox buried their West Coast jinx, the annoying Angels' "Rally Monkey," the monotonous drone of the Thunder Stix, and a 46-year pennant drought by whipping L.A. of Anaheim 6–3 on a drizzly Southern California evening. The Sox bullpen enjoyed another night off as Jose Contreras turned in the Sox's fourth-straight complete game.

With good command of his two-seam fastball and forkball, Contreras kept the Angels hitters off-stride all night. With an opportunity to launch another three-run homer in the first, Paul Konerko instead lined out to right field, giving the Angels and their followers momentary hope.

The enthusiasm was short-lived as the Sox reached the savvy Paul Byrd in the second inning, grabbing a run in textbook fashion: Aaron Rowand doubled down the right-field line; A.J. Pierzynski executed a sacrifice bunt; Joe Crede hit a deep fly ball to center field.

Juan Rivera led off the Los Angeles third with a double, and then Adam Kennedy stroked an RBI single to center. The inning ended when Vladimir Guerrero grounded into a fielder's choice with two aboard. The Angels star slugger would end up 1-for-20 in the series.

The Sox extended Paul Byrd's pitch count early and it cost him. In the fifth, Juan Uribe doubled, Podsednik walked, and Jermaine Dye drilled a two-out base hit to left, driving in the go-ahead run. Facing elimination, Scioscia went to his bullpen early, replacing junk-baller Byrd with the rubber-armed Scot Shields, who put out the fire.

Finally catching a break, L.A. moved ahead in their half of the frame. Kennedy's infield single down the third-base line started the rally. On a hit-and-run play, Chone Figgins swatted a ground-rule double into the right-field stands. The umpires conferred and ruled that Kennedy would have scored on the hit. Figgins then moved up on a grounder and came home on Garret Anderson's deep fly to right. It was the first lead for the Halos since winning Game 1.

Joe Crede opened the seventh with a booming homer to left against Kelvim Escobar to knot the seesaw affair at 3. It was Crede's seventh RBI of the postseason. The young Missourian had come of age, both as a hitter and fielder.

The umpires evened things out by ruling in favor of the Sox in the eighth. Aaron Rowand gamely battled the former Toronto closer to a full count, then drew a two-out walk.

Pierzynski, the series gnat, sent a sharp grounder down the first-base line. Escobar jumped off the mound, fielded the ball with his bare hand, but tagged Pierzynski with his empty mitt. First-base umpire Randy Marsh called Pierzynski out; but plate ump Ed Rapuano overruled him, allowing a smirking A.J. to remain at first base. There was no doubt about it. The umps made the right call, and now Escobar was done for the evening.

As Thunder Stix rained down on the field, Angels manager Mike Scioscia summoned closer Francisco "K-Rod" Rodriguez to face Angels-killer Joe Crede. On a full count, Joe bounced a seeing-eye single over the mound. Kennedy dove to stop the ball, then threw off balance much too late to stop the hard-charging Rowand from scoring the go-ahead run. Angel Stadium of Anaheim was suddenly very quiet.

Smelling victory, Iguchi led off the Sox ninth with a walk, then swiped second. K-Rod, wilting under the strain and obviously rattled by the turn of events, was overthrowing the ball. Jermaine Dye walked, bringing Paulie to the plate. Hitless for the game, Konerk rocketed an RBI double to the right-field wall to provide the Sox a critical insurance run. Then with one out, Aaron Rowand lofted a sacrifice fly to right, extending the lead to three. In the White Sox clubhouse, the champagne cart was rolled out.

Jose Contreras returned to the mound with a chance to make history. Not since the 1956 Yankees had a postseason pitching staff recorded four complete games. In Sox history, you have to go all the way back to the red pinstripe days of August 21–25, 1974, when Wilbur Wood, Jim Kaat, Bart Johnson, and Wood (again) last turned the trick.

L.A. went out meekly in their half of the ninth. Darin Erstad rolled out to short. Uribe made a good pickup on a tough hop and fired a strike to Konerko, who was named MVP of the ALCS. Bengie Molina was down 1–2 before he flew out to Rowand. And finally, Casey Kotchman, the last hope for the Angels, grounded out unassisted to Konerko, who stuffed the pennant-winning ball in his pocket. The Rally Monkey and the Comiskey Curse were dead and buried.

"We stick together," Ozzie Guillen said in the interview room. "They deserved it. They earned it. Enjoy it. Don't get too crazy in the street. Feel proud about this team. Feel proud about what we did."

"It's hard to believe where we are," exclaimed Jerry Reinsdorf. "When that 15-game lead was disappearing, there were a lot of people like me who were nervous." Pausing a moment, the chairman reflected on his other great success, the 1990s Chicago Bulls championship run. "It's like a repeat of the Bulls in '91. We lost the first game at home, and then won all the games in L.A."

It was raining in California, but the long draught was finally over in Chicago. About 2,000 die-hard, vocal White Sox fans, including Alderman James Balcer of the 11th Ward in the Bridgeport neighborhood of Chicago, gathered behind the visitors' dugout and celebrated with the White Sox after the trophy was presented and the champagne uncorked. It was just too bad the clincher had not come at home, but Mark Buehrle had this to say to the fans back home: "Don't go too crazy tearing up the city. But we're bringing it back to you guys!"

Game 1
October 11, at Chicago

Los Angeles	AB	R	H	RBI	BB	SO
Figgins, 3b	3	0	1	0	0	1
Cabrera, ss	4	0	1	1	0	0
Guerrero, dh	4	0	0	1	0	0
Anderson, lf	4	1	1	1	0	1
Molina, c	4	0	1	0	0	0
Erstad, 1b	4	0	1	0	0	0
Rivera, rf	4	0	0	0	0	0
Finley, cf	3	1	1	0	0	2
Kennedy, 2b	3	1	1	0	0	0
	33	3	7	3	0	4

Chicago	AB	R	H	RBI	BB	SO
Podsednik, lf	3	0	1	0	1	1
Iguchi, 2b	4	0	1	0	0	0
Dye, rf	4	0	1	0	0	0
Konerko, 1b	4	0	0	0	0	0
Everett, dh	4	1	1	0	0	0
a—Ozuna	0	0	0	0	0	0
Rowand, cf	3	0	0	0	0	0
Pierzynski, c	4	0	1	1	0	0
Crede, 3b	4	1	1	1	0	2
Uribe, ss	3	0	1	0	0	0
	33	2	7	2	1	3

Los Angeles	0	1	2	0	0	0	0	0	0—3
Chicago	0	0	1	1	0	0	0	0	0—2

a—ran for Everett in the ninth.

Los Angeles	IP	H	R	ER	BB	SO
Byrd (W)	6	5	2	2	1	1
Shields (H)	2	2	0	0	0	1
Rodriguez (S)	1	0	0	0	0	1

Chicago	IP	H	R	ER	BB	SO
Contreras (L)	8⅓	7	3	3	0	4
Cotts	⅔	0	0	0	0	0

E—Figgins. LOB—Los Angeles 4, Chicago 6. HR—Crede, Anderson. SB—Figgins, Erstad. HBP—by Byrd (Rowand). Umpires—Crawford, Eddings, Barrett, Kulpa, Rapuano, Marsh. Time—2:47, Attendance—40,659.

Game 2
October 12, at Chicago

Los Angeles	AB	R	H	RBI	BB	SO
Figgins, 3b	4	0	0	0	0	0
Cabrera, ss	4	0	2	0	0	0
Guerrero, dh	4	0	0	0	0	0
Molina, c	3	0	0	0	0	1
Anderson, lf	4	0	0	0	0	1
Quinlan, 3b	3	1	1	1	1	0
Erstad, 1b	3	0	1	0	0	0
Molina, c	3	0	1	0	0	0
a—Vanon, pr	0	0	0	0	0	0
Paul, c	0	0	0	0	0	0
Kennedy, 2b	2	0	0	0	0	0
	30	1	5	1	1	4

Chicago	AB	R	H	RBI	BB	SO
Podsednik, lf	4	1	1	0	0	1
Iguchi, 2b	2	0	0	0	0	1
Dye, rf	4	0	1	1	0	1
Konerko, 1b	4	0	1	0	0	2
Everett, dh	4	0	0	0	0	1
Rowand, cf	4	0	1	0	0	1
Pierzynski, c	3	0	0	0	1	2
b—Ozuna, pr	0	1	0	0	0	0
Crede, 3b	4	0	2	1	0	0
Uribe, ss	3	0	1	0	0	0
	32	2	7	2	1	9

Los Angeles	0	0	0	0	1	0	0	0	0—1
Chicago	1	0	0	0	0	0	0	0	1—2

a—ran for Molina in the eighth. b—ran for Pierzynski in the ninth.

Los Angeles	IP	H	R	ER	BB	SO
Washburn	4⅔	4	1	0	1	1
Donnelly	⅓	0	0	0	0	1
Shields	1	0	0	0	0	0
Escobar (L)	2⅔	3	1	0	0	5

Chicago	IP	H	R	ER	BB	SO
Buehrle (W)	9	5	1	1	0	4

E—Guerrrero, Paul, Washburn, Uribe. DP—Los Angeles, Chicago 2. LOB—Los Angeles 4, Chicago 7. 2B—Cabrera, Rowand, Crede 2, HR—Quinlan. SB—Ozuna. HBP—by Washburn (Iguchi), by Buehrle (Molina). Umpires—Crawford, Eddings, Barrett, Kulpa, Rapuano, Marsh Time—2:34, Attendance—41,013.

Game 3
October 14, at Los Angeles

Chicago	AB	R	H	RBI	BB	SO
Podsednik, lf	5	1	2	0	0	1
Iguchi, 2b	4	2	2	0	0	2
Dye, rf	2	1	1	1	2	1
Konerko, 1b	4	1	3	3	0	1
Everett, dh	4	0	1	1	0	1
Rowand, cf	4	0	0	0	0	0
Pierzynski, c	4	0	1	0	0	1
Crede, 3b	4	0	0	0	0	0
Uribe, ss	4	0	1	0	0	2
	35	5	11	5	2	9

Los Angeles	AB	R	H	RBI	BB	SO
Figgins, 3b	3	0	0	0	1	0
Cabrera, ss	4	1	1	2	0	2
Guerrero, rf	4	0	1	0	0	1
Anderson, lf	3	0	0	0	0	1
Molina, c	3	0	0	0	0	1
Erstad, 1b	3	0	1	0	0	1
Rivera, dh	2	0	0	0	0	1
a—Vanon, ph-dh	1	0	0	0	0	0
Finley, cf	3	0	0	0	0	0
Kennedy, 2b	3	1	1	0	0	0
	29	2	4	2	1	7

Chicago	3	0	1	0	1	0	0	0	0—5
Los Angeles	0	0	0	0	0	2	0	0	0—2

a—grounded out for J. Rivera in the eighth.

Chicago	IP	H	R	ER	BB	SO
Garland (W)	9	4	2	2	1	7

Los Angeles	IP	H	R	ER	BB	SO
Lackey (L)	5	8	5	5	1	3
Gregg	2	1	0	0	1	3
Donnelly	2	2	0	0	0	3

DP—Chicago 1, Los Angeles 2. LOB—Chicago 6, Los Angeles 1. 2B—Iguchi, Dye, Erstad. HR—Cabrera, Konerko. Umpires—Hirschbeck, Miller, Wegner, Carlson, Everitt, Iassogna. Time—2:42, Attendance—44,725.

Game 4
October 15, at Los Angeles

Chicago	AB	R	H	RBI	BB	SO
Podsednik, lf	2	2	1	0	3	0
Iguchi, 2b	4	1	0	0	0	2
Dye, rf	5	1	0	0	0	0
Konerko, 1b	4	1	1	3	1	0
Everett, dh	3	1	2	2	1	0
Rowand, cf	4	1	1	0	0	1
Pierzynski, c	4	1	1	1	0	2
Crede, 3b	4	0	2	2	0	1
Uribe, ss	3	0	0	0	1	0
	33	8	8	8	6	6

Los Angeles	AB	R	H	RBI	BB	SO
Figgins, 3b	4	0	0	0	0	2
Cabrera, ss	4	0	0	0	0	0
Izturis, ss	0	0	0	0	0	0
Guerrero, rf	4	0	0	0	0	0
Anderson, lf	4	1	1	0	0	2
Erstad, 1b	3	1	1	0	1	0
a—Vanon, pr	0	0	0	0	0	0
Kotchman, dh	4	0	2	1	0	0
Molina, c	3	0	1	1	0	0
Finley, cf	3	0	1	0	0	0
Kennedy, 2b	3	0	0	0	0	1
	32	2	6	2	1	5

Chicago	3	0	1	1	1	0	0	2	0—8
Los Angeles	0	1	0	1	0	0	0	0	0—2

a—ran for Erstad in the ninth.

Chicago	IP	H	R	ER	BB	SO
Garcia (W)	9	6	2	2	1	5

Los Angeles	IP	H	R	ER	BB	SO
Santana (L)	4⅓	3	6	6	3	2
Shields	1⅔	2	0	0	1	1
Donnelly	1	0	0	0	1	1
Yan	2	3	2	2	1	2

E—Garcia, Cabrera. DP—Chicago 1, Los Angeles 1. LOB—Chicago 5, Los Angeles 4. 2B—Rowand, Kotchman. 3B—Podsednik. HR—Pierzynski, Konerko. SB—Podsednik 2, Dye. HBP—by Santana (Iguchi). Umpires—Kulpa, Rapuano, Marsh, Crawford, Eddings, Barrett. Time—2:46, Attendance— 44,857.

Game 5
October 16, at Los Angeles

Chicago	AB	R	H	RBI	BB	SO
Podsednik, lf	3	0	0	0	2	2
Iguchi, 2b	3	1	0	0	1	1
Dye rf	4	1	2	1	1	1
Konerko, 1b	5	0	1	1	0	1
Everett, dh	5	0	1	0	0	2
Rowand, cf	3	2	1	1	1	0
Pierzynski, c	3	0	0	0	0	1
Crede, 3b	3	1	2	3	0	0
Uribe, ss	3	1	1	0	1	1
	32	6	8	6	6	9

Los Angeles	AB	R	H	RBI	BB	SO
Figgins, 3b	3	1	1	1	0	0
Cabrera, ss	4	0	0	0	0	0
Anderson, cf	2	0	1	1	1	0
Guerrero, rf	4	0	0	0	0	0
Erstad, 1b	4	0	0	0	0	1
Molina, c	4	0	0	0	0	0
Kotchman dh	3	0	0	0	1	1
Rivera, lf	3	1	1	0	0	0
Kennedy, 2b	3	1	2	1	0	0
	30	3	5	3	2	2

Chicago	0	1	0	0	1	0	1	1	2—6
Los Angeles	0	0	1	0	2	0	0	0	0—3

Chicago	IP	H	R	ER	BB	SO
Contreras (W)	9	5	3	3	2	2

Los Angeles	IP	H	R	ER	BB	SO
Byrd	4⅔	5	2	2	1	1
Shields	1⅓	0	0	0	0	1
Escobar (L)	1⅔	1	2	1	2	5
Rodriguez	1⅓	2	2	0	3	2

E—Contreras, Kennedy, Escobar. DP—Los Angeles 1. LOB—Chicago 9, Los Angeles 4. 2B—Dye, Konerko, Rowand, Uribe, Figgins, Rivera. HR—Crede. SB—Podsednik. HBP—by Bird (Iguchi). Umpires—Rapuano, Marsh, Crawford, Eddings, Barrett, Kulpa. Time—3:11, Attendance—44,172.

2005 World Series: White Sox versus Houston Astros

The White Sox moved into first place with a 1–0 win on Opening Day, remained in first place all season, then ended the playoffs as world champions, wrapping up a four-game sweep of Houston with a bookending 1–0 shutout. The White Sox were in exclusive company, joining only four other clubs to accomplish this wire-to-wire run, including the mighty 1927 Yankees.

The 2005 World Series, featuring two middle-market teams from the American heartland, was a refreshing affirmation that it was still possible for a couple of "dark horses" with payroll constraints to compete against one another on the national stage. Minus the tiresome presence of the Yankees, Boston, St. Louis, Atlanta, or one of the Southern California teams, TV ratings for the 101st World Series were way down. If smug viewers on the right and left coasts tuned out, it mattered little to the fans in Houston and Chicago, who were just happy to be there. As it turned out, it was an exciting and inspiring World Series. Manager Ozzie Guillen stuck with the same lineup for all eight games in the American League playoffs. He would adjust his lineup only slightly in the Houston series to accommodate the absence of a designated hitter. Again, the Sox were a well-rested club with five days off. The wild-card Astros, coming off a tough St. Louis series, had just two days to recoup.

Unlike the streaking White Sox, Houston was reminiscent of the 1914 "Miracle" Boston Braves. After a 15–30 start, and with a losing record on August 20, the Astros caught fire, finishing the season with a 36–10 run and a wild-card slot. On the road for most of the playoff games, Houston whipped Atlanta three games to one, then survived a dramatic ninth-inning homer by the Cardinals Albert Pujols in the fifth game of the NLCS to whip the Red Birds four games to two. It was the Astros' first trip to the big dance since their inaugural season of 1962.

The Astros had the best pitching staff the Sox had faced in some time. Roy Oswalt (20–12) won the NLCS clincher to earn MVP honors. Fishing buddies Roger Clemens (13–8) and Andy Pettitte (17–9) combined for 26 postseason wins while in New York. Bullpen reliever Brad Lidge (42 saves) was a top candidate for Fireman of the Year.

Mirroring the intensity of skipper Phil "Scrap Iron" Garner, Houston played a hustling brand of baseball. Contact hitters Willy Taveras, Lance Berkman, Morgan Ensberg, Jason Lane, and the "killer bees," Craig Biggio and Jeff Bagwell, sprayed balls to all the nooks and crannies of Houston's retro ballpark, the hitter-friendly Minute Maid Park.

But in the Series, the Astros failed time and again to deliver that clutch run, losing four games by a total of six runs. Each member of the vaunted pitching staff was knocked out of the box. Ozzie Guillen silenced his detractors by outmaneuvering Phil Garner in a number of key situations. Duplicating their playoff success, the White Sox won the clincher on the road.

Savoring this wonderful victory, the Sox players were honored in a motorcade, beginning near Midway Airport and zig-zagging its way through Bridgeport, Pilsen, Chinatown, and other White Sox enclaves, ending with a rally downtown attended by an estimated 2 million people taking part in celebrating the triumphal return of "the people's team."

Game 1

The Chicago fall sports season—basketball, football, and hockey—was put on hold. For the first time in 46 years, baseball reigned supreme in mid-October. The Sox were playing in the World Series.

Chicago was awash in a sea of silver and black. People proudly donned White Sox shirts and hats. White Sox flags were displayed on lampposts, flagpoles, and on the hoods of cars. Downtown Chicago was draped with White Sox banners; the Art Institute's lions sported White Sox caps. Cubs paraphernalia was nowhere in sight.

On opening night, the Chicago police established a security perimeter around U.S. Cellular Field, performing shakedowns and car inspections. The fans didn't mind the inconvenience as 41,206 of them filed into the Cell for Game 1.

Luis Aparicio, surrounded by 1959 teammates Jim Landis, Jim Rivera, J.C. Martin, Billy Pierce, and Bob Shaw, threw out the first pitch. Ozzie Guillen was the honorary catcher. Bo Jackson was on deck to do the opening pitch honors in Game 2.

There was something magical in the autumn air. It had to be the Sox. Small-ball big! The players seemed to gain strength from the encouragement of the fans and got by Houston 5–3, thereby gaining their fifth-straight postseason win.

Joe Crede was the "hero for a day," socking a game-winning homer and robbing Houston twice with fielding gems at third base.

In the sixth inning, with a runner on third, Crede fell across his body to nab a hot grounder and throw out the runner. He performed more body English in the seventh, diving to the ground to snare a ball headed for left with two Astros aboard.

There was no storybook ending for Astros starter and future Hall of Famer Roger Clemens. The aging "Rocket" left after two innings, suffering a strained left hamstring. Clemens threw 54 pitches, allowing three runs on four hits. Jermaine Dye started the Sox attack by swatting a two-out homer to right field in the first, after a nine-pitch battle with the Rocket Man.

After Sox starter Jose Contreras yielded a homer to Mike Lamb in the second, the White Sox came right back at Clemens, who had trouble pushing off the mound. Carl Everett and Aaron Rowand touched him for base hits. A.J. Pierzynski then punched a grounder to Lamb at first base. Everett bluffed a retreat to third. After checking Everett, Lamb started a slow-developing 3-6-3 double play. Everett tore home; Pierzynski beat the throw to first. Juan Uribe later placed a two-bagger in the left-field gap, scoring Pierzynski.

The Astros came right back and knotted the game at 3 on Lance Berkman's two-run double. Crede's eighth-inning blast off reliever Wandy Rodriguez put the Sox in front to stay. The Sox gained an extra tally in the frame on a Scott Podsednik triple.

The Sox bullpen, which had been idle for five games, went to work in the ninth. Neal Cotts rescued Contreras after Willy Taveras led off with a double. Lance Berkman drove a hard single to left, Taveras holding at third. Cotts fanned the next two batters. Ozzie Guillen then signaled for the big guy, rookie sensation Bobby Jenks (6′3″, 275 lbs.). Jenks, who hadn't pitched in 15 days, struck out Jeff Bagwell on a 100 mph dart to end the proceedings. Jenks walked off the mound delivering his customary arm pump, signaling another Sox win.

Bobby Jenks seals the deal in Game 1.

Game 2

Game 2 had the makings of another tense battle as Mark Buehrle (16–8), who had averaged 16 wins a season over the last five years, squared off against veteran Andy Pettitte, with 14 postseason wins and the most appearances ever in postseason play.

But it was the batters who were hot on a raw, rainy Sunday night in Chicago as the Sox edged the Astros 7–6 on a dramatic ninth-inning homer by Scott Podsednik.

In the mist and drizzle, Buehrle was tagged for four runs in seven innings; Pettitte, relying on his cut fastball, fared a little better, going six innings and yielding two runs.

Morgan Ensberg teed off on Buehrle's first pitch in the second inning, depositing the ball in the left-field seats. Two other hits did no damage. The Sox took a 2–1 lead in their half on consecutive base hits by Aaron Rowand, A.J. Pierzynski, and a "duck snort" single down the right-field line by the red-hot Joe Crede. An "unconventional" fielder's choice followed. Houston right fielder Jason Lane recovered second baseman Craig Biggio's muff of an easy pop fly in back of second base. He tossed the ball to shortstop Adam Everett for a force at second base.

Houston tied the game in the third on Willy Taveras' triple to right, then moved ahead 4–2 on Lance Berkman's two-run double in the fifth. The crowd was restless, but they expected the Sox to answer back.

Jermaine Dye narrowly missed a home run in the third when his long drive to left curved foul. Crede's fourth-inning bomb was even closer to the pole than Dye's, but still foul. Andy Pettitte picked off Tadahito Iguchi to end a mild threat in the Sox fifth; and in the sixth, Pettitte got Pierzynski to pop out, stranding two runners.

Paul Konerko circles the bases in triumph after his seventh-inning grand slam in Game 2.

Astros manager Phil Garner inexplicably turned the ball over to reliever Dan Wheeler in the seventh—a bad move. Juan Uribe stroked a one-out double to center to trigger the big comeback rally. After Scott Podsednik fanned on a tailing fastball, Iguchi walked after working the count full. Turning away from an inside pitch, Jermaine Dye claimed he was hit, shaking his hand in pain. Garner raced out of the dugout, protesting to umpire Jeff Nelson that the ball struck the barrel of the bat and not Dye. His protest fell on deaf ears, although television replays showed the ball hitting the bat. Then Paul Konerko stepped up to the plate and drilled the first pitch into the left-field stands for a grand slam off Chad Qualls, who had been brought in to pitch to the Sox slugger. It was the most important at-bat of his career, as pandemonium reigned at the Cell. Paulie was the man of the hour—a working-class South Side hero who cemented his place in team history with one swing of his mighty bat.

Bobby Jenks, claimed off of waivers by the Sox in the off-season, was looking to wrap things up in the ninth. But the big guy didn't have it this time. Jeff Bagwell punched a single to center. Jason Lane fanned. Chris Burke walked on four pitches. Both runners moved up on Brad Ausmus' infield grounder. Ex-Cubs infielder Jose Vizcaino delivered a two-out single to tie it. Chris Burke was safe by a hair on a close play at the plate.

The Sox answered the ex-Cubs factor in the ninth. With one out, Podsednik, who hadn't hit a homer in more than 500 regular season at-bats (becoming the second major league hitter to hit zero long balls for the season only to homer in the postseason), sent a low liner through the drizzle into the right-field seats off Brad Lidge.

Game 2 hero: Scotty Pods' walk-off homer

It was the 14th walk-off homer in Series history, earning Podsednik's bat a spot in Cooperstown and a delirious moment for White Sox fans toughing out the miserable 45-degree temperatures. The Astros were down for the count—upset with the umpires and with the White Sox celebrants after Craig Biggio's wife was allegedly swatted in the back of the head by an unruly spectator. Apologies were offered, but none were taken as the unhappy Astros sulked back to the land of Enron and horseflies, down 2–0.

Fans in the stands, Game 2 of the 2005 World Series

Game 3

The Sox beat Houston 7–5 in a five-hour, 41-minute, 14-inning game that ended at 1:20 AM. It was the longest World Series game in history.

The Astros, who tied for the best home record (53–28) in baseball, had lost a bit of the home advantage before the contest even started. Baseball Commissioner Bud Selig ruled the retractable roof at Minute Maid Park would have to remain open. When closed, the deafening roar made for an intimidating atmosphere. We'll never know if the "as-tough-on-the-road" White Sox (52–29) would have been distracted.

The Astros players sported beards when the playoffs started. After the two losses in Chicago, they switched to goatees. The Sox made their own luck, capitalizing on golden opportunities with clutch hitting and clutch pitching.

A couple of Cy Young candidates took the mound. Houston went with their best hurler, Roy Oswalt (12–2 at home). The Sox countered with Jon Garland (18–10). Designated hitter Carl Everett was relegated to the bench.

Garland didn't have his best stuff as Houston jumped to an early 4–0 lead. Houston's fourth run was a controversial homer by Jason Lane down the right-field foul line. Television replays seemed to indicate that the ball hit to the foul side of the yellow vertical line on the outfield wall. A mild dispute followed as the scoreboard erupted and the ornamental Minute Maid Park locomotive rumbled down the track high above the left-field wall. The umpires conferred and decided to allow the homer.

The evening turned bad for Oswalt as the Sox erupted for five runs in the fifth. Joe Crede started the rally with a home run over the right-field wall. Juan Uribe, Scott Podsednik, Tadahito Iguchi, and Jermaine Dye registered base hits; and A.J. Pierzynski capped the scoring with a two-run double.

Houston tied it at five on Jason Lane's eighth-inning double off the third Sox pitcher of the inning, Dustin Hermanson, who was making his first appearance in three weeks. As it turned out, this would be the last Houston tally of the series. The Astros stranded runners in the ninth, 10th, 11th, and 13th innings, as the Chicago bullpen held them in check.

The Sox settled matters in the 14th. Dye opened the frame with a single but was doubled up on Konerko's hot grounder to Morgan Ensberg. Acting on Ozzie Guillen's hunch, reserve infielder Geoff Blum, subbing for Tadahito Iguchi, was chosen over Pablo Ozuna and allowed to grab a bat with two down. The bases were empty when the 32-year-old former Astro sent a low whistling liner into the right-field stands off spot starter Ezequiel Astacio, relegated to bullpen duty in the Series. The Sox tagged the rattled pitcher for an insurance run on a bases-loaded walk to Chris Widger amid a loud and rhythmic chorus of "Let's go, White Sox!" from the vocal delegation of Chicago fans.

Damaso Marte, maligned by the fans and inconsistent in the regular season, took over in the 13th inning and earned the win, but he needed help. With two outs and two men on base, Mark Buehrle was rushed into the game to face Adam Everett. It was his first relief appearance since the 2000 playoffs, during his rookie year. The clock tolled 1:00 AM before the Sox ace induced Everett to pop up with two aboard. The 'Stros left 15 men on base for the game and could not blame the umpires or anyone else for their World Series misfortunes.

Addressing the media, Phil Garner called his team's performance "embarrassing.... We didn't hit the ball but still managed to stay in the game. I don't know how that happened. The story of this World Series is they're hammerin' on our mistakes and fouling off our good pitches. I got lots of emotions, but I'm really ticked off because we're not hitting well and we're not getting the job done."

In Chicago...no worries. The fans' only concern was whether or not the air-raid sirens would go off for the first time since 1959, now that a World Series championship was at hand.

Game 4

No team had ever come back from a three-game deficit to win a World Series. And none figured that this Houston team was up to the task. They simply didn't have the muscle to mount that kind of rally. As it turned out, the Astros could not deliver the clutch hit as the White Sox wrapped up the Series on Latino Night in Houston in front of former president George Bush, wife Barbara, and a large gathering of current and former Hispanic stars honored in pregame ceremonies with a fitting 1–0, small-ball win.

The win gave the White Sox their 11th win in 12 postseason games, and going back to the final week of the regular season, 16 of their last 17.

Sox workhorse Freddy Garcia, 2–0 in the postseason, allowed only four hits in seven innings of work and would have gone the distance if not for the absence of a designated hitter. Ironically, one of the seldom used bench players in the regular season ended up scoring the winning run and delivering the title to Chicago.

In the eighth inning of the scoreless tie, utility infielder Willie Harris pinch hit for Garcia and lined a single to left off Brad Lidge. Scott Podsednik brought his bat down on a high heater and sacrificed Harris to second. Pinch-hitter Carl Everett grounded out, Harris to third. Jermaine Dye, who would win series MVP honors (.438), poked a dribbler that snaked its way into left-center field. Dye clapped his hands as he left the plate—he knew he had tagged the clincher.

Ruining a gritty pitching performance by Brandon Backe (a 10–2 record at Minute Maid Park in 2005), Houston stranded nine more base runners. Desperate to score, they laid down a sacrifice bunt in the very first inning after Craig

Biggio led off with a single. Biggio remained at second base. The Astros tried to make a "Series" of it in the eighth. Reliever Cliff Politte hit Willy Taveras with a pitch, then wild-pitched him to second. Manager Ozzie Guillen ordered an intentional walk to Lance Berkman, putting the go-ahead run on base. Morgan Ensberg flew out, sending the runner to third. Neal Cotts relieved Politte. Jose Vizcaino sent a slow roller to Juan Uribe, who charged in and fired the ball to first a step ahead of the runner.

Uribe performed some more magic in the ninth as Houston gave it their last desperate shot. Jason Lane dumped a single to center off Bobby Jenks. Brad Ausmus, the catcher from Dartmouth, laid down the obligatory bunt. Chris Burke, on a 2–2 count, cued a foul ball to the left side. Uribe threw himself head-first into the stands and took the ball away from a fan, much to the amazement of the Astros players, who felt the Houston fans should have battled Uribe for the ball like Steve Bartman, the Wrigley Field fan, had done in the 2003 NLCS.

Orlando Palmeiro hit a slow bounding ball over Bobby Jenks' head that was fielded by the charging Juan Uribe, who fielded it cleanly and fired over to Paul Konerko, who, for the second time in the postseason, stuffed the souvenir ball into his pocket. (Paulie would hand over the ball to Sox owner Jerry Reinsdorf at the victory rally.)

In the Sox clubhouse, the players squirted the victory champagne at one another like fire extinguishers, soaking everyone to the skin with the expensive bubbly. A victory cigar askew in his mouth, Jerry Reinsdorf, who had won six titles with the Chicago Bulls, proclaimed this championship his greatest moment as commissioner Bud Selig handed over the trophy.

Back in Chicago, Sox strongholds on the South Side and in the south suburbs were aglow with firecrackers. A caravan of honking cars drove up and down 35th Street and Halsted. In Schaller's Pump, the famous South Side watering hole, joyous celebrants were singing and dancing to the new White Sox theme song: "Don't Stop Believin'" by the rock group Journey. Strangers traded high-fives. All across the South Side (and even some locations on the North Side), sports bars erupted in joyous celebration. Time to grab a beer! The White Sox were the champions of the universe for 2005, and no one could take it away.

Jermaine Dye: World Series MVP

A time to celebrate: the White Sox win the 2005 World Series.

Game 1
October 22, at Chicago

Houston	AB	R	H	RBI	BB	SO
Biggio, 2b	4	1	1	0	0	0
Taveras, cf	3	0	2	0	0	0
Berkman, lf	4	0	2	2	0	1
a—Burke, pr-lf	0	0	0	0	0	0
Ensberg, 3b	4	0	0	0	0	1
Lamb, 1b	4	1	1	1	0	2
Bagwell, dh	2	0	0	0	0	1
Lane, rf	4	0	0	0	0	1
Ausmus, c	3	0	1	0	0	0
A. Everett, ss	4	1	0	0	0	1
	32	3	7	3	0	7

Chicago	AB	R	H	RBI	BB	SO
Podsednik, lf	5	0	2	1	0	1
Iguchi, 2b	5	0	0	0	0	1
Dye, rf	2	1	1	1	2	0
Konerko, 1b	4	0	2	0	0	0
C. Everett, dh	3	1	1	0	0	1
Rowand, cf	3	0	1	0	1	1
Pierzynski, c	4	2	1	1	0	0
Crede, 3b	4	1	1	1	0	0
Uribe, ss	2	0	1	1	2	0
	32	5	10	5	5	4

a—Burke ran for Berkman in the eighth.

Houston	0	1	2	0	0	0	0	0	0—3
Chicago	1	2	0	1	0	0	0	1	x—5

Houston	IP	H	R	ER	BB	SO
Clemens	2	4	3	3	0	1
Rodriguez (L)	3⅓	4	1	1	5	1
Qualls	1⅔	0	0	0	0	2
Springer	1	2	1	1	0	0

Chicago	IP	H	R	ER	BB	SO
Contreras (W)	7	6	3	3	0	2
Cotts (H)	⅔	1	0	0	0	2
Jenks (S)	1⅓	0	0	0	0	3

E—A. Everett; DP—Houston 2, Chicago 1. LOB—Houston 6, Chicago 9. 2B—Taveras (2), Berkman, Uribe. 3B—Podsednik. HR—Crede, Dye, Lamb. SB—Burke, Podsednik, Pierzynski. HBP—by Contreras (Ausmus), by Contreras (Bagwell). Umpires—Nelson, Layne, Cousins, Cederstorm, Hernandez, West. Time—3:13, Attendance—41,206.

Game 2
October 23, at Chicago

Houston	AB	R	H	RBI	BB	SO
Biggio, 2b	4	0	0	0	0	1
Bruntlett, 2b	0	0	0	0	0	0
a—Lamb, ph-1b	1	0	0	0	0	0
Taveras, cf	4	2	2	0	0	0
Berkman, lf	3	0	1	3	0	2
Ensberg, 3b	4	1	1	1	0	1
Bagwell, dh	4	1	1	0	0	0
Lane, rf	4	0	1	0	0	2
Ausmus, c	4	1	2	0	0	0
Burke, 2b	0	1	0	0	1	0
A. Everett, ss	3	0	0	0	0	2
b—Vizcaino, ph-ss	1	0	1	2	0	0
	32	6	9	6	1	8

Chicago	AB	R	H	RBI	BB	SO
Podsednik, lf	5	1	1	1	0	1
Iguchi, 2b	3	1	1	0	1	1
Dye, rf	3	1	1	0	0	0
Konerko, 1b	4	1	1	4	0	1
C. Everett, dh	4	0	2	0	0	1
Rowand, cf	4	1	2	0	0	0
Pierzynski, c	4	1	1	0	0	1
Crede, 3b	4	0	1	1	0	0
Uribe, ss	4	1	2	1	0	0
	35	7	12	7	1	5

a—Lamb flied out for Brunlett in the ninth. b—Vizcaino singled for A. Everett in the ninth.

Houston	0	1	1	0	2	0	0	0	2—6
Chicago	0	2	0	0	0	0	4	0	1—7

Houston	IP	H	R	ER	BB	SO
Pettitte	6	8	2	2	0	4
Wheeler	⅔	1	3	3	1	1
Qualls	⅔	2	1	1	0	0
Gallo	⅔	0	0	0	0	0
Lidge (L)	⅓	1	1	1	0	0

Chicago	IP	H	R	ER	BB	SO
Buehrle	7	7	4	4	0	6
Politte	1	0	0	0	0	1
Jenks	⅔	2	2	2	1	1
Cotts (W)	⅓	0	0	0	0	0

LOB—Houston 4, Chicago 5. 2B—Berkman (2), Ausmus, Rowand, Uribe 2. 3B—Taveras. HR—Podsednik, Konerko, Ensberg. SB—Lane, Uribe. HBP—by Wheeler (Dye). Umpires—West, Nelson, Layne, Cousins, Cederstorm, Hernandez. Time—3:11, Attendance— 41,432.

Ozzie Guillen greets the fans during the 2005 World Series victory parade through the neighborhoods.

Game 3
October 25, at Houston

Chicago	AB	R	H	RBI	BB	SO
Podsednik, lf	8	1	2	0	0	2
Iguchi, 2b	7	1	2	1	0	0
Marte, p	0	0	0	0	0	0
Dye, rf	7	1	2	1	0	1
Konerko, 1b	4	0	1	0	2	0
Pierzynski, c	3	0	1	1	2	0
Hernandez, p	0	0	0	0	0	0
Vizcaino, p	0	0	0	0	0	0
a—Perez, ph	1	0	0	0	0	0
Jenks, p	0	0	0	0	0	0
Rowand, cf	5	1	1	0	1	3
Crede, 3b	4	1	2	1	1	0
Uribe, ss	6	1	1	0	0	0
Garland, p	3	0	0	0	0	2
b—C. Everett, ph	1	0	1	0	0	0
c—Harris, pr	0	0	0	0	0	0
Politte, p	0	0	0	0	0	0
Cotts, p	0	0	0	0	0	0
Hermanson, p	0	0	0	0	0	0
Widger, c	1	0	0	1	0	1
Blum, 2b	1	1	1	1	0	0
	51	7	14	6	6	9

Houston	AB	R	H	RBI	BB	SO
Biggio, 2b	5	2	2	1	1	1
Taveras, cf	5	0	0	0	0	1
Berkman, 1b-lf	4	0	2	1	0	0
Ensberg, 3b	5	1	1	1	1	2
Lamb, ph-1b	3	0	0	0	1	1
d—Bruntlett, pr	0	0	0	0	0	0
Lane, rf	5	1	2	2	1	0
Ausmus, c	5	0	0	0	0	0
A. Everett, ss	2	1	1	0	0	0
Oswalt, p	1	0	0	0	0	0
Springer, p	0	0	0	0	0	0
e—Bagwell, ph	1	0	0	0	0	0
Gallo, p	0	0	0	0	0	0
Burke, lf	0	0	0	0	1	0
Lidge, p	0	0	0	0	0	0
f—Palmeiro, ph	0	0	0	0	1	0
g—Vizcaino, ph	0	0	0	0	1	0
	36	5	8	5	7	5

a—Perez grounded out for Vizcaino in 11th. b—C. Everett singled for Garland in eighth. c—Harris ran for C. Everett. d—Brunlett ran for Lamb in eighth. e—Bagwell popped out for Springer in seventh. f—Palmeiro walked for Lidge in 10th. g—Vizcaino walked for Qualls in 13th.

Chicago	0	0	0	0	5	0	0	0	0	0	0	0	0	2—7
Houston	1	0	2	1	0	0	0	1	0	0	0	0	0	0—5

Chicago	IP	H	R	ER	BB	SO
Garland	7	7	4	2	2	4
Politte	⅔	0	1	1	1	1
Cotts	0	0	0	0	1	0
Hermanson	⅓	0	0	0	0	0
Hernandez	1	0	0	0	3	2
Vizcaino	1	0	0	0	1	0
Jenks	2	0	0	0	1	3
Marte (W)	1⅓	0	0	1	2	3
Buehrle (S)	⅓	0	0	0	0	0

Houston	IP	H	R	ER	BB	SO
Oswalt	6	8	5	5	4	3
Springer	1	0	0	0	0	1
Wheeler	1⅓	1	0	0	0	0
Gallo	⅓	0	0	0	0	0
Lidge	1⅓	0	0	0	0	3
Qualls	2	1	0	0	1	2
Astacio (L)	⅔	4	2	2	2	0
Rodriguez	⅓	0	0	0	0	0

E—Ensberg, Uribe (2), Hernandez. DP—Chicago 2, Houston 4. LOB—Chicago 15, Houston 15. 2B—Konerko, Pierzynski, Biggio, Lane. HR—Crede, Blum, Lane. SB—Burke, Podsednik, Harris. HBP—by Wheeler (Konerko), by Jenks (Taveras). Umpires—West, Nelson, Layne, Cousins, Cederstorm, Hernandez. Time—5:41, Attendance—42,848.

Game 4
October 26, at Houston

Chicago	AB	R	H	RBI	BB	SO
Podsednik, lf	3	0	1	0	0	0
Iguchi, 2b	3	0	0	0	0	0
a—C. Everett, ph	1	0	0	0	0	0
Politte, p	0	0	0	0	0	0
Cotts, p	0	0	0	0	0	0
Jenks, p	0	0	0	0	0	0
Dye, rf	4	0	3	1	0	1
Konerko, 1b	4	0	0	0	0	2
Pierzynski, c	4	0	1	0	0	1
Rowand, cf	4	0	1	0	0	2
Crede, 3b	3	0	1	0	0	2
Uribe, ss	4	0	0	0	0	2
Garcia, p	2	0	0	0	0	0
b—Harris, ph-2b	1	1	1	0	0	0
	33	1	8	0	0	10

Houston	AB	R	H	RBI	BB	SO
Biggio, 2b	3	0	1	0	0	0
Taveras, cf	4	0	1	0	0	0
Berkman, lf	1	0	0	0	3	1
Ensberg, 3b	3	0	0	0	0	2
Lamb, 1b	2	0	1	0	1	0
c—Vizcaino, ph-1b	1	0	0	0	0	0
Lane, rf	3	0	1	0	0	2
Ausmus, c	3	0	1	0	0	1
A. Everett, ss	3	0	0	0	0	0
d—Burke, ph	1	0	0	0	0	0
Backe, p	2	0	0	0	0	1
e—Bagwell, ph	0	0	0	0	0	0
Lidge, p	0	0	0	0	0	0
f—Palmiero, ph	1	0	0	0	0	0
	29	0	5	0	4	7

e—Bagwell grounded out for Backe in the seventh. b—Harris singled for Garcia in the eighth. a—C. Everett grounded out for Iguchi in the eighth. c—Vizcaino grounded out for Lamb in the eighth. e—Burke fouled out for A. Everett in the ninth. f—Palmeiro grounded out for Lidge in the ninth.

Chicago	0	0	0	0	0	0	0	1	0—1
Houston	0	0	0	0	0	0	0	0	0—0

Chicago	IP	H	R	ER	BB	SO
Garcia (W)	7	4	0	0	3	7
Politte	2/3	0	0	0	1	0
Cotts	1/3	0	0	0	0	0
Jenks (S)	1	1	0	0	0	0

Houston	IP	H	R	ER	BB	SO
Backe	7	5	0	0	0	7
Lidge (L)	2	3	1	1	0	3

DP—Chicago 1. LOB—Chicago 7 Houston 9. 2B—Dye, Pierzynski, Crede, Lamb. 3B—Podsednik. SB—Taveras, Berkman. WP—Politte; HBP—by Politte (Taveras). Umpires—West, Nelson, Layne, Cousins, Cederstorm, Hernandez. Time—3:20, Attendance—42,936

At last…88 years of frustration melts away.

Hail to the champs! LaSalle Street tickertape parade. (Photo courtesy of Karen Giammarese)

2008 ALDS: White Sox versus Tampa Bay Rays

Paul Konerko's leadoff homer in the ninth inning of Game 1 in Tampa Bay momentarily raised Sox hopes. (Courtesy of the Chicago White Sox)

Following a Sox 8–2 decision over the Detroit Tigers in a postseason makeup game, the 2008 AL Central Division ended in a deadlock between the White Sox and the other renowned midwestern scrapper, the Minnesota Twins.

The Sox went on to defeat the Twins 1–0 in a playoff match at U.S. Cellular Field before an enthusiastic crowd of 40,354 silver-and-black-clad fans. Jim Thome (solo home run) and John Danks (eight innings, two hits) padded their regular season stats and returned the Sox to the postseason for the third time in the decade. Outside the box score, newly acquired outfielder Ken Griffey Jr. preserved the victory by throwing out a Twins runner at home plate.

With the win, the never-say-die Sox entered the obscure record book by becoming the first team to win their final three games against three different opponents: 1) Sox 5, Indians 1 (regular season); 2) Sox 8, Detroit 2 (makeup game); and 3) Sox 1, Minnesota 0 (playoff game).

On the other side of town, the Cubs (97–64) romped to the NL Central Division title, marking the first time the two Chicago teams were in postseason play together since 1906.

After sending the Twins back to the Land of 10,000 Lakes, the White Sox flew down to the Sunshine State to do battle with the Tampa Bay Rays. (The Rays had exorcised the "Devil," literally, in November 2007, shortening their name from the fishy Devil Rays to just the Rays.) "A beacon of light that radiates throughout Florida," commented their majority owner Stuart Sternberg. Interestingly, Tampa Bay would become the fourth former AL expansion team the Sox would square off against in their postseason history, following Toronto (1993), Seattle (2000), and the Los Angeles Angels (2005). And by the time this one was over, the Sox had another compelling reason to oppose any further ideas of American League expansion into new markets, based on the unhappy results of their encounters with Toronto, Seattle, and Tampa Bay.

Smashing the Red Sox–Yankees oligarchy, the Rays turned things downside-up, jumping from last place in 2007 (66–96) to take the AL East (97–65). The 2008 Rays resembled the "2005 Small Ball" White Sox. Under Go-Go manager Joe Maddon, the surprising Rays stole a major league high 142 bases. Contact hitters Akinori Iwamura (.274), Carl Crawford (.273, 25 SB) and B.J. Upton (.273, 44 SB), and bottom-of-the-order gnats Dioner Navarro (.295) and Jason Bartlett (.286, 20 SB) set the table for run producers Carlos Pena (31 homers) and Evan Longoria (27 homers).

Nondescripts James Shields (14–8), Scott Kazmir (12–8), Matt Garza (11–9), and Andy Sonnanstine (13–9) were the Rays starters. Journeymen Grant Balfour, J.P. Howell, and ex-Sox farmhand Chad Bradford handled the bullpen chores for an expansion team that never had a winning season before 2008 and played before an empty house nearly every night of their entire existence.

The Sox, on the other hand, were the cracked-mirror image of the 2005 world champion team. Instead of a small-ball attack, the Sox lived and died with the longball, slugging a major league high 235 home runs. The Sox would be without two of their sluggers for the games: Carlos Quentin, suffering a wrist injury, and Joe Crede, with a career-ending back problem. Experiencing arm problems, hurler Jose Contreras had been out since mid-season. In a bit of baseball irony, the Rays' "go get-'em" outfielder Carl Crawford was ready to go after missing 10 weeks with a hand injury.

Tampa Bay hosted the first two games of the series at the domed Tropicana Field, where the Rays had posted baseball's best home record (57–24). The station-to-station Rays, tossing in some timely homers, quality starts, and splendid relief pitching, beat the Sox twice in Florida. Their spikes stuck in the spongy carpet, the White Sox lost both contests for the opposite reasons: poor pitching and a plodding offensive attack.

Back home in Chicago, the Sox staved off elimination with another miraculous do-or-die win at U.S. Cellular Field before bowing out of the series the following evening. Tampa Bay polished off the Boston Red Sox in the AL finals—another amazing accomplishment for the Cinderella expansion team. The Florida "whiz kids," however, ran out of gas in the World Series against the Phillies amid snow flurries at Citizen's Bank Ballpark in Philadelphia.

Though it did not end well for the injury-riddled White Sox, the ballclub gained the respect of Chicago baseball fans for their underdog fight. Drawing a measure of small consolation, the heavily favored and heavily followed Cubs lost three straight games to baseball's worst playoff entry, the Los Angeles Dodgers.

Game 1

Not starting where they left off, the White Sox ended an eight-game postseason winning streak, dating back to the 2005 championship year, with a 6–4 loss in the ALDS opener. The Pale Hose got off to a promising start. Left fielder Dewayne Wise, who was supposed to platoon with switch-hitter Nick Swisher, socked a three-run homer off Rays starter James Shields in the third to push the Sox in front 3–1.

Rays third-sacker Evan Longoria, living up to his star-studded billing—writers snapped up the Evan Longoria–actress Eva Longoria connection—drove a Javier Vasquez fastball into the left-field bleachers in his first at-bat. In his next at-bat in the third inning, following an Akinori Iwamura RBI triple and a sac fly, the golden boy Longoria deposited a Javier Vazquez hanging curveball up yonder into the left-field catwalk seats—a 465-foot "Roy Hobbs" shot.

Sox-tober in Chicago. The playoffs return to U.S. Cellular Field. (Courtesy of the Chicago White Sox)

Vazquez, a huge disappointment to Ozzie Guillen down the home stretch, gave way to reliever Clayton Richard in the Rays' two-run fifth. "Don't call me Eva" Longoria drove home the final run with an RBI single. The rookie Richard and Octavio Dotel held the Rays scoreless the rest of the way. Shields settled down after the Sox's initial burst in the third before a single, walk, and hit batsman loaded the bags with one down in the seventh. Grant Balfour came in and fanned Juan Uribe. The next hitter, shortstop Orlando Cabrera, tried to get into Balfour's head, and at the same time ignite his teammates. After taking a ball, Cabrera kicked some dirt toward the mound and yelled at Balfour to, "Throw it over the plate!"—which Balfour promptly did, three straight times as a matter of fact, retiring Cabrera. Leaving the mound, Balfour shouted at Cabrera to take a seat in the dugout. Touché.

Paul Konerko's leadoff homer in the ninth momentarily raised Sox hopes. But Ken Griffey Jr., ending an 0-for-4 night, flied out. Alexei Ramirez fanned. And A.J. Pierzynski flied out. Despite the opening loss, the Sox players remained upbeat: "We've been here before. We can build on Paulie's homer. We got Mark Buerhle on the mound tomorrow night."

Game 2

The postseason adage about gaining a split in the first two road games looked especially good for the White Sox as they pushed two runs across in the first inning against Scott Kazmir. Then, citing an old football adage, the drive stalled. On this night, Major League Baseball's reigning home run champs punched out 12 hits—all singles—leaving a dozen men on base, including a full house in the first inning. The heart of the order stranded six: Paul Konerko popped out with two aboard in the second inning; Jermaine Dye grounded out with two on in the fourth, as did A.J. Pierzynski with two on in the seventh, ending the Sox's final threat. In Dye's defense, he had four singles.

Sox ace Mark Buerhle yielded five runs on 10 hits over seven innings and was just ineffective. Stranding but five base runners, the Rays usually finished what they started. Tampa Bay cut into the Sox lead with a run in the second on catcher Dioner Navarro's base hit. They pulled in front 3–2 on infielder Akinori Iwamura's two-run blast in the fifth and pulled away after that. Buerhle exited in a Rays three-run eighth, which was ignited by B.J. Upton's triple on a 3–0 count. He was charged with two of the runs when Dotel and Matt Thornton failed in relief. The Rays' bullpen, on the other hand, was splendid. Kazmir, after a long pitch count, including 37 tosses in the first frame, turned the pitching chores over to Grant Balfour in the sixth, who retired the final two batters of the inning. When Balfour allowed the first two men to reach base in the seventh, southpaw J.P. Howell was rushed in and retired three in a row. For good measure, Howell struck out the side in the Sox eighth. The ex-Sox sidearm pitcher Chad Bradford put the Pale Hose down in order in the ninth to preserve the 6–2 win. Over the first two games, the Rays' pen had given up only one run, a Paul Konerko homer, in 6⅓ innings.

Throughout the game, cowbells echoed in Tropicana Field—the only distinctive trademark of that torpid, impersonal dome where the Sox would have landed in 1989 had the funding legislation to build the new Comiskey Park not passed in 1988.

Game 3

Sweet home Chicago never felt better as the White Sox whipped the Rays 5–3 before a packed house at U.S. Cellular. Observing "Sox blackout conditions," the fans dressed in black shirts, black slacks, black jackets, and, because of the nippy 58-degree weather, black hoodies. In getting by the Rays, the never-say-die White Sox avoided their fourth elimination game in a week, going back to the regular season. And, in doing so, remained the only game in town as the Cubs were swept in three games by the Los Angeles Dodgers. Jumping on the White Sox bandwagon was Cubs cheerleader Ronnie "Woo Woo" Wickers, who was spotted at the Cell dressed in black and silver. Incredible but true. Wickers is a lovable eccentric, but he is rarely seen around Chicago wearing anything but his replica Cubs uniform.

Dewayne Wise, the eighth man in the order, won player-of-the-game honors. In the third inning, he reached second base the small-ball way by drawing a walk then stealing second. He scored on A.J. Piersynski's base hit, knotting the score at 1. Wise then capped a Sox three-run third with a double, his fifth RBI of the series to go along with a .400 average. The Sox's No. 9 hitter, Juan Uribe, singled home an insurance run in the sixth, which was also developed in small-ball fashion—walk, stolen base, groundout. Besting Rays hurler Matt Garza, John Danks had a quality start, going deep into the seventh inning. After B.J. Upton's two out, two-run round-tripper and a hit by Carlos Pena, Sox manager Ozzie Guillen made a pitching change. Octavio Dotel fanned slugger Evan Longoria to end the inning. Matt Thornton and the big guy, Bobby Jenks, mopped up. For the moment, the Sox were back in business.

Pregame introductions. Juan Uribe and Ozzie Guillen. (Courtesy of the Chicago White Sox)

Game 4

Another feisty blackout crowd was on hand at U.S. Cellular Field expecting to see the miracle Sox knot the series at two games apiece. Instead, the black magic slowly dissipated in the chilly autumn night, as the No. 2 hitter, center fielder B.J. Upton, smashed solo homers off Sox starter Gavin Floyd in his first two at-bats. The gloom then turned to doom as designated hitter and ex-Cub Cliff Floyd, working the middle of a Rays two-run fourth, slapped an RBI double, then scored on Dioner Navarro's single to open up a Rays 4–0 lead. Rays first baseman Carlos Pena (who ended up hitting .500 for the series) hit RBI singles in the fifth and seventh inning off relievers Clayton Richard and Octavio Dotel.

The Sox could only answer with four hits. In keeping with their one-dimensional attack, two of their hits were solo homers off starter Andy Sonnanstine: Paul Konerko (fourth inning) and Jermaine Dye (sixth inning). After Dye's homer, Rays manager Joe Maddon handed the ball to J.P. Howell, who, after retiring his four men, handed the ball over to Grant Balfour, who shut out the Sox over the final two innings to preserve the Rays' 6–2 win. Both relievers ended up holding the Sox scoreless throughout the series.

Overall, the Rays bullpen gave up one run in 11⅔ innings. In support of their good arms, the speedy Rays had twice as many extra-base hits (10) and stolen bases (seven) as the Power Ball Sox (four and three, respectively). Avoiding their fourth elimination game in a week was perhaps just too much to ask of the White Sox at this late stage. Black slacks, black bats, good luck charms, and all the crossed fingers in the world couldn't help the Sox. The miraculous season-ending dash to the playoffs finally ran out of gas. A big disappointment? Not really. It wasn't 2005, but the working stiffs from 35th and Shields had themselves one heck of a year. As the game drew to an end, many in the house stood and applauded the scrappy, underdog Sox, whose fine effort in 2008 canceled out the memory of a disastrous 2007 season.

Game 1
October 2, at Tampa Bay

Chicago	AB	R	H	RBI	BB	SO
Cabrera, ss	4	0	0	0	0	1
Wise, lf	3	1	1	3	0	1
a—Anderson, ph-lf	1	0	0	0	0	1
Dye, rf	4	0	1	0	0	1
Thome, dh	4	0	0	0	0	0
Konerko, 1b	4	1	2	1	0	1
Griffey Jr., cf	4	0	0	0	0	2
Ramirez, 2b	3	1	1	0	1	1
Pierzynski, c	3	1	2	0	0	0
Uribe, 3b	2	0	0	0	0	1
	32	4	7	4	1	9

Tampa Bay	AB	R	H	RBI	BB	SO
Iwamura, 2b	4	1	2	1	1	1
Upton, cf	5	1	0	0	0	2
Pena, 1b	1	0	0	0	0	1
Aybar, 1b	2	1	1	1	0	0
Longoria, 3b	3	2	3	3	1	0
Crawford, lf	4	0	1	1	0	1
Floyd, dh	3	0	0	0	0	3
b—Baldelli, ph-dh	1	0	0	0	0	0
Navarro, c	4	0	1	0	0	1
Gross, rf	3	0	1	0	1	2
Bartlett, ss	4	1	2	0	0	1
	34	6	11	6	3	12

Chicago	0	0	3	0	0	0	0	0	1—4
Tampa Bay	0	1	3	0	2	0	0	0	x—6

a—struck out for Wise in the eighth. b—grounded out for Floyd in the eighth.

Chicago	IP	H	R	ER	BB	SO
Vazquez (L)	4⅓	8	6	6	1	6
Richard	3⅔	3	0	0	2	5
Dotel	⅓	0	0	0	0	1

Tampa Bay	IP	H	R	ER	BB	SO
Shields (W)	6⅓	6	3	3	1	4
Balfour	⅔	0	0	0	0	2
Howell	1	0	0	0	0	2
Wheeler (S)	1	1	1	1	0	1

LOB—Sox 4, Rays 8. 2B—Dye, Navarro. 3B—Iwamura. HR—Konerko,Wise, Longoria (2). SB—Longoria, Gross. HBP—by Shields (Pierzynski). Umpires—West, Bucknor, Kulpa, Kellogg, Darling, Cooper. Time—3:10. Attendance—35,041.

Game 2
October 3, at Tampa Bay

Chicago	AB	R	H	RBI	BB	SO
Cabrera, ss	4	1	2	0	0	0
Swisher, lf	3	1	1	0	2	1
Dye, rf	5	0	4	0	0	0
Konerko, 1b	5	0	1	0	0	0
Thome, dh	5	0	1	1	0	1
Ramirez, 2b	3	0	1	1	0	0
Pierzynski, c	4	0	1	0	0	1
Uribe, 3b	4	0	1	0	0	3
Anderson, cf	3	0	0	0	0	2
	36	2	12	2	2	8

Tampa Bay	AB	R	H	RBI	BB	SO
Iwamura, 2b	4	1	1	2	0	1
Upton, cf	4	1	1	0	0	1
Crawford, lf	4	1	2	1	0	0
Longoria, 3b	4	0	1	0	0	2
Aybar, 1b	3	1	2	0	0	0
Baldelli, dh	4	1	1	1	0	0
Navarro, c	4	0	2	2	0	0
Perez, rf	4	0	1	0	0	0
Bartlett, ss	3	1	1	0	0	0
	34	6	12	6	0	4

Chicago	2	0	0	0	0	0	0	0	0—2
Tampa Bay	0	1	0	0	2	0	0	3	x—6

Chicago	IP	H	R	ER	BB	SO
Buerhrle (L)	7	10	5	5	0	3
Dotel	⅔	1	1	1	0	1
Thornton	⅓	1	0	0	0	0

Tampa Bay	IP	H	R	ER	BB	SO
Kazmir (W)	5⅓	8	2	2	2	4
Balfour	⅔	2	0	0	0	0
Howell	2	1	0	0	0	3
Bradford	1	1	0	0	0	1

LOB—Sox 12, Rays 5. 2B—Aybar, Navarro. 3B—Upton. HR—Iwamura. SB—Crawford. DP—Sox 1, TB 1. Umpires—West, Bucknor, Kulpa, Kellogg, Darling, Cooper. Time—3:10. Attendance—35,257.

Game 3
October 5, at Chicago

Tampa Bay	AB	R	H	RBI	BB	SO
Iwamura, 2b	5	0	2	1	0	1
Upton, cf	5	1	2	2	0	2
Pena, 1b	5	0	2	0	0	2
Longoria, 3b	3	0	0	0	1	1
Crawford, lf	4	0	0	0	0	1
Aybar, dh	4	0	0	0	0	2
Navarro, c	3	1	2	0	1	0
Baldelli, rf	3	1	0	0	1	0
Gross, rf	0	0	0	0	0	0
Bartlett, ss	3	0	0	0	1	1
	35	3	8	3	4	10

Chicago	AB	R	H	RBI	BB	SO
Cabrera, ss	4	0	0	0	0	2
Pierzynski, c	3	0	2	1	1	0
Dye, rf	4	0	0	0	0	0
Thome, dh	3	1	1	0	1	1
Konerko, 1b	3	1	0	0	1	0
Swisher, 1b	0	0	0	0	0	0
Griffey Jr., cf	2	1	2	0	1	0
a—Anderson, pr-cf	1	1	0	0	0	1
Ramirez, 2b	3	0	0	1	0	0
Wise, lf	2	1	1	2	1	0
Uribe, 3b	3	0	1	1	0	1
	28	5	7	5	5	5

Tampa Bay	0	1	0	0	0	0	2	0	0—3
Chicago	0	0	1	3	0	1	0	0	x—5

a—ran for Griffey Jr. in the sixth

Tampa Bay	IP	H	R	ER	BB	SO
Garza (L)	6	7	5	5	4	4
Miller	0	0	0	0	1	0
Bradford	2	0	0	0	0	1

Chicago	IP	H	R	ER	BB	SO
Danks (W)	6⅔	7	3	3	3	7
Dotel	⅓	0	0	0	0	1
Thornton	1	0	0	0	1	1
Jenks	1	1	0	0	0	1

LOB—Rays 9, Sox 5. 2B—Pierzynski, Thome, Wise. HR—Upton. SB—Anderson, Wise, Uribe. DP—TB 2. Umpires—West, Bucknor, Kulpa, Kellogg, Darling, Cooper. Time—3:07. Attendance—40,142.

John Danks pumps his fist after getting an out in Game 3. (Courtesy of the Chicago White Sox)

Game 4
October 6, at Chicago

Tampa Bay	AB	R	H	RBI	BB	SO
Iwamura, 2b	5	1	2	0	0	1
Upton, cf	4	2	2	2	1	0
Pena, 1b	4	0	3	2	1	1
Longoria, 3b	5	0	0	0	0	3
Crawford, lf	2	1	0	0	2	0
Floyd, dh	2	1	1	1	0	0
a—Aybar, ph-dh	2	0	0	0	0	0
Navarro, c	4	0	1	1	0	1
Gross, rf	3	0	0	0	1	0
Bartlett, ss	4	1	1	0	0	1
	35	6	10	6	5	7

Chicago	AB	R	H	RBI	BB	SO
Cabrera, ss	4	0	0	0	0	0
Pierzynski, c	3	0	0	0	1	0
Dye, rf	3	1	1	1	1	2
Thome, dh	4	0	0	0	0	1
Konerko, 1b	4	1	2	1	0	0
Griffey Jr., cf	4	0	0	0	0	3
Ramirez, 2b	3	0	1	0	0	0
Wise, lf	2	0	0	0	0	1
b—Swisher, ph-lf	1	0	0	0	0	0
Uribe, 3b	3	0	0	0	0	0
	31	2	4	2	2	7

Tampa Bay	1	0	1	2	1	0	1	0	0—6
Chicago	0	0	0	1	0	1	0	0	0—2

a—flied out for Floyd in the sixth. b—popped out for Wise in the seventh.

Tampa Bay	IP	H	R	ER	BB	SO
Sonnanstine (W)	5⅔	3	2	2	1	4
Howell (H)	1⅓	1	0	0	0	1
Balfour	2	0	0	0	1	2

Chicago	IP	H	R	ER	BB	SO
Floyd (L)	3	5	4	4	2	4
Richard	3	2	1	1	1	1
Dotel	0	1	1	1	0	0
Thornton	2	1	0	0	1	1
Linebrink	1	1	0	0	1	1

LOB—Rays 7, Sox 4. 2B—Iwamura, Floyd, Bartlett. HR—Dye, Konerko, Upton. SB—Pena 2, Crawford 2. DP—Sox 1. Umpires—West, Bucknor, Kulpa, Kellogg, Darling, Cooper. Time—3:13. Attendance—40,454.

11

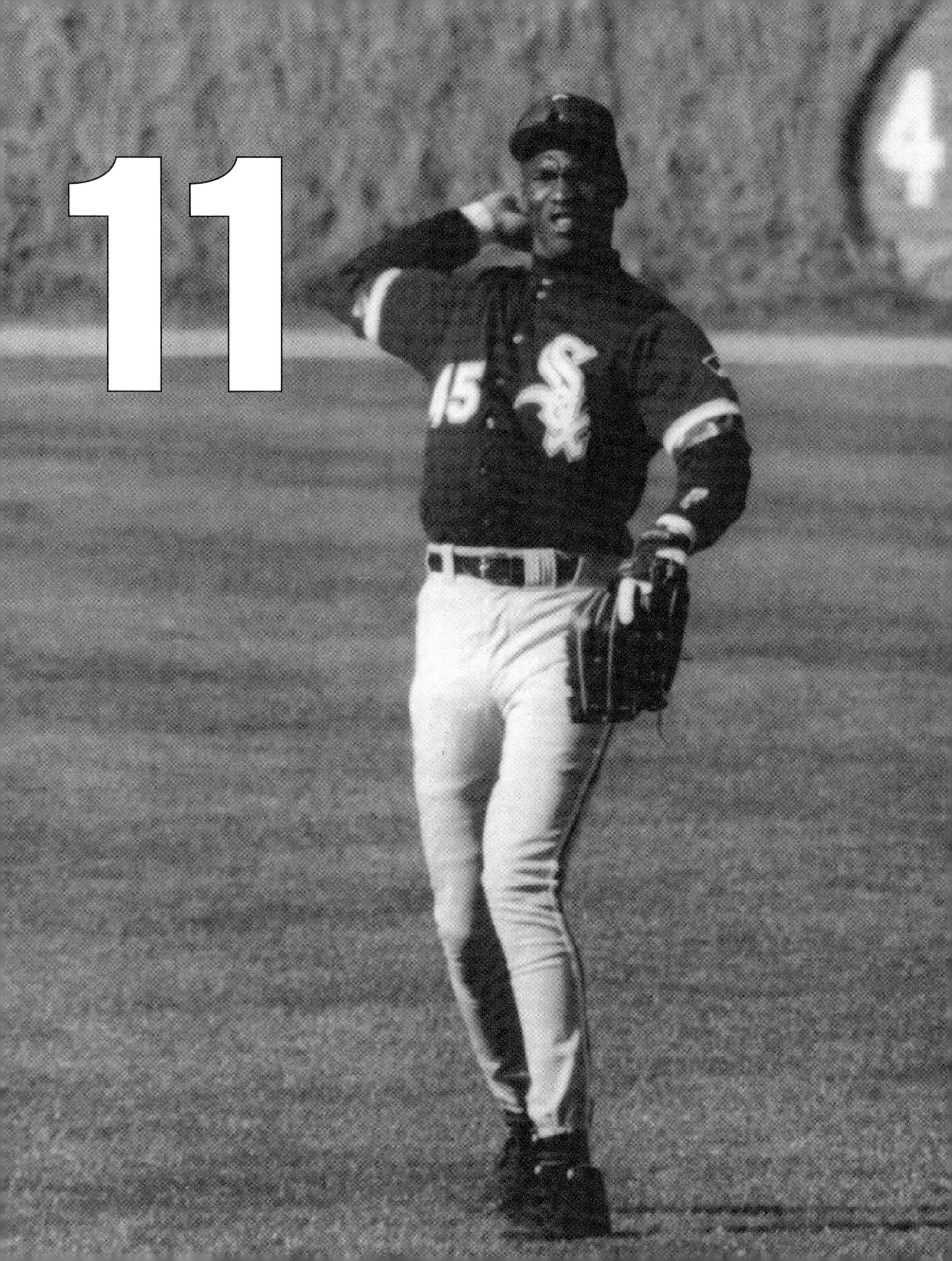

The City Series

by Biart Williams

The City Series (1903–1942) was Chicago's version of the World Series. The Cubs-Sox clashes were also a test of league strength, but, more importantly, the games were a battle for Windy City bragging rights. Boisterous crowds spurred the players on at both ballparks. Often, the local newspaper coverage of these contests dwarfed the World Series print.

South Side pride stirred, the Sox routinely dispatched the Cubs in these affairs (18–6–1). Usually it was a second-division Sox squad knocking off a pennant-contending Cubs team. It was said the Sox were just resting during the regular season, getting ready for the Cubs. Because of South Side domination, interest in the series lagged, and the games were called off in 1943.

1903

It appeared that the first Cubs-Sox series (14 games) would be a short-lived one as the Cubs' vaunted staff—Jack Taylor (21–14), Jake Weimer (21–9), and Bob Wicker (19–10)—held the Sox to one run and 10 hits over the first three contests. But Taylor became an easy mark. He lost his next three assignments helping the Sox gain a seven-game tie (one rainout), and an additional $2,500 team bonus from an elated Charles Comiskey.

Cubs president James Hart summarily dispatched Jack Taylor to St. Louis. He claimed Taylor boasted that he could get $500 for losing instead of Hart's $100 incentive for every game the series was shortened. Though the charges could not be substantiated, Hart stubbornly kept the Cubs out of the 1904 series.

Game 1

Sox	0	0	0	0	0	0	0	0	0— 0
Cubs	0	1	1	6	0	2	1	0	x—11

WP—Taylor
LP—Flaherty

Attendance: 8,000

Game 2

Cubs	2	0	3	0	0	0	0	0	0—5
Sox	0	0	0	0	0	0	1	0	0—1

WP—Weimer
LP—White

Attendance: 3,000

Game 3

Cubs	0	2	0	2	0	1	1	0	0—6
Sox	0	0	0	0	0	0	0	0	0—0

WP—Wicker
LP—Patterson

Attendance: 7,500

Game 4

Sox	2	0	1	0	2	0	1	0	4—10
Cubs	0	0	1	1	0	0	0	0	0— 2

WP—Owen
LP—Taylor

Attendance: 15,000

Game 5

Sox	0	0	0	2	0	0	1	0	0	1—4
Cubs	1	0	0	0	0	0	1	0	1	0—3

WP—Altrock
LP—Wicker

Attendance: 2,100

Game 6

Cubs	1	1	1	0	0	1	1	0	0—5
Sox	0	0	0	1	0	0	0	0	1—2

WP—Weimer
LP—Patterson

Attendance: 2,500

Game 7

Cubs	2	0	0	1	0	0	0	0	0—3
Sox	0	1	2	1	0	0	0	5	x—9

WP—White
LP—Taylor

Attendance: 700

Game 8

Sox	0	0	0	0	0	0	0	0	0—0
Cubs	0	0	0	0	0	0	0	0	1—1

WP—Lundgren
LP—Owen

Attendance: 3,000

Game 9

Sox	0	0	0	0	0	1	0	1	0—2
Cubs	0	4	0	0	0	0	0	0	x—4

WP—Weimer
LP—Altrock

Attendance: 6,500

The City Series was long over by the time Michael Jordan made his Chicago baseball debut in Wrigley Field for the 1994 Crosstown Classic, but the Sox-Cubs rivalry has never waned.

Game 10

Cubs	0	0	0	0	0	0	0	0	0—0
Sox	0	0	2	0	0	0	0	0	x—2

WP—White
LP—Lundgren

Attendance: 11,000

Game 11

Cubs	0	1	0	0	0	0	0	0	0—1
Sox	0	0	0	2	1	0	0	1	x—4

WP—Owen
LP—Taylor

Attendance: 1,200

Game 12

Sox	0	0	0	0	1	0	0	0	0—1
Cubs	2	0	0	0	0	1	2	0	x—5

WP—Wicker
LP—White

Attendance: 3,000

Game 13

Cubs	0	0	0	0	0	0	0	0	0—0
Sox	1	0	0	0	0	1	0	0	x—2

WP—Owen
LP—Weimer

Attendance: 2,200

Game 14

Cubs	0	0	0	0	0	0	0	0	0—0
Sox	2	0	0	0	0	0	0	0	x—2

WP—Altrock
LP—Lundgren

Attendance: 3,500

1905

A "dead-ball" showdown between baseball's best pitching staffs and tightest defenses turned out to be a slugfest (53 runs). The stronger-hitting Cubs captured four of five games.

The Sox had an opportunity to score the winning runs late in the first two contests, then blew a five-run lead in the fourth game. Sox owner Charles Comiskey called it his worst defeat up to that point in time. George Rohe, Frank Isbell, and Jiggs Donahue had gotten a taste of Cubs pitching and would feast on them in the '06 World Series. Ed Walsh, whose only appearance was as a pinch-hitter, was honing his spitter on the sidelines.

Game 1

Cubs	0	0	2	1	0	2	0	0	0—5
Sox	0	0	0	0	0	4	0	0	0—4

WP—Lundgren
LP—Owen

Attendance: 5,000

Game 2

Sox	4	1	1	0	0	0	0	0	1—7
Cubs	1	0	0	0	0	0	3	0	0—4

WP—Altrock
LP—Reulbach

Home run: Donahue (Sox)

Attendance: 9,500

Game 3

Cubs	0	3	0	0	0	0	0	0	0—3
Sox	0	0	1	0	0	0	0	1	0—2

WP—Weimer
LP—White

Attendance: 12,184

Game 4

Sox	5	0	0	0	0	0	0	0	0—5
Cubs	2	0	0	0	0	3	3	0	x—8

WP—Reulbach
LP—Owen

Attendance: 17,640

Game 5

Cubs	5	1	0	0	0	0	3	0	1—10
Sox	3	0	0	1	1	0	0	0	0— 5

WP—Weimer
LP—Smith
Save—Brown

Attendance: 16,121

Sox fans—"the Army of the South"—invade the Cubs' West Side Park, 1909. (Chicago Tribune)

1909

A stellar performance by Cubs pitchers (1.00 ERA) enabled the (Joe) Tinker to (Johnny) Evers to (Frank) Chance bunch to avenge their 1906 World Series loss to the White Sox. Ed Walsh lost two pitching duels to Orval Overall but gained the South Siders' only victory—won in Hitless Wonder fashion on a ninth-inning, bases-loaded balk by Ed Reulbach. Walsh's heroic counterpart, Mordecai Brown, won both his assignments.

Game 1

Sox	0	0	0	0	0	0	0	0	0—0
Cubs	2	0	0	1	0	0	0	1	x—4

WP—Overall
LP—Walsh

Attendance: 16,762

Game 2

Cubs	1	0	0	0	0	0	0	2	2—5
Sox	0	0	1	1	0	0	0	0	0—2

WP—Brown
LP—F. Smith

Home run: Purtell (Sox)
Attendance: 20,657

Game 3

Sox	0	1	0	0	0	0	0	0	1—2
Cubs	1	0	0	0	0	0	0	0	0—1

WP—Walsh
LP—Reulbach

Attendance: 24,034

Game 4

Cubs	1	0	1	0	0	0	0	0	0—2
Sox	0	0	0	1	0	0	0	0	0—1

WP—Overall
LP—Walsh

Attendance: 9,917

Game 5

Sox	0	0	0	0	0	0	0	0	0—0
Cubs	0	0	1	0	0	0	0	0	x—1

WP—Brown
LP—White

Attendance: 3,142

1911

Field generals Ed Walsh and Mordecai Brown finally met on the battlefield in the 1911 Civil War. In a Brown-Walsh opener, center fielder Solly Hofman misjudged a fly ball, opening the way for a Sox three-run, ninth-inning spurt. Out of the pen the next day, Walsh cleaned up an eighth-inning mess, then himself was saved on second sacker Amby McConnell's game-ending double-play stab. The Sox, sensing a sweep, started an every-other-inning run pattern with two in the first inning of the Brown-Walsh final. Big Ed retired the final nine in a row, then was carried off the field on the shoulders of Sox supporters.

Game 1

Cubs	0	0	0	1	0	2	0	0	0—3
Sox	0	0	0	0	0	0	0	1	3—4

WP—Walsh
LP—Brown

Attendance: 22,102

Game 2

Sox	0	3	0	0	1	2	0	2	0—8
Cubs	1	0	5	0	0	1	0	0	0—7

WP—Benz
LP—C. Smith
Save—Walsh

Attendance: 17,963

Game 3

Cubs	0	0	0	1	0	0	0	1	0—2
Sox	0	0	2	0	0	1	1	0	x—4

WP—White
LP—Cole

Attendance: 36,308

Game 4

Sox	2	0	2	0	2	1	0	0	0—7
Cubs	1	0	0	0	1	0	0	0	0—2

WP—Walsh
LP—Brown

Attendance: 22,986

1912

Following two postponements and a pair of rain-soaked draws—one a scoreless duel between Ed Walsh (one hit) and Jim Lavender—the first City Series decision was a 5-4 Sox loss. Snapping Walsh's five-game win streak and belting Ed Cicotte, the Cubs made it three straight. Walsh then piloted a heroic Sox comeback, taking an 11-inning nailbiter and preserving a victory to even the series. A Walsh 16–0 shellacking in Game 9 sparked rumors that the Cubs had laid down in support of lame-duck skipper Frank Chance—a charge adamantly denied by Chance and one that was never proven.

Game 1

Cubs	0	0	0	0	0	0	0	0	0—0
Sox	0	0	0	0	0	0	0	0	0—0

Cubs: Lavender
Sox: Walsh

Attendance: 16,012

Game 2

Cubs	0	0	0	0	1	0	0	2	0	0	0	0—3
Sox	1	0	0	0	0	0	0	0	2	0	0	0—3

Cubs: Cheney
Sox: Cicotte, Walsh

Attendance: 17,864

Game 3

Cubs	0	1	0	0	2	1	1	0	0—5
Sox	0	0	0	2	0	1	0	0	1—4

WP—Lavender
LP—White

Attendance: 30,149

Game 4

Sox	0	0	0	0	0	1	1	0	0—2
Cubs	0	0	0	0	0	1	3	0	x—4

WP—Reulbach
LP—Walsh

Home run: Schulte (Cubs)
Attendance: 30,323

Game 5

Cubs	3	0	3	0	0	0	0	0	2—8
Sox	0	0	0	0	0	1	0	0	0—1

WP—Cheney
LP—Cicotte

Attendance: 16,274

Game 6

Sox	0	3	0	0	0	0	0	1	0	0	1—5
Cubs	0	0	0	2	0	0	1	1	0	0	0—4

WP—Walsh
LP—Lavender

Home run: Schulte (Cubs)
Attendance: 10,297

Game 7

Cubs	1	2	0	0	0	1	0	0	1—5
Sox	0	0	1	0	0	2	0	4	x—7

WP—Benz
LP—Reulbach

Attendance: 12,438

Game 8

Sox	0	1	0	0	0	3	0	0	4—8
Cubs	1	0	0	2	0	0	0	2	0—5

WP—Lange
LP—Richie

Home runs: Zimmerman (Cubs), S. Collins (Sox), Weaver (Sox)

Attendance: 11,903

Game 9

Cubs	0	0	0	0	0	0	0	0	0— 0
Sox	1	2	8	2	3	0	0	0	x—16

WP—Walsh
LP—Lavender

Attendance: 14,985

1913

Closing out the 1913 series with three straight wins, the Sox took a 3–2 City Series lead—and would never look back! Outfielder Shano Collins led all batters with a .462 average. He accounted for half the Sox runs in the opener; his fourth hit of the match broke a scoreless duel in the pivotal fifth game; then his series-high 12th hit started things rolling in the last contest.

Game 1

Sox	2	0	0	1	0	2	1	0	0—6
Cubs	0	0	0	1	0	2	0	1	0—4

WP—Russell
LP—Cheney
Save—Scott

Home runs: Good (Cubs), Saier (Cubs)
Attendance: 16,936

Game 2

Cubs	0	0	0	4	1	0	0	0	0	0	0	0	1—6
Sox	0	0	0	3	0	1	0	1	0	0	0	0	0—5

WP—Vaughn
LP—Benz

Attendance: 29,368

Game 3

Sox	0	0	0	0	0	0	0	0	0—0
Cubs	0	0	0	0	0	3	5	0	x—8

WP—Humphries
LP—Scott

Attendance: 17,897

Game 4

Cubs	0	1	1	0	0	0	0	0	0—2
Sox	0	0	0	0	1	0	3	1	x—5

WP—Cicotte
LP—Pearce

Attendance: 32,707

Game 5

Sox	0	0	0	0	0	0	0	0	0	2—2
Cubs	0	0	0	0	0	0	0	0	0	0—0

WP—Benz
LP—Cheney

Attendance: 27,427

Game 6

Cubs	0	0	0	1	0	0	0	0	1—2
Sox	0	0	0	3	2	0	0	0	x—5

WP—Scott
LP—Humphries

Attendance: 29,484

1914

The White Sox concluded an expanded baseball year with an off-season world tour and still had something left for the Cubs. After falling behind three games to one, Jim Scott won two games. On Scott's behalf in Game 5, rookie Red Faber two-hit the Cubs over the final four innings. Ed Cicotte, rebounding from a Cubs double come-from-behind victory, earned a save and a win in the last two contests.

Game 1

Cubs	1	0	0	0	2	0	0	1	0—4
Sox	0	0	0	0	0	0	2	0	0—2

WP—Vaughn
LP—Wolfgang

Attendance: 21,744

Game 2

Sox	0	1	0	0	0	0	0	1	3—5
Cubs	0	2	0	0	0	0	0	0	0—2

WP—Scott
LP—Cheney

Attendance: 12,199

Game 3

Cubs	0	0	0	2	0	0	0	0	0—2
Sox	0	0	1	0	0	0	0	0	0—1

WP—Humphries
LP—Benz

Attendance: 17,377

Game 4

Sox	0	0	0	1	0	1	0	0	0	1—3
Cubs	0	0	0	0	0	0	0	0	2	2—4

WP—Lavender
LP—Cicotte

Attendance: 23,622

Game 5

Cubs	0	0	0	1	0	0	0	0	0—1
Sox	0	0	0	0	2	0	1	0	x—3

WP—Scott
LP—Cheney
Save—Faber

Attendance: 19,348

Game 6

Sox	0	1	0	0	4	0	0	0	0—5
Cubs	0	0	0	0	0	0	2	0	1—3

WP—Benz
LP—Vaughn
Save—Cicotte

Home run: Saier (Cubs)
Attendance: 6,601

Game 7

Cubs	2	0	0	0	0	0	0	0	0—2
Sox	0	0	0	3	0	0	0	0	x—3

WP—Cicotte
LP—Humphries

Attendance: 14,879

1915

After finishing the regular season with 11 straight wins, the Sox breezed past the Cubs. Playing in his first City Series, Hall of Famer Eddie Collins rallied the Sox from a 4–0 deficit in Game 1 against Hippo Vaughn. His namesake, Shano Collins, tagged Vaughn for an inside-the-park grand slammer (Game 4). Wrapping it up before a packed house at Comiskey Park, the Sox squared accounts with Jim Lavender, 11–3, chasing him in a five-run fifth.

Game 1

Cubs	3	0	0	1	1	0	0	0	0—5
Sox	0	0	0	2	0	0	4	3	x—9

WP—Russell
LP—Vaughn

Attendance: 19,513

Game 2

Sox	0	0	0	0	0	0	0	0	0—0
Cubs	0	1	0	0	0	3	0	0	x—4

WP—Lavender
LP—Benz

Home run: Zimmerman (Cubs)

Attendance: 5,211

Game 3

Cubs	0	0	0	0	0	0	0	0	2—2
Sox	0	0	0	0	0	0	0	5	x—5

WP—Faber
LP—Pearce

Attendance: 6,603

Game 4

Sox	0	0	5	0	0	0	0	0	0—5
Cubs	0	0	0	0	0	0	0	0	0—0

WP—Scott
LP—Vaughn

Home run: S. Collins (Sox)

Attendance: 11,963

Game 5

Cubs	0	0	1	0	0	0	1	1	0— 3
Sox	0	1	0	0	5	5	0	0	x—11

WP—Russell
LP—Lavender

Attendance: 32,666

1916

The White Sox swept past a conglomerate of Cubs and ex–Chicago Whales players (of the defunct Federal League) to make it six straight City Series triumphs. Each Sox starter went the distance. Shoeless Joe Jackson, held to one hit in the first two matches, closed with three doubles, two singles, and a home run. One of his two-baggers scorched the hand of a Cubs outfielder, taking him out of the game.

Game 1

Cubs	0	0	0	0	0	2	0	0	0—2
Sox	0	0	1	0	0	0	5	2	x—8

WP—Russell
LP—Vaughn

Attendance: 17,250

Game 2

Sox	0	0	0	3	0	0	0	0	0—3
Cubs	0	0	0	0	1	0	0	0	0—1

WP—Faber
LP—Lavender

Attendance: 11,649

Game 3

Cubs	0	0	0	0	0	0	0	0	0—0
Sox	0	1	1	0	0	1	0	0	x—3

WP—C. Williams
LP—Prendergast

Attendance: 10,916

Game 4

Sox	0	0	3	0	3	0	0	0	0—6
Cubs	1	0	1	0	1	0	0	0	0—3

WP—Cicotte
LP—Vaughn

Home run: J. Jackson (Sox)

Attendance: 16,798

1921

In the first series played in five eventful years (White Sox pennants in 1917 and 1919, a Cubs title in 1918, and the Black Sox scandal of 1920), a rebuilt Sox squad swept a five-game set. Red Faber wrenched his knee in Game 2, and catcher Ray Schalk bowed out in Game 3 with an injured finger. "Clean Sox" Dickie Kerr (1–0, 1 save) was called upon three times. His efforts pleased Sox fans but would not help in contract negotiations with Charles Comiskey, the stalemate ending Kerr's career.

Game 1

Cubs	0	0	0	0	0	0	0	0	0—0
Sox	0	0	1	0	0	1	0	0	x—2

WP—Kerr
LP—Alexander

Attendance: 16,000

Game 2

Sox	0	0	0	0	1	1	4	1	1—8
Cubs	1	0	0	0	0	0	1	2	1—5

WP—Faber
LP—Martin

Home run: Flack (Cubs)

Attendance: 12,859

Game 3

Cubs	2	0	0	0	0	0	0	1	0	0—3
Sox	0	0	0	0	0	0	0	0	3	1—4

WP—Hodge
LP—Jones

Attendance: 11,833

Game 4

Cubs	0	1	0	0	1	0	0	0	0—2
Sox	1	0	0	0	0	1	1	0	x—3

WP—Hodge
LP—Alexander

Attendance: 28,381

Game 5

Sox	2	0	0	0	5	0	0	1	1—9
Cubs	0	1	1	0	0	3	0	0	0—5

WP—Russell
LP—Cheeves
Save—Kerr

Home run: Sheely (Sox)

Attendance: 7,172

1922

The immortal Grover Cleveland Alexander bested Dixie Leverett in the seventh game, 2–0, giving the Cubs their first city title in 13 years. Following the South Siders' opening triumph (Red Faber's fourth straight win, the Sox' 13th), the Cubs' "Tiny" Osborne (6′4″, 215 lbs.) gained two wins. In his bid for a third victory, Osborne lost to Faber in a honey of a contest, 1–0. Earl Sheely touched the dish ahead of catcher Bob O'Farrell's tag on Ray Schalk's suicide bunt.

Game 1

Sox	0	0	0	0	1	3	0	1	1—6
Cubs	1	0	0	0	0	0	0	0	1—2

WP—Faber
LP—Aldridge

Home run: Mulligan (Sox)

Attendance: 17,434

Game 2

Sox	0	0	0	1	1	1	0	0	0— 3
Cubs	2	0	0	1	0	0	4	3	0—10

WP—Osborne
LP—Leverett

Home run: E. Collins (Sox)

Attendance: 14,516

Game 3

Cubs	3	0	0	0	2	0	3	0	0—8
Sox	2	0	1	0	0	2	0	0	0—5

WP—Osborne
LP—Wilkerson

Home runs: Hooper (Sox), Grimes (Cubs)

Attendance: 9,063

Game 4

Cubs	1	0	1	0	0	1	0	0	0—3
Sox	0	0	0	0	0	2	1	0	1—4

WP—Leverett
LP—Alexander

Attendance: 9,180

Game 5

Sox	0	0	0	1	0	1	0	0	0—2
Cubs	2	0	0	0	0	5	0	0	x—7

WP—Aldridge
LP—Blankenship

Attendance: 6,549

Game 6

Cubs	0	0	0	0	0	0	0	0	0—0
Sox	0	0	0	0	0	0	0	0	1—1

WP—Faber
LP—Osborne

Attendance: 14,677

Game 7

Sox	0	0	0	0	0	0	0	0	0—0
Cubs	0	0	0	0	0	1	1	0	0—2

WP—Alexander
LP—Leverett

Attendance: 32,842

1923

The series was about to be evened at three games apiece when Cubs second baseman George "Boots" Grantham mishandled a grounder in the ninth inning, allowing the Sox to rally back, then kicked another one in the 10th, thus handing the Sox a surprise victory.

In the joyous clubhouse, manager Kid Gleason interrupted the celebration to announce his retirement. Gleason, who had guided the team during the worst days of the Black Sox scandal, did not see a Sox revival but left town with yet another city title.

Game 1

Sox	0	0	1	0	2	1	0	0	0—4
Cubs	0	0	2	4	0	1	0	1	x—8

WP—Alexander
LP—Robertson

Home run: E. Collins (Sox)

Attendance: 24,038

Game 2

Cubs	1	0	0	2	0	1	0	0	0—4
Sox	0	0	0	0	0	0	1	2	0—3

WP—Aldridge
LP—Thurston
Save—Fussell

Attendance: 18,962

Game 3

Sox	1	0	0	0	2	0	1	0	0—4
Cubs	0	0	1	1	0	0	0	0	0—2

WP—Faber
LP—Keen

Home run: Friberg (Cubs)

Attendance: 26,128

Game 4

Cubs	0	0	0	0	3	0	0	0	0—3
Sox	2	0	1	0	0	0	0	0	2—5

WP—Thurston
LP—Kaufmann

Home run: Sheely (Sox)

Attendance: 41,825

Game 5

Sox	0	0	0	5	0	2	0	0	0—7
Cubs	0	1	0	0	0	0	1	2	0—4

WP—Robertson
LP—Aldridge

Home runs: Kamm 2 (Sox), E. Collins (Sox), Friberg (Cubs), Vogel (Cubs)

Attendance: 15,562

Game 6

Cubs	0	0	0	1	0	1	0	0	1	0—3
Sox	0	0	0	0	0	0	1	0	2	1—4

WP—Leverett
LP—Kaufmann

Home runs: Grantham (Cubs), Friberg (Cubs)

Attendance: 15,276

1924

Johnny Evers, let go by the Cubs for losing the 1913 City Series, piloted the cellar-dweller Sox to a power-laden win. Willie Kamm and Johnny Mostil had five extra-base hits apiece. Earl Sheely socked four roundtrippers, three off Grover Cleveland Alexander—he was the only Sox player to solve the mighty Alexander. The games were the first ever broadcast on local radio. Sen Kaney of WGN called the play-by-play from the roof of both stadiums.

Game 1

Sox	0	0	0	0	0	0	2	3	2— 7
Cubs	0	1	3	5	0	0	1	0	x—10

WP—Alexander
LP—Connally

Home runs: Sheely 2 (Sox), Grantham (Cubs), Weis (Cubs)

Attendance: 15,414

Game 2

Cubs	0	0	2	0	0	2	2	1	0— 7
Sox	1	2	0	0	5	0	2	2	x—12

WP—Thurston
LP—Keen

Home run: W. Barrett (Sox)

Attendance: 16,081

Game 3

Sox	0	0	0	0	0	4	0	0	2—6
Cubs	0	0	0	0	0	0	0	3	0—3

WP—Faber
LP—Jacobs

Home run: Sheely (Sox)

Attendance: 15,101

Game 4

Cubs	0	0	0	0	0	0	0	0	0— 0
Sox	3	0	0	0	4	0	2	4	x—13

WP—Blankenship
LP—Kaufmann

Attendance: 22,956

Game 5

Sox	0	2	0	0	0	1	0	0	0—3
Cubs	0	0	0	1	1	1	3	2	x—8

WP—Alexander
LP—Robertson

Home runs: R. Barrett (Cubs), Sheely (Sox), Heathcote (Cubs)

Attendance: 31,207

Game 6

Cubs	0	0	1	0	0	0	2	0	0—3
Sox	1	0	3	0	0	0	0	1	x—5

WP—Thurston
LP—Aldridge
Save—Lyons

Attendance: 12,996

1925

In a reversal of fortune, the modestly talented fifth-place Sox ballclub succumbed to a last-place Cubs team. The classic matchup of the series pitted Grover Cleveland Alexander against Ted Blankenship in a 19-inning opening-game draw. Blankenship yielded 11 hits, four over the final 10 frames. Alexander, rocked for 20 hits, allowed the lead-off man to reach in each of the last eight innings but survived. Rubber-arm Blankenship added nine more innings in Game 4 for the Sox' only win, but he failed in relief in the final.

Game 1

Cubs	0	0	0	1	1	0	0	0	0	0	0	0	0	0	0	0	0	0	0—2
Sox	0	0	2	0	0	0	0	0	0	0	0	0	0	0	0	0	0	0	0—2

Cubs—Alexander
Sox—Blankenship

Attendance: 10,265

Game 2

Sox	0	0	1	0	0	0	0	0	0—1
Cubs	1	0	0	0	0	1	0	0	x—2

WP—Cooper
LP—Lyons

Attendance: 14,073

Game 3

Sox	0	0	0	0	0	1	0	0	1—2
Cubs	4	0	0	0	2	0	0	2	x—8

WP—Blake
LP—Faber

Attendance: 13,693

Game 4

Cubs	0	1	0	0	1	0	0	0	0—2
Sox	4	0	0	0	1	2	0	0	x—7

WP—Blankenship
LP—Jones

Attendance: 13,901

Game 5

Sox	0	0	0	0	0	0	0	1	0—1
Cubs	0	0	0	2	0	0	1	0	x—3

WP—Kaufmann
LP—Lyons

Attendance: 11,101

Game 6

Cubs	0	0	1	0	0	3	0	3	0—7
Sox	0	0	0	0	0	0	3	1	0—4

WP—Cooper
LP—Faber

Attendance: 11,122

1926

The Cubs and Sox split four shutout contests. Two were won by the Pale Hose's Ted Blankenship, his second in the deciding seventh game.

The series featured seven future Hall of Famers: infielder Eddie Collins, catcher Ray Schalk, pitchers Red Faber and Ted Lyons, catcher Gabby Hartnett, outfielder Hack Wilson, and manager Joe McCarthy. A pair of roly-polies, Schalk and Wilson, met head-on in a play at home plate. Schalk was turned head over heels but held onto the ball for the putout.

Game 1

Sox	0	0	0	0	0	0	0	0	0—0
Cubs	0	0	2	0	0	4	0	0	x—6

WP—Root
LP—Faber

Attendance: 14,721

Game 2

Sox	2	0	0	0	0	1	4	3	0—10
Cubs	1	0	0	0	0	2	0	2	0— 5

WP—Lyons
LP—Kaufmann

Home runs: Falk (Sox), Wilson (Cubs), W. Barrett (Sox), Grimm (Cubs)

Attendance: 11,588

Game 3

Cubs	0	0	0	0	0	0	0	1	0—1
Sox	0	0	0	0	0	0	0	0	0—0

WP—Jones
LP—Thomas

Attendance: 20,396

Game 4

Sox	0	0	0	1	0	2	1	0	0—4
Cubs	0	0	0	0	0	0	0	0	0—0

WP—Blankenship
LP—Bush

Attendance: 37,141

Game 5

Cubs	0	0	0	0	0	0	0	0	0—1
Sox	0	0	0	1	1	0	1	0	x—3

WP—Faber
LP—Root
Save—Connally

Attendance: 5,770

Game 6

Cubs	0	2	0	0	0	2	0	0	0—4
Sox	0	0	0	0	0	0	0	1	0—1

WP—Jones
LP—Lyons

Attendance: 6,727

Game 7

Sox	0	0	0	1	1	0	1	0	0—3
Cubs	0	0	0	0	0	0	0	0	0—0

WP—Blankenship
LP—Root

Attendance: 16,835

1927

The Cubs did not issue a challenge to the Sox in 1927. Cubs officials were upset by the actions of Sox players who cheered every time the contending Cubs lost a September contest. The fifth-place Sox coveted the extra coin coming their way in an enlarged Comiskey Park.

"Nothing would be gained if the Sox beat the Cubs again," Sox owner Charles Comiskey remarked.

1928

A rising Cubs ballclub, just missing a league championship, squeaked by the fifth-place Sox. Tommy Thomas, following a tough 14-inning affair in Game 2 (sent into overtime by the Sox's porous infield), whitewashed the Bruins in Game 5, spoiling the series-clinching festivities at overflowing Wrigley Field (44,868). Rookie Art Shires forced a seventh game. The Sox, going with reliever George Connally, were thrashed 13–2.

The Sox triggered a mild uproar by voting a half share to rookie first sacker Art Shires. Shires, joining the Sox in August, had a robust series (.300). Under pressure from the commissioner's office, the players were forced to grant Shires a full share.

Game 1

Cubs	3	0	0	0	0	0	0	0	0—3
Sox	0	0	0	0	0	0	0	0	0—0

WP—Malone
LP—Faber

Attendance: 25,885

Game 2

Cubs	0	0	0	0	0	0	1	0	1	0	0	0	0	3—5
Sox	1	0	0	0	1	0	0	0	0	0	0	0	0	1—3

WP—Bush
LP—Thomas

Attendance: 15,629

Game 3

Sox	3	1	3	0	1	0	5	0	0—13
Cubs	3	5	0	1	1	0	1	0	0—11

WP—Walsh
LP—Jones
Save—Connally

Home run: Wilson (Cubs)

Attendance: 21,204

Game 4

Sox	0	1	0	0	0	0	0	1	0—2
Cubs	0	3	0	0	0	0	0	0	x—3

WP—Blake
LP—Faber

Home run: Falk (Sox)

Attendance: 30,965

Game 5

Sox	2	0	0	0	0	0	0	0	0—2
Cubs	0	0	0	0	0	0	0	0	0—0

WP—Thomas
LP—Malone

Attendance: 44,868

Game 6

Cubs	0	0	0	0	0	1	0	0	0—1
Sox	3	3	1	0	0	0	0	0	x—7

WP—Adkins
LP—Bush

Attendance: 11,710

Game 7

Cubs	6	0	0	0	6	0	1	0	0—13
Sox	0	0	0	0	0	0	0	0	2— 2

WP—Blake
LP—Connally

Attendance: 24,880

1930

The slugging Cubs garnered their second straight title and their first back-to-back wins in 20 years. Kiki Cuyler's three-run homer decided Game 2. National League home-run champ Hack Wilson blasted a round-tripper in each of the last two games and spurred a series-ending, ninth-inning rally with an RBI single.

Game 1

Cubs	0	0	0	0	0	0	0	0	1—1
Sox	3	0	0	0	0	0	0	2	x—5

WP—Lyons
LP—Malone

Attendance: 30,204

Game 2

Cubs	0	0	0	1	0	0	0	3	0—4
Sox	0	0	0	0	0	1	0	0	1—2

WP—Blake
LP—Caraway

Home run: Cuyler (Cubs)

Attendance: 21,334

Game 3

Sox	0	0	0	0	0	0	1	0	0— 1
Cubs	0	2	0	1	2	3	2	2	x—12

WP—Teachout
LB—Faber

Home run: Grimm (Cubs)

Attendance: 21,000

Game 4

Sox	1	3	0	0	0	0	1	3	0—8
Cubs	0	0	0	0	2	0	0	0	0—2

WP—Thomas
LP—Bush

Home run: Jolley (Sox)

Attendance: 28,547

Game 5

Sox	0	0	0	0	2	2	0	0	0—4
Cubs	2	1	0	0	2	0	1	0	x—6

WP—Malone
LP—Lyons

Home run: Wilson (Cubs)

Attendance: 45,104

Game 6

Cubs	0	0	0	1	1	0	0	1	3—6
Sox	0	0	0	0	2	1	0	1	0—4

WP—Petty
LP—Braxton

Home run: Wilson (Cubs)

Attendance: 16,729

1930: The Cubs win a rare one. The Sox catcher is Martin "Chick" Autry.

1931

Burrowed in the American League cellar, the White Sox rose up to thwart the Cubs. Red Faber, relying on slow curves and wicked spitters, bested Charlie Root twice. Both times Smead Jolley whaled on Root with a two-run homer and grand slam. Cubs hurler Pat Malone got his comeuppance in Game 4 after boasting that he could beat the Sox with eight bloomer girls from an old ladies home. Malone was pelted with a barrage of lemons. Then a crate of raspberries was sent over by the White Sox bench jockeys.

Game 1

Sox	0	0	0	0	0	7	2	0	0—9
Cubs	0	0	0	0	0	0	0	0	0—0

WP—Faber
LP—Root

Home run: Jolly (Sox)

Attendance: 16,641

Game 2

Sox	0	0	0	0	0	0	0	0	0—0
Cubs	0	0	0	0	0	0	0	0	1—1

WP—Bush
LP—Frasier

Attendance: 11,407

Game 3

Cubs	2	0	0	0	0	0	0	0	0—2
Sox	0	0	0	1	0	0	0	0	0—1

WP—Smith
LP—Lyons
Save—Root

Attendance: 14,245

Game 4

Cubs	0	0	0	0	0	0	0	2	1—3
Sox	1	0	0	0	3	0	0	0	x—4

WP—Thomas
LP—Malone
Save—Frasier

Home run: Fonseca (Sox)

Attendance: 22,747

Game 5

Cubs	1	0	0	2	0	1	1	0	1— 6
Sox	1	0	0	0	5	0	3	4	x—13

WP—Faber
LP—Root

Home runs: Jolley (Sox), Cissell (Sox), Cuyler (Cubs), Hemsley (Cubs)

Attendance: 41,523

Game 6

Sox	0	0	0	0	2	0	0	0	0—2
Cubs	0	1	0	0	0	0	0	0	2—3

WP—Root
LP—Frasier

Home run: D. Taylor (Cubs)

Attendance: 13,509

Game 7

Sox	0	1	0	6	0	0	0	0	0—7
Cubs	1	0	0	0	0	0	0	1	0—2

WP—Thomas
LP—Smith

Attendance: 17,379

1933

A solid Cubs team was again manhandled by a mediocre Sox squad. Four Sox pitchers contributed to the sweep: 41-year-old Sam Jones, 45-year-old Red Faber (taking leave with his 11th series win), Ted Lyons, and the nondescript Joe Heving. Newcomers Jimmy Dykes, Mule Haas, and Al Simmons played key roles. Dykes hit for a .563 average; Haas drove in the winning run in Game 1; Simmons accounted for both runs in Faber's shutout (Game 2); then together they KO'd Guy Bush (0–2).

Game 1

Sox	0	3	0	0	0	0	0	0	0—3
Cubs	0	0	0	1	0	0	0	0	1—2

WP—S. Jones
LP—Bush

Attendance: 14,565

Game 2

Sox	0	0	0	0	0	1	0	1	0—2
Cubs	0	0	0	0	0	0	0	0	0—0

WP—Faber
LP—Warneke

Attendance: 8,378

Game 3

Cubs	0	0	0	0	0	0	0	0	0—0
Sox	0	4	0	0	4	0	1	0	x—9

WP—Lyons
LP—Root

Home run: Kress (Sox)

Attendance: 9,152

Game 4

Cubs	0	0	0	0	0	0	0	0	1—1
Sox	2	0	0	0	0	0	1	2	x—5

WP—Heaving
LP—Bush

Attendance: 24,321

1934

In late August, the Cubs announced they would not challenge the Sox. Owner P.K. Wrigley, watching his club slip in a tight pennant race, felt the Cubs players were content with a first-division slice knowing a City Series awaited.

The Sox, mired in last place, saw the Cubs' refusal as a slap in the face, particularly in view of the beating administered by the White Sox in the 1933 City Series.

1936

Following their best finish (third; 81–70) in 15 years and a batting title for Luke Appling (.388), the Sox made it back-to-back sweeps. Again, it took only four Sox hurlers to complete the cycle. Larry Rosenthal (9-for-16) hit safely in each contest. Zeke Bonura closed with a perfect (5-for-5) day at the plate.

Owner P.K. Wrigley, snarling at his club's nonperformance, announced he would cut salaries in 1937 and ordered all players put on the trading block.

Game 1

Sox	0	0	0	0	5	0	0	0	0—5
Cubs	0	0	0	0	0	0	0	0	1—1

WP—Kennedy
LP—B. Lee

Home run: Radcliff (Sox)

Attendance: 12, 383

Game 2

Cubs	0	1	0	0	0	0	0	1	1— 3
Sox	3	0	0	0	0	8	0	0	x—11

WP—Stratton
LP—Warneke

Attendance: 13,990

Game 3

Cubs	0	0	1	0	1	0	0	0	0—2
Sox	1	0	3	0	0	0	0	0	x—4

WP—Lyons
LP—Davis

Attendance: 21,600

Game 4

Cubs	1	0	0	1	0	0	0	0	0—2
Sox	4	0	0	0	1	0	0	3	x—8

WP—Dietrich
LP—French

Attendance: 33,906

1937

In the interim years between the pennants of '35 and '38, the Cubs received the usual pasting from the White Sox. The Cubs ended a nine-game losing streak with a win in the opener, then behind Larry French (2–0) forced a seventh game. Outhit for the entire series, the Sox shut down the Cubs' offense turning four double plays (13 total), including a series-ending snuff.

Game 1

Cubs	0	0	0	0	1	3	0	3	0—7
Sox	0	2	0	0	0	0	0	1	0—3

WP—Carlton
LP—Lyons

Attendance: 14,589

Game 2

Cubs	0	0	0	0	0	0	0	1	0—1
Sox	0	0	0	1	0	0	0	2	x—3

WP—Kennedy
LP—Root

Attendance: 9,481

Game 3

Sox	0	0	0	0	0	0	0	1	0—1
Cubs	0	0	2	1	1	0	0	0	x—4

WP—French
LP—T. Lee

Home runs: Hartnett (Cubs), Hayes (Sox)

Attendance: 10,568

Game 4

Sox	0	2	3	0	4	2	0	0	3—14
Cubs	0	1	1	0	0	0	0	0	0— 2

WP—Whitehead
LP—W. Lee

Home run: Bonura (Sox)

Attendance: 12,947

Game 5

Cubs	0	0	1	0	0	0	2	0	1—4
Sox	1	0	2	0	1	0	2	0	0—6

WP—Stratton
LP—Carlton
Save—Brown

Home runs: Kreevich (Sox), Marty (Cubs)

Attendance: 11,575

Game 6

Cubs	1	2	0	0	1	0	0	1	1—6
Sox	0	0	0	2	0	0	0	0	0—2

WP—French
LP—Kennedy

Attendance: 4,241

Game 7

Sox	0	2	0	2	0	1	1	0	0—6
Cubs	1	0	0	0	0	0	0	0	0—1

WP—Whitehead
LP—Davis

Home run: Kreevich (Sox)

Attendance: 12,457

A quartet of Sox: Joe Kuhel, Marv Owen, Louis "Boze" Berger, and Luke Sewell prepare to lay it on the Cubs in Wrigley Field in a 1938 preseason match-up.

1939

Up three games to one, the Cubs blew a 5–0, fifth-inning lead and the series as they were outscored 21–2 over the last 24 innings for another in a long line of miraculous Sox comebacks.

Game 1

Cubs	0	1	0	1	0	2	3	0	2	1—10
Sox	0	0	0	0	3	0	5	1	0	0— 9

WP—Whitehill
LP—Brown

Home runs: G. Walker (Sox), Nicholson (Cubs)

Attendance: 42,767

Game 2

Cubs	0	0	1	0	1	0	0	0	0—2
Sox	1	3	0	2	0	0	3	0	x—9

WP—Lyons
LP—Root

Home runs: Kuhel (Sox), G. Walker (Sox), G. Russell 2 (Cubs)

Attendance: 6,131

Game 3

Sox	1	0	0	1	0	0	0	0	0—2
Cubs	0	0	0	0	1	1	1	1	x—4

WP—B. Lee
LP—T. Lee

Attendance: 9,484

Game 4

Sox	0	1	0	0	0	0	2	0	0—3
Cubs	1	0	0	1	0	0	0	0	3—5

WP—J. Russell
LP—Knott

Home runs: G. Russell (Cubs), Lieber (Cubs), E. Smith (Sox)

Attendance: 11,468

Game 5

Sox	0	0	0	0	0	2	0	3	0	3—8
Cubs	1	1	1	2	0	0	0	0	0	0—5

WP—Dietrich
LP—B. Lee

Home runs: Galan (Cubs), Kreevich (Sox)

Attendance: 17,227

Game 6

Cubs	1	0	0	0	0	0	0	0	0—1
Sox	0	0	0	1	1	1	0	3	x—6

WP—T. Lee
LP—Root

Attendance: 26,960

Game 7

Cubs	0	0	0	0	0	0	0	0	0—1
Sox	0	4	0	0	2	0	1	0	x—7

WP—Lyons
LP—Whitehill

Attendance: 14,781

1940

Outfielder Moose Solters (.375) led the White Sox to two wins and the City Series flag. His two-out, ninth-inning base hit decided the pivotal fifth game. Then, in the last contest, Solters keyed a late Sox rally with two hits, sending the game into overtime where Luke Appling's bases-loaded double became the title difference.

Game 1

Sox	0	3	1	0	1	0	0	0	0—5
Cubs	0	2	0	0	1	0	0	0	0—3

WP—Lyons
LP—Passeau

Home run: Solters (Sox)

Attendance: 9,929

Game 2

Sox	0	0	0	0	0	2	0	0	0—2
Cubs	0	1	1	0	3	3	0	0	x—8

WP—Olsen
LP—T. Lee

Attendance: 6,800

Game 3

Cubs	0	0	4	1	0	0	0	0	0— 5
Sox	0	2	3	0	2	1	3	0	x—11

WP—E. Smith
LP—French

Home run: Nicholson (Cubs)

Attendance: 39,625

Game 4

Cubs	0	0	1	1	0	0	1	0	1—4
Sox	0	0	0	0	0	0	0	0	0—0

WP—B. Lee
LP—Rigney

Attendance: 4,789

Game 5

Cubs	0	0	0	0	0	1	0	1—2
Sox	0	0	1	0	0	0	1	0	1—3

WP—Dietrich
LP—Raffensberger

Attendance: 37,383

Game 6

Sox	0	0	0	0	0	0	2	0	1	2—5
Cubs	0	1	0	2	0	0	0	0	0	1—4

WP—Lyons
LP—Olsen

Home runs: Leiber (Cubs), Bonura (Cubs)

Attendance: 12,075

1941

The jinxed Cubs were swept for the third time in six city matches. In a "here-we-go-again" opener, Claude Passeau was rocked for four runs in the ninth inning. The tying runs aboard, shortstop Luke Appling intercepted a Dom Dallesandro liner, ending Game 2. Jittery Cub fielders then handed the Sox eight unearned runs over the last two games. Topping all that, the Bruins suffered the ignominy of a triple play in Game 3 (second baseman Bill Knickerbocker to shortstop Luke Appling).

Game 1

Sox	0	0	0	0	0	0	0	0	4—4
Cubs	0	0	0	0	0	0	1	0	0—1

WP—Lyons
LP—Passeau

Attendance: 7,272

Game 2

Cubs	0	0	0	0	1	0	0	1	2—4
Sox	2	0	0	2	0	0	1	1	x—6

WP—E. Smith
LP—Olsen

Home runs: B. Kennedy (Sox), Wright (Sox)

Attendance: 27,169

Game 3

Sox	2	2	0	2	0	0	0	0	0—6
Cubs	0	0	0	0	0	0	0	0	0—0

WP—Rigney
LP—Erickson

Attendance: 17,774

Game 4

Cubs	0	1	0	0	0	0	0	0	0—1
Sox	0	2	0	0	0	0	1	0	x—3

WP—T. Lee
LP—Passeau

Attendance: 13,955

1942

White Sox domination and World War II brought about waning interest in the City Series. With sparse crowds watching the final match, the Sox scored another rout. Two home-front players figured prominently for the Sox: John Humphries (2–0) and Wally Moses (.360). Three days after enlisting in the Marines, 41-year-old Ted Lyons whitewashed the Cubs in the opener. Army-bound Don Kolloway tallied seven times over the first three contests.

Game 1

Sox	1	1	0	0	0	0	0	0	1—3
Cubs	0	0	0	0	0	0	0	0	0—0

WP—Lyons
LP—B. Lee

Attendance: 4,751

Game 2

Sox	3	0	0	1	0	0	1	4	0—9
Cubs	0	3	2	0	0	0	0	0	0—5

WP—Haynes
LP—Warneke

Home run: Kolloway (Sox)

Attendance: 3,320

Game 3

Cubs	1	0	0	1	0	0	0	0	0—2
Sox	1	0	2	0	0	0	0	0	x—3

WP—Humphries
LP—Passeau

Attendance: 20,819

Game 4

Sox	0	0	0	0	1	0	0	0	2—3
Cubs	0	1	1	1	0	0	1	1	x—5

WP—Bithorn
LP—T. Lee

Attendance: 3,360

Game 5

Cubs	0	0	0	0	0	0	0	1	0	1—2
Sox	0	0	0	0	0	0	0	0	1	0—1

WP—Passeau
LP—Lyons

Attendance: 5,963

Game 6

Cubs	0	0	1	0	0	0	0	0	0—1
Sox	0	0	0	2	1	0	1	0	x—4

WP—Humphries
LP—Warneke

Attendance: 7,599

The Boys' Benefit Games and The Crosstown Classic

Following the cancellation of the City Series, the White Sox and Cubs continued to meet in preseason games, many of them staged in cold April weather as a prelude to Opening Day. In 1949 the rivalry resumed with the first annual Boys' Benefit Game. The proceeds from the games were distributed to the various youth baseball leagues throughout the city and the selected charities the two teams sponsored. In those years, the Comiskeys donated their portion of the gate receipts to the White Sox Boys' Welfare Fund.

These mid-season Cubs-Sox matches were viewed by the fans as a battle for city bragging rights, although the managers generally took matters far less seriously, playing the veterans sparingly and bringing up unheralded rookie prospects from the minors, usually for a one-game audition. The players might have sensed their importance to the fans, however, as they played before large crowds at Wrigley Field and Comiskey Park in the steamy summer heat.

The Cubs, who fielded some terrible teams in the '50s and early '60s, used their underdog roll as a motivator, as the Sox had done through much of the City Series, and ended up on top in the final won-and-lost record (13–10) when the games ended in 1972. In 1981 Chicago mayor Jane Byrne sponsored a two-game charity series (resulting in a tie for the White Sox at Comiskey Park and a loss at Wrigley Field) on August 7–8, following the long and contentious player strike that year. But that was it until the Sox and Cubs resumed their intercity rivalry in the Crosstown Classic, which later became known as the Windy City Classic. The Sox brought their perceived second-team status to the ballpark for these encounters. However, these Cubs teams failed to knock the chip off the White Sox's shoulder. The Sox compiled a perfect record in these encounters in the years before interleague play began in 1997. All in all, it was a most satisfying run for the Sox as the North Siders lost 10 games and tied two.

Friendly crosstown rivals: Eddie Stanky and Leo Durocher settle bragging rights, 1966.

Beginning in 1997 there would be no more exhibition game preseason excuses—these next games were for keeps. Through the 2010 season, the Sox owned a 41–37 advantage in interleague play.

Boys' Benefit Games (1949–1972)

1949

Cubs 4, White Sox 2

Comiskey Park, July 11
Attendance—36,459

In a battle of southpaws, Johnny "Bear Tracks" Schmitz bested Bob "the Sarge" Kuzava, in the inaugural Boys' Benefit game to benefit the Chicago Park District playground facilities. Whereas the Sox missed numerous scoring opportunities, posting a base runner in all but one inning, the Cubs made the most of the opportunities handed to them by a wild and erratic Kuzava—three walks and a balk—plating three runners.

Cubs	1	0	2	1	0	0	0	0	0—4
Sox	0	1	0	1	0	0	0	0	0—2

WP—Schmitz
LP—Kuzava

1950

No game played—All-Star Game held at Comiskey Park

1951

White Sox 3, Cubs 2

Comiskey Park, July 9
Attendance—22,109

Outfielder Bud Stewart's first-inning, three-run homer off Bob Rush gave the White Sox all the runs they needed as they held on for a 3–2 win. Cubs catcher Mickey Owen grounded into a game-ending double play. Owen viewed the twin killing from the seat of his pants at home plate, where he landed after stumbling out of the batter's box.

Cubs	0	0	0	0	0	0	0	2	0—2
Sox	3	0	0	0	0	0	0	0	x—3

WP—Kretlow
LP—Rush

HR—Stewart (Sox)

1952

White Sox 5, Cubs 4

Comiskey Park, June 26
Attendance—32,405

After the Cubs knotted the game at 3 with two unearned runs in the top of the eighth, the Sox forged ahead for good with two runs in their half on Phil Masi's RBI triple and Sam Mele's base hit. Second-sacker Nellie Fox slugged his first career homer at Comiskey Park, staking the Sox to an early 3–1 lead. Luckless Howard Kolls Judson, who had pitched only 16 innings all year, tossed a complete game.

Cubs	1	0	0	0	0	0	0	2	1—4
Sox	2	1	0	0	0	0	0	2	x—5

WP—Judson
LP—Schultz

HR—Fox (Sox), Dente (Sox), Addis (Cubs)

1953

Cubs 4, White Sox 2

Wrigley Field, July 2
Attendance—12,403

In the first Boys' Benefit Game to be played in Wrigley Field, Cubs rookie right-hander Duke Simpson pitched seven innings of shutout ball and drove in what turned out to be the winning run with an RBI single in the fourth off Bob Keegan. Seven-time home run champ Ralph Kiner tagged a round-tripper in the third. Ex-Sox outfielder George "Catfish" Metkovich cleared the Wrigley Field ivy in the eighth, and Sam Mele pulled the Sox closer with a ninth inning blast, but it wasn't enough.

Sox	0	0	0	0	0	0	0	1	1—2
Cubs	1	0	1	1	0	0	0	1	x—4

WP—Simpson
LP—Keegan

HR—Kiner (Cubs), Metkovich (Cubs), Mele (Sox)

1954

Cubs 7, White Sox 6

Comiskey Park, July 1
Attendance—22,755

Ernie Banks' two-out, ninth-inning squibbler off shortstop Freddie Marsh's glove sent Hank Sauer scooting home with the winning run, capping a late Cubs rally. Sauer's RBI single and Ralph Kiner's pinch-hit homer off of veteran Sox reliever Harry Dorish knotted the game at 6 in the eighth. The game was interrupted when a near riot occurred in the center-field bleachers of Comiskey Park after Captain Rob Welling and Sergeant John L. Sullivan of the Deering Police District and a contingent of blue coats hustled nine bookmakers off to jail for clocking illegal bets. The bleacher crowd was unsympathetic and unruly as they hurled coffee cups at the police and chanted "Leave 'em alone!" The betting action in the cheap seats of old Comiskey was always legendary.

Cubs	0	4	0	0	0	0	1	1	1—7
Sox	0	0	0	4	0	2	0	0	0—6

WP—Klippstein
LP—Dorish

HR—Baker (Cubs), Kiner (Cubs)

1955

Cubs 7, White Sox 6 (10 Innings)

Comiskey Park, August 15
Attendance—26,028

With a time limit set because the Cubs had to catch a train to Cincinnati, their shortstop Eddie Miksis ("Miksis will fix us") and reliever "Fireman" Bill Tremel provided the heroics in a 10-inning barnburner. Mike Fornieles and Bob Keegan pitched brilliantly for the Pale Hose through the first five innings. But after Bob Speake worked Sox pitcher Jack Harshman for a two-out, 10th-inning walk, Miksis, on an 0–2 count, won it with a home run to left. With a run in and two on, Tremel put out the fire in the Sox half of the 10th.

Cubs	0	0	0	0	0	2	0	2	1	2—7
Sox	0	0	0	2	0	0	0	3	0	1—6

WP—Kaiser
LP—Harshman

HR—Miksis (Cubs)

1956

White Sox 4, Cubs 0

Comiskey Park, August 13
Attendance—23,438

Spot starter Millard "Dixie" Howell, scattering five hits and walking one, shut out the Cubs 4–0 to snap a Pale Hose three-game losing streak. Twenty-one-year-old Trinity College alum Moe Drabowsky, in his debut, had a rocky start, hitting two batters and issuing three walks in a two-run White Sox first. After that, he settled down, blanking the South Siders on two hits over the next six innings.

Cubs	0	0	0	0	0	0	0	0	0—0
Sox	2	0	0	0	0	0	0	2	x—4

WP—Howell
LP—Drabowsky

1957

Cubs 2, White Sox 0

Comiskey Park, August 12
Attendance—20,111

This was the game of "futures." The starting left fielder for the Cubs in the 1957 game was future Sox manager Chuck Tanner, who collected a hit and a walk for the day. Future Sox hurlers Jim Brosnan (who arrived in 1963) and ace reliever Turk Lown (1959–1962) combined on a three-hit shutout. Cubs outfielder Bob Speake scored both runs, driven home each time by Moose Moryn against Bill Fischer, a top Sox prospect who pitched seven innings a day *after* pitching three in relief.

Cubs	1	0	0	0	0	0	0	1	0—2
Sox	0	0	0	0	0	0	0	0	0—0

WP—Lown
LP —Fischer

1958

Cubs 1, Sox 0 Comiskey Park, June 16
Attendance—21,804

One week removed from his high school graduation, 18-year-old bonus baby Dick Ellsworth blanked the White Sox on four hits. Newly acquired Sox right-hander Bob Shaw (who had come over from Detroit just one day earlier in a big June trade) made his White Sox debut, giving up the only run of the game on three walks and a Moose Moryn base hit. Possessing a decent sinkerball, Ellsworth would toil for some dismal Cubs teams, accumulating an 84–110 record over seven seasons on the North Side.

Cubs	0	0	0	0	0	0	0	1	0—1
Sox	0	0	0	0	0	0	0	0	0—0

WP—Ellsworth
LP—Shaw

1959

Cubs 3, White Sox 2 Comiskey Park, June 22
Attendance—29,383

Starter Barry Latman disposed of the first two Cubs hitters he faced then lost it: a walk, an Ernie Banks single, then doubles from Moose Moryn and Bobby Thomson. In the Sox third, Cubs starter Bob Anderson also had the two-out jitters: a walk, then Harry "Suitcase" Simpson's double and a John Romano single. Romano, Norm Cash, and Johnny Callison—the three future stars of the 1960s the Sox let get away the next year—were in the starting lineup. Cubs relievers Seth Morehead and Moe Drabowsky shut down the Sox the rest of the way.

Cubs	3	0	0	0	0	0	0	0	0—3
Sox	0	0	2	0	0	0	0	0	0—2

WP—Anderson
LP—Latman

1960

White Sox 7, Cubs 0 (5½ innings) Comiskey Park, June 13
Attendance—28,408

A steady rain prompted the Cubs and White Sox to remove their regulars early. The game was subsequently canceled after five-and-a-half innings, the Sox on top 7–0. On the comeback trail, righty Herb Score pitched five scoreless innings and was aided by the non-rostered Mike Garcia, hanging on as a batting practice pitcher and struggling to catch on with the South Siders. Fenger High School alumnus Sammy Esposito punched a single and a double to key the Sox scoring.

Cubs	0	0	0	0	0	0—0
Sox	1	2	0	0	4	x—7

WP—Score
LP—Johnson

1961

Cubs 5, White Sox 1 Comiskey Park, June 26
Attendance—21,862

Cubs' hitters swatted 16 hits—15 singles and a double—in a 5–1 pasting of the Sox, who were in the midst of their 1961 12-game winning streak. Twelve of the Bruins' hits were off veteran Ned Garver, the ex–St. Louis Brown, who failed in his trial with the Sox after being waived by the Los Angeles Angels. Billy Williams, Ed Bouchee, and Jerry Kindall led the singles brigade with three hits apiece in a contest that featured some unruly young fans who were apprehended after tossing firecrackers at the feet of Cubs outfielders. George Altman stroked the only base hit—a first-inning ground-rule double that bounced into the center-field bullpen.

Cubs	2	0	0	0	0	2	0	1	0—5
Sox	0	0	0	0	0	1	0	0	0—1

WP—Brewer
LP—Garver

1962

Cubs 2, White Sox 1 Comiskey Park, May 14
Attendance—20,675

Rookie Dave DeBusschere, basketball star from the University of Detroit and a future NBA Hall of Famer, got the call from manager Al Lopez to start this one, and although he was wild, he was surprisingly effective for five innings. Billy Williams' triple, followed by Ernie Banks' sacrifice fly, broke a 1–1 tie in the eighth inning off of Russ Kemmerer to give the Cubs their ninth victory in 13 Boys' Benefit games.

Cubs	0	1	0	0	0	0	0	1	0—2
Sox	0	0	0	0	0	0	1	0	0—1

WP—Hobbie
LP—Kemmerer

HR—Roselli (Sox)

1963

Cubs 4, White Sox 2 Comiskey Park, July 1
Attendance—37,526

Erasing a two-run deficit, the Cubs erupted for three runs in the fifth and went on to beat the Sox and Indianapolis call-up Mike Joyce 4–2. This was the largest paid crowd of the 14 Benefit games played to date. Sox muscleman Dave Nicholson ignited the crowd with a two-run shot off of Dick LeMay into the left-field upper deck. But, in the bottom of the ninth with two on and two out, he rolled into a fielder's choice.

Cubs	0	0	0	0	3	1	0	0	0—4
Sox	0	0	2	0	0	0	0	0	0—2

WP—Brewer
LP—Joyce

HR—Nicholson (Sox), Williams (Cubs)

1964

White Sox 11, Cubs 1

Comiskey Park, June 26
Attendance—52,712

The largest crowd ever to view a crosstown match—52,712—watched the White Sox destroy the Cubs 11–1. Spilling onto the field, the fans were allowed to occupy a roped-off section along the center-field and right-field warning track. Overloading the exploding scoreboard, Ron Hansen, Tommy McCraw, and Gerry McNertney socked successive circuit breakers for the Sox in the third. Floyd Robinson kept the park vibrating with a four-bagger in the sixth. Ernie Banks broke the shutout with a blast off Frank Baumann. Then the Comiskey Park scoreboard erupted in tribute to "Mr. Cub."

Sox	0	1	6	1	0	1	0	0	2—11
Cubs	0	0	0	0	0	1	0	0	0—1

WP—Kruetzer
LP—Scott

HR—Banks (Cubs), Hansen (Sox), McCraw (Sox), McNertney (Sox), Robinson (Sox)

1965

White Sox 7, Cubs 2

Comiskey Park, July 26
Attendance—37,470

Just back from the Sox's disabled list, Juan Pizarro hurled five innings of shutout ball. J.C. Martin slugged a two-run homer off another returning DLer, the infamous Ernie Broglio (of Broglio-for-Lou Brock trade infamy), in a Sox four-run sixth. Chipping in, Pete Ward celebrated his 26th birthday with three base hits.

Cubs	0	0	0	0	0	0	0	1	1—2
Sox	0	0	1	0	0	4	0	2	x—7

WP—Pizarro
LP— Broglio

HR—Martin (Sox), Bailey (Cubs)

1966

White Sox 5, Cubs 4

Comiskey Park, July 25
Attendance—47,064

Before a near-capacity crowd at Comiskey Park—the second largest of the series—outfielder and 1966 Rookie of the Year Tommie Agee put on a one-man show in a thrilling 5–4 White Sox victory. Agee terminated a Cubs two-run first, doubling Ron Santo off first base on Ernie Banks' fly ball. He ended another threat in the fourth with a great running catch against the center-field wall. At the plate, Agee slugged a sixth-inning homer off Billy Hoeft for the fifth and final run. The presence of Sox manager Eddie Stanky, together again with his former boss Leo Durocher (now managing for the Cubs) for the first time in 13 years, was an added attraction for the fans. In the sixth inning, Durocher decided to coach third base—whereby the pugnacious Stanky had his players shower Leo with baseballs from the Sox dugout. Durocher retrieved the balls and threw them to the fans. Sox general manager Ed Short said afterward he was going to send Durocher a bill for $12.

Sox	0	0	4	0	0	1	0	0	0—5
Cubs	2	0	0	0	0	0	2	0	0—4

WP—Pizarro
LP—Hands

HR—Ward (Sox), Agee (Sox)

1967

White Sox 2, Cubs 0

Comiskey Park, June 22
Attendance—39,443

Four White Sox southpaws—rookie Fred Klages, the veteran Tommy John, Lynchburg call-up Andy Rubilotta, and knuckleballer Wilbur Wood—whitewashed the Cubs on five base hits. Eddie Stanky's dead-ball Sox socked 10 singles themselves. In the first, Ken Berry singled, stole second, then came around on Tommy McCraw's hit. Seven innings later, ex-Cub Jim King (3–4) tallied on two infield nubbers and a sacrifice fly. The ancient Smoky Burgess, pinch-hitter extraordinaire, gave the partisan Sox crowd a rare treat by catching the first three innings of the game, something he had not done in years.

Cubs	0	0	0	0	0	0	0	0	0—0
Sox	1	0	0	0	0	0	0	1	x—1

WP—Klages
LP —Koonce

1968

White Sox 1, Cubs 0

Comiskey Park, July 10
Attendance—23,994

A dismal second-division Sox team gained their fifth straight Boys' Benefit win, blanking the Cubs for the second year in a row to narrow the gap to one (10–9) in the overall competition. The lone run was unearned. With one down in the seventh, Tommy Davis singled and Buddy Bradford walked. Both runners advanced on a wild pitch by rookie hurler Darcy Fast. Sandy Alomar then lifted a popup to short right. Second baseman Lee Elia backpedaled, camped under the ball and dropped it, allowing Davis to score.

Sox	0	0	0	0	0	0	1	0	0—1
Cubs	0	0	0	0	0	0	0	0	0—0

WP—Smith
LP—Fast

1969

Cubs 2, White Sox 0

Comiskey Park, August 18
Attendance—33,333

Ernie Banks and Billy Williams slugged solo homers off 19-year-old rookie Bart Johnson, a call-up from the Appleton farm club, for the only runs of the game. After Banks' homer, the Comiskey Park scoreboard erupted, as it did in 1964, in honor of Mr. Cub. Cubs manager Leo Durocher had originally decided to rest his starters, only to change his mind under a storm of protest. The White Sox noted they had played their regulars in the games while they were involved in pennant races.

Cubs	0	1	0	1	0	0	0	0	0—2
Sox	0	0	0	0	0	0	0	0	0—0

WP—Reynolds
LP—Johnson

HR—Banks (Cubs), Williams (Cubs)

1970

Cubs 7, White Sox 6

Comiskey Park, May 21
Attendance—28,863

Jim Hickman sent a Gerry Arrigo fastball spiraling off the left-field rafters in the second inning. The Cubs then finished off Arrigo in a four-run fourth. This was a terrible year for the Sox. They lost 106 regular season games and compounded their misery before the largest crowd they managed to draw into Comiskey Park that entire season. A comely blonde slipped past the ushers and sat down in the Cubs dugout in the seventh inning. Umpire John Rice escorted her off the field amid a chorus of boos.

Cubs	0	2	0	4	0	0	1	0	0—7
Sox	1	0	0	0	0	2	0	1	0—4

WP—Reynolds
LP—Arrigo

HR—Hickman (Cubs), Hall (Cubs)

1971

White Sox 7, Cubs 3

Wrigley Field, June 24
Attendance—32,485

Down 3–0, the youthful White Sox team featuring rookies Bill Sharp (fresh off the Ohio State campus), Stan Perzanowski, Jim Magnuson, and Rich McKinney erupted for seven runs in the eighth inning at the Friendly Confines. Cubs relievers Burt Hooten and Ray Newman failed to retire a batter, issuing two walks, two base hits, and a three-run McKinney home run. Phil Regan restored order but not before Jay Johnstone ended the festivities with a two-run homer into the left-field basket. Another rookie call-up and a future Hall of Famer, Rich Gossage, made his White Sox debut in this game.

Sox	0	0	0	0	0	0	7	0	0—7
Cubs	0	0	0	3	0	0	0	0	0—3

WP—Kealey
LP—Newman

HR—McKinney (Sox), Johnstone (Sox)

1972

Cubs 3, White Sox 1

Comiskey Park, August 14
Attendance—38,153

In the final Boys' Benefit Game, Billy Williams broke a 1–1 tie in the fourth with a solo home run off Dennis O'Toole. It was Williams' third Boys' Benefit home run, tops for all players. Mr. Cub, Ernie Banks, came out of retirement to play the final three innings at first base. He fanned in his only plate appearance.

Cubs	1	0	0	1	0	0	1	0	0—3
Sox	0	0	1	0	0	0	0	0	0—1

WP—Phoebus
LP—O'Toole

HR—Williams

The Crosstown Classic Series (1985–1995)

1985

White Sox 7, Cubs 4

Comiskey Park, April 29
Attendance—42,600

Resuming their mid-season encounters after a 14-year hiatus, the Cubs and Sox provided their fans with plenty of thrills in Ozzie Guillen's rookie season. After a Julio Cruz single and Harold Baines' double put the Sox in front, the Cubs knotted it on Keith Moreland's double and Jody Davis' hit. Ray Fontenot set the table for a big Sox seventh-inning rally, issuing two walks and an infield hit. Ron Kittle and Daryl Boston base hits cleared the bags. Both then tallied on Tim Hulett's triple. The next inning, Scott Fletcher's three-bagger made it a six-run Sox bulge. The Cubs fought back with two in the eighth, and, on three straight hits, brought the tying run to the plate in the ninth. But Gary Woods and Davey Lopes flied out, and Gary Matthews fanned.

Cubs	0	0	0	0	1	0	0	2	1—4
Sox	0	0	1	0	0	0	5	1	x—7

WP—Hickey
LP—Fontenot

1986

White Sox 3, Cubs 0

Wrigley Field, May 19
Attendance—36,043

Twenty-five-mile-per-hour northerly winds, combined with temperatures in the low 50s, left the hitters at the mercy of the pitchers at frigid Wrigley Field. Joe Cowley, the first of four Sox hurlers and the author of a 1986 no-hitter, gained the victory, fanning seven over five innings. In the sixth, doubles by Joel Skinner and Bobby Bonilla (the one who got away!) gave the Sox the only run they needed.

Sox	0	0	0	0	0	0	0	0	0—3
Cubs	0	0	0	0	0	0	0	0	0—0

WP—Cowley
LP—Hall

1987

White Sox 10, Cubs 6

Comiskey Park, May 18
Attendance—42,006

On a foggy night on the South Side, Daryl Boston and Greg Walker led the White Sox over the Cubs 10–6. Boston singled and scored in the first inning. Two innings later, he was on base (single) along with Ron Karkovice (walk) when Walker dropped an unseen double through the pea-soup sky. Boston opened the fifth inning with a solo homer; Walker closed it with a 465-foot shot into the bullpen. The Cubs made it interesting against closer Bobby Thigpen in the ninth, scoring all of their six runs. Joel McKeon replaced Thigpen and struck out Brian Guinn for the final out. Guinn, however, was batting out of order, having moved up a notch for Bobby Dernier, who had showered and left the park.

Cubs	0	0	0	0	0	0	0	0	6—6
Sox	1	0	2	0	3	4	0	0	x—10

WP—Citarella
LP—Lancaster

HR—Boston (Sox), Walker (Sox), Fisk (Sox)

1988

White Sox 6, Cubs 6 (15 innings)

Wrigley Field, May 26
Attendance—25,034

Satisfying both sides of town, the Cubs and Sox fought to a 6–6, 15-inning draw. Thirty-five players got into the fray. Two position players—Cubs catcher Jim Sundberg and Sox third-sacker Steve Lyons—toed the pitching rubber. Both yielded one hit in their two-inning stint. Before Lyons went to the mound, he put the Sox ahead in the 13th with an RBI single. Damon Berryhill answered with a leadoff homer, knotting the game at 6. Lyons and Sundberg then breezed through the final two frames.

Sox	0	0	0	0	0	0	0	0	0	0	0	0	0	0	0—6
Cubs	0	0	0	0	0	0	0	0	0	0	0	0	0	0	0—6

HR—Sundberg (Cubs), Berryhill (Sox)

1989

White Sox 5, Cubs 4

Comiskey Park, May 18
Attendance—35,522

The White Sox remained undefeated in Windy City play, edging the Bruins 5–4 in an error-filled contest, giving rise to seven unearned runs. Cubs outfielder Phil Stephenson, having problems with the ball in the air and on the ground, handed the Sox three gift runs. Second-sacker Curtis Wilkinson kicked Ron Kittle's grounder, enabling Carlos Martinez to score the winner. This was the last Cub-Sox contest to be played in old Comiskey Park.

Cubs	0	0	0	0	3	0	1	0	0—4
Sox	0	0	0	2	0	0	2	1	x—5

WP—Kutzler
LP—Damian

HR—Karkovice (Sox), Pasqua (Sox)

1990

White Sox 6, Cubs 5

Wrigley Field, April 23
Attendance—37,135

In a bang-bang play at home plate, Sox center fielder Dave Gallagher threw out Rick Wrona, who was trailing Domingo Ramos home on Dwight Smith's ninth-inning, two-out single, enabling the Sox to squeak by the Cubs 6–5. Sox utility man Steve "Psycho" Lyons played all nine positions. On the mound, Lyons faced one batter, Lloyd McClendon, who reached on an error. The peripatetic Lyons took the collar in five at-bats.

Sox	0	2	1	1	1	0	0	0	1—6
Cubs	0	0	1	0	0	0	2	0	2—5

WP—Kutzler
LP—Damian

HR—Karkovice (Sox), Pasqua (Sox)

1991

White Sox 7, Cubs 2

Comiskey Park, May 16
Attendance—41,620

At the new Comiskey Park, the White Sox began where they left off in the old one—trouncing the Cubs again. Seldom-used Cory Snyder propelled a two-run homer in the second inning, walked and scored in a three-run third, and singled home a run in the seventh. Sox "Smurf" Lance Johnson banged out four base hits.

Cubs	0	0	0	0	0	0	0	0	0—2
Sox	0	0	0	0	0	0	0	0	0—7

WP—Wickman
LP—Wilson

HR—Snyder (Sox), McGinnis (Cubs)

1992

White Sox 5, Cubs 0

Wrigley Field, May 25
Attendance—33,410

Class A recruit Larry Thomas blanked the Cubs over the first six frames. Two more Sox minor leaguers—Jeff Schwarz and Frank Campos—extended the goose-egg line. Cubs stalwarts Sammy Sosa, Mark Grace, and Ryne Sandberg went hitless against the young trio as the Sox improved their Crosstown record to 7–0–2.

Sox	0	0	0	0	0	0	0	0	0—5
Cubs	0	0	0	0	0	0	0	0	0—0

WP—Thomas
LP—Boskie

HR—Pasqua

1993

White Sox 4, Cubs 3

Comiskey Park, May 6
Attendance—34,862

Bo knows the Cubs fold, or so it was said. Bo Jackson's two-run, eighth-inning homer off Frank Castillo knotted the game at 3. Steve Sax (single) and Frank Thomas (double) quickly disposed of Heathcliff Slocumb and the Cubs in the ninth.

Cubs	0	0	1	0	0	2	0	0	0—3
Sox	0	0	0	0	0	1	0	2	1—4

WP—Schwarz
LP—Slocumb

HR—Ventura (Sox), Jackson (Sox)

1994

White Sox 4, Cubs 4 (10 innings)

Wrigley Field, April 7
Attendance—37,825

Rookie phenom, one Michael Jeffrey Jordan, applied the whammy to the jinxed Cubs. Luring more than 37,000 to Wrigley Field, Jordan played the entire game, helping the Pale Hose overcome a 4–0 deficit. The Cubs tallied all their runs off North Side alumnus Scott Sanderson in a third inning smorgasbord of errors, hits, and walks. (Jordan received an *E* when he overran a ball in right field.) Jordan singled and scored in the sixth. In his next at-bat, he laced one off of third-sacker Craig Worthington's glove, doubling in the tying run. The Cubs stranded two runners in the 10th, and the game was called. "Air" Jordan then flew to Birmingham to begin his short-lived minor league baseball career.

Sox	0	0	0	0	0	3	1	0	0—4
Cubs	0	0	4	0	0	0	0	0	0—4

HR—Vinas (Sox)

1995

Game 1

White Sox 6, Cubs 3

Comiskey Park, April 24
Attendance—23,470

Cubs leadoff man Brian McRae connected on Wilson Alvarez's first pitch for a home run, after which the game fell into the usual Sox pattern. Craig Grebeck's sacrifice fly tied the game in the second. Ozzie Guillen's bases-loaded single, followed by a Ray Durham fly ball put the Sox on top for good in the fifth.

Cubs	1	0	0	0	0	0	1	0	1—3
Sox	0	1	0	0	2	0	3	0	x—6

WP—Fortugno
LP—Meyers

HR—McRae (Cubs), Pratt (Sox)

Game 2

White Sox 6, Cubs 2

Wrigley Field, April 25
Attendance—19,404

Taking the second game of a post-strike tune-up, the White Sox made it 12 straight games without a loss (10–0–2) to close out their crosstown cousins in the final Crosstown Classic. As in the waning years of the City Series (1903–1942), Cubs fans seemed resigned to their team's fate as only 19,000 fans attended the contest. Frank Thomas tagged a three-run homer. Chris Sabo and Mike Devereaux of the Sox added solo shots. Jim Baldwin and rookie Mike Bertotti combined on a four-hitter.

Sox	0	0	0	0	1	3	1	0	1—6
Cubs	0	0	0	0	2	0	0	0	x—2

WP—Baldwin
LP—Sturtze

HR—Thomas (Sox), Sabo (Sox), Devereaux (Sox)

12

Trades, Acquisitions, and Sales

In the early years of the 20th century, professional baseball teams looked to the independent minor leagues to procure the top-flight talent necessary to build their rosters and remain competitive. Minor league players were acquired through auction, direct purchase, waiver deals, or working agreements in place with the owners of teams in the various circuits. The annual winter meeting featuring the exchange of headlining players during the December confab of owners did not become an off-season ritual until the late 1920s and early 1930s—the time when the "hot-stove season" truly came alive.

Because the White Sox were considered a "western team" long before baseball expanded into markets west of St. Louis, it followed that owner Charles Comiskey shored up his roster by transacting business extensively with minor league operators in Iowa, Minnesota, Missouri, Western Canada, and the Dakotas, while occasionally reaching out into the distant hinterland of the Pacific Coast League.

The Old Roman often hosted the annual meetings of the Western League team owners at Comiskey Park in February. He formulated strong working relationships with old friends like Joseph Cantillon (1861–1930) of Janesville, Wisconsin, a successful entrepreneur with the Minneapolis team in the American Association, and Frank Isbell, his former Hitless Wonder second baseman, who purchased the Class A Des Moines team of the Western League in February 1912 and operated it as a quasi–farm team for his former employer, long before the system actually evolved.

Isbell, Cantillon, and others routinely sold their up-and-coming players to Comiskey and often agreed to take his veterans who were on the downgrade or approaching the tail end of their careers. The dearth of significant major league trades in the first two decades of team history makes it impossible to rank the Old Roman's "best and worst" player moves as easily as one could after 1930, when the modern farm system, the traditional winter meetings, and proscribed deadlines to complete trades were established and took root.

White Sox general managers, unlike other teams who practice a revolving-door policy of hiring and firing these men at will, have enjoyed greater job longevity than their counterparts. With the exception of Leslie O'Connor, Charley Comiskey, Hank Greenberg, Ken "Hawk" Harrelson, and Larry Himes, who were not around long enough for us to formulate a lengthy "best and worst" list for them (although Greenberg's disastrous 1960 trades ruined the team for decades to come), I offer on the following pages a "top five" list of the best and worst trades for each GM with more than five years of service to the White Sox organization, beginning with Harry Grabiner in the 1920s.

Tom Seaver, moments after winning his 300th game in Yankee Stadium on August 4, 1985, was selected by the Sox in the compensation draft on January 23, 1984.

Harry Grabiner (1915–1945) Five Best Trades

Date	Player(s) Acquired	Player(s) Traded	Team	Comment
December 8, 1936	Thornton Lee, P	Jack Salveson, P	Cleveland & Washington	Tricky three-cornered deal involving Washington. The Tribe sent future 20-game winner Lee to Chicago for ex-Yankees washout Salveson. By far, the best deal pulled off by the Grabiner-Dykes regime.
March 18, 1938	Joe Kuhel, IF	Zeke Bonura, IF	Washington	Straight-up swap of the worst-fielding first baseman in the league to Washington for the best. Advantage: White Sox.
December 8, 1938	Taft Wright, OF, & Pete Appleton, P	Gerald Walker, OF	Washington	Grabiner and Dykes redeemed their earlier blunder of trading Dixie Walker by sending the disappointing "Gee" Walker to the Nats for a solid contact hitter and excellent fielder in Wright, who gave the Sox six good seasons.
December 9, 1941	Wally Moses, OF	Mike Kreevich, OF, & Jack Hallett, P	Philadelphia (AL)	Two days after Pearl Harbor, Grabiner acquired A's speedster Moses, a career .300 hitter, for the fading Kreevich. Moses replaced Kreevich in center field and pilfered 56 bases in 1943, then a team record.
February 7, 1941	John Humphries, P	Clint Brown, P	Cleveland	Thirties bullpen ace Brown was at the end of his line when the Sox traded him for seldom-used Humphries, who was in the Cleveland manager's doghouse and desperate for a chance to work regularly. Dykes had his eye on the lad for several years, and he gave the Sox five workmanlike seasons before moving on.

Harry Grabiner (1915–1945) Five Worst Trades

Date	Player(s) Acquired	Player(s) Traded	Team	Comment
February 28, 1929	Martin Autry, C	Bibb Falk, OF	Cleveland	Reserve catcher Autry lasted barely two seasons. Falk had three more years of .300 hitting left in him.
April 27, 1932	Red Kress, IF	"Bump" Hadley, P, & Bruce Campbell, OF	St. Louis (AL)	The hard-hitting Campbell emerged as a star outfielder with the Tigers, Browns, and Indians for many years to come. Hadley enjoyed great success with the Yankees.
December 8, 1939	Julius "Moose" Solters, OF	"Rip" Radcliff, OF	St. Louis (AL)	The power-hitting Solters gave the Sox one good year (1940) but was plagued by an incurable charley horse and then refused to report to the St. Paul club to regain his strength after the Sox demoted him in 1942.
December 2, 1937	Gerald Walker, OF, Mike Tresh, C, & Marv Owen, IF	Vern Kennedy, P, "Dixie" Walker, OF, & Tony Piet, IF	Detroit	Manager Dykes pulled the pin on this deal, sending away "Dixie" Walker, who went on to became the "People's Cherce" in Brooklyn from 1940 to 1947 for the light-hitting Tresh and "Gee" Walker, a good-hit, no-field fly-chaser who lasted only two seasons in Chicago.
May 17, 1931	Lew Fonseca, OF	Willie Kamm, IF	Cleveland	Classy third baseman Kamm ran afoul with the Comiskeys and was dealt for the fading veteran Fonseca, who transitioned into the Sox manager's chair for two awful seasons.

Aaron Robinson (left) for Billy Pierce was one of the best trades GM Frank Lane ever made.

Frank C. Lane (1948–1955) Five Best Trades

Date	Player(s) Acquired	Player(s) Traded	Team	Comment
October 19, 1949	Nelson Fox, IF 	Joe Tipton, C 	Philadelphia (AL)	The mother-of-pearl trade of all-time. Tipton, a .236 career hitter and backup receiver was out of baseball after 1954. Fox, just a so-so infielder with the A's, blossomed under the tutelage of Paul Richards and coach Roger "Doc" Cramer in Chicago. "Those first two years [in Chicago] were nothing," Fox said. "They hired Richards, and he brought some terrific teachers to Chicago. When Richards got to Chicago, they straightened me around."
November 10, 1948	Billy Pierce, P	Aaron Robinson, C	Detroit	And the White Sox were paid $10,000 cash by Billy Evans, the Tigers' front-office boss, on top of it!
September 30, 1949	"Chico" Carrasquel, IF	Fred Hancock, IF, & Chuck Eisenmann, P	Fort Worth (Brooklyn affiliate)	International League umpire Ed Tatler had tipped Lane off about a sensational kid shortstop named Carrasquel during the 1948 Little World Series. Lane sprung into action. Branch Rickey talked trades with Lane during a 1949 visit to Comiskey Park, and slowly the wheels began to turn. More discussion followed. Names of other players filtered into the talks, including Negro Leaguer Sam Jethroe, until Rickey finally caved and let Chico slip through his hands. The first of three great Venezuelan shortstops was now on board to kick off the first half of the Go-Go Era.
November 28, 1951	Sherm Lollar, C, Al Widmar, P, & Tom Upton, P	Jim Rivera, OF, Gus Niarhos, C , Joe DeMaestri, IF, & Gordy Goldsberry, IF	St. Louis (AL)	The trade that launched the "St. Louis to Chicago Shuttle." Brownie owner Bill Veeck was a favorite trading partner of Lane's, who sent Rivera away, then reacquired him in a straight cash purchase in 1952. It was a fabulous arrangement for Chicago, akin to the Yankees–Kansas City Athletics dealings until Veeck moved the Browns to Baltimore in 1954.
April 30, 1951	Minnie Minoso, OF, & Paul Lehner, OF	Dave Philley, OF, & Gus Zernial, OF	Philadelphia & Cleveland	Three-way trade with Cleveland. Minoso was a great acquisition, but Lane overpaid. By admission, he could have kept Philley, but threw him in to sweeten the deal when it wasn't necessary. Minoso put the "go" in "Go-Go," and when he was traded in 1957 by Charley Comiskey, the Sox received Early Wynn in return.

Frank C. Lane (1948–1955) Five Worst Trades

Date	Player(s) Acquired	Player(s) Traded	Team	Comment
January 28, 1953	Ferris Fain, IF, & Bob Wilson, IF	Eddie Robinson, IF, Joe DeMaestri, IF, & Ed McGhee, OF	Philadelphia (AL)	The brash and temperamental Ferris "Burrhead" Fain, a two-time AL batting champion, flopped in Chicago after being awarded the highest salary believed to be paid to a Sox player up to that point in time—$35,000 for the 1953 season. Hot-headed and willing to duke it out with anyone who crossed him, Fain was involved in a nightclub brawl in 1953 and missed half of the 1954 season with a knee injury. Robinson had tied a White Sox team home record in 1951 and would be a durable power hitter through mid-decade.
May 3, 1952	Sam Mele, OF	Jim Busby, OF, & Mel Hoderlein, IF	Washington	This was a case of giving up too soon on a player. Busby went on to play for a number of teams but always put up the numbers. Lane was enticed into making this trade by Mele's torrid hitting in the first few weeks of the '52 season while Busby was slumping, but future Twins manager Mele was traded after just one year.
February 9, 1953	Vern Stephens, IF	Hal Brown, P, Marv Grissom, P, & Bill Kennedy, P	Boston	A bad youth-for-aging-veteran exchange. Hal "Skinny" Brown would have a solid career with the Red Sox and Orioles. Grissom provided good bullpen work with the Giants, while Stephens supplied no offense whatsoever in the cleanup spot for the Sox. He was benched and then sold back to Boston on July 29, 1953.
May 7, 1949	Earl Rapp, OF	Don Kolloway, IF	Detroit	Months of haggling over the coveted rookie Rapp resulted in Lane shuttling the dependable Kolloway for this overrated Tigers prospect who played a grand total of 19 games for Chicago before he was optioned out to Oakland of the PCL.
December 6, 1952	Mike Fornieles, P	Chuck Stobbs, P	Washington	Not a terrible deal, but one that certainly misfired. Stobbs, acquired from Boston a year earlier, went on to be a solid starting pitcher for some bad Senators teams in the mid-1950s. With Ray Berres' guiding hand, he might have become a standout with the pitching-rich Sox teams of the 1950s. Fornieles, a 20-year-old out of Havana, was fair-to-middling before being sent to Baltimore on May 21, 1956.

Edwin Short (1961–1970) Five Best Trades

Date	Player(s) Acquired	Player(s) Traded	Team	Comment
October 12, 1966	Wilbur Wood, P	Juan Pizarro, P	Columbus (Pittsburgh Affiliate)	Malcontent Juan Pizarro for Woody ranks as one of the greatest trades in Sox history. Wilbur perfected the knuckleball with Hoyt Wilhelm as his mentor, and the rest, as they say, is history.
January 20, 1965	Tommy John, P, John Romano, C, & Tommy Agee, OF	Mike Hersberger, OF, Jim Landis, OF, & Fred Talbot, P	Kansas City & Cleveland	In this three-team trade with Cleveland, Short picked the Tribe clean. Agee was the 1966 Rookie of the Year. John became an ace, and Romano returned home to provide some needed punch to a weak-hitting lineup in 1965.
December 14, 1966	Walt Williams, OF, & Don Dennis, P	John Romano, C, & Lee White, P	St. Louis	This unsung trade landed the Sox the hustling "No-Neck" Williams—who hit a robust .304 in 1969. Romano batted an anemic .121 for the Redbirds in '67 and was retired a year later.
January 14, 1963	Hoyt Wilhelm, P, Pete Ward, IF, Ron Hansen, IF, & Dave Nicholson, OF	Luis Aparcio, IF, & Al Smith, OF	Baltimore	Losing Aparicio was tough, but the Sox received the nucleus of the entire team that would hold for the next five seasons. Wilhelm alone was worth the cost.
November 29, 1961	John Buzhardt, P, & Charley Smith, IF	Roy Sievers, IF	Philadelphia	Ray Berres worked wonders with Buzhardt, a chronic loser with the Cubs and Phillies who became an excellent No. 4 starter at the back end of the White Sox rotation and famous "Yankees killer" for the next four seasons. Sievers closed out his career in 1965.

Edwin Short (1961–1970) Five Worst Trades

Date	Player(s) Acquired	Player(s) Traded	Team	Comment
June 8, 1969	Gary Bell, P	Bob Locker, P	Seattle	This was a real clunker, one of several Short made in his final years as GM. Sinkerballing Locker hung around until 1975—he was a very good bullpen man.
October 15, 1964	Bill Heath, C, & Joel Gibson, P	Rudy May, P	Philadelphia	Acquired from the Twins' scrap pile by the Sox in the 1963 first-year draft, May went on to win 152 games with the Angels, Expos, and Yankees in a career that spanned 14 years. One consolation: the Phillies also failed to hold on to him.
May 28, 1966	Wayne Causey, IF	Danny Cater, IF	Kansas City	A solid, .270-plus hitter for close to a decade, Cater was traded for the light-hitting and rapidly fading Causey, who was gone after 1967.
December 13, 1969	Jerry Janeski, P, Sid O'Brien, IF, & Billy Farmer, P (did not report)	Gary Peters, P, & Don Pavletich, C	Boston	A cost-cutting move to be sure. The Sox were not drawing flies and rebuilding wasn't going so well. But Short should have received a lot more in return for Peters, the grand old veteran, than the "Wheat Germ Kid" Janeski and O'Brien, an erratic-fielding second baseman. The Sox were so bad, Farmer decided to quit baseball rather than accept the trade to Chicago.
December 15, 1967	Jack Fisher, P, Tommy Davis, OF, Buddy Booker, C, & Billy Wynne, P	Tommie Agee, OF	New York (NL)	This one really stunk. Agee, of course, led the 1969 "Miracle" Mets to a World Series title. It might have worked out better if the Sox protected Davis in the 1969 expansion draft, but they didn't. He was claimed by Seattle and played another seven years after that.

Roland Hemond (1970–1985) Five Best Trades

Date	Player(s) Acquired	Player(s) Traded	Team	Comment
December 6, 1984	Ozzie Guillen, IF, Luis Salazar, IF, Tim Lollar, P, & Bill Long, P	Lamarr Hoyt, P, Kevin, Kristan, P, & Todd Simmons, P	San Diego	Cy Young–winner Hoyt was in decline, but the trade was still a huge gamble for Hemond and not a popular one when it was announced. Guillen anchored the middle of the infield for a dozen years and led the Sox to the World Series as manager. Long wasn't bad as a spot starter and middle reliever, but the other two were washouts.
April 4, 1977	Oscar Gamble, OF, Lamarr Hoyt, P, & Bob Polinsky, P	"Bucky" Dent, IF	New York (AL)	It isn't often the Sox exchange players with the Yankees, and even rarer when the deal makes an actual difference. This one did. Gamble gave us that one good year, but the rookie Hoyt was the sleeper in the deal.
December 15, 1975	Chet Lemon, OF, & Dave Hamilton, P	Stan Bahnsen, P	Oakland	The "Bahnsen Burner" had a great year in '72 but wasn't effective after that. Lemon was a top-flight A's prospect the Sox shifted from third base to the outfield. He achieved stardom with "Veeck's Wrecks."
October 13, 1970	Pat Kelly, OF	Gail Hopkins, IF, & John Matias, OF	Kansas City	One of the first Roland Hemond deals, and it was a dandy. The Sox acquired a bona fide leadoff man and All-Star in the speedy "P.K."
December 2, 1971	Dick Allen, IF	Tommy John, P, & Steve Huntz, IF	Los Angeles (NL)	Arguably the most famous but controversial trade in team history. Hemond likes to say that "Dick Allen saved the franchise," but he also nearly brought it down. Tommy John is a Hall of Fame candidate who was winning big games long after Allen had moved on. The jury is still out on this one.

Roland Hemond (1970–1985) Five Worst Trades

Date	Player(s) Acquired	Player(s) Traded	Team	Comment
December 5, 1977	Bobby Bonds, OF, Thad Bosley, OF, & Richard Dotson, P	Brian Downing, C, Chris Knapp, P, & Dave Frost, P	California	Bonds was another “rent-a-player” luxury Veeck could not afford to keep and was dealt to Texas early in the ’78 campaign. Dotson was labeled the “next Tom Seaver” by overly enthusiastic White Sox scouts, but injuries ruined his career. Meanwhile, Downing was moved to the outfield where he evolved into a star-caliber player in more favorable surroundings.
December 10, 1976	Richie Zisk, OF	Rich Gossage, P, & Terry Forster, P	Pittsburgh	Forget Zisk’s memorable “South Side Hit Men” year. He was strictly a one-year rent-a-player. The “Goose” is in the Hall of Fame now and should have entered as a career White Sox player. ’Nuff said.
December 3, 1971	Jerry Rodriguez, C	Bill Robinson, OF	Philadelphia	Exactly one year earlier Roland Hemond acquired Robinson from the Braves for pitcher Barry Moore—a great trade at the time. But Robinson languished in the minors and was traded to the Phillies for minor league catcher Rodriguez, who never played a game for the Sox. Robinson lasted 16 seasons in the National League, his best years were with the Pirates, from 1975 to 1977, when he hit over .300.
July 18, 1984	Roy Smalley Jr., IF	Kevin Hickey, P, & Doug Drabek, P	New York, (AL)	An embarrassing trade. Drabek was drafted by Chicago in the 11th round of the 1983 Amateur Draft but ended up as the “player to be named later” in the Smalley deal. With the Pirates, he won 22 games in 1990, and for his career he was 155–134.
November 27, 1981	Steve Kemp, OF	Chet Lemon, OF	Detroit	Getting Lemon was one of Roland’s best deals. Trading him, one of his worst. Chester stabilized the Tigers outfield and was a vital contributor to their 1984 title run.

Ron Schueler (1990–2000) Five Best Trades

Date	Player(s) Acquired	Player(s) Traded	Team	Comment
November 11, 1998	Paul Konerko, IF	Mike Cameron, OF	Cincinnati	Cameron, a 1991 18th-round draft pick, had a decent career, but Paulie is a franchise player—a great team leader who ranks high on nearly every White Sox All-Time Top 10 list and was one of the cornerstones of the 2005 championship season. The irony? No one had ever heard of Konerko, a Dodgers castoff, when the deal was consummated.
January 12, 2000	Jose Valentin, IF, & Cal Eldred, P	Jamie Navarro, P, & John Snyder, P	Milwaukee	Power-hitting shortstops are at a premium, but Valentin was one of them, and he complemented a Sox lineup that relied on the longball. Eldred, before his career-ending injury, shored up a weak starting rotation for the 2000 Division winners. Navarro was a disaster with the Sox start to finish, and it makes us wonder: what were the Brewers thinking?
July 29, 1998	Jon Garland, P	Matt Karchner, P	Chicago (NL)	Making amends for the disastrous Sammy Sosa deal, Schueler added Cubs prospect Garland, one of the building blocks of the 2005 champions, for Karchner, who had enjoyed short-lived success as a Sox setup man and closer in 1997.
December 24, 1990	Tim Raines, OF, Jeff Carter, P, & Mario Britto, P	Barry Jones, P, & Ivan Calderon, OF	Montreal	"Rock" Raines was one of the catalysts that turned the improving Sox into a contender and division winner early in the decade. Indicative of Montreal's coming misfortunes was their willingness to allow one of their all-time franchise players to go so cheaply.
December 8, 1998	Chris Singleton, OF	Rich Pratt, P	New York (AL)	Who is Rich Pratt? He was the minor leaguer to be named later. Anytime you can clip the Yankees in a deal like this, raise your glass and toast your success. Singleton gave the Sox three productive seasons before moving on to Baltimore on January 29, 2002, in the Willie Harris deal.

Ron Schueler (1990–2000) Two Worst Trades

Date	Player(s) Acquired	Player(s) Traded	Team	Comment
March 30, 1992	George Bell, OF	Sammy Sosa, OF, & Ken Patterson, P	Chicago (NL)	The worst trade ever made in White Sox history—right up there with the Red Sox sending Babe Ruth to the Yankees and the stupendous blunders of Bill Veeck and Hank Greenberg in 1960. Credit Larry Himes with making a great trade to acquire Sosa from Texas in 1989. Raspberries to Schueler for not only repudiating Himes and dealing Sosa, but he sent him to the Cubs no less—whose popularity and franchise value soared as a result. The issue goes well beyond the home runs Sosa didn't hit for the Sox, but speaks directly to the larger off-the-field PR and marketing setbacks endured by the South Siders in the 1990s.
January 10, 1992	Steve Sax, OF	Bob Wickman, P, Melido Perez, P, & Domingo Jean, P	New York (AL)	Sax was at the tail end of his stellar 14-year career and a shadow of his former self. His performance in 1992–1993 was miserable, and he was released by Chicago on April 21, 1994. Wickman saved 267 games in a 15-year career with a variety of teams. Like the Sosa giveaway, this one makes you want to weep.

Ken Williams (2000–) Five Best Trades

Date	Player(s) Acquired	Player(s) Traded	Team	Comment
June 27, 2004	Freddy Garcia, P, & Ben Davis, C	Miguel Olivo, C, Jeremy Reed, OF, & Mike Morse, OF	Seattle	The veteran Mariners ace was a key pick-up on the road to a championship. He anchored the staff through 2006 and was the bait that landed Gavin Floyd from Philadelphia and then re-signed with Chicago in 2009. Former top-rated prospect Reed ended up back with the White Sox in 2010 after many struggles.
December 23, 2006	John Danks, P, & Nick Masset, P	Jacob Rasner, P, Brandon McCarthy, P, & David Paisano, OF	Texas	Everyone in White Sox Nation was worried that McCarthy was just too valuable a prospect to give up on, when it was the Texas Rangers who should have been expressing the same concerns over their rookie, Danks—but they didn't, thank goodness, and Johnny blossomed into a great No. 2 starter in 2008.
December 6, 2006	Gavin Floyd, P, & Gio Gonzalez, P	Freddy Garcia, P	Philadelphia	Garcia enjoyed a career year in 2006 but was traded for two kids no one in Chicago had ever heard of. Then Freddy suffered shoulder tendinitis. Gavin Floyd answered the "Who's he?" question in 2008, his breakout year, by which time Freddy was already out of the Phillies organization.
March 20, 2006	Matt Thornton, P	Joe Borchard, OF	Seattle	Williams took Seattle to the cleaners a second time with this gem. Pitching coach Don Cooper worked his magic with Thornton and corrected some flaws in his delivery and became the best setup man Sox fans had seen in many years. Borchard was out of baseball a few years later.
July 31, 2004	Jose Contreras, P	Esteban Loiaza, P	New York (AL)	Contreras won a club-record 17 straight games from August 21, 2005, through July 4, 2006. He won Game 1 of the 2005 World Series and provided many other fine moments before age caught up with him. This was a great trade.

Ken Williams (2000–) Five Worst Trades

Date	Player(s) Acquired	Player(s) Traded	Team	Comment
Jan 3, 2008	Nick Swisher, OF	Ryan Sweeney, OF, Gio Gonzalez, P, & Fautino de Los Santos, P	Oakland	What was the greater blunder? Acquiring Swisher for Sweeney and Gonzalez, or trading Swisher to the Yankees for four Double A rookies? Either way, the Sox lost out.
July 25, 2002	Jon Adkins, P	Ray Durham, IF	Oakland	This was the most recent "white flag" trade by a Sox GM. Hopefully it will be the last, and the Sox will always be buyers and never again have to trade away a talented veteran in his prime like "Ray-Ray."
December 13, 2001	Todd Ritchie, P	Josh Fogg, P, Sean Lowe, P, & Kip Wells, P	Pittsburgh	The trade was a wash. Ritchie was a disaster, but the two vaunted Sox prospects, Fogg and Wells, didn't do much, either. Still, you have to wonder what Don Cooper might have done if he were around to improve their chances.
November 13, 2008	Wilson Betemit, IF, Jeff Marquez, P, & Jhonny Nunez, P	Nick Swisher, OF, & Kanekoa Texeira, P	New York (AL)	Getting Swisher was a bad idea; letting him go for three low-level Yankees prospects was worse. Swisher belted 29 homers in 2009 and made the All-Star team a year later. Betemit was terrible—but then got suddenly better with the Royals once he changed uniforms.
July 1, 2003	Carl Everett, OF	Frankie Francisco, P, Josh Rupe, P, & Anthony Webster, OF	Texas	Everett was a veteran presence who contributed to the 2005 title chase. But Francisco came into his own as the Rangers' closer in 2009 after ligament transplant surgery. Everett is long gone, but Francisco is still closing games for Texas.

Major Player Trades

1903, June 9
Infielder Tom Daly and outfielder Cozy Dolan to Cincinnati for infielder George Magoon.

1903, June 13–July 20
Pitcher Davey Dunkle to Washington (July 20) for outfielder Ducky Holmes (acquired June 13).

1909, May 16
Pitcher Nick Altrock, infielder Jiggs Donahue, and outfielder Gavvy Cravath to Washington for pitcher Bill Burns.

1910, August 10
Pitcher Frank Smith and infielder Billy Purtell to the Boston Red Sox for infielders Harry Lord and Ambrose McConnell.

1913, June 1
Infielders Babe Borton and Rollie Zeider to New York for first baseman Hal Chase.

1915, August 20
Outfielders Robert Roth and Larry Chappell, pitcher Ed Klepfer, and $31,500 to Cleveland for outfielder Joe Jackson.

1921, March 4
Outfielders Shano Collins and Nemo Leibold to the Boston Red Sox for outfielder Harry Hooper.

1927, January 13
Catcher John Grabowski and infielder Ray Morehart to the New York Yankees for infielder Aaron Ward.

1927, January 15
Pitchers Hollis Thurston and Leo Mangum to Washington for infielder Roger Peckinpaugh.

1929, February 28
Outfielder Bibb Falk to Cleveland for catcher Martin Autry.

1929, May 23
Outfielder Bill Barrett to Boston for outfielder Doug Taitt.

1930, June 16
Infielder Art Shires to Washington for pitcher Garland Braxton and catcher Bennie Tate.

1931, May 16
Infielder Willie Kamm to Cleveland for infielder Lew Fonseca.

1931, December 3
Infielder Johnny Kerr and outfielder Carl Reynolds to Washington for infielder Jackie Hayes and pitchers Bump Hadley and Sam Jones.
Pitcher Bob Weiland to the Boston Red Sox for pitcher Milt Gaston.

1932, April 24
Infielder Bill Cissell and outfielder Jim Moore to Cleveland for outfielder Bob Seeds and infielder Johnny Hodapp.

1932, April 27
Pitcher Bump Hadley and outfielder Bruce Campbell to St. Louis for shortstop Red Kress.

1932, April 29
Catcher Bennie Tate and outfielders Johnny Watwood and Smead Jolley to Boston for outfielder John Rothrock and catcher Charlie Berry.

1932, December 5
Outfielders Johnny Hodapp, Bob Seeds, and Fats Fothergill and infielder Greg Mulleavy to Boston for pitcher Bull Durham and infielder Hal Rhyne.

1933, June 2
Pitcher Vic Frasier to Detroit for pitcher Whitlow Wyatt.

1934, May 12
Infielder Red Kress to Washington for infielder Bob Boken.

1936, May 5
Pitcher Les Tietje to the St. Louis Browns for pitcher Merrit Cain.

1936, December 8
Pitcher Jack Salveson to Cleveland for pitcher Thornton Lee who came to Chicago from Cleveland in a three-cornered trade with Washington that sent pitcher Earl Whitehill to the Indians.

1937, December 2
Pitcher Vern Kennedy, infielder Tony Piet, and outfielder Dixie Walker to Detroit for catcher Mike Tresh, infielder Marv Owen, and outfielder Gee Walker.

1938, March 18
First baseman Zeke Bonura to Washington for first baseman Joe Kuhel.

1938, June 11
Pitcher Billy Cox to the St. Louis Browns for pitcher Jack Knott.

1938, December 21
Infielder Boze Berger to the Boston Red Sox for infielder Eric McNair.

1939, June 2
Pitcher John Whitehead to the St. Louis Browns for pitcher Johnny Marcum.

1939, December 8
Outfielder Gee Walker to Washington for outfielder Taft Wright and pitcher Pete Appleton.
Outfielder Rip Radcliff to the St. Louis Browns for outfielder Moose Solters.

1940, December 16
Pitcher Jack Knott to the Philadelphia A's for infielder Dario Lodigiani.

Dixie Walker

1940, December 31
Catcher Ken Silvestri to the New York Yankees for infielder Bill Knickerbocker.

1941, February 7
Pitcher Clint Brown to Cleveland for pitcher Johnny Humphries.

1941, December 9
Outfielder Mike Kreevich and pitcher Jack Hallett to the Philadelphia A's for outfielder Wally Moses.

1944, December 12
Infielder Skeeter Webb to Detroit for infielder Joe Orengo.
Infielder Eddie Carnett to Cleveland for outfielder Oris Hockett.

1944, December 15
Pitcher Jake Wade to the New York Yankees for outfielder John Johnson.

1946, January 2
Infielder Fred Vaughn to Washington for pitcher Alex Carrasquel.

1947, June 14
Infielder Murrell Jones to the Boston Red Sox for infielder Rudy York.

1948, January 27
Outfielder Thurman Tucker to Cleveland for catcher Ralph Weigel.

1948, February 24
Pitcher Eddie Lopat to the New York Yankees for catcher Aaron Robinson and pitchers Bill Wight and Fred Bradley.

1948, June 2
Infielder Bob Kennedy to Cleveland for outfielder Pat Seerey.

1948, June 9
Pitcher Earl Harrist to Washington for pitcher Marino Pieretti.

1948, November 10
Catcher Aaron Robinson to Detroit for pitcher Billy Pierce and $10,000.

1948, November 22
Pitcher Joe Haynes to Cleveland for catcher Joe Tipton.

1948, December 14
Pitcher Frank Papish to Cleveland for pitchers Bob Kuzava and Ernie Groth.

1949, May 7
Infielder Don Kolloway to the Detroit Tigers for outfielder Earl Rapp.

1949, September 30
Minor league infielder Fred Hancock, pitcher Chuck Eisenmann, and $25,000 to Montreal (International League) for infielder Chico Carrasquel.

1949, October 19
Catcher Joe Tipton to the Philadelphia A's for infielder Nelson Fox.

1950, May 31
Infielder Cass Michaels, pitcher Bob Kuzava, and outfielder John Ostrowski to Washington for infielders Eddie Robinson and Al Kozar and pitcher Ray Scarborough.

1950, December 11
Pitchers Bill Wight and Ray Scarborough to Boston for pitchers Joe Dobson and Dick Littlefield and outfielder Al Zarilla.

1951, April 30
Outfielders Dave Philley and Gus Zernial to Philadelphia for outfielders Paul Lehner and Minnie Minoso (coming from Cleveland in a three-way trade).

1951, May 16
Pitcher Bob Cain to Detroit for pitcher Saul Rogovin.

1951, October 24
Infielder Floyd Baker to Washington for infielder Willie Miranda.

1951, November 28
Outfielder Jim Rivera, infielders Joe DeMaestri and Gordie Goldsberry, and catcher Gus Niarhos to the St. Louis Browns for catcher Sherm Lollar and pitchers Al Widmar and Tom Upton.

1951, December 6
Infielder Rocky Nelson and cash to Montreal (International League) for infielder Hector Rodriguez.

1952, May 3
Outfielder Jim Busby and infielder Mel Hoderlein to Washington for outfielder Sam Mele.

1952, June 15
Infielder Willie Miranda and outfielder Al Zarilla to the St. Louis Browns for infielder Leo Thomas and outfielder Tom Wright.

1952, December 10
Pitcher Chuck Stobbs to Washington for pitcher Mike Fornieles.

1953, January 28
Infielders Eddie Robinson and Joe DeMaestri and outfielder Ed McGhee to the Philadelphia A's for infielders Ferris Fain and Bob Wilson.

1953, February 9
Pitchers Marv Grissom, Hal Brown, and Bill Kennedy to Boston for infielder Vern Stephens.

1953, June 14
Pitcher Lou Kretlow, catcher Darrell Johnson, and $50,000 to St. Louis for pitcher Virgil Trucks and infielder Bob Elliott.

1954, May 23
Infielder Grady Hatton and cash to Boston for infielder George Kell.

1954, December 6
Infielders Ferris Fain and Jack Phillips and pitcher Leo Cristante to Detroit for infielder Walt Dropo, outfielder Bob Nieman, and pitcher Ted Gray.
Pitchers Don Johnson and Don Ferarrese, catcher Matt Batts, and infielder Fred Marsh to Baltimore for catcher Clint Courtney, infielder Jim Brideweser, and pitcher Bob Chakales.

1955, October 25
Outfielder Jim Busby and shortstop Chico Carrasquel to Cleveland for outfielder Larry Doby.

1955, November 30
Pitcher Virgil Trucks to Detroit for infielder Bubba Phillips.

1956, May 21
Infielder George Kell, outfielder Bob Nieman, and pitchers Mike Fornieles and Connie Johnson to Baltimore for outfielder Dave Philley and pitcher Jim Wilson.

1957, June 13
Outfielder Dave Philley to Detroit for infielder Earl Torgeson.

1957, December 3
Outfielder Larry Doby, pitcher Russ Heman, and infielder Jim Marshall to Baltimore for infielder Billy Goodman, pitcher Ray Moore, and outfielder Tito Francona.

1957, December 4
Outfielder Minnie Minoso and infielder Fred Hatfield to Cleveland for pitcher Early Wynn and outfielder Al Smith.

1958, June 15
Outfielder Tito Francona and pitcher Bill Fischer to Detroit for pitcher Bob Shaw and first baseman Ray Boone.

1959, May 1
Pitcher Don Rudolph and infielder Lou Skizas to Cincinnati for outfielder Del Ennis.

1959, May 3
Infielder Ray Boone to Kansas City for outfielder Harry Simpson.

1959, August 25
Outfielder Harry Simpson and infielder Bob Sagers (assigned later) to Pittsburgh for infielder Ted Kluszewski.

1959, November 3
Infielder Ron Jackson to Boston for pitcher Frank Baumann.

Johnny Callison

1959, December 6
Infielders Bubba Phillips and Norm Cash and catcher John Romano to Cleveland for outfielder Minnie Minoso, catcher Dick Brown, and pitchers Don Ferarrese and Jake Striker.

1959, December 8
Outfielder Johnny Callison to Philadelphia for infielder Gene Freese.

1960, April 5
Catcher Earl Battey, infielder Don Mincher, and $150,000 to Washington for infielder Roy Sievers.

1960, April 18
Pitcher Barry Latman to Cleveland for pitcher Herb Score.

1960, December 14
Infielder Gene Freese to Cincinnati for pitchers Juan Pizarro and Cal McLish.

1961, June 10
Pitchers Bob Shaw and Gerry Staley, and outfielders Wes Covington and Stan Johnson to Kansas City for pitchers Ray Herbert and Don Larsen, infielder Andy Carey, and outfielder Al Pilarcik.

1961, November 28
Outfielder Minnie Minoso to St. Louis for infielder Joe Cunningham.

1961, November 29
Infielder Roy Sievers to Philadelphia for pitcher John Buzhardt and infielder Charley Smith.

1961, November 30
Pitchers Billy Pierce and Don Larsen to San Francisco for pitchers Eddie Fisher and Dom Zanni and outfielder Bab Farley.

1961, December 15
Pitcher Cal McLish, infielder Andy Carey, and minor leaguer Frank Barnes to Philadelphia for infielder Bob Sadowski and outfielder Taylor Phillips.

1962, June 22
Pitcher Russ Kemmerer to Houston for pitcher Dean Stone.

1963, January 14
Infielder Luis Aparicio and outfielder Al Smith to Baltimore for infielders Ron Hansen and Pete Ward, outfielder Dave Nicholson, and pitcher Hoyt Wilhelm.

1963, May 5
Pitcher Dom Zanni to Cincinnati for pitcher Jim Brosnan.

1963, December 10
Infielder Nellie Fox to Houston for pitcher Jim Golden, outfielder Danny Murphy, and cash.

1964, July 13
Infielder Joe Cunningham and pitcher Frank Kruetzer to Washington for infielder Bill "Moose" Skowron. Pitcher Carl Bouldin assigned to Sox later.

1964, October 15
Minor league pitcher Rudy May to Philadelphia for catcher Bill Heath. Pitcher Joel Gibson assigned to Sox November 24.

1964, November 30
Pitcher Ray Herbert and outfielder Jeoff Long to Philadelphia for infielders Danny Cater and Lee Elia.

1964, December 1
Pitcher Frank Baumann to the Cubs for catcher Jimmie Schaffer.

1965, January 20
Catcher Cam Carreon to Cleveland, outfielders Mike Hersberger, Jim Landis, and Fred Talbot to Kansas City for pitcher Tommy John, catcher John Romano, and outfielder Tommie Agee (three-team trade).

1966, May 28
Infielder Danny Cater to Kansas City for infielder Wayne Causey.

1966, June 12
Pitcher Eddie Fisher to Baltimore for infielder Jerry Adair.

1966, October 12
Pitcher Juan Pizarro to Columbus (International League) for pitcher Wilbur Wood.

1966, December 14
Catcher John Romano and pitcher Lee White to St. Louis for outfielder Walt Williams and pitcher Don Dennis.

1966, December 15
Outfielder Floyd Robinson to Cincinnati for pitcher Jim O'Toole.

1967, June 2
Infielder Jerry Adair to Boston for pitchers Don McMahon and Bob Snow.

1967, June 15
Outfielder Ed Stroud to Washington for outfielder Jim King.

1967, July 22
Catcher J. C. Martin (sent after the season) to the New York Mets for infielder Ken Boyer.

1967, July 29
Outfielder Jim King to Cleveland for outfielder Rocky Colavito.

1967, November 29
Infielder Don Buford and pitchers Bruce Howard and Roger Nelson to Baltimore for infielders Luis Aparicio and John Matias and outfielder Russ Snyder.

1967, December 15
Outfielder Tommie Agee to the New York Mets for outfielder Tommy Davis, pitchers Jack Fisher and Billy Wynne, and catcher Buddy Booker.

1968, February 13
Infielder Ron Hansen and pitchers Steve Jones and Dennis Higgins to Washington for infielder Tim Cullen and pitcher Buster Narum.

1968, June 13
Outfielder Russ Snyder to Cleveland for outfielder Leon Wagner.

1968, July 20
Infielder Wayne Causey to California for infielder Woodie Held.

1968, July 21
Pitcher Don McMahon to Detroit for pitcher Dennis Ribant.

1968, August 2
Infielder Tim Cullen to Washington for infielder Ron Hansen.

1968, December 6
Pitcher Jack Fisher to Cincinnati for catcher Don Pavletich and pitcher Don Secrist.

1969, January 20
Outfielder Bill Voss and pitcher Andy Rubilotta to California for pitcher Sammy Ellis.

1969, May 14
Pitcher Bob Priddy and infielder Sandy Alomar to California for infielder Bobby Knoop.

1969, June 8
Pitcher Bob Locker to Seattle for pitcher Gary Bell.

1969, December 13
Pitcher Gary Peters and catcher Don Pavletich to Boston for pitcher Billy Farmer (did not report), infielder Sid O'Brien, and pitcher Jerry Janeski (compensation for Farmer).

1969, December 18
Infielder Pete Ward to the New York Yankees for pitcher Ralph Scott.

1970, March 30
Pitcher Gerry Nyman to San Diego for pitcher Tommie Sisk.

1970, October 13
Infielders Gail Hopkins and John Matias to Kansas City for outfielder Pat Kelly and pitcher Don O'Riley.

1970, November 30
Outfielder Ken Berry and infielder Sid O'Brien to California for outfielder Jay Johnstone, catcher Tom Egan, and pitcher Tom Bradley.
Outfielder Jose Ortiz and infielder Ossie Blanco to the Cubs for pitchers Dave Lemonds and Pat Jacquez and infielder Roe Skidmore.

1970, December 1
Shortstop Luis Aparicio to Boston for infielders Mike Andrews and Luis Alvarado.

1970, December 3
Pitcher Barry Moore to the New York Yankees for outfielder Bill Robinson.

1971, February 8
Pitcher Jerry Janeski to Washington for outfielder Rick Reichardt.

1971, March 29
Infielder Tommy McCraw to Washington for outfielder Ed Stroud.

Earl Battey

1971, March 30
Catcher Duane Josephson and outfielder Danny Murphy to Boston for pitcher Vincente Romo and infielder Tony Muser.

1971, October 13
Pitcher Rich Hinton to the New York Yankees for outfielder Jim Lyttle.

1971, December 2
Pitcher Tommy John and infielder Steve Huntz to Los Angeles for first baseman Dick Allen.
Infielder Rich McKinney to the New York Yankees for pitcher Stan Bahnsen.

1971, December 3
Outfielder Bill Robinson to Philadelphia for minor league catcher Jerry Rodriguez.

1972, July 9
Pitcher Don Eddy and cash to San Diego for infielder Ed Spiezio.

1972, October 19
Outfielder Walt Williams to Cleveland for infielder Eddie Leon.

1972, October 28
Pitcher Vincente Romo to San Diego for outfielder John Jeter.

1972, November 19
Pitcher Tom Bradley to San Francisco for outfielder Ken Henderson and pitcher Steve Stone.

1973, August 29
Pitcher Steve Kealey to Cincinnati for pitcher Jim McGlothin.

1973, December 11
Pitchers Steve Stone, Jim Kremmel, and Ken Frailing and catcher Steve Swisher to the Cubs for infielder Ron Santo.

1974, April 27
Infielder Luis Alvarado to St. Louis for pitcher Ken Tatum.

1974, December 4
Infielder Eddie Leon to the New York Yankees for pitcher Cecil Upshaw.

1975, May 8
Outfielder Bill Sharp to Milwaukee for outfielder Bob Coluccio.

1975, June 15
Pitcher Stan Bahnsen to Oakland for outfielder Chet Lemon and pitcher Dave Hamilton.
Infielder Tony Muser to Baltimore for pitcher Jesse Jefferson.

1975, December 10
Pitchers Jim Kaat and Mike Buskey to Philadelphia for infielder Alan Bannister and pitchers Dick Ruthven and Roy Thomas.

1975, December 11
Infielder Bill Melton and pitcher Steve Dunning to California for infielder Jim Spencer and outfielder Morris Nettles.

1975, December 12
Outfielder Ken Henderson and pitchers Dick Ruthven and Dan Osborn to Atlanta for outfielder Ralph Garr and infielder Larvell Blanks.
Pitcher Rich Hinton and catcher Jeff Sovern to Cincinnati for pitcher Clay Carroll.
Infielder Larvell Blanks to Cleveland for infielder Jack Brohamer.

1976, May 18
Outfielder Carlos May to the New York Yankees for pitcher Ken Brett.

1976, June 15
Catcher Pete Varney to Atlanta for pitcher Blue Moon Odom.

1976, July 14
Infielder Rich Coggins to Philadelphia for outfielder Wayne Nordhagen.

1976, November 18
Outfielder Pat Kelly to Baltimore for catcher Dave Duncan.

1976, December 10
Pitchers Rich Gossage and Terry Forster to Pittsburgh for outfielder Richie Zisk and pitcher Silvio Martinez.

1977, March 23
Pitcher Clay Carroll to St. Louis for pitcher Lerrin LaGrow.

1977, April 5
Shortstop Bucky Dent to the New York Yankees for pitchers LaMarr Hoyt and Bob Polinsky, outfielder Oscar Gamble, and cash considerations.

1977, June 15
Pitcher Ken Brett and cash to California for pitchers Don Kirkwood and John Verhoeven and infielder John Flannery.

1977, August 18
Pitcher Larry Anderson to the Cubs for pitcher Steve Renko.

1977, August 20
Infielder Don Kessinger for pitchers Silvio Martinez and Dave Hamilton.

1977, December 5
Catcher Brian Downing and pitchers Chris Knapp and Dave Frost to California for outfielders Bobby Bonds and Thad Bosley and pitcher Richard Dotson.

1977, December 12
Infielder Jim Spencer, outfielder Tommy Cruz, and pitcher Bob Polinsky to the New York Yankees for pitchers Stan Thomas and Ed Ricks.

1978, March 30
Pitcher Steve Renko and catcher Jim Essian to Oakland for pitcher Pablo Torrealba.

1978, May 16
Outfielder Bobby Bonds to Texas for outfielders Claudell Washington and Rusty Torres.

1979, April 13
Pitcher Jack Kucek to Philadelphia for infielder Jim Morrison (assigned to Sox July 10).

1979, June 15
Infielder Eric Soderholm to the Texas Rangers for pitcher Ed Farmer and infielder Gary Holle.

1980, June 14
Infielder Alan Bannister to Cleveland for outfielder Ron Pruitt.

1980, December 12
Pitcher Richard Wortham to Montreal for infielder Tony Bernazard.

1981, March 28
Pitcher Ken Kravec to the Cubs for pitcher Dennis Lamp.

1981, August 30
Infielders Ivan Mesa and Ron Perry, outfielder Randy Johnson, and cash considerations to Minnesota for pitcher Jerry Koosman.

1981, November 27
Outfielder Chet Lemon to Detroit for outfielder Steve Kemp.

1981, December 11
Catcher Jim Essian, outfielder Rod Allen, and infielder Todd Cruz to Seattle for infielder Tom Paciorek.

1982, March 21
Pitcher Ross Baumgarten and Claude "Butch" Edge to Pittsburgh for infielder Vance Law and pitcher Ernie Camacho.

1982, March 30
Outfielder Cecil Espy and pitcher Burt Geiger to Los Angeles for outfielder Rudy Law.

1982, April 2
Outfielder Wayne Nordhagen to Toronto for infielder Aurelio Rodriguez.

1982, August 23
Infielders Leo Garcia and Wade Rowden to Cincinnati for pitcher Jim Kern.

1983, January 26
Pitchers Steve Trout and Warren Brusstar to the Cubs for infielders Scott Fletcher and Pat Tabler, and pitchers Randy Martz and Dick Tidrow.

1983, April 1
Infielder Pat Tabler to Cleveland for infielder Jerry Dybzinski.

1983, June 15
Infielder Tony Bernazard to Seattle for infielder Julio Cruz.

1983, December 6
Pitcher Jerry Koosman to Philadelphia for pitcher Ron Reed.

1984, June 21
Pitcher Jim Siwy (named later) to Cleveland for pitcher Dan Spillner.

1984, June 27
Pitcher Salome Barojas to Seattle for pitchers Gene Nelson and Jerry Don Gleaton.

1984, July 18
Pitchers Kevin Hickey and Doug Drabek (named later) to the New York Mets for infielder Roy Smalley.

1984, December 6
Pitchers LaMarr Hoyt, Kevin Kristan, and Todd Simmons to San Diego for infielders Ozzie Guillen and Luis Salazar, and pitchers Bill Long and Tim Lollar.

1984, December 7
Infielder Vance Law to Montreal for pitcher Bob James.
Pitcher Bert Roberge to Montreal for infielder Bryan Little.

1985, February 14
Infielder Roy Smalley to Minnesota for infielder Randy Johnson and outfielder Ron Scheer.

1985, July 11
Pitcher Tim Lollar to Boston for outfielder Reid Nichols.

1985, July 16
Infielder Tom Paciorek to the New York Mets for outfielder Dave Cochrane.

1985, November 24
Infielders Scott Fletcher and Jose Mota and pitcher Edwin Correa to Texas for pitcher Dave Schmidt and infielder Wayne Tolleson.

1985, December 12
Pitcher Britt Burns and infielders Mike Soper and Glen Braxton for pitcher Joe Cowley and catcher Ron Hassey.

1986, February 13
Catcher Ron Hassey and minor leaguers Matt Winters, Eric Schmidt, and Chris Alvarez to the New York Yankees for pitcher Neil Allen, catcher Scott Bradley, and minor league outfielder Glen Braxton.

1986, June 26
Catcher Scott Bradley to Seattle for outfielder Ivan Calderon.

1986, June 29
Pitcher Tom Seaver to Boston for outfielder Steve Lyons.

1986, July 23
Outfielder Bobby Bonilla to Pittsburgh for pitcher Jose DeLeon.

1986, July 29
Outfielder Ron Kittle, infielder Wayne Tolleson, and catcher Joel Skinner to the New York Yankees for infielder Carlos Martinez, catcher Ron Hassey, and catcher Bill Lindsey.

1986, December 10
Pitchers Gene Nelson and Bruce Tanner to Oakland for infielder Donnie Hill.

1986, December 22
Pitcher Bill Dawley to St. Louis for infielder Fred Manrique.

1987, January 5
Pitcher Pete Filson and infielder Randy Velarde to the New York Yankees for pitcher Scott Neilsen and infielder Mike Soper.

1987, August 26
Infielders Jerry Royster and Mike Soper to the New York Yankees for pitchers Ken Patterson and Jeff Pries.

1987, December 10
Pitcher Floyd Bannister and outfielder Dave Cochrane to Kansas City for pitchers Melido Perez, John Davis, Greg Hibbard, and Chuck Mount.

1987, March 26
Pitcher Joe Cowley to Philadelphia for outfielder Gary Redus.

1987, July 30
Minor league pitcher Bryce Hulstrom to St. Louis for pitcher Dave LaPoint.

1987, November 13
Pitchers Richard Dotson and Scott Neilsen to the New York Yankees for outfielder Dan Pasqua, pitcher Steve Rosenberg, and catcher Mark Salas.

1988, February 9
Pitcher Jose DeLeon to St. Louis for pitcher Rick Horton and outfielder Lance Johnson.

1988, August 13
Pitcher Dave LaPoint to Pittsburgh for pitcher Barry Jones.

1988, August 30
Pitcher Rick Horton to Los Angeles for pitcher Shawn Hillegas (named later).

1989, March 23
Outfielder Kenny Williams to Detroit for pitcher Eric King.

1989, July 29
Outfielder Harold Baines and infielder Fred Manrique to Texas for pitcher Wilson Alvarez, infielder Scott Fletcher, and outfielder Sammy Sosa.

1989, July 30
Pitcher Jerry Ruess to Milwaukee for pitcher Brian Drahman.

1989, August 3
Outfielder Mark Davis to California for pitcher Roberto Hernandez.

1990, April 30
Pitcher Bill Long to the Cubs for pitcher Frank Campos.

1990, July 30
Outfielder Ron Kittle to Baltimore for outfielder Phil Bradley.

1990, December 4
Pitchers Eric King and Shawn Hillegas to Cleveland for outfielder Cory Snyder and infielder Lindsey Foster.

1990, December 24
Outfielder Ivan Calderon and pitcher Barry Jones to Montreal for outfielder Tim Raines, pitcher Jeff Carter, and Mario Brito.

1991, March 31
Infielders Joey Cora and Kevin Garner and outfielder Warren Newson from San Diego for pitchers Adam Peterson and Steve Rosenberg.

1991, July 14
Outfielder Cory Snyder to Toronto for outfielder Shawn Jeter.

1992, January 10
Pitchers Melido Perez, Bob Wickman, and Domingo Jean to the New York Yankees for infielder Steve Sax and cash considerations.

1992, March 30
Outfielder Sammy Sosa and pitcher Ken Patterson to the Cubs for outfielder George Bell and cash considerations.

1992, August 10
Pitcher Keith Shepard to Philadelphia for infielder Dale Sveum.

1993, August 10
Pitcher Bobby Thigpen to Philadelphia for pitcher Jose DeLeon.

1993, July 31
Pitchers Johnny Ruffin and Jeff Pierce to Cincinnati for pitcher Tim Belcher.

1993, September 1
Pitcher Donn Pall traded to Philadelphia for a player to be named later.

1994, March 21
Pitcher Brian Boehringer to the New York Yankees for pitcher Paul Assenmacher.

1994, July 22
Pitcher Jeff Schwarz to California for catcher Bob Melvin.

1994, December 14
Pitcher Jack McDowell to the New York Yankees for pitcher Keith Heberling and outfielder Lyle Mouton.

1995, July 18
Outfielder Warren Newson to Seattle for pitcher Jeff Darwin (named later).

1995, July 27
Pitchers Jim Abbott and Tim Fortugno to California for minor league outfielder McKay Christensen, and pitchers Andrew Lorraine, Bill Simas, and John Snyder.

1995, August 25
Outfielder Mike Devereaux to Atlanta for outfielder Andre King.

1995, August 28
Pitcher Jose DeLeon to Montreal for pitcher Jeff Shaw.

1996, January 22
Pitcher Andrew Lorraine and minor league outfielder Charles Poe to Oakland for outfielder Danny Tartabull.

1996, August 22
Pitchers Luis Andujar and Allen Halley to Toronto for pitcher Tony Castillo and infielder Domingo Cedeno.

1996, August 31
Catcher Don Slaught from California for catcher Scott Vollmer.

1997, July 29
Designated hitter Harold Baines to Baltimore for a player to be named later, infielder Juan Bautista assigned to the Sox on August 18, 1997.

1997, July 31
Pitchers Wilson Alvarez, Roberto Hernandez, and Danny Darwin to San Francisco for pitchers Lorenzo Barcelo, Bob Howry, Keith Foulke, and Ken Vining, shortstop Mike Caruso, and outfielder Brian Manning.

1997, December 19
Pitchers Al Levine and Larry Thomas to Texas for infielder Benji Gil.

1998, July 29
Pitcher Matt Karchner to the Chicago Cubs for pitcher Jon Garland.

1998, November 11
Outfielder Mike Cameron to the Cincinnati Reds for infielder Paul Konerko.

1998, December 8
Pitcher Rich Pratt to the New York Yankees for outfielder Chris Singleton.

1999, February 9
Pitcher John Ambrose to St. Louis for pitcher Sean Lowe.

1999, March 25
Pitcher Jake Meyer to Cincinnati for catcher Brook Fordyce.

2000, January 12
Pitchers Jaime Navarro and John Snyder to Milwaukee for infielder Jose Valentin and pitcher Cal Eldred.

2000, May 29
Pitcher Tanyon Sturtze to Tampa Bay for infielder Tony Graffanino.

2000, July 29
Catcher Brook Fordyce and pitchers Miguel Felix, Juan Figueroa, and Jason Lakman to Baltimore for designated hitter Harold Baines and catcher Charles Johnson.

2000, November 7
Pitcher Scott Eyre to Toronto for pitcher Gary Glover.

2000, December 7
Pitcher Chad Bradford to Oakland for catcher Miguel Olivo.

2000, December 14
Pitchers Aaron Myette and Brian Schmack to Texas for infielder Royce Clayton.

2001, January 8
Designated hitter Harold Baines signed as a minor league free agent.

2001, January 14
Pitchers Mike Sirotka, Kevin Bierne, Mike Williams, and outfielder Brian Simmons to Toronto for pitchers David Wells and Matt DeWitt.

2001, July 26
Pitcher James Baldwin to Los Angeles for pitchers Gary Majewski, Onan Masaoka, and outfielder Jeff Barry.

2001, November 27
Infielder Herbert Perry to Texas for pitcher Corey Lee.

2001, December 13
Pitchers Josh Fogg, Sean Lowe, and Kip Wells to Pittsburgh for pitcher Todd Ritchie and catcher Lee Evans.

2002, January 29
Outfielder Chris Singleton to Baltimore for infielder Willie Harris.

2002, March 27
Infielder Edwin Yan and pitcher Matt Guerrier to Pittsburgh for pitcher Damaso Marte.

2002, July 25
Infielder Ray Durham to Oakland for pitcher Jon Adkins.

2002, July 28
Outfielder Kenny Lofton to San Francisco for pitchers Felix Diaz and Ryan Meaux.

2002, July 29
Catcher Sandy Alomar Jr. to the Colorado Rockies for pitcher Enemencio Pacheco.

2002, July 31
Pitcher Bob Howry to Boston for pitchers Frankie Francisco and Byeong Hak An.

2002, December 3
Pitchers Keith Foulke and Joe Valentine, and catcher Mark Johnson to Oakland for pitchers Billy Koch, Neal Cotts, and outfielder Daylon Holt.

2003, January 15
Pitchers Rocky Biddle and Orlando Hernandez, and outfielder Jeff Liefer to Montreal for pitcher Bartolo Colon and infielder Jorge Nunez. Hernandez was obtained briefly from the New York Yankees for pitcher Antonio Osuna and Delvis Lantigua.

2003, March 27
Pitcher Wade Parrish to Colorado for infielder Ross Gload.

2003, July 1
Pitchers Royce Ring, Edwin Almonte, and infielder Andrew Salvo to the New York Mets for infielder Roberto AloMarch.

2003, July 1
Pitchers Frankie Francisco, Josh Rupe, and outfielder Anthony Webster to Texas for outfielder Carl Everett.

2003, July 29
Pitchers Gary Glover, Scott Dunn, and Tim Bittner to Anaheim for pitchers Scott Schoeneweis and Doug Nickle.

2003, August 21
Infielder Tim Hummel (player to be named later) to Cincinnati for pitcher Scott Sullivan.

2003, December 2
Infielder Aaron Miles to Colorado for infielder Juan Uribe.

2004, March 27
Pitcher Matt Ginter to the New York Mets for outfielder Timo Perez.

2004, June 27
Catcher Miguel Olivo, outfielder Jeremy Reed, and infielder Michael Morse to Seattle for pitcher Freddy Garcia and catcher Ben Davis.

2004, July 18
Pitchers Jon Rauch and Gary Majewski to Montreal for outfielder Carl Everett.

2004, July 31
Pitcher Esteban Loaiza to the New York Yankees for pitcher Jose Contreras.

2004, December 13
Outfielder Carlos Lee to Milwaukee for outfielder Scott Podsednik, infielder Travis Hinton, and pitcher Luis Vizcaino.

2005, July 31
Pitcher Ryan Meaux to San Diego for infielder Geoff Blum.

2005, November 24
Outfielder Aaron Rowand to Philadelphia for infielder Jim Thome.

2005, December 7
Pitcher Damaso Marte to Pittsburgh for infielder Rob Mackowiak.

2005, December 14
Pitchers Orlando Hernandez and Luis Vizcaino, and outfielder Chris Young to Arizona for pitcher Javier Vazquez.

2006, March 8
Pitcher Jeff Bajenaru to Arizona for infielder Alex Cintron.

2006, March 20
Outfielder Joe Borchard to Seattle for pitcher Matt Thornton.

2006, June 15
Pitcher Javier Lopez to Boston for pitcher David Riske.

2006, July 23
Minor League pitcher B.J. LaMura to the Los Angeles Dodgers for catcher Sandy Alomar Jr.

2006, July 24
Minor League pitchers Tyler Lumsden and Daniel Cortes to Kansas City for pitcher Mike MacDougal.

2006, November 16
Pitcher Neal Cotts to the Cubs for pitchers David Aardsma and Carlos Vasquez.

2006, December 6
Pitcher Freddy Garcia to Philadelphia for pitchers Gavin Floyd and Gio Gonzalez (named on 12/7/07).

2006, December 16
Infielder Ross Gload to Kansas City for pitcher Andrew Sisco.

2006, December 23
Pitcher Brandon McCarthy and outfielder David Paisano to Texas for pitchers John Danks, Nick Masset, and Jacob Rasner.

2007, June 16
Infielder Aaron Cunningham to Arizona for infielder Danny Richar.

2007, July 27
Infielder Tadahito Iguchi to Philadelphia for pitcher Michael Dubee.

2007, July 31
Infielder Rob Mackowiak to San Diego for pitcher Jon Link.

2007, November 19
Pitcher Jon Garland to the Los Angeles Angels of Anaheim for infielder Orlando Cabrera.

2007, December 3
Infielder Chris Carter to Arizona for outfielder Carlos Quentin.

2008, January 3
Pitchers Gio Gonzalez, Fautino De Los Santos, and outfielder Ryan Sweeney to Oakland for outfielder Nick Swisher.

2008, July 31
Pitcher Nick Masset and infielder Danny Richar to Cincinnati for outfielder Ken Griffey Jr.

2008, November 13
Outfielder Nick Swisher and pitcher Kanekoa Texeira to the New York Yankees for infielder Wilson Betemit and pitchers Jhonny Nunez and Jeff Marquez.

2008, December 4
Pitchers Javier Vazquez and Boone Logan to Atlanta for catcher Tyler Flowers, infielder Brent Lillibridge, catcher Corky Miller, and pitcher Santos Rodriquez.

2009, March 22
Catcher Chris Stewart to the New York Yankees for future considerations.

Former NL Cy Young Award winner Jake Peavy joined the Sox in 2009 in a youth-for-experience trade with San Diego.

2009, May 29
Pitcher Lance Broadway and cash to the New York Mets for catcher Ramon Castro.

2009, July 7
Infielder Brandon Allen to Arizona for pitcher Tony Pena.

2009, July 28
Outfielder Brian Anderson to Boston for outfielder/infielder Mark Kotsay.

2009, July 31
Pitchers Clayton Richard, Aaron Poreda, Dexter Carter, and Adam Russell to San Diego for pitcher Jake Peavy.

2009, August 31
Designated Hitter Jim Thome to the Los Angeles Dodgers for infielder Justin Fuller.
Pitcher Jose Contreras to Colorado for pitcher Brandon Hynick.

2009, November 6
Infielders Chris Getz and Josh Fields to Kansas City for infielder Mark Teahen.

2009, December 15
Pitchers John Ely and Jon Link to the Los Angeles Dodgers for outfielder Juan Pierre.

2010, July 30
Pitchers Daniel Hudson and David Holmberg to the Arizona Diamondbacks for pitcher Edwin Jackson.

2010, December 3
Pitchers Scott Linebrink to the Atalanta Braves for pitcher Kyle Cofield.

Major Purchases, Waiver Deals, and Free-Agent Signings

1900, April 14
Outfielder Dummy Hoy signed as a free agent.

1901, March 1
Signed Colts (Cubs) pitcher Clark Griffith after he jumped his National League contract.

1901, March 14
Signed Brooklyn outfielder Fielder Jones after he jumped his National League contract.

1901, March 21
Signed Boston catcher Billy Sullivan after he jumped his National League contract.

1901, March 27
Signed Colts (Cubs) infielder Sandow Mertes after he jumped his National League contract.

1901, April 1
Signed Colts (Cubs) pitcher/outfielder James Callahan after he jumped his National League contract.

1901, July
Infielder Jimmy Burke purchased from Milwaukee.

1901, August 24
Pitcher Wiley Piatt purchased from the Philadelphia A's.

1901, October 24
Signed Colts (Cubs) outfielder Danny Green after he jumped his National League contract.

1903, January 18
Infielder Cozy Dolan signed as a free agent.

1903, February
Signed pitcher Doc White after he jumped his National League contract.

1903, July 7
Pitcher Nick Altrock claimed on waivers from the Boston Red Sox.

1906, May 10
Outfielder Eddie Hahn purchased from the New York Highlanders.

1906, July 6
Outfielder Patsy Dougherty purchased from the New York Highlanders on waivers.

1906, August 26
Outfielder Rube Vinson purchased from Cleveland.
Infielder George Rohe purchased from New Orleans (Southern League).

1907, August 1
Infielder Charles Hickman purchased from Washington.

1908, April
Infielder Freddy Parent purchased from the Boston Red Sox.

1908, September 23
Catcher Ossee Schreckengost purchased from the Philadelphia A's.

1912, May 8
Infielder Jacques Fournier purchased from the Boston Red Sox.

1912, July 10
Pitcher Ed Cicotte purchased from the Boston Red Sox.

1913, January 16
Outfielder Davy Jones purchased from Detroit.

1913, July 2
Pitcher Buck O'Brien purchased from the Boston Red Sox.

1913, August 25
Pitcher Red Faber purchased from Des Moines (Western League) for $3,500.

1914, August 8
Outfielder Oscar Felsch purchased from Milwaukee (American Association) for $12,000.

1914, December 8
Infielder Eddie Collins purchased from the Philadelphia A's for $50,000.

1915, July 7
Outfielder Nemo Leibold purchased from Cleveland on waivers.

1915, July 15
Outfielder Eddie Murphy purchased from the Philadelphia A's for $13,500.

1917, February 16
Infielder Chick Gandil purchased from Cleveland for $3,500.

1919, May 15
Pitcher Grover Lowdermilk purchased from the St. Louis Browns.

1919, August 6
Pitcher Erskine Mayer purchased on waivers for $2,500 from Pittsburgh.

1919, September 19
Pitcher Win Noyes claimed on waivers from the Philadelphia A's.

1920, July 23
Outfielder Amos Strunk purchased from the Philadelphia A's.

1922, February 4
Pitcher Jose Acosta purchased from Washington Senators.

1922, May 20
Pitcher Ferdie Schupp purchased from Kansas City (American Association).

1922, May 28
Infielder Willie Kamm purchased from San Francisco (Pacific Coast League) for $100,000 and pitcher Doug McWeeney.

1923, May 12
Pitcher Hollis Thurston purchased from the St. Louis Browns on waivers.

1930, July 18
Outfielder Bob Fothergill purchased on waivers from Detroit.

1931, April 3
Infielder Luzurne Blue purchased from the St. Louis Browns.

1932, September 28
Outfielders Al Simmons and Mule Haas and infielder Jimmie Dykes purchased from the Philadelphia A's for $150,000.

1933, May 9
Outfielder Earl Webb purchased from Detroit.

1934, May 15
Catcher Ed Madjeski purchased from the Philadelphia A's.

1935, January 22
Catcher Luke Sewell purchased from the St. Louis Browns.

1935, May 17
Pitcher Carl Fischer purchased from Detroit.

1935, June 4
Infielder Tony Piet purchased from Toronto (International League).

1935, June 16
Pitcher Jack Salveson purchased from Pittsburgh.

1935, September 20
Catcher Frank Grube purchased from the St. Louis Browns.

1936, April 11
Pitcher Clint Brown purchased from the Cleveland Indians.

1936, May 4
Outfielder Dixie Walker purchased from the New York Yankees.

1936, July 20
Pitcher Bill Dietrich claimed on waivers from Washington.

1938, May 2
Pitcher Frank Gabler purchased from the Boston Bees.

1939, April 27
Pitcher Edgar Smith purchased from the Philadelphia A's.

1940, April 30
Outfielder Myril Hoag purchased from the St. Louis Browns.

1941, January 4
Pitcher Joe Haynes purchased from Washington.

1941, April 30
Pitcher Lee Ross purchased from the Philadelphia A's.

1941, May 29
Outfielder Ben Chapman signed as a free agent.

1943, November 6
Infielder Hal Trosky purchased from Cleveland.

1944, December 30
Infielder Floyd Baker purchased from the St. Louis Browns.

1946, June 6
Pitcher Al Hollingsworth purchased on waivers from the St. Louis Browns.

1946, June 13
First baseman Joe Kuhel purchased from Washington.

1946, December 6
Pitcher Red Ruffing signed as a free agent.

1946, December 13
Infielder Jack Wallaesa purchased from the Philadelphia A's.

1950, February 9
Catcher Phil Masi purchased from Pittsburgh.

1950, June 27
Pitcher Gus Niarhos purchased from the New York Yankees.

1950, July 5
Pitcher Lou Kretlow purchased from the St. Louis Browns.

1951, May 16
Infielder Bob Dillinger purchased from Pittsburgh.

1952, July 28
Outfielder Jim Rivera purchased from the St. Louis Browns.

1953, March 6
Pitcher Earl Harrist purchased from the St. Louis Browns.

1953, March 18
Pitcher Gene Bearden purchased from the St. Louis Browns.

1953, May 12
Pitcher Sandy Consuegra purchased from Washington.

1953, December 8
Infielder Cass Michaels purchased from Philadelphia.

1954, May 24
Infielder Phil Cavarretta signed as a free agent.

1954, September 7
Pitcher Dick Donovan purchased from Atlanta (Southern Association).

1955, May 2
Infielder Vern Stephens signed as a free agent.

1955, June 8
Pitcher Dixie Howell purchased from Memphis (Southern Association).

1955, July 26.
Outfielder Bobby Adams purchased on waivers from Cincinnati.

1956, May 29
Pitcher Gerry Staley purchased from the New York Yankees.

1956, June 22
Pitcher Paul LaPalme purchased from Cincinnati on waivers.

1956, July 11
Pitcher Ellis Kinder purchased from St. Louis on waivers.

1958, June 23
Pitcher Turk Lown purchased from Cincinnati.

1959, May 13
Outfielder Larry Doby purchased from the Detroit Tigers for $20,000.

1959, December 11
Pitcher Mike Garcia signed as a free agent.

1960, May 18
Pitcher Russ Kemmerer purchased from Washington.

1961, May 10
Outfielder Wes Covington purchased on waivers from Milwaukee.

1962, June 25
Outfielder Charlie Maxwell purchased on waivers from Detroit (outfielder Bab Farley assigned to Detroit).

Pitcher Dean Stone purchased from Houston (pitcher Russ Kemmerer assigned to Houston).

1964, March 18
Pitcher Don Mossi purchased from Detroit for $20,000.

1964, September 12
Catcher Smoky Burgess purchased on waivers from Pittsburgh.

1965, July 7
Pitcher Frank Lary purchased on waivers from the New York Mets.

1965, August 23
Infielder Gene Freese purchased from Pittsburgh.

1965, December 1
Pitcher Jack Lamabe purchased from Houston (outfielder Dave Nicholson assigned to Houston later).

1967, August 15
Infielder Sandy Alomar purchased from the New York Mets.

1970, September 10
Outfielder Lee Maye purchased from Washington.

1970, September 11
Pitcher Steve Hamilton purchased on waivers from the New York Yankees.

1971, March 15
Pitcher Steve Kealey purchased from California.

1972, June 2
Pitcher Phil Regan purchased from the Cubs.

1973, August 14
Pitcher Jim Kaat claimed on waivers from Minnesota.

1975, April 5
Infielder Deron Johnson signed as a free agent.

1975, April 7
Pitcher Claude Osteen purchased on waivers from St. Louis.

1975, April 28
Catcher Gerry Moses purchased from San Diego.

1975, May 15
Catcher Jim Essian acquired from Atlanta as compensation for Dick Allen (signed by the Braves December 3, 1974).

Steve Stone

1976, November 24
Pitcher Steve Stone signed as a free agent. (Note: Stone was the first free agent signed by the White Sox following the Peter Seitz decision overturning the reserve clause.)

1976, November 26
Infielder Eric Soderholm signed as a free agent.

1976, December 2
Infielder Tim Nordbrook signed as a free agent.

1976, December 5
Outfielder Royle Stillman signed as a free agent.

1977, September 2
Outfielder Henry Cruz purchased from Los Angeles on waivers.

1977, September 8
Catcher Bill Nahorodny purchased on waivers from Philadelphia.

1977, September 23
Outfielder Bobby Molinaro claimed on waivers from Detroit.

1977, November 17
Pitcher Ron Schueler signed as a free agent.

Pitcher Jim Hughes signed as a free agent.

Infielder Ron Blomberg signed as a free agent.

1977, November 24
Infielder Junior Moore signed as a free agent.

1977, November 28
Infielder Greg Pryor signed as a free agent.

1978, April 5
Pitcher Jim Willoughby purchased from Boston.

1979, May 27
Catcher Milt May purchased from Detroit.

1979, December 4
Infielder Greg Walker selected from Philadelphia Phillies in the major league draft.

1980, November 21
Catcher Jim Essian signed as a free agent.

1980, December 6
Outfielder Ron LeFlore signed as a free agent.

1981, March 10
Catcher Carlton Fisk signed as a free agent.

1981, March 30
Outfielder Greg Luzinski purchased from Philadelphia.

1981, December 9
Pitcher Salome Barojas purchased from Mexico City Reds.

1982, December 13
Pitcher Floyd Bannister signed as a free agent.

1982, December 15
Outfielder Casey Parsons signed as a free agent.

1983, August 31
Infielder Aurelio Rodriguez signed as a free agent.

1984, January 23
Pitcher Tom Seaver selected in free-agent compensation draft.

1985, January 21
Pitcher Dave Wehrmeister signed as a free agent.

1986, April 15
Pitcher Bill Dawley signed as a free agent.

1986, August 12
Pitcher Steve Carlton claimed on waivers.

1986, August 15
Outfielder George Foster claimed on waivers.

1988, February
Pitcher Jerry Ruess signed as a free agent.

1990, December 20
Pitcher Charlie Hough signed as a free agent.

1991, April 3
Outfielder Bo Jackson signed as a free agent.

1991, July 15
Outfielder Mike Huff purchased on waivers from Cleveland.

1991, December 28
Pitcher Kirk McCaskill signed as a free agent.

1992, April 5
Pitcher Terry Leach signed as a free agent.

1992, August 6
Catcher Scott Hemond purchased on waivers from Oakland.

1992, December 8
Pitcher Dave Steib signed as a free agent.

1993, January 4
Outfielder Ellis Burks signed as a free agent.

1993, April 23
Catcher Mike LaValliere signed as a free agent.

1993, December 15
Infielder Julio Franco signed as a free agent.

1993, December 28
Outfielder Darrin Jackson signed as a free agent.

1994, March 1
Pitcher Scott Sanderson signed as a free agent.

1995, January 6
Pitcher Tim Fortugno claimed on waivers from Cincinnati.

1995, February 27
Pitcher Rob Dibble signed as a free agent.

1995, April 4
Outfielder Dave Martinez signed as a free agent.

1995, April 8
Outfielder Mike Devereaux signed as a free agent.
Pitcher Jim Abbott signed as a free agent.

1995, April 10
Infielder Chris Sabo signed as a free agent.

1995, May 14
Infielder John Kruk signed as a free agent.

1995, December 11
Designated hitter Harold Baines signed as a free agent.

1995, December 12
Outfielder Darren Lewis signed as a free agent.

1996, January 20
Outfielder Tony Phillips signed as a free agent.

1996, February 3
Pitcher Kevin Tapani signed as a free agent.

1996, February 6
Pitcher Joe Magrane signed as a free agent.

1996, July 27
Catcher Pat Borders signed as a free agent.

1996, November 19
Outfielder Albert Belle signed as free agent.

1996, December 11
Pitcher Jaimie Navarro signed as a free agent.

1997, January 14
Pitcher Doug Drabek signed as a free agent.

1997, December 7
Catcher Chad Kreuter signed as a free agent.

1998, January 9
Outfielder Ruben Sierra signed as a free agent.

1998, March 23
Infielder Wil Cordero signed as a free agent.

1998, May 31
Outfielder Jeff Abbott signed as a free agent.

1999, January 26
Infielder Darrin Jackson signed as a free agent.

1999, November 15
Pitcher Kelly Wunsch signed as a free agent.

2000, April 21
Infielder Herbert Perry claimed off of waivers from Tampa Bay.

2000, December 18
Catcher Sandy Alomar Jr. signed as a free agent.

2001, June 20
Outfielder/DH Jose Canseco signed as a free agent.

2002, February 1
Outfielder Kenny Lofton signed as a free agent.

2003, January 21
Pitcher Tom Gordon signed as a free agent.

2004, January 8
Pitcher Cliff Politte signed as a free agent.

2004, January 22
Pitcher Shingo Takatsu signed as a free agent.

2004, December 8
Pitcher Dustin Hermanson signed as a free agent.

2004, December 9
Outfielder Jermaine Dye signed as a free agent.

2004, December 17
Pitcher Bobby Jenks claimed off waivers from the Anaheim Angels.

2004, December 20
Infielder Pablo Ozuna signed as a free agent.

2004, December 22
Pitcher Orlando Hernandez signed as a free agent.

2004, December 23
Catcher Chris Widger signed as a free agent.

2005, January 6
Catcher A. J. Pierzynski signed as a free agent.

2005, January 27
Infielder Tadahito Iguchi signed as a free agent.

2006, November 3
Outfielder Luis Terrero signed as a free agent.

2006, December 17
Catcher Toby Hall signed as a free agent.

2007, January 25
Outfielder Darin Erstad signed as a free agent.

2007, May 21
Infielder Pedro Lopez claimed on waivers from Cincinnati.

2007, June 30
Catcher Gustavo Molina claimed on waivers from Baltimore.

2007, November 28
Pitcher Scott Linebrink signed as a free agent.

2008, January 22
Pitcher Octavio Dotel signed as a free agent.
Infielder Alexei Ramirez signed as a free agent.

2008, June 4
Pitcher Esteban Loiaza signed as a free agent.

2008, October 24
Infielder Jayson Nix signed as a free agent.

2008, December 12
Infielder Dayan Viciedo signed as a free agent.

2009, January 15
Pitcher Bartolo Colon signed as a free agent.

2009, April 14
Outfielder Scott Podsednik signed as a free agent.

2009, June 8
Pitcher Freddy Garcia signed as a free agent.

2009, August 10
Claimed outfielder Alex Rios on waivers from Toronto.

2009, October 21
Claimed infielder Alejandro De Aza on waivers from Florida.

2009, November 23
Infielder Omar Vizquel signed as a free agent.

2009, November 25
Outfielder Andruw Jones signed as a free agent.

2009, December 11
Pitcher J.J. Putz signed as a free agent.

2010, August 30
Outfielder Manny Ramirez acquired on waivers from Los Angeles (NL).

2010, December 2
Infielder Adam Dunn signed as a free agent.

2010, December 16
Pitcher Jesse Crain signed as a free agent.

2011, January 10
Pitcher Will Ohman signed as a free agent.

Players Released, Sold, or Lost to Other Teams

1901, March 17
Infielder Dick Padden "jumped" to the St. Louis Cardinals.

1901, September
Infielder Jimmy Burke sold to Pittsburgh.

1902, July 18
Pitcher Jack Katoll and outfielder Hermus McFarland transferred to Baltimore in an emergency league draft to allow the Orioles to complete the season.

1904, May 30
Outfielder Frank Huelsman sold to Detroit.

1904, June 5
Pitcher Patsy Flaherty released and signed by Pittsburgh.

1918, August 24
Pitcher John Picus Quinn awarded to the New York Yankees by the National Commission.

1923, May 31
Infielder Ernie Johnson sold to the New York Yankees.

1924, August
Outfielder Amos Strunk sold to the Philadelphia A's on waivers.

1925, December 31
Pitcher Charlie Robertson sold to the St. Louis Browns.

1926, July 6
Infielder Everett Scott sold to Washington.

1930, November
Outfielder Bill Hunnefield sold to Cleveland.

1931, April 2
Catcher Moe Berg sold to Cleveland.

1932, June 11
Pitcher Tommy Thomas sold to Washington.

1933, December 15
Catcher Frank Grube sold to the St. Louis Browns.

1935, December 10
Outfielder Al Simmons sold to Detroit for $75,000.

1938, December 20
Catcher Luke Sewell sold to the Brooklyn Dodgers.

1939, December 8
Infielder Marv Owen sold to the Boston Red Sox.

1940, December 18
Infielder Eric McNair sold to Detroit.

1941, May 29
Outfielder Larry Rosenthal sold to Cleveland.

1942, April 3
Infielder Bill Knockerbocker sold to the Philadelphia A's.

1943, November 24
First baseman Joe Kuhel sold to Washington.

1944, June 27
Outfielder Myril Hoag sold to Cleveland.

1945, December 7
Pitcher John Humphries sold to Philadelphia.

1946, July 23
Outfielder Wally Moses sold to the Boston Red Sox.

1948, February 2
Outfielder Rudy York released and claimed by the Philadelphia A's.

1948, November 15
Outfielder Taft Wright sold to the Philadelphia A's.

1948, December 14
Outfielder Jim Delsing sold to the New York Yankees.

1949, January 11
Catcher Mike Tresh sold to Cleveland.

1950, April 18
Pitcher Marino Pieretti sold to Cleveland.

1950, August 8
Pitcher Mickey Haefner sold to the Boston Braves.

1951, June 6
Outfielder Paul Lehner sold to the St. Louis Browns.

1952, June 16
Pitcher Ken Holcombe sold to the St. Louis Browns.

1953, June 11
Pitcher Tommy Byrne sold to Washington.

Eddie Stanky bids farewell to pitcher Jack Lamabe, sold to the Mets, April 26, 1967.

1953, July 31
Infielder Vern Stephens sold to the St. Louis Browns.

1959, May 9
Outfielder Don Mueller unconditionally released—then retires.

1959, June 15
Outfielder Del Ennis placed on waivers—then retires.

1960, June 13
Pitcher Ray Moore sold to Washington.

1960, December 14
Infielder Ted Kluszewski, catcher Earl Averill, pitcher Ken McBride, and outfielder Jim McAnany claimed by the Los Angeles Angels in the American League expansion draft. Pitchers Dick Donovan and Ed Hobaugh and outfielder Joe Hicks claimed by the Washington Senators.

1961, April 1
Pitcher Don Ferrarese purchased by the Philadelphia Phillies.

1961, May 9
Catcher Joe Ginsberg unconditionally released. (Signed by Boston on May 17, 1961.)

1961, June 6
Outfielder Jim Rivera unconditionally released. (Signed as a free agent by Kansas City on June 9, 1961.)

1961, September 2
Infielder Earl Torgeson claimed on waivers by the New York Yankees.

1962, May 9
Infielder Billy Goodman released and signed by Houston five days later.

1962, November 20
Pitcher Early Wynn released.

1963, April 8
Minor league pitcher Dennis McLain placed on waivers, claimed by Detroit a few days later.

1963, May 9
Infielder Sammy Esposito placed on waivers. (Signed by Kansas City on May 25, 1963.)

1965, October 20
Pitcher Frank Lary released unconditionally.

1967, April 26
Pitcher Jack Lamabe sold to the New York Mets.

1967, May 6
Infielder Moose Skowron sold to California on waivers.

1967, August 21
Pitcher John Buzhardt sold to Baltimore.

1967, October 13
Outfielder Jim Hicks sold to St. Louis.

1968, March 26
Outfielder Rocky Colavito sold to Los Angeles.

1968, May 2
Infielder Ken Boyer released; signed by Los Angeles on May 10.

1968, October 14
Outfielder Tommy Davis and catcher Gerry McNertney claimed by Seattle in the expansion draft. Pitchers Al Fitzmorris and Hoyt Wilhelm claimed by Kansas City in the expansion draft.

1971, March 24
Infielder Bobby Knoop sold to Kansas City.

1973, May 26
Infielder Rich Morales sold to San Diego.

1975, March 15
Pitcher Cy Acosta sold to Philadelphia.

1975, April 1
Catcher Ed Herrmann sold to the New York Yankees. (Sox also received three minor leaguers—none made it to the parent ballclub.)

1975, July 18
Catcher Gerry Moses sold to San Diego.

1975, August 1
Pitcher Lloyd Allen sold to St. Louis.

1975, September 21
Designated hitter Deron Johnson sold to Boston (pitcher Chuck Erickson assigned to the White Sox later).

1976, October 21
Catcher Phil Roof sold to Toronto.

1986, April 30
Pitcher Juan Agosto sold to Minnesota.

1990, August 1
Outfielder Dave Gallagher claimed on waivers by Baltimore.

1993, November 10
Pitcher Brian Drahman sold to Florida.

1993, November 30
Outfielder Ellis Burks signed as a free agent by Colorado.

1994, April 21
Infielder Steve Sax placed on waivers; claimed by Oakland April 30.

1995, June 3
Designated hitter Chris Sabo placed on waivers.

1995, July 16
Pitcher Rob Dibble placed on waivers.

1995, December 14
Outfielder Lance Johnson signed as a free agent by the New York Mets.

1996, January 23
Outfielder Tim Raines signed as a free agent by the New York Yankees.

1996, December 8
Alex Fernandez signed as a free agent by the Florida Marlins.

1996, December 13
Pitcher Kevin Tapani signed as a free agent by the Chicago Cubs.

1997, December 4
Outfielder Dave Martinez signed as a free agent by the Tampa Bay Devil Rays.

1998, November 13
Infielder Olmedo Saenz signed as a free agent by the Oakland A's.

1998, December 1
Infielder Robin Ventura signed as a free agent by the New York Mets.
Outfielder Albert Belle signed as a free agent by the Baltimore Orioles.

2000, December 18
Catcher Charles Johnson signed as a free agent by the Florida Marlins.

2001, January 5
Infielder Greg Norton signed as a free agent by the Colorado Rockies.

2002, January 10
Pitcher David Wells signed as a free agent by the New York Yankees after the White Sox declined to pick up his 2002 option.

2002, September 8
Shortstop Royce Clayton released. Signed by Milwaukee as a free agent on December 11.

2003, December 9
Pitcher Bartolo Colon signed as a free agent by the Anaheim Angels.
Pitcher Scott Sullivan signed as a free agent by the Kansas City Royals.

2003, December 16
Infielder Tony Graffanino signed as a free agent by the Kansas City Royals.

2003, December 23
Pitcher Tom Gordon signed as a free agent by the New York Yankees.

2004, December 31
Infielder Jose Valentin signed as a free agent by the Los Angeles Dodgers.

2005, February 7
Outfielder Magglio Ordonez signed as a free agent by the Detroit Tigers.

2005, August 1
Pitcher Shingo Takatsu placed on waivers and given his unconditional release.

2005, November 10
Infielder Geoff Blum signed as a free agent by the San Diego Padres.

2005, December 6
Designated hitter Frank Thomas declined arbitration by the club and was released. Signed by the Oakland A's on January 25, 2006.

2006, February 9
Outfielder Timo Perez signed to a minor league contract by the Cincinnati Reds.

2007, February 14
Pitcher Cliff Politte signed as minor league free agent by the Cleveland Indians.

2007, March 1
Pitcher Dustin Hermanson signed as a free agent by the Cincinnati Reds.

2007, December 7
Pitcher Ryan Bukvich signed as free agent by the Baltimore Orioles.

2007, December 27
Outfielder Darin Erstad signed as a free agent by the Houston Astros.

2008, February 8
Outfielder Scott Podsednik signed a minor league contract with the Colorado Rockies.

2008, July 20
Outfielder Pablo Ozuna signed as a free agent by the Los Angeles Dodgers.

2008, October 30
Option declined on outfielder Ken Griffey Jr. (Signed as a free agent by Seattle on February 18, 2009.)

2009, January 29
Outfielder Juan Uribe signed as a minor league free agent with the San Francisco Giants.

2009, March 6
Shortstop Orlando Cabrera signed as a free agent by the Oakland A's.

2009, April 29
Pitcher Mike MacDougal released on waivers. (Signed as a free agent by Washington on May 3, 2009.)

2009, May 4
Outfielder Jerry Owens signed as a free agent by the Seattle Mariners.

2009, October 9
Outfielder Dewayne Wise declared free agency in lieu of accepting a Triple A assignment.

2010, January 8
Outfielder Scott Podsednik signed as a free agent by the Kansas City Royals.

2010, January 13
Pitcher D.J. Carrasco signed as a minor league free agent by the Pittsburgh Pirates.

2010, January 21
Pitcher Octavio Dotel signed as a free agent by the Pittsburgh Pirates.

2010, June 17
Infielder Jayson Nix designated for assignment. (Signed as a free agent by Cleveland on June 24, 2010.)

2010, December 10
Pitcher J.J. Putz signed as a free agent by Arizona.

2010, December 16
Pitcher Bobby Jenks signed as a free agent by Boston.

13

U.S. Cellular Field
pepsi
CITY CHAMPIONS
CITY CHAMPIONS
IT WILL BLOW YOUR SOX OFF!
CHAMPIONS

Awards, Milestones, Honors, Stats, and Trivia

Major Award Winners

Most Valuable Player Award (Baseball Writers Association of America)

Year	Player	Position
1959	Nellie Fox	Second base
1972	Dick Allen	First base
1993	Frank Thomas	First base
1994	Frank Thomas	First base

Cy Young Award (Baseball Writers Association of America)

1959	Early Wynn
1983	LaMarr Hoyt
1993	Jack McDowell

***Sporting News* Pitcher of the Year Award**

1956	Billy Pierce
1957	Billy Pierce
1972	Wilbur Wood
1983	LaMarr Hoyt

Sporting News* Fireman of the Year Award

1965	Eddie Fisher
1968	Wilbur Wood
1974	Terry Forster
1975	Rich Gossage
1990	Bobby Thigpen

*As of 2001, the *Sporting News* Reliever of the Year Award

Rookie of the Year Award

Year	Player	Presenter
1951	Minnie Minoso	*Sporting News*
1956	Luis Aparicio	*Sporting News*/BBWAA
1963	Gary Peters	*Sporting News*/BBWAA
	Pete Ward	*Sporting News*
1966	Tommie Agee	*Sporting News*/BBWAA
1980	Britt Burns	*Sporting News*
1983	Ron Kittle	*Sporting News*/BBWAA
1985	Ozzie Guillen	*Sporting News*/BBWAA
2009	Gordon Beckham	*Sporting News*

Nellie Fox and Early Wynn receive the MVP award and Cy Young Award, respectively, in 1960.

Chicago's four most recent championship trophies displayed at U.S. Cellular Field, August 27, 2010. Jerry Reinsdorf represents the Bulls, and Mark Buehrle the White Sox. So where is the Cubs trophy? Oh, that's right, there is no Cubs trophy. (Courtesy of the Chicago White Sox)

Dick Allen and his 1972 MVP Award

Silver Slugger Award (Sporting News and Hillerich & Bradsby)

Year	Player	Position
1981	Carlton Fisk	Catcher
1985	Carlton Fisk	Catcher
1988	Carlton Fisk	Catcher
1991	Frank Thomas	First base
1993	Frank Thomas	First base
1994	Frank Thomas	First base
1994	Julio Franco	Designated hitter
1998	Albert Belle	Left field
2000	Magglio Ordonez	Right field
2000	Frank Thomas	Designated hitter
2002	Magglio Ordonez	Right field
2006	Joe Crede	Third Base
2006	Jermaine Dye	Right Field
2008	Carlos Quentin	Left field
2010	Alexei Ramirez	Shortstop

Manager of the Year (Associated Press, United Press International, Baseball Writers Association of America, *Sporting News*)

Year	
1959	Al Lopez (UPI)
1972	Chuck Tanner (*Sporting News,* AP)
1977	Bob Lemon (UPI)
1983	Tony LaRussa (*Sporting News,* AP, BBWAA)
1990	Jeff Torborg (AP, UPI, BBWAA, *Sporting News*)
1993	Gene Lamont (BBWAA)
2000	Jerry Manuel (TSN, AP, BBWAA)
2005	Ozzie Guillen (BBWAA, TSN)

Executive of the Year (United Press International)

1972	Roland Hemond
1977	Bill Veeck
1983	Roland Hemond

Rawlings Gold Glove Award

Year	Player	Position
1957	Sherm Lollar	Catcher
	Nellie Fox	Second base
1958	Sherm Lollar	Catcher
	Luis Aparicio	Shortstop
1959	Sherm Lollar	Catcher
	Luis Aparicio	Shortstop
	Nellie Fox	Second base
1960	Nellie Fox	Second base
	Luis Aparicio	Shortstop
1960	Minnie Minoso	Outfield
1961	Luis Aparicio	Shortstop
	Jim Landis	Center field
1962	Luis Aparicio	Shortstop
	Jim Landis	Center field
1963	Jim Landis	Center field
1964	Jim Landis	Center field
1966	Tommie Agee	Center field/ right field
1968	Luis Aparicio	Shortstop
1970	Luis Aparicio	Shortstop
	Ken Berry	Center field
1974	Jim Kaat	Pitcher
1975	Jim Kaat	Pitcher
1977	Jim Spencer	First base
1981	Mike Squires	First base
1990	Ozzie Guillen	Shortstop
1991	Robin Ventura	Third base
1992	Robin Ventura	Third base
1993	Robin Ventura	Third base
1996	Robin Ventura	Third base
1998	Robin Ventura	Third base
2009	Mark Buehrle	Pitcher
2010	Mark Buehrle	Pitcher

Comeback Player of the Year

Year	Player	Position	Award Presenter
1977	Eric Soderholm	Third Base	*Sporting News*
1993	Bo Jackson	Outfield	*Sporting News*
2000	Frank Thomas	DH	*Sporting News,* Player's Choice
2003	Esteban Loiaza	Pitcher	Player's Choice
2004	Paul Konerko	First Base	*Sporting News*
2006	Jim Thome	DH	*Sporting News,* Major League Baseball

2009 and 2010 Gold Glove winner, Mark Buehrle. (Courtesy of the Chicago White Sox)

Retired Numbers

Player	Number	Years with Sox	Year Retired
Nellie Fox	2	1950–63	1976
Harold Baines*	3	1980–89	1989
Luke Appling	4	1930–50	1975
Minnie Minoso	9	1951–56, 1960–61, 1964, 1976, 1980	1983
Luis Aparicio	11	1956–62, 1968–69	1984
Ted Lyons	16	1923–46	1987
Billy Pierce	19	1949–61	1987
Carlton Fisk	72	1981–93	1997
Frank Thomas	35	1990–2005	2010

*Baines' number was "unretired" in 1996.

American League All-Star Selections

1933 Al Simmons (of), Jimmie Dykes (3b)
1934 Al Simmons (of), Jimmie Dykes (3b)
1935 Al Simmons (of)
1936 Luke Appling (ss), Rip Radcliff (of), Ted Lyons (p)
1937 Luke Sewell (c), Monty Stratton (p)
1938 Mike Kreevich (of)
1939 Luke Appling (ss), Ted Lyons (p)
1940 Luke Appling (ss)
1941 Luke Appling (ss), Thornton Lee (p), Edgar Smith (p)
1942 Edgar Smith (p)
1943 Luke Appling (ss)
1944 Thurman Tucker (of), Orval Grove (p)
1946 Luke Appling (ss)
1947 Luke Appling (ss), Rudy York (1b)
1948 Joe Haynes (p)
1949 Cass Michaels (ss)
1950 Ray Scarborough (p)
1951 Chico Carrasquel (ss), Nellie Fox (2b), Jim Busby (of), Randy Gumpert (p), Minnie Minoso (of), Eddie Robinson, (1b)
1952 Eddie Robinson (1b), Nellie Fox (2b), Minnie Minoso (of)
1953 Chico Carrasquel (ss), Billy Pierce (p), Nellie Fox (2b), Ferris Fain (1b), Minnie Minoso (of)
1954 Minnie Minoso (of), Chico Carrasquel (ss), Sandy Consuegra (p), Nellie Fox (2b), Bob Keegan (p), Sherm Lollar (c), Virgil Trucks (p), George Kell (3b), Ferris Fain (1b)
1955 Nellie Fox (2b), Billy Pierce (p), Chico Carrasquel (ss), Sherm Lollar (c), Dick Donovan (p)
1956 Nellie Fox (2b), Billy Pierce (p), Sherm Lollar (c), Jim Wilson (p)
1957 Nellie Fox (2b), Minnie Minoso (of), Billy Pierce (p)
1958 Luis Aparicio (ss), Nellie Fox (p), Sherm Lollar (c), Billy Pierce (p), Early Wynn (p)
1959 Luis Aparicio (ss), Nellie Fox (2b), Early Wynn (p), Sherm Lollar (c), Billy Pierce (p)
1960 Minnie Minoso (of), Luis Aparicio (ss), Nellie Fox (2b), Sherm Lollar (c), Gerry Staley (p), Early Wynn (p), Al Smith (of)
1961 Nellie Fox (2b), Billy Pierce (p), Luis Aparicio (ss), Ray Herbert (p), Roy Sievers (1b)
1962 Luis Aparicio (ss), Jim Landis (of)
1963 Nellie Fox (2b), Juan Pizarro (p)
1964 Gary Peters (p), Juan Pizarro (p)
1965 Eddie Fisher (p), Bill Skowron (1b)

1966 Tommie Agee (of)
1967 Tommie Agee (of), Ken Berry (of), Joel Horlen (p), Gary Peters (p)
1968 Tommy John (p), Duane Josephson (c)
1969 Carlos May (of)
1970 Luis Aparicio (ss)
1971 Bill Melton (3b)
Wilbur Wood (p)
1972 Dick Allen (1b), Carlos May (of), Wilbur Wood (p)
1973 Dick Allen (1b), Pat Kelly (of)
1974 Dick Allen (1b), Wilbur Wood (p), Ed Herrmann (c)
1975 Bucky Dent (ss), Rich Gossage (p), Jim Kaat (p), Jorge Orta (2b)
1976 Rich Gossage (p)
1977 Richie Zisk (of)
1978 Chet Lemon (of)
1979 Chet Lemon (of)
1980 Ed Farmer (p)
1981 Carlton Fisk (c), Britt Burns (p)
1982 Carlton Fisk (c)
1983 Ron Kittle (of)
1984 Richard Dotson (p)
1985 Carlton Fisk (c), Harold Baines (of)
1986 Harold Baines (of)
1987 Harold Baines (of)
1988 Ozzie Guillen (ss)
1989 Harold Baines (dh)
1990 Ozzie Guillen (ss), Bobby Thigpen (p)
1991 Carlton Fisk (c), Ozzie Guillen (ss), Jack McDowell (p)
1992 Jack McDowell (p), Robin Ventura (3b)
1993 Jack McDowell (p), Frank Thomas (1b)
1994 Frank Thomas (1b), Jason Bere (p), Wilson Alvarez (p)
1995 Frank Thomas (1b)
1996 Roberto Hernandez (p)
Frank Thomas (1b)
1997 Frank Thomas (1b), Albert Belle (of)
1998 Ray Durham (2b)
1999 Magglio Ordonez (of)
2000 James Baldwin (p), Ray Durham (2b), Magglio Ordonez (of)
2001 Magglio Ordonez (of)
2002 Mark Buehrle (p), Paul Konerko (1b)
2003 Esteban Loaiza (p), Carl Everett (of), Magglio Ordonez (of)
2004 Esteban Loaiza (p),
2005 Mark Buehrle (p), Jon Garland (p), Scott Podsednik (of), Paul Konerko (1b)
2006 Mark Buehrle (p), Paul Konerko (1b), Jose Contreras (p), Jermaine Dye (of), Bobby Jenks (p), Jim Thome (1b), A.J. Pierzynski (c)
2007 Bobby Jenks (p)
2008 Joe Crede (3b), Carlos Quentin (of)
2009 Mark Buehrle (p)
2010 Matt Thornton (p), Paul Konerko (1b)

Nellie Fox and Harmon Killebrew at the 1961 All-Star Game in Boston

Al Lopez (left), managing the 1960 American League All-Stars, was reunited with his '59 World Series nemesis, Walt Alston.

White Sox in Chicago Sports Hall of Fame

Athletes

Dick Allen
Luis Aparicio
Luke Appling
Phil Cavarretta
Larry Doby
Ed Farmer
Bob Kennedy
Bill Melton
Minnie Minoso
Jim O'Toole
Billy Pierce
Jim Rivera
Scott Sanderson
Bob Shaw
Bill "Moose" Skowron
Tim Stoddard
Frank Thomas
Pete Ward
Wilbur Wood
Early Wynn

Builders

Charles A. Comiskey
Charley Comiskey
Grace Reidy Comiskey
Jimmie Dykes
Jerry Reinsdorf
Bill Veeck

In Memorium

Bob Elson
Nellie Fox
Sherm Lollar
Al Lopez
Ted Lyons
John Rigney

White Sox Runners-Up for MVP Award

Chalmers Award (presented 1911–14)

Player	Year	Votes Received	Winner's Votes
Ed Walsh	1911	35	64
Ed Walsh	1912	30	59

Most Valuable Player

Player	Year	Votes Received	Winner's Votes
Eddie Collins	1924	49	55
Johnny Mostil	1926	33	63
Luke Appling	1936	65	73
Luke Appling	1943	215	246
Luis Aparicio	1959	255	295*
Frank Thomas	2000	285	317

*Aparicio finished second to teammate Nellie Fox.

Sox Pitchers Who Were Runners-Up for Cy Young Award

Pitcher	Year	Votes Received	Winner's Votes
Dick Donovan	1957	1	15
Joel Horlen	1967	2	18
Wilbur Wood	1972	58	64

Pitcher	Year	Votes Received	Winner's Votes
Jack McDowell	1992	51	107
Esteban Loaiza	2003	63	136

Ted Lyons, Ray Schalk, Red Faber, and Luke Appling show off their Hall of Fame plaques at a 1964 old timers' reunion.

The Greatest White Sox Teams of All-Time

The 1949 Hall of Fame Poll (as determined in a poll of 5,000 fans in May 1949)

First base	Joe Kuhel
Second base	Eddie Collins
Third base	Jimmie Dykes
Shortstop	Luke Appling
Left field	Al Simmons
Center field	Johnny Mostil
Right field	Harry Hooper
Catcher	Ray Schalk/Billy Sullivan (tie)
Pitchers (4)	Ted Lyons
	Ed Walsh
	Red Faber
	Guy "Doc" White

The 1969 Major League Baseball Poll (conducted in a nationwide survey to select the all-time All-Star roster for each team)

First base	Eddie Robinson
Second base	Eddie Collins
Shortstop	Luke Appling
Third base	Willie Kamm
Left field	Al Simmons
Center field	Johnny Mostil
Right field	Harry Hooper
Catcher	Ray Schalk
RHP	Ted Lyons
LHP	Billy Pierce

The 2000 "Team of the Century" Commemorating 100 Years of White Sox History

Position Players	Pitchers
Dick Allen, 1b	Ed Cicotte
Luis Aparicio, ss	Red Faber
Luke Appling, ss	Ted Lyons
Harold Baines, of	Gary Peters
Chico Carrasquel, ss	Billy Pierce
Eddie Collins, 2b	Ed Walsh
Carlton Fisk, c	Doc White
Nellie Fox, 2b	Hoyt Wilhelm
Ozzie Guillen, ss	Wilbur Wood
Joe Jackson, of	
Jim Landis, of	
Sherm Lollar, c	
Bill Melton, 3b	
Minnie Minoso, of	
Ray Schalk, c	
Frank Thomas, 1b	
Robin Ventura, 3b	
Buck Weaver, 3b	

All-Time Pitching Leaders

Number of White Sox Victories

1.	Ted Lyons	260
2.	Red Faber	254
3.	Ed Walsh	194
4.	Billy Pierce	186
5.	Wilbur Wood	163
6.	Guy "Doc" White	159
7.	Ed Cicotte	158
8.	Mark Buehrle	148*
9.	Joel Horlen	113
10.	Jim Scott	111
11.	Frank Smith	107
12.	Thornton Lee	104
13.	Richard Dotson	97
14.	Gary Peters	91
	Jack McDowell	91
16.	Al "Tommy" Thomas	83
17.	Tommy John	82
	Roy Patterson	82
19.	Claude "Lefty" Williams	81
20.	Bill Dietrich	80

Number of White Sox Defeats

1.	Ted Lyons	230
2.	Red Faber	212
3.	Billy Pierce	152
4.	Wilbur Wood	148
5.	Ed Walsh	129
6.	Guy "Doc" White	123
7.	Joel Horlen	113
	Jim Scott	113
9.	Mark Buehrle	110*
10.	Thornton Lee	104
11.	Ed Cicotte	102
12.	Richard Dotson	95
13.	Al "Tommy" Thomas	92
14.	Bill Dietrich	91
15.	Edgar Smith	82
16.	Frank Smith	81
17.	Tommy John	80
18.	Ted Blankenship	79
19.	Gary Peters	78
20.	Joe Benz	76

*Through 2010

Complete Games

1.	Ted Lyons	356
2.	Red Faber	275
3.	Ed Walsh	247
4.	Doc White	206
5.	Billy Pierce	183
	Ed Cicotte	183
7.	Frank Smith	156
8.	Thornton Lee	142
9.	Jim Scott	125
10.	Roy Patterson	119

Innings Pitched

1.	Ted Lyons	4,161
2.	Red Faber	4,087
3.	Ed Walsh	2,946
4.	Billy Pierce	2,931
5.	Mark Buehrle	2,271*
6.	Wilbur Wood	2,524
7.	Doc White	2,516
8.	Ed Cicotte	2,322
9.	Joel Horlen	1,917
10.	Thornton Lee	1,888

Walks

1.	Red Faber	1,213
2.	Ted Lyons	1,121
3.	Billy Pierce	1,052
4.	Wilbur Wood	671
5.	Richard Dotson	637
6.	Thornton Lee	633
7.	Jim Scott	609
8.	Ed Walsh	608
9.	Bill Dietrich	561
10.	Edgar Smith	545

Games

1.	Red Faber	669
2.	Ted Lyons	594
3.	Wilbur Wood	578
4.	Billy Pierce	456
5.	Ed Walsh	426
6.	Bobby Thigpen	424
7.	Doc White	361
	Hoyt Wilhelm	361
9.	Mark Buehrle	359*
10.	Ed Cicotte	353

Shutouts

1.	Ed Walsh	58
2.	Doc White	43
3.	Billy Pierce	35
4.	Red Faber	30
5.	Ed Cicotte	28
6.	Ted Lyons	27
7.	Jim Scott	26
8.	Frank Smith	25
9.	Reb Russell	24
	Wilbur Wood	24

Strikeouts

1.	Billy Pierce	1,796
2.	Ed Walsh	1,732
3.	Red Faber	1,471
4.	Wilbur Wood	1,332
5.	Mark Buehrle	1,287*
6.	Gary Peters	1,098
7.	Doc White	1,095
8.	Ted Lyons	1,073
9.	Joel Horlen	1,007
10.	Ed Cicotte	961

Earned Run Average

1.	Ed Walsh	1.81
2.	Frank Smith	2.18
3.	Ed Cicotte	2.24
4.	Doc White	2.30
5.	Jim Scott	2.32
6.	Reb Russell	2.34
7.	Nick Altrock	2.40
8.	Joe Benz	2.42
9.	Frank Owen	2.48
10.	Roy Patterson	2.75

Games Started

1.	Red Faber	484
	Ted Lyons	484
3.	Billy Pierce	380
4.	Mark Buehrle	334*
5.	Ed Walsh	312
6.	Doc White	301
7.	Joel Horlen	284
8.	Richard Dotson	250
9.	Wilbur Wood	234
10.	Thornton Lee	232

Saves

1.	Bobby Thigpen	201
2.	Bobby Jenks	173
3.	Roberto Hernandez	161
4.	Keith Foulke	100
5.	Hoyt Wilhelm	98
6.	Terry Forster	75
7.	Wilbur Wood	57
8.	Bob James	56
9.	Ed Farmer	54
10.	Clint Brown	53

*Through 2010

Relief Appearances

1.	Bobby Thigpen	424
2.	Hoyt Wilhelm	358
3.	Keith Foulke	346
4.	Roberto Hernandez	342
5.	Matt Thornton	336*
6.	Bobby Jenks	329
7.	Scott Radinsky	316
8.	Wilbur Wood	292
9.	Bob Locker	271
10.	Gerry Staley	260

Relief Wins

1.	Hoyt Wilhelm	41
2.	Wilbur Wood	32
3.	Gerry Staley	31
4.	Clint Brown	29
5.	Bob Locker	28
	Bobby Thigpen	28
	Roberto Hernandez	28

Winning Percentage

1.	Lefty Williams	.648
2.	Juan Pizarro	.615
3.	Dickie Kerr	.609
	Ed Walsh	.609
5.	Ed Cicotte	.608
6.	Jack McDowell	.606
7.	LaMarr Hoyt	.602
8.	Dick Donovan	.593
9.	Eddie Fisher	.575
10.	Mark Buehrle	.574*

*Through 2010

All-Time Batting Leaders

Games

Luke Appling	2,422
Nellie Fox	2,115
Frank Thomas	1,959
Paul Konerko	1,849*
Ray Schalk	1,755
Harold Baines	1,670
Eddie Collins	1,670
Ozzie Guillen	1,601
Luis Aparicio	1,511
Carlton Fisk	1,421
Minnie Minoso	1,379
Harold Baines	1,378
Sherm Lollar	1,358
Shano Collins	1,335

At-Bats

Luke Appling	8,857
Nellie Fox	8,486
Frank Thomas	6,956
Paul Konerko	6,418*
Harold Baines	6,149
Eddie Collins	6,064
Luis Aparicio	5,856
Ozzie Guillen	5,577
Ray Schalk	5,304
Minnie Minoso	5,011
Carlton Fisk	4,896
Buck Weaver	4,810
Shano Collins	4,787

Hits

Luke Appling	2,749
Nellie Fox	2,470
Frank Thomas	2,136
Eddie Collins	2,007
Harold Baines	1,773
Paul Konerko	1,642*
Luis Aparicio	1,576
Minnie Minoso	1,523
Ozzie Guillen	1,488
Ray Schalk	1,345
Buck Weaver	1,310
Carlton Fisk	1,259
Shano Collins	1,254

Average

Joe Jackson	.339
Eddie Collins	.331
Carl Reynolds	.322
Zeke Bonura	.317
Bibb Falk	.315
Al Simmons	.315
Taft Wright	.312
Luke Appling	.310
Rip Radcliff	.310
Magglio Ordonez	.307
Earl Sheely	.305
Minnie Minoso	.304
Frank Thomas	.301

Runs

Frank Thomas	1,327
Luke Appling	1,319
Nellie Fox	1,187
Eddie Collins	1,063
Paul Konerko	950*
Minnie Minoso	893
Luis Aparicio	791
Harold Baines	786
Fielder Jones	695
Carlton Fisk	649
Ozzie Guillen	634
Buck Weaver	625
Johnny Mostil	618

Runs Batted In

Frank Thomas	1,465
Paul Konerko	1,127*
Luke Appling	1,116
Harold Baines	981
Minnie Minoso	808
Eddie Collins	803
Carlton Fisk	762
Nellie Fox	740
Sherm Lollar	631
Bibb Falk	627
Robin Ventura	624
Ray Schalk	594
Willie Kamm	587

*Through 2010

Total Bases

Frank Thomas	3,949
Luke Appling	3,528
Paul Konerko	3,238*
Nellie Fox	3,118
Harold Baines	2,844
Eddie Collins	2,567
Minnie Minoso	2,346
Carlton Fisk	2,143
Luis Aparicio	2,036
Frank Thomas	1,970
Shano Collins	1,740
Buck Weaver	1,719

Home Runs

Frank Thomas	448
Paul Konerko	358*
Harold Baines	221
Carlton Fisk	214
Magglio Ordonez	187
Robin Ventura	171
Jermaine Dye	164
Bill Melton	154
Carlos Lee	152
Ron Kittle	140
Jose Valentin	136

Doubles

Frank Thomas	447
Luke Appling	440
Nellie Fox	335
Paul Konerko	335*
Harold Baines	320
Eddie Collins	265
Minnie Minoso	260
Bibb Falk	245
Willie Kamm	242
Ozzie Guillen	240
Shano Collins	230
Luis Aparicio	223
Carlton Fisk	214

Triples

Nellie Fox	104
Shano Collins	104
Luke Appling	102
Eddie Collins	102
Johnny Mostil	82
Minnie Minoso	79
Joe Jackson	79
Lance Johnson	77
Buck Weaver	69
Ozzie Guillen	68
Willie Kamm	66
Mike Kreevich	65

Walks

Frank Thomas	1,466
Luke Appling	1,302
Eddie Collins	965
Paul Konerko	716*
Robin Ventura	668
Nellie Fox	658
Minnie Minoso	658
Ray Schalk	638
Willie Kamm	569
Harold Baines	565
Fielder Jones	551
Sherm Lollar	525

Slugging Percentage

Frank Thomas	.568
Jim Thome	.542
Magglio Ordonez	.525
Zeke Bonura	.518
Paul Konerko	.505*
Carl Reynolds	.499
Joe Jackson	.498
Carlos Lee	.488
Jose Valentin	.483
Ron Kittle	.470
Minnie Minoso	.468

Stolen Bases

Eddie Collins	366
Luis Aparicio	318
Frank Isbell	250
Lance Johnson	226
Ray Durham	219
Fielder Jones	206
Shano Collins	192
Luke Appling	179
Johnny Mostil	176
Ray Schalk	176
Buck Weaver	172
Rudy Law	171
Minnie Minoso	171

Extra-Base Hits

Frank Thomas	906
Paul Konerko	701*
Luke Appling	587
Harold Baines	585
Nellie Fox	474
Minnie Minoso	474
Carlton Fisk	442
Magglio Ordonez	442
Ray Durham	408
Robin Ventura	402
Eddie Collins	398
Shano Collins	350

Jerry Hairston

Pinch-Hits

Jerry Hairston	87
Smoky Burgess	50
Eddie Murphy	42
Walt Williams	37
Earl Torgeson	32
Sherm Lollar	30
Ralph Hodgin	27
Bud Stewart	26
Warren Newson	26
Ron Northey	24
Pete Ward	24

On-Base Percentage

Frank Thomas	.427
Eddie Collins	.426
Joe Jackson	.407
Luke Appling	.399
Minnie Minoso	.397
Zeke Bonura	.396
Jim Thome	.391
Earl Sheely	.391
Johnny Mostil	.386
Alex Metzler	.385

Strikeouts

Frank Thomas	1,165
Paul Konerko	1,052*
Harold Baines	918
Carlton Fisk	798
Ray Durham	758
Ron Karkovice	749
Robin Ventura	659
Jim Landis	608
Ron Kittle	606
Bill Melton	595

*Through 2010

Single-Season Pitching Records

Wins

40*	Ed Walsh	1908
29	Ed Cicotte	1919
28	Ed Cicotte	1917
27	Ed Walsh	1912
27	Ed Walsh	1911
27	Doc White	1907
25	Red Faber	1921
25	Frank Smith	1909
24	LaMarr Hoyt	1983
24	Wilbur Wood	1973
24	Wilbur Wood	1972
24	Red Faber	1915
24	Jim Scott	1915
24	Ed Walsh	1907
24	Clark Griffith	1901

*Under modern scoring rules Walsh would be credited with 36 wins.

Games

88	Wilbur Wood	1968
82	Eddie Fisher	1965
77	Bobby Thigpen	1990
77	Wilbur Wood	1970
77	Bob Locker	1967
76	Wilbur Wood	1969
74	Matt Thornton	2008
73	Scott Radinsky	1993
73	Hoyt Wilhelm	1964
72	Roberto Hernandez	1996
72	Hoyt Wilhelm	1968
72	Keith Foulke	2000
70	Roberto Hernandez	1993
70	Bob Locker	1968
70	Matt Thornton	2009
69	Bob James	1985

Strikeouts

269	Ed Walsh	1908
258	Ed Walsh	1910
255	Ed Walsh	1911
254	Ed Walsh	1912
215	Gary Peters	1967
213	Javier Vazquez	2007
210	Wilbur Wood	1971
209	Tom Bradley	1972
207	Esteban Loaiza	2003
206	Tom Bradley	1971
206	Ed Walsh	1907
205	Gary Peters	1964
200	Alex Fernandez	1996
200	Javier Vazquez	2008

Strikeouts per Nine Innings

8.85	Javier Vazquez	2007
8.69	Juan Pizarro	1961
8.46	Floyd Bannister	1985
8.23	Esteban Loaiza	2003
8.17	Javier Vazquez	2006
8.07	Jason Bere	1994
7.74	Bart Johnson	1971
7.66	Juan Pizarro	1962
7.44	Gary Peters	1967
7.36	Melido Perez	1990
7.32	Joe Cowley	1986
7.24	Jack McDowell	1990
7.23	Tom Bradley	1972
7.06	Billy Pierce	1954

Earned Run Average

1.27	Ed Walsh	1910
1.41	Ed Walsh	1909
1.42	Ed Walsh	1908
1.52	Doc White	1906
1.53	Ed Cicotte	1917
1.58	Ed Cicotte	1913
1.60	Ed Walsh	1907
1.72	Doc White	1909
1.76	Doc White	1905

Innings

464	Ed Walsh	1908
422	Ed Walsh	1907
393	Ed Walsh	1912
377	Wilbur Wood	1972
370	Ed Walsh	1910
369	Ed Walsh	1911
365	Frank Smith	1909
359	Wilbur Wood	1973
353	Red Faber	1922
347	Ed Cicotte	1917

Games Started

49	Wilbur Wood	1972
49	Ed Walsh	1908
48	Wilbur Wood	1973
46	Ed Walsh	1907
43	Wilbur Wood	1975
42	Wilbur Wood	1974
42	Stan Bahnsen	1973
42	Wilbur Wood	1971
41	Jim Kaat	1975
41	Stan Bahnsen	1972
41	Ed Walsh	1912
41	Frank Smith	1909

Complete Games

42	Ed Walsh	1908
37	Frank Smith	1909
37	Ed Walsh	1907
34	Frank Owen	1904
33	Ed Walsh	1911
33	Ed Walsh	1910
32	Red Faber	1921
32	Ed Walsh	1912
32	Frank Owen	1905
31	Red Faber	1922

Shutouts

12	Ed Walsh	1908
10	Ed Walsh	1906
8	Wilbur Wood	1972
8	Reb Russell	1913
8	Ed Walsh	1909
7	Wilbur Wood	1971
7	Ray Herbert	1963
7	Billy Pierce	1953
7	Ed Cicotte	1917
7	Jim Scott	1915
7	Ed Walsh	1910
7	Frank Smith	1909
7	Doc White	1907
7	Doc White	1906
7	Doc White	1904

Consecutive Scoreless Innings

45	Doc White	1904
40⅔	Ed Walsh	1910
39⅔	Billy Pierce	1953
38	Ray Herbert	1963
37	Joel Horlen	1968
35	John Humphries	1941
33	Jack Harshman	1954
31	Wilson Alvarez	1993
30	Britt Burns	1983
27	J.J. Putz	2010

Winning Percentage

.857	Jason Bere	1994
.842	Sandy Consuegra	1954
.806	Ed Cicotte	1919
.774	Clark Griffith	1901
.759	Richard Dotson	1983
.750	Bob Shaw	1959
.750	Monty Stratton	1937
.750	Doc White	1906
.731	Joel Horlen	1967
.727	Dick Donovan	1957
.727	Ed Walsh	1908

Hits per Nine Innings

5.89	Ed Walsh	1910
6.07	Joel Horlen	1964
6.39	Ed Cicotte	1917
6.42	Eddie Fisher	1965
6.44	Frank Smith	1908
6.47	Gary Peters	1967
6.49	Ed Walsh	1909
6.56	Joel Horlen	1967
6.57	Doc White	1906
6.63	Frank Smith	1905

Saves

57	Bobby Thigpen	1990*
42	Keith Foulke	2001
41	Bobby Jenks	2006
40	Bobby Jenks	2007
38	Roberto Hernandez	1996
38	Roberto Hernandez	1993
34	Keith Foulke	2000
34	Dustin Hermanson	2005
34	Bobby Thigpen	1989
34	Bobby Thigpen	1988
32	Roberto Hernandez	1995
32	Bob James	1985
30	Bobby Thigpen	1991
30	Ed Farmer	1980
30	Bobby Jenks	2008

*Major league record

Relief Wins

15	Eddie Fisher	1965
13	Gerry Staley	1960
13	Earl Caldwell	1946
12	Wilbur Wood	1968
12	Hoyt Wilhelm	1964
11	Barry Jones	1990
11	Clint Brown	1939
10	Cy Acosta	1973
10	Wilbur Wood	1969
10	Gordon Maltzberger	1944
9	Rich Gossage	1975

Single-Season Batting Records

Average

.388	Luke Appling	1936
.382	Joe Jackson	1920
.369	Eddie Collins	1920
.360	Eddie Collins	1923
.359	Carl Reynolds	1930
.353	Frank Thomas	1994
.352	Bibb Falk	1924
.351	Joe Jackson	1919
.349	Frank Thomas	1996
.349	Eddie Collins	1924
.348	Luke Appling	1940
.346	Eddie Collins	1925

Games

163	Albert Belle	1998
163	Greg Walker	1985
163	Don Buford	1966
162	Jim Morrison	1980
162	Ken Henderson	1974
162	Ron Hansen	1965
161	Dave Gallagher	1989
161	Harold Baines	1982
161	Robin Ventura	1998
161	Orlando Cabrera	2008

At-Bats

661	Orlando Cabrera	2008
651	Juan Pierre	2010
649	Nellie Fox	1956
648	Nellie Fox	1952
640	Harold Baines	1985
636	Jorge Orta	1976
636	Nellie Fox	1955
635	Ray Durham	1998
634	Ray Durham	1997
631	Nellie Fox	1954
630	Buck Weaver	1920
629	Tommie Agee	1966
625	Luis Aparicio	1961
624	Nellie Fox	1959
624	Nellie Fox	1953

Hits

222	Eddie Collins	1920
218	Joe Jackson	1920
210	Buck Weaver	1920
207	Rip Radcliff	1936
204	Luke Appling	1936
202	Carl Reynolds	1930
202	Joe Jackson	1916
201	Nellie Fox	1954
200	Albert Belle	1998
200	Al Simmons	1933
198	Harold Baines	1985
198	Nellie Fox	1955

Runs

135	Johnny Mostil	1925
126	Ray Durham	1998
125	Johnny Mostil	1925
121	Ray Durham	2000
120	Zeke Bonura	1936
120	Rip Radcliff	1936
120	Johnny Mostil	1926
120	Fielder Jones	1901
119	Tony Phillips	1996
119	Minnie Minoso	1954
119	Luzurne Blue	1931
118	Eddie Collins	1915
115	Eddie Collins	1920
112	Dummy Hoy	1901

Extra-Base Hits

99	Albert Belle	1998
87	Frank Thomas	2000
86	Magglio Ordonez	2002
78	Magglio Ordonez	2003
77	Frank Thomas	2003
77	Frank Thomas	1993
77	Jermaine Dye	2008
76	Albert Belle	1997
74	Joe Jackson	1920
74	Jermaine Dye	2006
73	Frank Thomas	1994
72	Ray Durham	2001
72	Magglio Ordonez	2001
72	Frank Thomas	1992

Slugging Percentage

.729	Frank Thomas	1994
.655	Albert Belle	1998
.626	Frank Thomas	1996
.625	Frank Thomas	2000
.622	Jermaine Dye	2006
.611	Frank Thomas	1997
.607	Frank Thomas	1993
.606	Frank Thomas	1995
.603	Dick Allen	1972
.598	Jim Thome	2006
.589	Joe Jackson	1920
.588	Oscar Gamble	1977
.584	Carl Reynolds	1930
.584	Paul Konerko	2010

Runs Batted In

152	Albert Belle	1998
143	Frank Thomas	2000
138	Zeke Bonura	1936
135	Magglio Ordonez	2002
134	Frank Thomas	1996
128	Frank Thomas	1993
128	Luke Appling	1936
125	Magglio Ordonez	2000
125	Frank Thomas	1997
121	Joe Jackson	1920
120	Jermaine Dye	2006
119	Al Simmons	1933
117	Eddie Robinson	1951
117	Paul Konerko	2004

Doubles

48	Albert Belle	1998
47	Magglio Ordonez	2002
46	Magglio Ordonez	2003
46	Frank Thomas	1992
45	Albert Belle	1997
45	Floyd Robinson	1962
44	Frank Thomas	2000
44	Ivan Calderon	1990
44	Chet Lemon	1979
43	Bibb Falk	1926
43	Earl Sheely	1925
42	Luke Appling	1937

Triples

21	Joe Jackson	1916
20	Joe Jackson	1920
18	Minnie Minoso	1954
18	Carl Reynolds	1930
18	Jacques Fournier	1915
18	Harry Lord	1911
17	Joe Jackson	1917
17	Eddie Collins	1916
17	Shano Collins	1915
17	Sandow Mertes	1901

Home Runs

49	Albert Belle	1998
44	Jermaine Dye	2006
43	Frank Thomas	2000
42	Frank Thomas	2003
42	Jim Thome	2006
41	Paul Konerko	2004
41	Frank Thomas	1993
40	Paul Konerko	2005
40	Frank Thomas	1995
39	Paul Konerko	2010
38	Magglio Ordonez	2002
38	Frank Thomas	1994
37	Carlton Fisk	1985
37	Dick Allen	1972

Total Bases

399	Albert Belle	1998
364	Frank Thomas	2000
352	Magglio Ordonez	2002
336	Joe Jackson	1920
335	Jermaine Dye	2006
333	Frank Thomas	1993
331	Magglio Ordonez	2003
330	Frank Thomas	1996
329	Carl Reynolds	1930
324	Frank Thomas	1997
321	Magglio Ordonez	2000
320	Paul Konerko	2010
319	Jermaine Dye	2008

On-Base Percentage

.487	Frank Thomas	1994
.474	Luke Appling	1936
.461	Eddie Collins	1925
.460	Eddie Collins	1915
.459	Frank Thomas	1996
.456	Frank Thomas	1997
.455	Eddie Collins	1923
.454	Frank Thomas	1995
.444	Joe Jackson	1920
.441	Eddie Collins	1924
.439	Frank Thomas	1992
.439	Luke Appling	1949
.437	Luke Appling	1935

Walks

138	Frank Thomas	1991
136	Frank Thomas	1995
127	Luzurne Blue	1931
125	Tony Phillips	1996
122	Frank Thomas	1992
122	Luke Appling	1935
119	Eddie Collins	1915
112	Frank Thomas	2000
112	Frank Thomas	1993
109	Frank Thomas	1996
109	Frank Thomas	1994
108	Ferris Fain	1953
105	Robin Ventura	1993
105	Luke Appling	1939
102	Larry Doby	1956

Walk Average

.216	Frank Thomas	1995
.215	Frank Thomas	1994
.198	Frank Thomas	1991
.197	Luke Appling	1949
.195	Ferris Fain	1953
.192	Frank Thomas	2000
.189	Luke Appling	1935
.188	Larry Rosenthal	1940
.186	Eddie Collins	1915
.181	Eddie Collins	1918
.181	Jim Thome	2008
.177	Tony Phillips	1996
.176	Frank Thomas	1992
.171	Frank Thomas	1996

Strikeouts

175	Dave Nicholson	1963
150	Sammy Sosa	1990
150	Ron Kittle	1983
147	Jim Thome	2006
147	Jim Thome	2008
139	Jose Valentin	2004
137	Ron Kittle	1984
135	Nick Swisher	2008
134	Jim Thome	2007
129	Tommie Agee	1967
128	Danny Tartabull	1996
127	Tommie Agee	1966
126	Ron Karkovice	1993
126	Dick Allen	1972
126	Dave Nicholson	1964

Strikeout Average

.390	Dave Nicholson	1963
.329	Ron Karkovice	1994
.313	Ron Karkovice	1993
.310	Jim Thome	2007
.300	Jim Thome	2006
.292	Jim Thome	2008
.288	Ron Kittle	1983
.282	Sammy Sosa	1990
.272	Nick Swisher	2008
.271	Danny Tartabull	1996
.260	Ron Karkovice	1995
.260	Jose Valentin	2001
.249	Dick Allen	1972
.244	Tommie Agee	1967

Stolen Bases

77	Rudy Law	1977
68	Juan Pierre	2010
59	Scott Podsednik	2005
56	Luis Aparicio	1959
56	Wally Moses	1943
53	Luis Aparicio	1961
53	Eddie Collins	1917
52	Gary Redus	1987
52	Frank Isbell	1901
51	Tim Raines	1991
51	Don Buford	1966

Pinch-Hits

21	Smoky Burgess	1966
20	Smoky Burgess	1965
18	Jerry Hairston	1984
17	Jerry Hairston	1983
17	Pete Ward	1969
15	Ron Northey	1956
14	Smead Jolley	1931
14	Jerry Hairston	1986
14	Jerry Hairston	1985

Pinch At-Bats

66	Smoky Burgess	1966
65	Smoky Burgess	1965
62	Jerry Hairston	1983
60	Smoky Burgess	1967
59	Jerry Hairston	1984
53	Jerry Hairston	1985
47	Jerry Hairston	1982
46	Jerry Hairston	1986
46	Pete Ward	1969

Pinch-Hit Batting Average

.467	Smead Jolley	1931
.394	Eddie Murphy	1920
.385	Ron Northey	1956
.371	Greg Walker	1983
.370	Pete Ward	1969
.355	Walt Dropo	1957
.318	Smoky Burgess	1966
.310	Tom Wright	1953

RBIs per Game

.95	Frank Thomas	1996
.93	Luke Appling	1936
.93	Albert Belle	1998
.93	Zeke Bonura	1936
.90	Frank Thomas	2000
.89	Frank Thomas	1994
.88	Julio Franco	1994
.88	Magglio Ordonez	2002
.87	Zeke Bonura	1934
.86	Zeke Bonura	1937
.86	Frank Thomas	1997
.84	Frank Thomas	1993
.83	Joe Jackson	1920
.82	Al Simmons	1933
.81	Oscar Felsch	1920

Runs per Game

.94	Frank Thomas	1994
.90	Fielder Jones	1901
.88	Johnny Mostil	1925
.87	Rip Radcliff	1936
.85	Dummy Hoy	1901
.82	Harry Hooper	1924
.81	Zeke Bonura	1936
.81	Johnny Mostil	1926
.80	Luke Appling	1936
.80	Ray Durham	2000
.80	Ray Durham	1998
.79	Minnie Minoso	1951
.79	Sammy Strang	1902

White Sox American League Leaders by Year

BATTING

Average

.388	Luke Appling	1936
.328	Luke Appling	1943
.347	Frank Thomas	1997

Home Runs

33	Bill Melton	1971
37	Dick Allen	1972
32	Dick Allen	1974

At-Bats

609	Jiggs Donahue	1907
648	Nellie Fox	1952
636	Nellie Fox	1955
624	Nellie Fox	1959
605	Nellie Fox	1960
607	Lance Johnson	1995

Runs

135	Johnny Mostil	1925
106	Frank Thomas	1994

Hits

192	Nellie Fox	1952
201*	Nellie Fox	1954
196	Nellie Fox	1957
187	Nellie Fox	1958
184	Minnie Minoso	1960
186	Lance Johnson	1995

* Tied for lead

Doubles

40	Don Kolloway	1942
35	Wally Moses	1945
36	Minnie Minoso	1957
45	Floyd Robinson	1962
44*	Chet Lemon	1979
46	Frank Thomas	1992

* Tied for lead

Triples

21	Joe Jackson	1916
20	Joe Jackson	1920
16*	Dixie Walker	1937
16*	Mike Kreevich	1937
12*	Wally Moses	1943
14	Minnie Minoso	1951
16	Jim Rivera	1953
18	Minnie Minoso	1954
11*	Minnie Minoso	1956
10	Nellie Fox	1960
13*	Lance Johnson	1991
12	Lance Johnson	1992
14	Lance Johnson	1993
14	Lance Johnson	1994

*Tied for lead

RBIs

113	Dick Allen	1972

Stolen Bases

52	Frank Isbell	1901
47	Patsy Dougherty	1908
33	Eddie Collins	1919
47	Eddie Collins	1923
42	Eddie Collins	1924
43	Johnny Mostil	1925
35	Johnny Mostil	1926
31*	Minnie Minoso	1951
22	Minnie Minoso	1952
25	Minnie Minoso	1953
25	Jim Rivera	1955
21	Luis Aparicio	1956
28	Luis Aparicio	1957
29	Luis Aparicio	1958
56	Luis Aparicio	1959
51	Luis Aparicio	1960
53	Luis Aparicio	1961
68	Juan Pierre	2010

*Tied for lead

Walks

86	Dummy Hoy	1901
119	Eddie Collins	1915
90*	Johnny Mostil	1925
90*	Willie Kamm	1925

99	Dick Allen	1972
138	Frank Thomas	1991
122	Frank Thomas	1992
109	Frank Thomas	1994
136	Frank Thomas	1995
125	Tony Phillips	1996

*Tied for lead

On-Base Percentage

.419	Luke Appling	1943
.422	Dick Allen	1972
.453	Frank Thomas	1991
.439	Frank Thomas	1992
.487	Frank Thomas	1994
.456	Frank Thomas	1997

Slugging Percentage

.491	Jacques Fournier	1915
.603	Dick Allen	1972
.563	Dick Allen	1974
.541	Harold Baines	1984
.729	Frank Thomas	1994
.655	Albert Belle	1998

PITCHING

Wins

27	Doc White	1907
40	Ed Walsh	1908
28	Ed Cicotte	1917
29	Ed Cicotte	1919
21*	Ted Lyons	1925
22*	Ted Lyons	1927
20*	Billy Pierce	1957
22	Early Wynn	1959
20*	Gary Peters	1964
24*	Wilbur Wood	1972
24	Wilbur Wood	1973
19	LaMarr Hoyt	1982
24	LaMarr Hoyt	1983
22	Jack McDowell	1993

*Tied for lead

Winning Percentage

.774	Clark Griffith	1901
.727	Ed Walsh	1908
.682	Ed Cicotte	1916
.750	Reb Russell	1917
.806	Ed Cicotte	1919
.842	Sandy Consuegra	1954
.727*	Dick Donovan	1957
.750	Bob Shaw	1959
.690	Ray Herbert	1962
.731	Joel Horlen	1967
.759	Richard Dotson	1983
.857	Jason Bere	1994

*Tied for lead

Earned Run Average

1.52	Doc White	1906
1.60	Ed Walsh	1907
1.27	Ed Walsh	1910
1.53	Ed Cicotte	1917
2.48	Red Faber	1921
2.80	Red Faber	1922
2.37	Thornton Lee	1941
2.10	Ted Lyons	1942
2.42	Joe Haynes	1947
2.48*	Saul Rogovin	1951
1.97	Billy Pierce	1955
2.67	Frank Baumann	1960
2.33	Gary Peters	1963
1.98	Gary Peters	1966
2.06	Joel Horlen	1967

*Tied for lead

Games

56	Ed Walsh	1907
66	Ed Walsh	1908
51	Frank Smith	1909
45*	Ed Walsh	1910
56	Ed Walsh	1911
62	Ed Walsh	1912
52	Reb Russell	1913
50*	Red Faber	1915
50	Dave Danforth	1917
53	Clint Brown	1937
61	Clint Brown	1939
40	Joe Haynes	1942
47	Bill Kennedy	1952
67	Gerry Staley	1959
82	Eddie Fisher	1965
77	Bob Locker	1967
88	Wilbur Wood	1968
76	Wilbur Wood	1969
77	Wilbur Wood	1970
77	Bobby Thigpen	1990
83	Kelly Wunsch	2000

*Tied for lead

Games Started

46	Ed Walsh	1907
49	Ed Walsh	1908
41	Frank Smith	1909
41	Ed Walsh	1912
38	Jim Scott	1913
40	Lefty Williams	1919
39	Red Faber	1920
36	Tommy Thomas	1927
37	Early Wynn	1959
49	Wilbur Wood	1972
48	Wilbur Wood	1973
42	Wilbur Wood	1974
43	Wilbur Wood	1975
35*	Jack McDowell	1991
25*	Jack McDowell	1994
35	Mark Buehrle	2004
34*	Mark Buehrle	2008

*Tied for lead

Complete Games

37	Ed Walsh	1907
42	Ed Walsh	1908
37	Frank Smith	1909
30	Ed Cicotte	1919
32	Red Faber	1921
31	Red Faber	1922
28	Hollis Thurston	1924
30	Ted Lyons	1927
24	Tommy Thomas	1929
29	Ted Lyons	1930
30	Thornton Lee	1941
21*	Billy Pierce	1956
16*	Billy Pierce	1957
16*	Dick Donovan	1957
19*	Billy Pierce	1958
15	Jack McDowell	1991
13	Jack McDowell	1992
9	Bartolo Colon	2003

*Tied for lead

Shutouts

5	Clark Griffith	1901
10	Ed Walsh	1906
11	Ed Walsh	1908
8	Ed Walsh	1909
7*	Jim Scott	1915
5	Ted Lyons	1925
4*	Ted Lyons	1940
5*	Virgil Trucks	1954
5	Jim Wilson	1957
4*	Early Wynn	1960
7	Ray Herbert	1963
6*	Joel Horlen	1967
6*	Tommy John	1967
4	Jack McDowell	1993
3*	Jon Garland	2005

*Tied for lead

Innings Pitched

422⅓	Ed Walsh	1907
464	Ed Walsh	1908
365	Frank Smith	1909
368	Ed Walsh	1911
393	Ed Walsh	1912
346⅔	Ed Cicotte	1917
306⅔	Ed Cicotte	1919
353	Red Faber	1922
307⅔*	Tommy Thomas	1927

307⅔*	Ted Lyons	1927
297⅔	Ted Lyons	1930
255⅔	Early Wynn	1959
376⅔	Wilbur Wood	1972
359⅓	Wilbur Wood	1973
245⅓	Mark Buehrle	2004
236⅔	Mark Buehrle	2005

Strikeouts

269	Ed Walsh	1908
177	Frank Smith	1909
255	Ed Walsh	1911
186	Billy Pierce	1953
179	Early Wynn	1958
207	Esteban Loaiza	2003

Hits per Nine Innings

7.97	Red Faber	1921
7.93	Tommy Thomas	1927
7.16	Billy Pierce	1953
6.07	Joel Horlen	1964
6.47	Gary Peters	1967

Walks per Nine Innings

1.18	Doc White	1907

1.49*	Ed Walsh	1910
1.47	Doc White	1911
1.43	Reb Russell	1916
1.52	Reb Russell	1917
1.35	Ed Cicotte	1918
1.44	Ed Cicotte	1919
2.23	Ted Lyons	1936
2.02	Monty Stratton	1937
1.36	Ted Lyons	1939
1.78	Ted Lyons	1941
1.92	Dick Donovan	1958
1.73	Jim Kaat	1973
1.07	LaMarr Hoyt	1983
1.64	LaMarr Hoyt	1984
1.49	Bill Long	1987

*Tied for lead

Strikeouts per Nine Innings

5.54	Lefty Williams	1916
6.17	Billy Pierce	1953
7.06	Billy Pierce	1954
8.69	Juan Pizarro	1961
7.66	Juan Pizarro	1962
7.99	Floyd Bannister	1983
8.46	Floyd Bannister	1985

Opponent Batting Average

.187	Ed Walsh	1910
.242	Red Faber	1921
.244*	Tommy Thomas	1926
.218	Billy Pierce	1953
.190	Joel Horlen	1964
.262*	Eddie Fisher	1965
.199	Gary Peters	1967

*Tied for lead

Saves

7	Ed Walsh	1908
6	Ed Walsh	1910
7	Ed Walsh	1911
10	Ed Walsh	1912
4	Red Faber	1914
7	Dave Danforth	1917
5	Dickie Kerr	1920
18	Clint Brown	1937
14	Gordon Maltzberger	1943
12	Gordon Maltzberger	1944
11	Harry Dorish	1952
15	Turk Lown	1959
24	Terry Forster	1974
26	Rich Gossage	1975
57	Bobby Thigpen	1990

The White Sox before Chicago: Western League Standings, 1894–99

1894

	Won	Lost	Pct
Sioux City*	**74**	**51**	**.592**
Toledo	67	55	.549
Kansas City	60	58	.508
Minneapolis	63	62	.504
Grand Rapids	62	65	.488
Indianapolis	60	66	.476
Detroit	56	69	.448
Milwaukee	50	74	.403

1895

	Won	Lost	Pct
Indianapolis	73	43	.629
St. Paul	**71**	**51**	**.581**
Kansas City	73	53	.579
Minneapolis	65	58	.520
Detroit	58	67	.464
Milwaukee	58	67	.464
Toledo/ Terre Haute	55	71	.436
Grand Rapids	38	86	.306

1896

	Won	Lost	Pct
Minneapolis	89	47	.654
Indianapolis	78	54	.594
Detroit	80	58	.580
St. Paul	**73**	**63**	**.537**
Kansas City	69	66	.511
Milwaukee	62	78	.443
Columbus	52	88	.371
Grand Rapids	45	94	.323

1897

	Won	Lost	Pct
Indianapolis	98	37	.725
Columbus	89	47	.654
St. Paul	**86**	**51**	**.627**
Milwaukee	85	51	.625
Detroit	79	66	.534
Minneapolis	43	95	.309
Kansas City	40	99	.287
Grand Rapids	35	100	.259

1898

	Won	Lost	Pct
Kansas City	88	51	.633
Indianapolis	84	50	.626
Milwaukee	82	57	.596
St. Paul	**81**	**58**	**.582**
Columbus	72	60	.549
Detroit	50	87	.364
Minneapolis	48	92	.342
St. Joseph	42	93	.311

1899

	Won	Lost	Pct
Indianapolis	75	47	.614
Minneapolis	76	50	.603
Detroit	64	60	.516
Grand Rapids	63	62	.504
St. Paul	**57**	**69**	**.452**
Milwaukee	55	68	.447
Kansas City	53	70	.430
Buffalo	53	70	.430

*Charles Comiskey purchased the Sioux City team after the 1894 season and moved it to St. Paul, Minnesota, where they played as the St. Paul Saints for the next five years before coming to Chicago in 1900 as a charter member of the American League.

Year by Year

Year	Pos.	W–L	Pct	GB–GA	Manager	Attendance
1901	1st	83–53	.610	+4	Clark Griffith	354,350
1902	4th	74–60	.552	8	Clark Griffith	337,898
1903	7th	60–77	.438	30½	Nixey Callahan	286,183
1904	3rd	89–65	.578	6	Nixey Callahan–Fielder Jones	557,123
1905	2nd	92–60	.605	3	Fielder Jones	687,419
1906	1st	93–58	.616	+3	Fielder Jones	585,202
1907	3rd	87–64	.576	5½	Fielder Jones	667,307
1908	3rd	88–64	.579	1½	Fielder Jones	636,096
1909	4th	78–74	.513	20	Billy Sullivan	478,400
1910	6th	68–85	.444	35½	Hugh Duffy	552,084
1911	4th	77–74	.510	24	Hugh Duffy	583,208
1912	4th	78–76	.506	28	Nixey Callahan	602,241
1913	5th	78–74	.513	17½	Nixey Callahan	644,501
1914	6th	70–84	.455	30	Nixey Callahan	469,290
1915	3rd	93–61	.604	9½	Clarence Rowland	539,461
1916	2nd	89–65	.578	2	Clarence Rowland	679,923
1917	1st	100–54	.649	+9	Clarence Rowland	684,521
1918	6th	57–67	.460	17	Clarence Rowland	195,081
1919	1st	88–52	.629	+3½	Kid Gleason	627,186
1920	2nd	96–58	.623	2	Kid Gleason	833,492
1921	7th	62–92	.403	36½	Kid Gleason	543,650
1922	5th	77–77	.500	17	Kid Gleason	602,860
1923	7th	69–85	.448	30	Kid Gleason	573,778
1924	8th	66–87	.431	25½	John Evers–Ed Walsh–Eddie Collins–John Evers	606,658
1925	5th	79–75	.513	18½	Eddie Collins	823,231
1926	5th	81–72	.529	9½	Eddie Collins	710,339
1927	5th	70–83	.458	39½	Ray Schalk	614,423
1928	5th	72–82	.468	29	Ray Schalk–Russ Blackburne	494,152
1929	7th	59–93	.366	46	Russ Blackburne	426,795
1930	7th	62–92	.403	40	Donie Bush	406,123
1931	8th	56–97	.366	51½	Donie Bush	403,550
1932	7th	49–102	.325	56½	Lew Fonseca	233,198
1933	6th	67–83	.477	31	Lew Fonseca	397,789
1934	8th	53–99	.349	47	Lew Fonseca–Jimmy Dykes	236,559
1935	5th	74–78	.487	19½	Jimmie Dykes	470,281
1936	3rd	81–70	.536	20	Jimmie Dykes	440,810
1937	3rd	86–68	.588	16	Jimmie Dykes	589,245
1938	6th	65–83	.439	32	Jimmie Dykes	338,278
1939	4th	85–69	.552	22½	Jimmie Dykes	594,104
1940	4th	82–72	.532	8	Jimmie Dykes	660,336
1941	3rd	77–77	.500	24	Jimmie Dykes	677,077
1942	6th	66–82	.466	34	Jimmie Dykes	425,734
1943	4th	82–72	.532	16	Jimmie Dykes	508,962
1944	7th	71–83	.461	18	Jimmie Dykes	563,539
1945	6th	71–78	.477	15	Jimmie Dykes	657,981
1946	5th	74–80	.481	30	Jimmie Dykes–Mule Haas–Ted Lyons	983,403
1947	6th	70–84	.455	27	Ted Lyons	876,948
1948	8th	51–101	.336	44½	Ted Lyons	777,844
1949	6th	63–91	.409	34	Jack Onslow	937,151
1950	6th	60–94	.390	38	Jack Onslow–Red Corriden	781,330
1951	4th	81–73	.526	17	Paul Richards	1,328,234
1952	3rd	81–73	.526	14	Paul Richards	1,231,675
1953	3rd	89–65	.578	11½	Paul Richards	1,141,353
1954	3rd	94–60	.610	17	Paul Richards–Marty Marion	1,231,629
1955	3rd	91–63	.591	9	Marty Marion	1,175,684
1956	3rd	85–69	.552	12	Marty Marion	1,000,090
1957	2nd	90–64	.584	8	Al Lopez	1,135,668
1958	2nd	82–72	.532	10	Al Lopez	797,451

HIS CHEEK BULGING WITH TOBACCO, CHICAGO'S NELSON FOX GETS TED WILLIAMS (9) AND THROWS FOR DOUBLE PLAY. AT LEFT IS SHORTSTOP CARRASQUEL

CHICAGO'S WHITE SOX ARE WHITE HOT

On Chicago's South Side last week the stockyards were empty and Comiskey Park was full. This was incredible enough, but the goings-on inside Comiskey Park, home of the White Sox, were stranger still. After 32 docile years the Sox suddenly had begun batting ferociously, running wild on the bases and ripping off slick double plays like the one above. They won 20 out of 24 games and vaulted into first place in the American League, a feat that astonished fans everywhere and brought South Siders scurrying into the open, some for the first time since the great 1919 "Black Sox" scandal.

At the ball park the Sox fans cast off their inferiority complexes and really cut loose. They howled, fought among themselves and lit fires in the stands. They kept an endless stream of torn paper fluttering down from the upper deck and threw lighted firecrackers at enemy outfielders. When a record 53,940 people jammed Comiskey Park one night last week to see Chicago play the Yankees, it was a fair indication of the happy hysteria the White Sox have aroused in fans of the underdog all over the country.

Life magazine, June 18, 1951, feature story about the amazing White Sox—resurrected from the dead.

Year	Pos.	W–L	Pct	GB–GA	Manager	Attendance
1959	1st	94–60	.610	+5	Al Lopez	1,423,144
1960	3rd	87–67	.565	10	Al Lopez	1,644,460
1961	4th	86–76	.531	23	Al Lopez	1,146,019
1962	5th	85–77	.525	11	Al Lopez	1,131,562
1963	2nd	94–68	.580	10½	Al Lopez	1,158,848
1964	2nd	98–64	.605	1	Al Lopez	1,250,053
1965	2nd	95–67	.586	7	Al Lopez	1,130,519
1966	4th	83–79	.512	15	Eddie Stanky	990,016
1967	4th	89–73	.549	3	Eddie Stanky	985,634
1968	8th-T	67–95	.414	36	Eddie Stanky–Les Moss–Al Lopez	803,775
1969	5th	68–94	.420	29	Al Lopez–Don Gutteridge	589,546
1970	6th	56–106	.346	42	Don Gutteridge–Bill Adair–Chuck Tanner	495,355
1971	3rd	79–83	.488	22½	Chuck Tanner	833,891
1972	2nd	87–67	.565	5½	Chuck Tanner	1,186,018
1973	5th	77–85	.475	17	Chuck Tanner	1,316,527
1974	4th	80–80	.500	9	Chuck Tanner	1,163,596
1975	5th	75–86	.466	22½	Chuck Tanner	770,800
1976	6th	64–97	.398	25½	Paul Richards	914,945
1977	3rd	90–72	.556	12	Bob Lemon	1,657,135
1978	5th	71–90	.441	20½	Bob Lemon–Larry Doby	1,491,100
1979	5th	73–87	.456	14	Don Kessinger–Tony LaRussa	1,280,702
1980	5th	70–90	.438	26	Tony LaRussa	1,200,365
1981	5th	54–52	.509	8½	Tony LaRussa	946,651
1982	3rd	87–75	.537	6	Tony LaRussa	1,567,787

Year	Pos.	W–L	Pct	GB–GA	Manager	Attendance
1983	1st	99–63	.612	+20*	Tony LaRussa	2,132,821
1984	5th-T	74–88	.457	10	Tony LaRussa	2,136,988
1985	3rd	85–77	.525	6	Tony LaRussa	1,669,888
1986	5th	72–90	.444	20	Tony LaRussa–Doug Rader–Jim Fregosi	1,424,313
1987	5th	77–85	.475	8	Jim Fregosi	1,208,060
1988	5th	71–90	.441	32½	Jim Fregosi	1,115,525
1989	7th	69–92	.429	29½	Jeff Torborg	1,045,651
1990	2nd	94–68	.580	9	Jeff Torborg	2,002,359
1991	2nd	87–75	.537	8	Jeff Torborg	2,934,154†
1992	3rd	86–76	.531	10	Gene Lamont	2,681,156
1993	1st	94–68	.580	+8	Gene Lamont	2,581,091
1994	1st	67–46	.593	+1	Gene Lamont	1,697,398
1995	3rd	68–76	.472	32	Gene Lamont–Terry Bevington	1,609,773
1996	2nd	85–77	.525	14½	Terry Bevington	1,676,416
1997	2nd	80–81	.497	-6	Terry Bevington	1,865,222
1998	2nd	80–82	.494	-9	Jerry Manuel	1,391,146
1999	2nd	75–86	.466	21.5	Jerry Manuel	1,338,851
2000	1st	95–67	.586	+5	Jerry Manuel	1,947,799
2001	3rd	83–79	.512	-8	Jerry Manuel	1,766,172
2002	2nd	81–81	.500	13.5	Jerry Manuel	1,676,804
2003	2nd	86–76	.531	4	Jerry Manuel	1,939,594
2004	2nd	83–79	.512	9	Ozzie Guillen	1,930,537
2005	1st	99–63	.611	+6	Ozzie Guillen	2,342,833
2006	3rd	90–72	.556	6	Ozzie Guillen	2,957,414
2007	4th	72–90	.444	24	Ozzie Guillen	2,684,395
2008	1st	89–74	.546	+1	Ozzie Guillen	2,500,648
2009	3rd	79–83	.488	7.5	Ozzie Guillen	2,284,163
2010	2nd	88–74	.543	6	Ozzie Guillen	2,194,378

*American League record
†White Sox record

Totals*

Games Played: 17,141
Games Won: 8,628
Games Lost: 8,413
Games Tied: 100

Three games ordered replayed:
September 3, 1915 vs. Cleveland; September 12, 1939, vs. Washington and June 20, 1940, vs. New York.

Four games forfeited:
May 2, 1901; September 9, 1917; April 26, 1925; July 12, 1979.

*Totals do not include the 1900 season when the American League was classified as a minor league and subject to National League governance.

Decade by Decade

Decade	Won	Lost	Tied	Percentage	Best Record
1901–10	812	660	35	.551	93–58, 1906
1911–20	826	664	15	.554	100–54, 1917
1921–30	697	838	7	.454	81–72, 1926
1931–40	698	821	11	.459	86–68, 1937
1941–50	685	842	10	.448	82–72, 1943
1951–60	874	666	11	.593	94–60, 1954, 1959

Decade	Won	Lost	Tied	Percentage	Best Record
1961–70	821	799	2	.506	98–64, 1964
1971–80	766	837	5	.477	87–67, 1972
1981–90	782	780	2	.501	99–63, 1983
1991–2000	817	734	2	.526	95–67, 2000
2001–2010	850	771	0	.522	99–63, 2005

All-Time Records against American League Opponents through 2010

EASTERN DIVISION	Year	Won	Lost	Tied	Pct
Baltimore	1954–	358	370	4	.491
Boston	1901–	919	954	11	.491
New York	1903–	800	1,035	13	.435
Toronto	1977–	160	183	0	.466
Tampa Bay	1998–	59	42	0	.584

CENTRAL DIVISION	Year	Won	Lost	Tied	Pct
Cleveland	1901–	1,024	986	17	.509
Detroit	1901–	996	1,009	15	.496
Kansas City	1969–	335	291	0	.535
Minnesota	1961–	360	407	3	.469

WESTERN DIVISION	Year	Won	Lost	Tied	Pct
Los Angeles/ Anaheim	1961–	343	336	1	.505
Oakland	1968–	260	283	0	.478
Seattle	1977–	205	181	0	.531
Texas	1972–	238	223	3	.516

DEFUNCT TEAMS

	Year	Won	Lost	Tied	Pct
Baltimore	1901–02	25	12	2	.676
Milwaukee	1901	16	4	0	.800
St. Louis	1902–53	619	491	13	.558
Philadelphia	1901–54	589	585	6	.502
Kansas City	1955–67	166	92	0	.643
Washington	1901–60	714	585	12	.550
Washington	1961–71	109	71	0	.606
Seattle	1969	10	8	0	.556

1900 American League (Minor League)

	Won	Lost	Tied	Pct
Buffalo	11	9	0	.555
Cleveland	13	7	1	.650
Detroit	10	10	0	.500
Indianapolis	12	5	0	.706
Kansas City	7	13	0	.350
Milwaukee	12	6	1	.667
Minneapolis	17	3	0	.607

All-Time Records against National League Opponents through 2010

EASTERN DIVISION	Year	Won	Lost	Tied	Pct
Atlanta	2002–	5	4	0	.555
Florida	2004–	4	5	0	.444
Montreal/ Washington	2002–	5	4	0	.555
New York	2002–	2	1	0	.666
Philadelphia	2002–	4	5	0	.444

CENTRAL DIVISION	Year	Won	Lost	Tied	Pct
Chicago Cubs	1997–	41	37	0	.525
Cincinnati	1997–	14	3	0	.823
Houston	1997–	10	8	0	.555
Milwaukee	1970–	199	174	0	.533
Pittsburgh	1997–	17	9	0	.653
St. Louis	1997–	8	10	0	.444

WESTERN DIVISION	Year	Won	Lost	Tied	Pct
Arizona	2003–	2	4	0	.333
Colorado	2005–	4	2	0	.666
Los Angeles	2003–	9	3	0	.750
San Diego	2003–	4	2	0	.666
San Francisco	2003–	4	2	0	.666

Sox on the road in 1956, Luis Aparicio coming up to the plate with Nellie Fox on deck

Best Single-Season Record against AL Opponents

EASTERN DIVISION

	Year	Record
Baltimore	1954	15–7
Boston	1906	18–4
Detroit	1920	19–3
New York	1990	10–2
Toronto	1977	8–3
Tampa Bay	2007	6–1

CENTRAL DIVISION

	Year	Record
Cleveland	1941	17–5
Kansas City	1997	11–1
Milwaukee	1989, 1990	10–2
Minnesota	1993, 1995	10–3

WESTERN DIVISION

	Year	Record
L.A./California	1980, 1983, 1992	10–3
Oakland	1977	10–5
Seattle	1983	12–1
Texas	1972	14–4

DEFUNCT TEAMS

	Year	Record
Baltimore	1901	14–4
Milwaukee	1901	16–4
St. Louis	1915, 1937, 1939	18–4
Philadelphia	1909	19–3
Kansas City	1964	16–2
Washington (1901–60)	1909	19–3
Washington (1961–71)	1961, 1963, 1965	13–5
Seattle	1969	10–8

Season-Series Results against Current and Defunct American League Opponents

Baltimore Orioles (1901–02)

1901	14–4
1902	11–8

New York Yankees (1903–)

1903	7–11
1904	12–10
1905	15–7
1906	12–10
1907	12–10
1908	16–6
1909	14–8
1910	8–13
1911	13–9
1912	13–9
1913	11–10
1914	12–10
1915	15–7
1916	10–12
1917	12–10
1918	12–6
1919	12–8
1920	10–12
1921	13–9
1922	9–13
1923	7–15
1924	6–16
1925	13–9
1926	8–14
1927	5–17
1928	9–13
1929	6–16
1930	8–14
1931	6–15
1932	5–17
1933	7–15
1934	5–17
1935	9–11
1936	7–14
1937	9–13
1938	8–14
1939	4–18
1940	11–11
1941	8–14
1942	7–15
1943	10–12
1944	10–12
1945	9–12
1946	8–14
1947	10–12
1948	6–16
1949	7–15
1950	8–14
1951	8–14
1952	8–14
1953	9–13
1954	7–15
1955	11–11
1956	9–13
1957	8–14
1958	7–15
1959	13–9
1960	10–12
1961	6–12
1962	8–10
1963	8–10
1964	6–12
1965	8–10
1966	9–9
1967	12–6
1968	6–12
1969	3–9
1970	5–7
1971	5–7
1972	7–5
1973	8–4
1974	4–8
1975	6–6
1976	1–11
1977	3–7
1978	1–9
1979	4–8
1980	5–7
1981	5–7
1982	8–4
1983	8–4
1984	7–5
1985	6–6

1986	6–6
1987	5–7
1988	3–9
1989	5–6
1990	10–2
1991	8–4
1992	8–4
1993	4–8
1994	4–2
1995	3–2
1996	6–7
1997	2–9
1998	4–7
1999	5–7
2000	8–4
2001	1–5
2002	2–4
2003	4–2
2004	3–4
2005	3–3
2006	2–4
2007	4–6
2008	2–5
2009	3–4
2010	2–4

Milwaukee Brewers (1901)

1901	16–4

St. Louis Browns (1902–53)

1902	9–9
1903	9–11
1904	14–8
1905	14–7
1906	13–7
1907	16–6
1908	11–10
1909	10–12
1910	12–10
1911	17–5
1912	13–9
1913	12–10
1914	13–9
1915	18–4
1916	15–7
1917	16–6
1918	5–5
1919	11–9
1920	14–8
1921	7–15
1922	8–14
1923	11–11
1924	13–8
1925	9–13
1926	13–9
1927	15–7
1928	10–12
1929	4–17
1930	12–10
1931	12–10
1932	8–14
1933	15–7
1934	7–14
1935	11–11
1936	13–8
1937	18–4
1938	13–8
1939	18–4
1940	13–9
1941	11–11
1942	6–13
1943	10–12
1944	8–14
1945	8–13
1946	12–10
1947	11–11
1948	8–13
1949	15–7
1950	12–10
1951	15–7
1952	14–8
1953	17–5

Baltimore Orioles (1954–)

1954	15–7
1955	12–10
1956	13–9
1957	12–10
1958	13–9
1959	11–11
1960	9–13
1961	7–11
1962	9–9
1963	11–7
1964	8–10
1965	9–9
1966	9–9
1967	11–7
1968	7–11
1969	3–9
1970	3–9
1971	4–8
1972	4–8
1973	4–8
1974	7–5
1975	4–7
1976	4–8
1977	5–5
1978	1–8
1979	3–8
1980	6–6
1981	6–3
1982	7–5
1983	5–7
1984	5–7
1985	4–8
1986	3–9
1987	4–8
1988	7–4
1989	6–6
1990	6–6
1991	8–4
1992	6–6
1993	8–4
1994	4–2
1995	1–6
1996	8–4
1997	6–5
1998	9–2
1999	3–7
2000	6–4
2001	4–3
2002	4–3
2003	4–2
2004	4–2
2005	6–2
2006	5–2
2007	3–5
2008	5–4
2009	4–5
2010	3–4

Washington Senators (1901–60)

1901	10–8
1902	12–7
1903	12–8
1904	18–4
1905	14–8
1906	15–7
1907	15–6
1908	15–6
1909	19–3
1910	9–13
1911	13–9
1912	9–13
1913	11–11
1914	12–10
1915	8–14
1916	12–10
1917	15–7
1918	6–13
1919	14–6
1920	17–5
1921	6–16
1922	7–15
1923	10–12
1924	5–17
1925	9–13
1926	11–11
1927	10–12

1928	10–12
1929	10–12
1930	8–14
1931	7–15
1932	4–18
1933	7–15
1934	9–13
1935	12–10
1936	16–5
1937	14–8
1938	10–11
1939	14–8
1940	12–10
1941	13–9
1942	13–7
1943	14–8
1944	16–6
1945	8–14
1946	10–12
1947	14–8
1948	9–12
1949	15–7
1950	8–14
1951	14–8
1952	13–9
1953	12–10
1954	15–7
1955	17–5
1956	13–9
1957	17–5
1958	16–6
1959	16–6
1960	14–8

Minnesota Twins (1961–)

1961	9–9
1962	8–10
1963	8–10
1964	9–9
1965	7–11
1966	4–14
1967	9–9
1968	10–8
1969	5–13
1970	6–12
1971	7–11
1972	8–6
1973	9–9
1974	7–11
1975	9–9
1976	7–11
1977	10–5
1978	8–7
1979	5–8
1980	5–8
1981	2–4
1982	7–6
1983	8–5
1984	8–5
1985	6–7
1986	6–7
1987	6–7
1988	4–9
1989	5–8
1990	7–6
1991	8–5
1992	8–5
1993	10–3
1994	2–4
1995	10–3
1996	6–7
1997	6–6
1998	6–6
1999	8–3
2000	7–5
2001	5–14
2002	8–11
2003	9–10
2004	9–10
2005	11–7
2006	9–10
2007	9–9
2008	9–10
2009	6–12
2010	5–13

Philadelphia Athletics (1901–54)

1901	12–8
1902	10–10
1903	6–14
1904	8–14
1905	9–12
1906	12–9
1907	10–12
1908	13–9
1909	12–10
1910	8–14
1911	9–11
1912	12–10
1913	11–11
1914	5–17
1915	19–3
1916	18–4
1917	15–7
1918	11–10
1919	17–3
1920	16–6
1921	14–8
1922	12–10
1923	10–12
1924	11–11
1925	8–14
1926	6–15
1927	8–14
1928	6–16
1929	9–13
1930	6–16
1931	3–19
1932	7–15
1933	12–10
1934	9–13
1935	12–10
1936	15–7
1937	15–7
1938	12–10
1939	11–11
1940	16–6
1941	10–12
1942	12–10
1943	18–4
1944	9–13
1945	12–10
1946	12–10
1947	11–11
1948	6–16
1949	6–16
1950	11–11
1951	9–13
1952	11–11
1953	10–12
1954	17–5

Kansas City Athletics (1955–67)

1955	14–8
1956	14–8
1957	14–8
1958	12–10
1959	12–10
1960	15–7
1961	14–4
1962	9–9
1963	12–6
1964	16–2
1965	13–5
1966	13–5
1967	8–10

Oakland Athletics (1968–)

1968	10–8
1969	8–10
1970	2–16
1971	11–7
1972	7–8
1973	6–12
1974	7–11
1975	9–9
1976	8–9
1977	10–5
1978	7–8
1979	9–4

1980	6–7
1981	7–6
1982	9–4
1983	8–5
1984	6–7
1985	8–5
1986	7–6
1987	9–4
1988	5–8
1989	5–8
1990	8–5
1991	7–6
1992	5–8
1993	7–6
1994	6–3
1995	7–5
1996	5–7
1997	8–3
1998	4–7
1999	3–7
2000	6–3
2001	1–8
2002	2–7
2003	4–5
2004	2–7
2005	2–7
2006	3–3
2007	4–5
2008	5–4
2009	4–5
2010	3–5

Detroit Tigers (1901–)

1901	10–10
1902	12–7
1903	10–9
1904	14–8
1905	11–11
1906	11–11
1907	13–9
1908	9–13
1909	6–15
1910	9–13
1911	8–14
1912	14–8
1913	13–9
1914	6–16
1915	7–15
1916	13–9
1917	16–6
1918	6–10
1919	11–9
1920	19–3
1921	8–14
1922	17–5
1923	9–13
1924	8–14
1925	13–9
1926	14–8
1927	13–8
1928	13–9
1929	10–12
1930	9–13
1931	11–11
1932	8–12
1933	10–12
1934	5–17
1935	11–11
1936	8–14
1937	8–14
1938	7–15
1939	12–10
1940	13–9
1941	12–10
1942	9–13
1943	9–13
1944	9–13
1945	10–12
1946	10–12
1947	7–15
1948	8–14
1949	8–14
1950	6–16
1951	12–10
1952	17–5
1953	14–8
1954	12–10
1955	14–8
1956	13–9
1957	11–11
1958	10–12
1959	13–9
1960	11–11
1961	6–12
1962	9–9
1963	11–7
1964	11–7
1965	9–9
1966	8–10
1967	8–10
1968	5–13
1969	3–9
1970	6–6
1971	7–5
1972	5–7
1973	5–7
1974	7–5
1975	5–7
1976	6–6
1977	4–6
1978	2–9
1979	3–9
1980	2–10
1981	3–3
1982	9–3
1983	8–4
1984	4–8
1985	6–6
1986	6–6
1987	3–9
1988	3–9
1989	4–8
1990	5–7
1991	4–8
1992	10–2
1993	7–5
1994	8–4
1995	8–4
1996	10–3
1997	4–7
1998	6–6
1999	7–5
2000	9–3
2001	13–6
2002	12–7
2003	11–8
2004	8–11
2005	14–5
2006	12–7
2007	11–7
2008	12–6
2009	9–9
2010	8–10

Cleveland Indians (1901–)

1901	13–7
1902	12–7
1903	10–10
1904	14–8
1905	13–9
1906	12–10
1907	10–11
1908	8–14
1909	8–13
1910	10–12
1911	6–15
1912	11–11
1913	9–13
1914	13–9
1915	16–6
1916	13–9
1917	14–8
1918	10–11
1919	12–8
1920	10–12
1921	7–15
1922	12–10
1923	9–13
1924	11–11
1925	14–8
1926	13–9
1927	8–14

1928	12–10
1929	9–12
1930	10–12
1931	7–15
1932	7–14
1933	9–13
1934	8–14
1935	10–12
1936	12–10
1937	10–12
1938	9–13
1939	12–10
1940	6–16
1941	17–5
1942	11–11
1943	7–15
1944	14–8
1945	11–8
1946	13–9
1947	11–11
1948	6–16
1949	7–15
1950	8–14
1951	12–10
1952	8–14
1953	11–11
1954	11–11
1955	10–12
1956	15–7
1957	14–8
1958	12–10
1959	15–7
1960	11–11
1961	12–6
1962	12–6
1963	11–7
1964	12–6
1965	10–8
1966	11–7
1967	12–6
1968	5–13
1969	8–4
1970	6–6
1971	3–9
1972	8–4
1973	7–5
1974	8–4
1975	7–5
1976	3–9
1977	6–4
1978	8–2
1979	6–6
1980	5–7
1981	2–5
1982	6–6
1983	8–4
1984	8–4
1985	10–2
1986	5–7
1987	7–5
1988	3–9
1989	7–5
1990	5–7
1991	6–6
1992	7–5
1993	9–3
1994	7–5
1995	5–8
1996	5–8
1997	5–7
1998	6–6
1999	3–9
2000	8–5
2001	10–9
2002	9–10
2003	11–8
2004	10–9
2005	14–5
2006	8–11
2007	7–11
2008	11–7
2009	10–8
2010	9–9

Boston Red Sox (1901–)

1901	8–12
1902	8–12
1903	6–14
1904	9–13
1905	16–6
1906	18–4
1907	11–10
1908	16–6
1909	9–13
1910	12–10
1911	11–11
1912	6–16
1913	11–10
1914	9–13
1915	10–12
1916	8–14
1917	12–10
1918	7–12
1919	11–9
1920	10–12
1921	7–15
1922	12–10
1923	13–9
1924	12–10
1925	13–9
1926	16–6
1927	11–11
1928	12–10
1929	11–11
1930	9–13
1931	10–12
1932	10–12
1933	7–11
1934	10–11
1935	9–13
1936	10–12
1937	12–10
1938	6–12
1939	14–8
1940	11–11
1941	6–16
1942	8–13
1943	14–8
1944	5–17
1945	13–9
1946	9–13
1947	6–16
1948	8–14

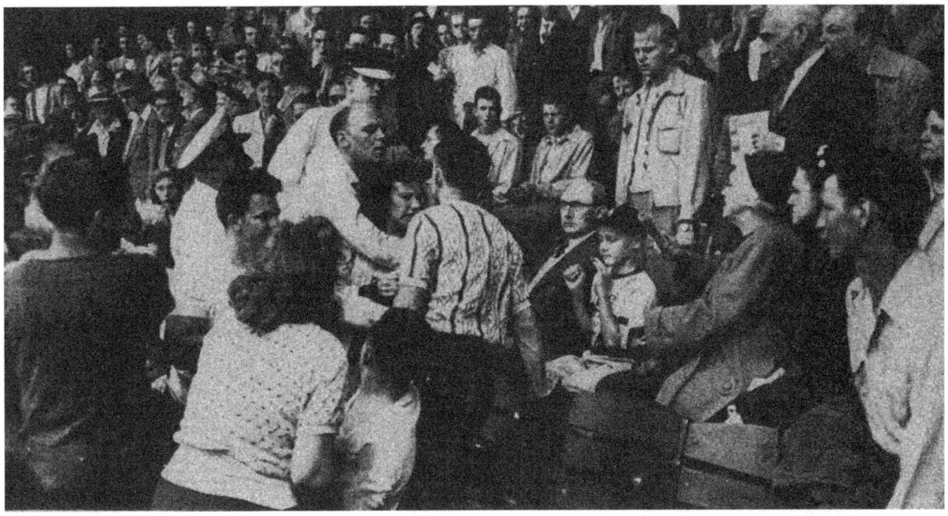

Life magazine took note of the White Sox in June 1951 with a lavish photo spread—including this grandstand photo of an angry White Sox fan about to square off against a Red Sox fan who dared to hold up a Boston banner in Comiskey Park.

1949	5–17
1950	7–15
1951	11–11
1952	10–12
1953	16–6
1954	17–5
1955	13–9
1956	8–14
1957	14–8
1958	12–10
1959	14–8
1960	17–5
1961	9–9
1962	10–8
1963	10–8
1964	14–4
1965	14–4
1966	7–11
1967	10–8
1968	4–14
1969	7–5
1970	4–8
1971	2–10
1972	6–6
1973	6–6
1974	4–8
1975	4–8
1976	6–6
1977	7–3
1978	3–7
1979	6–5
1980	4–6
1981	4–5
1982	8–4
1983	6–6
1984	5–7
1985	8–4
1986	5–7
1987	9–3
1988	5–7
1989	5–7
1990	6–6
1991	5–7
1992	6–6
1993	5–7
1994	4–2
1995	3–5
1996	6–6
1997	8–3
1998	6–5
1999	5–7
2000	5–7
2001	3–3
2002	4–2
2003	4–5
2004	2–4
2005	3–4
2006	5–2
2007	3–5
2008	5–4
2009	4–4
2010	6–1

Washington Senators (1961–71)

1961	13–5
1962	10–8
1963	13–5
1964	12–6
1965	13–5
1966	12–6
1967	8–10
1968	10–8
1969	4–8
1970	4–8
1971	10–2

Texas Rangers (1972–)

1972	14–4
1973	13–5
1974	9–7
1975	5–13
1976	7–11
1977	6–9
1978	11–4
1979	11–2
1980	6–7
1981	2–4
1982	8–5
1983	8–5
1984	5–8
1985	10–3
1986	2–11
1987	7–6
1988	8–5
1989	3–10
1990	7–6
1991	8–5
1992	5–8
1993	8–5
1994	4–5
1995	5–7
1996	8–4
1997	3–8
1998	5–6
1999	5–5
2000	5–5
2001	7–2
2002	5–4
2003	3–4
2004	6–3
2005	3–6
2006	5–5
2007	2–4
2008	3–3
2009	2–4
2010	4–5

Los Angeles/California/Los Angeles Angels of Anaheim (1961–)

1961	10–8
1962	10–8
1963	10–8
1964	10–8
1965	12–6
1966	10–8
1967	11–7
1968	10–8
1969	9–9
1970	6–12
1971	10–8
1972	11–7
1973	10–8
1974	8–10
1975	9–9
1976	7–11
1977	7–8
1978	7–8
1979	4–9
1980	10–3
1981	7–6
1982	5–8
1983	10–3
1984	5–8
1985	5–8
1986	6–7
1987	5–8
1988	4–9
1989	5–8
1990	8–5
1991	5–8
1992	10–3
1993	6–7
1994	5–5
1995	2–10
1996	6–6
1997	5–6
1998	6–5
1999	5–5
2000	6–4
2001	3–6
2002	3–6
2003	4–3
2004	4–5
2005	4–6
2006	6–3
2007	5–4
2008	5–5
2009	5–4
2010	7–2

Kansas City Royals (1969–)

1969	8–10
1970	7–11
1971	9–9
1972	8–9
1973	6–12
1974	11–7
1975	9–9
1976	8–10
1977	8–7
1978	8–7
1979	5–8
1980	5–8
1981	2–0
1982	3–10
1983	9–4
1984	5–8
1985	5–8
1986	7–6
1987	6–7
1988	7–6
1989	6–7
1990	9–4
1991	7–6
1992	7–6
1993	6–7
1994	3–7
1995	8–5
1996	7–5
1997	11–1
1998	8–4
1999	6–6
2000	5–7
2001	14–5
2002	11–8
2003	11–8
2004	13–6
2005	13–5
2006	11–8
2007	12–6
2008	12–6
2009	9–9
2010	10–8

Seattle Pilots (1969)

1969	10–8

Milwaukee Brewers (1970–)

1970	7–11
1971	11–7
1972	9–3
1973	3–9
1974	8–4
1975	8–4
1976	7–5
1977	6–5
1978	4–7
1979	5–7
1980	5–7
1981	4–1
1982	3–9
1983	4–8
1984	7–5
1985	5–7
1986	5–7
1987	6–6
1988	6–6
1989	10–2
1990	10–2
1991	7–5
1992	5–7
1993	9–3
1994	9–3
1995	6–7
1996	6–7
1997	4–7
1998	1–2
1999	1–2
2000	3–0
2001	3–0
2009	2–1

Seattle Mariners (1977–)

1977	10–5
1978	7–8
1979	5–8
1980	6–7
1981	3–3
1982	6–7
1983	12–1
1984	5–8
1985	9–4
1986	8–5
1987	6–7
1988	9–4
1989	7–6
1990	8–5
1991	7–6
1992	4–9
1993	9–4
1994	9–1
1995	4–9
1996	5–7
1997	5–6
1998	4–7
1999	4–8
2000	7–5
2001	2–7
2002	5–4
2003	2–7
2004	7–2
2005	6–3
2006	5–4
2007	1–7
2008	5–1
2009	4–5
2010	9–1

Toronto Blue Jays (1977–)

1977	8–3
1978	4–6
1979	7–5
1980	5–7
1981	7–5
1982	8–4
1983	5–7
1984	4–8
1985	3–9
1986	6–6
1987	4–8
1988	7–5
1989	1–11
1990	5–7
1991	7–5
1992	5–7
1993	6–6
1994	2–3
1995	6–5
1996	7–5
1997	5–6
1998	4–6
1999	6–5
2000	5–5
2001	3–3
2002	4–2
2003	6–3
2004	3–4
2005	4–2
2006	5–4
2007	3–4
2008	1–7
2009	1–6
2010	3–5

Tampa Bay Devil Rays/Rays (1998–)

1998	5–6
1999	6–4
2000	6–4
2001	5–2
2002	4–3
2003	3–3
2004	4–2
2005	4–2
2006	3–3
2007	6–1
2008	4–6
2009	6–2
2010	3–4

Highest Scoring Games (19 or more runs)

Score	Opponent	Date	Sox Pitcher of Record
29–6*	at Kansas City	April 23, 1955	Jack Harshman
22–13	at Boston	May 31, 1970	Floyd Weaver
21–7	Boston (2nd game)	June 26, 1960	Early Wynn
21–14	at Philadelphia	July 18, 1936	Clint Brown
20–6	St. Louis	June 20, 2006	Javier Vazquez
20–6	at Kansas City	April 22, 1959	Bob Shaw
20–2	Washington	June 17, 1956	Dick Donovan
20–10	Cleveland	April 30, 1934	Sam Jones
20–15	Detroit	September 9, 1921	Dickie Kerr
20–6	Washington	May 11, 1911	Doc White
20–8	at Milwaukee	May 15, 1996	Wilson Alvarez
19–11	Minnesota	August 4, 1992	Wilson Alvarez
19–7	Philadelphia	July 20, 1940	Edgar Smith
19–6	Philadelphia	July 28, 1936	Bill Dietrich
19–6	at St. Louis	May 11, 1936	John Whitehead
19–2	at Detroit	August 31, 1926	Red Faber
19–11	at Boston	August 15, 1922	Ted Blankenship
19–3	at Detroit	May 3, 1918	Lefty Williams
19–9	Detroit	May 1, 1901	Roy Patterson
19–3	at Kansas City	September 27, 2003	Bartolo Colon
19–10	Cleveland	September 2, 2001	Rocky Biddle
19–3	Seattle	August 9, 2000	Mike Sirotka

* American League record

Highest Scoring Innings (10 or more runs)

Runs	Opponent	Date	Inning
13	at Washington	September 26, 1943	4
12	at Philadelphia	June 10, 1952	4
11	St. Louis	June 20, 2006	3
11	at Kansas City	September 17, 2007	5
11	Seattle	April 18, 2000	5
11	Oakland	October 3, 1987	5
11	Seattle	September 15, 1983	6
11	California	May 31, 1978	5
11	at Boston	August 19, 1970	9
11	Boston	June 26, 1960	4

Runs	Opponent	Date	Inning
11	at Kansas City	April 22, 1959	7
11	Detroit	September 2, 1959	5
11	Baltimore	August 3, 1956	1
11	at New York	July 28, 1931	8
10	Detroit	May 9, 1953	4
10	at Cleveland	August 15, 1962	9
10	Boston	September 15, 1948	7
10	Philadelphia	May 23, 1940	8
10	at Cleveland	July 3, 1919	4
10	Arizona	June 15, 2005	6

Longest Games (17 or more innings)

Innings	Opponent	Date	Score	Sox Pitcher of Record
25*	Milwaukee	May 8–9, 1984	7–6	Tom Seaver
22	at Washington	June 12, 1967	5–6	John Buzhardt
21	Cleveland	May 26–28, 1973	6–3	Wilbur Wood
21†	Detroit	May 24, 1929	5–6	Ted Lyons
19	Boston	July 9, 2006	6–5	Cliff Politte
19	at Milwaukee	May 1, 1991	9–10	Wayne Edwards
19	at Oakland	August 11, 1972	3–5	Stan Bahnsen
19	Boston	July 13, 1951	5–4	Harry Dorish
19	at Cleveland	June 24, 1915	5–4	Red Faber
18	at Baltimore	August 6, 1959	1–1	None
18	Washington	June 18, 1947	0–1	Earl Harrist
18	New York	August 21, 1933	3–3	None

Innings	Opponent	Date	Score	Sox Pitcher of Record
18	at Washington	May 15, 1918	0–1	Lefty Williams
18	New York	June 25, 1903	6–6	None
17	at Kansas City	May 25, 1986	1–2	Bill Dawley
17	Cleveland	September 13, 1967	1–0	Don McMahon
17	New York	June 21, 1964	1–2	Don Mossi
17	Baltimore	July 25, 1959	3–2	Turk Lown
17	Baltimore	June 4, 1959	6–5	Bob Shaw
17	Boston	September 14, 1952	4–3	Luis Aloma
17	Boston	July 12, 1951	4–5	Saul Rogovin
17	Detroit	August 13, 1933	5–6	Ted Lyons
17	Boston	May 21, 1915	3–2	Red Faber
17	Detroit	May 25, 1912	5–4	Frank Lange
17	Washington	May 13, 1909	1–1	None
17	St. Louis	May 18, 1902	2–2	None

* American League record
† Complete game pitched by Lyons

The Best and Worst Season Starts (20 games)

BEST STARTS

Won	Lost	Year
16	4	2005
15	5	1912
15	5	1973
14	6	1907
14	6	1919
14	6	1920
14	6	1935
14	6	1965

WORST STARTS

Won	Lost	Year
4	16	1948
4	16	1942
5	15	1934
5	15	1950
6	14	1921
6	14	1932
6	14	1968

Consecutive Wins and Losses to Start a Season

WINS

Won	Dates
8	April 11–18, 1982
6	April 8–16, 1991
6	April 14–25, 1920
5	April 17–22, 1945
5	April 14–18, 1914
4	April 10–14, 1959
4	April 16–21, 1957

LOSSES

Lost	Dates
10	April 10–25, 1968
5	April 5–12, 1974
4	April 7–11, 1986
4	April 14–18, 1952
4	April 18–22, 1950
4	April 20–24, 1948
4	April 18–21, 1923
4	April 26–29, 1995

White Sox Home Runs off Walter Johnson, 1912–1926

Date	Place	Batter	Inning
5/8/12	Washington	Harry Lord	1
5/8/12	Washington	Ping Bodie	5
6/14/13	Washington	Ray Schalk	5
6/14/13	Washington	Buck Weaver	9
7/21/13	Chicago	Harry Lord	4
8/31/14	Washington	Jack Fournier	8
8/31/14	Washington	Jack Fournier	10
6/12/20	Chicago	Happy Felsch	6
9/23/22	Chicago	Johnny Mostil	5
6/15/23	Washington	Bibb Falk	7
8/13/23	Washington	Earl Sheely	8
6/16/24	Chicago	Harry Hooper	7
9/25/26	Chicago	Bill Barrett	9

White Sox Players Who Also Played for the Cubs

Player	Position	Sox Years	Cub Years
David Aardsma	Pitcher	2007	2006
Bobby Adams	Infield	1955	1957–59
Paul Assenmacher	Pitcher	1994	1989–93
Earl Averill Jr.	Catcher	1960	1959–60
Frank Baumann	Pitcher	1960–64	1965
George Bell	DH/outfield	1992–93	1991
Jason Bere	Pitcher	1993-98	2001–02
Hi Bithorn	Pitcher	1947	1942–46
Bobby Bonds	Outfield	1978	1981
Zeke Bonura	First base	1934–37	1940
Thad Bosley	Outfield	1978–80	1983–86
Jim Brosnan	Pitcher	1963	1954–58
Warren Brusstar	Pitcher	1982	1983–85
Smoky Burgess	Catcher	1964–67	1949–51
John Buzhardt	Pitcher	1962–67	1958–59
James Callahan	Pitcher/ outfield	1901–05, 1911–14	1897–1900
Johnny Callison	Outfield	1958–59	1970–71
Larry Casian	Pitcher	1998	1995–97
Phil Cavarretta	First base	1954–55	1934–53
Steve Christmas	Catcher	1984	1986
Lloyd Christopher	Outfield	1947	1945
Neal Cotts	Pitcher	2003–06	2007–09
Wes Covington	Outfield	1961	1966
Dick Culler	Infield	1943	1948
Mike Cvengros	Pitcher	1923–25	1929
Tom Daly	Catcher/ infield	1913–15	1887–88
Tommy Davis	Outfield	1968	1970, 1972
Steve Dillard	Infield	1982	1979–81
Miguel Dilone	Outfield	1983	1979
Jess Dobernic	Pitcher	1939	1948–49
Cozy Dolan	Outfield	1903	1900–01
Phil Douglas	Pitcher	1912	1915–19
Moe Drabowsky	Pitcher	1972	1955–60
Vallie Eaves	Pitcher	1939–40	1941–42
Hank Edwards	Outfield	1952	1949–50
Lee Elia	Infield	1966	1968
Johnny Evers	Infield	1922	1902–13
Scott Eyre	Pitcher	1997–2000	2006–08
Scott Fletcher	Infield	1983–85, 1989–91	1981–82
Ken Frailing	Pitcher	1972–73	1974–76
Oscar Gamble	DH	1977, 1985	1969
Ned Garvin	Pitcher	1902	1899–1900
Ross Gload	Infield	2004–06	2000
Wilbur Good	Outfield	1918	1911–15
Tom Gordon	Pitcher	2003	2001–02
Rich Gossage	Pitcher	1972–76	1988
Danny Green	Outfield	1902–05	1898–1901
Clark Griffith	Pitcher	1901–02	1893–1900
Warren Hacker	Pitcher	1961	1948–56
Steve Hamilton	Pitcher	1970	1972
Ralph Hamner	Pitcher	1946	1947–49
Erwin Harvey	Pitcher	1901	1900
Ron Hassey	Catcher	1986–87	1984
Grady Hatton	Infield	1954	1960
Bill Heath	Catcher	1965	1969
Ken Henderson	Outfield	1973–75	1979–80
Greg Hibbard	Pitcher	1989–92	1993
Guy Hoffman	Pitcher	1979–80,1983	1986
Bob Howry	Pitcher	1998–2002	2006–08; '10
Jim Hughes	Pitcher	1957	1956
Frank Isbell	Infield	1900–09	1898
Darrin Jackson	Outfield	1994; 99	1985, 1987–89
Elmer Jacobs	Pitcher	1927	1924–25
Lance Johnson	Outfielder	1988-95	1997-99
Jimmy Johnston	Outfield	1911	1914
Jay Johnstone	Outfield	1971–72	1982–84
Davy Jones	Outfield	1913	1902–04
Matt Karchner	Pitcher	1995–98	1998–2000
Jack Katoll	Pitcher	1901–02	1898–99
Don Kessinger	Infield	1977–79	1964–75
Bruce Kimm	Catcher	1980	1979
Jim King	Outfield	1967	1955–56
Fabian Kowalik	Pitcher	1932	1935–36
Ken Kravec	Pitcher	1975–80	1981–82
Mike Kreevich	Outfield	1935–41	1931
Jack Lamabe	Pitcher	1966–67	1968
Dennis Lamp	Pitcher	1981–83	1977–80
Don Larsen	Pitcher	1961	1967
Vance Law	Infield	1983–84	1988–89
Dave Lemonds	Pitcher	1972	1969
Darren Lewis	Outfielder	1996–97	2002
Dick Littlefield	Pitcher	1951	1957
Bob Locker	Pitcher	1965–69	1973, 1975
Kenny Lofton	Outfielder	2002	2003
Bill Long	Pitcher	1987–90	1990
Jay Loviglio	Infield	1981–82	1983
Grover Lowdermilk	Pitcher	1919–20	1912
Turk Lown	Pitcher	1958–62	1951–58
Robert Machado	Catcher	1996-98	2001-02
George Magoon	Infield	1903	1903
J. C. Martin	Catcher	1959–67	1970–72
Morrie Martin	Pitcher	1954–56	1959
Dave Martinez	Outfield	1995–97	1986–88
Randy Martz	Pitcher	1983	1980–82
Jim McAnany	Outfield	1958–60	1961–62
Chuck McElroy	Pitcher	1997	1991–93
Lynn McGlothen	Pitcher	1981	1978–81
Cal McLish	Pitcher	1961	1949
Lloyd Merriman	Outfield	1955	1955
Sandow Mertes	Infield	1901–02	1898–1900
George Metkovich	Outfield	1949	1953
Alex Metzler	Outfield	1927–30	1925
Bob Miller	Pitcher	1970	1970–71

Player	Position	Sox Years	Cub Years
Bobby Molinaro	Outfield	1977–78, 1980–81	1982
George Moriarity	Infield	1916	1903–04
Eddie Mulligan	Infield	1921–22	1915–16
Danny Murphy	Outfield	1969–70	1960–62
Wayne Nordhagen	Outfield/DH	1976–81	1983
Ron Northey	Pinch hitter	1955–57	1950
Emmett O'Neill	Pitcher	1946	1946
Jose Ortiz	Outfield	1969–70	1971
John Ostrowski	Outfield	1949–50	1943–46
Donn Pall	Pitcher	1988–93	1994
Ken Patterson	Pitcher	1988–91	1992
Reggie Patterson	Pitcher	1981	1983–85
Josh Paul	Catcher	1999–2003	2003
Taylor Phillips	Pitcher	1963	1958–59
Juan Pierre	Outfield	2010–	2006
Juan Pizarro	Pitcher	1961–66	1970–73
Whitey Platt	Outfield	1946	1942–43
Howie Pollet	Pitcher	1956	1953–56
Mike Proly	Pitcher	1978–80	1982–83
Jimmy Qualls	Outfield	1972	1969
Phil Regan	Pitcher	1972	1968–72
Steve Renko	Pitcher	1977	1976–77
Carl Reynolds	Outfield	1927–31	1937–39
Marv Rickert	Outfield	1950	1942, 1946–47
Bob Rush	Pitcher	1960	1948–57
Luis Salazar	Infield	1985–88	1989–92
Scott Sanderson	Pitcher	1994	1984–89
Ron Santo	Infield	1974	1960–73
Carl Sawatski	Catcher	1954	1948–50
Jimmy Schaffer	Catcher	1965	1963–64
Hank Schreiber	Outfield	1914	1926
Bob Shaw	Pitcher	1958–61	1967
Clyde Shoun	Pitcher	1949	1935–37
Charley Smith	Infield	1962–64	1969
Eddie Solomon	Pitcher	1982	1975
Sammy Sosa	Outfield	1989–91	1992–2004
Joe Stephenson	Catcher	1947	1944
Jimmy Stewart	Infield	1967	1963–67
Tim Stoddard	Pitcher	1975	1985
Steve Stone	Pitcher	1973, 1977–78	1974–76
Sammy Strang	Infield	1902	1900, 1902
Tanyon Sturtze	Pitcher	1999–2000	1995–96
Kevin Tapani	Pitcher	1996	1997–2001
Bennie Tate	Catcher	1930–32	1934
Zeb Terry	Infield	1916–17	1920–22
Dick Tidrow	Pitcher	1983	1979–82
Steve Trout	Pitcher	1978–82	1983–87
Vito Valentinetti	Pitcher	1954	1956–57
Luis Vizcaino	Pitcher	2005	2009
Earl Webb	Infield	1933	1927–28
Hoyt Wilhelm	Pitcher	1963–68	1970
Elwood Wirtz	Infield	1924	1921–23
Rick Wrona	Catcher	1993	1988–90
Rollie Zeider	Infield	1910–13	1916–18
Dutch Zwilling	Outfield	1910	1916

Ex-Cubs "Hi" Bithorn (left) and Joe Stephenson (right) show off their new uniforms to the Cubs' Micky Livingston in 1947.

Frank Grube played NFL football in 1928.

All-American Dave DeBusschere signed a Sox contract in 1962.

White Sox Players Who Also Played Professional Football

Player	Position	Years with Sox	Football Years	Team/League
Evar Swanson	of	1932–34	1924–27	Milwaukee Rock Isle Chicago Cardinals (NFL)
Charlie Berry	c	1932–33	1925–26	Pottsville (NFL)
Frank Grube	c	1931–33, 1935–36	1928	New York (NFL)
Bo Jackson	dh	1991–93	1987–90	Los Angeles Raiders (NFL)
Dean Look	of	1961	1962	New York (AFL)
Everett Purdy	of	1926	1926–27	Green Bay (NFL)
Joe Vance	p	1935	1931	Brooklyn (NFL)

White Sox Players Who Also Played Professional Basketball

Player	Position	Years with Sox	Basketball Years	Team/League
Bill Barrett	of	1923–29	1921–22	Worcester, Ill. (IL)
Louis Berger	if	1937–38	1938–39	Washington (ABL)
Dave DeBusschere	p	1962–63	1962–74	Detroit (NBA) New York (NBA)
Steve Hamilton	p	1970	1959–60	Minneapolis (NBA)
Charles Nash	1b	1967	1964–68	Los Angeles (NBA) San Francisco (NBA) Kentucky (ABA)
Ron Reed	p	1984	1965–67	Detroit (NBA)

Players with 50 or More Hits in a Month

Player	Month	Year	Hits
Eddie Collins	July	1920	52
Bibb Falk	June	1924	56
Smead Jolley	July	1930	52

Player	Month	Year	Hits
Rip Radcliff	July	1936	59
Gee Walker	August	1938	53
Luke Appling	July	1943	50

Top Home-Run Seasons (Team)

OVERALL		AT U.S. CELLULAR FIELD	
Year	Total	Year	Total
2004	242	2004	145
2006	236	2008	143
2008	235	2006	136
2003	220	2002	132
2002	217	2003	130
2000	216	2000	125
2001	214	2005	115
2005	200	2001	114
1998	198	2007	110
		1998	106

Most Home Runs at U.S Cellular Field and Old Comiskey Park

Homers	Player	Year
30	Frank Thomas	2000
29	Frank Thomas	2003
29	Paul Konerko	2004
29	Albert Belle	1998
27	Dick Allen	1972
25	Frank Thomas	1993
25	Jim Thome	2006
24	Frank Thomas	1991
24	Frank Thomas	2002
24	Magglio Ordonez	2002
23	Bill Melton	1970
23	Paul Konerko	2005

Winning and Losing Streaks of 10 or More Games

WINNING STREAKS

Wins	Dates
19	August 2–23, 1906
14	May 15–30, 1951
13	June 4–16, 1908
12	June 17–27, 1961
11	June 15–26, 2010
11	September 23–October 3, 1915
10	May 18–26, 1976
10	April 20–May 14, 1967
10	August 14–22, 1965
10	May 31–June 8, 1937
10	August 15–24, 1919
10	June 21–July 3, 1901

LOSING STREAKS

Losses	Dates
13	August 9–26, 1924
12	September 10–22, 1927
11	July 7–18, 1956
11	September 14–24, 1921
11	July 12–20, 1910
10	April 10–15, 1968
10	May 26–June 4, 1938
10	September 17–26, 1934
10	August 7–19, 1932
10	September 14–22, 1931

The 1906, 19-Game "Hitless Wonder" Winning Streak

Date	Opponent	Score	Winning Pitcher	Losing Pitcher
August 2	Boston	3–0	White	Young
August 3	Boston	4–0	Walsh	Harris
August 4	Boston	1–0	Patterson	Dinneen
August 5	Philadelphia	10–2	White	Bender
August 6	Philadelphia	7–2	Owen	Coombs
August 7	Philadelphia	4–0	Walsh	Waddell
August 8	Philadelphia	1–0 (10)	Patterson	Plank
August 9	Philadelphia	3–2 (10)	White	Dygert
August 10	New York	2–1	Walsh	Chesbro
August 11	New York	8–1	Owen	Hogg
August 12	New York	3–0	Walsh	Orth
August 13	New York	0–0 (9)	None	None
August 15	at Boston	6–0	Walsh	Tannehill
August 16	at Boston	9–4	Altrock	Harris
August 17	at Boston	4–3	White	Young
August 18	at New York	10–0	Walsh	Chesbro
August 20	at New York	4–1	White	Orth
August 22	at New York	6–1	Walsh	Chesbro
August 22	at New York	11–6	Owen	Hogg
August 23	at Washington	4–1	Patterson	Falkenberg

Position Players Who Also Pitched in One or More Games

Year	Player	Regular Position	Games	IP	Record	ERA
1901, 1902, 1906–07	Frank Isbell	Second base	4	4	0–0	4.15
1902	Sandow Mertes	Left field	1	7⅔	1–0	1.17
1907	Charles Hickman	Outfield	1	5	0–0	3.60
1929	Lena Blackburne	Manager	1	⅓	0–0	0.00
1932	Lew Fonseca	Manager	1	1	0–0	0.00
1944	Eddie Carnett	Outfield	2	2	0–0	9.00
1979	Wayne Nordhagen	Left field	2	2	0–0	9.00
1984	Mike Squires	First base	1	⅓	0–0	0.00
1990	Steve Lyons	Outfield	1	2	0–0	4.50
1995	Dave Martinez	Outfield	1	1	0–0	0.00

Playing Managers

Year	Manager	Years as a Playing Manager	Positions
1901–02	Clark Griffith	1901–1902	p
1903–04, 1912–14	Jimmy Callahan	1903–04, 1912–13	p-of
1904–08	Fielder Jones	1904–08	of
1909	Billy Sullivan	1909	c
1924, 1925–26	Eddie Collins	1924, 1925–26	2b
1927–28	Ray Schalk	1927–28	c
1934–46	Jimmie Dykes	1934–39	3b
1979	Don Kessinger	1979	ss

Jimmie Dykes played third for five years while managing the White Sox.

Fathers and Sons Who Played for the White Sox

Father	Years with Sox	Son(s)	Years with Sox
Sam Hairston	1951	Jerry Hairston	1973–77, 1981–90
Earl Sheely	1921–27	Hollis "Bud" Sheely	1951–53
Billy Sullivan Sr.	1901–14	Billy Sullivan Jr.	1931–33
Hal Trosky Sr.	1944, 1946	Hal Trosky Jr.	1958
Ed Walsh Sr.	1904–16	Ed Walsh Jr.	1928–32
Sandy Alomar	1966–68	Sandy Alomar Jr.	2001–04, 2006
		Roberto Alomar	2003, 2004

Catcher Sam Hairston was the first American-born black player with the Sox. His son, Jerry Jr., holds the team's record for career pinch-hits.

Ed Walsh Jr. (right) and Billy Sullivan Jr. reprise their famous fathers' battery.

Clark Griffith (left) and his son-in-law Joe Haynes

Brothers Who Played for the White Sox

	Years with Sox		Years with Sox
Dick Allen	1972–74	Hank Allen	1972–73
Ted Blankenship	1922–30	Homer Blankenship	1922–23
Nyls Nyman	1974–77	Chris Nyman	1982–83
Jim O'Toole	1967	Dennis O'Toole	1969–73
Frank Roth	1906	Robert "Braggo" Roth	1914–15
Bob Weiland	1928–31	Ed Weiland	1940–42
Sandy Alomar Jr.	2001–04, 2006	Roberto Alomar	2003, 04

Father-in-Law and Son-in-Law Who Played for the White Sox

Father-in-Law	Years with Sox	Son-in-Law	Years with Sox
Clark Griffith	1901–02	Joe Haynes	1941–48

Local Boys, Born in the Chicagoland Area Who Played for the White Sox

Player	Birthplace	Years with Sox	Position
Jerry Arrigo	Chicago	1970	p
Foster Blackburn	Chicago	1921	p
Milton Bocek	Chicago	1933	of
John "Jimmy" Breton	Chicago	1913	ss
Harold Bubser	Chicago	1922	ph
Ryan Bukvich	Naperville, Ill.	2007	p
Leon Cadore	Chicago	1933	p
George Caithamer	Chicago	1934	c
Bruce Campbell	Chicago	1930–32	of
Phil Cavarretta	Chicago	1954–55	1b
Bob Christian	Chicago	1969–70	of
John "Jocko" Conlan	Chicago	1934–35	of
Ed Corey	Chicago	1918	p
Mark Dalesandro	Chicago	2001	c
Joe Davenport	Chicago	1999	p

Player	Birthplace	Years with Sox	Position
John Davis	Chicago	1988–89	p
Johnny Dickshot	Waukegan, Ill.	1944–45	of
Tom Dougherty	Chicago	1904	p
Kelly Dransfeldt	Joliet, Ill.	2004	if
Fred Eichrodt	Chicago	1931	of
Sammy Esposito	Chicago	1952, 1955–63	if
Russ Evans	Chicago	1936	p
Ed Farmer	Evergreen Park, Ill.	1979–81	p
Marvin Freeman	Chicago	1996	p
Johnny Groth	Chicago	1954–55	of
Bert Haas	Naperville, Ill.	1951	1b
Chet Hajduk	Chicago	1941	ph
Spencer Heath	Chicago	1920	p

Player	Birthplace	Years with Sox	Position
Mike Heathcott	Chicago	1998	p
Kevin Hickey	Chicago	1981–83	p
Jim Hicks	East Chicago, Ind.	1964–66	of
Ed Hughes	Chicago	1902	c
Jim Hughes	Chicago	1956–57	p
Ira Hutchinson	Chicago	1933	p
Otto Jacobs	Chicago	1918	c
Ernie Johnson	Chicago	1912, 1921–23	ss
John Kane	Chicago	1925	ss
Charles Kavanaugh	Chicago	1914	ph
Bob Kennedy	Chicago	1939–48, 1955–56	3b
Ron Kittle	Gary, Ind.	1982–86, 1989–91	of-dh
Ted Kluszewski	Argo, Ill.	1959–60	1b
Don Kolloway	Posen, Ill.	1940–49	2b
Jerry Kutzler	Waukegan, Ill.	1990	p
Danny Lazar	East Chicago, Ind.	1968–69	p
Alan Levine	Park Ridge, Ill.	1996–97	p
Chuck Lindstrom	Chicago	1958	c
Merritt Lovett	Chicago	1933	ph
Greg Luzinski	Chicago	1981–84	dh
Rob Mackowiak	Oak Lawn, Ill.	2006–07	if-of
Eddie Malone	Chicago	1949–50	c
Phil Masi	Chicago	1950–52	c
Milt May	Chicago	1979	c
Tom McGuire	Chicago	1919	p
Doug McWeeney	Chicago	1921–22, 1924	p
George Meyer	Chicago	1938	if
George Moriarity	Chicago	1916	if
Johnny Mostil	Chicago	1918, 1921–29	cf
Jose Munoz	Chicago	1996	if
Mike Myers	Arlington Heights, Ill.	2007	p
Frank Naleway	Chicago	1924	if
John Ness	Chicago	1916	if
Dan Osinski	Chicago	1969	p
John Ostrowski	Chicago	1949–50	of
Dennis O'Toole	Chicago	1969–73	p
Jim O'Toole	Chicago	1967	p
Donn Pall	Chicago	1988–93	p
Josh Paul	Evanston, Ill.	1999–2003	c
John Perkowski	Chicago	1950	p
Stan Perzanowski	East Chicago, Ind.	1971, 1974	p
Al Pilarcik	Whiting, Ind.	1961	of
Lee "Skip" Pitlock	Chicago	1974–75	p
Brett Prinz	Chicago Heights, Ill.	2007	p
John Rigney	Oak Park, Ill.	1937–42, 1946–47	p
Marv Rotblatt	Chicago	1948, 1950–51	p
Frank Roth	Chicago	1906	c
LeRoy Schalk	Chicago	1944–45	if
Ray Schalk	Harvey, Ill.	1912–28	c
Walter "Biff" Schaller	Chicago	1913	of
Ken Silvestri	Chicago	1939–40	c
Mike Sirotka	Chicago	1995–96	p
Lou Skizas	Chicago	1959	of
Bill "Moose" Skowron	Chicago	1964–67	1b
Marv Staehle	Oak Park, Ill.	1964–67	if
Lee Stange	Chicago	1970	p
Tim Stoddard	East Chicago, Ind.	1975	p
Dick Strahs	Evanston, Ill.	1954	p
John Sullivan	Chicago	1919	p
Billy Sullivan Jr.	Chicago	1931–33	c
Charles Uhlir	Chicago	1934	of
Dave Wehrmeister	Berwyn, Ill.	1985	p
Ed Weiland	Evanston, Ill.	1940, 1942	p
Bob Weiland	Chicago	1928–31	p
Craig Wilson	Chicago	1998–2000	if
Mike Woodard	Melrose Park, Ill.	1988	if

White Sox Players Who Managed in the Major Leagues

Player	Teams Managed	Games Managed	Years
Luke Appling	Kansas City (AL)	40	1967
Ken Boyer	St. Louis (NL)	357	1978–80
James Callahan	Chicago (AL)	865*	1903–04
	Pittsburgh (NL)		1916–17
Phil Cavarretta	Chicago (NL)	384	1951–53
Hal Chase	New York (AL)	163	1910–11
Eddie Collins	Chicago (AL)	334	1924–26
Shano Collins	Boston (AL)	210	1931–32
Gavvy Cravath	Philadelphia (NL)	229	1919–20
George Davis	New York (NL)	252	1895, 1900–01
Bucky Dent	New York (AL)	89	1989–90
Jimmie Dykes	Chicago (AL)	2,960*	1934–46
	Philadelphia (AL)		1951–53
	Baltimore (AL)		1954
	Detroit (AL)		1959–60
	Cleveland (AL)		1960–61
Lee Elia	Chicago (NL)	539*	1982–83
	Philadelphia (NL)		1987–88
Jim Essian	Chicago (NL)	122	1991
Bibb Falk	Cleveland (AL)	1	1923
Kerby Farrell	Cleveland (AL)	153	1957
Clark Griffith	Chicago (AL)	2,916*	1901–02
	New York (AL)		1903–08
	Cincinnati (NL)		1909–11
	Washington (AL)		1912–20
Ozzie Guillen	Chicago (AL)	1,135	2004–
George Haas	Chicago (AL)	12	1946

Player	Teams Managed	Games Managed	Years
Grady Hatton	Houston (NL)	386	1966–68
Fielder Jones	Chicago (AL)	1,298*	1904–08
	St. Louis (FL)		1914–15
	St. Louis (AL)		1916–18
Bob Kennedy	Chicago (NL)	545*	1963–65
	Oakland (AL)		1968
Jim Lemon	Washington (AL)	168	1968
Eddie Lopat	Kansas City (AL)	214	1963–64
Harry Lord	Buffalo (FL)	107	1915
Ted Lyons	Chicago (AL)	434	1946–48
Sam Mele	Minnesota (AL)	948	1961–67
George Moriarity	Detroit (AL)	310	1927–28
Les Moss	Chicago (AL)	89*	1968
	Detroit (AL)		1979
Tony Muser	Kansas City (AL)	748	1997–2002
Tony Pena	Kansas City (AL)	483	2002–2005
Phil Regan	Baltimore	144	1995
Jerry Royster	Milwaukee	147	2002
Luke Sewell	St. Louis (AL)	1,260*	1941–46
	Cincinnati (NL)		1949–52
Ken Silvestri	Atlanta (NL)	3	1967
Joel Skinner	Cleveland (AL)	76	2002
Jack Slattery	Boston (NL)	31	1928
Billy Sullivan	Chicago (AL)	159	1909
Don Wakamatsu	Seattle (AL)	274	2009–2010
Ed Walsh	Chicago (AL)	3	1924
Rudy York	Boston (AL)	1	1959

*Total games managed for all teams

Most Wins by White Sox Managers

899	Jimmie Dykes
840	Al Lopez
600	Ozzie Guillen*
522	Tony LaRussa
500	Jerry Manuel
426	Fielder Jones
406	Paul Richards
401	Chuck Tanner
392	Kid Gleason
339	Clarence Rowland
309	James Callahan

*Through 2010 season

Highest Winning Percentages by White Sox Managers

.581	Clark Griffith
.578	Clarence Rowland
.576	Fielder Jones
.565	Marty Marion
.562	Al Lopez
.551	Gene Lamont
.529	Paul Richards
.529	Ozzie Guillen*
.525	Bob Lemon
.521	Eddie Collins
.519	Kid Gleason

*Through 2010 season

White Sox Coaches

Billy Adair*	1969–70
Jimmy Adair	1951–52
Luke Appling	1970–71
Jim Austin	1933–35, 1937, 1939–40
Loren Babe	1980, 1983
Harold Baines	2004–
Ray Berres†	1949–66, 1968–69
Albert "Chief" Bender	1926
Terry Bevington	1989–95
Lena Blackburne	1927–28
Dick Bosman†	1986–87
Ed Brinkman	1983–88
Jackie Brown†	1992–95
Bill Buckner	1996–97
Jim Busby	1976
John Butler	1932
Orlando Cepeda	1980
Ron Clark	1988–90
Nardi Contreras	1998–2002
John Cooney	1957–64
Don Cooper†	1995; 2002–
Joey Cora	2004–
Jeff Cox	2008–
John "Red" Corriden*	1950
Roger "Doc" Cramer	1951–53
Tony Cuccinello	1957–66, 1969
Bill Cunningham	1932
Roly de Armas	1995–96
Larry Doby	1977–78
Moe Drabowsky	1986
Dave Duncan†	1983–86
Arthur A. "Ben" Egan	1926
Sammy Ellis†	1989–91
Cal Emery	1988
Johnny Evers	1922, 1924
Urban "Red" Faber†	1947–48
Kerby Farrell	1966–69

Jimmie Dykes, Mule Haas

Barry Foote	1990–91
Terry Francona	1995
William "Kid" Gleason	1912–15, 1917
Marv Grissom†	1967–68
Don Gutteridge	1955–66, 1968–69
George "Mule" Haas*	1940–46
Luman Harris	1951–54
Willie Horton	1986
Walter Hriniak	1989–95
Ron Jackson	1995–98
Deron Johnson	1987
Wallace Johnson	1998–2002
Von Joshua	1998–2001
Bernie Kelly	1930–31
Bruce Kimm	2003
Bobby Knoop	1977–78
Art Kusyner	1980–87; 1997–2007
Dave LaRoche	1989–91
Tony LaRussa	1978
Charley Lau	1982–83
Bill Lauder	1925
Jim Leyland	1982–85
Brian Little	1997–2000
Joe Lonnet	1971–75
Mike Lum	1985
Jim Mahoney	1972–76
Doug Mansolino	1992–96
Marty Marion	1954
Freddie Martin†	1979
Charlie Metro	1965
Dyar Miller	1987–88
Ed Miller	1942–49
Colonel Buster Mills	1947–50
Minnie Minoso	1976–78, 1980
Al Monchak	1971–75
Les Moss*†	1967–70
Hugh Mulcahy†	1970
Omer Munoz	2010
George Myatt	1955–56
Dave Nelson	1981–84
Juan Nieves	2008–
Joe Nossek	1984–86, 1990–2003
Mike Pazik	1995–98
Rick Peterson	1994–95
Garry Pettis	2001–02
Vada Pinson	1981
Doug Rader*	1986–87, 1997
Tim Raines	2005–06
Grover Resinger	1967–68
Dewey Robinson	1993–94
Glen Rosenbaum	1974–75, 1986–89
Frank Roth	1927
Don Rowe	1988
Harold "Muddy" Ruel†	1936–45
Johnny Sain†	1971–75
Mark Salas	1995–1999; 2007–
Ron Schueler†	1979–82
Razor Shines	2007
Ken Silvestri	1976, 1982
Joe Sparks	1979
Mike Squires	1992
Monty Stratton	1940–41
Greg Walker	2003–
Ed Walsh*	1923–24, 1928–29
Gary Ward	2001–03
Billy Webb	1935, 1937–39
Del Wilber	1955–56
Stan Williams†	1977–78
Walt Williams	1988
Bobby Winkles	1979–81

*Briefly served as interim manager
†Served as pitching coach

Johnny Sain

Al Lopez (seated) and his brain trust, left to right: Ray Berres, Tony Cuccinello, Don Gutteridge, and John Cooney

Most Days the White Sox Spent in First Place

Year	Days	Last Day in First	Season Ended	Finish	Clinching Date
2005	183*		October 1	1st	September 29
2000	167		October 1	1st	September 24
2008	148		September 30	1st	September 30
1919	134		September 28	1st	September 24
1901	128		September 27	1st	September 21
1917	126		October 1	1st	September 21
1907	114	August 24	October 6	3rd	
1967	104	September 6	October 1	4th	
1993	103		September 30	1st	September 27
1959	101		September 27	1st	September 22
1900*	101		September 18	1st	September 12
1983	78		October 2	1st	September 17
1957	76	June 30	September 29	2nd	
1994	69		August 10	1st	August 10
1977	66	August 19	September 30	3rd	
1915	64	July 30	October 3	3rd	
1973	59	June 29	September 30	5th	
1951	57	July 20	September 30	4th	
1912	53	June 13	October 6	4th	
1960	42	August 15	October 2	3rd	
2010	33	August 11	October 3	2nd	
1965	30	May 29	October 3	2nd	

*American League was not recognized as a major league.

**The team was in first place wire-to-wire.

Four Home Runs in One Game

Player	Date	Opponent
Pat Seerey	July 18, 1948	at Philadelphia

Three Home Runs in One Game

Player	Date	Opponent
Carl Reynolds	July 2, 1930	at New York
Mervyn Connors	September 17, 1938	at Washington
Gus Zernial	October 1, 1950	St. Louis
Tommy McCraw	May 24, 1967	at Minnesota
Bill Melton	June 24, 1969	at Seattle
Claudell Washington	July 14, 1979	Detroit
Harold Baines	July 7, 1982	Detroit
Harold Baines	September 17, 1984	at Minnesota
Tim Raines	April 18, 1994	at Boston
Frank Thomas	September 15, 1996	at Boston
Jose Valentin	July 30, 2003	Kansas City
Paul Konerko	July 7, 2009	Cleveland

Four Stolen Bases in One Game

Player	Date	Opponent
George Davis	June 14, 1905	at Washington
Jimmy Callahan	September 16, 1905	St. Louis
Rollie Zeider	June 21, 1912	St. Louis
Lou Fraizer	April 19, 1998	Toronto
Scott Podsednik	May 7, 2005	Toronto
Scott Podsednik	May 14, 2005	Baltimore
Scott Podsednik	May 1, 2006	at Cleveland

Stole Second, Third, and Home in One Game

Player	Date	Opponent
Red Faber	July 14, 1915	Philadelphia
Buck Weaver	September 6, 1919	Cleveland
Don Kolloway	June 28, 1941	at Cleveland

White Sox Players with Six Hits in a Game

Player	Date	Hits/ At Bats	Opponent
Rip Radcliff	June 18, 1936	6–7	at Philadelphia
Hank Steinbacher	June 22, 1938	6–6	Washington
Floyd Robinson	July 22, 1962	6–6	at Boston
Lance Johnson	September 23, 1995	6–6	at Minnesota

Hank Steinbacher

White Sox Players Stealing Home

Player*	Date	Opponent
Sammy Strang	August 21, 1902	Washington
Frank Owen	August 2, 1904	Washington
Ducky Holmes	April 27, 1905	St. Louis
Billy Sullivan	October 8, 1905	St. Louis
Frank Owen	April 27, 1908	St. Louis
Ed Walsh	June 13, 1908	New York
Patsy Dougherty	June 15, 1908	New York
Patsy Dougherty	August 2, 1908	Washington
Ed Walsh	July 2, 1909	St. Louis
Billy Purtell	July 2, 1909	St. Louis
Freddy Parent	July 2, 1909	St. Louis
Rollie Zeider	June 24, 1910	Cleveland
Eddie Collins	July 9, 1915	Washington
Red Faber	July 14, 1915	Philadelphia
Reb Russell	August 7, 1916	Boston
Buck Weaver	June 1, 1919	Boston
Eddie Collins	September 17, 1919	New York
Dickie Kerr	July 8, 1921	New York
Red Faber	April 23, 1923	St. Louis
Bill Barrett	May 1, 1924 (twice)	Cleveland
Bill Cissell	April 19, 1929	St. Louis
Jimmie Dykes	July 5, 1933	Cleveland
Zeke Bonura	August 26, 1935	New York
Gee Walker	June 3, 1939	Washington
Joe Kuhel	June 25, 1941	Washington
Don Kolloway	August 5, 1942	Detroit
Wally Moses	May 5, 1943	Cleveland
Don Kolloway	June 3, 1943	Boston
Wally Moses	July 7, 1943	Boston
Thurman Tucker	July 29, 1943	Washington
Hal Trosky	May 11, 1944	Philadelphia
Joe Haynes	May 17, 1944	New York
Wally Moses	July 7, 1945	Philadelphia
Don Buford	September 4, 1965	Minnesota
Nyls Nyman	July 13, 1975	Milwaukee
Ellis Burks	May 14, 1993	Texas
Ray Durham	July 19, 1996	Kansas City
Brian Daubach	April 27, 2003	Minnesota
Pablo Ozuna	September 8, 2005	Kansas City
Jayson Nix	July 31, 2009	at New York
Juan Pierre	September 22, 2010	at Oakland
Juan Pierre	October 2, 2010	Cleveland

*Partial listing. Records are incomplete, but efforts continue to identify and catalog steals of home. In 1906, for example, the Sox set a record for stealing home 15 times.

Most Games Played by Position

Position	Player	Games	Years with Sox
1b	Paul Konerko	1,578*	1999–
2b	Nellie Fox	2,098	1950–63
ss	Luke Appling	2,218	1930–50
3b	Robin Ventura	1,220	1989–98
c	Ray Schalk	1,721	1912–28
lf	Minnie Minoso	1,262	1951–56, 1960–61, 1964, 1976, 1980
cf	Fielder Jones	1,158	1901–08
rf	Harold Baines	1,023	1980–89
p	Red Faber	669	1914–33
dh	Frank Thomas	959	1990–2005

FIRST BASE

Player	Games	Years with Sox
Paul Konerko	1,578*	1999–
Frank Thomas	972	1990–2005
Earl Sheely	938	1921–27
Joe Kuhel	880	1938–43
Tommy McCraw	735	1963–70
Greg Walker	689	1982–90

*Through 2010

SECOND BASE

Player	Games	Years with Sox
Nellie Fox	2,098	1950–63
Eddie Collins	1,654	1914–26
Ray Durham	1,124	1995–2002
Jackie Hayes	758	1932–40
Jorge Orta	688	1972–79
Don Kolloway	545	1940–49

THIRD BASE

Player	Games	Years with Sox
Robin Ventura	1,220	1989–98
Willie Kamm	1,157	1923–31
Bill Melton	867	1968–75
Lee Tannehill	669	1903–12
Pete Ward	562	1963–69
Jimmie Dykes	462	1933–39

SHORTSTOP

Player	Games	Years with Sox
Luke Appling	2,218	1930–50
Ozzie Guillen	1,724	1985–97
Luis Aparicio	1,506	1956–62, 1968–70
Chico Carrasquel	825	1950–55
Buck Weaver	822	1912–20

OUTFIELDERS

Player	Games	Years with Sox
Minnie Minoso	1,262	1951–56, 1960–61, 1964, 1976, 1980
Fielder Jones	1,158	1901–08
Jim Landis	1,035	1957–64
Bibb Falk	1,030	1921–28
Harold Baines	1,023	1980–89
Lance Johnson	945	1988–95
Shano Collins	937	1910–20
Jim Rivera	903	1952–61
Floyd Robinson	819	1960–66

CATCHERS

Player	Games	Years with Sox
Ray Schalk	1,721	1912–28
Sherm Lollar	1,241	1952–63
Carlton Fisk	1,236	1981–93
Billy Sullivan	1,032	1901–14
Mike Tresh	981	1938–48
Ron Karkovice	918	1986–97
A.J. Pierzynski	803*	2005–

*Through 2010

PITCHERS

Player	Games	Years with Sox
Red Faber	669	1914–33
Ted Lyons	594	1923–46
Wilbur Wood	578	1967–78
Billy Pierce	456	1949–61
Ed Walsh	426	1904–16
Bobby Thigpen	424	1986–93

Pete Ward

White Sox Players with the Shortest Careers

HITTING

One Game—No Official At-Bats

Player	Position	Year	Average
Ray Shook	ph	1916	.000

One Game—One Official At-Bat

Player	Position	Year	Average
Delos Brown	ph	1914	.000
Charles Jackson	ph	1915	.000
Francis Pratt	ph	1921	.000
John "Shine" Cortazzo	ph	1923	.000
Wyatt Snipes	ph	1923	.000
Merritt Lovett	ph	1933	.000
Bill "Dutch" Fehring	c	1934	.000
Chet Hajduk	ph	1941	.000
Lloyd Merriam	of	1955	.000
Chuck Lindstrom	c	1958	1.000
Mark Dalesandro	c	2001	.000

PITCHING

One Game—Two or Less Innings Pitched

Pitcher	Lefty/ Righty	Year	G	IP	Won– Lost	ERA
Tom Dougherty	R	1904	1	2	0–0	0.00
Fred Lamline	R	1912	1	2	0–0	31.50
Frank Miller	R	1913	1	1	0–0	27.00
Jim Scoggins	L	1913	1	0	0–0	0.00
Bob Smith	R	1913	1	2	0–0	13.50
Ed Corey	R	1918	1	2	0–0	4.50
Emmett Bowles	R	1922	1	1	0–0	27.00
Ernie Cox	R	1922	1	1	0–0	18.00
Bob Lawrence	R	1924	1	1	0–0	9.00
Webb Schultz	R	1924	1	1	0–0	9.00
Pryor McBee	L	1926	1	1⅓	0–0	6.75
Joe Brown	R	1927	1	0	0–0	0.00
Al Williamson	R	1928	1	2	0–0	0.00
Bob Uhle	L	1938	1	2	0–0	0.00
Rich Maloney	R	1970	1	1	0–0	0.00
Jose Paniagua	L	2003	1	⅓	0–0	8.00

Players Who Hit for the Cycle (Single, Double, Triple, Homer in One Game)

Player	Date	Opponent
Ray Schalk	June 22, 1922	at Detroit
Jack Brohamer	September 24, 1977	at Seattle
Carlton Fisk	May 16, 1984	Kansas City
Chris Singleton	July 6, 1999	Kansas City
Jose Valentin	April 27, 2000	Baltimore

Players with Eight RBIs in a Game

Player	Date	Opponent
Joe Jackson	August 4, 1920	New York
Carl Reynolds	July 2, 1930	at New York
Tommy McCraw	May 24, 1967	at Minnesota
Jim Spencer	May 14, 1977	Cleveland
Jim Spencer	June 17, 1977	Minnesota
Robin Ventura	September 4, 1995	at Texas

Hitting Streaks

Player	Games	Hits–At-Bats	Dates
Carlos Lee	28	45–118	May 13–June 15, 2004
Albert Belle	27	37–107	May 3–June 1, 1997
Luke Appling	27	34–99	Aug 6.–Aug. 31, 1936
Guy Curtright	26	43–105	June 6–July 2, 1943
Lance Johnson	25	43–98	July 18–Aug. 12, 1992
Chico Carrasquel	24	33–92	July 9–Aug. 5, 1950
Minnie Minoso	23	40–95	Aug. 9–Aug. 30, 1955
Sam Mele	22	29–84	June 27–July 19, 1953
Eddie Collins	22	39–87	Aug. 21–Sept. 13, 1920
Roy Sievers	21	32–79	June 23–July 18, 1960
Ken Berry	20	29–82	May 28–June 15, 1967
Rip Radcliff	20	33–83	July 31–Aug. 18, 1937
Eddie Collins	20	32–69	Sept. 3–Sept. 22, 1916
Frank Thomas	21	33–82	May 24–June 15, 1999

18 AND 19 GAME STREAKS

Player	Games	Year
Art Shires	19	1929
Cliff Watwood	19	1930
Roy Sievers	19	1961
Nellie Fox	19	1962
Lamar Johnson	19	1979
Chet Lemon	19	1979
Harold Baines	19	1983
Greg Luzinski	19	1984
Frank Thomas	19	1992
Bob Dillinger	18	1951
Pete Ward	18	1963
Ralph Garr	18	1977
Harold Baines	18	1987
Ozzie Guillen	18	1989
Frank Thomas	18	1993
Paul Konerko	18	2002
Magglio Ordonez	18	2003

Note: Efforts continue to track down and verify hitting streaks prior to 1950. Because of poor recordkeeping by the White Sox and other major league teams in the early years, many extended hitting streaks are simply lost to history. The Society for American Baseball Research (SABR), David Stephan of Los Angeles, and other baseball historians continue their diligent work.

Players Who Spent Their Entire Careers with White Sox

Player	Position	Years	Years with Sox
Ted Lyons*	p	21	1923–42, 1946
Luke Appling*	ss	20	1930–43, 1945–50
Red Faber	p	20	1914–33
Mike Squires	1b	10	1975, 1977–85
Orval Grove	p	10	1940–49
Johnny Mostil	cf	10	1918, 1921–29
Lee Tannehill	3b	10	1903–12
Ted Blankenship	p	9	1922–30
Buck Weaver	ss-3b	9	1912–20
Joe Benz	p	9	1911–19
Jim Scott	p	9	1909–17
Ron Karkovice	c	11	1986–97

* Service interrupted by World War II

Most Seasons with White Sox

Player	Position	Years	Years with Sox
Ted Lyons*	p	21	1923–42, 1946
Ted Lyons	p	21	1923–42, 1946
Luke Appling	ss	20	1930–43, 1945–50
Red Faber	p	20	1914–33
Ray Schalk	c	17	1912–28
Frank Thomas	1b/dh	16	1990–2005
Jerry Hairston	of/ph	15	1973–77, 1981–90
Nellie Fox	2b	14	1950–63
Carlton Fisk	c	13	1981–93
Billy Pierce	p	13	1949–61
Ed Walsh	p	13	1904–16
Eddie Collins	2b	12	1915–26
Sherm Lollar	c	12	1952–63
Minnie Minoso	of	12	1951–56, 1960–61, 1964, 1976, 1980
Paul Konerko	1b	12*	1999–

*Through 2010

Player	Position	Years	Years with Sox
Billy Sullivan Sr.	c	12	1901–13
Wilbur Wood	p	12	1967–78
Ozzie Guillen	ss	13	1985–97
Ron Karkovice	c	12	1986–97
Bill Dietrich	p	11	1936–46
Thornton Lee	p	11	1937–47
Mike Tresh	c	11	1938–48

Players Who Were with the White Sox on Two Different Occasions

Player	First Time	Second Time
Roberto Alomar	2003	2004
Sandy Alomar Jr.	2001–02	2003–04
Luis Aparicio	1956–62	1968–70
Harold Baines	1980–89	1996–97
Buddy Bradford	1966–70	1972–76
Jim Busby	1951–52	1955
Ivan Calderon	1986–90	1993
Jimmy Callahan	1901–05	1911–13
Bartolo Colon	2003	2009
George Davis	1902	1904–09
Jose DeLeon	1986–87	1993–95
Jim Delsing	1948	1956
Larry Doby	1956–57	1959
Richard Dotson	1979–87	1989
Jim Essian	1976–77	1981
Carl Everett	2003	2004–05
Eddie Fisher	1962–66	1972–73
Scott Fletcher	1983–85	1989–91
Vic Frazier	1931–33	1939
Gene Freese	1960	1965–66
Oscar Gamble	1977	1985
Chick Gandil	1910	1917–19
Freddy Garcia	2004–06	2009–10
Frank Grube	1931–33	1935–36
Jerry Hairston	1973–77	1981–90
Ron Hansen	1963–68	1968–1969
Earl Harrist	1947–48	1953
Mike Hershberger	1961–64	1971
Ernie Johnson	1912	1921–23
Barry Jones	1989–90	1993
Bob Kennedy	1939–42, 1946–48	1955–57
Ron Kittle	1982–86	1989–91
Joe Kuhel	1938–43	1946–47
Esteban Loaiza	2003–04	2008
Ed McGhee	1950	1954–55
Cass Michaels	1943–50	1954
Willie Miranda	1952	1952
Bobby Molinaro	1978	1980–81
Scott Podsednik	2005–07	2009
Aurelio Rodriguez	1982	1983
John Romano	1958–59	1965–66
Vern Stephens	1953	1955
Steve Stone	1973	1977–78
Ed Stroud	1966–67	1971
Pete Varney	1973–75	1976
Frank Wilson	1918	1927

Charles "Buddy" Bradford

Players Who Were with the White Sox on Three Different Occasions

Player	First Time	Second Time	Third Time
Sandy Alomar Jr.	2001–02	2003–04	2006
Lena Blackburne	1910–12	1914–15	1927, 1928–29
Dave Philley	1941	1946–51	1956–57
Rich Hinton	1971	1975	1978–79
Harold Baines	1980–89	1996–97	2000–01

Player Who Was with the White Sox on Four (or More) Occasions

Player	First Time	Second Time	Third Time	Fourth Time	Fifth Time
Minnie Minoso	1951–56	1960–61	1964	1976	1980

Home Runs Hit over the Roof at Old Comiskey Park (1927–90)

BY THE WHITE SOX

Player	Date	Opposing Pitcher/Team
Eddie Robinson	April 25, 1951	Al Widmar, St. Louis
Minnie Minoso	September 21, 1960	Bud Daley, Kansas City
Dave Nicholson	May 6, 1964	Moe Drabowsky, Kansas City
Buddy Bradford	April 25, 1969	Tom Hall, Minnesota
Tom Egan	July 25, 1971	Jackie Brown, Washington
Dick Allen	May 1, 1973	Mike Cueller, Baltimore
Richie Zisk	June 4, 1977	Don Gullett, New York
Greg Luzinski*	June 26, 1983	Brian Oelkers, Minnesota
Greg Luzinski*	August 1, 1983	Ray Fontenot, New York
Greg Luzinski*	August 28, 1983	Dennis "Oil Can" Boyd, Boston
Ron Kittle*	September 6, 1983	Chris Codiroli, Oakland
Ron Kittle*	September 19, 1983	Mike Walters, Minnesota
Ron Kittle*	April 29, 1984	Al Nipper, Boston
Ron Kittle*	July 2, 1984	Dave Rozema, Detroit
Greg Luzinski*	July 3, 1984	Jack Morris, Detroit
Ron Kittle*	August 1, 1984	Bob Ojeda, Boston
Carlton Fisk*	August 1, 1984	Bob Ojeda, Boston
Carlton Fisk*	May 30, 1985	Charlie Liebrandt, Kansas City
Ron Kittle*	August 8, 1985	Bob Ojeda, Boston
Harold Baines*	August 23, 1985	Tom Filer, Toronto
Dan Pasqua	May 30, 1989	Frank Tanana, Detroit
Ron Kittle	April 17, 1990	Rob Murphy, Baltimore

*Home runs hit during the period when home plate was moved eight feet closer to the outfield

Greg Luzinski hit three over the roof in one season.

BY OPPONENTS

Player/Team	Date	Sox Pitcher
Babe Ruth, New York	August 16, 1927	Alphonse "Tommy" Thomas
Lou Gehrig, New York	May 4, 1929	Urban "Red" Faber
Jimmy Foxx, Boston	June 16, 1936	Merritt "Sugar" Cain
Hank Greenberg, Detroit	April 21, 1938	Bill Dietrich
Jimmy Foxx, Boston	May 14, 1940	John Rigney

Player/Team	Date	Sox Pitcher
Ted Williams, Boston	May 7, 1941	John Rigney
Mickey Mantle, New York	June 5, 1955	Billy Pierce
Ted Williams, Boston	July 23, 1955	Harry Byrd
Bill Skowron, New York	July 24, 1956	Billy Pierce
Elston Howard, New York	July 15, 1961	Ray Herbert
Boog Powell, Baltimore	July 18, 1966	Juan Pizarro
Don Mincher, Oakland	May 24, 1970	Bart Johnson
Harmon Killebrew, Minnesota	July 1, 1973	Dave Lemonds
Sal Bando, Oakland	August 28, 1977	Wilbur Wood
Ruppert Jones, Detroit*	July 3, 1984	Tom Seaver
Kirk Gibson, Detroit*	May 10, 1985	Tom Seaver
George Bell, Toronto*	August 24, 1985	Tom Seaver
George Bell, Toronto*	August 25, 1985	Floyd Bannister
Brian Downing, California*	September 18, 1985	Jerry Don Gleaton
Jose Canseco, Oakland*	September 22, 1985	Joel Davis
Rob Deer, Milwaukee	April 7, 1986	Tom Seaver
Larry Sheets, Baltimore	May 9, 1987	Bob James

*Home runs hit during the period when home plate was moved eight feet closer to the outfield

Home Runs Hit into the Center-Field Bleachers at Old Comiskey Park (1927–90)

Player/Team	Date	Inning	Opposing Pitcher
Jimmy Foxx, Boston	May 18, 1934	6	Ted Lyons
Hank Greenberg, Detroit	May 27, 1938	3	Frank Gabler
Alex Johnson, California	Sept. 9, 1970	6	Billy Wynne
Dick Allen, White Sox	Aug. 23, 1972	7	Lindy McDaniel, New York
Richie Zisk, White Sox	May 22, 1977	8	Dave Rozema, Detroit
Tony Armas, Boston	April 28, 1984	7	Tom Seaver
George Bell, Toronto	August 23, 1985	7*	Dave Wehrmeister

*Second game

White Sox Grand-Slam Home Runs

Date	Player	Opponent
May 1, 1901	Hermus McFarland	Detroit
May 1, 1901	Dummy Hoy	Detroit
July 31, 1910	Lee Tannehill	Detroit
July 5, 1914	Ray Demmitt	Cleveland
June 18, 1915	Oscar Felsch	at Philadelphia
July 30, 1916	Joe Jackson	Philadelphia
September 30, 1916	Oscar Felsch	at Cleveland
June 2, 1918	Oscar Felsch	New York
June 5, 1919	Eddie Collins	at New York
July 16, 1920	Joe Jackson	at Washington
September 11, 1920	Joe Jackson	Boston
September 13, 1920	Oscar Felsch	Washington
May 22, 1921	Bibb Falk	Washington
July 1, 1922	Bibb Falk	at St. Louis
June 16, 1924	Harry Hooper	Washington
July 11, 1924	Bibb Falk	at New York
August 27, 1924	Harry Hooper	at Philadelphia
May 28, 1925	Willie Kamm	Detroit
July 28, 1925	Spencer Harris	at Washington
August 4, 1926	Bill Barrett	Boston
July 15, 1927	Bud Clancy	Philadelphia
September 6, 1927	Bill Barrett	at Detroit
August 23, 1933	Red Kress	Boston (2nd game)
May 8, 1934	Zeke Bonura	at Washington
June 16, 1934	Bob Boken	at Philadelphia
June 27, 1934	Al Simmons	at New York
September 9, 1934	Marty Hopkins	Washington
June 11, 1935	Al Simmons	Washington
June 14, 1935	Al Simmons	Washington
August 20, 1935	Luke Sewell	Philadelphia
June 7, 1936	Mike Kreevich	at Boston
August 4, 1937	Zeke Bonura	at New York
June 10, 1938	Monty Stratton	at Boston
July 3, 1940	Taft Wright	at Detroit
June 22, 1941	Ben Chapman	at Philadelphia (2nd game)
June 24, 1942	Tom Turner	Washington

Date	Player	Opponent
July 23, 1943	Vincent Castino	at Boston
August 27, 1945	Oris Hockett	at St. Louis
May 4, 1947	Jack Wallaesa	Philadelphia (1st game)
September 16, 1947	Jack Wallaesa	at Boston (2nd game)
September 15, 1948	Taft Wright	Boston
May 18, 1951	Bud Stewart	at New York
May 12, 1953	Chico Carrasquel	at Boston
May 16, 1953	Tommy Byrne	at New York
June 13, 1953	Sherm Lollar	Boston
July 8, 1953	Sam Mele	Detroit
May 4, 1954	Minnie Minoso	at Washington
May 28, 1954	Cass Michaels	at Baltimore
June 16, 1954	Ferris Fain	Philadelphia
August 4, 1954	Phil Cavarretta	Boston
April 16, 1955	Walt Dropo	Cleveland
April 24, 1955	George Kell	at Cleveland
June 5, 1955	Jim Rivera	New York
June 12, 1955	Bob Nieman	Washington (2nd game)
July 7, 1955	Walt Dropo	at Detroit
August 13, 1955	Bob Kennedy	at Detroit
May 2, 1957	Walt Dropo	Washington
May 31, 1957	Walt Dropo	Detroit
August 1, 1957	Larry Doby	at Washington
August 17, 1957	Minnie Minoso	at Detroit
July 12, 1958	Sherm Lollar	at Boston
July 18, 1958	Al Smith	at Washington
August 9, 1958	Sherm Lollar	at Detroit (2nd game)
June 27, 1959	Harry Simpson	New York
July 2, 1959	Al Smith	at Detroit
September 26, 1959	Johnny Callison	at Detroit
April 19, 1960	Minnie Minoso	Kansas City
May 7, 1961	Roy Sievers	Detroit
May 28, 1961	Wes Covington	at New York
June 13, 1961	Al Smith	Los Angeles (2nd game)
June 21, 1961	Roy Sievers	Cleveland
July 9, 1961	Sherm Lollar	at Cleveland
September 17, 1961	Al Smith	Los Angeles (1st game)
September 22, 1961	Floyd Robinson	Baltimore
April 19, 1962	Jim Landis	at Minnesota
August 19, 1962	Charlie Maxwell	Detroit (1st game)
April 20, 1963	Dave Nicholson	Minnesota
September 6, 1963	Dave Nicholson	Minnesota
May 23, 1964	Pete Ward	Washington
May 29, 1964	Pete Ward	at Detroit
June 30, 1964	Gerry McNertney	at Cleveland
July 12, 1964	Pete Ward	at Kansas City
June 28, 1965	Tommy McCraw	at Minnesota
July 25, 1965	John Romano	at Detroit (1st game)
June 16, 1966	Tommy McCraw	Kansas City

Date	Player	Opponent
September 14, 1967	Don Buford	Cleveland
May 5, 1968	Gary Peters	New York (1st game)
May 7, 1968	Tommy McCraw	at California
June 11, 1968	Russ Snyder	at New York
June 15, 1968	Ken Berry	Detroit
June 30, 1968	Bill Voss	at Detroit
August 20, 1968	Pete Ward	at Detroit (2nd game)
May 24, 1969	Bill Melton	Boston
June 2, 1969	Carlos May	at Boston
August 5, 1970	Ed Herrmann	Milwaukee
August 29, 1970	Ed Herrmann	Boston
April 7, 1971	Bill Melton	at Oakland (2nd game)
June 15, 1971	Bill Melton	at Detroit
June 20, 1971	Rick Reichardt	at Minnesota
August 6, 1971	Mike Andrews	at Oakland
September 18, 1971	Carlos May	California
April 26, 1972	Mike Andrews	Cleveland
April 30, 1972	Ed Herrmann	at Detroit
October 2, 1972	Buddy Bradford	at Minnesota
April 12, 1973	Ken Henderson	Oakland
June 4, 1974	Dick Allen	New York
June 8, 1974	Ron Santo	Boston
June 26, 1975	Bill Melton	Texas
July 19, 1975	Pat Kelly	Milwaukee
July 20, 1975	Bill Stein	Milwaukee
June 22, 1976	Kevin Bell	at Kansas City
May 14, 1977	Jim Spencer	Cleveland
July 2, 1977	Jim Spencer	Minnesota
September 19, 1978	Ron Blomberg	at Oakland
July 4, 1979	Wayne Nordhagen	at Cleveland
April 14, 1981	Carlton Fisk	Milwaukee
October 4, 1981	Jerry Hairston	Minnesota
April 27, 1982	Ron LeFlore	at Milwaukee
June 19, 1982	Steve Kemp	at California
July 7, 1982	Harold Baines	Detroit
July 11, 1982	Harold Baines	at Toronto
September 15, 1983	Harold Baines	Seattle
April 28, 1984	Julio Cruz	Boston
June 8, 1984	Greg Luzinski	Minnesota
June 9, 1984	Greg Luzinski	Minnesota
August 9, 1984	Harold Baines	at New York
July 2, 1985	Harold Baines	Seattle
July 8, 1985	Carlton Fisk	Detroit
September 13, 1985	Joe DeSa	at Seattle
June 23, 1986	Greg Walker	Minnesota
June 2, 1987	Greg Walker	at Texas
May 31, 1988	Gary Redus	at Detroit
June 4, 1988	Gary Redus	Texas
June 26, 1988	Daryl Boston	at Texas
April 8, 1989	Ivan Calderon	at Oakland
August 27, 1989	Ron Karkovice	at Cleveland
September 1, 1989	Daryl Boston	Baltimore
September 9, 1989	Steve Lyons	at Detroit
August 30, 1990	Ron Karkovice	at Minnesota

Date	Player	Opponent
June 18, 1991	Robin Ventura	Cleveland
June 24, 1991	Frank Thomas	Seattle
July 31, 1991	Robin Ventura	Texas
September 5, 1991	Ozzie Guillen	Kansas City
September 15, 1991	Craig Grebeck	at California
October 3, 1991	Carlton Fisk	Minnesota (2nd game)
April 11, 1992	Dan Pasqua	at Oakland
May 5, 1992	George Bell	Milwaukee
June 16, 1992	Steven Sax	at Seattle
July 5, 1992	George Bell	Boston
April 30, 1993	Frank Thomas	Toronto
May 16, 1993	Ellis Burks	at Texas
June 2, 1993	Ron Karkovice	at Detroit
June 20, 1993	George Bell	at California
June 26, 1993	Ellis Burks	Seattle
July 2, 1993	Robin Ventura	Baltimore
July 28, 1993	Robin Ventura	Cleveland
April 6, 1994	Robin Ventura	at Toronto
May 11, 1994	Ron Karkovice	Seattle
June 4, 1994	Norberto Martin	at Baltimore
June 7, 1994	Darrin Jackson	Toronto
July 31, 1994	Lance Johnson	Seattle
April 30, 1995	Ron Karkovice	at Boston
June 3, 1995	Dave Martinez	Detroit
July 5, 1995	John Kruk	New York
August 25, 1995	Ray Durham	at Toronto
September 4, 1995	Robin Ventura	at Texas
September 4, 1995	Robin Ventura	at Texas
May 4, 1996	Harold Baines	at New York
May 18, 1996	Ray Durham	at Detroit
May 19, 1996	Robin Ventura	at Detroit
May 19, 1996	Darren Lewis	at Detroit
August 4, 1996	Harold Baines	at Texas
August 13, 1996	Robin Ventura	New York
September 14, 1996	Danny Tartabull	at Boston
September 20, 1996	Frank Thomas	Minnesota
May 22, 1997	Albert Belle	Oakland
May 27, 1997	Albert Belle	Cleveland
August 22, 1997	Albert Belle	at Texas
September 19, 1997	Albert Belle	at Boston
April 29, 1998	Wil Cordero	Baltimore
July 31, 1998	Frank Thomas	at Texas
August 24, 1998	Robin Ventura	at Seattle
April 28, 1999	Magglio Ordonez	Tampa Bay
May 17, 1999	Carlos Lee	Cleveland
June 17, 1999	Paul Konerko	Baltimore
July 17, 1999	Magglio Ordonez	at St. Louis
October 1, 1999	Carlos Lee	Minnesota
April 26, 2000	Frank Thomas	Baltimore
June 18, 2000	Jose Valentin	at New York
July 16, 2000	Magglio Ordonez	Milwaukee
August 9, 2000	Tony Graffanino	Seattle
September 11, 2000	Frank Thomas	Detroit
September 20, 2000	Ray Durham	at Detroit
June 8, 2001	Carlos Lee	Chicago Cubs

Date	Player	Opponent
June 14, 2001	Paul Konerko	Cincinnati
July 21, 2001	Paul Konerko	Boston
September 23, 2001	Magglio Ordonez	Kansas City
April 16, 2002	Magglio Ordonez	Cleveland
June 16, 2002	Carlos Lee	at Chicago Cubs
July 2, 2002	Magglio Ordonez	Detroit
August 13, 2002	Jose Valentin	at Texas
August 27, 2002	Joe Crede	Toronto
September 9, 2002	Paul Konerko	at Kansas City
September 21, 2002	Carlos Lee	Minnesota
September 25, 2002	Jeff Liefer	Boston
April 17, 2003	Carlos Lee	Kansas City
May 25, 2003	Carlos Lee	Detroit
June 20, 2003	Miguel Olivo	at Chicago Cubs
July 4, 2003	Paul Konerko	at Kansas City
August 26, 2003	Frank Thomas	at New York
August 3, 2004	Paul Konerko	at Kansas City
August 18, 2004	Aaron Rowand	Detroit
September 21, 2004	Juan Uribe	Minnesota
September 29, 2004	Carlos Lee	at Detroit
May 16, 2005	A.J. Pierzynski	Texas
July 4, 2005	Jermaine Dye	Tampa Bay
May 3, 2006	Joe Crede	Seattle
May 20, 2006	Tadahito Iguchi	Chicago Cubs
June 16, 2006	Joe Crede	at Cincinnati
June 23, 2006	Scott Podsednik	Houston
June 24, 2006	Joe Crede	Houston
June 25, 2006	Tadahito Iguchi	Houston
July 6, 2006	Jim Thome	Baltimore
July 28, 2006	Ross Gload	at Baltimore
September 19, 2006	A.J. Pierzynski	Detroit
September 24, 2006	Juan Uribe	Seattle
September 29, 2006	Alex Cintron	at Kansas City
April 18, 2007	Jermaine Dye	Texas
May 20, 2007	A.J. Pierzynski	at Chicago Cubs
August 3, 2007	Juan Uribe	at Detroit
August 11, 2007	Josh Fields	Seattle

Bill Stein is congratulated by teammates after teeing off against the Milwaukee Brewers on July 20, 1975.

Date	Player	Opponent
August 17, 2007	Danny Richar	at Seattle
April 7, 2008	Joe Crede	Minnesota
April 13, 2008	Joe Crede	Detroit
April 13, 2008	Paul Konerko	Detroit
May 14, 2008	Carlos Quentin	at L.A. Angels
June 19, 2008	Jermaine Dye	Pittsburgh
June 27, 2008	Nick Swisher	Chicago Cubs
June 30, 2008	Nick Swisher	Cleveland
July 22, 2008	Alexei Ramirez	Texas
August 17, 2008	Alexei Ramirez	at Oakland
September 14, 2008	Dewayne Wise	Detroit
September 19, 2008	Alexei Ramirez	at Kansas City
September 28, 2008	Alexei Ramirez	Detroit
April 25, 2009	Alexei Ramirez	Toronto
May 2, 2009	A.J. Pierzynski	Texas
May 20, 2009	Jermaine Dye	Minnesota
July 7, 2009	Paul Konerko	Cleveland
July 17, 2009	Jim Thome	Baltimore
July 23, 2009	Josh Fields	Tampa Bay
September 19, 2009	Carlos Quentin	Kansas City
April 14, 2010	Carlos Quentin	at Toronto
May 30, 2010	Jayson Nix	at Tampa Bay
July 11, 2010	Carlos Quentin	Kansas City
September 12, 2010	Andruw Jones	Kansas City
September 30, 2010	Paul Konerko	Boston

Most Grand Slams in a Season

2008 (12)	2002 (8)	1993 (7)	2000 (6)
2006 (11)	1996 (8)	1961 (7)	1995, 1991 (6)

Most Grand Slams by a Player

Robin Ventura	(10)	Oscar Felsch	(4)
Paul Konerko	(9)	Sherm Lollar	(4)
Frank Thomas	(8)	Walt Dropo	(4)
Carlos Lee	(8)	Albert Belle	(4)
Harold Baines	(7)	Al Smith	(4)
Ron Karkovice	(5)	Pete Ward	(4)
Magglio Ordonez	(6)	Bill Melton	(4)
Joe Crede	(6)	Carlos Quentin	(4)
Alexei Ramirez	(5)		

Grand-Slam Home Runs by Sox Pitchers

Monty Stratton, June 1, 1938
Tommy Byrne, May 16, 1953
Gary Peters, May 5, 1968

Pinch-Hit Grand-Slam Home Runs

Taft Wright	July 3, 1940
Jack Wallaesa	May 4, 1947
Tommy Byrne	May 16, 1953
Walt Dropo	May 2, 1957
Roy Sievers	June 21, 1961
Sherm Lollar	July 9, 1961
Buddy Bradford	October 2, 1972
Joe DeSa	September 13, 1985
Juan Uribe	September 21, 2004
Dewayne Wise	September 14, 2008
Andruw Jones	September 12, 2010

Inside-the-Park Grand Slams

Player	Date	Opponent	Opposing Pitcher
Oscar Felsch	9/30/1916	at Cle.	Clarence Smith
Eddie Collins	6/5/1919	at N.Y.	Ernie Shore
Joe Jackson	716/1920	at Wash.	Eric Erickson
Bill Barrett	8/4/1926	Bos.	Fred Heimach
Bud Clancy	7/15/1927	Phila.	Rube Walberg
Ferris Fain	6/16/1954	Phila.	Sonny Dixon
Carlos May	9/18/1971	Cal.	Tom Murphy
Kevin Bell	6/22/1976	at K.C.	Steve Busby
Ron Karkovice	8/30/1990	at Minn.	David West

White Sox Players Who Homered From Both Sides of the Plate in the Same Game

Player	Date	Opponent	Pitcher	Inning
Ken Henderson	August 29, 1975	at Baltimore	Ross Grimsley	1st
			Wayne Garland	8th
Tim Raines	August 31, 1993	at New York	Sterling Hitchcock	5th
			Rich Monteleone	9th
Brian Simmons	September 26, 1998	at Kansas City	Brian Barber	4th
			Allen McDill	7th
Jose Valentin	September 30, 2000	Kansas City	Blake Stein	3rd
			Scott Mullen	8th

Player	Date	Opponent	Pitcher	Inning
Jose Valentin	August 13, 2002	at Texas	Dennys Reyes	4th
			Todd van Poppel	8th
Jose Valentin	July 30, 2003	at Kansas City	Runelvys Hernandez	2nd
			Runelvys Hernandez	3rd
			Jeremy Affeldt	5th
Nick Swisher	June 9, 2008	Minnesota	Glenn Perkins	4th
			Jesse Crain	6th
Nick Swisher	June 30, 2008	Cleveland	Jeremy Sowers	3rd
			Tom Mastny	6th

Single-Game Attendance Records at the Old Comiskey Park

Current Teams	Date	Attendance
1. Minnesota	May 20, 1973	55,555
2. New York	July 19, 1953	54,215
3. Cleveland	May 15, 1949	53,325
4. Boston	July 12, 1951	52,593
5. Milwaukee	April 14, 1981	51,560
6. California	June 13, 1982	50,892
7. Kansas City	July 31, 1977	50,412
8. Baltimore	September 4, 1977	48,952
9. Detroit	July 12, 1979	47,795
10. Seattle	September 17, 1983	45,646
11. Oakland	September 5, 1983	43,014
12. Texas	July 3, 1978	42,231
13. Toronto	April 10, 1979	41,043

Defunct Teams	Date	Attendance
1. St. Louis (1901–53)	April 27, 1952	42,040
2. Kansas City (1955–67)	April 19, 1960	41,661
3. Washington (1901–60)	May 10, 1925	40,000*
4. Philadelphia (1901–54)	May 4, 1947	39,544
5. Washington (1961–71)	June 25, 1961	29,584
6. Seattle (1969)	April 20, 1969	12,579

*Estimated figure. Crowd sizes for games prior to 1941 are generally not available, and when given, are usually rounded off to the nearest thousand.

Crowds of 50,000 or More at the Old Comiskey Park

Attendance	Opponent	Date
55,555	Minnesota*	June 20, 1973
54,215	New York*	July 19, 1953
53,940	New York*	June 8, 1951
53,325	Cleveland*	May 15, 1949
53,067	New York	July 27, 1954
52,712	Cubs†	June 25, 1964
52,593	Boston*	July 12, 1951
52,494	New York*	June 18, 1933
52,054	New York*	June 10, 1951
52,000	New York	May 8, 1927

Game day at Comiskey Park in the 1930s. Where are all the fans?

Attendance	Opponent	Date
51,904	New York*	June 4, 1972
51,599	Cleveland*	August 13, 1948
51,560	Milwaukee	April 14, 1981
51,178	New York*	July 23, 1939
50,990	New York*	August 28, 1955
50,911	New York*	August 23, 1931
50,892	California	June 13, 1982
50,754	Boston	April 7, 1978
50,412	Kansas City*	July 31, 1977
50,000	New York*	July 25, 1937

*Doubleheader
†Exhibition

Highest Single-Game Attendance at U.S. Cellular Field (1991–2010)

Attendance	Opponent	Date
46,246	Toronto (ALCS)	October 5, 1993
46,101	Toronto (ALCS)	October 6, 1993
46,027	Chicago Cubs	June 28, 2002
45,942	Chicago Cubs	June 29, 2002
45,936	Chicago Cubs	June 8, 2001
45,849	Chicago Cubs	June 9, 2001
45,527	Toronto (ALCS)	October 12, 1993
45,440	Chicago Cubs	June 28, 2003
45,383	Seattle (ALDS)	October 4, 2000
45,351	Chicago Cubs	June 30, 2002
45,290	Seattle (ALDS)	October 3, 2000
45,147	Chicago Cubs	June 27, 2003
45,079	Chicago Cubs	June 10, 2001

Single-Date Attendance Records on the Road

Date	Site	Attendance
1. August 20, 1948	Cleveland	78,382
2. July 29, 1951	New York	70,972
3. August 25, 1940	New York	70,740
4. August 11, 1951	Cleveland	70,619
5. August 30, 1959	Cleveland	66,586
6. June 7, 1970	New York	65,880
7. June 23, 1957	New York	63,787
8. June 11, 1967	New York	62,582
9. July 15, 1956	New York	61,351
10. June 19, 1951	New York	60,441

White Sox .300 Hitters (399 or more at bats)

Player	Year	Average
Fielder Jones	1901	.311
Fred Hartman	1901	.309
Fielder Jones	1902	.321
Danny Green	1902	.312
Danny Green	1903	.309
Matty McIntyre	1911	.323
Harry Lord	1911	.321
Eddie Collins	1915	.332
Jacques Fournier	1915	.302
Joe Jackson	1916	.341
Eddie Collins	1916	.308
Oscar Felsch	1916	.300
Oscar Felsch	1917	.308
Joe Jackson	1917	.301
Buck Weaver	1918	.300
Joe Jackson	1919	.351
Eddie Collins	1919	.319
Nemo Leibold	1919	.302
Joe Jackson	1920	.382
Eddie Collins	1920	.369
Oscar Felsch	1920	.338
Buck Weaver	1920	.333
Shano Collins	1920	.303
Eddie Collins	1921	.337
Amos Strunk	1921	.332
Harry Hooper	1921	.327
Earl Sheely	1921	.304
Eddie Collins	1922	.324
Earl Sheely	1922	.317
Harry Hooper	1922	.304
Johnny Mostil	1922	.303
Eddie Collins	1923	.360
Bibb Falk	1924	.352
Eddie Collins	1924	.349
Harry Hooper	1924	.328
Earl Sheely	1924	.320
Eddie Collins	1925	.346
Earl Sheely	1925	.315
Bibb Falk	1925	.301
Bibb Falk	1926	.345
Johnny Mostil	1926	.328
Bibb Falk	1927	.327
Alex Metzler	1927	.319
Willie Kamm	1928	.308
Alex Metzler	1928	.304
Carl Reynolds	1929	.317
Carl Reynolds	1930	.359
Smead Jolley	1930	.313
Cliff Watwood	1930	.302
Luzurne Blue	1931	.304
Al Simmons	1933	.331
Luke Appling	1933	.322
Evar Swanson	1933	.306
Al Simmons	1934	.344
Luke Appling	1934	.303
Zeke Bonura	1934	.302
Luke Appling	1935	.307

Player	Year	Average
Luke Appling	1936	.388
Rip Radcliff	1936	.335
Zeke Bonura	1936	.330
Jackie Hayes	1936	.312
Mike Kreevich	1936	.307
Zeke Bonura	1937	.345
Rip Radcliff	1937	.325
Luke Appling	1937	.317
Mike Kreevich	1937	.302
Dixie Walker	1937	.302
Rip Radcliff	1938	.330
Gee Walker	1938	.305
Eric "Boob" McNair	1939	.324
Mike Kreevich	1939	.323
Luke Appling	1939	.314
Joe Kuhel	1939	.300
Luke Appling	1940	.348
Taft Wright	1940	.337
Julius "Moose" Solters	1940	.308
Taft Wright	1941	.322
Luke Appling	1941	.314
Luke Appling	1943	.328
Ralph Hodgin	1943	.314
Tony Cuccinello	1945	.308
Johnny Dickshot	1945	.302
Luke Appling	1946	.309
Taft Wright	1947	.324
Luke Appling	1947	.306
Luke Appling	1948	.314
Cass Michaels	1949	.308
Luke Appling	1949	.301
Hank Majeski	1950	.309

Player	Year	Average
Minnie Minoso	1951	.326
Nellie Fox	1951	.313
Minnie Minoso	1953	.313
Minnie Minoso	1954	.320
Nellie Fox	1954	.319
George Kell	1955	.312
Nellie Fox	1955	.311
Minnie Minoso	1956	.316
Nellie Fox	1957	.317
Minnie Minoso	1957	.310
Nellie Fox	1958	.300
Nellie Fox	1959	.306
Al Smith	1960	.315
Minnie Minoso	1960	.311
Floyd Robinson	1961	.310
Floyd Robinson	1962	.312
Floyd Robinson	1964	.301
Walt Williams	1969	.304
Luis Aparicio	1970	.313
Dick Allen	1972	.308
Carlos May	1972	.308
Jorge Orta	1974	.316
Dick Allen	1974	.301
Jorge Orta	1975	.304
Ralph Garr	1976	.300
Ralph Garr	1977	.300
Chet Lemon	1979	.318
Lamar Johnson	1979	.309
Tom Paciorek	1983	.307
Harold Baines	1984	.304
Harold Baines	1985	.309
Dave Gallagher	1988	.303

Player	Year	Average
Frank Thomas	1991	.318
Frank Thomas	1992	.323
Frank Thomas	1993	.317
Lance Johnson	1993	.311
Tim Raines	1993	.306
Julio Franco	1994	.319
Frank Thomas	1994	.353
Frank Thomas	1995	.308
Lance Johnson	1995	.306
Frank Thomas	1996	.349
Dave Martinez	1996	.318
Harold Baines	1996	.311
Frank Thomas	1997	.347
Albert Belle	1998	.328
Mike Caruso	1998	.306
Frank Thomas	1999	.305
Magglio Ordonez	1999	.301
Carlos Lee	2000	.301
Magglio Ordonez	2000	.315
Frank Thomas	2000	.328
Magglio Ordonez	2001	.305
Paul Konerko	2002	.304
Magglio Ordonez	2002	.320
Magglio Ordonez	2003	.317
Aaron Rowand	2004	.310
Carlos Lee	2004	.305
Jermaine Dye	2006	.315
Paul Konerko	2006	.313
Scott Podsednik	2009	.304
A.J. Pierzynski	2009	.300
Paul Konerko	2010	.312

30 or More Home Runs in a Season

Player	Position	Year	Home Runs
Albert Belle	of	1998	49
Jermaine Dye	of	2006	44
Frank Thomas	dh	2000	43
Jim Thome	dh	2006	42
Frank Thomas	dh	2003	42
Frank Thomas	1b	1993	41
Paul Konerko	1b	2004	41
Frank Thomas	1b	1993	41
Frank Thomas	1b	1995	40
Paul Konerko	1b	2005	40
Paul Konerko	1B	2010	39
Frank Thomas	1b	1994	38
Magglio Ordonez	of	2002	38
Carlton Fisk	c	1985	37
Dick Allen	1b	1972	37
Carlos Quentin	of	2008	36
Jim Thome	dh	2007	35
Paul Konerko	1B	2006	35
Ron Kittle	of	1983	35

Player	Position	Year	Home Runs
Jermaine Dye	of	2008	34
Robin Ventura	3b	1996	34
Bill Melton	3b	1970	33
Bill Melton	3b	1971	33
Frank Thomas	1b	1991	32
Paul Konerko	1b	2001	32
Dick Allen	1b	1974	32
Magglio Ordonez	of	2000	32
Paul Konerko	1B	2007	31
Magglio Ordonez	of	2001	31
Carlos Lee	of	2003	31
Carlos Lee	of	2004	31
Oscar Gamble	dh	1977	31
Jermaine Dye	of	2005	31
Joe Crede	3B	2006	30
Jose Valentin	ss	2004	30
Richie Zisk	of	1977	30
Albert Belle	of	1997	30

10 or More Home Runs in a Month

Player	Position	Month and Year	Home Runs
Albert Belle	of	July 1998	16*
Carlos Lee	of	July 2004	13
Frank Thomas	dh	August 2003	13
Dick Allen	1b	July 1972	13
Paul Konerko	1b	June 2002	12
Frank Thomas	dh	June 2000	12
Frank Thomas	1b	May 1994	12
Robin Ventura	2b	July 1991	12
Ron Kittle	of/dh	September 1985	12
Bill Melton	3b	June 1971	12
Jim Thome	dh	September 2007	12
Bill Melton	3b	June 1969	12

Player	Position	Month and Year	Home Runs
Paul Konerko	1b	April 2010	11
Frank Thomas	1b	September 1996	11
Frank Thomas	1b	July 1993	11
Jim Thome	dh	April 2006	10
Jermaine Dye	of	August 2006	10
Frank Thomas	1b	August 1993	10
Carlton Fisk	c	July 1983	10
Bill Melton	3b	July 1974	10
Harold Baines	dh	June 1987	10
Paul Konerko	1b	June 2004	10
Magglio Ordonez	of	July 2002	10

*Major League record

Most Home Runs by Position

Player	Position	Year	Home Runs
Frank Thomas	1b	1993	41
Carlton Fisk	c	1985	37
Robin Ventura	3b	1996	34
Frank Thomas-T	dh	2003	42
Jim Thome-T	dh	2006	42
Albert Belle	of	1998	49

Player	Position	Year	Home Runs
Jermaine Dye	of	2006	44
Magglio Ordonez	of	2002	38
Jose Valentin	ss	2004	30
Alexei Ramirez	2b	2008	21
Jack Harshman	p	1956	6

Most RBIs by Position

Player	Position	Year	RBIs
Zeke Bonura	1b	1936	138
Luke Appling	ss	1936	128
Albert Belle	of	1998	152
Magglio Ordonez	of	2002	135
Magglio Ordonez	of	2000	126
Robin Ventura	3b	1996	105

Player	Position	Year	RBIs
Frank Thomas	dh	2001	143
Sandow Mertes	2b	1901	98
Carlton Fisk	c	1983, 1985	85*
Frank Smith	p	1909	20

*Fisk's RBI totals do not include designated hitter appearances. In 1985 his RBI output was 107. In games he actually caught, his RBI total for that season was 85, which stands as a single-season record for catchers.

200 or More Hits in a Season

Player	Position	Year	Hits
Eddie Collins	2b	1920	222
Joe Jackson	of	1920	218
Buck Weaver	3b	1920	210
Rip Radcliff	of	1936	207
Luke Appling	ss	1936	204

Player	Position	Year	Hits
Joe Jackson	of	1917	202
Carl Reynolds	of	1930	202
Nellie Fox	2b	1954	201
Al Simmons	of	1933	200
Albert Belle	of	1998	200

100 or More Walks in a Season

Player	Position	Year	Walks
Frank Thomas	1b	1991	138
Frank Thomas	1b/dh	1995	136
Luzurne Blue	1b	1931	127
Tony Phillips	of	1996	125
Frank Thomas	1b	1992	122
Luke Appling	ss	1935	122
Luke Appling	ss	1949	121
Eddie Collins	2b	1915	119
Frank Thomas	dh	2000	112

Player	Position	Year	Walks
Frank Thomas	1b	1993	112
Frank Thomas	1b	1996	109
Frank Thomas	1b	1994	109
Ferris Fain	1b	1953	108
Jim Thome	dh	2006	107
Robin Ventura	3b	1993	105
Luke Appling	ss	1939	105
Larry Doby	of	1956	102
Joe Cunningham	1b	1962	101
Cass Michaels	2b	1949	101

100 or More RBIs in a Season

Player	Year	RBIs
Oscar Felsch	1917	102
Oscar Felsch	1920	115
Joe Jackson	1920	121
Earl Sheely	1924	103
Earl Sheely	1925	111
Bibb Falk	1926	108
Smead Jolley	1930	114
Carl Reynolds	1930	100
Al Simmons	1933	119
Zeke Bonura	1934	110
Al Simmons	1934	104
Luke Appling	1936	128
Zeke Bonura	1936	138
Zeke Bonura	1937	100
Gee Walker	1939	111
Eddie Robinson	1951	117
Eddie Robinson	1952	104
Minnie Minoso	1953	104
Minnie Minoso	1954	116
Larry Doby	1956	102

Player	Year	RBIs
Minnie Minoso	1957	103
Minnie Minoso	1960	105
Floyd Robinson	1962	109
Dick Allen	1972	113
Richie Zisk	1977	101
Harold Baines	1982	105
Greg Luzinski	1982	102
Ron Kittle	1983	100
Harold Baines	1985	113
Carlton Fisk	1985	107
Frank Thomas	1991	109
Robin Ventura	1991	100
George Bell	1992	112
Frank Thomas	1992	115
Frank Thomas	1993	128
Frank Thomas	1994	101
Frank Thomas	1995	111
Frank Thomas	1996	134
Robin Ventura	1996	105
Danny Tartabull	1996	101

Player	Year	RBIs
Albert Belle	1997	116
Frank Thomas	1997	125
Albert Belle	1998	152
Frank Thomas	1998	109
Magglio Ordonez	1999	117
Frank Thomas	2000	143
Magglio Ordonez	2000	126
Magglio Ordonez	2001	113
Magglio Ordonez	2002	135
Paul Konerko	2002	104
Frank Thomas	2003	105
Carlos Lee	2003	113
Paul Konerko	2004	117
Paul Konerko	2005	100
Jermaine Dye	2006	120
Paul Konerko	2006	113
Jim Thome	2006	109
Carlos Quentin	2008	100
Paul Konerko	2010	111

30 or More Stolen Bases in a Season

Player	Year	Stolen Bases
Frank Isbell	1901	52
Sandow Mertes	1901	46
Fielder Jones	1901	38
Herm McFarland	1901	33
Fred Hartman	1901	31
Sandow Mertes	1902	46
Frank Isbell	1902	38
Sammy Strang	1902	38
Danny Green	1902	35
George Davis	1902	33

Player	Year	Stolen Bases
Fielder Jones	1902	33
George Davis	1904	32
Jiggs Donahue	1905	32
George Davis	1905	31
Frank Isbell	1906	37
Jiggs Donahue	1906	36
Patsy Dougherty	1907	33
Patsy Dougherty	1908	47
Patsy Dougherty	1909	36
Freddy Parent	1909	32

Player	Year	Stolen Bases
Rollie Zeider	1910	49
James Callahan	1911	45
Harry Lord	1911	43
Rollie Zeider	1912	47
Morrie Rath	1912	30
Shano Collins	1914	30
Eddie Collins	1915	46
Shano Collins	1915	38
Eddie Murphy	1915	33
Eddie Collins	1916	40

Player	Year	Stolen Bases
Ray Schalk	1916	30
Eddie Collins	1917	53
Eddie Collins	1919	33
Eddie Collins	1923	47
Johnny Mostil	1923	41
Eddie Collins	1924	42
Johnny Mostil	1925	43
Johnny Mostil	1926	35
Wally Moses	1943	56
Minnie Minoso	1951	31
Luis Aparicio	1959	56
Luis Aparicio	1960	51
Luis Aparicio	1961	53
Luis Aparicio	1962	31
Don Buford	1966	51
Tommie Agee	1966	44
Don Buford	1967	34
Pat Kelly	1972	32
Rudy Law	1982	36
Rudy Law	1983	77
John Cangelosi*	1986	50
Gary Redus	1987	52
Ozzie Guillen	1989	36
Lance Johnson	1990	36
Ivan Calderon	1990	32
Sammy Sosa	1990	32
Tim Raines	1991	51
Tim Raines	1992	45
Lance Johnson	1992	41
Steve Sax	1992	30
Lance Johnson	1993	35
Lance Johnson	1995	40
Ray Durham	1996	30
Ray Durham	1997	33
Ray Durham	1998	36
Ray Durham	1999	34
Scott Podsednik	2005	59
Scott Podsednik	2006	40
Jerry Owens	2007	32
Scott Podsednik	2009	30
Juan Pierre	2010	68
Alex Rios	2010	34

*Established new AL rookie record for stolen bases. Sox infielder Rollie Zeider had set the old record of 49 in 1910.

30 or More Doubles in a Season

Player	Year	Doubles
Lee Tannehill	1904	31
Shano Collins	1912	34
Shano Collins	1914	34
Joe Jackson	1916	40
Oscar Felsch	1919	34
Buck Weaver	1919	33
Joe Jackson	1919	31
Joe Jackson	1920	42
Oscar Felsch	1920	40
Eddie Collins	1920	37
Buck Weaver	1920	35
Bibb Falk	1921	31
Earl Sheely	1922	37
Harry Hooper	1922	35
Willie Kamm	1923	39
Johnny Mostil	1923	37
Harry Hooper	1923	32
Bibb Falk	1924	37
Earl Sheely	1924	34
Earl Sheely	1925	43
Johnny Mostil	1925	36
Bibb Falk	1925	35
Willie Kamm	1925	32
Ike Davis	1925	31
Bibb Falk	1926	43
Johnny Mostil	1926	41
Earl Sheely	1926	40
Eddie Collins	1926	32
Bill Barrett	1926	31
Bill Barrett	1927	35
Bibb Falk	1927	35
Willie Kamm	1927	32
Willie Kamm	1928	30
Willie Kamm	1929	32
Smead Jolley	1930	38
Red Kress	1932	42
Luke Appling	1933	36
George Haas	1933	33
Al Simmons	1934	36
Zeke Bonura	1934	35
Zeke Bonura	1935	34
Zeke Bonura	1936	39
Jackie Hayes	1936	34
Mike Kreevich	1936	32
Luke Appling	1936	31
Rip Radcliff	1936	31
Luke Appling	1937	42
Zeke Bonura	1937	41
Rip Radcliff	1937	38
Mike Kreevich	1939	30
Gee Walker	1939	30
Taft Wright	1940	31
Joe Kuhel	1941	39
Taft Wright	1941	35
Don Kolloway	1942	40
Luke Appling	1943	33
Hal Trosky	1944	32
Wally Moses	1945	35
Minnie Minoso	1951	34
Nellie Fox	1951	32
Eddie Robinson	1952	33
Nellie Fox	1953	31
Chico Carrasquel	1953	30
Minnie Minoso	1957	36
Nellie Fox	1959	34
Gene Freese	1960	32
Minnie Minoso	1960	32
Al Smith	1960	31
Floyd Robinson	1962	45
Joe Cunningham	1962	32
Pete Ward	1963	34
Ken Henderson	1974	35
Jorge Orta	1974	31
Chet Lemon	1977	38
Chet Lemon	1979	44
Claudell Washington	1979	33
Jim Morrison	1980	40
Chet Lemon	1980	32
Greg Luzinski	1982	37
Harold Baines	1983	33
Tom Paciorek	1983	32
Greg Walker	1985	38
Ivan Calderon	1987	38
Greg Walker	1987	33
Harold Baines	1988	39
Ivan Calderon	1989	34
Ivan Calderon	1990	44
Frank Thomas	1991	31
Frank Thomas	1992	46
Robin Ventura	1992	38
Frank Thomas	1993	36
Frank Thomas	1994	34
Ray Durham	1996	33
Robin Ventura	1996	31
Albert Belle	1997	45
Frank Thomas	1997	35
Albert Belle	1998	48
Frank Thomas	1998	35
Ray Durham	1998	35

Player	Year	Doubles
Robin Ventura	1998	31
Frank Thomas	1999	36
Magglio Ordonez	1999	34
Carlos Lee	1999	32
Paul Konerko	1999	31
Chris Singleton	1999	31
Ray Durham	1999	30
Frank Thomas	2000	44
Jose Valentin	2000	37
Ray Durham	2000	35
Magglio Ordonez	2000	34
Paul Konerko	2000	31
Ray Durham	2001	42
Magglio Ordonez	2001	40
Paul Konerko	2001	35
Carlos Lee	2001	33
Magglio Ordonez	2002	47
Paul Konerko	2002	30
Magglio Ordonez	2003	46
Carlos Lee	2003	35
Frank Thomas	2003	35
Joe Crede	2003	31
Aaron Rowand	2004	38
Carlos Lee	2004	37
Juan Uribe	2004	31
Aaron Rowand	2005	30
Joe Crede	2006	31
Paul Konerko	2006	30
Jermaine Dye	2007	34
Paul Konerko	2007	34
Orlando Cabrera	2008	33
Jermaine Dye	2008	41
A.J. Pierzynski	2008	31
Paul Konerko	2009	30
Paul Konerko	2010	30

300 or More Total Bases in a Season

Player	Year	Total Bases
Albert Belle	1998	399
Frank Thomas	2000	364
Magglio Ordonez	2002	352
Joe Jackson	1920	336
Jermaine Dye	2006	335
Frank Thomas	1993	333
Magglio Ordonez	2003	331
Frank Thomas	1996	330
Carl Reynolds	1930	329
Frank Thomas	1997	324
Magglio Ordonez	2000	321
Paul Konerko	2010	320
Jermaine Dye	2008	319
Magglio Ordonez	1999	318
Magglio Ordonez	2001	316
Paul Konerko	2006	312
Carlos Lee	2003	311
Carlos Lee	2004	310
Frank Thomas	1991	309
Harold Baines	1984	308
Frank Thomas	2003	307
Frank Thomas	1992	307
Dick Allen	1972	305
Minnie Minoso	1954	304
Smead Jolley	1930	303
Paul Konerko	2004	301
Oscar Felsch	1920	300

Leading Batting Average by Position

Player	Position	Year	Batting Average
Joe Jackson	lf	1920	.382
Eddie Collins	2b	1920	.369
Frank Thomas	1b	1994	.353
Oscar Felsch	cf	1920	.338
Taft Wright	rf	1940	.337
Luke Appling	ss	1936	.336
Buck Weaver	3b	1920	.333
George "Sarge" Connally	p	1927	.328
Frank Thomas	dh	2000	.321
A.J. Pierzynski	c	2009	.300

60 or More Extra-Base Hits (Doubles, Triples, Home Runs) in a Season

Player	Year	EB Hits
Albert Belle	1998	99
Magglio Ordonez	2002	86
Magglio Ordonez	2003	78
Frank Thomas	1993	77
Frank Thomas	2000	77
Frank Thomas	2003	77
Jermaine Dye	2008	77
Albert Belle	1997	76
Joe Jackson	1920	74
Jermaine Dye	2006	74
Frank Thomas	1994	73
Frank Thomas	1992	72
Magglio Ordonez	2001	72
Ray Durham	2001	72
Dick Allen	1972	70
Frank Thomas	1997	70
Paul Konerko	2010	70
Oscar Felsch	1920	69
Magglio Ordonez	2000	69
Ivan Calderon	1987	68
Carlos Lee	2004	68
Jim Thome	2006	68
Harold Baines	1984	67
Frank Thomas	1995	67
Robin Ventura	1996	67
Magglio Ordonez	1999	67
Paul Konerko	2001	67
Carlos Lee	2003	67
Smead Jolley	1930	66
Zeke Bonura	1934	66
Minnie Minoso	1954	66
Floyd Robinson	1962	66
Greg Walker	1985	66
Frank Thomas	1996	66
Frank Thomas	1998	66
Paul Konerko	2006	65

Player	Year	EB Hits
Paul Konerko	2007	65
Carl Reynolds	1930	65
Frank Thomas	1991	64
Joe Jackson	1916	64
Paul Konerko	2005	64
Joe Kuhel	1940	63
Chet Lemon	1979	63
Paul Konerko	2004	63
Carlos Quentin	2008	63
Zeke Bonura	1937	62
Pete Ward	1963	62
Harold Baines	1982	62
Greg Walker	1987	62
Ray Durham	1998	62
Jermaine Dye	2005	62
Jermaine Dye	2007	62
Al Simmons	1934	61
Minnie Minoso	1956	61
Al Smith	1961	61
Chet Lemon	1977	61
Carlton Fisk	1985	61
Ray Durham	2000	61
Joe Crede	2006	61
Johnny Mostil	1926	60
Ken Henderson	1974	60
Ivan Calderon	1990	60
Carlos Lee	2001	60
Juan Uribe	2004	60

10 or More Triples in a Season

Player	Year	Triples
Sandow Mertes	1901	17
Fred Hartman	1901	13
Dummy Hoy	1901	11
Frank Shugarts	1901	12
George Davis	1904	15
Danny Green	1904	10
Fielder Jones	1905	12
Frank Isbell	1905	11
Frank Isbell	1906	11
Patsy Dougherty	1909	13
Harry Lord	1911	18
Ping Bodie	1911	13
Matty McIntyre	1911	11
Harry Lord	1912	12
Shano Collins	1912	10
Rollie Zeider	1912	10
Hal Chase	1913	10
Harry Lord	1913	12
Ray Demmitt	1914	12
Jacques Fournier	1915	18
Shano Collins	1915	17
Oscar Felsch	1915	11
Buck Weaver	1915	11
Eddie Collins	1915	10
Robert "Braggo" Roth	1915	10
Joe Jackson	1916	21
Eddie Collins	1916	17
Shano Collins	1916	12
Oscar Felsch	1916	12
Joe Jackson	1917	17
Eddie Collins	1917	12
Oscar Felsch	1917	10
Shano Collins	1918	11
Joe Jackson	1919	14
Oscar Felsch	1919	11
Joe Jackson	1920	20
Oscar Felsch	1920	15
Eddie Collins	1920	13
Shano Collins	1920	10
Swede Risberg	1920	10
Eddie Mulligan	1921	12
Bibb Falk	1921	11
Eddie Collins	1921	10
Amos Strunk	1921	10
Johnny Mostil	1922	14
Eddie Collins	1922	12
Johnny Mostil	1923	15
Johnny Mostil	1925	16
Johnny Mostil	1926	15
Willie Kamm	1926	10
Willie Kamm	1927	13
Alex Metzler	1927	11
Alex Metzler	1928	14
Willie Kamm	1928	12
Bud Clancy	1928	11
Alex Metzler	1929	13
Bill Cissell	1929	12
Carl Reynolds	1929	12
Carl Reynolds	1930	18
Smead Jolley	1930	12
Luzurne Blue	1931	15
Carl Reynolds	1931	14
Luke Appling	1932	10
Luke Appling	1933	10
Al Simmons	1933	10
Mike Kreevich	1936	11
Mike Kreevich	1937	16
Dixie Walker	1937	16
Rip Radcliff	1937	10
Mike Kreevich	1938	12
Gee Walker	1939	11
Luke Appling	1940	13
Mike Kreevich	1940	10
Wally Moses	1943	12
Wally Moses	1945	15
Johnny Dickshot	1945	10
Dave Philley	1947	11
Minnie Minoso	1951	14
Nellie Fox	1951	12
Nellie Fox	1952	10
Jim Rivera	1953	16
Minnie Minoso	1954	18
Minnie Minoso	1956	11
Nellie Fox	1956	10
Nellie Fox	1960	10
Floyd Robinson	1962	10
Tommy McCraw	1968	12
Jorge Orta	1973	10
Jorge Orta	1975	10
Harold Baines	1984	10
Sammy Sosa	1990	10
Lance Johnson	1991	13
Lance Johnson	1992	12
Lance Johnson	1993	14
Joey Cora	1993	13
Lance Johnson	1994	14
Lance Johnson	1995	12
Ray Durham	2001	10

150 or More Singles in a Season

Player	Year	Singles
Eddie Collins	1920	169
Nellie Fox	1954	167
Buck Weaver	1920	165
Eddie Collins	1922	161
Rip Radcliff	1936	161
Luke Appling	1936	160
Nellie Fox	1958	160
Nellie Fox	1956	158
Luke Appling	1940	157
Nellie Fox	1952	157
Nellie Fox	1955	157
Nellie Fox	1957	155
Eddie Collins	1924	154
Luke Appling	1943	154
Matty McIntyre	1911	153
Taft Wright	1940	151
Luke Appling	1941	151
Fielder Jones	1902	150
Eddie Collins	1923	150

10 or More Doubles, Triples, Home Runs, and Stolen Bases in a Season

Player	Year	Doubles	Triples	Home Runs	Stolen Bases
Carl Reynolds	1929	24	12	11	19
Carl Reynolds	1930	25	18	22	16
Mike Kreevich	1937	29	16	12	10
Gee Walker	1939	30	11	13	17
Minnie Minoso	1951	34	14	10	31
Jim Rivera	1953	26	16	11	22
Minnie Minoso	1954	29	18	19	18
Minnie Minoso	1956	29	11	21	12
Jorge Orta	1977	26	10	11	16
Lance Johnson	1995	18	12	10	40
Ray Durham	2001	42	10	20	23

100 or More Runs in a Season

Player	Year	Runs
Dummy Hoy	1901	113
Fielder Jones	1901	120
Sammy Strang	1902	108
Harry Lord	1911	103
Matty McIntyre	1911	102
Morrie Rath	1912	104
Eddie Collins	1915	118
Joe Jackson	1920	105
Buck Weaver	1920	104
Harry Hooper	1922	111
Eddie Collins	1924	108
Harry Hooper	1924	107
Ike Davis	1925	105
Johnny Mostil	1925	135
Johnny Mostil	1926	120
Carl Reynolds	1930	103
Luzurne Blue	1931	119
Evar Swanson	1933	102
Al Simmons	1934	102
Zeke Bonura	1935	107
Luke Appling	1936	111
Zeke Bonura	1936	120
Rip Radcliff	1936	120
Rip Radcliff	1937	105
Dixie Walker	1937	105
Joe Kuhel	1939	107
Joe Kuhel	1940	111
Minnie Minoso	1951	112
Minnie Minoso	1953	104
Chico Carrasquel	1954	106
Nellie Fox	1954	111
Minnie Minoso	1954	119
Nellie Fox	1955	100
Nellie Fox	1956	109
Minnie Minoso	1956	106
Nellie Fox	1957	110
Tim Raines	1991	102
Frank Thomas	1991	104
Tim Raines	1992	102
Frank Thomas	1992	108
Frank Thomas	1993	106
Frank Thomas	1994	106
Frank Thomas	1995	102
Tony Phillips	1996	119
Frank Thomas	1996	110
Frank Thomas	1997	110
Ray Durham	1997	106
Ray Durham	1998	126
Albert Belle	1998	113
Frank Thomas	1998	109
Ray Durham	1999	109
Magglio Ordonez	1999	100
Ray Durham	2000	121
Frank Thomas	2000	115
Carlos Lee	2000	107
Jose Valentin	2000	107
Magglio Ordonez	2000	102
Ray Durham	2001	104
Magglio Ordonez	2002	116
Carlos Lee	2003	100
Carlos Lee	2004	103
Jim Thome	2006	108
Jermaine Dye	2006	103

Jim Scott (right)—shown with Buck Weaver (left) and Larry Doyle of the Cubs—won 24 games for the Sox in 1915. (Courtesy of the Amateur Athletic Foundation of Los Angeles)

White Sox 20-Game Winners

Year	Pitcher	Record
1901	Roy Patterson	20–16
1901	Clark Griffith	24–7
1902	Roy Patterson	20–12
1904	Nick Altrock	21–13
1904	Frank Owen	21–15
1905	Nick Altrock	22–12
1905	Frank Owen	21–13
1906	Frank Owen	22–13
1906	Nick Altrock	20–13
1907	Doc White	27–13
1907	Ed Walsh	24–18
1907	Frank Smith	22–11
1908	Ed Walsh	40–15
1909	Frank Smith	25–17
1911	Ed Walsh	27–18
1912	Ed Walsh	27–17
1913	Ewell "Reb" Russell	21–17
1915	Jim Scott	24–11
1915	Red Faber	24–14
1917	Ed Cicotte	28–12
1919	Ed Cicotte	29–7
1919	Claude "Lefty" Williams	23–11
1920	Red Faber	23–13
1920	Claude "Lefty" Williams	22–14
1920	Dickie Kerr	21–9
1920	Ed Cicotte	21–10
1921	Red Faber	25–15
1922	Red Faber	21–17
1924	Hollis Thurston	20–14
1925	Ted Lyons	21–11
1927	Ted Lyons	22–14
1930	Ted Lyons	22–15
1936	Vern Kennedy	21–9
1941	Thornton Lee	22–11
1956	Billy Pierce	20–9
1957	Billy Pierce	20–12
1959	Early Wynn	22–10
1962	Ray Herbert	20–9
1964	Gary Peters	20–8
1971	Wilbur Wood	22–13
1972	Wilbur Wood	24–17
1972	Stan Bahnsen	21–16
1973	Wilbur Wood	24–20
1974	Jim Kaat	21–13
1974	Wilbur Wood	20–19
1975	Jim Kaat	20–14
1975	Wilbur Wood	20–20
1983	LaMarr Hoyt	24–10
1983	Richard Dotson	22–7
1992	Jack McDowell	20–10
1993	Jack McDowell	22–10
2003	Esteban Loaiza	21–9

Pitchers with 200 or More Strikeouts in a Season

Year	Pitcher	Strikeouts
1907	Ed Walsh	206
1908	Ed Walsh	269
1910	Ed Walsh	258
1911	Ed Walsh	255
1912	Ed Walsh	254
1964	Gary Peters	205
1967	Gary Peters	215
1971	Wilbur Wood	210
1971	Tom Bradley	206
1972	Tom Bradley	209
1996	Alex Fernandez	200
2003	Esteban Loaiza	207
2007	Javier Vazquez	213
2008	Javier Vazquez	200

Pitchers Who Defeated Every Opponent at Least Once in a Season

1901	Clark Griffith
	Roy Patterson
1902	Roy Patterson
1903	Doc White
1904	Nick Altrock
	Frank Owen
1907	Doc White
	Ed Walsh
1908	Ed Walsh
	Frank Smith
1909	Ed Walsh
1910	Ed Walsh
	Doc White
1911	Ed Walsh
	Jim Scott
	Doc White
1912	Ed Walsh
	Joe Benz
1913	Ewell "Reb" Russell
	Jim Scott
	Ed Cicotte
1915	Jim Scott
	Red Faber
1916	Ewell "Reb" Russell
1917	Ed Cicotte
	Red Faber
1919	Ed Cicotte
	Claude "Lefty" Williams
1920	Red Faber
	Claude "Lefty" Williams
	Dickie Kerr
1921	Red Faber
	Dickie Kerr
1922	Red Faber
1923	Red Faber
	Charlie Robertson
1924	Hollis Thurston
1925	Ted Lyons
	Red Faber
1927	Ted Lyons
1928	Tommy Thomas
	Ted Lyons
1929	Tommy Thomas
	Red Faber
1930	Pat Caraway
1931	Vic Frasier
1934	George Earnshaw
1935	Ted Lyons
	John Whitehead
1936	Vern Kennedy
	John Whitehead
1937	Monty Stratton
	Vern Kennedy
1938	Monty Stratton
1941	Thornton Lee
	Johnny Rigney
1942	Ted Lyons
	John Humphries
1943	Bill Dietrich
	Orval Grove
1944	Orval Grove
1945	Thornton Lee
1945	Orval Grove
1949	Bill Wight
1950	Ray Scarborough
1951	Billy Pierce
1952	Billy Pierce
1953	Billy Pierce
	Virgil Trucks
	Saul Rogovin
1954	Virgil Trucks
	Sandy Consuegra
	Bob Keegan
1955	Billy Pierce
1956	Billy Pierce
	Jim Wilson
1957	Billy Pierce
	Jim Wilson
1958	Billy Pierce
	Dick Donovan
1959	Early Wynn
	Bob Shaw
	Turk Lown
1960	Billy Pierce
	Frank Baumann
	Turk Lown
1962	Ray Herbert
1964	Juan Pizarro
1967	Joel Horlen
1972	Wilbur Wood
1975	Jim Kaat

Pitchers with a .650 Winning Percentage in One Season

Year	Pitcher	Pct
1901	Clark Griffith	.774
1901	James Callahan	.652
1906	Doc White	.750
1907	Frank Smith	.667
1907	Doc White	.675
1908	Ed Walsh	.727
1913	Ed Walsh	.727
1916	Ed Cicotte	.697
1916	Claude "Lefty" Williams	.650
1917	Ed Cicotte	.700
1917	Claude "Lefty" Williams	.680
1917	Ewell "Reb" Russell	.706
1917	Dave Danforth	.714
1919	Ed Cicotte	.806
1919	Claude "Lefty" Williams	.676
1919	Dickie Kerr	.650
1920	Ed Cicotte	.677
1920	Dickie Kerr	.700
1925	Ted Blankenship	.680
1925	Ted Lyons	.656
1935	Ted Lyons	.652
1936	Vern Kennedy	.700
1939	John Rigney	.652
1939	Ted Lyons	.700
1941	Thornton Lee	.667
1942	Ted Lyons	.700
1943	Joe Haynes	.778
1944	Gordon Maltzberger	.667
1946	Earl Caldwell	.765
1947	Joe Haynes	.700
1952	Harry Dorish	.667
1953	Virgil Trucks	.714
1954	Sandy Consuegra	.842
1955	Dixie Howell	.727
1956	Billy Pierce	.690
1957	Dick Donovan	.727
1957	Jim Wilson	.652
1959	Early Wynn	.688
1959	Bob Shaw	.750
1960	Billy Pierce	.667
1960	Frank Baumann	.684
1960	Dick Donovan	.857
1960	Russ Kemmerer	.667
1961	Juan Pizarro	.667
1961	Early Wynn	.800
1961	Don Larsen	.778
1962	Ray Herbert	.690
1963	Gary Peters	.704
1963	Juan Pizarro	.667
1963	John Buzhardt	.692
1964	Gary Peters	.714
1964	Juan Pizarro	.679
1965	Tommy John	.667
1965	Eddie Fisher	.682
1965	Juan Pizarro	.667
1965	Bob Locker	.714
1966	Hoyt Wilhelm	.714
1967	Joel Horlen	.731
1967	Wilbur Wood	.667
1967	Hoyt Wilhelm	.727

Year	Pitcher	Pct
1968	Tommy John	.667
1972	Rich Gossage	.875
1977	Francisco Barrios	.667
1977	Lerrin LaGrow	.700
1979	Francisco Barrios	.727
1980	LaMarr Hoyt	.750
1981	LaMarr Hoyt	.750
1982	Britt Burns	.722
1983	LaMarr Hoyt	.706
1983	Richard Dotson	.759
1986	Neil Allen	.778
1990	Eric King	.750
1990	Barry Jones	.846
1992	Jack McDowell	.667
1993	Jason Bere	.706
1993	Jack McDowell	.688
1993	Alex Fernandez	.667
1994	Jason Bere	.857
1998	James Baldwin	.684
2000	Cal Eldred	.833
2000	Jim Parque	.684
2000	James Baldwin	.667
2001	Mark Buehrle	.667
2003	Esteban Loaiza	.700
2004	Freddy Garcia	.692
2005	Cliff Politte	.875
2005	Jose Contreras	.682
2006	Jon Garland	.720
2006	Freddy Garcia	.654
2007	Javier Vazquez	.652
2008	Gavin Floyd	.680
2010	Freddy Garcia	.667

300 or More Innings Pitched in a Season

Year	Pitcher	Innings
1901	Roy Patterson	312⅓
1903	Doc White	300
1903	Patsy Flaherty	338
1907	Ed Walsh	422⅓
1907	Frank Smith	310
1908	Ed Walsh	464
1909	Frank Smith	365
1910	Ed Walsh	369⅔
1911	Ed Walsh	368⅔
1912	Ed Walsh	393
1913	Ewell "Reb" Russell	316
1913	Jim Scott	312⅓
1917	Ed Cicotte	346⅔
1919	Ed Cicotte	306⅔
1920	Red Faber	319
1920	Ed Cicotte	303⅓
1921	Red Faber	330⅔
1921	Dickie Kerr	308⅔
1922	Red Faber	353
1927	Ted Lyons	307⅔
1927	Tommy Thomas	307⅔
1941	Thornton Lee	300⅓
1971	Wilbur Wood	334
1972	Wilbur Wood	376⅔
1973	Wilbur Wood	359⅓
1974	Wilbur Wood	320
1975	Jim Kaat	303⅔

10 or More Saves in a Season

Year	Pitcher	Saves
1912	Ed Walsh	10
1937	Clint Brown	18
1939	Clint Brown	18
1940	Clint Brown	10
1943	Gordon Maltzberger	14
1944	Gordon Maltzberger	12
1952	Harry Dorish	11
1953	Harry Dorish	18
1959	Gerry Staley	14
1959	Omar "Turk" Lown	15
1960	Gerry Staley	10
1961	Omar "Turk" Lown	11
1963	Hoyt Wilhelm	21
1963	Jim Brosnan	14
1964	Hoyt Wilhelm	27
1965	Eddie Fisher	24
1965	Hoyt Wilhelm	20
1966	Bob Locker	12
1967	Bob Locker	20
1967	Hoyt Wilhelm	12
1968	Wilbur Wood	16
1968	Bob Locker	10
1969	Wilbur Wood	15
1970	Wilbur Wood	21
1971	Bart Johnson	14
1972	Terry Forster	29
1973	Terry Forster	16
1973	Cecilio Acosta	18
1974	Terry Forster	24
1975	Rich Gossage	26
1976	Dave Hamilton	10
1977	Lerrin LaGrow	25
1978	Jim Willoughby	13
1978	Lerrin LaGrow	16
1979	Ed Farmer	14
1980	Ed Farmer	30
1981	LaMarr Hoyt	10
1981	Ed Farmer	10
1982	Salome Barojas	21
1983	Dennis Lamp	15
1983	Salome Barojas	12
1984	Ron Reed	12
1985	Bob James	32
1986	Bob James	14
1987	Bobby Thigpen	10
1988	Bobby Thigpen	34
1989	Bobby Thigpen	34
1990	Bobby Thigpen	57
1991	Bobby Thigpen	30
1992	Bobby Thigpen	22
1992	Scott Radinsky	15
1992	Roberto Hernandez	12
1993	Roberto Hernandez	38
1994	Roberto Hernandez	14
1995	Roberto Hernandez	32
1996	Roberto Hernandez	38
1997	Roberto Hernandez	27
1997	Matt Karchner	15
1998	Billy Simas	18
1999	Bob Howry	28
2000	Keith Foulke	34
2001	Keith Foulke	42
2002	Keith Foulke	11
2002	Antonio Osuna	11
2002	Damaso Marte	10
2003	Tom "Flash" Gordon	12
2003	Billy Koch	11
2003	Damaso Marte	11
2004	Shingo Takatsu	19
2005	Dustin Hermanson	34
2006	Bobby Jenks	41
2007	Bobby Jenks	40
2008	Bobby Jenks	30
2009	Bobby Jenks	29
2010	Bobby Jenks	27

White Sox Teams That Led the League in ERA

Year	Team ERA	Year	Team ERA	Year	Team ERA
1901	2.98	1941	3.52	1967	2.45
1905	1.99	1946	3.10	1993	3.70
1907	2.22	1959	3.29	1994	3.96
1913	2.33	1963	2.97	2005	3.61 (tie)
1916	2.36	1964	2.72		
1917	2.16	1966	2.68		

Pitching Staffs Recording More Than 1,000 Strikeouts in a Season

Year	K	Year	K	Year	K
1985	1,023	2004	1,013	2008	1,147
1996	1,039	2005	1,040	2009	1,119
2000	1,037	2006	1,012	2010	1,149
2003	1,056	2007	1,015		

Pitchers with 13 or More Strikeouts in a Game

K	Player	Date	Opponent
16	Jack Harshman	7/25/1954	at Boston
15	Ed Cicotte	8/26/1914	New York
15	Jim Scott	6/22/1913	St. Louis
15	Ed Walsh	8/11/1910	Boston
15	Ed Walsh	10/2/1908	at Cleveland
14	Jason Bere	6/28/1995	at Minnesota
14	Jason Bere	6/13/1994	Oakland
14	Juan Pizarro	7/31/1964	at Washington
14	Early Wynn	5/1/1959	Boston
14	Saul Rogovin	9/14/1952 (17 IP)	Boston
14	Jim Scott	9/27/1913	St. Louis
13	Jose Contreras	6/17/2006	at Cincinnati
13	Javier Vazquez	8/5/2006	at Toronto
13	Javier Vazquez	9/7/2007	at Kansas City
13	Alex Fernandez	6/12/1996	Boston
13	Jason Bere	9/8/1993	Boston
13	Chris Knapp	9/11/1997	at California
13	Juan Pizarro	8/23/1965 (13 IP)	Baltimore
13	Juan Pizarro	5/22/1962	Washington
13	Gary Peters	7/15/1963	Baltimore
13	Juan Pizarro	9/29/1961	at Baltimore
13	Juan Pizarro	8/25/1961	Cleveland
13	Marv Grissom	9/13/1952	New York
13	Thornton Lee	6/12/1945	Cleveland
13	Red Faber	5/17/1922	at Philadelphia
13	Jim Scott	4/20/1912 (15 IP)	at St. Louis
13	Frank Lange	9/20/1910	New York
13	Ed Walsh	9/13/1910	St. Louis
13	Ed Walsh	5/1/1910 (15 IP)	Detroit
13	Doc White	6/9/1905 (14 IP)	at Philadelphia

One-Hitters

Date	Opponent	Score	Winner	Loser
August 1, 1901	Detroit	4–0	Jim Callahan	Yeager
May 16, 1902	St. Louis	2–1	Wiley Piatt	Powell
September 6, 1903	Cleveland	1–0 (10 IP)	Doc White	Glendon
September 16, 1904	at St. Louis	1–0	Doc White	Siever
May 21, 1905	Washington	2–1	Frank Smith	Patten
August 31, 1905	Washington	2–0	Frank Smith	Hughes
May 6, 1906	Cleveland	6–0	Ed Walsh	Joss
June 5, 1906	Philadelphia	7–1	Doc White	Waddell
July 3, 1906	St. Louis	3–0	Doc White	Jacobson
August 3, 1906	Boston	4–0	Ed Walsh	Harris
May 19, 1908	at Washington	2–0	Doc White	Smith

Date	Opponent	Score	Winner	Loser
June 20, 1909	Cleveland	4–0	Ed Walsh	Young
July 31, 1909	at Washington	1–0	Bill Burns	Johnson
April 14, 1910	St. Louis	3–0	Frank Smith*	Graham
June 6, 1910	Boston	1–0	Ed Walsh	Hall
September 8, 1910	at St. Louis	1–0	Fred Olmstead	Lake
August 14, 1911	Detroit	2–0	Ed Walsh	Willett
July 14, 1913	Boston	8–0	Reb Russell	Foster
May 19, 1914	at Philadelphia	3–0	Ed Cicotte	Shawkey
June 4, 1914	Cleveland	2–0	Jim Scott	Blanding
June 10, 1914	Washington	2–0	Joe Benz	Johnson
June 17, 1914	Philadelphia	5–0	Red Faber	Bressler
May 17, 1915	Philadelphia	6–2	Jim Scott	Pennock
September 15, 1915	at Boston	3–1	Red Faber	Gregg
July 26, 1916	New York	2–0	Ed Cicotte	Mogridge
July 17, 1917	Washington	5–0	Ed Cicotte	Dumont
September 19, 1925	at Washington	17–0	Ted Lyons†	Zachary
May 26, 1929	Detroit	2–0	Red Faber	Carroll
June 13, 1933	St. Louis	6–1	Whit Wyatt†	Gray
July 20, 1935	at Washington	1–0	Carl Fischer	Hadley
May 29, 1941	St. Louis	4–0	Bill Dietrich	Caster
May 14, 1943	New York	3–0	Lee Ross	Wensloff
July 8, 1943	New York	1–0	Orval Grove†	Borowy
May 1, 1945	at Detroit	5–0	Joe Haynes	Wilson
June 15, 1950	New York	5–0	Billy Pierce	Lopat
April 16, 1953	St. Louis	1–0	Billy Pierce	Brecheen
May 1, 1954	at Boston	3–0	Virgil Trucks	Henry
July 6, 1954	at Detroit	4–0	Virgil Trucks	Aber
June 21, 1956	Baltimore	1–0	Jack Harshman‡	Johnson
May 25, 1957	at Cleveland	4–0	Dick Donovan	Wynn
July 20, 1957	Boston	4–0	Dick Donovon	Sisler
June 27, 1958	Washington	3–0	Billy Pierce†	Kemmerer
May 1, 1959	Boston	1–0	Early Wynn	Brewer
June 11, 1959	at Washington	3–1	Billy Pierce	Pascaul
July 15, 1963	Baltimore	4–0	Gary Peters	Roberts
August 11, 1965	Washington	7–0	Juan Pizarro	McCormick
May 30, 1966	Boston	11–0	Jack Lamabe	Santiago
May 14, 1967	California	3–1	Gary Peters	Coates
May 17, 1969	Washington	6–0	Gerry Nyman	Pasquel
August 21, 1973	at Cleveland	4–0	Stan Bahnsen†	Tidrow
May 26, 1976	at California	1–0	Ken Brett†	Kirkwood
July 2, 1980	California	1–0	Ross Baumgarten	Tanana
August 25, 1981	at Milwaukee	5–1	Dennis Lamp†	Slaton
May 18, 1983	at Baltimore	0–1	Martinez	Richard Dotson
September 9, 1983	California	11–0	Britt Burns	John
May 2, 1984	New York	3–0	LaMarr Hoyt	Rijo
September 13, 1987	at Seattle	2–0	Floyd Bannister	Langston
July 14, 1991	at Milwaukee	15–1	Jack McDowell	Knudson
May 4, 1992	Milwaukee	7–0	Alex Fernandez	Bones
August 3, 2001	Tampa Bay	4–0	Mark Buehrle	Bierbrodt
August 23, 2005	at Minnesota	0–1	Santana	Freddy Garcia
April 17, 2006**	Kansas City	9–0	Jose Contreras	Mays
September 13, 2006**	at Los Angeles	9–0	Freddy Garcia	Saunders
May 6, 2008**	Minnesota	7–1	Gavin Floyd	Blackburn

*Opening Day ** Combined one-hitter †No-hitter broken up in the 9th inning ‡Double one-hitter

Doc White and Ed Walsh lead the way with five one-hitters followed by Peters (4), Smith (3), and Cicotte (3). The prevalence of one-hitters before 1920 reflects the dead-ball style of play.

Doubleheader Shutouts

Date	Opponent	Score	Winning Sox Pitcher
September 6, 1905	at Detroit	2–0	Doc White
		15–0	Frank Smith*
July 31, 1909	at Washington	5–0	Jim Scott
		1–0	Frank Lange
August 11, 1914	Cleveland	2–0	Mellie Wolfgang
		2–0	Ed Cicotte
May 28, 1916	Cleveland	2–0	Jim Scott
		2–0	Red Faber
July 10, 1916	at Boston	4–0	Lefty Williams
		3–0	Reb Russell
July 13, 1940	at Boston	5–0	Ted Lyons
		7–0	Jack Knott
August 19, 1941	Philadelphia	4–0	Thornton Lee
		1–0	John Humphries
May 15, 1949	Cleveland	10–0	Bill Wight
		2–0	Alan Gettel
May 25, 1952	Detroit	3–0	Joe Dobson
		1–0	Marv Grissom
June 14, 1953	Boston	6–0	Billy Pierce
		1–0	Sandy Consuegra
June 15, 1958	at Baltimore	3–0	Jim Wilson
		4–0	Dick Donovan
June 5, 1960	Kansas City	2–0	Russ Kemmerer
		2–0	Frank Baumann
July 5, 1964	Cleveland	2–0	Juan Pizarro
		5–0	Joel Horlen
May 30, 1966	Boston	1–0	John Buzhardt
		11–0	Jack Lamabe†
September 10, 1967	Detroit	6–0	Joel Horlen*
		4–0	Cisco Carlos

*No-hitter
†One-hitter

Three Consecutive Shutouts

Dates	Opponent	Score	Sox Pitcher
July 31–August 2, 1901	Detroit	2–0	Clark Griffith
	Detroit	4–0	James Callahan
	Detroit	7–0	Roy Patterson
August 2–4, 1906	Boston	3–0	Doc White
	Boston	4–0	Ed Walsh
	Boston	1–0	Roy Patterson
April 25–27, 1909	St. Louis	1–0	Jim Scott
	St. Louis	1–0	Frank Smith
	St. Louis	1–0	Doc White
September 18–20, 1910	Boston	6–0	Ed Walsh
	Boston	1–0	Fred Olmstead
	New York	3–0	Frank Lange
August 19–20, 1941	Philadelphia	4–0	Thornton Lee
	Philadelphia	1–0	John Humphries
	Philadelphia	9–0	John Rigney
August 15–17, 1949	St. Louis	8–0	Bill Wight
	St. Louis	4–0	Bob Kuzava
	Detroit	1–0	Mickey Haefner
April 30–May 2, 1954	Boston	5–0	Bob Keegan
	Boston	3–0	Virgil Trucks
	Philadelphia	4–0	Connie Johnson
June 15–17, 1958	Baltimore	3–0	Jim Wilson
	Baltimore	4–0	Dick Donovan
	Boston	4–0	Billy Pierce
July 4–5, 1964	Cleveland	4–0	Gary Peters
	Cleveland	2–0	Juan Pizarro
	Cleveland	5–0	Joel Horlen
May 29–30, 1966	New York	2–0	Tommy John
	Boston	1–0	John Buzhardt
	Boston	11–0	Jack Lamabe
May 2–5, 1973	Baltimore	4–0	Wilbur Wood
	New York	5–0	Stan Bahnsen
	New York	4–0	Eddie Fisher

Participation in the Annual Hall of Fame Game at Doubleday Field, Cooperstown, NY

Date	Opponent	Score*	Sox Pitcher of Record
July 19, 1943	Brooklyn	5–7	Edgar Smith
July 27, 1953	Cincinnati	6–16	Bob Keegan
July 22, 1957	St. Louis	13–4	Jim Derrington
July 27, 1970	Montreal	6–10	Jim Magnuson
August 12, 1974	Atlanta	9–12	Larry Monroe
August 4, 1980	Pittsburgh	8–11	Ken Kravec
August 2, 1982	New York	4–4 (8)	—
August 3, 1992	New York	0–3	Scott Ruffcorn
July 29, 2002	Colorado	10–18	Jason Stumm

*Sox score given first

Great Pitching Rivalries

Ed Walsh versus Addie Joss of the Cleveland Indians

Date	Score	Winner	Loser	Site
May 6, 1906	6–0*	Walsh	Joss	Chicago
June 3, 1906	0–2	Joss	Walsh	Chicago
July 2, 1907	0–2	Joss	Walsh	Cleveland
April 21, 1908	1–5	Joss	Walsh	Cleveland
September 5, 1908	7–0	Walsh	Joss	Chicago
September 7, 1908	0–6	Joss	Walsh	Cleveland
October 2, 1908	0–1†	Joss	Walsh	Cleveland
June 22, 1909	2–3	Joss	Walsh	Cleveland
June 26, 1909	2–0	Walsh	Joss	Cleveland
September 13, 1909	2–0	Walsh	Joss	Chicago

Totals: Joss 6, Walsh 4

*One-hitter
†Perfect game

Ted Lyons versus Lefty Grove of the Philadelphia A's and Boston Red Sox

Date	Score	Winner	Loser	Site
June 15, 1927	6–4	Lyons	Grove	Philadelphia
July 13, 1927	5–7	Grove	Lyons	Chicago
August 22, 1929	4–3	Lyons	Grove	Chicago
June 3, 1931	1–2	Grove	Lyons	Philadelphia
July 9, 1932	7–0	Lyons	Grove	Philadelphia
August 7, 1932	3–1	Lyons	Grove	Chicago
July 10, 1933	2–3(11)	Grove	Lyons	Philadelphia
September 11, 1933	3–5	Grove	Lyons	Philadelphia
July 31, 1936	3–7	Grove	Lyons	Chicago
August 7, 1937	4–5	Grove	Lyons	Boston
June 18, 1938	3–4(12)	Grove	Lyons	Chicago
June 11, 1939	7–5	Lyons	Grove	Chicago
June 8, 1941	3–5(10)	Grove	Lyons	Chicago

Totals: Grove 8, Lyons 5

Ted Lyons versus Bob Feller of the Cleveland Indians

Date	Score	Winner	Loser	Site
August 22, 1937	5–2	Lyons	Feller	Chicago
May 30, 1938	2–5	Feller	Lyons	Cleveland
August 13, 1939	0–2	Feller	Lyons	Cleveland
July 7, 1940	3–1	Lyons	Feller	Cleveland
September 8, 1940	4–5	Feller	Lyons	Cleveland
August 17, 1941	8–2	Lyons	Feller	Chicago

Totals: Feller 3, Lyons 3

Billy Pierce versus Whitey Ford of the New York Yankees

Date	Score	Winner	Loser	Site
September 9, 1953	3–9	Ford	Pierce	New York
April 27, 1955	13–4	Pierce	Ford	Chicago
May 17, 1955	0–1	Ford	Pierce	New York
June 24, 1956	14–2	Pierce	Ford	Chicago
July 15, 1956	1–2	Ford	Pierce	New York
September 18, 1956	2–3 (11)	Ford	Pierce	Chicago
May 21, 1957	3–1	Pierce	Ford	New York
July 24, 1957	7–2	Pierce	Ford	New York
September 13, 1957	1–7	Ford	Pierce	New York
May 21, 1958	2–5	Ford	Pierce	Chicago
August 23, 1958	7–1	Pierce	Ford	New York
May 15, 1959	6–0	Pierce	Ford	New York
September 15, 1959	4–3	Pierce	Ford	New York
August 8, 1960	9–1	Pierce	Ford	Chicago

Totals: Pierce 8, Ford 6

Babe Ruth (as a Pitcher) versus the White Sox

Date	Score	Winner	Loser	Site
May 22, 1915	11–2	Joe Benz	Ruth	Chicago
September 14, 1915	1–2	Ruth	Joe Benz	Boston
June 17, 1916	5–0	Joe Benz	Ruth	Chicago
July 11, 1916	1–3	Ruth	Mel Wolfgang	Boston
September 17, 1916	2–6	Ruth	Red Faber	Chicago
May 18, 1917	8–2	Reb Russell	Ruth	Chicago
June 16, 1917	7–2	Ed Cicotte	Ruth	Boston
July 19, 1917	2–3	Ruth	Lefty Williams	Chicago
July 30, 1917	1–3	Ruth	Lefty Williams	Boston
August 21, 1917	2–0	Reb Russell	Ruth	Chicago
September 24, 1917	0–3	Ruth	Reb Russell	Boston
May 15, 1919	5–6 (12)	Ruth	Frank Shellenback	Chicago
June 10, 1919	5–3	Ed Cicotte	Ruth	Boston

Totals: Ruth 7, White Sox 6

Frank Thomas' Milestone Home Runs

Home Run Number	Date	Opponent	Pitcher
1	August 28, 1990	at Minnesota	Gary Wayne
100	August 31, 1993	at New York	Sterling Hitchcock
200	June 9, 1996	at Baltimore	Jimmy Haynes
300	August 7, 1999	at Oakland	Kevin Appier
400	July 25, 2003	Tampa Bay	Jorge Sosa
500*	June 28, 2007	at Minnesota	Carlos Silva

*Hit as a member of the Toronto Blue Jays

Ed Walsh's 40 Victories in 1908

Date	Opponent	Score	Losing Pitcher	IP	K	BB
April 18, 1908	St. Louis	3–0	Bill Graham	9	4	0
April 25, 1908	at St. Louis	6–2	Jack Powell	9	5	0
May 3, 1908	Cleveland	3–0	Charley Chech	9	9	0
May 9, 1908	St. Louis	6–3	Bill Graham	9	5	1
May 13, 1908	at Philadelphia	2–1	Jimmy Dygert	9	6	1
May 21, 1908	at New York	9–2	Joe Lake	9	3	0
May 25, 1908	at New York	9–3	Rube Manning	9	3	2
May 28, 1908	at Boston	2–1	Tex Pruitt	9	2	3
May 31, 1908	at Detroit	1–0	Ed Willett	9	1	1
June 4, 1908	at St. Louis	2–1 (11)*	Rube Waddell	⅔	2	1
June 8, 1908	Washington	2–1	Bill Burns	1	0	0
June 9, 1908	Philadelphia	10–0	Chief Bender	8	1	2
June 13, 1908	New York	5–1	Al Orth	9	3	2
June 16, 1908	New York	3–2	Fred Glade	9	3	1
June 20, 1908	Boston	1–0	Cy Young	9	6	1
July 2, 1908	St. Louis	5–1	Rube Waddell	9	2	1
July 4, 1908	St. Louis	8–4*	Harry Howell	3	4	0
July 11, 1908	at Philadelphia	5–4 (16)	Rube Vickers	16	9	1
July 15, 1908	at Philadelphia	3–1	Rube Vickers	9	8	0
July 18, 1908	at Boston	7–2	Tex Pruitt	9	4	0
July 21, 1908	at New York	6–3	Doc Newton	9	3	1
July 23, 1908	at New York	6–2	Joe Lake	9	7	0
July 26, 1908	Philadelphia	2–1 (10)	Jimmy Dygert	10	5	4
August 7, 1908	Boston	7–0	Fred Burchell	9	4	0
August 10, 1908	New York	2–1	Jack Chesbro	9	6	0
August 15, 1908	New York	6–1*	Joe Lake	4	5	0
August 15, 1908	at Washington	5–3* (15)	Burt Keeley	15	6	2
August 21, 1908	at Boston	8–7*	Elmer Steele	3⅔	1	0
August 25, 1908	at Boston	2–1	Frank Arellanes	9	3	0
August 28, 1908	at New York	2–1	Bill Hogg	9	4	1
September 2, 1908	at St. Louis	4–1	Bill Dineen	9	2	1
September 5, 1908	Cleveland	7–0	Addie Joss	9	5	1
September 11, 1908	at Detroit	4–2 (11)	George Mullin	11	5	1
September 13, 1908	Cleveland	1–0	Heinie Berger	9	6	0
September 18, 1908	Washington	1–0	Walter Johnson	9	7	3
September 21, 1908	Philadelphia	2–0	Biff Schlitzer	9	5	0
September 27, 1908	Boston	3–0	Ed Cicotte	9	8	1
September 29, 1908	Boston	5–1	Fred Burchell	9	10	0
September 29, 1908	Boston	2–0	Elmer Steele	9	5	1
October 5, 1908	Detroit	6–1	Ed Summers	9	9	1

*If modern scoring rules had been applied, Walsh would have been credited only with saves in the four games indicated. The *Chicago Tribune* agreed with this assessment in its October 7, 1908, postseason wrap-up, listing the 36 Walsh wins.

Doc White's Five Consecutive Shutouts

Date	Opponent	Score	Losing Pitcher	H	K	BB
September 12, 1904	Cleveland	1–0	Addie Joss	7	8	2
September 16, 1904	St. Louis	1–0	Ed Siever	1	6	1
September 19, 1904	Detroit	3–0	Frank Kitson	2	2	2
September 25, 1904	Philadelphia	4–0	Andy Coakley	4	6	2
September 30, 1904	New York	4–0	Jack Chesbro	3	7	3

Pitchers Who Hit .270 or Better in a Season

Pitcher	Year	Average	Hits	At-Bats*
Clark Griffith	1901	.303	27	89
Frank Smith	1906	.293	12	41
Frank Lange	1911	.289	22	76
Clarence "Shovel" Hodge	1921	.327	17	52
Hollis Thurston	1923	.316	25	79
Ted Blankenship	1924	.326	15	46
Hollis Thurston	1926	.311	19	61
George "Sarge" Connally	1927	.328	22	67
Ted Lyons	1930	.311	38	122
Ted Lyons	1933	.286	26	91
Vern Kennedy	1936	.283	32	113

Pitcher	Year	Average	Hits	At-Bats*
Ted Lyons	1939	.295	18	61
Johnny Marcum	1939	.281	16	57
Thornton Lee	1940	.274	23	84
Ted Lyons	1941	.270	20	74
John Humphries	1943	.290	20	69
Ed Lopat	1944	.309	25	81
Ed Lopat	1945	.293	24	82
Randy Gumpert	1951	.333	15	45
Jim Wilson	1956	.306	19	62

*40 or more at bats

Pitchers Who Hit Home Runs

Pitcher	Career Home Runs
Gary Peters	15
Jack Harshman	12
Ted Blankenship	9
Dick Donovan	8
Juan Pizarro	6
Ted Lyons	5
Dixie Howell	5
Ray Herbert	5
Monty Stratton	4
Thornton Lee	4
Bill Dietrich	4
Tommy John	4
Ed Walsh	3
Red Faber	3

Pitcher	Career Home Runs
Tommy Thomas	3
Early Wynn	3
Clark Griffith	2
Frank Owen	2
Vern Kennedy	2
Frank Baumann	2

One home run: Roy Patterson, Jack Katoll, John Skopec, Nick Altrock, Frank Smith, Jim Scott, Hollis Thurston, Charlie Barnabe, Jack Salveson, Orval Grove, Edgar Smith, Lee Ross, Eddie Lopat, Saul Rogovin, Hal Brown, Virgil Trucks, Tommy Byrne, Jim Wilson, Ray Moore, Don Larsen, Bob Priddy, Danny Murphy, Tom Bradley, Steve Kealey, Jon Garland, Mark Buehrle

All-Time Fielding Team

Position	Year	Player	Games	PO	A	E	TC	Pct
1b	1976	Jim Spencer	143	1,320	112	2	1,434	.998
1b	2003	Paul Konerko	119	889	80	2	971	.998
2b	1962	Nellie Fox	154	376	428	8	812	.990
3b	1947	Floyd Baker	101	84	253	7	344	.980
ss	1963	Ron Hansen	144	247	483	13	743	.983
of	1969	Ken Berry	120	215	7	0	222	1.000
of	1993	Tim Raines	112	200	5	0	205	1.000
of	1952	Sam Mele	119	157	8	0	N/A	1.000
of	1994	Lance Johnson	103	317	1	0	318	1.000
of	2004	Carlos Lee	148	282	11	0	293	1.000
c	1961	Sherm Lollar	116	939	67	2	1,008	.998
c	2007	A.J. Pierzynski	130	296	46	2	844	.998
p	1967	Joel Horlen	35	29	53	0	82	1.000
p	1969	Tommy John	33	16	66	0	82	1.000
p	2003	Mark Buehrle	35	15	38	0	53	1.000
p	2006	Javier Vazquez	33	7	29	0	36	1.000

White Sox Teams That Led the AL in Fielding Percentage

Year	Percentage
1902	.955
1904	.964
1905	.968
1907	.966
1908	.966
1909	.964
1922	.975
1926	.973
1927	.971
1952	.980
1953	.980
1954	.982
1956	.979
1957	.982
1959	.979
1960	.982
1962	.982
1984	.981 (tie)
1985	.982 (tie)

White Sox League Leaders in Fielding

FIRST BASEMEN

Fielding Percentage

Jiggs Donahue	1905	.988
Jiggs Donahue	1906	.988
Jiggs Donahue	1907	.994
Frank Isbell	1909	.994
Chick Gandil	1917	.995
Chick Gandil	1919	.997
Earl Sheely	1926	.995
Zeke Bonura	1934	.996
Zeke Bonura	1936	.996
Walt Dropo	1956	.993
Joe Cunningham	1962	.994
Jim Spencer	1976	.998
Mike Squires	1983	.996
Paul Konerko	2003	.998

Assists

Frank Isbell	1902	93
Jiggs Donahue	1906	118
Jiggs Donahue	1907	140
Earl Sheely	1921	119
Zeke Bonura	1936	107
Tommy McCraw	1968	93
Jim Spencer	1976	112

Putouts

Frank Isbell	1901	1,387
Jiggs Donahue	1905	1,645
Jiggs Donahue	1906	1,697
Jiggs Donahue	1907	1,846
Earl Sheely	1921	1,637
Earl Sheely	1923	1,563
Earl Sheely	1925	1,565
Luzurne Blue	1931	1,452
Zeke Bonura	1936	1,500
Joe Kuhel	1941	1,444
Tony Lupien	1948	1,436
Eddie Robinson	1951	1,296
Eddie Robinson	1952	1,329
Bill Skowron	1965	1,297

Double Plays

Frank Isbell	1902	97
Jiggs Donahue	1905	77
Earl Sheely	1921	121
Earl Sheely	1923	113
Earl Sheely	1925	136
Eddie Robinson	1951	143
Eddie Robinson	1952	145
Bill Skowron	1965	116
Tommy McCraw	1968	103

SECOND BASEMEN

Fielding Percentage

Gus Dundon	1905	.978
Ambrose McConnell	1911	.973
Morrie Rath	1912	.963
Eddie Collins	1915	.974
Eddie Collins	1916	.976
Eddie Collins	1920	.976
Eddie Collins	1921	.968
Eddie Collins	1922	.976
Eddie Collins	1924	.977
Nellie Fox	1952	.985
Nellie Fox	1954	.989
Nellie Fox	1956	.986
Nellie Fox	1959	.988
Nellie Fox	1962	.990
Nellie Fox	1963	.988

Assists

Morrie Rath	1912	463
Lena Blackburne	1914	433
Eddie Collins	1915	487
Jackie Hayes	1937	490
Cass Michaels	1949	484
Nellie Fox	1952	433
Nellie Fox	1955	483
Nellie Fox	1956	396
Nellie Fox	1957	453
Nellie Fox	1959	453
Nellie Fox	1960	447
Jim Morrison	1980	481

Louie Aparicio and Nellie Fox. (Courtesy of Gerry Bilek)

Jim Spencer was perfect at first base in 1976.

Putouts

Eddie Collins	1917	353
Eddie Collins	1919	347
Eddie Collins	1920	449
Jackie Hayes	1937	353
Nellie Fox	1952	406
Nellie Fox	1953	451
Nellie Fox	1954	400
Nellie Fox	1955	399
Nellie Fox	1956	478
Nellie Fox	1957	453
Nellie Fox	1958	444
Nellie Fox	1959	364
Nellie Fox	1960	412
Nellie Fox	1961	413
Mike Andrews	1972	354
Jim Morrison	1980	422

Double Plays

Tom Daly	1902	70
Eddie Collins	1916	75
Eddie Collins	1919	66
Cass Michaels	1949	135
Nellie Fox	1954	103
Nellie Fox	1956	124
Nellie Fox	1957	141
Nellie Fox	1958	117
Nellie Fox	1960	126
Jim Morrison	1980	117
Scott Fletcher	1990	115

SHORTSTOPS

Fielding Percentage

George Davis	1905	.948
Lee Tannehill	1911	.957
Chico Carrasquel	1951	.975
Chico Carrasquel	1953	.976
Chico Carrasquel	1954	.975
Luis Aparicio	1959	.970
Luis Aparicio	1960	.979
Luis Aparicio	1961	.962
Luis Aparicio	1962	.973
Bucky Dent	1975	.981
Ozzie Guillen	1985	.980

Assists

George Davis	1904	514
Buck Weaver	1913	520
Chalmer Cissell	1929	459
Luke Appling	1933	534
Luke Appling	1935	556
Luke Appling	1937	541
Luke Appling	1939	461
Luke Appling	1941	473
Luke Appling	1943	500
Luke Appling	1946	505
Chico Carrasquel	1951	477
Luis Aparicio	1956	474
Luis Aparicio	1957	449
Luis Aparicio	1958	463
Luis Aparicio	1959	460

Luis Aparicio	1960	551
Luis Aparicio	1961	487
Ron Hansen	1963	483
Ron Hansen	1964	514
Ron Hansen	1965	527
Ron Hansen	1967	482
Luis Aparicio	1968	535
Bucky Dent	1975	543
Ozzie Guillen	1988	570
Orlando Cabrera	2008	472

Putouts

George Davis	1904	347
Buck Weaver	1913	392
Chalmer Cissell	1929	357
Luke Appling	1935	335
Luke Appling	1940	307
Luis Aparicio	1956	250
Luis Aparicio	1957	289
Luis Aparicio	1959	282
Ron Hansen	1964	292
Bucky Dent	1975	279
Orlando Cabrera	2008	242

Double Plays

George Davis	1902	72
Lee Tannehill	1903	58
George Davis	1904	62
George Davis	1905	56
Buck Weaver	1913	73
Ike Davis	1925	97
Luke Appling	1936	119
Luke Appling	1937	111
Luke Appling	1946	99
Chico Carrasquel	1954	102
Luis Aparicio	1960	117
Ron Hansen	1964	105
Ron Hansen	1967	91
Luis Aparicio	1968	92
Bucky Dent	1974	108
Bucky Dent	1975	105
Ozzie Guillen	1987	105

THIRD BASEMEN

Fielding Percentage

Buck Weaver	1917	.949
Willie Kamm	1926	.978
Willie Kamm	1927	.972
Willie Kamm	1928	.977
Willie Kamm	1929	.978
Floyd Baker	1949	.977
George Kell	1955	.976
Eric Soderholm	1977	.978
Robin Ventura	1998	.966

Assists

Sammy Strang	1902	334
Lee Tannehill	1904	369
Lee Tannehill	1905	358
Lee Tannehill	1906	278
Lee Tannehill	1908	341
Willie Kamm	1924	312
Willie Kamm	1925	310
Willie Kamm	1926	323
Jimmie Dykes	1933	296
Robin Ventura	1992	392
Robin Ventura	1998	330

Putouts

Willie Kamm	1924	190
Willie Kamm	1926	177
Willie Kamm	1927	236
Willie Kamm	1928	243
Willie Kamm	1929	221
Bob Kennedy	1940	178
Eric Soderholm	1978	128
Robin Ventura	1991	135
Robin Ventura	1992	141
Robin Ventura	1996	133

Double Plays

Lee Tannehill	1904	22
Lee Tannehill	1905	17
Willie Kamm	1924	31
Steve Lyons	1988	36
Robin Ventura	1992	29

OUTFIELDERS

Fielding Percentage

Fielder Jones	1906	.988
Eddie Hahn	1907	.990
Oscar Felsch	1916	.981
Johnny Mostil	1925	.985
Bibb Falk	1926	.992
Mike Kreevich	1937	.988
Mike Kreevich	1941	.994
Thurman Tucker	1944	.991
Jim Landis	1963	.993
Ken Berry	1969	1.000
Pat Kelly	1975	.991
Rudy Law	1983	.994
Dan Pasqua	1988	.988
Tim Raines	1993	1.000
Lance Johnson	1994	1.000
Carlos Lee	2001	.969
Carlos Lee	2004	1.000
Aaron Rowand	2005	.992

Assists

Sandow Mertes	1902	26
Oscar Felsch	1919	32
Mike Kreevich	1939	18
Dave Philley	1948	22
Dave Philley	1949	16
Jim Rivera	1955	22
Tony Phillips	1996	13
Carlos Lee	2004	11

Putouts

Fielder Jones	1903	324
Fielder Jones	1905	337
Oscar Felsch	1917	440
Johnny Mostil	1923	422
Johnny Mostil	1926	440
Mike Kreevich	1940	428
Thurman Tucker	1943	399
Wally Moses	1945	329
Jim Landis	1959	420
Ken Berry	1965	331
Tommie Agee	1966	376
Ken Henderson	1974	462
Chet Lemon	1977	512
Lance Johnson	1993	427
Tony Phillips	1996	344
Albert Belle	1997	350
Albert Belle	1998	315
Jermaine Dye	2006	305

Double Plays

Danny Green	1903	3
Oscar Felsch	1919	15
Oscar Felsch	1920	10
Harry Hooper	1924	8
Mike Kreevich	1939	4
Dave Philley	1948	6
Dave Philley	1950	8
Jim Rivera	1955	7
Jim Landis	1957	4
Jim McAnany	1959	4

CATCHERS

Percentage

Billy Sullivan	1901	.967
Billy Sullivan	1906	.974
Billy Sullivan	1908	.985
Billy Sullivan	1911	.986
Ray Schalk	1915	.984
Ray Schalk	1916	.988
Ray Schalk	1920	.986
Ray Schalk	1921	.985
Ray Schalk	1922	.989
Phil Masi	1950	.996

Sherm Lollar	1953	.994
Sherm Lollar	1956	.993
Sherm Lollar	1960	.995
Sherm Lollar	1961	.998
Carlton Fisk	1989	.993

Assists

Billy Sullivan	1904	130
Ray Schalk	1916	166
Ray Schalk	1922	150
Luke Sewell	1936	87
Mike Tresh	1945	102
John Romano	1965	61
Duane Josephson	1968	86

Putouts

Ray Schalk	1913	599
Ray Schalk	1914	613
Ray Schalk	1915	655
Ray Schalk	1916	653
Ray Schalk	1917	624
Ray Schalk	1918	422
Ray Schalk	1919	551
Ray Schalk	1920	581
Ray Schalk	1922	591
Mike Tresh	1940	619
Mike Tresh	1941	488
Carlton Fisk	1981	470
Carlton Fisk	1983	709
Carlton Fisk	1985	801

Double Plays

Ray Schalk	1913	18
Ray Schalk	1920	19
Ray Schalk	1921	19
Ray Schalk	1923	20
Sherm Lollar	1955	12
Sherm Lollar	1959	14
Sherm Lollar	1960	12
John Romano	1965	10
Duane Josephson	1968	15
Carlton Fisk	1981	10
Carlton Fisk	1987	15

"Pudge" Fisk's No. 72 retired by Sox management

Most Double Plays in a Season (Team)

Year	Double Plays	Year	Double Plays	Year	Double Plays
2000	190*	1988	177*	1987	174*
1974	188*	1989	176*	1936	174*
1970	187*	1948	176	1937	173
1950	181	1960	175*	1982	173
1949	180				

*Led league

Triple Plays

Date	Opponent	Batter	Inning
May 4, 1907	at Detroit	Boss Schmidt	4
July 7, 1909	Boston	Doc Gessler	4
September 18, 1910	Boston	Bill Purtell	2
August 11, 1912	Philadelphia	Jack Coombs	7
April 29, 1916	at St. Louis	Burt Shotton	7
May 25, 1919	Washington	Howard Shanks	8
July 15, 1921	Washington	Eric Erickson	7
September 12, 1922	Cleveland	Larry Gardner	1
October 1, 1922	at St. Louis	Pat Collins	3
April 30, 1929	Cleveland	Carl Lind	7
July 23, 1931	Boston	Earl Webb	6
September 11, 1931	at New York	Babe Ruth	1
April 30, 1936	at Boston	Oscar Melillo	8
May 20, 1944	at Boston	Bob Johnson	1
August 10, 1944	at Boston	Jim Tabor	4
June 11, 1946	at Philadelphia	Irv Hall	1
April 27, 1947	at St. Louis	John Berardino	2
May 13, 1951	Cleveland	Jim Hegan	9
August 29, 1953	Boston	Karl Olson	9
August 10, 1957	Detroit	J. W. Porter	1
September 27, 1959	at Detroit	Boyd Harris	3
September 17, 1966	at Baltimore	Andy Etchebarren	9
August 6, 1967	at Baltimore	Brooks Robinson	5
June 22, 1980	Detroit	Duffy Dyer	5
August 31, 1981	Detroit	Al Cowens	2
June 15, 1986	at Seattle	Ken Phelps	2
June 6, 1996	at Boston	Tim Naehring	1
July 7, 2004	Anaheim	Bengie Molina	6
May 14, 2006	at Minnesota	Luis Castillo	6
September 18, 2006	Detroit	Carlos Guillen	1

Top Home-Run Hitters and Winning Pitchers by Decade

Decade	Player	Home Runs
1901–09	Frank Isbell	13
1910–19	Oscar "Hap" Felsch	24
1920–29	Bibb Falk	50
1930–39	Zeke Bonura	79
1940–49	Joe Kuhel	52
1950–59	Sherm Lollar	108
1960–69	Pete Ward	97
1970–79	Bill Melton	129
1980–89	Harold Baines	186
1990–99	Frank Thomas	301
2000–09	Paul Konerko	274

Decade	Pitcher	Wins
1901–09	Doc White	124
1910–19	Ed Cicotte	135
1920–29	Red Faber	149
1930–39	Ted Lyons	117
1940–49	Thornton Lee	64
1950–59	Billy Pierce	155
1960–69	Joel Horlen	99
1970–79	Wilbur Wood	136
1980–89	Richard Dotson	95
1990–99	Jack McDowell	83
2000–09	Mark Buehrle	135

White Sox Scouts

The Scouting System, 1900–24

Joseph Cantillon, Frank Isbell, Tip O'Neill, and Ted Sullivan were trusted associates of Charles Comiskey who were not necessarily paid by the ballclub for their advice and counsel. Comiskey was often alerted to promising young players in the Western League through Isbell, his former second baseman and friend who went on to complete a distinguished managerial career in Iowa. Sullivan was Comiskey's baseball mentor in college and a star of the 19th-century game. He maintained his close ties to the Old Roman through his early years in Chicago. Cantillon operated several minor league teams in Minnesota and was another trusted confidant of Comiskey. The same can be said of O'Neill.

In the first quarter of the 20th century, top minor league players were procured at auction during the annual winter meetings or through ongoing business relationships established between major league owners and minor league entrepreneurs like Isbell and O'Neill.

The Scouting System after 1924

For 15 years the husband-and-wife team of Bessie and Roy Largent comprised the nationwide White Sox scouting system. From 1924 to 1939 they cruised the dusty back roads of America in their beat-up sedan, sending their dispatches back to Harry Grabiner in Chicago. Roy was stone deaf. Bessie read lips and translated her husband's thoughts. It is hardly coincidental that some of the very worst White Sox teams of all time came to the fore during this period, which included the Great Depression years.

The Comiskey family, for lack of financial resources or because of the Old Roman's steadfast refusal to change with the times, vested their confidence in the Largents and wound up in the second division year in and year out. It wasn't until 1939, when Billy Webb, Bob Tarleton, and J. Lou Comiskey finally put in place the first White Sox farm system, that the scouting department finally expanded.

By the 1950s, the tree bore its fruit after Chuck Comiskey and John Rigney revitalized a dormant system that soon became the envy of the baseball world. By the late 1970s, however, the top scouts had left the organization and were not replaced. Dwindling attendance, economic problems at the major league level, and a growing sense of disillusionment within the organization hampered the team's ability to identify and sign top high school and college prospects to White Sox contracts. By 1978 there were only 15 scouts left on the payroll. It was the third year of Bill Veeck's ownership.

The Sox found themselves in essentially the same position as in the late 1930s when the Largents were still making the rounds. It was only after Jerry Reinsdorf and his partners bought the club in 1981 and reorganized the front office that this situation was properly addressed and new scouts hired. The improvement of the ballclub in the 1980s and 1990s mirrored this recommitment.

MEMPHIS—	ab.	r.	h.	po.	a.	e.
Flashkamper, ss.	4	3	1	4	1	1
Daughtry, lf.	5	2	1	1	0	0
Jeanes, cf.	3	1	1	3	0	0
Brazill, 2b.	5	1	3	3	2	0
Prothro, 3b.	5	0	1	1	1	0
Vick, rf.	5	2	2	4	0	0
McDaniel, 1b.	5	2	2	6	0	0
Berger, c.	4	1	3	5	1	0
Beck, p.	5	1	1	0	2	0
Totals	41	13	16	27	7	1

ATLANTA—	ab.	r.	h.	po.	a.	e.
Langford, cf.	5	2	2	3	0	0
Sheehan, 2b.	4	2	2	1	2	2
Rosenthal, rf.	4	1	3	3	0	0
Carlyle, lf.	5	0	1	2	0	0
Grimes, 1b.	5	0	1	11	0	1
Johnston, 3b.	4	0	1	1	3	0
Appling, ss.	4	0	0	3	2	1
Barrett, c.	4	1	1	3	1	0
Dumovich, p.	2	0	0	0	1	0
zPolvogt	1	0	0	0	0	0
Starling, p.	0	0	0	0	1	1
zzKnight	1	0	0	0	0	0
Totals	39	6	11	27	10	5

zBatted for Dumovich in seventh.
zzBatted for Starling in ninth.

Memphis ....000 210 523—13
Atlanta ....000 001 302— 6

Runs batted in—Jeanes, Brazill 2, Prothro 3, Vick, McDaniel, Berger, Sheehan 3, Rosenthal, Carlyle. Two-base hits—Jeanes, Berger, Flashkamper, Rosenthal, Carlyle, Langford, Sheehan. Three-base hits—McDaniel, Brazill, Grimes, Langford. Stolen bases—Flashkamper, Daughtry. Sacrifices—Daughtry, Jeanes, Berger. Left on bases—Memphis 7, Atlanta 9. Bases on balls—off Beck 3, off Dumovich 2, off Starling 1. Struck out—by Beck 4, by Dumovich 1, by Starling 1. Hits—off Dumovich 11 in 7 innings with 8 runs. Balk—Beck. Losing pitcher—Dumovich. Umpires—Shannon and Knaupp. Time of game—2:02.

Roy Largent's original scouting report on Atlanta rookie Luke Appling: "Good looking boy—will improve…" The notes were taken on May 30, 1930.

1940s

Scout	Region
Hal Beatty	Midwest
Frank Bridges	South
Ellsworth Brown	Midwest
William Buckley	Bird dog
M. A. Burgess	West
C. F. "Cap" Crossley	Northern California
John Donaldson	Negro Leagues
Jim Ferrante	New England
George Haas*	East
Paul Heil	West
Don Herget	Midwest
Harry Jenkins	Midwest
Irving Jeffries*	South
John Kerr*	West
Fred "King" Lear	East
Tony Lucadello	Midwest
Ed McLaughlin	East
Ray Meyers	Midwest
Doug Minor	Midwest
Eddie Onslow	Ohio
Emmet Ormsby	Midwest
Joseph L. O'Rourke	Midwest
Patsy O'Rourke	East
Maurice Robinson	Midwest
John Ryan	West
Charles San Huber	Midwest
George Senecker	Midwest
Fred Shaffer	Iowa
Earl Sheely*	West Coast
Len Tree	Midwest
Hal Trosky*	Midwest

*Played for the White Sox at one time

1950s

Scout	Region
Hugh Alexander	Southwest
Sam Allen	Georgia-Alabama-Florida
E. S. "Doc" Bennett	Central California
Ellsworth Brown	Midwest
Dave Day	West
Morris Deutsch	New Jersey
John Donaldson	Negro Leagues
Bill Fitzharris	St. Paul, Minnesota
Pat Gainey	North Carolina
Fred Hasselman	Midwest
Joe Holden	Western New York
Edward Holly	East
Bennie Huffman	New England
Ira Hutchinson*	Midwest
Jack Keilch	San Diego area
Vern Kennedy*	Missouri and Kansas
Bill Kimball	Iowa and Nebraska
Walter Laskowski	Iowa and Indiana
Fred Lent	Detroit area
Dario Lodigiani*	West
Joseph Lynch	Buffalo area
Ted Lyons*	South-Central
Robert Mattick	Northern California and Washington
Joe McManus	West
Benny Meyer	Missouri
Cass Michaels*	Midwest
Pete Milito	Midwest
Doug Minor	Allegheny region
Pat Monahan	Midwest
Johnny Mostil*	Midwest and Dakotas

Johnny Mostil became a White Sox scout after his playing days were over.

Scout	Region
Hugh Mulcahy	Pittsburgh area
Larry Murray	Washington, D.C., area
Herb Newberry	Baltimore area
Ron Northey*	New England
Harry O'Donnell	Western New York and Pennsylvania
Frank Parenti	Chicago area
Bob Pease	Los Angeles area
Harry Postove	Virginia and West Virginia
Mel Prebisch	Midwest
Eddie Ries	Upper Midwest
James Ross	Los Angeles area

Scout	Region
Eddie Schaak	Milwaukee area
Fred Shaffer	Midwest
Fred Schulte	Upper Midwest
Charles Seymour	West and Plains
J. Zack Taylor	South
Hollis Thurston*	West
Steve Vrablik	Illinois and Missouri
Robert Zuk	Northern California

*Played for the White Sox at one time

Field supervisors: Johnny Mostil, Harry Postove, Jack Sheehan and Hollis Thurston.

1960s

Scout	Region
Bruce Andrew	Southwest
Pel Austin	South
E. S. "Doc" Bennett	Southern California and Nevada
Ken Blackman	Midwest
Al Brown	South
Morris Deutsch	East
Bill Fitzharris	Minneapolis area
Pat Gainey	Southeast
Charles Gault	Chicago area
Sam Hairston*	South
Stanley "Bucky" Harris	Special assignment
Fred Hasselman	Midwest
Bennie Huffman	South
Grover "Deacon" Jones*	East
Bill Kearns	New England
Jack Keilch	Southern California
Bill Kimball	Northwest and Plains
Bill Lentini	California
Dario Lodigiani*	Northern California and Oregon
Ted Lyons*	South Central
Gordon Maltzberger*	Special assignment
Charlie Metro	Special assignment
Benny Meyer	Missouri
Pete Milito	Midwest
Les Moss*	Special assignment
Johnny Mostil*	Midwest and South
Hugh Mulcahy	Allegeheny region
Herb Newberry	East
George Noga	California
Bill Norman	Special assignment
Frank Parenti	Chicago area
Mel Preibisch	South
Steve Ray	East
Jim Robinson	St. Louis area
Charley Seymour	Southwest
Fred Shaffer	East
George Sobek	Chicago area
Steve Vrablik	Southern Illinois and Kentucky
Walt Widmayer	Southeast
Hugh Wise	Midwest

*Played for the White Sox at one time

Field supervisors: Hollis Thurston, Johnny Mostil, and Harry Postove.

1970s

Scout	Region
Carl Ackerman	Midwest
Bruce Andrew	West
Pel Austin	West
Loren Babe	West
Joe Begani	Chicago area
Ken Blackman	Midwest
Al Brown	South
Pat Gainey	Southeast
Charles Gault	Chicago area
Sam Hairston*	South
Bennie Huffman	South
Ira Hutchinson*	Chicago area
Joseph Ingalls	California
Gary Johnson	California
Grover "Deacon" Jones*	East
Jack Keilch	Southern California
Bill Kimball	Northwest and Plains
Eric Kitzman	Midwest
Jerry Krause	Chicago area
Bill Lentini	California
Leo Labossiere	New England
Dario Lodigiani*	Northern California and Oregon
Al Lynch	East
Luis Mayoral	Puerto Rico
Benny Meyer	Missouri
Pete Milito	Midwest
Hugh Mulcahy	Allegeheny region

Scout	Region
Mel F. Nelson	California
Herb Newberry	Baltimore area
George Noga	California
Fern Paredes	Southern California
Mel Preibisch	South
Silvano Quesada	Dominican Republic
Jim Robinson	St. Louis area
J. "Honey" Russell	East
Fred Shaffer	Special assignment
George Sobek	Chicago area
Steve Vrablik	Chicago area
Walt Widmayer	South
Hugh Wise	Midwest

*Played for the White Sox at one time

Field supervisors: Walt Widmayer, Steve Vrablik, and Gary Johnson.

1980s

Scout	Region
Loren Babe	Special assignment
Mike Becker	Part-time
Juan Bernhardt	Dominican Republic
Mark Bernstein	East
George Bradley	Missouri
Jim Busby*	Georgia
Tom Calvano	East
Baldemar Carmona	Texas
Orlando Cepeda	Puerto Rico
Ellis Clary	Advance scout
Alex Cosmidis	East
Bruce Dal Canton*	Pennsylvania
Preston Douglas	East
Jesse Flores	West
Ed Ford	East
Rod Fridley	West
Bobby Gardner Jr.	Ohio
Bill Gayton	South Dakota
Erick Glick	New York
Bill Haller	Chicago area
Mike Harris	Part-time
Edward Ben Hays	Part-time
Bennie Huffman	Virginia
Miguel Ibarra	Panama
Joe Ingalls	California
Bart Johnson*	Special assignment
Gary Johnson	California
Jerry Krause	Chicago area
Leo Labossiere	Rhode Island
Marvin Lane	Michigan
Reggie Lewis	Part-time
Dario Lodigiani*	Northern California
Terry Logan	Texas
Carlos Loretto	Venezuela
Jerry Manuel	California
Larry Maxie	West Coast supervisor
Vern McKee	West
Larry Monroe*	Chicago area
Dan Monzon	Eastern supervisor
Rich Morales*	California
Joe Nossek	Midwest
William Orr	Part-time
Jose Ortega	Part-time
Fern Paredos	California
Carlos Paz	Florida
Ed Pebley	West
Gary Pellant	West
Orlando Pena	Puerto Rico
Victor Puig	Puerto Rico
Mike Powers	Midwest
Silvano Quezeda	Dominican Republic
Mike Rizzo	East
Phil Rizzo	Midwest
Tom Roberts	California
Cucik Rodriguez	Puerto Rico
Mark Servais	Wisconsin
Duane Shaffer	California
Fred Shaffer	Special assignment/ Pennsylvania
Bob Sloan	Part-time
Lou Snipp	Midwestern supervisor
Mark Snipp	Midwest
George Sobek	Chicago area
Lynn Squires	Michigan
Ken Stauffeur	Texas
Mike Taylor	Midwest
Richard Taylor	Part-time
John Tumminia	Part-time
Henry Varlack	Part-time
Ron Vaughn	West
Angel Vazquez	Latin American supervisor
Walt Widmayer	Florida
Mike Woten	Part-time
Stan Zielinski	Chicago area

*Played for the White Sox at one time

Supervisors: Angel Vazquez, Ed Brinkman (American League), Larry Monroe, (National League), Bart Johnson (advance scout), Dan Monzon (East), Lou Snipp (Midwest), Larry Maxie (West), Walt Widmayer, and Gary Johnson.

1990s

Scout	Region
Steve Amieri	Midwest
Jose Bernhardt	Dominican Republic
Juan Bernhardt	Dominican Republic
Chuck Bizzell	Midwest
Kevin Burrell	South
Joseph Butler	Los Angeles area
Scott Cerny	California/Nevada
Brian Collins	Part-time
Herman Cortes	Venezuela
Marc Coseta	Part-time
Alex Cosmidis	South
Ed Crosby	Southern California
Preston Douglas	Florida
Jesse Flores	Southwest
Rod Fridley	South
Alonzo Ganther	Part-time
Nino Giarratano	Part-time
Larry Grefer	Midwest/South
Warren Hughes	South
Miguel Ibarra	Panama
Joe Ingalls	Part-time
Jack Jolly	Part-time
George Kachigan	Part-time
Bill Kahler	Part-time
Joe Karp	Western Canada, Far West
John Kazanos	West
Lou Lasio	Part-time
Doug Laumann	Midwest/South
Reggie Lewis	East
Dario Lodigiani*	Part-time
Gary Mader	Part-time

Scout	Region
Bill Meyer	Northern Florida
John Nilmeyer	Part-time
Jose Ortega	Puerto Rico
Al Otto	Part-time
Dave Owen	South Central states
J. D. Patton	Part-time
Gary Pellant	Hawaii/West Coast
Orlando Pena	Puerto Rico
Mike Powers	South
Paul Provas	Midwest
Victor Puig	Puerto Rico
Robert Rikeman	Part-time
Mike Rizzo	Midwest
Alberto Rondon	Venezuela
Mike Sgobba	Southern California
Bob Sloan	Part-time
Mike Taylor	South Dakota
Jun Teramotto	Far East
Joe Thurman	Part-time
John Tumminia	Canada/New England
Henry Varlack	Part-time
Mark Weidemaier	Double A
Bob Weinstein	Part-time
Kenny Williams*	Inner Cities

*Played for the White Sox at one time

Supervisors: Duane Shaffer (director), Dan Fabian (scouting administrator), Mark Bernstein (East), Doug Laumann (Midwest), Ed Pebley (West), Mike Wolever (West Coast), and George Bradley (national cross-checker).

2000s

Scout	Region
Amador Arias	Venezuela
Mike Baker	Southern California
Jaymie Bane	North & Central Florida
Scott Bikowski	North & Central Florida
Kevin Burrell	Georgia & South Carolina
Joe Butler	Southern California
Herman Cortes	Central Florida, Puerto Rico
Alex Cosmidos	North Carolina, Virginia
Ryan Dorsey	Eastern Seaboard
Dan Durst	Midwest & the Great Plains
Nathan Durst	Illinois, Northern Indiana, Michigan, Minn., North Dakota, South Dakota
Roberto Espinoza	Venezuela
Chuck Fox	Eastern Seaboard, Eastern Canada
Denny Gonzalez	Dominican Republic

Scout	Region
Larry Grefer	Kentucky, Ohio, West Virginia
Phil Gulley	Eastern Kentucky, Eastern Tennessee, West Virginia, Western Pennsylvania
Matt Hattabaugh	Southern California
Nick Hostetler	Georgia, North Carolina, South Carolina
Warren Hughes	Alabama, Florida, Mississippi
Miguel Ibarra	Panama
George Kachigan	San Diego, Nevada
John Kazanas	Arizona, Colorado, Montana, Utah, Wyoming
Larry Maxie	Southern California
Jeff McKay	Pacific Northwest & Western Canada

Scout	Region
Danny Ontiveros	Southern California
Jose Ortega	South Florida, Puerto Rico
Clay Overcash	Arkansas, Kansas, Missouri
Gary Pellant**	
Andrew Pinter	North Carolina, Virginia
Paul Provas	Western Louisiana
Mark Salas*	Southern California
Daraka Shaheed**	
Mike Shirley	Illinois, Indiana, Iowa
Alex Slattery	Georgia, North Carolina, South Carolina, Tennessee
Joe Siers	North Florida
Keith Staab	West Louisiana, Texas
John Tumminia	New England, Canada
Derek Valenzuela	Southern California
Adam Virchis	Northern California, Nevada, Oregon, Washington
Dedrick Williams**	
Gary Woods	Southern California
Bill Young**	

*Played for the White Sox at one time

** Classified as Professional Scouts—no assigned territory

Supervisors: Bob Fontaine Jr. (director of player development); Doug Laumann (director of scouting); Mike Sgobba (Latin America coordinator); Duane Shaffer Sr. (director of scouting); Ed Pebley (national crosschecker); Joe Butler and Rick Ingalls (West Coast supervisors); Nathan Durst (Midwest supervisor); Warren Hughes, Ken Stauffer, and John Tumminia (East Coast supervisors); Nick Capra (director of amateur scouting); J.J. Lally, Del Matthews (assistant directors of player development and scouting).

White Sox Spring Training Sites

Excelsior Springs, Missouri	1901–02
Mobile, Alabama	1903
Marlin Springs, Texas	1904
New Orleans, Louisiana	1905–06
Mexico City, Mexico*	1907
Los Angeles, California	1908
San Francisco, California	1909–10
Mineral Wells, Texas	1911
Waco, Texas	1912
Paso Robles, California	1913–15
Mineral Wells, Texas	1916–19
Waco, Texas	1920
Seguin, Texas	1922–23
Winter Haven, Florida	1924
Shreveport, Louisiana	1925–28
Dallas, Texas	1929
San Antonio, Texas	1930–32
Pasadena, California	1933–42
French Lick, Indiana†	1943–44
Terre Haute, Indiana†	1945
Pasadena, California	1946–50
Pasadena/Palm Springs, California	1951
Pasadena/El Centro, California	1952
El Centro, California	1953
Tampa, Florida‡	1954–59
Sarasota, Florida	1960–97
Tucson, Arizona	1998–2008
Glendale, Arizona	2009–

*The White Sox were the first team to conduct spring training outside U.S. borders. This trip was a prelude to Charles Comiskey's plan to take his team around the world on a goodwill tour—a goal accomplished in 1913–14.

†Wartime travel restrictions forced the Sox to headquarter in Indiana.

‡Shared facilities with the Cincinnati Reds.

March 1, 1944: Getting ready for spring training in the wartime years. Sox catcher Vince Castino (career average .228) and pitcher Orval Grove (left and center) engage in a game of "pepper" at the Englewood YMCA in Chicago with Nick Etten of the Yankees (wielding the bat).

February 23, 1941: The Sox arrive in Pasadena to begin spring training. The future is bleak, but the sun is shining. Traveling Secretary Joe Barry (sixth from right) is unconcerned.

Trainer A.F. Schacht leads calisthenics, 1939.

Grandstand of Payne Park in Sarasota, Florida. (Courtesy of Len Maybaum)

Game action at Payne Park, Sarasota, Florida—circa 1972. (Courtesy of Len Maybaum)

Beautiful Camelback Ranch in Glendale, Arizona, is the spring training home of the White Sox. (Courtesy of the Chicago White Sox)

The White Sox Farm System

Although the White Sox had established Des Moines, Iowa, as the team's first real "farm team" back in 1912, the minor league system officially launched in March 1939, when the first 81 recruits, many of them midwestern sandlot players, were dispatched to Longview, Texas, to tryout for positions with four new minor league Class D teams in Rayne, Louisiana; Longview and Lubbock, Texas; and Jonesboro, Arkansas, under the supervision of director Bob Tarleton and Doug Minor, White Sox scout. A year later, the first "graduates" of the system, Bob Kennedy and Orval Grove, arrived in spring training for a tryout with the parent club.

Billy Webb, soft-spoken, affable, and a former major league infielder, served as Jimmie Dykes' third-base coach for nearly five seasons before the Comiskeys asked him to take over minor league operations from Tarleton on January 1, 1940. Webb, patient and shrewd, was a great teacher and motivator for the young players, but leading the fledgling farm system was a tough job—and one that he accepted with the greatest reluctance. In 1942 the draft and World War II closed down the Three-Eye League, the Northern League, and other circuits where the Sox maintained their farm teams and working affiliates, making Webb's job nearly impossible.

The minor league operation was dealt a crippling setback by Billy's untimely death at age 46 on January 12, 1943. While motoring to Comiskey Park from his South Side home, Webb collapsed behind the wheel under the 35th Street railroad viaduct just a block west of the park and was pronounced dead—more bad luck in a long string of tragedies befalling the White Sox that seemed to affirm the superstitious belief that a "Comiskey Curse" haunted this ballclub.

The farm system, hampered by wartime restrictions, for all practical purposes was shut down until November 30, 1945, when general manager Harry Grabiner's incoming replacement, Leslie M. O'Connor, received approval from Mrs. Grace Comiskey to restart operations. New working agreements with affiliates were established, and the Waterloo, Iowa, team—a White Sox minor league mainstay where Chuck Comiskey, the Old Roman's grandson served his apprenticeship after the war—resumed play.

John Rigney, a former Sox pitcher and the husband of Dorothy Comiskey, took over as farm director in 1948, but Rigney relied on the keen intuition of the team's chief scout, Joseph "Patsy" O'Rourke, who, according to Frank Lane, "carried his office in his stuffed pockets." By 1948 the Comiskeys had entered into working agreements with 13 different teams—a high-water mark in franchise history. Over the next two years under Rigney and Lane, the bloated minor league system was paired down to nine teams and then six, a number that would remain constant through the 1960s.

However, the minor leagues were mostly a dry hole and remained that way through the early 1950s. Apart from slugger Gus Zernial, who emerged from the Hollywood, California, affiliate and attained stardom, success at the big-league level in the first half of the decade had more to do with the genius of Frank Lane's trades as general manager, than the over-hyped rookie recruits like third baseman Hector "Hot Rod" Rodriguez and pitcher Constantine "Gus" Keriazakos, the $67,000 high school bonus baby, both sent to the parent ballclub at a tender age, neither of whom could pass muster.

In 1956 Rigney was elevated to a full vice presidency and was succeeded in his duties as farm director by Glenn C. Miller, a Kaukauna, Wisconsin, native whose real genius was working with his scouts to procure top-notch talent—for every level and age. Miller devised a system of mid-winter tryout camps for high school– and college-age players; a midsummer baseball and sports camp sequestered deep in the northern Wisconsin woods near Eagle River, aimed at identifying talented grammar school kids; and in the 1960s he put into motion the "rotating special skills coaches" assigned to circulate through the minor league system to work with the young players. From 1956 through the end of the decade, Miller built it from scratch as the minor league system delivered an array of exciting prospects to the big leagues, including speedsters Louie Aparicio, Jim Landis, the diminutive Jack Kralick of Wyandotte, Michigan, who authored a no-hitter for the Twins in 1962, four years after the Sox released him outright; plus Barry Latman, Ken McBride, Norm Cash, John Romano, Earl Battey, Johnny Callison, and Don Mincher, who went on to star for other teams—although there were many more famous homegrown failures, too. In this category we find a collection of "can't miss" names—who simply missed: Stan Johnson, Bob Sagers, Joe Hicks, Jim McAnany, Chuck Lindstrom (who hit 1.000 in exactly one career plate appearance), the highly touted Joe Dahlke, Bill DuFour, Russ Heman, and Bill Fischer—and who can forget big Ron Jackson of Kalamazoo (who was tabbed as the next Babe Ruth) and Paul Stuffel?

Bill Veeck's disastrous trades in 1960 sent away Callison, Romano, Mincher, Battey, and Cash, leaving the farm system bereft of talent and in a mess at the time of Veeck's sale of the team to Art Allyn in June 1961. General manager Ed Short retrenched, exchanged veterans for younger players while developing some exceptional young pitchers in the early 1960s. Working very closely with Johnny Mostil (the old 1920s "fly-chaser" who left his mark on team history as a fine hitter and an even better talent scout), Joel Horlen, Gary Peters, Dennis McLain, and Bob Locker blossomed into stardom, although McLain was released on the last day of 1963 spring training and the pipeline for hitting talent was not nearly as plentiful as it had once been in the fruitful five-year period, 1956–1960.

Good contact hitters, particularly players with long-distance firepower, were nowhere to be found as the fortunes of the White Sox sagged in the late 1960s. Carlos May, Ken Berry, and Bill Melton emerged as true hitting stars, but Bill Voss, Berke Reichenbach, Bob Spence, Marv Staehli, Jim Hicks, Ed Stroud, Dick Kenworthy, and Ron Lolich—a cousin of Tigers ace Mickey Lolich—were among the more celebrated washouts of the decade. The talent pool of pitching—

something you could always count on in the salad years of Go-Go White Sox baseball—also declined as the decade rolled to an end. Greg Bollo; Roger Nelson; Brigham Young University grad Gerry Nyman; Cisco Carlos, a two-week wonder with the Sox in September 1967; Fred Rath, who posted a gaudy 17–3 record at Appleton in 1966 and a 7.75 ERA with the White Sox in 1969; the Chicago boy, Dennis O'Toole, a 1967 DeLaSalle graduate whose big brother Jim starred with the Reds; and Andy Rubilotta, who never made it up—all names that jog the memory of only the most diehard fan of a certain age—failed to match the earlier success of Peters and Horlen.

The 1970s were years of financial struggle and retrenchment. By 1975 the scouting system was pared down to just 18 men, with only four operating farm teams in Denver, Colorado; Knoxville, Tennessee; Appleton, Wisconsin; and Sarasota, Florida. In the last year of Bill Veeck's impoverished second ownership, the parent club maintained teams in only three locales—Des Moines, Iowa; Schenectedy, New York; and Appleton.

Sam Ewing, a first baseman/outfielder from the University of Tennessee; pitcher Rich Hinton, who flopped in at least a half-dozen tryouts in Chicago; and shortstop Lee "Bee Bee" Richard, out of Port Arthur, Texas, were drafted high and counted on for great things, but ended up as prized failures of the Arthur and John Allyn regimes during some of the darkest years of franchise history—1968–1970. Kevin Bell, Fran Mullins, Ricky Seilheimer, Randy Scarberry, "Tex" Wortham, Dewey Robinson, Guy Hoffman, Mike Eden, and Harry Chappas were products of Veeck's scaled-back operation in the late 1970s, and the results were what one might expect of an "also-ran" team with dwindling cash reserves.

Under the leadership of Jerry Reinsdorf and his ownership team, the White Sox made a significant investment in the minor league system beginning in the early 1980s by adding new affiliates, bolstering the scouting system, and hiring additional minor league instructors—and when his playing days ended, Ken Williams was brought in as an inner-cities scout. It took nearly a full decade before the investment bore its fruit—the affiliates were mostly barren of talent after many long years of neglect and budget cutbacks during the John Allyn and Bill Veeck regimes in the 1970s. But, beginning in the early 1990s, the White Sox minor league rebuilding plan began delivering future stars to the parent club, including Frank Thomas, Magglio Ordonez, Jack McDowell, Robin Ventura, Alex Fernandez, Mike Cameron, Ray Durham, and Carlos Lee—mostly the result of high draft picks. In the first decade of the new millennium, the trend continued, as Joe Crede, Aaron Rowand, and Mark Buehrle attained stardom, although the 10-year period 2000–09 was not nearly as productive as the first five years of the 1990s had been.

In February 2007 the White Sox promoted David Wilder to senior director of player personnel, as he continued to oversee the team's Latin American operations. Wilder was credited with the free agent signing of Jermaine Dye in 2004 and was a rising front-office star whose name was on the short list of several major league teams shopping for a new general manager when a scandal of major proportions torpedoed his baseball career. Wilder and two scouts were fired on May 16, 2008, following an investigation into Wilder's questionable dealings in the Dominican Republic involving bonuses that had allegedly been paid to the parents of several players. Wilder and the two scouts were accused of skimming a percentage of the bonus money, and the commissioner's office and the federal government stepped in to investigate the matter.

Buddy Bell, a former star third baseman, son of 1950s Reds outfielder Gus Bell, manager, and one of baseball's best talent scouts, rejoined the White Sox family in October 2007 and was appointed director of player development the following May, replacing Wilder. Bell had previously served as the White Sox's director of minor league instruction, a position he held from 1991 to 1993, and with Dan Fabian, Rick Hahn, and Doug Laumann working tirelessly behind the scenes, better results were immediate. In 2009 the system posted the third-best winning percentage in all of baseball.

Minor League Farm Directors

Bob Tarleton	1939–40
Billy Webb	1940–1943
John D. Rigney	1948–55
Glen C. Miller	1956–73
Carol V. Davis	1974–77
Paul Richards/Charles Evranian	1978–80
David M. Dombrowski	1981
Bobby Winkles	1982–85
Alvin Dark	1986
Al Goldis	1987–90
Steve Noworyta	1991–98
Jim Snyder	1999–2000
Bob Fontaine Jr.	2001–03
David Wilder	2003–08
Buddy Bell	2008–

Farm Clubs, 1939–50

Team	League
Albany, New York	International
Charleston, South Carolina	Southern, Class A
Dallas, Texas	Texas, Class A-1
Hot Springs, Arkansas	Cotton States, Class C
Fall River, Massachusetts	New England, Class B
Hollywood, California	Pacific Coast, Triple A
Hot Springs, Arkansas	Cotton States, Class C
Jonesboro, Arkansas	Northeast Arkansas League, Class D
Kingsport, Tennessee	Appalachian, Class D
Longview, Texas	East Texas, Class C
Lubbock, Texas	West Texas–New Mexico, Class D
Lima, Ohio	Ohio-Indiana, Class D
Madisonville, Kentucky	Kitty, Class D
Memphis, Tennessee	Southern, Double A
Milwaukee, Wisconsin	American Association, Triple A
Muskegon, Michigan	Central, Class D
Oil City, Pennsylvania	Middle Atlantic, Class D
Oklahoma City, Oklahoma	Texas, Class A-1
Portsmouth	Mid Atlantic
Rayne, Louisiana	Evangeline, Class D
Seminole, Oklahoma	Sooner State, Class D
Shreveport, Louisiana	Texas, Class A-1
Stockton, California	California, Class C
Superior, Wisconsin	Northern League, Class C
Waterloo, Iowa	Three-I, Class D
Wisconsin Rapids, Wisconsin	Midwest, Class D

Farm Clubs, 1950–60

Team	League
Charleston, South Carolina*	American Association, Class A South Atlantic, Class C
Clinton, Iowa	Midwest, Class D
Colorado Springs, Colorado	Western League, Class A
Danville, Illinois	Mississippi–Ohio Valley, Class D
Davenport, Iowa	Three-I, Class B
Dubuque, Iowa*	Mississippi–Ohio Valley, Class D Midwest, Class D
Duluth-Superior	Northern, Class C
Gastonia, North Carolina	Tri-States, Class B
Hot Springs, Arkansas	Cotton States, Class C
Holdrege, Nebraska	Nebraska State, Class D
Indianapolis, Indiana	American Association, Triple A
Lincoln, Nebraska	Three-I, Class B
Madisonville, Kentucky	Kitty, Class D
Memphis, Tennessee†	Southern, Double A
Sacramento, California	Pacific Coast, Triple A
Seattle, Washington	Pacific Coast, Triple A
Superior, Wisconsin	Northern, Class C
Topeka, Kansas	Western Association, Class B
Waterloo, Iowa†	Three-I, Class B
Wisconsin Rapids, Wisconsin	Wisconsin State, Class D

*The team changed leagues during the decade.
†The minor league ballclub was owned outright by the White Sox.

Farm Clubs, 1960–70

Team	League
Appleton, Wisconsin	Midwest, Class A
Charleston, South Carolina	South Atlantic, Class A
Clinton, Iowa	Midwest, Class D and A
Columbus, Georgia	Southern, Double A
Daytona Beach, Florida	Florida State, Class D
Deerfield Beach, Florida	Florida State, Class A
Duluth-Superior	Northern, Class A
Eugene, Oregon	Northwest, Class A
Evansville, Indiana	Southern, Double A
Harlan, Kentucky League	Appalachian, Rookie
Hawaii	Pacific Coast, Triple A
Hollywood, Florida	Minor league camp
Idaho Falls, Idaho	Pioneer, Class C
Indianapolis, Indiana*	American Association, Triple A
	Pacific Coast International
Lincoln, Nebraska	Three-I, Class B
Lynchburg, West Virginia*	Carolina, Class A
	South Atlantic, Double A
	Southern, Double A
Pensacola, Florida	Alabama–Florida, Class D
San Diego, California	Pacific Coast, Triple A
Sarasota, Florida*	Gulf Coast, Rookie
	Florida State, Rookie
Savannah, Georgia	South Atlantic, Class A
Tucson, Arizona	Pacific Coast, Triple A
Visalia, California	California, Class C

*The team changed leagues during the decade.

Farm Clubs, 1970–80

Team	League
Appleton, Wisconsin	Midwest, Class A
Asheville, North Carolina	Southern, Double A
Denver, Colorado	American Association, Triple A
Duluth-Superior	Northern, Class A
Iowa (Des Moines)	American Association, Triple A
Knoxville, Tennessee	Southern, Double A
Mobile, Alabama	Southern, Double A
Sarasota, Florida	Gulf Coast, Rookie League
Tucson, Arizona	Pacific Coast, Triple A

Hoover Stadium, Birmingham, Alabama, home of the Birmingham Barons, the Sox Double A affiliate

Farm Clubs, 1980–90

Team	League
Appleton, Wisconsin	Midwest, Class A
Birmingham, Alabama	Southern, Double A
Buffalo, New York	American Association, Triple A
Daytona Beach, Florida	Florida State, Class A
Denver, Colorado	American Association, Triple A
Edmonton, Alberta, Canada	Pacific Coast, Triple A
Glens Falls, New York	Eastern, Double A
Gulf Coast, Sarasota, Florida	Rookie League, Class A
Hawaii	Pacific Coast, Triple A
Niagara Falls, New York	New York–Penn, Class A
Peninsula, Virginia	Carolina, Class A
Sarasota, Florida	Gulf Coast, Rookie
Schenectady, New York	Eastern, Double A
South Bend, Indiana	Midwest, Class A
Tampa, Florida	Florida State, Class A
Utica, New York	New York–Penn, Class A
Vancouver, British Columbia, Canada	Pacific Coast, Triple A

Farm Clubs, 1990–2000

Team	League
Birmingham, Alabama	Southern, Double A
Bristol, Virginia	Appalachian, Class A
Gulf Coast, Sarasota, Florida	Gulf Coast, Rookie League
Hickory, North Carolina	South Atlantic, Class A
Nashville, Tennessee	American Association, Triple A
Prince William, Woodbridge, Virginia	Carolina, Class A
Sarasota, Florida	Florida State, Class A
South Bend, Indiana	Midwest, Class A
Utica, New York	New York–Penn, Class A
Vancouver, British Columbia, Canada	Pacific Coast, Triple A
Winston-Salem, North Carolina	Carolina, Class A
Calgary, Alberta	Triple A
Tucson, Arizona	Rookie
Charlotte, South Carolina	International, Triple A
Burlington, Iowa	Midwest League, Class A

Michael Jordan played for the Barons in 1994.

Farm Clubs, 2000–10

Team	League
Charlotte, North Carolina	International, Triple A
Birmingham, Alabama	Southern, Double A
Winston-Salem, North Carolina	Carolina League, Class A
Kannapolis, North Carolina	South Atlantic, Class A
Burlington, Iowa	Midwest League, Class A
Bristol, Virgina	Advanced Rookie
Great Falls, Montana	Advanced Rookie
Tucson, Arizona	Rookie
Phoenix, Arizona	Arizona League

In 2010 the Winston-Salem Dash, a White Sox Class A-Advanced minor league affiliate since 1997 (formerly known as the Warthogs), opened beautiful new BB&T Ballpark on Broad Street, near downtown Winston-Salem. (Courtesy of the Winston-Salem Dash)

Minor League Managers, 1946–2010

Manager	Team	Years Managed
Billy Adair	Hawaii	1968
	Tucson	1969
Bruce Andrew	Duluth	1968
	Sarasota	1969
Luke Appling*	Memphis	1951–53
	Indianapolis	1962
Roly de Armas	Sarasota	1997
Loren Babe	Denver	1975
	Iowa	1976
Don Bacon	Clinton	1963–64
	Sarasota	1965
	Deerfield Beach	1966
Wally Backman	Winston-Salem	2001
Bob Bailey	Peninsula	1986
	Hawaii	1987
Joe Becker	Charleston	1954
Ken Berry*	Birmingham	1989–90
Terry Bevington	Vancouver	1988
Tim Blackwell	Winston-Salem	2007–08
John Boles	Sarasota	1981–82
	Appleton	1983
	Glens Falls	1984
	Bufffalo	1985
Marc Bombard	Charlotte	2007–08
Jim Breazeale*	Appleton	1979
Nick Capra	Birmingham, Burlington, Bristol, Charlotte	1996–
Jack Cassini	Memphis	1955–56
Chris Chambliss	Charlotte	2009–
Bill Close	Madisonville	1955
Andy Cohen	Indianapolis	1957
Jack Conway	Colorado Springs	1955–56
Walker Cooper	Indianapolis	1958–59
Alex Cosmidis	Appleton	1967
	Lynchburg	1968
Chris Cron	Great Falls	2007–
	Hickory	1996–97
	Winston Salem	1998
	Birmingham	2006
Roy Dahlstrom	Oil City	1948
Brian Dayett	Winston-Salem	2000
Otto Denning	Oil City	1948–49
	Waterloo	1950–51
Steve Dillard*	Sarasota	1983–84, 1986–87
	Glens Falls	1985
	South Bend	1988
Fred Dorman	Waterloo	1955
J. C. Dunn	Pensacola	1960

Manager	Team	Years Managed
James Dykes*	Hollywood	1946–50
Sam Ewing*	Appleton	1981
Marvis Foley*	Peninsula	1987
	Tampa	1988
	Vancouver	1989–91
Pete Fox	Waterloo	1948
	Hot Springs	1949
Terry Francona	South Bend	1992
	Birmingham	1993–95
Tony Franklin	Sarasota	1989–90
	Birmingham	1991–92
	South Bend	1993
Adrian Garrett	Appleton	1982
	Glens Falls	1983
Mike Gellinger	Gulf Coast	1990
	Utica	1991
	South Bend	1994
	Gulf Coast	1995
Don Griffin	Memphis	1956
Don Gutteridge	Colorado Springs	1952–53
	Memphis	1954
	Indianapolis	1967
Tom Haller	Birmingham	1986
Jerry Hairston*	Bristol	2003–05
Joe Hauser	Duluth-Superior	1956–57
Mike Heath	Birmingham, Winston-Salem	1996–97
Rollie Hemsley	Indianapolis	1963
Marc Hill*	Daytona Beach	1987
Bennie Huffman	Waterloo	1948–49
	Superior	1950
Dave Huppert	Sarasota	1993
	Prince William	1994–96
Johnny Hutchings	Clinton	1959
Ira Hutchinson*	Wisconsin Rapids	1952
	Topeka	1953–54
	Dubuque	1955
	Waterloo	1956
	Colorado Springs	1957
	Davenport	1958
	Lincoln	1959–60
	Charleston	1961
	Clinton	1962, 1965
	Sarasota	1963–64
	Lynchburg	1966
	Duluth	1967
	Appleton	1970
Gary Johnson	Appleton	1968
	Columbus	1969
Al Jones	Portsmouth	1963–65
Chris Jones	Kannapolis	2007–08
Grover "Deacon" Jones*	Appleton	1973
Joe Jones	Sarasota	1970–78
Dave Keller	South Bend	1996

Ira Hutchinson

Manager	Team	Years Managed
Fred Kendall	Utica	1992
	Hickory	1993–94
	South Bend	1995
Dick Kinman	Clinton	1961
	Visalia	1962
Art Kusyner*	Sarasota	1988
Luis Lagunas	Niagara Falls	1985
Tony LaRussa	Knoxville	1978
	Iowa	1979
Vern Law	Denver	1984
Nick Leyva	Bristol	2002; 2006
Mickey Livingston	Colorado Springs	1954
Harry Lowrey	Idaho Falls	1960
Gordie Lund	Appleton	1974–75, 1977–78, 1980
	Knoxville	1976, 1979
	Edmonton	1981–82
Ever Magallanes	Birmingham	2009–
Jim Mahoney	Glens Falls	1981–82
	Denver	1983
Jim Marshall	Buffalo	1986
J. C. Martin*	Sarasota	1985
Gordon Maltzberger*	Lynchburg	1965
	Tucson	1970–71

Joe McEwing, the 2009 Carolina League Manager of the Year, guided the Winston-Salem Dash through the 2010 season. (Courtesy of the Winston-Salem Dash)

Manager	Team	Years Managed
Joe McEwing	Winston-Salem	2008–10
George Metkovich*	San Diego	1960
Walter Millies	Superior	1952
	Wisconsin Rapids	1953
	Waterloo	1954
Virl Minnis	Danville	1953
Les Moss*	Savannah	1962
	Lynchburg	1963
	Indianapolis	1964, 1966
Johnny Mostil*	Waterloo	1942–46
Omer Munoz	Kannapolis	2006
Jim Napier	Knoxville	1973–75, 1977
	Appleton	1976
Fred Nelson	Niagara Falls	1983–84
Ryan Newman	Bristol	2009–
George Noga	Dubuque	1956–57
	Holdrege	1958
	Duluth-Superior	1959
	Clinton	1960
	Lincoln	1961
	Sarasota	1962
	Eugene	1963
	Lynchburg	1964
	Indianapolis	1965
	Evansville	1966–67
Walter Novick	Superior	1955
Jack Onslow	Waterloo	1947
	Memphis	1948
John Orton	Bristol, Kannapolis, Great Falls	2001–05
Frank Parenti	Holdrege	1957, 1959
	Dubuque	1958
	Sarasota	1964–67
Rick Patterson	South Bend	1989–90
	Sarasota	1991–92
Mike Pazik	Schenectady	1980
Ed Pebley	Gulf Coast	1989
Tony Pena *	Tucson	1998
Rick Peterson	Utica	1988
Rico Petrocelli	Birmingham	1987–88
Jimmy Reese	San Diego	1961
Herman Reich	Idaho Falls	1961
Sal Rende	Appleton	1985
Rick Renick	Gulf Coast	1991
	Vancouver	1992
	Nashville	1993–94
R.J. Reynolds	Bristol	2000
Everett Robinson	Madisonville	1952–53
Mike Rojas	Gulf Coast	1992–94
	Hickory	1995
Red Ruffing*	Muskegon	1949
Tom Saffell	Sarasota	1968
	Appleton	1969
	Mobile	1970
Rafael Santana	Birmingham	2007–08
Frank Scalzi	Davenport	1957
	Colorado Springs	1958
	Charleston	1959–60
Larry Sherry	Asheville	1971
	Tucson	1972

George Noga

The Knights Castle in Fort Mill, South Carolina—home of the Charlotte Knights, the Triple A affilliate of the White Sox since 1999. (Photo by Bill Walker)

Manager	Team	Years Managed
Razor Shines	Kannapolis, Winston-Salem, Birmingham	2001–05
	Charlotte	2006
Duke Sims	Appleton	1986
Joe Sparks	Duluth	1970
	Appleton	1971
	Knoxville	1972
	Iowa	1973–74, 1977–78
Tom Spencer *	Calgary, Charlotte	1997–99
Carlos Subero	Birmingham	2008
Zack Taylor	Waterloo	1952–53
Jerry Terrell	Winston-Salem	1999
Tommy Thompson	Utica	1990
	South Bend	1991
	Bristol	1995
Dickie Thon	Gulf Coast	1996
Al Todd	Memphis	1949–50
Harold Van Pelt	Gastonia	1952
Ron Vaughn	Utica	1989
Pete Ward*	Iowa	1980
Stan Wasiak	Appleton	1966
	Lynchburg	1967–69
James "Skeeter" Webb*	Waterloo	1952
Ray Wilson	Daytona Beach	1961
Ernie Young	Kannapolis	2009–

*Played for the White Sox at one time

Chris Sale wore the uniform of the Knights ever so briefly in 2010. (Photo by Bill Walker)

Media

White Sox on the Radio

Baseball broadcasting in Chicago began during the 1923 City Series, described over the local airwaves by Sen Kaney.

The next season, 23-year-old Hal Totten was working on the rewrite desk of the old *Chicago Daily News* when his employer asked him to cover White Sox games over station WMAQ, owned by the newspaper. Totten was unsure about the future of this fledgling industry in 1924, but he jumped at the chance to attend baseball games for free. WMAQ was the first station to broadcast a game direct from the ballpark, and Totten became an instant celebrity. His signature sign-off—"G'bye now!"—was as famous in its day as Harry Caray's patented "Holy Cow!" Hal Totten lingered in Chicago through the 1940s, alternating his duties between the Cubs and White Sox. He later became president of the Three-I League of the Southern Association, after his Chicago broadcast career had run its course. He was a dyed-in-the-wool baseball man.

Then as now, the Cubs enjoyed greater local media exposure than the pallid White Sox teams of the 1920s, 1930s, and 1940s. Five stations carried the Cubs in the 1920s—only one covered the White Sox. This situation was not addressed until the ballclub gained a semblance of respectability in the mid-1930s, when additional local outlets picked up the broadcast.

Through depression and war, several other pioneering play-by-play men covered the local baseball scene with flair and style, including Johnny O'Hara, Pat Flanagan, Jimmy Dudley, and former Sox manager Lew Fonseca. O'Hara was a partisan White Sox fan who verbally taunted Cubs booster Flanagan over the airwaves of WJJD. Dudley was attached to the Cubs during the war years, providing backup to Totten, who had abandoned the South Side years earlier. Dudley came into his own later in the decade as the voice of Cleveland Indians baseball.

Cedar Rapids native Hal Totten was the first radio reporter to conduct live interviews with the players on the field. He was a fixture of early Chicago sports radio until his broadcasting career ended during World War II. In 1951 he took over the presidency of the Three-I League, where the White Sox maintained a farm club at Waterloo from 1941 to 1956. Totten continued on in this role until 1960, when he took over duties as president of the Southern League.

O'Hara and Flanagan shared announcing duties at the first All-Star Game from Comiskey Park in 1933. Shortly afterward O'Hara left Chicago to accept an announcing job with KMOX in St. Louis, leaving the market to Bob Elson, the voice of midwestern baseball for nearly four decades.

Harry Caray replaced Elson in 1971, helped revive the moribund franchise, and remained the radio and TV voice of White Sox baseball through the next 10 stormy years. Various combinations of announcers auditioned for Harry Caray's slot on the radio side after Harry severed ties with the White Sox and moved over to the North Side of town in 1982. Joe McConnell was the voice of the Chicago Bears, the Denver Broncos, and other NFL and college teams for 23 seasons and had called Minnesota Twins games for two seasons before joining Harry in the booth in 1980. He took over full-time, play-by-play duties in 1982, with South Sider Lorn Brown and former Sox and Indians great Early Wynn supplying color analysis.

McConnell was one of several "network guys" to fill the radio broadcast slot over the next few years. Because sports broadcasting jobs are often transitory assignments for nomadic announcers like McConnell, who have had national exposure or call other sports in other cities during the off-season, they are not anchored to one market or identified with one particular team year in and year out as, let's say, a Jack Brickhouse was. The delivery style of the network guys is more nonpartisan, and one easily senses a lack of enthusiasm or genuine feelings of warmth for the home team, the city, and the fans because the assignment is on a year-to-year contract basis. This year they are working in Chicago. Next year it might be Colorado or Arizona or whatever direction the four winds or the terms of their agreement push them. In this category of announcer Gary Thorne, Wayne Hagin, Bill Mercer, and Frank Messer all put in brief appearances in Chicago, but none left a lasting impression and all moved on rather quickly.

Many followers of the national pastime say they prefer a very straightforward and strictly nonpartisan approach to describing a ballgame, but in Chicago we are more accustomed to home-team announcers who are also ardent fans.

John Rooney of Richmond, Missouri, was another example of the nomadic announcer with many résumé credits to his name before checking into Chicago. He took over television play-by-play duties from Don Drysdale, who left to rejoin the Dodgers in 1988. Rooney shifted to the radio booth a year later to begin a long 18-year association with the team and his sidekick Ed Farmer while continuing on as a network announcer for CBS Radio, and later the USA Sports Radio Network.

Lacking the flamboyance of a Harry Caray or the personal charisma of Hawk Harrelson, Rooney provided an earnest, straightforward account of the game free of hyperbole. His most compelling show of emotion came after each Sox victory when he proclaimed, "That's a White Sox winner!" His home run call—"It's a goner!" was a personal Rooney trademark, but he was no cheerleader or hometown fan, and there are many in Chicago who questioned that. They might even call that style of announcing bland.

Rooney, who joined the Sox a year after calling the Twins games during their 1987 championship season, bowed out of the White Sox picture over a contract dispute with the new station, WSCR—"The Score"—replacing AM-1000, ESPN, as the Sox flagship station after the Sox won it all in 2005. The following year, he teamed up with Mike Shannon to broadcast Cardinals games over KTRS in St. Louis—replacing, of all people, the fired Wayne Hagin, his former White Sox sidekick on WMAQ from 1989 to 1991. Ed Farmer, a St. Rita High School graduate who grew up as a Sox fan and then closed games for "Veeck's Wrecks" in 1979–1980, moved into Rooney's vacated play-by-play slot and was joined by Chris Singleton, but the ex-Sox Singleton never gained traction as a color analyst. Darrin Jackson shifted over from the TV booth in 2009 to make room for Steve Stone.

Radio Play by Play, 1924–2010

Year	Station Affiliation	Announcer
1924–26	WMAQ	Hal Totten
1927–28	WGN	Quin Ryan
1929	WGN	Quin Ryan, Frank Dahm
1930	WGN	Quin Ryan, John Thompson
1931–33	WGN, WENR	Bob Elson
1934	WGN, WBBM, WIND, WMAQ*	Bob Elson
1935–36	WGN, WBBM, WIND, WCFL, WMAQ*	Bob Elson, Hal Totten, Russ Hodges
1937–38	WGN, WBBM, WJJD, WCFL, WIND	Bob Elson, Hal Totten, Russ Hodges
1939–40	WGN, WBBM, WIND, WCFL	Bob Elson
1941–42	WGN, WCFL, WJJD	Bob Elson
1943	WGN, WCFL, WJJD	Jack Brickhouse, Grayle Howlett
1944	WIND	Bob Elson
1945–51	WJJD, WFMF	Bob Elson
1952–56	WCFL	Bob Elson
1957–60	WCFL	Bob Elson, Don Wells
1961	WCFL	Bob Elson, Ralph Kiner
1962–65	WCFL	Bob Elson, Milo Hamilton
1966	WCFL	Bob Elson, Bob Finegan
1967–70	WMAQ	Bob Elson, Red Rush
1971–72	WTAQ, WEAW†	Harry Caray, Ralph Faucher
1973	WMAQ	Harry Caray, Gene Osborn
1974–75	WMAQ	Harry Caray, Bill Mercer
1976	WMAQ	Harry Caray, Lorn Brown
1977–79	WMAQ	Harry Caray, Jimmy Piersall, Lorn Brown, Mary Shane
1980	WBBM	Harry Caray, Joe McConnell, Jimmy Piersall, Rich King
1981	WBBM	Harry Caray, Joe McConnell, Rich King
1982	WMAQ	Joe McConnell, Early Wynn
1983	WMAQ	Joe McConnell, Early Wynn, Lorn Brown
1984	WMAQ	Lorn Brown, Joe McConnell
1985–88	WMAQ	Lorn Brown, Del Crandall

Hal Totten, broadcast pioneer, interviews Moe Berg.

Veteran WGN TV and radio broadcaster Vince Lloyd spends a few minutes with Chuck Tanner.

Year	Station Affiliation	Announcer
1989–91	WMAQ	Wayne Hagin, John Rooney
1992–95	WMAQ	John Rooney, Ed Farmer, Ken Korach (Sundays only)
1996–98	WMVP	John Rooney, Ed Farmer, Dave Wills (Sundays only)
1999–2005	ESPN Radio 1000	John Rooney, Ed Farmer
2006–08	WSCR, Chicago Sports Radio	Chris Singleton Ed Farmer
2009–	WSCR, Chicago Sports Radio	Ed Farmer, Darrin Jackson

*These stations shared the WGN feed. In the early years of radio there was no such thing as "exclusive rights" to major league broadcasts. Thus any station possessing a broadcast license and a transmission tower could cover the games without fear of reprisal.

†Because of fan apathy, dwindling attendance, and the disastrous 1970 results, WMAQ dropped the Sox from their format. With no other major AM outlet expressing interest, the ballclub was left with no other choice than to sell its broadcast rights cheaply to two low-wattage suburban affiliates: WTAQ-LaGrange and WEAW-Evanston.

White Sox on Television

Sox 1977 broadcast team, left to right: Jimmy Piersall, Harry Caray, Mary Shane, and Lorn Brown

Year	Station Affiliation	Announcer
1948–54	WGN/9	Jack Brickhouse, Harry Creighton
1955	WGN/9	Jack Brickhouse, Harry Creighton, Vince Lloyd
1956–64	WGN/9	Jack Brickhouse, Vince Lloyd
1965–67	WGN/9	Jack Brickhouse, Lloyd Pettit
1968	WFLD/32	Jack Drees, Dave Martin
1969	WFLD/32	Jack Drees, Mel Parnell
1970	WFLD/32	Jack Drees, Billy Pierce
1971–72	WFLD/32	Jack Drees, Bud Kelly
1973–74	WSNS/44	Harry Caray, Bob Waller
1975	WSNS/44	Harry Caray, J.C. Martin
1976	WSNS/44	Harry Caray, Lorn Brown
1977	WSNS/44	Harry Caray, Lorn Brown, Jimmy Piersall, Mary Shane
1978–80	WSNS/44	Harry Caray, Jimmy Piersall
1981	WGN/9	Harry Caray, Jimmy Piersall, Lou Brock
1982–85	WFLD/Sports Vision	Don Drysdale, Ken Harrelson
1986–87	WFLD/Sports Vision	Don Drysdale, Frank Messer
1988	WFLD/Sports Vision	John Rooney, Tom Paciorek
1989	WFLD/Sports Channel	Gary Thorne, Tom Paciorek

Year	Station Affiliation	Announcer
1990	WGN/Sports Channel	Jim Durham, Ken Harrelson, Tom Paciorek
1991–96	WGN/Sports Channel	Ken Harrelson, Tom Paciorek
1991–97	WGN/Sports Channel	Ken Harrelson, Tom Paciorek
1998–99	WGN-TV & FOX Sports Chicago	Ken Harrelson, Tom Paciorek
2000–05	WGN-TV/ FOX Sports Net/WCIU-TV	Ken Harrelson, Darrin Jackson
2006–08	WGN-TV/ Comcast SportsNet/ WCIU-TV	Ken Harrelson, Darrin Jackson
2009–	WGN-TV/ Comcast SportsNet/ WCIU-TV	Ken Harrelson–Steve Stone

From the playing field of Comiskey to the broadcast booth: the Hawk's one-time sidekick, Darrin "D.J." Jackson

Ken "Hawk" Harrelson and Steve Stone provide world-class play-by-play and commentary to Sox fans every game. (Courtesy of the Chicago White Sox)

Sources

Books

Allen, Dick, and Whitaker, Tim. *Crash: The Life and Times of Dick Allen.* New York: Ticknor & Fields, 1989.

Asinof, Eliot. *Eight Men Out: The Black Sox and the 1919 World Series.* New York: Holt, Rinehart & Winston, 1963.

Axelson, Gustav. *Commy: The Life Story of Charles A. Comiskey, The Grand Old Roman of Baseball and Nineteen Years the President and Owner of the Chicago White Sox.* Chicago: Reilly & Lee, 1919.

Brown, Warren. *The Chicago White Sox.* New York: G. P. Putnam's Sons, 1952.

Condon, David. *The Go-Go Chicago White Sox.* New York: Coward-McCann, 1960.

Cooper, Brian. *Ray Schalk: A Baseball Biography.* Jefferson, NC: McFarland, 2009.

———. *Red Faber: A Biography of a Hall of Fame Pitcher.* Jefferson, NC: McFarland, 2006.

Daguerrotypes: Complete Major and Minor League Record of Baseball's Immortals. St. Louis: The Sporting News, 1981.

Dykes, James J., and Deeter, Charles, ed. *You Can't Steal First Base.* Philadelphia: Lippincott, 1967.

Eskanazi, Gerald. *Bill Veeck: A Baseball Legend.* New York: McGraw-Hill, 1988.

Golenback, Peter. *Dynasty: The New York Yankees, 1949–1964.* New York: Prentice-Hall, 1975.

Gough, David, and Bard, Jim. *Little Nel—The Nellie Fox Story: An Up-Close & Personal Look at Baseball's "Mighty Mite."* Alexandria, VA: D.L. Megbec Publishing, 2000.

Gropman, Donald. *Say It Ain't So Joe: The True Story of Shoeless Joe Jackson and the 1919 World Series.* New York: Little Brown, 1979.

Helpingstine, Dan. *Through Hope and Despair: A Fan's Memories of the Chicago White Sox 1967–1997.* Highland, IN: Self Published, 2001.

Koppett, Leonard. *The Man in the Dugout.* New York: Crown, 1993.

Lindberg, Richard. *Sox. The Complete Record of Chicago White Sox Baseball.* New York: Macmillan, 1984.

———. *Stealing First in a Two-Team Town: The White Sox from Comiskey to Reinsdorf.* Champaign, IL: Sagamore Publishing, 1994.

———. *Stuck on the Sox.* Evanston, IL: Sassafrass Press, 1978.

———. *Who's on Third? The Chicago White Sox Story.* South Bend, IN: Icarus Press, 1983.

Logan, Bob. *Miracle on 35th Street: Winnin' Ugly with the 1983 White Sox.* South Bend, IN: Icarus Press, 1983.

Luhrs, Victor. *The Great Baseball Mystery: The 1919 World Series.* Cranbury, NJ: A.S. Barnes & Co., 1966.

Macmillan Baseball Encyclopedia (1st, 8th, and 9th editions). New York: Macmillan, 1969, 1990, 1993.

Minoso, Minnie, with Fagen, Herb. *Just Call Me Minnie: My Six Decades in Baseball.* Champaign, IL: Sagamore Publishing, 1994.

Moore, Joseph Thomas. *Pride against Prejudice: The Biography of Larry Doby.* Westport, CT: Praeger Publishing, 1988.

Palmer, Peter, and Thorn, John. *Total Baseball* (4th edition). New York: Viking, 1995.

Roeper, Richard. *Sox and the City: A Fan's Love Affair with the White Sox from the Heartbreak of '67 to the Wizards of Oz.* Chicago: Chicago Review Press, 2006.

Schnakenberg, Robert. *The Underground Baseball Encyclopedia,* Chicago: Triumph Books, 2010.

Seymour, Harold. *Baseball: The Early Years.* New York: Oxford University Press, 1960.

———. *Baseball: The Golden Age.* New York: Oxford University Press, 1971.

Shatzkin, Mike, ed. *The Ballplayers.* New York: Arbor House/William Morrow, 1990.

Smith, Curt. *Voices of the Game.* South Bend, IN: Diamond Communications, 1987.

Stein, Irving M. *The Ginger Kid: The Buck Weaver Story.* Dubuque, IA: Elysian Fields Press, 1992.

Thompson, S.C., and Turkin, Hy. *The Official Encyclopedia of Baseball.* New York: A.S. Barnes & Co., 1956.

Vanderberg, Bob. *From Lane and Fain to Zisk and Fisk.* Chicago: Chicago Review Press, 1982.

———. *Minnie and the Mick: The Go-Go White Sox Challenge the Fabled Yankee Dynasty, 1951–1964.* South Bend, IN: Diamond Communications, 1996.

———. *'59 Summer of the Sox.* Champaign, IL: Sports Publishing, 1999.

Veeck, Bill, and Linn, Ed. *The Hustler's Handbook.* New York: G.P. Putnam's Sons, 1965.

———. *Veeck as in Wreck.* New York: G.P. Putnam's Sons, 1962.

Ward, Arch. *The New Chicago White Sox.* Chicago: Henry Regnery & Co, 1951.

Whittingham, Richard. *The White Sox: A Pictoral History.* Chicago: Contemporary Books, 1983.

Team Publications

Chicago White Sox Postseason Statistical Summaries (1959–2008).

Chicago White Sox Press Guides (1948–2010).

Chicago White Sox Team Yearbooks (1952–70; 1982–84; 1991–2010).

Through the Years: A Commemorative Tribute to Comiskey Park (1910–90). Chicago: Sherman Media, 1990.

White Sox Yarns (newsletter, various years 1948–74).

Periodicals

Baseball Digest (various issues and years).

Baseball in Chicago, published by the Emil Rothe Chapter of the Society for American Baseball Research (SABR), 1986.

Baseball Research Journal (various issues and years, 1982–2010). Society for American Baseball Research (SABR).

Sport Magazine (various issues and years).

Sporting News (various issues and years).

Sporting News Guidebooks (various years).

Sports Illustrated (various issues and years).

Who's Who in the Major Leagues, ed. John P. Carmichael (various editions 1933–46).

Newspapers

Chicago American (1951–69)
Chicago Daily Journal (1900–10)
Chicago Daily News (1900–78)
Chicago Herald & Examiner (1922–40)
Chicago Herald-American (1940–48)
Chicago Inter-Ocean (1900–15)
Chicago Sun (1941–45)
Chicago Sun-Times (1948–2010)
Chicago Times (1945–48)
Chicago Today (1969–74)
Chicago Tribune (1900–2010)
New York Times (various years)
Northwest Herald (1982–2010)

Online Resources

www.baseball-reference.com
http://chicago.whitesox.mlb.com
www.whitesoxinteractive.com

Acknowledgments

Through three editions of *Total White Sox* (formerly *The White Sox Encyclopedia*), many talented individuals and dedicated Sox fans assisted us in this worthy endeavor over the years. As the author, I would first like to thank my two amigos, Mark Fletcher and Biart Williams, who worked closely with me in the development of this project from its inception back in 1994, through publication of *Total White Sox*, 2011—Mark, for procuring so many rare and interesting photographs and images; and Biart, for his work on the postseason section and the history of the Cubs-Sox rivalry. Mark thanks his daughters, Jenna and Hayley, and his dad, Dick Fletcher.

For this third edition, Mark and I particularly want to thank Gerry Bilek, Mike McCormick, Len Maybaum, and Mike McKay, who for the third time provided us with fresh images and historic photos that they had collected over the years. White Sox photographers Ron Vesely, Tony Inzerillo, and the late George Brace were of great help to us in prior editions. The Donaghues—Peter and Mike—shared with us a collection of images carefully preserved by their father, Donald, and a number of images culled from that collection formed the basis of the first book when it came out in 1997.

My relationship with the front office has been unique and rather special, dating back to the second Veeck era of the late 1970s, but one that really gained traction in the mid-1980s, when Paul Jensen headed media relations. The White Sox Communications and Marketing Department filled a number of important gaps and was generous in its support of my work for many years. Special thanks to Scott Reifert and Jeff Szynal. Jeff really is the keeper of the history and lore within the team organization and over the years has extended to me a number of courtesies. Scott has been a front-office man for over two decades, and it has been my great pleasure to work with him on a number of projects. Thanks also to Ray Garcia and Lou Hernandez, a part of Scott's team, Chris O'Reilly in community relations, and White Sox fan Steve Junge, who pointed out a few errors in the second edition that required correction.

I'll really miss Nancy Faust, the White Sox music lady for four decades until she retired in 2010. Gracious and charming—she made the ballpark experience something truly memorable for the fans.

Additional thanks to Mark Liptak—"the Lip"—who dives into White Sox history and posts interesting and well-researched articles and interviews on White Sox Interactive—a terrific Internet fan forum maintained by George Bova.

I extend a tip of the hat to Dr. Dave Fletcher, whose personal crusade to build and open a Chicago Baseball Hall of Fame Museum continues. It will be a very special and treasured repository of baseball history in the Windy City, once the funding is securely in place and the ceremonial ribbon is cut.

Author and journalist George Castle is a Cubs fan—arguably the most intense Cubs fan I have ever known in my life—but we have worked together closely through a number of joint appearances we have made at Chicago area libraries and community historical societies presenting our respective viewpoints and arguing the finer points of which team is better. The debate goes on, and the war will never end. George and I are alumni of the old Lerner Newspaper chain, and we have been doing this for a number of years, but George also covers the Sox for the *Times of Northwest Indiana* and has shared many rich baseball insights with me.

I always enjoy the company of the Sox Fans on Deck fan group. They organized in 1987 to fight for the stadium funding bill when it seemed evident the Sox were on the brink of leaving Chicago, and have hung together ever since. They meet once a month up on the northwest side of the City in various buffet restaurants where the food is always cheap, the conversation lively, and the room reserved. You'll often run into SFOD members on Sox road trips. The fans who follow the team around the circuit are the most devoted fans of all.

Finally, a big thank you to the Triumph Books team—Tom Bast, Josh Williams, and Don Gulbrandsen, plus Alex Lubertozzi and Jennifer Barrell of Prologue Publishing Services—for allowing us to update the 2005 edition and present it you now.

About the Authors

RICHARD LINDBERG is a noted Chicago historian who writes about true crime, politics, neighborhoods, ethnicity, and of course baseball in the Windy City. He is the award-winning author of 15 earlier books, including: *The Gambler King of Clark Street: Michael C. McDonald and the Rise of Chicago's Democratic Machine*; *Heartland Serial Killers: Belle Gunness, Johann Hoch, and Murder for Profit in Gaslight Era Chicago*; *Chicago Yesterday & Today*; *Shattered Sense of Innocence: The 1955 Murders of Three Chicago Children*; *Stealing First in a Two Team Town: The White Sox From Comiskey to Reinsdorf*; *Return to the Scene of the Crime: A Guide to Infamous Places in Chicago*; *Passport's Guide to Ethnic Chicago*; and *Chicago Ragtime: Another Look at Chicago, 1880–1920.* Over the years, he has provided commentary and historical interpretation on numerous radio and television programs of local and national origin, including *American Justice, Cities of the Underworld, History's Mysteries, Masterminds,* NPR's *All Things Considered, Deadly Women,* and *Mobsters.* Rich is a past president of the Society of Midland Authors and the winner of a 2010 Certificate of Excellence from the Illinois State Historical Society for his book *The Gambler King of Clark Street.* Since the mid-1980s he has been recognized as the official White Sox team historian, working on a number of noteworthy research projects for the ballclub, including the 200 greatest moments, which he provided for the Champions Plaza located outside of Gate 4, and as a research consultant to the production crew of the 1988 motion picture *Eight Men Out.*

Contributors

MARK FLETCHER is a commercial sports photographer and White Sox fan who lives in Alsip, Illinois, with his three daughters, Jenna, Marissa, and Hayley.

BIART WILLIAMS grew up on Chicago's South Side during the White Sox's cherished Go-Go period. After serving in the U.S. Marines, he attended Governor's State University, where he earned a degree in business. He currently resides in Frankfort, Illinois.

The Last Word

Buried somewhere in this wall at Wrigley Field is a brick from old Comiskey Park. It was cemented in place late one winter's night by ardent Sox fan Peter Donaghue. The Cubs are oblivious. Can you find the brick?